9900390

Nineteenth-Century Literature Criticism

Topics Volume

Guide to Gale Literary Criticism Series

For criticism on	Consult these Gale series
Authors now living or who died after December 31, 1959	*CONTEMPORARY LITERARY CRITICISM (CLC)*
Authors who died between 1900 and 1959	*TWENTIETH-CENTURY LITERARY CRITICISM (TCLC)*
Authors who died between 1800 and 1899	*NINETEENTH-CENTURY LITERATURE CRITICISM (NCLC)*
Authors who died between 1400 and 1799	*LITERATURE CRITICISM FROM 1400 TO 1800 (LC)* *SHAKESPEAREAN CRITICISM (SC)*
Authors who died before 1400	*CLASSICAL AND MEDIEVAL LITERATURE CRITICISM (CMLC)*
Black writers of the past two hundred years	*BLACK LITERATURE CRITICISM (BLC)*
Authors of books for children and young adults	*CHILDREN'S LITERATURE REVIEW (CLR)*
Dramatists	*DRAMA CRITICISM (DC)*
Hispanic writers of the late nineteenth and twentieth centuries	*HISPANIC LITERATURE CRITICISM (HLC)*
Native North American writers and orators of the eighteenth, nineteenth, and twentieth centuries	*NATIVE NORTH AMERICAN LITERATURE (NNAL)*
Poets	*POETRY CRITICISM (PC)*
Short story writers	*SHORT STORY CRITICISM (SSC)*
Major authors from the Renaissance to the present	*WORLD LITERATURE CRITICISM, 1500 TO THE PRESENT (WLC)*

ISSN 0732-1864

Volume 56

Nineteenth-Century Literature Criticism

Topics Volume

*Excerpts from Criticism of Various
Topics in Nineteenth-Century Literature,
including Literary and Critical Movements,
Prominent Themes and Genres, Anniversary
Celebrations, and Surveys of National Literatures*

Denise Evans
Mary L. Onorato
Editors

GALE

DETROIT • NEW YORK • TORONTO • LONDON

STAFF

Denise Evans and Mary L. Onorato, *Editors*

Dana Ramel Barnes, *Contributing Editor*

Ondine Le Blanc, *Associate Editor*

Susan M. Trosky, *Managing Editor*

Marlene S. Hurst, *Permissions Manager*
Margaret A. Chamberlain, Maria Franklin, Kimberly F. Smilay, *Permissions Specialists*
Diane Cooper, Edna Hedblad, Michele Lonoconus, Maureen Puhl, Susan Salas,
Shalice Shah, *Permissions Associates*
Sarah Chesney, Jeffrey Hermann, *Permissions Assistants*

Victoria B. Cariappa, *Research Manager*
Julia C. Daniel, Tamara C. Nott, Michele P. Pica,
Tracie A. Richardson, Cheryl Warnock, *Research Associates*

Mary Beth Trimper, *Production Director*
Deborah L. Milliken, *Production Assistant*

Sherrell Hobbs, *Macintosh Artist*
Randy Bassett, *Image Database Supervisor*
Mikal Ansari, Robert Duncan, *Imaging Specialists*
Pamela A. Hayes, *Photography Coordinator*

This book is printed on acid-free paper that meets the minimum requirements of American National Standard for Information Sciences—Permanence Paper for Printed Library Materials, ANSI Z39.48-1984.

Library of Congress Catalog Card Number 84-643008
ISBN 0-8103-7005-0
ISSN 0732-1864
Printed in the United States of America

10 9 8 7 6 5 4 3 2 1

0102101184764

Contents

The Novel of Manners

Preface

Since its inception in 1981, *Nineteenth-Century Literature Criticism* has been a valuable resource for students and librarians seeking critical commentary on writers of this transitional period in world history. Designated an "Outstanding Reference Source" by the American Library Association with the publication of its first volume, *NCLC* has since been purchased by over 6,000 school, public, and university libraries. The series has covered more than 300 authors representing 29 nationalities and over 17,000 titles. No other reference source has surveyed the critical reaction to nineteenth-century authors and literature as thoroughly as *NCLC*.

Scope of the Series

NCLC is designed to introduce students and advanced readers to the authors of the nineteenth century, and to the most significant interpretations of these authors' works. The great poets, novelists, short story writers, playwrights, and philosophers of this period are frequently studied in high school and college literature courses. By organizing and reprinting commentary written on these authors, *NCLC* helps students develop valuable insight into literary history, promotes a better understanding of the texts, and sparks ideas for papers and assignments. Each entry in *NCLC* presents a comprehensive survey of an author's career or an individual work of literature and provides the user with a multiplicity of interpretations and assessments. Such variety allows students to pursue their own interests; furthermore, it fosters an awareness that literature is dynamic and responsive to many different opinions.

Every fourth volume of *NCLC* is devoted to literary topics that cannot be covered under the author approach used in the rest of the series. Such topics include literary movements, prominent themes in nineteenth-century literature, literary reaction to political and historical events, significant eras in literary history, prominent literary anniversaries, and the literatures of cultures that are often overlooked by English-speaking readers.

NCLC continues the survey of criticism of world literature begun by Gale's *Contemporary Literary Criticism (CLC)* and *Twentieth-Century Literary Criticism (TCLC)*, both of which excerpt and reprint commentary on authors of the twentieth century. For additional information about *TCLC, CLC,* and Gale's other criticism series, users should consult the Guide to Gale Literary Criticism Series preceding the title page in this volume.

Coverage

Each volume of *NCLC* is carefully compiled to present:

- criticism of authors, or literary topics, representing a variety of genres and nationalities
- both major and lesser-known writers and literary works of the period
- 5-8 authors or 4-6 topics per volume
- individual entries that survey critical response to an author's work or a topic in literary history, including early criticism to reflect initial reactions, later criticism to represent any rise or decline in reputation, and current retrospective analyses.

Organization

An author entry consists of the following elements: author heading, biographical and critical introduction, list of principal works, excerpts of criticism (each preceded by a bibliographic citation and an annotation), and a bibliography of further reading.

- The **Author Heading** consists of the name under which the author most commonly wrote, followed by birth and death dates. If an author wrote consistently under a pseudonym, the pseudonym will be listed in the author heading and the real name given in parentheses on the first line of the biographical and critical introduction. Also located at the beginning of the introduction to the author entry are any name variations under which an author wrote, including transliterated forms for an author whose language uses a nonroman alphabet.

- The **Biographical and Critical Introduction** outlines the author's life and career, as well as the critical issues surrounding his or her work. References are provided to past volumes of *NCLC* in which further information about the author may be found.

- Most *NCLC* entries include a **Portrait** of the author. Many entries also contain reproductions of materials pertinent to an author's career, including manuscript pages, title pages, dust jackets, letters, and drawings, as well as photographs of important people, places, and events in an author's life.

- The list of **Principal Works** is chronological by date of first publication and identifies the genre of each work. In the case of foreign authors with both foreign-language publications and English translations, the English-language version is given in brackets. Unless otherwise indicated, dramas are dated by first performance, not first publication.

- **Criticism** in each author entry is arranged chronologically to provide a perspective on changes in critical evaluation over the years. All titles of works by the author featured in the entry are printed in boldface type to enable the user to easily locate discussion of particular works. Also for purposes of easier identification, the critic's name and the publication date of the essay are given at the beginning of each piece of criticism. Unsigned criticism is preceded by the title of the journal in which it appeared. Publication information (such as publisher names and book prices) and some parenthetical numerical references (such as page and line references to specific editions of works) have been deleted at the editors' discretion to provide smoother reading of the text.

- A complete **Bibliographic Citation** provides original publication information for each piece of criticism.

- Critical excerpts are prefaced by **Annotations** providing the reader with a summary of the critical intent of the piece. Also included, when appropriate, is information about the critic's reputation, individual approach to literary criticism, and particular expertise in an author's works, as well as information about the relative importance of the critical excerpt. In some cases, the annotations cross-reference excerpts by critics who discuss each other's commentary.

- An annotated list of **Further Reading** appearing at the end of each entry suggests secondary sources on the author. In some cases it includes essays for which the editors could not obtain reprint rights.

Cumulative Indexes

■ Each volume of *NCLC* contains a cumulative **Author Index** listing all authors who have appeared in Gale's Literary Criticism Series, along with cross-references to such biographical series as *Contemporary Authors* and *Dictionary of Literary Biography*. Useful for locating authors within the various series, this index is particularly valuable for those authors who are identified with a certain period but who, because of their death dates, are placed in another, or for those authors whose careers span two periods. For example, Fyodor Dostoevsky is found in *NCLC*, yet Leo Tolstoy, another major nineteenth-century Russian novelist, is found in *TCLC* because he died after 1899.

■ Each *NCLC* volume includes a cumulative **Nationality Index** which lists all authors who have appeared in *NCLC*, arranged alphabetically under their respective nationalities.

■ Each new volume in Gale's Literary Criticism Series includes a cumulative **Topic Index**, which lists all literary topics treated in *NCLC, TCLC, LC 1400-1800*, and the *CLC* Yearbook.

■ Each new volume of *NCLC*, with the exception of the Topics volumes, contains a **Title Index** listing the titles of all literary works discussed in the volume. In response to numerous suggestions from librarians, Gale has also produced a **Special Paperbound Edition** of the *NCLC* title index. This annual cumulation lists all titles discussed in the series since its inception. Additional copies of the index are available on request. Librarians and patrons have welcomed this separate index: it saves shelf space, is easy to use, and is recyclable upon receipt of the following year's cumulation. Titles discussed in the Topics volume entries are not included in the *NCLC* cumulative index.

Citing *Nineteenth-Century Literature Criticism*

When writing papers, students who quote directly from any volume in Gale's Literary Criticism Series may use the following general forms to footnote reprinted criticism. The first example pertains to material drawn from periodicals, the second to material reprinted from books:

[1]T.S. Eliot, "John Donne," *The Nation and Athenaeum*, 33 (9 June 1923), 321-32; excerpted and reprinted in *Literature Criticism from 1400-1800,* Vol. 10, ed. James E. Person, Jr. (Detroit: Gale Research, 1989), pp. 28-9.

[2]Clara G. Stillman, *Samuel Butler: A Mid-Victorian Modern* (Viking Press, 1932); excerpted and reprinted in *Twentieth-Century Literary Criticism,* Vol. 33, ed. Paula Kepos (Detroit: Gale Research, 1989), pp. 43-5.

Suggestions Are Welcome

In response to suggestions, several features have been added to *NCLC* since the series began, including annotations to excerpted criticism, a cumulative index to authors in all Gale literary criticism series, entries devoted to criticism on a single work by a major author, more illustrations, and a title index listing all literary works discussed in the series.

Readers who wish to suggest authors, single works, or topics to appear in future volumes, or who have other suggestions, are cordially invited to write: The Editors, *Nineteenth-Century Literature Criticism,* 835 Penobscot Bldg., 645 Griswold St., Detroit, MI 48226-4094; call toll-free at 1-800-347-GALE; or fax to 1-313-961-6599.

Acknowledgments

The editors wish to thank the copyright holders of the excerpted criticism included in this volume and the permissions managers of many book and magazine publishing companies for assisting us in securing reprint rights. We are also grateful to the staffs of the Detroit Public Library, the Library of Congress, the University of Detroit Mercy Library, Wayne State University Purdy/Kresge Library Complex, and the University of Michigan Libraries for making their resources available to us. Following is a list of the copyright holders who have granted us permission to reprint material in this volume of *NCLC*. Every effort has been made to trace copyright, but if omissions have been made, please let us know.

COPYRIGHTED EXCERPTS IN *NCLC*, VOLUME 56, WERE REPRINTED FROM THE FOLLOWING PERIODICALS:

Critical Inquiry, v. 12, Autumn, 1985 for "Three Women's Texts and a Critique of Imperialism." © 1985 by Gayatri Chakravorty Spivak. All rights reserved. Reprinted by permission of the author.—*Essays in Arts and Sciences,* v. x, March, 1982. Copyright © 1982 by the University of New Haven. Reprinted by permission of the publisher.—*The New England Quarterly,* v. xxix, March, 1956 for "The Machine in the Garden" by Leo Marx. Copyright 1956, renewed 1984 by *The New England Quarterly.* Reprinted by permission of the publisher and the author.—*Nineteenth-Century Contexts,* v. 13, Spring, 1989 for "Race, Gender, and Imperial Ideology: In the Nineteenth Century" by Zohreh R. Sullivan. Reprinted by permission of the author.—*Tulsa Studies in Women's Literature,* v. 6, Spring, 1987. © 1987, The University of Tulsa. Reprinted by permission of the publisher.

COPYRIGHTED EXCERPTS IN *NCLC*, VOLUME 56, WERE REPRINTED FROM THE FOLLOWING BOOKS:

Baldick, Chris. From *In Frankenstein's Shadow: Myth, Monstrosity, and Nineteenth-Century Writing.* Oxford at the Clarendon Press, 1987. © Chris Baldick 1987. All rights reserved. Reprinted by permission of Oxford University Press.—Beer, Patricia. From *Reader, I Married Him: A Study of the Women Characters of Jane Austen, Charlotte Brontë, Elizabeth Gaskell and George Eliot.* Barnes & Noble Books, 1974. © Patricia Beer 1974. Reprinted by permission of Macmillan, London and Basingstoke.—Brantlinger, Patrick. From *Rule of Darkness: British Literature and Imperialism, 1830-1914.* Cornell, 1988. Copyright © 1988 by Cornell University. Used by permission of the publisher, Cornell University Press.—Callow, James T. From *Kindred Spirits: Knickerbocker Writers and American Artists.* The University of North Carolina Press, 1967. Copyright © 1967 by The University of North Carolina Press. Reprinted by permission of the publisher.—Castle, Terry. From *The Apparitional Lesbian: Female Homosexuality and Modern Culture.* Columbia University Press, 1993. Copyright © 1993 Columbia University Press, New York. All rights reserved. Reprinted with the permission of the publisher.—Colby, Vineta. From *Yesterday's Woman: Domestic Realism in the English*

Colonialism in Victorian English Literature

INTRODUCTION

The Victorian period in British history marks the high point of British imperialism. Though the British policy of colonial expansion had begun earlier, during the nineteenth century Britain not only consolidated its existing empire, but also experienced an unprecedented expansion in its colonial possessions. This process began after the 1857 Mutiny in India, when India was placed under the direct control of the Crown, and continued through the scramble for Africa in the late 1800s, so that by the end of the century it could be proudly proclaimed that "the sun never sets on the British Empire." The tremendous upsurge of imperial activity during the nineteenth century, though physically taking place in areas distant from British shores, had a broad and pervasive impact on British culture. The literature of the period is thus inextricably embroiled in the imperialist project. In the view of many critics, irrespective of the direct involvement of individual literary works with the colonial enterprise, the overall contours of Victorian literature are consistently shaped by the influence of colonial ideology, which informed the collective unconscious of the British public during the entire period.

The most obvious influence of colonialism on Victorian literature is evident in the colonial novels of writers like H. Rider Haggard, Rudyard Kipling, and Joseph Conrad. These novels, which include works like Haggard's *She* (1889) and Kipling's *Kim* (1901), are usually set in the distant lands that Britain colonized and attempt to expose the insular domestic public to the exotic strangeness of their country's colonial possessions. The reality of colonialism enters these texts as the necessary background that makes possible their narratives of adventure and romance. The linking of colonialism with the genre of the romantic adventure story is also evident in the abundant children's fiction of the time, which includes works by Robert Louis Stevenson and R. M. Ballantyne. While using Britain's colonial enterprise as the setting of their narratives, such novels also participate in the construction and propagation of colonial ideology by providing an implicit justification for British imperialism. Colonialism, therefore, appears in these colonial novels not only as the literal backdrop for their narrative action, but also as the ideological framework that provides the raison d'être of the action.

The impact of colonialism, however, is not restricted to the so-called colonial novels. The nineteenth century's dominant genre of domestic fiction is also implicitly informed by colonial ideology. Though the novels of writers like Jane Austen, Charlotte Brönte, Charles Dickens, and George Eliot focus on domestic British society, Britain's overseas possessions frequently play an important role in the action. Thus, Sir Thomas Bertram's estate in *Mansfield Park* is maintained by his possessions in Antigua while *David Copperfield*'s Mr. Micawber achieves success in Australia and St. John Rivers in *Jane Eyre* leaves for India to fulfill his missionary aspirations. Colonialism thus provides an expanded canvas even to the domestic novels, which reveal the inextricable involvement of domestic British society in the colonial enterprise. At the same time, the implicit presence in these novels of ideas such as the savage nature of natives and the white man's burden of bringing civilization to them also involves these texts in the dissemination of racial and colonial ideologies that provided the conceptual framework for colonialism.

Though an awareness of the colonial presence in Victorian literature is evident in critical studies during the first half of the twentieth century, such criticism is usually restricted to an examination of colonial novels and an evaluation of the authors' differing attitudes to the colonial enterprise as reflected in their writings. It is only in the latter half of the twentieth century, in the so-called postcolonial period, that critics have explored the pervasive influence of colonial ideology throughout nineteenth-century British culture and society. Edward Said's *Orientalism* (1978) is a seminal work in this respect, providing an exhaustive analysis of the West's construction of the Orient as its "other." Such a construction, Said argues, is not motivated by any desire to represent faithfully the reality of the colonized cultures and their people. Instead, it works as a form of ideological control, allowing the West to create a series of Manichean oppositions between the colonizer and the colonized that make the latter manageable and provide a moral justification for the colonial enterprise. Even literary works like Conrad's *Heart of Darkness* (1902) that overtly question the validity of colonialism are informed by this Manichean aesthetic, which problematizes their critique of imperialism. In such cases, while the colonized "other" functions as a vantage point for a self-critique of Western civilization, it is still not allowed to articulate a distinct subject-position of its own.

The use of the "other" for self-critique and the construction of alternative subject-positions within the British context is also explored by feminist postcolonial critics like Gayatri Spivak and Jenny Sharpe. These critics analyze the relationship between colonial ideology and the growth of British feminism in Victorian England evident in the works of writers like Jane Austen and Charlotte Brönte. Similarly, colonial ideology is also seen to have an impact on the representation of domestic class relations, whereby the lower classes are frequently portrayed as internal "others" who share the characteristics of the colonized and hence require similar strategies of control. By thus exploring the class, gender, and racial politics that inform colonial ideology, postcolonial critics reveal the complexities of colonialism and its multi-faceted influence on Victorian society and literature. At the same time, such criticism reveals a contemporary relevance to the literary output of the nineteenth century. The exploration of the ideological complicities and resistances that characterize Victorian literature provides an insight into the complex ideological configurations of neo-colonialism that are an inescapable reality of late-twentieth-century culture and politics.

REPRESENTATIVE WORKS

Jane Austen
Mansfield Park (novel) 1814

R. M. Ballantyne
Coral Island (novel) 1857

Charlotte Brönte
Jane Eyre (novel) 1847

Lewis Carrol
Alice's Adventures in Wonderland (novel) 1865
Through the Looking Glass (novel) 1871

Joyce Cary
The African Witch (novel) 1936
Mr. Johnson (novel) 1939

Joseph Conrad
The Nigger of the "Narcissus" (novel) 1898
Lord Jim (novel) 1900
Heart of Darkness (novel) 1902

Charles Dickens
David Copperfield (novel) 1849-50
Great Expectations (novel) 1860-61

Sir Arthur Conan Doyle
The Lost World (novel) 1912

George Eliot
Middlemarch (novel) 1871-72

E. M. Forster
A Passage to India (novel) 1924

Aeneas Gunn
The Little Black Princess (novel) 1905
We of the Never-Never (novel) 1908

H. Rider Haggard
King Solomon's Mines (novel) 1885
She (novel) 1889

Rudyard Kipling
Plain Tales from the Hills (short stories) 1888
Barrack-Room Ballads (poetry) 1892
Kim (novel) 1901

Anna Leonowen
The English Governess at the Siamese Court (memoir) 1870

Mary Shelley
Frankenstein (novel) 1818

Robert Louis Stevenson
Treasure Island (novel) 1882

Bram Stoker
Dracula (novel) 1897

Lord Alfred Tennyson
Ballads and Other Poems (poetry) 1880

William Makepeace Thackeray
Vanity Fair (novel) 1847

OVERVIEWS

Susanne Howe

SOURCE: "The Happy Years," in *Novels of Empire*, Columbia University Press, 1949, pp. 38-64.

[*In the following extract, Howe explores the depiction of British men and women in India in Victorian novels, focusing on the representation of women, younger sons, missionaries, and Anglo-Indians.*]

We should not believe, of course, that novels about India have always been peopled exclusively with psychoneurotics, white or brown. There were many happy years before the middle of the nineteenth century when one could read novels with Indian settings from the Minerva Press and Mudie's and still sleep quietly of nights. We may return to those days for a while and see how the Anglo-Indian stories, like so much other English colonial fiction, fitted into the well-established patterns of the English novel.

The novelists had thirty or forty "quiet" years of the earlier nineteenth century in which to do this, years in which scarcely anyone at home, as was so often the case while "reluctant" British expansion was going on, needed to be conscious of India at all. No one needed to be uncomfortably aware of her as a "problem." If we may believe the novelists, the apathy and ignorance about India prevailing at home are the despair of soldier and civilian alike. Many distinguished Governors-General, before the Crown took over India from the East India Company in 1858, had come and gone— aggressive Wellesley, capable Lord Hastings, energetic Bentinck, Russo-phobe Auckland and fabulous Dalhousie. We hear about them all in novels of a later date. But at the time during which they were establishing "subordinate cooperation" among the native states surrounding John Company's territories, or fighting the first Afghan and Sikh Wars, or suppressing the Thugs, no one at home or in India itself felt impelled to write a whole novel about India in terms of Anglo-Indian life and events for their own sake.

During these years, too, the trading monopolies and commercial privileges of the old East India Company were quietly being swept away with each renewal of the Charter, in 1813, 1833, and 1853. Nabobs, "blackamoor colonels" and other arrivals from India, who battened on the Company and its declining fortunes, continue to be props of the Minerva Press novelists into the nineteenth century. But these "old Indians" belong to a vanished eighteenth century and most readers have the impression that no one before Thackeray is interested in writing about their successors, the "Qui Hais" of the years before the Mutiny in 1857. But W. D. Arnold, John Lang, H. S. Cunningham, and J. W. Kaye wrote about them too. These novelists knew a good deal more about India than Thackeray did, but somehow it is only Colonel Newcome, Mr. Binnie, and that unpleasant symptom of the decay of the old order, Jos Sedley, whom we have become familiar with. The others, nevertheless, have their significance too, with the added interest of being contemporary with the events and people they describe. It is a mistake to think of Thackeray as the only creator of these Anglo-Indian figures of the early and mid-century.

Edification. Among five or six kinds of novels in vogue during these years that were preliminary to the Mutiny and to Empire, the didactic and pedagogic books written partly for and partly about children, are easily distinguishable. Mrs. Barbauld, Hannah More, Mrs. Trimmer, Maria Edgeworth, Mrs. Sherwood, and countless other women wrote them. These tract-like stories seem to have been the almost exclusive province of the Evangelical woman writer. Novels one can scarcely call them; indeed their authors feared and disapproved of the novel as such and did what they could to undermine it. The Evangelicals were beginning to form the moral attitudes of a new Victorian world in which the middle class was to legislate on matters of conduct. It was to decree standards of behavior more decorous than the rowdy and uncouth manners of the old eigh-

teenth century world which Victoria's "wicked uncles" inhabited. Since children and their training are important in the establishment of any new order, juvenile reading formed a new and special concern for the Evangelical mind, and ushered in, with the backing, of course, of Rousseau and Thomas Day, what might be called The Century of the Child.

In this Evangelical fortifying of national morals, Mrs. Sherwood and India played an important but depressing part. She was in active missionary work of an educational kind for many years, off and on, at Meerut in the Province of Delhi. Journeys home, which took four months "and an extra four weeks" in those early years (she went out first in 1812) punctuated her long stays in the Upper Provinces. From a personal point of view they were melancholy years, and her life and letters make gloomy reading. She lost several children in India and the index at the back of F. J. Harvey Darton's book about her (1910) is full of grim little entries under their several names, reading "beauty of," "illness of," "death of," "grave of." One would like to think that the poor lady had a little fun writing her stories about children in India, *The History of Little Henry and His Bearer* (1812), and *The History of Little Lucy and Her Dhaye* (1822), but it seems improbable.

No doubt her morbid and edifying fables with a strong Sunday School flavor did much to acquaint the youth of England with Indian ways and atmosphere. By such missionary pieces as these, widely circulated, the foundations of Empire were being laid. They fitted in with the current taste for the pedagogic and didactic and moralistic tone in fiction, and used the Indian scene to lend savor and novelty to the lessons of missionary zeal which they taught. The end, we must hope, justified the means. A more repulsive pair of little ones than Henry and Lucy would be hard to find. They go into gentle declines, induced by the Indian climate, quoting more and more frequently from John 14, Job 19, and Luke 10, in neat, memorizable texts. They recite parts of the catechism at a moment's notice. Each finally succeeds in converting his native servant to Christianity, and then slips, with touching smiles, into a Clarissa-like deathbed finale. It is all perfectly terrible. But in terms that its ever-increasing audience in its own day could understand and appreciate, this sort of thing was fine publicity at home for British India, and for the Church Missionary Society abroad.

Mrs. Sherwood wished little English children to think of converting the heathen in India as an admirable lifework, but if this lesson did not "take," she was not the woman to overlook other possibilities. Her English readers might as well learn some of the Hindostani words most commonly in use—dobie, kamsamah, punkah, goreewallah, kitmutgar, and so on. She translates each one in a footnote at the bottom of the page. Anyone setting up an English household in India would have to know them, and they lent atmosphere to the story. Generations of writers about India have, unfortunately, since Mrs. Sherwood's day, relied too heavily on the same device for achieving "color," and without the painstaking and somehow oddly touching little footnotes. We can understand how Edward Lear felt when he wrote his famous poem "The Cummerbund" published in *Nonsense Songs*:

> She sat upon her Dobie,—
> She heard the Nimmak hum,—
> When all at once a cry arose:
> "The Cummerbund is come!"

Too many novelists, alas, never took the hint.

Mrs. Sherwood, however, was much lionized at the Presidency in Calcutta because new arrivals from England had heard much of *Little Henry*. "Such religious persons as came out that year (1815) to India, were all anxious to find out the author, supposed to be a man." The English edition was brought to Calcutta by the wife of a Baptist missionary, and, Mrs. Sherwood tells us, the little volume passed from hand to hand in the small religious society there. "It was lent to me, and I must say it brought tears to my eyes." It did the same for her many readers at home. Not only missionary zeal but the future gospel of empire was watered by such tears.

She wrote in 1825 another story of the Indian scene, but a more worldly one this time, *The Lady of the Manor*. This has no out-and-out missionary flavor, but is still a novel of purpose, a species of conduct-and-etiquette book combined. It delivers itself, with a primness all its own, of certain lessons regarding the behavior of young English ladies who come out to the east. The wholesome English standards of the heroine, Olivia, are undermined by her life in her semi-orientalized uncle's Indian household. (He is not exactly a nabob, but an Old Indian, or Qui Hai). Olivia finally marries—oh, shame!—for "worldly advantage."

Ladies in Exile. The problem of the Englishwoman in India fascinates every novelist who writes about that unhappy country. These "improving" writers of the earliest years of the century, while using India as a fresh and piquant setting for the lessons with which they catered to the popular taste for the didactic in fiction, also managed incidentally to pose certain questions destined to be of perennial interest to novelists of empire in the following decades. The disintegration of female character and personality in hot climates is one of these. The treatment of it becomes more complicated as the century advances in psychological sophistication.

At first, like Olivia, the ladies in exile are merely passive, unresisting victims of bad example and bad

climate. They stop dressing for dinner, they give up their music, embroidery, and water colors. If they were frivolous at home, they become doubly so in India. William Brown Hockley's novels describe this process as seen in the thirties and Sir J. W. Kaye does it for the forties. By the fifties, they are often pictured as ruthless little husband-hunters, flirts, and jilts. Florence Marryat, in several pieces about India for *Temple Bar* in 1867, divides her sisters into "the very gay, the very religious, and the very inane." Life in India for them is both boring and dangerous. Their husbands are away for long periods of time and "strange men do not have to have permission to call," as they would in England. They may call on whom they please. The round of balls and dinners and dancing, and the enervating weather "drains the mind of all desire to improve itself."

G. O. Trevelyan agrees with her pronouncements in his interesting "Letters from a Competition Wallah" in *Macmillan's Magazine* in 1863. He too feels that "the ladies, poor things, get the worst of it." Without plenty of work, India is unbearable. The women are bound to suffer more than the men from "languor and depth of ennui of which a person who has never left Europe can form no conception." Because of the climate they must spend the hours from eight to five indoors. "Good novels are limited in numbers, and it is too much to expect that a lady should read history and poetry for six hours every day." Trevelyan, indeed, is very tolerant; he has every sympathy with the poor creatures on the day when the "book-club has sent nothing but Latham's *Nationalities of Europe* and three refutations of Colenso . . . and the post brings only a letter from your old governess." Only a very brave or a very stupid woman, he concludes, can endure India for long without suffering "in mind, health and tournure. If a lady becomes dowdy, it is all up with her."

It is possible, of course, for a lady to be both brave *and* stupid, and perhaps this is why Kipling's exiled women do so well for the most part. He is hard on the spoiled and the mischievous (Mrs. Gadsby and Mrs. Hauksbee, respectively) and so is Maud Diver, whose books, however, also abound in the brave and the stupid of her sex. Pamela Hinkson's *Golden Rose* features them too, and most novels about the Mutiny have at least one upright, leathery-faced spinster or well-weathered soldier's wife with a heart of gold and not too much imagination. Perhaps Bromfield's fine Scottish nurse, Miss McDaid in *The Rains Came*, is about the best of this kind.

The brave and the stupid among Frenchwomen do not come out to Indo-China, if we may believe the novelists. (It is not a common Gallic combination anyway, but rather a feature of Anglo-Saxondom, if one may ever be justified in making such racial generalizations.) An old resident and colonial expert, Eugène Pujarniscle,

K, k.

MEN of different trades and sizes
Here you see before your eyeses:
Lanky sword and stumpy pen,
Doing useful things for men:
When the Empire wants a stitch in her
Send for Kipling and for Kitchener.

Rudyard Kipling and Lord Kitchener, as depicted by
F. Carruthers Gould.

gives us most unflattering pictures of French and other European ladies at Hanoï. They are as bad, or worse than, Bromfield's Mrs. Hoggett-Eggbury in *The Rains Came*. They are "dames" while the native girls are "femmes" and they are the cause of many happy and fruitful and generally pleasant relationships of colonial Frenchmen with "les brunes," he explains in *Philoxène* (1931). De Vogüé in *Les Morts qui parlent* (1901) feels that young French wives, no matter how devoted, should be left at home. Let the English take *their* women out; they can risk it; "elles ont le diable au corps." But French girls would be homesick so far from France. Daguèrches in *Le Kilomêtre 83* (1913) seems to bear him out; French colonial women cannot stand the climate of Siam-Cambodge, and they get jealous, if not of other women, then of a man's work. (Kipling's *The Gadsbys* provided a pretty useful pattern for unhappy colonial tangles in all languages—that of the child-wife who wants to be "first.") If your really nice "jeune fille" like Selysette Sylva in Farrère's *Les Civilisés* (1905) does by any chance live in Saïgon,

she is under the decorous family supervision that she would have in France, and she had better not fall in love with corrupted, though courageous, young colonial officers like Jacques Fièrce. It will make them both unhappy. Altogether, it is better that she should stay at home and mind her children and her "foyer" if she is married, and if she is a "jeune fille" then let her seek a husband elsewhere than in the insidious atmosphere of Saïgon or Hanoï.

This atmosphere is even more seductively presented by French writers than its Indian equivalent by the British. Of course it is all on a much smaller scale; there is less vastness and more of the "mysterious East." The dark leafy streets, the strings of harbor lights, the charming "brunes," the impassive and intriguing native "boys," the psychological mysteries of opium and cocaine, one is often glad to exchange for these all the odors of jasmine-cum-cowdung-smoke, all the dusty and brilliant sunsets and dawns, all the saris and sun helmets of British India.

But as the century wears on, English sophistication increases and Edwardian morals tend to loosen up what the Indian atmosphere had not already got to work on, in the English female character. French literature, too, had made sin fashionable. More and more the exiles come out brazenly to seek for husbands (England is full of superfluous women), or if already married they are discontented and pass from "flirting" or "playing with fire" in the nineties (in the vocabulary of Alice Perrin and Flora Annie Steel) to the activities of the coldly promiscuous vixen of the twenties and the high-class siren of the thirties, like Bromfield's Lady Esketh. Sometimes they take to solitary drinking. As the type of amorous adventuress comes to be taken more and more for granted in modern fiction, India comes more and more to be used as a playground for her exploits. So in modern times this character is the downright predatory female, unscrupulous, treacherous, tragic in varying degrees, and sometimes repentant, joining forces with the missionaries, the nursing nuns, or the "sensible" people, but usually too late. Typhus and cholera take a high toll of these sirens, whose role is played over and over again as one corner of the triangle that gives shape, or merely incident, to countless novels of Anglo-Indian life. In *Indigo* Mrs. Macbeth is "fluttery" and elopes with Captain Ponsonby. The lady may be merely unstable and undecided, like Barbara Wingfield-Stratford's *Beryl in India* (1920), and not really vicious at all, but brewing trouble for others nevertheless. But "tough" or not, she has come a long way from Mrs. Sherwood's comparatively decorous and ladylike Olivia in 1825.

Less in the sanctimonious vein of Mrs. Sherwood and more in the line of Miss Edgeworth's *Moral Tales* is another early and exemplary story about India called *The Young Cadet; or, Henry Delamere's Voyage to*

India. This was written by Mrs. Hofland (Barbara Hoole) about 1827-28, and illustrates again the easy use of Indian material by those who felt that chatty and persuasive books loaded with information and instruction could not fail to please the young. But here we have no exhortations to convert the heathen and no censoriousness about wayward young ladies. Everything has a sunny, sensible Church of England atmosphere. The book tells about Henry's travels in Hindostan, his experiences in the Burmese War (the first one, 1824-26), and his impressions of the wondrous caves of Elora. It is dutifully based on books of travel, histories, and the authentic reminiscences of Captain Snodgrass, who took part in the Burmese campaigns. But its real interest lies in the glimpses it affords of English views on the subject of the budding Empire, and the clear connection it makes between large families at home and dominion abroad.

Younger Sons. This aspect of imperial expansion accounts for the beginnings of many an Indian career more distinguished than that of Henry Delamere. The background is usually stated for us in Chapter I:

> 'You have indeed a numerous and lovely family,' said Mr. Wingrove to Mr. Delamere, as his lady and her eight children were quitting the dining-room, 'but you must frequently feel great anxiety on the subject of providing for so many in such a manner as their birth and education entitle them to expect.'

Here, in essence, we have the classic problem, posed with neatness and propriety by our capable authoress. What to do with too many younger sons? India, in many cases, became the answer. It relieved the pressure. Younger sons are often the heroes of novels about India, all through the century. They could not inherit the land, and it was getting more and more difficult to place them well at home and more and more expensive to train them for the professions. So, in the early nineteenth century novels they are often the traders and adventurers, with or without benefit of a connection with the East India Company. Toward the middle of the century they begin to be "competition-wallahs," young hopefuls of a rejuvenated and democratized Indian Civil Service, to which for a long time Indians themselves might not aspire. Oakfield in Arnold's novel of 1853 is reluctant to believe that "the English message to India is civil-engineering simply," but Middleton of the Civil Service is among the most admirable people in an Indian scene where the high moral expectations of Arnold allow him to find very few people admirable at all. (The younger sons in the regiments, of whom Vernon is an example, he finds pitiable indeed. They are "wretchedly blackguard." But presumably Arnold did not know the gallant Hodson of "Hodson's Horse," like himself a younger son, an old Rugbeian, and in India at about the same time.)

Not all Competition Men are agreeable fellows in the eighteen fifties, however. John Lang's *Too Clever by Half* (1853), almost exactly contemporary with *The Newcomes* and *Oakfield* by the way, has some very disagreeable ones indeed, and one at least is also a younger son. This is, in fact, one of the most disagreeable books about India to be found in this period, an ugly blend of Samuel Warren at his worst, with the facetiousness of Dickens and the archness of Thackeray at less than their best.

H. S. Cunningham does not quite commit himself on the younger son question in his amusingly satirical novel, *Chronicles of Dustypore, a Tale of Modern Anglo-Indian Society* (1875). It stands out as one of the few humorous novels on the too sad Indian question, in its own or any period of the century. A book which can poke fun at British rule and those endearing little British foibles in the very decade in which Disraeli, that great romantic, made the Queen into the Empress of India, is a rare phenomenon indeed. Cunningham, perhaps the best of the links between Thackeray and Kipling, makes one of his New Civilians, or Competition Men, jeer at the Old Regime. It consisted, according to the modern view (but perhaps not Cunningham's necessarily) of "all the stupidest sons of the stupidest families of England for several generations, like the pedigree wheat, you know, on the principle of selection; none but the blockheads of course would have anything to do with India."

Young Oakfield's friend Middleton in Arnold's novel tells the hero that a good officer is a blessing to his District; the new system was placing many younger sons as District Officers in the fifties. But Cunningham, in the book we have just mentioned, does not find Boldero admirable at all.

Other D.O.'s of the same overzealous kind appear in W. W. Hunter's *The Old Missionary*. This was published in 1897, but is set in the fifties after the Mutiny. In fact it would seem that the D.O. did not become a hero and martyr until Kipling got hold of him and made him one of the noblest of the Sons of Martha. Hunter allows us to see the admirable qualities of these bumptious young men, but they are impatient of government red-tape and full of ideas about schools, law, public works, tramways, and so on. Old Lieutenant-Governors of the "early time" find them very bothersome. According to Trevelyan in his letters to *Macmillan's Magazine* in 1863, the natives feel that the new Competition Men are of "another caste," having less *savoir-faire* than the old Haileybury crowd. Trevelyan himself is rather snobbish about them. He inclines to agree with the up-country magistrates who regard these young men as parvenus in a service where birth and breeding have hitherto been all in all. They lack the "physical dash and athletic habits" so essential to young men who may have to rule over an Indian province as large as Saxony. If they cannot drive a "series of shying horses and ride across country" they are useless. Your Competition Wallah has not been brought up in the tradition of field sports, poor fellow, and is not of the true "imperial race." The individual members of this race, Trevelyan reminds us must be "men of their hands" to command the necessary prestige. Ideas about building tramways are not enough.

Younger sons from many of those "numerous and lovely" families which Mrs. Hofland holds up for our regard are always among the more daring soldiers. Before Kipling, they are more attractive heroes than their civilian brothers. They appear dashingly in many novels about the Mutiny, the Afghan or Sikh or Burmese wars. They are exemplary and talkative in the Henty books, of godlike stature in Flora Annie Steel's books, desperately silent and incredibly gallant as the subalterns and captains of Kipling's Own. The younger son is cut loose from home. He is reckless because he has little to lose; defiant because he has probably been underestimated and misunderstood at home. He excels at taking risks. Often he is a disappointed and world-weary but lovable roué, or a sentimental, mysteriously "broken" man, like Louis Bromfield's Tom Ransome in *The Rains Came* (1937). Sometimes he is living down a dark past, because an older brother has "inherited" and he himself has spent his patrimony in riotous living in England where his extravagance has got him into trouble.

But Mrs. Hofland's Henry Delamere is not of these. For his edification, and that of the good lady's young readers, Henry's father holds forth on the history of the East India Company, of Hindostan, of Tamerlane, Hyder Ali, and Tippoo Sahib. It is all very Maria Edgeworth. But the low rumble of imperial ambition begins to be heard in odd ways under this demure surface. Father fairly smacks his lips over the "extension of British power in Asia" and the virtuous way in which it is being used. He is probably thinking of the 1813 act to limit the Company's trading monopoly, and of Lord Hastings' upright administration as Governor-General, when he says contentedly that British plundering of India is at an end now, and the bribery of officials too:

> India will be no longer the nurse of luxury, the reward of enterprize, the temptation to extortion and tyranny, which it has been in days past. A new and better order of things has sprung up, and will increase, arising from equitable laws duly administered, regular trade properly pursued and proportioned; and above all, from that sense of humanity and self-subjugation, commanded by our religion, which is now taught with most happy effect to the higher classes of society throughout British India.

The Church of England was a going concern by this time in India. But after the many sight-seeing tours

which Henry manages to make before and after his participation in the war to subdue those "contemptible" Burmese—who have somehow persisted in their determination to make trouble for the English—he is obliged to admit that native superstitions and idols still hold sway and that "there are in fact few, very *few* converts to Christianity, but there is a general amelioration of prejudice." Just what he means by this is not clear, except that he is hopeful. It is better to go slowly with attempts at conversion, he adds. In this conclusion most missionaries, in and out of novels, would probably agree with him. Mrs. Steel, Maud Diver, Louis Bromfield, and E. J. Thompson certainly do. Apropos of the conqueror's uneasy sense in India of something amiss, something vaguely hostile and aloof in the native attitude, the book is interesting. Henry feels the Burmese attitude of resentment keenly. They are lying and deceitful, he writes his people at home, and furthermore they "treat us with that contempt it is no part of John Bull's character to bear." There is the basic difficulty! Like so many of the large problems that beset the conqueror in India throughout the century, this one is recurrent and perhaps eternal. Mrs. Hofland had the luck, or the insight, or the common sense, to touch on several of them in her unpretentious little book about Henry.

Beside this dominant problem of racial mistrust and misunderstanding the smaller problems of the younger son and the marriageable miss in India seem of minor importance. Younger sons and marriageable misses have their difficulties in English life and English fiction all through the nineteenth century, against domestic and continental settings of all sorts. Their dilemmas are merely by-products of empire, and India merely serves to intensify their troubles. But one question of some real importance to the spread of empire is raised by both Mrs. Sherwood and Mrs. Hofland when they write about India: that is the question of the missionary.

In the Lord's Vineyard. For besides the military activities of the Governors-General, the decline of John Company, and the steadily growing predominance of British economic advantage in India at India's expense, it should be noted that the men of God were also at work. They were among the best trail-blazers for empire during these long, so-called "quiet" years before the storm of the Mutiny broke about astonished English ears. Unlike the military and mercantile men contemporary with them, the missionaries, both Catholic and Protestant, British and foreign, sit for their portraits quite early in the century. They were more closely associated with Indian life in concrete and visible ways than Governors-General or officials of the East India Company could possibly be. They were present on occasions of sickness and birth and death. Their knowledge of native conditions was gained from a personal daily struggle against these conditions.

While Mrs. Sherwood and Mrs. Hofland were writing their bland little books, stirring together Evangelical or Anglican fervor with pedagogy and moral etiquette and social observation into that odd mixture which entranced such a large public, the missionaries, like Mrs. Sherwood herself, were not idle. They were up and doing in India by 1801 when the Society for the Promotion of Christian Knowledge and the Church Missionary Society took over the excellent schools started by Danish missionaries in the eighteenth century. By 1813, when James Stephen (father of Sir Leslie) became a power in the Colonial Office, and imports of Lancashire cotton goods were beginning to undermine India's principal industry, all sorts of workers in the vineyard were permitted in the Company's territories.

Commerce, politics, and evangelism have always been comfortable bedfellows in England's overseas possessions, and the East India Company was nothing if not realistic. It kept everybody happy, or at least placated, by the sensible device of contributing to Mohammedan and Hindu temples at the same time, and by giving sturdy backing to the establishment of the Church of England in India. It did not neglect other denominations either, but by 1852—Dalhousie's time, that is, and Thackeray's and Arnold's—the Anglicans had outstripped all other denominations and held a comfortable lead. But of whatever persuasion, the missionaries rose on the wave of Christian humanitarianism that followed the French Revolution and became extremely busy in jungle and desert, making straight the pathway for additional gods—the telegraph, railway, irrigation and sanitation projects, famine control. As these other gods began to spread throughout India, the missionary became a more effective social worker. In return for this, he has always lent a helping hand to conquest.

In fiction he becomes less fanatical and more practical as the century wears on. He and his wife or his sister—they needed to suffer in pairs for the most part—no longer sit in the verandah reasoning with little children or converting native bearers. They tramp or bicycle along the dusty roads, like Alden in Thompson's *Farewell to India,* or Mr. and Mrs. Nair in Maud Diver's *Far to Seek.* They are inured to filth, ridicule, discouragement, and climate, and they are willing to cooperate with almost any agency that is making headway for the native good against these powerful forces.

Sometimes they are conscientious spinsters like Miss Williams in *Golden Rose.* The woman's rights movement that grew into the cause of suffrage, and the general nineteenth century emancipation of English "superfluous" women that sent the tough-minded ones into medical schools and settlements sent them also out to India. There they slaved as medical missionaries or nurses in health centers, or as hospital supervisors, or as teachers in mission schools. The backward state

of women in India, the suffering of the child wives, the aspiration of the "new" Indian woman, the frightful condition of thousands of undernourished children—all this made India a field especially engaging to female interest and sympathy and sacrifice. Flora Annie Steel's novels speak for the force of this appeal.

The missionaries' situation in India was, if possible, more equivocal and difficult than in Africa or Australia. They were up against conflicting sets of ancient, deeply rooted faiths which grew up again, like the jungle, the minute one looked away. Hinduism and Islam are more than faiths; they include a way of life, a system of education, morals, politics, and manners. People nurtured for centuries in these traditions could not be pushed about spiritually like children or the "naive" races of darkest Africa and aboriginal Australia. English and European missionaries of all sects found them baffling. The Anglo-Saxon sense of humor wavers and breaks before them. The articulate Indians are likely to be sophistical and disingenuous; they disappoint you and turn out not to have been converts at all. The uneducated and inarticulate are dead weight. They are so childishly bewildered, or so deeply oppressed by caste and starvation as to be practically inaccessible to missionary efforts. But they respond to social work.

So, while we have many "good" missionaries in fiction about India, we have those who are so much at a loss or so thick-skinned that they are the butts of the gentle, or not too gentle, cynicism aimed at all their kind. Bromfield neatly balances his "good" ones, the Smileys, against his "bad" ones, the Simons. Kipling does not give missionaries much space, but in "The Judgment of Dungara" (*Plain Tales*) he makes hilarious game of the defeat of their assurance by one wrong step.

Christine Weston in *Indigo* is skeptical about them. Her Scottish pair could not compete with India's antiquity and fertility, and it is the French Catholic priest, Father Sebastien, bigoted though he may be, who comes to the best terms with the country and its people. He is tranquil and tolerant and does not expect too much of human nature. (The Catholics, as both French and English novelists agree, made in general a better job of converting the "heathen"; what they had to offer was more ceremonious and colorful than the Protestant inducements to Christianity, and they were more patient and understanding with backsliders.) Forster's *Passage to India* is concerned with larger questions, but he has one former nurse in a Native State, "a stupid woman," say that she is all for chaplains and all against missionaries. Natives after all should not get into heaven, she says; the kindest thing for them was to let them die, then if the missionaries have got hold of them they might indeed slip into heaven somehow, whereas a chaplain—But she is a stupid woman, and Forster allows her to be interrupted at this point.

Though Forster was no missionary, his amusement at the "philosophical" mind of the Maharajah whom he visited with Lowes Dickinson in 1912 gives us the clue to what must have been many a missionary's exasperations and despairs. This Maharajah, who loved Dickinson and philosophy, keeps asking Dickinson, "Where is God? Can Herbert Spencer lead me to him, or should I prefer George Henry Lewes? Oh when will Krishna come and be my friend? Oh Mr. Dickinson!" And Ackerley's Maharajah of Chhokrapur in *Hindu Holiday* (1932) is obsessed by the same large questions and the same positivist Victorian reading which held wide sway in India among people of his kind, an inheritance from Macaulay no doubt: "Is there a God, or is there no God?" rapped out his Highness impatiently. "That is the question. That is what I want to know. Spencer says there *is* a God. Lewes says no. So you must read them, Mr. Ackerley, and tell me which is right."

This is the same Maharajah who turned the car around in order to behold a mongoose on the *left* side of the road, because that was a good omen. And E. J. Thompson testifies in one of his novels that the English missionaries have not paid enough attention to the superstitions and the Ghosts (*bhuts*) that are so important in India, and have overlooked the rich confusion of native deities. His hero Alden has kept his sanity only by occasionally exploring the jungles and by interesting himself in "the quaint and often very engaging beliefs of the heathen." *Le Kilomètre 83* is also emphatic about French neglect of native beliefs in Siam.

Of the actual services rendered to Empire by the missionaries, less is made in the novels than one might expect. But it was a real service. Their work among the "depressed" classes whom the higher castes of natives and many English officials would not bother about, their heroic labors in hospitals and schools, did much throughout the century to delay the mounting antagonism against England. But ironically they played their part in furthering the Indian nationalist movement against England, by helping the industrializing and educational forces that were opening up India to the West.

Of the missionaries in fiction before Mr. Thompson's broadminded Robert Alden, not many are well educated enough to see the value of taking native beliefs into account or realistic enough not to claim too much success with their "converts." But W. W. Hunter, himself an Indian Civilian and a historian and publicist who knew a great deal about Bengal, wrote his novel *The Old Missionary* (1890) about an actual Reverend James Williamson of the Baptist Mission who was apparently an exception to all the rules. He worked among the Bengal hill tribes in that "early time of promise" shortly after the Crown took over from the

Company. He came originally from Cumberland and was a veteran of Trafalgar. He is a noble, patriarchal figure of great reputation among the hillmen. But "real Christianity," he says, can only grow up among the native converts in the second generation. He has been of great service to the British Empire in keeping the hill tribes from revolt at times that were critical for England, and in making with other tribes certain peace agreements that have been advantageous to England.

This singular old warrior is also interested in scholarship and in the native dialect. He is making a dictionary of the hill language, with the help of a native Sanskrit scholar and an Oxford philologist. As a youth he has been fascinated by Cook's *Voyages,* and presumably, in these earlier days before the rise of strenuous professionalism among missionaries as well as other people, many a man of God had been drawn by just such reading to a life of adventure and globe-trotting mixed with Evangelism. The Reverend Mr. Williamson had soon discovered however, that Evangelism alone would accomplish little in India, and so, like many a less intelligent man after him, he had become a medical missionary.

He does Empire a final good turn, at the end of his career, by settling a dispute between Jesuits and Scottish Presbyterians as to which shall move into a certain factory settlement in lower Bengal. Both groups want to keep their hold on it. Through sheer force of faith, judiciously mingled with diplomacy and knowledge of the native mind, the missionary persuades half of the people to migrate to new homes, and the Presbyterians are victorious. The old man is strenuous and fanatical, but also very practical about his work. After his saintlike death he becomes a kind of legend in the district, something like Mrs. Moore in Forster's *Passage to India,* after the people hear of her death at sea.

But men of his kind are rare, both in life and in fiction. In the early novels of the century the missionaries are either detestable, as in Mrs. Sherwood's stories, or frankly fantastic and impossible, like the Spanish priest who tries to convert a Brahmin princess in *The Missionary* (1811) by Lady Morgan. (Lord Castlereagh is the only person known to have liked this warmly colored but inconsequential semi-Gothic effort by that ebullient Irish spirit, who did other kinds of fiction much more effectively.) In modern novels like E. J. Thompson's or Edmund Candler's, the missionaries are beginning to come into their own as civilized and well-rounded though often disillusioned and weary human beings, not very different from the teachers or the doctors who toil and wilt in the great nightmare of India.

But in the fiction of the middle years that come between the very early and the modern novels, the missionaries are pictured as poor and shy and provincial and "worthy," with a distressing taste for making up to influential people—the comfortable bureaucrats or the gracious wives of Residents of Native States, who play lady bountiful and are wise and winning in an aroma of eau-de-cologne and general elegance. In the historical novels, like those about the Mutiny, the missionaries are handled rather perfunctorily as part of the scenery and the properties in a drama that really belongs to the military characters involved. In romantic books like Flora Annie Steel's, the missionaries are too mystical and exalté for the ordinary reader. Many of the most sympathetic ones in all these novels are Scottish, wanderers and adventurers by nature, who took time out from being expert Presbyterians to be expert gardeners also. Around their compounds the desert blossoms, and they make a great point of raising all the flowers that are hardest to raise in tropical climates.

Dorothy Hammond and Alta Jablow on the characteristics of British "novels of empire":

In general, the novels of empire expressed the British devotion to country and dedication to the civilizing mission in Africa. They expressed as well the characterological virtues which reflected British values. In these respects they were similar to and supported the contemporaneous nonfiction. Nor did the major themes of the novels differ from those of the factual accounts; in both the descriptions of the land, sport, beasts, and people were the same. Where the novels differ from the nonfiction was in affording greater literary freedom to elaborate on the mystique of Africa and to proliferate all the images. Most significantly, the fictional embellishments presented even more dramatically the case for empire.

Dorothy Hammond and Alta Jablow, in The Africa That Never Was: Four Centuries of British Writing about Africa, *Twayne Publishers, 1970.*

In fact, not only the Scots but—unless the novelists mislead us completely—missionaries of all nationalities in India are fanatical gardeners. A passion for horticulture is meant to be, apparently, one of their attractive traits, a redeeming feature in the eyes of possibly unsympathetic readers who might feel that these hard-working liaison-officers between jungle and Empire would do better to stay at home and mind their own business. Yet all that these crisp bright gardens seem to accomplish is to accentuate for the reader the stubborn perversity of the missionary mind. One can see the gardens more charitably, of course, as part of the great Homesickness Cult or complex that thrives so richly among Europeans in India; the nostalgia of

exile is deepened and at the same time assuaged by the smell of mignonette or wallflowers or stock. But the same obstinacy that insists upon making Christians out of Hindus and Moslems, insists also upon making primroses and pinks grow where no self-respecting pink or primrose should. It is an involuntary gesture of defiance against the whole East to make the simple, cheerful little plants that do best in cottage gardens at Home thrive in a climate completely alien to them. But people who feel justified in wanting to uproot and transplant whole races from the faiths on which their civilization has rested for ages have to be hardy and obtuse; difficulty of any sort, horticultural or spiritual, is a challenge. These tidy English flowers blooming after the monsoon rains speak the missionary mind; they symbolize its qualities wherever it is found. It does not like jungle gardens of the kind that Mrs. Lyttleton, the courageous Englishwoman in *Indigo,* allows to run wild on her property, preferring cottage tulips to jasmine, and cottage tulips it will have, come flood, famine, drought, or cholera.

Some novelists ask us to find this imperviousness touching, or quixotic, or "crotchety" in a Dickensian sort of way. Others imply that it is quaint and funny. Some pay grudging tribute to the hardihood and courage, however misplaced, of these single-track minds in India. Only a few are so churlish as to suggest that it is downright officious. But whether presented as quaint or picturesque or sentimental or thick-skinned, the missionaries are generally dependable walk-on characters, always good for local color. And they are quite rightly given their due as part of the great "lift" that missions in general gave to the prestige of Empire. The Lord's cause was also that of the Raj.

The French, with their usual adaptability, provided the kind of Catholic missionaries in Indo-China who could make a success of their job without arrogance. In many and many a novel about French engineers or scientists or soldiers in "Siam-Cambodge" the missionary-priest is a sympathetic character, often able to help bridgebuilders, explorers, or financiers to avoid disastrous clashes with native superstitions. He understands these, and the native dialects as well, something many of his English confrères have not bothered about. He pours oil upon the troubled waters, making allowances for what the climate can do to white men in the way of susceptibility to opium, loose women, and other "moral microbes" that may beset them. Your typical English or American missionary is a hard and selfless worker; his French colleague never makes the mistake of being overzealous or "pressing" too hard, and he has the advantage of a finer degree of psychological insight into people in general and natives in particular. He may be a bit of a schemer, but he is never obtuse. He is typical of the entire difference of attitude toward colonial situations that makes such a wide cleavage between English and French colonial policy. Even in English novels where

French "religious" figure now and again, as in Pamela Hinkson's *Golden Rose* (1944), the French nuns have built up the most efficient nursing orders, profiting by a calm and shrewd knowledge of the native mind and an appreciation of the natives as people.

Half and Half. Another character that proved of perennial interest in novels about India throughout the century, was started on his way even earlier than the missionaries. This is the half-caste or Eurasian, or, as he is more often called nowadays, the Anglo-Indian. He has always been a difficult and uncomfortable by-product of empire. In the eighteenth century stories about the old-fashioned Nabobs, he is taken more or less for granted. The cheerfully earthy minds of the time were not squeamish about Anglo-native alliances and their resulting troops of brown children. There were a few such alliances in the early history of the Thackerays in India. But with the rise of Evangelical and middle-class morality, the attitude changed. To be sure, a certain amount of liberal feeling about the dark races prevailed after the antislavery campaigns of Wilberforce and his cohorts, and after the equalitarian doctrines of the French Revolution had swept a few dark-skinned little orphan boys or beautiful and virtuous Indian maidens into the novels of such large-minded radicals—often Unitarians or Quakers—as Amelia Opie, Mary Wollstonecraft, Robert Bage, or Thomas Holcroft. But by 1834 when William Brown Hockley is lamenting the situation of these hybrids in *The Widow of Calcutta,* the *Half-Caste Daughter and Other Sketches* it is clear that Rousseau and St. Pierre and all the "Noble Savages" have lost ground. Colonel Berners is about to welcome his child who is returning from England, but alas!

> His daughter was a half-caste! However gifted by nature,—by an education which wealth had spared no cost to perfect,—by loveliness, or by intellect—*still* a half-caste subjected to all the stain and stigma under which that unhappy race withers,—under which its very virtues become the instruments to render that stigma less tolerable.

The stigma has not been removed for the little Indian boy, Chandranath, in Maud Diver's *Far to Seek* (1921). He is rescued from bullies at school by Lance, son of Desmond (Miss Diver's favorite hero), and by Roy, himself of mixed English and Indian blood. But it is the right *kind* of Indian blood and that makes the difference. Chandranath, it seems, is not of the right "jat." Even Roy, the son of an Indian princess, is advised by Lance not to talk to the other boys about his mother.

Kipling, in one of his gentler and more touching stories, "Without Benefit of Clergy," can allow nothing but a tragic ending for his ill-starred pair—the young English officer and the beautiful Mohammedan girl—even though the tale was written in the early years

when he was still able to see such unblessed unions as simply a part of India's great human panorama. He becomes progressively less sympathetic with them and more censorious as time goes on, and his work is increasingly dominated by the gospel of Empire. For Somerset Maugham, the Anglo-Malay alliances, in many a fine short story, produce sharp dramatic situations, but they must of necessity be developed in a furtive and sultry moral atmosphere that leads to violent and tragic endings. Such an ending overtakes George Orwell's more modern hero in *Burmese Days* (1935).

In modern fiction the half-caste is still amazingly stereotyped. He might as well be the weak and wily misfit of Flora Annie Steel's books. Miss Murgatroyd in *The Rains Came* is pitiable perhaps, but uneasy, over-ingratiating, vaguely repulsive to almost everyone. So is the tougher and more complicated Thelma in Hitrec's excellent *Son of the Moon* (1947). So is the foreman Boodrie in *Indigo,* even when seen through the eyes of the French boy Jacques, who has no color prejudice when it comes to Indians in general.

As in the case of the successful French missionaries, the French, like the Dutch, feel less called upon than the British to draw the color line in their colonial possessions. The tolerant attitude toward Annamese or Cambodian liaisons with French officers or engineers is merely one example of the generally casual and easy-going view which prevailed in all parts of the French Empire of which the French novelists have written so colorfully. In Algeria, Madagascar, Malaya, the South Seas, or wherever the young Frenchman may find himself, no ugly whispers or pointing fingers ruin his peaceful little idylls with "les brunes" of whatever shade or caste or tribe. These romantic episodes, though they may end on a nostalgic or wistful note, are cheerful and comforting and natural enough while they are going on. Perhaps Rousseau and Bernardin, or merely Loti and Gauguin, had something to do with this attitude. In this respect the French novels of empire have a refreshing freedom from the tensions and inhibitions of the Anglo-Saxon code. A more relaxed atmosphere breathes through them.

The edifying and pedagogic novels, then, managed to raise, all unwittingly, some problems and themes and characters larger than themselves and destined to a longer life in better books. Most of these books were to be wholly preoccupied with India, instead of with a moral edification which the Indian setting was merely supposed to drive home or to coat with a little glamor. The frivolous ladies engulfed by their Indian ennui, the relegated younger sons, the zealous men of God, the Eurasians—all were to survive this prelude to empire and carry over into the days of empire itself and the books about it. As a setting for further conquest, India did not yet interest the general public at home, but as a setting for lessons in Evangelical morality it did.

Blood and Thunder. The novels combining blood-and-thunder history with the adventures of a rogue-hero were a more romantic vehicle for bringing a savor of oriental novelty to middle-class readers. Scott, himself responsible for the great vogue of historical novels, did not disdain this more sensational off-shoot of the genre. Richard Middlemas, the noble bastard, but a proud, unpleasant, and tricky fellow nevertheless, makes Scott's *The Surgeon's Daughter* (1827) into a melodrama of an eighteenth century adventurer in the service of the East India Company. In order to win his Scottish sweetheart, this not very genial rascal must spend three years of probation as a doctor. And what likelier proving ground for character, and for the knack of picking up a fortune, than India? She came to serve this purpose for generations of writers who were to feel, as Scott did no doubt, that intrigue and mystery, with a smattering of historical fact for substance, could be nowhere more easily combined than in the kingdom of Mysore, which the Company had determined to snatch from the usurper Hyder Ali by military force. It was a formula that "had everything," including trained elephants who crush people, unscrupulous potentates living in more than Oriental splendor, and the innocent Scottish maiden who is snatched at the eleventh hour from the zenana of Tippoo Sultan.

This was a recipe that served well a variety of writers from William Browne Hockley and Colonel Meadows-Taylor to their more sophisticated descendants like Talbot Mundy. Hockley and Taylor, whose books flourished from the 1820s to the 1840s, were able to take advantage of the vogue of the criminal hero. Widely popular in English fiction since Defoe, this daring figure was revived in the thirties by Ainsworth and Bulwer. Hockley's *The Memoirs of a Brahmin; or, The Fatal Jewels* (1843) and his earlier *Pandurang Hari; or, Memoirs of a Hindoo* (1826) purport to let the rogue or criminal tell his own story. Against an Indian background such a villain-hero need not be romanticized or sentimentalized after the fashion of Bulwer's and Ainsworth's highwaymen, who so aroused and annoyed Thackeray. His background absolves him at once of cheapness and sentimentality. He may hold the reader's interest and credulity without having to engage his sympathy, since all manner of villainy must obviously be possible in India, where it is at such a safe distance as to be inoffensive.

Many of these books about criminals were a strange compound of claptrap, research, and a dash of Gothic horror to add spice to the mixture. But Meadows-Taylor's *Confessions of a Thug* (1837) was a good deal better than that. It became a genuine Victorian thriller of classic dimensions, providing an authentic Indian theme for many mystery stories, even, as Edmund

Wilson believes, for Dickens's unfinished *Edwin Drood.* It mixed India and its horrifying cult of Thuggee so thoroughly into the materials of the Victorian adventure story, the thriller, and the detective story that it will probably never be outgrown or worn out. These novels did a service to Empire in publicizing the heroic efforts of British soldiers and administrators to root out the criminals; they were a talking point for the advocates of British rule as a pacifying and purifying force in its dominions.

Meadows-Taylor was the first serious historical novelist about India and surely one of the first serious-minded adventurers in what became practically the land of his adoption (he spent forty years there). He was far ahead of his time in seeing the necessity of learning native languages, and by sheer integrity, sagacity, and courage became the first "career man" in India to take the native seriously and respectfully as a civilized being. That he did so, we know through his autobiography and novels. Recently published letters show that he was not well-informed about India as a whole. But he gives a lift to English prestige of the better kind. He was, furthermore, independent of Company patronage. At eighteen he was assistant police superintendent over a large district, taking part in running down Thugs and robbers, and in several military expeditions. So his trilogy of novels about Indian history carries more weight than most. His exciting narrative of a Thug's career, told as though by the protagonist himself, is far better than the ordinary run of first-person crime stories, whether set in England or India. During several "placid" Victorian decades it satisfied the reader's thirst for violence. And murder, so the Victorians believed, is cleaner than sex. . . .

Susanne Howe on English fiction about India:

Novels about India provide more vicarious discomfort than anyone is entitled to. They are among the unhappiest books in the language. They are long on atmosphere, but short on humor and on hope. And what an atmosphere it is! Heavy with the sense of futility and failure, gluey with homesickness, and cloudy with puzzlement, it clogs the reader's mind with second-hand misery. It smells at some seasons of the drought and dust, at others of the steaming rains, and always of too many millions of unhealthy, caste-ridden people too close to the famine line. It breathes out the unhappiness of the conquered and of the insensitive Western conqueror in an alien and resentful Eastern world. The growth of his naively surprised "nobody-loves-me" attitude is sometimes touching, more often just annoying, to the reader who follows his fortunes in novels.

Susanne Howe, in Novels of Empire, *Columbia University Press, 1949.*

Martin Green

SOURCE: "Popular Literature and Children's Literature," in *Dreams of Adventure, Deeds of Empire,* Basic Books, Inc., Publishers, 1979, pp. 203-34.

[In the following extract, Green examines the different forms of heroism represented in popular boys' fiction during the nineteenth century.]

Tolstoy gives us the sense—proper to high culture and especially to art—that he is questioning and testing whatever he describes; both the modern system, and the adventures of its expansion. Now we must look to narratives and discussions which seem not to test but to advertise their values, which work at a lower artistic and cultural level.

Turning to popular literature will bring out the importance of the how-to-do-it strain of adventure, the Defoe/merchant-caste strain, which gets overshadowed by the chivalric romance when we restrict our attention to works of literary value (serious art being reactionary, and often allied to the aristocracy) but which was very powerful at the popular level. That strain of feeling was also more powerful in nonfiction than in even "democratic" fiction, because art at its purest recoils from predominant truisms, and perhaps especially from mercantile ones. It is in popular biographies and advice books that Defoe's adventurer lived on and inspired others, not in brilliant novels.

Books of this kind had been appearing ever since Defoe's time, though they are meagerly represented in the histories of literature. I have mentioned one or two eighteenth-century writers like Dilworth; there were the stories of the sea and sailors; and of course there was the unending sequence of reissues and adaptations of *Robinson Crusoe.* But in the nineteenth century, this literature changed its character somewhat, as did more serious literature, in response to changing cultural forces, and also found new forms of expression. In the first half of this chapter, then, I shall not be tracing the development of fictional motifs, or evoking the historical background that gave those motifs resonance, but categorizing the culture heroes of the time—those that were in effect variants on the adventurer theme, and reinforcements of that idea. In the second half I shall describe motifs in the children's and popular literature of the time, or that part of it that was adventurous.

My discussion in the other chapters is restricted to writers of first-class intelligence and sensibility. Even Cooper, though far from being a great novelist, a man of great intelligence. Since we are dealing with a cultural image as it got expressed in literature, and dealing with it in a literary way, it was necessary to choose material one can respect from that point of view. But it is necessary also to remember the other expressions of that image, less respectable and substantial from that point of view, but as effective or more so as a cultural influence. (For evidence of that effectiveness I rely on sales figures; no one seems to know what happens to books once bought—what they do inside the reading audience's heads.)

First of all, the work of Samuel Smiles, who was born in 1812, and became famous in 1859 with a book called *Self-Help,* which sold 25,000 copies in its year of publication, and 250,000 by 1900. It was translated into nearly every European language, and several Indian ones, plus Japanese, Arabic, and Turkish. In Italy there was an edition which substituted examples of self-help from Italian history for those British anecdotes which Smiles had chosen—anecdotes which made up nine-tenths of his book. This book was subtitled "Illustrations of Conduct and Perseverance," and it promised in effect to explain the secret of the superior energy and success of the Anglo-Saxons, their superior adaptation to the modern system. The *Revue des Deux Mondes* review took it as that, and only feared that Frenchmen's chauvinist prejudice might deny them access to this new source of moral energy. In his *Autobiography,* Smiles said that he wrote it to illustrate PERSEVERANCE, the great word of George Stephenson, the railway engineer.

Smiles was a Scotsman, a Utilitarian, and something of a radical in early life. Not an adventurer, then, but something of a Puritan. (He was a friend of Ebenezer Elliott, the Corn Law Rhymer of Sheffield.) And what this book teaches is how to acquire, by making a cult of these examples of great men and great actions, the standard virtues of Victorian England. What those are is perhaps sufficiently indicated by the titles of his later books: *Character,* 1871, *Thrift,* 1875, and *Duty,* 1880. They contain much warning against drink, and praise of savings banks; but basically these are collections of anecdotes about great men, noble boys, and Mothers (no need for an honorific for *them*). Some of the men most often cited are Washington, Wallerstein, Wellington, and Scott—a list somewhat equivalent to Defoe's list of Protestant heroes. Cobbett is described as the typical Englishman in character, and contrasted with Herder and Fichte; he was coarse and vulgar, compared with such Continental intellectuals, but had a strong undercurrent of poetry in his nature, and the tenderest regard for the character of women; though anything but refined, he was a true Englishman—pure, temperate, self-denying, industrious, vigorous, and energetic.

In the intellectual line, the greatest man who ever lived was Newton. (This is what Defoe and the Encyclopaedists said, but it's worth recalling that Swift dismissed Newton as a mechanic; Smiles is clearly on Defoe's side—the Encyclopaedists' side—in the Swift-Defoe battle.)

More controversial choices of exemplars of virtue, but characteristic of Smiles, are Savonarola and Grace Darling, the lifeboat heroine. Both of these are puritan, and in their different ways, modernist figures. On the other side, Goethe, though a great poet, is not a man to copy, because he was amoral and an aesthete. Smiles has his suspicions of art, and warns us against certain kinds of literature—the leprous book, the scrofulous book, and even the giggling book. (Petronius? Pope? Nabokov?)

Edward Said on the importance of representation to Orientalism:

Orientalism is premised upon exteriority, that is, on the fact that the Orientalist, poet or scholar, makes the Orient speak, describes the Orient, renders its mysteries plain for and to the West. He is never concerned with the Orient except as the first cause of what he says. What he says and writes, by virtue of the fact that it is said or written, is meant to indicate that the Orientalist is outside the Orient, both as an existential and as a moral fact. The principal product of this exteriority is of course representation: as early as Aeschylus's play *The Persians* the Orient is transformed from a very far distant and often threatening Otherness into figures that are relatively familiar (in Aeschylus's case, grieving Asiatic women). The dramatic immediacy of representation in *The Persians* obscures the fact that the audience is watching a highly artificial enactment of what a non-Oriental has made into a symbol for the whole Orient. My analysis of the Orientalist text therefore places emphasis on the evidence, which is by no means invisible, for such representations *as representations,* not as "natural" depictions of the Orient. This evidence is found just as prominently in the so-called truthful text (histories, philological analyses, political treatises) as in the avowedly artistic (i.e., openly imaginative) text. The things to look at are style, figures of speech, setting, narrative devices, historical and social circumstances, *not* the correctness of the representation nor its fidelity to some great original. The exteriority of the representation is always governed by some version of the truism that if the Orient could represent itself, it would; since it cannot, the representation does the job, for the West, and *faute de mieux,* for the poor Orient.

Edward W. Said, in Orientalism, *Pantheon Books, 1978.*

Considerably more interesting are his *Lives of the Engineers,* which began with *The Life of George Stephenson,* the great railway pioneer, who lived from 1781 to 1848. Smiles complained that history had been monopolized by kings and warriors and war, and claimed attention for engineers, the heroes of peace. Some phrases from the English reviews will indicate the kind of interest this biography has. "Few romances possess so strong an interest as this life, so brave, so simple, so strenuous in its faith . . . the true history of a working man." Stephenson was a true Victorian hero, and his rise from poverty to fame and fortune was felt to be adventure in the best sense—something in competition with, though not in hostility to, literal adventure in the Crusoe sense. "We see the vast achievements and the epic story of this age of ours more than half comprised in the feats of its strongest and most successful worker . . . we may designate him a hero . . . To young men faltering, it gives lessons which should supply fresh vigour. The continuous effort, the persistent valour, the daring ingenuity, and ever-active intellect of this collier boy . . ." Crusoe's virtues are seen at work in a somewhat different setting.

Smiles's importance is that he was so typical of nineteenth-century opinion. It is easy to recognize in his idea of manliness a vulgarized version of Emerson's, and indeed of other Victorian moralists. Stephenson was a *man*; he hated foppery and frippery above all things; he didn't drink, but ran and wrestled, and above all, worked. Emerson in fact, as Smiles tells us, said it was worth crossing the Atlantic just to meet Stephenson, he had such native force of character and intellect.

Smiles connects the cult of manliness, again in no unique way, with the cult of machinery. The ideas of work and workman subsume both. "There is indeed a peculiar fascination about an engine, to the intelligent workman who watches and feeds it. It is almost sublime in its untiring industry and quiet power; capable of performing the most gigantic work, yet so docile that a child's hand may guide it" (p. 28). Such a workman often speaks of his machine "with glowing admiration." All the improvements to machinery have come from workmen, not from scientists or philosophers. "This daily contemplation of the steam engine, and the sight of its steady action, is an education of itself to the ingenious and thoughtful workman." Defoe, I want to suggest, would have assented, would almost certainly have come to some such judgment, had he lived in the nineteenth century. It is a suggestive crystallization of the technocratic idea, which was powerful all through the century, though it rarely reached high levels of expression, literarily.

It figured largely in Mark Twain's life, however (his experience with the Paige type-setting machine constitutes a sardonic comment on the last sentence quoted), and he developed it literarily in *Connecticut Yankee* and other stories. It was also quite brilliantly expressed in fiction by Kipling and Wells; and commented on by Henry Adams, in "The Virgin and the Dynamo." The cult of the engineer may be said to have replaced in the nineteenth century Defoe's eighteenth-century cult of the merchant, as the former came to seem more the hero of peace, constructiveness, and the modern system.

Smiles's later *Lives of the Engineers* are particularly interesting for us because, alongside the biographies, they include histories of particular cities from a point of view very close to Defoe's, and continue the imaginative work he did in *The Tour*. We are shown England from a modern system point of view. Thus, in the Introduction we are told that England is not fertile—it has been *made* fertile by its industry, its canals, and other works of its engineers and improvers (p. 74). This work is moreover quite new. Not long ago, our wool was made into cloth in Flanders, our mines dug by Germans, our windmills built by the Dutch, and so on. Our apparent luck is based on our self-help—and will last only as long as our virtue does. This is exactly the approach Defoe took in his *Tour,* and his *Essay on Projects,* and Smiles emphasizes exactly what Defoe emphasized. He tells us for instance that the roads recently built in the Highlands of Scotland have had a moral influence. Telford, the engineer in charge, called the road-building a Working Academy, which turned out eight hundred improved workmen every year, and he meant improved as citizens too. (The image, and the tone, are very close to Twain's "factory of men" in *Connecticut Yankee*.) The change this road-building has made to Scotland can be measured in the fact that back in the 1745 Rebellion, when the district of Balmoral was remote from civilization, a whole regiment of Jacobite rebels was raised there, in a district "where *now* our Queen is so beloved."

Volume I is mostly about James Brindley, who built his first canal in 1761, but it also gives an account of Manchester in 1740. Volume II is mostly about Rennie and Smeaton—the latter built his first lighthouse in 1759—but it also gives a history of docks and bridges, and of the pirates who flourished before these modernizations. Volume III is mostly about Telford and Scotland; and it is notable how many of these men were Scots. Volume IV is about Watt and Boulton—Watt's first steam engine was built in 1766, and Arkwright's spinning jenny was built three years later; but also about Birmingham. Thus these four volumes are a history of England during its Industrial Revolution, complete with exempla and heroes, exactly what Defoe wanted, and very like what Defoe produced in that line.

In *Self-Help* Smiles also took many examples of heroism from the suppression of the Indian Mutiny, which had only just occurred; and in *Duty* he praised Sir Charles Napier, John and Henry Lawrence, and Outram, as military heroes of the Indian Service. This gives us the cue to put that kind of Victorian hero beside Smiles's engineers; such kinds of men surround and support figures like Stanley—perhaps the most famous

Victorian adventurer—in a cultural pantheon. The Indian soldiers are not Cortes or Clive types, military conquerors on the grand scale. They are suitable heroes for merchants, and their allies in the modern world system. But they assimilate as much of the conquistador material as could be assimilated into a Crusoe form.

As our example of the Indian hero let us take the Lawrence brothers, and their work in the Punjab in the mid-nineteenth century. They administered this province, after England took it away from the Sikhs in 1848, and made it the showpiece of British India. It was 74,000 square miles, of which the population was only one-fifth Sikh, though they were dominant. The British built the Grand Canal of the Punjab, nearly 250 miles long; and in four years built 3,000 miles of road, and surveyed 5,000 more, that was to be the Grand Trunk Road which Kipling celebrated.

The Lawrences were a Scots-Irish military family, very poor and in most senses underprivileged. John was the sixth son and eighth child, and said that at school "I was flogged every day of my life, except one, and then I was flogged twice" (Bosworth-Smith, *Life of Lord Lawrence,* p. 15). But it must have been a ruling-caste training place, for there were other boys at the school who were to become Indian heroes—besides the Lawrence brothers themselves. There was, for instance, Lord Gough, later to be the victor of Chillianwallah and conqueror of Gujerat. It was a school like Kipling's United Services College, in effect. These poor but ruling-caste Ulstermen (like but unlike the Ulstermen prominent on the American frontier) provided much of England's imperialist strength.

Bosworth-Smith's characterization of John Lawrence in his official biography is particularly interesting. Of Herculean physique, we are told, he had the cut of the Jats he ruled, with their handsome prominent features and tall bony frames; and the Jats are said to be descended from the ancient Goths. There was no ounce of superfluous fat upon John Lawrence, and he could hold a cannonball at arm's length. His friends, we are told, called him Oliver, after Cromwell, "the greatest and most downright and God-fearing of Englishmen" (p. 100). It was of course Carlyle's *Heroes and Hero-Worship* essay on Cromwell that they and Bosworth-Smith were thinking of. And the latter's whole account draws heavily on Carlyle's value-images.[1]

Lawrence was brave and strong and rough as a giant, but tender as a woman and simple as a child. He was heroically simple; he had the rough humor, the boisterous pranks, the wild spirit of adventure we associate with the Norwegian troll. When the rugged lineaments and deep furrows of his grand countenance are described, Bosworth-Smith quotes Milton's lines describing Satan. But the Satanic associations could be misleading. Lawrence was above all things a moral hero.

Smiles says, in *Self-Help,* that Delhi was taken and India saved during the Mutiny by the personal character of Sir John Lawrence. His eye glared terribly when he saw anything mean or cowardly or wrong. They called him King John on the frontier. He was made Viceroy in 1864, and came home a peer in 1869, one of the great Victorian heroes.

Comparing the Lawrence brothers, Bosworth-Smith (a schoolmaster at Harrow) categorized John as Scots in character, Henry as Irish. The latter was, it seems, the more imaginative, the gentler, the more literary. He married a rather literary woman, his second cousin Honoria, a governess who had been a great friend of his sister Letitia, who herself was an Evangelical in the circle of Wilberforce and Thornton. (This illustrates the range of ruling-class types, and the alliance between them.) John, we are told, was passionately fond of Scott, but otherwise seems to have been aesthetically philistine. Henry and Honoria were more imaginative. The brothers quarreled over the administration of the Punjab, though with great dignity and mutual respect. Henry went into semiretirement, but he emerged again to be Resident at Lucknow, where he died, a martyr, during the Mutiny.

Henry gathered around him a number of young men, who were destined to have remarkable careers in India. There were, for instance, William Hodson, famous for the corps he formed, Hodson's Foot; John Nicholson, famous for the relief of Delhi during the Mutiny; and James Abbott, who was, we are told, accepted as prophet, priest, and king, by the fierce Yusupzais of the Hozara country. This phrasing I take from Maud Diver's biography of Honoria Lawrence, and it reminds us of Kipling, but more importantly it reminds us of the enormous imaginative charge of these Indian careers, where it seemed that everyone English was a Man Who Could Be King. Another of Henry Lawrence's young men was Herbert Edwardes, who was sent to Jummu to be, as he said, a Lieutenant of Foot advising the King of the Mountains. Edwardes, who wrote remarkably well, again and again in his letters names that kind of excitement. "I found five countries oppressed by one tyrant—and I removed him. I found three chiefs in exile—and I restored them. Those countries and those chiefs rallied round me in the hour of need. When I held up my hand for soldiers, they came. When I left the province, during an imperial war, peace reigned behind me" (Maud Diver, *Honoria Lawrence,* p. 319). John Nicholson was literally worshiped by a sect, the Nikkulseynites, whom he cursed and flogged for doing so. Edwardes's obituary comment on Henry was as Carlylean as Bosworth-Smith's on John: "How much of the *man* there was in him. How unsubdued he was. How his great purposes, his fierce will, generous impulses, and strong passions raged within him, making him the fine, genuine character we knew. . . ."

One final quotation from Edwardes will make clear the moral and imaginative tone of the Victorian cult of Empire itself. In a letter of 1846, after a satirical description of some Sikhs, he continues, "These barbarous phases of society, into which an educated man descends as into a pit of lions, have, after all, a wild, almost terrible interest. There is something noble in putting the hand of civilization on the mane of a nation like the Punjab (if I may borrow Spenser's allegory) and *looking down* brute passions. What a victory! to bind a bullying people with a garland—to impose security of life, good order, and law as fine, upon a whole nation." The military impulse and military pride were sanctified and subdued to other caste values.[2]

There we have a kind of Victorian hero, obviously carrying a very potent image, who might have seemed quite unrelatable to the engineer and the merchant. In fact, India was a theater of empire where the military caste provided the leading actors, and even quite displaced the merchants from public view. But administrative civilians were heroes in India; their tasks more constructive, but their powers still exhilarating. I take as an example H. M. Kisch, whose letters were published as *A Young Victorian in India* in 1957. Mr. Kisch, who was born in 1850, arrived in India in 1873, and immediately found himself in charge of "198 square miles of famine" (p. 24). He wrote home that he gave employment to 5000 people every day, and fed another 3000 a day free. He had an establishment of 300 and ruled a population of 100,000. In 1874 he recalled with pride that when he arrived he couldn't dig a tank, build a grain store, or anything else. And a little later he wrote, "Since I last wrote, I have dammed several of the rivers in my circle. . . ." (p. 45). In 1876, his subdivision was 782 square miles, and contained a population of 154,000—mostly of an aboriginal tribe, "far superior to Bengalis." (That prejudice against the Hindus, and particularly the Bengalis, was a large feature of English rule in India; an imperial power prefers to deal with a primitive or aboriginal tribe.) They treated even his music box as a god.

It was in India that the institution of Guides originated; although guides and scouts were obviously famous long before, in the American colonies; perhaps I should say, it was in India that something was instituted on the British side which was called Guides. In 1839 Henry Lawrence proposed such a corps, trained to work in forest and jungle (to discover enemy positions) where regular troops could not operate. In 1845-1846 Harry Lumsden created the Queen's Corps of Guides (he himself being only twenty-five) and Hodson was his second in command.

The institution much struck the general imagination; Kipling for instance always found such irregular troops much more exciting than the regulars. (This excitement was a fraction of that attaching to the Cossacks in Russia, for the Cossacks were irregulars.) And after the Boer War Colonel Baden-Powell, with Kipling's advice, set out to create such an institution for boys, to save England from the softness and degeneracy threatening it. Baden-Powell designed the Boy Scouts to foster specifically English-boy qualities. He wrote, "Your Englishman . . . is endowed by nature with a spirit of practical discipline. . . . Whether it has been instilled into him by his public school training, by his football and his fagging, or whether it is inbred from previous generations of stern though kindly parents, one cannot say" (Ellis, *The Social History of the Machine Gun*, p. 105). That practical discipline was what the Empire required of its administrators, and the public schools supplied. He set out to develop that English quality by means of simulated and controlled adventures. The Boy Scouts and the public schools are examples of those institutions of large cultural effectiveness which did not operate through books, and which were hardly at all expressed or reflected in serious literature.

One final hero-type in the Victorian constellation is the missionary. In *Self-Help* Smiles tells, for instance, the story of John Williams, a London Society missionary, who died a martyr on Erromanga, a South Seas island. And a book-length version of that sort of narrative is James Paton's *The Story of John G. Paton: or 30 Years Among South Seas Cannibals*. The hero was born in 1824, and after a very severe and pious Scots Presbyterian childhood, set off as a missionary for the New Hebrides in 1858. There he engaged in a thirty-year-long and more or less fruitless struggle with naked savages, who practiced horrid heathen rites, including cannibalism. And the whites he encountered were nearly all rough, swearing traders, who mocked and jostled him. It is an intensely grim life that is described, but it is offered as a call to imitation; John G. Paton is a Christian hero of Christian adventure.

But in Smiles's book there is also much about Livingstone, which gives quite a different image of missionary work; stressing how Livingstone dug canals, built houses, cultivated fields, as he labored among the Bechuanas; he taught them to work as well as to worship. It was by using this stress on the missionaries' work that a man like Smiles could best assimilate it to the work of the explorers and administrators—the work of civilization. And this was a stress by no means foreign to the missionaries themselves; they sometimes took copies of *Robinson Crusoe* with them as well as Bibles. The practice, and later theory, was that the missionary should be a trustee for Western civilization. He taught his tribe habits of work, of justice, of reason, and collected information about their language, culture, natural habitat.

Seen as such, he was first cousin to the heroes of adventure stories; and in fact R. M. Ballantyne blended both images. In his very popular boys' stories, including *Coral Island* itself, he included a strong strain of missionary feeling, quite like that of *The Story of John G. Paton.*

Beside the missionary stood the colporteur, of whom the most famous and the most literary was George Borrow. His *The Bible in Spain,* 1842, told the adventures of an Englishman, attempting to circulate the Scriptures in Spain; but it was also full of picaresque adventures, romantic settings, and chauvinist opinions. "Yes, notwithstanding the misrule of the brutal and sensual Austrian, the doting Bourbon, and above all, the spiritual tyranny of the court of Rome, Spain can still maintain her own. . . ." And it might be Defoe himself who tells us that for two hundred years Spain was the she-butcher of malignant Rome.

Borrow learned to read on *Robinson Crusoe,* and maintained a kind of cult of it. For months, he tells us, "the wondrous volume was my only and principal source of amusement. For hours together I would sit poring over a page till I had become acquainted with the import of every line. . . ." (*Lavengro,* p. 10). Borrow was described as an Elizabethan born out of his time, and in fact illustrates that revival of primitive WASP energies in Victorian England. He traveled far and riskily with his Bibles; he went to Russia in 1823 for the London Missionary Society, and to Spain in 1835, where he told everyone that the Pope was Satan's prime minister, and that they weren't Christians, for they were ignorant of Christ and his teaching. It can give one a valuable insight into the imperialist aspect of the Victorian temperament to remember that Borrow was a pupil at grammar school together with James Brooke, who became Rajah Brooke of Sarawak.

Moreover, people in the nineteenth century continued to read the travel literature of earlier times, which made the explorer one of the great heroes of nineteenth-century culture. One reader we happen to know about is Thoreau, thanks to the researches of J. A. Christie, reported in his *Thoreau as World Traveller.* Thoreau read the collections of Hakluyt, Purchas, and Drake; but also the works of the Spaniards, like Columbus, Balboa, and Ponce de Leon; and also Frobisher, de Soto, Cartier, Hudson. But three-quarters of his travel-reading was written after 1800, and half of that was contemporary—written between 1832 and 1865. This meant books about travels in Japan, the Arctic and Antarctic, the West and South America, and, more latterly, Africa and Asia. He read, Mr. Christie calculates, about twelve such books a year.

One favorite was Alexander Henry, whose *Travels in Canada 1760-76,* Thoreau said, was "like the argument to a great poem on the primitive state of the country and its inhabitants." This—the relation to legend and myth—was Thoreau's main interest in such reading. In his *Journal* for March 16, 1852, he writes, "The volumes of the 15th, 16th, and 17th centuries, which lie so near us on the shelf, are rarely opened, are effectually forgotten and not implied by our literature and newspapers. When I looked into Purchas's *Pilgrims,* it affected me like looking into an impassable swamp, ten feet deep with sphagnum, where the monarchs of the forest, covered with mosses, and stretched out along the ground, were making haste to become peat. These old books suggested a certain fertility, an Ohio soil, as if they were making a humus for new literature to spring in." His language implies fertility even when it asserts decay. And indeed a new literature did spring up—that of Kingsley and Kipling. Whether Thoreau would have approved of that literature we cannot say; but it is clear that he was concerned for the tradition of thought we are following. (We should note a certain likeness between life at Walden and life on Crusoe's island; and a certain fondness in Thoreau for guns and hunting.) He read even the boys' books of the period; notably those of Captain Mayne Reid, whom we shall come to. He read each Reid tale, *Desert Home, Boy Hunters,* and *Forest Exiles,* as they came out in the '50s. (The last is a Swiss Family Robinson set in Peru.) He read and reread Reid's *Young Voyagers; The Boy Hunters in the North.*

Thus the engineer, the explorer, the missionary, and the Indian soldier, all in different ways continued and developed the Crusoe image of heroism. Nineteenth-century readers, at many levels of literacy, made a cult of those heroes. And at the end of the century, boys were urged to do the same, by a variety of institutional means.

If we turn now to fiction, we can begin with Captain Marryat, who wrote very popular books, first for men and then for boys, in the first half of the nineteenth century. He and Cooper together invented the genre of sea fiction at a significant level of intelligence and taste. Marryat was often said to be the best recruiting officer the British Navy had. His *Mr. Midshipman Easy* (1836) is an adventure tale of the kind we have studied, but set on shipboard. The hero's father had been mad about equality and other French Revolutionary ideas, so Jack has some hard lessons in discipline to learn when he joins a ship of the Royal Navy, but he is fundamentally good-natured—being a typical adventure hero. Thus in the course of many adventures he acquires a Black Prince, Mesty, who has tales to tell of savage despotism; a devoted friend and comrade, Gascoigne; and an exotic bride, Donna Agnes, whom he rescues from the clutches of wicked priests. Marryat used several of the motifs that Cooper used (in *The Prairie,* for instance) and which Defoe or Scott had used before him. He modified rather than transformed the energizing myth of the system.

But *Mr. Midshipman Easy* had something of Regency jauntiness, and in 1841 Marryat showed his alertness to the new Victorian mood by writing a more serious, an *Evangelical* adventure tale for children, *Masterman Ready.* This is the story of the Seagrave family who are shipwrecked on to a desert island while on their way to Australia. They learn to survive there in Robinson Crusoe fashion, their adventures rising to a climax with a battle against savages and a last-minute rescue. The differences from Defoe's book largely arise from the fact that the central figure is not an individual but a family. This change was introduced by Wyss in *Swiss Family Robinson* and Marryat consciously set out to improve on Wyss. The change brought with it not only a domestic life-style in the wilderness, but a narrative change, in the more moralistic differentiation of roles played by the different children (and the adults, but they are less important). Here William is definitively a good boy, while Tommy is naughty, and precipitates the catastrophe. By letting the water out of the drinking cask the family relies on while it is besieged by savages, he creates a critical emergency; Masterman Ready saves them by crawling out of the stockade to get water for Mrs. Seagrave and the babies, but is killed.

Ready is Marryat's crucial invention, and one that opened the way for many Victorian adaptations of the adventure tale. He is a common seaman, who has been fifty years at sea, and attaches himself to the genteel Seagrave family, and especially to William, even before the wreck; after the wreck he is their instructor in the practical arts of survival. He is a Natty Bumppo figure, except that he has a wild past to repent—which he narrates serially and edifyingly to William—and that he holds by a more Evangelical morality. His function is indicated by the name "Masterman"; he introduces the principle of social hierarchy even into the wilderness and adventure setting.

The book's Victorian prudence is indicated by its teaching about Empire and about discipline. Ready tells William, " . . . there is more work got out of men in a well-conducted man-of-war than there can in the merchant service in double the time . . . I should never have known what could be done by order and arrangement, if I had not been pressed on board a man-of-war. . . . I found that everything was done in silence" (p. 120). And William is even taught that all empires grow old and decay, that the British Empire will, too, and one day it may be the turn of black races to be great. This, then, is a highly moralized version of modernist adventure. The balance between Brahmin and merchant has shifted in favor of the former, and aristomilitary values are largely repudiated.

That story reflected the early Victorian mood, full of the vigor of English Puritanism, but at odds with the imperial situation. It was replaced in the second half of the century by something almost opposite. English readers soon passed from semi-Defoe adventure to ultra-Scott romance; to, for instance, Charles Kingsley, another extremely popular Victorian writer, and with higher intellectual claims. [3] His Elizabethan adventure tale, *Westward Ho!* was published in 1855, but reprinted very often. It was, for instance, officially distributed to English troops in the Crimean War, and after a new edition in 1857, it was reprinted three times in the '60s, twelve times in the '70s, eight times in the '80s, and altogether thirty-eight times by 1897. It was dedicated to two men, Rajah Brooke of Sarawak, and Bishop Selwyn of New Zealand, both of whom possessed "a virtue even purer and more heroic than the Elizabethan." That suggests Kingsley's key contribution to Victorianism and to the adventure tale—the idea of recapturing Elizabethan vigor (in somewhat purified form)—of assimilating the two ages to each other.

The hero is a "glorious lad," Amyas Leigh, who is much closer to the fiery hero of chivalric romance than to the prudent Crusoe-type, but who represents a new stress, derived from the sagas, on primitive and simple-minded strength. Kingsley describes him as a savage but simple-hearted giant, but also "a symbol of brave young England longing to wing its way out of its island prison, to discover and to traffic, to colonize and to civilize, until no wind can sweep the earth which does not bear the echoes of an English voice" (p. 10). The shout that greeted Amyas's victory was, we are told, "the birth-paean of North America, Australia, New Zealand, the Pacific Isles, of free commerce and free colonization over the whole earth." He is contrasted with his clever consumptive brother, Frank, and his hysterical Catholic cousin Eustace, who has been corrupted by Jesuit teachers, and whose face often writhes with envy, malice, and revenge. Amyas has been brought up by his widowed and martyred mother, and by stately Sir Richard Grenville. There is a lot of North Devon scenery and legend, and many historical characters, with elaborately Elizabethan language, verse, pageants, etc. (Kingsley's method is derived from Scott at his most "historical.") Defoe-virtues are represented only in the merchant, Mr. Salterne, a minor character and not much favored by the author. Romantic chivalry is the keynote of the author's values, and Spenser, Raleigh, and Sidney are his historical heroes.

Unlike Scott, Kingsley is very Protestant and even anti-Catholic. This, like the saga influence, derives from Carlyle, and reflects a recharging of the modern world system with moral righteousness of a more imperialist and military kind. Rose Salterne is the beauty of North Devon, and Amyas and five other glorious lads who love her form a chivalric Brotherhood of the Rose, and take an oath to all go away for three years and not court her, for fear that mutual competition may injure their mutual brotherhood. (This curious way to express their love is to be explained by the author's covert malevolence against Rose, and women, and sex.) While they are away, Rose is seduced by a Spaniard, Don Guzman, and elopes with him to Spain, and subsequently to South America, where Don Guzman is associated with the rape of Peru. Amyas sets off in pursuit of her, but she has been abandoned by Don Guzman and fallen a prey to the Inquisition, in whose hands she dies. Amyas then pursues Don Guzman, finally kills him in the battle that defeated the Armada, and—having been blinded in that battle, and so reduced to a status for which marriage is not inappropriate—marries Ayancora. She is a new and much-to-be repeated motif—adapted from Cortes's Marina; Ayancora is an Indian princess Amyas picked up in his travels, but is really an English girl abandoned in the jungle as a baby and worshiped by the savages because she is white. Marrying her, Amyas incorporates—without any real miscegenation—primitive powers. *Westward Ho!* tells the story of the ousting of Spain by England from the leadership of the modern system, one of the key episodes in the history of that system. But morally and aesthetically it is a lurid fantasy of power and revenge and hatred, on quite a different, and lower, level, from the other adventure tales.

It is worth taking a brief look at some nonfiction by Kingsley, because he was a central figure in the Victorian propaganda for empire and adventure. In *The Heroes or Greek Fairy Tales for My Children* (1868) he says that "heroes" used to mean (when nations were young) men who dared more than other men. Then it came to mean men who helped their countries. And now it means men who suffer pain and grief. (This idea is linked, paradoxically, to the atavistic worship of animal vigor in Amyas Leigh; Kingsley's moral imagination accords the primacy to pain and grief—to passivity—and as a result his historical and political imagination has no effective moral component.)

And his *The Roman and the Teuton* (1864) warns England against the fate of Rome and other empires. In the early years of Christendom, the Teutons were "Forest Children," a young and strong race, like English sailors and navies now, while the Romans were subtle and sophisticated. (William Morris took up this story in his late romance, *The House of the Wolfings.*) The Roman palace was "a sink of corruption," where eunuchs, concubines, spies abounded. Kingsley warns his listeners, who were the undergraduates at Cambridge, where he was Professor of History, to beware of a similar corruption at home. "Forget for a few minutes that you are Englishmen, the freest and bravest nation upon earth, strong in all that gives real strength, and with a volunteer army which is now formidable by numbers and courage. . . ." (p. 32). It can happen in England, too. Unbridled indulgence of the passions produces frivolity and effeminacy, as we see in the French noblesse of the ancien régime, in the Spaniards in America, and in the Italians in their once-great cities. National life is grounded in morality, that is, on the life of the family. "The muscle of the Teuton" was always combined with moral purity, and this gave him, "as it may give you, gentlemen, a calm and steady brain, and a free and loyal heart; the energy which springs from health; the self-respect which comes from self-restraint" . . . and so on (p. 38). Here we see the late Victorian version of the WASP hero, containing recognizable elements of Defoe and Scott, but also something else. That hero now embodies racist and atavistic energies.

Kingsley draws several contrasts between the Roman Empire and the British Empire in India, where the moral roles of imperial power and native population are reversed. "The Goth was very English; and the overcivilized, learned, false, profligate Roman was the very counterpart of the modern Brahmin" (p. 114). Only the English among the Goths' descendants preserved the Gothic heritage of freedom, and so they are anti-imperialist even in India. Kingsley's main hero in this book is Dietrich of Bern, who "went adventures." Dietrich, he says, has been criticized on the grounds that his civilized qualities only went skin-deep; that if you scratched him you'd find a barbarian. But this is really a high compliment, he argues. For Kingsley's message is always to cultivate the barbaric qualities in the individual and the nation; and that is one of the messages of most nineteenth-century adventure tales after him.[4]

That call sounds loud and clear in Kipling and Haggard, who form the climax to this chapter, but there are several other writers who modified or extended the range of the adventure-myth, before I come to them. For instance, there is Alexandre Dumas, one of the adventure tellers with the most international and long-lasting audiences. He will remind us of the pan-European character of modernist imperialism. Dumas was born in 1803, the son of one of Napoleon's generals, and though he lost his father at the age of three, he grew up on the tales of his father's exploits, and on the tales of adventure and bloodshed which the Napoleonic era left behind. His work is a literary equivalent to his father's career. Hippolyte Parigot said, "If Danton and Napoleon were exemplars of Gallic energy, Dumas, in *The Three Musketeers,* is the national novelist who puts it into words."

Having read Scott, and seen Shakespeare performed in Paris, Dumas wrote *Henri III et sa Cour* (staged in 1830), and set out to do for French history what the English writers were doing for English, and the American writers for America. (In 1838 he adapted Cooper's *The Pilot* as a serial for *Le Siècle,* and it attracted five thousand new subscribers in three weeks.) In 1844 he produced *The Three Musketeers,* also as a serial; drawing his historical material, incidentally, from Courtilz, the French Defoe.[5] The confrontation at the heart of that book, between Cardinal Richelieu, compact of old-man wisdom—cold, inhuman, unhealthy—and the four healthy young men, who are a composite representation of France's young-man vitality, is an important new motif of adventure. It reconstitutes the framework of the story of the brothers. That motif was to be repeated again and again, notably by Kipling, in the *Puck of Pook's Hill* stories.

Then Dumas's *Count of Monte Cristo* (1846) made triumphant use of that romantic revenge motif which was employed by later adventure writers, like Jules Verne in *Twenty Thousand Leagues Under the Sea.* And Dumas himself was another example of the writer as entrepreneur, on the largest possible scale. From the beginning he planned to put all French history into fiction; he made a fortune, built himself a great house (called Monte Cristo) like Scott and Twain; and went bankrupt, like Scott and Twain. He translated into literary terms (though terms which literature-as-a-system rejected) the energies of nineteenth-century France. And he distilled a version for child-reader—the new class of readers.

The Critical History of Children's Literature says "During the years from 1840 onward, boys were exploring remote regions, sailing the high seas, escaping from cannibals or redskins in the company of heroes . . ." (p. 237). This was something radically new. The genre of children's literature had been invented, we may roughly say, by the Puritans; in verse quite explicitly by Bunyan and Watts; Bunyan's *Book for Boys and Girls,* 1686, and Watts's *Divine and Moral Songs for Children,* 1715, which was influenced by Bunyan's example; in prose, more accidentally, by Bunyan and Defoe, with *Pilgrim's Progress* and *Robinson Crusoe,* not written for children, but soon given to them to read. The only Tory who contributed was Swift, in *Gulliver's Travels,* and that was read as if Defoe had written it. Later in the eighteenth century there were big successes like *Giles Gingerbread* and *Goody Two-Shoes,* but the message and the myth remained the same. Prudence and piety were the values recommended. The new nineteenth-century development (apart from *Alice in Wonderland,* which stands by itself) was in stories which operated on almost opposite values.

The middle of the nineteenth century saw a very striking and very significant change in the culture's idea of children. Their literature was in effect captured by the aristomilitary caste. Adventure took the place of fable; and the adventure took on the characteristics of romance. Children's literature became boys' literature; it focused its attention on the Empire and the Frontier; and the virtues it taught were dash, pluck, and lionheartedness, not obedience, duty, and piety. For instance, "Oliver Optic" in America (where children's literature had been *very* pious), wrote a Starry Flag series 1867-1869, and an Army and Navy series 1865-

1894. Another dominant interest was science and invention, and that was only slightly indirect in its support of the same values. Edward Stratemeyer wrote a long series about Tom Swift, boy adventurer, full of grit and ginger, who goes up in balloons, drives an electric car, fires an electric rifle, and so on. Stratemeyer started a syndicate of writers to use his name in 1903, because he was so successful. In 1926, 98 percent of the children questioned in a survey listed a Stratemeyer title as a favorite and in the '20s and '30s the Tom Swift series sold fifteen million.

Kingsley, and for that matter Scott, were read also by children, but some authors were read only by them, and these authors too were aristomilitary by affiliation. Among English writers of boys' adventure books, one of the most notable was George Alfred Henty. He wrote nearly eighty such books, with titles like *With Clive in India, With Roberts to Pretoria,* and so on, stories of the achievements of the British army in colonial settings. Henty borrowed a good deal from standard histories and geographies, so his books were also educational. They rely on Anglo-Saxon racism, assigning stereotype identities to Latins, Easterners, and "natives." *By Sheer Pluck* describes Africans as being "just like children. . . . They are always laughing or quarrelling. They are good-natured, and passionate, indolent, but will work hard for a time, clever up to a point, densely stupid beyond."[6] (It is the idea implicit in Defoe's *Four Year Voyage of Captain Roberts*.)

Most of Henty's books begin with a letter addressed to "My dear lads," and teaching some homely truth. He had himself been a puny and sickly boy, who spent most of his childhood in bed, and was bullied at school. Then he took up boxing and yachting, became a man and a war correspondent; and as a writer, became a preacher of manliness. His biography by G. Manville Fenn (published in 1910) says, "There was nothing namby-pamby in Henty's writings. . . . 'No,' he said, 'I never touch on love interest.'" His study was full of pipe-smoke and native weapons, and he had a "Johnsonian" manner with the effete and impudent. When met in the Strand, he had always just returned from wide open spaces, and was sternly silent about subjects of mere chatter. Fenn says his books are "essentially manly, and he used to say that he wanted his boys to be bold, straightforward, and ready to play a young man's part, not to be milksops. He had a horror of a lad who displayed any weak emotion and shrank from shedding blood, or winced at any encounter" (p. 334). He contributed stories to boys' magazines like *Captain, Chums, Great Thoughts, Young England,* and *Union Jack.*

In *The Great War and Modern Memory* Paul Fussell says that the soldiers in that war had learned the language of patriotic duty from Henty and Rider Haggard among the novelists, and from Robert Bridges and Henry Newbolt among the poets. Newbolt was famous for "Lampaida Vitae," with the famous refrain, "Play up, play up, and play the game." He will remind us of the important part played in this manliness propaganda by the public schools. In that poem, and many others, the subject moves from a public school to a colonial battle, and the first is shown to be essentially a preparation for the second. Newbolt was the poet of Clifton College, and wrote a famous poem, "Clifton Chapel," which begins with the stanza,

> This is the Chapel: here, my son,
> Your father thought the thoughts of youth,
> And heard the words that one by one
> The touch of life has turned to truth.
> Here in a day that is not far,
> You, too, may speak with noble ghosts
> Of manhood and the vows of war
> You made before the Lord of Hosts.

(We should not take this school militarism for granted. It was something new, and Thomas Arnold would have been shocked by it.)

At the end Newbolt added a note, "Thirty-seven Old Cliftonian officers served in the campaign of 1887 on the Indian frontier, of whom twenty-two were mentioned in dispatches and six recommended for the D.S.O. Of the 300 Cliftonians who served in the war in South Africa, 30 were killed in action and 14 died of wounds or fever." Then he added a supplementary stanza.

> Clifton remember thy sons who fell
> Fighting far oversea,
> For they in a dark hour remembered well
> Their warfare learned of thee.

Fussell tells us that General Haig, Commander in Chief during the Great War, was a lifelong friend of Newbolt's, and that the latter sneered at Wilfred Owen and poets of that kind as "broken men."

Literature of this kind was spread largely by means of the boys' magazines to which Henty contributed so much. The most famous of these was G. A. Hutchinson's *Boys' Own Paper,* which brought Henty, Ballantyne, Michael Fenn, and W. H. G. Kingston to a large audience, and, as *The Literature and Art of the Empire* says, made patriots of its readers. It began in 1879, belonged to the Religious Tract Society, but was above all patriotic, though it printed foreigners like Jules Verne as well as all the famous English ones. A typical title from Volume I is Kingston's *From Powder-Monkey to Admiral;* the navy had a whole chapel to itself in the cathedral of British patriotism. There were also publishing projects like a series of biographies, edited by Sir Harry Wilson, called "The Builders of Greater Britain" and another edited by Sir William Hunter, called "The Rulers of India." (This is the background against which to see Kipling.) There was, this volume says, a literary empire, consisting of Kipling's India, Haggard's South Africa, Gilbert Parker's Canada, and inspired by the songs of Tennyson, Henley, Newbolt, and Masefield.

Comparable with Henty in popularity, and even more popular internationally, was Captain Mayne Reid, 1818-1883, for a time the most popular English author in Russia, for instance; also translated into French, German, Italian, Spanish. He was born in Ireland of Presbyterian parents, and left for America in 1839. Reid was a militant and indeed military liberal. He fought in the Mexican War, and was the first man in the U.S. force to enter Mexico City. In 1848 he published *The Rifle Rangers,* his first romance, read and admired by Dumas and Lamartine. In 1849, stirred by the news of the revolutions in Europe, he organized a legion to go to Kossuth's support in the revolt of Hungary against Austria. Then his romance *The Scalp Hunters* sold a million copies in England, and was translated into as many languages as *Pilgrim's Progress.* Another book of his published that year, *The Desert House or The English Family Robinson,* began a series.

But he also continued his political activities, and it is important to note their anti-imperialist character. He had become Kossuth's friend, and in 1852 they planned to go together to Milan to fight against the Austrians for Italian freedom. In Reid the connection between book adventure and real-life adventure was especially close. But though he was a Liberal, and Kipling a Tory, both men established rifle clubs, so that young Englishmen should get some military training; and there is no real discontinuity between them culturally, despite the political difference. Like Henty's, Reid's books care as much about geography and history as about moral ideas or narrative—*The Castaways,* 1870, for instance, quotes Wallace and Livingstone for a page at a time, and has a trivial plot that seems not seriously meant. Indeed, because of the predominance of the killer albatross and the hammerhead shark over the human characters, the book produces an effect quite like those of Crane and Conrad.

A very important development in the boys' books of the second half of the century was the synthetic, framework story, like *The Three Musketeers.* One very popular example was W. H. G. Kingston's *The Three Midshipmen.* Kingston (1814-1880) wrote 150 books for children. This one begins at a school, and puts together an English, a Scots, and an Irish boy, who were to appear again and again in a whole series of books. The English boy, Jack Rogers, takes the lead; he is a squire's son, solid and pugnacious; Alick Murray is serious, clever, and cautious; while Paddy Adair is full of fun, lovable, but thoughtless. This trio is the United Kingdom in literary form, and they act out the same function—of dominating the rest of the empire.

At school the boys have to deal with a soft, fat sneak called Bully Pigeon, who embodies the least attractive aspects of Englishness and turns up later in their lives as a cowardly civilian in the Mediterranean, and then as a would-be sophisticate on their ship to China. Bully Pigeon boasts himself an atheist, but whines when he gets into trouble, and soon dies. Aboard ship, Honest Dick Needham, of the lower classes, comes to the help of the young gentlemen time and time again. In the Mediterranean, the three chase Greek pirates and smash Mehmet Ali on the Sultan of Turkey's behalf. Their adventures frequently lead to explosions, in which human limbs mingle with fragments of stone and iron. Then they go to Sierra Leone, where they chase slavers, and first meet the Portuguese villain, Dom Diogo, whom they pursue through several episodes. (England had gained great moral prestige by suppressing the slave trade in its own dominions, and Portugal great infamy by not doing so.) They meet a Black Prince and acquire a faithful Friday-style Negro, Wasser. Later they go to Singapore and Hong Kong, where they chase opium clippers. Thus they cover the whole empire, and make it, by their adventures, vivid and glorious to their readers.

Rather similar in synthetic form is R. M. Ballantyne's *Coral Island.* In this adventure three boys are wrecked on an island; Jack Martin is eighteen and a natural leader; Ralph, who tells the story, is fifteen and serious and "old-fashioned," and Peterkin Gay is thirteen or fourteen, little and quick and mischievous.[7] Like Crusoe, they land with an axe, an oar, an iron hoop, a telescope, some whipcord and a broken penknife, and have to make do. But Ballantyne puts much more stress than Defoe does on the Paradisal beauty of both land and sea, and the heroes are seen more romantically and chivalrically than Crusoe. (Ballantyne was much influenced by Scott.) Jack is lion-like; tall, strapping, broad-shouldered, handsome, good-humored; Peterkin expects him to become king of a native population. When cannibals arrive (looking more like demons than human beings) Jack goes berserk while fighting them. (The idea of an Englishman going berserk, when pushed too far, was a much-repeated device, derived from the sagas.) Later they get to Fiji, where the natives, being pagans, feed their eels with babies, and fill their temple with human bones. The story contains some Evangelical teaching, but puts more stress on the related secular virtues, for instance, cold bathing and training in observation. (This is the book which William Golding transvalued to write *Lord of the Flies,* one of the clearest cases of post-1945 reversal of sentiment.)

Another major force in fiction and ideas at the popular level in the nineteenth century was Jules Verne, and his followers. Though Verne imitated Dumas to begin with, he had more in common with Defoe than with Scott, while Dumas's affinity was the reverse. Verne's work is thought of usually as science fiction, but it is just as much adventure fiction, and his heroes are adventurers. And his case is an interesting one for us because there have been some studies of his work, in French, which are not too far removed from ours in point of view.

Jules Verne was born in 1828, and though he trained in law, always wanted to write. He met Dumas in 1849, sat in his box for the first stage performance of *Three Musketeers,* and became a sort of secretary to him. But he also made friends with Jacques Arago, a blind explorer, whose brother was an astronomer. Verne had always loved science, and also the sea and ships. In 1862 he wrote *Cinq Semaines en Ballon,* the story of a British eccentric, Dr. Ferguson, who floats across Africa in a balloon. He took this novel to a publisher, Jules Hetzel, a liberal who had been Lamartine's Chef de Cabinet in his Ministry in 1848, and thereafter for a time exiled by Napoleon III. (This liberal connection expresses an important tendency in the books.)

Hetzel gradually saw the immense potential in Verne's work. In 1866 the latter produced *Les Aventures du Capitaine Hatteras,* about an English explorer, who races against his American rival, Altamont, to discover the North Pole; and for this book Hetzel wrote an advertising explanation of Verne's work in general: "Son but est, en effet, de résumer toutes les connaissances géographiques, géologiques, physiques, astronomiques, amassées par la science moderne, et de faire, sous la forme attrayante et pittoresque qui lui est propre, l'histoire de l'univers" (M-H. Huet, in *L'Histoire des Voyages Extraordinaires,* p. 20).

He used as models for his heroes mostly explorers like Livingstone, Stanley, Burton, De Brazza, the heroes of the nineteenth century. It is notable how many of his leading figures were Anglo-Saxon; Huet counts ninety Americans, eighty English, thirty Russians, and so on. The French tend to appear as comic savants, like Paganel, or comic servants, like Passepartout. But Verne had in fact strong anti-English prejudices; though he admired their tunnels and bridges, and their energy, sense, and progress, he hated their cruelty and love of profit.[8] But still he judged them only by their own, modern system standards.

So it is not surprising that Verne wrote several Robinsonaden: *L'Oncle Robinson, L'Ecole des Robinsons, La Seconde Patrie* (an avowed continuation of *The Swiss Family Robinson*), and *Deux Ans de Vacances.* And his work is largely an energizing myth of the modern system. It is similar to Defoe's in emotional character. His works cannot be said to be novels, someone says, because they do not deal with love. He always declared he couldn't handle that subject; on the

other hand he was proud of and conscientious about the science he included. Michel Corday says (quoted by Jean Jules-Verne) that he helped young readers to escape their "stupid jail. . . . He inspired in us a desire to know about the universe, a taste for science, a dedication to masculine forms of energy."

When Chesneaux says that Verne is a Utopian Socialist, he is thinking of the Saint-Simonian brand of socialism; and in particular of the technocrats. The Saint-Simonian, Enfantin, became administrator of the French railways under the Third Empire, and other Saint-Simonians were employed in big projects like the Suez Canal and the plan for a Channel tunnel. Verne's friend Nadar, who is depicted in some of the novels, was de Lesseps's secretary. He often describes possible engineering projects, like a giant lighthouse on Cape Horn, or a canal to irrigate the Sahara. Many of his friends were polytechnicians, and he assigned that status to some of his favorite characters. "Paganel" was an avowed Saint-Simonian, and *Indes Noires* is a technocratic fantasy.

This line of imagination, which runs through much science fiction, is one we can only assume that Defoe would have found very congenial, as did H. G. Wells, the modern Defoe. Chesneaux says that Verne was, like Wells, an author of politics fiction as much as of science fiction. And though Wells had a much more literary imagination than Verne, it is fair to bracket them together. What strikes one about *The War of the Worlds* is the vivid way England is imagined—and imagined as vulnerable; Wells evokes the anxiety of riches and a panic at the rout of civilization. He presents London as an enormous magnificent city, about to be destroyed, and England as an entirely tamed country, at the mercy of fierce invaders. This is of course the vision of much imperialist fiction—a soft, rich, splendid mother country, inviting rape by the hardy savage tribes outside. It is Kipling's vision; while on the other hand the narrative structure of Wells's book is that of Defoe's *Journal of the Plague Year.*

An interesting book which connects Verne with Defoe is Emile Cammaerts's *Discoveries in England,* of 1930. Cammaerts was a Frenchman long resident in England. He says he was struck as a child by the number of Englishmen who played leading roles in Verne's stories, and finally realized that his hero, Phileas Fogg (in *Around the World in 80 Days*), was just another version of Robinson Crusoe, whom he had been in love with a long time. Crusoe was for him as a child "the ideal type of adventurer—courageous, patient, as well as wise and just in his relations with the savages"; whereas Cammaerts knew that temperamentally he couldn't emulate d'Artagnan's bravado, or the military dash of French adventure heroes in general. (He was pointing to a contrast between mercantile and military heroes as well as between English and French.) Crusoe was a settler, and carried, "in a kind of frog, instead of a sword and dagger, a little saw and a hatchet, one on one side, one on the other." This is a highly significant contrast, for Cammaerts. The English adventure novel, he says, is geographical, where the French is historical; the English dream is in a sense outside history—at least the history of militarism and domination.

Cammaerts mentions Robert Louis Stevenson's voyages as an example of the compulsion felt by every English author to live out something of an adventure himself; and Stevenson was a symbolic figure as man as well as author to many readers of adventure at the turn of the century. His family were famous consulting engineers, who had built lighthouses all around Scotland, and harbors all around the world. They were examples of Defoe's and Smiles's engineer-heroes. He had difficulty in reconciling his parents to his vocation to be a writer, but in fact he turned their engineering work to fictional images as much as Dumas turned his father's military exploits into fiction.

Stevenson finished *Treasure Island* in 1882, and it was a tremendous success, both accepting and changing the conventions of adventure. In "How This Book Came To Be," he shows how much it was a composite of earlier books in that tradition. The parrot came from *Robinson Crusoe,* the stockade from *Masterman Ready,* the chest from Washington Irving, and so on. There is much reference to Scott, whom Stevenson was very conscious of rivaling, and in fact there is much more of him than of Defoe. Stevenson's is *historical* expertise rather than practical. He said that the story began with the drawing of a map and that it was told to his stepson, with his father's collaboration. It is palpably the fantasy of men-being-boys. There is no real interest in large historical forces. What is strikingly new about it in a generic way is that a boy plays the leading part and tells the story; and that the violence is much more open and important.

The end of this sort of adventure romance was announced by another Scots writer whom it is suitable to connect with Stevenson in many ways, J. M. Barrie. The servitor imperialism of the Scots writers from Scott on has played an important part in the reinforcement of modernist values in England, as we have seen.[9] (John Buchan, another Scot, was the last of the old-style adventure writers.) Barrie was no conscious or intentional rebel against tradition. As a boy, he read Defoe, Cooper, Stevenson, and at the end of his life, when he was guardian of the boys for and about whom he wrote *Peter Pan,* he was, they tell us, always eager for them to be involved in sports and athletics, and reluctant to see them concerned with the arts. He wanted Kims and Hucks about him, not Little Lord Fauntleroys.

But his own temperament, which was expressed in *Peter Pan,* was purely whimsical and playful, and deeply averse from serious adventure or violence of any kind. *Peter Pan,* 1904, is about a Boy Who Would Not Grow Up, and though it uses all the devices of the boys' adventure story, the Indians, the hollow tree, the underground house, the lost boys, the pirates, it treats them all as conscious fantasy, and so denies their connection with the real world, a connection which is the life line of any energizing myth. But of course a work so purely playful has a thousand faces, and this one was not what most people, or Barrie himself, saw. To them *Peter Pan* seemed like a continuation of *Treasure Island,* the same themes transposed into another key. But the end of Empire was at hand, as far as England was concerned, and that feeling is transmitted, all innocently, through Barrie's work.

Treasure Island had been a very great success of the old kind; W. E. Henley called it the best boys' book since *Robinson Crusoe,* and Andrew Lang said, "Except for *Tom Sawyer* and *The Odyssey,* I never liked a romance so much." (Implicitly that comment conjures up a whole scheme of literary tradition, which would relate literature closely to imperialism, and relegate the serious domestic novel to the periphery of the system.) It prompted, amongst other things, *King Solomon's Mines,* which Rider Haggard published in 1885. This too was very popular; it sold 31,000 copies in twelve months, was praised by literary men, and read aloud in public schools. And though Haggard didn't have Stevenson's finished artistry, nor anything like Kipling's talent and taste, still some parts of his work have some literary importance.

Haggard was born in 1856, and went out to Natal with Sir Henry Bulwer, when the latter became Lieutenant Governor in 1875. When England annexed the Transvaal in 1877, it was Haggard who ran up the Union Jack there. Then he went back to England in 1881, published *Cetewayo and His White Neighbors* (which urged the Government to be aggressive in South Africa) and *King Solomon's Mines* in 1885 and *She* in 1889. *She* is a curiosity from our point of view, because the myth is implicitly erotic and in some sense feminist—the major character being an immortal incarnation of femininity; it is the sort of idea D. H. Lawrence played with, and *The Plumed Serpent* is not totally dissimilar from *She;* and yet Haggard employs many of the traditional adventure motifs, which are so tied to opposite values. (The result is to embarrass the characterization of the young man hero, whom the story keeps turning into Chéri, despite the story-teller's determination to make him stay Tom Brown.) This is the only time when one of these adventure romances is told—in part—in the service of the Mother Goddess.

King Solomon's Mines is not very interesting, though one should note the treasure motif, taken over from Stevenson, and from now on standard; and the introduction of the old-hunter narrator, Allan Quatermaine.

There is no striking similarity between him and Natty Bumppo. His literal model is probably African hunters like Frederick Courtney Selous, who advised Rhodes, and planted the Union Jack in Mashonaland in 1891— "the king of the white hunters." In literary effect, the important thing about Quatermaine is a certain almost-Cockney tone, a self-deprecating and antiromantic humor which proved an effective literary crystallization of the modern man's self-awareness in the presence of primitive grandeur and savagery. It combined intimations given by both Defoe and Scott, and was developed further by Kipling and Edgar Wallace.

Haggard was deeply impressed with both the grandeur and the savagery of tribal life, and felt them to be in some sense truer than the civilized ideas of Victorian England. "Nineteen parts of our nature are savage, the twentieth civilized, but the last is spread over the rest like the blacking over a boot, or the veneer over a table; it is on the savage that we fall back in emergencies" (*Allan Quatermaine*, p. 16). The deeper philosophic note of Haggard's romances is thus quite strongly stoic and melancholy. *King Solomon's Mines* introduced, as well as an old hunter, a Black Prince, Umslopogaas (modeled, Haggard tells us, on a Swazi aide-de-camp he knew in 1860). In *Allan Quatermaine*, in which the main characters of the earlier novel return, Umslopogaas says, "Man is born to kill. He who kills not when his blood is hot is a woman and no man." And in tendency the story endorses this.

For instance, even in *King Solomon's Mines,* Sir Henry Curtis, who is usually described as an Arthurian knight in Victorian dress, in battle turns back into a Viking and a Berserker. And on page 108 of *Allan Quatermaine* we are told, "The Englishmen are adventurers to the backbone; the colonies which will in time become a great nation, will testify to the value of this spirit of adventure, which seems at first sight mere luxury." Like Kingsley, Haggard saw the value of savagery, especially for a ruling race.

Like Kipling, Haggard was deeply impressed by Rhodes, his achievements and his ideas; Haggard's fiction is in effect propaganda in Rhodes's service. *Allan Quatermaine,* published in 1887, begins in England, and the narrator's picture of the country is charged with anxiety and indeed anger. "This prim English country, with its prim hedgerows and cultivated fields . . . now for several years I have lived here in England, and have in my own stupid manner done my best to learn the ways of the children of light . . . and found civilization is only savagery silvergilt. . . . It is on the savage that we fall back in emergencies. . . . Civilization should wipe away our tears, and yet we weep and cannot be comforted. Warfare is abhorrent to her, and yet we strike out for hearth and home, for honour and fair fame, and can glory in the blow" (p. 16).

Haggard's most impressive book is *Nada the Lily,* which came out in 1892, and was inspired by the story of Chaka the Zulu king, who ruled from 1800 to 1828, and is said to have caused the deaths of over a million people. This subject also inspired Bertram Mitford's *The King's Assegai,* which was published in 1894, and has a similar epic grandeur and ferocity. The translations of Homer taught in the public schools, and even more the Norse and Germanic sagas that aroused so much interest in the nineteenth century, provided a literary model for which these African subjects were perfect.

Haggard compares Chaka to Napoleon and Tiberius, and then dedicates his book, in Zulu style, to "Sompsen, my father," the white man who had 3000 black warriors shouting for his blood, but calmly replied that for every drop of blood they shed of his, a hundred avengers should rise from the sea; so that they gave him the Bayete and said that the spirit of Chaka dwelt in him. This is a key idea—to show natives that white heroes have as savage a splendor as they.

In his Preface Haggard says that his intention is to convey "the remarkable spirit that animated these kings and their subjects." The Zulu military organization, "perhaps the most wonderful thing the world has seen," is already a thing of the past. He says he has learned to think and speak like a Zulu, in order to tell this story. The story is told to a white man by Chaka's witch doctor, Mopo, who has known Chaka from childhood. Mopo has some of Quatermaine's antiheroic realism. Umslopogaas is Chaka's son, but is brought up as Mopo's, and consequently as Nada's brother, since Chaka always has his children killed. Umslopogaas wins a comrade, Galazi the Wolf, who has won a great club by passing the night in a cave inside Ghost Mountain, where the Stone Witch sits forever, waiting for the world to die. In the cleft between her breasts are the bones of human sacrifice. Umslopogaas also wins a great weapon, an axe, but to get it has to marry, which spoils their comradeship. "Galazi was also great among the people, but dwelt with them little, for best he loved the wild woods and the mountain's breast, and often, as of old, he swept at night across the forest and the plains, and the howling of the ghost wolves went with him" (p. 153). (Galazi was the inspiration for Mowgli, Kipling said.) When disaster finally comes, and the comrades know they must die, Umslopogaas says, "May we one day find a land where there are no women, and war only, for in that land we shall grow great. But now, at the least, we will make a good end to this fellowship and the Grey People shall fight their fill, and the old stone witch who sits aloft, waiting for the world to die, shall smile to see that fight, if she never smiled before" (p. 285). This is *not* in the spirit of Defoe or Scott; but it takes something from Kingsley, Morris, and Carlyle.

The most impressive passages are those describing battle, or meditating on it. Their stychomythic dialogues and ritual and rhythmic formulas are not original, but they have some power.

> Ah, the battle!—the battle! In those days we knew how to fight, my father! All night our fires shone out across the valley; all night the songs of soldiers echoed down the hills. Then the grey dawning came, the oxen lowed to the light, the regiments arose from their bed of spears; they sprang up and shook the dew from their hair and shields—yes! they arose! The glad to die! . . . The morning breeze came up and found them, their plumes bent in the breeze; like a plain of seeding grass they bent, the plumes of soldiers ripe for the assegai. Up over the shoulder of the hill came the sun of Slaughter; it glowed red upon the red shields; red grew the place of killing; the white plumes of chiefs were dipped in the blood of heaven. They knew it; they saw the omen of death, and, ah! they laughed in the joy of the waking of battle. What was death? Was it not well to die on the spear? What was death? Was it not well to die for the king? Death was the arms of Victory. Victory should be their bride that night, and ah! her breast is fair. (pp. 48-49)

The feeling that passage expresses—and there is much of it in *Nada the Lily* and Haggard's other books—is rare in English literature. That literature on the whole, and certainly in the nineteenth century, had been in the keeping of what Haggard called "the children of light"; let us say George Eliot, Matthew Arnold, John Stuart Mill, and the novelists Tolstoy approved in *What is Art?* What Haggard introduced was a lyrical or threnodic militarism, better fitting an army-focused culture like Prussia or Russia; and in *King Solomon's Mines* there is also a new emphasis upon regiments— their organization and training, but also their pride and glory.

There was to be something of this in Kipling, too; it was the two together who demonstrated in literary terms what Hannah Arendt called the Boomerang effect. The values by which the English on their frontier lived and imagined life, though the opposite of those which they proclaimed at home, crept home in novel form. The liberal values of the modern system, productivity and enlightened self-interest, etc., are undermined. The oppositeness itself took its toll, as we see in Quatermaine's alienation from England. The two effects together produced a kind of pessimism echoed in Mopo's remark, "Nothing matters, except being born. That is a mistake, my father!" (p. 39). The story of the Zulus made a particularly strong impression on the English imagination; they seemed terrible but noble, above all "worthy adversaries." They so appear, for instance, in one of Lady Butler's most famous battle pictures, "The Defence of Rourke's Drift"; and Cetewayo, who paid a visit to England,

became a figure in the popular vocabulary—in music-hall jokes, for instance.

Haggard's friend, Andrew Lang, spoke in 1901 of a new "exotic" literature, "whose writers have at least seen new worlds for themselves; have gone out of the streets of the overpopulated lands into the open air; have sailed and ridden, walked and hunted; have escaped from the smoke and fog of towns. New strength has come from fresher air into their brains and blood . . ." (Brian Street's *The Savage in Literature,* p. 11). And it is significant that Lang was an anthropologist. There was a strong racist interest in anthropology then. The Anthropological Society itself declared in 1864 that black children develop only up to the age of twelve—an idea you can find in both Henty and Kipling. To such ideas Darwin's influence added others, of man's nearness to the apes, the struggle for survival, the persistence or sudden development of monstrous specimens, and so on. This made "primitive man" seem very horrifying but very exciting. It has been proposed to call a whole group of novels that arose in the 1870s with Henty's book on the Ashanti, "the ethnographic novel." And there is also the "anthropological romance" genre which Leo J. Henkin discusses in *Darwinism and the English Novel*; these are novels written between 1890 and 1940 about fossil races of men or near-men. And then there is the whole Tarzan oeuvre. These all expressed and reinforced the trepidation of the imperialist race at the height of its powers. The anxiety of possession we noted in Defoe was an individual thing; by the time of Wells and Haggard it was national.

Notes

[1] According to Smith, scores of newspaper articles and periodicals and sermons also pointed out the likeness between Lawrence and Cromwell; both men cared naught for appearances, spoke freely, swept obstacles from their paths, worked like heroes, and made others work.

[2] Two more examples of this kind of adventure tale are Michael Scott's *Tom Cringle's Log* (Paris, 1836) and E. H. Trelawney's *Adventures of a Younger Son* (London, 1831). The first, though vigorous and stirring, is formally enchained to Smollett. The second is Romantic; as Byron said, Trelawney was "the personification of my *Corsair.* He sleeps with the poem under his pillow and all his past adventures and present manners aim at his personification" (Quoted in the Introduction to the Oxford English Novels edition of *Adventures*.). One point of interest is Trelawney's masculinism; in this, as in many other ways, he usefully exaggerates tendencies implicit in the adventure and romance forms. He wanted to call the book *A Man's Life,* and when Mary Shelley told him that women would not read the manuscript he showed her, he replied, "My life . . . is

not written for the amusement of women . . . it is to men I write, and my first three volumes are principally adapted to sailors. England is a nautical nation . . ." (Introduction, *Adventures*).

[3] Max Müller, in his memorial Preface to *The Roman and The Teuton,* described Kingsley as the ideal man. He recalled those " . . . features which Death had rendered calm, grand, sublime . . . How children delighted in him! How young, wild men believed in him, and obeyed him too! How women were captivated by his chivalry!" His funeral in 1875 collected men of all sorts, gypsies and farm-laborers, sailors, bishops, and governors. He will be missed "wherever Saxon speech and Saxon thought is understood."

[4] In that message Kingsley was of course very unlike Macaulay and James Mill and the Utilitarians. But his view of India was not so remote from theirs. James Mill's *History of British India* gives a very Hobbesian idea of the state's origin, says J. W. Burrow, in his *Evolution and Society*. The state is seen as a machine, and the civil philosophy is as demonstrable as geometry is. His Books II and III try to determine the stage of civilization reached by native India. His criterion is as follows: "Exactly in proportion as Utility is the object of every pursuit may we regard a nation as civilized." (Quoted in Burrows, p. 45.) In India, of course, he found that many pursuits did not have Utility as their object. So Mill blamed the Orientalist scholars (like Sir William Jones) for inducing the West to overrate Indian culture, which was really very backward. "By conversing with the Hindus of today we in some manner converse with the Chaldeans and Babylonians." Mill, Macaulay, and the Whigs of the *Edinburgh Review,* were very rough in their judgments on the East in general—in conscious dissent from the eighteenth-century high-culture fondness for the exotic. Their line of thought may be associated with merchant-caste low culture—the cultural tendency to which Defoe belonged.

[5] Indeed, Dumas's portrait of Richelieu is like Defoe's. Both portraits are composed of phrases like "exquisite subtlety" and "finished art." In the second issue of his *Review,* Defoe described Richelieu as "the most exquisite master of politics, Cardinal Richelieu, whose life and management may hereafter take up a considerable part of these papers . . . the most refined statesman in the world." And writing to Harley, Defoe recommended to the English statesman Richelieu's arrangement of having a series of three offices, each one more secret than the one before, and the third so private that no one was admitted except in the dark (Defoe, *The Letters,* p. 39). Another letter to Harley makes it clear how personally fascinated Defoe was; for he compares himself in Edinburgh, hiring people to betray their friends, with Richelieu. Richelieu was for Defoe what Macchiavelli was for the Elizabethans; and

the fascination continued throughout the life of the modern system, as Dumas's success makes plain.

[6] That book is credited with beginning the "ethnographic novels" which filled the penny dreadfuls after 1874. (See Brian V. Street, *The Savage in Literature.*) It is also the book in which Henty describes his trip up river with Stanley.

[7] Ballantyne is an interesting figure, in a number of ways. He was son and nephew to the Ballantyne brothers who were close friends of Scott. They printed *The Waverley Novels,* and even copied the manuscripts out so that their employees should not see and recognize Scott's handwriting. Thus he was brought up in the Waverley cult, and was much influenced by it. But at sixteen he was sent out to work in the Hudson's Bay Company, and stayed there six years, 1841-1847. His first book, published in 1848, was entitled *Hudson's Bay;* while his first fiction, published in 1856, *The Young Fur Traders,* had the same setting. Thus he embodied two of the major ideas of Scotland, from our point of view; and from 1856 to 1894 he poured out a stream of very popular boys' fiction, which combined the two, and carried the message of adventure.

[8] And this became stronger during his second period, according to Huet's classification. Between 1878 and 1879 his stories were mostly about colonization, and not about the adventures of colonizers but about native rebellions against them. He wrote about the Greek insurrection of 1826, the French-Canadian insurrection of 1837, the Indian Mutiny of 1857, the Bulgarian independence movement, and so on. His work became more literary, and made more reference to Scott. According to Jean Chesneaux (*Une Lecture Politique de Jules Verne*), there are three main strands to Verne's liberalism. He was in the tradition of 1848; that shows itself in Captain Nemo's gallery of heroes, in *20,000 Leagues Under the Sea,* which included Kosciusko, Botzaris, O'Connell, Washington, Lincoln and Brown. (Compare Defoe's list of Protestant heroes, and Smiles's.) But he was also a utopian socialist, whose heroes work for a scientific and fraternal exploitation of the earth. And he was finally an anarchic libertarian—against the police and for outlaws in general; his books show a strong interest in mutinies, and in islands which are *milieux libres*—alternatives to society.

In the third period, 1898 to 1905, according to Huet, he returned to the subject of voyages, but the mood of his work was much grimmer. *L'Etonnante Aventure de la Mission Barsac,* not published until 1914, tells of Henry Killer's wonderfully efficient settlement in Africa called Blackland, which makes use of ingenious ideas devised by the scientist Marcel Camaret, but works by slave labor. This is a dystopia, and all the enthusiasm for science of the earlier books has gone sour.

Of these three periods, the most important from our point of view is the first. Besides the titles already cited, it is worth mentioning *Les Enfants du Capitaine Grant,* 1867-1868, a three-volume odyssey about those children in search of their captain-father, who was shipwrecked while founding a Scots colony in Patagonia. The theme must remind us of Defoe, and it is worth nothing also the fondness of Verne for captains. After Captain Singleton and Captain Roberts, we have to wait until Verne began writing to meet such a concentration on this figure in fiction. The story of Captain Nemo, 1870, owes more to Dumas in the revenge motif, and is more politically motivated. Nemo is an Indian prince in disguise, and he sinks a British cruiser as part of his revenge. But *L'Ile Mystérieuse* (1873) is closer to the Crusoe pattern; an engineer, a journalist, a seaman, and a child are wrecked together, and are saved by the expertise of the engineer. He is an American called Cyrus Smith, who has as much skill of hand as ingenuity of mind, and they name the place Lincoln Island. It is, Chesneaux says, an Anglo-Saxon parable, a hymn to work.

[9] Take for instance Andrew Lang, who played a large literary role, as the friend of Twain, Kipling, and Haggard, and who edited the Border Edition of Scott. In his introduction to *Ivanhoe,* 1894, Lang defended Scott thus—against Ruskin: "Perhaps Mr. Ruskin was never a boy. Scott, like Thackeray, had been a boy, and never forgot that happy company of knights, ladies, dragons, enchanters, all the world of Ariosto . . ." Lang's identification of boyhood with chivalry was of the first importance in the history of children's literature. So was his identification of romance with self-indulgence, in opposition to intelligence and criticism. He continues, "We cannot all be old and melancholy . . . There shall be cakes and ale, though all the critics be virtuous, and recommend stuff 'rich in heart-break'. Still shall the greenwood trees be green . . ." That pouting whimsy was so often employed by Scots writers that it comes to seem inherently Scottish.

John McClure

SOURCE: "Problematic Presence: The Colonial Other in Kipling and Conrad," in *The Black Presence in English Literature,* edited by David Dabydeen, Manchester University Press, 1985, pp. 154-67.

[*In the following essay, McClure compares Kipling and Conrad to explore the conflicting racist and anti-imperialism discourses that inform their fictional works.*]

Serious fiction, as M. M. Bakhtin tells us, dramatises the play of discourses, the competition between different ideologically loaded 'languages' each attempting to set its mark on the world, establish its definitions as authoritative. At the end of the nineteenth century, when Kipling and Conrad were writing some of the most impressive colonial fiction in English, the ethics of imperial expansion was being seriously debated. One issue in the debate was the status of the colonised peoples, the Indians about whom Kipling wrote, the Malays and Africans of Conrad's fiction. Social scientists, liberal humanitarians, missionaries, colonial administrators and planters—each group defined the subject peoples of empire in its own way. But a strong consensus in the west held all peoples of other races to be morally, intellectually and socially inferior to white Europeans, and saw their ostensible inferiority as a justification for domination.

Artists tend to write both within the conventional discourses of their times, and against them. So it is with Kipling and Conrad. Their portraits of other peoples are, to borrow a term from *Heart of Darkness,* inconclusive: drawn now in the conventional terminology of racist discourses, now in terms that challenge these discourses and the image of the other they prescribe. Conrad's especially, is what Kenneth Burke calls 'a disintegrating art': it 'converts each simplicity into a complexity', 'ruins the possibility of ready hierarchies,' and by so doing 'works corrosively upon . . . expansionist certainties'.[1] Conrad persistently questions the two basic propositions of European racism: the notion that, as Brian Street puts it, 'a particular "character" could be attributed to a whole people . . . a "race" might be gullible, faithful, brave, childlike, savage, bloodthirsty';[2] and the notion that the races are arranged hierarchically, with the white race, or perhaps the Anglo-Saxon race, at the top. In novel after novel Conrad breaks down the crude dichotomies (white/black, civilised/savage, benevolent/blood-thirsty, mature/childish, hardworking/lazy) of racist discourses, ruins the ready racial hierarchies they underwrite, and so undermines the expansionistic certainties of imperialism. In his stories, written in the 1880s and '90s, Kipling uses many of these same crude dichotomies to defend imperialism, but in *Kim* (1901) he breaks with convention, offering instead a powerful criticism of racist modes of representation. In both Kipling's *Kim* and Conrad's Malay novels, we find powerfully persuasive representations of the colonised peoples, representations that identify them neither as innocents nor as demons, but as human beings, complex and difficult, to be approached with sympathy, respect, and caution.

In the much neglected 'Author's Note' to his first novel, *Almayer's Folly* (1895), Joseph Conrad describes a project of representation that informs much of his colonial fiction. Europeans, he insists in the 'Note', have the wrong picture of 'strange peoples' and 'far-off countries.' They 'think that in those distant lands all joy is a yell and a war dance, all pathos is a howl and a ghastly grin of filed teeth, and that the solution of all problems is found in the barrel of a revolver or in the point of an assegai.' But 'it is not so': the 'picture of

life' in these far-off lands is essentially 'the same picture' as one sees in Europe, equally elaborate and many-
sided. And the 'common mortals' who dwell there
deserve respect and sympathy. In short, the fashionable European 'verdict of contemptuous dislike' for
these peoples 'has nothing to do with justice.' [3]

The far-off land that Conrad portrays in *Almayer's Folly*
is the Malay Archipelago, the strange peoples Malays
and Arabs. In spite of its ringing preface, *Almayer's
Folly* is full of conventionally dismissive descriptions
of these peoples: the omniscient narrator makes much
of their 'savage nature' (p. 69) and 'half-formed, savage minds' (p. 116), and uses 'civilised' as if the word
referred to a radically different and manifestly superior
mode of existence. But the story related by the
narrator tends to cast doubt on such dismissive
characterisations. The novel's protagonist, a Dutch
colonialist named Almayer, prides himself on being,
as a white, infinitely superior to the Malays among
whom he dwells. But the story is about Almayer's
folly, and events show him to be intellectually and
psychologically weaker than the Malays who oppose
him.

Almayer's daughter Nina, whose mother is a Malay,
occupies a pivotal position between the two opposed
communities. She has been given 'a good glimpse of
civilised life' (p. 42) in Singapore and an equally intense exposure to Malay culture in the up-river settlement where Almayer works as a trader. Conrad, having established her divided allegiance and unique authority, uses her to challenge Almayer's claims of
superiority. Comparing the two communities, Nina at
first fails to sees any difference: 'It seemed to Nina',
the narrator reports, that 'whether they traded in brick
godowns or on the muddy river bank; whether they
reached after much or little; whether they made love
under the shadows of the great trees or in the shadow
of the cathedral on the Singapore promenade' there
was no difference, only 'the same manifestations of
love and hate and of sordid greed' (p. 43). If Nina has,
as the narrator claims, 'lost the power to discriminate'
(p. 43), she has gained the power to recognise essential similarities that Europeans such as the narrator are
anxious to overlook. This passage is the first of many
in Conrad's fiction that insist on the existence of such
similarities and dismiss European claims to all but
absolute difference and superiority.

Although Nina can find at first no essential difference
between 'civilised' and 'savage' ways of life, she ultimately comes to prefer the latter, and her choice has
the force of a judgement against European pretences.
Nina's mother, who influences her decision, makes her
own articulate case against these pretences. Her bitter
accusations, dismissed by the narrator as 'savage rav-
ings' (p. 151), reveal the prejudices of the oppressed
as well as those of their oppressors. Whites, she tells

Nina, ' "speak lies. And they think lies because they
despise us that are better than they are, but not so
strong" ' (p. 151). Racism, Conrad suggests, is not
an exclusively white phenomenon; but the distinction
between speaking lies and thinking them marks Nina's
mother's speech as something more than savage raving, and the narrator, by dismissing it as such, only
lends weight in the woman's charges.

Almayer's Folly is something of a literary curiosity: I
can think of no other novel in which an omniscient
narrator's commentaries are consistently undermined
by the actions and observations of characters he dis-
parages. Whether Conrad intended to produce this effect or not, he never produces it again. In the novels
that follow *Almayer's Folly* the narrators distance themselves from the discourses of racism, adopting them,
when they adopt them at all, only provisionally.

An Outcast of the Islands (1896) is set like its prede-
cessor in the remote Malayan settlement of Sambir.
Once again the action centres on a successful Malay
counter-offensive against western domination, and once
again Conrad depicts the Malays who lead the
campaign as patient, resourceful and determined men.
Babalatchi, who plans and directs the campaign against
Captain Tom Lingard, the English adventurer who
monopolises commercial and political power in Sambir,
is richly and respectfully drawn. He has been a pirate,
his methods are unscrupulous, but they are also brilliantly effective. When Conrad calls him a 'statesman',
then, there may be a slightly ironic inflection to his
voice, but the irony is pointed at the western reader,
not at Babalatchi. Syed Abdulla, Babalatchi's Arab ally,
is even more impressive. Conrad speaks of 'the un-
swerving piety of his heart and . . . the religious so-
lemnity of his demeanour', of 'his ability, his will—
strong to obstinacy—his wisdom beyond his years',
and of his 'great family', which with its various successful trading enterprises lies 'like a network over the
islands'. [4] Thus when white characters refer to Asians
as 'miserable savages' (p. 126) and boast of their own
'pure and superior descent' (p. 271), the vicious stupidity of racist discourse becomes evident.

Once again in this novel Malay characters offer eloquent and devastating assessments of the white men
who rule them. Aissa, a Malay woman courted, compromised and then scorned by Willems, the European
'outcast' of the novel's title, refers repeatedly to Europe as a 'land of lies and evil from which nothing but
misfortune ever comes to us—who are not white' (p.
144). Babalatchi's rejoinders to Captain Lingard are
even more corrosive of European certainties. Lingard,
defending his domination of Sambir, asserts that if he
ever spoke to its nominal Malay ruler 'like an elder
brother, it was for your good—for the good of all'.
'This is a white man's talk', responds Babalatchi, 'with
bitter exultation',

I know you. That is how you all talk while you load your guns and sharpen your swords; and when you are ready, then to those who are weak, you say: 'Obey me and be happy, or die!' You are strange, you white men. You think it is only your wisdom and your virtue and your happiness that are true. (p. 226)

Babalatchi's searing indictment of European hypocrisy and ethno-centricism is corroborated in a number of ways. The narrator makes it clear, for instance, that Europeans do feel racial antipathy and that the sources of this feeling are irrational. Thus when Willems dreams of escaping from Sambir, his desire is attributed to 'the flood of hate, disgust, and contempt of a white man for that blood which is not his blood, for that race that is not his race' (p. 152). This flood of feeling, which overmasters Willems' 'reason', resembles the 'feeling of condemnation' that overcomes Lingard when he imagines Willems' illicit relation with Aissa. And this reaction, too, is described as 'illogical'. It is an 'accursed feeling made up of disdain, of anger, and of the sense of superior virtue that leaves us deaf, blind, contemptuous and stupid before anything which is not like ourselves' (p. 254).

If Conrad challenges the European representation of Malays as uniformly savage and inferior, he does not do so in order to replace that representation with an idyllic one. Babalatchi and his comrades, Lakamba and Omar, are Malay adventurers, blood-thirsty, lawless men who consider 'throat cutting, kidnapping, slave-dealing' to be 'manly pursuits' (p. 52). The peace Lingard enforces seems in many ways preferable to the anarchy they admire. But Lingard's peace is also a kind of tyranny, and Adulla's ascension to power seems to restore some degree of freedom without destroying that peace. In the end, then, Conrad suggests that any generalised ennoblement of one race or another is as inappropriate as generalised dismissal: there are certainly differences of custom and belief between cultures, but the most important differences cut across racial lines and render racial affiliation meaningless as an indicator of intelligence, character, or virtue.

This same line of argument is developed in *Lord Jim* (1900),[5] which explores, among other things, the relation between a Malay community and its genuinely popular English ruler. When Jim, another European outcast, arrives in Patusan, another upriver settlement in the Malay Archipelago, three local factions are struggling for dominance: Rajah Allang's local Malays, Doramin's party of Malay settlers from Celebes, and Sherif Ali's forces, drawn from the tribes of the interior. Ambitious and utterly reckless, Jim quickly earns a reputation for valour, allies himself with Doramin's faction, and engineers a military victory over Sherif Ali so dramatic that no second campaign is necessary. By this means he becomes the actual ruler of Patusan,

and a widely admired ruler. As a white, a member of the race which has conquered the Archipelago, he is automatically feared and, however grudgingly, respected by the Malays. As a fearless warrior, a successful military leader, a peace-maker, and an even-handed governor, he is widely venerated. Conrad describes Jim's triumph, then, in a manner that makes the Malays' acquiescence and approval seem reasonable, a sign not of innate inferiority but of a reasonable reaction to a complex situation. If a 'Jim-myth' (p. 171) arises, it does so because Jim has saved the community from the bloody deadlock of factional strife, in which 'utter insecurity for life and property was the normal condition' (p. 139).

But Conrad, having exposed the logic of colonial acquiescence, goes on to elucidate the logic of rebellion. Like Lingard in *An Outcast of the Islands*, Jim proclaims his unqualified dedication to the Malay community he rules: 'He declared . . . that their welfare was his welfare, their losses his losses, their mourning his mourning' (p. 238). And once again, Conrad tests and refutes this claim to absolute identification. Jim, for reasons that include a misguided sense of racial allegiance, refuses to lead a necessary campaign against piratical white intruders, and these intruders, set free, slaughter a company of Malay warriors, including Doramin's noble son. Conrad's point here, as in *An Outcast of the Islands*, is clear: even the most well-intentioned white ruler will experience a conflict of cultural interests, will be torn between allegiance to his native European community and allegiance to the community he rules. And the resolution of that conflict will be at the expense of his subjects, will justify, ultimately, their resistance to his continued domination.

Conrad makes this point once again in *Heart of Darkness* (1902), but in a most unfortunate way. For here it is the European novelist, Conrad himself, who succumbs to the interests of his own community and betrays his colonial subjects, the Africans he 'represents'. Speaking through Marlow, Conrad identifies the Africans, not consistently but emphatically, as demons and fiends, insists that 'the picture of life' in the Congo forests is appallingly different from the picture in Europe.

In the early stages of Marlow's narrative, the familiar invitations to sympathetic identification with the colonised are still in play. The Congolese are described as victims of a particularly brutal imperialism, compared favourably to their European masters, depicted in ways that stress their kinship with other men. Noting that the villages along the trail to the Central Station are deserted, Marlow remarks, 'Well, if a lot of mysterious niggers armed with all kinds of fearful weapons suddenly took to travelling on the road between Deal and Gravesend, catching the yokels right and left to carry heavy loads for them, I fancy every farm and cottage thereabouts would get empty very soon'.[6] And he suggests that African drumming, 'a sound weird, appealing, suggestive, and wild', may have for Africans 'as profound a meaning as the sound of bells in a Christian country' (p. 20). This is identification with a vengeance.

But as Marlow recounts his voyage up the river to Kurtz at the Inner Station, these familiarising comparisons cease and the emphasis falls more and more emphatically on the savage otherness of the Congolese. Their speech is described as a 'fiendish row' (p. 37) and they are no longer represented as individuals, but rather as 'a whirl of black limbs, a mass of hands clapping, of feet stamping, of bodies swaying, of eyes rolling' (p. 36). When the idea of kinship is suggested, it is with horror: 'No, they were not inhuman. Well, you know, that was the worst of it—this suspicion of their not being inhuman' (p. 36).

The last images of the Congolese are the most thoroughly distancing: 'Deep within the forest, red gleams partially illuminate many men chanting each to himself some weird incantation' (p. 65) and 'a black figure', a 'sorcerer' with 'horns—antelope horns, I think— on its head' (p. 66). This nightmare vision of 'horned shapes' and the equation of the Congolese with a 'conquering darkness' (p. 75) haunt Marlow long after his return to Europe, and they seem intended to haunt the reader as well.

One could attribute the difference between Conrad's representation of the colonised peoples in the Malay novels and his treatment of them in *Heart of Darkness* to social and biographical factors. The Congo basin, ravaged by centuries of slaving, was undoubtedly horrific, and Conrad seems to have had little opportunity, while he was there, to familiarise himself with the Congolese. Certainly Marlow does not: he insists on more than one occasion that he could not get a clear picture of the Africans, the kind of picture, in other words, that might have enabled him to do justice to them as fellow mortals.

But if Conrad cooperates in the familiar misrepresentation of Africans as demonic others, he does so too, I think, because his commitment to accurate representation comes into conflict with another commitment. The nature of that commitment, which has only recently been recognised by Conrad critics,[7] is best brought out in two passages, one from the manuscript of *Heart of Darkness*, the other from the novel itself. The first has to do with events on board the yacht 'Nellie', where Marlow tells his tale. Just before Marlow begins, the frame narrator recalls,

> A big steamer came down all a long blaze of lights like a town viewed from the sea bound to the

uttermost ends of the earth and timed to the day, to the very hour with nothing unknown in her path, no mystery on her way, nothing but a few coaling stations. She went fullspeed, noisily, an angry commotion of the waters followed her . . . And the earth suddenly seemed shrunk to the size of a pea spinning in the heart of an immense darkness. (p. 7 n.)

The steamer makes a perfect figure of the forces of rationalisation: of science, industrial technology, planning and regimentation. And its voyage offers a powerful image of the consequences of these forces. The ship produces, by its precisely calculated passage to the very ends of the earth, the effect that Max Weber called 'disenchantment': it erases from the world, or from the narrator's imagination of the world, all sense of 'mystery' and wonder, leaves it barren and diminished. Marlow's story, which follows immediately, seems designed as an antidote to this diminution, his steamboat voyage as a counterthrust which reconstitutes, or reenchants, the world shrunk by the steamer. The conclusion of the novel signals the success of this project: looking down the Thames, the frame narrator now remarks that the river 'seemed to lead into the heart of an immense darkness' (p. 79).

By deleting the description of the steamer from the published version of *Heart of Darkness*, Conrad partially obscures this aspect of his fictional design. But some sense of what he is up to is conveyed by a fascinating passage early in the novel. Reminiscing about his childhood passion for maps, Marlow remembers that 'at that time there were many blank spaces on the earth'. Africa was one, 'a blank space of delightful mystery—a white patch for a boy to dream gloriously over' (p. 8). By the time he had grown up, Marlow continues, most such spaces had been filled in, but a sense of the unknown still hung over the upper Congo; it was still not quite charted: still a place of enchantment.

Marlow goes up the river, then, in part because he is dedicated to enchantment, drawn to a world radically different from the world of everyday, predictable familiarity. But this attraction, this need for mystery (which grew ever stronger in Europe as the domain of technological rationalisation expanded) impells Marlow to make something of the Africans that is quite inconsistent with Conrad's project of familiarisation. To preserve a domain of enchantment for himself and his European readers, Conrad has Marlow write 'zone of the demonic' across the 'blank space' of Africa, thus consigning the Africans to a familiar role as demonic others. He sacrifices their needs for adequate representation to his own need for mystery. That Marlow also writes 'zone of the human' across Africa is indisputable, but he does so in fainter script, and by the end of *Heart of Darkness* this script is all but illegible.

Heart of Darkness, then, offers a cruel corroboration of Conrad's warning that no European can be trusted to represent the colonised. Torn between his dedication to accurate and sympathetic representation and his need to affirm the existence of radical moral and epistemological darkness, Conrad makes his African characters bear the burden of that darkness and thus perpetuates identifications that justify European contempt and domination. It is a shame that his most widely read novel should contain his most pejorative representations of the colonised, but a consolation that it offers as well perhaps the most powerful indictment of imperial exploitation in English.

In their time, Kipling and Conrad were frequently compared, but from the distance of some eighty years the differences between their works are more apparent than the similarities. Conrad wrote about the raw edges of empire, Kipling about its great heart. Conrad's fiction is aesthetically ambitious, psychologically oriented, politically sceptical; Kipling's is more conventional, less interested in innerness, and basically affirmative in its treatment of imperial rule. It is not, in other words, a 'disintegrating' art: it sets out to celebrate and defend certain established positions, rather than to work corrosively on them. For the most part the certainties defended are those of imperial ideology. When Kipling criticises the crudest European representations of Indians, he does so on the basis of more sophisticated racist beliefs that still sustain white superiority and right to rule. But Kipling, like Conrad, is inconsistent. In *Kim,* his greatest Indian work, he celebrates a set of certainties that have nothing to do with race, certainties which in fact are directly antagonistic to all doctrines of racial superiority. The reversal becomes apparent when one approaches *Kim* by way of the two decades of stories that precede it.

In 'The Head of the District' (1890), a dying English official, ruler of a frontier district, addresses the Afghan tribesmen he has subdued:

> Men, I'm dying . . . but you must be good men when I am not here. . . . Tallantire Sahib will be with you, but I do not know who takes my place. I speak now true talk, for I am as it were already dead, my children—for though ye be strong men, ye are children.

'And thou art our father and our mother',[8] the Afghan chief replies, apparently satisfied with what Conrad's Babalatchi would have quickly dismissed as 'white man's talk'. But this consensus for dependency is threatened when a Bengali is sent to rule the district. The appointment is interpreted as an insult by the Afghans, who have consented to be ruled by the militarily superior English, but despise Bengalis as weaklings (here, as elsewhere in the stories, Kipling makes much of communal rivalries in India, and mocks the claims of

western-educated Bengalis to be ready for posts of responsibility in the Indian Civil Service). 'Dogs you are', a fanatical blind Mullah declares to the Afghans, 'because you listened to Orde Sahib and called him father and behaved as his children' (p. 180). But the Mullah's rebellion, unlike that sponsored by Babalatchi in *An Outcast of the Islands,* fails miserably and is morally, as well as pragmatically, discredited. In the end, after the Mullah has been killed and the unmanly Bengali has fled, the same tribal chief is shown listening, and assenting, to the same paternalistic and racist rhetoric: 'Get hence to the hills—go and wait there, starving, till it shall please the Government to call thy people out for punishment—children and fools that ye be!' (p. 203). The ready hierarchy of imperial domination is thus reconfirmed; the challenge, which is Conrad's work would be authentic and would remain unanswered, is only a pretext for its dramatic re-affirmation.

Indian dependency is affirmed in a different manner in 'His chance in life' (1887), the story of Michele D'Cruze, a young telegraph operator 'with seven-eighths native blood'.[9] A riot breaks out in the town where D'Cruze is posted while the English administrator is away. (Kipling pauses at this point in the story for a cautionary admonition to his audience: 'Never forget that unless the outward and visible signs of Our Authority are always before a native he is as incapable as a child of understanding what authority means' (p. 88).) The Indian police inspector, 'afraid, but obeying the old race instinct which recognizes a drop of White blood as far as it can be diluted' (p. 89), defers to D'Cruze, who astonishes everyone, including himself, by taking charge and putting down the rioters. When an English administrator appears, however, D'Cruze feels 'himself slipping back more and more into the native . . . It was the White drop in Michele's veins dying out, though he did not know it' (p. 91). Once again, the contrast to Conrad is instructive: while Conrad uses characters of 'mixed blood' to challenge European claims to superiority, Kipling finds in one such character a pretext for parading racist notions of the distribution of the faculty of rule: responsibility.

A third story, 'The enlightenment of Pagett, M.P.' (1890), shows Kipling working again to make a case for English domination of India. The MP of the story's title is a liberal who has come out to study (and embrace) the National Congress movement, newly founded in 1885. Congress, the organisation that eventually brought independence to India, represented the newly emerging Indian community of western-educated and oriented professionals, men who believed, often correctly, that they were being denied positions in government because of their race. It was only one of a number of nationalist and reform-minded organisations that sprang up in India in the last quarter of the nineteenth century.

But in 'Pagett', Kipling writes as if Congress were an isolated and idiotic institution. Pagett, visiting an old school friend now in the Indian civil service, is 'enlightened' by a series of Indian, British and American witnesses who appear on business and testify enthusiastically against Congress. Some of their criticisms seem plausible, but by no means all of them. And the onesideness of the testimony ultimately betrays the partiality of the whole proceeding: Kipling's unwillingness to let the Congress position be heard at all. Significantly, the only witness to defend Congress, an organisation which numbered among its members numerous well-educated Indians and Englishmen, is a callow school boy, enthusiastic but ill-informed, who impresses even the sympathetic Pagett unfavourably.

The other witnesses testify not only against Congress but to the innumerable failings of the Indian people: their religious and racial hatreds, caste exclusiveness, political indifference, corruption, sexism and 'utter indifference to all human suffering'.[10] These disabilities, Kipling suggests, make any talk of equality or of elections mere madness. And they are ineradicable, a kind of racial fatality, 'eternal and inextinguishable' (p. 354).

The racist rhetoric of these three stories, with their stereotypic characterisations, their talk of 'blood', their designation of Indians as 'children', their rejection of all claims to equality, and their refusal to enter into serious dialogue, is typical of Kipling's short fiction in general, the scores of short stories he turned out in the eighties and early nineties. There are impressive Indian characters in a few of these stories, and occasional criticisms of the most brutally dismissive forms of racism. But the good Indians are all also good servants of the raj, and Kipling's own attitude substitutes paternal condescension for contempt. He represents the subject peoples from within the discourse of dependency, the paternalistic rhetoric of racist societies from the American South to the Gangetic Plain.[11]

Something of this tone of condescension lingers in *Kim*. Once again, the positively portrayed Indian characters are all loyal servants of the raj; Congress and the forces it represented seem to have disappeared altogether from the Indian scene. But in *Kim* there is none of the insistence on racial difference and English superiority that we find in so many of the stories. Indeed, in this single work Kipling presses as hard against racist modes of perception and representation as Conrad ever does.

Thus the Church of England chaplain who views the authentically holy lama 'with the triple ringed uninterest of the creed that lumps nine-tenths of the world under the title of "heathen" '[12] is depicted as a fool. And so, too, is the young English soldier who calls 'all natives "niggers" ' (p. 108) and doesn't know a word of any Indian language. Kipling, who in his stories routinely casts Bengalis as cowardly weaklings, now presents a Bengali secret agent whose feats of courage and endurance 'would astonish folk who mock at his race' (p. 268).

The novel not only repudiates racist modes of characterisation, it dramatises this repudiation. Character after character—the Sahiba, Huree Babu Mokerjee, the Woman of Shamlegh—overcomes his or her racial prejudices. Even Mahbub Ali, the roguish Pathan horse trader and spy, grows more tolerant as he develops, as Mark Kinkead-Weekes has pointed out, 'away from the Pathan . . . whose opening words were always "God's curse on all unbelievers" . . . towards the Lama's tolerance, [learns] to stop himself with an effort from using his instinctive curse on the "other".'[13] If Kim, 'The Little Friend of All the World' (p. 23), is in one sense the catalyst of all this coming together, he also participates in it, shedding his own prejudices and sense of racial superiority. Throughout the novel, then, Kipling repudiates the hierarchical constructs of racist thinking. What is taken for granted in the earlier fiction is taken down in *Kim*.

Kipling is dreaming, of course, to imagine that the kind of interracial co-operation and comradeship he portrays in *Kim* could take root and grow under British imperial rule: this is E. M. Forster's point in *A Passage to India*. But by blinding himself in this one respect, Kipling is able to see beyond the horizon of his times and portray a world of yet to be realised interracial harmony. For this reason, *Kim* may well be a more effective antidote to racial antipathies than any of Conrad's works which by their great gloominess tend to corrode at once any belief in racist modes of vision and any hope that they may be abolished.

Notes

[1] Kenneth Burke: *Counter-Statement* (1931; Reprinted Berkeley, California, 1968), p. 105.

[2] B. V. Street: *The Savage in Literature* (London, 1975), p. 7.

[3] Joseph Conrad: *Almayer's Folly* (1895; reprinted New York, 1923), pp. ix-x. Subsequent references to this edition will appear in the text.

[4] Joseph Conrad: *An Outcast of the Islands* (1896; reprinted New York, 1926), pp. 109-10. Subsequent references to this essay will appear in the text.

[5] Joseph Conrad: *Lord Jim* (1900; reprinted New York, 1968). Subsequent references to this edition will appear in the text.

[6] Joseph Conrad: *Heart of Darkness* (1902; reprinted New York, 1963), p. 20. Subsequent references to this edition will appear in the text.

[7] See Allon White: *The Uses of Obscurity* (London, 1981) and Jacques Darras: *Joseph Conrad and the West* (London, 1982).

[8] Rudyard Kipling: 'The Head of the District', in *In Black and White* (1895; reprinted New York, 1898), p. 172. Subsequent references to this edition will appear in the text.

[9] Rudyard Kipling: 'His chance in life', in *Plain Tales From the Hills* (1888; reprinted New York, 1898), p. 86. Subsequent references to this edition will appear in the text.

[10] Rudyard Kipling: 'The enlightenments of Pagett, M.P.', in *In Black and White*, p. 383. Subsequent references to this edition will appear in the text.

[11] 'There is no originality in Kipling's rudeness to us', wrote Nirad C. Chaudhiri, 'but only a repetition, in the forthright Kiplingian manner, of what was being said in every mess and club.' Nirad C. Chaudhiri: 'The finest story about India—in English', in *Encounter*, VII (April 1957), p. 47.

[12] Rudyard Kipling: *Kim* (1901; reprinted New York, 1959), p. 90. Subsequent references to this edition will appear in the text.

[13] Mark Kinkead-Weekes: 'Vision in Kipling's novels', in *Kipling's Mind and Art,* ed. Andrew Rutherford (Stanford, California, 1964), p. 225. For further discussion of Kipling's change of attitude in *Kim,* see K. Bhaskara Rao: *Rudyard Kipling's India* (Norman, Oklahoma, 1967).

COLONIALISM AND GENDER

Gayatri Chakravorty Spivak

SOURCE: "Three Women's Texts and a Critique of Imperialism" in *Critical Inquiry,* Vol. 12, No. 1, Autumn, 1985, pp. 243-61.

[In the following essay, Spivak examines Jane Eyre, Wide Sargasso Sea, *and* Frankenstein *to reveal the manner in which imperialist ideology structures the expression of nineteenth-century feminist individualism.]*

It should not be possible to read nineteenth-century British literature without remembering that imperialism, understood as England's social mission, was a crucial part of the cultural representation of England to the English. The role of literature in the production of cultural representation should not be ignored. These two obvious "facts" continue to be disregarded in the reading of nineteenth-century British literature. This itself attests to the continuing success of the imperialist project, displaced and dispersed into more modern forms.

If these "facts" were remembered, not only in the study of British literature but in the study of the literatures of the European colonizing cultures of the great age of imperialism, we would produce a narrative, in literary history, of the "worlding" of what is now called "the Third World." To consider the Third World as distant cultures, exploited but with rich intact literary heritages waiting to be recovered, interpreted, and curricularized in English translation fosters the emergence of "the Third World" as a signifier that allows us to forget that "worlding," even as it expands the empire of the literary discipline.[1]

It seems particularly unfortunate when the emergent perspective of feminist criticism reproduces the axioms of imperialism. A basically isolationist admiration for the literature of the female subject in Europe and Anglo-America establishes the high feminist norm. It is supported and operated by an information-retrieval approach to "Third World" literature which often employs a deliberately "nontheoretical" methodology with self-conscious rectitude.

In this essay, I will attempt to examine the operation of the "worlding" of what is today "the Third World" by what has become a cult text of feminism: *Jane Eyre.*[2] I plot the novel's reach and grasp, and locate its structural motors. I read *Wide Sargasso Sea* as *Jane Eyre's* reinscription and *Frankenstein* as an analysis—even a deconstruction—of a "worlding" such as *Jane Eyre's.*[3]

I need hardly mention that the object of my investigation is the printed book, not its "author." To make such a distinction is, of course, to ignore the lessons of deconstruction. A deconstructive critical approach would loosen the binding of the book, undo the opposition between verbal text and the biography of the named subject "Charlotte Bronte," and see the two as each other's "scene of writing." In such a reading, the life that writes itself as "my life" is as much a production in psychosocial space (other names can be found) as the book that is written by the holder of that named life—a book that is then consigned to what *is* most often recognized as genuinely "social": the world of publication and distribution.[4] To touch Bronte's "life" in such a way, however, would be too risky here. We must rather strategically take shelter in an essentialism which, not wishing to lose the important advantages won by U.S. mainstream feminism, will continue to honor the suspect binary oppositions—book and author, individual and history—and start with an assurance of the following sort: my readings here do not seek to undermine the excellence of the individual artist. If even minimally successful, the readings will incite a degree of rage against the imperialist narrativization of history, that it should produce so abject a script for her. I provide these assurances to allow myself some room to situate feminist individualism in its historical determination rather than simply to canonize it as feminism as such.

Edward Said on the relationship between the novel and imperialism:

I am not trying to say that the novel—or the culture in the broad sense—"caused" imperialism, but that the novel, as a cultural artefact of bourgeois society, and imperialism are unthinkable without each other. Of all the major literary forms, the novel is the most recent, its emergence the most datable, its occurrence the most Western, its normative pattern of social authority the most structured; imperialism and the novel fortified each other to such a degree that it is impossible, I would argue, to read one without in some way dealing with the other.

Nor is this all. The novel is an incorporative, quasi-encyclopedic cultural form. Packed into it are both a highly regulated plot mechanism and an entire system of social reference that depends on the existing institutions of bourgeois society, their authority and power. The novelistic hero and heroine exhibit the restlessness and energy characteristic of the enterprising bourgeoisie, and they are permitted adventures in which their experiences reveal to them the limits of what they can aspire to, where they can go, what they can become. Novels therefore end either with the death of a hero or heroine . . . who by virtue of overflowing energy does not fit into the orderly scheme of things, or with the protagonists' accession to stability. . . .

Edward Said, in Culture and Imperialism,
Vintage Books, 1993.

Sympathetic U.S. feminists have remarked that I do not do justice to Jane Eyre's subjectivity. A word of explanation is perhaps in order. The broad strokes of my presuppositions are that what is at stake, for feminist individualism in the age of imperialism, is precisely the making of human beings, the constitution and "interpellation" of the subject not only as individual but as "individualist."[5] This stake is represented on two registers: childbearing and soul making. The first is domestic-society-through-sexual-reproduction cathected as "companionate love"; the second is the imperialist project cathected as civil-society-through-social-mission. As the female individualist, not-quite/not-male, articulates herself in shifting relationship to what is at stake, the "native female" as such (*within*

discourse, *as* a signifier) is excluded from any share in this emerging norm.[6] If we read this account from an isolationist perspective in a "metropolitan" context, we see nothing there but the psychobiography of the militant female subject. In a reading such as mine, in contrast, the effort is to wrench oneself away from the mesmerizing focus of the "subject-constitution" of the female individualist.

To develop further the notion that my stance need not be an accusing one, I will refer to a passage from Roberto Fernandez Retamar's "Caliban."[7] José Enrique Rodó had argued in 1900 that the model for the Latin American intellectual in relationship to Europe could be Shakespeare's Ariel.[8] In 1971 Retamar, denying the possibility of an identifiable "Latin American Culture," recast the model as Caliban. Not surprisingly, this powerful exchange still excludes any specific consideration of the civilizations of the Maya, the Aztecs, the Incas, or the smaller nations of what is now called Latin America. Let us note carefully that, at this stage of my argument, this "conversation" between Europe and Latin America (without a specific consideration of the political economy of the "worlding" of the "native") provides a sufficient thematic description of our attempt to confront the ethnocentric and reverse-ethnocentric benevolent double bind (that is, considering the "native" as object for enthusiastic information-retrieval and thus denying its own "worlding") that I sketched in my opening paragraphs.

In a moving passage in "Caliban," Retamar locates both Caliban and Ariel in the postcolonial intellectual:

> There is no real Ariel-Caliban polarity: both are slaves in the hands of Prospero, the foreign magician. But Caliban is the rude and unconquerable master of the island, while Ariel, a creature of the air, although also a child of the isle, is the intellectual.
>
> The deformed Caliban—enslaved, robbed of his island, and taught the language by Prospero—rebukes him thus: "You taught me language, and my profit on't / Is, I know how to curse." ["C," pp. 28, 11]

As we attempt to unlearn our so-called privilege as Ariel and "seek from [a certain] Caliban the honor of a place in his rebellious and glorious ranks," we do not ask that our students and colleagues should emulate us but that they should attend to us ("C," p. 72). If, however, we are driven by a nostalgia for lost origins, we too run the risk of effacing the "native" and stepping forth as "the real Caliban," of forgetting that he is a name in a play, an inaccessible blankness circumscribed by an interpretable text.[9] The stagings of Caliban work alongside the narrativization of history: claiming to *be* Caliban legitimizes the very individualism that we must persistently attempt to undermine from within.

Elizabeth Fox-Genovese, in an article on history and women's history, shows us how to define the historical moment of feminism in the West in terms of female access to individualism.[10] The battle for female individualism plays itself out within the larger theater of the establishment of meritocratic individualism, indexed in the aesthetic field by the ideology of "the creative imagination." Fox-Genovese's presupposition will guide us into the beautifully orchestrated opening of *Jane Eyre*.

It is a scene of the marginalization and privatization of the protagonist: "There was no possibility of taking a walk that day. . . . Out-door exercise was now out of the question. I was glad of it," Bronte writes (*JE*, p. 9). The movement continues as Jane breaks the rules of the appropriate topography of withdrawal. The family at the center withdraws into the sanctioned architectural space of the withdrawing room or drawing room; Jane inserts herself—"I slipped in"—into the margin— "A small breakfast-room *adjoined* the drawing room" (*JE*, p. 9; my emphasis).

The manipulation of the domestic inscription of space within the upwardly mobilizing currents of the eighteenth- and nineteenth-century bourgeoisie in England and France is well known. It seems fitting that the place to which Jane withdraws is not only not the withdrawing room but also not the dining room, the sanctioned place of family meals. Nor is it the library, the appropriate place for reading. The breakfast room "contained a book-case" (*JE*, p. 9). As Rudolph Ackerman wrote in his *Repository* (1823), one of the many manuals of taste in circulation in nineteenth-century England, these low bookcases and stands were designed to "contain all the books that may be desired for a sitting-room without reference to the library."[11] Even in this already triply off-center place, "having drawn the red moreen curtain nearly close, I [Jane] was shrined in double retirement" (*JE*, pp. 9-10).

Here in Jane's self-marginalized uniqueness, the reader becomes her accomplice: the reader and Jane are united—both are reading. Yet Jane still preserves her odd privilege, for she continues never quite doing the proper thing in its proper place. She cares little for reading what is *meant* to be read: the "letter-press." *She* reads the pictures. The power of this singular hermeneutics is precisely that it can make the outside inside. "At intervals, while turning over the leaves of my book, I studied the aspect of that winter afternoon." Under "the clear panes of glass," the rain no longer penetrates, "the drear November day" is rather a one-dimensional "aspect" to be "studied," not decoded like the "letter-press' but, like pictures, deciphered by the unique creative imagination of the marginal individualist (*JE*, p. 10).

Before following the track of this unique imagination, let us consider the suggestion that the progress of *Jane Eyre* can be charted through a sequential arrangement of the family/counter-family dyad. In the novel, we encounter, first, the Reeds as the legal family and Jane, the late Mr. Reed's sister's daughter, as the representative of a near incestuous counter-family; second, the Brocklehursts, who run the school Jane is sent to, as the legal family and Jane, Miss Temple, and Helen Burns as a counter-family that falls short because it is only a community of women; third, Rochester and the mad Mrs. Rochester as the legal family and Jane and Rochester as the illicit counter-family. Other items may be added to the thematic chain in this sequence: Rochester and Céline Varens as structurally functional counter-family; Rochester and Blanche Ingram as dissimulation of legality—and so on. It is during this sequence that Jane is moved from the counter-family to the family-in-law. In the next sequence, it is Jane who restores full family status to the as-yet-incomplete community of siblings, the Riverses. The final sequence of the book is a *community of families,* with Jane, Rochester, and their children at the center.

In terms of the narrative energy of the novel, how is Jane moved from the place of the counter-family to the family-in-law? It is the active ideology of imperialism that provides the discursive field.

(My working definition of "discursive field" must assume the existence of discrete "systems of signs" at hand in the socius, each based on a specific axiomatics. I am identifying these systems as discursive fields. "Imperialism as social mission" generates the possibility of one such axiomatics. How the individual artist taps the discursive field at hand with a sure touch, if not with transhistorical clairvoyance, in order to make the narrative structure move I hope to demonstrate through the following example. It is crucial that we extend our analysis of this example beyond the minimal diagnosis of "racism.")

Let us consider the figure of Bertha Mason, a figure produced by the axiomatics of imperialism. Through Bertha Mason, the white Jamaican Creole, Brontë renders the human/animal frontier as acceptably indeterminate, so that a good greater than the letter of the Law can be broached. Here is the celebrated passage, given in the voice of Jane:

> In the deep shade, at the further end of the room, a figure ran backwards and forwards. What it was, whether beast or human being, one could not . . . tell: it grovelled, seemingly, on all fours; it snatched and growled like some strange wild animal: but it was covered with clothing, and a quantity of dark, grizzled hair, wild as a mane, hid its head and face. [*JE*, p. 295]

In a matching passage, given in the voice of Rochester speaking *to* Jane, Brontë presents the imperative for a shift beyond the Law as divine injunction rather than human motive. In the terms of my essay, we might say that this is the register not of mere marriage or sexual reproduction but of Europe and its not-yet-human Other, of soul making. The field of imperial conquest is here inscribed as Hell:

> "One night I had been awakened by her yells . . . it was a fiery West Indian night. . . .
>
> "'This life,' said I at last, 'is hell!—this is the air— those are the sounds of the bottomless pit! *I have a right* to deliver myself from it if I can. . . . Let me break away, and go home to God!' . . .
>
> "A wind fresh from Europe blew over the ocean and rushed through the open casement: the storm broke, streamed, thundered, blazed, and the air grew pure. . . . It was true Wisdom that consoled me in that hour, and showed me the right path. . . .
>
> "The sweet wind from Europe was still whispering in the refreshed leaves, and the Atlantic was thundering in glorious liberty. . . .
>
> "'Go,' said Hope, 'and live again in Europe. . . . You have done all that God and Humanity require of you.'" [*JE*, pp. 310-11; my emphasis]

It is the unquestioned ideology of imperialist axiomatics, then, that conditions Jane's move from the counter-family set to the set of the family-in-law. Marxist critics such as Terry Eagleton have seen this only in terms of the ambiguous *class* position of the governess.[12] Sandra Gilbert and Susan Gubar, on the other hand, have seen Bertha Mason only in psychological terms, as Jane's dark double.[13]

I will not enter the critical debates that offer themselves here. Instead, I will develop the suggestion that nineteenth-century feminist individualism could conceive of a "greater" project than access to the closed circle of the nuclear family. This is the project of soul making beyond "mere" sexual reproduction. Here the native "subject" is not almost an animal but rather the object of what might be termed the terrorism of the categorical imperative.

I am using "Kant" in this essay as a metonym for the most flexible ethical moment in the European eighteenth century. Kant words the categorical imperative, conceived as the universal moral law given by pure reason, in this way: "In all creation every thing one chooses and over which one has any power, may be used *merely as means*; man alone, and with him every rational creature, is an *end in himself*." It is thus a moving displacement of Christian ethics

from religion to philosophy. As Kant writes: "With this agrees very well the possibility of such a command as: *Love God above everything, and thy neighbor as thyself.* For as a command it requires respect for a law which *commands love* and does not leave it to our own arbitrary choice to make this our principle."[14]

The "categorical" in Kant cannot be adequately represented in determinately grounded action. The dangerous transformative power of philosophy, however, is that its formal subtlety can be travestied in the service of the state. Such a travesty in the case of the categorical imperative can justify the imperialist project by producing the following formula: *make* the heathen into a human so that he can be treated as an end in himself.[15] This project is presented as a sort of tangent in *Jane Eyre,* a tangent that escapes the closed circle of the *narrative* conclusion. The tangent narrative is the story of St. John Rivers, who is granted the important task of concluding the *text.*

At the novel's end, the *allegorical* language of Christian psychobiography—rather than the textually constituted and seemingly *private* grammar of the creative imagination which we noted in the novel's opening— marks the inaccessibility of the imperialist project as such to the nascent "feminist" scenario. The concluding passage of *Jane Eyre* places St. John Rivers within the fold of *Pilgrim's Progress.* Eagleton pays no attention to this but accepts the novel's ideological lexicon, which establishes St. John Rivers' heroism by identifying a life in Calcutta with an unquestioning choice of death. Gilbert and Gubar, by calling *Jane Eyre* "Plain Jane's progress," see the novel as simply replacing the male protagonist with the female. They do not notice the distance between sexual reproduction and soul making, both actualized by the unquestioned idiom of imperialist presuppositions evident in the last part of *Jane Eyre:*

> Firm, faithful, and devoted, full of energy, and zeal, and truth, [St. John Rivers] labours for his race. . . . His is the sternness of the warrior Greatheart, who guards his pilgrim convoy from the onslaught of Apollyon. . . . His is the ambition of the high master-spirit[s] . . . who stand without fault before the throne of God; who share the last mighty victories of the Lamb; who are called, and chosen, and faithful. [*JE*, p. 455]

Earlier in the novel, St. John Rivers himself justifies the project: "My vocation? My great work? . . . My hopes of being numbered in the band who have merged all ambitions in the glorious one of bettering their race—of carrying knowledge into the realms of ignorance—of substituting peace for war—freedom for bondage—religion for superstition—the hope of heaven for the fear of hell?" (*JE*, p. 376). Imperial-

Rudyard Kipling's writings explored the British colonization of India.

ism and its territorial and subject-constituting project are a violent deconstruction of these oppositions.

When Jean Rhys, born on the Caribbean island of Dominica, read *Jane Eyre* as a child, she was moved by Bertha Mason: "I thought I'd try to write her a life."[16] *Wide Sargasso Sea*, the slim novel published in 1965, at the end of Rhys' long career, is that "life."

I have suggested that Bertha's function in *Jane Eyre* is to render indeterminate the boundary between human and animal and thereby to weaken her entitlement under the spirit if not the letter of the Law. When Rhys rewrites the scene in *Jane Eyre* where Jane hears "a snarling, snatching sound, almost like a dog quarrelling" and then encounters a bleeding Richard Mason (*JE*, p. 210), she keeps Bertha's humanity, indeed her sanity as critic of imperialism, intact. Grace Poole, another character originally in *Jane Eyre*, describes the incident to Bertha in *Wide Sargasso Sea*: "So you don't remember that you attacked this gentleman with a knife? . . . I didn't hear all he said except 'I cannot interfere legally between yourself and your husband'. It was when he said 'legally' that you flew at him'" (*WSS*, p. 150). In Rhys' retelling, it is the dissimulation that Bertha discerns in the word

"legally"—not an innate bestiality—that prompts her violent *re*action.

In the figure of Antoinette, whom in *Wide Sargasso Sea* Rochester violently renames Bertha, Rhys suggests that so intimate a thing as personal and human identity might be determined by the politics of imperialism. Antoinette, as a white Creole child growing up at the time of emancipation in Jamaica, is caught between the English imperialist and the black native. In recounting Antoinette's development, Rhys reinscribes some thematics of Narcissus.

There are, noticeably, many images of mirroring in the text. I will quote one from the first section. In this passage, Tia is the little black servant girl who is Antoinette's close companion: "We had eaten the same food, slept side by side, bathed in the same river. As I ran, I though, I will live with Tia and I will be like her. . . . When I was close I saw the jagged stone in her hand but I did not see her throw it. . . . We stared at each other, blood on my face, tears on hers. It was as if I saw myself. Like in a looking glass" (*WSS*, p. 38).

A progressive sequence of dreams reinforces this mirror imagery. In its second occurrence, the dream is partially set in a *hortus conclusus,* or "enclosed garden"—Rhys uses the phrase (*WSS*, p. 50)—a Romance rewriting of the Narcissus topos as the place of encounter with Love.[17] In the enclosed garden, Antoinette encounters not Love but a strange threatening voice that says merely "in here," inviting her into a prison which masquerades as the legalization of love (*WSS*, p. 50).

In Ovid's *Metamorphoses,* Narcissus' madness is disclosed when he recognizes his Other as his self: "Iste ego sum."[18] Rhys makes Antoinette see her *self* as her Other, Brontë's Bertha. In the last section of *Wide Sargasso Sea*, Antoinette acts out *Jane Eyre's* conclusion and recognizes herself as the so-called ghost in Thornfield Hall: "I went into the hall again with the tall candle in my hand. It was then that I saw her—the ghost. The woman with streaming hair. She was surrounded by a gilt frame but I knew her" (*WSS*, p. 154). The gilt frame encloses a mirror: as Narcissus' pool reflects the selfed Other, so this "pool" reflects the Othered self. Here the dream sequence ends, with an invocation of none other than Tia, the Other that could not be selfed, because the fracture of imperialism rather than the Ovidian pool intervened. (I will return to this difficult point.) "That was the third time I had my dream, and it ended. . . . I called 'Tia' and jumped and woke" (*WSS*, p. 155). It is now, at the very end of the book, that Antoinette/Bertha can say: "Now at last I know why I was brought here and what I have to do" (*WSS*, pp. 155-56). We can read this as her having been brought into the England of Brontë's novel: "This

cardboard house"—a book between cardboard covers—
"where I walk at night is not England" (*WSS,* p. 148).
In this fictive England, she must play out her role, act
out the transformation of her "self" into that fictive
Other, set fire to the house and kill herself, so that
Jane Eyre can become the feminist individualist heroine of British fiction. I must read this as an allegory of
the general epistemic violence of imperialism, the construction of a self-immolating colonial subject for the
glorification of the social mission of the colonizer. At
least Rhys sees to it that the woman from the colonies
is not sacrificed as an insane animal for her sister's
consolation.

Critics have remarked that *Wide Sargasso Sea* treats
the Rochester character with understanding and sympathy.[19] Indeed, he narrates the entire middle section
of the book. Rhys makes it clear that he is a victim
of the patriarchal inheritance law of entailment rather
than of a father's natural preference for the firstborn:
in *Wide Sargasso Sea,* Rochester's situation is clearly
that of a younger son dispatched to the colonies to
buy an heiress. If in the case of Antoinette and her
identity, Rhys utilizes the thematics of Narcissus, in
the case of Rochester and his patrimony, she touches
on the thematics of Oedipus. (In this she has her finger on our "historical moment." If, in the nineteenth
century, subject-constitution is represented as childbearing
and soul making, in the twentieth century psychoanalysis allows the West to plot the itinerary of the
subject from Narcissus [the "imaginary"] to Oedipus
[the "symbolic"]. This subject, however, is the normative male subject. In Rhys' reinscription of these
themes, divided between the female and the male
protagonist, feminism and a critique of imperialism
become complicit.)

In place of the "wind from Europe" scene, Rhys substitutes the scenario of a suppressed letter to a father,
a letter which would be the "correct" explanation of
the tragedy of the book.[20] "I thought about the letter
which should have been written to England a week
ago. Dear Father . . ." (*WSS,* p. 57). This is the first
instance: the letter not written. Shortly afterward:

> Dear Father. The thirty thousand pounds have been
> paid to me without question or condition. No
> provision made for her (that must be seen to). . . .
> I will never be a disgrace to you or to my dear
> brother the son you love. No begging letters, no
> mean requests. None of the furtive shabby
> manoeuvres of a younger son. I have sold my soul
> or you have sold it, and after all is it such a bad
> bargain? The girl is thought to be beautiful, she is
> beautiful. And yet . . . [*WSS,* p. 59]

This is the second instance: the letter not sent. The
formal letter is uninteresting; I will quote only a part
of it:

> Dear Father, we have arrived from Jamaica after an
> uncomfortable few days. This little estate in the
> Windward Islands is part of the family property and
> Antoinette is much attached to it. . . . All is well
> and has gone according to your plans and wishes.
> I dealt of course with Richard Mason. . . . He
> seemed to become attached to me and trusted me
> completely. This place is very beautiful but my
> illness has left me too exhausted to appreciate it
> fully. I will write again in a few days' time. [*WSS,*
> p. 63]

And so on.

Rhys' version of the Oedipal exchange is ironic, not a
closed circle. We cannot know if the letter actually
reaches its destination. "I wondered how they got their
letters posted," the Rochester figure muses. "I folded
mine and put it into a drawer of the desk. . . . There
are blanks in my mind that cannot be filled up" (*WSS,*
p. 64). It is as if the text presses us to note the analogy
between letter and mind.

Rhys denies to Brontë's Rochester the one thing that
is supposed to be secured in the Oedipal relay: the
Name of the Father, or the patronymic. In *Wide Sargasso Sea,* the character corresponding to Rochester
has no name. His writing of the final version of the
letter to his father is supervised, in fact, by an image
of the *loss* of the patronymic: "There was a crude
bookshelf made of three shingles strung together over
the desk and I looked at the books, Byron's poems,
novels by Sir Walter Scott, *Confessions of an Opium
Eater* . . . and on the last shelf, *Life and Letters of* . . .
The rest was eaten away" (*WSS,* p. 63).

Wide Sargasso Sea marks with uncanny clarity the
limits of its own discourse in Christophine, Antoinette's
black nurse. We may perhaps surmise the distance
between *Jane Eyre* and *Wide Sargasso Sea* by remarking that Christophine's unfinished story is the tangent
to the latter narrative, as St. John Rivers' story is to
the former. Christophine is not a native of Jamaica;
she is from Martinique. Taxonomically, she belongs to
the category of the good servant rather than that of the
pure native. But within these borders, Rhys creates a
powerfully suggestive figure.

Christophine is the first interpreter and named speaking subject in the text. "The Jamaican ladies had never
approved of my mother, 'because she pretty like pretty
self' Christophine said," we read in the book's opening paragraph (*WSS,* p. 15). I have taught this book
five times, once in France, once to students who had
worked on the book with the well-known Caribbean
novelist Wilson Harris, and once at a prestigious institute where the majority of the students were faculty
from other universities. It is part of the political argument I am making that all these students blithely stepped
over this paragraph without asking or knowing what

Queen Victoria's reign saw the height of British imperialism.

Christophine's patois, so-called incorrect English, might mean.

Christophine is, of course, a commodified person. "'She was your father's wedding present to me'" explains Antoinette's mother, "'one of his presents'" (*WSS*, p. 18). Yet Rhys assigns her some crucial functions in the text. It is Christophine who judges that black ritual practices are culture-specific and cannot be used by whites as cheap remedies for social evils, such as Rochester's lack of love for Antoinette. Most important, it is Christophine alone whom Rhys allows to offer a hard analysis of Rochester's actions, to challenge him in a face-to-face encounter. The entire extended passage is worthy of comment. I quote a brief extract:

> "She is Creole girl, and she have the sun in her. Tell the truth now. She don't come to your house in this place England they tell me about, she don't come to your beautiful house to beg you to marry with her. No, it's you come all the long way to her house—it's you beg her to marry. And she love you and she give you all she have. Now you say you don't love her and you break her up. What you do with her money, eh?" [And then Rochester, the white man, comments silently to himself] Her voice was

still quiet but with a hiss in it when she said "money." [*WSS*, p. 130]

Her analysis is powerful enough for the white man to be afraid: "I no longer felt dazed, tired, half hypnotized, but alert and wary, ready to defend myself" (*WSS*, p. 130).

Rhys does not, however, romanticize individual heroics on the part of the oppressed. When the Man refers to the forces of Law and Order, Christophine recognizes their power. This exposure of civil inequality is emphasized by the fact that, just before the Man's successful threat, Christophine had invoked the emancipation of slaves in Jamaica by proclaiming: "No chain gang, no tread machine, no dark jail either. This is free country and I am free woman" (*WSS*, p. 131).

As I mentioned above, Christophine is tangential to this narrative. She cannot be contained by a novel which rewrites a canonical English text within the European novelistic tradition in the interest of the white Creole rather than the native. No perspective *critical* of imperialism can turn the Other into a self, because the project of imperialism has always already historically refracted what might have been the absolutely Other into a domesticated Other that consolidates the imperialist self.[21] The Caliban of Retamar, caught between Europe and Latin America, reflects this predicament. We can read Rhys' reinscription of Narcissus as a thematization of the same problematic.

Of course, we cannot know Jean Rhys' feelings in the matter. We can, however, look at the scene of Christophine's inscription in the text. Immediately after the exchange between her and the Man, well before the conclusion, she is simply driven out of the story, with neither narrative nor characterological explanation or justice. "'Read and write I don't know. Other things I know.' She walked away without looking back" (*WSS*, p. 133).

Indeed, if Rhys rewrites the madwoman's attack on the Man by underlining of the misuse of "legality," she cannot deal with the passage that corresponds to St. John Rivers' own justification of his martyrdom, for it has been displaced into the current idiom of modernization and development. Attempts to construct the "Third World Woman" as a signifier remind us that the hegemonic definition of literature is itself caught within the history of imperialism. A full literary reinscription cannot easily flourish in the imperialist fracture or discontinuity, covered over by an alien legal system masquerading as Law as such, an alien ideology established as only Truth, and a set of human sciences busy establishing the "native" as self-consolidating Other.

In the Indian case at least, it would be difficult to find an ideological clue to the planned epistemic violence of imperialism merely by rearranging curricula or syllabi within existing norms of literary pedagogy. For a later period of imperialism—when the constituted colonial subject has firmly taken hold—straightforward experiments of comparison can be undertaken, say, between the functionally witless India of *Mrs. Dalloway,* on the one hand, and literary texts produced in India in the 1920s, on the other. But the first half of the nineteenth century resists questioning through literature or literary criticism in the narrow sense, because both are implicated in the project of producing Ariel. To reopen the fracture without succumbing to a nostalgia for lost origins, the literary critic must turn to the archives of imperial governance.

In conclusion, I shall look briefly at Mary Shelley's *Frankenstein,* a text of nascent feminism that remains cryptic, I think, simply because it does not speak the language of feminist individualism which we have come to hail as the language of high feminism within English literature. It is interesting that Barbara Johnson's brief study tries to rescue this recalcitrant text for the service of feminist autobiography.[22] Alternatively, George Levine reads *Frankenstein* in the context of the creative imagination and the nature of the hero. He sees the novel as a book about its own writing and about writing itself, a Romantic allegory of reading within which Jane Eyre as unself-conscious critic would fit quite nicely.[23]

I propose to take *Frankenstein* out of this arena and focus on it in terms of that sense of English cultural identity which I invoked at the opening of this essay. Within that focus we are obliged to admit that, although *Frankenstein* is ostensibly about the origin and evolution of man in society, it does not deploy the axiomatics of imperialism.

Let me say at once that there is plenty of incidental imperialist sentiment in *Frankenstein.* My point, within the argument of this essay, is that the discursive field of imperialism does not produce unquestioned ideological correlatives for the narrative structuring of the book. The discourse of imperialism surfaces in a curiously powerful way in Shelley's novel, and I will later discuss the moment at which it emerges.

Frankenstein is not a battleground of male and female individualism articulated in terms of sexual reproduction (family and female) and social subject-production (race and male). That binary opposition is undone in Victor Frankenstein's laboratory—an artificial womb where both projects are undertaken simultaneously, though the terms are never openly spelled out. Frankenstein's apparent antagonist is God himself as Maker of Man, but his real competitor is also woman as the maker of children. It is not just that his dream of the death of mother and bride and the actual death of his bride are associated with the visit of his monstrous homoerotic "son" to his bed. On a much more overt level, the monster is a bodied "corpse," unnatural because bereft of a determinable childhood: "No father had watched my infant days, no mother had blessed me with smiles and caresses; or if they had, all my past was now a blot, a blind vacancy in which I distinguished nothing" (*F,* pp. 57, 115). It is Frankenstein's own ambiguous and miscued understanding of the real motive for the monster's vengefulness that reveals his own competition with woman as maker:

> I created a rational creature and was bound towards him to assure, as far as was in my power, his happiness and well-being. This was my duty, but there was another still paramount to that. My duties towards the beings of my own species had greater claims to my attention because they included a greater proportion of happiness or misery. Urged by this view, I refused, and I did right in refusing, to create a companion for the first creature. [*F,* p. 206]

It is impossible not to notice the accents of transgression inflecting Frankenstein's demolition of his experiment to create the future Eve. Even in the laboratory, the woman-in-the-making is not a bodied corpse but "a human being." The (il)logic of the metaphor bestows on her a prior existence which Frankenstein aborts, rather than an anterior death which he reembodies: "The remains of the half-finished creature, whom I had destroyed, lay scattered on the floor, and I almost felt as if I had mangled the living flesh of a human being" (*F,* p. 163).

In Shelley's view, man's hubris as soul maker both usurps the place of God and attempts—vainly—to sublate woman's physiological prerogative.[24] Indeed, indulging a Freudian fantasy here, I could urge that, if to give and withhold to/from the mother a phallus is *the* male fetish, then to give and withhold to/from the man a womb might be the female fetish.[25] The icon of the sublimated womb in man is surely his productive brain, the box in the head.

In the judgment of classical psychoanalysis, the phallic mother exists only by virtue of the castration-anxious son; in *Frankenstein*'s judgment, the hysteric father (Victor Frankenstein gifted with his laboratory—the womb of theoretical reason) cannot produce a daughter. Here the language of racism—the dark side of imperialism understood as social mission—combines with the hysteria of masculism into the idiom of (the withdrawal of) sexual reproduction rather than subject-constitution. The roles of masculine and feminine individualists are hence reversed and displaced. Frankenstein cannot produce a "daughter" because "she might become ten thousand times more malignant than her mate . . . [and because] one of the first results of those sympathies for which the demon thirsted would be children, and a race of devils would be propagated upon the earth who might make the very existence of the species of man a condition precarious and full of terror" (*F*, p. 158). This particular narrative strand also launches a thoroughgoing critique of the eighteenth-century European discourses on the origin of society through (Western Christian) man. Should I mention that, much like Jean-Jacques Rousseau's remark in his *Confessions*, Frankenstein declares himself to be "by birth a Genevese" (*F*, p. 31)?

In this overly didactic text, Shelley's point is that social engineering should not be based on pure, theoretical, or natural-scientific reason alone, which is her implicit critique of the utilitarian vision of an engineered society. To this end, she presents in the first part of her deliberately schematic story three characters, childhood friends, who seem to represent Kant's three-part conception of the human subject: Victor Frankenstein, the forces of theoretical reason or "natural philosophy"; Henry Clerval, the forces of practical reason or "the moral relations of things"; and Elizabeth Lavenza, that aesthetic judgment—"the aerial creation of the poets"—which, according to Kant, is "a suitable mediating link connecting the realm of the concept of nature and that of the concept of freedom . . . (which) promotes . . . *moral* feeling" (*F*, pp. 37, 36).[26]

This three-part subject does not operate harmoniously in *Frankenstein*. That Henry Clerval, associated as he is with practical reason, should have as his "design . . . to visit India, in the belief that he had in his knowledge of its various languages, and in the views he had taken of its society, the means of materially assisting the progress of European colonization and trade" is proof of this, as well as part of the incidental imperialist sentiment that I speak of above (*F*, pp. 151-52). I should perhaps point out that the language here is entrepreneurial rather than missionary:

> He came to the university with the design of making himself complete master of the Oriental languages, as thus he should open a field for the plan of life he had marked out for himself. Resolved to pursue no inglorious career, he turned his eyes towards the East as affording scope for his spirit of enterprise. The Persian, Arabic, and Sanskrit languages engaged his attention. [*F*, pp. 66-67]

But it is of course Victor Frankenstein, with his strange itinerary of obsession with natural philosophy, who offers the strongest demonstration that the multiple perspectives of the three-part Kantian subject cannot co-operate harmoniously. Frankenstein creates a putative human subject out of natural philosophy alone. According to his own miscued summation: "In a fit of enthusiastic madness I created a rational creature" (*F*, p. 206). It is not at all farfetched to say that Kant's

categorical imperative can most easily be mistaken for the hypothetical imperative—a command to ground in cognitive comprehension what can be apprehended only by moral will—by putting natural philosophy in the place of practical reason.

I should hasten to add here that just as readings such as this one do not necessarily accuse Charlotte Brontë the named individual of harboring imperialist sentiments, so also they do not necessarily commend Mary Shelley the named individual for writing a successful Kantian allegory. The most I can say is that it is possible to read these texts, within the frame of imperialism and the Kantian ethical moment, in a politically useful way. Such an approach presupposes that a "disinterested" reading attempts to render transparent the interests of the hegemonic readership. (Other "political" readings—for instance, that the monster is the nascent working class—can also be advanced.)

Frankenstein is built in the established epistolary tradition of multiple frames. At the heart of the multiple frames, the narrative of the monster (as reported by Frankenstein to Robert Walton, who then recounts it in a letter to his sister) is of his almost learning, clandestinely, to be human. It is invariably noticed that the monster reads *Paradise Lost* as true history. What is not so often noticed is that he also reads Plutarch's *Lives*, "the histories of the first founders of the ancient republics," which he compares to "the patriarchal lives of my protectors" (*F*, pp. 123, 124). And his *education* comes through "Volney's *Ruins of Empires*," which purported to be a prefiguration of the French Revolution, published after the event and after the author had rounded off his theory with practice (*F*, p. 113). It is an attempt at an enlightened universal secular, rather than a Eurocentric Christian, history, written from the perspective of a narrator "from below," somewhat like the attempts of Eric Wolf or Peter Worsley in our own time.[27]

This Caliban's education in (universal secular) humanity takes place through the monster's eavesdropping on the instruction of an Ariel—Safie, the Christianized "Arabian" to whom "a residence in Turkey was abhorrent" (*F*, p. 121). In depicting Safie, Shelley uses some commonplaces of eighteenth-century liberalism that are shared by many today: Safie's Muslim father was a victim of (bad) Christian religious prejudice and yet was himself a wily and ungrateful man not as morally refined as her (good) Christian mother. Having tasted the emancipation of woman, Safie could not go home. The confusion between "Turk" and "Arab" has its counterpart in present-day confusion about Turkey and Iran as "Middle Eastern" but not "Arab."

Although we are a far cry here from the unexamined and covert axiomatics of imperialism in *Jane Eyre*, we will gain nothing by celebrating the time-bound pieties that Shelley, as the daughter of two antievangelicals, produces. It is more interesting for us that Shelley differentiates the Other, works at the Caliban/Ariel distinction, and *cannot* make the monster identical with the proper recipient of these lessions. Although he had "heard of the discovery of the American hemisphere and *wept with Safie* over the helpless fate of its original inhabitants," Safie cannot reciprocate his attachment. When she first catches sight of him, "Safie, unable to attend to her friend [Agatha], rushed out of the cottage" (*F*, pp. 114 [my emphasis], 129).

In the taxonomy of characters, the Muslim-Christian Safie belongs with Rhys' Antoinette/Bertha. And indeed, like Christophine the good servant, the subject created by the fiat of natural philosophy is the tangential unresolved moment in *Frankenstein*. The simple suggestion that the monster is human inside but monstrous outside and only provoked into vengefulness is clearly not enough to bear the burden of so great a historical dilemma.

At one moment, in fact, Shelley's Frankenstein does try to tame the monster, to humanize him by bringing him within the circuit of the Law. He "repair[s] to a criminal judge in the town and . . . relate[s his] history briefly but with firmness"—the first and disinterested version of the narrative of Frankenstein—"marking the dates with accuracy and never deviating into invective or exclamation. . . . When I had concluded my narration I said, 'This is the being whom I accuse and for whose seizure and punishment I call upon you to exert your whole power. It is your duty as a magistrate'" (*F*, pp. 189, 190). The sheer social reasonableness of the mundane voice of Shelley's "Genevan magistrate" reminds us that the absolutely Other cannot be selfed, that the monster has "properties" which will not be contained by "proper" measures:

> "I will exert myself [he says], and if it is in my power to seize the monster, be assured that he shall suffer punishment proportionate to his crimes. But I fear, from what you have yourself described to be his properties, that this will prove impracticable; and thus, while every proper measure is pursued, you should make up your mind to disappointment." [*F*, p. 190]

In the end, as is obvious to most readers, distinctions of human individuality themselves seem to fall away from the novel. Monster, Frankenstein, and Walton seem to become each others' relays. Frankenstein's story comes to an end in death; Walton concludes his own story within the frame of his function as letter writer. In the *narrative* conclusion, he is the natural philosopher who learns from Frankenstein's example. At the end of the *text,* the monster, having confessed his guilt toward his maker and ostensibly intending to immolate himself, is borne away on an ice raft. We do

not see the conflagration of his funeral pile—the selfimmolation is not consummated in the text: he too cannot be contained by the text. In terms of narrative logic, he is "lost in darkness and distance" (*F*, p. 211)—these are the last words of the novel—into an existential temporality that is coherent with neither the territorializing individual imagination (as in the opening of *Jane Eyre*) nor the authoritative scenario of Christian psychobiography (as at the end of Brontë's work). The very relationship between sexual reproduction and social object-production—the dynamic nineteenth-century topos of feminism-in-imperialism—remains problematic within the limits of Shelley's text and, paradoxically, constitutes its strength.

Earlier, I offered a reading of woman as womb holder in *Frankenstein*. I would now suggest that there is a framing woman in the book who is neither tangential, nor encircled, nor yet encircling. "Mrs. Saville," "excellent Margaret," "beloved Sister" are her address and kinship inscriptions (*F*, pp. 15, 17, 22). She is the occasion, though not the protagonist, of the novel. She is the feminine *subject* rather than the female individualist: she is the irreducible *recipient*-function of the letters that constitute *Frankenstein*. I have commented on the singular appropriative hermeneutics of the reader reading with Jane in the opening pages of *Jane Eyre*. Here the reader must read with Margaret Saville in the crucial sense that she must *intercept* the recipient-function, read the letters *as* recipient, in order for the novel to exist.[28] Margaret Saville does not respond to close the text as frame. The frame is thus simultaneously not a frame, and the monster can step "beyond the text" and be "lost in darkness." Within the allegory of our reading, the place of both the English lady and the unnamable monster are left open by this great flawed text. It is satisfying for a postcolonial reader to consider this a noble resolution for a nineteenth-century English novel. This is all the more striking because, on the anecdotal level, Shelley herself abundantly "identifies" with Victor Frankenstein.[29]

I must myself close with an idea that I cannot establish within the limits of this essay. Earlier I contended that *Wide Sargasso Sea* is necessarily bound by the reach of the European novel. I suggested that, in contradistinction, to reopen the epistemic fracture of imperialism without succumbing to a nostalgia for lost origins, the critic must turn to the archives of imperialist governance. I have not turned to those archives in these pages. In my current work, by way of a modest and inexpert "reading" of "archives," I try to extend, outside of the reach of the European novelistic tradition, the most powerful suggestion in *Wide Sargasso Sea*: that *Jane Eyre* can be read as the orchestration and staging of the self-immolation of Bertha Mason as "good wife." The power of that suggestion remains unclear if we remain insufficiently knowledgeable about the history of the legal manipulation of widow-sacrifice in the entitlement of the British government in India. I would hope that an informed critique of imperialism, granted some attention from readers in the First World, will at least expand the frontiers of the politics of reading.

Notes

[1] My notion of the "worlding of a world" upon what must be assumed to be uninscribed earth is a vulgarization of Martin Heidegger's idea; see "The Origin of the Work of Art," *Poetry, Language, Thought,* trans. Albert Hofstadter (New York, 1977), pp. 17-87.

[2] See Charlotte Brontë, *Jane Eyre* (New York, 1960); all further references to this work, abbreviated *JE,* will be included in the text.

[3] See Jean Rhys, *Wide Sargasso Sea* (Harmondsworth, 1966); all further references to this work, abbreviated *WSS,* will be included in the text. And see Mary Shelley, *Frankenstein; or, The Modern Prometheus* (New York, 1965); all further references to this work, abbreviated *F,* will be included in the text.

[4] I have tried to do this in my essay "Unmaking and Making in *To the Lighthouse,*" in *Women and Language in Literature and Society,* ed. Sally McConnell-Ginet, Ruth Borker, and Nelly Furman (New York, 1980), pp. 310-27.

[5] As always, I take my formula from Louis Althusser, "Ideology an Ideological State Apparatuses (Notes towards an Investigation)," *"Lenin and Philosophy" and Other Essays,* trans. Ben Brewster (New York, 1971), pp. 127-86. For an acute differention between the individual and individualism, see V. N. Vološinov, *Marxism and the Philosophy of Language,* trans. Ladislav Matejka and I. R. Titunik, Studies in Language, vol. 1 (New York, 1973), pp. 93-94 and 152-53. For a "straight" analysis of the roots and ramifications of English "individualism," see C. B. MacPherson, *The Political Theory of Possessive Individualism: Hobbes to Locke* (Oxford, 1962). I am grateful to Jonathan Rée for bringing this book to my attention and for giving a careful reading of all but the very end of the present essay.

[6] I am constructing an analogy with Homi Bhabha's powerful notion of "not-quite/not-white" in his "Of Mimicry and Man: The Ambiguity of Colonial Discourse," *October* 28 (Spring 1984): 132. I should also add that I use the word "native" here in reaction to the term "Third World Woman." It cannot, of course, apply with equal historical justice to both the West Indian and the Indian contexts nor to contexts of imperialism by transportation.

[7] See Roberto Fernández Retamar, "Caliban: Notes towards a Discussion of Culture in Our America," trans.

Lynn Garafola, David Arthur McMurray, and Robert Márquez, *Massachusetts Review* 15 (Winter-Spring 1974): 7-72; all further references to this work, abbreviated "C," will be included in the text.

[8] See José Enrique Rodó, *Ariel,* ed. Gordon Brotherston (Cambridge, 1967).

[9] For an elaboration of "an inaccessible blankness circumscribed by an interpretable text," see my "Can the Subaltern Speak?" *Marxist Interpretations of Culture,* ed. Cary Nelson (Urbana, Ill., forthcoming).

[10] See Elizabeth Fox-Genovese, "Placing Women's History in History," *New Left Review* 133 (May-June 1982): 5-29.

[11] Rudolph Ackerman, *The Repository of Arts, Literature, Commerce, Manufactures, Fashions, and Politics,* (London, 1823), p. 310.

[12] See Terry Eagleton, *Myths of Power: A Marxist Study of the Brontës* (London, 1975); this is one of the general presuppositions of his book.

[13] See Sandra M. Gilbert and Susan Gubar, *The Madwoman in the Attic: The Woman Writer and the Nineteenth-Century Literary Imagination* (New Haven, Conn., 1979), pp. 360-62.

[14] Immanuel Kant, *Critique of Practical Reason, The "Critique of Pure Reason," the "Critique of Practical Reason" and Other Ethical Treatises, the "Critique of Judgement,"* trans. J. M. D. Meiklejohn et al. (Chicago, 1952), pp. 328, 326.

[15] I have tried to justify the reduction of sociohistorical problems to formulas or propositions in my essay "Can the Subaltern Speak?" The "travesty" I speak of does not befall the Kantian ethic in its purity as an accident but rather exists within its lineaments as a possible supplement. On the register of the human being as child rather than heathen, my formula can be found, for example, in "What Is Enlightenment?" in Kant, *"Foundations of the Metaphysics of Morals," "What Is Enlightenment?" and a Passage from "The Metaphysics of Morals,"* trans. and ed. Lewis White Beck (Chicago, 1950). I have profited from discussing Kant with Jonathan Rée.

[16] Jean Rhys, in an interview with Elizabeth Vreeland, quoted in Nancy Harrison, *An Introduction to the Writing Practice of Jean Rhys: The Novel as Women's Text* (Rutherford, N. J., forthcoming). This is an excellent, detailed study of Rhys.

[17] See Louise Vinge, *The Narcissus Theme in Western European Literature Up to the Early Nineteenth Century,* trans. Robert Dewsnap et al. (Lund, 1967), chap. 5.

[18] For a detailed study of this text, see John Brenkman, "Narcissus in the Text," *Georgia Review* 30 (Summer 1976): 293-327.

[19] See, e.g., Thomas F. Staley, *Jean Rhys: A Critical Study* (Austin, Tex. 1979), pp. 108-16; it is interesting to note Staley's masculist discomfort with this and his consequent dissatisfaction with Rhys' novel.

[20] I have tried to relate castration and suppressed letters in my "The Letter As Cutting Edge," in *Literature and Psychoanalysis; The Question of Reading: Otherwise,* ed. Shoshana Felman (New Haven, Conn., 1981), pp. 208-26.

[21] This is the main argument of my "Can the Subaltern Speak?"

[22] See Barbara Johnson, "My Monster/My Self," *Diacritics* 12 (Summer 1982): 2-10.

[23] See George Levine, *The Realistic Imagination: English Fiction from Frankenstein to Lady Chatterley* (Chicago, 1981), pp. 23-35.

[24] Consult the publications of the Feminist International Network for the best overview of the current debate on reproductive technology.

[25] For the male fetish, see Sigmund Freud, "Fetishism," *The Standard Edition of the Complete Psychological Works of Sigmund Freud,* ed. and trans. James Strachey et al., 24 vols. (London, 1953-74), 21:152-57. For a more "serious" Freudian study of *Frankenstein,* see Mary Jacobus, "Is There a Woman in This Text?" *New Literary History* 14 (Autumn 1982): 117-41. My "fantasy" would of course be disproved by the "fact" that it is more difficult for a woman to assume the position of fetishist than for a man; see Mary Ann Doane, "Film and the Masquerade: Theorising the Female Spectator," *Screen* 23 (Sept.-Oct. 1982): 74-87.

[26] Kant, *Critique of Judgement,* trans. J. H. Bernard (New York, 1951), p. 39.

[27] See [Constantin François Chasseboeuf de Volney], *The Ruins; or, Meditations on the Revolutions of Empires,* trans. pub. (London, 1811). Johannes Fabian has shown us the manipulation of time in "new" secular histories of a similar kind; see *Time and the Other: How Anthropology Makes Its Object* (New York, 1983). See also Eric R. Wolf, *Europe and the People without History* (Berkeley and Los Angeles, 1982), and Peter Worsley, *The Third World,* 2d ed. (Chicago, 1973); I am grateful to Dennis Dworkin for bringing the latter book to my attention. The most striking ignoring of the monster's education through Volney is in Gilbert's otherwise brilliant "Horror's Twin: Mary Shelley's Monstrous Eve," *Feminist Studies* 4 (June 1980): 48-73. Gilbert's essay reflects the absence of race-determinations in a certain sort of feminism. Her present work has most convincingly filled in this gap; see, e.g., her recent piece on H. Rider Haggard's *She* ("Rider Haggard's Heart of Darkness," *Partisan Review* 50, no. 3 [1983]: 444-53).

[28] "A letter is always and *a priori* intercepted, . . . the 'subjects' are neither the senders nor the receivers of messages. . . . The letter is constituted . . . by its interception" (Jacques Derrida, "Discussion," after Claude Rabant, "Il n'a aucune chance de l'entendre," in *Affranchissement: Du transfert et de la lettre,* ed. René Major [Paris, 1981], p. 106; my translation). Margaret Saville is not made to appropriate the reader's "subject" into the signature of her own "individuality."

[29] The most striking "internal evidence" is the admission in the "Author's Introduction" that, after dreaming of the yet-unnamed Victor Frankenstein figure and being terrified (through, yet not quite through, him) by the monster in a scene she later reproduced in Frankenstein's story, Shelley began her tale "on the morrow . . . with the words 'It was on a dreary night of November'" (*F,* p. xi). Those are the opening words of chapter 5 of the finished book, where Frankenstein begins to recount the actual making of his monster (see *F,* p. 56).

Zohreh T. Sullivan

SOURCE: "Race, Gender, and Imperial Ideology: In the Nineteenth Century," in *Nineteenth-Century Contexts,* Vol. 13, No. 1, Spring, 1989, pp. 19-32.

[In the following essay, Sullivan argues that though the imperial subject was constructed in monolithic patriarchal and racist terms, the multiple discourses of imperialism disrupted this construction and provided a space for the voice of the "other," as is seen in Frankenstein.]

When the Monster created by Mary Shelley's Frankenstein learns to read, his first lessons include an ordering of the world at once racist, imperialist, and sexist—an oppositional, hierarchic structure finally and ironically reenforced by his own exile away from the company of man. Looking at his first family, he learns the gendering of morality and the moral ordering of nineteenth century class, caste and nationalism: Agatha, the girl with the golden hair and "gentle demeanour" who weeps, is "unlike" common farm-house servants (102); the "strange system of human society" consists of "the division of property . . . of rank, descent, and noble blood" (115); with either money or blood, a man, he knows, might be respected, but, wonders the Monster "what was I?" The answer that some readers have found is that in his inadequacy and self-loathing, the Monster is indeed not a Man but a woman. As nameless, suffering, and powerless object, the Monster is, like Woman, an incomplete and therefore "flawed opposite of man" (Suleiman, 147); and as textual Other, he carries, like Woman, a double status as powerful destroyer and as "miserable . . . abandoned . . . abortion" (219).

What the Monster learns from his Eurocentric and patriarchal texts are the reactionary and conservative lessons befitting the angelic ladies in the novel. "Through this monster," says Judith Weissman, "Mary Shelley begins what has become another battle cry of conservative politicians for the last two centuries—the real danger in radical change is that it will destroy the nuclear family, father, mother, and children" (133). In learning his first lessons in history, government and religion, he follows stages in the construction of Imperial masculinity: he is led to admire those "peaceable lawgivers Numa, Solon, and Lycurgus" (MS, 125) also favored by Rousseau, to transcend feeling by moving from Werther to Plutarch who "taught me high thoughts . . . elevated me above the wretched sphere of my own reflections, to admire and love the heroes of past ages" (124); he learns the lessons of Orientalism by opposing the "stupendous genius" of the Greeks against the "slothful Asiatics" (125), whose evidence of social power over women is seen in Safie's father, a version of the "Lustful Turk" (see Marcus Ch. 5). Safie, the "sweet Arabian" must flee from Asia and the bondage of the "treacherous Turk" whose religion, we are told, forbids "independence of spirit" to women (119). The Monster learns that geography, history, culture, and religion are all gendered along polarized, language lines—the "gentle," "slothful," female, Asiatic, and Islamic are opposed to the "stupendous genius" of the Greek world and by extension of Christian Europe. The Monster's deformity poses the colonial question of racial difference and is a cultural reminder of 19th-century anxieties about the proximity and fluidity of racial and sexual Otherness. His exile, therefore, is fit reward for upstart deviants who threaten, with terror, energy, or mere difference, the enclosed domestic and national family. But the Monster's rejection by the established family of man is also a symptom of nineteenth-century cultural hegemony that insulates by separating the normal from the deviant, man against monster, and the manly from the effeminate.

I introduce this essay with the story of Shelley's Monster because its unexpected and persistent hold on the English imagination reveals the anxieties of a culture (and gender) that in its preoccupation with defense against the Other constructs the stereotype as fixed reality, fantasy and fetish. "The scene of fetishism," says Bhabha, "is also the scene of the reactivation and repetition of primal fantasy—the subject's desire for a pure origin that is always threatened by its division

(161ff.)." Frankenstein's "fetishized" relationship to his creature—that of man to his (female) possession and of subject to object, to be made, displayed, and dismissed—bears obvious resemblance to that of the colonizer to the colonized with all the attendant problems of alienation from "product," projection of desire and contempt, denial of subjectivity, and denial of connection or responsibility for the creature he has tried to make in his own image. Yet, the oppositional and monological structure necessary for the creation of such racial stereotypes dissolves and is problematized when the Monster is allowed to speak his story. The image and fantasy of the Other, whether monster, immigrant, Jew, or "Oriental" fueled the British conviction that their island and unitary identity was imperilled by encroaching hordes of inefficient and physically undesirable aliens (see Rosenthal 131ff.). That fear, compounded by popular science and pamphleteers, predicted the impending degeneration of Empire and the mongrelization of the white race. Frankenstein's refusal to produce a female creature, of course, echoes not only Prospero's fear of peopling his island with Calibans and later fears of racial pollution expressed by Eugenicists, but is psychologically necessary for defense against the hegemonic and male fear of self-loss or castration. Or, as Gayatri Spivak puts it:

> "the phallic mother exists only by virtue of the castration-anxious son; in *Frankenstein's* judgment, the hysteric father . . . cannot produce a daughter. Here the language of racism—the dark side of imperialism understood as social mission—combines with the hysteria of masculism into the idiom of (the withdrawal of) sexual reproduction rather than subject-constitution. (255)

But the story also introduces the multiple and dialogic problems of colonial discourse in the language of the Monster, in his complicity with the lessons of patriarchy, and in the scenes of what Said would call both latent and manifest Orientalism. The Monster's introduction to the history of the world and to knowledge itself is to Patriarchy; the Orient, represented by the silent subaltern Safie, is typically described, to use Said's words, "as feminine, its riches as fertile, its main symbols the sensual woman, the harem and the despotic—but curiously attractive—ruler" (*Theory*, 225). The Oriental female is doubly oppressed, caught between her tyrannical father and foreign patriarchy, between native and foreign imperialism. The Monster too is doubly oppressed, caught between his own rejecting father/creator yet internalizing the knowledge of the world as constructed by the race of the Father; denied as son he is, like the native Caliban, able to recover a voice that simultaneously resists yet confirms and colludes in the repressions of the State.

The construction of the Monster in the position of nameless, fetishized lack allowed to occupy center stage, to speak and then in spite of its destructive and pitiful pleas for recognition, to be exiled into frozen silence, therefore demonstrates how hierarchies of race and class, ideologies of empire, and gender oppositions are actively interdependent on one another. Critics now working on Orientalism, Race theory or Imperialism draw on feminist criticism along with psychoanalytic and cultural criticism in order to raise further questions about margins and centers, about the construction of sexual and political identity, about the connections between power, family, and nationhood and the construction of the male imperial subject. The feminist critique of representation, therefore, has problematized not only the ambivalent image of the Monster, but also of women, of Otherness, and the Imperial and colonized subject.

We probably need no reminders of how theology, science, and ideology grew increasingly interdependent during the seventeenth, eighteenth, and nineteenth centuries as the Great Chain of Being evolved into the ladder of Darwinian evolution. Justifying class, race, and gender inequality by locating its cause in "Nature" rather than society or God, biology became not only the "science of the political right, but the science of those who suspected science, reason and progress" (Hobsbawm 252). And Darwin's theory of the survival of the fittest, now joined with his differentiation between "weaker" and "stronger" races, resulted in a racist anthropology which presumed that Western survival and Empire were proof enough of racial superiority. Empowered by language and his civilization, the European could define, erase, exoticize, and violate the people and space he entered.

The history of Imperialism is inseparable from (though not identical with) nineteenth century racism and the gender-coded moral oppositions and hierarchies which inform its judgments. Although the intersection between race, political power and gender can be traced to the earliest literary tracts on the "Other" (Said takes us back to Euripides' *The Bacchae* and Aeschylus' *The Persians*), it is to Count Joseph Arthur de Gobineau (1816-82) that modern writers point as the father of modern racism. As ethnographer, scientist, and aristocrat, Gobineau's fear of miscegenation, democracy, and mongrelization revealed itself through his construction of an elite race as defense against the catastrophe he foresaw of the end of the human race. His *Essay on the Inequality of Human Races* (1853), considered by Hannah Arendt and others as the standard text of the century for race theory in history, sees the decay of race and the mixing of blood as the cause of the fall of civilizations. Gobineau distinguishes between the white, the black, and the yellow in terms of the relative limitations of reason, thought, and intellect in nonwhite races and the predominance of energy, desire, and intensity, combined paradoxically with passivity, to be found in the black and yellow races. The split-

ting of racial virtues according to familiar class and gender polarities was as apparent to nineteenth-century readers as it is today. By opposing the masculine instincts of civilization, organization, law, and discipline, to the feminine instincts of creativity, art, and passive receptivity, Gobineau mapped the newly emerging science of man on to earlier philosophical (Rousseau) and theological theories. Other theories of race were less sinister than Gobineau's and in some cases were directed to defending the essential humanity of other races despite their difference. But even these functioned to preserve sharp distinctions between "us" and "them" and served to police the sexual and social imagination of nineteenth-century male imperialist ideology.

Across the channel, Edmund Burke denounced the "abstraction" of human rights and the horror of the French Revolution by defending the "national" rights of Englishmen against what he perceived to be the non-existent "natural" rights of men, thereby bestowing nobility onto an entire nation as opposed to a race. Historians debate the relative claims of Carlyle and Dilke to be known as the father of British Imperialism (see Arendt 180 and Bodelsen 22ff.). But both aimed to define Saxon character in terms of masculine virtues as essential to "leaders," to "heroes" and to what Dilke called that "grandeur of race." Constructions of heroic masculinity were conflated with myths of cultural origins and common inheritance in order to create a unified idea of the Imperial mission.

But while the English were creating images of newly acquired colonies as extensions of their idealized Family with Queen Victoria as androgynous protector, the "ma-baap" (Mother-Father) to native children, the working class family in England, deprived of protection against exploitation, was being subjected to an unregulated labor market with ten-to-eight-hour working days for men, women, and children. The rhetoric of fear eventually used against extended female employment in factories was not unlike that used to describe undesirable Others: Lord Anthony Ashley warned (in 1844) that women became too independent if they had the means to support families, that they were already forming "various clubs and associations, and gradually acquiring all those privileges which are held to be the proper portion of the male sex," that they were "leaders and exciters of the young men to violence," and that, when demoralized, they "contaminate all that comes within their reach" (quoted in Gallager 124). The future of England and of domestic peace, he added, rests on limiting the labor hours for factory women. By the end of the century, women found themselves in increasingly exploitative jobs in large scale manufacture or in sweat-shops such as match-making or sewing machine factories; or women returned to more underpaid and diminishing domestic industries (lace and dress-making, frame-work knitting) that sustained them before the factory age and that allowed them to work while also caring for families and homes. It was this gradual separation of home and work that encouraged patterns of gender-economic division and began a new kind of dependence and inequality between husbands and wives (Hobsbawm 198). But the growth of technology and industrialization also increased work possibilities for women and by the 1880's and 1890's, teaching and clerical and shop positions in Britain and other European countries were predominantly feminized (Hobsbawm 200ff.). Although most women stayed away from emancipation movements, those who formed the vanguard expected a new politics to transform traditional relationships between the sexes and classes, saw class and abolitionist struggles as versions of their own struggle against patriarchy, and formed a substantial part of labor unions, abolitionist and socialist movements. Queen Victoria, of course, opposed "'this mad wicked folly of 'Women's Rights'" for fear that they would, as they unsexed themselves, grow "'hateful, heartless—and *disgusting*'" (quoted in Miles 187).

As was the case in economics, so too were the politics of Imperialism and education dominantly masculine. The discourse of Imperialism, gendered by hierarchy and trope, mapped domestic ideology to social paternalism, repeated familiar antinomies and confirmed Victorian myths of manhood and of Empire as paternalistic enterprise that in turn informed the myths of manliness so constructed as to oppose the ordered, disciplined, rational and masculine to the chaotic, childlike, irrational and feminine. Ideas of "character" as secret keys to racial and colonial superiority were popularized by such propagandists as Samuel Smiles, whose *Self-Help* (1859), *Character* (1871), *Thrift* (1875), and *Duty* (1887) were enormously influential, easily assimilated, widely translated into almost every European and Indian language, as well as Japanese, Arabic, and Turkish. More importantly, they sold more than any of the great nineteenth-century novels. The virtues he extolled were part of his gospel of work, discipline and physical exercise—all part of the cult of manliness and Empire:

> Wonderful is the magic of drill! Drill means discipline, training, education . . . These soldiers—who are ready to march steadily against vollied fire, against belching cannon—or to beat their heads against bristling bayonets . . . were once tailors, shoemakers, mechanics, weavers and ploughmen: with mouths gaping, shoulders stooping, feet straggling, arms and hands like great fins hanging by their sides; but now their gait is firm and martial, their figures are erect, and they march along to the sound of music with a tread that makes the earth shake. (quoted in Briggs 127-8)

So too for Baden-Powell, constructor of the masculine schoolboy Imperial subject, the founder of the Boy

Scouts and inventor of the patent on English character as defense for the imperiled island, the key ingredients were discipline and obedience. The hidden agenda in Baden-Powell, as Michael Rosenthal has shown us, is the self-interested voice of the middle class defending its right to established privileges while justifying the inequalities of the class system (9). The concerns of scouting extend to the rigid and specific masculine codes that inform the mythology of Imperialism. The consensus about the ideal appearance of the Englishman weeded out those who were inefficient, narrow-chested, stunted, individualistic, excitable, or easily wearied (Rosenthal 131-3). The persistent myth of decadence, of a falling Empire, of an imperiled island, allowed a collusion between the Baden-Powells, the Eugenicists, the conservative politicians, and the ethnologists who conflated race degeneration, lost manhood, and loss of Empire. Men like Admiral Beresford, the Earl of Dunraven, and other well placed public figures supported, first, the Society for the Suppression of the Immigration of Destitute Aliens and then the British Brothers League that collected "all those who already shared his [William Shaw's] belief that the alien snatched the Englishman's bread from this lips, in order to agitate for a measure of restriction" (Gainer 68).

Whether written by missionaries, scientists, historians, or novelists, Imperial or colonial discourse struggles with the Other as a text upon which to project fantasy, fear, and desire. The historian Thomas Macaulay writes history using such familiar rhetorical tropes (reminiscent of Conrad's first narrator in "Heart of Darkness," who recalls early imperialists and sea pirates as "jewels flashing in the night of time") as exploits of romantic, strong masculine heroes against weak, feminine Others. Describing, for instance, a particular Brahmin Nuncomar in an essay on Warren Hastings, Macaulay writes "What the Italian is to the Englishman, what the Hindoo is to the Italian, what the Bengalee is to other Hindoos, that was Nuncumar to the Bengalees. The physical organization of the Bengalee is feeble even to Effeminancy" (quoted in Green 32). The eighteenth-century historian Abbé Demanet uses comparable tropes: "The African appears to be a machine, wound and unwound by springs, similar to soft wax, which can be made to take on any figure one wishes . . . eager to be instructed, he fervently grabs on to whatever is given him . . . he has nothing to hold him in place" (quoted in Miller 48). Both these passages share elements common to colonial discourse: race, class, masculinity, and power seem naturally interchangeable; and the Other in each becomes an Object to be scrutinized, classified, infantilized, and marked as "female." The popular representation of Africans from 1800-1850 is predominantly one of darkness, nullity, absence, a lack. By mid-century, evolutionary anthropology had blurred the lines between ape and African, by its very denial encouraged the popular acceptance of Africans as the "missing link," and focused on cannibalism as evidence of the unimaginable depths of African barbarism. But Victorians were equally happy with the myth of African as Child, and Sir Frederick Lugard, governor of Nigeria at the turn of the century, was one of many to describe the "typical" African as "a happy, thriftless, excitable person, lacking self-discipline and foresight, naturally courageous and naturally courteous and polite . . . the virtues and defects of this race-type are those of attractive children" (*The Dual Mandate in British Tropical Africa* quoted in Mangan 112). George Romannes' *Mental Evolution in Man* (1889), Winwood Reade's *Savage Africa* (1863), John Lubbock's *The Origin of Civilisation* (1870), and Henry Stanley's *Through the Dark Continent* (1878) are examples of but a few of the popular texts that informed and conflated such racist and Imperialist ideas of the age.

To be perceived as blank, empty, passive, and child-like suggests a sexual, geographic, and social ordering that is at once seductive and threatening. And while the British imperialists were out finding blank spaces on maps to call their own, their novelists were metonymically engaged in other conquests—the martial conquests and wars for domestic survival. The drawing room novel of the early nineteenth-century defined itself against the intruder or alien and denied the realities of empire even as it obscured the sources of wealth that sustained its propertied heroes; and while Jane Austen was writing of Pemberly and Mansfield Park, Admiral Austen, her brother, was engaged in the First Burmese war and the eventual annexation of Burma to the British Empire.

But there was another genre of popular fiction in the age whose writers acknowledged the world of Imperial conquest, the colonial, and the colonized female even as they revealed the deepest anxieties of Imperial culture—loss of manhood, identity, and racial purity. Charlotte Brontë's Bertha Mason, Joseph Conrad's Mrs. Almayer, Rider Haggard's Ayesha, or She-Who-Must-Be-Obeyed, and Kipling's native women are all products of English anxieties, primarily about erotic desire and domination, but also about sexually taboo encounters with darker races whose embrace will result in terminal boundary disintegration. Bertha, Rochester's West Indian wife, as so many readers have reminded us, is a nightmare figure, a racial monstrosity: "What it was, whether beast or human being, one could not, at first sight, tell: it grovelled, seemingly, on all fours; it snatched and growled like some strange wild animal: but it was covered with clothing; and a quantity of dark, grizzled hair, wild as a mane, hid its head and face" (Brontë, 258). Rider Haggard, however, worked his way around the problem of miscegenation even in darkest Africa: his solution was either to kill the African girl before love could be consummated (*King Solomon's Mines*), or to have his Europeans discover, in "darkest" Africa, a lost white civilization with an

almost white female at its heart (*Allen Quatermain* and *She*). In *She* (1887) however, the exquisite, near-immortal, and learned queen meets with a death more hideous than any other in nineteenth-century literature. Sandra Gilbert suggests that the frightful image of the female in Haggard may also be the consequence of anxiety over a new socio-cultural phenomenon—the emancipated New Woman: Ayesha, or She-Who-Must-Be-Obeyed may, she suggests, have been half-consciously modelled on other nineteenth-century works about female assertiveness and the New Woman such as Tennyson's *The Princess* (1847) and Olive Schreiner's *The Story of an African Farm* (1883). Conrad's Almayer (1895) is destroyed by two women—his native wife and his daughter, an unthinkable type of the new half-breed woman. Although he imagines his marriage to the native Malay will evolve into a bourgeois western family with traditional power divisions, Mrs. Almayer, the "savage tigress," with witchlike claws, instead sets fire to curtains and furniture, moves outside his house into her own hut and defies all his efforts to civilize her into domesticity. Yet, Conrad does not simply caricature her. His ambivalence towards miscegenation, imperialism, and gender roles is seen in his dialogical internalization of both the racist and anti-imperialist discourses of his time (see McClure 154). Denied speech for the major part of the novel, the native woman is momentarily, but significantly, restored into both language and history as she rejects her European husband and his civilization, articulates the forbidden wish to expel the colonizer, and is finally indulged by having all her desires met even as Almayer is allowed to die of opium and a broken heart. Even more important for this genre, Conrad allows the mixed marriage to produce a daughter who is not only beautiful, but allowed to speak, smarter than the Europeans and independent enough to choose native Malay life over western civilization.

Other colonial writers did not deal easily with the products of such miscegenation. Kipling, for instance, killed both child and mother in his greatest story of mixed marriage: "Without Benefit of Clergy (1890)." But not before he represents such a union in terms of Imperialist erotic fantasy: the woman is at once his servant, his slave and his "endless delight," able to love him even as he masters her. In his other stories, passion between Englishmen and Indian women meets with equally disastrous results: "Beyond the Pale (1888)" ends with the gruesome vision of the girl's arms held out in the moonlight: "both hands had been cut off at the wrist, and the stumps were nearly healed." In "Lisbeth" (1886), the girl who is seduced and abandoned meets a fate common to her lot: she ages badly, and we are told, marries a native who abuses her. But in spite of the scene of "white" writing and narrative control, she is not entirely silenced and recuperates her story and speech in *Kim* (1901). In "To Be Filed for Reference" (1888), the Oxford scholar Jellaludin

Macintosh slides from marriage to his silent native wife into drugs, alcohol, and death. Dravot's desire for marriage to a native woman in "The Man Who Would be King" (1889) results in his decapitation, in Carnehan's crucifixion, and in the end of their empire. What Kipling ironically sees in this story and others is that the King's desire (for a native woman) is incompatible with the System he has constructed that denies desire. And the King must die. In the battle between nature/desire and culture/imperialism, it is the second and by extension the masculine member of the binary opposition that will survive. And the last surviving image in the story is the decapitated shrivelled head of Dravot crowned with a shining circlet of gold. In all these encounters, then, the love affair between the European and the Native plays out the larger Imperial design that insists, while using a discourse that questions that very insistence, on the need to retain moral, racial, and gender superiority. Love only appears to conquer the male who "falls;" each story reveals an ideological necessity to maintain boundaries, one that confirms the love as transgression, as an alien intrusion into the world of the Ruler; if the story contains a death, its cause is often the native woman, the eroticized object of the colonizer's fantasy life.

These works reveal the stresses and tensions of a culture in which race and gender roles are at once polarized as part of a scientific hierarchy, but also undermined by a plurality of discourses that disrupt and question its hierarchic and moral certainties. The hysterical masculinity of the dominant ideology, so constructed to see the Other only in terms of difference and threat, fulfilled its destiny by compelling recognition, subjugation and fealty; in the process, however, it produced and depended on the existence of the Other, of a system and a desire that, like Frankenstein's Monster, chose to refuse silence, and instead threatened to displace, decenter and destroy its creator.

Notes

[1] Lata Mani and Gayatri Spivak draw attention to such double oppression in their studies of Sati and the silent subaltern. In questioning the "parameters within which colonial discourse works," Benita Parry, in a splendid overview, discusses some of the limitations (inadvertent neglect of the native as historical subject, of alternative traditions, of anti-imperialist texts written by national liberation movements) in the deconstructive strategies of Spivak and Bhabha.

For further reading on the social construction and experiences of female subjects in English society, see Barbara Kanner's and Susan Balley's useful guides to resources, Sara Ellis's 19th century handbooks to women, and the historical and critical work of Catherine Gallagher, Margaret Hewitt, Eric Hobsbawm, Barbara Kanner, Steven Marcus, Wanda Neff, and Ivy Pinch-

beck. Eric Hobsbawm's *The Age of Empire* has a fine chapter on women, and Rosalind Miles's *Women's History of the World* has a chapter on the role of women as weapons of empire and reproduction designed to "keep the master-race pure" (166), as instruments of dominion and domination, as wives, missionaries and teachers. For other works that address the role of women in English empire, see Francis Hutchins, J.A. Mangan, A. P. Thornton and Rupert Wilkinson. Because their work studies official masculine Imperial administration, the lives and writings of real women in the British Empire await further study. Nigel Nicolson's biography of Mary Curzon (1977) though an important contribution, focuses chiefly on her role as wife of the notoriously anti-feminist Viceroy of India, Lord Curzon.

Works Cited

Arendt, Hannah. *The Origins of Totalitarianism.* New York: Harcourt, 1973.

Bailey, Susan P. *Women and the British Empire: An Annotated Guide to Sources.* New York: Garland, 1983.

Bhabha, Homi K. "The Other Question: Difference, Discrimination and the Discourse of Colonialism", *Literature, Politics and Theory,* ed. Francis Barker et. al. New York: Methuen, 1986.

Bodelsen, C.A. *Studies in Mid-Victorian Imperialism.* New York: Howard Fertig, 1968.

Brontë, Charlotte. *Jane Eyre* [1847], ed. Richard J. Dunn. New York: Norton Critical Edition, 1971.

Briggs, Asa. *Victorian People.* Chicago: U of Chicago P, 1970.

Ellis, Sara. *The Mothers of England.* New York: Appleton, 1843.

———. *The Women of England.* New York: Appleton, 1839.

———. *The Daughters of England.* New York: Appleton, 1843.

———. *The Wives of England.* New York: Appleton: 1843.

Gainer, Bernard. *The Alien Invasion: The Origins of the Aliens Act of 1905.* London: Heinemann, 1972.

Gallagher, Catherine. *The Industrial Reformation of English Fiction: 1832-1867.* Chicago: U of Chicago P, 1985.

Gilbert, Sandra. "Rider Haggard's Heart of Darkness," *Partisan Review* 50 (1983): 444-53.

Green, Martin. *Dreams of Adventure, Dreams of Empire.* New York: Basic Books, 1979.

Hewitt, Margaret. *Wives and Mothers in Victorian Industry.* London: Salisbury, 958.

Hobsbawn, Eric. *The Age of Empire: 1875-94.* New York: Vintage, 1989.

Hutchins, Francis. *The Illusion of Permanence: British Imperialism in India.* Princeton: Princeton UP, 1967.

Kanner, Barbara. *The Women in England from Anglo-Saxon Times to the Present: Interpretive Bibliographical Essays.* Hamden: Conn.: Archon, 1979.

————. *Women in English Social History 1800-1914: A Guide to Research.* 3 Vols. New York: Garland, 1987.

Kipling, Rudyard. *Plain Tales from the Hills [1888].* Oxford: Oxford UP, 1987.

Mangan, J. A. *The Games Ethic and Imperialism: Aspects of the Diffusion of an Ideal.* New York: Viking, 1986.

Mani, Lata. "The Production of an Official Discourse of SATI in Early Nineteenth-Century Bengal." *Europe and Its Others,* ed. Francis Barker et. al. Colchester: U of Essex P, 1985, 107-27.

Marcus, Steven. *The Other Victorians: A Study of Sexuality and Pornography in Mid-Nineteenth-Century England.* New York: Basic Books, 1974.

McClure, John. "Problematic Presence: The Colonial Other in Kipling and Conrad." *The Black Presence in English Literature,* ed. David Dabydeen. Manchester: Manchester UP, 1985.

Miles, Rosalind. *The Women's History of the World.* Topsfield, Mass: Salem House, 1989.

Miller, Christopher L. *Blank Darkness: Africanist Discourse in French.* Chicago: U of Chicago P, 1985.

Neff, Wanda. *Victorian Working Women: An Historical and Literary Study of Women in British Industries and Professions, 1832-1850.* New York: Columbia UP, 1929.

Parry, Benita. "Problems in Current Theories of Colonial Discourse." *The Oxford Literary Review* 9 (1987): 27-58.

Pinchbeck, Ivy. *Women Workers and Industrial Revolution, 1750-1850.* London: Virago, 1969.

Rosenthal, Michael. *The Character Factory: Baden-Powell and the Origins of the Boy-Scout Movement.* New York: Pantheon, 1986.

Said, Edward. *Orientalism.* New York: Random House, 1978.

————. "Orientalism Reconsidered." *Literature, Politics and Theory,* ed. Francis Barker et. al. New York: Methuen, 1986.

Shelley, Mary. *Frankenstein, or The Modern Prometheus.* New York: Bobbs-Merrill, 1974.

Spivak, Gayatri Chakravorty. "Three Women's Texts and a Critique of Imperialism." *Critical Quarterly* 12, no. 1 (Autumn 1985): 243-61.

Suleiman, Susan Rubin. ""Nadja, Dora, Lol V. Stein: Women, Madness and Narrative." *Discourse in Psychoanalysis and Literature,* ed. Shlomith Rimmon-Kenan. London: Methuen, 1987, 124-51.

Thornton, A. P. *The Habit of Authority: Paternalism in British History.* London: Allen & Unwin, 1966.

Weissman, Judith. *Half Savage and Hardy and Free.* Middletown, Conn.: Wesleyan UP, 1987.

Wilkinson, Rupert. *Gentlemanly Power: British Leadership and the Public School Tradition.* London: Oxford UP, 1964.

MONSTERS AND THE OCCULT

Patrick Brantlinger

SOURCE: "Imperial Gothic: Atavism and the Occult in the British Adventure Novel, 1880-1914," in *Rule of Darkness: British Literature and Imperalism, 1830-1914,* Cornell, 1988, pp. 227-53.

[In the book-length study excerpted below, Brantlinger examines the genre he identifies as "imperial gothic," which uses spiritualism to emphasize the themes of regression, invasion, and the lack of British heroism. In this excerpt, the critic argues that the genre is symptomatic of the gradual disintegration of British imperialism towards the end of the nineteenth century.]

In "The Little Brass God," a 1905 story by Bithia Croker, a statue of "Kali, Goddess of Destruction," brings misfortune to its unwitting Anglo-Indian possessors. First their pets kill each other or are killed in accidents; next the servants get sick or fall downstairs; then the family's lives are jeopardized. Finally the statue is stolen and dropped down a well, thus ending the curse.[1] This featherweight tale typifies many written between 1880 and 1914. Its central feature, the magic statue, suggests that Western rationality may be subverted by the very superstitions it rejects. The destructive magic of the Orient takes its revenge; Croker unwittingly expresses a social version of the return of the repressed characteristic of late Victorian and Edwardian fiction, including that blend of adventure story with Gothic elements—imperial Gothic, as I will call it—which flourished from H. Rider Haggard's *King Solomon's Mines* in 1885 down at least to John Buchan's *Greenmantle* in 1916. Imperial Gothic combines the seemingly scientific, progressive, often Darwinian ideology of imperialism with an antithetical interest in the occult. Although the connections between imperialism and other aspects of late Victorian and Edwardian culture are innumerable, the link with occultism is especially symptomatic of the anxieties that attended the climax of the British Empire. No form of cultural expression reveals more clearly the contradictions within that climax than imperial Gothic.

Impelled by scientific materialism, the search for new sources of faith led many late Victorians to telepathy, séances, and psychic research. It also led to the far reaches of the Empire, where strange gods and "unspeakable rites" still had their millions of devotees. Publication of Madame Blavatsky's *Isis Unveiled* in 1877 marks the beginning of this trend, and the stunning success of Edwin Arnold's *The Light of Asia* (1879) suggests the strength of the desire for alternatives to both religious orthodoxy and scientific skepticism.[2] For the same reason, A. P. Sinnett's *Esoteric Buddhism* (1883) was widely popular, as was his earlier *The Occult World* (1881).[3] The standard explanation for the flourishing of occultism in the second half of the nineteenth century is that "triumphant positivism sparked an international reaction against its restrictive world view." In illustrating this thesis, Janet Oppenheim lists some manifestations of that reaction: "In England, it was an age of . . . the Rosicrucian revival, of cabalists, Hermeticists, and reincarnationists. In the late 1880s, the Hermetic Order of the Golden Dawn first saw the light of day in London, and during its stormy history, the Order lured into its arcane activities not only W. B. Yeats, but also the self-proclaimed magus Aleister Crowley. . . . Palmists and astrologers abounded, while books on magic and the occult sold briskly."[4] Oppenheim's thesis that "much of the attraction of these and related subjects depended on the dominant role that science had assumed in modern culture" (160) is borne out by the testimony of those drawn to occultism, among them Arthur Conan Doyle, Annie Besant, Arthur J. Balfour, and Oliver Lodge. At the same time an emphasis on the occult aspects of experience was often reconciled with "science" and even with Darwinism; such a reconciliation characterizes Andrew Lang's interests in both anthropology and psychic research, as well as the various

neo-Hegelian justifications of Empire. Thus in *Origins and Destiny of Imperial Britain* (1900), J. A. Cramb argues that "empires are successive incarnations of the Divine ideas," but also that empires result from the struggle for survival of the fittest among nations and races. The British nation and Anglo-Saxon race, he contends, are the fittest to survive.[5]

Imperialism itself, as an ideology or political faith, functioned as a partial substitute for declining or fallen Christianity and for declining faith in Britain's future. The poet John Davidson, for instance, having rejected other creeds and causes, "committed himself to a cluster of ideas centering on hero worship, and heroic vitalism," according to his biographer, which led him to pen ardent celebrations of the Empire.[6] In "St. George's Day," Davidson writes:

> The Sphinx that watches by the Nile
> Has seen great empires pass away:
> The mightiest lasted but a while;
> Yet ours shall not decay—

a claim that by the 1890s obviously required extraordinary faith.[7] The religious quality of late Victorian imperialism is also evident in much of Rudyard Kipling's poetry, as in "Recessional":

> God of our fathers, known of old,
>   Lord of our far-flung battle-line,
> Beneath whose awful Hand we hold
>   Dominion over palm and pine—
> Lord God of Hosts, be with us yet,
> Lest we forget—lest we forget![8]

In his study of William Ernest Henley, who did much to encourage the expression of imperialism in fin-de-siècle literature, Jerome Buckley remarks that "by the last decade of the century, the concept of a national or racial absolute inspired a fervor comparable to that engendered by the older evangelical religion."[9]

Imperialism and occultism both functioned as ersatz religions, but their fusion in imperial Gothic represents something different from a search for new faiths. The patterns of atavism and going native described by imperialist romancers do not offer salvationist answers for seekers after religious truth; they offer instead insistent images of decline and fall or of civilization turning into its opposite just as the Englishman who desecrates a Hindu temple in Kipling's "Mark of the Beast" turns into a werewolf. Imperial Gothic expresses anxieties about the waning of religious orthodoxy, but even more clearly it expresses anxieties about the ease with which civilization can revert to barbarism or savagery and thus about the weakening of Britain's imperial hegemony. The atavistic descents into the primitive experienced by fictional characters seem often to be allegories of the larger regressive movement of civi-

The first step towards lightening

The White Man's Burden

is through teaching the virtues of cleanliness.

Pears' Soap

is a potent factor in brightening the dark corners of the earth as
civilization advances, while amongst the cultured of all nations
it holds the highest place—it is the ideal toilet soap.

The Empire was a pervasive presence in Victorian life.

lization, British progress transformed into British back-sliding. So the first section of Richard Jefferies's apocalyptic fantasy *After London* (1885) is entitled "The Relapse into Barbarism." Similarly, the narrator of Erskine Childers's spy novel *Riddle of the Sands* (1903) starts his tale in this way: "I have read of men who, when forced by their calling to live for long periods in utter solitude—save for a few black faces—have made it a rule to dress regularly for dinner in order to . . . prevent a relapse into barbarism."[10] Much imperialist writing after about 1880 treats the Empire as a barricade against a new barbarian invasion; just as often it treats the Empire as a "dressing for dinner," a temporary means of preventing Britain itself from relapsing into barbarism.

After the mid-Victorian years the British found it increasingly difficult to think of themselves as inevitably progressive; they began worrying instead about the degeneration of their institutions, their culture, their racial "stock." In *Mark Rutherford's Deliverance* (1885), William Hale White writes that "our civiliza-tion is nothing but a thin film or crust lying over a volcanic pit," and in *Fabian Essays* (1889), George Bernard Shaw contends that Britain is "in an advanced state of rottenness."[11] Much of the literary culture of the period expresses similar views. The aesthetic and decadent movements offer sinister analogies to Roman imperial decline and fall, while realistic novelists— George Gissing and Thomas Hardy, for instance—paint gloomy pictures of contemporary society and "the ache of modernism" (some of Gissing's pictures are explicitly anti-imperialist). Apocalyptic themes and images are characteristic of imperial Gothic, in which, despite the consciously pro-Empire values of many authors, the feeling emerges that "we are those upon whom the ends of the world are come."[12]

The three principal themes of imperial Gothic are individual regression or going native; an invasion of civilization by the forces of barbarism or demonism; and the diminution of opportunities for adventure and heroism in the modern world. In the romances of Stevenson, Haggard, Kipling, Doyle, Bram Stoker, and John Buchan the supernatural or paranormal, usually symptomatic of individual regression, often manifests itself in imperial settings. Noting that Anglo-Indian fiction frequently deals with "inexplicable curses, demonic possession, and ghostly visitations," Lewis Wurgaft cites Kipling's "Phantom Rickshaw" as typical, and countless such tales were set in Burma, Egypt, Nigeria, and other parts of the Empire as well.[13] In Edgar Wallace's *Sanders of the River* (1909), for example, the commissioner of a West African territory out-savages the savages, partly through police brutality but partly also through his knowledge of witchcraft. Says the narrator: "You can no more explain many happenings which are the merest commonplace in [Africa] than you can explain the miracle of faith or the wonder of telepathy."[14]

In numerous late Victorian and Edwardian stories, moreover, occult phenomena follow characters from imperial settings home to Britain. In Doyle's "The Brown Hand" (1899), an Anglo-Indian doctor is haunted after his return to England by the ghost of an Afghan whose hand he had amputated. In "The Ring of Thoth" (1890) and "Lot No. 249" (1892), Egyptian mummies come to life in the Louvre and in the rooms of an Oxford student.[15] In all three stories, western science discovers or triggers supernatural effects associated with the "mysterious Orient." My favorite story of this type is H. G. Wells's "The Truth about Pyecraft," in which an obese Londoner takes an Indian recipe for "loss of weight" but instead of slimming down, begins levitating. The problem caused by oriental magic is then solved by western technology: lead underwear, which allows the balloonlike Mr. Pyecraft to live almost normally, feet on the ground.

The causes of the upsurge in romance writing toward the end of the century are numerous, complex, and often the same as those of the upsurge of occultism. Thus the new romanticism in fiction is frequently explained by its advocates—Stevenson, Haggard, Lang, and others—as a reaction against scientific materialism as embodied in "realistic" or "naturalistic" narratives. The most enthusiastic defender of the new fashion for romances was Andrew Lang, who thought the realism of George Eliot and Henry James intellectually superior but also that the romances of Stevenson and Haggard tapped universal, deep-rooted, "primitive" aspects of human nature which the realists could not approach. "Fiction is a shield with two sides, the silver and the golden: the study of manners and of character, on one hand; on the other, the description of adventure, the delight of romantic narrative."[16] Although he sees a place for both kinds of fiction, Lang has little patience with, for example, Dostoevsky's gloomy honesty: "I, for one, admire M. Dostoieffsky so much . . . that I pay him the supreme tribute of never reading him at all" (685). Lang prefers literature of a middlebrow sort, on a level with his own critical journalism, or, farther down the scale of cultural value, he prefers adventure stories written for boys: "'Treasure Island' and 'Kidnapped' are boys' books written by an author of whose genius, for narrative, for delineation of character, for style, I hardly care to speak, lest enthusiasm should seem to border on fanaticism" (690). Lang feels that Haggard is by no means so sophisticated a writer as Stevenson, but this is almost an advantage: the less sophisticated or the more boyish, the better.

All the same, Lang believes, realism in fiction should coexist with romanticism just as the rational, conscious side of human nature coexists with the unconscious. Lang can appreciate realistic novels intellectually, but "the natural man within me, the survival of some blue-painted Briton or of some gipsy," is "equally pleased with a *true* Zulu love story" (689). He therefore declares that "the advantage of our mixed condition, civilized at top with the old barbarian under our clothes, is just this, that we can enjoy all sorts of things" (690). Romances may be unsophisticated affairs, but because they appeal to the barbarian buried self of the reader, they are more fundamental, more honest, more natural than realism. In Lang's criticism, romances are "'savage survivals,' but so is the whole of the poetic way of regarding Nature" (690).

An anthropologist of sorts, Lang acquired his theory of savage survivals from his mentor Edward Burnett Tylor, who contends that occultism and spiritualism—indeed, all forms of superstition (and therefore, implicitly, of religion)—belong to "the philosophy of savages." Modern occultism, according to Tylor, is "a direct revival from the regions of savage philosophy and peasant folk-lore," a reversion to "primitive culture."[17] At the same time Tylor associates poetry with the mythology of primitive peoples: "The mental condition of the lower races is the key to poetry, nor is it a

small portion of the poetic realm which these definitions cover" (2:533). Literary activity in general thus appears to be a throwback to prerational states of mind and society. Similarly, Arthur Machen, author of numerous Gothic horror stories from the 1890s onward, defines literature as "the endeavour of every age to return to the first age, to an age, if you like, of savages."[18]

Robert Louis Stevenson, who echoes Lang's defenses of romances as against novels, discovered sources of "primitive" poetic energy in his own psyche, most notably through the nightmare that yielded *Dr. Jekyll and Mr. Hyde.* Stevenson entertained ambivalent feelings toward the popularity of that "Gothic gnome" or "crawler," in part because *any* popular appeal seemed irrational or vaguely barbaric to him. Although not overtly about imperial matters, *Jekyll and Hyde,* perhaps even more than *Treasure Island* and *Kidnapped,* served as a model for later writers of imperial Gothic fantasies. Because "within the Gothic we can find a very intense, if displaced, engagement with political and social problems," it is possible, as David Punter argues, to read *Jekyll and Hyde* as itself an example of imperial Gothic: "It is strongly suggested [by Stevenson] that Hyde's behaviour is an urban version of 'going native.' The particular difficulties encountered by English imperialism in its decline were conditioned by the nature of the supremacy which had been asserted: not a simple racial supremacy, but one constantly seen as founded on moral superiority. If an empire based on a morality declines, what are the implications . . . ? It is precisely Jekyll's 'high views' which produce morbidity in his *alter ego*."[19] Jekyll's alchemy releases the apelike barbarian—the savage or natural man—who lives beneath the civilized skin. Not only is this the general fantasy of going native in imperial Gothic, but Hyde—murderous, primitive, apelike—fits the Victorian stereotype of the Irish hooligan, and his dastardly murder of Sir Danvers Carew resembles some of the "Fenian outrages" of the early 1880s.[20]

Imperial Gothic is related to several other forms of romance writing which flourished between 1880 and 1914. Judith Wilt has argued for the existence of subterranean links between late Victorian imperialism, the resurrection of Gothic romance formulas, and the conversion of Gothic into science fiction. "In or around December, 1897," she writes, "Victorian gothic changed—into Victorian science fiction. The occasion was . . . Wells's *War of the Worlds,* which followed by only a few months Bram Stoker's . . . *Dracula.*"[21] A similar connection is evident between imperial Gothic and the romance fictions of the decadent movement, as in Oscar Wilde's *Picture of Dorian Gray,* which traces an atavistic descent into criminal self-indulgence as mirrored by a changing portrait. Both Stoker's and Wells's romances can be read, moreover, as fanciful versions of yet another popular literary form, invasion-scare stories, in which the outward movement of imperialist adventure is reversed, a pattern foreshadowed by the returned convict theme in Botany Bay eclogues. *Dracula* itself is an individual invasion or demonic possession fantasy with political implications. Not only is Stoker's bloodthirsty Count the "final aristocrat," he is also the last of a "conquering race," as Dracula explains to Jonathan Harker:

> We Szekelys have a right to be proud, for in our veins flows the blood of many brave races who fought as the lion fights, for lordship. Here, in the whirlpool of European races, the Ugric tribe bore down from Iceland the fighting spirit which Thor and Wodin gave them, which their Berserkers displayed to such fell intent on the seaboards of Europe, aye, and of Asia and Africa, too, till the peoples thought that the were-wolves themselves had come. Here, too, when they came, they found the Huns, whose warlike fury had swept the earth like a living flame, till the dying peoples held that in their veins ran the blood of those old witches, who, expelled from Scythia, had mated with the devils in the desert. Fool, fools! What devil or what witch was ever so great as Attila, whose blood is in these veins? . . . Is it a wonder that we were a conquering race?[22]

The whirlpool of the Count's own ideas, confounding racism with the mixing of races, pride in pure blood with blood-sucking cannibalism, and aristocratic descent with witchcraft and barbarism, reads like a grim parody of the "conquering race" rhetoric in much imperialist writing, a premonition of fascism. In common with several other Gothic invaders in late Victorian fiction, moreover, Dracula threatens to create a demonic empire of the dead from the living British Empire. "This was the being I was helping to transfer to London," says Jonathan Harker, "where, perhaps for centuries to come, he might, amongst its teeming millions, satiate his lust for blood, and create a new and ever widening circle of semi-demons to batten on the helpless" (67).

A similar demonic invasion is threatened in Haggard's *She:* Ayesha plans to usurp the British throne from Queen Victoria, though fortunately her second dousing in the flames of immortality kills her before she can leave the Caves of Kôr for London.[23] Horace Holly, the principal narrator of Haggard's romance, explains the situation: "Evidently the terrible *She* had determined to go to England, and it made me shudder to think what would be the result of her arrival. . . . In the end, I had little doubt, she would assume absolute rule over the British dominions, and probably over the whole earth, and, though I was sure that she would speedily make ours the most glorious and prosperous empire that the world has ever seen, it must be at the cost of a terrible sacrifice of life."[24] Though Haggard

resurrects Ayesha in later romances, his archetype of feminine domination grows tamer and never travels to Britain. Several critics have seen in both *She* and *Dracula* the threat of the New Woman to Victorian patriarchy, and Queen Tera, the mummy who comes to life in Stoker's *Jewel of the Seven Stars* (1903), represents the same threat. Norman Etherington calls Ayesha "a Diana in jack-boots who preaches materialism in philosophy and fascism in politics" (47), while Nina Auerbach notes that Ayesha's dream of eternal love and immortality is fused with the nightmare of universal empire. In Ayesha's case, "love does not tranquilize womanhood into domestic confinement, but fuels her latent powers into political life."[25] Although the New Woman is one of the threats underlying the demonism of Ayesha and also of Dracula and his female victims, however, Haggard's and Stoker's apocalyptic fears are comprehensive: the demons who threaten to subvert the Empire and invade Britain are of both sexes and come in many guises.

Often Wells's translations of Gothic conventions into quasi-scientific ones also suggest demonic subversions of the Empire or—what amounts to the same thing in late Victorian and Edwardian writing—of civilization. "It occurred to me that instead of the usual interview with the devil or a magician, an ingenious use of scientific patter might with advantage be substituted," Wells writes of his "scientific romances." "I simply brought the fetish stuff up to date, and made it as near actual theory as possible."[26] *The War of the Worlds* is the classic science fiction, invasion-from-outer-space fantasy, though Wells wrote many related stories—"The Empire of the Ants," for example, in which superintelligent, poisonous ants from the Amazon Basin threaten to overwhelm first British Guiana and then the entire world, founding their insect empire upon the ruins of human ones.

Numerous invasion fantasies were written between 1880 and 1914 without Gothic overtones. The ur-text is Sir George Chesney's *The Battle of Dorking*, which first appeared in *Blackwood's Magazine* in 1871. In the bibliography to *Voices Prophesying War*, I. F. Clarke lists dozens of "imaginary war" novels published between 1871 and 1914, many of them following an invasion-of-Britain pattern. Among them are T. A. Guthrie's *The Seizure of the Channel Tunnel* (1882), H. F. Lester's *The Taking of Dover* (1888), and the anonymous *The Sack of London in the Great French War of 1901* (1901). Several novels also appeared, both in Britain and elsewhere, with titles along the lines of *Decline and Fall of the British Empire*, as well as invasion-of-India stories.[27] Clearly this was not the fiction of a generation of writers confident about the future of Britain or its Empire. The essence of the genre is captured in P. G. Wodehouse's 1909 parody *The Swoop . . . A Tale of the Great Invasion*, in which Britain is overwhelmed by simultaneous onslaughts of

Germans, Russians, Chinese, Young Turks, the Swiss Navy, Moroccan brigands, cannibals in war canoes, the Prince of Monaco, and the Mad Mullah, until it is saved by a patriotic Boy Scout named Clarence Chugwater. The only question left to the reader's imagination is why these various forces of barbarism should want to invade so decrepit a country.[28]

Invasion-scare stories often intersect with spy stories. David Stafford gives 1893 as the date of "the birth of the British spy novel," with publication of William Le Queux's *The Great War in England in 1897,* and the subgenre includes many stories, among them Childers's *Riddle of the Sands,* that contain elements of imperial Gothic.[29] Spy stories can be as upbeat as Kipling's *Kim,* full of an evident delight in playing the Great Game in Asia, with little to fear from the bungling French and Russian agents whom Kim helps to foil, or as fear-ridden as Buchan's *Thirty-Nine Steps,* characterized by a breathless paranoia as the hero flees his would-be assassins through a British countryside where no one is to be trusted. Even *Kim,* however, fits Stafford's general description of spy fiction: "The world presented by these novels is a . . . treacherous one in which Britain is the target of the envy, hostility, and malevolence of the other European powers" (497-98).

All of these popular romance formulas—imperial Gothic, Wellsian science fiction, invasion fantasies, spy stories—betray anxieties characteristic of late Victorian and Edwardian imperialism both as an ideology and as a phase of political development. To Wilt's and Stafford's mainly literary perspectives can be added a socioeconomic one, related to those theories of J. A. Hobson and Joseph Schumpeter which treat imperialism itself as an atavistic stage of economic and political development. Although Schumpeter argues against the economic imperialism espoused by Hobson and later, in modified forms, by Lenin and other Marxists, his contention that "imperialism is . . . atavistic in character" fits both imperial Gothic and the flourishing of occultism.[30] Schumpeter identifies capitalism with progress through rational self-interest and therefore fails to see it as a source of social irrationality and regression. Hobson, on the other hand, sees imperialism as a direct result of underconsumption at home and capitalism's consequent search for ever-expanding markets abroad. But in terms of ideological and cultural effects, both Schumpeter and Hobson view imperialism as a retrograde social development, a backsliding toward barbarism.

Hobson locates the causes of "national hate" and international aggression as much in cultural as in economic factors, though for him culture and economics are finally inseparable.[31] Hobson was as much influenced by John Ruskin as by Richard Cobden (the best book on Ruskin published during the nineteenth century is Hobson's); his condemnation of industrialism is less

sweeping than Ruskin's, but his "economic humanism" nevertheless echoes *Unto This Last* and *Fors Clavigera.*[32] Ruskin, however, like his own mentor Carlyle, celebrated war as a supreme social value and offered little criticism of British overseas aggression, whereas Hobson contends that uncontrolled industrial capitalism generates wars and leads to the imperialization of preindustrial peoples. Ruskin saw that so-called industrial progress adversely affected nature, town life, workers, owners, the arts; Hobson sees that it also entails an expansive militarization that rides roughshod over older patterns of democracy and liberal nationalism toward an era of ruinous wars.

Both Ruskin and Hobson interpret in terms of regression much that their contemporaries understand as progress. According to Hobson, "the rapid and numerous changes in the external structure of modern civilization have been accompanied by grave unsettlement of the inner life; a breaking up of time-honoured dogmas, a collapse of principles in politics, religion, and morality have sensibly reduced the power of resistance to strong passionate suggestions in the individuals of all classes. Hence the common paradox that an age of universal scepticism may also be an age of multifarious superstitions, lightly acquired and briefly held, but dangerous for character and conduct while they hold their sway."[33] By superstitions Hobson appears to mean a variety of ideological phenomena, including both imperialism and occultism. In any event, he is especially distressed that universal education and the new mass literacy have failed to increase democratic rationality but instead seem to have undermined the intelligence of public opinion. "The popularization of the power to read has made the press the chief instrument of brutality. . . . A biassed, enslaved, and poisoned press has been the chief engine for manufacturing Jingoism" (29, 125). The very machinery that makes mass literacy possible Hobson sees as having deleterious side-effects. The "terse, dogmatic, unqualified, and unverifiable cablegram," for example, seems to represent technological progress but is instead, Hobson believes, a source of "emotional explosive" and mob sentiment (11). On the one hand, industrialization has created "mechanical facilities for cheap, quick carriage of persons, goods, and news"; on the other, a newly literate but poorly educated urban population is easy prey for sensational journalists and warmongering financiers. These new shapers of public opinion diffuse a potent ideological mix consisting of adulterated versions of social Darwinism, the chauvinistic ethos of the public schools and universities, the "khaki Christianity" of the churches, and above all the racism and narrow-mindedness of the music halls: "The glorification of brute force and an ignorant contempt for foreigners are ever-present factors which . . . make the music-hall a very serviceable engine for generating military passion" (2).

For Hobson, therefore, the path of social regression is marked by the signs of a corrupting, degenerate mass culture. He believes that "the physical and mental conditions of . . . town-life" breed "the very atmosphere of Jingoism. A coarse patriotism, fed by the wildest rumours and the most violent appeals to hate and the animal lust of blood, passes by quick contagion through the crowded life of cities, and recommends itself everywhere by the satisfaction it affords to sensational cravings" (8-9). Hobson is thinking partly of the riotous celebrations in London and other British cities which followed the lifting of the sieges of Ladysmith and Mafeking during the Boer War. Something was at work in those mob scenes far more destructive than the breaking of the Hyde Park railings which had distressed Matthew Arnold in 1866, even though the later rioters were presumably patriots celebrating British victories. Jingoism fused with the social imperialism of Joseph Chamberlain in the 1890s to emerge as the chief rival to liberalism and socialism for the allegiance of the new working- and lower middle-class voters, foreshadowing fascism. In *The Psychology of Jingoism,* Hobson interprets the ideological success of imperialism as threatening the entire project of civilizing humanity, including British humanity at home. During mob expressions of jingoism, Hobson declares, "the superstructure which centuries of civilization have imposed upon . . . the individual, gives way before some sudden wave of ancient savage nature roused from its subconscious depths" (19). If such a regression is possible for the individual who joins the mob, then it is also possible for an entire society—even the seemingly most civilized, most progressive society—and for Hobson one name for such a reversion to barbarism is imperialism, "a depraved choice of national life" transforming democratic civilization into a savage anarchy clamoring for war. "For the purposes of the present study . . . the hypothesis of reversion to a savage type of nature is distinctly profitable. The [modern] war-spirit . . . is composed of just those qualities which differentiate savage from civilized man" (19).

Numerous travel writers from about 1870 onward lament the decline of exploration into mere tourism. In "Regrets of a Veteran Traveller" (1897), Frederic Harrison declares: "Railways, telegraphs, and circular tours in twenty days have opened to the million the wonders of foreign parts." These signs of technological progress, however, conceal losses: "Have they not sown broadcast disfigurement, vulgarity, stupidity, demoralisation? Europe is changed indeed since the unprogressive forties! Is it all for the better?"[34] The old ideal of opening up the dark places of the world to civilization, commerce, and Christianity fades into the tourist trade: "Morally, we Britons plant the British flag on every peak and pass; and wherever the Union Jack floats there we place the cardinal British institutions—tea, tubs, sanitary appliances, lawn tennis, and churches; all of them excellent things in season. But the missionary zeal of our people is not always according to knowledge and discretion" (241). Before the ugly American came the ugly Briton, clutching a Baedeker or a Cook's travel guide. Harrison thinks it has all become too easy, too common, too standardized to be heroic or adventuresome—"We go abroad, but we travel no longer."

Imperial Gothic frequently expresses anxiety about the waning of opportunities for heroic adventure. With regression and invasion, this is the third of its major themes (ironic today, given Hollywood's frequent regressions to Haggard and Kipling for its adventure tales, as in *Raiders of the Lost Ark*). Early Victorian adventure writers—Marryat, Chamier, Mayne Reid, R. M. Ballantyne—took as self-evident the notion that England was the vanguard nation, leading the world toward the future. As one of the marooned boys in Ballantyne's *Coral Island* (1856) says, "We'll take possession of [this island] in the name of the King; we'll . . . enter the service of its black inhabitants. Of course we'll rise, naturally, to the top of affairs. White men always do in savage countries."[35] Upbeat racism and chauvinism continued to characterize boys' adventure fiction well into the twentieth century, but in imperial Gothic white men do not always rise to the top—just as often they sink into savagedom, cowardice, or exotic torpor, as in Tennyson's "Lotos Eaters." Conrad's fictions frequently read like botched romances in which adventure turns sour or squalid, undermined by moral frailty, and the same is true also of Stevenson's most realistic stories—*The Beach of Falesá, The Wreckers, Ebb-Tide.* Lord Jim's failure to live up to his heroic self-image has analogues in many imperial Gothic stories that are not ostensibly critical of imperialism.

The fear that adventure may be a thing of the past in the real world led many writers to seek it in the unreal world of romance, dreams, imagination. "Soon the ancient mystery of Africa will have vanished," Haggard laments in an 1894 essay appropriately titled "'Elephant Smashing' and 'Lion Shooting.'" Where, he dolefully asks, "will the romance writers of future generations find a safe and secret place, unknown to the pestilent accuracy of the geographer, in which to lay their plots?"[36] In similar fashion, in both *Heart of Darkness* and his autobiographical essays, Conrad registers his youthful excitement over the blank places on the map of Africa and the disillusionment he felt when he arrived at Stanley Falls in 1890: "A great melancholy descended on me . . . there was . . . no great haunting memory . . . only the unholy recollection of a prosaic newspaper 'stunt' and the distasteful knowledge of the vilest scramble for loot that ever disfigured the history of human conscience and geographical exploration. What an end to the idealized realities of a boy's daydreams! I wondered what I was doing there."[37]

The stunt was Stanley's 1871 trek into Central Africa in search of Livingstone for the *New York Herald,* the scramble for loot that Conrad saw at first hand King Leopold's rapacious private empire in the Congo.

Arguments defending theosophy and spiritualism often sound like Haggard's and Conrad's laments for the waning of geographical adventure: the disappearance of earthly frontiers will be compensated for by the opening of new frontiers in the beyond. Not only were occultists seeking proofs of immortality and of a spiritual realm above or beneath the material one, they were also seeking adventure. The fantasy element in such adventure seeking is its most obvious feature, as it is also in the literary turn away from realism to romanticism. According to Lang: "As the visible world is measured, mapped, tested, weighed, we seem to hope more and more that a world of invisible romance may not be far from us. . . . The ordinary shilling tales of 'hypnotism' and mesmerism are vulgar trash enough, and yet I can believe that an impossible romance, if the right man wrote it in the right mood, might still win us from the newspapers, and the stories of shabby love, and cheap remorses, and commonplace failures."[38] But even a well-written impossible romance, as Lang well knows, carries with it more than a hint of childish daydreaming.

If imperialist ideology is atavistic, occultism is obviously so, a rejection of individual and social rationality and a movement backward to primitive or infantile modes of perception and belief. "Ages, empires, civilisations pass, and leave some members even of educated mankind still, in certain points, on the level of the savage who propitiates with gifts, or addresses with prayers, the spirits of the dead"—so Lang writes in *Cock Lane and Common Sense* (1894), intended in part to expose the spurious aspects of spiritualism.[39] Lang believes that much of what goes by that name is fraudulent: "As to the idea of purposely evoking the dead, it is at least as impious, as absurd, as odious to taste and sentiment, as it is insane in the eyes of reason. This protest the writer feels obliged to make, for while he regards the traditional, historical, and anthropological curiosities here collected as matters of some interest . . . he has nothing but abhorrence and contempt for modern efforts to converse with the manes, and for all the profane impostures of 'spiritualism'" (*Cock Lane,* 22).

Like many other well-known Victorians, Lang participated in the Society for Psychical Research, founded in 1882, and even served as its president. But his opinions about psychic phenomena always retain a healthy skepticism. Stopping short of supernatural explanations, Lang favors instead explanations in terms of extraordinary, hitherto unidentified mental powers, including the power of "unconscious cerebration" to create illusions of ghosts or spirits and to perform tele-

pathic feats. If we assume psychic phenomena do occur, then the theory that they emanate from the subconscious is the chief alternative to what Lang calls "the old savage theory" of "the agency of the spirits of the dead."[40]

Just how the subconscious works—how to explain its mechanisms of projection, hallucination, dreams, and forgetting—was a major issue in late nineteenth-century psychology. British psychologists followed paths similar to those that led to psychoanalysis, and their explanations of psychic phenomena, in common with Freud's, tend toward ideas of regression and unconscious cerebration.[41] In *The Future of an Illusion,* Freud writes that the beliefs of the "spiritualists" are infantile: "They are convinced of the survival of the individual soul. . . . Unfortunately they cannot succeed in refuting the fact that . . . their spirits are merely the products of their own mental activity. They have called up the spirits of the greatest men . . . but all the pronouncements and information which they have received . . . have been so foolish . . . that one can find nothing credible in them but the capacity of the spirits to adapt themselves to the circle of people who have conjured them up."[42] Freud interprets spiritualist beliefs, as he does all of the "fairy tales of religion," as backsliding from adult, conscious rationality into the irrational depths of the subconscious.

Such an explanation of superstitions might do for the psychologists and also for Lang, who as an anthropologist was more interested in the products of myth making and religion than in experiencing the miraculous himself. For many of Lang's colleagues in psychic research, however, the realm of spirit was not reducible to that of the unconscious, even though the latter might contain unknown, potentially miraculous powers. In his *Encyclopedia Britannica* article on psychical research, Lang notes F.W.H. Myers's various studies; regrettably, Myers "tended more and more to the belief in the 'invasion' and 'possession' of living human organisms by spirits of the dead." He points to the same tendency in the work of the physicist and psychic researcher Oliver Lodge, and adds: "Other students can find, in the evidence cited [by Lodge and Myers], no warrant for this return to the 'palaeolithic psychology' of 'invasion' and 'possession'" (547).

Other late Victorians and Edwardians moved in the direction Lang held to be retrograde—away from an early skepticism toward increasing and occasionally absolute faith in occult phenomena, including demonic invasions and possessions of reality. Obviously the will-to-believe in such cases was powerful. A. J. Balfour, for example, Conservative prime minister from 1902 to 1905, produced several "metaphysical" essays—*A Defence of Philosophic Doubt* (1897), *The Foundations of Belief* (1895), and others—that make the case for faith by sharply dividing science and religion.

Balfour argues that the two are separate, equally valid realms; the methods and discoveries of science cannot invalidate those of religion. That his sympathies lie with religion is obvious. In his presidential address to the Society for Psychical Research in 1894, Balfour expresses his joy that the society's work demonstrates "there are things in heaven and earth not hitherto dreamed of in our scientific philosophy."[43] Small wonder that in 1916, when the former prime minister (aided by several automatic writers, including Kipling's sister Alice Fleming) began to receive spirit communications from the love of his youth, Mary Lyttelton, he came to believe that the messages were genuine. Small wonder, too, given his political career, that among the themes in the three thousand messages directed to him from the beyond is the establishment of a harmonious world order (Oppenheim 133).

Several early modern writers followed roughly similar paths from doubt to faith. In Kipling's case, the faith was perhaps never firm. While lightly tossing off such ghost stories as "The Phantom Rickshaw" (1888) and "The Return of Imray" (1891), the young Kipling showed what he actually thought of occultism in "The Sending of Dana Da" (1888)—and what he thought was skeptical to the point of sarcasm: "Once upon a time, some people in India made a new Heaven and a new Earth out of broken teacups, a missing brooch or two, and a hair-brush. These were hidden under bushes, or stuffed into holes in the hillside, and an entire Civil Service of subordinate Gods used to find or mend them again; and every one said: 'There are more things in Heaven and Earth than are dreamt of in our philosophy.'"[44] Kipling's satire, perhaps inspired by recent exposures of Mme. Blavatsky's fraudulence, takes aim at all branches of occultism including theosophy. The new "Religion," he says, "was too elastic for ordinary use. It stretched itself and embraced pieces of everything that the medicine-men of all ages have manufactured," including "White, Gray, and Black Magic . . . spiritualism, palmistry, fortune-telling by cards, hot chesnuts, double-kernelled nuts, and tallow droppings." It would even "have adopted Voodoo and Oboe had it known anything about them" (308).

In the story that follows this introduction, Dana Da, a magus from Afghanistan or parts unknown, is hired by an unnamed Englishman to produce a psychic sending or visitation to annoy the Englishman's enemy, Lone Sahib. Because Lone Sahib hates cats, the sending takes the form of an invasion of his bungalow by a plague of supposedly spirit kittens. Lone Sahib and his "co-religionists" see the kittens as materializations from the beyond, write up a report on them "as every Psychical Observer is bound to do," and grow ever more convinced that "spirits . . . squatter up and down their staircases all night" (313). At the story's end the Englishman who has paid for the sending asks Dana Da how he produced it; the alleged magus replies that

he gave Lone Sahib's servant "two-eight a month for cats—little, little cats. I wrote, and he put them about— very clever man" (320).

Just when Kipling put aside skepticism and began to be something of an occultist himself is not clear, though some accounts attribute the change to the death of his daughter Josephine in 1899. Certainly her death inspired Kipling to write the psychic story "They" (1904), in which the protagonist communicates with ghostly children in a ghostly country-house setting. But by that time Kipling had also written stories dealing with reincarnation—"The Finest Story in the World" (1891) and "Wireless" (1902)—a subject of increasing interest also to his friend Haggard, whose views about spiritual matters are easier to trace because he was always less defensively ironic than Kipling. Some critics dismiss the problem, suggesting that Kipling occasionally includes supernatural elements in his stories merely for artistic purposes, but this approach seems no more explanatory than arguing that Dante writes about heaven and hell for artistic purposes. Nor did Kipling drop the supernatural after the early 1900s: several stories in *Debits and Credits* (1926) deal with the supernatural—"The Gardener," "The Madonna of the Trenches," and "The Wish House"—and so do other works among his late fiction.[45]

Haggard was interested in occultism from the time when, as a young man in London, he attended séances at the house of Lady Paulet, who gave him his "entree to the spiritualistic society of the day."[46] The apparitions that he saw were not exactly spirits, he thought, but rather the products of "some existent but unknown force" (1:41). Occultism shows up in his first novel, *Dawn* (1884), which combines realism with, as George Saintsbury put it, the "elements of occult arts and astral spirits."[47] Haggard's second novel, *The Witch's Head* (1884), also supposedly realistic, touches upon the theme of reincarnation. After about 1900, according to Norman Etherington, Haggard dwelt with "increased fervor on the truth of reincarnation. The idea he had first tentatively expressed in *Witch's Head,* that lovers worked out their relationships in successive lives and literally eternal triangles, became a dominant theme in his later novels. He believed he had caught glimpses of his own previous existences in dreams and visions" (17). In *The Days of My Life,* Haggard describes a series of these visions of former lives, which might almost, Etherington says, "be tableaux from the ethnographic section of a museum," similar to "displays on 'the ascent of man' from the Stone Age to the Iron Age" (17). In the first reincarnation Haggard is a primitive man, perhaps of the Stone Age; in the second he is black, again primitive, defending his rude home against attackers who kill him; in the third he is an ancient Egyptian, in love with a "beautiful young woman with violet eyes"; and in the fourth he is probably an early medieval barbarian, living in "a timber-built hall" in a land of "boundless snows and great cold," though again in love with a violet-eyed woman, the same "as she of the Egyptian picture." Haggard believes that these "dream-pictures" can be explained in one of three ways: "(1) Memories of some central incident that occurred in a previous incarnation. (2) *Racial* memories of events that had happened to fore-fathers. (3) Subconscious imagination and invention" (2:168). The third explanation is the easiest to accept, he says, but he clearly favors the first or the second.

Kipling and Haggard often discussed telepathy, ghosts, and reincarnation. Although it is likely that Kipling believed—perhaps always with a certain ambivalence or ironic distance—in some version of occultism at least from 1904 onward, Haggard later opined that he converted Kipling to faith in reincarnation in the 1920s. "He is now convinced," Haggard wrote in his diary in 1923, "that the individual human being is not a mere flash in the pan, seen for a moment and lost forever, but an enduring entity that has lived elsewhere and will continue to live, though for a while memory of the past is blotted out" (quoted in Cohen, 122). This may have been only wishful thinking on Haggard's part. In any event, it seems likely that the very ambivalence with which Kipling approached any belief in the su-pernatural made him all the more ardent an imperialist. On political issues Haggard often seems more supple and thoughtful than Kipling, though always also ar-dently imperialistic.[48] Thus Haggard was not prepared to blame "all our Russian troubles" on "the machina-tions of the Jews." Puzzled by Kipling's often bellig-erent antisemitism, Haggard wrote in 1919: "I do not know, I am sure, but personally I am inclined to think that one can insist too much on the Jew motive, the truth being that there are Jews and Jews. . . . For my own part I should be inclined to read Trade Unions instead of Jews" (quoted in Cohen, 110-11). In con-trast, Kipling, ambivalent about so many matters, is often dogmatic about politics: "Any nation save our-selves, with such a fleet as we have at present, would go out swiftly to trample the guts out of the world," Kipling declaimed to Haggard in 1897; "and the fact that we do not seems to show that even if we aren't very civilized, we're about the one power with a glim-mering of civilization in us" (quoted in Cohen, 33). The only ambivalence here has to do with the meaning of civilization: perhaps it is a weakness, a disease; perhaps the brave if not civilized thing to do would be to "trample the guts out of the world."

Haggard's comparative uncertainty about politics is dimly reflected in the romance conventions he em-ploys in most of his fictions. In common with other advocates of the romance as against the novel, Hag-gard hesitates at defending his tales as truer than real-istic fictions or even as somehow true. He agrees with Lang that he is expressing universal, mythic concerns—writing about what Jung would later call archetypes.

But he also knows that his landscapes shade into the fantastic and are therefore highly subjective landscapes of the mind. Just as Lang is inclined to attribute psy-chic phenomena to the unconscious, so Haggard often suggests that his stories refer more to his own—or perhaps to universal—dream states than to outward reality. Haggard shares this emphasis on fantasy with all Gothic romancers, whose stories always veer to-ward dreams and the subliminal reaches of the mind.

The subjectivism of Gothic romance as a genre thus intersects with the atavistic character of both imperial-ist ideology and occultist belief. According to Theodor Adorno, "occultism is a reflex-action to the subjectifi-cation of all meaning, the complement of reification." Adorno contends that "occultism is a symptom of regression in consciousness," diagnosing it specifically as a "regres-sion to magic under late capitalism" whereby "thought is assimilated to late capitalist forms" (239).

> The power of occultism, as of Fascism, to which it is connected by thought-patterns of the ilk of anti-semitism, is not only pathic. Rather it lies in the fact that in the lesser panaceas, as in superimposed pictures, consciousness famished for truth imagines it is grasping a dimly present knowledge diligently denied to it by official progress in all its forms. It is the knowledge that society, by virtually excluding the possibility of spontaneous change, is gravitating towards total catastrophe. The real absurdity is reproduced in the astrological hocus-pocus, which adduces the impenetrable connections of alienated elements—nothing more alien than the stars—as knowledge about the subject.[49]

Adorno's analysis of the interior parallelism between occultism and fascism suggests also the interior sig-nificance (the political unconscious) of imperial Gothic fantasy. The subjective nature of the genre is more or less apparent to all of its best practitioners. The motif of the exploration of the Dark Continent or of other blank spaces of external reality whose meaning seems inward—the fabled journey into the unconscious or the heart of darkness of the explorer—is omnipresent in late Victorian and Edwardian literature. Graham Greene is writing at the end of a long tradition when, in *Journey without Maps* (1936), he likens African travel to a landscape of the mind, a dream geography, to be understood as much in psychoanalytic as in geo-graphical terms.[50] Africa, India, and the other dark places of the earth become a terrain upon which the political unconscious of imperialism maps its own desires, its own fantastic longitudes and latitudes.

All of Haggard's romances, from *King Solomon's Mines* onward, can be interpreted as journeys into the dreams of the protagonists and ultimately of Haggard himself. "I closed my eyes," says Horace Holly in *She*, "and imagination, taking up the thread of thought, shot its swift shuttle back across the ages, weaving a picture on their blackness so real and vivid in its detail that I could almost for a moment think that I had triumphed over Time, and that my vision had pierced the mystery of the Past" (141). After describing his fantasy of Ayesha in her youthful power and glory, Holly adds: "Let him who reads forgive the intrusion of a dream into a history of fact" (141). Or, as Captain John Good says after the battle with the Masai in *Allan Quatermain,* "the whole thing seemed more as though one had enjoyed a nightmare just before being called, than as a deed done" (485). Over and over Haggard's adventurers liken their experiences to dreams as they leave the actual geography of Africa or Asia for landscapes that obviously have more affinity to the world of fantasy than to the real one. For Haggard, it requires merely a flip-flopping of the equation to claim the reality of reincarnation and the spirit world that dreams appear to shadow forth.

Haggard's fantasy landscapes often refer less to mental processes than to downright visceral ones, as his characters are swallowed up or temporarily entombed in chasms, tunnels, crypts, and caves: the Place of Death in *King Solomon's Mines,* the underground river down which the explorers plummet to the land of the Zu-Vendis in *Allan Quatermain,* the Caves of Kôr in *She.* As Holly and Leo Vincy escape the midnight storm that shipwrecks them on the coast of Africa, "we shot out between the teeth-like lines of gnashing waves into the comparatively smooth water of the mouth of the sea" (*She,* 43). As Conrad recognized, the basic regression fantasy of imperial Gothic involves a reverse cannibalism: the nightmare of being swallowed by the world's dark places has as its obverse side the solipsistic fantasy of swallowing the world. In *Heart of Darkness,* Marlow describes Kurtz as an eloquent voice, though uttering emptiness, "the horror, the horror." The restraint of the African "cannibals" who serve as Marlow's crew stands in obvious contrast to the fact that "Mr. Kurtz lacked restraint in the gratification of his various lusts."[51] At one point Marlow describes Kurtz opening "his mouth wide—it gave him a weirdly voracious aspect, as though he had wanted to swallow all the air, all the earth, all the men before him" (61). George Gissing, too, sensed in late Victorian imperialism a cannibalism in reverse. In *The Whirlpool* (1897), after his friend Carnaby has ironically mentioned "nigger-hunting" as an excellent modern sport, Harvey Rolfe responds: "There's more than that to do in South Africa. . . . Who believes for a moment that England will remain satisfied with bits here and there? We have to swallow the whole, of course. We shall go on fighting and annexing until—until the decline and fall of the British Empire. That hasn't begun yet. Some of us are so over-civilized that it makes a reaction of wholesome barbarism in the rest. We shall fight like blazes in the twentieth century."[52]

Gissing here captures the tone of much late Victorian imperialist propaganda. Rolfe's statement, though ironi-

cally made, seems almost to echo Cecil Rhodes's grandiose claims about painting the map of Africa red, or his famous assertion that he "would annex the planets if I could."[53] The latter assertion, often quoted out of context, seems much less self-assured when read in relation to what proceeds it—a near-lament about the closing off of global frontiers, a lament suspiciously close to spiritualist concerns with astral bodies and astrology: "The world . . . is nearly all parcelled out, and what there is left of it is being divided up, conquered, and colonised. To think of these stars . . . that you see overhead at night, these vast worlds which we can never reach. I would annex the planets if I could; I often think of that. It makes me sad to see them so clear and yet so far" (190). Rhodes made this statement to the journalist W. T. Stead, who quotes it in his hagiographic *Last Will and Testament of Cecil John Rhodes* (1902). About the only criticism Stead has is that Rhodes was a social Darwinist who never crossed the invisible line between secular ideology and spiritualism. Nevertheless, Stead does his best to bring Rhodes into the occultist fold, attributing an imaginary chain of reasoning to Rhodes which couples survival of the fittest with God's will. Assuming that God *does* exist, Stead makes Rhodes speculate, then in a social Darwinian world He would no doubt make it His will that Britain and the British, the fittest nation and race that history has ever known, should annex as much of the globe as possible, if not the stars. "If there be a God, I think that what He would like me to do is to paint as much of the map of Africa British red as possible, and to do what I can elsewhere to promote the unity and extend the influence of the English-speaking race" (98).

Of all late Victorian and Edwardian occultists, none was more sanguine than Stead about the truth of his convictions. He believed that God had given him a personal mission as a journalist, to defend the Empire and to trumpet the truths of spiritualism through the world. In reporting the news, he made innovative use of interviews with the great and powerful, and when the great were not available—when they happened to be dead, for example—he questioned them anyway through what he called "automatic interviews." Thus be was able to publish the opinions of Catherine the Great on the Russian Question and those of Gladstone's ghost on the budget of 1909. The headline on the front page of the *Daily Chronicle* for 1 November 1909 read: "Amazing Spirit Interview: The Late Mr. Gladstone on the Budget." In her study of spiritualism Ruth Brandon notes that "Mr. Gladstone, as it happened, had not much of interest to say; but the news (to paraphrase Dr. Johnson) lay in his saying it at all" (201).

Through the urgings of his dead friend Julia Ames, Stead made plans to open better communications with the spirit world. In his occultist journal *Borderland* and elsewhere, Stead projected a highly original sort of news agency—one that would transmit news of the beyond through spirit mediumship and that would be named Julia's Bureau. "What is wanted is a bureau of communication between the two sides," Julia's ghost told Stead. "Could you not establish some sort of office with one or more trustworthy mediums? If only it were to enable the sorrowing on the earth to know, if only for once, that their so-called dead live nearer them than ever before, it would help to dry many a tear and soothe many a sorrow. I think you could count upon the eager co-operation of all on this side."[54]

Over the years Julia sent Stead many spirit letters containing news from the borderland, and she often exhorted him to open a bureau of communication. He saw these exhortations as a great opportunity but also, considering the numbers of both dead and living who might want to avail themselves of the bureau's services, as an enormous undertaking. On this score Julia was reassuring. In a communiqué dated 6 October 1908, four years before Stead went down in the *Titanic,* Julia acknowledged that the population of the spirit world was vast—of course far larger than the one and a half billion in the world of the living. But the desire of the dead to communicate with the living tended to wane quickly; therefore "I should say that the number of the 'dead' who wish to communicate with the living are comparatively few." Julia's ghost then offers what to any imperialist must have seemed an obvious analogy:

> It is with us as with immigrants to my former country [Australia]. When they arrive their hearts are in the old world. The new world is new and strange. They long to hear from the old home; and the post brings them more joy than the sunrise. But after a very little time the pain is dulled, new interests arise, and in a few years . . . they write no more. . . . The receipt of letters and telegrams has taken away the death-like edge of emigration. "We shall hear from them again." "Write soon." These are the consolations of humanity even on the physical plane. What the Bureau will do is to enable those who have newly lost their dead to write soon, to hear messages. (175-76)

The emigration analogy suggests once again the complex, unconscious interconnections between imperialist ideology and occultism. To the ardent imperialist, "away" can never be "away"; nothing is foreign, not even death; the borderland itself becomes a new frontier to cross, a new realm to conquer. And with the help of friendly spirits like the Australian Julia, how easy the conquest seems! Just at the moment actual frontiers were vanishing, late Victorian and Edwardian occultist literature is filled with metaphors of exploration, emigration, conquest, colonization. Nor is the news agency metaphor of Julia's Bureau unique. An imagery of telegraphy and cablegrams, telephone and radio, permeates the millennial expectations of the spiritualists, as Kipling shows in "Wireless." According to the persistent modernist Stead: "The recent applications of

electricity in wireless telegraphy and wireless telephony, while proving nothing in themselves as to the nature or permanence of personality, are valuable as enabling us to illustrate the difficulties as well as the possibilities of proving the existence of life after death" (xii). But though hard to prove, the discoveries of the spiritualists are at least as immense as those of Christopher Columbus: "In order to form a definite idea of the problem which we are about to attack, let us imagine the grave as if it were the Atlantic Ocean" (xii). Using similar language in *Phantom Walls,* Lodge writes of his hope "to be able to survey the ocean of eternity from Darien-like peaks," while Arthur Conan Doyle often seems willing to don armor and go crusading in order to conquer death or convince doubters of the truths of spiritualism: "The greater the difficulty in breaking down the wall of apathy, ignorance, and materialism, the more is it a challenge to our manhood to attack and ever attack in the same bulldog spirit with which Foch faced the German lines."[55]

Both Doyle's and Stead's "sublime self-certainty" in their spiritualist writings, Brandon speculates, is a reflection of imperial domination (193). But they frequently express fears about foreign rivals and British slippage in the real world, so the self-certainty of their spiritualism must be largely compensatory. In any event, Brandon reports that three weeks after Stead drowned in the *Titanic,* "he appeared in his inner sanctuary in Mowbray House, where his daughter, his secretary and other devoted ladies were waiting. His face (so they said) shone out; and as it faded his voice rang through the room saying: 'All I told you is true'" (205). Stead's ghost showed up a few years later, at one of the Doyle family séances, announcing that he had "looked into the eyes of Christ with Cecil Rhodes by my side and he said tell Arthur that his work on Earth is holy and divine—that his Message is Mine" (quoted by Brandon, 220). This message came after the death of Doyle's son Kingsley, who had been wounded in combat during the world war and, while recovering, contracted the pneumonia that killed him.

Doyle's path to spiritualism was much like the one traversed by many late Victorians and Edwardians. In his *Memories and Adventures* (1924), he writes that his youthful education had trained him in "the school of medical materialism," formed by "the negative views of all my great teachers" (77). At first he was generally skeptical about occultism:

> I had at that time the usual contempt which the young educated man feels towards the whole subject which has been covered by the clumsy name of Spiritualism. I had read of mediums being convicted of fraud, I had heard of phenomena which were opposed to every known scientific law, and I had deplored the simplicity and credulity which could deceive good, earnest people into believing that such bogus happenings were signs of intelligence outside

our own existence. . . . I was wrong and my great teachers were wrong, but still I hold that they wrought well and that their Victorian agnosticism was in the interests of the human race, for it shook the old iron-clad unreasoning Evangelical position which was so universal before their days. For all rebuilding a site must be cleared. (77)

From the 1890s onward, Doyle became increasingly interested in the spiritualist rebuilding of nothing less than world civilization. He engaged in psychic research, experimenting with telepathy and searching for poltergeists in haunted houses, at first with a skeptical air but later with growing belief in an invisible realm of spirits just beyond the boundaries of material reality. If it seemed evident that adventure was vanishing from the modern world, Doyle for one rebelled against the evidence. True, his reinventions of adventure in fiction have about them the same compensatory quality that characterizes most late Victorian romance writing, which senses its inferiority to realistic narration. Romance writers indicate in a variety of ways that their adventure stories are for adolescents; and occultist pursuits are also somehow, even to occultists themselves, childish and subrational. As a young man, at least, Doyle perceived these difficulties but plunged ahead anyway, toward the blinding light (he thought) at the end of the long tunnel of world history.

In Doyle's 1911 novel *The Lost World,* the journalist hero Malone is told by his girlfriend that he must go adventuring and become a hero before she will marry him. The demand seems to him next to impossible because, as his editor exclaims, "the big blank spaces in the map are all being filled, in, and there's no room for romance anywhere."[56] But there is room—or Doyle at least will make room—for romance in a fantasy version of the Amazon basin, where the British adventurers regress through a Darwinian nightmare to the days of the dinosaurs. The characters in the story, including the atavistically apelike Professor Challenger, reappear next in *The Poison Belt* of 1913, where adventure shrinks: they watch the end of the world from the windows of an airtight room in Challenger's house. But the world does not end, the poisonous cloud lifts, people revive, and Doyle's band of fantasy adventurers live on to appear in a third novel, *The Land of Mist,* published in 1925, the same year as Yeats's *A Vision.* Challenger and the rest are now participants in what Doyle believes to be the greatest adventure of all, beyond the borders of the material world. Exploration and invasion metaphors abound. Lord John Roxton's newspaper ad sets the tone: Roxton is "seeking fresh worlds to conquer. Having exhausted the sporting adventures of this terrestrial globe, he is now turning to those of the dim, dark and dubious regions of psychic research. He is in the market . . . for any genuine specimen of a haunted house."[57] While the crumbling of the Empire quickened after World War I, Doyle

himself turned obsessively to haunted houses, séances, lands of mysticism and mist. The skeptical Challenger exclaims that the "soul-talk" of the spiritualists is "the Animism of savages," but Doyle himself was no longer skeptical (19). He believed in magic, he believed in fairies, he believed in ectoplasmic projections. He believed Spiritualism with a capital S was the successor to Christianity, the new advent of the City of God after the fall of the City of Man. The creator of that great incarnation of scientific rationalism Sherlock Holmes devoted himself to the spiritualist movement, becoming one of its leaders, and it became for him a substitute for all other causes—for imperialism itself. Just as his friend Stead felt that he had received a call from God, so Doyle after the world war felt that the meaningful part of his life had begun. He had received the call; it was his duty to save the world. "In the days of universal sorrow and loss [after World War I], when the voice of Rachel was heard throughout the land, it was borne in upon me that the knowledge which had come to me thus was not for my own consolation alone, but that God had placed me in a very special position for conveying it to that world which needed it so badly" (*Memories,* 387).

Doyle's version of "Heaven was rather like Sussex, slightly watered down," says Brandon (222), but his plans for the future of the world were somewhat larger than Sussex. He believed the spirit world was arranged in a marvelous, infinite bureaucratic hierarchy very much like the British Raj in India.[58] In 1923 an "Arabian spirit" named Pheneas began to communicate with him through his wife's automatic writing, telling him that the old world would end soon and a glorious new one dawn. Doyle was no doubt reassured to learn that "England is to be the centre to which all humanity will turn. She is to be the beacon light in this dark, dark world. The light is Christ, and all humans will strive to get to that light in the great darkness" (*Pheneas Speaks,* 79). Sherlock Holmes cannot tolerate a mystery without solving it, nor can Doyle: the darkness of this world will soon disperse, and light, radiating especially from England and Sussex, will be universal. Doyle experienced a glimmer of embarrassment toward the end of the decade, shortly before his death, when Pheneas's predictions did not seem to be coming true on schedule, but it was only a minor setback. Material adventure in the material Empire might be on the wane, but over the ruins was dawning the light of the great spiritualist adventure.

As far as geopolitical arrangements were concerned, Doyle believed, the programs of all governments would have to be revised. In spiritualist armor, slaying the dragons of Bolshevism and materialism, Doyle sometimes felt that the future was his. Like the souls of the dead, the glories of the imperialist past would be reborn, purified or rarefied, for they were eternal. In his *History of Spiritualism,* Doyle writes: "I do not say to

[the] great and world-commanding . . . powers . . . open your eyes and see that your efforts are fruitless, and acknowledge your defeat, for probably they never will open their eyes . . . but I say to the Spiritualists . . . dark as the day may seem to you, never was it more cheering . . . never . . . more anticipatory of ultimate victory. It has upon it the stamp of all the conquering influences of the age."[59] But the ultimate victory of spiritualism was prefigured for Doyle in the demise of the empires of this world, the precondition for the invasion and reconquest of reality by the realm of spirit, or perhaps of our transubstantiation—a kind of psychic emigration and colonization—into the world beyond reality, an invisible, even more glorious empire rising ghostlike out of the corpse of the old.

As cultural formations, both imperialism and spiritualism have roots in "the dark powers of the subconscious, [and call] into play instincts that carry over from the life habits of the dim past. Driven out everywhere else, the irrational" seeks refuge in imperialism, Schumpeter contends (14), and, I would add, in late Victorian and early modern occultism. Imperial Gothic expresses the atavistic character of both movements, shadowing forth the larger, gradual disintegration of British hegemony. Doyle's phantom empire—and the imperial Gothic themes of regression, invasion, and the waning of adventure—express the narrowing vistas of the British Empire at the time of its greatest extent, in the moment before its fall.

Notes

[1] Bithia M. Croker, *The Old Cantonment; with Other Stories of India and Elsewhere* (London: Methuen, 1905), 48-63.

[2] See Brooks Wright, *Interpreter of Buddhism to the West: Sir Edwin Arnold* (New York: Brookman Associates, 1957).

[3] A brief account of the development of late-Victorian romanticism in conjunction with occultism appears in Tom Gibbons, *Rooms in the Darwin Hotel: Studies in English Literary Criticism and Ideas, 1880-1920* (Nedlands: University of Western Australia Press, 1973), 1-24. See also Ruth Brandon, *The Spiritualists: The Passion for the Occult in the Nineteenth and Twentieth Centuries* (New York: Knopf, 1983); Janet Oppenheim, *The Other World: Spiritualism and Psychical Research in England, 1850-1914* (Cambridge, Cambridge University Press, 1985); and Frank M. Turner, *Between Science and Religion: The Reaction to Scientific Naturalism in Late Victorian England* (New Haven: Yale University Press, 1974).

[4] Oppenheim, *Other World*, 160.

[5] J. A. Cramb, *The Origins and Destiny of Imperial Britain* (New York: Dutton, 1900), 230.

[6] Carroll V. Peterson, *John Davidson* (New York: Twayne, 1972), 82.

[7] John Davidson, "St. George's Day," in *The Poems of John Davidson*, ed. Andrew Turnbull, 2 vols. (Edinburgh: Scottish Academic Press, 1973), 1:228.

[8] Rudyard Kipling, "Recessional," in *Works*, 36 vols., Pocket Edition (London: Methuen, 1923), 34:186.

[9] Jerome Hamilton Buckley, *William Ernest Henley: A Study in the "Counter-Decadence" of the 'Nineties* (Princeton: Princeton University Press, 1945), 134. See also John Lester, *Journey through Despair, 1880-1914: Transformations in British Literary Culture* (Princeton: Princeton University Press, 1968), 9: both the imperialism and the socialism of the turn of the century "became charged with an overplus of fervor which exalted each at times almost to religion."

[10] Erskine Childers, *The Riddle of the Sands: A Record of Secret Service* (1903; New York: Dover, 1976), 15.

[11] Both White and Shaw are quoted by Lester, *Journey through Despair*, 50n and 5.

[12] Lester (*Journey through Despair*, 3) notes that this quotation from 1 Corinthians 10:11 "crops up recurrently in the literature of the time."

[13] Lewis S. Wurgaft, *The Imperial Imagination: Magic and Myth in Kipling's India* (Middletown: Wesleyan University Press, 1983), 57.

[14] Edgar Wallace, *Sanders of the River* (1909; Garden City, N.Y.: Doubleday, Doran, 1930), 277.

[15] For these and other examples see *The Best Supernatural Tales of Arthur Conan Doyle*, ed. E. F. Bleiler (New York: Dover, 1979). An interesting variant is W. Somerset Maugham's *The Magician* (1908), based on the career of Aleister Crowley.

[16] Andrew Lang, "Realism and Romance," *Contemporary Review* 52 (November 1887), 684. Page numbers are given parenthetically in the next two paragraphs of the text. See also Joseph Weintraub, "Andrew Lang: Critic of Romance," *English Literature in Transition* 18:1 (1975), 5-15.

[17] Sir Edward Burnett Tylor, *Primitive Culture*, 2 vols. (1871; New York: Harper & Row, 1970), 1:155, 142.

[18] Quoted by Wesley D. Sweetser, *Arthur Machen* (New York: Twayne, 1964), 116.

[19] David Punter, *The Literature of Terror: A History of Gothic Fictions from 1765 to the Present Day* (London: Longman, 1980), 62, 241.

[20] See Patrick Brantlinger and Richard Boyle, "The Education of Edward Hyde: Stevenson's 'Gothic Gnome' and the Mass Readership of Late-Victorian England," in *Jekyll and Hyde after 100 Years,* ed. William Veeder (Chicago: University of Chicago Press, 1987).

[21] Judith Wilt, "The Imperial Mouth: Imperialism, the Gothic and Science Fiction," *Journal of Popular Culture* 14 (Spring 1981), 618-28.

[22] Bram Stoker, *Dracula* (Harmondsworth: Penguin, 1979), 41. Punter (*Literature of Terror,* 257) calls Dracula "the final aristocrat."

[23] See Norman Etherington, *Rider Haggard* (Boston: Twayne, 1984), 47.

[24] H. Rider Haggard, *Three Adventure Novels: She, King Solomon's Mines, Allan Quatermain* (New York: Dover, 1951), 192-93.

[25] Nina Auerbach, *Woman and the Demon: The Life of a Victorian Myth* (Cambridge: Harvard University Press, 1982), 37. See also Sandra M. Gilbert, "Rider Haggard's Heart of Darkness," *Partisan Review* 50 (1983), 444-53, and Carol A. Senf, "*Dracula:* Stoker's Response to the New Woman," *Victorian Studies* 26 (Autumn 1982), 33-49.

[26] Quoted by Brian Aldiss, *Billion Year Spree: The True History of Science Fiction* (New York: Schocken, 1976), 8-9.

[27] See I. F. Clarke, *Voices Prophesying War, 1763-1984* (London: Oxford University Press, 1966), 227-39. See also Samuel Hynes, *The Edwardian Turn of Mind* (Princeton: Princeton University Press, 1968), 34-53.

[28] P. G. Wodehouse, *The Swoop! and Other Stories,* ed. David A. Jasen (New York: Seabury, 1979).

[29] See David A. T. Stafford, "Spies and Gentlemen: The Birth of the British Spy Novel, 1893-1914," *Victorian Studies* 24 (Summer 1981), 489-509.

[30] Joseph Schumpeter, *Imperialism and Social Classes* (1919; New York: Augustus M. Kelley, 1951), 84.

[31] J. A. Hobson, *The Psychology of Jingoism* (London: Grant Richards, 1901), 19, and *Imperialism: A Study* (1902; Ann Arbor: University of Michigan Press, 1965). See also John Allett, *New Liberalism: The Political Economy of J. A. Hobson* (Toronto: University of Toronto Press, 1981).

[32] See J. A. Hobson, *John Ruskin: Social Reformer* (Boston: Dana Estes, 1898).

[33] Hobson, *Psychology of Jingoism,* 13. Page numbers in parentheses refer to this volume.

[34] Frederic Harrison, *Memories and Thoughts* (London: Macmillan, 1906), 233.

[35] Robert M. Ballantyne, *The Coral Island* (London: Nelson, n.d.), 22.

[36] Quoted by Etherington, *Rider Haggard,* 66.

[37] Joseph Conrad, "Geography and Some Explorers," in *Last Essays* (London: Dent, 1926), 17.

[38] Andrew Lang, "The Supernatural in Fiction," in *Adventures in Books* (1905; Freeport, N.Y.: Books for Libraries Press, 1970), 279-80.

[39] Andrew Lang, *Cock Lane and Common Sense* (London: Longmans, Green, 1894), 2.

[40] Andrew Lang, "Psychical Research," *Encyclopedia Britannica,* 11th ed., 22:544-47.

[41] See L. S. Hearnshaw, *A Short History of British Psychology, 1840-1940* (New York: Barnes & Noble, 1964), especially chaps. 9 and 10, and Ed Block, Jr., "James Sully, Evolutionist Psychology, and Late Victorian Gothic Fiction," *Victorian Studies* 25 (Summer 1982), 443-67.

[42] Sigmund Freud, *The Future of an Illusion,* trans. James Strachey (New York: Norton, 1961), 28.

[43] Quoted by Oppenheim, *Other Worlds,* 132.

[44] Rudyard Kipling, "The Sending of Dana Da," in *Works* 6:307.

[45] Charles Carrington believes that "They" contains a warning against engaging in "psychical research," and J. M. S. Tompkins thinks Kipling grew less rather than more interested in the supernatural. But "They" clearly describes a supernatural experience. Perhaps all that Kipling quit doing was writing "ghost stories" of the skeptical, frivolous, "Phantom Rickshaw" variety. Carrington, *Rudyard Kipling, His Life and Work* (London: Macmillan, 1955), 373; Tompkins, *The Art of Rudyard Kipling* (Lincoln: University of Nebraska Press, 1965), 204. See also Elliot L. Gilbert, *The Good Kipling: Studies in the Short Story* (Manchester: Manchester University Press, 1972), 80.

[46] See Sir H. Rider Haggard, *The Days of My Life: An Autobiography,* 2 vols. (London: Longmans, Green,

1926), 1:37-41. Hereafter volume and page numbers are given parenthetically in the text.

[47] Saintsbury quoted in *Rudyard Kipling to Rider Haggard: The Record of a Friendship,* ed. Morton Cohen (London: Hutchinson, 1965), 4.

[48] Alan Sandison's contention in *The Wheel of Empire: A Study of the Imperial Idea in Some Late Nineteenth and Early Twentieth-Century Fiction* (London: Macmillan, 1967) that Haggard in *King Solomon's Mines* "as in every other [book] he wrote on Africa . . . repudiates without fuss the whole arrogant notion of the white man's burden" (31) is misleading. Haggard's frequent criticisms of the behavior of white settlers—especially Boers—toward black Africans lead to arguments for strengthening rather than weakening imperial authority. Haggard was a keen admirer of Theophilus Shepstone and Sir Charles Buller, and he patterned his imperialist thinking after theirs.

[49] Theodor Adorno, "Theses against Occultism," in *Minima Moralia: Reflections from Damaged Life,* trans. E. F. N. Jephcott (London: Verso, 1978), 240.

[50] Graham Greene, *Journey without Maps* (1936; London: Heinemann, 1978), 104: "The method of psychoanalysis is to bring the patient back to the idea which he is repressing: a long journey backwards without maps. . . . This is what you have feared, Africa may be imagined as saying, you can't avoid it."

[51] Joseph Conrad, *Heart of Darkness,* ed. Robert Kimbrough (New York: Norton, 1963), 58.

[52] George Gissing, *The Whirlpool* (Hassocks: Harvester, 1977), 16.

[53] *The Last Will and Testament of Cecil John Rhodes,* ed. W. T. Stead (London: Review of Reviews Office, 1902), 190.

[54] W. T. Stead, *After Death: A Personal Narrative* (New York: George H. Doran, 1914), 50.

[55] Sir Oliver Lodge, *Phantom Walls* (New York: Putnam's, 1930), xi; Sir Arthur Conan Doyle, *Memories and Adventures* (Boston: Little, Brown, 1924), 390.

[56] Sir Arthur Conan Doyle, *The Lost World* (New York: Review of Reviews, 1912), 13.

[57] Sir Arthur Conan Doyle, *The Land of Mist* (New York: Doran, 1926), 132.

[58] Sir Arthur Conan Doyle, *Pheneas Speaks: Direct Spirit Communication in the Family Circle* (London: Psychic Press, n.d.), 10.

[59] Sir Arthur Conan Doyle, *The History of Spiritualism,* 2 vols. (New York: Doran, 1926), 1:173.

Thomas Richards

SOURCE: "Archive and Form," in *The Imperial Archive: Knowledge and the Fantasy of Empire,* Verso, 1993, pp. 45-65.

[*In the following extract, Richards explores the connections between the discourses of morphology and monstrosity in Victorian fiction.*]

This chapter is about the place of monstrosity in the nineteenth-century imperial imagination. Until Bram Stoker's *Dracula,* there are few monsters in Victorian fiction. In Victorian literature ghosts, those images of a nether world replete with human significance, are more common than monsters, and it is worth asking why. Victorian travellers like Richard Burton and Henry Stanley never saw monsters. In his *Voyage of the Beagle* (1831-36) Darwin travelled around the world without seeing one. Thomas Henry Huxley doubted whether monsters ever existed, even in the distant past. In Poe 'monstrous' is always an adjective, never a noun, and monstrosity resides in the behavioral perversions of the self, as it does in Lombroso, where the monster is the criminal. In Victorian gothic it is the natural landscape that is monstrous. Even in the murky world of imperial gothic, as in Haggard's *She* (1887), there are no monsters of nature save for a woman who lives on eternally in a dead city. Why are there no monsters in Victorian literature?

This chapter looks at the role the science of form, or morphology, played in imagining a unitary natural world in which there would no longer be any place for monstrosity. Throughout the nineteenth century the practice of biology relied overwhelmingly on the techniques of morphology, the science concerned with the problems of form, function, and transformation in matter.[1] The immediate heirs to the work of the great taxonomists of the eighteenth century, the Victorian morphologists saw all life as an organized succession of forms capable of being derived from a unitary apparatus of constants and variables. The nineteenth-century and early-twentieth-century morphology of Owen and Darwin and D'Arcy Thompson represented life as unfolding within a Cartesian mechanism of vectors and coordinates, but it also moved the old Linnaean hierarchies into a new and completely different register. It fashioned not a hierarchy of general forms but a lineage of specific ones. No less an authority than Auguste Comte located the discipline of morphology perfectly at the juncture of the general and the particular, the abstract and the concrete.[2] In morphology the project of a complete and unravelled representation of existence became the ally of the positivist project of comprehensive knowledge. More than anything else, the work of morphology was to construct lines to join together the established points of positive knowledge into a projected network of comprehensive knowledge; for many years there was nothing in the geological record linking *mesopithecus* and *homo sapiens* but the fictions of morphology. A method for locating continuity within discontinuity, morphology provided filler for the great gaps of knowledge the Victorians were continually discovering in their own global schemes. Morphology put all beings on the same imperial family tree. In the heyday of Victorian morphology, there were no longer any singular beings in the universe other than those which human beings created for themselves; as in Mary Shelley's novel, the Victorian monster is made, not born. Even ghosts, as in James's *Turn of the Screw* (1898), came to be seen less as independent beings than as projections of human psychology. The Victorian morphologists shared a common conviction that the day was coming when the relationship of all living beings could be traced in a great common genealogy. When that day came, there would no longer be any creature unable to fit anywhere on the great chain of beings. The Victorian search for the mythical 'missing link' presaged not so much a new kind of monster as an end to all monstrosity. The search for the missing link was the search for the final link in the evolutionary chain. At the point at which the missing link shored up the great chain once and for all, nothing could ever be monstrous again because everything would then be known, fixed in a continuous reconstruction of serial descent.

Victorian morphology saw its origins in certain debates about natural form going back to the eighteenth century. The science of form began as an explicitly universal science devoted to the task of preparing scientific directories of the natural world. In his *Systema naturae* (1735) Linnaeus uses an empirical method of nomination to construct an ideal taxonomy of pure forms. He claims to include all known species of plants, but he also advances the idea that the study of matter can be anchored in philosophical first principles. The problem of form was to be solved by constructing a calculus of four variables in which 'every note should be a product of number, of form, of proportion, of situation.'[3] Linnaeus did everything he could to construct a work of natural history without undertaking to write an actual history of nature. For him nature always made manifest certain irreducible forms of order, forms which he attempted to call forth using an intricate system of symbols that resembled magic characters. Despite this emphasis on nature as a self-contained structure—what came to be called 'the natural order'—natural form tended most easily to assume the form of logic, and his conception of the wholeness of nature assumed that nature would always somehow resolve itself into a synchronic logical arrangement. Form in Linnaeus meant taxidermy; single specimens in little boxes defined in terms of one generalized ru-

bric, however defined. Any form that fell outside the purview of the logical definition was, by definition, a singularity, a fluke, a freak of nature, and the best that could be done was to place it in a bottomless category for all the deviations from logic traversed by nature, the special category of the monstrous.

In the nineteenth century the Linnaean metaphysics of the fixed form, the *forma formata,* gave way to the new field of the changing form, the *forma formans.* The problem of form no longer entailed the tabulation of synchronies; it now began to be equated with the diachronic reconstruction of lines of formal development. Linnaeus believed that since the forms of living beings were fixed, he did not need to delve into the past to study them. The new evolutionary reconstruction, however, extended into the past, the past of the fossil record. The fossil record equipped biology with a historical archive potentially capable of accounting for every form that had ever existed; all the exceptions that the old taxonomies had once relegated to the category of the monstrous could theoretically be rehabilitated using the new historical method in morphology. Just as, within philology, the desire to understand living languages led to a fixation on dead languages, in morphology the desire to understand living matter led to the residues of the fossil record. Victorian texts abound in representations of decaying residues, and in a classic morphological text, *The Formation of Vegetable Mould through the Action of Worms* (1881) Darwin would go so far as to attribute the life of the earth's topsoil to an ecology saturated with decomposing residues. In a great variety of ways the new nineteenth-century morphology was most concerned with constructing a lineage not of the present but of the past. The creatures that evolution had passed by were strange at first but, safely dead, they could be easily domesticated. Unearthed as fragments of bone, they became skulls and spines reconstructed in some museum of natural history, no longer monstrous, little capable of inspiring fear or awe, not warnings or portents but destinations for family outings, dinosaurs for children. Life on earth was always changing, and once you knew how to follow out the changes throughout all time, there would be no monsters save somewhere in the past, buried in the vast geological archive of the fossil record.

In the course of the nineteenth century it became clear that there was no longer any place for monstrosity within the biology of living matter. If the motto of Renaissance humanism was 'nothing human is alien,' the motto of Victorian morphology now became 'nothing alive is alien.' There was a confidence that all forms, however monstrous they might at first appear to the examining eye, would at last be discovered to be related by serial descent to other, less alien forms. Deviations from normative forms could now be explained merely by adjusting the focus of a historical reconstruction. Monsters, once considered singular forms, were now placed in active relation to other forms, whether presently living or long dead. The order of things went from being the order of ordered things to being the order of all things that had ever existed. Thus did the one characteristic move of all formal explanation in the nineteenth century—the ranking of all species by historical descent and modification—wipe out in one broad stroke the conditions of possibility for the stores of monsters that had once abounded in texts of literature, travel, natural history, and natural philosophy. Henceforth the forces of monstrosity would have to be located outside the Darwinian world-view, for within it, all monsters were our distant relatives.

This chapter shows that by the turn of the century a new form of monstrosity arose to outwit Darwin. These new monsters were essentially mutants, capable of sudden and catastrophic changes of form, a kind of change outlawed and virtually unknowable under the Darwinian system. Even at the height of Darwinism in late-Victorian Britain, writers began to imagine a great variety of monsters that fell outside the sureties of lineage enshrined in morphology. These monsters were beings capable of sudden changes of form. They were threats to the global claim of Darwinism, disrupting the very order of things and even threatening to bring about the end of Empire. The end was widely figured as a global morphology turned upside down, a state in which monsters that do not follow, and cannot be understood by, the ordinal system of morphological development, disrupt and finally overwhelm the harmonious Darwinian archive of Empire. The functioning British monopoly over knowledge ends in Bram Stoker's *Dracula* (1897), where a colonial alterity comes to be closely aligned with forms refusing to follow the ordinal scheme of historical morphological development. The abiding figure for this representation of morphological alterity is of course the vampire, a figure that first achieved full prominence at the close of the nineteenth century. H.G. Wells also hit on the idea of the mutant in his *Island of Dr. Moreau* (1898), a narrative in which an evil doctor incubates mutants on a remote island. Stoker, however, chose to place his monster in a larger international context and play out the problem of mutation on a much larger scale. He adapted an existing story rather than fabricating a new one, and his powerful new turn on the old Dracula story cannot be understood without a sense of how thoroughly he made his monster violate the doctrines of Darwinian morphology and so turn the natural world upside down. The narrative of *Dracula* makes it clear that there are some species whose origins cannot be understood using the Darwinian model, and that these originless species, impossible according to Darwin, had become the archetypal monsters of the twentieth century. After Dracula the monster stood once again outside science, not safely immured in the descent of man.

In common with the other chapters in this book, what follows has been laid out to trace a cultural course of development running parallel to the imperial trajectory of colonization, occupation, and decolonization. It shows the establishment, failure, and reconsolidation of a variant on the central organizing myth of comprehensive knowledge, the myth of the positive knowledge of form. The first part of the chapter reconstructs the central position which the notion of form occupied in pre-imperial discourse and considers Lewis Carroll's *Alice in Wonderland* (1865) and *Through the Looking Glass* (1871) as an anatomy of the problem of positive knowledge of exceptional forms within mid-Victorian morphology. The Alice books are about a little girl dropped into a world of monsters, monsters whose world changes in accordance with the dictates of logical form. The second part looks at a fully imperial morphology in a sequence of turn-of-the-century texts and places Bram Stoker's *Dracula* (1897) in the context of morphological theories of monstrosity and decay. The third examines J.G. Ballard's *The Crystal World* (1966), a text that links African decolonization with the rapid spread of an unknown crystalline form, and that testifies to the continuing presence of morphological assumptions in modern British literature. It will be seen that the search for the positive knowledge of form passed, as was the case with so many other positivist projects of comprehensive knowledge in the late nineteenth century, first from the domain of science into the domain of myth, and last into the domain of ideology. Yet at all points it preserved something of the essential character of the Victorian desire for the unification of all knowledge, a squaring of all departments of knowledge into a circle of concordant knowledges. In biology the project of constructing universal taxonomies of form remains very much alive, one of the last surviving emblems of the Victorian imperium, the project of a positive and comprehensive knowledge of the world.

For two centuries the science of morphology has worked to dissociate itself from the traditional fictions of metamorphosis. Alterations of form in morphology have none of the overt caprice of transformation in Ovid, where catastrophic changes issue from the summonses of gods. It was only in the nineteenth century that the science of form even began to concern itself with the mechanics of formal transformation. Rather the project of scientific morphology, idealistic or empirical, continuous or discontinuous, deductive or inductive, has always rested on a fundamental assumption of consonant wholeness. The system of form that developed within eighteenth-century botany asserted the priority of the whole, the idea that without the whole the parts are nothing, even as it allowed for the manifestation of growth in the extension of the plant, the assimilation or conversion of materials external to the plant into substances useful to the plant, the shaping of the plant according to the dictates of its own internal plan, and the interdependence between parts as constitutive of the whole plant. So influential was this matrix of organic form that, when Darwin toured South America in the early 1830s, the immense variety of new plant forms he saw, 'plants assuming most fantastical forms,' forms falling outside of all existing structures of forms, scarcely disturbed his center of gravity.[4] He had a confidence that everything would eventually come together with the precision of geometry. All relative magnitudes of formal difference would be subject to explanation by rectilinear coordinates (to make his taxonomies seem less mathematical and more organic, Darwin, like most of his nineteenth-century contemporaries, called them 'trees'). The loss of a complete knowledge of the world was always a temporary matter, for in the fullness of time the whole would be regained. [5]

In some respects, then, the demands of the whole in Darwin remain little changed from the Linnaean hierarchy. To overcome the separatist tendencies in his botanic material, Linnaeus had constructed classes to force variegated evidence into prescribed categories. He saw himself as a kind of technical writer supplying the specifications of a finished and complete product inspired by one logical and uniform Design. For Linnaeus, the form of logic dictated the logic of form, and the weight of design dictated the scale of designation. Though Darwin no longer accepted the argument from logical design, he was far from willing to abolish the typologies of classification derived from it. In fact he wanted to extend them. He devoted a long chapter in *The Origin of Species* (1859) to arguing for a great increase in the number of categories used to classify beings, all the while preserving most of Linnaeus's genera as families or still higher groups and advancing the project of an attainable holistic order.[6] The crucial difference is that the construction of the whole to which Darwin subscribed understood nature as a global rather than a universal totality. Darwin saw nature as the natural *world*. It is worth remembering that while Linnaeus spent his career in the confines of his native Sweden, Darwin began his by circumnavigating the globe. In Linnaean nature form is horizontal; it has a name and a position but not a local habitation and a place. In Darwin the project of comprehensive knowledge loses its universal inflection; the world of nature becomes a vertical world, a specific world, a relational world, an instrumental world, above all, a colonial world.

The corollary to the Linnaean postulate of the absolute whole is that such a whole, though it forms a unitary field of order, is not ordinally manipulable. The claim to certainty that Linnaean order makes is, purely and simply, a claim to the inherent certainty of order. The purpose of order is not to exert order over non-ordered areas of the world but to infer a universal order from the evidence at hand. Operating as it did by inference

and interpolation, Linnaean order had no colonial aspirations whatsoever. Rather, in the eighteenth century the science of form was a particular lineage of the absolutist state. An absolute whole is a conception well suited to the requirements of the absolutist state in which colonies tend to be viewed as subordinate parts of a sovereign whole, as 'new' Englands in which economic and political transformation somehow issue as if by fiat from the numen of the original state. The unitary field of order favored by the absolutist state does not require manipulation to stay ordered, for order is universal and cannot be affected by contingent action. The world does not need to be converted to a new order of Empire for the simple reason that it has already been ordered, at every time and in every place. Form in a colonial world is at best a mutilated copy of form in the metropolitan world.

The sole representation of the colonial within the Linnaean system is the order of the monstrous. Monsters in Linnaeus rise only from the colonial world and display only a contingent alterity. Monsters are figures for alterity outside of European systems of order, an alterity consistently figured as deformation. The monster ensures the placement of difference within the general science of order.[7] The monster is the joker in the Linnaean deck of cards, the undefined addendum, the blind spot in an otherwise compact system of order. In the 1930s the physicist Kurt Gödel offered a simple but convincing explanation for why projects of comprehensive knowledge such as Linnaeus's fail to achieve their ends. Gödel stated simply that a system of axioms cannot encompass all possible variations on that system. It cannot, in other words, foresee which variation will succeed in disturbing the system along its fault lines.[8] The central position of the monster in the eighteenth-century science of form turns out at last to be the Gödel-moment in all taxonomy when the ordering impulse admits its own inexactitude. By resolving irresolution into a category of its own, the monster-category is a tacit admission that all knowledge is neither comprehensive in scope nor logical in form. It is an admission that new and unusual modifications arise from time to time that cannot be derived from a system of systems. As a category it bears silent witness to the existence of unforeseen transformations even as it attempts to lay to rest a much larger problem, the problem of the catastrophic mutation of form.

It was exactly this problem of ordering a disordered nature that led Lewis Carroll, a mathematician whose work on the mathematics of form still commands attention, to construct a lasting burlesque of the general science of ordered form. *Alice in Wonderland* and *Through the Looking Glass* represent form as indomitable. A hundred years after the death of Linnaeus, Carroll's Alice stories laid bare the structure of what had become an obsolete science of form. Carroll structures his fantasy as a questioning of the received categories of morphology by performing a single and striking operation: he links the catastrophic mutation of form to the deconstruction of established logical categories. Unquestionably the most basic feature of the Alice texts is Carroll's linking of logical to natural form. Carroll goes to the end of his wits to make the Linnaean link—the basic assumption of eighteenth-century morphology that the form of logic dictates the logic of form—completely untenable. The mutations that Alice witnesses and undergoes make it impossible to maintain the fidelity of natural to logical form. But Carroll does not restrict his parody to highlighting unaccountable changes in form. Rather, the Alice stories are an anatomy of the very monstrosity of logic itself in dictating form. Logic, the Linnaean logic of form, is the only monster in the Alice books. The shapes the monsters assume there—cards, chessmen, cats—tend toward the domestic and the serene, not the strange and the portentous. Nothing in *Alice in Wonderland* and *Through the Looking Glass* turns out to be more truly monstrous than the operation of logic itself, which dictates shape and configuration at every instant.

Most of Alice's adventures among the being of Wonderland devolve on reversals of the logical order of common sense. Everything moves in both directions at once, prompting Alice to repeat like a mantra her pointed question, 'Which way, which way?' Alice becomes larger and she becomes smaller. She crosses from the day before to the day after, passing over the present: 'Jam tomorrow and jam yesterday—but never jam *to-day*.' She reverses more and less, as when five nights are five times hotter than a single night, 'but they must be five times as cold for the same reason.' Active and passive switch positions, as 'do cats eat bats?' becomes 'do bats eat cats?' And, perhaps most prominently, cause and effect change places as beings receive punishment before committing crimes, cry before wounding themselves, and serve food before dividing up the servings.[9] This series of reversals makes it virtually impossible to group morphological phenomena into general propositions. In no way does the surface of things mutate according to some presumed inner plan; morphology is no longer morpho-logical. Alice cannot perform the two operations most characteristic of the eighteenth-century science of form: she cannot fix the visible world in stable logical categories, and just as importantly, she cannot remember her own name. The loss of the proper name deals a final and crushing blow to the language of logical morphology, which, more than anything else, had been founded on the certainty of designation. In the Alice stories the very possibility of a unitary formulation for the science of form has become doubtful and remote.

The Alice stories also cast doubt on the certainty of allied absolutist conceptions of order. At all points Carroll makes it clear that Wonderland is an absolutist state that has lost its bearings. Wonderland is ruled by an imperious Queen who has adopted the cry of the Terror of the French Revolution, 'Off with their heads!' The state and the control it exerts are purely a matter of rhetoric; as in morphology, the absolutist form of order has lost its structural stability. The dictates of Wonderland's absolutist state are completely unrelated to the world of forms it actually contains. The Queen has no control over the forms that the beings in her kingdom assume, for the simple reason that everything in Wonderland is singular and nothing is repeatable. Form is indomitable, the world is full of functionless beings. At the croquet game the hedgehogs and flamingoes and card soldiers do not long retain their functions as equipment in the game. They take up one function only to relinquish it quickly and move to another. The croquet game must be seen as a carnival of form and function, a coming apart of form and a rebelling against function. In the Alice stories nothing is more fragile than the link joining form to function (unlike the animals in most Victorian children's books, forms do not even begin to assume the functions they actually perform in the natural world). In *Alice in Wonderland* and *Through the Looking Glass* form is at best imperfectly manipulable. The state cannot control it. Carroll sees an excess at the heart of form that unsettles it into a state of measureless mad becoming.

The Alice stories of Lewis Carroll can be taken as a negative picture of the emergence of a Darwinian morphology in mid- and late-Victorian Britain (a positive picture, less devoted to parody of the Linnaean system, can be found in Charles Kingsley's parable of selective metamorphosis, *The Water Babies* [1862-63]). Wonderland is everything that the mid-Victorian project of the positive knowledge of form sought to drive underground once and for all. At all points the Alice stories fail to provide a causal explanation of development. The project of Darwinian morphology rather fixed its sights on the grey areas between forms. It sought to verify the existence of forms between forms. As advanced by Darwin in *The Origin of Species* (1859), and later consolidated by E.S. Russell in *Form and Function* (1916) and D'Arcy Thompson in *On Growth and Form* (1917), the project of the positive knowledge of form designated form as the slow process of adaptation to new function. As confused as matters become in the Alice stories, Alice never loses form and slides into a state of formlessness, though there is a hint of this when she admits to being afraid that her neck will grow beyond its capacity for growth (soon the example of the giraffe's neck would become paradigmatic within the new Darwinian morphology). At times she is afraid that she will burst, but her body apparently conforms to internal limits. Overwhelmingly morphology came to be concerned with these limits to development. 'At what point will I burst?' is a question which Alice consciously decides not to pursue, but which morphologists inspired by Darwin now set themselves to answer. The Darwinian morphology closely replicated Alice's concern with the limits of scale in formal transformation as it began to pose the question of the area between forms—how to understand it, how to represent it, how to manipulate it.

The Alice stories, then, occupy a transitional space between Linnaean and Darwinian morphologies. If Wonderland had made the world of the old logical morphology seem impossible, the new Darwinian morphology would make Wonderland seem doubly impossible. In Wonderland everything changes suddenly in accordance with the logic of language. In Darwin's morphology everything changes gradually, imperceptibly, the outcome of many random events ultimately selected out according to function. Ignorant of genetics, Darwin did not yet know why things changed gradually, but he firmly believed that evolution proceeds by slow and gradual stages. Once reconstructed, the complete sequence of organisms would be absolutely continuous throughout. There is no longer any place in Darwin's morphology for the catastrophic mutation of form. Monsters of form no longer have any place in a system which works out thoroughly the relationship of forms using the minima and maxima of calculus. Unusual, deviant, or monstrous forms can now be fixed on a vast index of change, a book of all changes. In Darwin's scheme, monsters either disappear forever or mutate themselves into a form which eventually becomes the norm. Change itself is stable and can be represented using what came to be known as 'topology.'

A topology is a reconstruction of the form of forms. The serial drawings showing apes gradually straightening their spines and breaking into a human gait were the first and most familiar topologies, but by the turn of the century topology had become abstract and multidimensional. It entailed the representation of what D'Arcy Thompson, the great elaborator of differential topology that came to characterize late-Victorian morphology, once called 'a difference of relative magnitudes, capable of tabulation by numbers and of complete expression by means of rectilinear coordinates.'[10] The ability to classify and manipulate all types of form was achieved only by giving up quantitative concepts of exact measurement such as employed by Linnaeus. Victorian morphology became largely a labor of guesswork, scraping the ground for a past for which little hard evidence existed, but which had necessarily to exist if Darwin was right. Every small shard of bone thus bore immense hermeneutic weight, and paleontologists came to be known for their abilities to piece together a whole animal from a single surviving bone.

The Darwinian morphology thus managed to open up a new era of positive knowledge without forsaking entirely the traditional assumption of the consonant whole. Darwinian morphology was equally a project of comprehensive knowledge, a theory of variation that

nevertheless presupposed the inherent stability of biological processes. 'The form of the entire structure under investigation should be found to vary in a more or less uniform manner,' wrote Thompson, such that 'a comprehensive law of growth has pervaded the whole structure in its integrity, and that some more or less simple and recognizable system of forces has been in control.'[11] The emphasis on the control of the whole is striking. Though Thompson begs the question of what exactly is in control and how control is achieved and maintained, he assumes that control is unitary and comprehensive, exercised by a single 'system of forces.' The next section of this chapter will show how, in the late nineteenth century, this idea of a controlled whole derived from morphology began to take on an explicitly global, and finally imperial, coloration. The wholeness of the natural world became a figuration, in other words, for a united Empire. The assumption of the whole, which began almost as a matter of faith, thus ended as a central myth of imperial knowledge. In a great variety of ways the morphological idea of the earth as a single family tree acted as a new and vital counterpoint to the central myth of the British Empire, the myth traced in detail in the first chapter, the myth of the world as understandable by one conjoined imperial archive. A reading of Bram Stoker's *Dracula* will cast light on the process by which morphology became an imperial science of form that, beginning in the 1890s, began to imagine form coming apart at the seams, torn by the greatest threat that late-Victorian morphology saw to the whole, the specter of discontinuous mutation.

The new monsters were beings that had undergone, or were capable of undergoing, catastrophic mutations of form. They could pass from form to form, moving not one form at a time but skipping many forms in a single jump. In evolutionary theory, no form could finally remain fully separate from other forms. These monsters could do so. They introduced into morphology chasms of unbridgeable difference. Darwin had been actively concerned with trying to arrive at a comprehensive view of species as the product of gradual and small-scale mutation. In a great variety of ways, these beings were a new construction of monstrosity well suited to the blind spot in the Darwinian paradigm. They were what had just begun to be called 'mutants.'[12]

Certainly mutants were monstrous for the traditional reason that, even within the liberal guidelines for classification laid out by Darwin in *The Origin of Species,* they fell outside the domain of existing knowledge. But the mutant was something more than a being that eluded all existing structures of classification. A mutant is a being without a history. It has no past, no progenitors, no lineage, no putative position on a reconstructed time-line. A mutant cannot be understood topologically as a displacement and redistribution of a stable aggregate of formal features. The mutant eludes science's quantitative grasp of number and magnitude: it signals the presence of irrational, rather than rational, modes of changing form. The Darwinian worldview had encouraged a one-sided view of change that harmonized with other nineteenth-century views of the essential continuity of matter: the smoothly curving paths of planets around the sun, the continuously varying pressure of a gas as it heated and cooled, the quantitative increase of the sugar level in the bloodstream. The mutant entailed another kind of change, less suited to the assumption of a comprehensive knowledge regulating the behavior of all phenomena, a form of change like the abrupt bursting of a bubble or the discontinuous transition from ice at its melting point to water at its freezing point. This new mutantcy meant the sudden death of form. A mutant did not develop according to the calculus of variations, a form of forms; it was a form outside form.

This precise emphasis on discontinuous mutation led Bram Stoker to create a new and particularly imperial inflection of the myth of Dracula, lord and master of the Undead. Stoker erected a new mythology around an old myth because he made his Dracula into a single dense locus of all that the Darwinian world-view had found inexplicable. In particular, Stoker's Dracula forcibly undoes the assumptions of Darwinian morphology in the form of a creature capable of both *sudden* and *lasting* mutations of form. Stoker's vampire lurks in these two blind alleys of Darwinism. He is the origin of his own species, a human being suddenly transformed into the progenitor of a terrifying new species. And he is a being whom his opponents openly view as a mutant capable of the catastrophic mutation of form. He is an ideal invader of England for the simple reason that he cannot be understood according to the usual patterns of recurrence of form in nature. A mutant capable of singlehandedly and successfully crossing the boundary between species was entirely unknowable within the Darwinian frame of knowledge. Dracula represents a species having no gradual, composed origin. Little wonder that Stoker finds in his resuscitated vampire the material for a kind of Darwinian invasion novel. To the usual elements of the Dracula myth—the Transylvania setting, the wolves, the kisses of blood— he adds three elements: the sense of Dracula as a mutant; the association of Dracula with vegetable mould; and the shipment of the boxes of mould containing Dracula from the periphery of Europe to one of its centers, London. As a mutant, Count Dracula poses a direct threat to the order of things and, by extension, to the general order of an empire figured as knowable within a Darwinian frame of comprehensive morphological knowledge.

In Darwin the word 'mutation' had had an almost neutral connotation. All species originate by mutation, but mutation always remains safely subordinate to the functional criterion of natural selection. In Darwin the emphasis on adaptive function almost totally restricts the range of variant form. By the turn of the century, however, the Dutch plant breeder Hugo de Vries performed a number of botanical experiments with the evening primrose that proved decisively that new species could originate in a large, single jump. In the short space of one generation de Vries observed that the primrose changed leaf shape, incision, and color. In *The Mutation Theory* (1901-03) de Vries maintained that new species arose in one generation through the occurrence of large-scale variations, which he termed 'mutations.' Darwin had recognized the possibility of such a process in what he called 'sports' or 'monsters,' but he had rejected this mechanism as having little or no significant role in the production of species. The genius of Stoker's construction of Dracula is that, like de Vries, he realizes that the mutant is by no means a reproductive dead-end, that it has an immense potential for propagation. The narrative of *Dracula* takes on incredible suspense for the simple reason that Dracula must be stopped before he multiplies beyond the point where he can be extinguished. According to Van Helsing, the scientist who scrupulously observes Dracula's habits in Stoker's novel, the most fearsome feature of the vampire is the speed at which he mutates. He learns quickly, changes forms quickly. This sense of large-scale jumps between forms gives a new sense to the old adage, 'The dead travel fast.'[13] Van Helsing comes right out and says that Dracula has been 'experimenting, and doing it well; and if it had not been that we had crossed his path he would be yet—he may be yet if we fail—the father or furtherer of a new order of beings, whose road must lead through Death, not Life' (302).

The consistent figure for death throughout Stoker's novel, and the one element with which Dracula is repeatedly associated, is vegetable mould. Previous Dracula stories had always likened the Vampire's lair to dust, but Stoker is very specific about his Dracula's preference for mould. When Jonathan Harker happens upon Dracula's sarcophagus in Transylvania he notices 'the odour of old earth newly turned' (47). The cargo Dracula ships to London consists of 'a number of great wooden boxes filled with mould' (80). This unlikely element was the subject of one of Darwin's most popular and practical books, *The Formation of Vegetable Mould through the Action of Worms* (1881). The relevant feature of vegetable mould is that, in Darwin's definition, it is matter that consists exclusively of the decaying residue of what was once living matter. Vegetable mould is matter in the median stage between life and death, matter that exists in a state of fertility. The role of worms is to fertilize the soil by turning over the earth like a plough, mixing the soil with leaves, twigs, the bones of dead animals, the harder parts of insects, the shells of land molluscs. Worms accelerate decay by subjecting the particles of earth 'to conditions eminently favourable for their decomposition and disintegration.'[14]

The representation of death as decomposition thus holds no mystery whatsoever for Darwin. Here as elsewhere Darwin sees decay as the primordial constituent of life on earth; the earth thrives on spent life, for the successive generations of life passing into death ensure the fertility of the topsoil. In the Victorian order of things the frightful thing about Dracula is not that he lives in a cemetery amidst dead things (the Victorians viewed cemeteries as familiar places) but that he lives in a purgatory of decay instead of just passing through it. Victorian popular culture was full of horror stories about the undecayed bodies of remarkable people, Paganinis and Lincolns whose bodies remained mysteriously immune to decay after death. In Stoker's novel the most terrifying moments come when his characters view the undecomposed bodies of vampires—when Jonathan Harker flees the sight of Dracula in his stone box, when the four men confront the dead Lucy in her tomb, when Van Helsing slays the three weird sisters in their Transylvanian crypt. Van Helsing goes so far as to say that even the sight of an undecomposed body is enough to cast a spell. The slight alteration the vampire makes in the Darwinian scheme, the one that makes him into an archetype of monstrosity within it, is that he does not complete the developmental process that forms the very precondition for life on earth. He dies without decaying, and flaunts his condition elementally by living in mould.

The new direction in which Stoker takes the Dracula myth also entails placing his Darwinian monster in a specifically imperial economy and making him pose a specifically imperial threat. Like so many other Victorian biologists, Darwin located the great incubators of mutation in the colonial world (even Wonderland, after all, is *under* England and contains colonial creatures like the hookah-smoking hookworm). Overwhelmingly the mutation tends to be represented as the revenge of the colonial world on the colonizer. Then as now, mutations at the periphery of the world—new forms, new creatures, new diseases—come back to haunt the world at its center. Transylvania was of course never a British colony, but Stoker makes his Dracula into the very type of the alienated colonial intellectual later analyzed with such acumen by Frantz Fanon.[15] In Stoker's narrative Dracula, a Magyar noble incensed at centuries of external domination that had reduced Transylvania to a Turkish colony, invades England from Transylvania. The basic movement of *Dracula* reverses the customary direction of colonization: in Stoker's novel the periphery attempts to colonize the center. Dracula brings with him not only an almost unlimited capacity for reproduction but also an association with the traditional carriers of the West's own ecological imperialism—rats, flies, mice, and vermin.[16] He proves a master at using Britain's imperial system of transport to his own advantage. He invades using the very shipping lines upon which Britain depended for receiving raw material from the colonial world. Most adeptly of all, he has mastered certain imperial practices of knowledge and power. He has worked at amassing a comprehensive knowledge of Britain, in Van Helsing's words, learning 'new social life; new environment of old ways, the politic, the law, the finance, the science, the habit of a new land and a new people who have come to be since he was' (321). In a sense he is pointing to a possibility that turn-of-the-century Britain could not bring itself to contemplate in the light of day: the possibility that the former colonist would emerge as the new immigrant, that Britain itself would emerge as a destination for immigrants from the colonial world. To prevent this from ever happening Stoker's characters adopt an unequivocal policy: 'We must sterilize all the imported earth' (274).

How could such a creature, a colonial creature capable of appropriating so many of the means of imperial domination to his own ends, ever be defeated? Dracula is defeated because, though he can control the transport of bodies and things, he cannot control the flow of information. At every point Stoker makes it crushingly clear that Dracula must be defeated through a mastery of the means of information. Dracula himself cannot move long distances; through out the novel he is less a moving body than a point of inertia. Because Dracula must hire intermediaries to carry him from place to place, his movements can be traced through invoices, memoranda, and other documents. He uses transport without realizing that what he is confronting is a new kind of empire, an imperial archive already seen on view in Kipling's *Kim,* an empire in which all transport entails the production of data. His movements from place to place leaves traces in a language that his opponents can decipher, the language of information. 'Accurate note was made of the state of things' (79). It does not even occur to him to destroy documents that give his enemies some knowledge of him, like Jonathan Harker's journal. While Dracula moves in a state of stillness, waiting out the interval between arrival and departure, his opponents send and receive messages in the space of seconds using telegraphy. Distances mean nothing to Van Helsing and his crew of vampire-killers; they seem to traverse them in a flash. The spatial distance between central and peripheral zones makes way for temporal distance fixed by the imperial certainty of the train timetable. Even Lord Godalming's old-boy network joins the imperial archive, conveying messages rapidly from consulate to consulate in order to defeat Dracula. The dead travel fast but data travels faster.

In a great variety of ways, then, Stoker's narrative figures the defeat of a kind of colonial uprising. *Dracula* enacts the domination of a once-indomitable mutation by the imperial archive. The novel ends with an expedition to Transylvania in which the rebellious form is put to death. Like Lewis Carroll, Stoker takes care to represent indomitable form as despotic and absolutist, embodied in the form of Count Dracula, who 'spoke almost in the plural, like a king speaking' (28). Far from being represented as the wave of the future, the colonial uprising has been represented here, as it soon would be by the British all over their Empire, as the recrudescence of an obsolete form, absolutism. The monologues recorded by Jonathan Harker in his journal read like an inventory of the modes of control invented by the absolutist state; speaking of Transylvanian history, Dracula tells of the introduction of standing armies, a permanent bureaucracy, national taxation, a codified law, and the beginnings of a unified market.[17] Dracula is clearly a feudal lord who, over time, has come to think of himself as an absolutist monarch.

Van Helsing counters Dracula's universalism by slowly picking it apart. Like Auguste Comte, who sought to liberate politics from the influence of parties insisting on the divine right of kings by establishing a positive social science, Van Helsing counters Dracula's absolutism with a simple emphasis on the positive knowledge of form. Form for Van Helsing is not absolute and universal but particular and positive. He defeats Dracula by studying the functions of Dracula's form. He makes careful note of the vampire's habits and habitat. His manner of investigation is a model of experimental method, and he refuses to explain to the others that the mysterious occurrences in the novel have been caused by a supernatural phenomenon until he can supply them with sufficient proof. Even though he is dealing with vampires, Van Helsing preserves all the assumptions of the positive knowledge of form, maintaining the presumed integrity of the world though what can be called an imperialism of particulars. In *Dracula* 'the habit of entering accurately' (36) along with 'power of combination' (238) ensure the reach of the Empire. At stake throughout the novel are the methods and procedures for controlling the imperial whole, and the primary vehicle for the control of the whole, a whole that can now comprise the irrational as well as the rational, is the procedure of positive knowledge.

Despite the defeat of Dracula by a smoothly functioning imperial archive, however, the novel has a prospective and unmistakably postcolonial character, for in it the boundaries of Empire have contracted. The boundaries of Empire have fallen back from Africa and India to an obscure danger zone at the edge of Europe. Contrary to Kipling, the novel begins at the place where East and West actually meet. At Budapest, Harker has the impression that 'we were leaving the West and entering the East,' entering 'one of the wildest and least known portions of Europe' (1). He represents the Balkan region using the stock figures of orientalism: the trains run late as 'in China,' the people

remind him of 'some old Oriental band of brigands,' all in all the region is 'the centre of some sort of imaginative whirlpool' in which is gathered 'every known superstition in the world' (2-3). Throughout the nineteenth century the Balkans were like a trip wire waiting to be crossed. The famous 'Eastern Question' came into being to address the fall of the Ottoman and Persian empires and the emergence of superpower rivalry among successor states in the region.[18] The narrative of *Dracula* runs along the retaining wall that separated imperial Europe from the imagined deluge of the colonial world, but it also points to the source of a very real catastrophe. The liminal zone of the Balkans, marked off by Stoker as the home of vampires, the site of mutation and locus of monstrosity, is the very place where the First World War began, the very place where the great colonial empires of the late nineteenth century began to end.

For nearly one hundred years the myth of Dracula has fed off this precise tension between continuous and discontinuous mutation, between an imperial order figured as continuous and a colonial disorder figured as formal discontinuity. In Stoker's novel the threat of discontinuity turns out at last to be manageable. Dracula is defeated, but only just. The triumph of the forces of Darwinian order over the forces of mutant disorder requires a last-minute high-speed chase in which the outcome is uncertain until the very last page. After two debilitating world wars it would no longer be possible to imagine the defeat of such a prodigy of mutation spawned in the colonial world. As a myth of knowledge the mutation would rise again in the imagination of postcolonial Britain. . . .

Notes

[1] Darwin once said of morphology, 'This is the most interesting department of natural history, and may be said to be its very soul' (quoted in George Gaylord Simpson, 'Anatomy and Morphology: Classification and Evolution: 1859 and 1959,' in *Proceedings of the American Philosophical Society,* vol. 103, no. 23, April 1959, p. 289).

Basic introductions to the position of morphology in nineteenth-century biology can be found in William Coleman, *Biology in the Nineteenth Century: Problems of Form, Function, and Transformation* (Cambridge 1977); Ernst Mayr, *The Growth of Biological Thought: Diversity, Evolution, and Inheritance* (Cambridge 1982); and Ernst Cassirer, 'The Ideal of Knowledge and its Transformation in Biology,' in *The Problem of Knowledge* (New Haven 1950). The reaction against morphology in twentieth-century biology receives attention in Garland Allen, *Life Science in the Twentieth Century* (Cambridge 1978).

The classic text announcing 'the cleavage between morphology and biophysics or biochemistry' is Joseph Needham, *Order and Life* (Cambridge 1936).

[2] See Auguste Comte, 'General View of Biology' (from *Cours de Philosophie Positive* [1838-1842]), in *Auguste Comte and Positivism: The Essential Writings* (Chicago 1983), pp. 163-81.

[3] Linnaeus, *Philosophie botanique,* Section 299, quoted in Michel Foucault, 'Classifying,' in *The Order of Things: An Archaeology of the Human Sciences* (New York 1973), p. 134.

[4] Charles Darwin, *The Voyage of the Beagle* (New York 1988), p. 17.

[5] The later Darwin preserves this taxonomic optimism: 'We could not . . . define the several groups; but we could pick out types, or forms, representing the characters of each group, whether large or small, and thus give a general idea of the value of the differences between them. This is what we should be driven to if we were ever to succeed in collecting all the forms in any class which have lived throughout all time and space. We shall certainly never succeed in making so perfect a collection: nevertheless, in certain classes, we are tending in this direction . . .' (quoted in George Gaylord Simpson, 'Anatomy and Morphology,' p. 299).

[6] Charles Darwin, 'Mutual Affinities of Organic Beings: Morphology: Embryology: Rudimentary Organs,' in *The Origin of Species* (Harmondsworth 1968; orig. pub. 1859), pp. 397-434.

[7] Michel Foucault says that 'the monster ensures the *emergence* of difference' (my emphasis), but I believe that this formulation must be altered. What ensures the emergence of difference is the expansion of Europe into the colonial world. The position of the monster within the Linnaean scheme allows only for the placement of difference in a taxonomy, where its emergence is effectively confined and prevented from becoming a very threatening event. See 'Classifying,' in *The Order of Things,* pp. 155-7.

[8] See Kurt Gödel, 'On Formally Undecidable Propositions in [Alfred North Whitehead's] *Principia Mathematica* [1911]' (1931).

[9] This sequence of logical reversals in Alice's adventures follows the analysis of Gilles Deleuze in *The Logic of Sense* (New York 1990), pp. 2-3. Because most of the quotations from the Alice texts are quite familiar, I have dispensed with page citations.

[10] D'Arcy Thompson, *On Growth and Form* (Cambridge 1961; orig. pub. 1917), p. 293.

[11] Ibid., pp. 274-5.

[12] The idea of the 'mutant' at first encompassed primarily the possibility of discontinuous variation. The possibility of artificial cloning began with the 1891 experiments of Hans Driesch, which showed that organisms may develop not only out of eggs but also out of certain cells caught at an early embryonic phase. The science of H.G. Wells's *The Island of Dr. Moreau* (1896) strikes an uneasy balance between Driesch's findings and the emphasis within late-Victorian morphology on discontinuous variation. One of the earliest texts on the viability of cloning is Jacques Loeb, *The Organism as a Whole from a Physiochemical Viewpoint* (1916).

[13] Bram Stoker, *Dracula* (Oxford 1983; orig. pub. 1897), p. 10. Subsequent citations appear in the text.

[14] Charles Darwin, *The Formation of Vegetable Mould through the Action of Worms* (Ontario, California 1976), p. 145. Stoker was obsessed by the functions of worms and returned to them in his 1911 novel, *The Lair of the White Worm.*

[15] Fanon quite frequently uses the image of living death to describe the plight of colonial peoples. 'The culture once living and open to the future, becomes closed, fixed in the colonial status, caught in the yoke of oppression. Both present and mummified, it testifies against its members. . . . The cultural mummification leads to a mummification of individual thinking. . . . As though it were possible for a man to evolve otherwise than within the framework of a culture that recognizes him and that he decides to assume.' Frantz Fanon, 'Racism and Culture,' in *Toward an African Revolution* (London 1970), p. 44. Fanon's classic anatomy of the alienated colonial intellectual is *Black Skin White Masks* (London 1970).

[16] See Alfred W. Crosby, *Ecological Imperialism: The Biological Expansion of Europe, 900-1900* (Cambridge 1986). Stoker's text has a prospective character for the twentieth century: it reverses the flow of disease to the colonial world and figures the biological *contraction* of Europe. On the problem of Dracula's coming to England, see Stephen Arata, 'The Occidental Tourist: Dracula and the Anxiety of Reverse Colonization,' *Victorian Studies,* vol. 33, no. 4 (1990), pp. 621-45.

[17] These are of course the classic functions of absolutism as enumerated by Perry Anderson in *Lineages of the Absolutist State* (London 1974).

[18] Any number of agreements, foremost among them the Berlin Congress of 1878, contrived to keep the edge of Europe secure so that the great powers could concentrate on expansion in the colonial world. On the centrality of the Eastern Question in nineteenth-cen-

tury politics, see Franz Ansprenger, *The Dissolution of the Colonial Empires* (London 1989); Richard Millman, *Britain and the Eastern Question, 1875-1878* (Oxford 1979); and G. D. Clayton, *Britain and the Eastern Question: Missolonghi to Gallipoli* (London 1971).

FURTHER READING

Bhabha, Homi K. "The other question: difference, discrimination and the discourse of colonialism." In *Literature, Politics and Theory*, edited by Francis Barker, Peter Hulme, Margaret Iversen, and Diana Loxley, pp. 148-72. London: Methuen, 1986, 259 p.

> Uses the writings of Frantz Fanon to argue that the construction of the colonial stereotype of the "other" is characterized by an ambivalence which reflects the contradictions inherent in colonial discourse.

Bivona, Daniel. *Desire and Contradiction: Imperial Visions and Domestic Debates in Victorian Literature*. Manchester: Manchester University Press, 1990, 153 p.

> Reveals the pervasive influence of imperialist ideology by tracing its impact on domestic novels where constructions of the "other" act as a form of self-reflection.

Bratton, J. S. "Of England, Home and Duty: The Image of England in Victorian and Edwardian Juvenile Fiction." In *Imperialism and Popular Culture*, edited by John M. MacKenzie, pp.73-93. Manchester: Manchester University Press, 1986.

> Focuses on children's fiction as a vehicle for indoctrination of England's youth into imperialist ideology.

David, Deirdre. "Children of Empire: Victorian Imperialism and Sexual Politics in Dickens and Kipling." In *Gender and Discourse in Victorian Literature and Art*, edited by Antony H. Harrison and Beverly Taylor, pp. 124-42. Dekalb, IL: Northern Illinois University Press, 1992, 286 p.

> Analyzes Dickens' *Old Curiosity Shop* and Kipling's *Kim* to reveal the mutually constitutive nature of gender and imperialist politics throughout the Victorian period.

Donaldson, Laura E. *Decolonizing Feminisms: Race, Gender, and Empire-Building*. Chapel Hill: The University of North Carolina Press, 1992, 175 p.

> Explores the problematic connections between colonialism and western feminism to emphasize the necessity of combining feminist and anti-racist postcolonial analysis in our readings of Victorian fiction.

Ferguson, Moira. *Colonialism and Gender Relations from Mary Wollstonecraft to Jamaica Kincaid*. New York: Columbia University Press, 1993, 175 p.

> Analyzes the connections between race, gender and colonial politics in representations of the East Caribbean by British and Caribbean women writers.

Green, Martin. *Dreams of Adventure, Deeds of Empire*. New York: Basic Books, 1979, 429 p.

> Argues that adventure is a central myth of empire-building, and explores the functioning of this myth in fiction in a broad historical context. A portion is excerpted above.

Hammond, Dorothy, and Alta Jablow. *The Africa That Never Was: Four Centuries of British Writing about Africa*. New York: Twayne, 1970, 251 p.

> Relates the portrayal of Africa and Africans by British writers to British political and economic interests.

Howe, Susanna. *Novels of Empire*. New York: Columbia University Press, 1949, 186 p.

> Broad review of novels on imperial themes set in India and Indo-China, Africa, Australia, and New Zealand. A portion of Chapter 2 is excerpted above.

Kiernan, V. G. *The Lords of Human Kind: Black Man, Yellow Man, and White Man in an Age of Empire*. New York: Columbia University Press, 1986, 336 p.

> Places nineteenth-century European colonialism in the long historical tradition of empire-building from the beginning of human civilization.

Lane, Christopher. *The Ruling Passion: British Colonial Allegory and the Paradox of Homosexual Desire*. Durham: Duke University Press, 1995, 326 p.

> Uses psychoanalysis to reveal the multiple formulations of homosexual desire in the Victorian period and their complex supporting/conflicting relationship with colonial ideology.

McClintock, Anne. *Imperial Leather: Race, Gender and Sexuality in the Colonial Contest*. New York: Routledge, 1995.

> Combines a psychoanalytical analysis of the domestic sphere with a historical analysis of the politics of Victorian England to trace the intersection of the discourses of race, gender, and colonialism during this period.

McClure, John A. *Kipling and Conrad: The Colonial Fiction*. Cambridge, MA: Harvard University Press, 1981, 182 p.

> Through a reading of the novels of Kipling and Conrad, traces the two novelists' changing attitudes towards the imperialist project.

Melman, Billie. *Women's Orients: English Women and the Middle East, 1718-1918*. London: Macmillan, 1992, 417 p.

> Analyzes British women's travels to the Middle East and the resultant writings to reveal the multiplicity of orientalist discourse and the differences between the relationship of British men and women with colonial ideology.

Meyer, Susan L. "Colonialism and the Figurative Strategy of *Jane Eyre*." *Victorian Studies* 33, No. 2 (Winter 1990): 247-68.

> Through a reading of *Jane Eyre*, explores Brönte's conflicting attitudes towards race relations.

Meyers, Jeffrey. *Fiction and the Colonial Experience*. Totowa, NJ: Rowman and Littlefield, Inc., 1968, 147 p.

> Analyzes how works by Kipling, Conrad, Forster, Cary, and Greene represent the cultural dynamics of the colonial encounter from the viewpoints of both colonizer and colonized and use colonial settings to re-evaluate Western civilization from an external perspective.

Nayder, Lillian. "Robinson Crusoe and Friday in Victorian Britain: 'Discipline,' 'Dialogue,' and Collins's Critique of Empire in *The Moonstone*." In *Dickens Studies Annual* Vol. 21, edited by Michael Timko, Fred Kaplan, and Edward Guiliano, pp. 213-31. New York: AMS Press, 1992, 339 p.

> Analyzes Collins's *The Moonstone* as an ideological critique of social and racial oppression in *Robinson Crusoe*.

Perera, Suvendrini. "'Fit Only for a Seraglio': The Discourse of Oriental Misogyny in *Jane Eyre* and *Vanity Fair*." In *Reaches of Empire: The English Novel from Edgeworth to Dickens*, pp. 79-102. New York: Columbia University Press, 1991.

> Examines *Jane Eyre* and *Vanity Fair* to explore the use of the discourse of oriental womanhood in the construction of the feminist individual subject in British fiction.

Raskin, Johan. *The Mythology of Imperialism*. New York: Random House, 1971, 335 p.

> Analyzes conflicts and compromises with respect to imperialism and resistance in the fiction of Kipling, Conrad, Forster, Lawrence, and Cary.

Said, Edward W. *Orientalism*. New York: Pantheon Books, 1978, 368 p.

> A ground-breaking work that argues that the West constructed the "orient" as its "other," underground self in both discursive and material terms as a means of controlling its colonial possessions.

——. *Culture and Imperialism*. New York: Vintage Books, 1993, 380 p.

> Explores the relationship between imperialism and narrative fiction, and argues that representations of imperialism are always accompanied by strategies of resistance.

Sandison, Alan. *The Wheel of Empire: A Study of the Imperial Idea in Some Late Nineteenth and Early Twentieth-Century Fiction*. New York: St. Martin's Press, 1967, 213 p.

> Looks at the writings of Kipling, Conrad, Haggard, and Buchan to analyze the moral, rather than the political, implications of the imperial idea as it functions in the fictional works of these writers.

Sharpe, Jenny. *Allegories of Empire: The Figure of Woman in the Colonial Text*. Minneapolis: University of Minnesota Press, 1993, 190 p.

> Argues that nineteenth-century racial ideology, which acted as a form of containment for threats to colonial authority, was appropriated by British women for their own feminist agenda.

Spurr, David. *The Rhetoric of Empire: Colonial Discourse in Journalism, Travel Writing, and Imperial Administration*. Durham: Duke University Press, 1993, 292 p.

> Analyzes the rhetorical modes of writing about the "other" as tropes of colonial discourse in non-fictional writings of the Victorian period.

Sullivan, Zohreh T. *Narratives of Empire: The Fictions of Rudyard Kipling*. Cambridge: Cambridge University Press, 1993, 199 p.

> Explores the ambivalence generated by the combination of power and desire in colonial discourse through a reading of Kipling's fiction and its conflation of the political and the familial.

Viera, Carol. "The Black Man's Burden in Anticolonial Satire." *CLA Journal* 26, No. 1 (September 1982): 1-22.

> Examines lesser-known British writers during the latter half of the nineteenth century who produced anti-colonial satire and thus provided an internal challenge to the colonial enterprise.

Wurgaft, Lewis D. *The Imperial Imagination: Magic and Myth in Kipling's India*. Middletown, CT: Wesleyan University Press, 1983, 211 p.

> A psychoanalytical study of the British relationship with India in the latter part of the nineteenth century through a reading of Kipling's fiction and its embodiment of the heroic mythology about British achievements in India.

Young, Robert. "Colonialism and the Desiring Machine." In *Liminal Postmodernisms: The Postmodern, the (Post-)Colonial, and the (Post-)Feminist*, edited by Theo D'haen and Hans Bertens, pp. 11-34. Amsterdam: Rodopi, 1994, 357 p.

> Examines the racial and sexual framework that formed the theoretical framework for colonial discourse during the Victorian period.

Homosexuality in Nineteenth-Century Literature

INTRODUCTION

Homosexual content in nineteenth-century literature manages to be at once rare and pervasive: while it makes virtually no explicit appearance in mainstream fiction, it nonetheless maintains a persistent implicit presence. That obscurity reflects nineteenth-century culture. The sexual morés of Victorian England, for example, allowed for little overt discussion of homosexuality outside of the legal and medical fields. Early in the century, when homosexual activity was perceived almost exclusively as a crime, a sin, or both, men who engaged sexually with one another were most often labelled "sodomites." Other terms gained currency as the century proceeded, including "inverts" and "Uranians"; each term reflected a different conception of same-sex desire. This array of labels and meanings consolidated into the pervasive "homosexuality" only after the 1895 trial of Oscar Wilde for his liaisons with other men. At its inception, the word "homosexual" expressed a largely medical notion of sexual desire, reflecting its first use by the Swiss doctor Karoly Bankert in 1869. Through the efforts of Bankert and other sexologists, the public gradually became familiar with an idea of homosexuality as inherent to an individual, a quality that encompassed but also outstripped sexual acts. In the twentieth century, this trend would develop into the image of gay and lesbian identity we find most familiar today.

The general silence about sexuality in Victorian culture fostered a corresponding muteness in literature. Rather than being completely absent, however, homosexual desire and activity emerged in literature and in culture through socially acceptable and heavily disguised forms, such as the romantic friendship. Emily Dickinson and George Eliot, for example, enjoyed significant emotional relationships with other women. Romantic friendships between women were integral to Victorian culture since they were entirely compatible with Victorian notions of female sexuality, which was considered almost nonexistent. Historians have disagreed about the extent to which such friendships were actually platonic, some arguing that chaste Victorian women would have maintained asexual attachments. Others insist that at least some of these relationships—which often lasted a lifetime and involved not only a shared home but also a shared bed—must have included a sexual component.

Such bonds between men were also accepted in a way unfamiliar to twentieth-century culture. Walt Whitman celebrated male-male attachments in *Leaves of Grass* and did not shy from investing them with physicality. Alfred, Lord Tennyson's *In Memoriam* has long been recognized as a tribute to the author's profound emotional connection with another man. Thus experienced and valorized by many of the century's writers, these intimate same-sex relationships filled Victorian literature without ever prompting the charge of homosexuality. Where these descriptions masked physical desire, the disguise was necessary to avoid social and legal condemnation.

British law—and American law in its shadow—maintained a vehement condemnation of homosexual activity throughout the century, even as reforms relaxed measures that had oppressed other minorities for centuries. Slavery, for example, was abolished throughout the United Kingdom in 1833, and laws punishing English Catholics were eased considerably. The death penalty was revoked for many crimes—including rape—in the 1836 law reform. For the "nameless offense of great enormity," however, the death penalty remained intact and was regularly enforced: through the first third of the century, men went to the gallows for sexual activity with other men almost every year. When the death penalty was abolished in 1861, it was replaced by life imprisonment. The Criminal Law Amendment Act of 1885, aimed primarily at reducing heterosexual prostitution, once again redefined measures against sodomy, heterosexual and homosexual: an offender convicted of sodomy would receive a minimum of ten years; for "attempted sodomy" an offender could receive ten years maximum; for specifically homosexual "gross indecency," public or private, the sentence was two years with hard labor. It was on this last charge that Oscar Wilde went to prison. No such laws addressed lesbianism, however, since authorities appeared to consider it too unimaginable or unmentionable even to condemn. Occasionally, women were prosecuted for "masquerading" in male attire and thereby usurping male social and economic prerogatives.

Despite the heavy persecution of male-male sexual activity, homosexual subcultures thrived as they had for centuries. Underground institutions provided space and an economic basis for this subculture, much the way pubs and clubs might service a man's platonic social activities. The most visible subcultural activity occurred among middle- and lower-class men, many of whom were exclusively homosexual, usually passive in sex, occasionally transvestite, and whose social life consisted of participation in this subculture. Some historians contend that these men did not represent the majority of the male population who engaged in homosexual sex, but simply the most visible. Court documents suggest that most male homosexuals were married men who maintained conventionally masculine manners and families, like Captain Henry Nicholas Nicholls, a war veteran and member of a respectable family who was executed for sodomy in 1833.

In general, homosexual men of the upper-middle class and the aristocracy belonged to this less visible milieu, insulated to some degree by wealth and social status. When an explicit subculture emerged later in the century among these men, it contributed to the development of homosexual identity and social rights. Historians attribute this to the influence of two phenomena: the development of a medical definition of homosexuality and the intellectual reevaluation of classical literature. The first, a medical discourse that classified individuals according to their sexual desires, owed its development to the work of sexologists throughout Europe, including Karl Heinrich Ulrichs, Richard von Krafft-Ebing, and Havelock Ellis. The latter owed its development largely to the efforts of Benjamin Jowett, who reintroduced the teaching of Plato and other classical authors at Oxford University as part of the Oxford Great Works Curriculum. This training allowed homosexual undergraduates—including such influential intellectuals as Wilde, Walter Pater, and J. A. Symonds—to validate their desires as the resurrected spirit of Hellenism: noble, aesthetic, intellectually rigorous, even martial and athletic. Symonds and Edward Carpenter, in particular, dedicated themselves to defining a positive and coherent image of homosexual identity. Their efforts began to have some effect in the 1880s and 1890s, coexisting with a long-standing conviction that "effeminacy" and "corruption" characterized male-male desire. The traditional condemnation re-emerged in 1895 in response to Wilde's trial. While the trial brought the discussion of homosexual desire into the open, it also catalyzed the kind of active persecution that had been for some time dormant. Many homosexual men, particularly those of high social status, resettled at least temporarily on the continent, seeking to avoid scandal and prosecution. Even the ambiguous forms of same-sex love that had so far been integral to Victorian culture became suspect, and homoaffectional literature became both more explicit in its sexuality and much less common.

The tentative changes that began in the nineteenth century would not blossom until the twentieth century, and until then homosexual desire remained a largely unacknowledged phenomenon. Aside from sexually explicit texts that were a part of a thriving underground Victorian taste for pornography, homosexuality in books, as in real life, was "closeted"—or hidden beneath the trappings of heterosexuality and acceptable same-sex affection. Consequently, it has been the work of recent literature criticism—which put forth a branch of gay and lesbian studies in the mid-1980s—to point out the same-sex desire evident in much of Victorian literature.

REPRESENTATIVE WORKS

Alcott, Louisa May
Work (novel) 1873

Anonymous
Don Leon (poetry) 1866

Anonymous
The Sins of the Cities of the Plain (novel) 1881

Anonymous
Teleny (novel) 1890

Baudelaire, Charles
"Femmes damnées" (poetry) 1857

Coleridge, Samuel Taylor
Christabel (poetry) 1816

Converse, Florence
Diana Victrix (novel) 1897

Douglas, Lord Alfred
"Two Loves" (poetry) 1894

Gautier, Theophile
Mademoiselle de Maupin (novel) 1835

James, Henry
The Bostonians (novel) 1886

Lee, Vernon
Miss Brown (novel) 1884

Meredith, George
Diana of the Crossways (novel) 1885

Pater, Walter
Marius the Epicurian (novel) 1885

Rossetti, Christina
"Goblin Market" (poetry) 1859

Swinburne, A. C.
Poems and Ballads (poetry) 1866

Taylor, Bayard
Poems of the Orient (poetry) 1854

Tennyson, Alfred, Lord
In Memoriam (poetry) 1850

Whitman, Walt
Leaves of Grass (poetry) 1855

Wilde, Oscar
The Picture of Dorian Gray (novel) 1891

DEFINING HOMOSEXUALITY

Havelock Ellis

SOURCE: "The Theory of Sexual Inversion," in *Sexual Inversion,* 1897. Reprint by Arno Press, 1975, pp. 128-40.

[*When sexologist Havelock Ellis first published* Sexual Inversion *in 1897, his study became one of the standard authorities in English on the subject. Considered a highly scientific and generally sympathetic perspective for its time, Ellis's work presents the view that most homosexuals are the product of an inborn condition that inverts their gender identities, coupling male personalities with female bodies and vice versa. Although largely discredited among professionals today, Ellis's theory still resonates in popular stereotype, and many students of gay and lesbian history study it as an important document. In the following excerpt, Ellis explains his central theory.*]

. . . What is sexual inversion? Is it, as many would have us believe, an abominable acquired vice, to be stamped out by the prison? or is it, as a few assert, a beneficial variety of human emotion which should be tolerated or even fostered? Is it a diseased condition which qualifies its subject for the lunatic asylum? or is it a natural monstrosity, a human "sport," the manifestations of which must be regulated when they become anti-social? There is probably an element of truth in more than one of these views. I am prepared to admit that very widely divergent views of sexual inversion are largely justified by the position and attitude of the investigator. It is natural that the police official should find that his cases are largely mere examples of disgusting vice and crime. It is natural that the asylum superintendent should find that we are chiefly dealing with a form of insanity. It is equally natural that the sexual invert himself should find that he and his inverted friends are not so very unlike ordinary persons. We have to recognise the influence of professional and personal bias and the influence of environment, one investigator basing his conclusions on one class of cases, another on a quite different class of cases. Naturally, I have largely founded my own conclusions on my own cases. I believe, however, that my cases and my attitude towards them justify me in doing this with some confidence. I am not in the position of one who is pleading *pro domo,* nor of the police official, nor even of the physician, for these persons have not come to me for treatment. I approach the matter as a psychologist who has ascertained certain definite facts, and who is founding his conclusions on those facts.

The first point which impresses me is that we must regard sexual inversion as largely a congenital phenomenon, or, to speak more accurately, as a phenomenon which is based on congenital conditions. This, I think, lies at the root of the right comprehension of the matter. There are at the present day two streams of tendency in the views regarding sexual inversion: one seeking to enlarge the sphere of the acquired (represented by [Alfred] Binet—who, however, recognises predisposition—[Baron von] Schrenck-Notzing, and others), the other seeking to enlarge the sphere of the congenital (represented by [R. von] Krafft-Ebing, [Albert] Moll, and others). There is, as usually happens, truth in both these views. But inasmuch as those who represent the acquired view often emphatically deny any congenital element, I think we are specially called upon to emphasise this congenital element. The view that sexual inversion is entirely explained by the influence of early association, or of "suggestion," is an attractive one, and at first sight it seems to be supported by what we know of erotic fetichism, by which a woman's hair, or foot, or even clothing, becomes the focus of a man's sexual aspirations. But it must be remembered that what we see in erotic fetichism is merely the exaggeration of a normal impulse; every lover is to some extent excited by his mistress's hair, or foot, or clothing; even here, therefore, there is really what may fairly be regarded as a congenital element; and, moreover, there is reason to believe that the erotic fetichist usually displays the further congenital element of hereditary neurosis. Therefore, the analogy with erotic fetichism, does not bring much help to those who argue that inversion is purely acquired. It must also be pointed out that the argument for acquired or suggested inversion logically involves the assertion that normal sexuality is also acquired or suggested. If a man becomes attracted to his own sex simply because the fact or the image of such attraction is brought before him, then we are bound to believe that a man becomes attracted to the opposite sex only because the fact or the image of such attraction is brought before him. This theory is wholly unworkable. In nearly every country of the world men associate with men, and women with women; if association and suggestion were the only influential causes, then inversion, instead of being the exception, ought to be the rule throughout the human species, if not, indeed, throughout the whole zoological series. We should, moreover, have to admit that the most fundamental human instinct is so constituted as to be equally well adapted for sterility as for that propagation of the race which, as a matter of fact, we find dominant throughout the whole of life. We must, therefore, put aside entirely the notion that the direction of sexual impulse is merely a suggested phenomenon; such a notion is entirely opposed to observation and experience, and will with difficulty fit into a rational biological scheme.

The rational way of regarding the normal sexual impulse is as an inborn organic impulse, developing about the time of puberty. At this period suggestion and association may come in to play a part in defining the object of the emotion; the soil is now ready, but the variety of seeds likely to thrive in it is limited. That there is a greater indefiniteness in the aim of the sexual impulse at this period we may well believe. This is shown not only by occasional tentative signs of sexual emotion directed towards the same sex, but by the usually vague and non-sexual character of the normal passion at puberty. But the channel of sexual emotion is not thereby turned into an utterly abnormal path. Whenever this permanently happens we are, I think, bound to believe—and we have many grounds for believing—that we are dealing with an organism which from the beginning is abnormal. The same seed of suggestion is sown in various soils; in the many it dies out, in the few it flourishes. The cause can only be a difference in the soil.

If, then, we must postulate a congenital abnormality in order to account satisfactorily for at least a large proportion of sexual inverts, wherein does that abnormality consist? [Carl Heinrich] Ulrichs explained the matter by saying that in sexual inverts a male body coexists with a female soul: *anima maliebris in corpore virili inclusa*. Even writers with some pretension to scientific precision, like Magnan and Gley, have adopted this phrase in a modified form, considering that in inversion a female brain is combined with a male body or male glands. This is, however, not an explanation. It merely crystallises into an epigram the superficial impression of the matter. As an explanation it is to a scientific psychologist unthinkable. We only know soul as manifested through body; and, although if we say that a person seems to have the body of a man and the feelings of a woman we are saying what is often true enough, it is quite another matter to assert dogmatically that a female soul, or even a female brain, is expressing itself through a male body. That is simply unintelligible. I say nothing of the fact that in male inverts the feminine psychic tendencies may be little if at all marked, so that there is no "feminine soul" in the question; nor of the further important fact that in a very large proportion of cases the body itself presents primary and secondary sexual characters that are distinctly modified.

We can probably grasp the nature of the abnormality better if we reflect on the development of the sexes and on the latent organic bi-sexuality in each sex. At an early stage of development the sexes are indistinguishable, and throughout life the traces of this early community of sex remain. The hen fowl retains in a rudimentary form the spurs which are so large and formidable in her lord, and sometimes she develops a capacity to crow, or puts on male plumage. Among mammals the male possesses useless nipples, which occasionally even develop into breasts, and the female possesses a clitoris, which is merely a rudimentary penis, and may also develop. The sexually inverted person does not usually possess any gross exaggeration of these signs of community with the opposite sex. But, as we have seen, there are a considerable number of more subtle approximations to the opposite sex in inverted persons, both on the physical and the psychic side. Putting the matter in a purely speculative shape, it may be said that at conception the organism is provided with about 50 per cent. of male germs and about 50 per cent. of female germs, and that as development proceeds either the male or the female germs assume the upper hand, killing out those of the other sex, until in the maturely developed individual only a few aborted germs of the opposite sex are left. In the homosexual person, however, and in the psychosexual hermaphrodite, we may imagine that the process has not proceeded normally, on account of some peculiarity in the number or character of either the original male germs or female germs, or both; the result being that we have a person who is organically twisted into a shape that is more fitted for the exercise of the inverted than of the normal sexual impulse, or else equally fitted for both.

Thus in sexual inversion we have what may fairly be called a "sport" or variation, one of those organic aberrations which we see throughout living nature, in plants and in animals.

It is not here asserted, as I would carefully point out, that an inverted sexual instinct, or organ for such instinct, is developed in early embryonic life; such a notion is rightly rejected as absurd. What we may reasonably regard as formed at an early stage of development is strictly a predisposition, that is to say, such a modification of the organism that it becomes more adapted than the normal or average organism to experience sexual attraction to the same sex. The sexual invert may thus be roughly compared to the congenital idiot, to the instinctive criminal, to the man of genius, who are all not strictly concordant with the usual biological variation (because this is of a less subtle character) but who become somewhat more intelligible to us if we bear in mind their affinity to variations. [J.A.] Symonds compared inversion to colour-blindness; and such a comparison is reasonable. Just as the ordinary colour-blind person is congenitally insensitive to those red-green rays which are precisely the most impressive to the normal eye, and gives an extended value to the other colours—finding that blood is the same colour as grass, and a florid complexion blue as the sky—so the invert fails to see emotional values patent to normal persons, transferring their values to emotional associations which for the rest of the world are utterly distinct. Or we may compare inversion to such a phenom-enon as coloured-hearing in which there is not so much defect, as an abnormality of nervous tracks producing new and involuntary combinations. Just as the colour-hearer instinctively associates colours with sounds, like the young Japanese lady who remarked when listening to singing, "That boy's voice is red!" so the invert has his sexual sensations brought into relationship with objects that are normally without sexual appeal. And inversion, like colour-hearing, is found more common-ly in young subjects, tending to become less marked, or to die out, after puberty. Colour-hearing, while an abnormal phenomena, it must be added, cannot be called a diseased condition, and it is probably much less fre-quently associated with other abnormal or degenera-tive stigmata than is inversion. There is often a con-genital element, shown by the tendency to hereditary transmission, while the associations are developed in very early life, and are too regular to be the simple result of suggestion.

All these organic variations, which I have here men-tioned to illustrate sexual inversion, are abnormalities. It is important that we should have a clear idea as to what an abnormality is. Many people imagine that what is abnormal is necessarily diseased. That is not the case, unless we give the word disease an inconvenient-ly and illegitimately wide extension. It is both incon-venient and inexact to speak of colour-blindness, crim-inality and genius, as diseases, in the same sense as we speak of scarlet-fever or tuberculosis or general paral-ysis as diseases. Every congenital abnormality is doubt-less due to a peculiarity in the sperm or oval elements or in their mingling, or to some disturbance in their early development. But the same may doubtless be said of the normal dissimilarities between brothers and sis-ters. It is quite true that any of these aberrations may be due to ante-natal disease, but to call them abnormal does not beg that question. If it is thought that any authority is needed to support this view, we can scarcely find a weightier than that of Virchow, who has repeat-edly insisted on the right use of the word "anomaly," and who teaches that, though an anomaly may consti-tute a predisposition to disease, the study of anoma-lies—pathology, as he would call it, teratology as we may perhaps prefer to call it—is not the study of dis-ease, which he would term nosology; the study of the abnormal is perfectly distinct from the study of the morbid. Virchow considers that the region of the ab-normal is the region of pathology, and that the study of disease must be regarded distinctly as nosology. Whether we adopt this terminology, or whether we consider the study of the abnormal as part of teratol-ogy, is a secondary matter, not affecting the right understanding of the term "anomaly", and its due dif-ferentiation from the term "disease". . . .

Sexual inversion, therefore, remains a congenital ab-normality, to be classed with the other congenital ab-

Havelock Ellis.

normalities which have psychic concomitants. At the very least such congenital abnormality usually exists as a predisposition to inversion. It is probable that many persons go through the world with a congenital predis-position to inversion which always remain latent and unroused; in others the instinct is so strong that it forces its own way in spite of all obstacles; in others, again, the predisposition is weaker, and a powerful exciting cause plays the predominant part.

We are thus led to the consideration of the causes that excite the latent predisposition. A great variety of causes has been held to excite to sexual inversion. It is only necessary to mention those which I have found influ-ential. The most important of these is undoubtedly our school system, with its segregation of boys and girls apart from each other during the important periods of puberty and adolescence. Many congenital inverts have not been to school at all, and many who have been, pass through school life without forming any passion-ate or sexual relationship; but there remain a large number who date the development of homosexuality from the influences and examples of school life. The impressions received at the time are not less potent because they are often purely sentimental and without any obvious sensual admixture. Whether they are suf-ficiently potent to generate permanent inversion alone may be doubtful, but if it is true that in early life the sexual instincts are less definitely determined than when adolescence is complete, it is conceivable, though unproved, that a very strong impression, acting even on a normal organism, may cause arrest of sexual development on the psychic side. It is a question I am not in a position to settle.

Another important exciting cause of inversion is seduction. By this I mean the initiation of the young boy or girl by some older and more experienced person in whom inversion is already developed, and who is seeking the gratification of the abnormal instinct. This appears to be a not uncommon incident in the early history of sexual inverts. That such seduction—sometimes an abrupt and inconsiderate act of mere sexual gratification—could by itself produce a taste for homosexuality is highly improbable; in individuals not already predisposed it is far more likely to produce disgust, as it did in the case of the youthful Rousseau. "He only can be seduced", as Moll puts it, "who is capable of being seduced". No doubt it frequently happens in these, as so often in more normal "seductions", that the victim has offered a voluntary or involuntary invitation.

Another exciting cause of inversion, to which little importance is usually attached but which I find to have some weight, is disappointment in normal love. It happens that a man in whom the homosexual instinct is yet only latent, or at all events held in a state of repression, tries to form a relationship with a woman. This relationship may be ardent on one or both sides, but—often, doubtless, from the latent homosexuality of the lover—it comes to nothing. Such love-disappointments, in a more or less acute form, occur at some time or another to nearly everyone. But in these persons the disappointment with one woman constitutes motive strong enough to disgust the lover with the whole sex and to turn his attention towards his own sex. It is evident that the instinct which can thus be turned round can scarcely be strong, and it seems probable that in some of these cases the episode of normal love simply serves to bring home to the invert the fact that he is not made for normal love. In other cases, doubtless—especially those that are somewhat feeble-minded and unbalanced—a love disappointment really does poison the normal instinct, and a more or less impotent love for women becomes an equally impotent love for men. The prevalence of homosexuality among prostitutes must certainly be in large extent explained by a similar and better founded disgust with normal sexuality.

These three influences, therefore,—example at school, seduction, disappointment in normal love,—all of them drawing the subject away from the opposite sex and concentrating him on his own sex, are powerful exciting causes of inversion; but they mostly require a favourable organic predisposition to act on, while there are a large number of cases in which no exciting cause at all can be found, but in which from the earliest childhood the subject's interest seems to be turned on his own sex, and continues to be so turned throughout life.

At this point I conclude the analysis of the psychology of sexual inversion as it presents itself to me. I have sought only to bring out the more salient points, neglecting minor points, neglecting also those groups of inverts who may be regarded as of secondary importance. The average invert, moving in ordinary society, so far as my evidence extends, is most usually a person of average general health, though very frequently with hereditary relationships that are markedly neurotic. He is usually the subject of a congenital predisposing abnormality, or complexus of minor abnormalities, making it difficult or impossible for him to feel sexual attraction to the opposite sex, and easy to feel sexual attraction to his own sex. This abnormality either appears spontaneously from the first, by development or arrest of development, or it is called into activity by some accidental circumstance.

EVIL WOMEN AND ROMANTIC FRIENDS

Jeannette H. Foster

SOURCE: "From the Romantics to the Moderns," in *Sex Variant Women in Literature: A Historical and Quantitative Survey,* Vantage Press, 1956, pp. 60-80.

[*In 1956, Foster published the first exhaustive study of lesbian content in literature,* Sex Variant Women in Literature. *The following excerpt presents some of her findings on the nineteenth century, demonstrating the ways in which authors—most of them French men—presented lesbian characters and encounters.*]

The Novel Before 1870

For the first three-quarters of the nineteenth century variant fiction was so nearly an exclusive product of France that traces appearing elsewhere may be left for separate consideration. The first pertinent French item was a typical Romantic Period novel of indifferent literary quality, Philip Cuisin's *Clémentine, Orpheline et Androgyne* (1819). As its title indicates, intersexual anatomy is responsible for the heroine's variant personality, which is used merely as mainspring for a plot of the wildest extravagance. *Clémentine* is a beautiful child of unknown antecedents cast ashore near Carcassone as sole survivor of a shipwreck. With the approach of puberty her ambiguous sex makes her the object of so much superstitious hostility among the peasants of the neighborhood that she is sent by her wealthy protector to a physician in Cadiz who is glad of the chance to observe such an anomaly.

A child's unawareness of her own peculiarity had betrayed her to the peasants of Carcassone. Shocked into neurotic prudery she manages in Cadiz to avoid suspicion though not curiosity on the part of the physician's daughter, who becomes strongly attached to her and is hurt by her refusal of the easy intimacy common among growing girls. Clémentine canalizes her waxing male eroticism into strenuous physical exercise and becomes a proficient fencer. This unfeminine skill and her habit of going about occasionally in men's clothing produce violent infatuation in a bold young woman of the neighborhood who believes her to be a man, and who plays thereafter the role of villain in the piece. Because of this woman's advances, Clémentine is forced to leave her second home in Cadiz and is subsequently involved in a series of stormy adventures. She is too feminine to live out her life disguised as a man, too relentlessly pursued by her evil adorer to settle down as an independent woman and win a man she has come to love. An interim in a convent, where she takes refuge from the law after killing a man in a duel, naturally only produces fresh complications. Here she, herself, is passionately drawn to the urbane Superior who cherishes her, and a novice is similarly attracted to her; but she resists all temptations (and they are many) to give way to her feelings. At last obstacles are overcome according to the best romantic pattern—she marries her male beloved, who understands and accepts her anomaly, encourages her to fence and hunt with him, and enjoys her love, which has "la force réuni des deux sexes." The author must have read the contemporary literature on hermaphroditism, but was evidently shy of attributing his heroine's passionate intensity to her anomaly after once he had her settled as a married woman, and so lays it in part to prenatal influence. Her mother, we are told, had during pregnancy been very friendly with a Persian ambassador to the French court, and had been "saturated" with his oriental tales. Thus, the daughter was predestined to love "avec l'exaltation d'une Persane."

The second and slightly more artistic French narrative is a two-volume novel by Henri de Latouche entitled *Fragoletta* (1829), which is concerned primarily with the Napoleonic wars and anti-British propaganda. Emotional interest centers about the hero's love for the title figure, whom he first meets as a boyish girl of fourteen, daring, brilliant, and free of coquetry. Her Sicilian guardian, knowing himself pursued by political assassins, implores d'Hauteville to marry and care for Fragoletta, but d'Hauteville feels that his love for her has roused no response save lively friendship and so waits for her emotions to mature. On the guardian's death he becomes her protector until the misfortunes of war separate them. Later he hears she has returned to her native Austria from which she was removed as an infant.

She writes him of discovering there a twin brother, Adriani, who eventually visits d'Hauteville in his Paris home and falls in love with his sister, an untouched innocent a year Adriani's senior. Sent as a spy to Naples, d'Hauteville sees Fragoletta there at a court ball given by Queen Caroline, at which Lady Hamilton is a guest. He hears that Adriani is a spy on the English-Neapolitan side, but because of the need for concealing his own identity he can neither reveal himself to Fragoletta nor penetrate the mystery of her presence among the English and her brother's treasonous activity.

He then learns from a frantic letter from his sister that Adriani has seduced her and that she no longer wishes to live. Her mother also has fallen gravely ill of the shock. D'Hauteville pursues the boy to Paris only to find him gone again and his sister on her deathbed. Subsequently, he tracks the traitor-seducer back to Naples and challenges him to a duel. Fragoletta, still in Naples, begs him not to expose himself to certain capture by the enemy merely in order to avenge "un tort exagéré ou peut-être imaginaire," implying that only his sister's naïvete led her to believe herself ravished. D'Hauteville persists in duelling, however, and overcomes his opponent without effort. Adriani retreats almost without resistance over the edge of a cliff and falls to death in the sea below with a feminine cry which reveals to d'Hauteville that Fragoletta and her twin are one. The reader is left in doubt whether Fragoletta was, like Clémentine, a hermaphrodite, or (as seems more probable) was simply an exclusively lesbian woman. (Similarly the Chevalier d'Eon moved in international diplomatic circles alternately as man and woman, his true sex being known only upon his death in 1810.) In the course of the story the author incorporates a scene between Queen Caroline and Emma Hamilton which takes place in the former's sunken marble bath. The queen first plays the part of lady's maid in disrobing her beautiful friend, and later indulges in erotic play until the two drowse off in one another's arms in the warm pool. Latouche may have intended this lax court background to account for Fragoletta's transformation from a rather engaging tomboy into an active lesbian.

Far superior from a literary viewpoint to either of these novels was Balzac's first venture in the intersexual field, *Seraphitus-Seraphita* (1834). The heroine of this tale has been mentioned by Natalie Clifford Barney, a twentieth century writer of lesbian verse, as one of those androgynes who lend rarity to the Human Comedy, but Seraphita was not, like Clémentine, a physical anomaly. The novel of which she is the title figure is a lengthy excursion into Swedenborgian philosophy, and the girl is raised in an undiluted atmosphere of that particular mysticism. The result is a sexless and wholly ascetic personality. To the man who loves her she seems the perfect woman. To a younger girl whom she leads in fearless ascents of rocky heights above the fjords and who loves her equally, she seems the perfect man, although there is never any mystery about her true sex. With neither man nor girl does she exchange even the most innocent of physical caresses. After her early death the girl and the man marry one another, their common half-mystical worship of her constituting a stronger bond than exists between ordinary lovers.

In the following year Balzac published his much better-known novel, *The Girl with the Golden Eyes,* a romantic tale involving an overt lesbian, though the latter enters the story only at the end, the main theme being her effect upon her passive victim. The story describes the conquest, by the very flower of Byronic heroes, of a mysterious beauty sequestered in a Paris mansion with all the vigilance surrounding a caliph's harem. Once reached by the hero, the golden-eyed girl proves a paradox of virginity and voluptuous sophistication until a *lapsus linguae* betrays that it is a lesbian of enormous wealth who has initiated her sexually and kept her hidden from the world of men. This woman, returning from an absence which made the adventure possible, at once detects the girl's infidelity and, in a jealous and sadistic frenzy, kills her. She then discovers that her rival is her own half-brother and almost physical twin (they were both illegitimate, their father but one step removed from royalty), and, consequently, it was his resemblance to her that made his fatal conquest of the girl so easy.

In the extravagance of the plot and the description of the hero, which occupies a good quarter of the tale, one might suspect satire upon the Byronism which was sweeping Europe, except for the romantic seriousness of the whole. Another long interpolated essay is an arraignment, mordant in brilliance, of the cruelty, stupidity, and license of Parisian life, in which one detects echoes from Rousseau: in such an "unnatural" milieu excesses of evil are only to be expected. Such romantic social philosophy concerned Balzac here more than the psychology of either woman. That the golden-eyed girl, sold by her mother at the age of twelve and a passive partner throughout, should first learn complete love from the hero, is barely credible. That after a decade in which she has suffered neither physical nor nervous ill-health she should be so instantly changed as to prefer death to her former life might be questioned by the modern psychologist. The lesbian Marquise is hardly better accounted for. Her cool purchase and long imprisonment of the girl, whose physical beauty is the only tie suggested between them, make poor preparation for her heartbreak and sudden desire for convent life because she has lost "that which seemed the infinite." Possibly her half-Spanish, half-royal blood are intended to account for both her lesbianism and her vagaries of temperament, for gossip credited the Spanish ruling dynasty

as well as the house of Orléans with tendencies toward homosexuality.

In *Cousin Bette* (1846), Balzac, with a realism in sharp contrast to both his earlier tales and in keeping with literary trends of the intervening dozen years, presents rather casually the half-realized infatuation of the thwarted spinster, Bette, for Madame Marneffe, the human instrument she employs to satisfy her much stronger passion for revenge upon the family who have humiliated her. Valérie Marneffe, who "spent her days upon a sofa, turning the lantern of her detective spirit on the obscurest depths of souls, sentiments and intrigues . . . had discovered the true nature of this ardent creature burning with wasted passion, and meant to attach her to herself." Both women have had lovers, Bette having striven in vain to hold a Polish artist several years her junior. But "in this new affection she had found food . . . far more satisfying than her insane passion for Wenceslas, who had always been cold to her." Little of physical intimacy is implied between the two women beyond frequent kisses, and since Balzac is not particularly reticent about such details, it is not safe to assume any such relation as existed in *The Girl with the Golden Eyes*. But later in the book he speaks of such attachments as "the strongest emotion known, that of a woman for a woman."

Thus, the faithful observer of the Human Comedy presented three contrasting types of emotional variance and offered three distinct explanations of it. In the first, intellectual conditioning was the causal factor; in the second, a possible inheritance of temperament plus the certain freedom for self-indulgence provided by limitless wealth; and in the third, poverty of both circumstance and emotional opportunity. The resulting experiences also show the writer's imaginative range. The first seraphic heroine is as innocent and passionless as the biblical Ruth. The Spanish Marquise is violent to the point of melodrama. The warped spinster is confused and groping in expression as well as feeling.

In the same year that *The Girl with the Golden Eyes* appeared, Gautier published *Mlle de Maupin*. The former enjoyed a few months' priority, but Gautier's volume had been promised to the publisher a year before its appearance, and as the two men's long friendship began only with Balzac's reading of the younger man's story, there is no question of influence in either direction.

From the standpoint of modern psychology Gautier's is the more careful and complete study. Indeed, having humor, vitality, and a tolerant bisexual attitude, it is probably the most generally popular of all variant "classics." In it an orphaned heiress dons men's clothes and sets out to discover how men live when uninhibited by the presence of ladies. In the course of her adventures

Maupin is loved by a young man of poetic temperament who has had mistresses but found them physically satisfying only, and by a young woman of good social standing who has been one of those mistresses. Maupin also has with her for a time a young girl disguised as a page whom she has rescued from exploitation by an old rake and on whom she lavishes a devotion both erotic and maternal. The young man suffers from believing his passion abnormal until he learns Maupin's true sex, but then recognizes that for the first time he has found complete love because he has so many more tastes in common with this girl than with his previous feminine paramours.

As to the young woman, her passion survives the revelation of Maupin's sex, her persistent caresses prove as exciting as the man's, and Maupin finishes by spending half the final night depicted with each of them and by riding off in the morning with markedly unfeminine detachment. Physically, we have for the first time in modern fiction the explicit description of a type which has since become associated with homosexual tendencies in women—the tall, wide shouldered, slim hipped figure endowed with perfect grace and with great skill in riding and fencing. Temperamentally we have Maupin's own description of herself as "of a third sex, one that has as yet no name above or below." As a girl she was "six months older but six years less romantic" than her bosom friend, for whom her friendship had "all the characteristics of a passion," but for years she "burned in her little skin like a chestnut on the stove" to satisfy what is described as an intellectual curiosity about the lives of men away from women and their real attitude toward women. It is this unemotional detachment which Gautier emphasizes as peculiarly masculine.

Scattered through the story is a quantity of very canny analysis of intersexual characteristics, and though the tale is supposedly based upon the life of a seventeenth-century actress, it departs so far from the known facts about her that it must stand as a monument to the author's physchological acumen alone. Since he wrote it at the age of twenty-four, one cannot escape the suspicion that it was drawn from personal or at least close secondhand acquaintance with George Sand, so newly come to Paris in her male costume and so prominent in literary circles at that moment. It certainly marks a long step forward in the serious study of a variant personality. (The actual history of Madeleine Maupin d'Aubigny, late seventeenth-century singer and actress, is perhaps worth attention because of its contrast to Gautier's artistic modification. As a young woman Maupin came to Paris from the provinces determined upon a stage career, and married her vocal teacher, d'Aubigny, who was connected with the Opera and who got her the position upon which she was set. The marriage was apparently a mere strategic move on her part and was short-lived. A tall woman, and a

fencer of extraordinary ability, Mme d'Aubigny frequently played young men's parts, and soon took to wearing men's costume off as well as on the stage. One of her diversions was roaming the streets at night and provoking men to cross swords with her for the pleasure of worsting them. She inspired passion in many young women, one of whom, a girl of good family, ran away with her when her repeated embroilments forced her to leave Paris. The girl's parents overtook the eloping couple and put their daughter into a convent at Avignon.

Being apparently infatuated herself, Maupin resumed woman's dress and gained entry to the convent as a novice for the purpose of manoeuvering her friend's escape. The means which presented themselves were macabre enough. A nun died and was buried within the convent enclosure; Maupin exhumed the body, put it in her friend's bed, and set fire to the cell; during the resulting confusion the two young women escaped. But their subsequent precarious vagabondage apparently cured the girl of her taste for bohemian freedom and for Maupin; she returned to her parents. Maupin's later career was comparatively seamy and unromantic.)

In 1851 Lamartine included in *Nouvelles Confidences* an innocent infatuation between two adolescent girls which is reminiscent of Wollstonecraft's Mary and Balzac's *Seraphita*. (Though a reference in Havelock Ellis seems to place Regina among Lamartine's poetic works, it is actually prose. His statement that here the theme is treated with "more or less boldness" also appears unjustified.) Although the initial attachment between the heroine, Regina, and her school friend, Clothilde, might be considered "normal," since it occurs between the ages of fourteen and seventeen, its later effects compel attention. The two girls, thrown together in a declining Roman convent school where supervision is lax, contrive regularly to spend their nights together. Lamartine describes their hours of long talk and tenderness with such skill and delicacy that one can doubt neither the basic innocence of both girls nor the ultimate passion in their embraces.

During their years together Clothilde talks so much of a twin brother Saluse that Regina falls half in love with him vicariously, but at seventeen she is married unwillingly to a titled dotard. In the same year Clothilde's mother dies, and Clothilde does not long survive this double loss of her only parent and beloved friend. At Clothilde's grave Regina and Saluse meet and fall in love at sight. Their passion runs a stormy but blameless course, which leads eventually to Regina's seeking formal release from her marriage. While she is away from Rome her petition is granted by the church, but only on condition of Saluse's permanent exile from the city. Saluse decides in her absence on exile for her sake rather than on elopement and public scandal. On learning of his decision the girl cries out that he who would sacrifice love to conscience cannot be the brother of Clothilde. 'At Clothilde's tomb it was not she I found again, it was a phantom. . . . He had her features but not her heart.'

Lamartine's effort to explain the girls' passionate friendship is interesting if seemingly somewhat confused. Primarily, like Diderot, he lays responsibility upon the convent environment, where not only are women segregated but every aspect of their life—music, incense, pageantry, solitude and idleness—inflames the 'imagination,' while the feeble pretense at education includes nothing to stimulate or discipline the intellect. Such life produces 'veritable orientals, fit only for the harem.' The specific occasion of their emotional involvement, however, he says, is Regina's identification of Clothilde with the unknown brother of whom the latter talks so eloquently. 'I should never have believed in this phenomenon, which reflects and thus redoubles the beloved object, I should have taken it for the imaginative creation of poets, had I not seen it with my own eyes in the spirit of Regina.' This seems a rather feeble attempt to gloss over any homosexual implication, for Clothilde, though more intellectual and less passionate than Regina, is in no way masculine. And, in the end, it was precisely the masculine element in Saluse's sacrifice of their love which repelled Regina. It was a man's decision and not a woman's, 'of the head and not the heart.' Lamartine's treatment here of the variant theme gains added interest from the fact that earlier, in *Jocelyn,* he had sailed perilously close to the implication of male variance. In this story, popular enough to supply the libretto for Godard's opera, a hermit priest becomes so attached to the "boy" left in his charge that he suffers agonies of conscience before discovering that his ward is a disguised girl. Evidently the whole matter of possible intrasexual attraction held a kind of fascination for Lamartine, though he treated it with a reserve more Victorian than French.

Toward the end of this decade (1858) a novel appeared, *La Sapho,* cited by Lewandowski in *Das Sexual Probleme . . .* as definitely lesbian, and of added interest in that it was written by a woman, Céleste Venard comtesse de Chabrillan; but unhappily this has not been available for examination.

At the beginning of the following decade (1862) Flaubert published *Salammbo,* of which Krafft-Ebing says that the author made his heroine homosexual. If this is true at all by modern standards the condition is latent and of short duration, but because of the expressed judgment of so prominent an early authority on sex variance the story will be examined in some detail. It will also be interesting to see with what "pitiless method" Flaubert dissects the emotional economy of an inhibited girl. To be sure Salammbo's adolescent devotion to the virgin moon-goddess Tanit (comparable to the Greek Astarte and the Roman Diana, and allied also to the Roman Bona Dea) verges upon passion, but it is so described as to suggest the sexual overtones in any ecstatic religious experience rather than to imply a variant element.

Daughter of Hamilcar of Carthage, Salammbo grows up in a time of such peril that she is raised in solitary seclusion; her only companions are an aged nurse and the eunuch who is chief priest in the temple of Tanit. She would like to become a "devotee," but Hamilcar designs a politically profitable marriage for her, and forbids her initiation into the inner mysteries of the cult (which would involve ritual defloration, though Flaubert does not mention this fact).

> She had grown up in abstinence, in fastings and purifications, always surrounded by exquisite and solemn things, her body saturated with perfumes and her soul with prayers. . . . Of obscene symbols she knew nothing . . . (she) worshipped the Goddess in her sidereal aspect.

She says to the priest:

> It is a spirit that drives me to this love of mine. . . . [The other gods] are all too far away, too high, too insensible; while She—I feel her as a part of my life, she fills my soul. . . . I am devoured with eagerness to see her body.

This may seem suggestive, but she denies physical interest when under the fires of spring and the full moon, she cries out to her nurse:

> Sometimes gusts of heat seem to rise from the depths of my being. . . . Voices call me . . . fire rises in my breast; it stifles me, I feel that I am dying . . . it is a caress folding about me and I feel crushed. . . . Oh! that I might lose myself in the night mists . . . that I could *leave my body* [author's italics] and be but a breath, a ray, then float up to thee, O Mother [Tanit].

Her nurse, wise in the signs of physical ripening, does not take this for religious ecstasy.

> 'You must choose a husband from the sons of the Elders, since it was [your father's] wish,' she says. 'Your sorrow will vanish in the arms of a man.' 'Why?' asked the young girl. All the men she had seen had horrified her with their wild bestial laughter and their coarse limbs.

These men are her father's barbarian mercenaries, and Flaubert's picture of their drunken orgy after victory would revolt a stronger spirit than that of a sheltered girl. Her first direct encounter is with Matho the Libyan, "his great mouth agape, his necklet of silver moons tangled in the hairs on his chest." Crazed with passion for her, he steals the Zaimph [sacred veil of Tanit] from the temple as a love charm, breaks into Salammbo's chambers at midnight, and attempts to ravish and abduct her. Naturally terrified, she summons aid in time to save herself, but she does not understand what it is he wants of her. Later she tells him: "Your words I did not understand, but I knew you wished to drag me toward something horrible, to the bottom of some abyss. . . ."

The story then centers around her personal conflict between her desire to retrieve the Zaimph and her horror of the barbarian who has fled the city without returning it. Finally, under religious compulsion to save Carthage by regaining its sacred talisman, she makes her way to the Libyan's tent. She has been instructed by the high priest to resist Matho in no way, and consequently she submits to his embrace.

> Salammbo, who was accustomed to eunuchs, yielded to amazement at the strength of this man. . . . A feeling of lassitude overpowered her . . . all the time she felt that she was in the grip of some doom, that she had reached a supreme and irrevocable moment. . . . Some power from within and at the same time above her, a command from the gods, forced her to yield to it; she was borne up as on clouds, and fell back swooning.

But on being questioned subsequently by her father as to what occurred, she is evasive.

> Salammbo told no more, perhaps through shame, or else because in her extreme ingenuousness she attached but little importance to the soldier's embraces. . . . Then she examined the Zaimph and when she had well considered it, she was surprised to find that she did not experience that ecstasy which she had once pictured to herself. Her dream was accomplished; yet she was melancholy.

Although she does not see Matho again and feels only hatred for him " . . . the anguish from which she formerly suffered had left her, and a strange calm possessed her. Her eyes were not so restless, and shone with limpid fire. . . . She did not keep such long or such rigid fasts now. . . . In spite of her hatred of him, she would have liked to see Matho again."

This is a master's account of the effect of physical release on an unawakened girl.

Considerably later Salammbo is married, according to her father's plan, to the effete prince, Narr' Havas.

> He wore a flower-painted robe fringed with gold at the hem; his braided hair was caught up at his ears by two arrows of silver. . . . As she watched him, she was wrapped about with a host of vague thoughts. This young man with his gentle voice and

woman's figure charmed her by the grace of his person and seemed like an elder sister sent by the Baalim to protect her. She did not understand how this young man could ever become her master. The thought of Matho came to her and she could not resist the desire to learn what had become of him. . . . Although she prayed every day to Tanit for Matho's death, her horror of the Libyan was growing less. She was confusedly aware that there was something almost like religion in the hatred [sic] with which he had persecuted her, and she wished to see in Narr' Havas a reflection, as it were, of a violence which still bemused her.

These two passages indicate quite the opposite of homosexual emotion.

When, after months of carnage, Matho is taken captive and literally torn to pieces by the people of Carthage, Salammbo is witness to his terrible death. Instead of sharing in the shrieking triumph of the populace, she "could once more see him in his tent, clasping his arms about her waist, stammering gentle words. She thirsted to feel and hear those things again and was at the point of screaming aloud." And when Matho "fell back and moved no more," Salammbo also collapsed into unconsciousness from which she never recovered. The concluding words of the book are: "So died Hamilcar's daughter, because she had touched the mantle of Tanit." Flaubert's novel carries symbolic overtones not apparent in brief summary, and since Tanit was allied to the Roman Bona Dea, goddess of sexual fulfillment and fertility, her Zaimph doubtless represents heterosexual passion. Salammbo, conditioned to asceticism throughout her early life, dies of the unresolved conflict between these two dominating drives.

A minor novel which Krafft-Ebing mentions as also "mainly lesbian in theme" may shed some light on what he intended by the term. It is Ernest Feydeau's *La Comtesse de Chalis* (1867), in which a dashing Parisian beauty neglects her children and tubercular husband for a spectacular career in *le haut monde*. An idealistic and infatuated professor of the new *Ecole Normale,* who is keenly aware of belonging to a lower social class, ruins himself financially in his attempt to maintain a place in the countess's world. The story, told by him, is chiefly concerned with his efforts to save her from the frivolous and corrupt life of her circle. Her evil genius is a fabulously wealthy Prince Titiane, diseased and depraved at twenty-one, whom she repeatedly promises to dismiss from her life but to whose influence she continuously succumbs. She goes gradually from bad to worse, and ends by consorting *à trois* with him and one of the city's celebrated courtesans, his long-time mistress; however, this situation develops only in the last pages of a lengthy volume. The Prince is described throughout as so effeminate in appearance, dress, and appurtenances that it would be easy to imagine him a woman in disguise, but there is no textual support for such an inference. Late in the story it develops that it is solely his use of the whip which binds the countess to him, and that this flagellation is without sexual sequel, since Titiane is impotent.

Aside from being unusually tall and arrogant, the countess has no masculine attributes whatever, either physical or psychological, and it is never she who wields the lash. Her dominant motive is an egotistic compulsion to be the most dazzling figure in Paris. Since the fantastic young Croesus, Titiane, is the arbiter of social destinies in her particular world, she is slavishly submissive to him. Her interest in the courtesan, though it is charged with emotion throughout, appears to be the obsession of an ambitious woman with the techniques of a serious rival, and the emotion is predominantly jealousy. Her final indulgence in sexual promiscuity results from her determination to be outdone by that rival in no field whatsoever. Analyzed by a modern psychiatrist, the countess would be diagnosed as a complete narcissist, unable to care the slightest for anyone but herself.

Consideration of these two novels suggests that to Krafft-Ebing any failure of feminine heterosexual adjustment was included in that "contrary sexual feeling" which was equated throughout his later study with active homosexuality. As we have seen, modern psychoanalysts consider narcissism and homosexuality as closely related in etiology; yet it is confusing to have the more specific term applied to experiences which, like Salammbo's and the countess's, include relations with men and none with their own sex. "Mainly lesbian in theme" *La Comtesse de Chalis* certainly is not.

The fact that in a contemporary novel . . . , Feydeau's *La Comtesse* was bracketed with Gautier's *Mlle Maupin* and Balzac's *Girl with the Golden Eyes* may also have contributed to Krafft-Ebing's thinking it more "lesbian" than it is. Indeed, the modern investigator sometimes suspects that scientific writers had not read all of the belletristic titles they referred to but were satisfied to rely on the word of others with respect to them. Another detail which might have strengthened an impression of similarity to Balzac is Feydeau's denunciation of *le haut monde* in imitation of Balzac's earlier indictment of metropolitan life in general. The new element in Feydeau is acute class consciousness in his condemnation of the "idle rich." However second-rate from an artistic standpoint *La Comtesse de Chalis* may be, it is a remarkably exact contemporary record of "the mixture of splendor and misery . . . the sense of uneasy satiety, of restless torpor, of indefinable dread" described by the modern Albert Guérard as prevailing in the late Second Empire.

Evidence from Poets

Although fiction made up so preponderant a part of variant writing in the nineteenth century, poetry also made a sizable contribution. In 1816, Coleridge, who with Wordsworth is generally thought of as initiating the Romantic Period in England, published two parts of a narrative poem, *Christabel,* which was never finished. All college students of literature know that eerie fragment of medieval romance with its occult overtones.

Christabel, the innocent heroine whose betrothed is "far away" on a knightly quest, steals out from her father's castle at midnight to pray for her lover beneath a giant oak hung with mistletoe—a test of maidenly courage in the face of both natural and occult darkness, for oak and mistletoe still retain pre-Christian connotations. In the moonlit wood she finds a distressed lady, Geraldine, who tells a story of kidnaping and violence designed to win her sympathy. As she helps the fainting lady into the castle certain signs forebode evil to a reader acquainted with demonic lore: Geraldine's eyes gleam in the dark like an animal's, she is so faint that she requires Christabel's aid in crossing the sill, and once she is inside a mastiff moans in its sleep and embers on the hearth shoot out tongues of flame.

In Christabel's maiden chamber while the two are disrobing Geraldine (and she alone) sees the "spectre" of Christabel's dead mother come to guard her child, and bids the hovering spirit be off. Though she has shown fear at sight of a carven angel in the room and has made poor work of feigning prayer, Geraldine still has power to prevent Christabel's seeing the vision or being warned, and presently the two lie down together "in appropriate medieval nudity." With fascinated loathing Christabel notes that Geraldine's "breast and side" are those of a withered hag; still she is powerless to resist the other's spell, and in Geraldine's arms she falls into a trance.

> With open eyes (ah woe is me!)
> Asleep and dreaming fearfully,
> Fearfully dreaming, yet, I wis,
> Dreaming that alone, which is—
> O sorrow and shame! Can this be she
> The lady [Christabel] who knelt at the old oak
>   tree?

Afterward "Her limbs relax, her countenance Grows sad and soft," and in her sleep she both smiles and weeps, while Geraldine "Seems to slumber still and mild As a mother with her child."

In the morning Christabel wakes to find her guest already clothed, but "fairer yet and yet more fair!" for now her shriveled bosom has the fullness of a young woman's, a subtle allusion to the wide-spread folk superstition that sexual contact with innocent youth heals sickness and restores old age. Christabel is troubled by "such perplexity of mind As dreams too lively leave behind," and delivers her morning greeting in "low faltering tones." "Sure I have sinned!" she feels, but is uncertain precisely how, and prays merely that "He who on the cross did groan Might wash away her sins unknown."

Roy Basler, in his *Sex, Symbolism and Psychology in Literature,* devotes a long chapter to the poem which is recommended to the reader for its minute analysis of Coleridge's skill in handling the whole episode. As he points out, it is "too realistic psychologically . . . for one to avoid an erotic implication." The remainder of the poem contains nothing further of variant significance. The spell of Geraldine's touch has made it impossible for Christabel to give her father anything beyond the simplest objective account of how the woman came there, and the action merely prepares for later events never written.

Of the content of these three projected "books" we have only a brief account by Dr. James Gilman, with whom Coleridge lived later while undergoing treatment for his addiction to opium. The relevant points follow: Complications force Geraldine to abandon her feminine form and to assume that of Christabel's absent lover. In this guise she woos the girl and gains the father's consent to a marriage, even though Christabel is filled with inexplicable loathing for her at the altar. Had Coleridge carried through this outlined narrative, he could scarcely, as Basler says, "have avoided even more harrowing suggestions of a sexual nature" in Geraldine's disguised courtship. Significant of her sexual duality are repeated references to her height and her arrogant bearing.

Basler points out that after 1801, Coleridge's moral reputation was precarious because of his opium habit, and that "no man ever feared calumny more keenly." Although the poet began *Christabel* and had the entire plot worked out at that time, he published none of it for fifteen years. When it finally appeared, the *Edinburgh Review* attacked it with "charges of obscenity" and "implications of personal turpitude," while "parodies and vulgar continuations of the poem made the most of leering improbabilities." The dread of further personal attack discouraged Coleridge from completing the work, and no other English poet seems to have approached the subject of variance for nearly a half century.

The next poem that appeared in England, however—Christina Rossetti's *Goblin Market,* written in 1859—is so akin to *Christabel* in its overtones of folk magic and so alien to the temporally intervening French poetry on variant themes that it is best to examine it here. It is generally regarded as variant or even lesbian, but

the vivid narrative is too symbolic for precise sexual interpretation. On the surface it recounts that two sisters, Laura and Lizzie, as they stroll at dusk are daily tempted by "goblin men" to buy the most luscious of ripe fruits. Though knowing the fruits to be forbidden, Laura succumbs, pays with a curl of her golden hair (having no money), and partakes alone, Lizzie having fled. "She sucked their fruit globes fair or red . . . sucked and sucked and sucked . . . until her tongue was sore. . . ." After this indulgence she can no longer see or hear the goblins, and wastes away with pining for their delicacies.

When she seems "knocking at Death's door," Lizzie, aware that another girl in like case has recently died, goes to purchase fruit for her sister with honest coin. The goblins refuse her money and use every means to force their wares between her own lips, but she resists and returns so dripping with crushed fruit that she is hopeful of bringing some satisfaction to her sister. Laura kisses her hungrily, but more in gratitude for the dreadful risk she has run than in greed for what lingers "in dimples of her chin." Indeed, the fruit now scorches Laura's lips and is wormwood on her tongue, so that from loathing she is seized with violent convulsion and falls unconscious. In the morning she awakes cured, and Lizzie suffers no ill effects at all.

As a translation of voluptuous experience into decorous terms the poem cannot be equaled, but any attempt at literal reconstruction of the experience bogs down in the symbolic details. Certain points however are implicit in the text: Laura's experience is a complete sexual release which it needs no acquaintance with Freud to recognize as oral-erotic. All the goblins are male, but they are grotesque, repulsive, more animal than human save for their ability to hawk their wares, and these irresistible wares take the shapes of ripe cherries, peaches, plums, melons, "figs that fill the mouth"—in short, the whole catalog of age-old symbols for female charms. Although the sisters are described as "Sleeping in their curtained bed Cheek to cheek and breast to breast," there is no more incestuous lesbian implication here than in Sidney's *Arcadia.* These embraces are plainly symbols of the innocence from which Laura lapses and to which she returns by virtue of Lizzie's steadfast purity. Perhaps the only safe inference is that Laura's "fall" is solitary, even subjectively induced (psychiatric records prove fantasy to be an adequate agent). Her subsequent neurotic inhibition is the product of guilt, and ends in a releasing hysteric convulsion somehow brought about by Lizzie's ministrations.

This mundane analysis of an exquisite work of art does reveal its author's emotional pattern. It is known that Miss Rossetti had a somewhat cloistered life, largely spent in the company of a mother to whom she was intensely devoted and a sister who later became an

Anglican nun, all three women being almost fanatically devout. She was twice passionately in love with men, but refused them both on the grounds of religious incompatibility. The first of these episodes occurred when she was barely seventeen. The man, a recent convert to Catholicism, returned to the Church of England when he discovered that Christina would not marry a papist, but later reverted to Rome, and the whole affair seems to have constituted a two-year span of acute emotional disturbance in the girl's life. (She subsequently fainted upon meeting him unexpectedly in the street.) It may well have been that any man's ability to switch religious camps so readily under the stress of passion produced a reaction to the whole business of sex such as we find in *Goblin Market,* which was written when its author was nearing thirty. Tragically enough, her life-long ascetic repression broke during her last illness in a protracted delirium which revealed at what cost it had been maintained.

France was as always more tolerant of sexual latitude in literature than England, but even there the open-mindedness which made *Mlle de Maupin* acceptable in 1835 was not constant. Since it is impossible to give in short compass any account of the alternating waves of liberalism and conservative reaction that swayed public opinion there during the middle decades of the century, it must suffice to note that Charles Baudelaire published his *Fleurs du Mal* during an interim of clerical dominance, and in consequence the volume was condemned by the *Tribunal Correctionnel* in August 1857. As early as 1846 the publisher Levy had announced on advertising pages of other works a forthcoming title by Baudelaire, *Les Lesbiennes,* which never appeared as such, probably because the title was too daring. Only three poems in the *Fleurs* touch upon lesbianism, but the longest of these was one of the six which were ordered removed from the volume and which were not publicly printed again until 1911.

This poem, "Femmes Damnées, I," some twenty-six quatrains in length, describes rather explicitly the conquest of a feminine and passive young girl, half reluctant because still dreaming of heterosexual love, by a more aggressive feminine partner who decries the physical brutality and spiritual incompatibility of any male lover. In "Femmes Damnées, II" the poet watches a band of lesbians at a shore resort behaving much as any uninhibited heterosexual group might do, and accords them more than even his customary despairing compassion. Such love as theirs is doomed to go unsated, and they themselves, he says, will pass progressively to drink and drugs and "loveless loves that know no pity." And yet in "Lesbos" he holds Sappho guilty of a "crime of the spirit" when, faithless to her own earlier teaching and practice, she "flung the dark roses of her love sublime To a vain churl (Phaon.)" (Note: "Lesbos" had appeared in 1850 in an anthology, *Les Poétes de l'Amour,* published by Lemerre. It was omitted from the 1858 edition of that volume, but reappeared in the edition of 1865.) The Catholic Baudelaire was essentially a mystic, not a romantic with that faith in Love which had been the gospel of the preceding decades. Obsessed as he was by the failure of all passion to satisfy the human craving for perfection, it is natural that homosexual passion, inevitably "unassuageable, sterile and outcast," should seem to him the essence of pitiable futility. This negative judgment, however, is not given in terms of conventional morality.

Within a decade the wave of conservatism had so far receded that Paul Verlaine's *Les Amies, Scènes d'Amour Sapphique* (1867), though published in Brussels for safety, apparently encountered in France no harsher judgment than a comment in the *Bulletin Trimestriel* that they were by a poet of the school of M Leconte de Lisle, and were "fort singuliers." The slim sheaf of sixteen pages contained six poems, subsequently included in his volume *Parallèlement,* which described lesbian love and its overt expression more explicitly than Baudelaire's condemned verses, or indeed than any other non-erotic work up to that time. The "Pensionnaires" are sisters in the middle teens, the younger of whom still 'smiles with innocence' despite the elder's far from innocent ministrations. The pair in "Sur le Balcon," dreaming only of the love between women, are 'a strange couple, pitied by other heterosexual couples.' "Printemps" and "Eté" reproduce the situation in Baudelaire's "Femmes Damnées, I" except that here the younger and more innocent girl is neither reluctant nor apprehensive. In "Per Amica Silentia" the poet applies for the first time the adjective "esseulées"—solitary, left alone—to those who 'in these unhappy times' are set apart by "le glorieux stigmate," thus foreshadowing the social isolation lamented sixty years later in the *Well of Loneliness,* but indicating by the adjective "glorieux" that his sentiment, unlike Baudelaire's, is one of championship. In the final "Sappho" he describes the poet, hollow-eyed, pacing a cold shore, restless as a she-wolf, weeping and tearing her hair over Phaon's indifference until finally she plunges into the sea in despair at the contrast between her present state and the 'young glory of her early loves.' It is more than likely that it was from this poem that Rilke derived his interpretation of Sappho's "Lament.". . .

During the preceding year (1866) there had appeared in England Swinburne's *Poems and Ballads: First Series,* which raised an outcry on several counts—its general "paganism," its evidence of French influence (particularly that of Baudelaire), and its scattering of poems with a homosexual tinge. Swinburne had, in his youth, been intimate with the much older Sir Richard Burton, famous translator of the *Arabian Nights* and author of an appendix on that "sotadic zone" in the Mediterranean region which in his opinion favored the development of homosexual tendencies. Later Swinburne fell under the influence of Richard Monckton-Milnes, famous for a library of variant erotica. As both of these friendships were matters of common knowledge, when *Poems and Ballads* appeared, attention focussed naturally on such poems as "Erotion," "Hermaphroditus," "Fragoletta," "Hesperia," and the fairly numerous group with a lesbian coloring, though none of these were explicit or described a realistic contemporary situation in the manner of Verlaine.

"Anactoria" is a ten-page plaint from Sappho to a girl who no longer reciprocates her love, but it differs little from Swinburne's many laments celebrating all love as pain. The "Sapphics" describe life on Mitylene, "place whence all gods fled . . . full of fruitless women and music only." A half dozen stanzas scattered through other poems—notably "Dolores," "Faustine," and "Masque of Queen Bersabe"—echo the same note. Swinburne's attitude is unsympathetic, colder even than Baudelaire's and more scornful, with emphasis always upon the barrenness of lesbian love, as might be expected from a poet who occasionally made almost a fetish of baby-worship.

All of the longer biographies of Swinburne give some account of a projected narrative in mixed prose and verse upon which he worked intermittently between 1864 and 1867 but never finished. What remains of manuscript and galley proof is now in the British Museum, after a half-century in the possession of the notorious rare-book dealer and literary forger, Thomas Wise. It was finally edited and given private publication in 1952 by Langdon Hughes, an idolatrous admirer of Swinburne, for whom it held the promise of becoming, if completed, one of the greater English novels. Unhappily, neither the scant surviving text nor Mr. Hughes's overwhelming volume of annotation and championship convey to the reader much of that promise or of the author's projected intent. As Swinburne himself gave it no title it is generally known by the suggestive name of its central figure: *Lesbia Brandon.* Georges Lafourcade, in his scholarly two-volume study of Swinburne, suggests that this character was drawn from Jane Faulkner, daughter of one of the poet's friends, who also inspired "The Triumph of Time" (fifteen pages of bitter reproach for failure to love him and save him from other fateful loves). For this dark, spirited young girl he seems to have nursed briefly his only "normal" passion; she responded to his half-hysterical romantic proposal with a helpless burst of laughter, and it needed but the one touch of ridicule to snuff out the hardly lighted spark. Lafourcade believes that Jane herself "avait quelque chose d'anormal," and certainly the description of Lesbia is suggestive: dark, heavy-lidded, taciturn, Byronically proud, with a pathological hatred of men. When, on her deathbed, she is tenderly embraced by the man who adores her she shows only "mad repugnance, blind absolute horror." In her youth she had loved a governess and threatened

suicide when the woman talked of marrying. Later she was an enthusiastic student of Sappho and wrote many love poems from the masculine viewpoint.

The emotional life of the hero, Hubert, up to the time of his meeting with Lesbia is said to be a quite frank parallel of Swinburne's own. The critical first encounter occurs while Hubert is dressed as a girl, and this disguise is responsible for Lesbia's immediate interest. Their subsequent relations are not developed in the portions of the story that Swinburne committed to paper, nor is much of Lesbia's experience save her eventual slow suicide by opium, in an atmosphere heavily fragrant with flowers and eau de cologne. Among the disconnected residual fragments are two: "Turris Iburnea" and "La Bohème Dédorée," in which the poet presents Leonora Harley, a beautiful but vulgar and stupid demi-mondaine. This character was said to be drawn directly from Adah Isaacs Menken, who was also the original of his "Dolores"—a fifteen page description of an insatiable nymphomaniac. There is reason, as will appear later, to believe that Menken's temperament included a variant strain. That Swinburne intended to make use of this in his plot is strongly suggested by the following:

> Over their evening Leonora Harley guided with the due graces of her professional art [that of courtesan]. It was not her fault if she could not help asking her young friend [Hubert] when he had last met a dark beauty: she had seen him once with Lesbia.

Further evidence that he planned to incorporate a lesbian element in the story is found in his correspondence of 1866, where he boasted that having won an undeservedly scandalous reputation because of that element in *Poems and Ballads,* he meant to live up to it in his current effort, which would give his countrymen real cause for Philistine horror.

It is known that Swinburne was still at work on the manuscript in 1867 when his meeting with Mazzini deflected his interests into new channels. After the years of political discipleship which produced *Songs Before Sunrise,* he returned to the interrupted narrative. Following that, its history becomes confused. Certain passages in the hands of his publishers reached the stage of galley proof but became mixed with proofs of other incomplete work. Sections of manuscript entrusted to his good friend, Watts-Dunton, were "mislaid," and the poet's repeated pleas and complaints never stimulated him to find them. Though Langdon Hughes finds Watts-Dunton guilty of criminal rascality, one cannot help wondering whether all this apparent carelessness may not have been well-meant discretion.

The text as it now stands is almost wholly in prose, and the few songs it contains have, like "The Triumph of Time" and "Dolores," been published among Swinburne's other poems. Nothing in it is at all daring; there is nothing to account for Lesbia's variance, nor any indication of how far the relations between her and Leonora would have gone. But it is clear that Swinburne, like his hero, worshipped the repressed, intense and melancholy Lesbia, and despised Leonora, the bisexual wanton. A reasonable conjecture is that Lesbia's early passions had been innocent; that even though despising Leonora she was unable to resist the other's seduction; and that self-contempt motivated her suicide—a plot allowing plenty of latitude for the author's intent to shock the British reading public.

Lillian Faderman

SOURCE: "Kindred Spirits," in *Surpassing the Love of Men: Romantic Friendship and Love Between Women from the Renaissance to the Present,* William Morrow and Company, Inc., 1981, pp. 157-77.

[*Faderman's* Surpassing the Love of Men *constituted a landmark in the progress of feminist and lesbian studies on its publication in 1981. The book's scope ranges from the sixteenth century to the present, examining the nature and images of both sexual and platonic female relationships. The chapter on the nineteenth century, excerpted below, puts forth Faderman's argument that the "romantic friendships" of the era were an integral part of mainstream culture. Such attachments were in fact valorized as a testament to feminine virtue, since popular belief saw women as passionless or asexual.*]

Throughout much of the nineteenth century, women moved still farther from men as both continued to develop their own even more distinct sets of values. Men tried to claim exclusively for themselves the capacity of action and thought, and relegated women to the realm of sensibility alone. Women made the best of it: They internalized the only values they were permitted to have, and they developed what has been called the Cult of True Womanhood.[1] The spiritual life, moral purity, sentiment, grew in importance. But with whom could they share these values?

In America and England during the second half of the nineteenth century, as more women began to claim more of the world, the reasons for bonding together against men who wished to deny them a broader sphere became greater. When men wrote about female attachments in literature, they tended to see the same sentimental pictures that were prevalent in eighteenth-century fiction: Two sweet females uplifting each other morally, but ultimately entirely dependent on men whether that dependence brought them joy or tragedy. What they did not see was how female relationships could sustain a woman intellectually and make her strong enough to engage in the battle for more of the world. But they also did not suspect—any more than the women themselves did—that such an emotional and even physical closeness was "lesbian," at least in a twentieth-century definition. They did not treat it as an abnormality because it was common enough to be a norm.

Since men and women occupied separate spheres, particularly among the great middle classes, they considered themselves virtually different species. Men believed a woman could command no rational thought as a man could, although, at her best, she dwelt in the realm of the heart and might be an "Angel in the House," as the English writer Coventry Patmore calls her in his mid-nineteenth-century poem. But whatever she was, she was not male and thus not as human as man. The observation regarding women that Tennyson's protagonist makes in "Locksley Hall" (1842) was probably echoed by many men: "Nature made them blinder motions bounded in a shallower brain: woman is the lesser man."

Men saw women as what Simone de Beauvoir has called "the Other," and for that reason they could attribute to them magical properties (sometimes beneficial, sometimes dangerous) which the real human beings, men, do not have; e.g., they believed that if a syphilitic man raped a virgin he would be cured.[2] Such absurdity was not limited to folk wisdom. For example, in 1878 there was a serious debate, which lasted over several issues among correspondents in the *British Medical Journal,* about whether or not ham would be spoiled if cured by a menstruating woman. Several of the doctors who joined the debate agreed that it would.

Such views of women as being something other than human were by no means peculiar to Britain. G. J. Barker-Benfield shows that in nineteenth-century America, the estrangement between men and women was even worse than in Britain, since it had an immediate practical purpose in men's minds: The American male must not be distracted from his "desire of prosperity" by the softness and seductiveness of the female. He "had to be above sex" to succeed. Stronger bonds were formed between father and son, and male and male in general, because men needed the assistance of other men to realize their ardent material passion.[3] Male "muscle values" and "rational values" were fostered to the exclusion of women. The converse of this situation was, of course, that mother and daughter, and female and female, also formed stronger bonds largely based on "heart values," since male-directed society permitted them little else.

Female chastity which was held to be vital in earlier centuries took on even greater importance in nineteenth-century America, since an unchaste woman could distract a man from his larger purpose. Accordingly, an 1808 writer warns young men to test the virtue of a woman whom they wish to marry by making sexual advances to her. If she does not respond with "becoming abhorrence," she is not a proper girl and would not make a good wife.[4] In this way women were taught to deny any heterosexual urge. The lesson was often extended to sexual appetites not only outside of marriage but in marriage as well. By the mid-nineteenth century a number of authorities warned that even in lawful marriage, too much intercourse caused the male "general debility, weakness, and lameness of the back" as well as a predisposition to "almost innumerable diseases." It afflicted the female with "uterine inflammation, and ulceration, leucorrhea, deranged menstruation, miscarriage, barrenness as well as debility, hysteria, and an endless train of nervous and other diseases."[5] Since heterosexual indulgence was declared to be dangerous to both social standing and health, we can believe the author of *Plain Talk on Avoided Subjects* (1882) when he states that not infrequently so great a shock is administered to a young woman's sensibilities on her wedding night "that she does not recover from it for years" and that she often "forms a deeply rooted antipathy" toward heterosexuality.[6]

Women understood that they must not be open with men. They must not show heterosexual feeling even to a beloved fiancé before marriage, and once married they must be very restrained or they risked grave disease. They knew too, in an era when birth control was not effective and when the risks of childbirth were high, that heterosexual intercourse might mean they were taking their lives into their hands. To love a man meant pain and burdens and potential death. What Nancy Cott has called "passionlessness" was soundly impressed upon them.[7] Since middle and upper-class women were separated from men not only in their daily occupations, but in their spiritual and leisure interests as well,[8] outside of the practical necessities of raising a family there was little that tied the sexes together. But with other females a woman inhabited the same sphere, and she could be entirely trusting and unrestrained. She could share sentiment, her heart—all emotions that manly males had to repress in favor of "rationality"—with another female. And regardless of the intensity of the feeling that might develop between them, they need not attribute it to the demon, sexuality, since women supposedly had none. They could safely see it as an effusion of the spirit. The shield of passionlessness that a woman was trained to raise before a man could be lowered with another woman without fear of losing her chastity and reputation and health. Men too were encouraged to form intense friendships with other men. Thoreau was speaking for his time when he observed in his mid-nineteenth-century essay, *Friendship,* that intimacy was much more possible "between two of the same sex" than "between the sexes."[9]

William Taylor and Christopher Lasch ("Two 'Kindred Spirits': Sorority and Family in New England, 1839-1846") and Carroll Smith-Rosenberg ("The Female World of Love and Ritual: Relations Between Women in Nineteenth Century America")[10] have amply demonstrated that deeply felt friendships between women were casually accepted in American society, primarily because women saw themselves, and were seen as, kindred spirits who inhabited a world of interests and sensibilities alien to men. During the second half of the nineteenth century, when women slowly began to enter the world that men had built, their ties to each other became even more important. Particularly when they engaged in reform and betterment work, they were confirmed in their belief that women were spiritually superior to men, their moral perceptions were more highly developed, and their sensibilities were more refined. Thus if they needed emotional understanding and support, they turned to other women. New England reform movements often were fueled by the sisterhood of kindred spirits who were righting a world men had wronged.[11] In nineteenth-century America close bonds between women were essential both as an outlet for the individual female's sensibilities and as a crucial prop for women's work toward social and personal betterment in man's sullied and insensitive world.

What was the nature of these same-sex bonds that so many twentieth-century historians have observed? Margaret Fuller, an early feminist, saw same-sex love as far superior to heterosexuality. She wrote in her journal in the 1840's, "It is so true that a woman may be in love with a woman, and a man with a man." Such love, she says, is regulated by the same law that governs love between the sexes, "only it is purely intellectual and spiritual, unprofaned by any mixture of lower instincts, undisturbed by any need of consulting temporal interests." Presumably what she means by "lower instincts" is stark sex, and by "temporal interests" the practicalities one must take into consideration when choosing a spouse. To a nineteenth-century woman the first must have been ugly and the second an embarrassing necessary evil. While the unpleasant aspects of heterosexual love are lacking in love between women, nothing of value or joy is, at least as Fuller experienced that love herself. She admits to having loved another woman "passionately": "Her face," Fuller writes, "was always gleaming before me; her voice was echoing in my ear; all poetic thoughts clustered round the dear image. This love was for me a key which unlocked many a treasure which I still possess; it was the carbuncle (emblematic gem!) which cast light into many of the darkest corners of human nature."[12]

Female autobiographies and memoirs throughout the century suggest that Fuller's elevated view of passionate love between women was not atypical. Anna Cogswell Wood, for example, recounts her thirty-three-year relationship with another woman, characterizing it as a "true friendship" which "unites in its pure flame all other loves, that of parent and child, of brothers, as well as of the chosen companion."[13] Her relationship with Irene Leache is indistinguishable from a perfect marriage. She rhapsodizes for four pages over the eyes of the other woman, but spends more time discussing their happy life together, which was much like that of the Ladies of Llangollen. "Before six in the morning we were in the garden, where, seated under a pear tree, we passed the hours between sunrise and breakfast occupied with a book and needlework or with conversation."[14] Wood prizes her relationship with Irene Leache especially because it permitted her to develop, to blossom forth; Leache, she says, had the "power to draw beauty out of the commonplace" and to make her do it too; she stirred her "inmost depths." Through her relationship with the other woman, Wood was able to grow in ways she had never before imagined, even to perceive "sublimity in abstract thought, because love completed my circle of existence and raised things to their highest power."[15]

Nineteenth-century women were taught to expect to find what Fuller and Wood did in their love relationships with other females. Love between women could be both passionate and spiritually uplifting. It could cast one into a state of euphoria and yet unlock the secrets of life and the intellect. William Alger in *The Friendships of Women* (1868) cites one historical example after another of love between women (in America and Europe), which was characterized by the same enthusiasm described in Wood's memoir—a love which "largely constituted the richness, consolation, and joy of their lives." Typically the women wrote each other, "I feel so deeply the happiness of being loved by you, that you can never cease to love me," "I need to know all your thoughts, to follow all your motions, and can find no other occupation so sweet and so dear," "My heart is so full of you, that, since we parted, I have thought of nothing but writing to you," "I see in your soul as if it were my own." They did not need to play games with each other such as in heterosexual relationships—they shared perfect trust: "I fear no misunderstanding with you; my gratitude alone can equal the perfect security with which you inspire me."[16] Alger encourages his unmarried women readers to form such relationships, and promises that passionate friendships bring to life "freshness, stimulant charm, noble truths and aspirations."[17]

What made a male writer so sensitive to the glories of romantic friendship between women? Alger's motives were mixed. Writing in 1868, shortly after the American Civil War had increased even further through male mortality the large surplus of females, he recognized that many women would remain unmarried. He drew for them the solace of passionate friendship as a "rich and noble" resource which would occupy them and compensate happily for the lack of a family.[18] But he also saw female friendship as a means of keeping women in their place by encouraging their self-image as primarily sentient beings, too pure for the material world. Alger believed that women must stay out of men's sphere, but how to convince them that "it is simple blindness to fail to see that the distinctively feminine sphere of action is domestic life, and the inner life,—not the brawling mart and caucus," especially if they had no husbands and families?[19] women needed some diversion that would occupy their time and emotion. In his chapters entitled "Friendships of Women with Women" and "Pairs of Female Friends," Alger offers the solution of romantic friendship which permits women to be emotional, spiritual creatures together. Perhaps this trivializing view of romantic friendship accounts for why American men continued to be fairly tolerant of it throughout much of the twentieth century.

Englishmen were also tolerant, undoubtedly for the same reasons, since England too had a large surplus of women and a generally strong determination to restrict them to their proper sphere.[20] In fiction the male view of romantic friendship was largely unchanged from what it had been the century before: Men found it charming and delightful and quite unthreatening. George Meredith, for example, in *Diana of the Crossways* (1885) presents Antonia (the Diana of the novel) and Lady Emma Dunstane as two lovely creatures who see no way out of the round of their tragic relationships with men, despite the fact that they have a powerful love for each other. Antonia tells Lady Dunstane, "Be sure I am giving up the ghost when I cease to be one soul with you, dear and dearest." She calls her "my beloved! my only truly loved on earth!" Like eighteenth-century heroines, they often talk of the possibility of a classic friendship between women, "the alliance of a mutual devotedness men choose to doubt of." However, also like eighteenth-century heroines, even Diana the chaste must attach herself to a man, even though she resents those forces "natural and social" which urge her to "marry and be bound." Although Meredith attributes feminist sentiments to her, he renders her incapable of acting on them. Throughout her unhappy marriage, she continues to think of Emma, again like in an eighteenth-century novel, as "the next heavenly thing to Heaven that I know." Male-female relationships are always a dismal failure in this novel, but the romantic friendship endures and offers refuge and sustenance to the end. It does not, however, go beyond the pattern we have already observed in most of the novels of the previous century.[21]

But Englishwomen, like their American counterparts, often viewed romantic friendship as much more. For instance, to Edith Simcox, the writer and reform leader, her passionate involvement with George Eliot (Mary Ann Evans) was not only emotional and uplifting, it was sensual, intellectually stimulating, and, in fact, her great reason for being. In Simcox's autobiography she states that she loved Eliot "my Darling, lover-wise";[22] she speaks repeatedly of kissing her "again and again," of murmuring "broken words of love." Eliot seems to have had little interest in Simcox as a lover, but she admired her as an intellect and cheered her on to achievements. Although Simcox lamented that "my life has flung itself at her feet—and not been picked up—only told to rise and make itself a serviceable place elsewhere," she vowed to take the life Eliot directed her toward and make it constructive. Much of her social work, her zeal on behalf of the oppressed, her almost religious commitment to causes were stimulated by the desire to please Eliot.[23] As Bonnie Zimmerman remarks in her study "My Whole Soul is a Longing Question: Edith Simcox and George Eliot," Simcox's love for Eliot, while unrequited, provided fuel to keep her writing, organizing, and lecturing. Edith Simcox founded a cooperative shirt-making factory, served on the London School Board, started a lodgers' league, organized trade unions for women and men, and lectured extensively on topics such as socialism, women's work, suffrage, and conditions in China. She wrote for intellectual journals and political newspapers, and she published several books. Such Herculean efforts by a woman born in the mid-nineteenth century were possible because she took Eliot for her muse and her model.[24] In a patriarchal culture like Victorian England, the worship which a romantic friend bestowed upon the object of her love, and her desire to be worthy of that love, may have been one of the few stimuli which motivated achievement in a woman's life.

In the same vein, women with ambition to make a name for themselves looked for kindred spirits to appreciate their achievements and sympathize with them for the coldness with which the world greeted their efforts. Such a relationship might be crucial to offset society's hostility, or what was at best society's indifference. It was thus charged with a warmth, a fervor, a passion that went beyond simple friendship. The letters of the nineteenth-century English writer, Geraldine Jewsbury, to the wife of Thomas Carlyle, Jane Welsh Carlyle, are representative. Jane, who prided herself on her intellect, was, according to her, generally neglected and disparaged by her husband. She complained constantly of her loneliness and feelings of worthlessness. Geraldine gave her both the affection and encouragement she needed. Her letters to Jane are those of a lover, such as Thomas Carlyle had neither the inclination nor the desire to be. They indicate also the frustration Geraldine must have felt in loving a woman who was bound in Victorian marriage: "O Carissima mia . . . you are never out of either my head or my heart. After you left on Tuesday I felt so horribly wretched, too miserable even to cry, and what could be done?" (July 1841);[25] "I love you my darling, more than I can express, more than I am conscious of

myself, and yet I can do nothing for you . . ." (October 29, 1841);[26] "I love you more than anything else in the world. . . . It may do you no good now, but it may be a comfort some time, it will always be there for you" (May 1842);[27] "If I could see you and speak to you, I should have no tragic mood for a year to come, I think, and really that is saying no little, for I have had a strong inclination to hang myself oftener than once within the last month" (c. 1843).[28]

Geraldine craved a Llangollen-like existence with Jane, which was unattainable, even if Jane had wished it, since she was legally and socially tied to her husband. But she begged Geraldine to come live near her—to which Geraldine responded that what she truly wished was "a cottage in the country with you," and painted a picture of an idyllic life in such a setting.[29]

It appears that Geraldine had heterosexual relationships, but she often informed Jane that they were insignificant compared with her love for Jane, "You are of infinitely more worth and importance in my eyes. . . . You come nearer to me."[30] Jane was usually furious over these heterosexual attachments, minor as they were.[31] But although it was sometimes stormy, the love between the two continued for more than twenty-five years until Jane's death in 1866.

Their love was reinforced by a mutual struggle to transcend the role allotted to Victorian women. Jane flagged in that struggle often, too overcome by Carlyle's overbearing personality to summon the energy to assert herself. Geraldine, who believed she was the luckier of the two because she was independent and could earn a livelihood through her writing, frequently exhorted Jane to such a healthy pursuit. In one letter, for example, she points out that Jane is depressed because she has no occupation. Writing would be ideal, but Geraldine understands that her friend will get no encouragement at home. She takes it upon herself to provide the encouragement:

> It is not . . . altogether for your own sake that I am anxious you should set to work upon a story or a book of any kind that you are moved to do. You have more sense and stronger judgment than any other woman I ever knew or expect to know. . . . Do not go to Mr. Carlyle for sympathy, do not let him dash you with cold water. You must respect your own work and your own motives; if people only did what others thought good and useful, half the work in the world would be left undone.[32]

Jane could not write because she felt that she would be ridiculed by her husband, and that in any case he would dwarf any production of hers. Geraldine, who had no such problem, nevertheless saw a similarity between herself and Jane, which perhaps bound them initially: While Geraldine had no husband to discourage her efforts, she had the world. However, she believed that the world was slowly changing, and that women of the intellectual caliber of herself and Jane were making it change. But their great tragedy was that the world had not yet changed enough—they were New Women before the era of the New Woman, as Geraldine suggests to Jane in a letter of 1849:

> I believe we are touching on better days, when women will have a genuine, normal life of their own to lead. There, perhaps, will not be so many marriages, and women will be taught not to feel their destiny *manqué* if they remain single. They will be able to be friends and companions in a way they cannot be now. . . . I do not feel that either you or I are to be called failures. We are indications of a development of womanhood which as yet is not recognized. It has, so far, no ready made channels to run in, but still we have looked, and tried, and found that the present rules for women will not hold us—that something better and stronger is needed. . . . There are women to come after us, who will approach nearer the fulness of the measure of the stature of a woman's nature. I regard myself as a mere faint indication, a rudiment of the idea, of certain higher qualities and possibilities that lie in women, and all the eccentricities and mistakes and desires and absurdities I have made are only the consequences of an imperfect formation, an immature growth. . . . I can see there is a precious mine of a species of womanhood yet undreamed of by the professors and essayists on female education, and I believe also that we belong to it.[33]

Geraldine saw that they were both out of place in their era, and that a remedy for their dislocation was to provide love and encouragement for each other while they awaited a new day.

If Geraldine could have written a novel about women's lives and their relationships with each other about fifty years from the time of the above letter, it probably would have resembled Florence Converse's novel *Diana Victrix* (1897), in which the world has become more ready for New Women, they need not feel themselves *manqué* if they remain single, and their love for each other can take on revolutionary dimensions as it could not in 1849.

Unlike Meredith's "Diana," Enid and Sylvia, the American Dianas of Converse's novel, never feel compelled to form a connection with a man. While one of them is tempted for a time to engage in a heterosexual liaison, she sees it ultimately as destructive and rejects it. The other, although she is pursued by a likable man, can think of no reason for marrying him—the "natural and social forces" of Diana of the Crossways do not exist for her. As the title of Converse's book suggests, Diana, embodied in these two women, can now be victorious to the end. However, for women without a profession and an overwhelming desire to succeed in

this world, the concept of Diana generally fails: Converse presents a foil character, Rosa Campion, who envies the relationship between Enid and Sylvia and wishes she had one too. But Rosa was born into great wealth and has had no reason to focus her energies on external accomplishments such as would confirm the conviction that a woman need not marry to feel herself complete. She reluctantly admits, "I am afraid I should feel as if I hadn't managed my life cleverly if I did not marry. I should feel ashamed of myself." Enid, however, speaks for the author when she tells Rosa, "I have been sorry for married women oftener than for old maids."

Converse is open about the physical closeness between her two heroines. For example, she places Enid and Sylvia in bed together and tells us, "Enid had her arms about her and was saying a great many things very softly in the dark." Male writers had often depicted such scenes. What they generally did not depict, however, and what women writers who lived the experiences themselves could depict, was strength and encouragement to achieve in the world which romantic friends of the late nineteenth century could give each other. Converse shows these women sustaining each other as a husband generally could not and would not. Not only do they encourage each other's worldly successes, but, when the relationship is at its best, they nurture each other in ways wives were taught to nurture husbands. Converse finds such relationships between professional women to be characteristic of her times, and she clearly indicates that she is not talking about Longfellow's "rehearsal in girlhood of the great drama of woman's life," but rather about solid, permanent attachments: "As a woman advances towards thirty unmarried, her women-friendships possess more and more a stability, an intensity, which were lacking in the explosively sentimental intimacies of her youth; they are to her instead of many things." Despite a woman's successes in the world, or perhaps because of them, she desperately requires the nurturing love that another woman can give her.

Nineteenth-century men, who generally did not have convenient labels to fall back on (i.e., lesbianism or perversion), simply could not understand such relationships. When a man proposes to Enid, she tells him she cannot marry him for two reasons: First of all, she is devoted to her work. This he doesn't understand, but he understands her second reason (which is inextricably bound up with her first) even less:

> "I do not need you. It is true I have no man friend whom I enjoy as much as I do you, but I have a woman friend who is dearer to me. . . . I share with her thoughts that I have no wish to share with you. I give to her a love surpassing any affection I could teach myself to have for you. She comes first. She is my friend as you can never be, and I could not marry you unless you were a nearer friend than she.

You would have to come first. And you could not, for she is first."

"And this is all that separates us," said Jacques, in a tone of amazement. "Only a woman?"

"The reason the woman separates us," said Enid, "is because the woman and I understand each other, sympathize with each other, are necessary to each other. And you and I are not. It is not simply her womanliness, it is her friendship. There might be a man who could give me the inspiration, the equalness of sympathy, I find in her,—there might be,—some women find such men. But there are not yet enough for all of us."

She expresses a mortal fear that a man would make her give up her work and offer "only his love in return, his love and his amiable domestic tyranny!", and she tells Jacques that his domestic tyrannies and the role they would cast her in would be destructive to all she values most—while her life with another woman gives her energy for what is most important to her:

> For a moment, because I was tired, I thought I wanted you—your home. But I do not! . . . I am not domestic the way some women are. I shouldn't like to keep house and sew. . . . It would bore me. I should hate it! Sylvia and I share the responsibility here, and the maid works faithfully. There are only a few rooms. We have time for our real work, but a wife wouldn't have. And, oh, I couldn't be just a wife! I don't want to! Please go away! I have chosen my life and I love it!

Enid is the New Woman, whose number is "increasing every day." The New Woman is firm in her purpose in life (in Enid's case she is a writer and lecturer involved with improving the lot of the masses), and nothing can distract her. As a human being she needs love, but she knows she must find it in a relationship that will strengthen her purpose instead of interfering with it.

Through the character of Jacques's father, Converse warns men away from the heroic New Woman while still encouraging respect for her. She is like Joan of Arc, he says: "That kind is not to be possessed by one man; she belongs to a cause. . . . [She is] to be worshipped—the great, the universal woman—but that is a different affair from a wife."

The novel ends happily with Enid and Sylvia in domestic bliss and in the joy of their professional success. Sylvia surfaces from a long depression, caused first by her feeling that she did not have enough talent to be a fine writer and then by her ambivalence over an unworthy man. At the conclusion Sylvia publishes a novel about a New Woman similar to Enid (who marries at the end of Sylvia's novel only because "the

public are more used to it"—but as Enid joyfully reminds Sylvia, "sometimes . . . I don't marry, even in books"), and presents Enid with a copy of the novel, which is dedicated to her.

But such a revolutionary aspect of romantic friendship went largely unobserved by American male novelists of the nineteenth century. Instead, their view was of sentimental and comfortably ephemeral relationships. Henry Wadsworth Longfellow's treatment of two female protagonists in *Kavanagh* (1849) and Oliver Wendell Holmes's presentation of a similar set of characters in *A Mortal Antipathy* (1885) are representative. Longfellow's Cecilia and Alice are permitted to indulge in a boundless affection for each other, sharing the kind of intimacy the eighteenth-century novel portrayed. The two were bosom friends at school, and afterward, "the love between them, and consequently the letters, increased rather than diminished." Longfellow is gently satirical about their verbal effusions, which he considers to be characteristic of female friendship. He has difficulty in understanding of what, specifically, intimacy between two young women might consist, so he limits himself generally to showing them baring their hearts: "These two young hearts found not only a delight, but a necessity in pouring forth their thoughts and feelings to each other." However, he also plays occasionally with the notion of a sensual relationship between his two heroines. In one scene he borrows imagery from *Cymbeline* and "The Eve of St. Agnes" to suggest a delicate sensuousness between them. Cecilia has just purchased a carrier pigeon to hasten delivery of their urgent communications (which Longfellow presents as nothing more than girlish secrets):

> "I have just been writing to you," said Alice; "I wanted so much to see you this morning!"
>
> "Why this morning in particular? Has anything happened?"
>
> "Nothing, only I had such a longing to see you!" And, seating herself in a low chair by Cecilia's side, she laid her head upon the shoulder of her friend, who, taking one of her pale, thin hands in both her own, silently kissed her forehead again and again . . .
>
> "I am so glad to see you, Cecilia!" she continued. "You are so strong and beautiful! Ah, how I wish Heaven had made me as tall, and strong, and beautiful as you are!"
>
> "You little flatterer! What an affectionate, lover-like friend you are! What have you been doing all morning?"
>
> "Looking out the window, thinking of you, and writing you this letter, to beg you to come and see me!"

"And I have been buying a carrier-pigeon, to fly between us and carry all our letters."

"That will be delightful."

"He is to be sent home today; and after he gets accustomed to my room, I shall send him here, to get acquainted with yours;—a Iachimo in my Imogen's bed-chamber, to spy out its secrets."

"If he sees Cleopatra in these white curtains, and silver cupids in these andirons, he will have your imagination."

"He will see the book with the leaf turned down, and you asleep, and tell me all about you."

Longfellow depicts such sensuous exchanges, making it clear that they are not very serious. While Alice and Cecilia are in love with each other, they both fall in love with a young minister, Kavanagh, and naturally the heterosexual love is more overwhelming. Longfellow can thus characterize love between two women as "a rehearsal in girlhood of the great drama of woman's life."

Oliver Wendell Holmes offers an identical explanation of the passion between Lurida and Euthymia, his two heroines. "The friendships of young girls," he remarks, "prefigure the closer relations which will one day come in and dissolve their earlier intimacies." After assuring the reader that all will end right, he presents the two women as a perfect couple:

> The two young ladies who had recently graduated at the Corinna Institute remained, as they had always been, intimate friends. They were the natural complements of each other. Euthymia represented a complete, symmetrical womanhood. Her outward presence was only an index of a large, wholesome, affluent life. . . . She knew that she was called The Wonder by the schoolmates who were dazzled by her singular accomplishments, but she did not over-value them. She rather tended to depreciate her own gifts, in comparison with those of her friend, Miss Lurida Vincent. The two agreed all the better for differing as they did. The octave makes a perfect chord, when shorter intervals jar more or less on the ear. . . . It was a pleasant thing to observe their dependence on each other.

He even suggests, as Longfellow did, a sensuous element in their attachment in brief exchanges:

> "It is a shame that you will not let your exquisitely molded form be portrayed in marble . . ." [Lurida said]. She was startled to see what an effect her proposal had produced, for Euthymia was not only blushing but there was a flame in her eyes which she had hardly ever seen before.

Despite their mutual involvement, the forces "natural and social" move the two young women toward a heterosexual selection. Both marry, although Lurida (who wanted to be a doctor until she discovered she could not stand the sight of blood) protests to the zero hour.[34] By 1885, when Holmes wrote this novel, New England women who were happy in their romantic friendships and had some sort of professional ambition did not need to opt for marriage. Their friendships often became lifelong relationships which were a source of great support in their occupational struggles. But Holmes was a romantic writer who had no interest in recognizing a revolutionary life-style for women.

There is yet another manifestation of the failure to recognize the revolutionary potential of romantic friendship: It is curious that so many English and American writers of the nineteenth century presented such explicit sensual descriptions of the affection between two female characters. In 1928, Radclyffe Hall's novel, *The Well of Loneliness,* was censored, although she shows nothing more about the physical relationship of her two female characters than one kissing the other's hand "very humbly" in a brief scene which concludes, "and that night they were not divided." In the 1860's, at the height of the Victorian era, Christina Rossetti could describe the two heroines of "Goblin Market" thus without the slightest fear of public objection:

> *Golden head by golden head,*
> *Like two pigeons in one nest,*
> *Folded in each other's wings,*
> *They lay down in their curtained bed:*
> *Like two blossoms on one stem,*
> *Like two flakes of new fall'n snow . . .*
> *Cheek to cheek and breast to breast*
> *Locked together in one nest.*

It was probably not the almost precious quality of the description alone that saved Rossetti from contumely. Thomas Hardy in *Desperate Remedies* (1871) presented, without being threatened by the censors, an even more detailed description of his two female characters in a bed:

> The instant they were in bed Miss Aldclyffe freed herself from the last remnant of restraint. She flung her arms round the young girl, and pressed her gently to her heart.

> "Now kiss me," she said. . . .

When Miss Aldclyffe discovers that the girl, Cytherea, whom she hired as a lady's maid, loves Edward Springrove, she cries:

> "Cytherea, try to love me more than you love him—do. I love you more sincerely than any man can. Do, Cythie: don't let any man stand between us.

O, I can't bear that!" She clasped Cytherea's neck again. . . . "Why can't you kiss me as I kiss you? Why can't you!"

Although Miss Aldclyffe's kisses are described, in spite of her passionate outburst, as being "motherly" (and Hardy sees no contradiction in that description), the sensual element in her interest in Cytherea is overt. For example, before Miss Aldclyffe hires the inexperienced Cytherea, she has some initial concern that it might be boring to instruct her in her duties as a lady's maid, but then she decides it will be worthwhile "in order to have a creature who could glide round my luxurious indolent body in that manner, and look at me in that way—I warrant how light her fingers are upon one's head and neck." Most surely an author who had written forty or fifty years later this explicitly would have had to stand trial for obscenity and would have found the pressure on him so uncomfortable that he would be forced to take a night boat to the Continent. But perhaps such descriptions were permissible in the nineteenth century because that era did not have our passion for placing people in sexual categories.

Widespread twentieth-century pseudoknowledge about sexual matters, beginning with the writings of the French aesthetes and the German sexologists in the middle and late nineteenth century, has made self-described sophisticated individuals certain that they understand what "lesbianism" is and how to identify it: Two women holding one another in bed, breast to breast, is "lesbianism"; one woman begging another to love her more than she loves a man is "lesbianism." To provide a label which has been charged with the connotations of sickness or sin, and then to apply that label to a particular situation, renders that situation sick or sinful regardless of its innate attributes.

But in nineteenth-century English and American writing, behavior and emotions were not as facilely defined as they are now. Even by 1912, Edward Carpenter, who was very familiar with the sexologists' theories, spoke nevertheless for the nineteenth century when he observed that "no hard and fast line can at any point be drawn effectively separating the different kinds of attachment." He states what any nineteenth-century person must have known, that there are "friendships so romantic in sentiment that they verge into love," and that there are "loves so intellectual and spiritual that they hardly dwell in the sphere of passion." He considers this phenomenon to be indicative of the immense diversity of human temperament in matters relating to sex and love.[35] The twentieth century has rejected such subtleties by insisting that a woman is either a lesbian or she isn't; and if she is, she is abnormal; therefore a woman who loves another woman passionately is abnormal.

Such a pat definition would probably have mystified the nineteenth century. Not having the "knowledge" of the French aesthetes or the German sexologists as a guide, writers could present the most passionate love scenes between two women and not be concerned that they were dealing with "abnormality." The American writer Elizabeth Wetherell can therefore show her young heroine in the popular girl's book, *The Wide, Wide World* (1852), as being ecstatic over the possibility of spending two nights in a row together with an older girl. Wetherell can tell the reader, "There was a long silence, during which they remained locked in each other's arms," and she can have the older girl request of her young friend, "Come here and sit in my lap again . . . and let your head rest where it used to."

Similarly, Louisa May Alcott, whose fame rested on her moral stories for children, can show in *Work: A Story of Experience* (1873), two young women, Christie and Rachel, casting amorous glances at each other. Christie "woos" Rachel "as gently as a lover might," proffering flowers and compliments. She tells Rachel, "I only want to feel that you like me a little and don't mind my liking you a great deal." When Rachel seems encouraging, Christie is ecstatic: "'Then I may love you, and not be afraid of offending?' cried Christie, much touched. . . . Then Christie kissed her warmly, whisked away the tear, and began to paint the delights in store for them in her most enthusiastic way, being much elated with her victory." The two women live together after Christie proposes to Rachel: "I must love somebody, and 'love them hard,' as children say; so why can't you come and stay with me?" Rachel's presence gives Christie purpose and happiness. When the two are separated for a time, and Christie believes she has lost Rachel for good, she marries. But at the conclusion Rachel, who it turns out is the sister of Christie's husband, comes back into her life. Christie's husband conveniently dies in the Civil War, and the two women presumably remain together forever. There is nothing covert about such relationships in nineteenth-century American fiction. The writers show the women laying bare their emotions in front of any third party without the least suggestion that there is any reason to hide such emotions.

In nineteenth-century American life as well, such intense emotional bonds were not unusual, and the expression of those feelings was often committed to paper. But what the nineteenth century saw as normal, our century saw as perverse. Twentieth-century biographers have not infrequently bowdlerized the letters of their nineteenth-century subjects in order to "save" those subjects' reputations. Emily Dickinson's letters to Sue Gilbert, the woman who became her sister-in-law, and the edited version of those letters by her niece, Martha Dickinson Bianchi, are perhaps the most dramatic illustration of this point. Emily's love letters to Sue were written in the early 1850's. Bianchi's editions appeared in 1924[36] and 1932.[37] Because Bianchi was Sue's daughter, she wished to show that Emily relied on Sue, that Sue influenced her poetry, and that the two were the best of friends. But working during the height of the popularization of Sigmund Freud, she must have known to what extent intense friendship had fallen into disrepute. She therefore edited out all indications of Emily's truly powerful involvement with her mother.[38] For example, on February 6, 1852, Emily wrote Sue:

> . . . sometimes I shut my eyes, and shut my heart towards you, and try hard to forget you because you grieve me so, but you'll never go away. Oh you never will—say, Susie, promise me again, and I will smile faintly—and take up my little cross of sad—*sad* separation. How vain it seems to *write,* when one knows how to feel—how much more near and dear to sit beside you, talk with you, hear the tones of your voice; so hard to "deny thyself, and take up thy cross, and follow me"—give me strength, Susie, write me of hope and love, and of hearts that *endured,* and great was their reward of "Our Father who art in Heaven." I don't know how I shall bear it, when the gentle spring comes; if she should come and see me and talk to me of you, Oh it would surely kill me! While the frost clings to the windows and the World is stern and drear; this absence is easier; the *Earth* mourns too, for all her little birds; but when they all come back again, and she sings and is so merry—pray, what will become of me? Susie, forgive me, forget all what I say.[39]

Bianchi reproduced only these lines of the passage:

> . . . Sometimes I shut my eyes and shut my heart towards you and try hard to forget you, but you'll never go away. Susie, forgive me, forget all that I say.[40]

In the letter of June 11, 1852, Bianchi tells us that Emily wrote:

> . . . Susie, forgive me darling, for every word I say, my heart is full of you, yet when I seek to say to you something not for the world, words fail me. I try to bring you nearer, I chase the weeks away till they are quite departed—three weeks—they can't last always, for surely they must go with their little brothers and sisters to their long home in the West![41]

But the complete letter reads:

> . . . Susie, forgive me Darling, for every word I say—my heart is full of you, *none other than you in my thoughts,* yet when I seek to say to you something not for the world, words fail me. *If you were here—and Oh that you were, my Susie, we need not talk at all, our eyes would whisper for us, and your hand fast in mine, we would not ask for language*—I try to bring you nearer, I chase the weeks away till they are quite departed, *and fancy you have come, and I am on my way through the green lane to meet you, and my heart goes scampering so, that I have much ado to bring it back again, and learn it to be patient, till that dear Susie comes.* Three weeks—they can't last always, for surely they must go with their little brothers and sisters to their long home in the West![42] (Italics mine)

Bianchi also includes an affectionate note that Emily sent to Sue on June 27, 1852:

> . . . Susie, will you indeed come home next Saturday? Shall I, indeed behold you, not "darkly, but face to face"—or am I *fancying* so and dreaming blessed dreams from which the day will wake me? I hope for you so much and feel so eager for you—feel I cannot wait. Sometimes I must have Saturday before tomorrow comes.[43]

But what Emily really said in that note places their relationship in quite a different light:

> . . . Susie, will you indeed come home next Saturday, *and be my own again, and kiss me as you used to?* Shall I indeed behold you, not "darkly, but face to face" or am I *fancying* so, and dreaming blessed dreams from which the day will wake me? I hope for you so much and feel so eager for you, feel that I *cannot wait, feel that now I must have you—that the expectation once more to see your face again, makes me feel hot and feverish, and my heart beats so fast—I go to sleep at night, and the first thing I know, I am sitting there wide awake, and clasping my hands tightly, and thinking of next Saturday, and "never a bit" of you.*
>
> Sometimes I must have Saturday before tomorrow comes.[44] (The words "fancying," "cannot," and "now" are italicized in the Johnson edition. All other italics are mine.)

Bianchi must have felt that if she did not censor the letters, her aunt's literary reputation could be at stake. Since love between women had become in her day an abnormality, if Emily Dickinson were suspected of lesbianism, the universality and validity of her poetic sentiments might even be called into question, just as Amy Lowell's were in the 1920's.[45]

But it would not have occurred to Americans (and to most of the English) of the previous century to regard such sentiments as abnormal. Perhaps love between women was permitted to flourish unchecked in the nineteenth century because the fact of the New Woman and her revolutionary potential for forming a permanent bond with another woman had not yet been widely impressed upon the popular imagination, as after World War I when New Women emerged in great numbers. It was then that love between women came to be generally feared in America and England. The emotional and sensual exchanges between women, which correspondence and fiction tell us were a common form of affectional expression for centuries, suddenly took on the character of perversion.

Notes

[1] See Barbara Welter, "The Cult of True Womanhood, 1820-1860," *Dimity Convictions: The American Woman in the Nineteenth Century* (Athens: Ohio University Press, 1976), pp. 21-41.

[2] Ronald Pearsall, *The Worm in the Bud: The World of Victorian Sexuality* (Toronto: Macmillan, 1969), p. 227.

[3] G. J. Barker-Benfield, *The Horrors of the Half-Known Life: Male Attitudes Toward Women and Sexuality in Nineteenth Century America* (New York: Harper and Row, 1976). See also a discussion of this male-female division in Ann Douglas, *The Feminization of American Culture* (New York: Alfred A. Knopf, 1977).

[4] Thomas Branagan, *The Excellence of Female Character Vindicated* (Philadelphia, 1808), p. 161.

[5] John Ellis, *Marriage and its Violations* (New York, 1860), p. 21.

[6] Henry N. Guernsey, *Plain Talk on Avoided Subjects* (Philadelphia: F. A. Davis, 1882), p. 103.

[7] Nancy F. Cott, "Passionlessness: An Interpretation of Victorian Sexual Ideology," *Signs: Journal of Women in Culture and Society,* Vol. IV, No. 2 (Winter 1978), pp. 219-36.

[8] See, for example, Douglas, *The Feminization of American Culture,* and Nancy F. Cott, *The Bonds of Womanhood: "Woman's Sphere" in New England, 1780-1835* (New Haven: Yale University Press, 1977).

[9] Henry David Thoreau, *Friendship* (reprinted New York: Thomas Crowell, 1906). The term "romantic friendship" was apparently used to describe male-male relationships as well as female-female relationships in mid-nineteenth century America. See Francis Parkman, *The Oregon Trail* (1846), quoted in Jonathan Katz, *Gay American History: Lesbians and Gay Men in the U.S.A.* (New York: Thomas Crowell, 1976), pp. 303-04.

[10] *New England Quarterly,* Vol. XXXVI, No. 1 (March 1963), pp. 23-41, and *Signs: Journal of Women in Culture and Society,* Vol. 1, No. 1 (Autumn 1975), pp. 1-29.

[11] See, for example, Judith Becker Ranlett, "Sorority and Community: Women's Answer to a Changing Massachusetts, 1865-1895," Ph.D. dissertation, Brandeis University, 1974 (especially the discussion of the views of female superiority, pp. 41-42 and pp. 120-21).

[12] Margaret Fuller Ossoli, *Women in the Nineteenth Century and Kindred Papers Relating to the Sphere, Condition and Duties of Women* (Boston, 1855), pp. 342-43. Fuller's love of other women is discussed at greater length in my review of Bell Chevigny, *The Woman and the Myth: Margaret Fuller's Life and Writings in Journal of Homosexuality,* Vol. IV, No. 1 (Fall 1978), pp. 110-12.

[13] Anna Cogswell Wood, *The Story of a Friendship: A Memoir* (New York: Knickerbocker Press, 1901), p. 4.

[14] Ibid., p. 22.

[15] Ibid., p. 311.

[16] William Rounseville Alger, *The Friendships of Women* (Boston: Roberts Brothers, 1868); see, for example, pp. 346-58. These expressions of trust were common in love letters between women. See, for example, Helen Morton to Mary Hopkinson, July 24, 1872: "I, the inside I, am at home, at ease, and clear with you, as if heart and soul had found blue sky and sunshine" (Radcliffe Women's Archives, Schlesinger Library, Radcliffe College, Cambridge, Mass.).

[17] Ibid., p. 364.

[18] Ibid., p. viii.

[19] Ibid., p. 365.

[20] See John Ruskin, "Of Queen's Gardens," in *Sesame and Lilies: Three Lectures* (1865) for one of the most popular nineteenth-century English discussions of what that sphere was.

[21] Meredith's contemporary, Edith Arnold (a niece of Matthew Arnold) also wrote about love between women which is complicated by the "natural force" of heterosexuality, but female love wins out in the end. In her novel *Platonics: A Study* (1894), two romantic friends, Kit and Susan, become interested for a time in a man. Kit, the younger of the two, marries him after Susan refuses his first proposal. But for these women the heterosexual passion is transitory or unsatisfactory, while their love for each other is immutable. Kit realizes, "There are some women whom no man's love can compensate for the loss of a woman's and Kit was one of them." Susan, too, comes to acknowledge her own priorities. During a fatal illness, she writes to Kit of her brief heterosexual interest, "All that has faded away. Passion has died as it must always die, and at the end of it all I am only conscious of my love for you. The past is all lit with it—I cannot realize the

time when it was not; it holds a torch up to the future—for its cessation is unthinkable."

[22] In K. A. McKenzie, *Edith Simcox and George Eliot* (New York: Oxford University Press, 1961), p. 102.

[23] Ibid., p. 38.

[24] Unpublished paper, 1979, Women's Studies Program, San Diego State University, Calif.

[25] *Selections from the Letters of Geraldine Endsor Jewsbury to Jane Welsh Carlyle,* ed. Mrs. Alexander Ireland (London: Longmans, Green and Co., 1892), p. 22. Jane Carlyle's letters to Geraldine Jewsbury were destroyed by Geraldine just before her death. See also Virginia Woolf's discussion of their relationship in "Geraldine and Jane," *Times Literary Supplement* (February 28, 1929).

[26] *Selections from the Letters of Geraldine Endsor Jewsbury . . .,* p. 38.

[27] Ibid., p. 58.

[28] Ibid., p. 88.

[29] Ibid., pp. 333-34.

[30] Ibid., p. 43.

[31] See, for example, a letter to Mrs. Russell, January 16, 1858, referring to Geraldine's involvement with a Mr. Mantell: "She has been making a considerable fool of herself, to speak plainly, and has got estranged from me utterly for the time being," quoted in Susanne Howe, *Geraldine Jewsbury: Her Life and Errors* (London: George Allen and Unwin, 1935), p. 162.

[32] Ibid., p. 57.

[33] *Selections from the Letters of Geraldine Jewsbury . . . ,* pp. 347-49.

[34] See a more extensive discussion of this work in my article, "Female Same-sex Relationships in Novels by Henry Wadsworth Longfellow, Oliver Wendell Holmes, and Henry James," *New England Quarterly,* Vol. LI, No. 3 (September 1978), pp. 309-32.

[35] Edward Carpenter, *The Intermediate Sex: A Study of Some Transitional Types of Men and Women* (New York: Mitchell Kinnerley, 1912), p. 18.

[36] Martha Dickinson Bianchi, *The Life and Letters of Emily Dickinson* (Boston: Houghton Mifflin and Co., 1924).

[37] Martha Dickinson Bianchi, *Emily Dickinson Face to Face: Unpublished Letters with Notes and Reminiscences* (Boston: Houghton Mifflin and Co., 1932).

[38] I discuss at greater length Dickinson's emotional involvement with Sue Gilbert and other women in my articles, "Emily Dickinson's Letters to Sue Gilbert," *Massachusetts Review,* Vol. XVIII, No. 2 (September 1977), pp. 197-225 and "Emily Dickinson's Homoerotic Poetry," *Higginson Journal,* Vol. 18 (June 1978), pp. 19-27.

[39] *The Letters of Emily Dickinson,* eds. Thomas H. Johnson and Theodora Ward (Cambridge: Harvard University Press, 1958), letter 73.

[40] Bianchi, *Emily Dickinson Face to Face,* p. 184.

[41] Ibid., p. 216.

[42] Johnson and Ward, *The Letters of Emily Dickinson,* letter 94.

[43] Bianchi, *Emily Dickinson Face to Face,* p. 218.

[44] Johnson and Ward, *The Letters of Emily Dickinson,* letter 96.

[45] Clement Wood, for example, argued in a study published one year after Lowell's death that she was not a good poet because many of her poems were homosexual and therefore did not "word a common cry of many hearts." Thus he concluded that she may qualify "as an impassioned singer of her own desires; and she may well be laureate also of as many as stand beside her," but nonlesbian readers will find nothing in her verse, *Amy Lowell* (New York: Harold Vinal, 1926), pp. 13, 173.

Terry Castle

SOURCE: "The Apparitional Lesbian," in *The Apparitional Lesbian: Female Homosexuality and Modern Culture,* Columbia University Press, 1993, pp. 28-65.

[*In the excerpt below, Castle surveys the history of lesbianism in literature—both covert and overt—to find a connection between the presence of apparitions and the presence, or erasure, of lesbian desire.*]

To try to write the literary history of lesbianism is to confront, from the start, something ghostly: an impalpability, a misting over, an evaporation, or "whiting out" of possibility. Take, for example, that first (and strangest) of lesbian love stories, Daniel Defoe's *The Apparition of Mrs. Veal* (1706). The heroine of this spectral yarn (which Defoe presents in typically hoaxing fashion as unvarnished "fact") is one Mrs. Bargrave, who lives in Canterbury with a cruel and unfeeling husband. While lamenting her sad state one morning, Mrs. Bargrave is amazed to see her oldest and dearest friend, Mrs. Veal, coming up the street to her door. The two friends have been estranged ever since Mrs. Veal, "a Maiden Gentlewoman of about 30 Years of Age," began keeping house for a brother in Dover. Overcome with joy, Mrs. Bargrave greets her long-lost companion and moves to kiss her. Just as the clock strikes noon, writes Defoe, "their Lips almost touched," but *"Mrs. Veal drew her hand cross her own Eyes, and said, 'I am not very well,'* and so waved it."[1]

The touch of lips deferred, the two nonetheless converse lovingly. Mrs. Veal tells Mrs. Bargrave she is about to set off on a journey, and wished to see her again before doing so. She begs Mrs. Bargrave's forgiveness for the lapse in their friendship and reminds her of their former happy days, when they read "Drelincourt's Book of Death" together and comforted one another in affliction. Moved, Mrs. Bargrave fetches a devotional poem on Christian love, "Friendship in Perfection," and they read it aloud, musing on God's will and the happiness to come in the hereafter. "Dear Mrs. *Bargrave*," exclaims Mrs. Veal, "I shall love you forever." Then she draws her hand once again over her eyes. *"Don't you think I am mightily impaired by my Fits?"* she asks. (Mrs. Veal has suffered in the past from falling sickness.) "No," Mrs. Bargrave replies, "I think you look as well as I ever knew you." Not long after, Mrs. Veal departs, as if in embarrassed haste.

It is not until the next day, when Mrs. Bargrave goes to look for Mrs. Veal at a nearby relative's, that the eerie truth is revealed: her friend has in fact been dead for two days, having succumbed to "fits" at exactly the stroke of noon on the day before Mrs. Bargrave saw her. The supposed "Mrs. Veal" was nothing less than an apparition. Suddenly it all makes sense. The spirit was undoubtedly heaven-sent, an excited Mrs. Bargrave now tells her friends, for all of its actions, including the mysterious "waving" off of her attempted kiss, displayed its "Wonderful Love to her, and Care of her, that she should not be affrighted." And Defoe himself, in his role of supposed reporter, concurs: the specter's great errand, he concludes, was "to comfort Mrs. *Bargrave* in her Affliction, and to ask her Forgiveness for her Breach of Friendship, and with a Pious Discourse to encourage her." From this we learn "that there is a Life to come after this, and a Just God who will retribute to every one according to the Deeds done in the Body" (preface).

Why call this bizarre little fable a lesbian love story? One could, conceivably, read into its sparse and somewhat lugubrious detail a richer, more secular, and sensational narrative—cunningly secreted inside the uplifting homily on Christian doctrine. Mrs. Bargrave, the unhappy wife, and Mrs. Veal, the maiden gentle-

woman—such a story might go—have in fact been clandestine lovers; they have been estranged by circumstances; Mrs. Veal dies; Mrs. Bargrave's vision is a kind of hysterical projection, in which the passion she feels for her dead friend is phantasmatically renewed. Defoe even gives a certain amount of evidence for this sort of fantasia. All the men mentioned in the story are either evil or unsympathetic: Mrs. Bargrave's husband is "barbarous"; Mrs. Veal's brother tries to stop Mrs. Bargrave from spreading the story of his sister's spectral visit. We are invited to imagine a male conspiracy against the lovers: they have been kept apart in life; they will be alienated (or so the brother hopes) in death. The fact that Defoe sometimes hints at erotic relationships between women elsewhere in his fiction—witness *Roxana*—might make such a "reading between the lines" seem even more enticing.[2]

And yet, this does not feel quite right: one is troubled by a certain crassness, anachronism, even narcissism in the reading. Is it not a peculiarly late twentieth-century moral and sexual infantilism that wishes to read into every story from the past some hidden scandal or provocation? And hasn't Defoe made it clear—more or less—that the relationship between Mrs. Bargrave and Mrs. Veal is strictly an incorporeal one? Mrs. Veal, after all, is an apparition—a mere collection of vapors—so much so that Mrs. Bargrave, as we are explicitly reminded, cannot even kiss her.

At the risk of dealing in paradoxes, I would like to argue that it is in fact the very ghostliness—the seeming ineffability—of the connection between Mrs. Bargrave and Mrs. Veal that makes *The Apparition of Mrs. Veal* an archetypally lesbian story. The kiss that doesn't happen, the kiss that *can't* happen, because one of the women involved has become a ghost (or else is direly haunted by ghosts) seems to me a crucial metaphor for the history of lesbian literary representation since the early eighteenth century. Given the threat that sexual love between women inevitably poses to the workings of patriarchal arrangement, it has often been felt necessary to deny the carnal *bravada* of lesbian existence. The hoary misogynist challenge, "But what do lesbians do?" insinuates as much: *This cannot be. There is no place for this.* It is perhaps not so surprising that at least until around 1900 lesbianism manifests itself in the Western literary imagination primarily as an absence, as chimera or *amor impossibilia*—a kind of love that, by definition, cannot exist. Even when "there" (like Stein's Oakland) it is "not there": inhabiting only a recessive, indeterminate, misted-over space in the collective literary psyche. Like the kiss between Mrs. Bargrave and Mrs. Veal, it is reduced to a ghost effect: to ambiguity and taboo. It cannot be perceived, except apparitionally.

But how, one might object, to recognize (enough to remark) something as elusive as a ghost effect? By way of answer let us turn to another work, also from the eighteenth century, in which a similar apparition-ality envelops—and ultimately obscures—the representational field. The work is Diderot's *La Religieuse* (1760), long recognized as a masterpiece of the erotic, though of what sort of eros its admirers (and detractors) have often been at a loss to specify.[3] We recall the story: Diderot's pathetic heroine, Suzanne Simonin, forced to become a nun by her selfish and obdurate family, is imprisoned within a series of corrupt convents, each worse than the last, where she is singled out for cruel and incessant persecution by her superiors. In letters smuggled out to various lawyers and secular officials, Suzanne recounts her sufferings and begs for release, though her cries for help go unheard. Diderot's first-person narrative itself masquerades as one of these letters, supposedly addressed to the Marquis de Croismare. Yet it also doubles as Diderot's own sensationalist assault on cloistered religious communities and the inhuman "wickedness" perpetrated within them.

As most of its modern commentators have remarked, a fear of sexual relations between women seems to suffuse—if not to rule—Diderot's story.[4] And yet how is this fear insinuated? Ineluctably, by shadow play—through a kind of linguistic necromancy, or calling up, of ghosts. Take Diderot's sleight-of-hand, for example, in the scene early in the novel in which the vicious mother superior at Longchamp, the first convent in which Suzanne is incarcerated, forces her to undergo a sadistic mock death as a punishment for disobedience. After being made to lie in a coffin, being drenched with freezing holy water, and trodden upon (as "a corpse") by her fellow nuns, the pitiful Suzanne is confined to her cell, without blankets, crucifix, or food. That night, at the behest of the superior, other nuns break into her room, shrieking and overturning objects, so that

> those who were not in the conspiracy alleged that strange things were going on in my cell, that they had heard mournful voices, shoutings and the rattlings of chains, and that I held communion with ghosts and evil spirits, that I must have made a pact with the devil and that my corridor should be vacated at once.[5]

A young nun, infected by the atmosphere of collective paranoia, sees Suzanne wandering in the corridor, becomes hysterical with terror, and flings herself into the bewildered Suzanne's arms. At this point, Suzanne tells the marquis, "the most criminal-sounding story was made out of it." Namely,

> that the demon of impurity had possessed me, and I was credited with intentions I dare not mention, and unnatural desires to which they attributed the obvious disarray of the young nun. Of course I am

not a man, and I don't know what can be imagined about one woman and another, still less about one woman alone, but as my bed had no curtains and people came in and out of my room at all hours, what can I say, Sir? For all their circumspect behaviour, their modest eyes and the chastity of their talk, these women must be very corrupt at heart—anyway they know that you can commit indecent acts alone, which I don't know, and so I have never quite understood what they accused me of, and they expressed themselves in such veiled terms that I never knew how to answer them.

An irrational yet potent symbolic logic is at work here: to be taken for a ghost is to be "credited" with unnatural desires. No other incriminating acts need be represented, no fleeting palpitation recorded—it is enough to become phantomlike in the sight of others, to change oneself (or be changed) from mortified flesh to baffled apparition. To "be a ghost" is to long, unspeakably, after one's own sex. At the same time—Diderot slyly suggests—the demonic opposite is also true: to love another woman is to lose one's solidity in the world, to evanesce, and fade into the spectral.

The notorious final section of *La Religieuse*—in which Suzanne is moved to a new convent and falls under the erotic sway of its depraved superior, "Madame ***"—shows this last uncanny transformation most powerfully. Suzanne, we recollect, after being half-seduced by Madame *** (who visits her nightly in her cell and excites her with ambiguous caresses), becomes afraid for her soul and begins to avoid her, on the advice of her confessor. Maddened by the young nun's rebuffs, Madame *** pursues her like a specter, day and night. "If I went downstairs," writes Suzanne, "I would find her at the bottom, and she would be waiting for me at the top when I went up again." Surprised by her on one occasion in the convent chapel, Suzanne actually mistakes the superior for an apparition, owing to what she calls a "strange effect" of the imagination, complicated by an optical illusion: "her position in relation to the church lamp had been such that only her face and the tips of her fingers had been lit up, the rest was in shadow, and that had given her a weird appearance."

As the superior's sexual obsession finally lapses into outright dementia—following upon a church inquiry instigated by Suzanne into abuses at the convent—her ghostly status is confirmed. As she passes "from melancholy to piety and from piety to frenzy," she becomes a nightwalker in the convent, raving, subject to terrible hallucinations, surrounded by imaginary phantasms. Sometimes, Suzanne tells the marquis, when she would come upon Madame ***—barefoot, veiled, and in white—in the convent corridors, or being bled in the convent infirmary, the madwoman would cover her eyes and turn away, as though possessed. "I dare not describe all the indecent things she did and said in her delirium," says Suzanne; "She kept on putting her hand to her forehead as though trying to drive away unwanted thoughts or visions—what visions I don't know. She buried her head in the bed and covered her face with her sheets. 'It is the tempter!' she cried, 'it is he! What a strange shape he has put on! Get some holy water and sprinkle it over me. . . . Stop, stop, he's gone now.'" Exiled to a world of diabolical spirits, surrounded by horrific shapes she tries feebly to "fend off" with a crucifix, the naked and emaciated Madame *** finally expires in an exhalation of curses—a ghost indeed of her former sensual and worldly self.

How are we to read such scenes? One is struck at once by the curious repetition of gesture: like the ghostly Mrs. Veal, putting hand to eyes and "waving" off the kiss of Mrs. Bargrave, Madame *** raises her hand repeatedly to her face to obliterate those visions—the ghosts of her former love—that haunt and torment her. As if in closeup in some lost avant-garde film, the isolated hand over the eyes, caught forever in Manichaean black and white, makes the gesture of blockage, as though to cede into the void the memory (or hope) of a fleshly passion. But somewhat more insistently than in *The Apparition of Mrs. Veal,* the blocking motion is visible here as an authorial gesture as well—as the displaced representation, or symbolic show, of Diderovian motive. What better way to exorcize the threat of female homosexuality than by treating it as ghostly? By "waving" off, so to speak, the lesbian dimension of his own story, even as his heroine Suzanne exculpates herself from any complicity in the superior's erotic mania, Diderot establishes his credentials as law-abiding, slightly flirtatious, homophobic man of letters—the same man who could jealously complain to his lover Sophie Volland about the unnaturally "voluptuous and loving way" in which her own sister often embraced her. [See, for example, Diderot's letter to Volland of September 17, 1760 (in *Diderot's Letters to Sophie Volland*), in which he animadverts on her sister's "curiously" erotic way with her. In a letter written August 3, 1759, Diderot coped with his imagined rival by transforming her, through simile, into airy nothingness. "It does not make me unhappy to be her successor," he wrote, "indeed it rather pleases me. It is as if I were pressing her soul between yours and mine. She is like a snowflake which will perhaps melt away between two coals of fire." And later, after warning Sophie not to kiss her sister's portrait too often lest he find out, he says: "I put my lips to yours and kiss them, even if your sister's kisses are still there. But no, there's nothing there; hers are so light and airy."]

The literary history of lesbianism, I would like to argue, is first of all a history of derealization. Diderot's blocking gesture is symptomatic: in nearly all of the art of the eighteenth and nineteenth centuries, lesbianism, or its possibility, can only be represented to the degree that it is simultaneously "derealized," through a blanching authorial infusion of spectral metaphors. (I speak here of so-called polite or mainstream writing; the shadow discourse of pornography is of course another matter, and demands a separate analysis.[6]) One woman or the other must be a ghost, or on the way to becoming one. Passion is excited, only to be obscured, disembodied, decarnalized. The vision is inevitably waved off. Panic seems to underwrite these obsessional spectralizing gestures: a panic over love, female pleasure, and the possibility of women breaking free—together—from their male sexual overseers. Homophobia is the order of the day, entertains itself (wryly or gothically) with phantoms, then exorcizes them.

One might easily compile an anthology of spectralizing moments from the eighteenth-, nineteenth-, and even early twentieth-century literature of lesbianism. After the melodramatics of *La Religieuse,* one might turn, for example, to Théophile Gautier's *Mademoiselle de Maupin,* a novel that, despite its different tone and sensibility (comical-fantastic rather than morbid-sublime), also presents the sexual love of woman for woman as an essentially phantasmatic enterprise. Rosette, the lover of the narrator D'Albert, has fallen in love with Théodore, a mysterious young visitor to her country estate. What she does not know (nor any of the other characters) is that Théodore is in reality a woman in disguise, the handsome adventurer Madeleine de Maupin. Clad only in the most apparitional of nightgowns ("so clinging and so diaphanous that it showed her nipples, like those statues of bathing women covered with wet drapery"), Rosette comes to Théodore/Madeleine's room one moonlit evening and pleads with her to make love to her. When "Théodore" (assuming that Rosette is deluded about her sex) is reluctant, Rosette takes matters into her own hands. Although, she explains, "you find it wearisome to see me following your steps like this, like a loving ghost which can only follow you and would like to merge with your body . . . I cannot help doing it."[7] Then she pulls Théodore/Madeleine toward her and their lips meet in a ghostly, "almost imperceptible kiss."

Aroused by Rosette to the point that she can no longer tell whether she is "in heaven or on earth, here or elsewhere, dead or living," "Théodore" now wonders for a fleeting instant what it would be like to give some "semblance of reality to this shadow of pleasure which my lovely mistress embraced with such ardour." But how to turn shadow into substance? Her question goes unanswered, for just as Rosette slips naked into her bed, Rosette's brother, Alcibiades, bursts farcically into the room, sword in hand, to prevent the rape he imagines to be taking place. His mocking accusations underline the already free-floating spectral metaphorics of the scene: "It appears, then, my very dear and very virtuous sister, that having judged in your wisdom that my lord Théodore's bed was softer than yours, you came to sleep here? Or perhaps there are ghosts in your room, and you thought that you would be safer in this one, under his protection?" After wounding Alcibiades in an impromptu duel and fleeing on horseback into the woods around Rosette's house, Théodore/Madeleine is herself pursued by seeming phantoms:

> The branches of the trees, all heavy with dew, struck against my face and made it wet; one would have said that the old trees were stretching out their arms to hold me back and keep me for the love of their chatelaine. If I had been in another frame of mind, or a little superstitious, I could easily have believed that they were so many ghosts who wanted to seize me and that they were showing me their fists.

Though carefully designed to maximize readerly titillation, Gautier's stagey scene of lesbian coitus interruptus is also a paradoxical statement on sexual ontology. Such spectral coupling as that between Rosette and Madeleine de Maupin must needs be interrupted, because otherwise *it might prove itself to exist.* What would happen, Gautier seems to ask, were Rosette to realize the true sex of her lover? The anxiety that pursues the novelist—or so his compulsive slippage into the language of the apparitional here suggests—is not so much that the ethereal Rosette might start back in blank dismay, but that the discovery of absence instead of presence (a haunting vacuity where the phallus should be) might bring with it its own perverse and unexpected joy. Yet Gautier can no more tolerate eros without a phallus than the dripping branches of the trees can hold back Madeleine de Maupin on behalf of their infatuated "chatelaine." Indeed, lest Rosette or her would-be lover bring into being some giddying new embodiment of love, the *amor impossibilia* must remain just that—a phantom or shadow in the comic narrative of desire. [The trees brushing Madeleine de Maupin's face bring to mind, of course, that waving gesture which I am suggesting often subverts the literary representation of lesbian desire. Yet here the gesture is displaced—with its meaning seemingly inverted—onto those anthropomorphic trees, which, like ghosts, want to *preserve* the possibility of a sexual union between Madeleine and Rosette. How to deal with the apparent contradiction? One way, it seems to me, would be to read "into" the narrative a second, unmentioned gesture: that of the rider, who finding her eyes momentarily blinded with dew, reflexively brushes back the very branches that brush her. In this second, hypothetical waving—so automatic as to preclude mention—will be found that motion of avoidance so often accompanying the literary threat of female homosexuality.]

Similar negations haunt the nineteenth-century poetry of lesbianism. In Baudelaire's "Femmes damnées," for example, one of the numerous lesbian-obsessed poems in *Les Fleurs du mal* (1857), Delphine and Hippolyte, the tortured lovers, are presented as damned spirits, enslaved by a sterile passion and doomed to wander ceaselessly in a hell of their own creation. Although Delphine's spectral kiss falls on Hippolyte's mouth—as Rosette's does on Madeleine de Maupin's—so "lightly" as to be barely perceptible ("Mes baisers sont légers comme ces éphémères / Qui caressent le soir les grands lacs transparents"), its psychic weight is enough to impel Hippolyte into haunting torments:

> Je sens fondre sur moi de lourdes épouvantes
> Et de noirs bataillons de fantômes épars,
> Qui veulent me conduire en des routes mouvantes
> Qu'un horizon sanglant ferme de toutes parts.

> [I bear a weight of terrors, and dark hosts
> Of phantoms haunt my steps and seem to lead.
> I walk, compelled, behind these beckoning ghosts
> Down sliding roads and under skies that bleed.][8]

Breathing "la fraîcheur des tombeaux" on her lover's breast, she longs for oblivion. But in a morbid excoriation in the concluding stanzas of the poem the poet himself addresses the ghost-ridden couple, condemning them forever to a world of shades:

> —Descendez, descendez, lamentables victimes,
> Descendez le chemin de l'enfer éternel!
> Plongez au plus profond du gouffre où tous les crimes,
> Flagellés par un vent qui ne vient pas du ciel,

> Bouillonnent pêle-mêle avec un bruit d'orage.
> Ombres folles, courez au but de vos désirs;
> Jamais vous ne pourrez assouvir votre rage,
> Et votre châtiment naîtra de vos plaisirs.
>
> (ll.85-92)

> [Hence, lamentable victims, get you hence!
> Hells yawn beneath, your road is straight and steep.
> Where all the crimes receive their recompense
> Wind-whipped and seething in the lowest deep

> With a huge roaring as of storms and fires,
> Go down, mad phantoms, doomed to seek in vain
> The ne'er-won goal of unassuaged desires,
> And in your pleasures find eternal pain!]

In Swinburne's would-be Baudelairean "Faustine" (1862), a similar fate is reserved for the wicked Roman empress Faustine, in whom "stray breaths of Sapphic song that blew / Through Mitylene" once "shook the fierce quivering blood" by night. Worn out by that "shameless nameless love" that makes "Hell's iron gin" shut "like a trap that breaks the soul," Faustine is surrounded in death by the phantoms of women she has debauched in life:

> And when your veins were void and dead,
>   What ghosts unclean
> Swarmed round the straitened barren bed
>   That hid Faustine?
>
> What sterile growths of sexless root
>   Or epicene?
> What flower of kisses without fruit
>   Of love, Faustine?[9]

And in "The Lesbian Hell" (1898), a bizarre poem by Baudelaire and Swinburne's turn-of-the-century epigone, the poet and occultist Aleister Crowley,

> Pale women fleet around, whose infinite
>   Long sorrow and desire have torn their
>   wombs,
> Whose empty fruitlessness assails the night
>   With hollow repercussion, like dim tombs
>   Wherein some vampire glooms.
>
> Pale women sickening for some sister breast;
>   Lone sisterhood of voiceless melancholy
> That wanders in this Hell, desiring rest
>   From that desire that dwells forever free,
>   Monstrous, a storm, a sea.[10]

Drawing "the unsubstantial shapes / Of other women" to them with kisses that burn cold "on the lips whose purple blood escapes," the inhabitants of "lesbian hell" roam the earth,

> Like mists uprisen from the frosty moon
> Like shadows fleeting in a seer's glass,
>   Beckoning, yearning, amorous of the noon
>   When earth dreams on in swoon.
>   (ll. 27-30)

When we turn to late nineteenth- and early twentieth-century fiction, the apparitional lesbian is equally ubiquitous—even in works such as Henry James's *The Bostonians* (1886) in which the homophobic fantasy that generates (and evacuates) her is disguised within a more realistic and neutral-seeming representational context. How else, perhaps, to regard the ineffable Olive Chancellor, defeated in her love for Verena Tarrant by the all-too palpable Basil Ransom, than as a more repressed version of those pale females, "sickening for some sister breast," who wander unappeased through late Victorian decadent fantasy? The ascetical Olive, who "glides" through rooms and greets strangers with a freezing touch of her slender white hand ("at once cold and limp") is indeed the ghost-woman of James's novel, chilling all around her with her preternatural-

seeming passion for the lovely and puerile Verena. (Her connection with Olive, Basil warns Verena, is "the most unreal, accidental, illusory thing in the world.")[11] And like the evil exhalations of Swinburnean afflatus, Olive too will ultimately be exiled to an asexual "land of vapors." When Basil, in the tumultuous last scene of the novel, comes to drag Verena away "by muscular force" from the Music Hall in Boston where she is about to give an oration on women's rights, Olive, at her creator's behest, lapses at once into impotent, agonized insubstantiality. "Dry, desperate, rigid," writes James, "yet she wavered and seemed uncertain; her pale, glittering eyes straining forward, as if they were looking for death." To the triumphant Basil she is a "vision"—an unearthly "presentment" of "blighted hope and wounded pride." Unable in the end to compete—in this most crudely embodied of Jamesian erotic struggles—Olive simply "disappears" on the last page of the novel, retreating to the unseen stage of the auditorium, where she will search for words to explain her loss. . . .

Why, since the eighteenth century, this phantasmagorical association between ghosts and lesbians? And why the seductive permutation of the metaphor in the twentieth century? The answer, it seems to me, is not far to seek. The spectral figure is a perfect vehicle for conveying what must be called—though without a doubt paradoxically—that "recognition through negation" which has taken place with regard to female homosexuality in Western culture since the Enlightenment. Over the past three hundred years, I would like to suggest, the metaphor has functioned as the necessary psychological and rhetorical means for objectifying—and ultimately embracing—that which otherwise could not be acknowledged.

Psychoanalytic theory offers an interesting analogy. Freud, in his famous essay on negation (published three years before *The Well of Loneliness*) argued that the most important way in which repressed thoughts entered into individual consciousness, paradoxically, was through disavowal. To seek to negate an idea—as when one says of an unknown person in a dream, "it was *not* my mother"—was in fact, according to Freud, to affirm the truth of the idea on another level:

> We emend this: so it *was* his mother. In our interpretation we take the liberty of disregarding the negation and of simply picking out the subject-matter of the association. It is just as though the patient had said: "It is true that I thought of my mother in connection with this person, but I don't feel at all inclined to allow the association to count."[36]

Precisely "by the help of the symbol of negation," Freud concluded, "the thinking-process frees itself from the limitations of repression and enriches itself with the subject-matter without which it could not work efficiently."[37]

One might think of lesbianism as the "repressed idea" at the heart of patriarchal culture. By its very nature (and in this respect it differs significantly from male homosexuality) lesbianism poses an ineluctable challenge to the political, economic, and sexual authority of men over women. It implies a whole new social order, characterized—at the very least—by a profound feminine indifference to masculine charisma. (In its militant or "Amazonian" transformation lesbianism may also, of course, be associated with outright hostility toward men.) One might go so far as to argue—along with Adrienne Rich, Gayle Rubin, and others—that patriarchal ideology necessarily depends on the "compulsory" suppression of love between women.[38] As Henry Fielding put it in *The Female Husband,* the vehemently antilesbian pamphlet he published anonymously in 1746, once women gave way to "unnatural lusts," there was no civil "excess and disorder" they were not liable to commit.[39]

Beginning in Western Europe in the eighteenth century, with the gradual attenuation of moral and religious orthodoxies, the weakening of traditional family structures, urbanization, and the growing mobility and economic independence of women, male authority found itself increasingly under assault. And not surprisingly, with such far-reaching social changes in the offing, the "repressed idea" of love between women—one can speculate—began to manifest itself more threateningly in the collective psyche. Eighteenth- and nineteenth-century ideologues were at once fascinated and repelled by the possibility of women without sexual allegiance toward men.[40] And ultimately a backlash set in—characterized as we have seen in the writings of Diderot, Gautier, James, and others, by an effort to derealize the threat of lesbianism by associating it with the apparitional.

From one angle this act of negation made a sort of morbid sense; for how better, one might ask, to exorcize the threat of lesbianism than by turning it into a phantom? The spectral metaphor had useful theological associations: witches, after all, dealt in spirits, and the witchcraft connection could be counted on to add an invidious aura of diabolism to any scene of female-female desire. ("Oh we wouldn't have stood a chance in that time," says Matt in Duffy's *Microcosm,* thinking of the Middle Ages; "sure sign of a witch to love your own sex." But more important by far was the way the apparitional figure seemed to obliterate, through a single vaporizing gesture, the disturbing carnality of lesbian love. It made of such love—literally—a phantasm: an ineffable anticoupling between "women" who weren't there.

—Or did it? As I have tried to intimate, the case could be made that the metaphor meant to derealize lesbian desire in fact did just the opposite. Indeed, strictly for repressive purposes, one could hardly think of a *worse* metaphor. For embedded in the ghostly figure, as even its first proponents seemed at times to realize, was inevitably a notion of reembodiment: of uncanny return to the flesh. "This image obsesses me, and follows me everywhere," says the narrator in Gautier's *Mademoiselle de Maupin,* "and I never see it more than when it isn't there." To become an apparition was also to become endlessly capable of "appearing." And once there, the specter, like a living being, was not so easily gotten rid of. It demanded a response. It is precisely the demanding, importuning aspect of the apparitional that Radclyffe Hall depicted to such striking allegorical effect in the last pages of *The Well of Loneliness.*

Though in the course of this essay I have, for rhetorical purposes, implied a break between older "homophobic" invocations of the apparitional lesbian and later revisionist ones, it is perhaps more useful in the end to stress the continuity between them. If it is true that the first stage of recognition is denial, then the denial of lesbianism—through its fateful association with the spectral—was also the first stage of its cultural recognition. In the same way that the act of negation, in Freud's words, "frees the thinking process from repression," so the spectral metaphor provided the very imagery, paradoxically, through which the carnal truth of lesbianism might be rediscovered and reclaimed by lesbian writers.

This process of "recognition through negation" may have something to do, finally, with one of the most intriguing features of modern lesbian-themed literature—its tendency to hark back, by way of embedded intertextual references, to earlier works on the same subject. I mentioned in passing Stephen Gordon's "haunted" reading of Krafft-Ebing in *The Well of Loneliness* and Maureen Duffy's lengthy citation from Charlotte Charke's 1755 *Life* in *The Microcosm,* but other examples abound. In both Colette's *Claudine à l'école* and Lillian Hellman's *The Children's Hour,* the characters are reading Gautier's *Mademoiselle de Maupin;* in Brigid Brophy's *The Finishing Touch,* the main character not only invokes Gautier but also Renée Vivien's *Une Femme m'apparut* and Proust's *Sodom et Gomorrhe.* In Christine Crow's *Miss X,* the narrator quotes (with irony) from Baudelaire's "Femmes damnées" and jokes compulsively about Radclyffe Hall's *Well of Loneliness.* In Sarah Schulman's *After Delores,* one of the narrator's friends is reading—and rewriting—Renault's *The Friendly Young Ladies.* For the reader attempting to proceed logically, as it were, through the canon of lesbian writing, such rampant intertextuality can bring with it an unsettling sense of déjà vu—if not a feeling of outright "possession" by the ghosts of the lesbian literary past. [The passage in Schulman's *After Delores* is exemplary in this respect.

Beatriz is describing a screenplay she is writing based on *The Friendly Young Ladies*. In Beatriz's new version, Leo and Helen are lesbians but do not acknowledge the fact to one another until an American woman seduces one of them. Then they are forced to confront the truth of their lives. As Beatriz says to the narrator, "You see, it forces them to confront the lie in their relationship and their complicity in that lie, a lie that has consumed ten years of their lives." The effect of this embedded invocation, even with Beatriz's critical reenvisioning of the plot, is to break down boundaries between Renault's novel and Schulman's own—to make the reader feel suspended, as it were, within a single lesbian Ur-text, replete with plots and counterplots, conjurings and reconjurings.]

Yet the haunted nature of modern lesbian writing attests directly, I think, to the process by which lesbianism itself has entered into the imaginative life of the West over the past two centuries. It is a curious fact that for most readers of lesbian literature, at least until very recently, it has seldom mattered very much whether a given work of literature depicted love between women in a positive or negative light: so few in number have such representations been over the years, and so intense the cultural taboo against them, that virtually any novel or story dealing with the subject has automatically been granted a place in lesbian literary tradition. (Thus even such negative-seeming works as Diderot's *La Religieuse,* James's *The Bostonians,* or Renault's *The Friendly Young Ladies* continue to hold an acknowledged, if not exactly esteemed, place in the underground lesbian literary canon.[41]) Like the analyst, who, in Freud's words, "takes the liberty of disregarding [any] negation," interested readers have tended simply to "pick out the subject-matter" of lesbianism, regardless of surrounding context, in order to retrieve it for their own subversive imaginative ends.

In the case of the apparitional lesbian, twentieth-century lesbian writers have been able for the most part to ignore the negative backdrop against which she has traditionally (de)materialized. By calling her back to passionate, imbricated life—by invoking her both as lover and beloved—they have succeeded in transforming her from a negating to an affirming presence. But they have altered our understanding of the homophobic literature of the past as well. For once apprised of the apparitional lesbian's insinuating sensualism—and her scandalous bent for return—we can no longer read, say, the novels of Diderot or James without sensing something of her surreptitious erotic power. Indeed, like Mrs. Veal, she may haunt us most when she pretends to demur. For even at her most ethereal and dissembling, as when seeming to "wave off" the intrusive pleasures of the flesh, she cannot help but also signal—as if by secret benediction—that fall into flesh which is to come.

Notes

[1] Daniel Defoe, *A True Relation of the Apparition of one Mrs. Veal* (London, 1706; rpt. William Andrews Clark Memorial Library, 1965), p. 3.

[2] On the hints of lesbianism in *Roxana* (1724), see my "'Amy, Who Knew my Disease.'"

[3] To sample some of the critical controversy see, for example, Vivienne Mylne, "What Suzanne Knew: Lesbianism and *La Religieuse,*" Jack Undank, "An Ethics of Discourse," Rita Goldberg, *Sex and Enlightenment,* pp. 169-204, Walter E. Rex, "Secrets from Suzanne," and Eve Kosofsky Sedgwick, "Privilege of Unknowing."

[4] Cf. Goldberg, in *Sex and Enlightenment,* on Diderot's distaste for the lesbian mother superior: "Her sexual desire is so easily stimulated that we are meant to think of it as a kind of disease. . . . She is, in fact, an example of the dreaded *homme-femme,* with the desires of a man and the body and supposed emotional weakness of a woman."

[5] Diderot, *The Nun* (Penguin, 1974), p. 85.

[6] The pornographic representation of lesbianism may nonetheless have influenced so-called mainstream representation more often—and more profoundly—than is commonly acknowledged. In a subsequent essay in this book ("Marie Antoinette Obsession"), I argue that various pornographic works written at the time of French Revolution depicting the supposed lesbian relationships of the French queen, Marie Antoinette, contributed directly—albeit covertly—to her incarnation in the nineteenth century as an icon of romantic female-female love. The distinction I make in the present essay between polite discourse and its pornographic "shadow," is in one sense an artificial one: from Diderot and Gautier to Zola and Djuna Barnes, mainstream writers taking up the theme of lesbianism have often, in fact, drawn upon the motifs and stock situations of pornographic discourse.

[7] Gautier, *Mademoiselle de Maupin* (Penguin, 1981), p. 304. Richardson's assertion in her introduction to the novel, that "the story is the least important part of the book," is characteristic, alas, of the way in which the majority of commentators have dealt with Gautier's crypto-lesbian plot line. For a somewhat less repressive view, see Sadoff, *Ambivalence, Ambiguity, and Androgyny.*

[8] Baudelaire, "Femmes damnées (Delphine et Hippolyte)," lines 45-48. The poem was one of those excluded, on grounds of indecency, from the 1861 edition of *Les Fleurs du mal.* It is reprinted in Baudelaire's *Oeuvres complètes* (Gallimard, 1975), pp. 152-55. All French citations are to this edition. The English translation here is by Aldous Huxley, rpt. in Marthiel and Jackson Mathews, eds., *The Flowers of*

Evil, pp. 115-23.

[9] Swinburne, "Faustine," lines 125-132, in *The Complete Works of Algernon Charles Swinburne* (William Heinemann, 1925), 1:238-43.

[10] Crowley, "The Lesbian Hell," lines 6-15, in Coote, *The Penguin Book of Homosexual Verse* (1983), pp. 273-75.

[11] James, *The Bostonians* (Oxford University Press, 1984), p. 325. . . .

. . . . .

[36] Freud, "Negation," p. 235.

[37] Freud, "Negation," p. 236.

[38] See Rich, "Compulsory Heterosexuality and Lesbian Existence," and Rubin, "The Traffic in Women." Society demands the suppression of same-sex love, argues Rubin, because such love destroys the distinction between "genders" on which patriarchal authority depends:

> Gender is not only an identification with one sex; it also entails that sexual desire be directed towards the other sex. The sexual division of labor is implicated in both aspects of gender—male and female it creates them, and it creates them heterosexual. The suppression of the homosexual component of human sexuality, and by corollary, the oppression of homosexuals, is therefore a product of the same system whose rules and relations oppress women.

See Rubin, "Traffic in Women," p. 180.

[39] Fielding, *The Female Husband,* p. 29.

[40] On the paradoxical male attitude toward lesbianism in the eighteenth century, see my "Matters Not Fit to be Mentioned." On nineteenth-century responses, see Faderman, *Surpassing the Love of Men,* especially pp. 277-94, and Katz, *Gay American History and Gay/Lesbian Almanac: A New Documentary, passim.*

[41] All three of these novels are featured prominently, for example, in Jeannette Foster's classic bibliographic study, *Sex Variant Women in Literature.*

GREEK LOVE

John Addington Symonds

SOURCE: "A Problem in Greek Ethics," in *Sexual Inversion,* 1897. Reprint by Arno Press, 1975, pp. 245-47.

[*In the late-nineteenth century, Symonds and sexologist Havelock Ellis discussed working together to produce a study of homosexuality. When Ellis published his finished work in 1897, Symonds's contribution, written several decades earlier, was relegated to the appendix. Excerpted below, his "A Problem in Greek Ethics" presents the thesis he had wanted to include in the larger work: like many homosexual men of his generation educated at Oxford, Symonds emphasized the importance of male-male love to Hellenistic culture—a world that all Victorian scholars, heterosexual and homosexual, venerated.*]

Sensitive to every form of loveliness, and unrestrained by moral or religious prohibition, [the Greeks] could not fail to be enthusiastic for that corporeal beauty, unlike all other beauties of the human form, which marks male adolescence no less triumphantly than does the male soprano voice upon the point of breaking. The power of this corporeal loveliness to sway their imagination by its unique æsthetic charm is abundantly illustrated in the passages which I have quoted above from the *Charmides* of Plato and Xenophon's *Symposium.* An expressive Greek phrase, . . . "youths in their prime of adolescence, but not distinguished by a special beauty", recognises the persuasive influence, separate from that of true beauty, which belongs to a certain period of masculine growth. The very evanescence of this . . . "bloom of youth" made it in Greek eyes desirable, since nothing more clearly characterises the poetic myths which adumbrate their special sensibility than the pathos of a blossom that must fade. When distinction of feature and symmetry of form were added to this charm of youthfulness, the Greeks admitted, as true artists are obliged to do, that the male body displays harmonies of proportion and melodies of outline more comprehensive, more indicative of strength expressed in terms of grace, than that of women. [The following passage may be extracted from a letter of Winckelmann (see Pater's *Studies in the History of the Renaissance,* p. 162): "As it is confessedly the beauty of man which is to be conceived under one general idea, so I have noticed that those who are observant of beauty only in women, and are moved little or not at all by the beauty of men, seldom have an impartial, vital, inborn instinct for beauty in art. To such persons the beauty of Greek art will ever seem wanting, because its supreme beauty is rather male than female." To this I think we ought to add that, while it is true that "the supreme beauty of Greek art is rather male than female", this is due not so much to any passion of the Greeks for male beauty as to the fact that the male body exhibits a higher organisation of the human form than the female.] I guard myself against saying—more seductive to the senses, more soft, more delicate, more undulating. The superiority of male beauty does not consist in these attractions, but in the symmetrical development of all the qualities of the human frame, the complete organisation of the body as the supreme instrument of vital energy. In the bloom of adolescence the elements of feminine grace, suggested rather than expressed, are combined with virility to produce a perfection which is lacking to the mature and adult excellence of either sex. The Greek lover, if I am right in the idea which I have formed of him, sought less to stimulate desire by the contemplation of sensual charms than to attune his spirit with the spectacle of strength at rest in suavity. He admired the chastened lines, the figure slight but sinewy, the limbs well-knit and flexible, the small head set upon broad shoulders, the keen eyes, the austere reins, and the elastic movement of a youth made vigorous by exercise. Physical perfection of this kind suggested to his fancy all that he loved best in moral qualities. Hardihood, self-discipline, alertness of intelligence, health, temperance, indomitable spirit, energy, the joy of active life, plain living and high thinking—these qualities the Greeks idealised, and of these . . . "the lightning vision of the darling" was the living incarnation. There is plenty in their literature to show that paiderastia obtained sanction from the belief that a soul of this sort would be found within the body of a young man rather than a woman. I need scarcely add that none but a race of artists could be lovers of this sort, just as none but a race of poets were adequate to apprehend the chivalrous enthusiasm for women as an object of worship.

The morality of the Greeks, as I have tried elsewhere to prove, was æsthetic. They regarded humanity as a part of a good and beautiful universe, nor did they shrink from any of their normal instincts. To find the law of human energy, the measure of man's natural desires, the right moment for indulgence and for self-restraint, the balance which results in health, the proper limit for each several function which secures the harmony of all, seemed to them the aim of ethics. Their personal code of conduct ended in . . . "modest self-restraint": not abstention, but selection and subordination ruled their practice. They were satisfied with controlling much that more ascetic natures unconditionally suppress. Consequently, to the Greeks there was nothing at first sight criminal in paiderastia. To forbid it as a hateful and unclean thing did not occur to them. Finding it within their hearts, they chose to regulate it, rather than to root it out. It was only after the inconveniences and scandals to which paiderastia gave rise had been forced upon their notice, that they felt the visitings of conscience and wavered in their fearless attitude.

In like manner the religion of the Greeks was æsthetic. They analysed the world of objects and the soul of man, unconsciously perhaps, but effectively, and called their generalisations by the names of gods and goddesses. That these were beautiful and filled with human energy was enough to arouse in them the sentiments of worship. The notion of a single Deity who ruled the human race by punishment and favour, hat-

ing certain acts while he tolerated others—in other words, a God who idealised one part of man's nature to the exclusion of the rest—had never passed into the sphere of Greek conceptions. When, therefore, paiderastia became a fact of their consciousness, they reasoned thus: If man loves boys, God loves boys also. Homer and Hesiod forgot to tell us about Ganymede and Hyacinth and Hylas. Let these lads be added to the list of Danaë and Semele and Io. Homer told us that, because Ganymede was beautiful, Zeus made him the serving-boy of the immortals. We understand the meaning of that tale. Zeus loved him. The reason why he did not leave him here on earth like Danaë was that he could not beget sons upon his body and people the earth with heroes. Do not our wives stay at home and breed our children? Our . . . ". . . favourite youths" are always at our side.

Linda Dowling

SOURCE: "The Higher Sodomy," in *Hellenism and Homosexuality in Victorian Oxford*, Cornell University Press, 1994, pp. 117-54.

[*In the excerpt that follows, Dowling investigates the culture that prevailed at Oxford University in the late nineteenth century. She contends that a Greek or Hellenistic idea of aesthetics advocated by many of the school's leading scholars—most notably Benjamin Jowett—facilitated a more positive sense of homosexual desire among such prominent Oxford students as Wilde, Pater, and Symonds. She notes that other scholars, including Matthew Arnold, attempted to valorize the Greek aesthetics while purging them of sexuality.*]

As Wilde was to declare in *De Profundis,* one of the two great turning-points of his life occurred "when my father sent me to Oxford" (*The Letters of Oscar Wilde*). Everything he encountered there seems to have been charged with a palpitating vibrancy of signification—such that Wilde could not regard the Cumnor hills, for instance, without imagining Arnold's Scholar-Gipsy or consider the river Isis without seeing Socrates and Phaedrus beside the Illisus—an aura of implication which was only to intensify for him in later years. Arriving in Oxford in the autumn of 1874, at the very moment Pater's "Conclusion" was being denounced from the university pulpit of St. Mary's, Wilde took up this fatal book—the book, as he was so memorably to tell Lord Alfred Douglas from prison, "which has had such a strange influence over my life"—and committed to heart its intoxicating command to end the crucifixion of the senses and begin the renaissance of joy.

Yet the impact on Wilde of Mallock's [W.H.] *New Republic* (1877) as the unintended handbook of a new Oxford aestheticism was only slightly less intense. For Mallock's extraordinary succès de scandale—achieved (as was widely believed) when he was still an Oxford undergraduate—represented to Wilde precisely the image of his own ambitions after literary and social success, here stunningly realized as fact. Learning from Mallock that an Oxford undergraduate could become a significant figure in English cultural life by writing a witty and scandalous book, Wilde then grasps the possibility, to be so brilliantly realized in his own later works, of rewriting Mallock's *New Republic,* as it were, from the inside out—of portraying the English social and artistic world with all the elegant and cynical verve of a Robert Leslie.

It is in this sense that the distinguishing characteristics of the brilliant public personae deployed by Wilde in the world beyond Oxford during his later life and in his literary works would always be meant to invoke the imprimatur and sanction of the Oxford Greats school as precisely the most Oxonian and prestigious institution at Oxford. Greats, as Wilde himself declared, was "the only fine school at Oxford, the only sphere of thought where one can be, *simultaneously,* brilliant and unreasonable, speculative and well-informed, creative as well as critical, and write with all the passion of youth about the truths which belong to the august serenity of old age" (*More Letters of Oscar Wilde*). The flexible comprehension of opposing viewpoints, the full appreciation of the "play of ideas," and the fearless pursuit of all questions beyond any prematurely closed conclusions had been inculcated as a mental discipline under the liberal regime of [Benjamin] Jowett, [Mark] Pattison, and the tutors teaching under their influence. It is, in turn, just this "Oxford temper"—this power of insouciant, apparently effortless play with ideas—which Wilde, after suitably enlarging its antinomian dimension—was to erect as his imperious standard in all intellectual and artistic matters.[18]

This is why we are able to see Wilde's later personae, and that movement of free play which was so brilliantly to characterize the movement of his critical dialogues, already taking form in his Oxford notebooks. Keeping such a commonplace book was a recommended and standard practice for honors candidates preparing for the Greats exam. Wilde's notations are unusual, however, in the way they continually strive to translate the conceptual language of one author or thinker into the intellectual system of another—so Darwin is brought to bear on Hegel, and Plato is made to confront Herbert Spencer.[19] Here we see commencing in rough outline the process that would culminate in *Decay of Lying* and *Critic as Artist,* when Wilde was to translate the Platonic doctrine of Ideas into the theory of aesthetic ontology which would later have such far-reaching consequences for twentieth-century literature and criticism.

At any such moment as this, Wilde is not so much studying Greek dialectical thinking as actively engaging in it, enacting its logic of discursive conflict repeatedly on the page. This he does, in turn, with a consciousness of the erotic tension shaping the Greek dialectic from within—in such discussions, as Wilde observes, "we wrestle to embrace, and embrace to wrestle."[20] To read Wilde's notations on Greek thought or Athenian education is thus to be constantly aware of his own excited sense of discovery, to see in his cognition an emergent self-recognition of the same sort that overtook Symonds when he first read the *Phaedrus* and the *Symposium.* "Philosophein met' erōtos," Wilde writes in his commonplace book, using the phrase so central to Pater. "Philosophein met' erōtos!" exclaims the narrator of Wilde's *Portrait of Mr. W. H.,* "How that phrase had stirred me in my Oxford days!"

At the same time, it is clear how fully embedded these materials of the emergently homosexual legitimation strategy yet remain within the ideological matrix of Oxford liberalism. For even as Wilde meditates in the familiar Paterian cadences upon "the refinement of Greek culture coming through the romantic medium of impassioned friendships, the freedom and gladness of the palaestra" (*Notebooks*), his eye has been led to these embracing dyads of Greek wrestling or paiderastia by the diversity ideal of Victorian Hellenism. Flexibility, versatility, many-sidedness—all that had been enunciated so compellingly by Pericles in the Funeral Oration as to have become some twenty-three centuries later the central authorizing text for the liberalism of Jowett and Arnold, Grote and Mill—are now hailed familiarly in Wilde's notebook as "eutrapelia."

In this context as well even those passages from Wilde's maturer works which from a twentieth-century perspective seem so obviously engaged with modern forms of forbidden experience—as when Eve Sedgwick, for instance, associates Wilde's recurrent use of "curious" and "subtle" in *Dorian Gray* with drug experimentation (*Epistemology of the Closet, 1990*)—demand further to be seen deriving in direct terms from the Oxford liberal agenda of such writers as Arnold and Pater. For the literary genealogy of "curious," which Sedgwick reasonably enough traces back to Pater, does not begin there. Instead it passes quite beyond Pater to originate in specific terms with Arnold's *Function of Criticism* (1856),[22] and more generally in the urgent conviction among Victorian liberals that such new capacities as "curiosity," "individuality," and "diversity"—all Mill had meant when he called for "variety not uniformity"—quite simply demanded to be developed as the best hope for national survival amid the crisis of the new social and industrial modernity.

As we have already seen, the Greats school as it had been reshaped by Jowett and Pattison and the other university reformers represented the translation of exactly those theoretical arguments of Victorian liberalism into specific institutional terms. The great complaint about the reformed Literae humaniores school had always been that it taught very young men how to sound fluent and plausible on the basis of very little experience of thought—to "write with all the passion of youth," as we have heard Wilde say, "about the truths which belong to the august serenity of old age." This sort of showmanship, however, was precisely the mode in which Wilde himself, who was gifted with a sumptuous power of intellect as well as an extraordinary memory, could perform brilliantly. Even had he never worn an aggressively elegant coat cut like a violincello or attempted to live up to his blue china, Wilde would have been famous beyond Oxford for his Newdigate and his Double First. As it was, his First was widely known to have been the best of his year, and supremely confident to begin with, Wilde was to launch his overwhelming personality upon the world from the uttermost pinnacle of Oxford celebrity.

By the time Wilde had completed his Oxford experience, ready to step forth as the most fearlessly original—even eccentric[23]—Oxonian of his time, the categories of Greek thought and literature would have become structuring categories of his literary and social imagination. Saturated in the language and literature of ancient Greece, Wilde would repeatedly grasp his own life in the terms supplied by such ancient Greek forms as the life of Socrates or the plays of Aeschylus—which were ever to him a reality more compelling than the lurid implausibilities published in the daily newspapers. This is why, when his anxious friends watched in bewildered suspense as the nets of the prosecution closed around him just before his arrest for sodimic indecency, they sensed in Wilde's puzzling inaction the inevitability of a Greek dramatic destiny.[24] Or why when Wilde summoned himself in prison to write the *De Profundis* letter to Douglas, it was the story of the lion cub from Aeschylus's *Agammemnon* which determined his understanding of his own relationship with this unreflectingly ferocious young man, whose fury at his own father had so recklessly and utterly destroyed Wilde's life and art (*Letters*).

In this sense the conventions of Greek life—*paiderastia, symposia, dialektikē*—would assume the status of lived categories for Wilde, ostentatiously flourished by him on the level of public presentation as a sign of his high Hellenic culture and Oxford credentials, yet simultaneously experienced by him on the level of ordinary existence as elements scarcely more remarkable than air or wine. "Between his mind and mine," as the young Wilde reports to one Oxford friend about another, "there is no *intellectual friction to rouse me up to talk or think,* as I used with you" (*Letters*; Wilde's emphasis), and beneath all the patent flattery of such a remark, we glimpse the Socratic ideal of mental intercourse between male friends. "You are the only one I would tell about it," Wilde writes the same friend

concerning an episode of boy-worship he has chanced to witness, "as you have a philosophical mind," and in the word "philosophical" we hear the rich manifold of accents—ironical, historicist, liberal, etymological—which were comprehended in Oxford Hellenism.

In the same way, the conventions of Greek paiderastia as mediated through the Oxford Greats school would visibly shape such literary works as *The Portrait of Mr. W. H.* There, in a long excursus on what Wilde calls the "soul" of neo-Platonism—by which he means the Platonic identification between "intellectual enthusiasm and the physical passion of love"—he portrays the progress of this "soul" from Ficino to Shakespeare to the Romantics and beyond as the same metempsychosis of cultural renewal which Pater had once so suggestively traced: homoerotic friendship repeatedly becoming "a vital factor in the new culture, and a mode of self-conscious intellectual development."

The great significance of Dorian Gray's given name becomes, in turn, the way it implicitly summons, with an elegantly offhand gesture of allusion, the legitimating authority of K. O. Müller's *Dorians* and, beyond it, a world of learned historical *Wissenschaft*—that "solid bedrock of classical scholarship," as Paul Cartledge has called it [in "The Importance of Being Dorian," *Hermathena* (1989-90)], upon which Wilde's seemingly airy Hellenism ultimately rests. This submerged body of Hellenic implication continuously operates in concert with other more visible systems of signification, as when Lord Henry Wotton, for instance, meditates upon the deep satisfaction he gains from influencing Dorian. For even as Wotton invokes experimental science and artistic creation as models for the pleasure he feels, the underlying basis for his desire to "project one's soul into some gracious form, and let it tarry there for a moment; to hear one's own intellectual views echoed back to one with all the added music of passion and youth" (*The Picture of Dorian Gray*) always remains, as Cartledge has reminded us, precisely the erotic and pedagogical pleasure generated within the hearer/inspirer relationship of Dorian paiderastia. So, too, does Lord Henry's "low, musical voice" always remain that of the Socratic corruptor of youth.[25]

Even to glance at recent gender criticism on *Dorian Gray* or Symonds or the Uranian poets is to see how fully such late-Victorian invocations of Hellenism and ancient Greece have by now been understood as legitimating gestures on behalf of "homosexuality," an appeal, as Sedgwick has justly characterized it, "to the virilizing authority of the Greeks" (*Between Men*, 1985). Yet such late-Victorian allusions to "Greek love" or Plato or Dorianism are further to be understood, on this account, as functioning within an ideological economy of repression, displacement, and resistance—Foucault's discarded law and sovereignty model of power here making its silent reappearance—by which reprobated ideas or expressions are suppressed outright or translated into forms that are the least intolerable to the socially dominant orders or, yet again, boldly redeployed against the prohibiting power itself.

In recent years, this critical approach has supplied a predictable interpretive context in which Wilde's failure in *Mr. W. H.* or *Dorian Gray,* for instance, to *name* the "love that dare not speak its name" as "homosexuality" or "inversion" or some other name will always be found to constitute either the sign of his ideological erasure from a dominant discourse that denies public forms of expression to male love or, alternatively, the sign of his opposition to that very discourse, the play of indeterminate or deferred naming in *Mr. W. H.,* for instance, constituting in Lawrence Danson's view "a necessary act of resistance" ["Oscar Wilde, Mr. W. H. and the Unspoken Name of Love," *ELH* (1991)]. Yet not to see that Wilde's very lack of specificity may itself constitute an aesthetic choice wholly independent of the mechanics of repression and resistance is to make the mistake of reductionism—as if Basil Hallward, to take one salient instance, employs such a phrase as "the visible incarnation of that unseen ideal that haunts us artists like an exquisite dream" simply because he somehow lacks a language of properly "homosexual" denotation.

By contrast, only when we reembed such phrases as Hallward's in their originary context of Oxford Hellenism is their genuine expressiveness thrust into view. For Hallward's phrase in this case marks a double allusion to Greek culture by treating the Platonic doctrine of eros as if it were operating according to the Platonic doctrine of reminiscence (*anamnēsis*)—homoerotic friendship as a remembered dream, "as though in some antenatal experience I had lived the life of a philosophical Greek lover," which had proved, as we have seen, so moving to Pater and Symonds alike. In the same way, such suggestive phrases of Lord Henry Wotton's as "the Hellenic ideal" or "the aim of life is self-development" become fully intelligible only when they are understood—not as evasions or euphemisms—but as perfectly expressive, in their unspecific amplitude of implication, of precisely that imaginative richness, that many-sidedness and "variety" so central to the sociocultural agenda of Victorian Hellenism.

This is not to say that certain homosexual apologists did not feel the contemporary limits on homoerotic expressiveness as a heavy further penalty. For indeed nothing more clearly represents this sense of expressive constraint, perhaps, than the case of Symonds. Even after his removal with his wife and daughters to Switzerland—far from either the disapprobations of Mrs. Grundy or the depredations of those professional blackmailers ("renters") whose career paths had been opened by the 1885 Criminal Law Amendment Act

later to be used to prosecute Wilde—Symonds chafed under these iron constraints as if they were, in the words of Lord Alfred Douglas's memorial tribute to him, "chains on the limbs of lovers and burdens on the wings of poets" (Timothy· d'Arch Smith *Love in Earnest,* 1970).[26]

At the same time, the problem posed by Symonds in this context demands to be understood as less a problem in expressive prohibition than one of excess expressive capacity. In fact, Symonds's sharpest sense of constraint arises only when he himself rejects the very language of the Platonic eros which had once served him as a medium of homoerotic self-revelation. For as Symonds establishes long-term and fully sexual relationships with working-class men outside of England in the 1880s, he begins to regard the nongenital or nonphysical eroticism of the Platonic doctrine of eros with a deepening mistrust. It is then that a Platonic love denying or devaluing or indefinitely deferring all genital release[27] becomes for him "a deeply rooted mysticism, an impenetrable Soofyism" ("Dantesque")—an iridescent web or maze into which such susceptible young men as himself had been led until they found themselves utterly lost. "It is a delusion to imagine," as Symonds declared in the 1890 essay that represents nothing less than his farewell to Platonic love, "that the human spirit is led to discover divine truths by amorous enthusiasm for a fellow-creature, however refined that impulse may be."

With this realization, Symonds comes to a bitter new assessment of his old teacher Jowett, as though Jowett's Socratic "corruption" had somehow consisted in tempting suggestible young men down the delusive path to spiritual procreancy rather than fleshly excess. Writing from Davos in 1889, Symonds confronts his old tutor across a crevass of ancient and mutual misunderstanding into which the bitter sufferings of thirty years now pour. When young men in whom the homoerotic passion is innate come into contact with the writings of Plato, as Symonds now tells Jowett, "they discover that what they had been blindly groping after was once an admitted possibility—not in a mean hole or corner—but that the race whose literature forms the basis of their higher culture, lived in that way, aspired in that way. . . . derived courage, drew intellectual illumination, took their first step in the path which led to great achievements and the arduous pursuit of truth." Symonds is making explicit here his sense of the cruel pedagogical contradiction within Oxford Hellenism which had harried him for so many years—his instruction in Platonic thought by the same teachers of Hellenism who denounced erotic relations between men as "unnatural": "those very men who condemn him, have placed the most electrical literature of the world in his hands, pregnant with the stuff that damns him."

Such a young man has learned the lesson of Oxford Hellenism only too well, trained to regard Plato as *"the greatest uninspired writing,"* as if it were indeed the surrogate scripture that can save him from an outworn Christian orthodoxy now imploding from the combined effects of superstition and science. Such a student now reads his *Symposium* or his *Phaedrus,* Symonds tells Jowett, "as you would wish him to read his Bible—i.e. with a vivid conviction that what he reads is the life-record of a masterful creative man-determining race, and the monument of a world-important epoch." Yet what in the end has been the result of all this deeply engaged, brilliantly historicist education? A class of perversely susceptible young men have been "injured" and "incriminated," raised up helplessly as victims to a Victorian Hellenism that works "by ensnaring the noblest part of them—their intellectual imagination."

No wonder Symonds in concluding *A Problem in Modern Ethics* (1891), the last of the homosexualist apologias he was to have printed during his lifetime, should suggest that those who insist on punishing homosexuals at law would do better instead to "turn their attention to the higher education" being carried on in English public schools and universities. For it was just there that the "best minds of our youth are . . . exposed to the influences of a paederastic literature at the same time that they acquire the knowledge and experience of unnatural practices."

Nor is it strange that Symonds, upon learning that Jowett lay gravely ill, should experience "the deepest strangest dreams of him," in which the Master of Balliol "came to me, and was quite glorified, and spoke to me so sweetly and kindly—as though he understood some ancient wrong he had not fathomed in me before." Jowett had known of Symonds's sexual "inversion" ever since the Shorting scandal in the early 1860s. Symonds's sense of an "ancient wrong" between them must therefore be understood to represent his desire that his own miseducation at Jowett's hands be at last acknowledged and righted—Jowett, the translator of Plato who had for so long denied what Symonds had come to know as a burning truth, that "Greek love was for Plato"—and much more painfully, "for modern students of Plato" not a mere figure of speech but nothing less than "a present poignant reality."

To glimpse Symonds in these last years, then, is to see him struggling to free himself and the English Uranians from one half of the inheritance of Oxford Hellenism while retaining the other half of its powerful ideological support. Attempting to discard the crippling sexual sublimations of the Platonic eros, Symonds fights at the same time to preserve the ideal of Dorian comradeship first discovered in K. O. Müller's *Dorians,* the ideal that so powerfully contested the ancient slur of "effeminacy" invariably raised in England and

America against men who loved men. Dorian comradeship, especially as this ideal had been unconsciously but completely realized by Whitman in the "Calamus" poems of *Leaves of Grass,* could strengthen the foundation, as Symonds believed, upon which "to regenerate political life and to cement nations" (*Walt Whitman: A Study,* 1893), by imparting to the amorphous old dreams of democratic "fraternity" a new basis in men's bodily experience.

The more immediate significance of Greek comradeship to Symonds, however, is its tremendous force as a counterweight to contemporary medical and psychiatric opinion. For by the early 1890s Symonds realizes that through a peculiar discursive irony, masculine love is in danger of being imprisoned by what once had seemed to be the means of its own liberation: the medical "science" Symonds had hoped to use to legitimate male love was in fact working to consign it to the category of disease. Such terms as "inverted sexual instinct" or "homosexuality" or "male sexual morbidity," for all their useful neutrality, possessed their own autonomous discursive life, projecting new theoretical models of pathology and abnormality which would become, as Symonds now recognizes, no less crippling for the individual lives formulated within them than the religious and social models of sin and vice currently being repudiated by "science." The theory of morbidity is "more humane," Symonds declares, "but it is not less false, than that of sin or vice" (*Letters*).[28]

Against this solidifying consensus of the "so-called scientific 'psychiatrists'," Symonds now urgently asserts that the historical study of ancient Greece could prove "absolutely essential to the psychological treatment of the subject" because it would confront the investigators of sexual "abnormality" with the inescapable historical evidence of precisely the broad and sane and socially enriching *normality* of Greek comradeship. Such psychiatrists fatally err, Symonds tells Havelock Ellis in 1892 when seeking him as a collaborator on the book that would become *Sexual Inversion,* "by diagnosing as necessarily morbid what was the leading emotion of the best and noblest men in Hellas." "Casper-Liman, Tardieu, Carlier, Taxil, Moreau, Tarnowsky, Krafft-Ebing"—the massive ignorance of all these men, Symonds insists, "is only equalled to their presumption. They not only do not know Ancient Greece, but they do not know their own cousins and club-mates."

Yet Symonds knows he cannot effectively intervene in the scientific discourse without the discursive permission of the scientists themselves—"Alone," as he tells his Uranian friend Edward Carpenter, "I could make but little effect—the effect of an eccentric." He needs "somebody of medical importance to collaborate with"—and Havelock Ellis possesses an M.D. It is, however, precisely in his capacity *as* medical "scientist" that Ellis would in the end redirect the emphasis of *Sexual Inversion* away from Symonds's historical dimension centered in the Greeks and toward the pole of neuropathy and morbidity and "science." The 1883 essay on Greek ethics which had constituted so momentous a step in Symonds's career as a homosexual apologist he now urged Ellis to install as the central core of their collaborative project. But driven first by the discursive momentum of "science" and later by the maelstrom of the Wilde catastrophe, Symonds's Greek essay would be pushed to the margins of *Sexual Inversion*—appearing as chapter 3 in the German translation (1896), as an appendix of the first English edition (1897), and in the second edition disappearing without a trace.

We tend today, almost inevitably, to interpret Symonds's struggle to develop a persuasive language of homosexual legitimation in light of the event we know is to come, the tragedy of Oscar Wilde. Yet in the cultural moment before the Wilde disaster there was no implication of an impending doom, only the gradual emergence into visibility of a new system of values and attitudes, associated with a variety of movements in art and society, having in common their relation to the inchoate counterdiscourse of "homosexuality." This is the moment in which "homosexuality" in the modern sense begins to be visible as such: the activities of a reprobated but largely invisible minority, given publicity by such scandals as the 1889 Cleveland Street affair, are at the same time being given positive status in various legitimated modes of action and expression. In the aesthetically charged atmosphere of the earlier 1890s the criminal homosexual subculture, with its houses of assignation, its cruising grounds in Leicester Square and Piccadilly,[29] and the "renters" whose activity had only been stimulated by the Criminal Law Amendment Act of 1885, are swept up in the momentum of a larger social and artistic movement that was, under Wilde's leadership, so energetically taking over the language of French avant-gardism to realize Pater's goal of cultural renaissance.

This is why, from a twentieth-century perspective, the Yellow Nineties, lasting as a cultural epoch a mere five years, has always seemed so pronouncedly a moment in which the distinctions between dominated and dominant sexual cultures, especially among the young—and "nobody," as Graham Robertson said [in *Life was Worth Living,* 1931] "was very old in the early 'nineties"—have blurred in a great onrush of aesthetic and social innovation. So it would happen, for instance, that the first-night audience at Wilde's *Lady Windermere's Fan* could include a score or more young men displaying green-carnation boutonnieres while totally unaware that the mystic green blossom had become the emblem of French homosexuals. Similarly, the young French poet Pierre Louÿs, writing home about his visits to the new English "school" gathered around

Wilde, seems to be expressing a characteristic fin de siècle delight in the sexually transgressive when he reports that "These young people are most charming. . . . You cannot imagine the elegance of their manners. . . . the first day I was introduced to them, X, to whom I had just been presented, offered me a cigarette; but, instead of simply offering it as we do, he began by lighting it himself and not handing it over until after he had taken the first drag. Isn't that exquisite?" (Jerusha Hull McCormack *John Gray,* 1991).

Here we encounter the Victorian fin de siècle which so much contemporary writing about homosexuality has wanted to see as a privileged world of momentarily permeable sexual categories, where Wilde can safely consort with his male prostitutes at public restaurants, even as such "cultural inverts" as John Gray, Max Beerbohm, Ernest Dowson—men uninterested in masculine love as a sexual outlet yet drawn to the ethos of its subculture—can safely, or with a lack of safety less dangerous than merely stimulating—consort with Wilde himself. Yet as John Stokes [*In the Nineties,* 1989] has recently made clear, the truth remains that this view of the 1890s is a modern construction, a myth produced in our own cultural moment and made persuasive only as it succeeds in projecting an as-yet-unthought-of polarization of "homosexual" versus "heterosexual"— Barthes's "binary prison" in its newest guise—backward upon an indeterminate welter of late-Victorian psychosocial categories. And the reason we now so readily impose our own categories on fin de siècle culture is not far to seek. For these dimensions of late-Victorian erotic experience—"ego-mania" and "zooerast" and "urolagnia" quite as much as "Urning" and "Uranian" and "inversion"—are precisely what so abruptly vanish in what Sedgwick has memorably called the "sudden, radical condensation of sexual categories" (*Epistemology*) which was to be precipitated by the Wilde catastrophe.

By the early twentieth century, such fossils of pre-Wildean Victorian discourse as "invert" and "zooerast" would thus seem merely incoherent or, in light of the growing influence of Freudian theory, crudely prescientific. Thus the genuine richness and complexity of late-Victorian psychocultural experience, that world of vanished categories to which George Chauncey ["From Sexual Inversion to Homosexuality," *Salmagundi* (1982-83)] has recently recalled our attention, becomes once again intelligible only when we gaze upon it in the moment before its condensation into any modern opposition between "homosexual" and "heterosexual." For it was only a counterdiscourse comprised as much of "male adhesiveness" and "Uranianism" as of "homosexuality" which had been able, given the exigencies of the cultural moment, to enter seamlessly into such late-Victorian formations as "the new" and "the artistic" and "the perverse," assuming, in Foucauldian terms, a thickening depth of discursivity.

Here may be glimpsed the roots of the modern homosexual identity, for during just this period the notion of Greek paiderastia made so vivid by Oxford Hellenism persuaded many late-Victorian "inverts" that the homoerotic emotions they themselves had felt in fearful isolation or confused disgust might instead belong to human experience in its fullest historicity and cultural density. And here we may begin to understand why, as well, it would become so crucial that the earlier tradition of Uranian love, now being eclipsed by a more generalized fin de siècle avant-gardism, had undertaken to deploy against the notion of a merely carnal homoeroticism certain ideals of undiseased psychological complexity and noble emotionality in male love.

Before these ideals would once again become available to "homosexuality" as a positive social identity, however, the Uranian modality of male love would be rejected by the avant-garde itself as an outworn fashion. This is the paradox: even as its ideals of spiritual procreancy and nongenital eroticism went on silently expanding the dimensions of intentionality and inwardness necessary to constitute "homosexuality" as a positive social identity, the Uranian ideal could in the early years of the twentieth century be contemptuously dismissed by such influential voices as that of Lytton Strachey as nothing more than a weak attempt to deny that physical desire now pronounced by Freud and others to be universal and all pervasive—as, in short, nothing more than "the higher sodomy."

In this sense Lionel Johnson's angry reaction to Symonds's call for a frankly genital view of male love—Johnson declaring Symonds "an absolute Priapus" (Ian Fletcher "Decadence and the Little Magazines," *Decadence and the 1890s,* 1979), or André Raffalovich's searching condemnation of Wilde in *Uranisme et unisexualité* (1896)—may be said to constitute events in the prehistory of "homosexuality" rather than mere occurrences in late-Victorian literary relations. The problem posed by such a remark as Johnson's, we might ordinarily say, is its disabling degree of self-hatred and its hypocrisy masquerading as moral criticism. Yet not to understand that Johnson is writing from within the Oxford tradition of pederastic Hellenism is to make the mistake of regarding his phrase "an absolute Priapus" as a simple expression of phobic detestation for the male body and the genital sexuality which Symonds himself regarded as "the central reality of human life" (*Whitman*). Instead, nothing more clearly illustrates the enriching complexity of these late-Victorian homoerotic and homosocial filiations, perhaps, than the moment in which Johnson of New College, Oxford, dismisses Symonds of Balliol or, again, applauds and then denounces Wilde of Magdalen—for Johnson's Latin poem praising the "creator" of Dorian Gray (1891) was soon followed by his searing poetic rebuke to Wilde as "To the Destroyer of a Soul" (1892).

To grasp the all but obliterated contextual situation out of which a poet such as Johnson writes is thus to locate him not simply within that rising generation of Oxford undergraduates—of Lord Alfred Douglas, Charles Sayle, Theodore Wratislaw, and J. F. Bloxam—whose contributions to such Uranian publications as *The Spirit Lamp, The Artist,* and *The Chameleon* seem so obviously to confirm Symonds's own sense of these young men as his successors in the struggle to legitimate masculine love. Nor is it to place Johnson within that still more famous and tragic generation of Rhymers' Club poets which Yeats was so sumptuously to enamber in literary myth. It is rather to situate him at the conjunction of both these formations precisely as they engage Oxford Hellenism, with its traditions of Tractarian friendship, Socratic education, spiritual procreancy, and cultural renewal.

This is in turn why Johnson can both praise Wilde in a witty Latin poem for the "sweet sins" of Greek love portrayed in *Dorian Gray* and yet execrate him so bitterly in another poem a few months later as the "destroyer" of Lord Alfred Douglas's soul: "Call you this thing my friend? this nameless thing? / This living body, hiding its dead soul?"[30] For the sustaining tradition of Oxford Hellenism within which Johnson is working both approves the spiritual procreancy represented by any such creator of fictions as Wilde and at the same time reprobates the failure of an erotic teacher such as Wilde genuinely to educate his beloved friend. Whatever his own feelings toward these two men may have been, Johnson is using the language of the Uranian ideal to condemn the betrayer of that ideal. For Wilde in his relation to Douglas has become in Johnson's eyes something hideously akin to Socrates' "nonlover" of *Phaedrus* 239—a man to whom the "defects of mind and more in the beloved are bound to be a source of pleasure . . . if they do not exist already as innate qualities, he will cultivate them." Here we see that Johnson, with the line "This living body, hiding its dead soul," is implicitly comparing his friend's changed nature to Dorian Gray's unapparent yet radical inward ruin. For Johnson's larger point will always be that the real perversion involved here has little to do with the outward physical transactions of male love: the destruction of his friend has come instead through the sodomic evacuation of the soul from the body.

The great significance of Johnson's work as a Uranian poet thus becomes his attempt to defend the older tradition of pederastic Hellenism in the face of the newer sexual realism in male love being asserted in the earlier 1890s by such writers as Symonds and Wratislaw and indeed by Douglas himself. This is why Pater had come to represent such a hero to Johnson, who hails his part in inspiring the new culture in a memorial poem to Pater which employs all Pater's own exquisite etymological care for words:

Momentous things he prized, gradual and fair,
　　Births of passionate air:

　　　　. . . . .

Some delicate dawning of a new desire,
　　Distilling fragrant fire
On hearts of men prophetically fain
　　To feel earth young again:

Pater is so eminently "Worthy Uranian song," as Johnson says, because the "births of passionate air" he prized are precisely the art and thought born of the spiritual procreancy of male love—"momentous" in arising *in* a moment and "simply *for* those moments' sake," as Pater himself had so unforgettably said in the "Conclusion" to *The Renaissance,* but "momentous" as well in their far-reaching significance for culture. At the same time, there runs through Johnson's poem the wistful, valedictory note of a larger farewell. For by the time of Pater's death in 1894 it was already becoming clear to Johnson just how impotent Oxford Hellenism might prove in any contest that pitted Oxford Greats culture against the clamorous sensuality of an urban modernity—against "these surging cries, / This restless glare!" as he says in his poem "Plato in London."

There is no question that Pater himself had sensed this shift in the aesthetic and erotic atmosphere. In the last story he published before he died—"Apollo in Picardy"—for instance, Pater traces with an extraordinary subtlety of reference the doubtful fate of the Uranian love that had been bred out of Oxford Hellenism. Re-creating the fictional situation Symonds had depicted when he wrote his allegory of Jowett's Oxford in *Gabriel,* Pater describes in "Apollo in Picardy" a small community of monks, "creatures of rule" whose severe life is transformed by the arrival of a handsome, pagan stranger whom they decide to call Apollyon. Commentators on Pater's fiction have from the first pointed to the homoerotic dimension of Apollyon's relationship with the young novice Hyacinth, for the youth's accidental death occurs in exactly the same manner as that of his famous Greek namesake—while playing quoits with his lover Apollo.

Yet this obvious parallel with the classical myth of Hyacinthus represents merely the superficial aspect of the homoerotic tradition Pater is drawing upon here. For when he says that in meeting Apollo/Apollyon both Hyacinth and the prior "come in contact for the first time in their lives with the power of untutored natural impulse, of natural inspiration," Pater means that both men engage with Greek culture under its homoerotic aspect—the word "natural" having by now come to signify "Greek" as automatically in the Oxford tradition of pederastic Hellenism as "inspiration" signifies the "hearer/inspirer" relationship of Greek paiderastia.

Walter Pater.

This ancient pederastic ethos explains why Hyacinth is able to assume all the physical grace and "immense gaiety" of Greek athletes when Apollyon teaches him wrestling and archery. Nonetheless, it is the older monk, the prior Saint-Jean—so often dismissed in modern Pater criticism as a repressed or maddened or even "homophobic" figure—who is even more deeply transformed by the pagan erotic energies flowing out of Apollo/Apollyon.

Here we glimpse the great significance of the pedagogical scene between the prior and Apollyon. For it is the ostensible teacher—the prior—who is in fact taught or inspired "at the contact of this extraordinary pupil or fellow-inquirer." In this moment the prior's relationship to his own knowledge is totally transformed: now he comprehends the old dry facts as living totalities, grasps the previously unimaginable as simple actuality, passing from a conventionally Ptolemaic view of the cosmos to a new vision of "the earth . . . moving round the sun."[31] His mind illuminated by "this beam of insight, or of inspiration!" the prior turns to write the last volume of his twelve-volume treatise on mathematics. Diverging radically from the earlier volumes, the argument of the new book is convulsed "as with the throes of childbirth," its pages fill with "line and figure bending, breathing, flaming, into lovely 'arrangements'" until the prior is declared mad by his monkish colleagues, and he breaks off the work to die.

It is precisely here that Pater shows Uranian love menaced by cruel incomprehension—as when the monks mistake the prior's homoerotic possession by Apollo/Apollyon for ordinary madness, or when the officers of justice mistake the outcome of Apollo/Apollyon's own homoerotic *mania*—the accidental death of Hyacinth—for the result of what they suppose to have been a "fit of mania" in the prior. In such misprisions as these Pater allows us to see his larger fears for homoerotic Hellenism. Quite simply, everything about what Socrates had called in the *Phaedrus* erotic "madness" (*mania*)—"the best of all forms of divine possession"—has been misunderstood in this monkish and unimpassioned world so like Oxford's own: Apollo is mistaken for Apollyon, the angel of the bottomless, sodomic pit; a dream of soft wintry auroras—"a low circlet of soundless flame, waving, licking daintily up the black sky, but harmless, beautiful"—is misinterpreted by the prior himself as "hell-fire!"; the prior's childbirth-like throes of intellectual, spiritual procreancy—those "births of passionate air"—are taken by his fellow monks for the convulsions of a diseased mind; and all the stir and ferment of genuine cultural renewal in medieval Picardy—the barn architecture changing from Gothic to neoclassical, the Gregorian chants "turned to real silvery music"—are dismissed as mere excesses owing to the winter solstice. This is doubtless why the silently flaming auroras that so continually reappear in "Apollo in Picardy" upon the prior's page as in the night sky, and foretell precisely what Lionel Johnson would call "Some delicate dawning of a new desire" about to be kindled in culture and the individual life by the ardent flame of the Platonic eros, are instead so repeatedly mistaken both within the story by Pater's characters and beyond the story by Pater's critics.[32]

All the painful burden of Pater's own experience at Oxford thus presses into view here—the intoxicating education, the fiery friendships, the hopes for cultural regeneration and a more liberal way of life, followed by the cold incomprehension, the hatred, the stony exile. Pater had made a celebrated career out of simultaneously uncovering and reveiling the homoerotic text within the cultural ideal of Victorian liberalism. Driven by scandal and satire at Oxford into a self-protective posture of covert resistance, "Mr. Rose" had had to begin again, in the beautiful, laborious historical fiction of *Marius the Epicurean* (1885), to attempt to vindicate himself and express the case for the cultural power of male love through all the elegant indirections of aesthetic humanism. Yet as this late story and some of his scattered remarks in the collected Oxford lectures known as *Plato and Platonism* (1893) repeatedly suggest, Pater never ceased to realize that the danger to

homoerotic Hellenism might in fact come not from the predictably uncomprehending barbarians alone but also from the Greeks themselves: Socrates' teaching had been corrupted by Alcibiades, his own had been mistaken by Wilde.[33]

When the Wilde scandal first erupted in March of 1895, Pater had been dead less than a year, Symonds less than two. The scandal, with its sordid arrests, trials, testimony, and incarcerations, assured that the hopes Pater and Symonds had once cherished for male love as the agent of personal and cultural transformation—for that "delicate dawning of a new desire"—were eclipsed in the ensuing controversy, completely overwhelmed by an extraordinary, lurid publicity. In this moment of March 1895 all the expanded scope Symonds had so cautiously, Pater so covertly, and Wilde so carelessly endeavored to win for homoerotic imagination and experience would seemingly vanish overnight. Yet even as it vanished, the apparent mechanism of its repression—the Victorian state apparatus of police and courts and prisons—would simultaneously be operating, as Foucault has taught us to understand, as a steady incitement to speech, the prosecution of the "love that dare not speak its name" impelling more people to speak more garrulously than ever before of this new thing now to be known as "homosexuality."

From the first moments of the scandal, Wilde was engulfed in a maelstrom of competing and meretricious fictions. Lord Alfred Douglas, Douglas's father the marquis of Queensberry, the lawyers, the newspapers—all the official and unofficial participants in the first trial sought to manipulate the available languages of legitimation to vindicate themselves and destroy their opponents. Queensberry, a poisonous atheist, debauché, and bully, fought to appear before the British public, as Wilde himself realized, "in an entirely new character, that of the affectionate father . . . a champion of purity," even as he transformed his son into "the good young man who was very nearly tempted into wrong-doing by the wicked and immoral artist, but was rescued just in time" (*Letters*). This ludicrously untrue yet deeply satisfying fiction would take on an autonomous life, becoming the version, as Wilde was to protest in *De Profundis,* that "has now actually passed into serious history: it is quoted, believed, and chronicled" (*Letters*).

When Wilde in turn was arrested and charged with gross indecency in the second trial, Queensberry's role as the defender of the innocent youth and the public interest was taken up by the Crown prosecutor, who sought to safeguard society . . . from a sodomic sore upon the body politic "which cannot fail in time to corrupt and taint it all." In Wilde's third trial, the prosecutor would marshal a still richer rhetorical display of invective, so effective a set of forensic fictions—"like a thing out of Tacitus, like a passage in Dante, like one of Savanarola's indictments of the Popes at Rome"—as to convince even Wilde himself, who would remember "being sickened with horror at what I heard."

On trial for his life—"All trials," as he was to declare in *De Profundis,* "are trials for one's life"—Wilde, with the masterful peroration we have heard him pronounce, would call upon the language of Oxford Hellenism to contest and disarm the enormous residual power of the ideological traditions so massively marshaled against him. Charged with corrupting youth, Wilde invokes Plato's pedagogic eros. Confronted with the sordid evidence of sodomic indecency, he appeals to a "pure" procreancy of the spirit. Condemned as effeminate and degenerate, he shows the intellectual fearlessness and commanding flexibility of mind so celebrated in Victorian liberal Hellenism as the only vitally regenerative powers still capable of saving England.

In the brief moment remade by his overwhelming personality, when the profound silence of the Old Bailey courtroom is broken by loud applause, Wilde thus realizes in his own person all that Symonds had ever said about the revelation of reading Plato—he reveals masculine love as dwelling "not in a mean hole or corner" but at the very heart of "the race whose literature forms the basis of [our] higher culture." When Wilde speaks, the discourse of Oxford Hellenism speaks through him, and in this dire moment of its compelling authority claims in the name of an undeformed humanity a hearing for a masculine procreancy to which culture itself owes an inextinguishable debt.

Yet the full measure of Wilde's achievement in the witness box finally becomes clear only when we read his meditation on his own life in *De Profundis* and realize how much he had despised Douglas's vapid phrase about "the love that dare not speak its name." For as Wilde realized, Douglas had indolently borrowed the notion of "two loves" for his poem of the same title from the Platonic doctrine of the Uranian and Pandemic eros—where its subtle axis is poised between a telos of intellectual aspiration and a telos of physical appetite. Douglas then transferred the notion of "two loves" to a banal new polarity organized around sexual object choice—of "true Love," as Douglas says, filling the "hearts of boy and girl with mutual flame" (*"Two Loves"*) versus an antagonistic "Love that dares not tell its name," as Wilde would slightingly misquote the line (*Letters*). When Douglas's poem is cited in court as evidence of a spreading sexual indecency at Oxford and elsewhere, Wilde, loyal to him even in this extremity, summons himself to defend Douglas's lame verse. Speaking his mighty peroration, Wilde briefly embodies the power of a mind saturated in Greek thought and Oxford Hellenism to stave off the invading horror, to overcome another man's intellectual in-

dolence and imaginative vulgarity, and to transfigure even vapidity into something eloquent and fine.

As Richard Ellmann's magisterial biography has made clear, the categories of Hellenic thought and experience which had so deeply informed Wilde's experience at Oxford—intensifying his pleasure, as we have heard him say, in *"intellectual friction to rouse me up to talk or think"*—never released their hold upon him. When some years after going down from Oxford, he was first seduced into homosexual practices by Robert Ross, Wilde understood their intercourse as proceeding along the Platonic ladder of love, passing from pandemic physical delight to Uranian intellectual friendship. With Ross, the Platonic ideal of an erotic procreancy of the spirit generating thought and art, as well as the frank Greek practice of "embracing to wrestle and wrestling to embrace," seemed to issue in a perfect fulfillment of Hellenism, for it was out of his conversation with Ross that Wilde achieved the ideas for both *Mr. W. H.* and *The Decay of Lying.*[34]

In the same way, the beauty and homage of younger men genuinely inspired Wilde, as when admiring groups of undergraduates at Oxford or Cambridge would call upon him for "Early Church" or some other of his *contes parlés*—"bright young faces, and grey misty quadrangles, Greek forms passing through Gothic cloisters" (*Letters*). Roused within the radiant circle of their admiration, Wilde would then begin to weave one of his entrancing verbal arabesques. Even Wilde's frankly commercial relations with male prostitutes were conducted within the transforming frame of the Socratic eros. Frank Harris's wonderful tale of finding Wilde at the Café Royal discoursing on the Olympic Games with two Cockney youths of dubious aspect— "talking as well as if he had had a picked audience"— achieves, for all its improbability, the deeper truth of fiction: "'Did you sy they was niked?' 'Of course,' Oscar replied, 'nude, clothed only in sunshine and beauty.'"

The full dimensions of his own catastrophe would become apparent to Wilde only as he wrote *De Profundis* during the final months of his prison term. For it was then, as the world he had lost yet remained intact to him—preserved in suspended animation by memory, and undiminished by the sordid world of social extinction, penury, and sickness which would rise around him once he was released—that Wilde was able to see his life with Alfred Douglas in its true relation to the ideal of Greek love. Cut off from the outside world, he writes his long letter to Douglas through a power of inertial momentum, drawing on the deep reserves of memory and imagination laid down in him by his Oxford experience: no other work of Wilde's, as Richard Jenkyns [*The Victorians and Ancient Greece,* 1980] has reminded us, is so full of Greek echoes and quotations as *De Profundis.* With his acute suffering in prison now illuminating his own earlier suffering at Douglas's hands—misery once all but invisible to him in the blaze of the younger man's beauty and his own triumphant success—*De Profundis* becomes in this context a moral epistle or essay on male friendship in the classical tradition of Cicero's *De Amicitia* or Aristotle's *Politics*.[35]

Beyond the very real likelihood that Wilde was convicted, as Ellmann has argued, for sexual acts Douglas had actually committed,[36] Wilde's overriding concern in the letter has little to do with sexual acts, which he regarded as trivial—"Sins of the flesh are nothing" (*Letters*). It is only as Douglas's own relentless interest in buggering boys approached "appetite without distinction" "desire without limit," only as his obsessive talk about boys and buggery drove out everything else, that Wilde recognized that the younger man's appetite for "the mire" had become a genuinely shameful "sin of the soul." As Wilde tells Douglas, "It was only in the mire that we met, and fascinating, terribly fascinating though the one topic round which your talk invariably centred was, still at the end it became quite monotonous I was often bored to death by it."

For Wilde, the great and salient fact about their love thus becomes that "during the whole time we were together I never wrote one single line. Whether at Torquay, Goring, London, Florence or elsewhere, my life, as long as you were by my side, was entirely sterile and uncreative." Here is the unmistakable language of the Platonic eros and spiritual procreancy, the native idiom of the high ideal which Wilde once believed, with the *anamnēsis* of the Oxford homoerotic imagination, had been miraculously reincarnated in Douglas, the Greek and gracious boy whom he so repeatedly hailed as "Hyacinth" and "Hylas" and "Narcissus." In *De Profundis* Wilde's genuine lovers, by contrast, are seen to have been such younger men as Robbie Ross, with whom Wilde shared both literary and sexual secrets, or Pierre Louÿs and John Gray, with whom he shared his art and probably nothing more: "My real life, my higher life was with them and such as they" (*Letters*).

As the corrupting instructor of Dorian Gray, Lord Henry Wotton represented, Wilde knew, all that the world imagined Wilde to be in his relation to Douglas. Yet the grotesque truth of their actual relationship would always remain that the "corruption" and fatal influence of "personality" had in fact worked all the other way. It was not Wilde who had ruined the younger man.[37] It was instead the younger man who had ruined Wilde with "an unintellectual friendship, a friendship whose primary aim was not the creation and contemplation of beautiful things," a bond "intellectually degrading to me," destroying the conditions for his art, and insisting upon the ruinous suit against Queensberry which had made public such evidence that the authorities could not in the end avoid prosecuting Wilde.[38]

The most damning of the evidentiary texts used to prosecute Wilde was a letter of fantastic literary conceits ("I know Hyacinthus, whom Apollo loved so madly, was you in Greek days"), a letter that could "only be understood," as he now says to Douglas, "by those who have read the *Symposium* of Plato, or caught the spirit of a certain grave mood made beautiful for us in Greek marbles." Its Uranian phrases caught from the Greats tradition, and gilded by Wilde's extravagant wit, such a letter was a Uranian eulogy to youthful beauty and promise which Wilde would have written "to any graceful young man of either University who had sent me a poem of his own making, certain that he would have sufficient wit or culture to interpret rightly its fantastic phrases." Carelessly misplaced by Douglas, and later stolen by one of Douglas' male sex partners, the letter entered the economy of extortion, of "renters" and blackmail victims and police, where it circulated as "an infamous letter," and "every construction but the right one is put on it," Douglas using it to taunt his dangerously inflammable father. So in the end the inescapable irony would always be not that the prosecutors or the respectable Victorian public could not understand what Wilde meant by a "pure" Platonic love or a "higher life" of spiritual procreancy, but that the Oxford Hyacinthus, Douglas himself, could not. "You had not yet been able to acquire," as Wilde now told him, "the 'Oxford temper' in intellectual matters, never, I mean been one who could play gracefully with ideas but had arrived at violence of opinion merely."

This is why Wilde has undertaken to write to Douglas the long letter of reproach and forgiveness that is *De Profundis* in the first place: to restore the true relations between older lover and younger beloved, *erastēs* and *erōmenos,* which had been so inverted in their actual friendship, returning it to the "hearer/inspirer" dyad of Dorian and Platonic love. For only by genuinely hearing what his lover now teaches will Douglas be rescued, so that the mean-spirited and hate-filled young man, whose golden beauty had once seemed to promise Wilde the very perfection of Greek love,[39] might at last, although with an appalling belatedness, truly realize himself as a man. "The only vice is shallowness," Wilde now counsels Douglas, appealing repeatedly to the presiding ideal of liberal Germano-Hellenism, to *Bildung* and human development in its richest diversity: "whatever is realised, is right." If Wilde, following his release from prison, was briefly to return to and live with Douglas on the old degraded terms of graceless excess and thankless exploitation, it is, as Ellmann has suggested, largely because his real life had ended in Reading Gaol ("I died in prison," "Something is killed in me," as Wilde would tell his remaining friends), and he was now condemned to relive all his past existence, but this time as a failure.

The symbolic point of rupture would thus always remain the trials for Wilde's life of April-May 1895, when the discourse of Oxford Hellenism still spoke so powerfully through him that it compelled an unwilling assent from the men in the Old Bailey courtroom. As they listened to a superbly confident expositor of the supremely confident tradition of Oxford Hellenism, these men recognized in Wilde's voice the language of their own aspiration—an aspiration that had been shaped for Victorians by Mill and Grote, Jowett and Arnold, Gladstone and Pater out of the tumult of the mid-Victorian cultural crisis.

To regard any such symbolic moment as this one is to see that Victorian Hellenism has here become powerful enough as a legitimating discourse to counter and momentarily to silence the ideological constructions of an ancient classical republicanism—*effeminatus* and "effeminacy," *virtus* and "corruption"—which had for so long determined so much that was now being discursively reconfigured as "homosexuality." It is, perhaps, one measure of the ideological potency of Victorian liberal Hellenism that it can in this moment speak without loss of persuasive power through the medium of precisely the most notorious dandy-aesthete-effeminatus of the day, a man who had flourished specifically those modes of dress, mannerism, and speech which had since the time of Pope's Sporus and Smollett's Whiffle signaled to the English that effeminacy and civic incapacity have once again minced forward within the polity and now threaten it with utter ruin.

Yet even as Wilde speaks his mighty peroration, Victorian Hellenism has already begun to slip into equivocality, a semantic shift we may hear beginning when Swinburne calls Simeon Solomon, the Pre-Raphaelite painter arrested 1873 for soliciting in a London urinal, "a Platonist" and a "translator . . . of Platonic theory into Socratic practice" [*The Swinburne Letters,* 1959]; and accelerating, when Benjamin Jowett tells Hallam Tennyson in 1892 that his father's feeling for Shakespeare's sonnets constituted "a sort of sympathy with Hellenism" (*Tennyson: A Selected Edition,* 1989); and approaching completion when George Ives, the secretive agitator for homosexualism, declares himself in 1903 to be "a cold disciplined Hellenist" (Ellmann).

Above all in later years, it would be Wilde's own hapless and sordid catastrophe that was to seem in the public imagination to have entered into indissoluble combination with the cultural values asserted by Pater and Symonds and the English Uranians, reducing any invocation of a high and "gracious" Hellenism to something half ridiculous and partially suspect.[40] It is because a writer such as Compton MacKenzie would ultimately be able to summon up a whole late-Victorian epoch at Oxford and Eton and such other "Arcadian" venues in the murmurous, flutelike speech of a single Hellenizing invert in *Sinister Street* (1913), or because G. Lowes Dickinson's little handbook on Greece would come to serve as much as a source of

information about paiderastia as about hubris or helots or the agora for generations of desperately ignorant English and American homosexual young men, that such recent defenders of Greek studies as Richard Jenkyns have only been able to regard the inheritance of Pater's Hellenism or Symonds and Wilde's with a deeply angry dismay.

In the same way, Wilde's late twentieth-century heirs have been able to see, as Eve Sedgwick has said, nothing more than "Oscar Wilde"—a largely empty, almost arbitrary name onto which law and journalism, medicine and theology, prejudice and ignorance would so ceaselessly project their theories and loathing and fears. But today, as Wilde is steadily becoming audible once again as a cultural hero rather than merely a homosexual martyr, it is the supreme confidence and the Dorian "manliness" of Oxford Hellenism which lifts his voice to be heard. For it is only now, perhaps, a century after the tragedy of Wilde's fall, that we are at last able to hear in the demand for a nonmedical or nonpsychiatric or unpathologized account of "homosexuality"—as a normality unencumbered by norms—precisely the recovery of a perspective that had originally entered Anglo-American consciousness through the spiritual procreancy ideal of Oxford Hellenism. If it has been inordinately difficult for late twentieth-century homosexual apologists to see this idealist dimension of Hellenism either in the formative moment of Victorian "homosexuality" or in Wilde, it is precisely because the salient forces fostered by that discourse—self-development, diversity, "liberty of the heart"—so completely survived the wreck of Wilde's life and art as to have become quite invisibly what we are.

Notes

. . . . .

[18] Wilde defines the "Oxford temper" in *De Profundis,* in the course of rebuking Lord Alfred Douglas for his utter lack of it, Douglas having left Oxford without taking a degree. Its importance to Wilde may be judged indirectly by reading Robert Ross's essay "The Brand of Isis," the amusing protest of a Cambridge man at the Oxford ascendancy. The battle of the two universities was a convention in the friendship between Ross and Wilde, and is alluded to in *The Portrait of Mr. W. H.:* "Yes, I am aware that Cambridge is a sort of educational institute," Wilde's narrator murmurs dismissively. "I am glad I was not there." "I always fancied," recalled Robert Sherard, who had matriculated at New College, Oxford, "that the fact that I did not take my degree seemed to [Wilde] to draw a line between us. There were certain subjects on which he would not listen to me; and when other graduates were present, a vague feeling of exclusion from his confidence communicated itself to me."

[19] See, for example, Wilde's *Oxford Notebooks* 148-49, where he quotes from the long passage about the Platonic eros, cited above in Chapter 3, from Jowett's introduction to Plato's *Symposium*. I follow the editors' dating of Wilde's college notebook and commonplace book to the period of 1874-79.

[20] Wilde is copying this phrase into his Oxford notebook from an essay by W. K. Clifford. Cf. also Wilde's notation: "*Erōs* and *dialektikē* as two sides of the same thing: *erōs*, the impassioned search after truth, as well the romantic side of that friendship so necessary for philosophy, because *discussion* was the primitive method" (*Notebooks*).

[21] Wilde strikes this characteristic Millian-Grotean note of Oxford liberalism again when he declares in his undergraduate essay *Hellenism* that "this intense individuality, if one might use the term, of each city saved the Greeks from the mediocre sameness of thought and feeling which seems always to exist in the cities of great empires." For the development of Wilde's Hellenism at Trinity College, Dublin, under the tutelage of the noted Greek scholar J. P. Mahaffy, see Stanford and McDowell; Pine; and Ellmann 27-30. Mahaffy was able to prevail upon a not unwilling Wilde to delay returning to Oxford in April 1877 and to visit Greece instead ("I stood upon the soil of Greece at last!" as the speaker of Wilde's "Impression de Voyage" exclaims in triumph [Bobby Fong "The Poetry of Oscar Wilde: A critical Edition," Ph. D. dissertation, 1978]). "Seeing Greece," Wilde announced to the Dean of Magdalen whose permission he needed for a late return to the college, "is really a great education for anyone and will I think benefit me greatly and Mr. Mahaffy is such a clever man that it is quite as good as going to lectures to be in his society" (*Letters*). After his return to Oxford, Wilde's Catholic friends became convinced he was changed by this experience, "become Hellenized, somewhat Paganized," as one of them, David Hunter-Blair, would later say (E. H. Mikhail *Oscar Wilde: Interviews and Recollections,* 1979). Nor did the effect of Greece in providing an alternative source of transcendental value to Wilde seem to diminish with time. Writing in October 1880 a letter now held in the Robert H. Taylor Collection of the Princeton University Libraries and quoted here by permission, the actor Kyrle Bellew told Wilde bluntly, "I am a Catholic—you would have been one too had you been spared Greece."

[22] Cf. Arnold: "It is noticeable that the word *curiosity,* which in other languages is used in a good sense, to mean, as a high and fine quality of man's nature, just this disinterested love of a free play of the mind on all subjects, for its own sake,—it is noticeable, I say, that this word has in our language no sense of the kind, no sense but a rather bad and disparaging one. But criticism, real criticism, is essentially the exercise of this very quality" (*Function*). Arnold was thinking of Ernest Renan's praise of curiosity in *Averroës et averroeisme* (1852). Pater emphasizes curiosity in the Leonardo essay of *The Renaissance* and, more especially, in the postscript to *Appreciations* 1889).

[23] Wilde's flamboyant self-presentation derived most immediately from his own personality and from his mother, with Ireland as an influence no very distant third. All these, however, need to be read within the larger sociocultural context established by the liberal sanction of eccentricity expressed so compellingly in Mill's *On Liberty:* "In this age the mere example of nonconformity, the mere refusal to bend the knee to custom, is itself a service. Precisely because the tyranny of opinion is such as to make eccentricity a reproach, it is desirable, in order to break through that tyranny, that people should be eccentric. Eccentricity has always abounded when and where strength of character has abounded; and the amount of eccentricity in a society has generally been proportional to the amount of genius, mental vigour, and moral courage which it contained. That so few now dare to be eccentric, marks the chief danger of the time."

[24] Cf. this reminiscence by an anonymous woman writer: "It was, as I believe, his sense of the Greek that carried him through [the trial], as it had brought him to its cause. He felt himself Socrates perhaps; but it is easier to drink hemlock than to return from prison" (Brian Reade *Sexual Heretics: Male Homosexuality in English Literature from 1850 to 1900: An Anthology,* 1970).

[25] Marc-André Raffalovich notes that by 1895 the word "musical" had attained a special Uranian inflection (*Uranisme et unisexualité,* 1896).

[26] Cf. Symonds's letter to Edmund Gosse of March 1890: "I must even sit down upon the ground & complain to heaven that Mrs Grundy's tyranny deprives us of the natural enjoyment of such works of art as [Gosse's poetic sequence "The Taming of Chimaera"] . . . I feel very bitter about this. Quoque tandem Domine? How long are souls to groan beneath the altar, & poets to eviscerate their offspring, for the sake of what— What shall I call it?—an unnatural disnaturing respect for middleclass propriety.—I find no phrase for my abhorrence."

[27] Foucault, characterizing the principle of "indefinite abstention" in the Platonic doctrine of eros as "the ideal of a renunciation, which Socrates exemplifies by his faultless resistance of [Alcibiades'] temptation [in the *Symposium*]" and which "has a high spiritual value by itself," has argued that such an asceticism served the Greeks as a means "of stylizing [the love of boys] and hence, by giving shape and form, of valorizing it" (*The History of Sexuality,* 1980-88).

[28] Symonds's rising dismay at the medical transformation of masculine love was soon to be echoed by Wilde. Not the least part of the social extinction Wilde felt after his release from prison was his knowledge that such works as Max Nordau's *Degeneration* had reduced his genius and personality to the banal statistical nullity of a "problem": The "fact that I am also a pathological problem in the eyes of German scientists," Wilde would say in 1897, "is only interesting to German scientists: and even in their work I am tabulated, and come under the law of *averages! Quantum mutatus!*" (*Letters*).

[29] This association provides the larger context for W. S. Gilbert's celebrated line about the effeminate aesthete Bunthorne in the comic opera *Patience* (1881): "If you walk down Piccadilly with a poppy or a lily in your medieval hand." The line appears in the stanza celebrating "An attachment à la Plato."

[30] Johnson's own erotic conduct is now difficult to trace with any certainty (see Fletcher's account in his edition of Johnson), but that he loved men, and perhaps specifically loved Douglas—his intimate friend, to whom he introduced Wilde—has always been suggested by a poem, dedicated to Douglas and published in 1890, praising youthful love in these terms:

> Their eyes on fire, their bright limbs flushed,
> They dominate the night with love:
> While stars burn and flash above,
> These kindle through the dark such flame,
> As is not seen, and hath no name:
> Can night bear more?
> Can nature bend
> In benediction without end,
> Over this love of friend for friend?
>
> ("Decadence")

The "nameless" love and "dark flame" here both point forward in unmistakable terms to two of the most famous 1890s poems of Uranian provenance—Douglas's "Two Loves" ("I am the love that dare not speak its name") and Johnson's own "Dark Angel."

[31] See Monsman, *Pater's Portraits,* and the Keefes, *Gods,* for the Copernican and Keplerian dimensions to the prior's vision of a heliocentric system.

[32] Richard Dellamora [*Masculine Desire: The Sexual Politics of Victorian Aestheticism,* 1990], for instance, imagines that the prior's dream of "a circlet of soundless flame, waving, licking daintily up the black sky, but harmless, beautiful, closing in upon that round dark space in the midst, which was the earth" represents the prior's "sexual fantasies of anilingus and anal copulation. The 'flame . . . licking daintily' refers to tongue and/or penis; 'the round dark space in the midst,' to the opening sphincter." Though the reading has been to some degree controversial, it is perhaps possible to agree with Dellamora that, in whatever case, all this "is a figment not just of the prior" (190).

[33] Cf. Pater's characterization of the "rhapsodist" in Plato "whose sensitive performance of his part is nothing less than an 'interpretation' of it, artist and critic at once" (*Plato*)—Wilde, of course, was known for his rhapsodies and *contes parlés*—and his critical dialogue *Critic as Artist* had appeared in 1891. Pater's discussion of Plato's Alcibiades also bears on his own relationship to Wilde: "the winning brilliancy of the lost spirit of Alcibiades . . . the nature of one by birth and endowments an aristocrat, amid the dangers to which it is exposed in the Athens of that day—the qualities which must make him, if not the saviour, the destroyer, of a society which cannot remain unaffected by his showy presence. *Corruptio optimi pessima!*"

[34] Ross's extensive collaboration with Wilde and other writers such as Siegfried Sassoon and Robert Graves has gone unnoticed in much recent work on male literary collaboration. He was, however, "one of the most *indirectly* creative [of] men," as Arnold Bennett told Sassoon (Margery Ross *Robert Ross: Friend of Friends,* 1952). Wilde's dedicatory inscription to Ross—"To the Mirror of Perfect Friendship: Robbie" (*Letters*)—written years after Wilde's release from prison in February 1899, shows that his belief in the Platonic ideal of Uranian love continued even after he had ceased to look for anything more for himself than "Passion with the mask of Love." Deriving from *Phaedrus* 255 d-e: "his lover is as it were a mirror in which he beholds himself . . . that counterlove [*anterōs*] which is the image of love," the notion of the male lover as ethical mirror would come to be represented by the figure of Narcissus, a symbol that, emptied of its classical ethical content, would in turn come to represent male love—Wilde and Mallock, as we have seen, both deploy it in this way. This form of the Narcissus figure would later assume a new and pathological meaning as "narcissism" within Freud's psychoanalytic account of homosexuality. Pater had given the title "Anteros" to chapter 10 of his unfinished work *Gaston de Latour.* See Monsman "Unpublished Chapters" [*Victorians Institute Journal* (1992)] For the origin of the Anteros figure in the athletic and pederastic rituals of the Greek *palaestra,* see Böttinger [*Kleine schriften archäologischen und antiquarischen Inhalts,* 1837-38].

[35] Cf. *De Profundis:* "Guildenstern and Rosencrantz are as immortal as Angelo and Tartuffe, and should rank with them. They are what modern life has contributed to the antique ideal of friendship. He who writes a new *De Amicitia* must find a new niche for them and praise them in Tusculan prose. . . . Of course I do not propose to compare you. There is a wide difference between you. What with [Rosencrantz and Guildenstern] was chance, with you was choice" (*Letters*). As

Wilde's warder at Reading Gaol was to recall, "He was no good for anything—except writing, and that as a rule has small place inside a prison. . . . He was so unlike other men. Just a bundle of brains—and that is all" (John Wyse Jackson, *Aristotle at Afternoon Tea*, 19).

[36] Richard Ellman [*Oscar Wilde*, 1987] assumes that Douglas, in informing Wilde's counsel of certain information prejudicial to himself, and offering to testify, was taking responsibility for the incidents of buggery established in the trial through the evidence of stained bedsheets, since, as Ellmann says, "Wilde did not practice this." Unable to refer to such a matter directly in a manuscript controlled by the prison authorities, Wilde himself appears to be referring to it guardedly in *De Profundis:* "The sins of another were being placed to my account. Had I so chosen, I could on either trial have saved myself at his expense, not from shame indeed but from imprisonment. Had I cared to show that the Crown witnesses—the three most important—had been carefully coached by your father and his solicitors, not in reticences merely but in assertions, in the absolute transference, deliberate, plotted, and rehearsed, of the actions and doings of someone else on to me, I could have had each one of them dismissed from the box by the Judge. . . . I could have walked out of court . . . a free man" (*Letters*).

Wilde presents his reproach here as arising not from the excruciating cost to himself of this sacrifice but from Douglas's complete moral obtuseness and ingratitude about it: "You had the sympathy and the sentimentality of the spectator of a rather pathetic play. That you were the true author of the hideous tragedy did not occur to you. I saw that you realised nothing of what you had done." In this context Douglas's charge that the government had engaged in a criminal conspiracy to convict Wilde becomes intelligible as a displacement of or psychic defense against his own complicity in Wilde's ruin.

[37] Initiated into homosexual practices at Winchester, Douglas first sought out Wilde for help in dealing with a "renter" who was blackmailing him at Oxford. As Wilde tells him in *De Profundis*, "Your defect was not that you knew so little about life, but that you knew so much. . . . The gutter and the things that live in it had begun to fascinate you" (*Letters*). Nor was Wilde alone in this opinion. George Ives, the poet and homosexual apologist whose immense and earnest diary provides a view into the Uranian half-world of the 1890s, regarded Douglas as the foremost activist for "the Cause" at Oxford ("he has made Oxford what it is") but was unnerved by Douglas's "difficult character, swayed by passion, shaken by impulse" (Stokes, "Wilde at Bay: The Diaries of George Ives," *English Literature in Transition* [1983]). After Douglas spent the night with Ives on 24 August 1894, and more especially after the

Wilde trials, Ives came to regard him as "that miserable traitor . . . I knew he had faults and more or less insanity all along, but I thought him rather the victim than the villain he proved to be."

[38] Cf. *De Profundis:* "Do you think I am here on account of my relations with the witnesses in my trial? My relations, real or supposed, with people of that kind were matters of no interest to either the Government or Society. . . . I am here for having tried to put your father into prison" (*Letters*). Ellmann has presented a compelling case for regarding Wilde's prosecution as more the result of grotesque accident and miscalculation than of specific judicial or social persecution.

Wilde himself trusted that the *De Profundis* letter would eventually vindicate him, telling Robert Ross in 1897, "When you have read the letter you will see the psychological explanation of a course of conduct that from the outside seems a combination of absolute idiocy with vulgar bravado. Some day the truth will have to be known: not necessarily in my lifetime or in Douglas's: but I am not prepared to sit in the grotesque pillory they put me into, for all time" (*Letters*).

The motives behind Wilde's prosecution have been central to much recent commentary on him and Victorian "homosexuality" generally (see, for example, Regenia Gagnier [*Idylls of the Marketplace*, 1986] and, following her, Dellamora). Responding to assertions by Jeffrey Weeks and others that the legal position of such "homosexuals" as Wilde greatly deteriorated in the later Victorian period as a result of changes in the law covering sodomy, attempted sodomy, and related offenses, Arthur Gilbert has argued that these historians have typically focused on the sodomy and attempted sodomy laws to the exclusion of the *application* of those laws. Gilbert's own studies of court records in the earlier nineteenth century have convinced him that the 1826 change in the sodomy statute (eliminating the requirement that emission as well as penetration be proved in sodomy cases, thereby making convictions easier to obtain) was followed by, if anything, a decrease in the number of sodomy convictions. With regard to the Labouchere amendment, under which Wide was tried for "gross indecency," Gilbert has similarly found no evidence that the new law brought about any substantial increase in actual prosecutions (Review in *The Journal of Homosexuality* 6 [1980-81]).

Proposing instead an explanation of English sodomy prosecutions and convictions as arising from a sense of imminent social catastrophe, Gilbert has argued that the historical record of England during the period 1749-1814 "seems to show that fear of disaster may be far more significant in general and in specific situations" than more general concerns about marriage, gender identity, and procreation ("Sexual Deviance" *Albion*

[1977]). He notes in particular that the 1749-92 period in London and Middlesex Country saw only one execution for sodomy, whereas during the much shorter Napoleonic Wars period of 1803-14 seven men were executed. Indeed, the rate of prosecutions for attempted sodomy spiked in 1810—the year of the "Vere Street conspiracy" involving the patrons of a male brothel—which was precisely the most difficult year of England's war with France.

The interpretation advanced in the present study argues that, beyond the search for scapegoats in times of national catastrophe posited by Gilbert, the intensified prosecution of suspected sodomites in times of war or danger represents a crisis response at the level of archaic civic consciousness as it identifies male weakness and "effeminacy" with the martial collapse of the collectivity. Amid the alarm over the Vere Street conspiracy, for instance, the *Morning Chronicle* could be heard invoking the familiar vocabulary of classical republicanism—Machiavelli's pervasive idiom of *corruzione* and *rovina*—when that newspaper called on the English to join those "zealously disposed to stemming a torrent of corruption that threatens to involve us in the gulf of infamy as well as ruin" (Louis Crompton *Byron and Greek Love*, 1985). A more recent sign of the remarkable persistence and residual power of the ancient civic response identifying male effeminacy with martial failure may be glimpsed in the American controversy over admitting declared homosexuals into the U.S. military.

[39] This valorization of male bodily beauty derives its ethical claims from the passage in *Symposium* 212a noted earlier, where Diotima instructs Socrates that "it is only when he discerns beauty itself through what makes it visible that a man will be quickened with the true, and not the seeming, virtue." Wilde's own visual sensitivity bordered on hyperaesthesia—cf. *De Profundis*: "There is not a single colour hidden away in the chalice of a flower, or the curve of a shell, to which, by some subtle sympathy with the very soul of things, my nature does not answer. Like Gautier I have always been one of those *pour qui le monde visible existe*" (*Letters*). Robert Sherard [*Oscar Wilde: The Story of an Unhappy Friendship*, 1970] considered Wilde's delight in visual beauty and corresponding horror at physical ugliness to have been entirely sincere if excessive: "I have heard him refuse to meet people who were ugly, however sympathetic to him, because of the real distress which their appearance caused to him. I have heard him excuse himself on such occasions in accents which left no doubt of his sincerity. 'I cannot do it—I really cannot.'"

[40] Cf. E. F. Benson's remark in his memoir *As We Were* (1930) that Wilde believed "he was realizing for a drab world the ancient Greek ideal of the joy and beauty of life. Nothing could have been less like what he was doing, for the Greek genius for exquisite living was founded on physical fitness and moderation in all things, while he based it on the unbridled gratification of animal appetites." An intimate friend of Alfred Douglas (who had by this time renounced all sodomy and Uranian themes), Benson sounds a note Wilde himself had taken up in *De Profundis* and in his post-prison letters: "I do not accept the British view that Messalina is better than Sporus: these things are matters of temperament, and both are equally vile, because sensual pleasures wreck the soul: but all my profligacy, extravagance, and worldly life of fashion and senseless ease, were wrong for an artist" (*Letters*). Although Wilde here is addressing an aesthetic former-clergyman, and hence is inclined to exaggerate his new regard for *sōphrosynē*, the theme recurs even with such correspondents as Ross from whom Wilde had little to hide.

Richard Dellamora

SOURCE: "Dorianism," in *Apocalyptic Overtures: Sexual Politics and the Sense of an Ending,* Rutgers University Press, 1994, pp. 43-64.

[*Dellamora, who also wrote* Masculine Desire: The Sexual Politics of Victorian Aestheticism, *offers a more condensed version of his studies in the essay that follows. Looking at several of the major figures of the era—including Wilde, Walter Pater, and J. A. Symonds—Dellamora considers the shifting notions of masculinity and male-male desire that traversed the century, focusing specifically on efforts to maintain the Greek ideal.*]

In this chapter I follow Neil Bartlett's example [*Who Was That Man? A Present for Mr. Oscar Wilde*, 1988] in looking back to the 1890s as a site at which key issues in relations between subjects of male-male desire become evident. As these subjects were increasingly specified as "homosexual," the old patterns that mobilized male-male libidinal energies in service of the nation-state or in the production of high culture came under severe pressure. I conclude this chapter with a discussion of works by male homosexuals in which are set in play reverse discourses that challenge the construction of desire in elite culture. Men like Pater, Wilde, and Carpenter were interested in drawing a distinction between emergent male homosexual culture and the male homosocial culture in which homosexual desire was regularly induced, then directed to hegemonic purposes. In order to be able to do so, such writers needed at some point to turn their attention to the critical analysis of the erotics of pedagogy in the public schools and at Oxford and Cambridge. Pater does so in one of his final works, "Emerald Uthwart" (1892). In this short fiction, he shows how two young Englishmen are drawn into love by the discipline of school life and the place in it of Greek studies. Subsequently, they place their devotion in service of Great Britain in the armed struggle against Napoleon, and both die. Similarly, in *The Picture of Dorian Gray* (1890), Wilde casts a skeptical eye on Basil Hallward's unsuccessful attempt to validate his attraction to a beautiful young aristocrat by placing it in the service of high art. In Wilde's novel too, both young men die.

The reverse discourses of Pater and Wilde pose a major question concerning sexual and emotional ties between men. If the traditional enlistment of these ties in cultural production of various sorts is to be challenged, what new rationales will be offered in its place? Or will writers, defending such ties on aesthetic grounds, argue that they are characterized—as Kant contends that art is characterized—by a *"finalité sans fin,"* a "finality without [moral, social, political or some other] end."[1] Late Victorian writers offer a variety of proposals. Pater, perhaps with Dorian and Basil in mind, deals with the question by arguing that desire between men needs to be translated from artistic commodification into existence, into the "real portrait of a real young" man. John Gray, a former friend and, probably, lover of Wilde, sees the idolization of young male beauty as leading inevitably first to sexual and gender inversion and then to death. Edward Carpenter attempts to validate homosexual desire by enlisting it in the service of the evolution of the race.

In order better to understand the argument in which these writers are involved, it is worthwhile to follow Bartlett's lead yet further in time to the very beginning of the century when apocalyptic anxieties and hopes were focused on the figure of Napoleon and his armies. In early nineteenth-century invocations of love between comrades-in-arms, three sorts of ends are invoked: the sacrifice of soldiers' lives, the moral purpose to which that sacrifice is devoted (that is, saving civilization from the enemy), and the catastrophic end that threatens if one's own party is defeated. The writers of the 1890s rejected this triple linkage of the ends of individual lives to the ethical and eschatological "ends" of humanity. During the Napoleonic period and afterward, sexual and emotional ties between men were mobilized in England, France, and Germany as a way to consolidate national brotherhood. Patriotic brothers were subject to a sacrificial logic in which their "collective casualties *within* war" validated the ideals— "freedom," "national sovereignty," and so on—in whose name the war was being fought.[2]

This set of factors was usually alluded to when what I call Dorianism was invoked in the nineteenth century. Dorianism refers to the institution of pederasty as it existed in the army of ancient Sparta. In Foucauldian terms, the idealization of love between soldiers might be described as yet another "technology of the self," "centering on the body as a machine: its disciplining, the optimization of its capabilities, the extortion of its forces, the parallel increase of its usefulness and its docility, its integration into systems of efficient and economic controls."[3] Between the defeat of Napoleon at Waterloo in 1815 and the early 1900s, writers in England frequently considered the subject of "Greek love," a phrase that David Halperin describes as a "coded phrase for the unmentionable term *paederasty*." In these discussions, pederasty, defined as "the sexual pursuit of adolescent males by adult males," usually means pederasty in the form of the educational, at times philosophic institution that existed at Athens.[4] This institution, whose meaning hinges on the induction of young male citizens into the privileges and responsibilities of adult citizenship through friendship with an older male, I refer to as Athenian-model pederasty. In ancient Greece, there was another form of pederasty, namely, the practice at Sparta of friendship and love between an adult male citizen/soldier and a younger one preparing to achieve the same status.[5] This relationship I refer to as Spartan-model pederasty.[6] Because nineteenth-century philologists associate it with the Dorian invaders of Lacedaemon, I refer to its invocation in painting and writing as *Dorianism*.

Framing their representations in terms of the social uses of desire between men, the apologists of Dorianism raised questions of continuing interest in relation to ethical aspects of desire between men. On the one hand, nineteenth-century approaches demonstrate how desire can be constructed in terms of nationalist and ethnic ambitions. These ends are served by invoking apocalyptic narratives and by other aesthetic means, especially the exploitation of sublime affects. On the other hand, the attempt by Pater and Wilde to sever emergent homosexuality from service to the state prompted urgent questions about how modes of sociality among homosexuals could be developed and sustained.

In the nineteenth century the willingness of some writers to validate sexual and emotional ties between men when these bonds were exercised in military action in effect effaces these relations. Desire between men is praiseworthy only when merged in nationalist fraternity or even, as in the painting of Jacques-Louis David, in a model of father-son relationship. When, as occurred later in the century, sexual ties between males began to become evident, they fell outside the normalizing representation of masculinity in nineteenth-century middle-class culture that links respectability with purity and virility. Under these circumstances, such ties were construed as signs of a criminal conspiracy against the state.[7]

Leonidas at Thermopylae

After one group of Dorian warriors gained ascendancy in ancient Lacedaemon, they found themselves surrounded by other Greeks. In order to guarantee the hegemony of this one group while suppressing conflict within it, the Spartan lawmaker Lycurgus followed the example of Crete by converting this group of Dorian fighting men into a permanent military corps.[8] He inscribed pederasty within the constitution as a prime means of socializing young men into this organization. This account of the origin of Spartan-model pederasty associates Dorianism with military expansion as well as with the dominance of one ethnic and class group over others within the boundaries of a particular state. The Lycurgan constitution was installed in the face of imminent internal collapse. Similarly Dorianism in the nineteenth century was usually invoked in the face of fears of catastrophic apocalypse. This atmosphere is readily reinforced by assumptions about cultural and social decadence, especially in the fin de siècle, and by invocations of a sacrificial logic that make a seductive appeal to subjects of male-male desire. Such men are subliminally offered an exchange: their lives for validation of their desires for other men.[9]

When the French state under Napoleon was extending its dominion across Europe, the French painter David glorified Dorianism. In the context of the German nationalism provoked by French expansionism, the philologist C. O. Müller did too. At Oxford, where Müller's *History and Antiquities of the Doric Race* became a standard undergraduate text, sages like Ruskin, Arnold, and Benjamin Jowett endorsed prescriptions drawn from the Spartan constitution as refracted through Plato in *The Republic*. These endorsements of the disciplinary organization of male sociality were underwritten by the general principle within late eighteenth-century humanism that the structure of individual psychology should mirror the structure of the state and vice-versa. As Paul de Man says of the end of Friedrich Schiller's *Letters on Aesthetic Education* (1795): "The 'state' that is here being advocated is not just a state of mind or of soul, but a principle of political value and authority that has its own claims on the shape and the limits of our freedom."[10] The metaphoric relationship between individual and corporate organization remained a potent one in nineteenth-century writing.

Apocalyptic narrative, decadence, ethnic prejudice, sacrificial logic, and the aesthetic ideology all figure in Immanuel Kant's representation of the sublime. In the immediate aftermath of the French Revolution, of which he was a partisan,[11] Kant includes in his analysis of the dynamic sublime the following paean to the military man:

> Even where civilization has reached a high pitch there remains this special reverence for the soldier; only that there is then further required of him that he should also exhibit all the virtues of peace— gentleness, sympathy and even becoming thought

for his own person; and for the reason that in this we recognize that his mind is above the threats of danger. And so, comparing the statesman and the general, men may argue as they please as to the pre-eminent respect which is due either above the other; but the verdict of the aesthetic judgement is for the latter. War itself, provided it is conducted with order and a sacred respect for the rights of civilians, has something sublime about it, and gives nations that carry it on in such a manner a stamp of mind only the more sublime the more numerous the dangers to which they are exposed, and which they are able to meet with fortitude. On the other hand, a prolonged peace favours the predominance of a mere commercial spirit, and with it a debasing self-interest, cowardice, and effeminacy, and tends to degrade the character of the nation.[12]

An interesting shift occurs in the course of this passage from "the soldier" *(der Krieger),* who is liable to die, and "the general" *(der Feldherr),* who will most likely survive. The experience of the sublime varies with one's position within a hierarchy. Kant endorses "civilization" as superior to the "mere commercial spirit," a phrase that alludes to the petty bourgeoisie and to Jews.[13] To achieve something higher, in the name of the state, renders the immolation of individual soldiers sublime and saves "the character of the nation" [*die Denkungsart des Volks*] from contamination by "effeminacy."

David's painting *Leonidas at Thermopylae* provides a paradigmatic example of the aesthetic inscription of Spartan pederasty within the rhetoric of the nation-state in crisis. Referring to the sheer mass of nude male flesh in this unusually large painting, Robert Rosenblum terms the scene "the Davidian equivalent of a classical locker room," offering "the sexualized male counterpart" of contemporary academic paintings of nude females in Turkish baths.[14] In David's painting, however, the male nude is enlisted against a racial Other. At the right center of the painting, David emphasizes the institutional role of pederasty within Spartan life by portraying a fully mature soldier tenderly embracing a male ephebe garbed in sword, scabbard, and garland. The only nude figure whose genitals are not partly or altogether concealed from view is another ephebe, tying his sandal in the left foreground. The suffusion of a wide range of male relations with desire and love is signaled by the young men who dance together to the left and right while the thoroughly masculinized body of Leonidas at center is the object of an admiring look from another male in full prime.[15] In these representations, sexualized desire includes a wide range of relations of age and body type. According to Müller, in Crete and Sparta "the youth . . . wore the military dress which had been given him . . .; and fought in battle next his lover, inspired with double valour by the gods of war and love . . . ; and even in man's age he was distinguished by the first place and rank in the course, and certain insignia worn about the body."[16]

Although the Napoleonic Code of 1810 retained the decriminalization of sodomy included in the penal code of 1791, the evident homoeroticism of David's painting is not due to a relatively tolerant attitude toward sexual intimacy between men. Rather, the painting provides at once a demonstration and an analysis of the inscription of desire in the public order, in part through the dance, whose members are of one sex only, in part by the look of the soldier seated at right center. This look pertains to male homosocial culture, which by visual address fixes in place the idealized and idealizing figure of Leonidas, the king of Sparta killed by the Persians at Thermopylae in 480 B.C. If look and gesture inscribe male homosocial relations of power, the process of inscription is figured in literal fashion in the soldier at upper left who incises into the wall of the defile the epitaph: "Passerby, go tell Sparta that her children have died for her."[17] This use of prosopopeia is particularly chilling when written by and for men who are still alive. In the dance, indeed, men offer themselves to this process of memorialization. Equally chilling is the attempt to construct individual and collective memory before the fact. In the cultural modernity of Charles Baudelaire and Marcel Proust, memory is represented as the most individual aspect of consciousness. But already at the beginning of the century, David regarded memory as to be written in stone before the birth of future children. David's painting is organized in accord with this operation, not only by virtue of the impact of its overwhelming size but also by how the viewer's attention is focused on the central figure. In this way, the viewer is positioned within a male homosocial system. If there is any space of resistance to these processes, it occurs in the exploitation of an aspect of the work which belongs to all painting; namely, its poignant silence.[18] This limitation of the medium permits the viewer to enter into the mute world of those who will soon be dead and in this way remember aspects of existence that the memory excludes.

The inscription of male love within a statist project ennobles aesthetically and morally both male relations and the political aim. The implicit apocalyptic narrative of the painting, the setting at Thermopylae where this panoply of flesh is about to be sacrificed, endows devotion with the sublime value of dying for the sake of civilization itself. This raising of levels is signified in Leonidas's upward glance, which can be described as the sublimating operator of the painting, and by the open sky behind the defile as well as by "the fortified city" in the distance, "which is supposed to represent Athens."[19] The Doric temple facade behind the king, which was to be favored for the facades of nineteenth-century institutions such as universities, museums, and banks, serves a like function, as do the movements of the dancing warriors, whose arabesque stance, invented in 1790 by Pierre Gardel, choreographer and ballet master of the Paris Opéra, was used in huge, outdoor pantomimes celebrating the Revolution. The arabesque, with its connotations of both flight and elevation, signified purity and transcendence in fin de sìecle French art and thought.[20]

Although David began working on this subject as early as 1799, by 1814, the year of its completion, when he showed the painting in his studio, the parallel between Leonidas and Napoleon, in exile at Elba, was evident, even to Napoleon when he visited David's studio during his brief return to Paris. During the earlier phase in which David had worked on the painting, he portrayed a number of the more lyrical figures: the ephebe tying his sandal and the young boy with the warrior. Only a decade later did David fix the position of Leonidas and his admirer and add the soldier with spear and helmet to the far left. In this shift in looks and body types, David registers the experience of ten more years of war. Vulnerability could be portrayed when one could still hope that young soldiers might return, alive and uninjured from battle. Later, the nude wears its musculature as though it were armor. This masculinizing of the body signifies casualties already incurred. Similarly, in inception, the painting included among its addressees David's son, who was instructed thereby in exemplary virtue. David returned to the subject shortly after his son, now grown to adulthood, was feared to have been lost in action at Leipzig.[21] The epitaph of the painting, then, is both prospective and retrospective: in 1800, David looks forward to victory, but by 1813 he was looking back on mass destruction and defeat.

Thinking Greek

German nationalism awoke in the resistance to French control of the German states in the opening years of the nineteenth century. Aryan "purity" was opposed to both English materialism and Jewish "effeminacy"—a construction that has survived well into this century.[22] After Waterloo, philologists like Friedrich Gottlieb Welcker and his successor at the university of Göttingen, Carl Ottfried Müller, invoked the Spartan model for their own ends. The idealization of Hellenic culture in the writings of Schiller and Johann Winckelmann had already guaranteed that it "would play a privileged role in the creation of German national identity and values."[23] For Welcker and Müller, there was the additional favorable association of the Dorians, northern invaders of the Peloponnesus, with Germany. Martin Bernal has argued that "the university of Göttingen, founded in 1734 by George II, Elector of Hanover and King of England, and forming a cultural bridge between Britain and Germany," was the prime source of the "Aryan Model" of Greek ethnic purity. Müller, who was "extreme in his Romanticism and ahead of his time in the intensity of his racialism and anti-Semitism," made use of modern source criticism in order to disavow North African and Semitic elements in Greek culture.[24] The attraction to Sparta was especially appropriate since "it was the Greeks themselves who first drew a sharp contrast between Asia and Europe, between 'Us' in the democratic West and the 'Barbarians' in the royal, imperial East." It was, as well, the Greek victories over the Persians between 490 and 479 B.C. that prompted Athenians to dreams of imperial grandeur that were soon to result in disaster.[25]

German responses to pederasty were both defensive and innovative. Welcker invoked the Greek poet Sappho as the model of a celibate *male* pederasty that provided one of "the foundations of Greek nationalism and the source of Greek artistic power."[26] In Welcker's desexualizing model, the attempt to achieve *Deutschheit* had homophobic, misogynistic, and erotophobic aspects.[27] Yet in his defense of *Männerliebe*, love of men, he extends his discussion to "the larger context of all homoerotic relations. Secondly, unlike many of his followers, Welcker refuses to deny completely the sensual content of 'love of men' by claiming that the phenomenon existed solely for pedagogical purposes." Müller seconded Welcker in "his history of the Dorians, in which he proposes this civilization as the model for the Greek genius and *pederastia* as the origin of that genius."[28] In this book, which in its English translation (1830, 1839) became a fixture of undergraduate education at Oxford, Müller expresses his intention to discuss pederasty "without examining it in a moral point of view, which does not fall within the scope of this work."[29] Müller considers pederasty without casting it in terms of a Christian antithesis between purity and "vice."[30] Instead he challenges his readers to discern the meaning of this institution within the terms of ancient Dorian existence or, in other words, to think Greek.[31] *Thinking Greek* in this sense becomes a permanent challenge (and problem) to latter-day Dorians. Although the tendency, as Müller himself in part exemplifies, is to relapse into a "Christian" view, through the remainder of the nineteenth century the problem of pederasty as Müller situates it remains central to Dorianism. The key questions are the ones that he implicitly poses: What is the Dorian understanding of pederasty? How do I as a modern man enter into that understanding? How does success in that effort change me and, potentially, my society? The questions have a utopian aspect, since implicit in the representations of Müller and others I consider is a metaphoric apprehension of the Dorian/modern analogy.

In *A Problem in Greek Ethics,* written for the most part in 1873 but published only posthumously in 1897 and then only until its publisher "was convicted on a charge of obscenity,"[32] Symonds associates pederasty with the Dorian invasions of the Peloponnesus: "To be loved was honourable, for it implied being worthy to be died for. To love was glorious, since it pledged the lover to self-sacrifice in case of need. In these conditions the paiderastic passion may have well combined manly virtue with carnal appetite, adding such romantic sentiment as some stern men reserve within their hearts for women. A motto might be chosen for a lover of this early Dorian type from the Aeolic poem ascribed to Theocritus: 'And made me tender from the iron man I used to be.'"[33] In Symonds's text, at least as later revised, Dorianism changes its character, since he speaks of utilizing "homosexual passions . . . for the benefit of society" with an eye not primarily to the needs of the nation but on behalf of himself and other homosexuals who sought to decriminalize sexual activities between men. Hence he addresses the text "to medical psychologists and jurists."[34] In contrast, Müller's discussion is compromised by the return of Christian moral conceptions. Still, Müller's final discussion does open a space for "this pure connexion": "In early times this proximity never would have been permitted, if any pollution had been apprehended from it."[35] *Thinking Greek* means apprehending this space, which exists between celibacy and *stuprum,* the Ciceronian term that Symonds translates with the word "outrage."[36]

Of course, for those less carefully decorous than Müller and Symonds, "pure connexion" could be basely parodied. The term "fellator," with which A. C. Swinburne peppers his correspondence, may be read as a transliteration of Müller's φιλήτωρ, the Cretan term for the male lover in pederasty.[37] Swinburne's point is not to specify which sexual practices were involved in Spartan-model pederasty. Rather, his abusive translation is designed to bring into view the general connection between intimate male bonding and sexual practices about which Müller is so discreet.

Müller's position, which Symonds draws on, is by no means the most daring one that exists in texts written in German. In *Mother Right* (1861), Johann Bachofen, a Swiss university professor and friend of Jakob Burckhardt and Friedrich Nietzsche, releases Sappho from the bonds of celibacy to which she had been relegated by Welcker and his successors. Declining to assess her "according to the ethical concepts of Christianity," Bachofen argues that "the love of women for their own sex was equivalent to the Orphic ἄρρενες ἔρωτες. Here again the sole purpose was to transcend the lower sensuality, to make physical beauty into a purified psychic beauty." Despite the sublimating rhetoric, purification in Bachofen's genuinely dialectical context means not celibacy but a fully embodied love in contrast to the "hetaerism" or profligacy that he associates with archaic or pre-Hellenic culture. Bachofen observes: "the madness of her heart . . . accomplished greater things than human reason." Sappho's eros, like Diotima's in the *Symposium,* is "not unitary and absolutely pure, but of twofold origin."[38] When Friedrich Engels drew on Bachofen's theory of mother right in his account of the genealogy of the family, he excluded this aspect of his thought. Instead, in an aside on Athenian pederasty, Engels condemns it as a corruption that issued from the reduced status of the wives of Athenian citizens: "This degradation of the women was avenged on the men and degraded them also till they fell into the abominable practice of sodomy."[39]

Discourse and Counterdiscourse at Oxford

In his introduction to *The Republic,* Benjamin Jowett writes: "The good man and the good citizen only coincide in the perfect State; and this perfection cannot be attained by legislation acting upon them from without, but, if at all, by education fashioning them from within."[40] The metaphoric relationship that Jowett draws between the structure of the state and the structure of the citizen is a commonplace of mid-Victorian social theory. John Ruskin makes use of it in *Unto This Last* (1860), as does Arnold in *Culture and Anarchy* (1869). All three writers draw on Plato's use of the metaphor in *The Republic.* Since Plato modeled his republic on Sparta, Victorian uses of the metaphor allude to Sparta. Given the importance that Plato and the Victorians both attach to "education," Dorianism, the special institution of Spartan pedagogy, is also implicated in these discussions. In "Emerald Uthwart," in which Pater analyzes the consciousness effects of Spartan-model pedagogy in nineteenth-century England, he comments at one point: "The social type [Plato] preferred, as we know, was conservative Sparta and its youth; whose unsparing discipline had doubtless something to do with the fact that it was the handsomest and best-formed in all Greece."[41] The surprising direction that this sentence takes from "discipline" to male beauty draws attention to the unspecified connections that exist between these two terms. Does "discipline" produce the "best-formed" body? Does a "handsome" face inspire disciplinary energy? The relations of cause and effect remain unspecified in Pater's deliberately vague phrasing.

Like the Plato of *The Republic,* Arnold in *Culture and Anarchy* appeals to a metaphoric relation between the structure of the subject and the structure of the state in order to provide a bulwark against the "anarchy" that he apprehends from the extension of the vote in 1867 to previously unenfranchised members of the middle, lower-middle, and working classes. Given the warring factions of Barbarians, Philistines, and Populace, as Arnold terms them, the extension of suffrage poses major challenges to civilization. These challenges can be met only by developing the idea of the State as subsuming and transcending particular persons and interests. "What if we tried to rise above the idea of class to the idea of the whole community, *the State,* and to find our centre of light and authority there? Every one of us has the idea of country, as a senti-

ment; hardly any one of us has the idea of *the State,* as a working power." In this context, individual culture is important primarily because the organization of the self provides an internal model of the discipline necessary to convert *the State* into "a working power." Whereas *Culture and Anarchy* does promise to enhance individual freedom, it proposes to achieve that end by turning the individual into a good citizen. Arnold proposes the State as the "organ of our collective best self, of our national right reason." Though this "reason" is to be formulated in cultural terms, persisting from Plato's adaptation of the Spartan model is the emphasis on "the power to respect, the power to obey."[42]

Arnold's reviews during the early 1870s of English translations of succeeding volumes of Ernst Curtius's *History of Greece* put national and imperial issues to the fore. Curtius was a proponent of Athenian democracy and a critic of Müller's claim of ethnic purity (and superiority) for the Dorians. In Arnold's reviews, democracy, which becomes synonymous with demagogy, accounts for the Sparta's ultimate triumph over Athens.[43] In his 1876 review of Curtius's fifth and final volume, Arnold asks "whether it is inevitable, then, that the faultier side of a national character should be always the one to prevail finally; and whether, therefore, since every national character has its faultier side, the greatness of no great nation can be permanent?" Faced with the prospect of decline, he concludes his review by urging his readers to "remain faithful to those moral ideas which, however they may be sometimes obscured or denied, are yet in the natural order of things the master-light for men of the Germanic race, for both Germans and Englishmen. And in our common, instinctive appreciation of those ideas lies the true, the indestructible ground of sympathy between Germany and England."[44] In the face of the rising tide of democracy, Arnold returns for comfort to the security of racial identity and recommends that England ally herself with the emergent Continental power of the 1870s.

Pater did not believe in such myths. In his account of ancient Sparta, he resists the validation of warfare that is fueled by the same beauty, love, and enthusiasm that it expends. In "Lacedaemon," published in the *Contemporary Review* in June 1892, he contrasts the operation of desire within Athenian- and Spartan-model pederasty by interpolating an interpretive figure, that of "some contemporary student of *The Republic,* a pupil, say! in the Athenian academy," who is "an admiring visitor" of Sparta and through whose eyes Lacedaemon is presented.[45] This figure opens the hermeneutic space known as "thinking Greek." In contrast are the "idle bystanders, . . . Platonic loungers after truth or what not," presumably practitioners or fantasists of what Cicero refers to as *stuprum,* whom the Spartans exclude from their gymnasia.[46] Pater insinuates his listeners into the subject-position of the young traveler, schooled in the institution of Athenian pederasty. But Pater also attempts to correct that position insofar as it participates in the regressive aspects of Dorianism. This correction is necessary historically since, as the Peloponnesian War devolved toward victory for Sparta, Athenians and in particular Plato in *The Republic,* had constructed Sparta as their imaginary (and superior) Other.[47] In Victorian terms, the correction is also necessary because, in the words of "Emerald Uthwart," "none" of the Greek models of pederasty "fits exactly."

"Emerald Uthwart" is a story of schoolboy friendship set at the time of Waterloo. In it, a pair of passionate but celibate friends embrace military service, are posted to the Continent, launch a raid of their own only to miss orders to advance, and are subsequently court-martialed. One is executed; the other dies shortly thereafter. Despite or perhaps in part by means of these individual apocalypses, Pater, in Lesley Higgins's term, *recodes* Plato's dialogue and makes it the eloquent expression of adolescent male romance.[48] For the protagonist and "James Stokes, the prefect, his immediate superior", *thinking Greek* means attempting to find a model for their "antique friendship" in the Latin and Greek "books they read together." In the story, the Athenian model vies with the Spartan one. Though the latter appears to win out, Pater's point is that perfect translation from the Greek is not possible.

James and Emerald's friendship has strong overtones of Athenian-model pederasty. As the narrator remarks:

> In every generation of schoolboys there are a few who find out, almost for themselves, the beauty and power of good literature, even in the literature they must read perforce; and this, in turn, is but the handsel of a beauty and power still active in the actual world, should they have the good fortune, or rather, acquire the skill, to deal with it properly. It has something of the stir and unction—the intellectual awaking with a leap—of the coming of love. So it was with Uthwart about his seventeenth year. He felt it, felt the intellectual passion, like the pressure outward of wings within him—ἡ πτεροῦ ὀύναμις, says Plato, in the *Phaedrus;* but again, as some do with everyday love, withheld, restrained himself.

At Emerald's school, the influence of texts like *Phaedrus* is overmastered by a "monastic" ("Hebraic" in Arnold's term) discipline that is repeatedly figured in the schoolboys' singing in choir. This singing, in turn, is both Christian and Greek, achieving the aesthetic effect of individual subordination within a larger unit that had earlier been produced in Lacedaemon. Athenian-model pederasty is subordinated to the Spartan model—so that, as the narrator observes—"It is of military glory that [the schoolboys] are really think-

ing." Indeed, the relation between the two models, the potentialities of each, and the process whereby one is subordinated to the other are central concerns of Pater's study. The result is a portrait of the construction of male-male desire within English schooling that is framed in silent irony by the ongoing discussion within late Victorian sexology of homosexuality as a perversion. The categorization of attraction between men as *abnormal* gives Pater reason for setting the events of the story two generations earlier during the romantic period, when the intensification of sentiment between men was celebrated in aesthetic discourses in England and Germany.[49] Yet for a polemicist on behalf of sexual and emotional ties between men such as Pater, the same pressure impels a latter-day effort to frame new relations between masculine desire and cultural and social formations.

Attempting to think Greek, the narrator of "Emerald Uthwart" chooses two Greek words to indicate the powerful effects of the Spartan model. In contrast to the love between two young men that dawns over shared schoolbooks and which leads to self-reflection on Emerald's part, the narrator stresses that ἄσκησις, the beauty associated with "discipline," exerts its determining power over the young man *unconsciously:* "It would misrepresent Uthwart's wholly unconscious humility to say that he felt the beauty of the ἄσκησις (we need that Greek word) to which he not merely finds himself subject, but as under a fascination submissively yields himself, although another might have been aware of the charm of it, half ethic, half physical, as visibly effective in him." "Another" here might be the narrator, who describes himself earlier as "the careful aesthetic observer." Or it might be his friend James, whose wish to pursue a military career encourages Emerald's similar wish. Or it might be a schoolmaster who consciously manipulates the blend of physical and moral charm, perhaps the same schoolmaster who helps seal Emerald's fate by "frankly" recommending that he relinquish his dawning intellectual ambitions. Or it might be "others" whom Emerald meets during his brief stay at Oxford and who likewise "tell him, as if weighing him, his very self, against his merely scholastic capacity and effects, that he would 'do for the army.'"

During their first year at Oxford, the two young men take "advantage of a sudden outbreak of war to join the army at once." Pater sets the period of their service in Europe immediately before Waterloo.[50] He does so in order to put in question the social utility of Spartan-model pederasty as well as the use of military service as a model of social organization generally in the opening chapter of Ruskin's *Unto This Last.* By setting the climax of the story in 1815, Pater concedes the maximum to his antagonists, since the final struggle against Napoleon can be construed as a supremely fitting moment of sacrifice. Yet even in this context he undercuts male sublimation. The narrator chooses a second Greek word to mark Uthwart's seemingly inevitable path, "a special word the Greeks had for the Fate which accompanied one who would come to a violent end. . . . *Κήρ*, the extraordinary Destiny, one's Doom, had a scent for distant blood-shedding; and, to be in at a sanguinary death, one of their number came forth to the very cradle, followed persistently all the way, over the waves, through powder and shot, through the rose-gardens;—where not? Looking back, one might trace the red footsteps all along, side by side." Although the mythic presentation of this fate poses it as individual, it is socially constructed, incised in the ideal of male self-sacrifice. Given how Uthwart's pedigree combines Anglo-Saxon antiquity, Norman supersession, and Druid prehistory, the shadowed cradle may well be that of English manhood itself and specifically of the aristocratic caste to which Emerald belongs.[51]

The suggestion of class catastrophe signals Pater's view that neither the Athenian nor the Spartan model are serviceable in the contemporary world. Rather, men like Emerald and James require space in which to live their relationship in a way that alters their social surround instead of making them vulnerable to destructive manipulation at the behest of national interest. The love that Emerald finds in *Phaedrus* "is but the handsel of a beauty and power still active in the actual world." The key words are "active" and "actual": desire between men can work to help transform everyday life. This passage introduces a second apocalyptic possibility in sharp contrast to the individual fates prescribed in the main line of the narrative. The second possibility is of a power between men capable of transforming the conditions of social existence. By 1892, when the story was published, this utopian vision could be termed, properly speaking, homosexual. But to achieve the power and beauty suggested to the two students by *Phaedrus* requires an ethical knowledge and a shared experience that is not given but earned. In other words, unlike some other projections of utopian existence in homosexual polemic, Pater's comes back to ordinary contingencies. The transformation is to be not just dreamt but accomplished.

In a number of later writings modeled on the myth of Dionysus, Pater repeatedly invokes the return of the idealized young male body from the grave. But in "Emerald Uthwart" he grows impatient with mortality and insists instead on the "skill" needed to *think Greek.* The narrator contends that the return of the "'Golden-haired, scholar Apollo'" is a delusion. One has to find something "better; . . . more like a real portrait of a real young Greek, like *Tryphon, Son of Eutychos,* for instance, (as friends remembered him with regret, as you may see him still on his tombstone in the British Museum) alive among the paler physical and intellectual lights of modern England." In this passage, Pater denies the possibility of the perfect "Englishing" of Greek. One is removed from the "real young Greek"

by a series of figures: of a sculpture in relief, of an epitaph written by friends, and by the fact that England is not Greece, that in "modern England" the light is "paler."[52] He also concedes a necessary mourning within what he takes to be the sculptural figure of desire. Loss is inseparable from memory and from apocalyptic hope. Together with this multiple resistance to metaphoric identification occurs Pater's insistence that one can find something "better" than the sublime figure of Apollo. One can find something or, rather, someone who is "alive" today.

Shades of Gray

Given Pater's critique of Dorianism, what is one to make of the proximity of Dorian style to the style that a public schooler might aspire to, including even "that expressive brevity of utterance" associated with the stiff upper lip? And, in a section of "Lacedaemon" in which Pater repeatedly refers to public schools, what is one to make of his emphasis on "youthful friendship, 'passing even the love of woman,' which, by system, . . . elaborated into a kind of art, became an elementary part of education?"[53] Partial answers to these questions may be found in *The Picture of Dorian Gray,* the novel by Oscar Wilde whose parodic critique of Pater's aestheticism helped impel Pater to the analysis of pedagogic eros that he makes in his writing of the early 1890s.

In its earlier, magazine version, the novel combines a moral fable that is intimately associated with pederastic idealization and a discussion of the good life reminiscent of the Platonic dialogues most closely associated with the Athenian model. The first key moment in Wilde's version of Platonic conversation combines both Athenian and Dorian elements. The painter Basil Hallward declares at once his faith in cultural renaissance and the central place in it of his devotion to Dorian Gray.

> I sometimes think, Harry, that there are only two eras of any importance in the history of the world. The first is the appearance of a new medium for art, and the second is the appearance of a new personality for art also. What the invention of oil-painting was to the Venetians, the face of Antinoüs was to late Greek sculpture, and the face of Dorian Gray will some day be to me. . . . His personality has suggested to me an entirely new manner in art, an entirely new mode of style. I see things differently, I think of them differently. I can now re-create life in a way that was hidden from me before. . . . Unconsciously he defines for me the lines of a fresh school, a school that is to have in itself all the passion of the romantic spirit, all the perfection of the spirit that is Greek. The harmony of soul and body—how much that is! We in our madness have separated the two, and have invented a realism that is vulgar, an ideality that is void. Harry! Harry! if you only knew what Dorian Gray is to me![54]

Hallward's representation of Dorian recalls the homo-erotic aesthetic culture of the essays on Leonardo and Winckelmann produced by Pater at Oxford in the 1860s. In these essays, desire works to desublimate what Hallward calls a false "ideality." Pater validates bodily existence, masturbation, and sexual and emotional ties between men both as valuable in themselves and as contributing to democratic change. In addition, in the years around 1867, Pater and other liberals hoped for legislative reform that would decriminalize sexual activities between men.[55] The loss of these hopes is a necessary precondition of the outcomes of pederasty in Wilde's novel. Following passage of the antihomosexual Labouchère amendment in 1885, Hallward's evocation is most remarkable for what is left unsaid: he dissociates masculine desire and the art it prompts from hope for social transformation.

Although the relation between culture and the state remains tacit, Basil reports that he has already painted Dorian in the guise of Antinoüs: "Crowned with heavy lotus-blossoms, he has sat on the prow of Adrian's barge, looking into the green, turbid Nile." Antinoüs was the beloved of the emperor Hadrian, who purportedly arranged the young man's death in the Nile before having him declared a god.[56] Represented in Hallward's portraiture as an object of the male homosocial gaze, Dorian's beauty connotes subjection, sacrifice, and idealization. These suggestions render Basil's cultural ideal ominous, a tone that echoes in Wilde's suggestion that Dorian sits for his portrait "with the air of a young Greek martyr." A "martyr" of and to what?[57]

In Basil's statement, absence of confidence in the civic meaning of Dorianism is matched by excessive attention to a renovating "passion." But Basil's will to celebrate "the harmony of soul and body" lacks a location in personal or social life. A process of aesthetic abstraction overtakes his relation with Dorian: "Dorian Gray," he says defensively to Sir Henry, "is merely to me a motive in art. . . . He is simply a suggestion, as I have said, of a new manner. I see him in the curves of certain lines, in the loveliness and the subtleties of certain colors. That is all." As to why Basil does not wish to exhibit the painting that reveals "the secret of my soul," in the manuscript he says, "Where there is merely love, [the world] . . . would see something evil. Where there is spiritual passion, they would suggest something vile." In these passages, the anxious sublimation of homosexual desire in aesthetic form becomes consciously closeting. Dorian's portrait must be kept secret lest its meaning be mediated by the "vile" representation of the Cleveland Street scandal of 1889-1890 in the popular press and by the emerging picture of homosexuality within sexology and criminology.[58] Under these pressures, Basil, contrary to his affirmations, loses the ability to *think Greek* that had been prompted by discussions earlier in the century. The loss is evident in the turn to aesthetic abstraction and,

later, to the antinomies of "Christian" morality. This inability negates Hallward's advocacy of "the spirit that is Greek." Congruent with this emptying as well is his double existence, which combines idealization of a young man, socially his superior, plus the undivulged details of Basil's stays in Paris. So much for "the harmony of soul and body."

In *The Picture of Dorian Gray,* masculine desire is presented in the context of Wilde's satire of male culture, especially as it existed at Oxford. Dorian himself is presented as representing an Oxford ideal: "Very young men . . . saw, or fancied that they saw, in Dorian Gray the true realization of a type of which they had often dreamed in Eton or Oxford days, a type that was to combine something of the real culture of the scholar with all the grace and distinction and perfect manner of a citizen of the world. To them he seemed to belong to those whom Dante describes as having sought to 'make themselves perfect by the worship of beauty.'" Dorian is also identified with an athletic Greek ideal: after discovering changes in the portrait, he exults that he himself will remain "like the gods of the Greeks . . . , strong, and fleet, and joyous. What did it matter what happened to the colored image on the canvas? He would be safe. That was everything." In a parody of Platonic love, Dorian has fallen for his peers' idolization of his beauty and privilege.[59] Like the young Spartan aristocrats of Pater's essay of two years later, Dorian turns himself into "a perfect work of art" functioning in a world of spectacle.[60] This position has its counterpart in the power that men like Dorian have to abuse others but likewise in the power of other men over them, which makes Dorian paranoid: late in the novel, he becomes "sick with a wild terror of dying. . . . The consciousness of being hunted, snared, tracked down, had begun to dominate him."

Dorian is, in fact, anything but "safe." His danger, including the growing fin de siècle danger of exposure as a homosexual, is one that he shares with his namesake, John Gray, the beautiful, gifted young man of working-class background, whom Wilde befriended after 1889 and probably took, for a time, as his lover.[61] In order to protect his position at the Foreign Office, early in 1892 Gray issued a writ for libel against a newspaper that had reported that he was "said to be the original Dorian of the same name."[62] Gray's career included conversion to Roman Catholicism; a correct but devoted relationship with Mark André Raffalovich, a writer who polemicized on behalf of celibate male homosexuality; and service as a pastor in Edinburgh.

After a long period of silence, in 1922 John Gray published *Vivis,* a little book of poems in an edition of fifty copies. Inserted in the volume on a separate sheet of paper is a vignette, "a drawing of what appears to be a female head, with a mask (a girl's face) tied over the lower half; but when it is turned upside down the picture shows a skull, with the mask, now in reverse, tied over the upper part of the skull. Below the skull is a scroll bearing the words *Non omnia novi*" (literally, "I do not know everything"). Gray's biographer remarks: "Possibly the idea that the drawing is meant to convey is that of careless youth heedless of the four last things—a notion apposite to Gray's own former life."[63] The dual aspect of the image lends it an affinity with the ending of Wilde's novel, which offsets the "exquisite youth and beauty" of the portrait with the "withered, wrinkled, and loathsome . . . visage" of the corpse on the floor. In the context of Dorianism, the image suggests the collapse of the sublime association of idealized male flesh with death on behalf of civilization. Here is no flesh, no masculinity, only a travesty of the feminine.

The female mask, face, or body that only partially conceals a death's head is familiar in the iconography of *vanitas*. Morris Meredith Williams, who provided Gray with the drawing, conceived it within a tradition whose erotophobia is specifically misogynistic. Nonetheless, the double image has an apt relation to Gray's disabused view of desire between men. Through Raffalovich's research into the theory of sexual inversion, Gray had access to "third-sex theories" of homosexuality, which "'regarded uranism, or homosexual love, as a congenital abnormality by which a female soul had become united with a male body—*anima muliebris in corpore virili inclusa.*'"[64] Gray provides a thoroughly ironic version of this metaphysical incongruity, in which the attractions of young male beauty, including his own seductive attractiveness when he was in his early twenties, are a feminine pretense covering moral and physical corruption. More pointed still, the double visage may represent a homosocial/homosexual gaze masked by the feminized mirror image that it proffers to attractive young men. In this reading, the image refers not to Gray's subjectivity (which remains unrepresented) but to the social construction of gender that proffers seductive lures to attractive young men.

Dorianism did not disappear in the new century. In Germany, its appeal continued in *Der Eigene,* a right-wing male homosexual periodical whose circulation reached 150,000 during the Weimar Republic. Promoting a masculinized model of desire between men in the service of Aryan ideals, Adolf Brand, the publisher of the journal, attacked the third-sex theory of homosexuality espoused by his Jewish socialist rival, Magnus Hirschfeld. Benedict Friedländer, a politically conservative, Jewish homosexual likewise argued that "attacks on homosexuals . . . were led by Jews determined to undermine Aryan virility and self-awareness."[65]

In England at the end of the century, the bond between masculine desire and the salvation of the state became inverted. In *L'Affaire Oscar Wilde* (1895), Raffalovich blames Wilde's debacle on national decadence: "La societé anglaise est coupable également."[66] But homosexual polemicists continued to invoke Dorianism. Why? Because it provided a defense of sexual and emotional ties between men. It likewise offered a defense against feminizing representations of men who desired other men. It provided a resonant answer to the difficult question about what utility sexual and emotional ties between men might possess. It validated homosexuals as equal to other men and gave meaning to sacrifice, something that many homosexual men found that their attachments to other men necessitated. Edward Carpenter hated modern war, but he had his own vision of the value of Dorianism. In *The Intermediate Sex* (1908), he writes:

> We have solid work waiting to be done in the patient and life-long building up of new forms of society, new orders of thought, and new institutions of human solidarity—all of which in their genesis must meet with opposition, ridicule, hatred, and even violence. Such campaigns as these—though different in kind from those of the Dorian mountaineers described above—will call for equal hardihood and courage, and will stand in need of a comradeship as true and valiant. And it may indeed be doubted whether the higher heroic and spiritual life of a nation is ever quite possible without the sanction of this attachment in its institutions, adding a new range and scope to the possibilities of love.[67]

Both Carpenter's rhapsody and the panicky image of the masked skull are transformations of the Dorianism of David's splendid painting. The emergence by the early 1890s of male homosexual existence and its representation within contemporary sexology undercut Dorian friendship. The conceptual space, carefully opened for Dorianism within bourgeois culture, narrowed. Despite the ascendancy in the public schools and the older universities of a humanism aligned with a national and imperial ethos, the sublime association of devotion between men with the interests of the state underwent a process of de-idealization that did not erase the connections between friendship and (military) service but which made them increasingly difficult to sustain. Nonetheless, as Carpenter's response shows, the revulsion expressed in the vignette from Gray's book is not the inevitable or the only end to which pederastic models could lead. Pater's mordant view in "Emerald Uthwart" of the social uses to which young male desire could be put and Wilde's satire of the attempt to validate pederastic desire by placing it in service of high culture and self-enclosure within a social elite both imply the need to complete the task of what John Addington Symonds had referred to as *aesthesis* in his *Studies of the Greek Poets.* The work of making desire and relationship between men a mode of ethical action, cultural reflection, and social existence was more important than ever.[68] This project has its own apocalyptic tenor in antagonistic relationship to Dorianism as it is memorialized in David's painting. Even Gray's turn to the priesthood may be interpreted not merely as a lapse into the conventional thinking that Müller had challenged long before but rather as an effort, within the very limited means available after the Wilde trials, to achieve a locus in which the work of *aesthesis* could continue.

Notes

[1] Quoted in Jacques Derrida, *The Truth in Painting,* 68n.

[2] Elaine Scarry, *The Body in Pain: The Making and Unmaking of the World,* 63. For studies of the ideological structure of nation-building, see Benedict Anderson, *Imagined Communities: Reflections on the Origins and Spread of Nationalism,* and Ernest Gellner, *Nations and Nationalism.*

[3] Michel Foucault, *The History of Sexuality. Volume I: An Introduction,* 139.

[4] David Halperin, *One Hundred Years of Homosexuality and Other Essays on Greek Love,* ix.

[5] In contrast to the Spartan model, Halperin points out that in a number of early texts "pair-bonding" within a military or political context is not sexualized (*One Hundred Years of Homosexuality,* 75). He instances the relationships of Achilles and Patroclus in the *Iliad,* of David and Jonathan in the Books of Samuel in the Old Testament, and of Gilgamesh and Enkidu in the Gilgamesh epic.

[6] See Paul Cartledge, "The Politics of Spartan Pederasty."

[7] George Mosse, *Nationalism and Sexuality: Middle-Class Morality and Sexual Norms in Modern Europe,* 88, chap. 2; Barry D. Adam, *The Rise of a Gay and Lesbian Movement,* 21-22.

[8] Ernst Curtius, *The History of Greece,* 1: 190-197.

[9] Hector Hugh Munro ("Saki"), a British writer who died in military action in World War I, was one such subject (Mosse, *Nationalism and Sexuality,* 43).

[10] Paul de Man, *The Rhetoric of Romanticism,* 264.

[11] Immanuel Kant, *On History,* xii.

[12] Immanuel Kant, *The Critique of Judgement,* 112-113.

[13] In his *Anthropology* (1798), Kant refers to Jews as "a nation of cheats, . . . a nation of traders" (Paul Lawrence Rose, *Revolutionary Antisemitism in Germany: From Kant to Wagner,* 94. See Rose's general discussion of Kant and Judaism, 91-97).

[14] Robert Rosenblum, "Reconstructing David," 196.

[15] In this sentence and in the remainder of the chapter, I observe the distinction that Kaja Silverman draws in *Male Subjectivity at the Margins* between the "look" or "eye" and the "gaze." She writes: "The relationship between eye and gaze is . . . analogous . . . to that which links penis and phallus; the former can stand in for the latter, but can never approximate it. Lacan makes this point with particular force when he situates the gaze outside the voyeuristic transaction, a transaction within which the eye would seem most to aspire to a transcendental status, and which has consequently provided the basis, within feminist film theory, for an equation of the male voyeur with the gaze" (130).

[16] C. O. Müller, *The History and Antiquities of the Doric Race,* 2:303.

[17] Luc de Nanteuil, *Jacques-Louis David,* 118.

[18] Cf. the discussion in de Man, *The Rhetoric of Romanticism,* chap. 4, esp. 77-78.

[19] De Nanteuil, *Jacques-Louis David,* 118.

[20] Stephanie Carroll, "Reciprocal Representations: David and Theater."

[21] Jack Lindsay, *Death of the Hero: French Painting from David to Delacroix,* 131.

[22] Sander Gilman, "Opera, Homosexuality, and Models of Disease: Richard Strauss's *Salome* in the Context of Images of Disease in the Fin de Siècle," in *Disease and Representation: Images of Illness from Madness to AIDS,* 155-181.

[23] Joan DeJean, *Fictions of Sappho: 1546-1937,* 206.

[24] Martin Bernal, *Black Athena: The Afroasiatic Roots of Classical Civilization,* 1:27, 33.

[25] Emily Vermeule, "The World Turned Upside Down," 40, 41. Although Vermeule is highly critical of the arguments that Bernal puts forward in the second volume of his study to justify his belief "that [black] Egypt and the Levant inspired the culture of the Greeks," she acknowledges Bernal's "justifiable condemnation" in the first volume "of the narrow-minded teaching of the classics that assumed the cultural superiority of the Greeks without reference to Egypt and the East" (40).

[26] DeJean, *Fictions of Sappho,* 204.

[27] On *Deutschheit* and related terms in advanced thinking of the period, see Jacques Derrida, "*Geschlecht* II: Heidegger's Hand."

[28] DeJean, *Fictions of Sappho,* 209, 214.

[29] Müller, *History and Antiquities of the Doric Race,* 2:300. Linda Dowling discusses this claim in "Ruskin's Pied Beauty and the Constitution of a 'Homosexual' Code," 2, as does DeJean in *Fictions of Sappho,* 214-215.

[30] Müller, *History and Antiquities of the Doric Race,* 2:304.

[31] This demand for a hermeneutic reading persists today. See the discussion in the afterword of my *Masculine Desire: The Sexual Politics of Victorian Aestheticism,* as well as in Halperin, *One Hundred Years of Homosexuality,* 10-11 and chap. 3.

[32] Halperin, *One Hundred Years of Homosexuality,* 154 n. 12; DeJean, *Fictions of Sappho,* 346 n. 16.

[33] John Addington Symonds, *Male Love: A Problem in Greek Ethics and Other Writings,* 17.

[34] Ibid., xxi.

[35] Müller, *History and Antiquities of the Doric Race,* 2:306.

[36] Symonds, *Male Love,* 14.

[37] Müller, *History and Antiquities of the Doric Race,* 2:302.

[38] Johann Jakob Bachofen, *Myth, Religion, and Mother Right,* 201, 204, 71, 205, 207. See DeJean's discussion in *Fictions of Sappho,* 220-222. For connections between Bachofen and anglophone writers, see Bachofen, li-lvi.

[39] Friedrich Engels, *The Origin of the Family, Private Property and the State,* 95.

[40] Benjamin Jowett, trans., *The Dialogues of Plato,* 2d rev. ed., 3:26.

[41] Walter Pater, *Miscellaneous Studies: A Series of Essays,* 181-182. Subsequent page citations to this work will be given in the text.

[42] Matthew Arnold, *Complete Prose Works,* 5:134, 136, 283.

[43] Ibid., 5:282.

[44] Ibid., 5:292, 294.

[45] Walter Pater, *Plato and Platonism,* 202, 198.

[46] Ibid., 220.

[47] William Shuter, "Walter Pater and the Academy's 'Dubious Name,'" 140.

[48] Used in conversation with the author, September 1990. Lesley Higgins has made clear to me the polemical relation between Pater's later writing about *Phaedrus* and Jowett's translation. In the introduction to his translation of *Phaedrus,* Jowett attempts to evade the emphasis on desire between males in Plato's text by substituting for male love a nearly asexual ideal of Victorian marriage (Benjamin Jowett, trans., *The Dialogues of Plato,* 3d rev. ed., 1:406-409).

[49] Pater refers to these discourses at the beginning of "Emerald Uthwart" when the narrator meditates on the epitaphs of "German students" who studied at Siena early in the eighteenth century. Pater links these men with the paintings of "Sodoma" (*Miscellaneous Studies,* 170; Rudolf Wittkower and Margot Wittkower, *Born under Saturn: The Character and Conduct of Artists—A Documented History from Antiquity to the French Revolution,* 173-175) in the same church and, allusively, with later German students—such as those who studied with Winckelmann in Rome or like the Nazarenes, Friedrich Overbeck, Peter Cornelius, and Franz Pforr, who made "friendship pictures" for each other early in the nineteenth century (*German Masters of the Nineteenth Century: Paintings and Drawings from the Federal Republic of Germany,* 176; Keith Andrews, *The Nazarenes: A Brotherhood of German Painters in Rome,* frontispiece; for an account of apologies for desire between men in late eighteenth-century German philosophy, see Gert Hekma, "Sodomites, Platonic Lovers, Contrary Lovers: The Backgrounds of the Modern Homosexual," 435-440).

[50] Gerald Monsman, *Pater's Portraits: Mythic Pattern in the Fiction of Walter Pater,* 178n. On 171-183 Monsman traces the connections between the portrait and *Plato and Platonism.*

[51] For the post-1870 history of British aristocracy, see Noel Annan, "The Death of 'Society.'"

[52] William Shuter discusses Pater's use of the Greek *stele* in a number of texts. See his "Arrested Narrative of 'Emerald Uthwart,'" 15-18.

[53] Pater, *Plato and Platonism,* 222, 231.

[54] Oscar Wilde, *The Picture of Dorian Gray,* 180. Henceforth cited in the text.

[55] See Dellamora, *Masculine Desire,* 114.

[56] See Royston Lambert, *Beloved and God: The Story of Hadrian and Antinous.*

[57] Richard Kaye is studying the fin de siècle interest, heterosexual and homosexual, in Saint Sebastian.

[58] Dellamora, *Masculine Desire,* 202.

[59] Halperin argues that the Platonic lover falls in love with the love of beauty pouring forth from the eye of the beloved. The latter responds to the reflection of this love in the look of the lover (David Halperin, "Plato and Erotic Reciprocity," 62-63, 75 n. 49).

[60] Pater, *Plato and Platonism,* 232.

[61] In Wilde's novel, Dorian appears to be attracted to both men and women. For Wilde's relationship with John Gray, see Richard Ellmann, *Oscar Wilde,* 291.

[62] Brocard Sewell, *In the Dorian Mode: A Life of John Gray, 1866-1934,* 18.

[63] Ibid., 138.

[64] Havelock Ellis, cited in Christopher Craft, "'Kiss Me with Those Red Lips': Gender and Inversion in Bram Stoker's *Dracula,*" 113. For Raffalovich, see Timothy d'Arch Smith, *Love in Earnest: Some Notes on the Lives and Writings of English 'Uranian' Poets from 1889 to 1930,* 29-30, 34.

[65] Mosse, *Nationalism and Sexuality,* 41, 42.

[66] Sewell, *In the Dorian Mode,* 79.

[67] Edward Carpenter, *Selected Writings, Volume One: Sex,* 217. Carpenter's *Intermediate Types Among Primitive Folk: A Study in Social Evolution* (1914) includes a chapter, "Military Comradeship Among the Dorian Greeks."

[68] Dellamora, *Masculine Desire,* 160-161.

Byrne R. S. Fone

SOURCE: "This Other Eden: Arcadia and the Homosexual Imagination," in *Literary Visions of Homosexuality,* The Haworth Press, 1983, pp. 13-34.

[*In the excerpt that follows, Fone suggests that gay male literature tends toward a certain image of Utopia. He substantiates his view with examples from the work of several nineteenth-century writers, including Gerard Manley Hopkins and Walt Whitman.*]

Those who would dwell in Arcadia seek out that secret Eden because of its isolation from the troubled world and its safety from the arrogant demands of those who would deny freedom, curtail human action, and destroy innocence and love. Arcadia can be a happy valley, a blessed isle, a pastoral retreat, or a green forest fastness. Those who search for that hidden paradise are often lovers, or the truly wise, trying, as one questing pilgrim put it, to escape from "the clank of the world."[1]

I would like to suggest that the Arcadian ideal has been used in the homosexual literary tradition in a fashion that speaks directly to the gay sensibility. The homosexual imagination finds a special value and a particular use for this ideal, employing it in three major ways: 1) to suggest a place where it is safe to be gay: where gay men can be free from the outlaw status society confers upon us, where homosexuality can be revealed and spoken of without reprisal, and where homosexual love can be consummated without concern for the punishment or scorn of the world; 2) to imply the presence of gay love and sensibility in a text that otherwise makes no explicit statement about homosexuality;[2] and 3) to establish a metaphor for certain spiritual values and myths prevalent in homosexual literature and life, namely, that homosexuality is superior to heterosexuality and is a divinely sanctioned means to an understanding of the good and the beautiful, and that the search for the Ideal Friend is one of the major undertakings of the homosexual life. Only in this metaphoric land can certain rituals take place, rituals that celebrate this mythology. These rites are transformational and involve the union of lovers, the loving and sexual fraternity of men, and the washing away of societal guilt. The symbolic events of the rituals include the offering of gifts, usually from nature, and the purification by water to prepare for an eternity of blissful habitation in the garden. . . .

In *Joseph and His Friend,* written by the American poet and novelist Bayard Taylor in 1869, Arcadia is described as:

a great valley, bounded by hundreds of miles of snowy peaks; lakes in its bed; enormous hillsides, dotted with groves of ilex and pine, orchards of orange and olive; a perfect climate, where it is bliss enough to breathe, and [where there is] freedom from the distorted laws of men, for none are near enough to enforce them. If there is no legal way of escape for you, here, at least there is no force which will drag you back, once you are there: I will go with you, and perhaps, perhaps. . . .[6]

The speaker, Joseph, says to his friend Philip: "We should be outlaws there, in our freedom!—here we are fettered outlaws." The two men determine that the time has not yet come for them to enter into their great valley, their Arcadia. But in the fullness of the vision, and against every canon of Victorian rectitude, they took each other's hands. The day was fading, the landscape silent, and only the twitter of nestling birds was heard in the boughs above them. Each gave way to the impulse of manly love, rarer, alas! but as tender and true as the love of woman, and they drew near and kissed each other. As they walked back and parted on the highway, each felt that life was not wholly unkind, and that happiness was not yet impossible.

Earlier in the book, Joseph met Philip when both were in a train wreck. Joseph's response to Philip's handsome face, and the intimacy that develops between them, are at odds with the fact that the plot of the book ostensibly has nothing to do with homosexuality. Rather, it is a midcentury novel of manners, detailing Joseph's misery in a loveless first marriage and his eventual happiness in a second (with, it ought to be noted, the look-alike sister of his friend Philip). But aside from the fact that much of Taylor's poetry is specifically homoerotic, his reference to "manly love" (a code word in Whitman and the nineteenth-century British Uranian poets) and his play upon the biblical story of David and Jonathan, whose love was "passing the love of women" as Philip and Joseph's is "rarer, alas, but as tender and true as the love of woman," provide a distinctly homosexual atmosphere that is only reinforced by the lengthy appeal to the happy-valley imagery, the happy valley as a place where two men can be free and "live as outlaws." The "great valley," of course, is Arcadia, the secret garden where their love can be consummated, far from the "distorted laws of men." . . .

Scenes of boys bathing are unquestionably a genre of homosexual art and literature. Tuke's celebrated painting *August Blue* (1894), a picture of four boys, nude and sunbathing in a boat on the river, was the occasion of several poems by English Uranians.[19] Alan Stanley's "August Blue" and Charles Kains-Jackson's "Sonnet on a Picture by Tuke" are examples; one of the best is Frederick Rolfe's melodic "Ballade of Boys Bathing." A prime example of the genre was printed in *The Artist,* a magazine that devoted itself, especially under the editorship of Kains-Jackson, to homosexual poetry and fiction. This was S. S. Saale's sonnet of 1890, which links the miracle of transformation by water, a kind of homosexual baptism, to legends of Greek mythology.

> Upon the wall, of idling boys in a row
>   The grimy barges not more dull than they,
>   When sudden in the midst of all their play
> They strip and plunge into the stream below:
> Changed by a miracle, they rise as though
>   The youth of Greece burst on this later day
>   As on their lithe young bodies many a ray
> Of sunlight dallies with its blushing glow.
> Flower of clear beauty, naked purity,

> With thy sweet presence olden days return,
> Like fragrant ashes from a classic urn,
> Flashed into life anew once more we see
> Narcissus by the pool, or 'neath the tree
>   Young Daphnis, and new pulses throb and
>   burn.[20]

The dull boys are transformed into Grecian youths and the grimy urban Thameside into a paradise resplendent with rural and Arcadian sunlight, the same sunlight that will later shine, incidentally, on the burnished body of Paul in *The Divided Path* as he walks with "Arcadian naturalness." If the poet recalls the pool of Narcissus, and Daphnis in his grove, so too are we reminded of Tadzio, who in "Death in Venice" will rise from the water "with dripping locks, beautiful as a tender young god."

The homosexual content of Saale's sonnet lies not in any overt sexuality but, first, in a code that includes phrases like "clear beauty," "sweet presence," and "naked purity"; second, in references to homosexual myth (Narcissus and Daphnis); and last, in the dominant metaphor of the poem, the transformation by water, turning dull boys into lithe ephebes. Similarly, such elements of homosexual discourse can be found in poetry even less obviously homosexual in content. For Gerard Manley Hopkins, the homosexual discourse was one that exerted considerable fascination and produced no inconsiderable pain and evasion. But in his "Epithalamion,"[21] an unfinished poem ostensibly written in celebration of heterosexual marriage, the dominant metaphor and attending imagery are concerned with just those matters under discussion here. Though Hopkins tacks onto the end of the poem a few incomplete and not entirely clear lines—perhaps fragmentary—about wedlock and spousal love, they are half-hearted and do not have the passionate force of the homosexual elements of the bulk of the poem.

To begin, Hopkins invokes the "hearer" to "hear what I do." Though the image is conventional in its invocation of a muse at first consideration, a muse is generally thought of as the inspirer, not the hearer. Not to put too fine a point on it, we might be reminded that in Greek custom and poetry the beloved youth was called the "hearer" and his lover the "inspirer." As Hans Licht, the pseudonymous Paul Brandt, notes in *Sexual Life in Ancient Greece:* "In the Dorian dialect, the usual word for the lover was . . . the 'inspirer,' which contains the hint that the lover, who indeed was responsible for the boy in every connection, inspired the young receptive soul with all that was good and noble. . . . with this the Dorian name for the loved boy, the 'listening, the intellectually receptive,' agrees."[22]

For his hearer, Hopkins the inspirer conjures up a truly wondrous greenwood. "Make believe," he says,

We are leafwhelmed somewhere with the hood
   of some branchy bunchy bushybowered wood
Southern dene or Lancashire clough or Devon
   cleave,
That leans along the loins of hills, where a
   candy-colored
   where a blue-brown
Marbled river, boisterously beautiful, between
Roots and Rocks is dance and dandled, all in
   froth
   and water
   blowbells, down.

In the river, "boys from the town" are bathing. "It is summer's sovereign good." Into this noisy scene comes a "listless stranger" who watches and is so inspired by the "bellbright bodies," the "garland of their gambols flashes in his breast / Into such a sudden zest," that he

hies to a pool neighboring; sees it is the best
   There; sweetest, freshest, shadowiest;
Fairyland; silk-beech, scrolled ash, packed
   sycamores
   wild wychelm, hornbeam fretty overstood
By.

While the boys from town bathe in the real world, the listless stranger's pool is in Fairyland, surely Arcadia, a happy valley surrounded by Virgilian forests and fragrant with Marlovian posies.

Of course, the listless stranger is one with the unhappy Corydon. And, like the boys in Saale's sonnet, and like the Reverend Beebe, he will strip and plunge into the miraculous pool.

Off with—down
   he dings
His bleached both and woolen wear:
Careless these in colored wisp
All lie tumbled-to; then loop-locks
Forward falling, forehead frowning, lips crisp
Over fingers teasing task, his twiny boots
Fast he opens, last offwrings
Till walk the world he can with bare his feet. . . .

Striding naked, in command of the world in sudden liberation, he dives into the water and into communion with the bathing boys and with the innocence of the happy valley:

Here he will then, here he will the
Flinty feet kindcold element let break across
   his limbs
Long. When we leave him, froliclavish, while
   he looks about
   him, laughs, swims

The image is striking. In one pool the naked boys frolic; in the next, the stranger. The naked stranger is inspired by the beauty of the boys; he enters the secret garden, Fairyland, and dives into the pool of miracles. He is transfigured. No longer listless, he is "froliclavish." He laughs and is liberated, purified by water.

"What is this delightful dene," Hopkins asks. "This is sacred matter that I mean." His answer is that the delightful dene is "wedlock." "What is water," he inquires. The answer: "Spousal love." The answers are curiously out of context in a poem where a naked male stranger is revived from his spiritual decline by the sight of bathing naked boys and in which he is drawn into refreshing communion with these boys in a baptismal pool, this all taking place in our now-classic homosexual Arcadian grove.

Hopkins compounds the confusion at the end with a fragmentary observation: "Father, mother, brothers, sisters, friends? Into fairy trees, wild flowers, wood ferns / Ranked round the bower." This is distinctly unhelpful; in fact, I think, deliberately misleading. Yet he tells the truth when he says that "This is sacred matter that I mean." For the poem describes one of the sacred rituals of Arcadia: wedlock. The poem celebrates a moment of revelation in the greenwood where young men and boys are united in spousal love, where the listless stranger is transformed by the purifying waters of homosexual passion. The poem is an epithalamion indeed, and we are hearers to Hopkins' inspirer if we only have the ears.

All of the elements of the Arcadian metaphor come together in two poems by Whitman, "In Paths Untrodden" and "These I Singing in Spring." Like Corydon, who seeks out his "beeches with their shady summits" to sing his passionate song, or like Hopkins' "listless stranger" who seeks out the "sweetest, freshest, shadowiest" pool, Whitman, who elsewhere is the "solitary singer," seeks out "paths untrodden, / In the growth by the margins of pond waters." His purpose in finding this isolated retreat is to "escape from the life that exhibits itself," and "from all the standards hitherto published, from the pleasures, / profits, conformities, / Which too long I was offering to feed my soul." In this place he is alone, "away from the clank of the world."

Two elements are present here: the world of real life, which demands a certain conformity of appearance, and the world of the spirit, which is ill fed by the standards of that world. Physical and spiritual yearnings, then, call Whitman to his untrodden paths, his hidden pond waters. The typical Arcadian paradigm is again established: the lonely retreat, and the miraculous pool. Why does he come here? Like all the others, "in this secluded spot I can respond as I would not dare elsewhere." But what is it that he would not dare to speak of amidst the conformity of the real world? Three things: "standards not yet published," the fact that he "rejoices in comrades," and that "strong upon

Walt Whitman.

me" is "the life that does not exhibit itself." That all three of these are references to homosexuality has been ignored by many critics, denied by several, and should be perfectly clear to all. The most obvious phrase, "rejoices in comrades," had such a general homosexual use in the nineteenth century that its meaning is almost unavoidable, even if Whitman did not make it even more clear at the end of the poem and in other poems in the "Calamus" group, such as "For you O Democracy," with its refrain "by the love of comrades, / By the manly love of comrades." More oblique than this are "the standards not yet published" and the "life that does not exhibit itself." Obvious to any gay person, the standards not published are the standards of homosexual life and all its works, manners, and feelings. The "standards hitherto published," standards of heterosexual morality, are not useful to the soul of a man like Whitman. The standards of his own soul, the qualities that make him homosexual not only in sexual orientation but in sensibility—what we now call gay— are not, indeed cannot be, openly published. Similarly, the "life that does not exhibit itself" is certainly Whit-

man's phrase for the hidden gay sensibility, and it is the life, necessarily secret and secretive, that any nineteenth-century homosexual had to lead. But not only that, it must also be the life of the spirit that Whitman has had to conceal, and which he reveals in his poems, especially in this poem, a manifesto declaring his homosexuality and its purpose. This hidden life, he says dramatically, "contains all the rest," a singular statement revealing Whitman's deep awareness of how homosexuality informs, and becomes a dominating metaphor for, each individual life. That all this cannot be spoken in the real world demands that he repair to this secluded spot.

Like Corydon inspired to song in his fastness, Whitman is "resolv'd to sing no songs to-day but those of manly / attachment." Here, surrounded by "tongues aromatic"—the calamus—and of course all that other fragrant verdure we have seen in so many other Arcadian moments, he discovers the purpose of his life and the reason for his homosexuality: to bequeath "hence types of athletic love." (These types are of course his poems about homosexual love. "Athletic love" was to become another nineteenth-century commonplace standing for homosexuality.[23]) His mission is to sing the songs of manly attachment and, like the Grecian inspirer, to "proceed for all who are or have been young men," that is, to be the spokesman for all those who have not dared to speak, to educate them into the proper meaning of the virtuous homosexual life. To do this, he determines to undertake the breathtaking task of telling the "secrets of my nights and days," to be the celebrant of the "need of comrades." For Whitman, the experience in the garden frees him and sets him upon his appointed path: a creator spirit, come from paths untrodden to sing the most remarkable coming-out poem in our literature.

But if Arcadia serves as the scene for personal discovery and revelation, we have seen that it is also the place where a spiritual voyager can find a safe haven with others like himself and celebrate their common rites. So, in "These I Singing in Spring," we find Whitman talking of what Hopkins called "sacred matter," what Forster described as "a holiness, a spell, a momentary chalice of youth." Whitman begins the ritual by collecting tokens "for lovers." He asks: "Who but I should understand lovers and all their sorrows and joy? / Who but I should be the poet of comrades?" The search for tokens, we recall, is common to many of the works we have examined; the tokens are the wedding gifts that Corydon, the passionate shepherd, and Daphnis collected. His search for tokens leads Whitman into the "garden of the world." And soon, he says, "I pass the gates" into the world of the greenwood. The magic of pastoral rules, "along the pondside . . . far, far, in the forest." He had thought himself alone, but "soon a troop gathers round me." This is his troop of bathing boys, his ideal friends. He distributes his tokens to them, moss from the live oak (which, as he has noted elsewhere in "I Saw in Louisiana a Live-Oak Growing," "Makes me think of manly love"), lilac, pine, and sage, tokens like those Corydon brings to his Alexis. The significant moment, the moment of revelation—here nearly a eucharistic climax—comes when he draws from the water the aromatic calamus root, symbol of phallic homosexuality, physical and spiritual. Whitman is reminded now of *his* lover, "him that tenderly loves me, and returns again never to separate from me." Memory and desire flood in as he offers the calamus to his troop of young men in a sacred ceremony. This calamus is the "token of comrades. . . . Interchange it youths with each other! never render it back." So complex is this moment that it combines communion in both a spiritual and a religious sense—in wedlock, of Whitman to his troop of young men and of Whitman to his lover who will soon return, and in a plighting of vows: "Interchange it youths! never render it back." The vow is to eternal fidelity not only to one another but to the homosexual life itself, for the calamus is the symbol of that life.

Of all the moments of climax and communion that we have seen in various manifestations in the Arcadian garden, this is the most intense because it is the most highly charged with ritual and myth. There, in the greenwood, in the "far, far forest," which Whitman describes as redolent with "twigs of maple and a bunch of wild orange and chestnut, / and stems of currants and plum blows, and aromatic cedar," this natural incense rising to heaven, Whitman celebrates his erotic communion. Like Hopkins' "riot of . . . boys from town," Whitman's acolytes are a "thick cloud of spirits." They stand in Arcadia at its altar, next to the water of calamus, Whitman's Ladon. Whitman distributes his sacred token, the sacrament of calamus. Hopkins was specific: this cleansing by water means wedlock and is sacred matter. Whitman is equally clear: the calamus he draws from his pond-side is given "only to them that love as I myself am capable of loving." The poet has bound himself and his troop of friends by tokens and sacred oaths to the love of comrades. His words are the testament; calamus is the symbol and outward sign of that inward grace which can only be found in the leafy greenwood bower of a secret Arcadia.

I hope that this paper will suggest to other students some areas for exploration in the examination of that term which seems to be so real to all of us who engage in the pursuit of gay history, but which so often seems difficult to define precisely: *the gay sensibility.* For surely the mythology and the symbolic acts of our literature contribute not only to the texture of that sensibility but to its definition as well.

Concerning the subject of this essay, it may be said that the myth of Arcadia is almost a quasi-religious requirement of the human psyche, in all climes and cultures, and whatever the sexual preference. But for gay people—or homosexuals, or Uranians, or whatever name we have used for ourselves at various times in history—Arcadia has seemed to be a special kind of metaphor, relevant to the conditions of our lives and spirits. We have adapted it to our own needs, to express the yearnings and secret desires of a sexual, emotional, and intellectual minority, embellishing it with the products of our pen. Thus, while the Arcadian myth is only one element in the much larger tapestry of the homosexual imagination, it is a myth that speaks directly to our minds and hearts.

Notes

[1] Walt Whitman, *Leaves of Grass,* ed. Sculley Bradley and Harold Blodgett (1965; rpt. New York: W. W. Norton, 1973). p. 112. All references to Whitman hereinafter are from this edition.

[2] Sometimes the implicit approaches the explicit. For example, in 1873, Walter Pater included an essay on Johann Winckelmann in his book *The Renaissance.* In what is one of the earliest, if oblique, references to the homosexual imagination, Pater notes that Winckelmann's "affinity for Hellenism was not merely intellectual. . . . The subtler threads of temperament were inwoven in it, as proved by romantic, fervent friendships with young men" (Walter Pater, *The Renaissance* [1873; rpt. New York: Modern Library, n.d.], p. 158). As an epigraph for this essay, Pater inscribed: "Et ego in Arcadia fui" (p. 147).

Some years before, John Addington Symonds had found himself involved in a fervent friendship with a young man. The youth was named G. H. Shorting, and we are told he had long and curling yellow hair. Symonds pursued Shorting, as he said, because he detected that they both shared similar tastes. "Arcadian tastes," he called them (Phyllis Grosskurth, *The Woeful Victorian: A Biography of John Addington Symonds* [New York: Holt, Rinehart and Winston, 1964], p. 58). Oscar Wilde, writing to Douglas from his prison cell, referred to "Sicilian and Arcadian airs" to get around the censors (Rupert Hart-Davis, ed., *The Letters of Oscar Wilde* [New York: Harcourt Brace, 1962]). See Wilde's remarkable letter to Douglas (pp. 423-511), which is an evocation of the themes of the homosexual sensibility. . . .

[6] Bayard Taylor, *Joseph and His Friend* (New York: 1870), p. 216. All reference to the novel are to this edition. For an excellent discussion of Taylor's presumed homosexuality, see Robert K. Martin, *The Homosexual Tradition in American Poetry* (Austin; Univ. of Texas, 1979), pp. 97 ff. . . .

. . . . .

[19] The best book on the English Uraninan poets and prose writers is *Love in Earnest* by Timothy d'Arch Smith (London; Routledge and Kegan Paul, 1970).

[20] S. S. Saale, "Sonnet," quoted in *Sexual Heretics,* ed. Brian Reade (New York: Coward McCann, 1970), p. 228.

[21] Gerard Manley Hopkins, *Poems and Prose: A Selection,* ed. W. H. Gardner (Harmondsworth: Penguin, 1953), p. 85. All references to Hopkins are to this edition.

[22] Hans Licht [pseud. of Paul Brandt], *Sexual Life in Ancient Greece* (London: Routledge and Kegan Paul, 1932), p. 415.

[23] The phrase appears often as a euphemism for homosexuality. Pater's essay, "The Age of Athletic Prizemen," from *Greek Studies* (1895) suggests it, and Forster in *Maurice* has Maurice know the "impossibility of vexing athletic love" (p. 111).

TRIAL AND DANGER

Jeffrey Meyers

SOURCE: "Wilde: The Picture of Dorian Gray," in *Homosexuality and Literature: 1890-1930,* The Athlone Press, 1977, pp. 20-31.

[*Meyers's* Homosexuality and Literature 1890-1930 *offered one of the first serious studies of gay male content in literature. In the chapter excerpted below, Meyers reassesses Oscar Wilde's* The Picture of Dorian Gray *in light of the author's sexuality, arguing that much of the novel's ambiguity is actually veiled reference to homosexual desire and activity. Although the specifics of Meyers's interpretation have been disputed by more recent scholars, his work apparently helped open the door for direct and extensive study of homosexual content in literature.*]

> For any man of culture to accept the standard of his age is a form of the grossest immorality.
>
> *The Picture of Dorian Gray*

Most critics of *The Picture of Dorian Gray* (1891) treat the book as a classical illustration of literary aestheticism and decadence or, like Roditi, concentrate on its heterogeneous sources, from the Gothic novel through Balzac and Poe to Pater and Huysmans.[1] Despite the abundant evidence, both external and internal, no critic has discussed the work as a homosexual novel. But this interpretation defines more precisely the nature of its decadence and its relation to Baudelaire and *Against Nature;* reveals a coherence and consistency in the uneven, loosely structured, melodramatic and sometimes absurd work; and suggests that the real meaning of the novel, like so many others on this subject, is more complex and interesting than it appears to be. It is really about the jealousy and pain, the fear and guilt of being a homosexual.

The most recent biographer of Wilde writes that the models for two of the principal characters in the novel were notorious homosexuals. Basil Hallward was 'Charles Shannon, the artist who for many years lived in marital bliss with Charles Ricketts, and Lord Henry Wotton . . . was Lord Ronald Gower', whom Croft-Cooke calls 'a thorough-paced queer who liked rough trade and found time, in spite of a public career, to enjoy it prodigally'.[2] Wilde himself emphasizes that the characters are also projections of his own personality and says that *Dorian Gray* 'contains much of me. Basil Hallward is what I think I am: Lord Henry what the world thinks of me: Dorian what I would like to be—in other ages, perhaps'.[3] Wilde thinks he is an artist and an idealist who loves beauty and handsome young men, and wants to be inspired by them as Socrates was inspired by Alcibiades. The world, encouraged by his wicked *persona,* believes he is a posturing, dissolute cynic. Wilde would like to be a beautiful youth, and he would also like to enjoy homosexual love without the severe and repressive legal penalties of the late Victorian age. For as Dorian

> looked back upon man moving through History, he was haunted by a feeling of loss. So much had been surrendered! and to such little purpose! There had been mad wilful rejections, monstrous forms of self-torture and self-denial, whose origin was fear, and whose result was a degradation infinitely more terrible than that fancied degradation from which, in their ignorance, they had sought to escape.

Wilde's condemnation of the repression of homosexuals—who are not specifically mentioned though they are clearly the subject of this passage—anticipates Freud's ideas about the irremediable antagonism between the demands of instinct and the restrictions of civilization in *Civilization and Its Discontents* (1930). Wotton also believes that repression is evil and argues that 'the only way to get rid of a temptation is to yield to it. Resist it, and your soul grows sick with longing for the things it has forbidden to itself, with desire for what its monstrous laws have made monstrous and unlawful'. In the novel Hallward and Wotton, the artistic and cynical aspects of Wilde, personify Dorian's conscience and instinct, the irresolvable conflict between his superego and his id.

But this triple projection of Wilde's personality leads to a split between the characters and the ideas they are meant to represent. The kindly and optimistic Hallward seems to come closest to the ideal of the novel— 'to teach man to concentrate himself upon the moments of a life that is itself but a moment . . . [and] find in the spiritualizing of the senses its highest relization'. But Hallward is killed by Dorian, whose descent into the 'vulgar profligacy' that dulls the senses and into the suicide that extinguishes them is the antithesis of the ideal that Wilde is trying to express through Hallward. The ideas of Wotton, who urges Dorian to realize his true nature and yield to temptation even though his passions might shame him, are discredited by Dorian's dissolute behaviour. Wotton epigrammatically expresses some fine and some bitter sentiments, but we cannot take him seriously because he is an essentially passive and negative character who vicariously experiences evil through Dorian and has no real life of his own. We are constantly told about the evil of Dorian, who also enjoys corrupting young men, but we never learn exactly what he has done because the theme cannot be overtly expressed and the characters hide as much as they reveal.

The original inspiration for the novel also evolved from Wilde's personal experience:

> When the sitting was over and Mr Wilde had looked at his portrait, it occurred to him that a thing of beauty, when it takes the form of a middle-aged gentleman, is unhappily not a joy forever. "What a tragic thing it is', he exclaimed. 'This portrait will never grow old, and I shall.' Then the passion of his soul sought refuge in prose composition, and the result was 'Dorian Gray'.[5]

This autobiographical incident is transposed directly into the novel when Dorian, staring at his finished portrait, remarks: 'How sad it is! I shall grow old, and horrible, and dreadful. But this picture will remain always young . . . If it were only the other way! If it were I who was to be always young, and the picture that was to grow old! . . . I would give my soul for that!' This fanciful yet fatal wish for eternal youth and beauty (since old age is horrible and dreadful), rather than for moral or intellectual or artistic qualities, is consummated by a devil's pact in which the face on the canvas bears the burdens of his passions and his sins in return for a final, Gothic retribution. This pact turns Dorian into an image without a soul and allows him to be loved by men (and women) without having to love them in return.

The opening paragraphs of the novel, with their evocation of opium-tainted cigarettes and Baudelairean *fleurs du mal* (an anodyne for pain that becomes a recurrent theme in the book, for Dorian sniffs a flower just before he murders Hallward), establishes an atmo-sphere of preciosity and corruption. And this ambience is reinforced by Hallward's description of his first meeting and subsequent relationship with Dorian:

> When our eyes first met I felt I was growing pale. A curious sensation of terror came over me. I knew that I had come face to face with someone whose mere personality was so fascinating that, if I allowed it to do so, it would absorb my whole nature, my whole *soul,* my very art itself . . . I have always been my own master; had at least always been so, till I met Dorian Gray. Then . . . something seemed to tell me that I was on the verge of a terrible crisis in my life. I had a strange feeling that Fate had in store for me exquisite joys and exquisite sorrows.

Though Dorian is young, innocent and beautiful—'a type that was to combine something of the real culture of the scholar with all the grace and distinction and perfect manner of a citizen of the world'—Hallward's first, intensely physical reaction, is of fear. And though Dorian's character has not yet come under Wotton's evil influence, Hallward immediately feels threatened, weak and subservient as he enters the sexual crisis that provides far more sorrows than joys.

Hallward enjoys confessing his literal idolatry and admits, 'I couldn't be happy if I didn't see him every day. He is absolutely necessary to me'. He compares his love for Dorian to the love of Michelangelo, of Winckelmann (whom Pater discussed in *The Renaissance*), and of Shakespeare (whose passion for the young man of the Sonnets is described by Wilde in his story, 'The Portrait of Mr W. H.'). Hallward needs Dorian not only as an artistic inspiration, but also as the dominant partner in their sado-masochistic relationship; and he explains that 'Dorian's whims are laws to everybody, except himself . . . He is horribly thoughtless, and seems to take a real delight in giving me pain'.

When Wotton (the corrupt homosexual) maliciously steals Dorian from Hallward (the idealistic homosexual), the latter is forced to make humiliating though ineffectual pleas for Dorian's company. As he had foreseen, his art declines as his passionate friendship ends, and as Dorian becomes weary of 'the painter's absurd fits of jealousy, his wild devotion, his extravagant panegyrics, his curious reticences'.

Lord Henry Wotton[6] is supposed to represent cynical hedonism, but as Hallward justly remarks (paraphrasing Rochester's famous epigram on Charles II who 'never says a foolish thing, nor ever does a wise one'). 'You never say a moral thing, and you never do a wrong thing. Your cynicism is simply a pose.' If Hallward is the masochistic creator of Dorian's aesthetic glorification, Wotton (who manipulates the vanity stimulated by the portrait) is the sadistic catalyst of his moral degeneration.

Wotton is an extreme misogynist who intensifies the homosexual theme by insisting on the need to escape from the horrible *ennui* of fashionable society ('My dear fellow, she tried to found a *salon,* and only succeeded in opening a restaurant'), from the overwhelming dreariness of heterosexual relations, and from the tedium of marriage, a 'bad habit' whose one charm is that it 'makes a life of deception absolutely necessary for both parties'.

One of the subtlest scenes in the novel occurs when Wotton's wife first meets Dorian. Though she is a gauche and even ludicrous character, and an easy target for satire ('Her name was Victoria, and she had a perfect mania for going to church'), her awkward intrusion into her own library reveals her estrangement from Wotton and his intimacy with Dorian, whose photographs fill the house. Though Wilde writes, 'She was usually in love with somebody, and her passion was never returned', she causes a scandal by running away with her musical lover and divorcing Wotton. He deceives his wife with Dorian and appears indifferent to her infidelity; but she merely laughs at his affair, for his extreme passivity is the emotional equivalent of impotence.

Gray is inevitably compared to 'the perfection of the spirit that is Greek', to Greek marbles, a young Adonis and a Greek martyr (Hallward's masochistic projection) in order to create an aesthetic tradition for the homosexual ideal. Though he is more elaborately Corinthian than austerely Dorian, he takes his name from a race whom John Addington Symonds calls 'those martial founders of the institution of Greek love'.[7]

The correspondence between Dorian's external beauty and internal corruption is a variation of a more important Greek idea. According to the Neoplatonic doctrine expressed, for example, in Sidney's *Astrophel and Stella* (1580), the face is the outward form of the soul. Because of the harmony between the body and the soul, a beautiful face reveals an inward spirituality and inspires 'those whom Dante describes as having sought to "make themselves perfect by the worship of beauty"' (144). This same connection exists in *Dorian Gray,* where one character states that 'wicked people were always very old and very ugly', and where the grotesque reflection of Dorian's spiritual state is transferred to the painting. Dorian's dualism is reflected in the attitudes of Hallward and Wotton. The former sees him as 'the visible incarnation of that unseen ideal whose memory haunts us artists like an exquisite dream', while the latter calls him the 'son of Love and Death'.

When Dorian attempts to love the young actress, Sibyl Vane, he ignores the warning in Juliet's speech: 'I have no joy of this contract tonight: / It is too rash, too unadvised, too sudden', and follows the pattern of Wotton's prediction: 'When one is in love, one always begins by deceiving oneself and one always ends by deceiving others'. Dorian deceives himself by believing that he is able to love a woman and that 'his unreal and selfish love would yield to some higher influence, would be *transformed* into some nobler passion'. He is attracted to Sibyl partly because she is an illusion who is idealized and distanced from him by the stage, and mainly because she is androgynous. For when she plays Rosalind in *As You Like It* she appeals to his homosexual tastes: 'she came out in her boy's clothes and was perfectly wonderful. She had never seemed to me more exquisite.'

Both Dorian and Sibyl have similarly sordid backgrounds which are meant to provide a melodramatic contrast to their youthful purity and to explain their bizarre behaviour. Both were children of a passionate but ill-considered love affair. When Dorian's father ran off with his mother, a beautiful heiress, he was forced into a duel and deliberately killed; and after the early death of Dorian's mother, the posthumous child was brought up by the same wicked grandfather who had arranged the duel and then replaced the man he had murdered. Sibyl was an illegitimate child whose father also died early in her life. His surrogate, at the time she meets Dorian, is a stereotyped 'hideous Jew' with greasy ringlets who has financial control over her and acts as her guardian and pander. The brief narration of their disturbed childhood attempts to account for their extreme sensitivity and vulnerability, their emotional instability, and their manic-depressive behaviour, for Dorian moves from adoration to hate and Sibyl from ecstasy to suicide. But none of these biographical details can make Dorian and Sibyl's relationship real, for the whole episode is merely symbolic.

Wilde suggests that Dorian rejects Sibyl when he discovers his preference for illusion to reality, and this polarity is similar to the art-life conflict expressed in Dorian's portrait. Hallward's early paintings of Dorian were 'unconscious, ideal and remote'; and when he first paints Dorian realistically, he reveals his love and Dorian's true nature, and destroys their friendship. Similarly, Dorian loves Sibyl as an actress, as an impersonator of romantic heroines in an unreal and artificial atmosphere. When her love for him freed her soul from her emotional prison and taught her to recognize reality, she saw the hollowness and sham of her empty performances. But when she began to 'live', she lost her ability to act and forced Dorian to accept her as a real woman, not as 'a dream or a phantom'. This change killed his 'love' because, in Huysmans' words, 'anyone who dreams of the ideal, prefers illusion to reality, and calls for veils to clothe the naked truth'.[8]

Dorian is never really in love with Sibyl because he is too narcissistic to love anyone but himself. He tries to love her because he believes it will be good for him to love a woman, but recoils when confronted with a real woman who loves him. Wilde associates reality with heterosexuality and illusion with homosexuality, and expresses Dorian's confirmation of his homosexuality through these associations. The ferocity of Dorian's reaction to Sibyl's love reveals the conflict between what he really feels and what society thinks he ought to feel.

Wilde derived these sexual and aesthetic associations from *Against Nature,* for Huysmans connects reality with bourgeois respectability and conventional morality, and equates art with imagination, refinement, sensuality and immoral love. In Huysmans and Wilde's scale of values homosexuality, which is anti-social and taboo, is related to art; and homosexuals surround themselves with rich and elaborate illusions to 'spiritualize the senses'.

Wotton completes his domination of Dorian by sending him a copy of *Against Nature* bound in yellow paper, for the 'whole book seemed to [Dorian] to contain the story of his own life, written before he had lived it'. Dorian responds passionately to Huysmans because he sanctifies the sensitive and *raffiné* mode of existence and provides an aesthetic justification of homosexuality. In view of Wilde's statement that *Dorian Gray* 'is a fantastic variation of Huysmans' over-realistic study of the artistic temperament in our unartistic age',[9] it is significant that Des Esseintes and Dorian are not real artists but dilettantes who express their artistic temperaments through Dandyism, hedonism (that is, childish self-indulgence) and homosexuality. The whole of Chapter 11 is a weak imitation of Huysmans, with successive paragraphs appropriately devoted to the more *recherché* aspects of perfumes, music, jewels, embroideries and ecclesiastical vestments, all used by Dorian as an aesthetic means of escape from the guilt of his sexual perversity. Though Dorian, in another weak attempt to rationalize his outrageous conduct, complains that he was 'poisoned' by the book, it is clear that Huysmans' novel did not change Dorian's life but merely accentuated tendencies that already existed in him.

Auden observes in his review of Wilde's *Letters* that 'the artist and the homosexual are both characterized by a greater-than-normal amount of narcissism',[10] and this trait is particularly prominent in the homosexual artist. Hallward rhapsodically tells Dorian: 'You had leant over the still pool of some Greek woodland, and seen in the water's silent silver the marvel of your own face'. And 'once, in boyish mockery of Narcissus', Dorian had kissed his portrait. But instead of falling in love, like Narcissus, with his own image, an aesthetic extension of himself, he comes to hate it and destroys himself as he attempts to destroy his portrait. In the modern age, the relation of the artist to society has been analogous to the relation of the homosexual to society, so that Dorian's image reflects his self-hatred as well as his self-love.

The numerous parallels between Hallward and Sibyl also emphasize Dorian's homosexuality. He tells Wotton about his adoration of Sibyl in the same way that Hallward told Wotton about his idealization of Dorian. And Sibyl assumes Hallward's self-abasing sexual posture, and expresses her love by flinging herself on her knees, trembling all over 'like a white narcissus' and sobbing at Dorian's feet. Hallward, who understands Dorian's true nature, finds his engagement to Sibyl 'Impossible'. But on reflection, though 'he could not bear this marriage, yet it seemed to him to be better than many other things that might have happened'. These other things could only refer to Dorian's liaison with another man. By contrast, Dorian's mad adoration of Sibyl did not cause Wotton the slightest pang of annoyance or jealousy because he knew that Dorian could never love a woman.

Dorian's rejection of Sibyl is as sudden and unexpected as his murder of Basil, and both crimes are inspired by the same motive. For Basil and Sibyl (both have Greek names, though he is not regal nor she prophetic) make a great emotional claim on Dorian who, because of the guilt about his homosexuality (the reason for his emphasis on purity), feels compelled to displace his self-hatred and to punish those who love him and attempt to redeem him. For Basil created the visible emblem of his conscience, and Sibyl's love might 'purify him, and shield him from those sins that seemed to be already stirring in spirit and in flesh—those curious *unpictured* sins whose very mystery lent them their subtlety and their charm'.

The irreconcilable conflict between art and life, between the homosexual and heterosexual modes of love, leads to the murder of Hallward just as it had led to the suicide of Sibyl and the corresponding signs of degeneration in Dorian's portrait. In the first chapter the artist says that he cannot exhibit the painting because 'I have put too much of myself into it', and he later adds that it would reveal the shameful secret of his idolatrous love for Dorian. The portrait also holds the secret of Dorian's life, for it teaches him to love his own beauty and to loathe his own soul, an impossible combination of homosexual narcissism and socially-conditioned self-hatred.

When Basil changes his mind and asks Dorian if he can exhibit the portrait, Dorian offers to exchange secrets about it. Though he discovers Hallward's secret, he never reveals his own until his friend visits him again on the night of the murder. Then, in response to the long sermon about his behaviour from Hallward, who has become an insufferable prig and a bore (and is killed, one suspects, partly for this reason), Dorian says, 'I shall show you my soul . . . You are the one man in the world entitled to know everything about me'—though Hallward already knows virtually everything there is to know. After revealing the visual evidence to Hallward and hearing his horrified response, Dorian is madly inspired by the overt image of evil and, pursuing a false logic, kills 'the friend who had painted the fatal portrait to which all his misery had been due'. It is significant that Dorian impulsively kills Hallward by driving a knife into the great *vein* behind the ear (the play in the novel on vein, vain and Vane is a weak attempt to achieve unity), and that he blackmails one of his homosexual acquaintances (who later commits suicide) and forces him to destroy the corpse with acid, for Sybil had also used prussic acid to destroy herself.[11]

Just as Basil haunts Dorian after his death through his portrait, so Sibyl posthumously pursues him through her brother James, who has sworn to kill her deceiver. James is motivated by jealousy as well as by revenge, for in the absence of their father, he developed an unusually close and protective relationship with his sister. When he left for Australia they parted like lovers: 'her arms were flung round his neck, and her fingers strayed through his hair, and he softened, and kissed her with real affection'. After James, like Dorian's father, is conveniently shot (during a hunting party), the way is clear for Dorian to kill himself, as he had killed Hallward, by stabbing.

The crimes of desertion and murder are the external manifestations of the inward corruption that is frequently hinted at but never defined, and Dorian's subsequent absorption in evil is essentially homosexual. He shares a house with Wotton in Algiers (where Wilde enjoyed the pleasures of pederasty without fear of the law), adopts (like Sibyl) the 'curious disguises' of a transvestite, frequents the low dens that cater to the perverse predilections of foreign sailors, and acquires an impressive list of male victims:

> There was that wretched boy in the Guards who committed suicide. You were his great friend. There was Sir Henry Ashton, who had to leave England, with a tarnished name. You and he were inseparable. What about Adrian Singleton, and his dreadful end? What about Lord Kent's only son, and his career? I met his father yesterday in St. James's Street. He seemed broken with shame and sorrow. What about the young Duke of Perth? What sort of life has he got now? What gentleman would associate with him?[12]

All these male friendships are described in terms of strong moral opprobrium—they are shameful, vile and degraded—and though Kent's son married a whore and Singleton forged a bill, all these men obviously practised what Lord Alfred Douglas called 'the love that

dare not speak its name'.[13] Dorian has again punished a succession of well-born and promising young men for his own sin, which caused women who had wildly adored him 'to grow pallid with shame or horror if [he] entered the room'. These women felt shame for allowing themselves to be deceived by him, and horror of his vice. If Dorian were merely a libertine he would not be, as Hallward says, 'a man whom no pure-minded girl should be allowed to know, and whom no chaste woman should sit in the same room with'. Though their purity and chastity would protect them from seduction, they could still be contaminated by his perversity.

Dorian's final, Faustian attempt to redeem himself as he slides from corruption to crime (and it is the crime that betrays the corruption) is a conscious repetition of his relationship with Sibyl. Dorian meets a working-class village girl named Hetty who 'was quite beautiful and wonderfully like Sibyl Vane. I think it was that which first attracted me to her'. He plans to run off with her but decides, suddenly and at the last moment, 'to leave her as flower-like as I had found her'. Wotton reinforces the parallel with Sibyl by insisting that Dorian's noble sacrifice has in fact broken her heart and possibly caused her to kill herself. And he compares her to Ophelia and Perdita just as Dorian had compared Sibyl to Juliet and Rosalind. Wotton quite rightly denies the morality of Dorian's renunciation, and his worldly and sophisticated analysis destroys the last flicker of idealism in Dorian and confirms his damnation. Though Dorian is more deliberately cruel to Sibyl, he treats both Sibyl and Hetty in the same way, commits the terrible Victorian crime of toying with a young girl's affections and ruins their lives. The greatest similarity in these two unconsummated affairs is, of course, Dorian's attempt to use a pure woman to rescue himself from homosexuality. In both cases, when he is forced to commit himself emotionally and sexually to a woman, he becomes frightened, abandons her and returns to his old way of life.

In *De Profundis* (1905) Wilde writes that homosexual love 'was like feasting with panthers. The danger was half the excitement'. But the legal danger cut both ways and diminished the pleasure at the same time that it intensified the excitement. This double aspect of ecstasy and fear is reflected in the many polarities that create a vital tension in Dorian, who keenly felt 'the terrible pleasure of a double life': the man and the portrait, youth and age, beauty and ugliness, body and soul, freedom and conscience, life and art. This ambivalence is also manifested in Dorian's intense emotions which lead both to his crimes and to his almost anaesthetic lack of feeling about them, in his extreme variation between ruthless behaviour and guilty repentance, and in his simultaneous desire to conceal his actions and to confess them.

The overt moral of *Dorian Gray* is not convincing. It is too heavy-handed, obvious and *de rigueur,* and too inconsistent with the defiant tone of the novel, which delights in the Baudelairean fascination of sin and authorization of evil. For as T. S. Eliot writes of Baudelaire, 'The recognition of the reality of Sin is a New Life; and the possibility of damnation is itself . . . an immediate form of Salvation—of Salvation from the ennui of modern life, because it gives some significance to living.'[14]

Though Wilde insisted in his somewhat posturing Preface, 'There is no such thing as a moral or an immoral book', he felt obliged to emphasize the moral ending in his letters. He writes in 1890, the year the book was serialized, that Dorian Gray ('what I would like to be') 'is extremely impulsive, absurdly romantic, and is haunted all his life by an exaggerated sense of conscience which mars his pleasures for him . . . In his attempt to kill conscience, Dorian Gray kills himself.'[15] Though Dorian moves directly from renunciation of women to excess with men, Wilde's supposed 'moral is this: All excess as well as all renunciation brings its own punishment'.[16] Wilde begins by pleading for sexual freedom and ends by equating homosexuality with undefined and pervasive evil.

Dorian Gray is a failure as a novel because Wilde was unable to resolve the conflict between his desire for homosexual freedom and his fear of social condemnation. Though the picture represents Dorian's conscience, it would be more accurate to say (despite Wilde's statement) that he is haunted by the fear that the visual evidence of the picture will lead to the *discovery* of his crimes and his corruption. As long as he feels the painting is securely hidden, he does exactly as he pleases. But when he feels threatened by exposure, he becomes convinced that if he kills the painting with the same knife he used to kill the painter, 'It would kill the past, and when that was dead he would be free'. But Dorian is already as free as it is possible to be—in the Victorian age—for he has regressed to a state of childish and narcissistic irresponsibility. The aesthetic point of the novel may be that if instinct overcomes restraint, it will destroy art. But the real subject of the book, where 'conscience' stands for law and 'soul' for body, is the impossibility of achieving homosexual pleasure without the inevitable accompaniment of fear, guilt and self-hatred.

Notes

1. See, for example: Edouard Roditi, *Oscar Wilde* (Norfolk, Conn., 1947); Graham Hough, *The Last Romantics* (London, 1949), pp. 194-204; Epifanio San Juan, 'The Picture of Dorian Gray and the Form of Fiction', *The Art of Oscar Wilde* (Princeton, 1967), pp. 49-73; Jan Gordan, '"Parody as Initiation": The Sad Education of "Dorian Gray"', *Criticism,* ix (1967), 355-71;

Houston Baker, 'A Tragedy of the Artist: *The Picture of Dorian Gray*', *Nineteenth Century Fiction,* xxiv (1969), 349-55; Louis Potect, '*Dorian Gray* and the Gothic Novel', *Modern Fiction Studies,* xvii (1971), 239-48; and Christopher Nassaar, 'The Darkening Lens', *Into the Demon Universe* (New Haven, 1974), pp. 37-72.

2. Rupert Croft-Cooke, *The Unrecorded Oscar Wilde* (London, 1972), p. 112, and *Feasting With Panthers* (London, 1967), p. 194.

3. Oscar Wilde, *Letters,* ed. Rupert Hart-Davis (London, 1962), p. 352 (12 February 1894).

4. Oscar Wilde, *The Picture of Dorian Gray* (London: Penguin, 1973), p. 145.

5. *St James Gazette,* 24 September 1890, quoted in Cooke, p. 27.

6. Henry Wotton is the namesake of the witty Elizabethan diplomat who defined an ambassador as a man who lies abroad for his country.

7. John Addington Symonds, *A Problem in Modern Ethics* (London, 1896), p. 118.

8. J.-K. Huysmans, *Against Nature,* trans. Robert Baldick (London: Penguin, 1959), p. 29.

9. Wilde, *Letters,* p. 313 (15 April 1892). For a discussion of Huysmans' novel see my book, *Painting and the Novel* (Manchester, 1975), which also has chapters on Mann, Proust, Forster and D. H. Lawrence.

10. W. H. Auden, 'An Improbable Life', *Forewords and Afterwords* (London, 1973), p. 323.

11. In one of the more incredible moments of the book, Dorian sends his servant to get the necessary chemicals and then gives him the day off so he will not discover the crime.

12. Wilde's attempt to lay on the sin rather thickly sometimes results in unintentional comedy. When Dorian enters a Baudelairean opium den, he spies one of his former victims: '"You here, Adrian?" muttered Dorian. "Where else should I be?" he answered, listlessly. "None of the chaps will speak to me now"' (207).

13. Lord Alfred Douglas, 'Two Loves' (1894), in *Sexual Heretics,* ed. Brian Reade (London, 1970), p. 362.

14. T. S. Eliot, 'Baudelaire', *Selected Essays, 1912-1932* (London, 1932), p. 343.

[15] Wilde, *Letters,* pp. 263-4 (1890).

[16] Ibid., p. 259 (26 June 1890).

Louis Crompton

SOURCE: "Epilogue: The Truth Appears," in *Byron and Greek Love: Homophobia in 19th-Century England,* University of California Press, 1985, pp. 343-61.

[*The following excerpt from Crompton's biography of Romantic poet Lord Byron looks at the explicitly homosexual poem* Don Leon. *The poem, which appeared in print soon after the poet's death, presents itself as a portion of Byron's memoirs. Crompton argues against Byron's authorship, but also takes the poem as a serious object of study, considering it an important document in gay history.*]

The authorship of *Don Leon* remains a riddle, but it is possible to understand why the poem was resolutely ignored by nineteenth-century writers on Byron. Part of the difficulty lay in the form in which the poet chose to convey his revelations. The obviously fabricated side of the publication suggested that it belonged to the extensive category of pseudo-Byroniana that appeared after Byron's death with no further aim than to titillate readers and relieve them of their shillings or francs. The title page describes the work as a "Poem by Lord Byron, Author of Childe Harold, Don Juan, &c. &c. and Forming Part of the Private Journal of His Lordship, Supposed to Have Been Entirely Destroyed by Thos. Moore." No knowledgeable contemporary reader would have been taken in by this claim. No one had ever suggested that Byron's memoirs were in rhymed couplets, and the poem makes reference to dozens of events that took place in the decade following Byron's death. This playful pretense that Byron himself is speaking the lines—an obvious impossibility—would in itself have militated against the credibility of these "confessions," though we now know that on many substantial points they come startlingly close to the truth.

The other consideration that led to the general dismissal of the poem as a record of fact stemmed from its shady provenance. Apparently some earlier printed version of these fifty rhymed pages existed, but the only copies known to us come from an edition printed by the London publisher William Dugdale in 1866.[8] Since Dugdale's main line was erotic "curiosa," this led readers to dismiss the lines as a purely fictive concoction prepared for the under-the-counter trade. Even so sophisticated an expert on sexuality as Henry Spencer Ashbee, the one nineteenth-century authority to take any notice of the work, assumed there could be no truth in the poem's implication that Byron was a bisexual.

But who was the poet who knew so much about Byron that he was able to write so revealingly? Knight has suggested that the author was the playwright George Colman the younger whose wit and conviviality Byron enjoyed during their work together at Drury Lane Theater in 1815, the year of his marriage.[9] The parallels between *Don Leon* and some of Colman's satires are striking, but ascriptions of authorship on stylistic grounds are always tenuous. Besides, Colman was old and ill at the time the poem was written—he died in 1836 at seventy-three. On these and other grounds Doris Langley Moore has argued against Colman's authorship and proposed another candidate.[10] At present the authorship must be regarded as an unsolved mystery.

Indeed, all we can say with certainty about the *Leon* poet is that he had a clever wit, a talent for writing forceful couplets, and a remarkable knowledge both of Byron's life (on its homosexual side) and of British parliamentary affairs in the decade following his death. Written with great verve and cleverness, *Don Leon,* though not quite the masterpiece it has been called, is nevertheless a work of real literary significance. The poem itself is full of ideas and information, much of which (especially the detailed parliamentary part) is inevitably obscure to the modern reader. Since the kaleidoscopic turns of thought of *Don Leon* are so many that even someone who has read it two or three times may have only a confused idea of its structure and logic, a fairly extended summary may be useful. It will also communicate, as no other approach can, the concentrated energy of the poem.

But before we look at these details, it is necessary to appreciate another side of the work, a side that was its real raison d'être. So far, commentary on *Don Leon,* on the few occasions that it has been noticed, has been concentrated on its Byronic aspects. Nevertheless, what moved the *Leon* poet to write was not, apparently, the revelations he had to make about Byron, sensational as they were, but the problem that had obsessed Jeremy Bentham, the problem of repealing the death penalty for sodomy. Bentham had died in 1832, the year of the Reform Bill. The next year, under the new dispensation, a new parliamentary commission on criminal law reform was set up under Lord John Russell, who had strong Benthamite views. It was this development and two other events of 1833 that seem to have moved the *Leon* poet to write his passionate plea for reform. One of these was the sentence of death pronounced on Captain Henry Nicholas Nicholls on August 12 of that year. Hangings for homosexual relations had continued unabated after Byron's death, despite their rapid decline for other crimes. In the years 1826-1830 there were seven; another took place in 1831, three in 1833 (including Nicholls's), four in 1834, and three in 1835. This was the case in spite of the fact that in this era of rapid reform the status of many minority groups in England had improved. Nonconformists had been relieved of their disabilities by the repeal of the Test Act in 1828, Catholic emancipation had come in 1829, and the reformed House crowned decades of agitation by finally ending black slavery in 1833. The death penalty had already been repealed for dozens of nonviolent crimes, but conviction in sodomy cases had actually been rendered easier by a change of the law in 1828, and the new reform commission seemed unwilling to brave public opinion on this matter.

With more rage and despair than hope, the *Leon* poet makes himself the spokesman for England's gay community by urging the abolition of hanging for sodomy. In the pursuit of this aim, he especially directs his arguments to members of Parliament. In the interval since Byron's death, several members of the House of Commons had joined him in exile, committed suicide, or faced trials. Besides Nicholls's hanging, the other event of 1833 that seems particularly to have spurred him to write was the arrest of Byron's Cambridge friend and fellow parliamentarian William Bankes, which had taken place on June 7. In the notes to the poem, which fill another fifty pages and were apparently written at different times between 1833 and 1959, the last date mentioned in them, legal matters and newspaper reports of scandals bulk far larger than references to Byron.

Thus it is that a poem purporting to be Byron's autobiography opens with a protest against a hanging that took place nine years after his death and against the continuing entrapment of homosexuals by the police:

> Thou ermined judge, pull off that sable cap!
> What! Can'st thou lie, and take thy morning
>   nap?
> Peep thro' the casement; see the gallows
>   there:
> Thy work hangs on it; could not mercy spare?
> What had he done? Ask crippled Talleyrand,
> Ask Beckford, Courtenay, all the motley band
> Of priest and laymen, who have shared his
>   guilt
> (If guilt it be) then slumber if thou wilt;
> What bonds had he of social safety broke?
> Found'st thou the dagger hid beneath his
>   cloak?
> He stopped no lonely traveller on the road;
> He burst no lock, he plundered no abode;
> He never wrong'd the orphan of his own;
> He stifled not the ravish'd maiden's groan.
> His secret haunts were hid from every soul,
> Till thou did'st send thy myrmidons to
>   prowl.[11]
>
>   (lines 1-16)

The sable cap is, of course, the black cap English judges wore when they were about to pronounce the sentence of death. The annotator of *Don Leon,* in his first footnote, preserves only the thinnest pretense that Byron had written these lines: "In reading the opening of this poem, it would almost seem that the author of it had in his eye Mr. Justice Park [who pronounced death on Nicholls] were it not that the supposed date of the poem would imply an anachronism." Because the *Leon* poet purports to be speaking in the person of Byron, I shall refer to him as "Byron" in the rest of my summary, though in fact the pseudo-Byronic mask is often all but completely dropped in the argumentative sections.

After the opening protest, "Byron" begs Moore to give a sympathetic ear to his "swelling rage" and to print his thoughts unaltered. (This is almost the only reference in the text to the pretense that the poem has some connection with the famous memoir.) England, he complains, tolerates the most open forms of prostitution but condemns "poor misogynists" to the gallows and vilifies them incessantly in the press. The Sodom story is urged against them, though many other ancient cities have vanished without anyone's interpreting their disappearance as instances of divine displeasure. The venal clergy approve only those unions that bring them marriage or baptismal fees and are blind to a love that will "Produce no other blossoms than its own" (line 126).

"Byron" now speaks of his own life and of his hidden affections. During his teens, he tells us, he was aware of an instinct that drew him to other boys. Social custom allowed him to express his love for Mary Chaworth and Margaret Parker, but not these other longings. Now, looking back, he realizes that his feelings for his page Robert Rushton, which once passed for lordly patronage, had a sexual element:

> Full well I knew, though decency forbad
> The same caresses to a rustic lad;
> Love, love it was, that made my eyes delight
> To have his person ever in my sight.
>
>   (lines 169-72)

At Cambridge, he feels alienated from the common revels and longs for a kindred soul who might return his affection. He hears John Edlestone singing in the choir, and friendship ripens into love:

>   Oh! 'tis hard to trace
> The line where love usurps tame friendship's
>   place.
> Friendship's the chrysalis, which seems to die,
> But throws its coils to give love wing to fly.
>
>   (lines 219-22)

(These lines echo Byron's youthful poem "L'Amitié est L'Amour Sans Ailes.") He is tormented by the intensity of his emotions and struggles to understand them. Moral law opposes his desires, but to him they seem natural since they spring from his inner being.

He begins to question traditional standards—after all, he is not about to ruin a virgin, betray a husband, or beget a bastard. He seeks to divert himself from these anxieties by losing himself in the pleasures of classical poetry but is inadvertently driven back to the question. Horace, he discovers, loved youths, Virgil sighed for Alexis, Socrates and Plato spoke openly of kissing ephebes, and Plutarch praised the love of Epaminondas for Cephidorus. He rejects these loves as pagan perversions, but when he turns to the history of Christianity, he discovers such attachments again in the lives of popes, devotees, kings, scholars, jurists, and poets:

> Nay, e'en our bard, Dame Nature's darling
> child,
> Felt the strange impulse, and his hours
> beguiled
> In penning sonnets to a stripling's praise,
> Such as would damn a poet now-a-days.
>
> (lines 315-18)

(Here the poet seems to draw on the comment on Shakespeare that Byron made to George Finlay, which Leiceister Stanhope had published in 1825.) Obviously, "the great, the wise, the pious, and the good" have had the same susceptibility. In alarm he rejects books and history as morally dangerous guides. But untutored schoolboys take the same path even if they are "in *Justine* unread." This may be better, however, than their risking disease through harlotry. School authorities should quietly ignore such "illicit play": only fools would make a public issue of it.

Edlestone dies (the poem is inaccurate in making this occur before Byron left England for Greece in 1809), and, weary of Cambridge, "Byron" seeks the freedom of the East, with admissions that parallel the real Byron's Falmouth letter to Matthews:

> Love, love, clandestine love, was still my
> dream.
> Methought there must be yet some people
> found,
> Where Cupid's wings were free, his hands
> unbound
> Where law had no erotic statutes framed,
> Nor gibbets stood to fright the unreclaimed.
>
> (lines 423-27)

The account of Byron in Greece is particularly full and striking. In Constantinople he is excited by the traditional tourist visit to taverns with dancing boys but hides his feelings from his friend Hobhouse, affecting to be horrified. (The *Leon* poet was either unaware that Hobhouse shared any knowledge of Byron's tastes or, if he knew, sought to protect him.) He feels alienated from his countrymen and is relieved when he parts from Hobhouse at Zea. "Byron" warmly praises the latter's political work for radical causes in England but

himself follows other pursuits: "A demon urged, and with Satanic force / Still goaded on" (lines 494-95). He is enraptured by the historical associations of Athens, moves to the capuchin convent, and then takes up residence in the nearby Lantern of Demosthenes.[12]

While searching through the ruins of the city, "Byron" is invited home by a citizen. There the man's son attends the guest in Oriental fashion. This, it turns out, is the poet's account of Byron's meeting with Nicolo Giraud, who is identified by name in line 678. (The *Leon* poet follows Moore in mistakenly assuming that Nicolo was Lusieri's son rather than his brother-in-law.) "Byron" is struck by the boy's beauty, courts him, and is urged by the father to take him as his page. He tries to cultivate the boy's mind, gazes on him with affectionate lust while he sleeps, and cares for him with tender solicitude. The dual fires of poetic inspiration and carnal desire rage in him. Though he has met the Macri sisters, they inspire him only poetically; his real passion is for this, boy, who finally gratifies him: "So boldly I set calumny at naught, / And fearless utter what I fearless wrought" (lines 690-91). (At this point, the poet comes strikingly close to Byron's "Greek epistles.") There follows a description of how the then Waiwode (or mayor) of Athens was attended by a beautiful catamite on public occasions; such openness, we are told, is common at every level of Turkish society.

The *Leon* poet, dropping any effort to relate his plea to the experience of the historical Byron, now embarks on a frank apology for homosexuality. First, Malthus has dramatically shown the danger of overpopulation, which must breed starvation if not controlled. One must also take into consideration the great diversity of sexual tastes. Some men (such as the English ambassador to Constantinople) are born exhibitionists. Others seek cunnilingus, flagellation, or fellation from women. Incest and lesbianism are not uncommon. Some women have died to preserve their virginity, but others, like the Countess of Blessington, have risen to wealth and social prominence by judiciously losing theirs. When bench and pulpit endlessly maintain that the sexual behavior of the English is morally superior to other nations, they are hypocritical and never more so than when, in the case of homosexuality, they give the impression

> That self-condemned, decried, ineffable,
> Innominate, this blackest sin of hell,
> Had fled dismayed to some Transalpine shore
> To sully Albion's pudic cliffs no more.
>
> (lines 854-57)

The press exposes arrested men with cruel glee and entertains its readers with scabrous police reports. The rich and secure feign horror, never taking into account what may have led a man into these paths: perhaps he was corrupted when young, perhaps he shrank from the idea of seducing a woman, perhaps he was ugly or shy or averse to the ribaldry or diseases of harlots.

Every rank of English society is involved. The average British soldier or tar is a priapist prone to take his pleasure where he finds it. Teachers relish flogging half-naked schoolboys. Parliament itself is not immune. Looking into the future, "Byron" prophesies that a member famed for his learning and book collecting will be forced to flee the country and later will be cruelly maligned in a libel suit brought by a father against an editor for having linked his son's name to the exile's. Another, a young officer who fought in Sicily, will be tragically drawn into the case. A third member, a pious advocate of prison reform and the rights of blacks, will also face the bitterness of exile.[13] The poet complains indignantly that Peel's revisions of the law have worsened matters. Liberal legislators such as Richard Martin, who led the movement to protect animals from cruelty, and legal reformers such as Sir James Mackintosh, remain callously indifferent to the plight of homosexuals.

Near the speaker's chair where Charles Manners-Sutton presides and waits for his peerage sits Sir Stephen Lushington, whom "Byron" curses for having turned Lady Byron against him. He recalls some of his happy moments with his wife; in a bedroom colloquy he describes Muslim manners to her and pictures the life of harem women and the Turkish passion for boys. Lady Byron expresses curiosity, and "Byron" enlightens her about Anacreon, Virgil, and Catullus. She is somewhat shocked but allows him to practice anal relations (which he extols) with her because her pregnancy makes ordinary relations awkward. Later, when they are estranged, Lady Byron is pressed to reveal this secret, and friends use it to separate her from her husband.[14]

After a second appeal by "Byron" to Thomas Moore to tell the truth and not bowdlerize his life—if Moore should ever write it—the poem abruptly flashes back to Parliament to cast a spotlight upon another figure, a friend (William Bankes) whom Byron had known since college days. Despite his wealth, the fame of his travels, and his high social standing, Bankes will eventually suffer Byron's fate. Bankes's friend Peel, when he passes Bankes's darkened house and remembers what a staunch supporter he has been in Parliament, may then regret his failure to reform the law.

In conclusion, "Byron" bitterly recalls what abuse he suffered as a man after being praised so highly as a poet. But England is not the universe: its prejudices cannot stand before the light of reason. God's law is higher than Parliament's; it is as outrageous to persecute sexual as religious heresy. Then with a final imp-

ish gesture the poet ends with a series of crude and exuberant epigrams on the pleasures of anal intercourse.

Obviously the "Byron" of this poem is something more than the historical Byron. Besides giving a candid account of his own pederastic experiences, Leon-Byron is a spokesman for a persecuted minority, a prophetic voice looking forward to future tragedies, a scandalmonger, and a purveyor of marital secrets. The *Leon* poet exploits Byron's reputation as an opponent of social injustice, plays on curiosity about the burned memoirs, and uses the poem for revelations about the side of Byron that Moore had tried to obscure. The poem's most striking features are, of course, the challenge it posed to contemporary prejudices against homosexuality and the new (and largely true) facts it revealed about Byron's own sexuality. There are, however, material facts the *Leon* poet was not aware of. He did not realize, for example, that the Thyrza lyrics were elegies on the death of Edlestone; and he had no inkling of Byron's love during the final months of his life for Lukas Chalandrutsanos. But whatever its source, the story is worked out with much sensitive detail. The gradations by which ardent friendship melts into erotic awareness are depicted with some subtlety. It is difficult to think of any comparable description of the awakening of homosexual feeling in English literature before the twentieth century. As a portrait of an adolescent struggling toward self-awareness, *Don Leon* adumbrates Forster's *Maurice*, which was not written until eighty years later. This sympathetic dramatization of the stages by which Byron realized his feelings for the male sex works in two ways—as a biographical revelation and as a rhetorical device to moderate homophobic sentiment by showing the anguish of a sensitive boy. The "argument from antiquity" is cleverly handled by having "Byron" discover the truth about Greek and Roman society from his reading.

As for the sociological arguments for tolerance, it is interesting to compare these to Bentham's. There is the same citing of Malthus (who did indeed list "unnatural acts" as a check to population): "Economists, who seek the world to thin, / 'Tis you who teach this so named deadly sin" (lines 775-76). Both protest strongly against the sensationalism and virulence of the British press. Like Bentham, the *Leon* poet also argues that homosexuality is less of a social evil than extramarital pregnancies and adultery. Bentham, in his prospectus addressed to William Beckford, painstakingly enumerated every kind of sexual conduct in order that prejudice might be "perplexed and weakened" by their sheer numbers. The *Leon* poet does something similar, dwelling on a variety of heterosexual techniques with some relish. This is perhaps the least acceptable part of the poem: there is something offensive in his lubricious bandying of names and initials. Where Bentham presents his list in a scientific spirit with dry logic, the *Leon* poet writes with a smirk that is rather reminiscent of Martial; his approach is too much like blackening the kettle to brighten the pot.

Once again, one is brought up short by the language. Like everything else published on homosexuality in its day, this passionately antihomophobic poem uses virulently homophobic expressions. This diction, however, is more difficult to explain than in Byron's Beckford stanza, Hobhouse's paragraph on the Albanians, or Bentham's early manuscript notes and essays. In other contexts such language might be explicable on rhetorical grounds or grounds of prudence. But such considerations would scarcely seem to hold for the *Leon* poet, who frankly celebrates the joys of same-sex intercourse. To find this enthusiasm coupled with references to homosexuality as a "morbid lust," "sport obscene," "rank disease," "impure delinquency," etc., is startling. G. Wilson Knight explains the anomaly as an attempt at "balance," but the effect is more like linguistic schizophrenia.

It is also difficult, given the deadly seriousness of the poem's plea for law reform, to account for the playful eroticism of some of the later pages. Though it is a minor element, there is enough in this vein to have tempted most nineteenth-century readers to dismiss the production as a mere essay in pornography, as the Victorians understood the term. This must have drastically limited its circulation and weakened its impact on all but the least prudish. One possibility is that the more glaring passages—the bedroom scene and the final peroration—were not added until after 1841, by which time all hopes for homosexual law reform, as we shall see, had been finally laid to rest. Perhaps the author felt that, given the circumstances, the only channels of distribution open to him were illicit sales in shops dealing in erotica. This may have prompted him to add these passages. Ironically, this spice, which, under Victorian law, would itself have justified the pamphlet's destruction by the authorities, in fact preserved it since the erotic sections seem to have been what motivated Dugdale to print his 1866 edition.

Some of the contrasts with Bentham, both in tone and argument, reflect the change that had taken place in the political situation between the Regency (when Bentham did most of his writing) and the 1830s. In 1818, when Bentham finished his most extensive notes in favor of the decriminalization of sodomy, criminal law reform in England was still in the future. By 1833, the death penalty had been abolished for many offenses. It was this movement, originating in the House of Commons, that had particularly aroused the hopes of homosexuals. The poem is consequently full of minutiae relating to Parliament and parliamentarians. Though these create many obscurities for the modern reader, they also give it substance and reality. As if specifically addressed to its members, *Don Leon* contains detailed accounts of four men in the House who found themselves threatened by the law in homosexual scandals, and a fifth is mentioned in the notes. Of these, two, Richard Heber and William Bankes, had connections with Hobhouse and Byron.

Writing from Ravenna in 1821, Byron had asked Hobhouse to congratulate Heber on his recent election as a member from Oxford.[15] When Heber, a famous book collector, died in exile twelve years later, the English press was full of lengthy obituaries, most of which ignored or made only veiled references to the ostracism he had suffered in his last years. Sir Walter Scott had praised him as "Heber the magnificent" for his library, rendered him thanks in the notes to the Waverley novels, and celebrated their friendship in the sixth canto of *Marmion*. Heber's collection of early English books was the most impressive yet assembled; he left eight houses full of volumes in England and on the Continent. Then in 1826, he was accused of homosexual relations, and he fled to Brussels. Scott noted in his journal that "his life was compromised but for the exertions of Hobhouse under Secy of State who detected a warrant for his trial passing through the office."[16] (This Hobhouse was, in fact, not John Cam but his cousin Henry.) In a long account of Heber's scholarship and politics, the *Annual Register* reported with unusual candor: "In the year 1831, he returned to England, but not into the society which he had left; for rumors had been in circulation degrading to his moral character. With the exception of his visits to the auction-rooms and booksellers' shops, he lived entirely secluded among his books at Pimlico or Hodnet."[17]

During his first year at Trinity College Byron identified William Bankes and Edward Noel Long as his closest student intimates. He called Bankes his "collegiate pastor, and master, and patron" and often joined him and Matthews in Bankes's rooms.[18] Later their paths crossed again under ironic circumstances. Bankes proposed to Annabella Milbanke shortly after Byron had made his first proposal and, like him, was turned down. When Bankes ventured on a long voyage to the East, Byron wrote recommendations for him in Albania and, impressed by his scholarly discoveries, took a vicarious pride in his "perilous researches."[19] "Bankes is a wonderful fellow," Byron wrote Murray in 1820, "I love and esteem him."[20] That same year Byron wrote an unusually warm invitation to Bankes to join him in Ravenna to celebrate the carnival. After his return to England, Bankes made his country house in Dorset a showplace for antiquities and became a close friend of the Duke of Wellington. From 1822 to 1826 he sat in Parliament as the member from Cambridge; later he represented Marlborough and Dorset. Then in June 1833, he was arrested and accused of sexual misconduct with a guardsman in a public convenience near the House of Commons. At his trial in December the duke testified as a character witness. So did the headmaster of Harrow and a phalanx of members from both houses. The jury, duly impressed, found both men not guilty and "without the least stain on their characters."[21] Eight years later, when Bankes was again arrested for a similar offense, he followed in Byron's footsteps by retiring to Venice, where he died in 1855.[22]

Don Leon was written to forward homosexual law reform, but the cause did not prosper. When the Commission on Criminal Law, appointed in 1833, issued their second report in June 1836, they recommended reducing capital offenses to eight crimes, all of which (except sodomy) involved violence or danger to life. But their only reference to homosexuality was a single sentence: "A nameless offense of great enormity we, at present, exclude from consideration."[23] A bill to abolish the death penalty for rape and sodomy passed the Commons in 1841 (where the debate touched only on rape), but the sodomy law reform was killed in the House of Lords. On June 17, the Earl of Wicklow argued that if the Lords passed such a law, "they would lower themselves in public opinion; for as the organ of the public voice, they would sanction what the people of this country would never confirm—that sodomy and rape were not crimes of so heinous a character as to deserve death." Next day, the Earl of Winchelsea proposed an amendment to retain capital punishment for homosexuality alone. "Their Lordships, he was convinced, would do great violence to the moral feelings of a very large class of the community, if they exempted this crime from the penalty of death."[24] Not until 1861, when a comprehensive measure consolidating and revising portions of the English criminal law was passed, was the death penalty for sodomy reduced to life imprisonment, a sanction that remained unchanged for more than a century.

Though it is impossible to speak with real certainty of the author and the date of *Don Leon*, certain considerations do suggest themselves. First, it seems altogether likely that, whatever additions or changes were made later, the poem was completed substantially in its present form sometime in the late summer or early fall of 1833.[25] The two cases that seem to have provoked the work were the arrest of William Bankes in June and the execution of Nicholls in August. The Bankes episode may have suggested to the poet that members of Parliament would now be ready to listen to reformist arguments since a distinguished Tory member of the lower house had become a victim of the law. Because Bankes's acquittal in December made his case moot, it is likely that the section of the poem devoted to Bankes (which is very near the conclusion) was finished before his trial took place. There is also the curious fact that the substantial list of arrests for 1833, in note 56, includes cases dated February, April, May, June, and early August, but none later. Probably, then, the note was compiled in late August or shortly afterward.

As for the author, one is struck by his minute knowledge of details pertaining to the Commons. He notes, for instance, that Sir Stephen Lushington sat near the speaker and that the "youth with courtly manners" (who may or may not have been James Stanhope) shared the same row with the "elder Bankes," that is, Bankes's father. No one who had not frequented the House often and been closely familiar with its membership would have been aware that these two obscure parliamentarians sat in the same row or could have told the reader that James Brogden spoke in a shy manner at certain moments (as in line 1012). If the author was not an elected representative, he was certainly someone whose duties or interests brought him into close relation with Parliament. His intimate knowledge of Byron's life also suggests that if he had not known Byron, he was at least a confidant of some friend of his. Possibly this friend was William Bankes himself, who, on visiting Byron in Italy on the way home from his Eastern travels in 1821, may have exchanged confidences with him.

But whoever he was, the *Leon* poet has left us a unique document. No further candid discussion of Byron's homosexuality appeared in English until 1935 when Peter Quennell published his *Byron: The Years of Fame*. Not only did the *Leon* poet set forth the main facts about Byron's homosexuality a full century before Byron's more conventional biographers dared to broach the subject; he also wrote, in a form that is telling and powerful, the earliest published protest against homosexual oppression in England that has survived and the first plea for understanding. . . .

Notes

. . . . .

[8] A correspondent signing himself "I. W." in *Notes and Queries* 7 (1853):66, refers to "a poem (about 1500 lines) which professes to be written by Lord Byron, is addressed to Thomas Moore, and was printed abroad many years since." This is the only evidence we have for the existence of an earlier edition, no copy of which has as yet been identified.

[9] G. Wilson Knight, "Who Wrote 'Don Leon'?" *Twentieth Century* 156 (1954):67-79; and G. Wilson Knight, "Colman and 'Don Leon,'" *Twentieth Century* 159 (1956):562-73.

[10] In the "Editorial Note" added to the 1977 edition of *The Late Lord Byron,* Moore identifies him (p. viii) as Richard Paternoster, of Madras, who contributed to a Byron monument fund in 1826 and then quarreled with the committee. See also Doris Langley Moore, *The Late Lord Byron: Posthumous Dramas,* rev. ed. 1977, pp. 210-13; and Doris Langley Moore, *Lord Byron: Accounts Rendered,* 1974, pp. 449-53.

[11] My earlier references to *Don Leon* have been to the Arno Press reprint of 1975 (a facsimile of the suppressed 1934 Fortune Press edition), the most readily accessible edition. For quotations from the text of the poem in this chapter, however, I have used the 1866 Dugdale version. The discussion of the poem that follows was published, in a somewhat fuller version, in "*Don Leon,* Byron, and Homosexual Law Reform," *Journal of Homosexuality* 8 (Spring-Summer 1983):53-71. This version has details on the history of law reform, parliamentary scandals, etc., not reprinted here.

[12] In n. 31, the annotator to *Don Leon* points out that this is a mistake; Byron wrote poems in the Lantern but did not live there.

[13] The annotator tells us the bibliophile is Hobhouse's friend, Richard Heber, member for Oxford, and conjectures that the officer who committed suicide was James Stanhope. The reformer is identified as Henry Grey Bennett, the well-known humanitarian (nn. 63, 65, 66).

[14] This theme of marital sodomy is central to *Leon to Annabella,* a companion piece to *Don Leon,* published with it in the 1866 edition, which deals entirely with this subject and ignores the question of homosexuality. Some contemporaries, including Hobhouse and Lord Holland, speculated that Byron had attempted anal intercourse with his wife and that this had been one reason for the separation (Leslie A. Marchand, *Byron: A Biography,* 1957, 2:587n.).

[15] September 12, 1821, *Byron's Letters and Journals,* 8:207.

[16] July 10, 1826, *The Journal of Sir Walter Scott,* ed. W. E. K. Anderson (Oxford: Clarendon Press, 1972), p. 170. Anderson wrongly identifies the undersecretary as John Cam Hobhouse.

[17] *Annual Register* (1833), p. 246.

[18] To John Murray, Ravenna, November 19, 1820, *Byron's Letters and Journals,* 7:230.

[19] To William Bankes, November 20, 1819, *Byron's Letters and Journals,* 6:243.

[20] August 31 and October 8, 1820, *Byron's Letters and Journals,* 7:168, 195.

[21] *Annual Register* (1833), p. 169.

[22] See n. 88 to *Don Leon.* There is more on Heber and Bankes in A. L. Rowse, *Homosexuals in History* (London: Weidenfeld & Nicolson, 1977), pp. 120-27; and in my essay, "*Don Leon,* Byron, and Homosexual Law Reform."

[23] "Punishments, and Particularly That of Death," in *Second Report from His Majesty's Commissioners on Criminal Laws* (British Sessional Papers, 1836), 36:219.

[24] June 17, 1841, *Hansard's Parliamentary Debates* (London: Hansard, 1841), 3rd ser., vol. 58, cols. 1557, 1568.

[25] There have been two principal arguments advanced for a date later than 1833. One is that Charles Manners-Sutton, the speaker, did not get the peerage (referred to in line 1041) until March 1835. But as I show in my article, "*Don Leon,* Byron, and Homosexual Law Reform," Manners-Sutton's longed-for peerage was a publicly debated issue in 1833 when the reform Parliament met. The other argument is that line 987 predicts that Henry Grey Bennett will die abroad. Bennett did die in Florence on June 16, 1836. But, as Knight points out, this may simply be a reasonable guess as to what would happen. It is also possible that the poem was revised at a later date.

Eve Kosofsky Sedgwick

SOURCE: "Homophobia, Misogyny, and Capital: The Example of *Our Mutual Friend,*" in *Between Men: English Literature and Male Homosocial Desire,* Columbia University Press, 1985, pp. 161-79.

[*Sedgwick's* Between Men: English Literature and Male Homosocial Desire *became a standard in the new field of gay and lesbian studies on its publication in 1985. In her work, Sedgwick argues that heterosexual culture depends on homosocial relations between men: that is, on a male-male sexual desire played out through exchange of women. In the following chapter, Sedgwick presents her thesis in relation to Charles Dickens'* Our Mutual Friend.*]

Eight years ago, writing a narrative poem about a musicologist with a writing block, I included a little literary joke: a fictional psychoanalyst in the poem was writing a fictional essay for *Thalassa: A* (fictional) *Journal of Genitality,* on the then-fictional topic,

"Sustained Homosexual Panic and Literary Productiveness" (which includes close readings from *Our Mutual Friend*). . . .

It didn't amount to much as a joke, but at any rate it does record the slightly incredulous beginnings of my thinking about this present project, and their inextricability from a reading of late Dickens. At that time I probably imagined a reading couched in more biographical terms than it now seems to me feasible to do well, or interesting to do speculatively. In a more historical and political framework, though, it still seems important to delineate the force of Dickens' contribution to the "Gothic" project: the psychologization and political naturalization of homophobia about men. . . .

By the time of *Great Expectations, Our Mutual Friend,* and *Edwin Drood,* . . . Dickens' writing had incorporated the concerns and thematics of the paranoid Gothic as a central preoccupation. Specifically, each of these novels sites an important plot in triangular, heterosexual romance—in the Romance tradition—and then changes its focus as if by compulsion from the heterosexual bonds of the triangle to the male-homosocial one, here called "erotic rivalry." In these male homosocial bonds are concentrated the fantasy energies of compulsion, prohibition, and explosive violence; all are fully structured by the logic of paranoia. At the same time, however, these fantasy energies are mapped along the axes of social and political power; so that the revelation of intrapsychic structures is inextricable from the revelation of the mechanisms of class domination.

In the half-century or so between the classic Gothic and Dickens, the terms of engagement between homophobia and class structure had become ever more differentiated. The normative status of the rural gentry in Hogg had to a large extent devolved onto (some version of) the English middle class—mediated by genealogical narratives like *Henry Esmond* and *The Princess*. And an anxious self-definition of that class, in male-homosocial terms, as against those both above and below on the social ladder, was effected, as well as critiqued, by neo-Gothic writers such as Dickens. In this chapter . . . I am going to be focusing on these political strains in Dickens' use of the paranoid Gothic. This chapter will make primary use of *Our Mutual Friend,* with some additional reference to other nineteenth-century English fiction, to explore the uses of homophobia in the domestic political terms of mid-Victorian England. . . .

Our Mutual Friend has had an emboldening effect on at any rate the thematic project of *Between Men,* because it is so thick with themes associated with male homophobia and homosexuality. After all, *Our Mutual Friend* is *the* English novel that everyone knows is about anality. The inheritance at the center of the plot is immensely valuable real estate that contains a cluster of what Dickens calls "dust heaps." Layers of scholarly controversy have been devoted to the contents of Victorian dust heaps; and, led by Humphry House's *The Dickens World,* many critics have agreed that human excrement was an important (and financially valuable) component of the mounds. Such critics as Earle Davis, Monroe Engel, J. Hillis Miller, and Sylvia Bank Manning have given this thematic element a good deal of play, often, as F. S. Schwarzbach says, "with the intention of establishing whether Dickens did or did not understand Freud's later formulation of the psychic relation between human waste and money."[3]

But although many of those who write about Dickens' conjunction of excrement and money refer to Freud, sometimes by way of Norman O. Brown, most of the substance of Freud's (and Brown's) argument is missing from their accounts. Their point is most often far simpler and essentially moralistic: that money and excrement are alike because (more or less) they are worthless, *bad.* Thus Earle Davis writes,

> Economically speaking, [Dickens'] world could see no difference between unearned increment and diffused excrement. . . . [I]n every part of London he saw mankind straining and struggling over a dung heap. . . . His pen became an excretory organ spouting out a sizzling cover for all the organic corruption which lay festering in the values that money set, the awful offal of Victorian standards.

Davis concludes his "post-Freudian" reading with the ancient favorite text of Chaucer's Pardoner:

> At the bottom of all is money, the love of money at the cost of everything else. It is the overweening desire for money which lands most people in the filth of Hell.[4]

Perhaps it would be more precise, then, to say that *Our Mutual Friend* is the only English novel that everyone *says* is about excrement in order that they may *forget* that it is about anality. For the Freudian insights, elided in the critics' moralistic yoking of filth and lucre, are erotic ones. They are insights into the pleasures, desires, bonds, and forms of eros that have to do with the anus. And it is precisely the repression of these pleasures and desires that, in Freud, turns feces into filth and filth into gold. A novel about the whole issue of anal eroticism, and not merely a sanitized invective against money or "filthy lucre" or what critics have come to call "the dust-money equation," would have to concern itself with other elements in the chain Freud describes: love between man and man, for instance; the sphincter, its control, and the relation of these to sadism; the relations among bodily images, material accumulation, and economic status. It would also offer some intimations, at least, of adult genital desire, and repression, in relation to the anus. Furthermore a novel that treated these issues would necessarily cast them in the mold of a particular, historical vision of society, class, power, money, and gender.

One curious thematic marker in *Our Mutual Friend* that has gone critically unnoticed, and that the novel itself tends to muffle, is a name. An important character in the novel chooses to call herself Jenny Wren, but we are told—just once—that that is not the name she was born with. Her real name is Fanny Cleaver. Unlike the later, funny, almost childishly deflationary name, Fanny Assingham, in *The Golden Bowl,* Fanny Cleaver is a name that hints at aggression—specifically, at rape, and perhaps at homosexual rape.[5] The pun would seem a trivial accident, were it not a small pointer to something much more striking: that there are two scenes in *Our Mutual Friend* whose language does indeed strongly suggest male rape.[6] These are Bradley Headstone's attack on Rogue Riderhood (discussed below), and the attack on John Harmon in chapter 13. . . . Another thematic "clue" functions at a different level to solicit the twentieth-century reader's attention to the male homosocial components in the book. One of the male protagonists lives in domestic happiness with another man, and at moments of particular intensity he says things like, "I love you, Mortimer."[7]

In some simple sense, therefore, this must be a novel that delineates something close to the whole extent of the male homosocial spectrum, including elements of homosexual genitality. Just what version of male homosociality most concerns it, however? The sweet avowal, "I love you, Mortimer," almost promises the sunny, Pickwickian innocence of encompassing homosocial love rendered in the absence of homophobia. At the same time, to give a *woman* a name like Fanny Cleaver may suggest something almost opposite: homophobia, in the absence of homosexuality. And those golden dust heaps are the emblem of a wholly abstracted anality: they do not refer us to any individual or sentient anus. To understand the very excess, the supervisibility of the homosocial/homophobic/homosexual thematics in this novel requires us to see that for Dickens the erotic fate of every female or male is also cast in the terms and propelled by the forces of class and economic accumulation.

Let me begin by tracing a chain of Girardian triangles within one of the novel's plots, a chain reaching from the lowest class up to the professional class. It begins with the three members of the Hexam family: Gaffer Hexam, the father, an illiterate scavenger who makes his living by fishing corpses from the Thames and robbing them; Lizzie Hexam, his beautiful, good, and loyal daughter; and Charley Hexam, his son, whom Lizzie protects from their father's violent resentment until Charley is old enough to run away and go to school. These three comprise the first triangle.

Charley is determined and industrious enough to go from a Ragged School to a National School, where he becomes a pupil-teacher under the sponsorship of a young schoolmaster, Bradley Headstone. Bradley, like Charley, began as a pauper, and Dickens says, "regarding that origin of his, he was proud, moody, and sullen, desiring it to be forgotten." Yet an intense bond soon develops between the schoolmaster and young Charley. After the father's death, Bradley advises Charley to have no more to do with his impoverished, illiterate sister. Charley begs Bradley to come meet Lizzie first, however, and Bradley finds himself, as if by compulsion, violently in love with her.

The triangles of the Hexam family and of Charley, Lizzie, and Bradley are complicated by another triangle. Eugene Wrayburn, a young barrister and one of the heroes of the novel, also falls in love with Lizzie. He, like Bradley, has an intense encounter with Charley before meeting Lizzie, although in this case the intensity takes the form of instant, almost allergic dislike on both sides. And Eugene has another, apparently non-triangular, love relationship—it is he who says, "I love you, Mortimer." Mortimer Lightwood is an old friend and protégé of Eugene's from public school, and the two, while making languid efforts to succeed in the law, make a household together.

Already contrasts of class are appearing under the guise of contrasts of personality and sexuality. One great evidence of class and control divides this little world in two as absolutely as gender does, though less permanently: the division of the literate from the illiterate. And after Gaffer's early death, only one of these people—Lizzie, the desired woman—remains illiterate. The quarrel between the schoolmaster and Eugene is over who will teach her to read. But even within the masculine world of literacy, the gradations of class are unforgiving. Charley's and Bradley's relation to knowledge is always marked by the anxious, compulsive circumstances of its acquisition. Dickens says of the schoolmaster,

> From his early childhood up, his mind had been a place of mechanical stowage. . . . There was a kind of settled trouble in the face. It was the face belonging to a normally slow or inattentive intellect that had toiled hard to get what it had won, and that had to hold it now that it was gotten.

Bradley seems always to be in pain, "like . . . one who was being physically hurt, and was unwilling to cry out"; his infliction of pain on others seems to come from even greater spasms of it within himself; talking to Lizzie about his desire to teach her to read, for example, he seems to be hemorrhaging internally:

> He looked at Lizzie again, and held the look. And his face turned from burning red to white, and from white back to burning red, and so for the time to lasting deadly white.

In fact, to borrow an image from a patient of Freud's, the schoolmaster behaves socially like a man with a hungry rat in his bowels. And for him, the rat represents not money but more specifically his small private capital of knowledge. Or rather it represents the alienation from himself of the profit of his knowledge. For the knowledge never makes *him* wiser; it is quite worthless outside the schoolroom; it merely places him, more decisively even than illiteracy would, in a particular, low position in the line of production of labor for a capitalism whose needs now included a literate, rather than merely a massive, workforce. Bradley's one effort to invest his nest egg for his own profit—to teach Lizzie to read, as part of that triangular transaction with Charley—is imperiously overruled by Eugene, who wants to pay for his own person to do the teaching. "Are you her schoolmaster as well as her brother's?" asks Eugene scornfully, and instead of using his name, will only call him, "Schoolmaster." Bradley, as usual, loses control of his composure and complexion—for he is merely "used to the little audience of a school, and unused to the larger ways of men."

Eugene, on the other hand, though not wealthy, is a gentleman and a public-school boy. His relation to his own store of knowledge is the confident one of inconspicuous consumption: he can afford to be funny and silly. He likes to say things like "But then I mean so much that I—that I don't mean." Or

> "You know that when I became enough of a man to find myself an embodied conundrum, I bored myself to the last degree by trying to find out what I meant. You know that at length I gave it up, and declined to guess any more."

Mortimer sees him affectionately as "this utterly careless Eugene." He has no consciousness of knowledge, or even of power, as something to be struggled for, although his unconscious wielding of them makes him not only more loveable and relaxed than Bradley but also much more destructive. The moral ugliness of Eugene's taunts against the schoolmaster is always less striking, in the novel's presentation, than the unloveliness of the schoolmaster's anxiety and frustration. Bradley the pauper, thinking to make himself independent by his learning, finds that he has struggled himself into a powerless, alienating position in an impervious hierarchical economy. Eugene Wrayburn, like Yorick imagining himself as marginal, passive, and unempowered in his relation to the economy, nevertheless speaks with the full-throated authority of a man near its very center.

Bradley's relation with Charley and Eugene's with Mortimer differ on the basis of class, and the position of Lizzie in each relationship is accordingly different. Charley's offer of Lizzie to his schoolmaster represents the purest form of the male traffic in women. Charley explains it to Lizzie this way:

> "Then *I* come in. Mr. Headstone has always got me on, and he has a good deal in his power, and of course if he was my brother-in-law he wouldn't get me on less, but would get me on more. Mr. Headstone comes and confides in me, in a very delicate way, and says, 'I hope my marrying your sister would be agreeable to you, Hexam, and useful to you?' I say, 'There's nothing in the world, Mr. Headstone, that I could be better pleased with.' Mr.

Headstone says, 'Then I may rely upon your intimate knowledge of me for your good word with your sister, Hexam?' And I say, 'Certainly, Mr. Headstone, and naturally I have a good deal of influence with her.' So I have; haven't I, Liz?"

> "Yes, Charley."

> "Well said! Now you see, we begin to get on, the moment we begin to be really talking it over, like brother and sister."

To Bradley, his triangle with Charley and Lizzie represents not access to power within the society but a dire sliding away from it; and this is true whether one takes his desire for Lizzie or for Charley to represent the main erotic bond. No wonder he says to Lizzie, in an example of his resentful style of courtship:

> "You are the ruin—the ruin—the ruin—of me. . . . I have never been quit of you since I first saw you. Oh, that was a wretched day for me! That was a wretched, miserable day!"

No; the closest relation to patriarchal power for Bradley in this tangle comes in the link of rivalry between himself and Eugene Wrayburn. And it soon emerges that this is, indeed, for him, the focus of the whole affair. In the painful scene with Lizzie I have been quoting, Bradley makes a threat against Eugene, and when she responds, indignantly, "He is nothing to you, I think," he insists, "Oh yes he is. There you mistake. He is much to me." What? she asks.

> "He can be a rival to me *among other things*. . . . I knew all this about Mr. Eugene Wrayburn, all the while you were drawing me to you. . . . With Mr. Eugene Wrayburn in my mind, I went on. With Mr. Eugene Wrayburn in my mind, I spoke to you just now. With Mr. Eugene Wrayburn in my mind, I have been set aside and I have been cast out."

> (emphasis added)

After Lizzie has refused Bradley and left London, the desiring relation between Bradley and Eugene, far from dissipating, becomes hotter and more reciprocal. The schoolmaster decides—wrongly—that he can find Lizzie by following Eugene everywhere he goes, and, Eugene says,

> "I goad the schoolmaster to madness. . . . I tempt him on, all over London. . . . Sometimes, I walk; sometimes, I proceed in cabs, draining the pocket of the schoolmaster, who then follows in cabs. I study and get up abstruse No Thoroughfares in the course of the day [while Bradley is teaching]. With Venetian mystery I seek those No Thoroughfares at night, glide into them by means of dark courts, tempt the schoolmaster to follow, turn suddenly, and catch him before he can retreat. Then we face one another,

and I pass him as unaware of his existence, and he undergoes grinding torments. . . . Thus I enjoy the pleasures of the chase. . . . just now I am a little excited by the glorious fact that a southerly wind and a cloudy sky proclaim a hunting evening."

In Surtees's *Handley Cross,* Mr. Jorrocks declaims that "'Unting" is "the image of war without its guilt, and only five-and-twenty per cent. of its danger," but it is less lucky than that for the men who are caught up in this chase. One day on a towpath Bradley attacks Eugene from behind; the two men struggle in an embrace, and Eugene, both arms broken, nearly drowns. Soon after that, another man, a lockkeeper with the sinister and important name Rogue Riderhood, who has been dogging and blackmailing Bradley Headstone, finds himself, too, attacked from behind. This is one of the scenes whose language is that of male rape:

> Bradley had caught him round the body. He seemed to be girdled with an iron ring. . . . Bradley got him round, with his back to the Lock, and still worked him backward. . . . "I'll hold you living, and I'll hold you dead! Come down!"

> Riderhood went over into the smooth pit, backward, and Bradley Headstone upon him. When the two were found, lying under the ooze and scum behind one of the rotting gates, Riderhood's hold had relaxed, probably in falling, and his eyes were staring upward. But, he was girdled still with Bradley's iron ring, and the rivets of the iron ring held tight.

Sphincter domination is Bradley Headstone's only mode of grappling for the power that is continually flowing away from him. Unfortunately for him, sphincter control can't give him any leverage at all with women—with Lizzie, who simply never engages with him, who eludes him from the start. It only succeeds in grappling more closely to him men who have already been drawn into a fascinated mirroring relation to him—Eugene, with whom he has been engaged in that reversible hunt, and Rogue Riderhood, in whose clothing he had disguised himself for the assault on Eugene. His initial, hating terror of Lizzie was a terror of, as he kept putting it, being "drawn" from himself, having his accumulated value sucked from him down the great void of her illiteracy and powerlessness. But, classically, he is the Pinchwife-like man who, fearing to entrust his relations with patriarchy to a powerless counter, a woman, can himself only be used as a woman, and valued as a woman, by the men with whom he comes into narcissistic relation.

In the novel's social mapping of the body, Bradley, like some other figures at the lower end of the respectable classes, powerfully represents the repressive divorce of the private thematics of the anus from the social forces of desire and pleasure. Dickens does precede Freud, Ferenczi, Norman O. Brown, and Deleuze/Guattari, among others, in seeing digestion and the control of the anus as the crucial images for the illusion of economic individualism: cross-culturally, Brown remarks, "the category of 'possession,' and power based on possession, is apparently indigenous to the magic-dirt complex."[8] One thematic portrayal of this exclusion is a splitting of the body between twin images of a distended gut and a distended disembodied head. Bradley Headstone (and note his name), the most wrackingly anal of the characters, also appears repeatedly as a floating "haggard head in the air"; Mr. Venus, a taxidermist and articulator of skeletons, with his shop full of hydrocephalic babies in jars, is himself given to "floating his powerful mind in tea"; illiterate "Noddy" Boffin dandles the head of his walking stick at his ear like the head of a floating "familiar spirit" or baby, and himself seems to turn into a great heavy-headed puppet at the end of the novel; and so on. The unanxious version of *homo digestivus* is the "hideous solidity" that the firmly bourgeois Podsnaps and their circle share with their "corpulent straddling" tableware:

> Everything said boastfully, "Here you have as much of me in my ugliness as if I were only lead; but I am so many ounces of precious metal worth so much an ounce; wouldn't you like to melt me down?" . . . All the big silver spoons and forks widened the mouths of the company expressly for the purpose of thrusting the sentiment down their throats with every morsel they ate. The majority of the guests were like the plate. . . .

This strain of imagery, of course, culminates in the monstrous dust-heaps themselves. In short, one thing that goes on when the human body is taken as a capitalist emblem is that the relation of parts to wholes becomes problematic; there is no intelligible form of circulation; the parts swell up with accumulated value, they take on an autonomous life of their own, and eventually power comes to be expressed as power over reified doubles fashioned in one's own image from the waste of one's own body. Power is over dolls, puppets, and articulated skeletons, over the narcissistic, singular, nondesiring phantoms of individuality.

For Bradley Headstone, dissociation, anxiety, toil, and a crippling somatic self-consciousness mark the transition into respectability, and make heavy and humiliating work of his heterosexual involvement. How differently they manage these things in the upper classes. While Bradley's intentions toward Lizzie, however uneasy, had been strictly honorable, Eugene Wrayburn has no intentions toward her at all. Mortimer asks him,

> "Eugene, do you design to capture and desert this girl?"

"My dear fellow, no."

"Do you design to marry her?"

"My dear fellow, no."

"Do you design to pursue her?"

"My dear fellow, I don't design anything. I have no design whatsoever. I am incapable of designs. If I conceived a design, I should speedily abandon it, exhausted by the operation."

This is the opposite of Bradley's compulsive, grasping relation to power. Eugene sees himself as a little leaf borne upon a stream; and an image that is often associated with him is the pretty river that supplies power to the papermill where Lizzie finally gets work. But Eugene's lack of will is enormously more potent than Bradley's clenched, entrapping will, simply because the powerful, "natural" trajectory of this stream is eternally toward swelling the exploitive power of ruling-class men over working-class women. Resolute and independent as Lizzie is, weak and passive as *he* is, Eugene barely has to make a decision, much less form a design, in order to ruin her.

> The rippling of the river seemed to cause a correspondent stir in his uneasy reflections. He would have laid them asleep if he could, but they were in movement, like the stream, and all tending one way with a strong current. . . . "Out of the question to marry her," said Eugene, "and out of the question to leave her."

It is traditional, in criticism of *Our Mutual Friend,* to distinguish two groups of thematic imagery, that surrounding the river and that surrounding the dust-heaps. If, as I have suggested, the dust-heaps can be said to represent an anthropomorphization of capital that is most closely responsive to the anxieties of the petit-bourgeoisie, then the river, in a sense, offers a critique of that in terms of a more collectively scaled capitalism, organized around alienation and the flow of currency. Its gender implications are pointed and odd: all the men in this waterside novel are strikingly incompetent about the water; there are seven drownings or near-drownings, all of males; men are always dragging each other into the river; and only one person, Lizzie, has the skill to navigate a rescue. At the same time, women are in control only in correctly understanding the current of power as always flowing away from themselves. Gazing into the river, both Lizzie and Eugene read in it the image of Lizzie's inability to resist ruin.

Just as Eugene's higher status enables his heterosexual relationship to be at once more exploitive and less guilty than Bradley's, so his desiring relationship with

a man can be at once much more open and much less embroiled in repressive conflict than any of Bradley's. Interestingly, though it is more open, it also seems much less tinged with the sexual. Imagery of the sphincter, the girdle, the embrace, the "iron ring" of the male grasp, was salient in those murderous attacks on men by Bradley Headstone. By contrast it is utterly absent from the tenderer love between Eugene and Mortimer. They live together like Bert and Ernie on Sesame Street—and who ever wonders what Muppets do in bed? This thematic reticence, if it is reticence, in contrast to the hypersaturation with anal thematics of Bradley's part of the story, can perhaps best be accounted for not by some vague invocation of "Victorian prudery," but by thinking about how the libidinal careers of Victorian gentlemen were distinguished, in fiction and in ideology at any rate, from those of males of higher and lower class.

The obstacles to mapping this territory have been suggested before. The historical research on primary sources that would add texture and specificity to generalizations is only beginning to be done, or at any rate published; at the same time, the paradigms available for understanding the history of sexuality are in rapid and productive flux. The best that I can attempt here is perhaps to lay out in a useful codified form what the "common sense" or "common knowledge" of the (essentially middle-class) Victorian reader of novels might be likely to have been, buttressed by some evidence from biographies. I wish to make clear how tentative and how thoroughly filtered through the ideological lens of middle-class literature these generalizations are, but still to make them available *for* revision by other scholars.

With respect to homosocial/homosexual style, it seems to be possible to divide Victorian men among three rough categories according to class. The first includes aristocratic men and small groups of their friends and dependents, including bohemians and prostitutes; for these people, by 1865, a distinct homosexual role and culture seem already to have been in existence in England for several centuries. This seems to have been a milieu, at once courtly and in touch with the criminal, related to those in which the usages of the term "gay" recorded by John Boswell occurred.[9] It seems to have constituted a genuine subculture, facilitated in the face of an ideologically hostile dominant culture by money, privilege, internationalism, and, for the most part, the ability to command secrecy. Pope's lines on Sporus in "Epistle to Dr. Arbuthnot" do, however, presuppose his audience's knowledge that such a role and culture exist. This role is closely related to—is in fact, through Oscar Wilde, the antecedent of—the particular stereotype that at least until recently has characterized American middle-class gay homosexuality; its strongest associations, as we have noted, are with effeminacy, transvestitism, promiscuity, prostitution, continental European culture, and the arts.

For classes below the nobility, however, there seems in the nineteenth century not to have been an association of a particular personal style with the genital activities now thought of as "homosexual." The class of men about which we know most—the educated middle class, the men who produced the novels and journalism and are the subjects of the biographies—operated sexually in what seems to have been startlingly close to a cognitive vacuum. A gentleman (I will use the word "gentleman" to distinguish the educated bourgeois from the aristocrat as well as from the working-class man—a usage that accords, not with Victorian ideology, but with Victorian practice) had a good deal of objective sexual freedom, especially if he were single, having managed to evade the great cult of the family and, with it, much of the enforcing machinery of his class and time. At the same time, he seems not to have had easy access to the alternative subculture, the stylized discourse, or the sense of immunity of the aristocratic/bohemian sexual minority. So perhaps it is not surprising that the sexual histories of English gentlemen, unlike those of men above and below them socially, are so marked by a resourceful, makeshift, *suit generis* quality, in their denials, their rationalizations, their fears and guilts, their sublimations, and their quite various genital outlets alike. Biographies of English gentlemen of the nineteenth and early twentieth centuries are full of oddities, surprises, and apparent false starts; they seem to have no predetermined sexual trajectory. Good examples include Lewis Carroll, Charles Kingsley, John Ruskin, and a little later, T. E. Lawrence, James M. Barrie, T. H. White, Havelock Ellis, and J. R. Ackerley, who describes in an autobiography how he moved from a furtive promiscuous homosexuality to a fifteen-year-long affair of the heart with a female dog.[10] The sexuality of a single gentleman was silent, tentative, protean, and relatively divorced from expectations of genre, though not of gender.

In fiction, a thematically tamer but structurally interesting and emotionally—very often—turbid and preoccupying relationship was common between single gentlemen: Pendennis and Warrington, Clive Newcome and J. J. Ridley, the two Armadales of Collins' *Armadale,* the gentlemen of the Pickwick Club, resemble Eugene and Mortimer in the lack of remark surrounding their union and in the shadowy presence of a mysterious imperative (physical debility, hereditary curse, secret unhappy prior marriage, or simply extreme disinclination) that bars at least one of the partners in each union forever from marriage.

Of the sexuality of English people below the middle class, reliable accounts are difficult to assemble. Both aristocratic and (early twentieth-century) middle-class

English male homosexuality seem to have been organized to a striking degree around the objectification of proletarian men, as we read in accounts by or of Forster, Isherwood, Ackerley, Edward Carpenter, Tom Driberg, and others; at the same time, there is no evidence (from these middle-class-oriented accounts) of a homosexual role or subculture indigenous to men of the working class, apart from their sexual value to more privileged men. It is possible that for the great balance of the non-public-school-educated classes, overt homosexual acts may have been recognized mainly as instances of violence: English law before the Labouchère amendment of 1885 did not codify or criminalize most of the spectrum of male bodily contacts, so that homosexual acts would more often have become *legally* visible for the violence that may have accompanied them than for their distinctively sexual content. In middle-class accounts of the working class, at any rate, and possibly within the working class itself, there seems to have been an association between male homosexual genitality and violence, as in Dickens' treatment of Bradley Headstone's anal eroticism in terms exclusively of murder and mutilation.

Since most Victorians neither named nor recognized a syndrome of male homosexuality as our society thinks of it, the various classes probably grouped this range of sexual activities under various moral and psychological headings. I have suggested that the working class may have grouped it with violence. In aristocrats—or, again, in aristocrats as perceived by the middle class—it came under the heading of dissolution, at the very time when dissolution was itself becoming the (wishful?) bourgeois-ideological name for aristocracy itself. Profligate young lords in Victorian novels almost *all* share the traits of the Sporus-like aristocratic homosexual "type," and it is impossible to predict from their feckless, "effeminate" behavior whether their final ruin will be the work of male favorites, female favorites, the racecourse, or the bottle; waste and wastage is the presiding category of scandal. . . . Fictional examples of this ambiguous style include Lord Frederick Verisopht (with his more "masculine," less aristocratic sidekick, Sir Mulberry Hawk), in *Nicholas Nickleby;* Count Fosco, (with his more "masculine," less aristocratic sidekick, Sir Percival Glyde) in *The Woman in White;* Lord Porlock, in *The Small House at Allington* and *Doctor Thorne;* in a more admiring version, Patrick, Earl of Desmond (with his more "masculine," less aristocratic sidekick, Owen Fitzgerald) in Trollope's *Castle Richmond;* and Lord Nidderdale (with Dolly Longstaffe) in *The Way We Live Now.* In each case there is explicit mention of only female erotic objects, if any; but in each case the allegedly vicious or dissolute drive seems more visibly to be directed at a man in more immediate proximity. Perhaps the most overtly sympathetic—at any rate the least grotesque, the closest to "normal"-seeming—of the men in this category is also one who is without a title, although within the context of the novel he represents the vitiated line of a rural aristocracy. That is Harold Transome, in *Felix Holt*. To his sexual history we receive three clues, each tantalizing in its own way: we hear—mentioned once, without elaboration—that the woman he had married in his Eastern travels was one whom he had bought as a slave;[11] we hear—mentioned once, without elaboration—that he has brought a (different) woman back with him from the East;[12] but the person of whom we hear incessantly in connection with Harold is his plangent, ubiquitous manservant-companion:

> "I don't know whether he's most of a Jew, a Greek, an Italian, or a Spaniard. He speaks five or six languages, one as well as another. He's cook, valet, major-domo, and secretary all in one; and what's more, he's an affectionate fellow. . . . That's a sort of human specimen that doesn't grow here in England, I fancy. I should have been badly off if I could not have brought Dominic."[13]

Throughout a plot elaboration that depends heavily on the tergiversations of a slippery group of servants-who-are-not-quite-servants, who have unexplained bonds from the past with Dominic, one waits for the omniscient, serviceable, ingratiating character of Dominic to emerge into its full sinisterness or glamor or sexual insistence—in vain, since the exploitive "oriental" luxuries of his master can be perceived only in a sexually irresolute blur of "decadence." . . . Perhaps similarly, the lurid dissipations of the characters in *The Picture of Dorian Gray* are presented in heterosexual terms when detailed at all, even though (biographical hindsight aside) the triangular relationship of Basil, Dorian, and Lord Henry makes sense only in homosexual terms.

Between the extremes of upper-class male homosocial desire, grouped with dissipation, and working-class male homosocial desire, grouped perhaps with violence, the view of the gentleman, the public-school product, was different again. School itself was, of course, a crucial link in ruling-class male homosocial formation. Disraeli (who was not himself an Etonian) offers the flattering ideological version of Eton friendships in *Coningsby*:

> At school, friendship is a passion. It entrances the being; it tears the soul. All loves of after life can never bring its rapture, or its wretchedness; no bliss so absorbing, no pangs of jealousy or despair so crushing and so keen! What tenderness and what devotion; what illimitable confidence; what infinite revelations of inmost thoughts; what ecstatic present and romantic future; what bitter estrangements and what melting reconciliations; what scenes of wild recrimination, agitating explanations, passionate correspondence; what insane sensitiveness, and what frantic sensibility; what earthquakes of the heart, and whirlwinds of the soul, are confined in that simple phrase—a school-boy's friendship![14]

Candid accounts agree that in most of the public schools, the whirlwinds of the soul, were often acted out in the flesh. Like the young aristocrat, the young gentleman at those same public schools would have seen or engaged in a variety of sexual activities among males; but unlike the aristocrat, most gentlemen found neither a community nor a shared, distinctive sexual identity ready for adults who wanted more of the same. A twentieth-century writer, Michael Nelson, reports asking a school friend, "Have you ever had any homosexual inclinations since leaving Eton?" "I say, steady on," his friend replied. "It's all right for fellows to mess one another about a bit at school. But when we grow up we put aside childish things, don't we?"[15]

David Copperfield, among other books, makes the same point. David's infatuation with his friend Steerforth, who calls him "Daisy" and treats him like a girl, is simply part of David's education—though another, later part is the painful learning of how to triangulate from Steerforth onto women, and finally, although incompletely, to hate Steerforth and grow at the expense of his death. In short, a gentleman will associate the erotic end of the homosocial spectrum, not with dissipation, not with viciousness or violence, but with childishness, as an infantile need, a mark of powerlessness, which, while it may be viewed with shame or scorn or denial, is unlikely to provoke the virulent, accusatory projection that characterizes twentieth-century homophobia.

This slow, distinctive two-stage progression from schoolboy desire to adult homophobia seems to take its structure from the distinctive anxieties that came with being educated for the relatively new class of middle-class "gentlemen." Unlike title, wealth, or land, the terms that defined the gentleman were not clearly and simply hereditary but had somehow to be earned by being a particular kind of person who spent time and money in particular ways. But the early prerequisites for membership in this powerful but nebulous class—to speak with a certain accent, to spend years translating Latin and Greek, to leave family and the society of women—all made one unfit for any other form of work, long before they entitled one to chance one's fortune actively in the ruling class.

The action of *Our Mutual Friend* brings to a close that long abeyance in Eugene's life between, so to speak, being *called* and being *chosen* for the professional work of empire. (For instance, he has been called to the Bar, but no one has yet chosen to employ him.) His position is awash with patriarchal authority, the authority of the law itself, but none of it belongs to him yet. In just the same way, having been removed from his family as a child, he will soon be required to return—and in the enforcing position of *paterfamilias,* a position that will lend a retroactive meaning and heterosexual trajectory to his improvised, provisional relationship with Mortimer and his apparently aimless courtship of Lizzie. In the violence at the end of the novel, we see the implacability with which this heterosexual, homophobic meaning is impressed on Eugene's narrative: Bradley, his rival, nearly kills him by drowning; Lizzie saves him; while he seems to be dying, Mortimer interprets his last wishes as being that he might marry Lizzie; and when he comes back to life, he is already a married man. "But would you believe," Lizzie asks afterwards, "that on our wedding day he told me he almost thought the best thing he could do, was to die?"

There is one character to whom this homophobic reinscription of the bourgeois family is even more crippling than it is to Eugene, who already, by the end of the novel, looks almost "as though he had never been mutilated." That person is, of course, Lizzie. The formal, ideological requirements for a fairytale "happy ending" for her are satisfied by the fact that she is not "ruined" by Eugene, not cast into the urban underclass of prostitution, but raised up into whatever class the wife of a Victorian barrister belongs to. Eugene is determined to fight for his right to have her regarded as a lady. But with all that good news, Dickens makes no attempt to disguise the terrible diminution in her personal stature as she moves from being the resentful, veiled, muscular, illiterate figure rowing a scavenger boat on the Thames, to being a factory worker in love, to being Mrs. Eugene Wrayburn *tout court*. Admittedly, Lizzie has been a reactionary all along. But she has been a blazing, courageous reactionary: she has defended and defied her violent father; she has sacrificed everything for her beastly brother; she gave up a chance to form an alliance with an older woman, a tavernkeeper, just because the woman would not accept her father; she took off for the countryside to save her honor from the man she loved; and she unhesitatingly risked her life to save his life. But all her reactionary courage meets with a stiflingly reactionary reward. Lizzie stops being Lizzie, once she is Mrs. Eugene Wrayburn.

As we see how unrelentingly Lizzie is diminished by her increasingly distinct gender assignment, it becomes clearer why "childishness," rather than femininity, should at that moment have been the ideological way the ruling class categorized its own male homosexuality. As Jean Baker Miller points out in *Toward a New Psychology of Women,* an attribution of gender difference marks a structure of *permanent* inequality, while the relation between adult and child is the prototype of the *temporary* inequality that in principle—or in ideology—exists only in order to be overcome: children are supposed to grow up into parents, but wives are not supposed to grow up into husbands.[16] Now, the newly significant class of "gentlemen," the flagship class of English high capitalism, was to include a very wide range of status and economic position, from plutocrats down to impoverished functionaries. In order to main-

tain the illusion of equality, or at any rate of meritocratic pseudoequality, *within* the class of gentlemen, and at the same time justify the magnification of distinctions within the class, it clearly made sense to envision a long, complicated period of individual psychic testing and preparation, full of fallings-away, redefinitions, and crossings and recrossings of lines of identification. This protracted, baffling narrative of the self, a direct forerunner of the twentieth-century Oedipal narrative, enabled the process of social and vocational sorting to occur under the less invidious shape of different rates of individual maturation.

Not until this psychologistic, "developmental" way of thinking had been firmly established was the *aristocratic* link between male homosexuality and *femininity* allowed to become an article of wide public consumption—a change that was crystallized in the Wilde affair . . . and that coincided (in the 1890s) with the beginnings of a dissemination across classes of language about male homosexuality (e.g., the word "homosexual"), and with the medicalization of homosexuality through an array of scientific "third sex" and "intersex" theories.

But during all this time, for women, the immutability of gender inequality was being inscribed more and more firmly, moralistically, and descriptively in the structure of bourgeois institutions. As the contrasting bodily images in *Our Mutual Friend* suggest, woman's deepening understanding, as she saw the current flowing away under her own image, came for the most part at the cost of renouncing individual ownership and accumulation. The division of cognitive labor that emerged with the bourgeois family was not a means of power for women, but another part of the edifice of master-slave subordination to men. Sentient middle-class women of this time perceive the triangular path of circulation that enforces patriarchal power as being routed through them, but never ending in them—while capitalist man, with his prehensile, precapitalist image of the body, is always deluded about what it is that he pursues, and in whose service. His delusion is, however, often indistinguishable from real empowerment; and indeed it is blindest, and closest to real empowerment, in his triangular transactions through women with other men.

Notes

[1] Sedgwick, "Trace at 46," *Diacritics* 10, No. 1, March, 1980, p. 14.

. . . . .

[3] Schwarzbach, *Dickens and the City,* 1979, pp. 198-99.

[4] Davis, *The Flint and the Flame,* 1963, pp. 266, 271.

[5] This is not a necessary inference from the pun, because of the gender ambiguity of the word "fanny": it apparently referred to female genitals throughout the nineteenth century in England, but cf., for example, Pope's portrayal of the homosexual Lord Hervey as "Lord Fanny" in the eighteenth century ("pure white curd of asses' milk"); and Fanny Assingham.

[6] On the whole I consider the term "male rape," where its meaning is clear in context, preferable to "homosexual rape," since men who rape men are often not homosexual either by self-attribution or by habitual sexual practice; the violent and often the specifically *homophobic* content of this crime are more relevant to our concerns here than its apparently *homosexual* orientation.

[7] Dickens, *Our Mutual Friend,* Bk. IV, ch. 10, p. 812. Further citations will be incorporated in the text and designated by book and chapter number.

[8] Brown, *Life Against Death,* 1959, p. 300. The association between possession and the control of the anus must have something to do with an odd feature of the male "rapes" discussed in this chapter and the next: except in the one case of literal rape, it is the participant who would ordinarily be termed passive—the one associated with the "iron ring" of the sphincter—who is presented as the *aggressor;* the phallus itself barely figures in these "rapes."

[9] Boswell, *Christianity, Social Tolerance, and Homosexuality,* 1980, p. 43.

[10] Ackerley, *My Father and Myself,* 1968.

[11] Eliot, *Felix Holt,* Bk. III, ch. 10.

[12] *Ibid.,* III, 3.

[13] *Ibid.,* I, 2.

[14] Disraeli, *Coningsby,* ch. 9.

[15] Nelson, *Nobs and Snobs,* 1976, p. 147.

[16] Miller, *Toward a New Psychology of Women,* 1976, ch. 1.

Christopher Craft

SOURCE: "'Descend, and Touch, and Enter': Tennyson's Strange Manner of Address," in *Another Kind of Love: Male Homosexual Desire in English Discourse, 1850-1920,* University of California Press, 1994, pp. 44-70.

[*In the following chapter from his book, Craft studies Tennyson's* In Memoriam *as a document of homosexual desire, looking at the poem in relation to its social context and contemporary notions of sexuality.*]

In the final chapter of *Sexual Inversion,* Havelock Ellis turns with measured circumspection to the difficult problem of the correction and consolation of the sexual invert. In the especially vexed case of the "congenital invert"—in the case, that is, of a person who is the "victim of abnormal [homosexual] impulses" that spring incorrigibly from "the central core of organic personality"—consolation through sublimation provides the only available palliation; and this because the invert's "inborn constitutional abnormality" remains, by definition, nonductile and fundamentally resistant to "psychotherapeutical [and] surgical treatment."[1] Still, the impossibility of effective medical remediation did not legitimate an active homosexual genitality. Instead, and for reasons less medical than political, Ellis prescribed the difficult consolation of a more than Penelopean patience: "it is the ideal of chastity, rather than normal sexuality, which the congenital invert should hold before his eyes."[2] Yet if the rigors of so sustained a meditation upon "the ideal of chastity" were likely to produce intense ocular strain, then perhaps this difficulty could be mitigated by the implementation of a practical program of displacement and surrogate satisfaction: a regimen of sublimation, a course of psychosexual exercises, or, as Ellis cheerfully calls it, a "method of self-restraint and self-culture, without self-repression."[3] A civilization, it would seem, without the burden of *much* discontent.

What does Ellis offer as his primary example of this "method of self-treatment?" By what "psychic methods" may the invert "refine and spiritualize the inverted impulse"? How else than by a course of corrective reading? And indeed Ellis proposes a list of books to read and imitate, a prophylactic mimesis. Such remedial homosexual reading, at once consolatory and disciplinary, would serve a double or ambivalent function: the verbal substitution would express the very desire it would also work to contain; the text would be at once the home of desire and the site of its exile. (*The Memoirs of John Addington Symonds,* . . . narrates a personal history of this agonistic Victorian belief that "literary and imaginative palliatives" would double as both "the vehicle and the safety valve for [the] tormenting preoccupations" that beset the victims of "this inexorable and incurable disease.")[4] First among the exemplary texts listed in Ellis's curriculum of literary palliation are, predictably enough, the dialogues of Plato, which "have frequently been found a source of great help and consolation by inverts." The reading of Plato, especially the *Phaedrus* and the *Symposium,* often had for nineteenth-century gay males the force of a revelation. Symond's case history in *Sexual Inversion,* transcribed by Ellis into the third person, is representative: "It was in his 18th year that an event which A [Symonds] regards as decisive in his development occurred. He read the *Phaedrus* and *Symposium* of Plato. A new world opened, and he felt that his own nature had been revealed."[5] This topos of self-recognition via Platonic texts is of course a staple in the cultural construction of nineteenth-century male homosexual subjectivity. Second in order of emphasis in Ellis's itinerary of inverted reading is, again predictably, Whitman's *Leaves of Grass,* with "its wholesome and robust ideal" of "manly love," although Whitman's exuberant sensuality and aboriginal stance rendered his poetry "of more doubtful value for general use." Again, Symonds on Whitman has representative value: *Leaves of Grass* "became for me a kind of Bible. Inspired by 'Calamus' I adopted another method of palliative treatment, and tried to invigorate the emotion I could not shake off by absorbing Whitman's conception of comradeship. . . . The immediate result of this study of Walt Whitman was the determination to write the history of paiderastia in Greece [Symonds's *A Problem in Greek Ethics*] and to attempt a theoretical demonstration of the chivalrous enthusiasm which seemed to me implicit in comradeship."[6] Here, in the transposition of desire into sexual discourse and of sexual discourse into *more* sexual discourse, we may see a paradigmatic example of Ellis's program of disciplinary reading and writing, itself a striking confirmation of Foucault's assertion that the nineteenth century worked assiduously to "put sex into discourse."

Yet if Ellis felt the rhetorical need to demur at Whitman's anatomical insistence, his barely veiled genital reference, he also had the advantage of an absolutely canonical counterexample, a Victorian text whose passionate discursivity and sexual obliquity everywhere marked its constitutive submission to the agonistic Victorian imperative "to refine and spiritualize" so problematic a desire. He turned with confidence to *In Memoriam:*

> Various modern poets of high ability have given expression to emotions of exalted or passionate friendship towards individuals of the same sex, whether or not such friendship can properly be termed homosexual. It is scarcely necessary to refer to *In Memoriam,* in which Tennyson enshrined his affection for his early friend, Arthur Hallam, and developed a picture of the universe on the basis of that affection.[7]

Ellis's sentences here pivot on an ambivalence we may recognize as our own: it may be "scarcely necessary" to adduce *In Memoriam* in this homosexual context, so famous is it as a site of exalted friendship and erotic displacement, yet Ellis equivocates, as indeed he must, as to "whether or not such friendship can properly be termed homosexual." Ellis's verbal equipoise here— his dichotomous need to affirm the homosociality of Tennyson's poem while refusing to specify the homosexuality of Tennysonian desire—responds faithfully

both to Ellis's own delicate discursive situation as a writer of suspect texts and to a certain strategic equivocation within *In Memoriam* itself, one accurately identified by Edward Carpenter when he described *In Memoriam* as being "reserved" and "dignified" "in [its] sustained meditation and tender sentiment" but as also "half revealing here and there a more passionate feeling."[8] Exactly this equivocation defines the critical and taxonomic problem of whether *In Memoriam* "can properly be termed homosexual." The issue here is not merely one of choosing specific terminologies, words like homosexual or heterosexual, but also of submitting (or refusing to submit) to the historically particular acts of conceptualization that make a taxonomic category like homosexuality intelligible at all. To make any definition is first to establish, and then to be governed by, a set of constitutive limits or boundaries. Obviously enough, this process of defining entails the inscription within specific vocabularies and discourses of the authorizing culture's signature, its particular impress of value and belief. Equally obviously, the category of homosexuality, with its inescapable residuary imputations of disease, dysfunction, and disorder, is manifestly incompetent to represent the complex, evasive, and beautiful manipulations that Tennyson's desire for Hallam receives in *In Memoriam.*

This is not to deny but rather to assume and affirm that *In Memoriam* revolves around Hallam as around "the centre of a world's desire."[9] Or, rather more accurately, around Hallam's absconded presence, for he is, as Carol T. Christ writes, "the absent center around which the poem moves."[10] But if Hallam is Tennyson's "central warmth diffusing bliss," the elegy negotiates its problematic desire less by a centering of its warmth than by the dispersion of its bliss, less by acts of specific definition than by strategies of deferral, truncation, and displacement, strategies that everywhere work to "refine and spiritualize" what otherwise would be "the wish too strong for words to name." But *In Memoriam* is more than a machine for the sublimation, management, or transformation of male homosexual desire; it is, rather, the site of a continuing problematization: the problem not merely of desire between men, but also of the desire (very urgent in the elegy) to speak it.

A certain anxiety attends the reading of *In Memoriam* and always has. The first reviews were, of course, largely laudatory, but a palpable dis-ease haunts particular early responses. An anonymous review in *The Times* (28 November 1851), now usually attributed to Manley Hopkins, father of Gerard Manley Hopkins, specifically complained of the elegy's erotic metaphorics, its "strange manner of address to a man, even though he be dead."[11] A "defect," this reviewer noted, "which has painfully come out as often as we take up the volume, is the tone of—may we say so!—amatory tenderness." "Very sweet and plaintive these verses are," Hopkins the elder continued, "but who would not give them a feminine application? Shakespeare may be considered the founder of this style in English." Here the reviewer's palpable gender anxiety, his fear of the unhinged gender within Tennyson's poetic voice, reflects the bewildering ease with which Tennyson employs heterosexual desire and marriage as a trope to represent his passion for lost Hallam, a tropological indiscretion, the reviewer assumes, derived from "floating remembrances of Shakespeare's sonnets," which "present the startling peculiarity of transferring every epithet of womanly endearment to a masculine friend—his master-mistress, as he calls him by a compound epithet, harsh, as it is disagreeable." This homoerotic linkage of *In Memoriam* to Shakespeare's sonnets is hardly anomalous. In another review published anonymously, Charles Kingsley found in *In Memoriam* a descendant of "the old tales of David and Jonathan, Damon and Pythias, Socrates and Alcibiades, Shakespeare and his nameless friend, of 'love passing the love of woman'," although recently Christopher Ricks has charged Kingsley with "recklessness" and has balked at the allusion to 2 Samuel, calling it "that perilous phrase."[12] By the 1890s, when Tennyson's son Hallam wrote his biography-cum-hagiography *Alfred Lord Tennyson: A Memoir* (1897), the perils of what Ricks defensively calls the "homosexual misconstruction" incited Hallam to a prudential pruning of any material that might conduce to equivocal interpretation. For example, as Ricks's biography of Tennyson informs us, when Hallam quoted Benjamin Jowett regarding "the great sorrow of [Tennyson's] mind," he carefully elided anything suggesting what Jowett called, with discreet indirection, "a sort of sympathy with Hellenism." Jowett's comment on Tennyson's grief, that "it would not have been manly or natural to have lived in it always," succumbed to Hallam's editorial vigilance and was cut from the *Memoir*.[13]

Very much the same critical propensity to keep Tennyson "manly and natural" has governed more recent criticism of *In Memoriam,* although modern evasions of the poem's disturbing sexuality have generally demonstrated more cunning than Hallam Tennyson's. Perhaps the simplest of contemporary critical circumventions of *In Memoriam*'s homoerotic discourse are those, like Jerome Buckley's *Tennyson: The Growth of a Poet* (1960), that don't find sexuality pertinent at all to the elegy's recuperative desiring; we have here the simple elision of the homosexual subject. A more intriguing strategy for negotiating the problematics of same-gender desire can be found in Harold Bloom's early essay "Tennyson, Hallam, and Romantic Tradition" (1966), in which Bloom declares, with a false assurance, that it "need disturb no one any longer" that "Tennyson's Muse was (and always remained) Hallam." Bloom's poetic/sexual centering of Hallam is of course substantially correct, but his cosmopolitan poise would be more convincing did he not directly exculpate himself from

further musing on homoerotic muses by saying, first, that "the sexual longings of a poet *qua* poet appear to have little relation to mere experience anyway" and second, that "the analytical sophistication in aesthetic realms that would allow a responsible sexual history of English poetry is not available to us."[14] There is therefore very little to say.

We may see in Bloom's passing acknowledgment of the homosexual subject an ambivalence characteristic of our tradition's reading of this poem. First, he specifies the inescapable homoerotics of *In Memoriam*'s elegiac desire, then precludes a sustained and detailed analysis of that desire by foreclosing critical access either to "mere experience" (which in the case of Tennyson and Hallam is unrevealing anyway) or to the "analytical sophistication" that would render such criticism "responsible." (Since 1966, of course, Bloom has been writing a brilliant and responsible "sexual history of English poetry": a history, not incidentally, in which a belated poet's creative potency—his power of speech as self-production or self-fathering—is tested not in a heterosexual embrace with a female muse but rather in a distinctly Oedipal tussle between men, during which the muscular ephebe may wrest from his father/precursor the power of seminal speech. It is precisely this gladiatorial wrestling—during which the ephebe, now giving what he had been forced to take, reverses the temporal hydraulics of influence—that enables his subsequently productive intercourse with the text-to-be, whose essentially "feminine" receptivity has been, until that moment, effectively forfended by the father's presence, by the Oedipal force of his prior inscriptions. In Bloom's agonistic reading, a text functions as an already inscribed mediatrix, an intervening distance or difference, between two competing familial male potencies whose displaced intercourse is poetry itself. The applicability of all this to *In Memoriam* is, to say the least, enticing, but as yet we have had from Bloom no revised misprision of Tennyson's elegy.)

But Bloom's blithe assurance in 1966 that Hallam's erotic centrality in *In Memoriam* "need disturb no one any longer" seems not to have had its pacifying effects, seems indeed to have gone unheeded, for in 1972 Christopher Ricks in his astute critical biography *Tennyson* paused for some ten pages to worry over precisely this issue. "But do we too," Ricks asks, "need to speak bluntly? Is Tennyson's love for Hallam a homosexual one"?[15] Ricks's answer—I doubt that I am betraying any suspense here—is no, although a number of equivocations beset this denial. His discussion of this anxiogenic question opens with a gesture that recalls Bloom's deferral of adequate discussion to that millennial day when analytic sophistication in aesthetic realms will enable intelligent discourse, but whereas Bloom's displacement is temporal, Ricks's is spatial. Disclaiming the authority of literary criticism altogeth-

Alfred, Lord Tennyson.

er, Ricks invokes another professional discipline, and a predictable one: "the crucial acts of definition will have to be left to the psychologists and psychiatrists, though it should be said that literary historians usually vitiate their arguments by conveniently jumbling the old severely differentiating view with the newer 'something of it in everybody' one." Such recourse to psychiatry and psychology does double duty: in submitting poetry to pathology, the literary critic escapes ultimate responsibility for what must remain a literary-critical decision about the representational function of desire in the text, while simultaneously and inescapably situating that decision within an ideological economy of disease, dysfunction, and presumptively desirable remediation. Implicit in this gesture is the normalizing hope that Tennyson was not "bluntly" "homosexual" or, in Ricks's odd locution, "abnormally abnormal." More importantly still, the deferral of literary decision to medical authority quite simply misses the point. The question at issue is neither the history of Tennyson's genitalia (which Tennyson's most recent biographer suggests would yield a rather brief and tedious narrative) nor the potentially psychopathic trajectories of an obviously tortured psyche. Rather, as we shall see, the issue that matters here is the function of represented sexual desire within the verbal economy we call *In Memoriam* and within the larger tradition of representation from which the poem arises, the tradition to which it continues to direct its strange manner of address.

Ricks's extended "defense" (so to speak) "of Tennyson" against imputations of homosexuality remains sympathetic to certain Tennysonian notions of an orderly and conventional androgyny, an androgyny that perhaps mitigates but never subverts the disciplinary bifurcation of gender characteristics, as when Tennyson admonishes that "men should be androgynous and women gynandrous, but men should not be gynandrous nor women androgynous."[16] A transparent ambivalence informs Tennyson's sentence: a desire to escape the containments of gender engages a desire to contain the escape. Tennyson's precise marshalling of prefixes and suffixes, of fronts and backs, of (to borrow one of Ricks's metaphors) "heads" and "tails," bespeaks an anxiety of gender inversion strong enough to require careful regulation at the level of the signifier. (If signifiers can be compelled into remaining "jubilantly straight" [Ricks again], perhaps signifieds will follow suit.) The disciplinary punctilio of gender enacted by Tennyson's sentence suggests one reason for the obliquity of sexual representation in *In Memoriam,* and it certainly anticipates the disease circulating throughout Ricks's defense of Tennyson's (hetero)sexuality. As a parting instance of this representative anxiety consider Ricks's response to the inclusion of selected stanzas of *In Memoriam* in an anthology of homosexual writing published by Brian Reade in 1970:

> Was Tennyson, so to speak, abnormally abnormal? A new anthology entitled *Sexual Heretics: Male Homosexuality in English Literature from 1850 to 1900* does not hesitate to quote extensively from ten sections of *In Memoriam;* its editor, anxious to enlist or if necessary pressgang Tennyson, quaintly says "the fact that Tennyson evolved an emphatically heterosexual image in later life does nothing to disqualify him as homosexual when he wrote *In Memoriam.*"

To read Ricks reading Reade is to disclose a confusion that in turn generates an anxiety: Reade's confusion is to fail to transcend the cultural agon of a fixed, bipolar opposition between the homo and the hetero (despite the familiar compromise trope of temporal oscillation), while Ricks's anxiety registers itself as a barely suppressed metaphor of homosexual rape by an editor "anxious to enlist or if necessary pressgang Tennyson" into a very dubious literary brotherhood. The rigors of such an enlistment are presumably unbearable, but for a poet laureate to be ganged upon and then pressed—

perhaps im-pressed as well as em-pressed—is to suffer at editorial hands the additional indignity of a sod-omitical intrusion. Better, obviously, to house *In Memoriam* in canonical—that is to say, heterosexual—anthologies.

The foregoing reading of *In Memoriam* criticism, how-ever fragmentary, suggests the conceptual and imagistic burden suffered by our culture's discourse on same-sex eroticism. *In Memoriam* remains a pivotal case in this regard precisely because the problematics of the poem's erotic representations are indistinguishable from readerly problems of interpretation and feeling. To mouth the Tennysonian "I," as the reader of this poem must repeatedly and obsessively do, is to bespeak (for the duration of the reading at least) an anxiogenic iden-tification with the poet's fierce reparational longing, which regularly presses to a transgressive homosexual verge. But *In Memoriam* approaches this verge only when compelled by an incommensurate grief; homo-sexual desire, in other words, is here constituted only elegiacally, once its object has been surpassed. Why, we must now ask, does *In Memoriam* disclose homo-sexual desire as indissociable from death? As itself a mode of mourning? Why this constitutive linking of desire and death?

In *In Memoriam* death discovers desire, the latter ar-riving in and as the wake of the former. The linkage between desire and death is not a casual metaphorical articulation; it is a causal narrative one. For in the highly personal erotic myth that *In Memoriam* so ex-tensively develops, the death of Hallam, when "God's finger touch'd him, and he slept," initiates in the poet both a recuperational homosexual desire—a desire to restore to its preschismatic unity the "divided hal[ves] of such / A friendship as had master'd Time"—and, what is worse, a desperate need to speak this potential-ly philosophic "desire and pursuit of the whole" under the aegis of a transgressive erotics.[17] "Descend, and touch, and enter," Tennyson dangerously pleads, and "hear / The wish too strong for words to name." The extremity of such expression, its desperate mode of erotic address, proceeds from the poet's belated recog-nition that no other human love will ever be "as pure and whole / As when he loved me here in Time"; correlative to this recognition of loss is the fear that "love for him [may] have drain'd / My capabilities of love." Thus desire's duration, the temporal and spatial extensions of this very distended text's poetic wooing (compare "I woo your love"), commences not with Arthur's desirable presence—for when Arthur is present desire and language are supernumerary—but rather with its opposite, with destitution: the poet recognizes that his "dear friend" has become in death's difference "my lost Arthur's loved remains." In a figure whose mur-derous implications will concern us repeatedly in the present study, the language of active homosexual de-siring discovers its origin in a death or terminus that

disrupts an ontologically prior wholeness whose uni-tary gender remains emphatically, inescapably, male. In what we may now correctly call the "hom(m)osexual" economy of *In Memoriam,* death and not gender is the differential out of which longing is so painfully born; it is death that breaches the perfect male couple and opens it to the circulations of desire.[18]

This structure of desire entrains certain disciplinary relations that are coextensive with, indistinguishable from, the desire itself. Because it established homo-sexual desire as always already elegiac, as originally grounded in the destitution of its object, *In Memoriam* both incites and contains homosexual desire in a single cunning articulation. The elegiac mode constrains the desire it also enables: the sundering of death instigates an insistent reparational longing, yet it claustrates the object of this desire on the far side of a divide that interdicts touch even as it incites the desire for touch-ing. An infinite desire is infinitely deferred, subject always to postponement, displacement, diffusion. Death works to inscribe a prophylactic distance, as Tennyson himself suggested in a related context. Commenting on the initial line of lyric 122 ("Oh, wast thou with me, dearest, then"), the poet said: "If anybody thinks I ever called him 'dearest' in his life they are much mistaken, for I never even called him 'dear.'" Ricks finds this statement "naïve perhaps, but not tonally suggestive of homosexuality."[19] Better to say that such "naïveté" marks Tennyson's perfectly Victorian strategy of lin-guistic displacement, precisely because it embeds ho-mosexual desire within an idealizing elegiac register. The elegy insists that desire and death conjugate out of tropological necessity: "Let Love clasp Grief lest both be drown'd." What is "saved" in this embrace is a poetic logic that instantiates homosexual desire as al-ready its own distantiation. "My prime passion [is] in the grave," and "so hold I commerce with the dead."

Of course, as Victorian and modern readers have been quick to notice, the formal solution to this problem is Christ. In a way that is so straightforward as to be transparent, Tennyson would master his unconvention-al desire for Hallam by figuring it as a subspecies of a very conventional desire for "the Strong Son of God" (prologue). A perfectly conventional trope of typolog-ical interpretation enables Tennyson to represent Hal-lam as a "noble type / Appearing ere the times were ripe" (epilogue)—as, that is, a medial character whose death repeats the ontologically prior sacrifice of the other "He that died," and whose earthly presence had pointed to the superior consummation of a second coming. Yet simply to identify Hallam and Christ as interpenetrated figures of erotic and religious devotion is to repeat what the criticism has already noticed. *"In Memoriam,"* Gerhard Joseph writes, "describes the transformation of Hallam into an analogue of Christ; to render this Hallam-Christ accessible Tennyson eroti-cizes him, giving him female attributes."[20] Joseph's sentence is of course summarily correct—correct, that is, as summary—but the pages to follow will argue that a more capacious understanding of Tennyson's fluent erotics demands that we pause at length to consider just how *In Memoriam* articulates its analogy between Hallam and Christ, and how that analogy operates to relieve the speaker's desperate erotic distress—a distress, as I have said, indistinguishable from his grief. To rush to the Christological or logocentric solution—to chant compliantly with Tennyson "Love is and was my lord and king"—risks another terminological reduction, one that, in its leap to the available comforts of a conventional faith, fails to register the anxious and fluctuant interfusion of sexual desire and religious faith in a poem justly more famous for the quality of its oscillations than for the force of its closural affirmation. *In Memoriam,* Eliot was right to say, "is not religious because of the quality of its faith, but because of the quality of its doubt."[21] If, making explicit what Eliot in his essay leaves implicit, we recognize doubt as a figure of desire, as a mode of suspension poised between the loss of Hallam and the promise of his restoration in a Christological embrace, we will have begun to trace the homoerotic basis of the elegy's extensive yearning.

In its most orthodox articulation, Tennyson's typological strategy represents Hallam as a beautiful but fallen simulacrum of the ontologically prior archetype of Christ himself. The disciplinary and transferential trajectory of such a figural strategy is clear: a desire that would seem to begin in Hallam is discovered to begin and end in Christ, whose forgiving body safely absorbs, relays, and completes a fierce homoerotic cathexis. The elegy's sustained appeal to the "conclusive bliss" of its Christological closure identifies apocalyptic death as the site of a deferred but certain erotic restoration. In the closural ecstasis of the "one far-off divine event / To which the whole creation moves," Christ will "take" the lovers' riven halves and restore them to a "single soul." *In Memoriam* thus solves the problem of desire's divisiveness by fantasizing a dissolving incorporation:

> Dear friend, far off, my lost desire
>   So far, so near in woe and weal;
>   O loved the most, when most I feel
> There is a lower and a higher;
>
> Known and unknown; human, divine;
>   Sweet human hand and lips and eye;
>   Dear heavenly friend that canst not die,
> Mine, mine, for ever, ever mine.
>
> (129)

The intermediate qualities identified in these quatrains refer equally or indistinguishably to Hallam and to Christ; the blended might of erotic and religious devotion both facilitates and idealizes the poet's indefatiga-

ble longing for "that dear friend of mine who lives in God" (epilogue). In this transfiguration the conventional topoi of a reparational theology subsume and discipline the transgressive force of Tennyson's elegiac desire.

Faithful to its consolatory structure, *In Memoriam* begins and ends with an orthodox stress upon this Christological figuration; begins and ends, that is, with promises of transcendence for the unappeasable homosexual longing that drives the poem's extended middle. For as *In Memoriam* opens, the problematics of elegiac desire—of desire for the dead and desire for death as recuperated sameness—have already found their solution and resolution in Christ; or so at least the pietistic voice of the prologue suggests:

> Strong Son of God, immortal Love,
>   Whom we, that have not seen thy face,
>   By faith, and faith alone, embrace,
> Believing where we cannot prove;
>
> Thine are those orbs of light and shade;
>   Thou madest Life in man and brute;
>   Thou madest Death; and lo, thy foot
> Is on the skull which thou hast made.
>
> Thou wilt not leave us in the dust:
>   Thou madest man, he knows not why,
>   He thinks he was not made to die;
> And thou hast made him: thou art just.

That the prologue, which was written last and postdates the composition of the earliest lyrics by some seventeen years, should offer the image of a Christocentric "embrace" as the elegy's apparently originary gesture very well figures the evasive dislocations, both temporal and spatial, required to manage the anxieties generated by Tennyson's "lost desire."[22] Indeed, part of the disciplinary work of the prologue specifically, as of the Christological figuration generally, is thus belatedly to install a fantasized terminus (the promise of Christ's restorative embrace) in the place of the origin (the rift opened by Hallam's death) in order thereby to mask the apostasy intrinsic to a personal love that is, to borrow Bloom's apt phrase, "about as restrained and societal as Heathcliff's passion."[23]

Within the figural economy of *In Memoriam*, the Christocentric impulse works its consolatory changes largely through the extended trope by which Christ's hand comes to substitute for Hallam's own; the oft-repeated images of "clasp," "touch," and "embrace" are all local variations on this trope. Indeed, as the criticism has already noticed, *In Memoriam* is almost obsessive in its concern for the human hand and in its desire for a restored male touch. Noting correctly that "Tennyson's love for Hallam is the overriding subject of *In Memoriam*," John D. Rosenberg continues: "Indeed, Tennyson's unending speculation on immortality is rooted in his inexhaustible impulse to visualize and to *touch* Hallam. Hence the ubiquitous image of the hand."[24] Ubiquitous indeed, Hallam's "sweet human hand" is at once this text's primary synecdoche for presence ("hands so often clasp'd in mine"); for absence ("A hand that can be clasp'd no more"); and for the medial condition between these two (that crepuscular state of "dreamy touch" during which the poet is left "waiting for a hand"). Nor is it surprising that "one of the great love poems in English," as Rosenberg correctly calls it, should identify the hand as a site of passional interchange, since the elegy's explicit recommendation that "Love clasp Grief lest both be drown'd" specifically cathects the hand with an erotic charge that oscillates obscurely between the homosocial and the homosexual. At times the poet's desire that Hallam "should strike a sudden hand in mine" takes on a startling sexual configuration:

> Tears of a widower, when he sees
>   A late-lost form that sleep reveals,
>   And moves his doubtful arms, and feels
> Her place is empty, fall like these;
>
> Which weep a loss for ever new
>   A void where heart on heart reposed;
>   And, where warm hands have prest and
>   closed,
> Silence, till I be silent too.

Tennyson's specification of the squeeze of the hand as a multivalent site of male homosocial communion is anything but anomalous in Victorian literature, although the extraordinary repetitiousness in his use of this figure may well be so. The utility of the hand as at once an overdetermined and unstable signifier is, I take it, manifest and obvious: on the one hand, the "manly" handshake and the "fraternal" embrace are respectable, disciplined, and sexually innocent gestures of Victorian male homosociality (imagine, for instance, counting the handshakes in Dickens); on the other hand, such gestures, given a slightly altered social context, readily take on the heat and the pressure of the sexual. A mobile figure, the hand ranges dexterously across the entire male homosocial spectrum. Consider what happens when fingers wander:

> I stripped him naked, and fed sight, touch and mouth on these things. Will my lips ever forget their place upon his breast, or of the tender satin of his flank, or on the snowy whiteness of his belly? Will they lose the nectar of his mouth—those opened lips like flower petals, expanding neath their touch and fluttering? Will my arms forget the strain of his small fragile waist, my thighs the pressure of his yielding thighs, my ears the murmur of his drowsy voice, my brain the scent of his sweet flesh and breathing mouth? Shall I ever cease to hear the metallic throb of his mysterious heart—calm and true—ringing little bells beneath my ear?

> I do not know whether, after all, the mere touch of his fingers as they met and clasped and put aside my hand, was not of all the best. For there is a soul in the fingers. They speak. The body is but silent, a dumb eloquent animated work of art made by the divine artificer.[25]

The ambivalent gesture that dominates this passage from *The Memoirs of John Addington Symonds* very well figures the cloven subjectivity of sexual inversion while it also tellingly exercises the ambivalence at hand here. "For [if] there is a soul in the fingers" and if "they speak," then what they bespeak is a rivenness so integral to soul that soul must celebrate its own alienation. The touch that repels touch touches fulfillment; to have one's hand "put aside" is indeed "all the best." As a self-nominated "invert" who understood himself to be "a compound of antagonistic impulses" and whose sexual praxis certainly included mutual masturbation, Symonds repeatedly inclined toward the hand as a figure, and a mode, of self-expression:

> I knew that my right hand was useless—firmly clenched in the grip of an unconquerable love, the love of comrades. But they [i.e., those who criticized "the languor of my temperament"] stung me into using my left hand for work, in order to contradict their prognostications [of failure].[26]

When one hand is busy at pleasure, the other may be stung by criticism into the compensation of good work. Clearly enough, the heterosexualizing semiotics of Victorian masculinity inscribe a developmental trajectory by which the boy's hand of pleasure must pass into the mature hand of work (a trajectory, obviously, that Symonds never quite mastered). What is understood to happen between boys in the dormitories of Harrow ("onanism, mutual masturbation, the sport of naked boys in bed together")[27] must not happen, as Wilde was to discover, between men in the private dining rooms of, say, the Savoy Hotel. Hence the maturing boy's growing hand must be lifted from the specific genitality of an institutionalized homosexual pedagogy and carefully steered forth into the business-like and sterilizing grip of a radically homophobic male homosociality. Handsome is as handsome does; fingers must not wander.[28]

If, as I have suggested, these passages from Symonds's *Memoirs* present genitally specific analogues to *In Memoriam's* fetishizing of the hand, then it is also clear that large differences of tact and tactility distinguish the two discourses. Part of *In Memoriam's* rhetorical finesse lies in its articulation of a desire whose intensities are sexual but whose modalities have already superseded the genital placement that Symonds's autobiography works to justify and explain. Indeed, the elegy's typological figuration works against the "deviations" that Symonds so breathlessly charts, especially so since *In Memoriam* curbs the longing of its hands by transfiguring Hallam's hands into Christ's own "shining hand." By way of a "metamorphosis of Hallam's hands into those of divinity,"[29] *In Memoriam* devises a trajectory by which a desire to touch Hallam is satisfied in Christ, as when late in the poem "out of darkness came the hands / That reach thro' nature moulding men." And in turn these consoling hands point to the closural embrace in which Christ's outstretched apocalyptic hand will redeem—or, more literally, re-member (restore the hand to)—the interrupted secular embrace between the poet and Hallam. In that good moment the poet and his beloved will

> Arrive at last the blessed goal,
>   And He that died in Holy Land
>   Would reach us out the shining hand,
> And take us as a single soul.

The singular virtue of Christ's apocalyptic hand is that its finishing touch finishes everything, and not the least what it finishes—completes and erases—is the constitutive ambivalence about intermasculine union that the metonymy of hands so ambidextrously conveys. In the rapture that comes at his second coming, the handy interchangeability of Hallam and Christ insures a taking so complete that it leaves nothing—no one—to be desired.[30]

But now we must clarify what Tennyson's orthodox typology works to obscure: this Christocentric embrace—which should at once be originary, medial, and terminal—is in fact secondary and irreducibly belated; only by a strategic misspeaking may such fulfillment be termed Christocentric at all. For the consoling pieties of a conventional typological reading cannot diminish the elegy's strong impression that Christ arrives as a belated lover who functions as the devotional succedaneum of which Hallam is the great original. Christ's otherwise redundant presence is fathered by Hallam's absence, since it is the loss of Hallam's hand and Hallam's embrace that alone motivates the re/pair/ational touch of Christ, whose hand must "shine" in order to obscure its transparent second-handedness. T. S. Eliot, who understood the anamorphic optics of Christological displacement well enough not to be blinded by the light, caught Tennyson at his sleight of hand. In what remains the best essay ever written on *In Memoriam*, Eliot handles this subject with characteristic and knowing finesse:

> [Tennyson] was desperately anxious to hold to the faith of the believer, without being very clear about what he wanted to believe: he was capable of illumination which he was incapable of understanding. "The Strong Son of God, immortal Love," with an invocation of whom the poem opens, has only a hazy connection with the Logos, or Incarnate God. Tennyson is distressed by the idea of a mechanical universe; he is naturally, in lamenting his friend,

> teased by the hope of immortality and reunion beyond death. Yet the renewal craved for seems at best but a continuance, or a substitute for the joys of friendship upon earth. His desire for immortality never is quite the desire for eternal life; his concern is for the loss of man rather than the gain of God.[31]

Eliot's circumspection here constitutes a brilliant tactical response to the failure of tact in Tennyson's account of Christological tactility. Gently reproving Tennyson for dubious or eccentric theology, Eliot clearly recognizes that the elegy's desire for Christ is "at best but a continuance, or a substitute for the joys of friendship upon earth." A stylistic chastisement is also implicit here. Consider, for instance, the revisionary subtlety with which Eliot redeploys Tennyson's language of desperate and anxious "holding," of "teasing," of "craving," and finally of "desiring." Performing a kind of postmortem refinement upon *In Memoriam's* language of desire, Eliot effectively chastens the precursor poet for the startling clarity of his longing to fill the "void where heart on heart [had once] reposed / And, where warm hands have prest and closed." Eliot's tact inherits and then reproves Tennyson's passionate failure of it.

In the opening pages of "Mourning and Melancholia," Freud explicates the libidinal work that mourning performs:

> Reality-testing has shown that the loved object no longer exists, and it proceeds to demand that all libido shall be withdrawn from its attachments to the object. This demand arouses understandable opposition—it is a matter of general observation that people never willingly abandon a libidinal position, not even, indeed, when a substitute is already beckoning to them. This opposition can be so intense that a turning away from reality takes place and a clinging to the object through the medium of hallucinatory wishful psychosis. Normally, respect for reality gains the day. Nevertheless its orders cannot be obeyed at once. They are carried out bit by bit, at great expense of time and cathectic energy, and in the meantime the existence of the lost object is psychically prolonged. Each single one of the memories and expectations in which the libido is bound to the object is brought up and hypercathected, and detach-ment of the libido is accomplished in respect of it. Why this compromise by which the command of reality is carried out piecemeal should be so extraordinarily painful is not at all easy to explain in terms of eco-nomics. It is remarkable that this painful unpleasure is taken as a matter of course by us. The fact is, however, that when the work of mourning is completed the ego becomes free and uninhibited again.[32]

In this compact synopsis of a libidinal dilemma that recalls Tennyson's own, Freud delineates the process of "normal" mourning: an excruciating, fluctuant, and piecemeal process through which the mourner is compelled by the reality of loss to abandon one object cathexis for another. "A substitute," after all, "is already beckoning." But this cruel process of abandonment and substitution is sometimes impeded by an intractable resistance, as the mourner refuses to abandon his attachment to the beloved object. An ambivalent memorialization ensues. "Each single one of the memories and expectations in which the libido is bound to the object is brought up and hypercathected." As Freud carefully stresses, this work of remembering performs a double or ambivalent function, a binding and an unbinding. The beloved object is revived and made present, even by "hallucinatory wish," to consciousness; in this way "the existence of the lost object is psychically prolonged." Conversely, and by way of an operation whose workings Freud leaves obscure, the same labor of remembering accomplishes "detachment of the libido" in respect to the lost beloved; somehow the "hypercathected" repetition unbinds or decathects desiring subject and desired object. Every act of vivifying memory, Freud seems to imply, entrains a corresponding death, a terminal forgetting, if only because the desiring subject cannot, short of psychosis, sustain the fantasmatic presence of the beloved. The lost object thus suffers a thousand posthumous deaths at the now-murderous hands of the mourner. Hence the duplicitous work of mourning: to "prolong" in order to "detach," to give birth in order to kill. Once this "work of mourning is completed"—once detachment overmasters prolongation—"the ego becomes free and uninhibited again." Free, that is, to become bound to a substitute object.

It is unnecessary, I think, to belabor the striking symmetries between Freud's account of mourning and Tennyson's elegy; each of Tennyson's lyrics operates like a hypercathected memory, working at once to prolong Hallam's presence and to facilitate his substitution in Christ. Freud's intuition regarding the ambivalence of memorialization may be employed to interrogate the divided work of *In Memoriam*'s homosexual figuration, to suggest, that is, the ways in which *In Memoriam* resists its own ideology of recuperative substitution, Christological or otherwise, and the ways in which this resistance ensures the intractable circulation of male homosexual desire. For *In Memoriam* works to postpone the conclusive bliss it also wants to complete. Thus at odds with its own desire to end desiring, the elegy wards off, even as it employs, an (eroto)logic of efficient surrogation. Until that far-off and divine event enfolds the poet and his beloved in its closural embrace, the poet must endure the empty and passive space of grief, the same space in which "the existence of the lost object is psychically prolonged." It is, finally, this medial space of unclosed longing that *In Memoriam* memorializes. But there is compensation here too. Because disseminated Hallam inseminates everything, Tennyson as desiring subject partakes of

an equivocal expansion that helps him endure his subjection to desire:

> Thy voice is on the rolling air;
>   I hear thee where the waters run;
>   Thou standest in the rising sun,
> And in the setting thou art fair.
>
> What art thou then? I cannot guess;
>   But tho' I seem in star and flower
>   To feel thee some diffusive power,
> I do not therefore love thee less:
>
> My love involves the love before;
>   My love is vaster passion now;
>   Tho' mix'd with God and Nature thou,
> I seem to love thee more and more.

Not the least beauty of *In Memoriam,* nor its least cultural utility, can be traced in these lines, which very well enact the equivocal process of substitution that Freud anatomizes in "Mourning and Melancholia." Hallam is prolonged even as he is dispersed into simulacra whose "more and more," Tennyson says, involves and extends "the love before." This ambivalent procedure subjects male homosexual desire to an almost sanitizing mediation. An intense desire for another male submits itself, or is taught by privation to submit, to a mediating force, or "diffusive power," that generates the difference of a "vaster passion" whose very differences will in turn recondense (if Tennyson's promise of the good moment holds) into the closural bliss of an absolutely androcentric embrace. From sameness to sameness, then, but only *through* difference. If this is a disciplinary trajectory (and of course it is), its particular strength resides in the quality of its ambivalence: on the one hand a startling and sometimes abrupt acknowledgment of intermasculine desire and its right to bliss; on the other, the submission of this desire to mediation by substitutes that bespeak a more conventional erotics of difference.

Of course the most obvious instance of such differentiating substitution is what Ricks aptly calls "the reiterated metaphor of man and wife,"[33] which both sexualizes and heterosexualizes the perduring grief whose extreme painfulness seems to have neutralized whatever disciplinary anxiety would otherwise have forestalled the use of an even heterosexually figured homosexual desire. Perhaps the sheer straightforwardness of the requisite gender inversion is this figure's most disarming quality:

> Two partners of a married life—
>   I look'd on these and thought of thee
>   In vastness and in mystery
> And of my spirit as of a wife.

As *In Memoriam* repeats this swerve toward heterosexual (only sometimes marital) figuration, the gender assignments within the figure vary. In lyric 13, "Tears of a widower," which specifically recalls Milton's sonnet on the seeming return of his dead wife, Tennyson identifies himself as a male, though a weeping one; but it is more characteristic, given both the passivity of his grief and the feminization of passivity within Victorian gender codes, that Tennyson should feminize his longing for Hallam as a "perpetual maidenhood" that expects "no second friend." Like Marianna, who fixedly grieves for the arrival of a male lover who "cometh not," Tennyson, as the speaker of *In Memoriam,* can only yearn in a perpetual—and here "heterosexual"—stasis.

Yet the metaphor of heterosexual embrace remains—at least for Tennyson and Hallam—a figure of separation, interdiction, distance. In *In Memoriam* woman indeed "exists only as an occasion for mediation, transaction, transition, transference, between man and his fellow man, indeed between man and himself."[34] The very presence of woman signifies the rift or gap in sameness that the hetero, by definition, cannot heal, or perhaps even help. Hence the elegy most characteristically represents the heterosexual embrace as always already interrupted, and therefore as a sign or structure whose primary service is painfully to repeat loss without ever recuperating loss into gain. Of course to say even this much is to refute the recuperative or reparational value of the thumpingly symbolic heterosexual marriage that so famously and unconvincingly closes—or almost closes—the elegy. Tennyson himself made the point didactically enough: "the poem," he said, "concludes with the marriage of my youngest sister [to Edward Lushington]. It was meant to be a kind of *Divina Commedia,* ending with happiness."[35] If Tennyson's argument for this particular variety of terminal bliss seems a little forced—more formal than felt—this is because the overweighted marriage quite obviously leaves the elegy's two central lovers still halved by desire, still unwed, the distantiated participants (Hallam's spirit, Tennyson conjectures, is present as a silent "stiller guest") at a wedding whose symbolic recompense quite openly ignores the poem's primary erotic schism. Even Tennyson himself seems unconvinced by this account of heterosexual closure; his "posture in the closing epithalamium is mannered and false."[36] When the poem quite correctly dismisses the newlyweds ("But they must go . . . and they are gone"; epilogue) and Tennyson "retire[s]" to his enduring loss, he must then dream (or dream up) the abundant recompense of this poem's other dream of closure: its prolepsis of the "one far-off divine event" whose Christocentric erotics we have already examined. In a very linear way, therefore, the epilogue repeats the elegy's double or contrary relations to longing: its desire to put an end to desire and its countervailing desire to exceed all such endings. Hence the epilogue goes on to supersede its own account of satisfactory heterosexual closure, requiring its speaker once again to fanta-

size the conclusive bliss that is offered only by—and only in the deferral of—that divine embrace with the compound "Christ that is to be." A promise, then, of homosexual closure rather than the thing itself. Or better: a promise indistinguishable from its own deferral.

In Memoriam may be Victorian poetry's preeminent example of this aesthetic regime of hygenic deferral, but it is hardly the only one. Consider, for instance, the febrile equivocations of Coventry Patmore's little-noted poem "The Unknown Eros" (1878), a text that obliquely narrates both the advent of pedophilic desire and its subsequent sublimation. Consisting largely of an extended series of interrogatives, Patmore's seventy-five-line poem nervously questions the meaning of the "blind and unrelated joy" that seizes the poet/speaker when he is unexpectedly subject to the descent of an "Unknown Eros"—that is, of an insufficiently celebrated homoerotic Cupid ("which not a poet sings") whose promise of "rumour'd heavens" provokes in Patmore an otherwise "unguess'd want" "to lie / Between those quivering plumes that thro' fine ether pant."[37] Teased into an anxious sentience by the flirtations of this fluttering boy-god, the speaker begins his speculation upon the problem of homosexual desire by presenting, coyly but recognizably, his genital response to the unknown deity's (semi)divine bottom:

> O, Unknown Eros, sire of awful bliss,
> What portent and what Delphic word,
> Such as in the form of snake or bird,
> Is this?
> In my life's even flood
> What eddies thus?
> What in its ruddy orbit lifts the blood
>
> Like a perturbed moon of Uranus
> Reaching to some great world in ungauged
>   darkness hid;
> And whence
> This rapture of the sense
> Which, by thy whisper bid,
> Reveres with obscure rite and sacramental sign
> A bond I know not of nor dimly can divine?

If the obliquity with which the lifted blood of the poet's genitalia (itself figured, by way of an astronomical pun, as "a perturbed moon of Uranus") stands and tracks the hovering boy's "ruddy orbit" seems more than a little comic, it is clear that Patmore intended no laughter. The gravity of tone and diction in these lines implicitly counterspeak the indignity of their latent anal implications. Indeed the nervously, or even unconsciously, embedded pun on "your anus" accurately figures the poet's anxious oscillation between the exalted pedophilia, or Aphrodite Uranos, as encomiastically described by Pausanias in Plato's *Symposium,* and the specifically anal desire to reach into "some great world in ungauged darkness hid."

If one hears a residually Satanic resonance in the temptation of a great world in darkness hid, it will come as no surprise that the speaker renounces the boy-god's body as a "compulsive focus" that must lead to "Nought." The poet's errant and culturally transgressive desire to gauge this darkness yields, not unexpectedly, to a conventional fear of the anus as a site of decreation; and this fear in turn moves the poet to refuse or renounce his "meaningless desire." But, by way of a familiar paradox whose ideological investments still require unpacking, this act of renunciation is said to entail a benefit, a recompense, in the form of an enabling sublimation. In the poem's closing lines, Patmore discloses the "enigma," or constitutive ambivalence, that structures this representative Victorian renunciation (the quotation marks are Patmore's):

> "There lies the crown
> "Which all thy longing cures.
> "Refuse it, Mortal, that it may be yours!
> "It is a spirit, though it seems red gold;
> "And such may no man, but by shunning,
>   hold.
> "Refuse it, though refusing be despair;
> "And thou shalt feel the phantom in thy hair."

As in the more subtle and beautiful example of *In Memoriam,* these programmatic lines deploy a compensatory logic of substitution that both excites and curtails homosexual desire by identifying renunciation as itself a deferred mode of possession: "Refuse it, Mortal, that it may be yours!" And in a substitution too funny to be intentional, the poet renounces "the Crown / Which all thy longing cures" in return for the endless tickle of a heady sublimation: "And thou shalt feel the phantom in thy hair."

But any desire that must be shunned in order to be held might indeed be occasion for despair. The extreme personal cost inherent in Patmore's phantom logic has already been registered for us by a self-declaredly "complete and undoubtedly congenital" homosexual who discovered in Patmore's verse a copytext for the conversion of his own "inverted nature" into "transcendental interpretations." The individual to whom I refer is "R.S., aged 31, American of French descent," also known as "History IX" in Ellis's *Sexual Inversion*.[38] As is typical of these case histories, which seem to have been patterned after a questionnaire developed by John Addington Symonds, R.S. begins his narrative with a personal genealogy ("Upon the question of heredity I may say that I belong to a reasonably healthy, prolific, and long-lived family . . . my father was a very masculine man."); moves next to a history of childhood and adolescence ("It was always the *prince* in fairy tales who held my interest or affection."); and

then expatiates at some length upon the process that "stirred me to a full consciousness of my inverted nature." In this context and in a striking parallel to the erotic situation in *In Memoriam,* R.S. describes the self-revelatory effects of a passionate but nongenital friendship that is prematurely terminated by the death of the friend:

> It was now that I felt for the first time the full shock of love. He returned my affection but both of us were shy of showing our feelings or speaking of them. Often when walking together after nightfall we would put our arms about each other. Sometimes, too, when sleeping together we would lie in close contact, and my friend once suggested that I put my legs against his. He frequently begged me to spend the night with him; but I began to fear my feelings, and slept with him but seldom. We neither of us had any definite ideas about homosexual relations, and, apart from what I have related above, we had no further contact with each other. A few months after our amorous feelings had developed my friend died. His death caused me great distress, and my naturally religious temperament began to manifest itself quite strongly. At this time, too, I first read some writings of Mr. Addington Symonds, and certain allusions in his work, coupled with my recent experience, soon stirred me to a full consciousness of my inverted nature.

After the passage of some years, during which he continued to "couple" his "recent experience" with his "allusive" reading, an anguished R.S. developed "what, for lack of a better name, I term my homosexual Patmorean ideal":

> Three or four years ago a little book by Coventry Patmore fell into my hands, and from its perusal resulted a strange blending of my religious and erotic notions. The desire to love and be loved is hard to drown, and, when I realized that homosexually it was neither lawful nor possible for me to love in this world, I began to project my longings into the next. By birth I am a Roman Catholic, and in spite of a somewhat skeptical temper, manage to remain one by conviction.
>
> From the doctrines of the Trinity, Incarnation, and Eucharist, I have drawn conclusions which would fill the minds of the average pietist with holy horror; nevertheless I believe that (granting the premises) these conclusions are both logically and theologically defensible. The Divinity of my fancied paradise resembles in no way the vapid conceptions of Fra Angelico, or the Quartier St. Sulpice. His physical aspect, at least, would be better represented by some Praxitilean demigod or Flandrin's naked, brooding boy.
>
> While these imaginings have caused me considerable moral disquietude, they do not seem wholly reprehensible, because I feel that the chief happiness

I would derive by their realization would be mainly
from the contemplation of the loved one, rather than
from closer joys.

If R.S. circumspectly omits the title of that "little book
by Coventry Patmore," we may with reasonable certainty identify it, a little belatedly, as *The Unknown
Eros,* the 1878 volume whose title Patmore derived
from the coyly pedophilic poem we have already read.
Like *In Memoriam,* it is a volume preeminent for its
"strange blending of religious and erotic notions," a
process in which the considerable work of homosexual
deferral can be completed only by a diffusion of these
otherwise inadmissible erotics into a Christocentric
"Desire of Him whom all things love."[39] As we have
seen, this implicitly disciplinary process is not without
its agonistic benefits, as when in the volume's final
poem, "The Child's Purchase," Patmore deploys an
elaborate trope of feminine mediation in order himself
to share, with Christ, "the spousal rapture of the sharp
spear's head." But even as a way of forestalling "closer joys," these pleasures are not innocent of individual
expense. "To project [one's] longing into the next
[world]" may itself constitute a project of self-desicca-
tion. These are the last sentences of History IX:

> Since the birth and development within me of what,
> for lack of a better name, I term my homosexualized
> Patmorean ideal, life has become, in the main, a
> weary business. I am not despondent, however,
> because many things still hold for me a certain
> interest. When that interest dies down, as it is wont
> from time to time, I endeavor to be patient. God
> grant that after the end here, I may be drawn from
> the shadow, and seemingly vain imaginings into
> the possession of their never-ending reality hereafter.

Displacement may have its place, but it also has its
costs.

But what is the place of displacement, short of that
"never-ending reality hereafter"? Exactly this question
intervenes between R.S.'s finally disheartened account
of the bleak housing offered to desire by the "homo-
sexualized Patmorean ideal" and Tennyson's altogether more bullish accounting of the compensatory economics that fund *In Memoriam's* strategy of erotic
deferral. *In Memoriam* more deeply invests, and is more
deeply invested in, the practices of postponement and
sublimation. The sheer extensiveness of Tennyson's
discourse of desire (no one ever wished the poem longer) writes against desire's own desire to end. And if it
is true that *In Memoriam* concludes with one of Victorian poetry's most famous promises of satisfaction—
that "one far-off divine event / To which the whole
creation moves"—it is conversely true that it is this
movement, rather than this event, that the whole creation of *In Memoriam* memorializes. For the very
medium of Tennyson's spoken desire to embrace Hal-

lam in Christ and Christ in Hallam depends upon the
same enabling rupture or scission that this desire also
wants rapturously to terminate; the very desire to speak
the end leaves one stranded in the desiring middle,
where "[a] use in measured language lies." This paradoxical condition can be readily measured into orthodox uses: a potentially transgressive desire is obsessively evoked in order that it may be just as obsessively repeated in words that "half reveal / And half conceal the soul within." The desiring subject is thus held
back, by language as by death, from his proper place,
but in some sense he loves that displacement:

> O days and hours, your work is this
>   To hold me from my proper place,
>   A little while from his embrace,
> For fuller gain of after bliss:
>
> That out of distance might ensue
>   Desire of nearness doubly sweet;
>   And unto meeting when we meet,
> Delight a hundredfold accrue,
>
> For every grain of sand that runs,
>   And every span of shade that steals,
>   And every kiss of toothed wheels,
> And all the courses of the suns.

Here, in a totalizing eroticism that would be difficult
to exceed, Tennyson submits all things to desire in
order thereby to achieve the submission of desire itself. As Hallam had once been "the centre of a world's
desire," its "central warmth diffusing bliss," so in these
lines he becomes diffusion itself, as Tennyson dutifully deploys the whole of creation—every grain, every
span, all suns—to facilitate the good Victorian work of
interdicting the homoerotic embrace that is nonetheless acknowledged to be "my proper place." It may
have been death alone that set Tennyson to his specifically reparational wooing, but these lines suggest the
poet's own complicity with the duty of differentiation;
for just as it is the "work" of the world both to separate and remember lovers by incarnating difference, so
it is the poet's work to distribute his desire as meaning—indeed, as the most overdetermined of meanings—
through the differentiae of an otherwise blank scape.
The diffusive power of imagination thus perfectly fe-
tishizes the world: where Hallam emphatically is not,
Hallam therefore everywhere is.

In a strategically double way, then, Tennyson retains
the ontological primacy of his desire for Hallam while
simultaneously dispersing the perils of gender sameness into the prophylactic difference of an absolute
heterocosm; the inescapable residuum of this process
is that "every kiss" of this therefore secondary hetero
remains but the disfigured memorial of a banished
originary homo. The erotics of such a substitutive structure are irreducibly ambivalent: since the homo is lost

or banished only to be rediscovered in and as the het-ero, all longing remains longing for the homo even as it submits to the differences intrinsic to mediation. Difference itself thus bespeaks a desire for sameness—speaks, like the poet, in memoriam. No surprise, then, that the work of mediation is double: time ("O days and hours") and "distance" "work" to "hold" the poet "a little while" from his proper "embrace", yet this deferral recenters and heightens the desire for that "meeting when we meet." Within this transparently compensatory structure, distance (here the aporia of death) is said to double the sweetness of desire, even as the postponement of desire's closural embrace yields, in due time, that "fuller gain of afterbliss."

It was, I think, to this strategic ambivalence that Ellis alluded when he recommended *In Memoriam* as a primary literary exemplar of how "by psychic methods to refine and spiritualize the inverted impulse." In the extremity of his grief, Tennyson had authored a virtual copytext for the recognition and articulation of a homosexual desire whose subjective effects were palpable in their intensity, but whose distantiated object had always already been exiled to a realm beyond touch if not beyond the desire for touching. In figuring Hallam's death as the terminus in which desire discovers its origin, Tennyson's discourse of homosexual longing instructs the desiring subject in the affined Victorian virtues of heroic patience and active surrogation, virtues that alone make it possible to endure a desire otherwise impossible of fulfillment. (They also serve who only stand and wait.) And in his figuration of the hetero as the diffused or encoded expression of the homo, as in his subsumption of erotic privation within an economy of symbolic reparation, Tennyson had in effect devised a translation machine for the conversion of the desire otherwise too strong for words to name; by 1850 he had provided a personal and exacting version of what Ellis, more than fifty years later, was still struggling to formulate: "a method of self-restraint and self-culture, without self-repression." Revaluing the easy optimism of Ellis's last phrase, we may say that Tennyson transvalued his passionate grief into a semiotics of homosexual desire in which the painful but presumably liberating work of recognition and accommodation blends indistinguishably into the work of discipline and containment; incitement and repression are complicit and coeval here.

But to have said even this much is already to have overvalued the disciplinary register at the expense of its revisionary or oppositional complement; and it would be wrong to leave *In Memoriam* with so compliant an acceptance of its normalizing significations, important as it is for criticism to acknowledge these. For Tennyson's elegy retains much of the transgressive force that so unsettled some of its first readers. Whatever bliss or agony the poem owns it owes to its insuperable desire for Hallam; nor can the manifold dispersions of that

"vaster passion" displace Hallam as the affective center of *In Memoriam's* world of desire. In this sense, *In Memoriam* refuses to complete its work of mourning; refuses, that is, the work of normal, and normalizing, substitution. Thus, in the sheer ferocity of its personal loss, as in the extreme extensiveness of its reparational hungering, Tennyson's elegy manages to counterspeak its own submission to its culture's heterosexualizing conventions. In this view, our departing view, *In Memoriam* remains at its end what it had been at its beginning: a desiring machine whose first motive is the restitution of lost Hallam. As such *In Memoriam* continues to do what it has always done best: it keeps its desire by keeping its desire desiring.

Notes

[1] Havelock Ellis, *Sexual Inversion,* 3rd ed. (Philadelphia, 1931), 328. See note 38 below.

[2] Ibid., 341.

[3] Ibid., 341.

[4] Symonds, *Memoirs,* 194, 189, 190.

[5] Ellis and Symonds, *Sexual Inversion,* 60-61.

[6] Symonds, *Memoirs,* 189.

[7] Ellis, *Sexual Inversion,* 339.

[8] Edward Carpenter, *Iölaus: An Anthology of Friendship* (1917; reprint, New York, 1982), 181. My use of the notion of "homosociality" is derived from Eve Kosofsky Sedgwick's *Between Men: English Literature and Male Homosocial Desire* (New York, 1985). Following Sedgwick I understand "male homosociality" to denote an entire spectrum of male bonds, only some of which are sexual; and I understand this spectrum or continuum to be historically marked by a phobic disruption that would severely disjoin the homosocial from the directly homosexual. It might be said of the intensity of *In Memoriam's* elegiac desire that it problematically overrides or elides the disjunction that conventionally intervenes, so phobically, between what is social and what is sexual.

[9] Alfred, Lord Tennyson, *In Memoriam,* lyric 64; I have used the Norton Critical Edition, ed. Robert H. Ross (New York, 1973). Subsequent citations of *In Memoriam* refer to this edition and appear in parentheses.

[10] Carol T. Christ, *Victorian and Modern Poetics* (Chicago, 1984), 117.

[11] This contemporary review is most readily accessible in John Dixon Hunt, ed., *In Memoriam: A Casebook* (London, 1970), 100-12.

[12] Charles Kingsley's unsigned review of *In Memoriam* first appeared in *Fraser's Magazine* (September 1850), 245-55; it is most readily available in *Tennyson: The Critical Heritage,* John D. Jump, ed. (London, 1967), 172-85. Christopher Ricks's remarks may be found in his *Tennyson* (New York, 1972), 215.

[13] Ricks, *Tennyson,* 215.

[14] Harold Bloom, "Tennyson, Hallam, and Romantic Tradition" in *Ringers in the Tower* (Chicago, 1971), 149-50.

[15] Ricks, *Tennyson,* 215.

[16] Quoted in Ricks, *Tennyson,* 218.

[17] I take the phrase "the desire and pursuit of the whole" from Benjamin Jowett's translation of Plato's *Symposium,* where it is employed by Aristophanes to explicate a problematically sexual desire whose recuperative energy seeks to restore a lost ontological wholeness. David M. Halperin, in "One Hundred Years of Homosexuality," *Diacritics* 16 no. 2 (1986): 34-45, explains:

> According to Aristophanes, human beings were originally round, eight-limbed creatures, with two faces and two sets of genitals—both front and back—and three sexes (male, female, and androgyne). These ancestors of ours were powerful and ambitious; to put them in their place, Zeus had them cut in two, their skin stretched over the exposed flesh and tied at the navel and their heads rotated so as to keep that physical reminder of their daring and its consequences constantly before their eyes. The severed halves of each former individual, once reunited, clung to one another so desperately and concerned themselves so little with their survival as separate entities that they began to perish for lack of sustenance; those who outlived their mates sought out persons belonging to the same gender as their lost complements and repeated their embraces in a foredoomed attempt to recover their original unity. Zeus at length took pity on them, moved their genitals to the side their bodies now faced, and invented sex, so that the bereaved creatures might at least put a terminus to their longing and devote their attention to other, more important matters.

From this narrative Aristophanes extracts, as Halperin says, "a genetic explanation of the observable differences among human beings with respect to sexual object-choice," an explanation that clearly establishes a formal isomorphism between female-female, male-male, and male-female desire. As Aristophanes says, "the reason is that human nature was originally one and we were whole, and the desire and pursuit of the whole is called love." *The Dialogues of Plato,* ed. and trans. Benjamin Juwett, 3 vols. (Oxford, 1875), 2:43-44). For an excellent analysis of the relation between the Aristophanic myth and modern notions of homosexuality, see Halperin.

[18] The cross-lingual pun "hom(m)osexual" comes from Luce Irigaray, *This Sex Which Is Not One,* where it is used to designate the androcentric assumptions grounding Western notions of same-sex desire. See especially "Commodities among Themselves," 192-98.

[19] Ricks, *Tennyson,* 218.

[20] Gerhard Joseph, *Tennysonian Love* (Minneapolis, 1969), 68.

[21] T. S. Eliot, "In Memoriam," from *Essays Ancient and Modern* (London, 1936), 186-203. This essay is also available in Hunt, ed., *A Casebook,* 129-37.

[22] Although the first lyrics in memory of Hallam were composed as early as 1833, the prologue was not composed until 1849, as Tennyson arranged and assembled the individual elegies into the long poem we know as *In Memoriam.*

[23] Bloom, "Tennyson," 154.

[24] John D. Rosenberg, "The Two Kingdoms of *In Memoriam,*" *Journal of English and Germanic Philology* 58 (1959), 228-40; reprinted in Ross, ed., *In Memoriam,* 206-19.

[25] Symonds, *Memoirs,* 209-10.

[26] Ibid., 119-20.

[27] Ibid., 94.

[28] Other Victorian texts, specifically two canonical American ones, offer comic and comically displaced versions of Tennyson's fellowship of hand; if the examples I am about to cite are already familiar, they nonetheless merit our brief recognition. The first of these examples, chapter 94 of *Moby Dick,* coyly entitled "A Squeeze of the Hand," literally expresses—that is, presses out or fluidly extrudes—its almost homosexual homosociality by way of the exuberant topos of "spermatic" immersion. As part of the Pequod's systematic capitalist transfiguration of natural object into commodity, of whale into product, of sperm oil into money, the members of the crew are compelled by "business" and "unctuous duty" into the blissful hiatus of a good squeeze. After "the baling of the Heidelburgh Tun, or Case," the sperm thus removed

> had cooled and crystallized to such a degree that when, with several others, I sat down before a large Constantine's bath of it, I found it strangely concreted into lumps, here and there rolling in the

liquid part. It was our business to squeeze the lumps back into fluid.

The immediate effect of the "carefully manipulated" sperm is a subjective sense of benign metamorphosis ("After having my hands in it for only a few minutes, my fingers felt like eels and began, as it were, to serpentine and spiralize") which in turn mediates a fluid masculine intersubjectivity:

> I squeezed that sperm till I myself almost melted into it; I squeezed that sperm till a strange sort of insanity came over me; and I found myself unwittingly squeezing my colaborer's hands in it, mistaking the hands for the gentle globules. Such an abounding, affectionate, friendly, loving feeling did this avocation beget; that at last I was continually squeezing their hands and looking up into their eyes sentimentally. . . . Come; let us squeeze hands all around; nay, let us squeeze ourselves into each other; let us squeeze ourselves universally into the very milk and sperm of kindness.

If the rhetorical densities and fluidities of this passage are so manifold and interfluent as to preclude comprehensive analysis here, we are nonetheless constrained to remark the figural duplicity by which the self-evident homoerotics of such a vision of intermasculine community are rendered visible by an occulting that is at once ocular (Ishmael cannot see the squeeze he loves to feel) and auricular (the homosexual valence of this passage is, as it were, pun-buried in a comic homophone—in, that is, the handy wordplay on, in, of "sperm"). We should also note, if only again in passing, Ishmael's claim that the opulent tactility exercised here releases or "discharges"—his verb not mine—a specific renovatory effect, a direct counterfluence to the brutalizing and suicidal homosocial pact, or "indissoluble league," explicit in the crew's promise to man the harpoon of Ahab's vengeance. "In that inexpressible sperm," says Ishmael in recalling the moment on the quarterdeck, "I forgot all about our horrible oath" and "I washed my hands and heart of it."

When Melville has Ishmael dream that he might squeeze himself and his fellows "into the very milk and sperm of kindness," he is deploying a particular cultural fantasy about the body's dark hydraulics: a fantasy of what Thomas Laqueur calls "the fungibility of [bodily] fluids" in "Orgasm, Generation, and the Politics of Reproductive Biology," *Representations* 14 (Spring 1986): 1-41, a belief that the body's base fluid, blood, may under particular conditions of heat and pressure be "concocted" or expressed into other bodily fluids—milk and semen most particularly. And when that cultural fantasy is conjoined with its masculist writerly analogue (most familiar in its Freudian version) that a telling half pun obtains between pen and penis, and between semen and semantics, then there are large implications for the hands of the writer and the reader,

specific implications for the craft of writing and for the semiotics of reading. "I find it hard to write of these things," Symonds writes in the erotic diary entry I have already quoted, "yet I wish to dwell on them and to recall them, pen in hand."

If Symonds is comically *un*selfconscious here, if the trope works him rather than he the trope, then this was never the case with Symonds's "Master," Whitman, who very self-consciously exploited this analogy to considerable cultural effect. The assault that Whitman launched on literary culture derived in fair part from his refusal to subdue this trope, from a specific refusal to idealize the difference between textual production and bodily discharge: "bathing [his] songs in sex," he then presses the reader with the texts, that are for him indistinguishable from the "limitless jets" of his "slow rude muscle." ("Enfants D'Adam," poems 12, 3, 4). Obviously, this strategy was calculated to disrupt idealizations of reading by putting a problematic text directly into the hands of the reader, who must hereafter equivocate over just what it is that he or she is holding now. The (homo)erotics of this readerly dilemma are specifically thematized in the third poem of the "Calamus" sequence:

> Whoever you are holding me now in hand,
> Without one thing all will be useless,
> I give you fair warning, before you attempt
> me further
> I am not what you supposed, but far different.

If the quotidian dynamics of reading require a certain tactility—if, after all, we must hold the books we read and touch the texts we also see—then it is also implicitly the case that these dynamics open within the primarily ocular trope of reading another aperture for the writer's promiscuous address. The reader reading thus touches, retouches, the writer's touch, even touches back, and in doing so finds himself (the implied reader of "Calamus" is, I would argue, male) implicated in the comic Melvillian topos we have just explicated: finds himself squeezing hands squeezing sperm, and staring sentimentally into the eyes of the poet. Here, from stanza 5 of "Calamus" 3, is another, or rather the same, trope of reading:

> Or, if you will, thrusting me beneath your
> clothing,
> Where I may feel the throbs of your heart, or
> rest upon your hip,
> Carry me when you go forth over land or sea;
> For thus, merely touching you, is enough—is
> best,
> And thus, touching you, would I silently sleep
> and be carried eternally.

By way of a fatal trajectory characteristic of Whitman, the palpable "thrusting" of these lines touches or taps into a desire for death's cradling, as if the writer could die into the reader, thereafter to be "carried eternally." Whitman very capably exercised the ambivalence that the metonymy of hands conveys: if he liked to finger pulses, he also said "my tap is death" ("Sleep-Chasings"). In "Calamus" 3 this ambivalence, partly self-protective, is figured by the reversal of touch that closes the poem, closes it by leaving its grasp open:

> But these leaves conning, you con at peril
> For these leaves, and me, you will not
>   understand—
>
>   . . . . .
>
> Even while you should think you had
>   unquestionably caught me, behold!
> Already you see I have escaped from you.

And then the poem's last line:

> Therefore release me, and depart on your way.

Whitman's writing exuberantly exercises the same hands that shake and haunt Tennyson in *In Memoriam,* but pivotal differences in tact intervene to separate their discourses on tactility: Whitman specifies what Tennyson prefers to diffuse, just as he incarnates what Tennyson instead drives into the recesses of the incarnation. But these are differences that serve to texturize the therefore palpable sameness that otherwise we would not be able to feel. Herman Melville, *Moby Dick* (New York, 1972). Walt Whitman, *Leaves of Grass,* facsimile edition of the 1860 text (Ithaca, 1961).

[29] Rosenberg, "The Two Kingdoms," 214.

[30] In broad terms of Christocentric desire the strong parallel to Tennyson is Hopkins, who finds in Christ both "beauty's self and beauty's giver" and whose sermons on the body and the blood of Christ—"of our noble lover, our prince, our champion"—describe a theology of desire with unembarrassed sensuality:

> I leave it to you, brethren, then to picture him, in whom fullness of the godhead dwelt bodily, in his bearing how majestic, how strong and yet how lovely and lissome in his limbs, in his look how earnest grave but kind. In his Passion all this strength was spent, this lissomeness crippled, this beauty wrecked, this majesty beaten down. But now it is more than all restored, and for myself I make no secret I look forward with eager desire to seeing the matchless beauty of Christ's body in the heavenly light.
>
>   (*Sermons,* 34-38.)

Hopkins's eager desire for "the matchless beauty of Christ's body" can be borne only because it is contrapuntally and agonistically matched with, or wedded to, Hopkins's own matchless passion for substitute satisfaction and submission to his "mastering me/God." In the complex and beautiful way that J. Hillis Miller has explicated in *The Disappearance of God,* the world for Hopkins is so radically inscribed with the grandeur of God that phenomenal things are literally—that is, as letters—the dispersed fragments of the originary integral word:

> All things therefore are charged with love, are charged with God, and if we know how to touch them give off sparks and take fire, yield drops and flow, ring and tell of him. (*Sermons,* 175)

Right perception—luminous, fluid, harmonic—is sacramental reading.

And what the perceiver reads when reading is right are the literal traces of Christ's blood—his "lessons" "written upon lovely limbs / In bloody letters." The figural mechanism that so charges Hopkins's world is, very explicitly, the saving "discharge" of Christ's "dense" and "driven Passion" ("The Wreck of the Deutschland," stanza 7). By way of a powerful temporal inversion, Hopkins deploys a historical event, the crucifixion, as the only trope adequate to represent the otherwise inaccessible, ahistorical moment of the "great sacrifice" of God's own selving—of, that is, the fracturing or "cleaving" of Christ out of God that Hopkins calls "the Incarnation proper." For Hopkins this originary fracture creates flesh, invents time, enables redemption, and sets desire to its reparational yearning. But because this moment is ontologically prior to the divisiveness it is in the process of creating, it can only be figured belatedly and retrospectively by a reversal of origin and terminus. Thus Hopkins interpolates Jesus' last moment where Christ's first one should be; the sensations of the crucifixion bespeak the incarnation:

> The first intention then of God outside himself or, as they say, *ab extra,* outwards, the first outstress of God's power was Christ; and we must believe the next was the Blessed Virgin. . . . It is as if the blissful agony or stress of selving in God forced out drops of sweat and blood, which drops were the world. (*Sermons,* 197)

Here Christ's originary self-expression must take as its expressive figure the terminal moment of "the piercing of Christ's side," when "the sacred body and sacred heart seemed waiting for an opportunity of discharging themselves." (*Sermons,* 255). This tropological inversion is predictably double. It is epistemologically negative in the deconstructive sense that the presumptively originary origin must submit to the belatedness of historical figuration. Thus the Christocentric origin is already blocked or decentered by the writhing body of Christ himself. But it is phenomenologically positive in the sense that the world and the things in it are spectacularly reified as the sacramental distillations of Christ's saving effluence; thus "bathe[d] in his fall-gold mercies," "this world then is the word, expression, news of God" ("The Wreck of the Deutschland," stanza 23; *Sermons,* 129). Exactly this extreme incarnationism, with its celebratory corollary that "Christ plays in ten thousand places / lovely in limbs, and lovely in eyes not his" (poem 57, "As kingfishers catch fire"), enables Hopkins to sustain himself on the supplemental satisfactions that intervene between the patient time of writing and the eager time when the poet will be restored "to the dearest him that lives alas! away)" (poem 67, "I wake and feel the fell of dark"). In the parallel cases of Hopkins and Tennyson, that distanced and dearest him—that "first, fast, last friend" (poem 40, "The Lantern Out of Doors")—is an ambivalent figure or compound ghost, a copula who conjoins both Christ and that other "He that died": in the case of Tennyson, Hallam obviously; in the less renowned case of Hopkins, the boy-poet Digby Mackworth Dolben. *The Poems of Gerard Manley Hopkins,* 4th ed., ed. W. H. Gardener and N. H. MacKenzie, (Oxford, 1970); and *Sermons and Devotional Writings,* ed. Christopher Devlin (London, 1959).

[31] Eliot, "In Memoriam," 133.

[32] Sigmund Freud, "Mourning and Melancholia," in *The Standard Edition,* 14:244-45.

[33] Ricks, *Tennyson,* 216.

[34] Irigaray, *This Sex Which Is Not One,* 193.

[35] Tennyson, quoted in Hallam, Lord Tennyson, *Alfred, Lord Tennyson: A Memoir,* 2 vols. (London, 1897), 1:300.

[36] Rosenberg, "The Two Kingdoms," 216.

[37] Coventry Patmore, *The Unknown Eros* (London, 1878), 8-12. In the streamlined analysis offered here, I have somewhat simplified Patmore's rather more elusive sexual representation in order to foreground the poem's homosexual/pedophilic valences. Not surprisingly, Patmore embeds such valences within a rhetoric that is idealizing, interrogative, sometimes downright obscure. There is, furthermore, some shifty gender identification that permits the "Unknown Eros" to be figured sometimes as male ("bashful love, in his own way and hour") and sometimes, though less emphatically, as female. Of course anything like a complete account of Patmore's poem and volume would have to negotiate these differences.

[38] R.S. is "History IX" in the third American edition (1931) of Ellis's *Sexual Inversion,* 111-15. Readers interested in this citation should note that different editions of *Sexual Inversion* have differently numbered case histories; revising his text for each edition, Ellis both added and deleted individual case histories. The Ellis-Symonds English edition of 1897 does not contain R.S.'s history.

[39] Patmore, "The Child's Purchase," *Unknown Eros,* 208-9.

FURTHER READING

Anthologies

Faderman, Lillian, ed. *Chloe Plus Olivia: An Anthology of Lesbian Literature from the Seventeenth Century to the Present.* New York: Viking, 1994, 812 p.

> Arranges extensive selection of fiction, non-fiction, poetry, and letters according to several topics, including romantic friendship, inversion, and exoticism.

Bibliographies

Grier, Barbara. *The Lesbian in Literature.* Tallahasee: Naiad Press, 1981.

> Lists works written by lesbian authors and/or that present lesbian characters, focusing primarily on fiction in the twentieth century.

Young, Ian. *The Male Homosexual in Literature: A Bibliography.* 2d ed. Metuchen NJ: Scarecrow Press, 1982, 349 p.

> Gathers titles of fiction, drama, autobiography, and poetry "concerned with male homosexuality or having male homosexual characters" from the last five centuries. Also includes genre-specific essays by writers and critics.

Criticism

Bristow, Joseph. "Wilde's Fatal Effeminacy." In *Effeminate England: Homoerotic Writing after 1885,* pp. 16-54. New York: Columbia UP, 1995.

> Uses Wilde's life and writings as a case study in the impact of Victorian ideals of masculinity on notions of homosexuality.

D'Arch Smith, Timothy. *Love in Earnest: Some Notes on the Lives and Writings of English "Uranian" Poets from 1889 to 1930.* London: Routledge and Kegan Paul, 1970, 280 p.

> Documents the idealization of adolescent masculinity and male-male bonding that influenced a substantial body of nineteenth- and early twentieth-century poetry.

Dellamora, Richard. *Masculine Desire: The Sexual Politics of Victorian Aestheticism.* Chapel Hill and London: University of North Carolina Press, 1990, 276 p.

> Examines nineteenth-century, English notions of masculinity and desire as manifested in the works of various authors, including Tennyson, Hopkins, Ruskin, and Pater.

Dynes, Wayne R. and Stephen Donaldson. *Homosexual Themes in Literary Studies.* New York and London: Garland, 1992, 389 p.

> Reprints critical studies of homoerotic literature, many of them central to the burgeoning of gay and lesbian studies in the 1980s.

Fone, Byrne R. S. *A Road to Stonewall: Male Homosexuality and Homophobia in English and American Literature, 1750-1969.* New York: Twayne, 1995, 303 p.

> Presents a study of the literature—central and marginal—against a detailed backdrop of social history, particularly in relation to ideas of gender and desire.

Kellogg, Stuart. *Literary Visions of Homosexuality.* New York: Haworth Press, 1983, 171 p.

> Contains essays by literary critics on several nineteenth-century authors, including Byron, Edward Carpenter, and Henry James.

Kopelson, Kevin. "Wilde's Love-Deaths." *Love's Litany: The Writing of Modern Homoerotics.* Stanford CA: Stanford University Press, 1994, 194 p.

> Contends that the nineteenth-century association of homosexual desire with death stems from the mandated death penalty for homosexual acts. Kopelson's study goes beyond *The Picture of Dorian Gray* to less studied texts, including *Salomé, The Happy Prince*, and the explicitly pornographic *Teleny.*

Lane, Christopher. *The Ruling Passion: British Colonial Allegory and the Paradox of Homosexual Desire.* Durham and London: Duke University Press, 1995, 311 p.

> Investigates popular nineteenth-century works of fiction and poetry to suggest that "sexual desire between men frequently ruptured Britain's imperial allegory by shattering national unity."

Martin, Robert K. *The Homosexual Tradition in American Poetry.* Austin: University of Texas Press, 1979.

> Demonstrates the presence of male-male desire in American poetry throughout its history, although it was often disguised in the nineteenth century.

Reade, Brian. *Sexual Heretics: Male Homosexuality in English Literature from 1850 to 1900.* New York: Coward McCann, 1970.

> Argues that male homosexual desire, embedded in much of late nineteenth-century literature, constituted a subversive element in Victorian culture.

Sedgwick, Eve Kosofsky. *Epistemology of the Closet.* Berkeley: University California Press, 1990, 258 p.

> Examines late nineteenth-century literature for its evidence of the culture of the "closet" that gave shape to twentieth-century straight and gay culture.

The Industrial Revolution in Literature

INTRODUCTION

The rapid industrial growth that began in Great Britain during the middle of the eighteenth century and extended into the United States for the next 150 years provided a wide range of material for many nineteenth-century writers. The literature of the Industrial Revolution includes essays, fiction, and poetry that respond to the enormous growth of technology as well as the labor and demographic changes it fostered. Having observed the adoption of such new technologies as the steam engine and the blast furnace, the Scottish intellectual Thomas Carlyle described this period as the "Mechanical Age," reflecting his belief that the machine was the dominant symbol of his era, one representing a profound change in both the physical and mental activities of his society. The Industrial Revolution figured prominently across a broad range of literary genres. While social critics such as Carlyle, John Ruskin, Matthew Arnold, and Henry Adams examined the cultural changes that accompanied the machine, novelists ranging from Charles Dickens and Elizabeth Gaskell to Rebecca Harding Davis and Herman Melville provided a realistic treatment of modern working conditions. Meanwhile, poets such as William Wordsworth and Walt Whitman contemplated the artist's role in such a world.

During the initial stages of the Industrial Revolution in England, the literati, for the most part, supported the new discoveries of science, often promoting their application in literary reviews. By the close of the eighteenth century, however, the early romantics began to view the emerging technology in a different light. In his *Letters upon the Aesthetical Education of Man* (1795), Friedrich Schiller argued that the machine was a threat to individual freedom and a destructive force on contemporary culture. Likewise, William Wordsworth, in his *Preface to the Second Edition of "Lyrical Ballads"* (1800), asserted that the rise of technology blunted the mind "to a state of almost savage torpor." Carlyle's influential essay, "Signs of the Times" (1829), in which he decried the encroachment of "mechanical genius" into the "internal and spiritual" aspects of life, continued the critique of industrialism and set the stage for the social-problem novels of the mid-nineteenth century. Charles Dickens's realistic and ironic depictions of industrial towns in *Hard Times* (1854), for example, underscored the deleterious affects of urbanization on the working class. Works by Benjamin Disraeli, Elizabeth Gaskell, the Brontë sisters, and W. M. Thackeray also presented accurate accounts of the industrialism of Victorian society.

The transfer of new technologies across the Atlantic also shaped the development of literature in the United States. As in England, many of the initial responses welcomed the new technology, finding it indispensable to the economic growth of the fledgling nation. Thomas Jefferson, for instance, writing near the close of the eighteenth century, believed that the machine would blend harmoniously into the open countryside of the American Republic rather than produce the overcrowded and polluted cities of Europe. Critic Leo Marx contended that, with the exception of apologists for the Southern slavery system, there was little effective opposition to the forces of urbanization and industrialism. The abundance of land and scarcity of labor had intensified the demand for machinery, and by the time Carlyle's essay reached America, the economy was expanding at such a phenomenal rate that his attack on the machine was not widely accepted by the American populace. Writers such as Walt Whitman and Ralph Waldo Emerson, for the most part, embraced the new technology, finding in the railroad a vehicle for uniting the country and furthering democratic ideals. However, such a response was not universally shared. Nathaniel Hawthorne, Herman Melville, and Mark Twain, among others, provided alternative perspectives, often critiquing the materialistic value systems that accompanied industrialism through the metaphors, themes, and details of their works.

The issues surrounding the relationship between technology and culture have continued to interest critics and writers well into the twentieth century. Not only have scholars concentrated on the canonical works by major authors of the period, but they have increasingly focused their attention on contemporary reactions found in magazines, newspapers, and popular novels in an effort to better understand the culture of the period. Contemporary writers also look to literary figures of the Industrial Revolution as they address similar concerns of the role of the machine in society.

REPRESENTATIVE WORKS

Henry Adams
The Education of Henry Adams 1918

Matthew Arnold
Essays in Criticism 1865

Honoré de Balzac
The Quest of the Absolute 1834

William Blake
The Four Zoas 1797

Charlotte Brontë
Jane Eyre 1847

Emily Brontë
Wuthering Heights 1848

Thomas Carlyle
Sartor Resartus 1833-34
Critical and Miscellaneous Essays 1873

Rebecca Harding Davis
Life in the Iron Mills 1861

Charles Dickens
Bleak House 1853
Hard Times 1854

Benjamin Disraeli
Coningsby 1844
Sybil, or The Two Nations 1845
Tancred 1847

Ralph Waldo Emerson
Nature 1836

Elizabeth Gaskell
North and South 1855

Nathaniel Hawthorne
Mosses from an Old Manse 1846

Thomas Huxley
Science and Culture and Other Essays 1881

Thomas Jefferson
Notes on Virginia 1785

Herman Melville
Moby-Dick 1844
The Piazza Tales and Other Prose Pieces 1839-
1860

John Stuart Mill
On Liberty 1859

Friedrich Schiller
Letters upon the Aesthetical Education of Man 1795

Mary Shelley
Frankenstein 1818

Percy Bysshe Shelley
The Defence of Poetry 1840

W. M. Thackeray
Vanity Fair 1847

Henry David Thoreau
Walden 1854

Mark Twain
The Gilded Age 1873
A Connecticut Yankee in King Arthur's Court 1889

Walt Whitman
Democratic Vistas 1871
Leaves of Grass 1855, 1856, 1860-61, 1867, 1871,
1876, 1881-82, 1888, 1891-2

William Wordsworth
Preface to the Second Edition of "Lyrical Ballads"
1800

HISTORICAL AND CULTURAL PERSPECTIVES

Henry Adams

SOURCE: "The Dynamo and the Virgin," in *The Education of Henry Adams,* The Modern Library, 1931, pp. 379-90.

[*In the following essay written in 1905 and first published in 1918, Adams examines the influence of the machine on the Western world, suggesting that it functions like a religious symbol carrying a "moral force."*]

Until the Great Exposition of 1900 closed [the Trocadero's] doors in November, Adams haunted it, aching to absorb knowledge, and helpless to find it. He would have liked to know how much of it could have been grasped by the best-informed man in the world. While he was thus meditating chaos, Langley came by, and showed it to him. At Langley's behest, the Exhibition dropped its superfluous rags and stripped itself to the skin, for Langley knew what to study, and why, and how; while Adams might as well have stood outside in the night, staring at the Milky Way. Yet Langley said nothing new, and taught nothing that one might not have learned from Lord Bacon, three hundred years before; but though one should have known the "Advancement of Science" as well as one knew the "Comedy of Errors," the literary knowledge counted for nothing until some teacher should show how to apply it. Bacon took a vast deal of trouble in teaching King James I and his subjects, American or other, towards the year 1620, that true science was the development or economy of forces; yet an elderly American in 1900 knew neither the formula nor the forces; or even so much as to say to himself that his historical business in the Exposition concerned only the economies or developments of force since 1893, when he began the study at Chicago.

Nothing in education is so astonishing as the amount of ignorance it accumulates in the form of inert facts. Adams had looked at most of the accumulations of art in the storehouses called Art Museums; yet he did not know how to look at the art exhibits of 1900. He had studied Karl Marx and his doctrines of history with profound attention, yet he could not apply them at Paris. Langley, with the ease of a great master of experiment, threw out of the field every exhibit that did not reveal a new application of force, and naturally threw out, to begin with, almost the whole art exhibit. Equally, he ignored almost the whole industrial exhibit. He led his pupil directly to the forces. His chief interest was in new motors to make his airship feasible, and he taught Adams the astonishing complexities of the new Daimler motor, and of the automobile, which, since 1893, had become a nightmare at a hundred kilometres an hour, almost as destructive as the electric tram which was only ten years older; and threatening to become as terrible as the locomotive steam-engine itself, which was almost exactly Adams's own age.

Then he showed his scholar the great hall of dynamos, and explained how little he knew about electricity or force of any kind, even of his own special sun, which spouted heat in inconceivable volume, but which, as far as he knew, might spout less or more, at any time, for all the certainty he felt in it. To him, the dynamo itself was but an ingenious channel for conveying somewhere the heat latent in a few tons of poor coal hidden in a dirty engine-house carefully kept out of sight; but to Adams the dynamo became a symbol of infinity. As he grew accustomed to the great gallery of machines, he began to feel the forty-foot dynamos as a moral force, much as the early Christians felt the Cross. The planet itself seemed less impressive, in its old-fashioned, deliberate, annual or daily revolution, than this huge wheel, revolving within arm's-length at some vertiginous speed, and barely murmuring—scarcely humming an audible warning to stand a hair's-breadth further for respect of power—while it would not wake the baby lying close against its frame. Before the end, one began to pray to it; inherited instinct taught the natural expression of man before silent and infinite force. Among the thousand symbols of ultimate energy, the dynamo was not so human as some, but it was the most expressive.

Yet the dynamo, next to the steam-engine, was the most familiar of exhibits. For Adams's objects its value lay chiefly in its occult mechanism. Between the dynamo in the gallery of machines and the engine-house outside, the break of continuity amounted to abysmal fracture for a historian's objects. No more relation could he discover between the steam and the electric current than between the Cross and the cathe-dral. The forces were interchangeable if not reversible, but he could see only an absolute *fiat* in electricity as in faith. Langley could not help him. Indeed, Langley seemed to be worried by the same trouble, for he constantly repeated that the new forces were anarchical, and specially that he was not responsible for the new rays, that were little short of parricidal in their wicked spirit towards science. His own rays, with which he had doubled the solar spectrum, were altogether harmless and beneficent; but Radium denied its God—or, what was to Langley the same thing, denied the truths of his Science. The force was wholly new.

A historian who asked only to learn enough to be as futile as Langley or Kelvin, made rapid progress under this teaching, and mixed himself up in the tangle of ideas until he achieved a sort of Paradise of ignorance vastly consoling to his fatigued senses. He wrapped himself in vibrations and rays which were new, and he would have hugged Marconi and Branly had he met them, as he hugged the dynamo; while he lost his arithmetic in trying to figure out the equation between the discoveries and the economies of force. The economies, like the discoveries, were absolute, supersensual, occult; incapable of expression in horse-power. What mathematical equivalent could he suggest as the value of a Branly coherer? Frozen air, or the electric furnace, had some scale of measurement, no doubt, if somebody could invent a thermometer adequate to the purpose; but X-rays had played no part whatever in man's consciousness, and the atom itself had figured only as a fiction of thought. In these seven years man had translated himself into a new universe which had no common scale of measurement with the old. He had entered a supersensual world, in which he could measure nothing except by chance collisions of movements imperceptible to his senses, perhaps even imperceptible to his instruments, but perceptible to each other, and so to some known ray at the end of the scale. Langley seemed prepared for anything, even for an indeterminable number of universes interfused—physics stark mad in metaphysics.

Historians undertake to arrange sequences,—called stories, or histories—assuming in silence a relation of cause and effect. These assumptions, hidden in the depths of dusty libraries, have been astounding, but commonly unconscious and childlike; so much so, that if any captious critic were to drag them to light, historians would probably reply, with one voice, that they had never supposed themselves required to know what they were talking about. Adams, for one, had toiled in vain to find out what he meant. He had even published a dozen volumes of American history for no other purpose than to satisfy himself whether, by the severest process of stating, with the least possible comment, such facts as seemed sure, in such order as seemed rigorously consequent, he could fix for a familiar moment a necessary sequence of human movement.

The result had satisfied him as little as at Harvard College. Where he saw sequence, other men saw something quite different, and no one saw the same unit of measure. He cared little about his experiments and less about his statesmen, who seemed to him quite as ignorant as himself and, as a rule, no more honest; but he insisted on a relation of sequence, and if he could not reach it by one method, he would try as many methods as science knew. Satisfied that the sequence of men led to nothing and that the sequence of their society could lead no further, while the mere sequence of time was artificial, and the sequence of thought was chaos, he turned at last to the sequence of force; and thus it happened that, after ten years' pursuit, he found himself lying in the Gallery of Machines at the Great Exposition of 1900, his historical neck broken by the sudden irruption of forces totally new.

Since no one else showed much concern, an elderly person without other cares had no need to betray alarm. The year 1900 was not the first to upset schoolmasters. Copernicus and Galileo had broken many professorial necks about 1600; Columbus had stood the world on its head towards 1500; but the nearest approach to the revolution of 1900 was that of 310, when Constantine set up the Cross. The rays that Langley disowned, as well as those which he fathered, were occult, supersensual, irrational; they were a revelation of mysterious energy like that of the Cross; they were what, in terms of mediæval science, were called immediate modes of the divine substance.

The historian was thus reduced to his last resources. Clearly if he was bound to reduce all these forces to a common value, this common value could have no measure but that of their attraction on his own mind. He must treat them as they had been felt; as convertible, reversible, interchangeable attractions on thought. He made up his mind to venture it; he would risk translating rays into faith. Such a reversible process would vastly amuse a chemist, but the chemist could not deny that he, or some of his fellow physicists, could feel the force of both. When Adams was a boy in Boston, the best chemist in the place had probably never heard of Venus except by way of scandal, or of the Virgin except as idolatry; neither had he heard of dynamos or automobiles or radium; yet his mind was ready to feel the force of all, though the rays were unborn and the women were dead.

Here opened another totally new education, which promised to be by far the most hazardous of all. The knife-edge along which he must crawl, like Sir Lancelot in the twelfth century, divided two kingdoms of force which had nothing in common but attraction. They were as different as a magnet is from gravitation, supposing one knew what a magnet was, or gravitation, or love. The force of the Virgin was still felt at Lourdes, and seemed to be as potent as X-rays; but in America neither Venus nor Virgin ever had value as force—at most as sentiment. No American had ever been truly afraid of either.

This problem in dynamics gravely perplexed an American historian. The Woman had once been supreme; in France she still seemed potent, not merely as a sentiment, but as a force. Why was she unknown in America? For evidently America was ashamed of her, and she was ashamed of herself, otherwise they would not have strewn fig-leaves so profusely all over her. When she was a true force, she was ignorant of fig-leaves, but the monthly-magazine-made American female had not a feature that would have been recognized by Adam. The trait was notorious, and often humorous, but any one brought up among Puritans knew that sex was sin. In any previous age, sex was strength. Neither art nor beauty was needed. Every one, even among Puritans, knew that neither Diana of the Ephesians nor any of the Oriental goddesses was worshipped for her beauty. She was goddess because of her force; she was the animated dynamo; she was reproduction—the greatest and most mysterious of all energies; all she needed was to be fecund. Singularly enough, not one of Adams's many schools of education had ever drawn his attention to the opening lines of Lucretius, though they were perhaps the finest in all Latin literature, where the poet invoked Venus exactly as Dante invoked the Virgin:—

Quae quoniam rerum naturam *sola* gubernas.

The Venus of Epicurean philosophy survived in the Virgin of the Schools:—

Donna, sei tanto grande, e tanto vali,
Che qual vuol grazia, e a te non ricorre,
Sua disianza vuol volar senz' ali.

All this was to American thought as though it had never existed. The true American knew something of the facts, but nothing of the feelings; he read the letter, but he never felt the law. Before this historical chasm, a mind like that of Adams felt itself helpless; he turned from the Virgin to the Dynamo as though he were a Branly coherer. On one side, at the Louvre and at Chartres, as he knew by the record of work actually done and still before his eyes, was the highest energy ever known to man, the creator of four-fifths of his noblest art, exercising vastly more attraction over the human mind than all the steam-engines and dynamos ever dreamed of; and yet this energy was unknown to the American mind. An American Virgin would never dare command; an American Venus would never dare exist.

The question, which to any plain American of the nineteenth century seemed as remote as it did to Adams, drew him almost violently to study, once it was posed;

and on this point Langleys were as useless as though they were Herbert Spencers or dynamos. The idea survived only as art. There one turned as naturally as though the artist were himself a woman. Adams began to ponder, asking himself whether he knew of any American artist who had ever insisted on the power of sex, as every classic had always done; but he could think only of Walt Whitman; Bret Harte, as far as the magazines would let him venture; and one or two painters, for the flesh-tones. All the rest had used sex for sentiment, never for force; to them, Eve was a tender flower, and Herodias an unfeminine horror. American art, like the American language and American education, was as far as possible sexless. Society regarded this victory over sex as its greatest triumph, and the historian readily admitted it, since the moral issue, for the moment, did not concern one who was studying the relations of unmoral force. He cared nothing for the sex of the dynamo until he could measure its energy.

Vaguely seeking a clue, he wandered through the art exhibit, and, in his stroll, stopped almost every day before St. Gaudens's General Sherman, which had been given the central post of honor. St. Gaudens himself was in Paris, putting on the work his usual interminable last touches, and listening to the usual contradictory suggestions of brother sculptors. Of all the American artists who gave to American art whatever life it breathed in the seventies, St. Gaudens was perhaps the most sympathetic, but certainly the most inarticulate. General Grant or Don Cameron had scarcely less instinct of rhetoric than he. All the others—the Hunts, Richardson, John La Farge, Stanford White—were exuberant; only St. Gaudens could never discuss or dilate on an emotion, or suggest artistic arguments for giving to his work the forms that he felt. He never laid down the law, or affected the despot, or became brutalized like Whistler by the brutalities of his world. He required no incense; he was no egoist; his simplicity of thought was excessive; he could not imitate, or give any form but his own to the creations of his hand. No one felt more strongly than he the strength of other men, but the idea that they could affect him never stirred an image in his mind.

This summer his health was poor and his spirits were low. For such a temper, Adams was not the best companion, since his own gaiety was not *folle*; but he risked going now and then to the studio on Mont Parnasse to draw him out for a stroll in the Bois de Boulogne, or dinner as pleased his moods, and in return St. Gaudens sometimes let Adams go about in his company.

Once St. Gaudens took him down to Amiens, with a party of Frenchmen, to see the cathedral. Not until they found themselves actually studying the sculpture of the western portal, did it dawn on Adams's mind that, for his purposes, St. Gaudens on that spot had more interest to him than the cathedral itself. Great men before great monuments express great truths, provided they are not taken too solemnly. Adams never tired of quoting the supreme phrase of his idol Gibbon, before the Gothic cathedrals: "I darted a contemptuous look on the stately monuments of superstition." Even in the footnotes of his history, Gibbon had never inserted a bit of humor more human than this, and one would have paid largely for a photograph of the fat little historian, on the background of Notre Dame of Amiens, trying to persuade his readers—perhaps himself—that he was darting a contemptuous look on the stately monument, for which he felt in fact the respect which every man of his vast study and active mind always feels before objects worthy of it; but besides the humor, one felt also the relation. Gibbon ignored the Virgin, because in 1789 religious monuments were out of fashion. In 1900 his remark sounded fresh and simple as the green fields to ears that had heard a hundred years of other remarks, mostly no more fresh and certainly less simple. Without malice, one might find it more instructive than a whole lecture of Ruskin. One sees what one brings, and at that moment Gibbon brought the French Revolution. Ruskin brought reaction against the Revolution. St. Gaudens had passed beyond all. He liked the stately monuments much more than he liked Gibbon or Ruskin; he loved their dignity; their unity; their scale; their lines; their lights and shadows; their decorative sculpture; but he was even less conscious than they of the force that created it all—the Virgin, the Woman—by whose genius "the stately monuments of superstition" were built, through which she was expressed. He would have seen more meaning in Isis with the cow's horns, at Edfoo, who expressed the same thought. The art remained, but the energy was lost even upon the artist.

Yet in mind and person St. Gaudens was a survival of the 1500; he bore the stamp of the Renaissance, and should have carried an image of the Virgin round his neck, or stuck in his hat, like Louis XI. In mere time he was a lost soul that had strayed by chance into the twentieth century, and forgotten where it came from. He writhed and cursed at his ignorance, much as Adams did at his own, but in the opposite sense. St. Gaudens was a child of Benvenuto Cellini, smothered in an American cradle. Adams was a quintessence of Boston, devoured by curiosity to think like Benvenuto. St. Gaudens's art was starved from birth, and Adams's instinct was blighted from babyhood. Each had but half of a nature, and when they came together before the Virgin of Amiens they ought both to have felt in her the force that made them one; but it was not so. To Adams she became more than ever a channel of force; to St Gaudens she remained as before a channel of taste.

For a symbol of power, St. Gaudens instinctively preferred the horse, as was plain in his horse and Victory of the Sherman monument. Doubtless Sherman also felt it so. The attitude was so American that, for at least forty years, Adams had never realized that any other could be in sound taste. How many years had he taken to admit a notion of what Michael Angelo and Rubens were driving at? He could not say; but he knew that only since 1895 had he begun to feel the Virgin or Venus as force, and not everywhere even so. At Chartres—perhaps at Lourdes—possibly at Cnidos if one could still find there the divinely naked Aphrodite of Praxiteles—but otherwise one must look for force to the goddesses of Indian mythology. The idea died out long ago in the German and English stock. St. Gaudens at Amiens was hardly less sensitive to the force of the female energy than Matthew Arnold at the Grande Chartreuse. Neither of them felt goddesses as power—only as reflected emotion, human expression, beauty, purity, taste, scarcely even as sympathy. They felt a railway train as power; yet they, and all other artists, constantly complained that the power embodied in a railway train could never be embodied in art. All the steam in the world could not, like the Virgin, build Chartres.

Yet in mechanics, whatever the mechanicians might think, both energies acted as interchangeable forces on man, and by action on man all known force may be measured. Indeed, few men of science measured force in any other way. After once admitting that a straight line was the shortest distance between two points, no serious mathematician cared to deny anything that suited his convenience, and rejected no symbol, unproved or unproveable, that helped him to accomplish work. The symbol was force, as a compass needle or a triangle was force, as the mechanist might prove by losing it, and nothing could be gained by ignoring their value. Symbol or energy, the Virgin had acted as the greatest force the Western world ever felt, and had drawn man's activities to herself more strongly than any other power, natural or supernatural, had ever done; the historian's business was to follow the track of the energy; to find where it came from and where it went to; its complex source and shifting channels; its values, equivalents, conversions. It could scarcely be more complex than radium; it could hardly be deflected, diverted, polarized, absorbed more perplexingly than other radiant matter. Adams knew nothing about any of them, but as a mathematical problem of influence on human progress, though all were occult, all reacted on his mind, and he rather inclined to think the Virgin easiest to handle.

The pursuit turned out to be long and tortuous, leading at last into the vast forests of scholastic science. From Zeno to Descartes, hand in hand with Thomas Aquinas, Montaigne, and Pascal, one stumbled as stupidly as though one were still a German student of 1860. Only with the instinct of despair could one force one's self into this old thicket of ignorance after having been repulsed at a score of entrances more promising and more popular. Thus far, no path had led anywhere, unless perhaps to an exceedingly modest living. Forty-five years of study had proved to be quite futile for the pursuit of power; one controlled no more force in 1900 than in 1850, although the amount of force controlled by society had enormously increased. The secret of education still hid itself somewhere behind ignorance, and one fumbled over it as feebly as ever. In such labyrinths, the staff is a force almost more necessary than the legs; the pen becomes a sort of blind-man's dog, to keep him from falling into the gutters. The pen works for itself, and acts like a hand, modelling the plastic material over and over again to the form that suits it best. The form is never arbitrary, but is a sort of growth like crystallization, as any artist knows too well; for often the pencil or pen runs into side-paths and shapelessness, loses its relations, stops or is bogged. Then it has to return on its trail, and recover, if it can, its line of force. The result of a year's work depends more on what is struck out than on what is left in; on the sequence of the main lines of thought, than on their play or variety. Compelled once more to lean heavily on this support, Adams covered more thousands of pages with figures as formal as though they were algebra, laboriously striking out, altering, burning, experimenting, until the year had expired, the Exposition had long been closed, and winter drawing to its end, before he sailed from Cherbourg, on January 19, 1901, for home.

Jacquetta Hawkes

SOURCE: "The Industrial Revolution and the Common Man," in *Ideas in Context,* edited by Joseph Satin, Houghton Mifflin, 1958, pp. 7-14.

[In the following essay first published in 1951, Hawkes outlines various causes and effects of the Industrial Revolution, emphasizing the destruction of eighteenth-century rural culture and the predominance of scientific thought.]

The pattern of settlement was no longer to be decided by the character of the soil, the surface features of the land and the climate, but by the distribution of the deposits which time had left far below the surface. Huge numbers left farms and villages and swarmed to the places where coal and metal ores lay hidden; once there they showed an extraordinary fecundity. The population doubled and doubled again. By the middle of the nineteenth century half the people of Britain were living in towns, a situation new in the history of great nations.

Those town dwellers, cut off from the soil and from food production, soon lost all those arts and skills which had always been the possession if not of every man, then of every small community. The sons and daughters of the first generation of town dwellers were not taught how to use eye and hand in the traditional skills, and, a loss of absolute finality, they could not inherit all the traditional forms, the shape for an axe handle, a yoke, for a pair of tongs; the proportions of cottage doors and windows, the designs for smocking, lace making, embroidery. Some of these forms, because they had achieved fitness for their purpose as complete as the unchanging bodies of the insects, had remained constant for centuries or millennia; others were always evolving yet maintained their continuity. Now all of them, or almost all, were to fade from the common imagination, to become extinct. I know of only one traditional form for an everyday tool which has been adapted without loss to machine production; this is the exquisitely curved and modulated handle of the woodcutter's axe.

With the extinction of ancient arts and skills there went also countless local rites, customs, legends and histories. All these, whether or no they had been adapted to Christianity, were survivals of a paganism that helped to unite country people with nature and their own ancestors. Stories and names for fields and lanes recalled men and women who had worked the land before them; legends still commemorated local deities who had lived in wood, water, and stone; many customs recognized and assisted in the main crises of individual lives; rites helped to harmonize these individual rhythms with the greater rhythms of nature— they celebrated the return of the sun, the resurrection of the corn, harvest, and the return of death.

Without these immemorial ties, personal and universal, relating men to their surroundings in time and space, the isolation of human consciousness by urban life was a most violent challenge. It gave opportunity for the heightening of consciousness and the sharpening of intellect, but human weakness and material circumstances made it impossible for any but the few gifted or fortunate to respond. The urban masses having lost all the traditions I have just named which together make up the inheritance which may be called culture, tended to become, as individuals, cultureless. The women were in better case, for all except the most downtrodden could rear children, clean, launder, sew, and cook after a fashion, though all their work was dulled and robbed of distinction by the standardization and poor quality of their materials. (It is one of the more bizarre results of industrialism that the rich will now pay great sums to obtain goods that were once taken for granted by quite humble people. Such things as real honey, fresh butter and eggs, hand needlework, tiles made of real stone, reed thatch.) For the men it was far worse. Usually they could do only one thing, and that without direct relation to their own lives; when they returned from the set hours of "work" there was nothing for hand or imagination to do. So, when

at last leisure was won for them, it proved to be a barren gift.

I do not wish to suggest that there was any lessening of man's dependence on the land, of his struggle to extract a living from it; that is the stuff of existence and cannot be reduced. It is not true either that industry is lacking in its own bold regional variations; the collieries with hoists and slag heaps, the steel furnaces, the clustering chimneys of the brick kilns, the potteries, all create their own landscape. But the individual life, the individual culture, was not sensitively adjusted to locality, and the nature of the relationship was profoundly changed. It ceased to be creative, a patient and increasingly skilful lovemaking that had persuaded the land to flourish, and became destructive, a grabbing of material for man to destroy or to refashion to his own design. The intrusion of machines between hand and material completed the estrangement.

By this new rapacious treatment of the land man certainly made himself abundantly productive of material goods. But he cannot be sure of getting what he wants from the great cauldron of production. Meanwhile the land, *with which he must always continue to live,* shows in its ravaged face that husbandry has been succeeded by exploitation—an exploitation designed to satisfy man's vanity, his greed and possessiveness, his wish for domination.

As a starting point for the Revolution I shall choose the time about two hundred years ago, when men began to smelt iron with coke. Earlier attempts to use coal instead of wood had failed, but now, largely through the efforts of generations of one family, the Darbys of Shropshire, the new process was mastered and the coal-and-iron age of Victorian England was already within sight. It is, of course, possible to say that the real revolution, the tipping of the balance from agriculture to manufacture, took place later than this. Equally, or indeed with more justification, it can be claimed that it began much earlier with Tudor commerce and the scientific ferment of the seventeenth century. I would agree, I would even willingly push it back to the depths of the Carboniferous forests; there is never a beginning. But I prefer to select the mating of coal and iron, for with the thought of it the weight and grime of the Black Country, the bustle and energy of material activity, at once take shape in the imagination. Besides, it was a time when the intellect, sharpened by the new scientific, analytical modes of thought, was achieving many other of the devices that made industrialism possible. In one year, 1769, Arkwright gave the water frame to the cotton industry and Watt patented the steam engine. Within another ten years the gorge of the Severn which had been cut in the Ice Age by the overflowing waters of Lake Lapworth was spanned by the first iron bridge to be built in the world. Together these closely consecutive events well represent the new forces of the Revolution: coal and iron, mechanical power, mechanization, and the corresponding development of transport.

The Industrial Revolution was certainly in part brought about by the scientific mode of thought that had grown from the Renaissance intellect. Yet it was not itself a rational episode. To me it seems an upsurge of instinctive forces comparable to the barbarian invasions, a surge that destroyed eighteenth-century civilization much as the Anglo-Saxons destroyed that of Roman Britain. No one planned it, no one foresaw more than a tittle of the consequences, very few people said that they wanted it, but once begun the impetus was irresistible; more and more individual lives became helplessly involved, drawn into the vortex. It went forward as irresistibly as the evolution of the dinosaurs and in it was included the roaring of *Tyrannosaurus*. It seems indeed that *Tyrannosaurus* and Apollo of the Intellect worked together for the Revolution and no combination could be more powerful or more dangerous.

It lent to its instruments an astonishing strength. It enabled this chip of the earth's surface, the small fund of human mind, will and energy that it supported, momentarily to dominate the whole surface of the planet and in so doing, like a gigantic, slow explosion, to disperse fragments of itself all over that surface. It seems possible that had there not been this association of coal and iron, growing population and intellectual ferment within the bounds of a temperate island, the industrialization that in two centuries has totally changed human life might never have assumed its present forms.

They were there, and the new way of life developed with a speed that is almost unbelievable when it is compared with any other experience of human history. In south Wales, south Yorkshire, and Tyneside, all those regions where past events had left iron and coal in close proximity, there sprang up foundries whose crimson glare by night repeats something of the volcanic furies of other ages. With them there grew to colossal stature the manufacture of metal goods, a manufacture centred on Birmingham in a region that had remained longer than almost any other under the peaceful covering of the forests. On the moist western side of the Pennines the cotton industry, the first to be wholly dependent on material produced outside the island, grew up in obscene relationship with the trade in African slaves. The little mills once turned by the Pennine streams, family cottage manufacture, were soon abandoned for the factories of Manchester and the neighbouring towns that were growing round it. Away on the east of the central mountains, the ancient conservatism of the wool trade long resisted the new methods; in time, however, first spinning and then weaving left the rural valleys and moved to towns like Bradford, where the foamy white wool is combed and spun in

mills of blackened rock, and to Leeds and Huddersfield, where it is woven on looms whose descent from those of the Bronze Age it is hard to credit. The salt that the evaporation of the Triassic lakes and lagoons had left under the Cheshire plain became the source of a chemical industry, a thing new even among so much innovation. One other industry there was which I will mention because it shows how, exceptionally, a few individuals may impose themselves on the land, creating something from their own wills that is not dictated by circumstances. There was no material reason beyond a supply of coal for his furnaces why Josiah Wedgwood and his family should have built up the pottery business in Staffordshire. Much of his material was dug in Cornwall (where the glistening white heaps of kaolin look so alien, so improbable among the soft, warmly coloured granite moorlands), and his kilns were inconveniently far from the coast for the carriage of both the raw clay and the finished china. However, Wedgwood lived there and started his work there and so the existence of the Five Towns was determined. The craft that even in Britain had a history of four and a half millennia now went into mass production largely through the inspiration of one man. It was appropriate that for a time his name was identified with that of the clay he manipulated—that "common Wedgwood" should become the accepted term for the people's crockery. Because of their history, the Potteries have remained more patriarchal in organization, more personal in feeling than other industries, just as from its nature the work itself remains exceptionally individual and unmechanized. I will not leave the Potteries without commenting on the extraordinary forethought that nature seems to me to have shown in the formation of kaolin; nearly two hundred million years after its deposition, it has proved that this substance can be used for making china, for fulling cloth, for keeping the shine from women's faces, for papermaking, and as a cure for diarrhoea.

Transport was of course one of the keys of industrialism. Upon it depended a state of affairs in which men no longer made things for local use and in which a locality no longer provided the food for its people. By the eighteenth century Britain was more closely unified by roads than it had been since Roman times and soon this was reinforced by the canals, a quiet, deliberate form of carriage that came to have its own nomadic population. Then down the ringing grooves of change came the railway engine begotten by Watt and Stephenson on the iron-and-coal age. Gangs of navies were moved about the country embanking, cutting, tunnelling, bridge-building; thousands of tons of metal were laid across our meadows, along our valleys, round our coasts. The incidental result of this activity in stimulating consciousness in its search for its origins has already been demonstrated in the life of William Smith, the Father of Stratigraphy.

The shift in population was the fourth and infinitely the greatest that had taken place since Mesolithic times. The north of England and southern Wales, formerly rather thinly settled, soon had the bulk of a sharply rising population. As mills, factories, foundries, and kilns multiplied, the little streets of the workers' houses spread their lines over hills that belonged to wild birds and mountain sheep, and up valleys where there was nothing busier than a rushing beck. Without intention or understanding the greater part of the people of Britain found themselves living in towns, uprooted, and in a strange, unstable environment. The growths of brick and stone, later of concrete, whose ragged outer edges were always creeping further, might coalesce one with another in urban areas so large that it was difficult for the inhabitants to set foot on grass or naked earth. The results were grim, but sometimes and particularly in the Pennine towns they had their own grandeur. Where houses and factories are still built from the local rocks and where straight streets climb uncompromisingly up hillsides, their roofs stepping up and up against the sky, they have a geometric beauty that is harsh but true, while the texture of smoke-blackened lime or sandstone can be curiously soft and rich, like the wings of some of our sombre night-flying moths. Nor do such cities ever quite lose the modelling of their natural foundations. On my first visit to the industrial north I rode on the top of a tram all the way from Leeds to Batley and all the way I rode through urban streets. In the last daylight it seemed a melancholy and formless jumble of brick and stone, but as darkness closed and a few smoky stars soothed and extended my thoughts, the lamps going up in innumerable little houses restored the contours of hill and dale in shimmering lines of light.

William N. Parker

SOURCE: "The Pre-History of the Nineteenth Century," in *Europe, America, and the Wider World: Essays on the Economic History of Western Capitalism,* Vol. 1, Cambridge University Press, 1984, pp. 15-57.

[*In this excerpt from an essay originally published in 1979, Parker discusses the spread of industrialization throughout Western Europe during the first half of the nineteenth century, emphasizing the economic conditions and the technological advances of the period.*]

THE SPREAD OF MODERN INDUSTRY[11]

The spread of mechanical techniques through industries and through geographical regions is a pair of processes with many common characteristics. The mechanisation of a new industry required adaptation of the power and inventions to harness power to specific operations. The spread of a given machine technique, e.g. mechanical spinning, from one region re-quired interested entrepreneurs, favourable factor cost conditions, suitable government policy, and supplies of capital and workers adaptable to the machine process. It too required minor inventions to adapt the equipment to specific raw materials, markets, climate, and labour force. The timing, speed, and form of the diffusion in both cases depended on special technical, economic or sociological conditions of the industry or region in question. In the competitive economy of northern Europe, the spread of mechanisation among industries was in one sense the more fundamental sort of diffusion since the minimum physical cost locations of new industries were determined by cost characteristics of the new technique. Given these characteristics, the ultimate dispersion of an industry was largely a matter of economic geography. Social and economic differences—the availability of capital, the training and immobility of the local labour force, the policy of the region's government—determined the lags, however, before the 'natural' economic factors and the force of competition took effect. This was especially true where the natural locational advantage of one region over another was rather small. In textiles, for example, differences in the location of enterprise, capital, cheap labour, and close relations with overseas outlets could set the advantage.

Diffusion among industries. [By indicating the path of the Industrial Revolution among industrial processes, one] may observe certain clusterings in the history of its progress. One was the spread of the power process from cotton-spinning through other branches of the textile industry—to wool and linen, and after a delay to mechanised weaving. Hand processes in the garment industry—e.g. shoemaking and sewing—presented specific technical problems which yielded, one after another between 1800 and 1850, to British and American ingenuity and enterprise. All this development was brought on partly by the force of economic pressures within the structure of textile and clothing production which focussed inventive activity, and partly by the rise in the level of technical opportunity for solving problems through improvements in materials, machine tools and control mechanisms. The history of the development of the sewing machine may be cited as a notable example of the eco-technic process at work.

Beyond the 'light' industries—textiles, boots and shoes, machine tools, and farm machinery—the latter developing more rapidly under favourable market and terrain conditions in North America after 1850—there lay the engineering problems of heavier equipment in transport and power generation. Continuous improvements in the steam engine increased its efficiency and extended the range of capacities and pressures generated and contained. Such improvements occurred at all the locations where engines were used and produced, in England, Wales, Belgium, Germany—even on the banks of the Ohio in America. The adaptation of steam

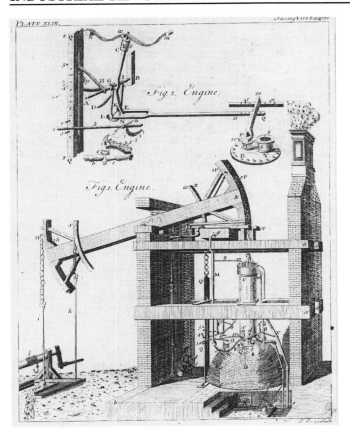

Inventions like the steam engine transformed the economy and society.

make machines, a large market for machinery is essential. The increase in the productivity of machinery and in its durability when iron was used worked in exactly the reverse direction. A market for machinery of unusual scale must have been present to give the impetus. This is true in early nineteenth-century northeastern United States, where the level of income, its distribution, the protection afforded by distance from English competition and (some allege) the scarcity of labour relative to capital, and of both relative to the ambitions of the population, helped also to allow an industry of specialised machine tool manufacture to grow quickly out of the machine shops of the textile mills. Once developed, the machine tool industry, employing water or steam power, improved and cheapened iron, and better and more closely machined parts in its own equipment could lift machine production out of the workshop of the mechanic and make it too a factory industry. The cheapening of machinery, rather than a fall in the rate of interest, has been largely responsible for the greater physical capital intensity of modern processes.

In England and Belgium, the close link of machinery production to the local iron industry cannot fail to be observed. With the possibilities of steam-powered machinery, an engineering industry was growing up around iron works, and the massive fuel requirements of coke smelting and puddling brought iron works to locations at coal beds. In Britain by 1850 most major coal beds were thus the site of iron smelting and fabricating industries. There can be little doubt that even before the steel inventions of the 1850s, the coal-based industrial complex was an economic unit. Because of the saving in fuel transport costs and the further advantages of agglomeration and communication in a concentrated area, its products could undersell those of producers at scattered locations. By 1850 the Industrial Revolution, as a revolution in both technology and plant and enterprise organisation, had spread from cotton-spinning to other 'light' easily mechanised industries, then to the heavier industries of transport equipment and machine production itself, the latter based also on the improvements in the iron industry that were part of the eighteenth-century development. Lodged between light and heavy industries, the machine tool companies expanded and extended the varieties and uses of their products. As these industries, particularly those using coal and iron, clustered around coal or ore mining areas, the typical industrial complex of the later nineteenth century was formed. The railroad added to the advantage of these dark and smoky districts even as it increased the demand for their products, and the Bessemer and open-hearth processes coming in after the 1850s ensured their stability for the half-century following 1870, not only in Britain and Belgium, but around the coal beds of the valleys tributary to the lower Rhine, and the upper Ohio.

to water navigation is a classic story in the history of invention, and from Trevithick to Stephenson, the development of locomotives, braking mechanisms, and all the vast array of railroad inventions created the mid-century transformation of land transportation. In stationary engines, the first half of the nineteenth century saw the development of the water and steam turbine in France and England through the inventions of Fourneyron and the thorough investigation of the science of thermodynamics by Carnot.[12]

We have seen that mechanical inventions, as they spread to various industries and locations in northern Europe and North America, presupposed a large interconnected industrial region. This was required to ensure both adequate market size and the mass of intercommunicating inventive activity necessary to keep economic expansion and technical change in motion. In the eighteenth century, it appears that central England itself was a large enough area. A striking fact about the Industrial Revolution is the speed with which improvement extended from iron and machinery production to the manufacture of machine tools. Machine tools lie deep in the production processes of modern industry. To make it worthwhile to devote efforts to improve the machines which

One must remember that the Industrial Revolution was based on a certain group of inventions and an accompanying organisational form, which could not spread beyond the industries where coal, iron and machinery could be introduced. In Britain in 1850 many industries and operations were not power driven, or mechanised. The largest component of the non-agricultural labour force in 1850 was, after all, domestic service, and the mechanisation of the household lay beyond anyone's imagination. Construction, including ship-building and road-building, was relatively untouched, similarly most food-processing operations and, of course, agriculture. The very growth of the larger-scale industries, and the swarming of populations to new locations gave occupation to vast numbers of small-scale producers, and furnishers of service. Office work, too—except for the development of the typewriter and the telephone and telegraph after 1850—experienced no productivity increases, and the way was laid in all these respects not only for the perpetuation of the class of small shopkeepers and professionals, but also for the growth of the 'white collar' staff of the larger establishments. The whole society then was not industrialised, much less proletarianised. Industry, industrial capital, industrialists, and industrial wage workers assumed a place on the front bench of society and politics, constituting a special 'interest' alongside the interests of the mercantile community, the bankers, the professional and white collar class and the landed interest of ancient origin. It assumed a place beside the others, but did not crowd them off the scene.

Diffusion among regions of north-western Europe. The advances in the cotton, iron and machinery industries between 1780 and 1840 were the whole bases on which the English Midlands, with extensions in South Wales and Scotland, in 1850 rested a remarkable industrial leadership over the long-established industrial regions of the Continent. In textiles, technical obstacles which lay in the way of mechanising operations in flax, silk, or even wool did not obstruct the application of machinery to cotton. England's lead in the cotton industry then must be attributed to her superior trading position and access to markets and to raw cotton supplies. Possibly also, the long experience in wool made an easier transition to cotton than could be achieved by silk or linen producers. The development of a cotton industry on the Continent had to depend initially on the importation of English machinery and a few English workmen and plant designers—an expensive and unsatisfactory way to overtake a foreign competitor. Still machinery was eventually applied to the branches of textiles in which continental producers specialised and the slower pace of development in machinery and the iron industry on the Continent cannot be attributed to technical reasons. Clearly before 1840 the continental industrial regions—the cities with their workshops and the rather widely separated and disconnected areas of rural industry—lacked the inten-sity in industrial activity closely linked to machine shops, which gave British industry the critical mass necessary to a continuous and self-reinforcing economic and industrial development. The imported English spinning machinery at Ratingen in the Rhineland, in Normandy along the Seine tributaries, and later in Ghent, were sparks of modernisation which did not light a fuse to set off the fireworks.

The Belgian case is the exception on the Continent which proves the point at issue here.[13] In Flanders the dense textile industrial district lay close to a large foreign market and to the iron-and coal-based industry of Liège and the Belgian coalfield. Even under Napoleon, industrial development began, when the area was joined with the Dutch provinces in 1815, overseas markets were opened and access given to Dutch capital. The Dutch areas themselves failed to industrialise—possibly because of a history and social structure based solely on commerce, possibly also because of lack of cheap coal. Instead, the Dutch king invested in the Belgian areas which lay under his government between 1815 and 1830, and a little borrowing of workmen and machinery from England developed mechanised spinning and a domestic machinery industry. By 1850—twenty years after the separation from Dutch rule, the Belgian Netherlands had become the world's second coal-based industrial district in which the light and heavy industries of the Industrial Revolution were joined.

The persistence of traditional and typically 'early modern' barriers to industrialisation on the Continent is shown best in France. The Revolution had swept away the remains of feudal forms—feudal land tenures and the power of the guilds in cities. It had destroyed, indeed it had confirmed, governmental centralisation and mercantilist policies of the state. The revolutionary governments and Napoleon had strengthened the state much as Louis XIV had done, though more intelligently, and much was provided for the new (and not so new) commercial and industrial bourgeoisie. Commercial and property law was regularised through the *Code Napoléon,* scientific and technical education was extended and strengthened. An educated scientific and engineering élite was enlarged. The Bank of France helped stabilise the currency and brought French public finance up to the degree of modernity that England had achieved a hundred years earlier. Modernisation and regularisation of the tax system added greatly to the regularity with which business expectations could be pursued. By reducing its personal and arbitrary character, the post-Revolutionary government helped to create a climate of reduced uncertainty for mercantile and business interests.

The regimes from Napoleon I to Napoleon III offered also many direct opportunities to business enterprise. Interruption of trade with England from 1790 to 1815 reserved the Continental market to Continental—and largely to French or Belgian—producers. The inflation and the wars themselves offered the usual opportunity for short-term and individual gains. Enough venality was present, enough luxury demand, enough waste to nourish the greediest entrepreneur. Yet for all that, one cannot speak of any French government until the parliamentary democracy of the Third Republic, as an oligarchy like that in seventeenth-century Netherlands or eighteenth-century England. The peasantry, the church, the remaining aristocracy, the army, the bureaucracy—all were too strong to furnish a clear climate for modern capitalism. If the balance in England by 1780 was about right to allow an eco-technic, industrial revolution to proceed, the balance lay in France a bit too strongly on the side of what Marxists call pre-industrial economic formations. Much is made in history books of England's political gradualism, in contrast to France's recurrent revolutions. But in economic modernisation, it was in France that gradualism prevailed. Napoleonic government and its successors under the Restoration and the July Monarchy maintained a stance which combined liberalisation, protection, and paternalism until more classic liberal policies were introduced. By that time, industrialisation had developed into something different from what it had been seventy years earlier, and what France had preserved of the older forms and values—the system of technical education, the aristocratic spirit of scientific research, the balance between population growth and her own food supplies—began to pay off.[14] The nation then could lay the base for continued economic progress as a national unit, even up to the present day, through all the devastations of war and political and moral catastrophe.

The situation in the scattered German textile and metalworking regions of the eighteenth century was not greatly different from that in France.[15] But they lacked two developments that English and French regions had experienced: incorporation in a national state, and within it a political revolution. Even by 1700, the physical depredations of the Thirty Years War had been repaired, but within the notoriously numerous political districts, a mixed medieval and Renaissance political economy survived and flourished. The states were not inactive in efforts to advance industry; they encouraged it by all the best principles of mercantilist economic policy. Nor was there any lack of skill or enterprise in many areas; we have seen earlier how extensive was the diffusion of the Renaissance technology in the south, central and western German states. Rhine merchants and bankers were active throughout the whole period before 1850, and in south-west Germany, the activity and ambitions of apothecaries, along with the princely sponsorship of 'pure' science in the universities, laid the foundations for Germany's later successes in chemicals. The tariff history, of which so much has been written, indicates that barriers to internal trade were overcome, but the Zollverein, too, was

a mercantilist measure pursued from political motives, not only on the part of Prussia but also of the petty princes who hoped, in typically seventeenth-century fashion, to increase net revenues from a source outside the control of assemblies and nobility. Even after the industrialisation got under way in the Prussian territories and in the Empire, no one would ever have mistaken the Imperial German government for a businessman's state.

By 1850 what was lacking in both Germany and France in 1800 had been partially supplied. The social and political basis for modern capitalistic industry had inched its way toward a condition which could tolerate capitalist expansion without the continual drag of medieval or mercantilist restrictions or the unexpected and disrupting assertions of authority of divine right monarchs and their bureaucracies. Then between 1850 and 1870 two decades of classical liberal policies in both France and Prussia expanded trade, strengthened financial institutions, encouraged capital accumulation. What had been lacking in the earlier textile industrialisation was the opportunity to make the link with the iron industries, and this the railroad had only partly supplied. But the social and physical elements in modern industry were present—the intangible social capital of laws, skilled mechanics and engineers, educational institutions, a still disciplined labour force, and the physical capital of transport improvements. As contact between regions improved, the disadvantages of the small- and scattered-scale of the earlier textile and light machinery industries began to be overcome.

Into this atmosphere in the 1860s came as a supplement and substitute for wide geographical scale, the opportunity for heavy industry localisation. Through the accidents of politics north-western Europe's coal was distributed in bits across all of the major north-western countries. It had long been known and mined in spots—in the Saar, in the Liège region, and at a few shallow diggings in France. With the opportunity opened by market growth and the steel inventions of the 1860s, the clustering around these deposits began to take shape, and the immense industrial strength of the Franco-German-Belgian area began to make itself felt.

The development of coal, steel, chemicals and electricity on the continent belongs to the history of the latter part of the nineteenth century. It would take another chapter, or another book, to fill it in. It exhibits similarities in form and timing to the American development south of the Great Lakes, between Chicago and Pittsburgh in these same decades. But European industrial history prior to 1850 shows that it grew up on an industrial base very different from that of both England and the USA. Unlike the eighteenth- and early nineteenth-century developments in England, continental industrialisation after 1850 was not based simply on the scale economics of wide textile markets, and the accompaniment of a mechanical engineering technology. That was a combination which the continental locations, for reasons of economic and social organisation in the late eighteenth century, had not been able to achieve. But at length after half a century of sporadic, artificial, and pale imitations of British technology, continental industry hit upon a rich vein which its own tools and traditions were able to mine. In the technology of coal-based chemistry, in metallurgy scientifically developed, and in inventions leading into the lighter but even more science-based industry of the twentieth century, the Continent's long industrial traditions and its institutions of pure scientific research and of applied training could at last come into their own. With the concentration of activity around coalfields, the industrial strength was developed which, by permitting further developments away from coalfields, could lead continental industry into its upsurge after the calamities of the 1940s.

Notes

[11] W. O. Henderson, *Britain and Industrial Europe 1770-1870* (2nd edn, Leicester, Leicester University Press, 1965) traces some of the direct lines of connection from Britain to the Continent. Rondo Cameron's original and well-researched book, *France and the Economic Development of Europe 1800-1914* (Princeton, New Jersey, Princeton University Press, 1961) and the monumental work of Maurice Lévy-Leboyer, *Les Banques Européennes et l'Industrialisation Internationale* (Paris, Presses Universitaires de France, 1964) treat the Continental industrialisation, as does the earlier work of A. L. Dunham, *The Industrial Revolution in France 1815-1848* (New York, Exposition Press, 1955) and the essays by Jan Craeybeckx and Claude Fohlen in Rondo Cameron (ed.), *Essays in French Economic History* (Homewood, Illinois, Richard D. Irwin, Inc., 1970). To the classic textbook of J. H. Clapham, *The Economic Development of France and Germany 1815-1914* (4th edn, London, Cambridge University Press, 1963) and David Landes' treatment of the western European area as a whole (see *The Cambridge Economic History of Europe*, vol. VI, part 2, H. J. Habbakuk and M. M. Postan (eds.) (London, Cambridge University Press, 1965) and *The Unbound Prometheus* (London, Cambridge University Press, 1969) have now been added very good chapters in A. S. Milward and S. B. Saul, *The Economic Development of Conti-Europe 1780-1870* (London, George Allen & Unwin Ltd., 1973) and in C. M. Cipolla (ed.), *The Fontana Economic History of Europe*, vol. IV, especially chapter 1, 'France 1700-1914' by Claude Fohlen, and 2, 'Germany 1700-1914' by Knut Borchardt. The conference volume of the International Economic Association, edited by W. W. Rostow, *The Economics of Take-off into Sustained Growth* (New York, St Martin's Press, 1965) also contains a number of valuable articles on early development in various countries as well as an evaluation of the 'take-off' hypothesis of W. W. Rostow.

[12] D. S. L. Cardwell, *From Watt to Clausius* (Ithaca, New York, Cornell University Press, 1971).

[13] [See the] excellent chapter in Rondo Cameron's *France and the Economic Development of Europe 1800-1914* (Princeton, New Jersey, Princeton University Press, 1961) [and] a recent treatment of the Belgian 'case' by Joel Mokyr, *Industrialization in the Low Countries 1795-1850* (New Haven, Connecticut, Yale University Press, 1976).

[14] French technical education is interestingly treated in F. B. Artz, *The Development of Technical Education in France 1500-1850* (Cambridge, Massachusetts, The M.I.T. Press, 1966). A recent dissertation by Bernard Gustin, 'The German Chemical Profession: 1824-1867' (Department of Sociology, University of Chicago, 1975) throws needed light on German chemical training and research before Liebig, and the role of the apothecaries in the development.

[15] See the articles by Herbert Kisch, 'The Impact of the French Revolution on the Lower Rhine Textile Districts—Some Comments on Economic Development and Social Change,' *Economic History Review*, 2nd ser., 15 (1962), 304-27, and 'Textile Industries in The Rhineland and Silesia, A Comparative Study,' *Journal of Economic History*, 19 (1959), 541-69, and also Gerhard Adelmann, 'Structural Change in the Rhenish Linen and Cotton Trades at the Outset of Industrialization' in Francois Crouzet, W. H. Chaloner and W. M. Stern (eds.), *Essays in European Economic History 1789-1914* (London, Edward Arnold Ltd., 1966). On metallurgy, see N. J. G. Pounds and W. N. Parker, *Coal and Steel in Western Europe* (Bloomington, Indiana, Indiana University Press, 1957).

Paul C. Wilson

SOURCE: "Playing the Role: Howe and Singer as Heroic Inventors," in *Beyond the Two Cultures: Essays on Science, Technology, and Literature*, edited by Joseph W. Slade and Judith Yaross Lee, Iowa State University Press, 1990, pp. 275-85.

[*In the following essay, Wilson examines the self-portraits of the sewing machine inventors Elias Howe and Isaac Singer, suggesting that both men shaped their accounts according to the romantic stereotypes of inventors found in the popular literature of nineteenth-century America.*]

Popular literature in nineteenth-century America was filled with stories about inventors. When Elias Howe and Isaac Singer were asked to tell how they invented their sewing machines, they knew exactly what their audiences expected, and naturally enough they were delighted to represent themselves as the conventional heroes of the age. In their self-portraits as inventors and in their accounts of how they built their first sewing machines, both men shaped historical fact to bring it closer to the stereotypes found in newspaper features, fiction, and drama.

The public's notion of inventors and their work was drawn largely from the newspapers, which reached a wide readership and carried articles about people who devised almost every kind of obscure device. In the standard formula of these articles the inventor is usually penniless, eccentric in manner or dress, and unsuccessful in his trade. One day he has a sudden inspiration, and the invention appears to him like a vision. He quickly perfects it but then has a long struggle with unsympathetic capitalists who fail to recognize its value. In the end the inventor either dies, victim of the world's injustice, or is rewarded by fabulous riches.

An article published in the *Boston Daily Advertiser* in early 1841 illustrates the conventional views of the inventive character and the process of invention. It focuses on Aloys Senefelder, the inventor of lithography. "Fifty years ago," the story explains, "there lived at Munich a poor fellow, by name Aloys Senefelder, who was in so little repute as an author and artist, that painters and engravers refused to publish his works at their own charges, and so set him upon some plan for doing without their aid."[1] Ostracized and ridiculed by his neighbors, the inventor typically has mixed motives of greed and self-justification. He begins making experiments, but the solution always arrives by accident. The circumstances of Senefelder's inspiration were typical of the genre: "One day, it is said, that Aloys was called upon to write—rather a humble composition for an author and artist—a washing bill." Happening to write out the bill on a stone, he chanced upon the process of lithography. It would work well, he thought, if he made a few refinements; in the words of the article, "he did, and succeeded." Suddenly, the invention was complete.

Like most popular accounts of invention, this story stresses the dramatic moment of inspiration and virtually ignores the long process of development that usually follows it. A true genius is supposed to be not a dogged eliminator of petty problems, but a superior being whose imagination is suddenly blessed with a divine vision of truth. Divine visions are never imperfect. The conclusion of Senefelder's story emphasizes the writer's lack of interest in narrative development and reveals the extraordinary assumption that most of his audience had heard the story of Aloys Senefelder before: "such is the story, which the reader most likely knows well—and having alluded to the origin of the

art, we shall not follow the stream through the windings and enlargements after it issued from the little parent rock, or fill our pages with the rest of the pedigree."

An equally typical account of an inventor's struggle to introduce his invention appears in a brief report on John Slocom, inventor of a pinmaking machine: "The inventor of the pin making machine, row in successful operation, at Pokeepsie [*sic*], is Mr. John Slocom, or Slocum, of Pawtucket. He invented it some years ago; but as he had no funds to carry it into operation, and could not find any one to take hold of the 'experiment,' he moved to Bristol, hoping that some of the capitalists of that place would assist him. In this he was disappointed; and finally got someone in Pokeepsie, to 'take hold with him.'"[2] Where possible, the stories conclude with a detailed account of the inventor's wealth. Slocom was one of the lucky ones: we are told that he was "now carrying on the business with entire success," having produced fifty tons of pins in the previous year.

Popular fiction and drama repeated the clichés found in newspaper features about inventors and their work, generally without adding anything significant to the standard pattern. But they show even more clearly a view of life that is implicit in the *Advertiser*'s account of Senefelder. In this perspective life is not progressive but discontinuous: a character is penniless in the first act but a millionaire in the last through sudden shifts in fortune that are associated more with luck than steady application. Life is reduced to pivotal moments, when a character faces a dilemma on which his or her whole future depends. Scenes like this one from the melodramatic tale "The Wings of Icarus" were typical:

> "Do you swear to me," said she, "that I should not know any of the men who visit this woman?"
>
> At this moment the countenance and the voice of Isaura had an expression too significant to be mistaken, and Deslandes could no longer be deceived. . . . He found himself between two rocks equally to be dreaded. To speak the truth was to provoke the hatred of the counsellor of state. To speak falsely, was to justify the anger of his patroness. But he needed them both, what means should he find to offend neither?[3]

Newspapers regularly carried fiction of this sort, often novels in serialized form, the mid-nineteenth-century equivalent of television soap operas.

"The Wings of Icarus" and the features on Slocom and Senefelder were published in the *Boston Daily Advertiser* early in 1841, when Elias Howe was first beginning work on his sewing machine. Howe was then living in Cambridge, and though he may not have read these issues of the *Daily Advertiser,* he did read a newspaper regularly[4] and seems to have shared the outlook on life that he found there. An aura of stage melodrama and pulp fiction clings to almost every account of his life, including a long article by James Parton based on interviews with the inventor.[5] Parton's account of Howe's childhood emphasizes the humble farm life, whose poverty and rural simplicity instill the appropriate Yankee values. Then comes the pivotal moment of inspiration, when Howe overhears a chance remark and has a vision of the wealth that inventing a sewing machine might bring. After years of experiments and frustration, when the inventor is near despair, the solution suddenly comes to him in a dream. The machine is patented, but a long struggle with adversity follows. The next scenes prominently feature the ailing but ever-faithful wife and the children dressed in rags, who show their thrift and stoicism in many situations of picturesque poverty. After persecution by a heartless villain, a series of heart-rending tragedies, and coincidences heavy with irony, the inventor is finally vindicated and becomes immensely rich. He now amuses himself with anonymous acts of charity and patriotism. Through it all the significant moments are punctuated by memorable aphorisms, and the moral is firmly pointed out to us—that in a democracy, virtue (defined as thrift, industry, and perseverance) is in the end rewarded by public recognition and lots of money.

In analyzing Howe's story we need to remember that we are looking for two kinds of information—on the one hand, Howe's view of life and his role as an inventor and, on the other, the historical facts. Both areas are of interest, but they must be distinguished. Perhaps the clearest example of the way Howe shaped his recollection of events (he was an enthusiastic and skillful teller of anecdotes) is in the account of his original inspiration. First told to a reporter for the *New York Daily Tribune,*[6] the story is repeated in fuller form by Parton. Howe was working in a machine shop that made watches, nautical instruments, and "philosophical apparatus"—that is, laboratory equipment. It was run by Ari Davis, whom Parton depicts as the eccentric genius of popular myth: "he gave way to the foible of affecting an oddity of dress and deportment. It pleased him to say extravagant and nonsensical things, and to go about singing, and to attract attention by unusual garments." One day a rich capitalist and an inventor, who were working together to develop a knitting machine, came to the shop to consult with Davis. Here is Parton's account of what happened:

> Davis, in his wild, extravagant way, broke in with these words: "What are you bothering yourselves with a knitting machine for? Why don't you make a sewing machine?"

> "I wish I could," said the capitalist; "but it can't be done."

> "O, yes it can," said Davis; "I can make a sewing machine myself."

> "Well," said the other, "you do it, Davis, and I'll insure you an independent fortune."[7]

The twenty-year-old Howe, who overheard the conversation, was much impressed by the capitalist and resolved on the spot that he would himself make the machine—and reap the fortune.

The story sounds like something taken directly from "The Wings of Icarus," and in a sense it was. A more sober account of the episode was given by Thomas Hall, who shared Howe's bench at the shop and witnessed the incident.[8] According to Hall, the would-be inventor of a knitting machine did come to the shop and did discuss the possibility of a sewing machine with the proprietor. But the romantic elements of Howe's story are absent. The rich capitalist, the source of most of the story's dramatic tension, was recruited from popular literature; he was not present in actual fact. The shop was run by the prosaically named Daniel Davis, assisted by his brother Asa (whose name was perhaps transmuted to the exotic Ari when his eccentricities were embellished). When the inventor came, Asa Davis looked over the plans for the knitting machine, pointed out weaknesses, and said that when the design was corrected he could build the model. As the two men discussed the technical problems of the knitting machine they were led to speculate about a sewing machine, and Davis remarked that a usable sewing machine would be worth a fortune, if it could be built. No bold assurances were given that the machine was feasible. No dramatic promises of reward were made.

Howe's famous dream, in which the idea of using an eye-pointed needle first occurred to him, also closely follows the fairy-tale pattern.

> He might have failed altogether [goes the tale] if he had not dreamed he was building a sewing machine for a savage king in a strange country. . . . He thought the king gave him twenty-four hours in which to complete the machine and make it sew. If he was not finished in that time, death was to be his punishment. Howe worked and worked, and puzzled, and finally gave it up. Then he thought he was taken out to be executed. He noticed that the warriors carried spears that were pierced near the head. Instantly came the solution to his difficulty, and while the inventor was begging for time he awoke. It was 4 o'clock in the morning. He jumped out of bed, ran to his workshop, and by 9, a needle with an eye at the point had been rudely modeled. After that it was easy.[9]

So goes the legend. But did Howe really dream all this, or did he make it up later? Or did he have a dream, but shape his recollection of it to the point where little was left of the original? The legend gives internal evidence for all of these interpretations. Its psychology follows the familiar pattern of an anxiety dream, and the pressures it expresses symbolically were certainly present in Howe's waking life. In a broader sense it accurately represents the process of creative thought. Solutions to difficult questions do often present themselves when the mind is relaxed and ideas can associate more freely.

For all that the basic features of Howe's dream are not improbable, however, it follows the folklore of invention so closely that its authenticity is dubious. The notion that great discoveries spring from the subconscious has been a commonplace since antiquity and was repeated countless times in the stories of invention that Howe must have read. It would have been tempting for Howe to include a dream in his account to make it more authentic. Certainly there are many features of his story that come straight from a fairy tale: the brief period given to the hero to solve his dilemma, for example, is always carefully specified by ogres and wicked kings. The assumptions of the dream reflect the same origin. It shows life not as a gradual and ill-defined process, but as a series of concentrated moments in which issues are sharply focused. Will the invention succeed or fail? Will the inventor live or die? Radical simplification of life is of course necessary to achieve this focus. The long and exhausting work of invention is reduced to a single flash of insight verified by a quick experiment: "After that," concludes the story, "it was easy." And like the proverbial princess, they lived happily ever after.

According to the folklore of invention, the inventive genius is supposed to have a revelation in which the complete design of the invention is presented to his mind, leaving only the translation of the mental image into tangible form. Like so many clichés about the heroic inventor, this conception of the creative process is typically romantic and reflects some of the same assumptions as Coleridge's famous preface to "Kubla Khan." Writing of himself in the third person, as "the poet," Coleridge describes how he fell asleep while reading, "during which time he has the most vivid confidence, that he could not have composed less than from two to three hundred lines; if that indeed can be called composition in which all the images rose up before him . . . without any sensation or consciousness of effort. On awaking he appeared to himself to have a distinct recollection of the whole, and taking his pen, ink, and paper, instantly and eagerly wrote down the lines that are here preserved."[10] Howe's story is similar to Coleridge's in the dream and also in its insistence that the vision required almost no later modification. "His conception of what he intended to produce was so clear and complete," wrote Parton, whose account is based mainly on what Howe told him, "that he was little delayed by failures, but worked on with almost as much certainty and steadiness as though he had a model before him."[11]

This assertion seems dubious not only because of its fidelity to the stereotype, but also because Howe's expenses in building his machine were several times what they would have been if the machine had worked well immediately. "At the present time," Parton wrote in 1867, "with a machine before him for a model, a good mechanic could not, with his ordinary tools, construct a sewing machine . . . at a less expense than three hundred dollars."[12] In 1845 the cost of the tools, and hence the expense, would have been roughly comparable, so if few modifications had been necessary, the five hundred dollars Howe's partner had originally promised to provide for materials and tools should have been just about sufficient. Yet before his work was done Howe had received closer to two thousand dollars.[13] Some of this money, to be sure, was used to support his family, but a large amount must also have gone toward the machine. It is likely that Howe, like other inventors, had to overcome a lengthy series of setbacks on the way to successful realization of his ideas.

Singer's fullest account of his invention shows some of the same notions about genius and the inventive process that we have seen in Howe's story, but whereas Howe drew his ideas mainly from newspapers, Singer was influenced more strongly by popular drama. Singer's lifelong dream was to be a famous actor, and he pursued a stage career for fourteen years, including five years as the manager of his own troupe, the Merritt Players. Though his repertory included Shakespeare (his favorite play was *Richard II*), Singer was not in the usual sense a literary man. He was in fact barely able to write an intelligible letter, and the performances of Shakespeare put on by the Merritt Players probably resembled those of the Duke and the Dauphin in *Huckleberry Finn*. The rest of the bill was made up of temperance dramas and stage versions of pulp fiction like "The Wings of Icarus."

Singer knew all the scripts by heart, and even when he was not on stage he carried on his life as if he were playing a role from a play. His wife's brother once noted that "most of his time was spent giving performances."[14] Thus when asked during the course of some patent litigation to describe how he had made his invention, he shaped his story to create melodrama and to accentuate the parallels between himself and what the public expected of a romantic genius.

Like Howe, Singer was well aware of the romantic convention that great creative ideas are supposed to flash suddenly upon the artist in complete and final form and was resolved that his story would follow the same pattern. Molding his experience into the expected narrative form was particularly difficult, however, because though life in the melodramas proceeds in discontinuous jumps, the process through which Singer conceived, built, and developed his sewing machine was unusually systematic and progressive. Singer first saw a sewing machine in the spring of 1850, and his associates Orson Phelps and George Zieber, recognizing his skill in mechanical contrivance, urged him for months to build an improved version of it. Singer, however, insisted that he had never put his mind to the problem or taken their suggestions seriously until one momentous day in September 1850. His account reduces the process of redesigning the earlier machine to one night of intense creative thought: "I took the matter into consideration that night and satisfied myself that I could so improve sewing machines as to render them applicable to the sewing of all kinds of work. . . . Upon seeing Phelps and Zieber the next day I told them that I had considered the matter and had the general plan worked out in my mind, and I proceeded at once to make a rough sketch of the machine I proposed to make."[15] Singer knew, of course, that to fulfill the requirements of the myth heroic inventors must face a twenty-four-hour deadline at some point, and this seems to have been the most convenient place in his story to include it. His claim that the sketch showed all the principal features of the completed machine is not improbable, however, since he had actually played with the problem for three or four months.

In describing how the prototype was built, Singer continued his self-portrait as a romantic hero in the grip of a creative frenzy. "I worked at the matter day and night," he said, "sleeping but three or four hours out of the twenty-four and eating generally but once a day." He exaggerated the project's real limitations of money and time in order to create the kind of sharply defined dilemma so popular in the melodramas. He recalled that his financial backer, George Zieber, had only forty dollars left, and in the manner of the hero in "The Wings of Icarus" he explained, "I knew that I must get a machine made for the $40, or not get it at all."[16] Singer's story of superhuman effort seemed a bit exaggerated to one lawyer, who later asked Phelps's foreman Jott Grant about it. "Was he there all day and all night for a fortnight?" asked the lawyer. "What I meant in speaking of all day and all night," Grant conceded, "was the usual day's work of a man, and up to 10 or 11 o'clock at night." "He did not sleep there?" "No, sir."[17]

One detail that makes Singer's account of heroic endeavor seem slightly ludicrous is that he could actually do very little to help when the machine was being built. In his four-month apprenticeship as a machinist he had mastered few of the basic skills, and thus while Jott Grant and one or two of Phelps's other workmen made the parts of the machine, Singer paced restlessly around the shop, unable to put his terrific nervous energy to use. He spent much of his time putting on

dramatic performances, which were well received, for the workmen in the shop. "Did he have a company there to assist him in entertaining the workmen?" a lawyer asked Grant. "No, no, he was alone. . . . It was a solo: he would speak different parts at different times."

"Declaim?"

"Declaim."

"Did that materially assist you in the construction of the sewing machine?"

"It rather amused anybody that was at work night and day, especially if they were not particularly interested in the machine."[18]

More than anything else, Singer's impatience seems to have been the reason why the first machine was built in such a desperate hurry. Limited funds were available for it, but since the men would have been paid for the hours they worked in any case, the machine would have cost about the same if it had been made during the usual working hours. No matter: creative geniuses are supposed to work at a terrific pace, and Singer's later telling of the story emphasizes the pressure of an implied deadline: "the machine was completed the night of the eleventh day from the day it was commenced," he remembered.[19]

The conventions of melodrama also require a last-minute difficulty to heighten the suspense, and the story Singer and Zieber later told does not disappoint us: "About nine o'clock that evening we got the parts of the machine together and commenced trying it. The first attempts to sew were unsuccessful and the workmen, who were tired out with almost unremitting work left me intimating that it was a failure. I continued trying the machine with Zieber to hold a lamp for me, but in the nervous condition to which I had been reduced by incessant work and anxiety, was unsuccessful in getting the machine to sew tight stitches."[20] In Singer's story he and Zieber thought of the solution as they "sat on a pile of boards" resting on the way to their hotel that night, but Zieber's recollection that they were in bed before it occurred to them is more probable. Zieber asked him if he had noticed that the loose loops of thread on the upper side of the cloth came from the needle, and "it then flashed upon me," Singer said, "that I had forgotten to adjust the tension on the needle thread." Zieber described Singer's reaction: "'By God' (he was much addicted to profanity), 'do you think so,' he said. 'Let's go back to the shop and try it again.'"[21]

The important point about Singer's account of a deadline and a last-minute difficulty is not that it is factually inaccurate, but rather that it is an *interpretation* of the facts showing an awareness of literary models, and that it is shaped in a way that expresses certain assumptions that another viewer of the same events might not have held. That it is a deliberate distortion is unlikely because it is taken from a deposition Singer gave under oath, and indeed the basic facts are not improbable. In a crash program the machine could certainly have been built in eleven days, and fatigue could well have prevented the wrought-up Singer from seeing the problem until he began to relax. The workmen's desertion no doubt occurred, too—it was, after all, late evening—though their gloomy judgment of the machine, which Singer took seriously, might only have been Jott Grant's way of having some fun at the expense of the feverish inventor. Grant had a sly sense of humor that on occasion could turn to sarcasm, and after a long day of putting up with Singer's frequently violent temper, he might have offered a poker-faced opinion that the machine was a failure for the pleasure of seeing Singer's face go purple with frustration. Singer, who never was sensitive to humor or nuance anyway, would have been too deeply immersed in his project to detect the tone.

But even though the raw outlines of the story are accurate, it is misleading in its suggestion that after two weeks of effort and a few flashes of inspiration the essential work of invention was completed. Unlike ordinary mortals, the genius is never supposed to have tentative or partially developed ideas; the concept springs into his mind fully formed. "Zieber and I went back to the shop," Singer continued. "I adjusted the tension, tried the machine, and sewed five stitches perfectly, when the thread broke. The perfection of these stitches satisfied me that the machine was a success, and I stopped work, went to the hotel and had a sound sleep. By three o'clock the next day I had the machine finished."[22] It was "finished," said Singer, and so it should have been, according to the conventions of this kind of story. But in fact at that point it worked scarcely better than the Blodgett & Lerow machine that it was based on. A particularly serious defect still remaining was precisely the feature that Singer suggests he perfected in this last moment of inspiration, the tension device for the needle thread. Compression of the process of invention into a few large steps makes a tidy story, but reality is often far different. It certainly was different in Singer's case, in which the final excellence of the machine was due to his painstaking elimination of innumerable small weaknesses over a period of several years. Since the problem with the tension mechanism was similar to so many others encountered during construction of the machine, it made no special impression on Jott Grant, though he certainly would have known about it. "Have you any recollection of the time when the machine was finished?" a lawyer later asked him, clearly fishing for the story of its triumphant completion. "I remember of it being finished," Grant replied vaguely, "and that we exper-

imented with it once or twice after it was finished. I don't remember any particular time."[23]

The accounts given by both Howe and Singer show that they were strongly aware of popular ideas about their role as inventors and were willing to select and adapt the facts of their own lives to conform to the expected pattern. In particular, they put extreme emphasis on the moment of inspiration, reducing the essential activity of invention to a single flash of insight verified by a quick experiment and suggesting (very inaccurately, in both cases) that their original conceptions required little modification or development before they were perfect. Not only the inventive process but life itself is shown in their narratives as discontinuous rather than evolutionary: their accounts exaggerate and focus events in order to create the kind of sharply defined dilemmas that were popular in the melodramas. And in their self-portraits they borrowed from conventional notions of the romantic genius, Howe stressing the visionary qualities of the type, Singer his titanic passions. But even though their narratives are sometimes not reliable as historical fact, they do express the dreams of the inventors and thus have much interest for us. Stories of invention can have many endings, but all of them start with a dream.

Notes

[1] "The Inventor of Lithography," *Boston Daily Advertiser,* 13 Jan. 1841.

[2] Untitled article on John Slocom, inventor of the pin-making machine, *Boston Daily Advertiser and Patriot,* 30 April 1841.

[3] "The Wings of Icarus, or, The Provincial in Paris," *Boston Monthly Chronicle,* reprint, in the *Boston Daily Advertiser,* 25 March 1841.

[4] George Arrowsmith, Testimony given for *Howe v. Hunt,* in Singer and Co. Archives, State Historical Society of Wisconsin, Madison.

[5] James Parton, "History of the Sewing Machine," *The Atlantic Monthly,* May 1867, 527-44.

[6] "The Sewing Machine," *New York Daily Tribune,* 23 May 1862.

[7] Parton, "History of the Sewing Machine," 527.

[8] Thomas Hall to Dr. Alonzo Bemis, 8 Dec. 1910, in Percy H. Epler, "Elias Howe, Jr., Inventor of the Sewing Machine, 1819-1919, A Centennial Address," *Proc. of the Cambridge Historical Society,* Oct. 1919, 128-29.

[9] Thomas Waln-Morgan Draper, *The Bemis History and Genealogy, Being an Account, in Greater Part, of*

the Descendants of Joseph Bemis of Watertown, Mass. (San Francisco: Stanley Taylor, 1900), 160.

[10] Samuel Taylor Coleridge, *The Complete Poetical Works,* 2 vols. (Oxford: Clarendon Press, 1912), 1:296.

[11] Parton, "History of the Sewing Machine," 530.

[12] Parton, "History of the Sewing Machine," 530.

[13] George Fisher, Testimony given for *Howe v. Hunt,* in extension files for Howe patent of 1846, National Archives.

[14] Ruth M. Brandon, *A Capitalist Romance: Singer and the Sewing Machine* (Philadelphia: Lippincott, 1977), 20.

[15] Isaac Singer, Testimony given for *Singer v. Walmsley,* in extension files for Singer 1851 patent, National Archives.

[16] Singer, Testimony.

[17] Jott Grant, Testimony given for Extension Files for Singer 1851 Patent, in extension files for Singer 1851 patent, National Archives.

[18] Grant, Testimony.

[19] Singer, Testimony.

[20] Singer, Testimony.

[21] Singer, Testimony; Zieber's remarks from his memoirs, quoted in Brandon, *A Capitalist Romance,* 48.

[22] Singer, Testimony.

[23] Grant, Testimony.

CONTEMPORARY REACTIONS TO THE MACHINE

Thomas Carlyle

SOURCE: "Signs of the Times," in *Critical and Miscellaneous Essays,* D. Appleton and Company, 1873, pp. 187-96.

[*In the following essay, originally published in 1829 in the* Edinburgh Review, *Carlyle describes what he observes to be the largely negative influence of modern technology on the action, thought, and feeling of nineteenth-century society.*]

It is no very good symptom either of nations or individuals, that they deal much in vaticination. Happy men are full of the present, for its bounty suffices them; and wise men also, for its duties engage them. Our grand business undoubtedly is, not to *see* what lies dimly at a distance, but to *do* what lies clearly at hand.

> Know'st thou *Yesterday,* its aim and reason?
> Work'st thou well *To-day,* for worthy things?
> Then calmly wait the *Morrow's* hidden season,
> And fear not thou, what hap soe'er it brings!

But man's "large discourse of reason" *will* look "before and after;" and, impatient of "the ignorant present time," will indulge in anticipation far more than profits him. Seldom can the unhappy be persuaded that the evil of the day is sufficient for it; and the ambitious will not be content with present splendour, but paints yet more glorious triumphs, on the cloud-curtain of the future.

The case, however, is still worse with nations. For here the prophets are not one, but many; and each incites and confirms the other; so that the fatidical fury spreads wider and wider, till at last even Saul must join in it. For there is still a real magic in the action and reaction of minds on one another. The casual deliration of a few becomes, by this mysterious reverberation, the frenzy of many; men lose the use, not only of their understandings, but of their bodily senses; while the most obdurate, unbelieving hearts melt, like the rest, in the furnace where all are cast as victims and as fuel. It is grievous to think, that this noble omnipotence of Sympathy has been so rarely the Aaron's-rod of Truth and Virtue, and so often the Enchanter's-rod of Wickedness and Folly! No solitary miscreant, scarcely any solitary maniac, would venture on such actions and imaginations, as large communities of sane men have, in such circumstances, entertained as sound wisdom. Witness long scenes of the French Revolution! a whole people drunk with blood and arrogance, and then with terror and cruelty, and with desperation, and blood again! Levity is no protection against such visitations, nor the utmost earnestness of character. The New England Puritan burns witches, wrestles for months with the horrors of Satan's invisible world, and all ghastly phantasms, the daily and hourly precursors of the Last Day; then suddenly bethinks him that he is frantic, weeps bitterly, prays contritely, and the history of that gloomy season lies behind him like a frightful dream.

And Old England has had her share of such frenzies and panics; though happily, like other old maladies, they have grown milder of late: and since the days of Titus Oates, have mostly passed without loss of men's lives, or indeed without much other loss than that of reason, for the time, in the sufferers. In this mitigated form, however, the distemper is of pretty regular recurrence; and may be reckoned on at intervals, like other natural visitations; so that reasonable men deal with it, as the Londoners do with their fogs,—go cautiously out into the groping crowd, and patiently carry lanterns at noon; knowing, by a well grounded faith, that the sun is still in existence, and will one day reappear. How often have we heard, for the last fifty years, that the country was wrecked, and fast sinking; whereas, up to this date, the country is entire and afloat! The "State in Danger" is a condition of things, which we have witnessed a hundred times; and as for the church, it has seldom been out of "danger" since we can remember.

All men are aware, that the present is a crisis of this sort; and why it has become so. The repeal of the Test Acts, and then of the Catholic disabilities, has struck many of their admirers with an indescribable astonishment. Those things seemed fixed and immovable; deep as the foundations of the world; and lo! in a moment they have vanished, and their place knows them no more! Our worthy friends mistook the slumbering Leviathan for an island; often as they had been assured, that intolerance was, and could be nothing but a Monster; and so, mooring under the lee, they had anchored comfortably in his scaly rind, thinking to take good cheer; as for some space they did. But now their Leviathan has suddenly dived under; and they can no longer be fastened in the stream of time; but must drift forward on it, even like the rest of the world; no very appalling fate, we think, could they but understand it: which, however, they will not yet, for a season. Their little island is gone, and sunk deep amid confused eddies; and what is left worth caring for in the universe? What is it to them, that the great continents of the earth are still standing; and the polestar and all our loadstars, in the heavens, still shining and eternal? Their cherished little haven is gone, and they will not be comforted! And therefore, day after day, in all manner of periodical or perennial publications, the most lugubrious predictions are sent forth. The king has virtually abdicated; the church is a widow, without jointure; public principle is gone; private honesty is going; society, in short, is fast falling in pieces; and a time of unmixed evil is come on us. At such a period, it was to be expected that the rage of prophecy should be more than usually excited. Accordingly, the Millenarians have come forth on the right hand, and the Millites on the left. The Fifth-monarchy men prophesy from the Bible, and the Utilitarians from Bentham. The one announces that the last of the seals is to be opened, positively, in the year 1860; and the other assures us, that "the greatest happiness principle" is to make a heaven of earth, in a still shorter time. We know these symptoms too well, to think it necessary or safe to interfere with them. Time and the hours will bring relief to all parties. The grand encourager of Delphic or other noises is—the Echo. Left to themselves, they will soon dissipate, and die away in space.

Meanwhile, we too admit that the present is an important time; as all present time necessarily is. The poorest day that passes over us is the conflux of two Eternities! and is made up of currents that issue from the remotest Past, and flow onwards into the remotest Future. We were wise indeed, could we discern truly the signs of our own time; and by knowledge of its wants and advantages, wisely adjust our own position in it. Let us then, instead of gazing idly into the obscure distance, look calmly around us for a little, on the perplexed scene where we stand. Perhaps, on a more serious inspection, something of its perplexity will disappear, some of its distinctive characters, and deeper tendencies, more clearly reveal themselves; whereby our own relations to it, our own true aims and endeavours in it, may also become clearer.

Were we required to characterize this age of ours by any single epithet, we should be tempted to call it, not an Heroical, Devotional, Philosophical, or Moral Age, but, above all others, the Mechanical Age. It is the Age of Machinery, in every outward and inward sense of that word; the age which, with its whole undivided might, forwards, teaches, and practises the great art of adopting means to ends. Nothing is now done directly, or by hand; all is by rule and calculated contrivance. For the simplest operation, some helps and accompaniments, some cunning, abbreviating process is in readiness. Our old modes of exertion are all discredited, and thrown aside. On every hand, the living artisan is driven from his workshop, to make room for a speedier, inanimate one. The shuttle drops from the fingers of the weaver, and falls into iron fingers that ply it faster. The sailor furls his sail, and lays down his oar, and bids a strong, unwearied servant, on vapourous wings, bear him through the waters. Men have crossed oceans by steam; the Birmingham Fire-king has visited the fabulous East; and the genius of the Cape, were there any Camoens now to sing it, has again been alarmed, and with far stranger thunders than Gama's. There is no end to machinery. Even the horse is stripped of his harness, and finds a fleet fire-horse yoked in his stead. Nay, we have an artist that hatches chickens by steam; the very brood-hen is to be superseded! For all earthly, and for some unearthly purposes, we have machines and mechanic furtherances; for mincing our cabbages; for casting us into magnetic sleep. We remove mountains, and make seas our smooth highway; nothing can resist us. We war with rude nature; and, by our resistless engines, come off always victorious, and loaded with spoils.

What wonderful accessions have thus been made, and are still making, to the physical power of mankind; how much better fed, clothed, lodged, and, in all outward respects, accommodated, men now are, or might be, by a given quantity of labour, is a grateful reflection which forces itself on every one. What changes, too, this addition of power is introducing into the social system; how wealth has more and more increased, and at the same time gathered itself more and more into masses, strangely altering the old relations, and increasing the distance between the rich and the poor, will be a question for Political Economists, and a much more complex and important one than any they have yet engaged with. But leaving these matters for the present, let us observe how the mechanical genius of our time has diffused itself into quite other provinces. Not the external and physical alone is now managed by machinery, but the internal and spiritual also. Here, too, nothing follows its spontaneous course, nothing is left to be accomplished by old, natural methods. Every thing has its cunningly devised implements, its pre-established apparatus; it is not done by hand, but by machinery. Thus we have machines for Education: Lancastrin machines: Hamiltonian machines; Monitors, maps, and emblems, Instruction, that mysterious communing of Wisdom with Ignorance, is no longer an indefinable tentative process, requiring a study of individual aptitudes, and a perpetual variation of means and methods, to attain the same end; but a secure, universal, straight-forward business, to be conducted in the gross, by proper mechanism, with such intellect as comes to hand. Then, we have Religious machines, of all imaginable varieties; the Bible Society, professing a far higher and heavenly structure, is found, on inquiry, to be altogether an earthly contrivance, supported by collection of moneys, by fomenting of vanities, by puffing, intrigue, and chicane; and yet, in effect, a very excellent machine for converting the heathen. It is the same in all other departments. Has any man, or any society of men, a truth to speak, a piece of spiritual work to do, they can nowise proceed at once, and with the mere natural organs, but must first call a public meeting, appoint committees, issue prospectuses, eat a public dinner; in a word, construct or borrow machinery, wherewith to speak it and do it. Without machinery they were hopeless, helpless; a colony of Hindoo weavers squatting in the heart of Lancashire. Then every machine must have its moving power, in some of the great currents of society: Every little sect among us, Unitarians, Utilitarians, Anabaptists, Phrenologists, must each have its periodical, its monthly or quarterly magazine,—hanging out, like its windmill, into the *popularis aura,* to grind meal for the society.

With individuals, in like manner, natural strength avails little. No individual now hopes to accomplish the poorest enterprise single-handed, and without mechanical aids; he must make interest with some existing corporation, and till his field with their oxen. In these days, more emphatically than ever, "to live, signifies to unite with a party, or to make one." Philosophy, Science, Art, Literature, all depend on machinery. No Newton, by silent meditation, now discovers the system of the world from the falling of an apple; but some quite other than Newton stands in his Museum, his Scientific Institution, and behind whole batteries of retorts,

digesters, and galvanic piles imperatively "interrogates Nature,"—who, however, shows no haste to answer. In defect of Raphaels, and Angelos, and Mozarts, we have Royal Academies of Painting, Sculpture, Music; whereby the languishing spirit of art may be strengthened by the more generous diet of a Public Kitchen. Literature too, has its Paternoster-row mechanism, its Trade dinners, its Editorial conclaves, and huge subterranean puffing bellows; so that books are not only printed, but, in a great measure, written and sold, by machinery. National culture, spiritual benefit of all sorts, is under the same management. No Queen Christina, in these times, needs to send for her Descartes; no King Frederic for his Voltaire, and painfully nourish him with pensions and flattery: but any sovereign of taste, who wishes to enlighten his people, has only to impose a new tax, and with the proceeds establish Philosophic Institutes. Hence the Royal and imperial Societies, the Bibliothèques, Glyptothèques, Technothèques, which front us in all capital cities, like so many well-finished hives, to which it is expected the stray agencies of Wisdom will swarm of their own accord, and hive and make honey. In like manner, among ourselves, when it is thought that religion is declining, we have only to vote half a million's worth of bricks and mortar, and build new churches. In Ireland, it seems they have gone still farther; having actually established a "Penny-a-week Purgatory Society!" Thus does the Genius of Mechanism stand by to help us in all difficulties and emergencies; and, with his iron back, bears all our burdens.

These things, which we state lightly enough here, are yet of deep import, and indicate a mighty change in our whole manner of existence. For the same habit regulates not our modes of action alone, but our modes of thought and feeling. Men are grown mechanical in head and in heart, as well as in hand. They have lost faith in individual endeavour, and in natural force, of any kind. Not for internal perfection, but for external combinations and arrangements, for institutions, constitutions,—for Mechanism of one sort or other, do they hope and struggle. Their whole efforts, attachments, opinions, turn on mechanism, and are of a mechanical character.

We may trace this tendency, we think, very distinctly, in all the great manifestations of our time; in its intellectual aspect, the studies it most favours, and its manner of conducting them; in its practical aspects, its politics, arts, religion, morals; in the whole sources, and throughout the whole currents, of its spiritual, no less than its material activity.

Consider, for example, the state of Science generally, in Europe, at this period. It is admitted, on all sides, that the Metaphysical and Moral Sciences are falling into decay, while the Physical are engrossing, every day, more respect and attention. In most of the European nations, there is now no such thing as a Science of Mind; only more or less advancement in the general science, or the special sciences, of matter. The French were the first to desert this school of Metaphysics; and though they have lately affected to revive it, it has yet no signs of vitality. The land of Malebranche, Pascal, Descartes, and Fenelon, has now only its Cousins and Villemains; while, in the department of Physics, it reckons far other names. Among ourselves, the Philosophy of Mind, after a rickety infancy, which never reached the vigour of manhood, fell suddenly into decay, languished, and finally died out, with its last amiable cultivator, Professor Stewart. In no nation but Germany has any decisive effort been made in psychological science; not to speak of any decisive result. The science of the age, in short, is physical, chemical, physiological, and, in all shapes, mechanical. Our favourite Mathematics, the highly prized exponent of all these other sciences, has also become more and more mechanical. Excellence, in what is called its higher departments, depends less on natural genius, than on acquired expertness in wielding its machinery. Without undervaluing the wonderful results which a Lagrange, or Laplace, educes by means of it, we may remark, that its calculus, differential and integral, is little else than a more cunningly-constructed arithmetical mill, where the factors being put in, are, as it were, ground into the true product, under cover, and without other effort, on our part, than steady turning of the handle. We have more Mathematics certainly than ever; but less Mathesis. Archimedes and Plato could not have read the *Mécanique Céleste;* but neither would the whole French Institute see aught in that saying, "God geometrizes!" but a sentimental rodomontade.

From Locke's time downwards, our whole Metaphysics have been physical; not a spiritual Philosophy, but a material one. The singular estimation in which his Essay was so long held as a scientific work, (for the character of the man entitled all he said to veneration,) will one day be thought a curious indication of the spirit of these times. His whole doctrine is mechanical, in its aim and origin, in its method and its results. It is a mere discussion concerning the origin of our consciousness, or ideas, or whatever else they are called; a genetic history of what we see in the mind. But the grand secrets of Necessity and Free-will, of the mind's vital or nonvital dependence on matter, of our mysterious relations to Time and Space, to God, to the universe, are not, in the faintest degree, touched on in these inquiries; and seem not to have the smallest connection with them.

The last class of our Scotch Metaphysicians had a dim notion that much of this was wrong; but they knew not how to right it. The school of Reid had also from the first taken a mechanical course, not seeing any other. The singular conclusions at which Hume, setting out from their admitted premises, was arriving, brought this school into being; they let loose Instinct, as an undiscriminating ban-dog, to guard them against these conclusions;—they tugged lustily at the logical chain by which Hume was so coldly towing them and the world into bottomless abysses of Atheism and Fatalism. But the chain somehow snapped between them; and the issue has been that nobody now cares about either,—any more than about Hartley's, Darwin's, or Priestley's contemporaneous doings in England. Hartley's vibrations and vibratiuncles one would think were material and mechanical enough; but our continental neighbours have gone still farther. One of their philosophers has lately discovered, that "as the liver secretes bile, so does the brain secrete thought;" which astonishing discovery Dr. Cabanis, more lately still, in his *Rapports du Physique et du Morale de l'Homme,* has pushed into its minutest developments. The metaphysical philosophy of this last inquirer is certainly no shadowy or unsubstantial one. He fairly lays open our moral structure with his dissecting-knives and real metal probes; and exhibits it to the inspection of mankind, by Leuwenhoek microscopes and inflation with the anatomical blowpipe. Thought, he is inclined to hold, is still secreted by the brain; but then Poetry and Religion (and it is really worth knowing) are "a product of the smaller intestines!" We have the greatest admiration for this learned doctor: with what scientific stoicism he walks through the land of wonders, unwondering; like a wise man through some huge, gaudy, imposing Vauxhall, whose fire-works, cascades, and symphonies, the vulgar may enjoy and believe in,—but where he finds nothing real but the saltpetre, pasteboard, and catgut. His book may be regarded as the ultimatum of mechanical metaphysics in our time; a remarkable realization of what in Martinus Scriblerus was still only an idea, that "as the jack had a meat-roasting quality, so had the body a thinking quality"—upon the strength of which the Nurembergers were to build a wood and leather man, "who should reason as well as most country parsons." Vaucanson did indeed make a wooden duck, that seemed to eat and digest; but that bold scheme of the Nurembergers remained for a more modern virtuoso.

This condition of the two great departments of knowledge—the outward, cultivated exclusively on mechanical principles; the inward finally abandoned, because, cultivated on such principles, it is found to yield no result—sufficiently indicates the intellectual bias of our time, its all-pervading disposition towards that line of inquiry. In fact, an inward persuasion has long been diffusing itself, and now and then even comes to utterance, that, except the external, there are no true sciences; that to the inward world (if there be any) our only conceivable road is through the outward; that, in short, what cannot be investigated and understood mechanically, cannot be investigated and understood at all. We advert the more particularly to these intellectual propensities, as to prominent symptoms of our age; because Opinion is at all times doubly related to Action, first as cause, then as effect; and the speculative tendency of any age will therefore give us, on the whole, the best indications of its practical tendency.

Nowhere, for example, is the deep, almost exclusive faith, we have in Mechanism, more visible than in the Politics of this time. Civil government does, by its nature, include much that is mechanical, and must be treated accordingly. We term it, indeed, in ordinary language, the Machine of Society, and talk of it as the grand working wheel from which all private machines must derive, or to which they must adapt, their movements. Considered merely as a metaphor, all this is well enough; but here, as in so many other cases, the "foam hardens itself into a shell," and the shadow we have wantonly evoked stands terribly before us, and will not depart at our bidding. Government includes much also that is not mechanical, and cannot be treated mechanically; of which latter truth, as appears to us, the political speculations and exertions of our time are taking less and less cognisance.

Nay, in the very outset, we might note the mighty interest taken in *mere political arrangements, as itself* the sign of a mechanical age. The whole discontent of Europe takes this direction. The deep, strong cry of all civilized nations—a cry which every one now sees, must and will be answered—is, Give us a reform of Government! A good structure of legislation,—a proper check upon the executive,—a wise arrangement of the judiciary, is *all* that is wanting for human happiness. The Philosopher of this age is not a Socrates, a Plato, a Hooker, or Taylor, who inculcates on men the necessity and infinite worth of moral goodness, the great truth that our happiness depends on the mind which is within us, and not on the circumstances which are without us; but a Smith, a De Lolme, a Bentham, who chiefly inculcates the reverse of this,—that our happiness depends entirely on external circumstances; nay, that the strength and dignity of the mind within us is itself the creature and consequence of these. Were the laws, the government, in good order, all were well with us; the rest would care for itself! Dissentients from this opinion, expressed or implied, are now rarely to be met with; widely and angrily as men differ in its application, the principle is admitted by all.

Equally mechanical, and of equal simplicity, are the methods proposed by both parties for completing or securing this all-sufficient perfection of arrangement. It is no longer the moral, religious, spiritual condition of the people that is our concern, but their physical, practical, economical condition, as regulated by public laws. Thus is the Body-politic more than ever worshipped and tended: but the Soul-politic less than ever. Love of country, in any high or generous sense, in any other than an almost animal sense, or mere habit, has

little importance attached to it in such reforms, or in the opposition shown them. Men are to be guided only by their self-interests. Good government is a good balancing of these; and, except a keen eye and appetite for self-interest, requires no virtue in any quarter. To both parties it is emphatically a machine: to the discontented, a "taxing machine;" to the contented, a "machine for securing property." Its duties and its faults are not those of a father, but of an active parish constable.

Thus it is by the mere condition of the machine; by preserving it untouched, or else by re-constructing it, and oiling it anew, that man's salvation as a social being is to be insured and indefinitely promoted. Contrive the fabric of law aright, and without farther effort on your part, that divine spirit of freedom, which all hearts venerate and long for, will of herself come to inhabit it; and under her healing wings every noxious influence will wither, every good and salutary one more and more expand. Nay, so devoted are we to this principle, and at the same time so curiously mechanical, that a new trade, specially grounded in it, has arisen among us, under the name of "Codification," or code-making in the abstract; whereby any people, for a reasonable consideration, may be accommodated with a patent code,—more easily than curious individuals with patent breeches, for the people does *not* need to be measured first.

To us who live in the midst of all this, and see continually the faith, hope, and practice of every one founded on Mechanism of one kind or other, it is apt to seem quite natural and as if it could never have been otherwise Nevertheless, if we recollect or reflect a little, we shall find both that it has been, and might again be, otherwise. The domain of Mechanism,—meaning thereby political, ecclesiastical, or other outward establishments,—was once considered as embracing, and we are persuaded can at any time embrace but a limited portion of man's interests, and by no means the highest portion.

To speak a little pedantically, there is a science of *Dynamics* in man's fortunes and nature, as well as of *Mechanics*. There is a science which treats of, and practically addresses, the primary, unmodified forces and energies of man, the mysterious springs of Love, and Fear, and Wonder, of Enthusiasm, Poetry, Religion, all which have a truly vital and *infinite* character; as well as a science which practically addresses the finite, modified developments of these, when they take the shape of immediate "motives," as hope of reward, or as fear of punishment.

Now it is certain, that in former times the wise men, the enlightened lovers of their kind, who appeared generally as Moralists, Poets, or Priests, did, without neglecting the Mechanical province, deal chiefly with the Dynamical; applying themselves chiefly to regulate, increase, and purify the inward primary powers of man; and fancying that herein lay the main difficulty, and the best service they could undertake. But a wide difference is manifest in our age. For the wise men, who now appear as Political Philosophers, deal exclusively with the Mechanical province; and occupying themselves in counting up and estimating men's motives, strive by curious checking and balancing, and other adjustments of Profit and Loss, to guide them to their true advantage: while, unfortunately, those same "motives" are so innumerable, and so variable in every individual, that no really useful conclusion can ever be drawn from their enumeration. But though Mechanism, wisely contrived, has done much for man, in a social and moral point of view, we cannot be persuaded that it has ever been the chief source of his worth or happiness. Consider the great elements of human enjoyment, the attainments and possessions that exalt man's life to its present height, and see what part of these he owes to institutions, to Mechanism of any kind; and what to the instinctive, unbounded force, which Nature herself lent him, and still continues to him. Shall we say, for example, that Science and Art are indebted principally to the founders of Schools and universities? Did not Science originate rather, and gain advancement, in the obscure closets of the Roger Bacons, Keplers, Newtons; in the workshops of the Fausts and the Watts; wherever, and in what guise soever Nature, from the first times downwards, had sent a gifted spirit upon the earth? Again, were Homer and Shakespeare members of any beneficial guild, or made Poets by means of it? Were Painting and Sculpture created by forethought, brought into the world by institutions for that end? No; Science and Art have, from first to last, been the free gift of Nature; an unsolicited, unexpected gift: often even a fatal one. These things rose up, as it were by spontaneous growth, in the free soil and sunshine of Nature. They were not planted or grafted, nor even greatly multiplied or improved by the culture or manuring of institutions. Generally speaking, they have derived only partial help from these: often have suffered damage. They made constitutions for themselves. They originated in the Dynamical nature of man, and not in his Mechanical nature.

Or, to take an infinitely higher instance, that of the Christian Religion, which, under every theory of it, in the believing or the unbelieving mind, must be ever regarded as the crowning glory, or rather the life and soul, of our whole modern culture: How did Christianity arise and spread abroad among men? Was it by institutions, and establishments, and well-arranged systems of mechanism? Not so; on the contrary, in all past and existing institutions for those ends, its divine spirit has invariably been found to languish and decay. It arose in the mystic deeps of man's soul; and was spread abroad by the "preaching of the word," by simple, altogether natural and individual efforts; and flew,

like hallowed fire, from heart to heart, till all were purified and illuminated by it; and its heavenly light shone, as it still shines, and as sun or star will ever shine, through the whole dark destinies of man. Here again was no Mechanism; man's highest attainment was accomplished, Dynamically, not Mechanically. Nay, we will venture to say, that no high attainment, not even any far-extending movement among men, was ever accomplished otherwise. Strange as it may seem, if we read History with any degree of thoughtfulness, we shall find, that the checks and balances of Profit and Loss have never been the grand agents with man; that they have never been roused into deep, thorough, all-pervading efforts by any computable prospect of Profit and Loss, for any visible, finite object; but always for some invisible and infinite one. The Crusades took their rise in Religion; their visible object was, commercially speaking, worth nothing. It was the boundless, Invisible world that was laid bare in the imaginations of those men; and in its burning light, the visible shrunk as a scroll. Not mechanical, nor produced by mechanical means, was this vast movement. No dining at Freemasons' Tavern, with the other long train of modern machinery; no cunning reconciliation of "vested interests," was required here: only the passionate voice of one man, the rapt soul looking through the eyes of one man; and rugged, steel-clad Europe trembled beneath his words, and followed him whither he listed. In later ages, it was still the same. The Reformation had an invisible, mystic, and ideal aim; the result was indeed to be embodied in external things; but its spirit, its worth, was internal, invisible, infinite. Our English Revolution, too, originated in Religion. Men did battle, in those days, not for Purse sake, but for Conscience sake. Nay, in our own days, it is no way different. The French Revolution itself had something higher in it than cheap bread and a Habeas-corpus act. Here, too, was an Idea; a Dynamic, not a Mechanic force. It was a struggle, though a blind and at last an insane one, for the infinite, divine nature of Right, of Freedom, of Country.

Thus does man, in every age, vindicate, consciously or unconsciously, his celestial birthright. Thus does nature hold on her wondrous, unquestionable course; and all our systems and theories are but so many forth-eddies or sand-banks, which from time to time she casts up and washes away. When we can drain the Ocean into our mill-pounds, and bottle up the Force of Gravity, to be sold by retail, in our gas-jars; then may we hope to comprehend the infinitudes of man's soul under formulas of Profit and Loss; and rule over this too, as over a patent engine, by checks, and valves, and balances.

Nay, even with regard to Government itself, can it be necessary to remind any one that Freedom, without which indeed all spiritual life is impossible, depends on infinitely more complex influences than either the extension or the curtailment of the "democratic interest?" Who is there that, "taking the high *priori* road," shall point out what these influences are; what deep, subtle, inextricably entangled influences they have been, and may be? For man is not the creature and product of Mechanism; but, in a far truer sense, its creator and producer: it is the noble people that makes the noble Government; rather than conversely. On the whole, Institutions are much; but they are not all. The freest and highest spirits of the world have often been found under strange outward circumstances: Saint Paul and his brother Apostles were politically slaves; Epictents was personally one. Again, forget the influences of Chivalry and Religion, and ask,—what countries produced Columbus and Las Casas? Or, descending from virtue and heroism, to mere energy and spiritual talent: Cortes, Pizarro, Alba, Ximenes? The Spaniards of the sixteenth century were indisputably the noblest nation of Europe; yet they had the Inquisition, and Philip II. They have the same government at this day; and are the lowest nation. The Dutch, too, have retained their old constitution; but no Siege of Leyden, no William the Silent, not even an Egmont or De Witt, any longer appears among them. With ourselves, also, where much has changed, effect has nowise followed cause, as it should have done: two centuries ago, the Commons' Speaker addressed Queen Elizabeth on bended knees, happy that the virago's foot did not even smite him; yet the people were then governed, not by a Castlereagh, but by a Burghley; they had their Shakespeare and Philip Sidney, where we have our Sheridan Knowles and Beau Brummel.

These and the like facts are so familiar, the truths which they preach so obvious, and have in all past times been so universally believed and acted on, that we should almost feel ashamed for repeating them; were it not that, on, every hand, the memory of them seems to have passed away, or at best died into a faint tradition, of no value as a practical principle. To judge by the loud clamour of our Constitution builders, Statists, Economists, directors, creators, reformers of Public Societies; in a word, all manner of Mechanists, from the Cartwright up to the Code-maker; and by the nearly total silence of all Preachers and Teachers who should give a voice to Poetry, Religion, and Morality, we might fancy either that man's Dynamical nature was, to all spiritual intents, extinct, or else so perfected, that nothing more was to be made of it by the old means; and henceforth only in his Mechanical contrivances did any hope exist for him.

To define the limits of these two departments of man's activity, which work into one another, and by means of one another, so intricately and inseparably, were by its nature an impossible attempt. Their relative importance, even to the wisest mind, will vary in different times, according to the special wants and dispositions of these times. Meanwhile, it seems clear enough that only in the right co-ordination of the two, and the vigorous forwarding of *both,* does our true line of action lie. Undue cultivation of the inward or Dynamical province leads to idle, visionary, impracticable courses, and, especially in rude eras, to Superstition and Fanaticism, with their long train of baleful and well-known evils. Undue cultivation of the outward, again, though less immediately prejudicial, and even for the time productive of many palpable benefits, must, in the long run, by destroying Moral Force, which is the parent of all other Force, prove not less certainly, and perhaps still more hopelessly, pernicious. This, we take it, is the grand characteristic of our age. By our skill in Mechanism, it has come to pass that, in the management of external things, we excel all other ages; while in whatever respects the pure moral nature, in true dignity of soul and character, we are perhaps inferior to most civilized ages.

In fact, if we look deeper, we shall find that this faith in Mechanism has now struck its roots deep into men's most intimate, primary sources of conviction; and is thence sending up, over his whole life and activity, innumerable stems,—fruit-bearing and poison-bearing. The truth is, men have lost their belief in the Invisible, and believe, and hope, and work only in the Visible; or, to speak it in other words, This is not a Religious age. Only the material, the immediately practical, not the divine and spiritual, is important to us. The infinite, absolute character of Virtue has passed into a finite, conditional one; it is no longer a worship of the Beautiful and Good; but a calculation of the Profitable. Worship, indeed, in any sense, is not recognised among us, or is mechanically explained into Fear of pain, or Hope of pleasure. Our true Deity is Mechanism. It has subdued external Nature for us, and, we think, it will do all other things. We are Giants in physical power: in a deeper than a metaphorical sense, we are Titans, that strive, by heaping mountain on mountain, to conquer Heaven also.

The strong mechanical character, so visible in the spiritual pursuits and methods of this age, may be traced much farther into the condition and prevailing disposition of our spiritual nature itself. Consider, for example, the general fashion of Intellect in this era. Intellect, the power man has of knowing and believing, is now nearly synonymous with Logic, or the mere power of arranging and communicating. Its implement is not Meditation, but Argument. "Cause and effect" is almost the only category under which we look at, and work with, all Nature. Our first question with regard to any object is not, What is it? but, How is it? We are no longer instinctively driven to apprehend, and lay to heart, what is Good and Lovely, but rather to inquire, as onlookers, how it is produced, whence it comes, whither it goes. Our favourite Philosophers have no love and no hatred; they stand among us not to do, nor to create any thing, but as a sort of Logic-mills to grind out the true causes and effects of all that is done and created. To the eye of a Smith, a Hume, or a Constant, all is well that works quietly. An Order of Ignatius Loyola, a Presbyterianism of John Knox, a Wickliffe, or a Henry the Eighth, are simply so many mechanical phenomena, caused or causing.

The *Euphuist* of our day differs much from his pleasant predecessors. An intellectual dapperling of these times boasts chiefly of his irresistible perspicacity, his "dwelling in the daylight of truth," and so forth; which, on examination, turns out to be a dwelling in the *rush*-light of "closet-logic," and a deep unconsciousness that there is any other light to dwell in; or any other objects to survey with it. Wonder indeed, is, on all hands, dying out: it is the sign of uncultivation to wonder. Speak to any small man of a high, majestic Reformation, of a high, majestic Luther to lead it, and forthwith he sets about "accounting" for it! how the "circumstances of the time" called for such a character, and found him, we suppose, standing girt and road-ready, to do its errand; how the "circumstances of the time" created, fashioned, floated him quietly along into the result; how, in short, this small man, had he been there, could have performed the like himself! For it is the "force of circumstances" that does every thing; the force of one man can do nothing. Now all this is grounded on little more than a metaphor. We figure Society as a "Machine," and that mind is opposed to mind, as body is to body; whereby two, or at most ten, little minds must be stronger than one great mind. Notable absurdity! For the plain truth, very plain, we think, is, that minds are opposed to minds in quite a different way; and *one* man that has a higher Wisdom, a hitherto unknown spiritual Truth in him, is stronger, not than ten men that have it not, or than ten thousand, but than *all* men, that have it not; and stands among them with a quite ethereal, angelic power, as with a sword out of Heaven's own armory, sky-tempered, which no buckler, and no tower of brass, will finally withstand.

But to us, in these times, such considerations rarely occur. We enjoy, we see nothing by direct vision; but only by reflection, and in anatomical dismemberment. Like Sir Hudibras, for every Why, we must have a Wherefore. We have our little *theory* on all human and divine things. Poetry, the workings of genius itself, which in all times, with one or another meaning, has been called Inspiration, and held to be mysterious and inscrutable, is no longer without its scientific exposition. The building of the lofty rhyme is like any other masonry or bricklaying: we have theories of its rise, height, decline, and fall,—which latter, it would seem, is now near, among all people. Of our "Theories of Taste," as they are called, wherein the deep, infinite, unspeakable Love of Wisdom and Beauty, which dwells in all men, is "explained," made mechanically visible, from "Association," and the like, why should we say

any thing? Hume has written us a "Natural History of Religion;" in which one Natural History, all the rest are included. Strangely, too, does the general feeling coincide with Hume's in this wonderful problem; for whether his "Natural History" be the right one or not, that Religion must have a Natural History, all of us, cleric and laic, seem to be agreed. He indeed regards it as a Disease, we again as Health; so far there is a difference; but in our first principle we are at one.

To what extent theological Unbelief, we mean intellectual dissent from the Church, in its view of Holy Writ, prevails at this day, would be a highly important, were it not, under any circumstances, an almost impossible inquiry. But the Unbelief, which is of a still more fundamental character, every man may see prevailing, with scarcely any but the faintest contradiction, all around him; even in the Pulpit itself. Religion in most countries, more or less in every country, is no longer what it was, and should be,—a thousand-voiced psalm from the heart of Man to his invisible Father, the fountain of all Goodness, Beauty, Truth, and revealed in every revelation of these; out for the most part, a wise, prudential feeling grounded on a mere calculation; a matter, as all others now are, of Expediency and Utility: whereby some smaller quantum of earthly enjoyment may be exchanged for a far larger quantum of celestial enjoyment. Thus Religion, too, is Profit; a working for wages; not Reverence, but vulgar Hope or Fear. Many, we know, very many, we hope, are still religious in a far different sense; were it not so, our case were too desperate: But to witness that such is the temper of the times, we take any calm observant man, who agrees or disagrees in our feeling on the matter, and ask him whether our *view* of it is not in general well-founded.

Literature, too, if we consider it, gives similar testimony. At no former era has Literature, the printed communication of Thought, been of such importance as it is now. We often hear that the Church is in danger; and truly so it is,—in a danger it seems not to know of: For, with its tithes in the most perfect safety, its functions are becoming more and more superseded. The true Church of England, at this moment, lies in the Editors of its Newspapers. These preach to the people daily, weekly; admonishing kings themselves; advising peace or war, with an authority which only the first Reformers and a long-past class of Popes were possessed of inflicting moral censure; imparting moral encouragement, consolation, edification; in all ways, diligently "administering the Discipline of the Church." It may be said, too, that in private disposition, the new Preachers somewhat resemble the Mendicant Friars of old times: outwardly full of holy zeal; inwardly not without stratagem, and hunger for terrestrial things. But omitting this class, and the boundless host of watery personages who pipe, as they are able, on so many scrannel straws, let us look at the higher regions of

Literature, where, if anywhere, the pure melodies of Poesy and Wisdom should be heard. Of natural talent there is no deficiency: one or two richly-endowed individuals even give us a superiority in this respect. But what is the song they sing? Is it a tone of the Memnon Statue, breathing music as the *light* first touches it? a "liquid wisdom," disclosing to our sense the deep, infinite harmonies of Nature and man's soul? Alas, no! It is not a matin or vesper hymn to the Spirit of all Beauty, but a fierce clashing of cymbals, and shouting of multitudes, as children pass through the fire to Molech! Poetry itself has no eye for the Invisible. Beauty is no longer the god it worships, but some brute image of Strength; which we may well call an idol, for true Strength is one and the same with Beauty, and its worship also is a hymn. The meek, silent Light can mould, create, and purify all Nature; but the loud Whirlwind, the sign and product of Disunion, of Weakness, passes on, and is forgotten. How widely this veneration for the physically Strongest has spread itself through Literature, any one may judge, who reads either criticism or poem. We praise a work, not as "true," but as "strong;" our highest praise is that it has "affected" us, has "terrified" us. All this, it has been well observed, is the "maximum of the Barbarous," the symptom, not of vigorous refinement, but of luxurious corruption. It speaks much, too, for men's indestructible love of truth, that nothing of this kind will abide with them: that even the talent of a Byron cannot permanently seduce us into idol-worship; but that he, too, with all his wild syren charming, already begins to be disregarded and forgotten.

Again, with respect to our Moral condition: here also, he who runs may read that the same physical, mechanical influences are every where busy. For the "superior morality," of which we hear so much, we too, would desire to be thankful: at the same time, it were but blindness to deny that this "superior morality" is properly rather an "inferior criminality," produced not by greater love of Virtue, but by greater perfection of Police; and of that far subtler and stronger Police, called Public Opinion. This last watches over us with its Argus eyes more keenly than ever; but the "inward eye" seems heavy with sleep. Of any belief in invisible, divine things, we find as few traces in our Morality as elsewhere. It is by tangible, material considerations that we are guided, not by inward and spiritual. Self-denial, the parent of all virtue, in any true sense of that word, has perhaps seldom been rarer: so rare is it, that the most, even in their abstract speculations, regard its existence as a chimera. Virtue is Pleasure, is Profit; no celestial, but an earthly thing. Virtuous men, Philanthropists, Martyrs, are happy accidents; their "taste" lies the right way! In all senses, we worship and follow after Power; which may be called a physical pursuit. No man now loves Truth, as Truth must be loved, with an infinite love; but only with a finite love, and as it were *par amours*. Nay, properly speaking, he does not *believe* and know it, but only "*thinks*" it, and that "there is every probability!" He preaches it aloud, and rushes courageously forth with it,—if there is a multitude huzzaing at his back! yet ever keeps looking over his shoulder, and the instant the huzzaing languishes, he too stops short. In fact, what morality we have takes the shape of Ambition, of Honour; beyond money and money's worth, our only rational blessedness is popularity. It were but a fool's trick to die for conscience. Only for "character," by duel, or in case of extremity, by suicide, is the wise man bound to die. By arguing on the "force of circumstances," we have argued away all force from ourselves; and stand leashed together, uniform in dress and movement, like the rowers of some boundless galley. This and that may be right and true; *but* we must not do it. Wonderful "Force of Public Opinion!" We must act and walk in all points as it prescribes; follow the traffic it bids us, realize the sum of money, the degree of "influence" it expects of us, *or* we shall be lightly esteemed; certain mouthfuls of articulate wind will be blown at us, and this, what mortal courage can front? Thus, while civil Liberty is more and more secured to us, our moral Liberty is all but lost. Practically considered, our creed is Fatalism: and, free in hand and foot, we are shackled in heart and soul, with far stratier than Feudal chains. Truly may we say with the Philosopher, "the deep meaning of the laws of Mechanism lies heavy on us;" and in the closet, in the marketplace, in the temple, by the social hearth, encumbers the whole movements of our mind, and over our noblest faculties is spreading a nightmare sleep.

These dark features, we are aware, belong more or less to other ages, as well as to ours. This faith in Mechanism, in the all-importance of physical things, is in every age the common refuge of Weakness and blind Discontent; of all who believe, as many will ever do, that man's true good lies without him, not within. We are aware also, that, as applied to ourselves in all their aggravation, they form but half a picture; that in the whole picture there are bright lights as well as gloomy shadows. If we here dwell chiefly on the latter, let us not be blamed: it is in general more profitable to reckon up our defects, than to boast of our attainments.

Neither, with all these evils more or less clearly before us, have we at any time despaired of the fortunes of society. Despair, or even despondency, in that respect, appears to us, in all cases, a groundless feeling. We have a faith in the imperishable dignity of man; in the high vocation to which, throughout this his earthly history, he has been appointed. However it may be with individual nations, whatever melancholic speculators may assert, it seems a well-ascertained fact that, in all times, reckoning even from those of the Heracleids and Pelasgi, the happiness and greatness of mankind at large have been continually progressive. Doubtless this age also is advancing. Its very unrest, its ceaseless activity, its discontent, contains matter of promise. Knowledge, education, are opening the eyes of the humblest,—are increasing the number of thinking minds without limit. This is as it should be; for, not in turning back, not in resisting, but only in resolutely struggling forward, does our life consist. Nay, after all, our spiritual maladies are but of Opinion; we are but fettered by chains of our own forging, and which ourselves also can rend asunder. This deep, paralyzed subjection to physical objects comes not from Nature, but from our own unwise mode of *viewing* Nature. Neither can we understand that man wants, at this hour, any faculty of heart, soul, or body, that ever belonged to him. "He, who has been born, has been a First Man;" has had lying before his young eyes, and as yet unhardened into scientific shapes, a world as plastic, infinite, divine, as lay before the eyes of Adam himself. If Mechanism, like some glass bell, encircles and imprisons us, if the soul looks forth on a fair heavenly country which it cannot reach, and pines, and in its scanty atmosphere is ready to perish,—yet the bell is but of glass; "one bold stroke to break the bell in pieces, and thou art delivered!" Not the invisible world is wanting, for it dwells in man's soul, and this last is still here. Are the solemn temples in which the Divinity was once visibly revealed among us, crumbling away? We can repair them, we can rebuild them. The wisdom, the heroic worth of our forefathers, which we have lost, we can recover. That admiration of old nobleness, which now so often shows itself as a faint *dilettantism,* will one day become a generous emulation, and man may again be all that he has been, and more than he has been. Nor are these the mere daydreams of fancy; they are clear possibilities; nay, in this time, they are even assuming the character of hopes. Indications we do see, in other countries and in our own, signs infinitely cheering to us, that Mechanism is not always to be our hard taskmaster, but one day to be our pliant, all-ministering servant; that a new and brighter spiritual era is slowly evolving itself for all men. But on these things our present course forbids us to enter.

Meanwhile, that great outward changes are in progress can be doubtful to no one. The time is sick and out of joint. Many things have reached their height; and it is a wise adage that tells us, "the darkest hour is nearest the dawn." Whenever we can gather any indication of the public thought, whether from printed books, as in France of Germany, or from Carbonari rebellions and other political tumults, as in Spain, Portugal, Italy, and Greece, the voice it utters is the same. The thinking minds of all nations call for change. There is a deep-lying struggle in the whole fabric of society; a boundless, grinding collision of the New with the Old. The French Revolution, as is now visible enough, was not the parent of this mighty movement, but its offspring. Those two hostile influences, which always exist in human things, and on the constant intercommunion of

which depends their health and safety, had lain in separate masses, accumulating through generations, and France was the scene of their fiercest explosion; but the final issue was not unfolded in that country: nay, it is not yet anywhere unfolded. Political freedom is hitherto the object of these efforts; but they will not and cannot stop there. It is towards a higher freedom than mere freedom from oppression by his fellow-mortal that man dimly aims. Of this higher, heavenly freedom, which is "man's reasonable service," all his noble institutions, his faithful endeavours, and loftiest attainments, are but the body, and more and more approximated emblem.

On the whole, as this wondrous planet, Earth, is journeying with its fellows through infinite space, so are the wondrous destinies embarked on it journeying through infinite time, under a higher guidance than ours. For the present, as our astronomy informs us, its path lies towards *Hercules,* the constellation of *Physical Power:* But that is not our most pressing concern. Go where it will, the deep HEAVEN will be around it. Therein let us have hope and sure faith. To reform a world, to reform a nation, no wise man will undertake; and all but foolish men know that the only solid, though a far slower reformation, is what each begins and perfects on *himself.*

S. C. Chase

SOURCE: "Effects of Machinery," in *The North American Review,* Vol. XXXIV, No. LXXIV, January, 1832, pp. 220-46.

[*In the following excerpt, Chase praises the accomplishments of the Industrial Revolution, suggesting that problems usually associated with it are only "temporary inconveniences."*]

[*The Working Man's Companion, No. 1. The Results of Machinery; being an Address to the Working Men of the United Kingdom*] was published under the superintendence of the Society for the Diffusion of Useful Knowledge. Its object is to convince the working men of the United Kingdom, of the folly and wickedness of attempting to arrest the progress of improvement, by the destruction of machinery. It is written in a plain, unadorned style, but it is replete with valuable facts, and strong and persuasive reasoning. We commend the book to all croakers,—to all praisers of the past and revilers of the present time. We ask a careful perusal of it, of those venerable grand-mothers who see misery and ruin close at hand, because the sound of the spinning-wheel and the loom is no longer heard in all our farm-houses.

In the present article, we shall attempt an independent and somewhat enlarged discussion of the principal questions, presented in this work. We shall not confine our attention to 'cheap production and increased employment,' alone; but shall endeavor to trace the influence of machinery farther, in its effects on society. The question is, is this influence,—confessedly, and beyond calculation, vast,—good or evil? This has been said to be 'a far more difficult and complex question, than any that political economists have yet engaged with.' Its importance and interests are certainly not exceeded by its difficulty and complexity. The first arise from the intimate connexion of the influence of machinery with every other influence, that affects the social condition of man, and the last are shared by it in common with every other question, relating to matters yet imperfectly understood. It is embarrassed by being complicated with a number of considerations, not necessarily belonging to it, and because it requires, in those who would resolve it, a larger amount of contemporary information, than is generally, or can be easily, acquired.

We look upon the knowledge of the present circumstances of society, of the transactions of our own age and country, of modern science and modern art, as more important than any other. Yet it is precisely the sort of knowledge, of which, until very recently, we have had least. We would not be understood to undervalue any species of knowledge. Every kind of information is precious. We would only say, that that which instructs us, where we are, what we are, and how we are, has peculiar value. It is true, that to know the present, we must be, in some degree, acquainted with the past. To understand the result, we must have knowledge of the cause. To foresee consequences, it is necessary to know how consequences have been heretofore produced. What we complain of is, not that we know too much of what has been, but that we do not know enough of what is;—not that we are too familiar with the past, but that we are not familiar enough with the present. And we would go so far as to say, that, if any part of knowledge were to be given up, it would be better to let alone the study of what happened before we were born, and the conjecture of what is to happen after we are dead, and confine our view within the horizon of our present existence. It was demanded of the Spartan king, 'what study is fittest for the boy?' His answer was, 'that of the science most useful to the man.' Utility measures the value of knowledge, as of every thing else; and surely, on the scale of utility, the knowledge of what is all around us, affecting us, physically, intellectually, and morally, in countless ways, ranks far higher than the knowledge of the circumstances of preceding generations.

It has not been the fact, however, that men have applied themselves to the study of their own times, with as much earnestness, as to the investigation of the records of the past. It has always been extremely difficult to obtain contemporary information of events.

Intelligence has been transmitted from point to point very slowly. And when it has finally reached its destination, it has come in so questionable a shape, that its authenticity could by no means be relied on. The consequence has been, that men of learning and study have turned away from so unpromising a field of research. Almost all writers, except those whose business was politics, have occupied themselves in other tasks. It was a natural consequence, that science became speculative, rather than practical. The object of study was rather to gratify the instinctive desire of knowledge, than to strike out a light to guide the conduct, or to discover the means of improving the condition of man. And thus men, instead of believing that they were intrusted by Providence with the care of their own fates, have been accustomed to think of themselves, as embarked, without a rudder, without a sail, without an oar, upon the stream of destiny, hurried on, they know not how, and destined to arrive, they know not whither.

But there is a better philosophy than this,—a philosophy that attributes more to men and less to circumstance. It teaches that knowledge is for use, and not for ostentation. It teaches that the great events, which crowd the historian's page, are beacons kindled by those who have gone before us, illumining the scene of present things, and dispelling, partially at least, the shadows, clouds and darkness, that overhang the future. Intelligence of recent events is now communicated with a degree of certainty and rapidity, utterly unknown hitherto. The best intellects are employed in the observation of the passing pageant of existence. The importance of each occurrence is immediately ascertained; its proper place in the system of events is fixed, and the fact, with the reasoning that links it to the past and the future, is communicated to the public, through the periodical press. It is true that the fact is yet frequently misstated, and the reasoning about it often erroneous; but, on the whole, truth greatly prevails; and the present age is doubtless better acquainted with itself, than any which have preceded it.

Still, this acquaintance, this self-knowledge, an attainment, by the way, quite as important to nations as to individuals, is extremely imperfect and superficial. A reflecting man who looks around him, upon the countless agencies, operating with different degrees of energy, for good or for evil, upon the condition and character of men, wherever man exists, cannot help feeling how little is known of things as they are. What we hear about the age in which we live, is quite too vague and general, to satisfy a rational curiosity. We hear it called the age of improvement, the enlightened age, the age of practical benevolence. But we want a deeper and more extensive knowledge, than these epithets convey. We want something more, than a mere map of the surface of society. We want a deep, intimate, pervading knowledge of the circumstances of man's actual condition, and of the influences, whether friendly or adverse, which are acting on his character. Men are divided now into a far greater number of classes, than they have ever before been. We want to know why this is so. All the classes stand much more nearly on the same level, than formerly. Rulers are no longer more, and the ruled are no longer less, than men. The divisions now are not so much of high from low, as of equals from equals. This is a glorious change for the better. We want to understand its nature, cause and extent. But this understanding we have not yet fully attained. We are yet very far from having attained it. And it is this imperfection of our knowledge, rather than any inseparable obscurity belonging to them, that darkens so many questions of deep and vital importance. It is this that makes it so difficult, to point to the cause and effect of a contemporary event, and to decide upon the complexion and tendency of existing circumstances.

Of the questions, relating to the present interests and deeply affecting the present happiness of society, not one, probably, gathers into itself a greater consequence, and certainly, not one ought to excite a livelier concern, than that which we now propose to discuss. This subject is intimately connected with the great topic of human progress. The experiment of machinery has multiplied relations to the condition and prospects of our race. It is a new and almost infinite power, brought to bear on the action of the social system. And, in proportion as it would be consoling and delightful to have reason to believe, that, under the influence of these new impulses, society is advancing and will continue to advance, with swift and constantly accelerating progress, towards the ultimate limits of human improvement; so would it be mortifying, and beyond expression painful, to be driven to acquiesce in the gloomy doctrine, which represents all these new and powerful agents as only working out for man, deeper and deeper wretchedness and degradation.

This question may be more advantageously discussed in our country, than in any other. The experiment of machinery may have a fairer trial here, than elsewhere. The natural course of industry is not obstructed here, in any great degree, by unwise legislation. The profits of labor are secured to the laborer. The burdens of taxation are light. The highest motives to exertion operate upon every man in the community. In short, a nearer approach has been made here, than any where else, to a Government that protects all, and injures none; that leaves every one at full liberty to benefit himself, so far as it can be done without injury to others; that takes off every weight and fetter from individual energy, while it restrains all hurtful excesses, and restrains them rather by the fear of public opinion, than the fear of punishment. In such a state of society, every new impulse given to the public mind,—every new agent introduced to further the operations of la-

bor,—exhibits at once its real character and tendency. In such a state of society, the moral action of machinery is not liable to what natural philosophers call the influence of disturbing forces. It operates without restraint, and produces its appropriate effects. It is not complicated with other influences. It has a simple unmodified action of its own, unaffected by the movements around it. Here, therefore, we may ascertain, with comparative facility, what this action is, and what are likely to be its results.

Some of our readers may be surprised, that so much importance and difficulty should be ascribed to this question. They live in the midst of machinery. They see machinery at work on every side, abridging the processes of labor, and making the difficult easy. They are accustomed to regard this subjection of the powers of nature to the will and direction of man, as a splendid triumph of the intellect, and as altogether and unquestionably beneficial in all its tendencies. It is natural, therefore, that they should be astonished when it is made a question. It seems to them quite too plain a matter to admit of argument. But let these persons look abroad. There they will find men, and men too held in high repute for wisdom and honesty, who think and say, that, to those who depend upon their daily labor for their daily bread, or, in other words, to four fifths of almost every nation on the globe, the introduction of labor-saving machinery is a grievous curse. These men will bid them look for a commentary on the influence of machinery, to the condition of the English laborers. They will bid them to ask the half-clothed and half-fed workman, what is his opinion on this subject? They will say to them, 'Inquire of those distracted parents, why they deny food to their famishing offspring? Demand of the whole body of the working classes, what is the cause of this deep, wide-spread distress, which pervades the land like a pestilence, carrying dread to every bosom? Why is Government alarmed? Why is the Church directed to offer up supplications to Heaven, to avert from England the horrible calamities of intestine discord and war? A glance at the condition of the country will answer these questions. There are multitudes of workmen, who either have no employment at all, or labor for wages altogether inadequate to the necessities of existence. This want of employment, and these low wages, are occasioned by the introduction of machinery. The laborers have, of course, become uneasy and discontented. Their irrepressible discontent has at length broken out into open violence. They begin to destroy the machinery. The sure instinct of revenge directs them to the cause of their sufferings. But they do not stop here. They attack the property of their employers, or rather, as they think, their tyrants. Those conflagrations, converting midnight darkness into unnatural day, are their work. There is reason that Government should be alarmed. They are alarmed. They have made strong efforts to arrest the progress of dis-affection. The iron arm of power has been stretched out to punish the excesses of these wretched men. Nothing is pardoned to ignorance. Nothing is forgiven to misery. Many have been sentenced to transportation,—many to imprisonment,—many to death. Yet all this avails nothing. Disaffection and disquiet still spread and strengthen. No man is able to foresee what will be the end of these things. This,' these honest and intelligent persons will say, 'is in truth a terrible picture of present and impending calamity. But it is only a faint shadow of the real state of things. And if the vengeance of those unfortunate men be not mis-directed,—if, as we believe, machinery be the fruitful mother of all these woes, then, surely, its introduction into such general use cannot be too earnestly deplored.'

It requires no effort of the imagination to suppose this to be the present language of that numerous and highly respectable class of men, who think that the influence of machinery on society is evil and pernicious. There is, however, another class, equally numerous and respectable, who hold the contrary opinion. These persons ascribe the distress, that afflicts the laboring classes of England, and some other portions of Europe, to other and more deep-lying causes, than the introduction of machinery. 'The real springs of all these evils are to be sought for,' they say, 'in vicious political institutions, in unequal laws, and grinding taxation. These are the true fountains, which send forth poisonous and bitter waters. Machinery multiplies the comforts and conveniences of life. Is this an evil? Machinery lightens the burthens of labor. Is relief from the necessity of hard work, a grievance to the laboring classes? No doubt, like every other great power, machinery may be converted into an instrument of great oppression. But it is not such naturally. In itself it has been always, and, under well regulated Governments, it always will be a source of great good,—of good almost unmixed. The evils necessarily incident to its introduction, are slight, partial, and transient. They reach only the surface of society, affect but small portions of the community, and speedily pass away. The benefits arising from the same source, are substantial, universal, permanent. They are seen every where, felt every where, and must abide forever.'

Such is the conflict of opinions on this subject. Where there is so much disagreement, it becomes him, who would share in the discussion, to advance his sentiments with diffidence. We do not dogmatize. We assume the attitude of inquirers rather than of teachers. We shall be satisfied, though none should be convinced by our labors, if we induce any to examine the subject for themselves,—a subject, which it is important that every man in our community should thoroughly understand. It has not been much discussed, particularly in this country. The general sentiment is decidedly, so far as we have been able to ascertain it, in favor of machinery. A few apostles of the opposite doctrine have

arisen here and there; but their converts have not been numerous. Recently, we have observed in some quarters, a disposition to make machinery bear the sins of the tariff; to establish the fact of a partnership between the two, and to make the former responsible for all the faults, real or imaginary, of the latter. We apprehend, that it would not be difficult to demonstrate the absurdity of this notion. We cannot, however, spare more space than is required for the simple statement, that it is groundless. And now, we shall let alone the opinions of others, and proceed to put our readers in possession of our own views on this important subject.

In the earliest ages of society, machinery was unknown. Man was created in a climate where the earth yielded bountifully at all seasons of the year, her productions for his use. Then, his only labor was to gather from Nature's abundant store, the supply of his present want. Afterwards, he began to cultivate the soil, and then, probably, some simple instrument of culture was invented. At a still later period, his Creator invested him with dominion over the life of living creatures; and, to enable himself to exercise this new authority, he invented, also, rude instruments of hunting and fishing. These are all arts of absolute necessity. Without them, man could not exist, except in the mildest climates, and there only in small numbers. Beyond these arts, a large proportion of the human race have made no great advances. The only additional skill, yet attained by many tribes of the human family,—the skill to make rude clothing and to build rude huts to protect them from the inclemency of the weather,—has been taught them by stern necessity. In their circumstances, each individual of the society must labor for his own subsistence, and all hope of intellectual or moral improvement seems entirely cut off.

From time to time, however, in different parts of the world, there have been communities, which have risen far above this condition. Assyria, Persia, Egypt, Greece and Rome felt, by turns, the genial influence of improvement. And it is worthy of remark, that, wherever, over the whole earth, the light of civilization has once dawned, some rays of that light linger yet,—the utter darkness of absolute barbarism has never returned. It cannot wholly return. The law of man's nature, impressed on him by his God, is onward progress; and let a nation but once rise into the light of civilization, and then, however low adverse circumstances may afterwards thrust them down, they will never sink into utter night, nor will they ever cease to strive to re-ascend to day. It is also worthy of remark, as illustrative of this law, that these nations made different degrees of progress, and that each advanced farther in improvement than the preceding. The light shone faintest, where it first dawned, on Assyria,—its brightest effulgence illuminated Rome. It was a progressive illumination,—faint and hardly perceptible at first,—then gradually receiving grater and greater accessions of splendor. Now, in

Workers leaving a textile mill in Lawrence, Massachusetts, 1869.

our day, it has flashed out into a broad, bright, and glorious effulgence, encompassing and illuminating more than half the globe. But of this hereafter. Our present business is with the cause of all this. Civilization never takes place without the accumulation of the material products of labor. Different causes may produce this accumulation. The hand of violence may gather the spoils of rapine, and manual labor or mechanical contrivance may heap up the store of industry. The two first of these causes, but more particularly the first, procured an abundance of the necessaries and luxuries of life to the states of antiquity; and were, therefore, the principal agents in the work of civilizing those states. Mechanical contrivance exerted a similar, but, at first, almost imperceptible influence, increasing the stores of wealth, and thus helping forward the progress of civilization. The experiment of machinery, however, as a substitute for human labor, employed in producing and increasing the comforts of life, was never tried on a great scale by the nations of antiquity. That was reserved to be the distinction of modern times. The glory of compelling the powers of Nature into the service of man, was destined to grace our own age. And, as the spoils of these bloodless victories have been far greater than ancient conquest ever gained,— as the accumulation of wealth, by the new agents that have been employed in the task, has been far more rapid than was ever known in former times, through the instrumentality of any agent whatever, so civiliza-

tion has, in these latter days, spread far more widely, and penetrated much more deeply, than ever before; reaching, not one nation only, but many, and bestowing its invaluable benefits, not upon a favored portion merely, but upon the whole of society. We would not say, that machinery has been the only efficient agent of modern civilization. We do not so believe. There have been moral agents at work. They have effected much; but without the aid of machinery, they could not have effected much. What we claim for machinery is, that it is in modern times by far the most efficient physical cause of human improvement; that it does for civilization, what conquest and human labor formerly did, and accomplishes incalculably more than they accomplished. And how different are the characters of these three agents! War, the direst curse of humanity, must necessarily precede conquest; and the structure of civilization, reared by this agent, rises upon the spoil, the desolation, and the anguish of the vanquished. Human labor, when urged to excessive efforts, must necessarily, to a considerable extent, prevent intellectual and moral improvement. But machinery, doing the work, without feeling the wants of man; taking from none, yet giving to all, produces almost unmingled benefit, to an amount and extent, of which we have as yet, probably, but a very faint conception.

There are several objections to this general view of the effects of machinery, which we shall now examine.

The first and principal one is, that all labor-saving inventions diminish the demand for human industry, and, consequently, deprive multitudes of laborers of employment. We meet this objection by denying the fact. It is not true, that the demand for human industry is diminished. It is not true, that multitudes of laborers are absolutely deprived of employment. It is true, however, that many laborers are sometimes compelled to change their employment, by the introduction of new and improved machinery into a branch of industry, where a great deal of human labor had been previously required. And it is true, that sometimes, while this change is in progress, a great deal of suffering is experienced. All this we shall attempt to explain.

The earth is the great primary source of the supply of human wants. It is the great laboratory, where the dust we tread upon is converted into life-sustaining nutriment. Whatever we eat, or drink, or wear, comes originally from her bosom. In the earliest stages of society, as has been already said, men consume her productions in their simple state. The springs supply them with water to drink. They eat the fruits of the field, and clothe themselves with leaves and skins. In this savage state, each one supplies his own wants, and it takes all his time to do it. But, after a while, some one more lazy or more ingenious than the rest, discovers some method of lightening his individual labor. Then others imitate him;—and, in time, machines are invented, that seem likely to supersede the necessity of human labor altogether. This would, in fact, be the result, if, in this condition of things, men should consume no more of the products of industry than before; and, of course, a multitude who had been actively employed would be employed no longer. But such is not the fact. The cravings of desire are never satisfied. Extend the supply as you may, the wish for the enjoyments of life will still go beyond it, and will find its only limit in the means of gratification. The only effect, therefore, of increasing the productive energies of labor, by the introduction of machinery, is to distribute it into more numerous departments. A few years ago, those, who roamed through the regions in which we now dwell, exercised, all of them, the same employments. Each one performed his own labor. No one was, in any great degree, dependent on another. How different is the condition of things now! Hardly an individual, of the millions congregated here, produces, himself, the hundredth part of what is required for his own subsistence. The departments of industry are multiplied. The laborers in each are under a tacit obligation to contribute their proportion to the great fund of human subsistence and enjoyment. Each one works for all the rest, and all the rest work for him. In the savage state, all were hunters and fishers; now, some cultivate the ground, some construct machines, some make clothing, some build houses, some make laws, and some preach sermons. Each fills his appropriate place, the amount and the products of human industry are incalculably increased, and the action of the great social system goes on safely and harmoniously.

The effect machinery upon labor may be illustrated by an example. We will take the printing-press. It is difficult to conceive what was the condition of society, when there was no printing. We can almost as easily imagine the condition of the world, when there was no light. Yet we know that there was such a time. Then the copyist performed the printer's work. Books were published by copying them out with a pen. A considerable number of persons were employed in this business, and a considerable number more found employment in the preparation of the materials for copying. Books published in this way were, of course, very expensive. The whole annual income of a man in moderate circumstances would hardly buy a Bible. None but princes and very rich men could afford to purchase libraries. Hence, the demand for books was extremely limited, and the number of persons employed in furnishing them, must have been regulated by the state of the demand.

When the printing-press was introduced, an extensive change took place. Books were multiplied. The price fell. Readers became more numerous. The demand for information became more urgent. Knowledge began to diffuse her healing beams every where, and an impulse was given to society, that has ever since continued to grow in energy and power. But this is not the result,—though an important and a glorious one,—that claims our consideration now. What we would now press upon the attention of our readers, is the effect of this machinery upon human industry. Is there more or less of human labor employed in furnishing books, since the press has lent its mighty aid to the work, than before? Where was then one author, there are now, at least, one hundred. It has been calculated that in Germany, one out of every hundred of the whole population, is an author. Instead of a few hundred copyists, and a few hundred manufacturers of materials for copying, there are thousands and tens of thousands of persons, who obtain a living by making types, presses, and paper, by printing books, by binding them when they are printed, and by selling them when they are bound. It is no exaggeration to say, that this business employs many hundred times as much human labor, as it did before the printing-press was invented.

In this instance, then, the demand for human industry has not ceased nor diminished, but is greatly augmented in consequence of the introduction of machinery. Nor does it seem to be possible that any other effect than this can be produced, until every department of industry,—when industry shall have subdivided itself into the greatest possible number of departments, whether moral, intellectual, or physical,—shall be overstocked, and every want of man more than supplied. This can happen only when man shall cease to improve;—a period, to which no philanthropist would wish to look forward.

But if this be so, some may urge, why is it that almost everywhere, when machinery has been introduced on a large scale, the working classes have uniformly evinced dissatisfaction and hostility? Why did they destroy the spinning-jennies in Normandy? Why are they now destroying the threshing machines in England? Why did the printers of Paris, after the recent revolution, go about destroying the steam-presses? Why did they petition the Legislature, that their use might be prohibited by law? The obvious answer to all questions of this sort is, that the working classes, especially of Europe, are not apt to distinguish between present inconvenience and permanent evil. They are not very far-sighted. They do see and feel the drenching and pelting storm; but they do not see, even in remote anticipation, the renovated beauty of nature, when the storm has gone by. No well-informed person ever denied, that the introduction of machinery may occasion temporary inconvenience. If a man, who has been accustomed to employ twenty workmen, procure a machine, which, with the aid of one, will do the work of the twenty, nineteen, of course, must be deprived of employment. When this takes place on a small scale, the inconvenience is not great. The little labor that is turned out of its accustomed channels, is almost immediately absorbed by other employments. Every trace and vestige of evil at once disappears. When, however, the experiment is made on a grander scale,—when a great number of machines, superseding the necessity of a vast quantity of human labor, are suddenly brought into use, the consequences are more serious. A multitude of laborers are, at once, thrown out of work. They find it difficult to obtain other employment, and in fact are, in some measure, unfitted for it by their previous occupations. They have no resources but their labor. Their daily wages supply their daily sustenance. Want of work instantly reduces them to beggary; and, sometimes, under these circumstances, their distress is great. The same effect is produced by over-production. A farmer may grow as much in one year, as he can dispose of in two. A manufacturer may, in like manner, have a superabundant stock of goods on his hands. Neither will be likely to go on producing at the same rate as before. Some of their workmen must be discharged; and then the same consequences follow, as upon the introduction of labor-saving machines. These consequences will be imperceptible, if the over-production be slight and partial; but if it be great and general, they will be plainly seen and deeply felt. Sometimes both the causes we have mentioned concur. Machinery substitutes bodies of iron, with souls of steam, to do the work of living men; and the prospect of immense gain stimulates production to such an excess, that the markets of the whole world are glutted. This was the case with the cotton manufacture in 1825. Almost the whole of the machinery employed in this manufacture, has been invented within the last fifty years. When it had been introduced into general use, the same effects upon human labor followed, as in the case of the printing-press. The price of cotton fabrics was reduced. The demand for consumption increased, and the supply was extended to meet the demand. Some, who had been accustomed to spin and weave at home, lost their work; but a greater number found employment in the factories. On the whole, the number of persons employed in this business, instead of diminishing, considerably increased. The inventions of 1816 had a great effect upon this state of things. Among other improvements, the power-loom was introduced. Requiring only the superintendence of a single individual, it performed the labor of numbers. Then, to use the language of an English writer, 'on every hand the living artisan was driven from his work-shop, to make room for a speedier inanimate one. The shuttle dropped from the fingers of the weaver, and fell into iron fingers, that could ply it faster.' These improvements in machinery, of course, occasioned a good deal of inconvenience and distress among the workmen; and before these evils could be wholly cured by the natural operation of the causes which produced them, a heavier calamity was to happen. The manufacture, aided by the new inventions, went on with unabated,—with increased activity. The disproportion between the cost of production and the price of the manufactured article, gave immense profits. Millions were added to the millions already invested in the business. The production of the raw material kept pace with the extension of the manufacture. At length, the supply far exceeded the demand. The warehouses of the world were filled. Prices suddenly fell to half of what they had been before. Multitudes were ruined. Thousands of families were reduced to beggary. Some manufacturers discharged a part of their workmen, while they retained the rest at reduced wages. Many ceased to struggle with the adverse torrent, and discharged all their hands, and shut up their factories. The distress that ensued may, perhaps, be imagined. We are not competent to describe it. To aid the conception of our readers, however, we will quote the language of one, who was an eye-witness of a scene of distress, occasioned by a similar, but slighter cause.

'Within a small distance of my house,' says this person, 'is a large manufactory, the machinery of which extends nearly half a mile. I passed by it one morning, after its operations were suspended, and was exceedingly affected by the sight. A little while before, it was all animation and industry, affording honorable means of livelihood to many thousands of my fellow-creatures. The silence that now pervaded it spoke more eloquently and impressively to my heart, than any language could possibly do; it was the silence of unmingled desolation. I visited a row of houses occupied by the workmen. The doors were used to be open, inviting the eye of the stranger to glance, as he went along, at their neatness, cleanliness, and felicity. Little groups of healthful children were accustomed to appear about the cottages, full of merriment and joy; and the inhabitants, strong and healthy, saluted you as they went by. But the scene was lamentably changed. The cottages were closed. The inhabitants could not bear to have it known that they were stripped of their little ornaments. No children played about the doors. The very plants that were trained up in their windows, had pined and died. One man only appeared, emaciated and ghastly, a frightful spectre, as if the sepulchre had sent forth its inhabitants, to fill with terror the abodes of the living.'

It is not at all wonderful, that distress so sore as this should drive men to do what afterwards they are sorry for. Extreme misery impairs the moral sense. The distinctions of right and wrong are apt to be obscured and lost sight of, in the tumult and tempest of passion. Resentment is almost always blind. Its violence generally expends itself on the apparent cause of injury; while it seldom reaches the real cause. It so happened in this case. The laboring classes cried out against machinery, and some statesmen, too, joined in the cry, when the principal source,—by far the most fruitful source,—of calamity, was an imprudent and excessive production, stimulated by high prices. Even this, however, is but a transitory evil. The bright and cheering beams of prosperity are intercepted only by a temporary eclipse. They are not quenched. They are not extinguished. When production ceases to be profitable, a part of the industry employed in it will be withdrawn. When other employment is found for it, the distress will vanish. And this will take place in a longer or shorter time, according to the circumstances of the nation, and the amount of labor thrown out of employment. In our country, neither the introduction of machinery, nor over-production, can occasion any extensive or permanent evil. The demand for labor is so urgent, that no man need be long out of work. Whenever the current of industry receives a check in one direction, the overflowing waters will immediately find an outlet in another. If machinery bear a part in occasioning distress, it also helps to remove it. If over-production do not irritate the wound, it will soon heal. The man who employs a machine, produces as much as he who employs living workmen. If there be a difference of expense in favor of the machinery, the former will make larger profits than the latter. He will grow rich faster. But he will not put his riches into a strong box. He will surround himself with additional comforts. He will employ a school-master. He will patronize the printer. He will travel and become better acquainted with his race. And thus, while he makes himself a far more useful and valuable member of society than before, he gives employment, in one way and another, to quite as much human industry, as his machine deprived of employment. Thus, from the same cause that produced partial evil, flows also universal good. The amount of productive industry of every sort is, in the end, vastly increased. It has been estimated,

that the people of the United States and Great Britain, aided by the improved machinery of the present day, do as much work as could be done by the whole population of the earth, without that aid. And it needs but a glance at the condition of the working classes, (an epithet, which we use for want of one more appropriate to our meaning,) in our country, to convince the candid, that its influence, so far as its ultimate effect on human industry is concerned, is altogether salutary and beneficial.

We have given quite as much attention to the argument against machinery, derived from its effects on labor, as it deserves. It is the strongest and most striking argument that occurs to us on that side of the question, and we wished to state it as fully, fairly, and forcibly as we could. But after all, is it certain that machinery occasions any distress, greater than would have existed, had machinery never been invented? We speak now of that improved machinery, which has, within the last century, so changed the aspect of the civilized world. Before this era, in many countries, the most affluent hardly enjoyed more comforts, than the poorest do now. The poorest classes depended upon servile labor, or an unskilful cultivation of the soil, for a scanty subsistence. They were miserably fed, clothed, and lodged. If they did not feel the wretchedness of their condition so acutely, as men similarly situated would now, it was because none of their neighbors fared much better. They

'Saw no contiguous palace rear its head,
To shame the meanness of their humble shed;
No costly lord the sumptuous banquet deal,
To make them loathe their vegetable meal;
But poor, and bred in ignorance and toil,
Each wish contracting bound them to the soil.'

But their ignorance was all their bliss. If the thick gloom which involved them, were not a darkness that might be felt, it was because there was no neighboring land of Goshen, where there was light. And to us, their lot seems to be far more worthy of commiseration, because far less susceptible of improvement than that of those, who, at the present day, occasionally experience temporary inconvenience and suffering from want of employment.

The next objection to machinery is, that its tendency is to gather wealth into masses, and widen the distance between the rich and the poor. It is easy to see how this may be the fact in England, where the statute of descents transmits the possessions of the father, almost unimpaired, to the eldest son. The accumulated acquisitions of one generation are handed down to the next, almost unbroken. The eldest son of a rich man must himself be wealthy; and, if he conduct his affairs with prudence, will leave his own eldest son master of a large fortune. The law closes up many of the outlets, by which wealth would otherwise be distributed through the community, and gathers it into the hands of a few. Thus a new order of nobility is created, who have been styled, not inappropriately, the lords of the spinning jenny. It is not machinery, therefore, that widens the distance between the rich and the poor, into an almost impassable gulf, but this law,—a law hardly to be vindicated upon principles of sound policy, under any circumstances, but pernicious and dangerous in the extreme, to a manufacturing and commercial community. In our country, we have no such law, and no such consequences have attended the introduction of machinery. If a rich man, in these States, invest a large fortune in fixed machinery, when he dies, it becomes the property of all his children. Death relaxes the grasp that held the mass of acquisition together, and the law does not put forth its stronger grasp to prevent its natural dissolution. On the contrary, the statute of distribution pulls down the pile of wealth, which the father's industry had accumulated, and divides it among his offspring. It can seldom happen, that there will be enough to make them all rich. The consequence is, that nearly all the individuals of each successive generation, start in the race of life from about the same point; and they are the most successful in that race, who are the most intelligent and the most industrious. It is thus plainly impossible, that, while this statute continues in force, machinery can enrich the few and impoverish the many. Almost all of us have an equal chance to be benefited by its introduction. A machine feels no partialities. It works for one just as vigorously and efficiently as for another. And if any man in this country have no direct interest in machinery, it is simply because he can employ his means more advantageously in some other way. In nearly every instance, where machinery is extensively employed, there is a joint-stock concern. The property is divided into shares, and these shares are held by various individuals. The workmen themselves, who are employed in the manufactory, may, and not unfrequently do, possess an interest in the establishment. It is then little less than absurd to say, that machinery accumulates for the rich alone, while it still farther impoverishes those who are already poor.

A far more serious objection than this remains to be considered. It is alleged, that machinery gathers men together in large masses, confines them in unhealthy apartments, ruins their health, contracts their minds, and depraves their morals; that its wages, like the wages of sin, is death,—moral, intellectual, physical death. This is true in part, and in part it seems to us to be false. It is true, that modern machinery can hardly be used to advantage, especially for manufacturing purposes, without collecting together large numbers of workmen. But it is not true, that these workmen must inevitably be 'crowded in hot task-houses by day, and herded together in damp cellars by night;' that they must toil in unwholesome employments twelve hours

a day, and frequently a much longer time; that they must live without decency, and die without hope; that they must sweat night and day, keeping up a perpetual oblation of body and soul, to the demons of gain, 'before furnaces which are never suffered to cool, and breathing in vapors which inevitably produce disease and death.' To all these charges, in behalf of machinery we plead not guilty. They are not true. If they were, well might the genius of humanity be represented as looking on with drooping wings, and a countenance of mingled pity and despair. There would be room for pity. There would be reason to despair. If we admit these allegations to be just, we are driven to the conviction, that the fabric of national greatness, power, and prosperity, however goodly it may seem in its outward show, is but a gorgeous sepulchre, in which are buried the intelligence, the virtue, and the freedom of the mass of the population; that national wealth and national misery go hand in hand, linked together by the strong compulsion of fate, in gloomy yet inseparable companionship. It were better that a nation should remain forever poor and barbarous. Better, far better, that society should make no progress, than that a few should advance and ascend, by treading on the necks of all the rest.

But it is not a necessary, nor a natural consequence of the introduction of machinery, that this state of things should exist. Wherever it does exist, there must be bad laws or a bad Government. We witness no such scenes in our country. The poet, who should search those districts of our country, where machinery is most extensively employed, for images of wretchedness and want, would return disappointed from his quest. The political economist, who should go there for facts to sustain the gloomy theory we have alluded to, would perhaps become a convert to the opposite opinion. There, beautiful villages spring up suddenly, as if the earth had been touched by an enchanter's wand. There, are large and commodious buildings, filled with active machinery, and with intelligent and contented human beings. Around, are their neat and convenient dwellings. There are a few shops, to supply them with a number of little foreign luxuries, which they can well afford to buy; and a tavern, it may be, to furnish, not a resort for the idle and the dissipated, but rest and a temporary home to the weary traveller. There are the schools, in which the children and young persons are instructed how to act well their parts, as free citizens on a free republic. And there, last and best of all, is the church, where, on the sabbath, all, old and young, assemble reverently to worship God. This is no picture drawn from fancy. We have ourselves beheld the real scene, and can attest the verisimilitude of the sketch. And though, in the larger manufacturing towns and cities, a part of these advantages can hardly be enjoyed, yet we may safely appeal to the character and condition of our manufacturing population throughout the whole country, as a standing and unanswerable refutation of the objection, which we have been considering.

We have now done with objections, and will pass to other considerations. We will now say something of the more general effects of machinery; and first, of the vast accession which has been made to the productive energies of labor, and the consequent vast augmentation of the products of industry. The necessaries, the comforts, and the luxuries of life are now produced in unparalleled profusion. The effect of abundant supply is to make articles cheap. Every man can now provide for his wants, and the wants of those dependant on him, in a much easier way, and at a much cheaper rate, than ever before; and the happy consequences of this state of things are visible in the improved condition of all classes of civilized society. But it is not in this point of view, that we chiefly delight to contemplate the effects of machinery. Its influence on the physical condition of man is doubtless very great; but its influence on his intellectual condition is greater. Not only are men in general better fed, better clothed, and better lodged than formerly, but, what seems to us to be a matter of infinitely greater moment, they are far better taught than formerly. Machinery has released some from hand-work, who have applied themselves to head-work. Machinery has supplied them with the means of communicating the results of their industry to the world. Thought is no longer restricted to the narrow circle around the thinker. Machinery has furnished better methods of sending it abroad, than speech. Art has been called in to assist nature. The speaker yields to the writer. The tongue is vanquished by the pen. No power can long preserve, or extensively diffuse spoken words, however eloquent. Write them out and give them to the printer, and if they are worthy of it, they will spread every where and live forever. Formerly, Cicero thundered in the Roman forum, in the midst of the proud monuments of his country's victories, and surrounded on all sides by the altars of his religion, to an audience, that shuddered, and kindled, and quailed, and burned, as he spoke. But when his oration was ended, it was forgotten by the multitude. Some burning thought might be stamped upon the memory. It might pass into a proverb, and be handed down by tradition. But that would not transmit his fame to future times. Had not Cicero written his orations, we should have known little more of him, than that he was a great orator, and that he lived and died in the latter ages of the Roman republic. He did write them, however; but even then, how limited was the circulation, which the copyist alone could give them!

Very different is the case now. A great orator rises in the British parliament. Every word, as it falls from his lips, is caught and written down. Early the next morning, the press gives wings to his thoughts, and sends them abroad, by the aid of the multiplied machinery of conveyance, to traverse regions, and to kindle minds, where Cicero did not even dream that it was possible for man to exist. The epithet, 'winged words,' seems no longer Homeric, but familiar and common-place. In a month's time, they reach New York. In less than a fortnight more, they are descending the Ohio and the Mississippi. In the mean time, they have been passing across the channel, into France, Spain, and Germany, learning new languages as they rush along. They make the circuit of the world. They are heard in India, in Australia, and in the isles of the Pacific ocean. Thus a great thinker and speaker, without the press can do little, against it, nothing; but with its aid he is like the sun, light radiates from him in all directions, and diffuses itself through space. It may be said of him, without hyperbole, that his words go into all the world, carrying with them a momentous influence for evil or for good. By the side of this tremendous energy, every other power becomes insignificant. It proceeds from mind, and acts upon mind, and it is the chief glory of machinery, that it conveys its impulses to the remotest quarters of the globe. And this power is not conferred only on the great orator and statesman, who stands conspicuously out from the mass of his fellow-men. It is shared, in different degrees, by all who have thoroughly awakened their own immortal energies of mind and spirit. It may emanate from the closet of the poorest student, and be of force to revolutionize and empire. It has been truly, as well as forcibly said, by an illustrious man of our own age and nation, that 'one great and kindling thought, from a retired and obscure man, may live when thrones are fallen, and the memory of those who filled them obliterated, and, like an undying fire, illuminate and quicken all future generations.'

But not only has machinery set free from the necessity of labor, many to teach, but a far greater number to be taught. Let the machines, which now supply the wants of the nations, be destroyed, and it requires no prophetic skill to foresee, that, at the same time, the school-houses will be emptied. Let it be imagined, if any are able to imagine, that every machine, for the furtherance of the operations of labor, is destroyed, and that all memory of the mode of their construction is blotted from the mind, and then let us be told, whether we should not, almost at once, sink back into barbarism. Now, thousands are instructed, where one was formerly. Knowledge is diffused widely through all classes of society, and is yet to be diffused far more widely. An unprecedented demand for useful information is every where made. Through the instrumentality of the press, and the modern engines of swift conveyance, sympathies are established between individuals, and between communities of individuals, who entertain similar sentiments, though residing in opposite hemispheres. It is a remarkable illustration of this, that the friends of freedom and knowledge throughout the globe, seem now to constitute but one great party. Wherever a struggle is made for liberty, wherever a contest is begun with that worst of tyrants, ignorance,—that spot concentrates and fixes the attention of multitudes in every civilized nation. Unnumbered minds watch the progress of the contest, with deep anxiety. Thus a universal public opinion is formed. This opinion has strength in its own nature. It is spiritual, wide-reaching, and mighty. It dethrones kings, it abrogates laws, it changes customs. It is stronger than armies. Barriers and *cordons* cannot shut it out. Fortresses and citadels are no defence against it. It spreads every where, and conquers wherever it spreads. God grant, that it may continue to spread and to conquer, till every throne of tyranny shall be overturned, and every altar of superstition broken down!

But the most wonderful consequence resulting from the introduction of machinery is, that it has, to all intents and purposes, greatly prolonged the term of human existence. This is not fancy, but fact; not imagination, but reality. Human life should be measured by deeds, rather than by years. He lives long, who accomplishes much; and he lives longer than other men, who accomplishes more than they. And how much more can he accomplish, whose active existence is but beginning now, than was performed, or could have been performed by one, who lived fifty years ago! The multiplied facilities of intercourse, and the cunningly abbreviated methods of doing every thing at the present day, have introduced extraordinary despatch into all the operations of life, and increased a hundred fold the active power of each individual. Whole communities feel the power of these strong exciting influences. Not only are more important and numerous private acts performed by individuals, than have ever before been done in the compass of one life, but public events, more astonishing and of greater consequence, than were wont to happen in former times in the course of centuries, are now crowded into the history of a single generation. And when we look around us, and behold these strong agents of improvement, acting, at the present moment, with greater energy than ever, and producing every day still more wonderful results, we confess, we are filled with astonishment and admiration. We do not claim, as we have already said, for machinery, the sole agency in producing these magnificent effects. We know that they are principally owing to the operation of moral causes. But we say, that it is machinery, which has removed obstructions out of the way of their action, and brought them into contact with the objects on which they are to act; and that, without the aid of machinery, these causes, whatever inherent energy they might possess, could have produced little or no effect on the condition of society.

We have mentioned some of the general results, which machinery has contributed to produce. There is one particular consequence, that should never be forgotten when machinery is spoken of. It was the inventions of two mechanics, that carried England triumphantly through the contest with Napoleon. Arkwright invented a machine for spinning cotton, and Watt perfected the application of steam power to manufacturing purposes. These inventions conquered Bonaparte. They enabled Great Britain to manufacture for the world. Wealth flowed into her treasury in copious streams, from every quarter. With this wealth she maintained her own armies, and subsidized those of almost all the nations on the continent. She took the lead in the struggle that ensued, and maintained it, until the battle of Waterloo finally decided the fate of Napoleon and of Europe. These inventions made no great show. They attracted little of popular admiration. No laurels bound the brows of the inventors, though, in our esteem, they were far worthier of the laurel wreath, than the proudest conqueror that ever desolated the earth. Their names have not been blazoned in song. The historian honors them but with a cursory notice. Yet did these men, by their astonishing genius, confer on England power to control the issue of the most momentous and fearful struggle, that ever put in peril the best interests of man.

How does machinery produce these almost miraculous results? How long have these strong influences been acting on society? A few words by way of answer to these questions, shall conclude this article. We have already remarked, that the invention of some machines of a simple construction, is dated far back in remote antiquity; but these were all helps to individual labor, and are never thought of now, when machinery is named. Then, almost every thing was done by hand. Navigation clung timidly to the shore. Labor performed its task tediously and imperfectly. Knowledge was diffused in scanty measures and by tedious processes. Human improvement advanced, if indeed it did advance, imperceptibly. It is but recently, that any great change has taken place. The era of machinery may be said to have commenced within the last fifty years. Man has called upon the unwearied powers of nature to bear his burdens, and they have obeyed the call. Whatever agency expands, contracts, impels, retards, uplifts, or depresses, is set at work. We confine elasticity in our watches, and bid it measure our time. With pulleys and levers, we compel gravitation to undo its own work. We arrest the water as it flows onward to the ocean. It must do so much spinning, so much weaving, or so much grinding, before it can be allowed to pass on. With the help of pumps and other machinery, we force the very atmosphere we live in, to raise our water from the wells and from the rivers, and to aid in an uncounted and countless variety of other operations. Last, and most wonderful of all, by the application of fire we transform water into that most potent of all agents, steam. Man, as it were, yokes the hostile elements of fire and water, and subjects them to his bidding. It is hardly a metaphor, to call steam the vital principle, the living soul of modern machinery. There is hardly any sort of work, in which this mighty agent may not be employed. It is equal to the vastest operations, and it will perform the most minute. It delves in the mines, it lifts the ore to the surface, and converts it into a thousand forms. It helps to make the engine, which it afterwards inhabits. It brings the cotton to the manufactory, picks it, cards it, spins it, weaves it, stamps it, and then distributes the fabrics for sale. It works on the land and on the water, on the rivers and on the seas. It is found on the Rhine and on the Danube, driving huge fabrics impetuously along through the echoing forests, and by the old castles of chivalrous ages, accustomed to behold far different scenes; and it performs on land the work of many thousand hands. It quickens the activity of commerce on the Indian seas, at the very moment when it is doing the same on the Mississippi and the Ohio. Invention seems to rest from the effort to discover new forces, and to bend all her energies to multiply the applications of this. Friction and gravity alone continue to oppose the dominion of steam over space. Numberless subtle contrivances have been resorted to, to evade the power of these stubborn antagonists of motion. Railways are constructed, stretching over mountains and plains, linking together and making near neighbors of distant territories. Long trains of cars, moving on wheels so peculiarly constructed, that their friction is scarcely perceptible, are placed on them. The horse is unharnessed. He is too slow and too weak to perform the required service. At command, the whole moves, hurrying on, under the strong impulse of an invisible power, with a velocity that defies description. The lover need no longer pray for wings to bear him through the air. A railway car will bear him swifter than the swiftest wing. The exclamation of the poet no longer startles us. His description of the physical achievements of man's 'genius, spirit, power,' are no longer extravagant. It falls far short of the reality.

> Look down on Earth!—What seest thou?—
>   Wondrous things!
> Terrestrial wonders that eclipse the skies!
> What lengths of labored lands! What loaded
>   seas!
> Loaded by man for pleasure, wealth or war!
> Seas, winds and planets, into service brought,
> His art acknowledge, and subserve his ends.
> Nor can the eternal rocks his will withstand;
> What levelled mountains! and what lifted
>   vales!
> High through mid air, *here,* streams are taught
>   to flow;
> Whole river, *there,* laid by in basins, sleep.
> *Here,* plains turn oceans; *there,* vast oceans
>   join
> Through kingdoms, channelled deep from
>   shore to shore.
> Earth's disembowelled! Measured are the
>   skies!
> Stars are detected in their deep recess!

> Creation widens! Vanquished Nature yields!
> Her secrets are extorted! *Art* prevails!
> What monument of genius, spirit, power!

This was a just description when it was written; and it describes splendid triumphs of the intellect over matter. Let our readers add to it all the wonders which have been achieved by steam, and they will have a tolerably accurate idea of what the mechanical powers have done, and are doing for man.

THEMES AND SYMBOLS IN LITERATURE

Elémire Zolla

SOURCE: "The Fruits of Industry," in *The Eclipse of the Intellectual,* translated by Raymond Rosenthal, Funk & Wagnalls, 1956, pp. 3-19.

[In the following excerpt, Zolla provides a chronology of literary responses to the Industrial Revolution, ranging from Blake to Melville.]

> When we heard talk about the Encyclopedists or opened a volume of their enormous work, we felt we were making our way among the innumerable spools and looms of a huge factory, and before all that clatter and loud rolling of wheels, before that mechanism which disorients the eye and the sensibility, before the incomprehensibility of a plant which has so many diverse ramifications, contemplating everything that is required to make a piece of cloth, we felt that the very suit we wore was spoiled.
>
> Goethe, *Poetry and Truth*

One of the commonplaces which plague us is the statement: "Industry and technique can of course be harmful to the spirit, but that is only due to their improper use." In truth, the machine does not by itself become tyrannical; it does so simply because of a certain "spirit" which pervades, accompanies, and spreads its aura around it. To detach the object from the effect it has on the subject is already tantamount to being subjugated by the spirit of the Industrial Revolution. Whoever tries to discover the Archimedean point from which to overturn its pernicious power, whether by the Luddite destruction of machines or by the redemption of the "spirit" with which machines are used, is already its victim. In fact, as Goethe perceived, an ordering of reality along technical lines was already immanent in Encyclopedism, just as Encyclopedism could not have arisen without the development of factories. Modern armies already had a factory-like structure, the bureaucracies of the absolutist regimes were already being mechanized, and Western science was already excluding every ritual and meditative element.

Why is it that at the peak of Greek scientific thought, which possessed the scientific knowledge to permit it, an industrial revolution was not born? Why didn't Greek science become the servant of the mercantile spirit? Why didn't the isolated and desperate application of science to the invention of burning glasses, or Heron's steam engine, divest science of its sacramental purity? Hanns Sachs has shown that neither economic nor social reasons were responsible for this,[1] and he has pointed, in explanation, to the psychological attitude of the Greeks, their "narcissistic investment" in the body, their spontaneous erotic relationship to the flesh, which made it impossible for them to conceive of technical exploitation or to create a utilitarian world. Among the archetypes of the ancient world figured certain mythical situations—for example, Athena's aristocratic nature and Aphrodite's dominion over Hephaestus—which are the expression of the orientation Sachs formulates in narrowly psychoanalytical terms. These were certainly not the myths that the European bourgeoisie lived through *en masse* during the eighteenth century.

The first signs of the Industrial Revolution did not trouble the literati. On the contrary, the interest in scientific discoveries and their application was often promoted by the literary reviews. In Italy the *Conciliator* published articles on the new machines and the applications of steam, and Vincenzo Monti, the neoclassicist poet, extolled the conquests of a progressive humanity with the same suavity with which he had celebrated the first foreshadowings of the centralized modern state in the Napoleonic regime. At most, Count Gasparo Gozzi complained that the future god and regulator of industrial civilization, the clock, had become too invasive, rendering impossible a lovers' rendezvous, by its nature inimical to such a tyrannical calculation of minutes.

Only the forerunners of romanticism in England were able to discern the real face of the Industrial Revolution. It was William Blake who foresaw all the horrors that lay in store and sensed the threat that hung over man's very hand, condemned by machines to lose its ability to shape matter directly and to create freely and beautifully the objects destined for daily use. He perceived the relationship between machines on the one hand and Newtonian physics and sensist philosophy on the other; he foretold the destruction of beauty that the factories would bring at a time when industries were still confined to the Lancashire valleys and did not yet exist in his native London.

Here is William Blake's prophecy in his poem "The Four Zoas," written between 1795 and 1804:

> The Villages lament! they faint, outstretch'd
>   upon the plain.
> Wailing runs round the Valleys from the Mill
>   and from the Barn.

> But most the polish'd Palaces, dark, silent,
>   bow with dread,
> Hiding their books & pictures underneath the
>   dens of Earth.
> The Cities send to one another saying: 'My
>   sons are Mad
> With wine of cruelty. Let us plat a scourge,
>   O Sister City.'
> Children are nourished for the Slaughter; once
>   the Child was fed
> With Milk, but wherefore now are Children
>   fed with blood?
> The Horse is of more value than the Man. The
>   Tyger fierce
> Laughs at the Human form; The Lion mocks
>   and thirsts for blood.
> They cry, O Spider, spread thy web! Enlarge
>   thy bones & fill'd
> With marrow, sinews and flesh, Exalt Thyself,
>   attain a voice.
> 'Call to thy dark arm'd hosts; for all the Sons
>   of Men muster together
> To desolate their cities! Man shall be no
>   more! Awake, O Hosts!'

Only Blake's prophetic images were adequate to the Revolution: his vision of the spider which grew gigantic, the loss of the image of man, the insatiable beasts which would impose the laws of oppression on the new world. Later, Wordsworth, too, intoned a lament, more meditative yet incapable of discerning the mythological presences behind the spectacle of brutalization. He was, however, the first to see that "a multitude of causes, unknown to former times, are now acting with a combined force to blunt the discriminating powers of the mind, and, unfitting it for all voluntary exertion, to reduce it to a state of almost savage torpor. The most effective of these causes are the great national events which are daily taking place, and the increasing accumulation of men in cities, where the uniformity of their occupations produces a craving for extraordinary incident which the rapid communication of intelligence hourly gratifies."[2]

"The Excursion" is dated 1814:

> . . . I have lived to mark
> A new and unforeseen creation rise
> From out the labours of a peaceful land
> Wielding her potent enginery to frame
> And to produce, with appetite as keen
> As that of war, which rests not night or day,
> Industrious to destroy! . . .
>   At social industry's command,
> How quick, how vast an increase! From the
>   germ
> Of some poor hamlet, rapidly produced
> Here a huge town, continuous and compact,
> Hiding the face of the earth for leagues—and
>   there,

Where not a habitation stood before,
Abodes of men irregularly massed
Like trees in forests—spread through spacious
        tracts,
O'er which the smoke of unremitting fires
Hangs permanent, and plentiful as wreaths
Of vapour glittering in the morning sun.
    . . . I grieve when on the darker side
Of this great change I look; and there behold,
Such outrage done to nature as compels
The indignant power to justify herself;
    . . . Then, maidens, youths,
Mothers and little children, boys and girls,
Enter, and each the wonted task resumes
Within this temple, where is offered up
To Gain, the master idol of the realm,
Perpetual Sacrifice. Even thus of old
Our ancestors, within the still domain
Of vast cathedral or conventional church,
Their vigils kept; where tapers day and night
On the dim altar burned continually,
In token that the House was evermore
Watching to God . . .

Triumph who will in these profaner rites
Which we, a generation self-extolled
As zealously perform! I cannot share
His proud complacency:—yet do I exult,
Casting reserve away, exult to see
An intellectual mastery exercised
O'er the blind elements; a purpose given,
A perseverance fed; almost a soul
Imparted—to brute matter.

Yet in fact Wordsworth retreated from the austere beauty which, he felt, he should have seen behind the desolation of the new factories, and preferred to turn with even more tremulous emotion to the beauty of the still untouched fields, the pastoral life as yet spared by the Leviathan. This anxious feeling for landscape in English romantic poetry derives its vibration of fear, its self-isolating rapture, its sense of an obscure threat to its contemplation, precisely from the precarious nature of its rural consolations. It is in this nuance of its vision of landscape that the horrors of the new industrial agglomerates make themselves felt, indirectly, secretly, affecting those who ignore them and turn their minds to some other sight. Only in Southey and Coleridge is there a vivid awareness of the new state of affairs, for they recognize in the periodic unemployment a consequence of the anarchic development of industrial production. Indeed, Coleridge notes that what Wordsworth called the new idol, profit, causes a pernicious transformation in man himself, converting him into a commodity, since the worker sells that which should above all be *extra commercium:* "the worker's health, life and well-being."

The initial phases of the Industrial Revolution found their clearest expression in the novel. After Gaskell's descriptions of Manchester's proletariat, it is Dickens who presents the truest picture of industrial conditions. In *Hard Times,* published in 1854, he observes the squalor of the industrial towns which had by now invaded England like a plague. Especially memorable is the description of Coketown, the city where imagination has been banished and the reign of "hard facts" has been installed.

> Coketown . . . was a triumph of fact. . . . It was a town of red brick, or of brick that would have been red if the smoke and ashes had allowed it; but as matters stood it was a town of unnatural red and black like the painted face of a savage. It was a town of machinery and tall chimneys, out of which interminable serpents of smoke trailed themselves for ever and ever, and never got uncoiled. It had a black canal in it, and a river that ran purple with ill-smelling dye, and vast piles of buildings full of windows where there was a rattling and a trembling all day long and where the piston of the steam engine worked monotonously up and down, like the head of an elephant in a state of melancholy madness. It contained several large streets all very like one another, and many small streets still more like one another, inhabited by people equally like one another, who all went in and out at the same hours, with the same sound upon the same pavements, to do the same work, and to whom every day was the same as yesterday and tomorrow, and every year the counterpart of the last and the next . . . The perplexing mystery of the place was, who belonged to the eighteen denominations? Because, whoever did, the laboring people did not. It was very strange to walk through the streets on a Sunday morning, and note how few of *them* the barbarous jangling of bells that was driving the sick and nervous mad, called away from their own quarters, from their own close rooms, from the corners of their own streets, where they lounged listlessly, gazing at all the church and chapel going, as at a thing with which they had no manner of concern. Nor was it merely the stranger who noticed this, because there was a native organization in Coketown itself, whose members were to be heard of in the House of Commons every session, indignantly petitioning for acts of parliament that should make these people religious by main force. Then came the Teetotal Society, who complained that these same people *would* get drunk . . . Then came the chemist and druggist, with (other) tabular statements, showing that when they didn't get drunk, they took opium. Then came the experienced chaplain of the jail, with more tabular statements (outdoing all the previous tabular statements) and showing that the same people *would* resort to low haunts, hidden from the public eye, where they heard low singing and saw low dancing, and mayhaps joined in it; and where A.B., aged twenty-four next birthday, and committed for eighteen months solitary, had himself said (not that he had ever shown himself particularly worthy of belief) his ruin began, as he was perfectly sure and confident that otherwise he would have been a tiptop moral specimen.

This is one of the first accurate and ironic descriptions of an industrial city of the period. The farmers and uprooted artisans, transported to the new cities and forced to work eighteen hours a day, forced to keep their wives and children in the same dreadful places and at the same senseless labor—indeed reduced to regarding their children as commodities to be sold as soon as possible—had lost all interest in their ancestral traditions. Indifferent to the religion which had once step by step marked off the rural year, they turned to whiskey for solace and during the first half of the century, as Dickens remarks and Thomas de Quincey minutely describes, began to use opium. The spectacle of a mob of rootless, anonymous people began to dominate and move the poets' imaginations even more than the outrages to the beauty of nature. It was the same mob that packed London and Paris, the demonic horde that had been foreseen by William Blake and was now omnipresent. Confronted by this industrial mob, this succession of silent faces dominated by squalor, plaintive laments over Cyclops persecuting the nymphs, enthusiasm for nature conquered by science, and nostalgia for salubrious air and open glades were no longer acceptable literary reactions.

One of the first to realize this was a French publicist, Saint-Marc Girardin. His famous essay *Les Barbares* was published in 1831. He compared the revolt of the textile workers of Lyon to the revolt of San Domingo. "The barbarians who threaten our society are not in the Caucasus or on the steppes of Tartary, but in the settlements surrounding the industrial cities. These barbarians should not be insulted, for they are worthy of pity, not of reproach."

The bourgeoisie will pay dearly, Saint-Marc Girardin warns, if it permits the masses to enter the National Guard. What is interesting here, however, are not the political considerations but the invitation to consider the uprooted in the midst of bourgeois society as a horde of barbarians. At the opposite pole from this reaction of the pitying, frightened bourgeois stands Friedrich Engels, who experienced the same phenomenon in his *Condition of the Working Class of England:*

> London is unique, because it is a city in which one can roam for hours without leaving the built-up area and without seeing the slightest sign of the approach of open country. This enormous agglomeration of population on a single spot has multiplied a hundred fold the economic strength of the two and a half million inhabitants concentrated there . . . It is only later that the traveller appreciates the human suffering which has made all this possible. He can only realize the price that has been paid for all this magnificence after he has tramped the pavements of the main streets of London for some days and has tired himself out by jostling his way through the crowds and by dodging the endless stream of coaches and carts which fills the streets. It is only when he has visited the slums of this great city that it dawns upon him that the inhabitants of modern London have had to sacrifice so much that is best in human nature in order to create those wonders of civilization with which their city teems. The vast majority of Londoners have had to let so many of their potential creative faculties lie dormant, stunted and unused in order that a small, closely-knit group of their fellow citizens could develop to the full the qualities with which nature has endowed them. The restless and noisy activity of the crowded streets is highly distasteful, and it is surely abhorrent to human nature itself. Hundreds of thousands of men and women drawn from all classes and ranks of society pack the streets of London. Are they not all human beings with the same innate characteristics and potentialities? Are they not all equally interested in the pursuit of happiness? . . . Yet they rush past each other as if they had nothing in common. They are tacitly agreed on one thing only—that everyone should keep to the right of the pavement so as not to collide with the stream of people moving in the opposite direction. No one even thinks of sparing a glance for his neighbor on the streets. The more that Londoners are packed into a tiny space, the more repulsive and disgraceful becomes the brutal indifference with which they ignore their neighbors and selfishly concentrate upon their private affairs.

Engels is describing the trauma of someone who finds himself submerged in an anonymous crowd, where each person's features have long been shaped in the withered lines of selfishness and indifference. The industrial city, with its flamboyant stores and its colorless miseries, offers through the spectacle of the crowd a vivid expression, an immediate image, of that humanity which the industrial revolution had lumped together and fragmented, animated and parched. This is the trauma which will strike at all of the century's poets and novelists. Reactions will range from Balzac's enthusiastic effervescence to the Romantics' pleasure in escape and Baudelaire's immersion in symbols of aridity and sterility.

In Balzac's *Lost Illusions* the vitality of Paris in the throes of becoming an industrial city is caught in all of its nuances: exaltation before the spectacle of a life whose rhythm has been accelerated and dismay at the cruelty of this life without solidarity.

In Dickens as in Balzac one sees an apparent realism as the response to the new human condition. In fact, in order to respond to the inhuman leveling, to the transformation of small communities into mass agglomerates, and to the cold domination of private interest, both these novelists have recourse to grandiose deformations. Exaggerating their characters' tics, they placate their fury by means of the grotesque. For the first time, deformation and the grotesque cease to be artistic forms in a light genre, or forms suited only to expressing a world of unearthly terrors; they become the exact equivalent of daily life. This relationship has been noticed by the critic Theodore Adorno, who pointed out:

> Dickens and Balzac reveal not only romantic and pre-bourgeois traits, but in fact Balzac's entire *Comedie Humaine,* which not without reason had been compared to Daumier's caricatures, proves to be a reconstruction of an alienated reality, that is, a reality no longer shared by the observer.

In Balzac even more than in Dickens, there is an attempt to compensate for the coldness of industrial life by an outpouring of sentiment, so blatantly displayed that it becomes abject sentimentality.

The only great novelist of the century who became thoroughly aware of the trauma of the industrial mob and resolved it in a completely original poetic world, following in Blake's footsteps and shaping his enigmatic, Medusa-like vision in a vast allegory, was Herman Melville. In his novel *Redburn* an autobiographical scene recalls a visit to the industrial quarter of Southampton, where the protagonist comes upon a hovel in which a family is dying. Here one sees again the mute squalor and desperation of De Quincey's cities. In a later novel, *Israel Potter,* Melville expresses the trauma of the mob in a fashion that presages the poetry of the twentieth century, indeed, of Eliot's *The Waste Land*. To represent London on the point of industrializing itself, the London already prophetically divined by Blake, he employs images which in ancient times were reserved for the description of other-worldly sufferings. Israel Potter, a young American, reaches the great metropolis. "For forty years he never recovered from (the) surprise" at the new city of Dis that swarmed with hordes of the damned in a whirling, demonic dance:

> Whichever way the eye turned, no tree, no speck of any green thing was seen—no more than in smithies. All labourers, of whatever sort, were hued like men in foundries. The black vistas of streets were galleries in coal mines; the flagging, as flat tombstones, minus the consecration of moss, worn heavily down, by sorrowful tramping, as the vitreous rocks in the cursed Galápagos, over which the convict tortoises crawl. . . .

Melville conjures up another vision of industrial horror in his short story "The Tartarus of Maids," in which a lugubrious paper mill in one of New England's once beautiful valleys is populated with consumptive girls stirring a nauseous pulp of rags. The reduction to the machine-like is similar, Melville senses, to the reduction to the merely biological; and so the factory becomes for him an inexhaustible source of allegory: the pulp is similar to the human seed that must become man, yet it is also destined to become paper on which

will be written the impressions that form a rootless man—the *tabula rasa* of Lockian philosophy which in fact presaged tomorrow's rootless man.

But Melville did not limit himself to the present; he also envisaged the future, and in his late work *The Confidence Man* he was able to deduce our whole epoch, including automation, from the facts of his own time. One of the novel's characters, a promoter, says:

> I'm now on the road to get me made some sort of machine to do my work. Machines for me. My cider mill—does that ever steal my cider? My mowing machine—does that ever lay a-bed mornings? My corn husker—does that ever give me insolence? No: cider mill, mowing machine, corn husker—all faithfully attend to their business. Disinterested, too; no board, no wages; yet doing good all their lives long; shining examples that virtue is its own reward—the only practical Christians I know . . . Sir, a corn husker, for its patient continuance in well-doing, might not unfitly go to heaven. Do you suppose a boy will?

The interlocutor of this typical entrepreneur, consternated by the lack of Christian virtues in his employees, like a character in Dickens but even more marvelously grotesque, replies:

> Respected sir, this way of talking as if heaven were a kind of Washington patent-office museum—oh! oh! oh!—as if mere machine work and puppet work went to heaven—oh! oh! oh! Things incapable of free agency, to receive the eternal reward of well-doing—oh! oh! oh!

The entrepreneur is not deflected by these horrified outcries and goes on to affirm that man, from the standpoint of work, is a total loss, less to be trusted than the ox, while from the standpoint of conscience, he is inferior to the dachshund. In the coming era, machines will do all of man's work, and he will become a fossil, a superfluous curio. All that will then be left will be to hunt him with guns as though he were a possum.

Just as in *Israel Potter* Melville describes the real reason for the Napoleonic wars, that is, the need to check the great growth of pauperism and overpopulation brought about by the periodical crises of the industrial system, so in this passage of *The Confidence Man* he describes the inevitable combinations of the industrial era's social mechanics in the remote future. And haven't we witnessed hunts of men-possums after crises of unemployment? Melville foresaw all the consequences of complete industrialization and, in his long poem *Clarel,* even the lonely crowd of today:

> The world clean fails me, still I yearn,
> This side the dark and hollow bound
> Lies there no unexplored rich ground?

Some other world: well, there's the New—
Ah, joyless and ironic too!

   But in the New World things make haste:
Not only things, the *state* lives fast—
Fast breed the pregnant eggs and shells,
The slumberous combustibles
Sure to explode. 'Twill come, 'twill come!
One demagogue can trouble much:
How of a hundred thousand such? . . .
Indeed, whose germs one now may view:
Myriads playing pigmy parts—
   Debased into equality:
In glut of all material arts
A civic barbarism may be:
Man disennobled—brutalized
By popular science—Atheized
Into a smatterer—

Yet knowing all self need to know
In self's base little fallacy;
Dead level of rank commonplace:
An Anglo-Saxon China, see,
May on your vast plains shame the race
In the Dark Ages of Democracy . . .
Your arts advance in faith's decay:
You are but drilling the new Hun
Whose growl even now can some dismay;
Vindictive in his heart of hearts,
He schools him in your mines and marts—
A skilled destroyer . . .

                              (IV, xxi)

The Anglo-Saxon . . .
Who in the name of Christ and Trade
Deflower the world's last sylvan glade! . . .
                              (IV, ix)

The impieties of 'Progress' speak;
What say *these,* in effect, to God?
'How profits it? And who art Thou
That we should serve Thee? Of Thy ways
No knowledge we desire; *new* ways
We have found out, and better, Go—
Depart from us!'
And if He do?
(And that He may, the Scripture says)
Is aught betwixt us and the hells?

                              (IV, xxi)

Melville's attitude is wholly dictated by a vivid recognition of the consequences of the new industrial epoch. In order to represent its desperation he had recourse to allegory, calling to his aid the most profound myths of his culture—Leviathan and the Calvinist God—just as Blake had evoked the gigantic spider and the tiger.

Precisely while industrial civilization was taking over America, transforming it even more rapidly than Eu-

rope, the poet had arisen who was capable of looking the new reality in the face. Indeed, he wasn't the artist invoked by the optimists, nor the artist summoned by Emerson, who had written:

> Time and nature yield us many gifts, but not yet the timely man, the new religion, the reconciler, whom all things await. Dante's praise is that he dared to write his autobiography in colossal cipher, or into universality. We have yet had no genius in America, with tyrannous eye, which knew the value of our incomparable materials, and saw, in the barbarism and materialism of our times, another carnival of the same gods whose picture he so much admired in Homer: then in the Middle Ages; then in Calvinism. Banks and tariffs, the newspaper and caucus, Methodism and Unitarianism, are flat and dull to dull people, but rest on the same foundations of wonder as the town of Troy and the temple of Delphi . . . For as it is dislocation and detachment from the life of God that makes things ugly, the poet, who reattaches things to nature and the Whole,—reattaching even artificial things and violation of nature, to nature, by a deeper insight,—disposes very easily of the most disagreeable facts.

Melville carried out Emerson's program and told the story of the attempt to link oneself again to the whole—the hunt for Moby Dick, the white whale. In his novel *Pierre* he also told the story of the shipwreck of man in the new metropolis, where the situation seen in Balzac's *Lost Illusions* reappears.

From America was to come another voice capable of sounding the lament—Edgar Allan Poe. The trauma of the industrial mass appears in his short story "The Man of the Crowd," in which the London crowd is described. Just as Engels came from an as yet patriarchal society in Germany and fully experienced the feeling of dismay, so Poe imagines a man kept in solitude by an illness who suddenly finds himself again in the heart of the industrial metropolis. He sits at the window of a tavern and observes:

> But as the darkness came on, the throng momently increased; and by the time the lamps were well lighted, two dense and continuous tides of population were rushing past the door. At this particular period of the evening I had never before been in a similar situation, and the tumultuous sea of human heads filled me, therefore, with a delicious novelty of emotion. I gave up, at length, all care of things within the hotel, and became absorbed in contemplation of the scene without.

He tries in vain to find an individual face, but the mass is a mixture of inane types, of marionettes. Poe attempted to escape from his vision through exasperation and crime, which are ways of separating oneself from the crowd. His is a poetic which derives from the trauma of the crowd and which weeps:

> . . . and driven the hamadryad from the wood
> To seek a shelter in some happier star?

But unlike Melville, Poe tried to adjust to the times and invent new genres suited to the new style of existence. Thus he wrote in a letter to Longfellow in 1841: "I need not call your attention to the signs of the times in respect to Magazine literature. You will admit that the tendency of the age lies in this way—so far at least as regards the lighter letters. The brief, the condensed, and the easily circulated will take the place of the diffuse, the ponderous, and the inaccessible."

In "The Philosophy of Furniture," he wrote: " . . . the *display of wealth* has here to take the place and perform the office of the heraldic display in monarchical countries. By a transition readily understood, and which might have been as readily foreseen, we have been brought to merge in a simple *show* our notions of taste itself."

In creating the detective story, Poe sensed a secret need of the mass which he had described in "The Man of the Crowd," the need for a crude, stereotyped stimulus.

The real poet of the trauma was Charles Baudelaire. But before tracing the process which in Baudelaire absorbs and expresses the new civilization, it is worthwhile to point to another case of fundamental trauma in the literature of the nineteenth century. In 1863 an article by Fyodor Dostoevsky was published in the magazine *Vremia* [*Time*], which proves that he too had had much the same experience as Melville, Poe, and Engels. He speaks of London:

> Here you see the tenacious, subterranean and by now inveterate struggle of the principle of the individual, as it is conceived in the West, and of the necessity of living together in some way, forming a society, of transforming oneself into an ant-eater, and yet of coming to some agreement so as not to devour each other . . . A city which, immense as an ocean, seethes day and night with the screams and shrieks of machinery, with railroads running above the roofs and soon under the ground—this audacious, false disorder which is bourgeois order. The Thames poisoned, the air saturated with coal, the horrible sections of the city, like Whitechapel with its half-naked and starving inhabitants; the City with its millions and its world trade; the Crystal Palace and the Universal Exposition. Indeed, this exposition of goods is impressive . . . It requires strength of spirit and great abnegation not to succumb, not to give in to its overwhelming effect, not to succumb to the *fait accompli*, that is, not to mistake what exists for the ideal, not to adore Baal.

What struck Dostoevsky most of all was that now he was face to face with the mass. The mass is not a numerical fact but derives its character from the form of its social relations. A mass exists wherever profound indifference reigns between one person and another and both general and particular movements are coordinated by external forces, most often anonymous. Coordinated by the God Baal, Dostoevsky claims, as he describes the spectacle of alcoholism and prostitution and depicts the humiliation and general oppression.

Melville had divined a further truth beyond the visible presence of misery, that is, the lack in the masses of any customs, of a traditional and consecrated way of handling their passions. And it is worth reading *Israel Potter* again:

> Nor marble, nor flesh, nor the sad spirit of man, may in this cindery City of Dis abide white . . . one after the other they [the pedestrians] drifted by, uninvoked ghosts in Hades. Some of the wayfarers wore a less serious look; some seemed hysterically merry; but the mournful faces had an earnestness not seen in the others. . . .

Here the character of the industrial mass is perfectly grasped: it sways between hysteria and gloom, for among these coerced worshippers of Baal the emotions are formless.

Whitman defines the function of the artist in the industrial society (1851):

Among such a people as the Americans, viewing most things with an eye to pecuniary profit—more for acquiring than for enjoying or well developing what they acquire—ambitious of the physical rather than the intellectual; a race to whom matter of fact is everything, and the ideal nothing—a nation of whom the steam engine is no bad symbol—he does a good work who, pausing in the way, calls to the feverish crowd that in the life we live upon this beautiful earth, there may, after all, be something vaster and better than dress and the table, and business and politics.

There was an idle Persian hundreds of years ago who wrote poems; and he was accosted by one who believed more in thrift.—"Of what use are you?" inquired the supercilious son of traffic. The poet turning plucked a rose and said, "Of what use is this?" "To be beautiful, to perfume the air," answered the man of gains. "And I," responded the poet, "am of use to perceive its beauty and to smell its perfume."

It is the glorious province of Art, and of all Artists worthy the name, to disentangle from whatever obstructs it, and nourish in the heart of man, the germ of the perception of the truly great, the beautiful and the simple. . . .

Walt Whitman, in The Uncollected Poetry and Prose of Walt Whitman, *edited by Emory Holloway, Peter Smith, 1932.*

Leo Marx

SOURCE: "The Machine in the Garden," in *The Pilot and the Passenger: Essays on Literature, Technology, and Culture in the United States,* Oxford University Press, 1988, pp. 113-26.

[*In the following essay, originally published in 1956 in* The New England Quarterly, *Marx examines the themes and images employed by American authors such as Emerson, Thoreau, Hawthorne, and Melville to indirectly respond to industrialization during the years before 1860. Marx also studies the influence of the Industrial Revolution on the literature of the time.*]

> . . . the artist must employ the symbols in use in his day and nation to convey his enlarged sense to his fellow-men.
>
> Ralph Waldo Emerson[1]

I

The response of American writers to industrialism has been a typical and, in many respects, a distinguishing feature of our culture. The Industrial Revolution, of course, was international, but certain aspects of the process were intensified in this country. Here, for one thing, the Revolution was delayed, and when it began it was abrupt, thorough, and dramatic. During a decisive phase of that transition, our first significant literary generation, that of Hawthorne and Emerson, came to maturity.[2] Hence it may be said that our literature, virtually from the beginning, has embodied the experience of a people crossing the line which sets off the era of machine production from the rest of human history. As Emerson said, speaking of the century as the "age of tools," so many inventions had been added in his time that life seemed "almost made over new."[3] My aim here is to demonstrate one of the ways in which a sense of the transformation of life by the machine has contributed to the temper of our literature. The emphasis is upon the years before 1860, because the themes and images with which our major writers then responded to the onset of the Machine Age have provided us with a continuing source of meaning.

Some will justifiably object, however, that very little of the work of Emerson, Thoreau, Hawthorne, or Melville actually was *about* the Industrial Revolution. But this fact hardly disposes of the inquiry; indeed, one appeal of the subject is precisely the need to meet this objection. For among the many arid notions which have beset inquiries into the relations between literature and society, perhaps the most barren has been the assumption that artists respond to history chiefly by making history their manifest subject. As if one might adequately gauge the imaginative impact of atomic power by seeking out direct allusions to it in recent literature.

Our historical scholars do not sufficiently distinguish between the setting of a literary work (it may be institutional, geographical, or historical) and its subject-matter or theme. A poem set in a factory need be no more about industrialism than *Hamlet* about living in castles. Not that the setting is without significance. But the first obligation of the scholar, like any other reader of literature, is to know what the work is about. Only then may he proceed to his special business of elucidating the relevance of the theme to the experience of the age.

But here a difficulty arises: the theme itself cannot be said to "belong" to the age. It is centuries old. The Promethean theme, for example, belongs to no single time or place; history periodically renews man's sense of the perils attendant upon the conquest of nature. This obvious fact lends force to the view, tacit postulate of much recent criticism, that what we value in art derives from (and resides in) a realm beyond time, or, for that matter, society. Yet because the scholar grants his inability to account for the genesis of themes, he need not entertain a denial of history. True, he should not speak, for example, of *the* literature of industrialism, as if there were serious works whose controlling insights originate in a single, specific historical setting. But he has every reason to assume that certain themes and conventions, though they derive from the remote past, may have had a peculiar relevance to an age suddenly aware that machines were making life over new. That, in any case, is what seems to have happened in the age of Emerson and Melville. Because our writers seldom employed industrial settings until late in the century we have thought that only then did the prospect of a mechanized America affect their vision of life.[4] My view is that an awareness of the Machine Revolution has been vital to our literature since the eighteen thirties.

But what of a man like Hawthorne, whom we still regard as the "pure" artist, and whose work apparently bears little relation to the Industrial Revolution of his age? In his case it is necessary to demonstrate the importance for his work of matters about which he wrote virtually nothing. Here is "Ethan Brand," a characteristic story developed from an idea Hawthorne recorded in 1843: "The search of an investigator for the Unpardonable Sin;—he at last finds it in his own heart and practice."[5] The theme manifestly has nothing to do with industrialization. On the contrary, it is traditional; we correctly associate it with the Faust myth.[6] Nevertheless, some facts about the genesis of the tale are suggestive. For its physical details, including characters and landscape, Hawthorne drew upon notes he had made during a Berkshire vacation in 1838. At that time several new factories were in operation along the mountain streams near North Adams.[7] He was struck by the sight of machinery in the green hills; he took elaborate notes, and conceived the idea of a malignant steam engine which attacked and killed its human at-tendants.[8] But he did nothing with that idea, or with any of his other observations upon the industrialization of the Berkshires. And the fact remains that nowhere, in "Ethan Brand" or the notebooks, do we find any explicit evidence of a direct link between Hawthorne's awareness of the new power and this fable of the quest for knowledge of absolute evil.

II

Nevertheless this connection can, I believe, be estab-lished. What enables us to establish it is the discovery of a body of imagery through which the age repeatedly expressed its response to the Industrial Revolution. This "imagery of technology" is decisively present in "Ethan Brand."

Although the theme is traditional, some components of the tale take on their full significance only when we consider what was happening in America at the time. Between 1830 and 1860 the image of the machine, and the idea of a capitalist society founded upon machine power suddenly took hold of the public imagination. In the magazines, for example, images of industrial-ism, and particularly images associated with the power of steam, were widely employed as emblems of Amer-ica's future.[9] They stood for progress, productivity, and, above all, man's new power over nature. And they invariably carried a sense of violent break with the past. Later, looking back at those years, Henry Adams compressed the essential feeling into his account of the way "he and his eighteenth century . . . were sud-denly cut apart—separated forever . . ." by the rail-road, steamship, and telegraph.[10] It is the suddenness and finality of change—the recent past all at once a green colonial memory—to which American writers have persistently called attention. The motif recurs in our literature from *Walden* to *The Bear*.

But at first our writers did not respond by writing *about* the Industrial Revolution. Long before they knew enough to find concepts for the experience, as Adams later could do, they had invested their work with ideas and emotions it provoked. To this end they drew upon images of technology already familiar to the public. Such collective representations, or "cultural images," allowed them to express what they could not yet fully understand. And at times they heightened these images to the intensity of symbols. The symbolism of Haw-thorne and Melville was, after all, designed to get at circumstances which gave rise to conflicting emotions, and which exceeded, in their complexity, the capaci-ties of understanding.[11] Indeed, there is reason to be-lieve that the unprecedented changes then taking place may have provided a direct impetus to the use of sym-bolic techniques.[12] Hawthorne admitted as much in explaining why he required the image of the railroad to convey that sense of loneliness in the crowd he

thought characteristic of the new America. This image, he said, enabled him to present the feeling of a "whole world, both morally and physically, . . . detached from its old standfasts and set in rapid motion."[13]

Now, as the statements of Emerson, Adams, and Haw-thorne suggest, the evocative power of the imagery of industrialism is not to be attributed to any intrinsic feature of machines. What gives rise to the emotion is not the machine, but rather its presence against the felt background of the older historic landscape. The Amer-ican landscape, in fact, accounts for another singular feature of the response to our Industrial Revolution. In this country mechanization had been arrested, among other things, by space—the sheer extent of the land itself. Then, suddenly, with the application of mecha-nized motive power to transport, this obstacle had been overcome. Hence the dramatic decisiveness of the changes in Hawthorne's time, when steam power was suddenly joined to the forces already pressing to occu-py the virgin land. In America machines were pre-eminently conquerors of nature—nature conceived as space. They blazed across a raw landscape of wilder-ness and farm.

Now it is hardly necessary to discuss the high value, aesthetic, moral, and even political, with which the landscape had so recently been invested. Henry Nash Smith has indicated how central a place images of the landscape occupied in the popular vision of America's future as new Garden of the World.[14] The sudden appearance of the Machine in the Garden deeply stirred an age already sensitive to the conflict be-tween civilization and nature. This symbolic tableau recorded the tension between two opposed concep-tions of man's relations with his universe. The soci-ety prefigured by the myth of the Garden would celebrate a passive accommodation to nature's law. There, survival would depend upon organic produc-tion or growth. But the machine foretold an economy designed by human intelligence, and it implied an active, indeed proud, assertion of humanity's domin-ion over nature. Hence the writers of the American "renaissance," not unlike Shakespeare's contemporar-ies, confronted one of the more rewarding situations history bestows upon art: the simultaneous attraction of two visions of a people's destiny, each embodying a discrete view of human experience, and each, more-over, accompanied by fresh and vivid symbols. The theme was as old as the story of Prometheus and Epimetheus, but its renewed vitality in Hawthorne's day may be attributed to the power with which fire was making life over new.[15]

III

In 1838, five years before Hawthorne had formulated the moral germ of "Ethan Brand," he had been struck by an actual sight of this change in American society.

"And taking a turn in the road," he wrote, "behold these factories. . . . And perhaps the wild scenery is all around the very site of the factory and mingles its impression strangely with those opposite ones." Here was history made visible. What most impressed Hawthorne was a "sort of picturesqueness in finding these factories, supremely artificial establishments, in the midst of such wild scenery."[16] Nevertheless, ten years later, when Hawthorne so thoroughly mined this Berkshire notebook for "Ethan Brand," he passed over these impressions. The factories do not appear in the story. Nor is there any overt allusion to industrialization. To speculate about the reasons for this "omission" would take us far afield.[17] Whatever the reason, the important fact is not that "Ethan Brand" contains no mention of the factories themselves, but that the ideas and emotions they suggested to Hawthorne are central to the story.

A sense of loss, anxiety, and dislocation hangs over the world of "Ethan Brand." The mood is located in the landscape. At the outset we hear that the countryside is filled with "relics of antiquity." What caused this melancholy situation becomes apparent when Hawthorne describes the people of the region. Brand has returned from his quest. Word is sent to the village, and a crowd climbs the mountain to hear his tale. From among them Hawthorne singles out several men: the stage-agent, recently deprived of his vocation; an old-fashioned country doctor, his useful days gone by; and a man who has lost a hand (emblem of craftsmanship?) in the "devilish grip of a steam-engine." He is now a "fragment of a human being." Like the Wandering Jew and the forlorn old man who searches for his lost daughter (said to have been a victim of Ethan's experimental bent), all are derelicts. They are victims of the fires of change. Like the monomaniac hero himself, all suffer a sense of not belonging.

This intense feeling of "unrelatendness" to nature and society has often been ascribed to the very historical forces which Hawthorne had observed in 1838. Discussing the intellectual climate of that era, Emerson once remarked that young men then had been born with knives in their brains. This condition was a result, he said, of the pervasive "war between intellect and affection." He called it "detachment," and found it reflected everywhere in the age: in Kant, Goethe's *Faust,* and in the consequences of the new capitalist power. "Instead of the social existence which all shared," he wrote, "was now separation."[19] Whatever we choose to call it—"detachment" or "alienation" (Karl Marx), or "anomie" (Emile Durkheim) or "dissociation of sensibility" (T. S. Eliot)—this is the malaise from which Ethan suffered.[20] Though there are important differences of emphasis, each of these terms refers to the state of mind of an individual cut off from a realm of experience said to be an indispensable source of life's meaning. The source may vary, but it is sig-

nificant that the responsible agent, or *separator,* so to speak, is invariably identified with science or industrial technology. In this sense Hawthorne's major theme was as vividly contemporary as it was traditional. He gave us the classic American account of the anguish of detachment.

The knife in Ethan's brain was a "cold philosophical curiosity" which led to a "separation of the intellect from the heart."[21] Now it is of the utmost significance that this scientific obsession is said to have literally emanated from the fire. There was a legend about Ethan's having been accustomed "to evoke a fiend from the hot furnace." Together they spent many nights by the fire evolving the idea of the quest. But the fiend always retreated through the "iron door" of the kiln with the first glimmer of sunlight. Here we discover how Hawthorne's earlier impressions of industrialization have been transmuted in the creative process. Here is the conduit through which thought and emotion flow to the work from the artist's experience of his age. In this case the symbolic contrast between fire and sun serves the purpose. It blends a traditional convention (we think of Milton's Hell)[22] and immediate experience; it provides the symbolic frame for the entire story. "Ethan Brand" begins at sundown and ends at dawn. During the long night the action centers upon the kiln or "furnace" which replaces the sun as source of warmth, light, and (indirectly) sustenance. The fire in the kiln is at once the symbolic source of evil and of the energy necessary to make nature's raw materials useful to man. Moreover, it can be shown that the very words and phrases used to describe this fire are used elsewhere, by Hawthorne, in direct reference to industrialization.[23] In the magazines of the day fire was repeatedly identified with the new machine power.[24] Hence fire, whatever its traditional connotations, is here an emblem, or fragment of an emblem, of the nascent industrial order. The new America was being forged by fire.

But if fire cripples men and devastates the landscape in "Ethan Brand," the sun finally dispels anxiety and evil, restoring man's solidarity with nature. When Ethan dies, his body burned to a brand by the satanic flames which had possessed his soul, the fire goes out and the ravaged landscape disappears. In its stead we see a golden vision of the self-contained New England village. The sun is just coming up. The hills swell gently about the town, as if resting "peacefully in the hollow of the great hand of Providence." In pointed contrast to the murky atmosphere of Ethan's Walpurgisnacht, there is no smoke anywhere. The sun allows perfect clarity of perception. Every house is "distinctly visible." At the center of this pastoral tableau the spires of the churches catch the first rays of the sun. Now the countryside is invested with all the order and serenity and permanence which the fire had banished. This harmony between man and nature is then projected beyond time in the vision of a stepladder of clouds on which it seemed that (from such a social order?) "mortal man might thus ascend into heavenly regions." Finally, though he had already hinted that stage coaches were obsolete, Hawthorne introduces one into this eighteenth-century New England version of the Garden of Eden.

Beneath the surface of "Ethan Brand" we thus find many of the ideas and emotions aroused by the Machine's sudden entrance into the Garden. But this is not to say that the story is *about* industrialization. It is about the consequences of breaking the magic chain of humanity. That is the manifest theme and, like the symbols through which it is developed, the theme is traditional. His apprehension of the tradition permits Hawthorne to discover meanings in contemporary facts. On the other hand, the capacity of this theme and these images to excite the imagination must also be ascribed to their vivid relevance to life in modern America. This story, in short, is an amalgam of tradition, which supplies the theme, and experience, which presents the occasion, and imagery common to both.

IV

But it may be said that, after all, this is merely one short story. The fact remains, however, that the same, or related, images may be traced outward from this story to Hawthorne's other work, the work of his contemporaries, the work of many later writers, and the society at large.

It is revealing, for example, that Hawthorne so often described his villains as alchemists, thereby associating them with fire and smoke. We recall that Aylmer, the scientist in "The Birthmark," made a point of building his laboratory underground to avoid sunlight.[25] Or consider Rappaccini, whose experiments perverted the Garden itself. His flowers were evil because of their "artificialness indicating . . . the production . . . no longer of God's making, but the monstrous offspring of man's depraved fancy. . . ."[26] From Hamilton's "Report on Manufactures" in 1791 until today, American thinking about industrialism, in and out of literature, has been tangled in the invidious distinction between "artificial" and "natural" production.[27] These adjectives, like so much of American political rhetoric, along with Hawthorne's theme of isolation, are a characteristic legacy of pre-industrial experience. They are expressions of our native tradition of pastoral, with its glorification of the Garden and its consequent identification of science and technology with evil. To Hawthorne's contemporaries, Emerson, Thoreau, and Whitman, the sun also represented the primal source of redemption.[28] "The sun rose clear," Thoreau tells us at the beginning of *Walden*; though he notes that the smoke of the train momentarily obscures its rays, the book ends with a passionate affirmation of the possi-

bility of renewed access, as in "Ethan Brand," to its redeeming light: "The sun is but a morning star."[29]

In *Moby-Dick,* published three years after "Ethan Brand," the identical motif emerges as a controlling element of tragedy. The "Try-Works," a crucial chapter in Ishmael's progressive renunciation of Ahab's quest, is quite literally constructed out of the symbols of "Ethan Brand."[30] Again it is night, and vision is limited to the lurid light of a "kiln" or "furnace." Fire again is a means of production, rendering the whale's fat, and again it is also the source of alienation. Ishmael, at the helm, controls the ship's fate. Like Ethan he momentarily succumbs to the enchantment of fire, and so nearly fulfills Ahab's destructive destiny. But he recovers his sanity in time, and tells us: "Look not too long in the face of the fire, O Man! . . . believe not the *artificial fire* when its redness makes all things look ghastly. Tomorrow, in the *natural sun,* the skies will be bright; those who glared like devils in the forking flames, the more will show in far other, at least gentler relief; the glorious, golden, glad sun, the only true lamp—all others but liars!"[31]

From this passage we may trace lines of iconological continuity to the heart of Melville's meaning.[32] When the *Pequod* sailed both Ahab and Ishmael suffered the pain of "detachment." But if the voyage merely reinforced Ahab's worship of the power of fire, it provoked in Ishmael a reaffirmation of the Garden. Ahab again and again expressed his aspiration in images of fire and iron, cogs and wheels, automata, and manufactured men. He had his "humanities," and at times was tempted by thoughts of "green land," but Ahab could not finally renounce the chase.[33] In *Moby-Dick* space is the sea—a sea repeatedly depicted in images of the American landscape. The conquest of the whale was a type of our fated conquest of nature itself. But in the end Ishmael in effect renounced the fiery quest. He was cured and saved. His rediscovery of that pastoral accommodation to the mystery of growth and fertility was as vital to his salvation as it had been to the myth of the Garden.[34] The close identity of the great democratic God and the God of the Garden was a central facet of Melville's apocalyptic insight.

His was also a tragic insight. Ahab and Ishmael, representing irreconcilable conceptions of America's destiny, as indeed of all human experience, were equally incapable of saving the *Pequod*. From Melville to Faulkner our writers have provided a desperate recognition of this truth: of the attributes necessary for survival, the Ahabs alone have been endowed with the power, and the Ishmaels with the perception. Ishmael was saved. But like one of Job's messengers, he was saved to warn us of greater disasters in store for worshippers of fire. In this way imagery associated with the Machine's entrance into the Garden has served to join native experience and inherited wisdom.

Notes

1 "Art," *Complete Works* (Boston, 1904), II, 352.

2 The decisive character of technological change in this period has been set forth in detail by George R. Taylor; see *The Transportation Revolution, 1815-1860* (New York, 1951). Edward C. Kirkland, in a symposium on "The Flowering of New England," suggested the close relationship between the literary and technological developments at this time. See *The Cultural Approach to History,* edited by Caroline Ware (New York, 1940).

3 "Works and Days," *Works,* VII, 158.

4 Edmund Wilson, for example, criticized Maxwell Geismar for suggesting that the criticism of industrial society in the literature of the 1930s was "something quite new." Wilson contended that this was a point of view to be found in our literature in the period from 1870-1900. Most standard histories of American literature accept the same chronology. For Wilson's comment, see his review of Geismar's *The Last of the Provincials* in *The New Yorker,* XXIII (1947), 57.

5 Randall Stewart, ed., *The American Notebooks* (New Haven, 1932), 106.

6 This connection has been thoroughly explored by William Bysshe Stein, *Hawthorne's Faust* (Gainesville, Florida, 1953).

7 According to some accounts, the production of textiles in the North Adams area had increased by over 400 percent between 1829 and 1837, the year before Hawthorne's visit. See John W. Yeomans, "A History of the Town of Adams," in *A History of the County of Berkshire, Massachusetts, . . .* (Pittsfield, Mass., 1839), 422-42.

8 *American Notebooks,* 42. This idea follows Hawthorne's record of a visit to a shop for the manufacture of marble. The press at this time featured stories of such industrial accidents. And it is worth remarking that similar images later caught the attention of Emerson (*Works,* VI, 115) and Henry James (*The American* (London, 1921), 263).

9 A survey of this material has been made possible by a grant from the Research Fund of the Graduate School, University of Minnesota, and by the assistance of Mr. Donald Houghton.

10 *The Education of Henry Adams* (New York, 1931), 5.

11 According to Carl Jung, the very essence of symbolism is that it "attempts to express a thing for which there exists *as yet* no adequate verbal concept." It conveys perceptions which can "*as yet,* neither be apprehended better, nor expressed differently." The emphasis upon "as yet" is the present author's, and is intended to call attention to the temporal, or historic, factor in this conception of symbolism. The implication is that the elements of experience which most urgently demand symbolic expression are the novel elements. For Jung's formulation, see *Contributions to Analytical Psychology* (London, 1928), 225-49.

12 The common concern of our writers with symbolism, so far from indicating an essentially aesthetic (or technical) turn of mind, might profitably be re-examined as a response to needs presented by the age. This suggestion is made as a possible alternative to the views of Charles Fiedelson. In *Symbolism and American Literature* (Chicago, 1953), Fiedelson argues that the "really vital common denominator" among our writers of the age was their "devotion to the possibilities of symbolism." His account of their symbolic vision is convincing, but he suggests that the concern with technique on the part of these men is a measure of their "purely" literary bent. Here he is taking issue with such critics as F. O. Matthiessen, who have insisted upon the decisive significance of the cultural context. There is no need, however, for forcing a choice between a technical (aesthetic) and a cultural (historic) interpretation of our literature. We need an awareness of both.

13 "The Old Apple Dealer," *The Complete Works of Nathaniel Hawthorne* (Boston, 1883), II, 502. Hawthorne later used virtually the same image in *The House of the Seven Gables.* For Hawthorne's development of the railroad symbol, see Leo Marx, "Hawthorne and Emerson: Studies in the Impact of the Machine Technology Upon the American Writer," unpublished dissertation (Harvard, 1950).

14 *Virgin Land, The American West as Symbol and Myth* (Cambridge, 1950). Though he does not explicitly develop the idea, Smith's material suggests that the myth may have taken shape, or at least reached its fullest development, under pressure from industrialization.

15 The contrast between Epimetheus and Prometheus offers a particularly close analogue to the theme under discussion. Epimetheus, whose name may actually have connoted a concern with the past, was committed to tradition, to a passive, some would say "feminine," celebration of the organic. But Prometheus, who stole fire from the gods, was oriented toward the future, and a technology in the service of man. His attitude was aggressively man-centered; Epimetheus was reverent toward the gods. It is highly probable that the literary interest in this myth in modern times must be understood in relation to the development of technology in

general, and to the use of fire in particular. The most exact parallel is the antithesis, suggested below, of Ahab and Ishmael. But with this difference: Ahab was concerned not with mankind, as in the case of Prometheus, but with himself. In this sense Ahab represents a perversion of the Promethean quest, as Richard Chase (*Herman Melville* (New York, 1949)) and M. O. Percival (*A Reading of Moby Dick* [Chicago, 1950]) have suggested.

[16] *American Notebooks,* 34-35. Hawthorne's comment illustrates the close affinity between this characteristic experience of the age and the symbolic technique our writers developed at the time. (See note 11, above.) When confronted by this tableau of the Machine in the Garden, Hawthorne is most fascinated by the mingling of opposite impressions. Such polarizations of meaning within a single object of sense were precisely what called forth the symbolic method of the period. As Melville explained in expounding upon the symbolic power of the whiteness of the whale, the essential circumstance was the "bringing together [of] two . . . opposite emotions in our minds." The age dramatized such polarizations of meaning, and the symbolic technique was designed to encompass them.

[17] One plausible explanation is suggested by Hawthorne's initial effort to describe the factories as aspects of the "picturesque." He was committed to the picturesque convention as a basis for selecting and treating the physical background of his fiction. However, this convention, with its stress upon the "natural" and the archaic, was hardly a congenial medium through which to present such radically new phenomena as the new technology. "In one way or another," he wrote in 1843, " . . . the inventions of mankind are fast blotting the picturesque, the poetic, and the beautiful out of human life." ("Fire Worship," *Works,* II, 160.) Hence we might conclude that Hawthorne's well-known difficulty in handling such characteristic aspects of the modern environment as the factories is to be accounted for by an unwillingness to step outside the bounds set by a literary convention; that he saw the choice as one between the literary convention on the one hand and the new subject matter on the other. If so, it is clear that he habitually chose the convention, and that the ideas and emotions he did feel in the presence of the new factories had to be invested, if they were to be given any expression, in other subjects. Hence they were expressed "covertly," or, as it were, symbolically.

But this is not to say that Hawthorne's difficulty in writing about the new material world was therefore "merely" aesthetic. On the contrary, the decision to continue working inside the convention was itself an indirect response to the changing environment. Why did he choose to work inside the convention when he found it unsuitable for presenting such obviously fascinating material? His choice here, it would seem, is as revealing of his underlying emotions as more direct

expressions of anxiety such as the fantasy of the malignant steam engine. He was uneasy about the changes foretold by the new technology, as a study of the imagery of industrialism in his work would bear out. He invariably used such images to convey a sense of menace, brutality, and generalized hostility to the human and the beautiful. Thus his attachment to the picturesque convention, which implicitly rejected the new technology, was a manifestation of the same emotions, and merely a special aspect of his total response to reality.

[18] *Works,* III, 478. Subsequent references to "Ethan Brand" appear in the text.

[19] "Historic Notes of Life and Letters in New England," *Works,* X, 307-47. See especially 307-311.

[20] For the Marxian concept of "alienation" see Karl Marx and Friedrich Engels, *The German Ideology,* Parts I and III, edited by R. Pascal (New York, 1939).

Durkheim develops the conception of "anomie" in *The Division of Labor in Society,* tr. George Simpson (Glencoe, Ill., 1947); see especially pages 353-74.

For Eliot's conception of "dissociation of sensibility" see T. S. Eliot, "The Metaphysical Poets," *Selected Essays* (New York, 1950), 241-50.

[21] *American Notebooks,* 106.

[22] Francis D. Klingender has indicated that industrial imagery was being used in illustrations of Milton's Hell in editions of *Paradise Lost* published early in the nineteenth century. See *Art and the Industrial Revolution* (London, 1947), 103-8, 192-96. As Klingender suggests, this tendency to identify Satan with industrialism is to be found in the poem itself. Blake saw this and made it explicit in his *Milton* (1804-1808). In addition to the factories in Hell, *Paradise Lost* is relevant here for the marked use Milton made of the traditional opposition of fire (associated with human technology) and sun (associated with the divine creation). The poem was one of Hawthorne's favorite works of literature. The connection is particularly apparent in Milton's view that before the fall of Adam and Eve there were in the garden only such tools "as art yet rude, / Guiltless of fire had formed." (IX, 391-92.) After the fall, however, Adam and Eve resorted, among other techniques of self-preservation, to fire. (X, 1060-93.) *The Poems of John Milton,* edited by James Holly Hanford (New York, 1953).

[23] The associative continuity between Hawthorne's emotions about the Industrial Revolution and "Ethan Brand" can be established. Here are a few of several instances of images which appear both in "Ethan Brand" and elsewhere in explicit reference to the new technology. (For further details see Marx, "Hawthorne and Emerson.")

A₁ "Fire Worship" (see note 17, above) is an essay on the changes which result from certain new inventions. There the stove is referred to as an "iron prison."

A₂ "Ethan Brand": the kiln is called the "hollow prison-house of the fire."

B₁ In "The Celestial Railroad," a satire on America's commitment to salvation by (technological) works, the narrator sees fire and smoke issuing from a hillside. There is some doubt as to whether this is the "mouth of the infernal region" or a place where "forges" have been "set up for the manufacture of railroad iron." (*Works,* II, 221.) The Bunyan aspect is explicit.

B₂ "Ethan Brand": the smoke and flame of the lime kiln is said to resemble "nothing so much as the private entrance to the infernal regions" in Bunyan. (III, 478.)

Other words in this cluster of technological association are *furnace, forge, coal, smoke,* and *iron*. Most of them are important in "Ethan Brand." Of the entire group, however, the word which seems to carry these implications closest to the center of Hawthorne's work is *iron*. In *The Scarlet Letter* and wherever he dealt with Puritanism, Hawthorne repeatedly used the word *iron* to convey the cold strain of utilitarianism in the Puritan character. In *The House of the Seven Gables,* the connection between Puritanism and the new industrial power is made clear.

In the magazines in Hawthorne's day this association of *iron* with the new power of steam was widespread. "The age may . . . be called an age of iron . . . ," said one writer, "for it is the supreme agent in motive-power, which may be truly said at the present time to govern the world. It is the ponderous machinery, instinct with the life which steam gives it, that connects countries. . . ." *Hunt's Merchants Magazine,* XXIII (Oct. 1850), 463.

24 Writing on the "Effects of Machinery," a contributor to the *North American Review* praised the new technology, and characteristically stressed the rôle of fire in the Revolution: "Last, and most wonderful of all, by the application of fire we transform water into that most potent of all agents, steam. Man, as it were, yokes the hostile elements of fire and water, and subjects them to his bidding. It is hardly a metaphor, to call steam the vital principle, the living soul of modern machinery." XXXIV (Jan. 1832), 244.

It should also be noted that lime kilns figured prominently in early industrial landscapes. See, for example, J. M. W. Turner, "Colebrook Dale, View of the Lime Kilns," reproduced in Klingender, 176.

25 *Works,* II, 56.

26 *Works,* II, 128.

27 Although Hamilton, in his celebrated Report, was stating the case for industrial development, he could not avoid the distinction. It was virtually a part of the language. "Report on Manufactures," *Industrial and Commercial Correspondence of Alexander Hamilton,* edited by Arthur Harrison Cole (Chicago, 1928), 247-322. See esp. 247-56.

28 Consider, for example, the "Introduction" to Emerson's *Nature*: "The sun shines to-day also." *Works,* I, 3. Or the second section of "Song of Myself," Whitman's lines: "Stop this day and night with me and you shall possess the origin of all poems, / You shall possess the good of the earth and sun (there are millions of suns left,)." In each case the sun is presented as a source of redemption peculiarly accessible to Americans. But when Whitman came to recognize that, due to urbanization, the myth of the Garden no longer was relevant to the experience of most Americans, he announced his own rejection of the myth with the refrain, "Keep your splendid silent sun." See "Give Me the Splendid Silent Sun."

29 Henry Thoreau, *Walden,* Modern Library Edition (New York, 1937), 8, 297.

30 "The Try-Works," Chapter XCVI. The parallel to "Ethan Brand" is discussed by Howard P. Vincent, *The Trying Out of Moby-Dick* (New York, 1949), 335. There is no doubt that Melville had read and was impressed by "Ethan Brand" before completing *Moby-Dick.* See his letter to Hawthorne in *The Portable Melville,* edited by Jay Leyda (New York, 1952), 429-34. Leyda estimates that the letter was written about June 1, 1851.

31 *Moby-Dick,* edited by Willard Thorp (New York, 1947), 398. My italics.

32 Here and throughout this essay I am indebted to Erwin Panofsky for the method of iconological analysis. See *Studies in Iconology* (New York, 1939).

33 See especially, "The Symphony," Chapter CXXXII.

34 In the first chapter Ishmael asks whether the green fields are gone, and in Chapter XCIV Ishmael identifies the "meadow" with a series of organic and domestic images of man's attainable felicity.

Thomas Reed West

SOURCE: "The Shapes Arise," in *Flesh of Steel: Literature and the Machine in American Culture,* Vanderbilt, 1967, pp. 3-20.

[*In the excerpt that follows, West examines various British and American authors' treatment of industrialism as a form of power and discipline.*]

The machine proves itself increasingly fecund not only in the economic goods but in its own symbolism. Its twentieth-century forms—the assembly line, the power plant, the skyscraper, the automobile, even the wrist watch, at once dictatorial and fastidiously unobtrusive—connote with striking effectiveness the extent of its control over society and the meticulousness of that control. The symbolism is endless: it is inherent in the closer fusion of the factory with the higher sciences; in the transformation of city traffic into a function of the machine, its inner motions rhythmically meshed like those within an engine or a factory room; in a new polish of surfaces, a diffusion of light, and a pure line that Lewis Mumford, in *Technics and Civilization,* has held to characterize the latest, "neotechnic" stage of industrialism. Quite possibly, machine sketches of the sort that are to be found in the work of Sherwood Anderson could not have been drawn a century ago; there is too much cool light, too many fine precise lines and harmonies in the factories and technological minds he portrayed: the shy inventor Hugh McVey in the novel *Poor White,* or the craftsmanlike technicians and delicate factory machinery of *Perhaps Women.*

But if the steam-and-smoke mechanics and the looser meshings of industry in the Victorian age provided only an imperfect imagery of the discipline to which the machine might attain over itself and over men, the discipline and its imagery were present. In his *Capital,* Marx was able to expound at length upon the division of labor and the subservience of the laborer to the speed and uniformities of the factory.[1] Well before the present century, of course, literature had come to strike a series of elaborate postures toward its mechanical surroundings, and the twentieth-century writer has had an opportunity to draw upon these, as well as upon the technological sophistication of his own immediate environment. The works of Thomas Carlyle, Charles Dickens, John Ruskin, Walt Whitman, and Henry Adams give some clues to the impressions that the machine was making upon the consciousness of the nineteenth and early twentieth centuries, and of what might be handed on, by way of intellectual inheritance, to writers of more recent decades.

"'Coal and iron, so long close unregardful neighbours, are wedded together; Birmingham and Wolverhampton, and the hundred Stygian forges, with their fire-throats, and never-resting sledge-hammers, rose into day,'" wrote Carlyle in "Chartism," an essay of 1839.[2] In this manner the industrial era presented itself to Carlyle. It was an affair of Stygian forges and fire-throats, a thrust of Saxon energy turned to the subduing of iron and cotton; it was a more perfect expression of an eternal work-ethic, and even a heightened application of intelligence to the act of labor—but never, or at least not typically, did machine industry appear in Carlyle's writings as a totally new method, a new habit of minute calculation, a timed pace of work or the complete subjugation of the individual and his skill to the demands of a machine.

It was a vision of the industrial age consistent with Carlyle's roughhewn perception of things. Philosophically, he saw existence as a surge and fusion of forces, whether the crude power of physical nature or the purer force of Christianity; visually, he grasped scenes and events in their rougher lines and dominant colors, in great blocks and chunks; normally, he admired directness, honesty in the confronting of existence, and despised subtlety and facile wit. Hence, the hero or prophet is strong, Carlyle thought, in the *force* rather than the cleverness of his insight; in the plainness and sincerity with which he fronts the universe and lets it teach its truths to him.[3] And while Carlyle conceived of the task of man as one of ordering the still untamed element of existence ("Wheresoever thou findest Disorder, there is thy eternal enemy; attack him swiftly, subdue him; make Order of him, the subject not of Chaos, but of Intelligence, Divinity and Thee!"),[4] order never seemed to signify a nicety of proportion—it was, rather, the kind of order that the form of a great shaggy mountain fixes upon broken rock.

The gigantic energies and bold shapes of the industrial age therefore would have for Carlyle their appeal, and industrialism would be for him essentially a phenomenon of force, needing only to be freed from its bondage to Mammon to fulfill its destiny.

> The Saxon kindred burst forth into cotton-spinning, cloth-cropping, iron-forging, steamengineing, railwaying, commercing and careering towards all the winds of Heaven,—in this inexplicable noisy manner; the noise of which, in Power-mills, in progress-of-the-species Magazines, still deafens us somewhat. Most noisy, sudden![5]

Industrialism did appear to Carlyle a moral discipline, but no different in kind from all other labors and disciplines whereby a man gets into a true relationship with Force, and an honest relationship with the laws of existence that must be obeyed in the act of work. He wrote in *Past and Present* (1843):

> The grim inarticulate veracity of the English people, unable to speak its meaning in words, has turned itself silently on things; and the dark powers of Material Nature have answered, "Yes, this at least is true, this is not false!"

The labors of England were "the one God's Voice we have heard in these two atheistic centuries."[6] So we cannot look to Carlyle to furnish any detailed account of the methods of industry, or of the more minute adjustments, mental and physical, that the machine might force upon its servants. Instead, he demonstrates how the rougher and more striking images to which industrialism gives form might impress themselves upon the consciousness of its observers and provides a contrast to those writers who would inquire more closely into the nature of industrialism as a specific technique and discipline.

Yet while Carlyle seldom concerned himself with the technique of industry, he did see in the machine one potential danger to the human spirit—a danger posed not so much by the machine itself and the order of labor and life it brings about as by the sterile analogies and false lessons to which it could give rise. Carlyle complained of the utilitarian and rationalistic philosophies, the corrupted uses of science that would measure and dissect existence by logic alone and hold the universe a machine and the human soul a weighing balance for pleasure and pain. These philosophies meant the denial of wonder, the devitalization of thought and experience[7]—the machine become a symbol not of life-force but of spiritual death.

In a single novel of Dickens, the reader is brought concretely into the smoky industrial world that Carlyle viewed only in its more general massive outline. Like other novels of Dickens, *Hard Times* (1854) is at once a bit of extravagant and romantic characterization and a work of social criticism. But there is about it a rather unexpected austerity; the narrative is relatively short and very much to the point, there is little fatness and ruddiness of descriptive detail, the social message is stark and direct. And in its analysis of industrialism as a social force and as a repressive discipline of the human personality, *Hard Times* is strikingly modern.[8]

The novel analyzes mid-nineteenth century industrialism in its two complementary and mutually illustrative forms—physical and intellectual. Materially, the industrial system resides in Coketown, a murky inferno of monotonous, unending factory labor, monotonous streets, grim uniformity. Intellectually, it resides in the Gradgrind household, where children are brought up on Fact and science and utilitarian philosophy and every thought is a polemic in defense of Coketown. Coketown and Thomas Gradgrind are the closest of allies, and each is an explanation of the other.

Coketown

> had a black canal in it, and a river that ran purple with ill-smelling dye, and vast piles of building full of windows where there was a rattling and a trembling all day long, and where the piston of the steam-engine worked monotonously up and down, like the head of an elephant in a state of melancholy madness.

Streets were similar; days were all alike. "These attributes of Coketown were in the main inseparable from the work by which it was sustained. . . ."[9] The Coke-

town thread of the novel is a tale, dreary as its setting, of an honest millhand burdened with a drunken wife, persecuted by his employer—the blustering "self-made" Bounderby—and ostracized by his fellow workers, a victim finally of a mine accident. And while the laborers of Coketown are seen to struggle under all the conventionally recognizable forms of economic oppression, Dickens did not set forth their problem simply or even primarily as one of poverty or child labor or industrial hazard, but as a spiritual starvation.

Against the story of Coketown Dickens played the story of the Gradgrind family. Here individualist industrialism and political economy can find their spokesman in the utilitarian dogmatist, Thomas Gradgrind. Here also the sterile material existence of Coketown is reflected in the sterile abstractions by which Gradgrind lives, and in the scientific education given his children—trained from earliest years always to seize upon the rigid blunt Fact and never to wonder or to toy with fancy. Especially modern in its implications is Dickens's portrayal of Louisa Gradgrind, her life almost destroyed through the suppression and maiming of her human feelings; it is a psychological study suggestive of the diagnoses that post-Freudian writers would make of the repressed industrial personality. In sum, the Gradgrind philosophy and the Gradgrind system of education constitute a discipline, iron-hard and iron-cold, that clamps itself upon the mind as the factory environment settles upon the operatives.[10]

But while Dickens maintained a harmony and a correspondence between Coketown and Gradgrindism, he clearly placed the greater responsibility for the ills of industrialism at the account of the Gradgrinds and the Bounderbys, the intellectual and business representatives of the new era. Mechanism itself has its role to play—"the noon bell rang. . . . The looms, and wheels, and Hands all out of gear for an hour";[11] but there is no real suggestion that technology might be the prime mover, the self-sustained arbiter of new social forms. Other Victorian writers would attack more directly the machine, the factory, and the new technology of labor. Among the most important was John Ruskin.

In one of the essays gathered in *Unto This Last,* Ruskin wrote:

> In fact, it may be discovered that the true veins of wealth are purple—and not in Rock, but in Flesh—perhaps even that the final outcome and consummation of all wealth is in the producing as many as possible full-breathed, bright-eyed, and happy-hearted human creatures.

And in the same series:

> No scene is continually and untiringly loved, but one rich by joyful human labour; smooth in field;

fair in garden; full in orchard; trim, sweet, and frequent in homestead; ringing with voices of vivid existence.[12]

Here, as clearly as in any of Ruskin's more elaborate statements of social reform, can be found the substance of his dream for the good society. It is a vision not of a civilization reconstructed in due accordance with scientific reform theory, efficiently administered and economically progressive, but of a society virtuous, sociable, and happy in the concrete details of its daily life—a society of peasants and good craftsmen; and its ultimate bond would be that of Christian love. This grasp of the social situation is at the heart of the argument in *Unto This Last.* For the work is an attack upon the conventional theories of political economy; and the essence of the argument is that the liberal economists had misdefined the true nature of wealth and, therefore, the true means to its achievement—had failed to see that the value of goods and services lies, not in the price they are artificially assigned under a market economy, but in their possibilities for the enrichment of life. From this concrete sense of wealth stemmed all of Ruskin's more explicit schemes for social reconstruction: for child education, for government regulation of the economy, for the acknowledgment of kingship and class distinction.

The main force of Ruskin's social reformist argument was therefore directed against the laissez faire economics of Victorian Britain, and against every institution of the nineteenth century—whether in its politics, its economics, its methods of labor, or its aesthetic— that appeared poor in earthy life-value. Specifically, he attacked the industrial disciplines of labor; for he believed that the division of labor and the demand for a mechanical perfection in workmanship eliminate all expressiveness from labor and prevent the laborer from translating his vital self into the materials he handles. The point is made with great thoroughness in one of the most famous of Ruskin's writings—the essay on "The Nature of Gothic," which appeared in the second volume of *The Stones of Venice,* published in 1853.

The essential mistake of the industrial regime, insisted Ruskin, is its requirement that every manufactured product be perfect in finish, an exact fulfillment of specifications rigidly established. But if a worker of living flesh and groping spirit is to approach such perfection, he must contradict his own imperfect nature, submerge his personality, and become a tool:

> Men were not intended to work with the accuracy of tools, to be precise and perfect in all their actions. If you will have that precision out of them, and make their fingers measure degrees like cog-wheels, and their arms strike curves like compasses, you must unhumanize them. . . . The eye of the soul must be bent upon the finger-point, and the soul's force must fill all the invisible nerves that guide it,

> ten hours a day, that it may not err from its steely precision, and so soul and sight be worn away. . . . On the other hand, if you will make a man of the working creature, you cannot make a tool. Let him but begin to imagine, to think, to try to do anything worth doing; and the engine-turned precision is lost at once. Out come all his roughness, all his dulness, all his incapability; shame upon shame, failure upon failure, pause after pause: but out comes the whole majesty of him also. . . .

And through the intensification, in modern times, of the division of labor, the workers themselves are atomized:

> Divided into mere segments of men—broken into small fragments and crumbs of life; so that all the little piece of intelligence that is left in a man is not enough to make a pin, or a nail, but exhausts itself in making the point of a pin, or the head of a nail.[13]

In contrast to the sterile perfection of modern workmanship Ruskin placed the grandeur of Gothic architecture.

The essay "The Nature of Gothic" is of the greatest significance. Its own influence has been considerable— most notably, perhaps, upon William Morris;[14] and it expresses a kind of objection to the industrial order that became increasingly vocal in the late nineteenth century and after—in Morris, in G. D. H. Cole and Guild Socialism, in Eric Gill. Among American novelists, Sherwood Anderson has explored with special sensitivity the antagonism between craftsmanship and the industrial method.

In "The Nature of Gothic," the industrial era comes into the sharpest focus; the meaning of the era is discovered in an examination of the factory itself and of the specific discipline the factory represents. In the work of Walt Whitman, American contemporary to Ruskin, the focus is again widened—and blurred, and we view the machine age, as Carlyle viewed it, in its larger outlines.

Material and soul, appearance and Idea, multiple and One: the Platonic dualism that the American Transcendentalists carried over, as did Carlyle, in part from Germanic metaphysics gives the philosophic clue to the poetic mysticism of Whitman. On the one side stands the Whitmanesque zest for the concrete, the diverse, the vital; on the other, the assertion of a spirit that is the "ever-tending, the finalè of visible forms."[15] And this intuition suffuses the poems, so that the universe they create appears in almost kaleidoscopic motion, flinging itself momentarily apart into the most discordant hues and shapes as its substances are agitated, assuming some new quiet and harmony, only to fracture again into multiplicity.

From among the discrete and merging images that pass before the reader, a few glimpses are caught of the machine; but they are glimpses only, shifting and suggestive rather than distinct. In "To a Locomotive in Winter" (1876) the impression is of a keen and reckless force:

> *Type of the modern—emblem of motion and*
> *   power—pulse of the continent,*
>
> . . . . .
>
> *Fierce-throated beauty!*
> *Roll through my chant with all thy lawless*
> *   music, thy swinging lamps at night. . . .*[16]

In other passages, industrial activities are seen as expressions of a vast, swift-moving and creative American democracy. Here there may be no clear separation between industrial occupations and the crafts; both are revelations of a democratic impulse and belong to the phenomenal world at its most concrete, its most energetic; both are material reflections of a spirit, an American Idea. In "Song of the Broad-Axe" (1856), the axe becomes the symbol of an acting America; out of its wielding emerge the structures, physical and social and even spiritual, of American life. Yet among these, only a few are distinctively of the order of machine industry.

> *The axe leaps!*
> *The solid forest gives fluid utterances,*
>
> . . . . .
>
> *The shapes arise!*
> *Shapes of factories, arsenals, foundries,*
> *   markets,*
> *Shapes of the two-threaded tracks of*
> *   railroads,*
> *Shapes of the sleepers of bridges, vast*
> *   frameworks, girders, arches,*
> *Shapes of the fleets of barges, tows, lake and*
> *   canal craft, river craft,*
>
> . . . . .
>
> *The main shapes arise!*
> *Shapes of Democracy total, result of centuries,*
> *Shapes ever projecting other shapes,*
> *Shapes of turbulent manly cities,*
> *Shapes of the friends and home-givers of the*
> *   whole earth,*
> *Shapes bracing the earth and braced with the*
> *   whole earth.*

And "Song of the Exposition" (1871) makes poetry of America's inventive and industrial activity—the material outpouring of the American soul.[17]

"Passage to India" (1868) carries a broader conception. The poem interprets the engineering labors of the modern world as representing a march toward the unity of the earth: the binding of regions and peoples through the canal, the railroad, and the cable, and the return of Western man to the Orient, the ancient. After the physical union is to come a mystic fusion of parts, and a fulfillment of the soul.[18] Finally, it is significant that Whitman discovered in some of the industrial creations of his nineteenth century the cleanliness of design that is more readily associated with the industrial architecture of a later day; in the eighteen sixties he could discern "the strong light works of engineers," the "high growths of iron, slender, strong, light" that graced Manhattan.[19]

Whitman made little direct contribution to a conception of the machine: he never treated industrialism in any major or even particularly coherent manner. But indirectly his effect may have been considerable. He taught American writers to disregard traditional literary forms and to report the energy and variety of life—to look to the strong raw facts of American society and relate them to the diversity and potentiality of democracy. These predilections shaped Whitman's own understanding of American industrialism; and many a later author, celebrating the industrial force of the American Middle West or the democracy of the skyscraper, might draw upon the Whitman heritage to strengthen the insight and invigorate the expression. The connection seems most apparent in the poems of Sandburg, with their Whitmanesque though original renderings of an imagery taken from democratic and industrial sources.

The Education of Henry Adams was printed privately in 1906. Adams's great autobiography might almost be considered as among the writings of main concern in this essay rather than as a precursor; it was contemporary to some of the work of Veblen and preceded by only a few years the earliest work of Frank, Anderson, and Lewis. But the *Education* can serve a more useful purpose in illustrating the continuities and discontinuities between the nineteenth-century insights of Carlyle, Ruskin, and Whitman, and the viewpoints of the writers whose industrial milieu has been more advanced. Born in 1838, Adams was fully a Victorian—or even, so he thought, an anachronism out of the colonial period—and was therefore a historian, not only of the industrial conditions of the twentieth century, but of rapid industrial change; the philosophy he expounded in the *Education* represents an immediate intellectual reaction to the new sciences of energy which by the turn of the century were revising the mechanical physics of the past; the entire tone of the work conveys an impression of an industrial civilization quickened in its tempo, more completely expressive of mammoth resistless energies than was the society of Carlyle and Whitman, or of Adams's own earlier years.

The *Education* is a puzzling work and can be taken in more than one way. The ironic posture, the cutting references to politics and business suggest that possibly it is at heart simply a commentary upon the decline of the republic following the political defeat of the Adams family and the principles they had sustained. The scientific-philosophical framework upon which Adams built his narrative might then be little more than a jest, a satirical method for the measurement of an acceleration into anarchy; or it could be a bitter conviction stemming from a narrow set of concerns. Yet Adams took his historical philosophy too seriously for this and spent too much of his later life in its careful statement and application. *Mont-Saint-Michel and Chartres* (1904), his study of thirteenth-century faith and architecture, had been planned as a companion to the story of Adams's own times; together they would define two historical points from which to plot and measure scientifically the movement of force in history.[20] And in two essays of 1909 and 1910, later published by Brooks Adams in *The Degradation of the Democratic Dogma,* Henry Adams gave further definition to his historical philosophy. That philosophy is worth consideration; for it is inseparable from Adams's interpretation of industrialism and is in itself a testament to a new scientific era.

Adams's philosophy of history amounts to the conviction that society is no more or less than a function of physical energy and that human history repeats the tendency of all existence toward an ever-accelerated release of energy, a progression from compact force to force in diffuse complexity. Man, who seeks order, has striven again and again to control new elements of chaotic energy as they appear, to maintain against the anarchy a workable unity; but it is a fragile unity that can only be defended along a widening front. For the nineteenth century, the increase in force had expressed itself in the volume and intensity of coal power, and in the unleashing of the other great forces of industrial civilization; only recently "a new universe of force had been revealed in radiation."[21]

In the later chapters of the *Education,* Adams sketched the revolutionary developments in science, toward the last years of the nineteenth century, that had contributed to his radical interpretation of existence and of history; and in the essays published in *The Degradation of the Democratic Dogma* he buttressed his ideas with the terms and findings of the new science: the law of the dissipation of energy, the recognition that energy might exist in supersensory phases, the discovery of radium. The power of Adams's historical philosophy, however, lies not in any inherent scientific merit but in the artistic form it imparts to the *Education.* The work is a chronicle of historical movement during the lifetime of its author, from the relative stability of Adams's Boston-Quincy childhood—a little

out of date even for its own time, he implied—to the anarchic upheaval of industrial and social energy that confronted Adams at the beginning of the twentieth century; and by setting the historical development against a wider background of natural forces in accelerating thrust and complexity, he brought dramatic integrity and continuity to his tale and sharply intensified its feeling. Energy and multiplicity become inevitable; society assumes an irresistible motion of its own, increasing into infinity. The dramatic scheme moves to a fitting climax—in an impression of New York City in 1904:

> The outline of the city became frantic in its effort to explain something that defied meaning. Power seemed to have outgrown its servitude and to have asserted its freedom. The cylinder had exploded, and thrown great masses of stone and steam against the sky. The city had the air and movement of hysteria, and the citizens were crying, in every accent of anger and alarm, that the new forces must at any cost be brought under control. Prosperity never before imagined, power never yet wielded by man, speed never reached by anything but a meteor, had made the world irritable, nervous, querulous, unreasonable and afraid. All New York was demanding new men, and all the new forces, condensed into corporations, were demanding a new type of man—a man with ten times the endurance, energy, will and mind of the old type—for whom they were ready to pay millions at sight. As one jolted over the pavements or read the last week's newspapers, the new man seemed close at hand, for the old one had plainly reached the end of his strength, and his failure had become catastrophic.[22]

In conceiving industrialism in its energy and bulk, Adams was in the company of Carlyle and of Whitman. But the energy he perceived, particularly in its twentieth-century forms, was of a nature at once subtler and more gigantic than the simple rugged force that Carlyle had depicted. It was an energy that had spilled out of the factory and overrun the whole of society; it was paced, and unimaginably complex; it issued from mysterious substances and compounds unknown to the contemporaries of Carlyle; and it was uncovered, for immediate or future use, not through the crude mechanics of the earlier nineteenth century, but through science perfected to the finest edge. He had seen, said the author,

> the number of minds, engaged in pursuing force— the truest measure of its attraction—increase from a few scores or hundreds, in 1838, to many thousands in 1905, trained to sharpness never before reached, and armed with instruments amounting to new senses of indefinite power and accuracy, while they chased force into hiding-places where Nature herself had never known it to be, making analyses that contradicted being, and syntheses that endangered the elements.

tion in complex energy. And despite the pessimism with which Adams viewed the future, he did not fail to respect the mind that would come to grips with the emergent forces of the twentieth century.

> At the rate of progress since 1800, every American who lived into the year 2000 would know how to control unlimited power. He would think in complexities unimaginable to an earlier mind. He would deal with problems altogether beyond the range of earlier society.

In face of a staggering expansion in natural and social energies, only an expansion in human energy, intelligence, and endurance would suffice.[24]

In the work of Carlyle, of Whitman, and of Henry Adams, industrialism appears in the form of energy; in the work of Dickens, Ruskin, and again Adams, it appears in the form of discipline. As an energy, industrialism projects itself upon a magnificent scale. It assumes weight and ruggedness of contour; all its acts are exhibitions of a massive power, wielded against massive materials. As a discipline, industrialism becomes tighter and more exacting in its method. It subjects the workman to the ordered routines of the factory and demands of his imperfect spirit a relentless perfection in labor; it drills the intellect in science and grim mechanical Fact and in the precise understanding and mastery of expanding complexities. In these forms the machine would continue to confront writers of a more recent day: its disciplines, still subtler; its energies, more multiple and swift.

Notes

[1] *Capital, the Communist Manifesto and Other Writings,* edited, with an introduction, by Max Eastman (New York: Random House, The Modern Library, 1932), pp. 78, 85, 115-128.

[2] *The Works of Thomas Carlyle* (Centenary Edition; New York: Charles Scribner's Sons, 1898-1901), XXIX, 185.

[3] *On Heroes, Hero-Worship and the Heroic in History* (1841), in *Works,* V, 45, 54.

[4] *Past and Present* (1843), in *Works,* X, 201.

[5] "Chartism," in *Works,* XXIX, 184.

[6] *Works,* X, 168-169.

[7] *Sartor Resartus* (1833), in *Works,* I, 53-54; *Heroes,* in *Works,* V, 20-21, 76; "Signs of the Times" (1829), in *Works,* XXVII, 56-82.

[8] See the introduction by John H. Middendorf in *Hard Times* (New York: Harper and Brothers, 1960), pp. v-xx.

Walt Whitman's poetry often dealt with technological change and its meaning for humanity.

The new scientific formulations, in themselves the basis of Adams's philosophy, were of the very fiber of the industrial civilization of the twentieth century as Adams saw its beginnings and imagined its future; they would supply its energies, train its intellect and, it seems, in the very fact of revealing the multiplicity of existence, would hurl the twentieth-century mind even further into multiplicity.[23] They would be, in effect, the intellectualization and epitome of twentieth-century energy, as the steam-engine had been the symbol of energy in Carlyle's day.

In still another manner, the *Education* may be contrasted to the work of Carlyle. While the Scots historian saw the machine age only in its mass and force, and Ruskin was concerned only with its disciplines, in the machine world of Adams the distinction is obliterated: energy at its most anarchic is the instrument of discipline. The tempo of the new civilization is set by its greater energies, and man adjusts himself to that tempo; through its own impetus, complexity begets a larger complexity, and the mind schools itself to some grasp of the expanding whole; the human personality strains and tenses in response to every new accelera-

[9] *Ibid.,* pp. 28-29.

[10] *Ibid.,* p. 32.

[11] *Ibid.,* p. 92.

[12] *Unto This Last* (London: G. Allen and Unwin, 1923), pp. 64-65, 167-168. The essays were first published in 1860.

[13] *The Stones of Venice* (New York: John Wiley and Sons, 1888), II, 161-162, 165. Originally published in 1853.

[14] For a careful appraisal of the effect of *The Stones of Venice* upon Morris, see Lloyd Wendell Eshleman, *A Victorian Rebel: The Life of William Morris* (New York: Charles Scribner's Sons, 1940), pp. 164-167.

[15] "Starting from Paumanok" (1860), in *The Complete Poetry and Prose of Walt Whitman,* with an introduction by Malcolm Cowley (New York: Pellegrini and Cudahy, 1948), I, 53.

[16] *Poetry and Prose,* I, 407-408.

[17] *Ibid.,* pp. 186-204.

[18] *Ibid.,* pp. 361-369.

[19] "Passage to India," in *ibid.,* p. 361; "Mannahatta" (1860), in *ibid.,* p. 409.

[20] *The Education of Henry Adams: An Autobiography* (Boston and New York: Houghton Mifflin Company, 1946), pp. 434-435. Appeared privately in 1906.

[21] *Ibid.,* pp. 460-461, 490-491.

[22] *Ibid.,* p. 499.

[23] *Ibid.,* pp. 457-458, 494-495.

[24] *Ibid.,* pp. 496-497, 499.

Herbert L. Sussman

SOURCE: "Introduction," in *Victorians and the Machine: The Literary Response to Technology,* Cambridge, Mass.: Harvard University Press, 1968, pp. 1-12.

[*In the essay that follows, Sussman examines the machine as a prominent symbol in Victorian literature, addressing various critiques and celebrations of technology in works by such authors as Carlyle, Wordsworth, Mill, and Kipling.*]

When the eight locomotives, drawing six hundred persons, including the Duke of Wellington, Robert Peel, and the ill-fated Mr. Huskisson, puffed down the tracks at the public opening of the Liverpool and Manchester Railway in 1830, high fences were erected, constables and soldiers called out "to keep off the pressure of the multitude, and prevent them from falling over in their eagerness to witness the opening ceremony."[1] Earlier technology had aroused no such general enthusiasm; for all their usefulness, the canal, the macadam road, the stagecoach were only refined versions of techniques that had existed from primitive times. But the steam locomotive, constructed almost wholly of iron, moving steadily along an iron track, throwing clouds of smoke and sparks into the air, was a sight entirely new to human experience. So, too, was the stationary engine, the steam engine without wheels, whose massive beam regularly rising and falling had become a familiar sight outside the red brick mills of northern cities. The technological revolution, then, differed from other historical events. Gods may change, churches remain very much the same; but the machine transformed the very appearance of the visible world. Not only was there the new machinery itself, there were now entire landscapes created by the machine: slag heaps, red brick factories, red brick houses for the factory workers. Even the countryside was marked by railway tracks, viaducts, and embankments.

The first question for the Victorian writer facing this new world was whether or not these images could be considered appropriate subjects for literature. And most often, the answer was no. With very few exceptions, during the Victorian period the machine appears in the minor works of major poets or the major works of minor poets.[2] Such poems as Charles Tennyson Turner's "Steam Threshing-Machine" or the "grooves of change" passage in his brother's "Locksley Hall" are distinct anomalies in Victorian poetry. The more typical attitude is that of William Morris who, for all his zeal in recasting the conditions of mechanized work, considered poetry a means of calling up a beauty vanished from the mechanized world:

> Forget six counties overhung with smoke,
> Forget the snorting steam and piston stroke,
> Forget the spreading of the hideous town;
> Think rather of the pack-horse on the down,
> And dream of London, small, and white, and
>   clean.[3]

It was not until the very end of the nineteenth century that Rudyard Kipling could advocate a new poetry celebrating the essential beauty of the machine.

Even the novelists, whom the Victorians felt should be more concerned with life as it is than as it might be, shied away from confronting the mechanized world. George Eliot writes *Middlemarch* as an historical novel set at the moment when the railway is about to disrupt the traditional order. The concern of Thackeray and Meredith is with the novel of society rather than the novel of industrial society. And Hardy follows the Wordsworthian theme of Victorian literature in finding the "essential passions of the heart" in people removed from the mechanized world. Thus, in the earlier part of the Victorian period the machine is found only in the novel of reform, in Dickens and the "industrial novelists." Only later in the century does there emerge, in H. G. Wells and in Kipling, prose fiction that celebrates technology and scientific speculation.

Primarily, the machine appears in those Victorian writers most directly concerned with immediate social problems. For Carlyle, Ruskin, and Morris, as well as for Dickens, Wells, and Kipling, the machine is important not merely as an image, a representation of a visual experience, but as a symbol, an image that suggests a complex of meanings beyond itself. For it is the fortuitous quality of the machine as symbol that it includes the central themes of Victorian culture. First, it was clear to all, from the compilers of Parliamentary bluebooks to the worker watching the power loom, that technological progress was creating the immense social and economic upheavals taking place. As a metonymy for the constellation of changes that we, like the Victorians, call "progress," the machine, especially the railroad, was the most public, the most visual of emblems. As Mill says in his review of de Tocqueville's *Democracy in America:* "The mere visible fruits of scientific progress in a wealthy society, the mechanical improvements, the steam-engines, the railroads, carry the feeling of admiration for modern and disrespect for ancient times, down even to the wholly uneducated classes."[4]

Combined with the use of the machine as metonymy for progress was another perception, commonplace now only because it was first articulated by Victorian writers, that the rhythms created by the machine itself had a profound and primarily destructive effect on the psychic life. This idea, that as mechanization expands the affective life declines, shapes the form as well as the content of much Victorian writing. In its simplest form, it is the sense that the age is dull, and with ease has come softness; in a more subtle form, that the very qualities which make for the success of the machine, its power, its precision, its unwearied ability to repeat the same action, pose the greatest danger to the psyche. Literature consistently suggests that the rhythms of the machine are unnatural and, as such, destructive. The machine thus becomes both cause and symbol for what writers saw as the declining emotional vitality of their age.

But to use the machine as a symbol for what is unnatural is to evoke a complex of philosophical assumptions for which the machine is also symbol. Long before the railway and the power loom, in its primeval form as watch, to use Samuel Butler's evolutionary terms,

the machine had served as a philosophical model. Modern scholarship defines romanticism as the replacing of this mechanistic intellectual model by another intellectual metaphor, that of the living organism.[5] The machine as metaphor for the cosmos implies a natural order, once created by a God, but now fixed, moving by regular laws and therefore deterministic; changing the metaphor to an organism suggests a developing universe, infused with a vital, usually divine, energy and therefore not subject to determinism. Applying the machine metaphor to the mind suggests that mental processes are orderly and therefore determined, and that the highest faculty is the reason; the organic metaphor suggests irregularity and freedom, a mind whose highest power is intuitive. The state as machine is also orderly, explicable by rationalistic laws; an organic society is free of restrictive external form, held together by ties of loyalty or love, and beyond rational creation or explanation.

In the sense that it consistently opposes the organic to the mechanistic, Victorian literature can be said to continue the romantic tradition. But if a major theme of Victorian writing is, like the earlier romantic literature, opposition to the deterministic, abstracting method of science, then the Victorians found this mechanistic mode of thought not only in abstract philosophical theory but manifested in the machine technology beginning to regulate their daily lives. In the Victorian period, the machine becomes simultaneously a tangible influence and a philosophical symbol. And the opposition of the machine, considered in this double sense, to the organic becomes one of the dominant patterns in Victorian literature. A well-known passage from Mill's *On Liberty* gives explicit and eloquent expression to this theme:

> Supposing it were possible to get houses built, corn grown, battles fought, causes tried, and even churches erected and prayers said, by machinery— by automatons in human form—it would be a considerable loss to exchange for these automatons even the men and women who at present inhabit the more civilized parts of the world, and who assuredly are but starved specimens of what nature can and will produce. Human nature is not a machine to be built after a model, and set to do exactly the work prescribed for it, but a tree, which requires to grow and develop itself on all sides, according to the tendency of the inward forces which make it a living thing.[6]

The complexity in the use of the machine as symbol indicates a corresponding complexity in perception, an awareness that technological progress, the transformation of emotional life, and the growth of scientific thought are interdependent. For this new quality of life there is no single word. "Mechanization" applies to the tangible fact of technological progress, "mechanistic" to a mode of thought. Only the literary symbol of the machine can express this complex interrelationship which defines Victorian life; for, as symbol, it eradicates the misleading antithesis of external technological change to internal emotional and intellectual change. As Thomas Carlyle stated in 1829: "It is the Age of Machinery, in every outward and inward sense of that word."[7]

For many Victorian authors, this interrelation between the "outward and inward sense" becomes the central theme of their work. But it would be a mistake to see the literary response to the machine solely in terms of opposition. The proper metaphor for culture, as Lionel Trilling suggests,[8] is that of tension, the attempt to hold together contradictory ideas. And in confronting machine technology, the Victorians did hold directly contradictory ideas. The machine is both the unwearied iron servant and the sacrificial god to whom mankind has offered its soul. And as each writer criticizes the destructive union of mechanization and philosophic mechanism, he also admires his age for its technological skill. None are Luddites. Rather they see the machine as a servant who would be terribly useful if he would only not insist on ordering the household according to his own needs.

From this ambivalent attitude toward the machine develop the two antithetical literary modes of treating technology. Through nineteenth-century literature, as through nineteenth-century architecture,[9] there run two distinct styles, each of which can be defined by its attitude toward the machine. The first either attempts to escape what it considers the ugliness of the mechanized world or works in a realistic mode which describes this ugliness. The second, which culminates in Wells and Kipling, seeks to celebrate the machine in a language and through a set of values derived from the machine itself.

Examining the relationship between mechanistic thought and mechanization, whether in cosmology, aesthetic theory, the production of art, or biological science, is a central concern of Victorian intellectual prose. The conflict between the organic and the mechanistic, the new dangers and the new heroism of the machine age are major themes of Victorian imaginative writing. This study will discuss the literary forms developed to express these various, often ambivalent attitudes toward the machine and suggest that whatever consistency may be found in the Victorian literary response lies not so much in a dislike of technology as in a more general opposition to mechanistic modes of thought.

Although the symbolic implications of the machine remain generally consistent throughout the century, the imaginative treatment of the machine continued to change in response to advances in technology itself. Among the earliest visible signs of mechanization in England were the textile mills. But the Victorian vi-

sion of the mill surrounded by smoke and flame was not a reality until the stationary engine was first geared to provide the rotary motion necessary to turn spinning machinery. Early in the century, most mills depended upon water power and were thus confined to rural areas. The romantic poets, when they wrote of the machine at all, took up the contrast between the factory and its pastoral surroundings as a figure for what they saw as the profound unnaturalness of mechanization. In Blake the "dark, Satanic Mills" are seen destroying the divine, almost sacramental order of "England's green and pleasant Land."[10] In Wordsworth's *Excursion*, the textile mills of Cumberland destroy the natural rhythms once preserved in pastoral life:

> In full many a region, once like this
> The assured domain of calm simplicity
> And pensive quiet, an unnatural light
> Prepared for never-resting Labour's eyes
> Breaks from a many-windowed fabric huge.[11]

And the central theme of nineteenth-century machine literature, the destruction of the emotional life by mechanization, is expressed in the isolation of the child from the natural world. Wordsworth speaks of the child

> In whom a premature necessity
> Blocks out the forms of nature, preconsumes
> The reason, famishes the heart, shuts up
> The infant Being in itself, and makes
> Its very spring a season of decay![12]

But machine technology did not truly engage the literary imagination until the coming of the railway. Before the spread of the railway through England in the 1830's, steam-powered manufacturing was confined largely to the North, a long and difficult journey from London. The only signs of the machine in London itself before the railway arrived were a few steamboats on the Thames. But even after the railway connected North and South, few of the London-based writers had a felt sense of life in a mechanized factory or in the manufacturing towns. The standard picture of the industrial world in Victorian literature consists of smoke and flame seen from a distance. And of the machines themselves only the most fantastic or grotesque creations, such as the steam hammer or the stationary engine, caught the literary imagination.

But everyone understood the railway. It was, as Mill notes, the most public of symbols. The railway spread with amazing rapidity; the first company to use modern high-speed locomotive began operations in 1830, and by 1850 there were six thousand miles of track. But figures alone only suggest the extent of the railway revolution. Social life was transformed as travel became easy and inexpensive, economics transformed as the railway moved coal to the factories and finished products from the factory to the consumer. Add to this the new feeling of speed, the new optical sensations of railway travel and it becomes clear why most early Victorians saw theirs as the railway age.

But for all their novelty, for all their power, the stationary engine and the locomotive were unquestionably ugly. The stationary engine threw out clouds of smoke that hung over the industrial towns; railway passengers had to choose between suffocation and opening the windows to let in the soot and cinders. But the visual despair of the age of steam, which Lewis Mumford calls the Paleotechnic age,[13] began to lessen when, in the 1880's, the source of power shifted first from coal and steam to electricity and, finally, to the internal-combustion engine. So, for the late victorians, Wells and Kipling, the image of the machine became the dynamo and the airplane. The new sleekness, above all the new cleanliness of the machine in, to use Mumford's term again,[14] the Neotechnic age did much to suggest to these later writers the possibilities of a literature celebrating the beauty of the machine.

In spite of the changing appearance of the machine, the attitudes toward it, from Carlyle to Wells, from Dickens to Kipling, remain generally consistent. This study, then, will concentrate on the work of seven writers who use the symbol of the machine to express the interrelationships of technological change, psychic well-being, and mechanistic thought. This emphasis on the effects of technological change necessarily omits major figures who express the more general Victorian literary opposition to mechanistic thought. The figure of the machine is central to Matthew Arnold's thought and rhetoric. When he asks in *Culture and Anarchy* "What is freedom but machinery? what is population but machinery? what is coal but machinery? what are railroads but machinery? what is wealth but machinery? what are, even, religious organisations but machinery?"[15] the figure points to the interdependence of the zeal for individualism, the decline of intellectual certainty, and the new wealth created by mechanized industry. And to "machinery" he opposes the organic process of culture, in which the mind grows by fusing ethics and intellect. But "machinery" remains primarily a metaphor. Arnold has little concern with the relation of technological change to the liberal ideology and even less with the psychological effects of mechanized labor. For him the villain is the Zeitgeist rather than the steam engine.

For similar reasons, Mill must be omitted also. For although the antithesis between the organic and the mechanistic pervades his writing, Mill, like Arnold, saw causal principles in political rather than technological terms. In *On Liberty*, individualism may be limned by its contrast to the figure of man as machine, but it is analyzed in its relation to majority rule, not to the factory system. But for Carlyle, Dickens, Ruskin, Morris, Butler, Wells, and Kipling, the belief that the tangible fact of mechanization shapes the intellectual, aesthetic, and emotional life of their time lies at the center of their thought and of their art.

Notes

[1] Samuel Smiles, *The Life of George Stephenson* (London, 1868), p. 262.

[2] See the Victorian selections in the excellent collection of poetry of the machine edited by Jeremy Warburg, *The Industrial Muse* (London, 1958).

[3] "Prologue" to *The Earthly Paradise,* in *Works of William Morris,* ed. May Morris (London, 1910-1915), III, 3.

[4] *Essays on Politics and Culture,* ed. Gertrude Himmelfarb (New York, 1962), p. 262.

[5] The most important statement of this theory is Alfred North Whitehead, *Science and the Modern World* (New York, 1925), chap. v.

[6] *Three Essays by John Stuart Mill* (London, 1912), p. 73.

[7] "Signs of the Times," *The Works of Thomas Carlyle* (London, 1896-1899), XXVII, 59.

[8] "Reality in America," *The Liberal Imagination* (Garden City, 1957), p. 7.

[9] The two styles in architecture are discussed by Sigfried Giedion, *Space, Time and Architecture* (Cambridge, Mass., 1949).

[10] Preface to *Milton.*

[11] Bk. VIII, 11. 164-169.

[12] *The Excursion,* Bk. VIII, 11. 287-291.

[13] *Technics and Civilization* (New York, 1934), chap. iv.

[14] *Ibid.,* chap. v.

[15] *Culture and Anarchy,* ed. J. Dover Wilson (Cambridge, Eng., 1961), p. 50.

David E. E. Sloane

SOURCE: "A Connecticut Yankee and Industrial America: Mark Twain's Lesson," in *Essays in Arts and Sciences,* Vol. X, No. 2, March, 1982, pp. 197-205.

[In this essay, presented in 1980 as part of a series of lectures titled "Nineteenth-Century Industry and Culture in Connecticut," Sloane discusses Mark Twain's

favorable impression of American industrialism as seen in A Connecticut Yankee in King Arthur's Court, *which he calls "Twain's most ambitious attempt to make a comprehensive dramatization of the issues surrounding democracy and industrial progress."*]

Mark Twain, in 1871, wryly observed of a "medieval" tournament in Brooklyn, N.Y., that it was absurd to introduce the sentimentalized brag, vanity, and mock-heroics of the medieval joust into the broad-awake city of New York and the rolling mills and factories of the Northeast.[2] Mark Twain was not alone among Northeastern humorists in his progressive viewpoint, for lesser writers like Max Adeler, B. P. Shillaber, and John Phoenix had also pointedly remarked on the social advances which characterized "modern" America.[3] These writers, and others like William Cox in the 1830's and Will Carleton in the 1870's, and Mark Twain particularly as an adopted son and Connecticut Yankee, fancied that principles of American life were uniquely embodied in the material advances of the machine age beyond those benighted cultures which were held back by monarchical absolutism, religious superstition, and technical ignorance. Twain's assumption was that modern man was a natural ally of mechanical progress, helping populate a world of democratic principles, professional responsibility, and humane dealings. When he saw the opposite in corporate dealings, as in the corruption depicted in *The Gilded Age,* he resolved the contradictions through dramatic action and humor. Whether or not Twain's solutions really fit the problems he defines is a moot point, as the resolution of *A Connecticut Yankee in King Arthur's Court* suggests, and his practice as a novelist raises some ethical questions that remain pertinent to American society today.

As early as the 1830's, American writers were showing an awareness of the implications of technology for their own lives. William Cox, in "Steam" as early as 1833, took a conventional tack in decrying the loss of peace and pastoral calm to railroads and steam-driven automatons.[4] Cox describes a world of steam power in which rapid transit much like subways whisks people along so rapidly that they suffocate from lack of oxygen. "Vegetable nature," in his Romantic pastoral view, is bisected by "iron gangways," "monstrous machines," and even dancing, singing, love-making, marriage, and resurrection are all "done in a hurry . . . upon the high-pressure principle." The narrator is roused to fury by the inhumanity of the crowd of passersby who ignore a workman fallen from a scaffold and weltering in his own blood; on closer inspection, the workman is "only a steam man," working on the "locomotive" principle and easily repaired. When a steam-man replaces the "rosy-cheeked chambermaid" and *Hamlet* is played by steam, the narrator escapes from his dream vision by waking up. Cox is not dealing with technology itself as much as he is projecting his own anxiety about a

failure to manage its changes. Writing expressionistically, he finds in machines a metaphor for a world which dominates individuals, even while seeming to serve mankind; John Dos Passos' *Manhattan Transfer* (1925) and *U.S.A.* (1938), among a host of other works in the 1920's and 1930's, prove Cox's themes to be continuing ones.

Cox's position is an *interpretation* of technology, and it was by no means clear to American industrial pioneers that industry and technology were incompatible with the Athenian idealism of Federal New England. At Lowell and Andover, Massachusetts, lyceums were provided, and the moral growth and protection of the Yankee mill girls was carefully attended to.[5] Eli Whitney's development of the interchangeability system was consistent with the egalitarian ideal of farmers and artisans sharing the capability of making workable objects through machine tooling. Even the buildings he created show Federal designs and local building materials testifying to his aesthetic order in conjunction with manufacturing objectives. As time passed, in fact, many American writers saw American mechanical progress in favorable terms.

Will Carleton and Mark Twain are two writers who saw American industrialism and American technology in patriotic and humanistic terms. The Midwestern poet Will Carleton was one of the most beloved of the dialect poets of the 1870's, famed throughout the country for his defense of familial virtues and loyalty in "Over the Hill to the Poorhouse" and "Betsy and I are Out," published in *Harper's Monthly* and in his *Farm Ballads* (1873). Carleton found himself in lyrical abandon on spying a McCormick reaper in the wheat fields of Great Britain. Although his poem is laced with Romantic images of pastoral life such as abound in Wordsworth, his declaration is clearly in favor of the patriotic supremacy of American mechanical progress:

> The clang of the Yankee reaper,
>   On Salibury Plain!
> A music sweeter—deeper—
>   Than many a nobler strain.
>
> Across that British prairie
>   I tramped one summer day;
> The breeze was free and merry—
>   White lamb clouds were at play;
>
> With fleecy wealth was teeming
>   The shepherd's paddock fold;
> And ripened grain stood gleaming
>   Like lakes of melted gold; . . .
>
> And never the sea's wide reaches
>   Seemed half the fathoms o'er,
> Or the West-land's shining beaches
>   So far away before.

When, richer, sweeter, deeper
   Than a distant music strain,
Came the clang of the Yankee reaper
   On Salisbury Plain!

As when the heart is weeping
   'Neath slowly crushing hours,
The fragrance soft comes creeping
   Of memory-hallowed flowers;

As when, with sudden gleaming,
   Above some foreign dome,
Against the sky goes streaming
   The flag of our nation-home; . . . [6]

Carleton's poem identifies the machine with a complex of patriotic and natural feelings. The personal and ideological identification is emotional even more than it is philosophical or pragmatic. Nor is Carleton alone among American humorous writers. Whereas Dickens, in *Hard Times* (1854), saw English spinning jennies as melancholy elephants, Benjamin Taylor, in *The World on Wheels* (1873) finds that New York's advances in the application of the wheel embody "pretty much everything in the Nineteenth Century but the Christian Religion and the Declaration of Independence. Having thought about it a minute more, I am inclined to except the exceptions, and say they translate the one and transport the other."[7] Considering these views, it is not surprising that Twain's Connecticut Yankee would declare that "The first thing you want in a new country, is a patent office."[8]

For Mark Twain, industrialism is the enemy of vice, ignorance, and poverty. The American vandal of *The Innocents Abroad* (1869) is an outright exponent of technological progress as an alternative to the forces of reaction. In the Azores, the traveling reporter Mark Twain protests, "There is not a wheelbarrow in the land—they carry everything on their heads. . . . There is not a modern plow in the islands, or a threshing-machine. All attempts to introduce them have failed. The good Catholic Portuguese crossed himself and prayed God shield him from all blasphemous desire to know more than his father did before him."[9] Twain's profound rejection of Catholic reaction and technological ignorance is close to Will Carleton's enthusiasm for the Yankee reaper. Twain appears more pragmatic, but in other respects, the sentiments are almost identical.

In burlesque, later in *The Innocents Abroad,* Twain reversed his viewpoint, pretending to be a Roman traveling in America and writing home to Catholic Italy. Reporting beyond his "modern Roman sloth, modern Roman superstition, and modern Roman boundlessness of ignorance," the narrator describes fire engines, fashions, the rich and the poor—"a senator, no matter how ignorant an ass he is" and rich men are invited "to

drink complicated beverages; but if he be poor and in debt, they require him to do that which they term to 'settle.'" More significantly, however, common people read books and newspapers printed by "a great machine," and, finally:

> In America the people are absolutely wiser and know much more than their grandfathers did. *They* do not plow with a sharpened stick, nor yet with a three-cornered block of wood. . . . Those people have no holy reverence for their ancestors. They plow with a plow that is a sharp, curved blade of iron, and it cuts into the earth full five inches. And this is not all. They cut their grain with a horrid machine that mows down whole fields in a day. If I dared, I would say that sometimes they use a blasphemous plow that works by fire and vapor and tears up an acre of ground in a single hour.[10]

Morse, Jenner, Howe, Fulton, and Daguerre are among those praised by Twain, a representative mix of mechanical and humane inventiveness. In fact, a lengthy catalog of material goods and political rights expands considerably on the items cited above, overtly linking knowledge, political beliefs, and economic progress. Twain's own investments in the ill-fated Paige typesetting machine were consistent with all of these attitudes.

A Connecticut Yankee in King Arthur's Court, in 1889, is Twain's most ambitious attempt to make a comprehensive dramatization of the issues surrounding democracy and industrial progress. The two most prominent symbols in the novel are the Colt revolver and the Gatling gun, products of the nineteenth-century industrial age having great destructive potential. The Yankee, Hank Morgan, is the symbolic American entrepreneur-industrialist, an amalgam of Andrew Carnegie and P. T. Barnum. Like Frederic Tudor, the early nineteenth-century American who not only recognized the commercial potential of New England's ice harvesting but then went on to develop the technology and even the markets for his million-dollar enterprise over twenty-five years, the Connecticut Yankee is the "go getter," the representative of the "go ahead" spirit of the universal Yankee nation.[11] Like other representatives of the "go getter" spirit in the American West, however, occasions arise when the immensity of his own designs overwhelms conventions of law and morality, demonstrating a complex issue which Twain admits in the plot of the novel but does not discuss.

From Hank Morgan's introduction and his initial decision to bust Brer Merlin's stock flat at the Round Table, the Yankee is a symbol of irreverent inventiveness, from his mistaking Camelot for Bridgeport and his labelling of Raphael as "a bird" to his announcement that he would bring to the serfs of feudal England a "New Deal," the origin of Franklin D. Roosevelt's famous phrase. Repeatedly, the Yankee asserts his national identity in relation to his mechanical ability, claiming "I am an American . . . a Yankee of the Yankees—and practical. . . . I went over to the great arms factory and learned my real trade; learned all there was to it; learned to make everything; guns, revolvers, cannon, boilers, engines, all sorts of labor-saving machinery . . . if there wasn't any quick new-fangled way to make a thing, I could invent one." Hank Morgan thus becomes the personal embodiment of American industry in the nineteenth century.[12]

From the opening pages of *A Connecticut Yankee,* Twain built ambiguities into his plot, superficially symbolized by the coat of mail with a bullet hole, presumed to be from Cromwellian times but really made by the Yankee. The Yankee notes in Arthurian England the absence of modern conveniences—bells, speaking tubes, gas and even candle light, books, pens, paper, glass ("It is a little thing—glass is—until it is absent, then it becomes a big thing"), and sugar, tea, tobacco: "I saw that I was just another Robinson Crusoe cast away on an uninhabited island, with no society but some more or less tame animals, and if I wanted to make life bearable I must do as he did—invent, contrive, create, reorganize things; set brain and hand to work, and keep them busy. Well, that was in my line." His laudable industrial ambition complements an equally strong intention to educate the English peasantry up to revolution grade, even though he realizes that goody-goody talk cannot replace the rule that successful revolutions must begin in blood. It seems that Hank's sense of medieval people as animals and his hostility to the political machines of church and state represents a source of irreconcilable conflict with his inventiveness.

As a true industrial entrepreneur, Hank establishes a "Man-Factory" (*passim*) in which he can make the materials of an American-style industrial democracy complete with stock boards and baseball teams. There the principle could be established that "A man *is* a man, at bottom. . . . bound out to some useful trade, universal suffrage instituted, and the whole government placed in the hands of the men and women of the nation, there to remain." Unfortunately, as Henry Nash Smith has shrewdly pointed out, the Yankee's financial and industrial empire is virtually without a system in the novel; money has no relation to power; Hank Morgan represents a spirit of democratic horse-play as much as he represents a reasoned form of technology or industrial capitalism.[13] Consequently, progress takes an uncomfortable turn as the conflicts broaden between the Connecticut Yankee and the Catholic Church and feudal knights led by Merlin. Originally, Hank had defended himself against a knight with a dynamite bomb, and later in the "Valley of Holiness" he reintroduces bathing to the monks by opening up a well with a dynamite torpedo like those used to reopen oil wells

in America; but by the time Hank must make his last stand against Arthurian chivalry, his "civilization factories" and delegations of knights must be exploded in acts of desperate self-defense.

Almost from the moment when Yankee industrialism is at its highest point, it is threatened by its own success. Hank Morgan's pride in his cultural achievements expands even on Will Carleton's sentimentalism:

> Slavery was dead and gone; all men were equal before the law; taxation had been equalized. The telegraph, the telephone, the phonograph, the type-writer, the sewing machine, and all the thousand willing and handy servants of steam and electricity were working their way into favor. We had a steamboat or two in the Thames, we had steam war-ships, and the beginnings of a steam commercial marine; I was getting ready to send out an expedition to discover America.

However, with success comes awareness on the part of the Church, which attacks Hank's power with an Interdict against England, and the forces of feudalism are mobilized. Hank retreats to a cave with fifty-four boys and prepares to defend himself with electric fences and Gatling guns. Hank had previously killed a knight with his Colt revolver, accounting for the hole in the chain-mail beginning the story. In the final chapter, electrocution—supposed to be a humane way of killing—and the Gatling gun—supposed to be a weapon to end wars because of its horrible efficiency—become his primary tools:[14]

> So I touched the button and set fifty electric suns aflame on the top of our precipice.

> Land, what a sight! We were enclosed in three walls of dead men! All the other fences were pretty near filled with the living, . . . while even that slight fragment of time was still unspent, I shot the current through all the fences and struck the whole host dead in their tracks! *There* was a groan you could *hear*! It voiced the death-pang of eleven thousand men. . . .

> "Stand to your guns, men! Open fire!"

> The thirteen gatlings began to vomit death into the fated ten thousand. They halted, they stood their ground a moment against that withering deluge of fire, then they broke. . . . Twenty-five thousand men lay dead around us.

The technical magician and democratic champion has become a tremendous destroyer. At least one modern critic has commented that Hank has substituted the politics of the Western gunman with his "High Noon" confrontations to prove he is the better man.[15]

Any attempt to interpret American industrialism as a cultural phenomenon needs to take into consideration a variety of disparate elements. Biographies of men such as Eli Whitney are studded with ambiguities like those captured in Twain's Hank Morgan. So Whitney's cotton gin, designed to save labor, is credited with reinforcing the slave labor system in the South. Nor are all the surprises on the negative side, as when atomic power yields medical cures. For Mark Twain, as with several of the other humorists referred to, technical progress and American political ideology seemed to be combined in ways which guaranteed humane uses of technology. It may well be that they were not sufficiently wary of the openness of technology as a system to any directive use.[16] In relating Twain to nineteenth-century industry, we find that his tendency to see conflicts in terms of dramatic confrontation brought about a sort of warfare which Hank Morgan himself had been at pains throughout the novel to reject. A modern reader might well note the ambiguities in Twain's approach to industrialism, for Mark Twain's rejection of the violence which the plot demands seems to call for a careful and thoughtful control of mechanical progress in order that it really serve the ends for which it is contrived.

Notes

. . . . .

[2] Mark Twain, "The 'Tournament' in A.D. 1870," *Contributions to "The Galaxy," 1868-1871 by Mark Twain,* ed., Bruce R. McElderry (Gainesville: Scholars' Facsimiles and Reprints, 1961), pp. 59-60: "It is hard to tell which is the most startling, the idea of that highest achievement of human genius and intelligence, the telegraph, prating away about the practical concerns of the world's daily life in the heart and home of ancient indolence, ignorance, and savagery, or the idea of that happiest expression of the brag, vanity, and mock-heroics of our ancestors, the 'tournament,' coming out of its grave to flaunt its tinsel trumpery . . . in the high noon of the nineteenth century, and under the patronage of a great broad-awake city and an advanced civilization."

[3] Max Adeler [Charles Heber Clark] treated the modern civilization/feudalism contrast explicitly in *The Fortunate Island* (1881), which anticipates Twain's *A Connecticut Yankee;* see Edward M. Foster, "*A Connecticut Yankee* Anticipated: Max Adeler's *Fortunate Island,*" *Ball State University Forum,* 9 (1968), 73-6. John Phoenix was the pen-name of George H. Derby, author of *Phoenixiana* (1855) and *The Squibob Papers* (1859).

[4] William Cox, "Steam," *Crayon Sketches* (New York: Conner & Cooke, 1833). The version referred to here is in *The Cyclopedia of Wit and Humor,* ed., William

E. Burton (New York: Appleton, 1875 [1855]), pp. 91-3.

[5] Daniel Boorstin, *The Americans/The National Experience* (New York; Vintage Books, 1965), pp. 28-35, relates mill life to the "uniformity" or "Whitney" system revolutionizing New England. The sorry outcome of this early progressivism in the lumber mills of Everett, Washington, is chronicled in Norman H. Clark's *Mill Town* (Seattle: U. of Washington Press, 1970).

[6] Will Carleton, "The Clang of the Yankee Reaper," *Farm Ballads* (New York: Harper & Bros., 1873), pp. 101-2, verses 4-6, 13 are omitted.

[7] Charles Dickens, *Hard Times* (New York: Holt, Rinehart, and Winston, 1963), *passim.* Benjamin F. Taylor, *The World on Wheels* (Chicago: S. C. Griggs & Co., 1874), p. 13.

[8] Mark Twain, *A Connecticut Yankee in King Arthur's Court* (San Francisco: Chandler Publishing Co., 1963 [1889]), p. 109.

[9] Mark Twain, *The Innocents Abroad* (New York: Harper & Bros., 1911), p. 40.

[10] *Ibid.,* pp. 274-80.

[11] See Boorstin, *The Americans/The National Experience,* pp. 10-16. The "go getter" spirit is discussed in relation to the Johnson County War between law-abiding sheep herders and "outlaw" cattle ranchers backed by lawmen, in Daniel Boorstin's *The Americans/The Democratic Experience* (New York: Vintage Books, 1974), pp. 3-87. The "go ahead" spirit is a more common term in comic journals of the 1850s and 1860s such as *Yankee Notions.*

[12] For a fuller treatment of *A Connecticut Yankee* as literary comedy see David E. E. Sloane, *Mark Twain as a Literary Comedian* (Baton Rouge: L.S.U. Press, 1979), pp. 146-67.

[13] Henry Nash Smith, *Mark Twain's Fable of Progress: Political and Economic Ideas in "A Connecticut Yankee"* (New Brunswick: Rutgers U. Press, 1964), pp. 90-104.

[14] I am indebted to Professor Louis J. Budd of Duke Univ. for bringing my attention to these points.

[15] Chadwick Hansen in a paper to the national convention of the Modern Language Association (1973) titled "The Politics of the Gunman: A Connecticut Yankee."

[16] Richard Rubenstein, in *The Cunning of History* (New York: Harper & Row, 1975), has applied this point to the extermination camps of World War II in a way

which should impress interested readers as horrifyingly logical; readers are recommended to this outstanding study.

Chris Baldick

SOURCE: "Tales of Transgression, Fables of Industry: Hoffmann, Hawthorne, Melville, and Gaskell," in *In Frankenstein's Shadow: Myth, Monstrosity, and Nineteenth-Century Writing,* Oxford at the Clarendon Press, 1987, pp. 63-91.

[In the essay that follows, Baldick examines "stories of doomed experimenters" found in works by Hoffmann, Hawthorne, Melville, and Gaskell, suggesting that these authors portray various forms of production as self-destructive activities.]

Mary Shelley was not alone in fictionalizing the various preoccupations which we find at work in *Frankenstein;* stories of doomed experimenters and obsessive chemists were favourites with early nineteenth-century readers. In France Balzac himself tried his hand at this kind of tale in his *La Recherche de l'Absolu* (1834), in which the protagonist Balthazar Claes, who has studied chemistry under Lavoisier, encounters a Polish chemist who inspires him to search for 'the Absolute'—the single element to which all matter can be reduced. The quest is of course fatal in its consequences, especially for Claes's domestic peace, as his wife foresees. She accuses Claes of regarding people merely as mechanisms animated by electrical fluid, and warns him against the Pole: 'Did you look at him closely? Only the tempter could have those yellow eyes, blazing with the fire of Prometheus.' Claes's science is, she warns, encroaching on God's power just as Satan had done in his reckless pride.[1]

The more familiar home of such Frankensteinian themes, though, lay in the European and American short-story tradition, where the emergent sub-genres of horror story, science fiction, and detective tale mingled productively in the early part of the century. Many of the most impressive short stories of this period are tales of transgression which show a particular interest in production—whether artistic, craft, or scientific—as an obsessive and self-destructive activity. The model for most of these Romantic fables is of course the Faust myth, but in these versions the Faustian figure is radically modernized, his former acquisition of merely abstract knowledge now rewritten as the perfecting of productive technique.[2] These stories are often also explorations of the Romantic crisis of artistic identity, self-reflexive fictions of creative aspiration and its uncertainties. In many of the best tales of E. T. A. Hoffmann and Nathaniel Hawthorne, artists of various kinds discover the destructive and damning qualities of their own creations,

which typically develop autonomous powers and overwhelm their creators. As we are not yet dealing with a conscious or clearly defined 'science fiction' (the word 'scientist' itself does not appear before 1834), the kind of creator-figure we find in these stories is a peculiar mixture of artist, philosopher, craftsman, and chemical experimenter. Through these versatile and obsessive creators, Romantic story-tellers offered their own artistic dilemmas as metaphors for the production and reproduction of life in every domain from the sexual to the industrial.

Given the then incipient division of art from technology, Romantic authors could better subsume the full range of human activity under their sense of the 'creative' by using a conventional figure of creativity drawn from economically retarded societies in which a cherished integration of imagination and manual skill was still embodied in a single person. This would seem to explain partly the strong Germanic influence on the short-story tradition in the nineteenth century, and why the protagonists in Hoffmann, Hawthorne, and their imitators are so often skilled craftsmen; theirs are tales of mystery in the archaic sense of 'mystery' as a skilled and secretive trade. So we find in these stories a gallery or arcade of watchmakers, jewellers, violin-makers, goldsmiths, architects, opticians, and assorted experimenting doctors or professors, all of them obsessively independent producers who create marvels from their private researches, usually without Mephistophelean assistance. These figures are, in short, classical petty-bourgeois producers whose special knowledge and skill have allowed them to become their own masters, answerable to nobody and often feared by their fellow burghers.

What is repeatedly shown in these tales of transgression is how the secret skill which makes the protagonist independent and severs his social ties becomes an obsessional end in itself and masters the master. In particular, the pursuit of craft skills to the point of artistic perfectionism is often shown—especially by Hoffmann—to stand in direct competition with sexual love. Hoffmann's young protagonists typically find themselves distracted from their fiancées by some delusion associated with their work or that of their masters, in the same pattern by which Victor Frankenstein neglects Elizabeth for his workshop. This element of sublimating distraction is one of the few original features of the tale most carefully preserved in stage and film versions of *Frankenstein;* Victor as a kind of secretive Bluebeard thus stands as one of the more popular components from which the cliché of the Mad Scientist will be constructed. The products of similarly obsessed creators in Hoffmann and Hawthorne are often poisonous or otherwise blighted, mocking the ideals of artistic perfectionism and metaphorically revealing the blighting of the creator as he seals himself off from the sources of life in other people.

Nathaniel's fiancée Clara in Hoffmann's 'The Sandman' takes the experimenter's syndrome for granted when she writes to her intended of his recent experiences:

> The uncanny night-time activities with your father were no doubt nothing more than secret alchemical experiments . . . and your mother can hardly have been pleased about it, since a lot of money was undoubtedly wasted and, moreover, as is always supposed to be the case with such laboratory experimenters, your father, altogether absorbed in the deceptive desire for higher truth, would have become estranged from his family.[3]

True to the same pattern, Nathaniel is seduced away from the devoted Clara by the sinister optician Coppola and by the charms of Professor Spalanzini's perfect clockwork doll Olympia, with whom he falls in love. Finally driven insane by a series of delusions, Nathaniel almost kills Clara before leaping to his death from a tower. Similarly the artist Berthold in 'The Jesuit College at Glogau', who speaks of his art in terms of Promethean struggle, finds his life divided sharply between his obsessive work and his love, and is suspected of killing his wife and child to remove all distractions from his painting. Councillor Krespel, who dismantles violins to discover their secrets, throws his pregnant wife out of a window when she interrupts his music, and metonymically 'kills' his daughter by dismantling a violin especially associated with her.

The pattern of fatal oppositions between love and work is repeated in a particularly fascinating story by Hoffmann, 'The Mines at Falun' (1819), upon which Wagner once planned to base an opera. The tale is a kind of *Moby Dick* in reverse: a melancholic and introspective sailor, Elis Fröbom, meets an old miner and is ensnared by the attractions of subterranean life. As in Melville's novel, the industry is endowed with a metaphysical value beyond its financial rewards, and it is this lure of higher aspirations which draws the protagonist on to his eventual destruction.

> Elis Fröbom was almost terrified by the old man's words. 'What are you advising me to do?' he cried. 'Am I to leave the beautiful earth and the sunlit sky and go down into the dreadful depths and burrow like a mole, grubbing for ores and minerals, for the sake of vile profit?'

> 'People despise what they want to know nothing about!' the old man cried angrily. 'Vile profit! As if the horrors perpetrated on the face of the earth by trade and commerce were nobler than the work of the miner, whose indefatigable industry opens up nature's most secret treasure-houses. You speak of vile profit, Elis Fröbom!—well, something higher than that might be involved. If the blind mole burrows by blind instinct, it may be that the eyes of

man acquire more penetrating sight in the deepest depths of the earth, until they can recognize in the wonderful stones they find a reflection of that which is hidden above the clouds. You know nothing about mining, Elis; let me tell you about it.'

As the old man describes the world of mining, Elis begins to feel the charm of a world whose magic has been known to him from earliest boyhood in strange and secret presentiments. They are perhaps not so strange if we remember that he is being invited to penetrate Mother Nature; and indeed that night Elis is conquered in a dream by the huge and terrifying subterranean 'Queen' at the same time that he hears the voice of his dead mother.

Repelled at first by the chasm of the open-cast mine and its resemblance to Dante's Inferno, Elis bashfully falls in love with Ulla, the daughter of a mine overseer, and becomes a miner himself. But the mysterious old miner reappears to warn him that the Prince of Metals jealously demands an exclusive devotion with which Elis's love for Ulla conflicts. Other miners tell him that the old man is the ghost of the bachelor Torbern, whose understanding of 'the hidden powers which rule in the womb of the earth' had transcended mere material greed, but who had been killed in a collapse; his ghost recruits miners in times of labour shortage and guides them to the best veins of ore. When it appears that Ulla is accepting the advances of a rich merchant, Elis rushes to the mine to devote himself to it instead; in a vision, he discovers the richest veins, and is clasped to the breast of the Queen. Ulla's apparent betrayal turns out to have been staged by her father to force a proposal from Elis, so their engagement can now go ahead. In the midst of their bliss, though, Elis feels haunted by his commitment to the Queen, while Ulla senses something pulling him away from her as he raves about 'the paradise which shone in the womb of the earth.' As the wedding day nears, Elis's state improves, but on the nuptial morning he sets off again to the mine to find, as a bridal gift, a blood-red carbuncle which he has seen in a dream and which reflects 'the heart of the Queen at the mid-point of the earth' (where Lucifer is placed in Dante's Inferno). Elis is then killed in a landslide.

In this tale Hoffmann outlines, almost at the same time as Mary Shelley, a series of Frankensteinian problems, most obviously a complex involving the fusion of productive labour and sexual obsession. As in *Frankenstein,* the hero is clearly gripped by fantasies of his dead mother, and the tale is almost too overtly a 'mine' for depth psychology. Yet, like other tales of Hoffmann, it pursues the conflict between normal bonds of affection and a professional 'mystery' which exacts a single-minded devotion from its followers. It gives us not just a Freudian nuptial trauma but an image of the world of work as a rival to the sexual claims of the fiancée. Only when Elis hears that there is more to mining than the mundane value of 'vile profit' does he become embroiled in its fantasized appeal. Thus it is suggested (as it is in *Moby Dick,* as we shall see) that Elis's self-destruction follows from his aspiring beyond the bourgeois safety of the balance-sheet, in ardent pursuit of Nature's secrets. Hoffmann hints at a mysterious force of attraction which entices young men into frantic labours apparently unjustified by the simple market value of the ores extracted. The brilliant gems and metals seen in Elis's visions seem to reflect all his desires both sexual and spiritual, and it is worth noting that although he starts by scorning vile profit, his obsession is put in motion by the prospect of marrying his overseer's daughter. Elis's industry is rewarded in just this way by Ulla's father, so his frantic accumulation can be seen as a means towards a respectable end. At the close of the tale, though, what seems to Ulla and her father to be a means has become an end in itself. In this kind of concern with the obsessional appeal of production, 'The Mines at Falun' stands alongside *Frankenstein* as another remarkable modern parable of the industrial condition.

Nathaniel Hawthorne, in his many fictional studies of self-destructive artists, craftsmen, alchemists, and other alienated producers, is clearly an imitator of Hoffmann, although the American's tales show a more measured and artistically finished quality. Often, as in 'The Artist of the Beautiful', it is apparent that Hawthorne's central concern is with the dilemmas of the Romantic artist, yet in this and in many closely related tales he also brings into focus wider questions of society, science, and solitude which are posed in ways which are strikingly familiar to the reader of *Frankenstein*. Hawthorne's stock figure in these allegorical sketches is an isolated man whose mentality and special pursuits tear him from the warmth of (usually female) society until he hardens into a frozen or petrified monster. Indeed, the protagonist of 'The Man of Adamant' literally turns to stone after rejecting the sympathies of woman; conversely, the 'monstrous egotism'[4] of Roderick Elliston in 'Egotism, or the Bosom Serpent' is finally cured by woman's love. Hawthorne repeatedly plays upon a contrast between the human warmth of domesticity and the self-defeating coldness and abstraction of egotistical endeavour, as in 'The Ambitious Guest' or 'The Christmas Banquet'. Similar patterns of characterization are at work in the longer romances too: in the prying heartlessness of Chillingworth in *The Scarlet Letter,* and in Hollingsworth's pseudo-philanthropic egoism in *The Blithedale Romance.*

> Hollingsworth had a closer friend than ever you could be. And this friend was the cold, spectral monster which he had himself conjured up, and on which he was wasting all the warmth of his heart, and of which, at last—as these men of mighty purpose so invariably do—he had grown to be the bond-slave. It was his philanthropic theory![5]

Before this Frankensteinian narcissism destroys the warm-blooded Zenobia, she accuses Hollingsworth of being a monster and a 'cold, heartless, self-beginning and self-ending piece of mechanism'.[6]

Hawthorne's interests extend beyond the spectres conjured up by egotism, to take in similarly alienated figures who are not just heartless individualists but also producers in a more practical sense: alchemists, artists, or both. 'The Artist of the Beautiful' is unusual in the sympathy which Hawthorne extends to its hero, the poetical watchmaker Owen Warlock; the tale is less a critique of egotism than an indulgent self-examination of the artist's predicament, but it is still worth noting how Hawthorne makes Owen lose the girl Annie, as a result of his creative obsession, to a more earthly blacksmith and suffer 'a sensation of moral cold that makes the spirit shiver as if it had reached the frozen solitudes around the pole.' Trying to improve upon nature by manufacturing a butterfly-like automaton, Owen cuts himself off from the blessings of truly humanized nature. Appropriately it is Annie's child who finally crushes Owen's painstakingly constructed model butterfly.

Owen's malign counterpart in Hawthorne is the physician Rappaccini, whose exile from human sympathies fits more closely the developing stereotype of the Mad Scientist: the hero Giovanni is told by Professor Baglioni that Rappaccini 'cares infinitely more for science than for mankind. His patients are interesting to him only as subjects for some new experiment.' In Hawthorne's works clinical detachment of this kind is always a symptom of moral disease. Rappaccini is not just a sinister experimenter, though, but a creator whose works are fabricated on recognizably Frankensteinian principles. The plants in his poisonous artificial garden

> would have shocked a delicate instinct by an appearance of artificialness indicating that there had been such commixture, and, as it were, adultery, of various vegetable species, that the production was no longer of God's making, but the monstrous offspring of man's depraved fancy, glowing with only an evil mockery of beauty. They were probably the result of experiment, which in one or two cases had succeeded in mingling plants individually lovely into a compound possessing the questionable and ominous character that distinguished the whole growth of the garden.

Taking individually beautiful components, as Victor Frankenstein had done, Rappaccini has combined them to produce not an abortive Adam but a poisonous Garden of Eden, which similarly exhibits the nature of the temperament behind its creation. And for Rappaccini's crime it is his creature who suffers: his daughter (and finest 'flower') Beatrice, who is condemned to solitude by her poisonous constitution and who regards herself as a monster when she infects Giovanni.

Perhaps a more interesting figure among Hawthorne's deluded creators is Aylmer in 'The Birthmark'. Like Owen Warlock and like Frankenstein, Aylmer is a modern disciple of Albertus Magnus and a latter-day rival to Pygmalion. Seeking to improve upon nature, he attempts to correct the only blemish in his wife's otherwise perfect beauty—a hand-shaped birthmark which comes to symbolize earthly imperfection in general. In this story too we see 'the love of science . . . rival the love of woman in its depth and absorbing energy'. So strong is the rivalry, in fact, that Aylmer's attempt to eradicate the birthmark succeeds in killing his wife along with her supposed blemish.

Several of these characteristics of heartless isolation and abortive production are united in the most Frankensteinian figure in Hawthorne's fiction, that of Ethan Brand. In his story we can detect a significant shift from a Faustian to a Promethean model of transgression. The legend which surrounds Brand in the tale attributes to him the conjuring of a devil from the furnace of his lime-kiln, but the activity which he and the devil are alleged then to pursue is described as if it were a process of production, 'the man and the fiend each laboring to frame the image of some mode of guilt which could neither be atoned for nor forgiven.' A lime-burner by trade, Ethan is a maker, and a suitably Promethean one at that, as his fiery surname hints. Although he is for a while led off on a fruitless quest for the Unpardonable Sin, he finds it at last only by making it. Hawthorne shows in Brand's project a familiar process of dehumanization which is revealed at last to be a process of transgressive production.

> So much for the intellect! But where was the heart? That, indeed, had withered,—had contracted,—had hardened,—had perished! It had ceased to partake of the universal throb. He had lost his hold of the magnetic chain of humanity. He was no longer a brother-man, opening the chambers or the dungeons of our common nature by the key of holy sympathy, which gave him a right to share in all its secrets; he was now a cold observer, looking on mankind as the subject of his experiment, and, at length, converting man and woman to be his puppets, and pulling the wires that moved them to such degrees of crime as were demanded for his study.

> Thus Ethan Brand became a fiend. He began to be so from the moment that his moral nature had ceased to keep the pace of improvement with his intellect. And now, as his highest effort and inevitable development,—as the bright and gorgeous flower, and rich, delicious fruit of his life's labor,— he had produced the Unpardonable Sin!

By 'producing' the Unpardonable Sin, Brand has produced himself too, remaking himself as a man whose heart, after his final self-immolation, is so hard as to withstand the furnace. His long search for the Unpardonable Sin has been a wasted effort, more pointless even than the spinnings of the dog in the story who chases his own tail, since Brand's goal too is in himself. Ethan Brand's activity combines all those disorders which Hawthorne habitually analyses: individualism, isolation from human sympathies, intellectual irresponsibility, and an instrumental attitude to others. Brand comes to define the Unpardonable Sin as the one he has himself practised: 'The sin of an intellect that triumphed over the sense of brotherhood with man and reverence for God, and sacrificed everything to its own mighty claims!'

As if to emphasize the fact that Brand's sin is a misdirected labour, Hawthorne takes care to contrast with him the figure of Lawyer Giles. Whereas Brand has risen from manual to intellectual labour, Giles has gone the other way.

> This poor fellow had been an attorney . . . but flip, and sling, and toddy, and cocktails, imbibed at all hours, morning, noon, and night, had caused him to slide from intellectual to various kinds and degrees of bodily labor, till at last, to adopt his own phrase, he slid into a soap-vat. In other words, Giles was now a soap-boiler, in a small way. He had come to be but the fragment of a human being, a part of one foot having been chopped off by an axe, and an entire hand torn away by the devilish grip of a steam engine.

If Ethan Brand's intellectual labour condemns him to burn in his own kiln, Giles's manual labour dismembers him in the grip of a mechanical devil; his soap-boiling and Brand's lime-burning both hint at the infernal. As Leo Marx has pointed out, this macabre vision of manual labour as dismemberment seems to arise from Hawthorne's visit in 1838 to the new factories in the Berkshires.[7] Hawthorne addresses in 'Ethan Brand' the problem of Schiller's fragmented humanity, allegorizing that division of labour which the Transcendentalists of Brook Farm had tried to overcome in their Utopian schemes, under the sceptical eye of Nathaniel Hawthorne himself.

Thanks to R. W. Emerson and his associates, the problem of modern fragmentation as formulated in German Idealist and Carlylean terms was to become a central preoccupation of mid-century American writing, the novelty of the American adventure having called forth fundamental questions about life, labour, and human ambition in an individualist and scientific age. Emerson's own anxiety, expressed in 'The American Scholar', was that the advanced division of labour in modern industrial society was fragmenting any sense of human integrity:

The state of society is one in which the members have suffered amputation from the trunk, and strut about so many walking monsters,—a good finger, a neck, a stomach, an elbow, but never a man.

Man is thus metamorphosed into a thing, into many things. . . . The priest becomes a form; the attorney a statute-book; the mechanic a machine; the sailor a rope of the ship.[8]

This kind of Transcendentalist social criticism emphasizes both the dismemberment of the body politic and the subordination of men and women to their own creations, under the new reign of the commodity. As Emerson lamented in his 'Ode Inscribed to W. E. Channing',

'Tis the day of the chattel,
Web to weave, and corn to grind;
Things are in the saddle,
And ride mankind.

There are two laws discrete,
Not reconciled,—
Law for man and law for thing;
The last builds town and fleet,
But it runs wild,
And doth the man unking.[9]

This running wild of the huge productive energies of the nineteenth century, particularly in the unprecedented conquests of nature going forward in Britain and America, is a recurrent nightmare for the mid-century writer. The feeling that 'things are in the saddle' reappears in the paradoxical formulations of H. D. Thoreau, whose hut at Walden adjoined a new railroad track. 'We do not ride on the railroad', Thoreau wrote, 'it rides upon us.' Reflecting on his neighbours' enslaved existence, he believes that 'men are not so much the keepers of herds as herds are the keepers of men', and again that 'when the farmer has got his house, he may not be the richer but the poorer for it, and it be the house that has got him'. Thoreau summarizes the incompatibility of liberty and property by agreeing with Emerson that 'men have become the tools of their tools'.[10]

The prospect which so troubled these Transcendentalist writers was that the 'Adam' of Tom Paine's new world would turn out to be a miscreant, and that the created wealth of the New World would turn (or had already turned) against 'Man', its supposed master. Instead of conquering nature, Americans would find themselves becoming the slaves of their own products, whose power would run wild. Frankensteinian forebodings of this kind were prompted not just by railroads or machinery but also by larger problems of nationhood in the United States. Another of Emerson's Transcendentalist associates, the feminist Margaret

Fuller, applied the Frankenstein myth to the prospects of American literature itself. Arguing against premature attempts to synthesize a peculiarly national literature, Fuller contended that such an achievement would have to await the further fusion of races on the American continent and the advent of greater leisure alongside material progress; 'national ideas shall take birth' only then, she maintains. 'Without such ideas', Fuller warns, 'all attempts to construct a national literature must end in abortions like the monster of Frankenstein, things with forms, and the instincts of forms, but soulless, and therefore revolting.'[11] Fuller's analogy is not quite clear, but it appears to warn against assembling a literature from the existing cultural *disjecta membra* available in the United States before a unified American 'soul' has emerged. The almost unavoidable corollary is that the United States themselves form already a Frankenstein monster, the federal attempt to make one from many (*e pluribus unum*) having proved either abortive or, at best, embryonic. America itself might become a colossal, powerful, but alarmingly uncontrolled creation running wild.

It is partly out of this ferment of ideas in mid-century America that the major writings of Herman Melville emerge, and partly too from the example of his literary hero and sometime neighbour Nathaniel Hawthorne. Melville's focus of interest, like Hawthorne's, is usually on the outcast or *isolato,* often a fatherless figure doomed to wander the world. And like Emerson and Thoreau, Melville is particularly alert to the contradictory promise of America's new empire of productive forces: 'Seeking to conquer a larger liberty,' he wrote, 'man but extends the empire of necessity.' This striking aphorism appears as one of the epigraphs to a short story, 'The Bell-Tower', in which Melville most concisely reproduces the themes of *Frankenstein*. The tale is often regarded as a reworking of Hawthorne's 'Ethan Brand', but it is likely to have been based also on *Frankenstein,* a copy of which was sent to Melville by his publisher in 1849. The meaning of 'The Bell-Tower' is summarized, rather too emphatically and proverbially, in its final paragraph: 'So the blind slave obeyed its blinder lord; but, in obedience, slew him. So the creator was killed by the creature. So the bell was too heavy for the tower. So the bell's main weakness was where man's blood had flawed it. And so pride went before the fall.'[12] The pride of the protagonist Bannadonna takes, as so often in Melville, a phallic form: he erects a tower to house his perfect bell, but this bell is in fact blemished by a fragment of flesh from a foundry worker killed in anger by Bannadonna during its casting. To chime the hours, Bannadonna secretly constructs an automaton whose hammering action kills him. The bell later crashes down and is finally destroyed along with the tower by an earthquake.

Bannadonna's dream, described by Melville as Promethean and compared with those of Albertus Magnus and Cornelius Agrippa, has been to construct a superior creature as a helot. 'All excellences of all God-made creatures, which served man, were here to receive advancement, and then to be combined in one.' The difference from Frankenstein or Faust is, as Melville is at pains to stress, that Bannadonna does not believe in a mysterious secret of life; he is 'a practical materialist' aiming to achieve Frankensteinian ends by means of applied mechanics:

> In short, to solve nature, to steal into her, to intrigue beyond her, to procure some one else to bind her to his hand;—these, one and all, had not been his objects; but, asking no favors from any element or any being, of himself, to rival her, outstrip her, and rule her. He stooped to conquer. With him, common sense was theurgy; machinery, miracle; Prometheus, the heroic name for machinist; man, the true God.

It is as if Melville were criticizing *Frankenstein* for being too Faustian, too alchemical to be a fully modern version of the Prometheus myth. Despite the tale's setting in Renaissance Italy, Bannadonna's 'utilitarian ambition' more accurately represents the nineteenth-century Prometheanism of industry. It attempts no romantic seduction or inveigling of Nature but an individualistic effort of competition against her, carried on in what Melville implies is a 'stooping' mechanical efficiency rather than in transcendental aspiration.

Melville's response to *Frankenstein* is not to convert it again into a moral fable—although he does his worst in the last lines of 'The Bell-Tower'—but to outstrip it himself, to make it both more secular and yet more potently mythical too. The achievement of the earlier and far greater *Moby Dick* follows this paradoxical pattern, representing the Prometheanism of modern industry in almost pedantic realist reportage while at the same time inflating it mythically into the grandest of Titanic enterprises. Through such a paradoxical design can be shown the larger contradictions behind the self-destructiveness of Melville's age—both the mechanical inventiveness of the nineteenth century and the restless ambition which drives it.

Like *Frankenstein* but more ostentatiously, Melville's *Moby Dick* is an assemblage and pastiche of older myths. Most obviously, the novel recalls the myths of Job and Jonah along with other biblical tales, and employs—like earlier Gothic novels—a clearly Shakespearian tragic pattern in its plotting. *Moby Dick* is an allusive omnivore, digesting myths as remote as those of Osiris or Narcissus and as recent as *Paradise Lost* or *Robinson Crusoe,* but among the more prominent of the myths which the novel absorbs and reworks is that of Prometheus. Like Victor Frankenstein, Captain Ahab embodies both the transgressive and the creative aspects of Prometheus, in such a contradictory manner that Captain Peleg has to describe him as 'a grand,

ungodly, god-like man'.[13] Ahab's Promethean traits extend beyond his rebellion against divine power to include a tormented capacity for remaking himself, most strikingly apparent in this account of his obsession:

> . . . it must have been that, in Ahab's case, yielding up all his thoughts and fancies to his one supreme purpose; that purpose, by its own sheer inveteracy of will, forced itself against gods and devils into a kind of self-assumed, independent being of its own. Nay, could grimly live and burn, while the common vitality to which it was conjoined, fled horror-stricken from the unbidden and unfathered birth. Therefore, the tormented spirit that glared out of bodily eyes, when what seemed Ahab rushed from his room, was for the time but a vacated thing, a formless somnambulistic being, a ray of living light, to be sure, but without an object to color, and therefore a blankness in itself. God help thee, old man, thy thoughts have created a creature in thee; and he whose intense thinking thus makes him a Prometheus; a vulture feeds upon that heart for ever; that vulture the very creature he creates.

Ahab's obsessive purpose is seen here to be an independent creature of his own fashioning, which now feeds upon the remaining human elements within him. He is caught here in the process of becoming his own self-created monster.

Ahab is of course already partly an artificial man, recognizable by the ivory leg which is both a reminder of and a defiant challenge to the divine malevolence he detects behind the White Whale. In a sequence of more or less comic scenes involving the replacement of this leg, Ahab elaborates upon the myth of Prometheus in his dialogues with the ship's carpenter and blacksmith, whom he nicknames 'manmaker' and 'Prometheus' respectively. 'I do deem it now a most meaning thing,' he says, 'that that old Greek, Prometheus, who made men, they say, should have been a blacksmith, and animated them with fire; for what's made in fire must properly belong to fire; and so hell's probable.' Warming to his hellish theme, Ahab himself tries on the role of Prometheus by imagining the creation of an artificial man:

> Hold; while Prometheus is about it, I'll order a complete man after a desirable pattern. Imprimis, fifty feet high in his socks; then, chest modelled after the Thames Tunnel; then, legs with roots to 'em, to stay in one place; then, arms three feet through the wrist; no heart at all, brass forehead, and about a quarter of fine brains; and let me see— shall I order eyes to see outwards? No, but put a sky-light on top of his head to illuminate inwards.

Behind the foolery here is a grandiose self-portraiture, an enlarged projection of Ahab's own ambition, complete with its heartlessness and its solipsism. Like the ship's surgeon and anatomist Dr Cuticle in *White-Jacket,* 'a curious patch-work of life and death, with a wig, one glass eye, and a set of false teeth',[14] Ahab's willed resistance to common human sympathies has refashioned him as an artificial being, the creature and plaything of his own monomania. He is both sides of the Promethean creation at once, both obsessed creator and outcast creature.

To emphasize his Promethean role Ahab becomes a blacksmith himself and forges his own harpoon, which we foresee will bring about his death ('have I been but forging my own branding-iron, then?'), baptizing it in the name of the Devil. He has already described himself as an iron artefact, indeed as the all-conquering and world-embracing railroad engine. 'The path to my fixed purpose is laid with iron rails, whereon my soul is grooved to run. Over unsounded gorges, through the rifled hearts of mountains, under torrents' beds, unerringly I rush! Naught's an obstacle, naught's an angle to the iron way!' Beneath this expansionist brag lies an ironic admission that Ahab has re-created himself in the image of a mechanical beast of burden, enslaving himself to what he imagines is a conquest of nature. Ahab's Promethean self-making is both heroic and pathetic, for in seeking a larger liberty he has but extended the realm of necessity.

Victor Frankenstein's first disciple is a navigator, Robert Walton, who attempts with Frankenstein's help to inspire his crew to complete a dangerous voyage. He is saved from the consequences of his ambition by the threat of mutiny by his sailors, who have been recruited, as it happens, from whaling ships. *Moby Dick* can be read as a study of what happens when the crew fails to mutiny against Frankensteinian leadership. The crew of the *Pequod* allows itself to be welded into another instrument of Ahab's mania. The old captain regards the mentality of his sailors as that of the 'manufactured man', while in the preparations for the final chase the men around him appear to Ishmael as if their human feelings had been 'ground to finest dust, and powdered, for the time, in the clamped mortar of Ahab's iron soul. Like machines, they dumbly moved about the deck, ever conscious that the old man's despot eye was on them.' Melville had explained in *White-Jacket* that a ship's captain regards his subordinates as 'disintegrated parts of himself, detached from the main body';[15] Ahab has remade from such parts a disciplined organic instrument subordinate to his will. As he exclaims at the climax of the chase, 'Ye are not other men, but my arms and legs; and so obey me.'

Animated by Ahab's controlling will, the arms and legs of the crew, and their separate racial and personal identities, are brought together to compose a floating body politic.

> They were one man, not thirty. For as the one ship that held them all; though it was put together of all

contrasting things—oak, and maple, and pine wood; iron, and pitch, and hemp—yet all these ran into each other in the one concrete hull, which shot on its way, both balanced and directed by the long central keel; even so, all the individualities of the crew, this man's valor, that man's fear; guilt and guiltiness, all varieties were welded into oneness, and were all directed to that fatal goal which Ahab their one lord and keel did point to.

It is the crew as a whole which is the 'manufactured man' shaped by Ahab in his role as the Prometheus of nineteenth-century industry. The crew is deliberately and allegorically presented to us as a medley of different races and temperaments, all of its members being islanders, individualists, and *isolatoes.* 'Yet now, federated along one keel, what a set these Isolatoes were!' They stand, in short, for the federated American republic, afloat upon Melville's allegorical waters. But they do not form a federation of equals; the red man, the brown man, and the black boy are all mere instruments subordinate to the white captain and his white obsession. The nineteenth-century American whaling ship, as H. Bruce Franklin reminds us,[16] combined many of the worst features of Northern wage-slavery with those of Southern chattel-slavery, driving its victims—Melville included—to desertion or mutiny.

That reactionary relapse into concealed feudal tyrannies imagined in Gothic novels is also the concern of *Moby Dick,* which envisages the possibility of America's federated parts being reassembled in the service of a guiding principle—a 'keel'—both oppressive and self-destructive. The danger is the same as that announced in *White-Jacket:* a 'monstrous grafting of tyranny upon freedom'.[17] The individuals or *isolatoes* of the *Pequod*'s crew succumb to a Shakespearian rhetoric and to a resurgent European mode of hierarchy in which Ahab galvanizes them through 'the Leyden jar of his own magnetic life.' Rather than squeeze hands in that democratic brotherhood dreamed of by Ishmael, they surrender their destinies to a 'head' who turns them into mere arms and legs. Since Ahab is waging war against Nature in the shape of the White Whale, he requires a prior conquest over his men; called into life as a collective instrument, their task is to suffer for their captain's transgression. While Ahab attempts to subdue Nature, pursuing her to her hiding-places like Frankenstein, the crew is expected to suffer the consequences. The fate of the *Pequod* asks us to question the logic of industrial development stirring into life in America and across 'the all-grasping western world.'

Read in a Frankensteinian perspective, *Moby Dick* can be seen to harbour three monsters: the dehumanized Ahab, the 'manufactured man' which is the crew, and finally the White Whale itself. Moby Dick is frequently referred to as a monster, often simply because of his huge size and destructive capacity, but he has other claims to the title. In the episode of 'The Spirit-Spout', Ishmael and the rest of the crew sense a malevolence in the whale's appearance, 'as if it were treacherously beckoning us on and on, in order that the monster might turn round upon us, and rend us at last in the remotest and most savage seas.' This ambiguous point at which the quarry becomes a trapper and the hunter becomes the hunted is precisely that of *Frankenstein*'s closing episodes, in which the monster appears to flee Victor but leaves him food and directions in order to lure him to the Arctic. In both novels the effect of the confusion between pursuer and pursued is to cast the antagonists as twin 'moments' within a single self-destructive complex, in which revenge can be revealed as suicide and heroism as folly pursuing its own tail. As in *Caleb Williams* and *Frankenstein,* the quest turns in upon itself statically, and the antagonists of *Moby Dick* confront one another as mirror images. That the White Whale acts, or at least appears to the Puritan paranoiac, as Ahab's 'double' has often been remarked by readers of *Moby Dick;* the two share the same wrinkled brow and the same solitary and maimed grandeur. Yet their equivalence is ultimately a figment of Ahab's obsessed mind: as a white whale, Ahab's quarry is simply a whale, a dumb brute, but as Moby Dick—humanly named and adorned with legend—he becomes a 'monster', apparently wilfil in provoking and mocking Ahab's urge to subdue Nature.

If the monstrous quality of the White Whale is a projection of Ahab's persecution mania, then it should come as no surprise to find Ahab blending into this mirror image, and becoming a vengeful monster himself. On the other hand the whale, with the help of Ishmael's bragging cetology, appears in heroic guise, and even as an inscrutable divinity towards whom Ahab is acting as a presumptuous blasphemer. By the end of the story Moby Dick has become a fully American hero by resisting and eluding the Europeanized tyranny of Ahab's monomania. His human counterpart and panegyrist Ishmael also slips away from the despotic nightmare and offers through his narrative a fraternal and pastoral alternative to Ahab's lust for conquest. The whale is a mute 'monster', but he is given a displaced voice through his advocate Ishmael, a virtuoso of rhetorical energy and style. Between them, these two survivors offer the dialogical rebuttal of Ahab's obsession, as the monster does to Victor's. Goaded into self-defence, the whale remains innocent because dumb; forced to become, in human eyes, a 'monster', he is never truly part of the human world. His articulate equivalent is Ishmael, a fellow-victim and outcast orphan, while the true monster is the Frankensteinian figure of Ahab himself, dismembered, unnaturally vengeful, self-enslaved, and self-exiled from land and from women.

Even more than *Frankenstein, Moby Dick* is a novel which excludes women from its action, yet it manages

similarly, if less pointedly, to problematize the masculine heroism which its setting isolates. Melville's men appear to be redeemed to the extent that they are feminized: Ishmael and Queequeg are seen to be bound together in what is almost a parody of the marriage-bed and its harmony, and they are later 'wedded' by the monkey-rope, while Queequeg acts as a 'midwife' to Tashtego. By contrast, Ahab's regime aboard the *Pequod* bristles with phallic menace. Only in the chapter entitled 'The Symphony' does his rigour unbend as he observes the sexualized heavings of sea and sky. Here he admits to Starbuck that his forty years at sea have been a 'desolation of solitude'. For the first time, Ahab mentions

> that young girl-wife I wedded past fifty, and sailed for Cape Horn the next day, leaving but one dent in my marriage pillow—wife? wife?—rather a widow with her husband alive! Aye, I widowed that poor girl when I married her, Starbuck . . .

The image of his wife and child which he sees in Starbuck's eye is the last lifeline by which Ahab could pull himself back to his 'humanities'. In rejecting it, he joins Victor Frankenstein, Elis Fröbom, and Hawthorne's transgressors as another victim of industrial sublimation.

The earliest and most outspoken champions of the modern Melville revival rightly stressed the connections between *Moby Dick* and the dynamic energies of territorial and industrial expansion in mid-century America. Both D. H. Lawrence in *Studies in Classic American Literature* and Charles Olson in *Call Me Ishmael* read the *Pequod* as an image of American industry, and Ahab as the white American urge to subdue Nature by mechanical efficiency. Many critics have seen Ahab as a latter-day Faust, but Olson recognizes that after the industrial revolution Faust could never be the same again.[18] Faust has become Prometheanized; and in the nineteenth-century world of industrial development, transgression and damnation have become identified less with devilry than with production. The world of *Moby Dick* is no alchemical laboratory but an authentic and exhaustively catalogued American whaling ship setting out to convert real spermaceti and blubber into dollars for its owners. The problem of defining Ahab's transgression, however, is that his project is not simply an over-reaching extension of capitalist enterprise as such; on the contrary, it appears to be a hijacking or usurpation of the *Pequod* for private purposes at odds with those of mundane profit-making. As in 'The Mines at Falun', it is the conversion of the industrial into a route to 'higher' goals which proves fatal.

Starbuck, the pious and (as his name suggests) dollar-orientated first mate, voices the horror of the respectable New England bourgeois at Ahab's motives.

I am game for his crooked jaw, and for the jaws of Death too, Captain Ahab, if it fairly comes in the way of the business we follow; but I came here to hunt whales, not my commander's vengeance. How many barrels will thy vengeance yield thee even it thou gettest it, Captain Ahab? it will not fetch thee much in our Nantucket market.

Ahab scorns this as an accountant's view of the world, and it is only then that Starbuck resorts to moral objections, condemning Ahab's pursuit as blasphemous. From the point of view of the *Pequod's* owners, Ahab is a profitable instrument who has now rebelled in pursuit of his own higher goal, diverting the lucrative resources of the crew and the ship towards the symbolic conquest of Nature's malevolence in the shape of the White Whale. Yet Starbuck, the loyal representative of the company's interests, is forced nevertheless to obey the man to whom the supreme powers of captain and industrial manager have been delegated. Ahab's maritime *coup d'état* may be illegal, but to the impotent Starbuck it is also irresistible, because all he can offer the crew, in competition with Ahab's inspiring heroic purpose, is a frugal and drily legalistic accountancy. Melville is, in effect, enquiring into the possibility that simple capitalist enterprise can harbour within it—in its acquisitive mentality, in its forms of labour-discipline and delegated power—tendencies towards untrammelled despotism and destructive energy which its sober guardians are powerless to resist once they are unleashed.

The good Quakers of Nantucket are obliged by the law of the market to employ heathen harpooners and a satanic captain, because their labour is more productive. Once out of their sight, though, the Quakers' ship becomes a weapon to strike at their own God in open rebellion. Starbuck seems quite unprepared for this transformation, having failed to discern beneath the *Pequod's* innocent commercial status a power susceptible to irrational development. What Ahab's usurpation represents is the subordination of simple commercial transactions to an underlying thirst for capital *accumulation,* an uncontrolled expansionist drive which uses each transaction or productive act merely as a step to the next. This process was still very much a mystery even to those who were most eagerly practising it, and so it can only be represented symbolically, in the somewhat lurid and melodramatic terms of biblical or Shakespearian vengeance, in pseudo-Masonic rituals and other codes incompatible with Starbuck's mercantile common sense. Even Ahab cannot understand the nature of the force which drives him; like Queequeg, who cannot decipher the hieroglyphs tattooed upon his own skin, the captain is inscrutable to himself.

What is it, what nameless, inscrutable, unearthly thing is it; what cozzening, hidden lord and master,

and cruel, remorseless emperor commands me; that against all natural lovings and longings, I so keep pushing, and crowding, and jamming myself on all the time; recklessly making me ready to do what in my own proper, natural heart, I durst not so much as dare? is Ahab, Ahab?

Never stably identical with himself, Ahab is indeed not Ahab but the instrument of an accumulative frenzy which grips nineteenth-century industry, possessing the possessor and commanding the commander. Ahab's combination of technical efficiency with general loss of control and purpose, of localized tyranny with generalized anarchy, encapsulates perfectly the very logic of capitalist accumulation and expansion: 'all my means are sane,' he realizes, 'my motive and my object mad.'[19]

The singular achievement of *Moby Dick* is now generally acknowledged as an unprecedented combination of high tragic dignity and mythological resonance with the meticulous, even pedantic realism of reportage, in which Melville plays off Ahab the mythic quester and tragedian against Ishmael the encyclopaedic cetologist and practical mariner. The novel's divergent registers somehow balance one another, the central chapters on the parts and dimensions of the whale and on the bloody details of its exploitation serving as a 'ballast'—as many critics have expressed it—to the symbolic and metaphysical soaring which is the book's countermovement. This cetological material holds what would otherwise be transcendental freewheeling down to the observable facts of the nineteenth-century world, while on the other hand the anatomizing of the whale and the inventory of the ship are lifted and propelled beyond the merely documentary by the impetus of the book's mythic, symbolic, and romance elements. Yoked together in *Moby Dick* are two contrary impulses—of documentary realism and of symbolic romance—which tend to pull in opposite directions throughout the history of the novel form, and whose magnetic repulsion was especially powerful in the nineteenth century as an ugly, urbanized, industrial world proved increasingly indigestible to the traditions of literary romance.

Melville's ability thus to digest fictionally the hard facts of nineteenth-century industry relies to a great extent on his use of transgression myths—those of Frankenstein and Faust, with the stories of Ethan Brand and others—as the foundation for *Moby Dick's* design and narrative movement. It is the mobilization of such myths which gives the novel a means (perhaps the only means) of grasping imaginatively the new complexities of the modern world and especially the motive forces of industrial expansion; forces whose impersonal and invisible movements concealed themselves behind the phenomena they produced and which were therefore not readily accessible to realist representation. Melville's resort to myth in *Moby Dick* is not an atavistic invocation of primeval archetypes but a remarkably modern effort to dramatize the dynamics of nineteenth-century industrial expansion.

In many respects the achievement of *Moby Dick* invites comparison with that of a contemporary work which also attempts to assimilate romance and industrial life: Elizabeth Gaskell's *Mary Barton*. According to Gaskell's preface, this novel was born from the realization of 'how deep might be the romance in the lives of some of those who elbowed me daily in the busy streets of the town in which I resided'.[20] The strength of its earlier chapters lies in a realist commitment to reproducing the speech, manners, domestic environment, and personal histories of the Manchester factory-workers and their families. Yet along with this element in *Mary Barton* goes an element of romance, of the kind which rapidly curdles into melodrama. These two sides of the novel sit so uneasily together that it is almost possible to divide *Mary Barton* into a first half of powerful and sympathetic reportage and a second half of melodramatic degeneration. The crucial dividing line falls, very significantly, across the discussion in Chapter 15 of John Barton's support for Chartism.

Gaskell had originally intended John Barton to be the hero of the novel and the central object of our sympathies but, partly under her publishers' pressure and partly because of her own problems with the character, she discarded this plan as the book took shape. The first part of *Mary Barton* tries to lead readers to understand the disaffection and protests of workers like John Barton, but it reaches a conclusion and a crisis of a kind which obliges Gaskell to dislodge this character from the centre of sympathy and to substitute for him his daughter Mary, who takes over as the beautiful romance heroine. The discarding of John Barton is a rapid and even spectacular operation: he becomes an opium addict, a Chartist, and a trade-unionist in quick (and, we are left to infer, logical) succession. Gaskell's commentary reveals several of her motives for the sudden change of direction:

> John Barton's overpowering thought, which was to work out his fate on earth, was rich and poor; why are they so separate, so distinct, when God has made them all? It is not His will, that their interests are so far apart. Whose doing is it?

> And so on into the problems and mysteries of life, until, bewildered and lost, unhappy and suffering, the only feeling that remained clear and undisturbed in the tumult of his heart, was hatred to the one class and keen sympathy with the other.

> But what availed his sympathy? No education had given him wisdom; and without wisdom, even love, with all its effects, too often works but harm. He acted to the best of his judgement, but it was a widely-erring judgement.

> The actions of the uneducated seem to me typified in those of Frankenstein, that monster of many human qualities, ungifted with a soul, a knowledge of the difference between good and evil.

> The people rise up to life; they irritate us, they terrify us, and we become their enemies. Then, in the sorrowful moment of our triumphant power, their eyes gaze on us with a mute reproach. Why have we made them what they are; a powerful monster, yet without the inner means for peace and happiness?

In a novel which offers a considered response to the sufferings of the Manchester workers, and an effort to sympathize with them, such a passage has considerable significance. It is the point at which a class at first represented as suffering passively now 'rises up into life' in protest, and has therefore to be distanced and reinterpreted as a monster, strong but childishly misguided. The working class now becomes 'the uneducated'; at the moment when it tries to overcome its subordination it has to be told that its actions are based upon a fundamental ignorance of Manchester Political Economy and its eternal truths: 'Distrust each other as they may, the employers and employed must rise or fall together. There may be some difference as to cronology, none as to fact.'[21]

In Gaskell's allusion to *Frankenstein* we have a prominent example of a creative misreading which wrenches the myth into new patterns while applying it directly to the central tensions of an industrializing social order. The misreading here is more than just a matter of calling the monster by the name of his maker; it brings in too the stage versions' redefinition of the monster as a soulless being and as an inarticulate child. This allows Gaskell to represent the working class as an unfortunate but morally irresponsible creature which lashes out blindly and mutely at its begetter in the deluded belief that the employers are in some way to blame for its misery. It is no more human than Mary Wollstonecraft's blind elephant, although Gaskell does allow it the charitable condescension due to a child. If the employers are to blame, it is, according to Gaskell, only for failing to provide their workers with 'soul' in the form of religious example, and with an education which could explain that their miseries are the necessary consequences of immutable market forces, their prosperity tied forever to that of their masters. The repeated refrain which Gaskell raises against working-class violence in *Mary Barton* is 'They know not what they do.' What begins as an account of the sufferings of the working class ends by equating the passion of the crucified Christ with that of the Manchester bourgeoisie.[22]

In this extraordinary series of mythological displacements Gaskell herself manages to double up as both Victor Frankenstein and Pontius Pilate. While her intended message in *Mary Barton* is one of sympathy and brotherhood, ironically she comes to wash her hands of her proletarian hero and to recoil from him as a monster when he appears to be asserting his independence from his employers and from his literary creator. Gaskell enacts, in other words, the same repudiation of the monster and his claims of which Victor Frankenstein had been guilty. She accompanies this gesture with a litany of disclaimers on behalf of the employers' class, shifting responsibility to the eternal laws of supply and demand, which her ideology identifies in turn with the injunctions of Christian charity: when it is weak and incapable, the working class deserves pious sympathy, but when it is in a position to assert itself, it is to be reviled as a monstrous beast. The result is that just when John Barton is about to transform himself from passive victim to articulate champion of his class, Gaskell has to drug him and turn him into a mute and vengeful monster. His form of class resistance is narrowed into a personal grudge and dramatized as the reflex savagery of an inarticulate assassin. *Mary Barton* falls asunder into reportage on the one side and lurid melodrama on the other, split apart by Gaskell's recoiling from and silencing of the working-class monster.

That Melville is able to overcome the danger of such a split in *Moby Dick,* that he can mythicize the everyday reality of the whaling industry while preserving its authenticity, can be attributed ultimately to his radical-democratic reinterpretation of the grand style and of tragic propriety.

> If, then, to meanest mariners, and renegades and castaways, I shall hereafter ascribe high qualities, though dark; weave round them tragic graces; if even the most mournful, perchance the most abased, among them all, shall at times lift himself to the exalted mounts; if I shall touch that workman's arm with some ethereal light; if I shall spread a rainbow over his disastrous set of sun; then against all mortal critics bear me out in it, thou just Spirit of Equality, which has spread one royal mantle of humanity over all my kind!

Melville is able to elevate his mariners in this way because he believes in their 'democratic degnity', and because he himself has been formed by their experiences, viewing the world of his novels from the forecastle rather than from the bridge. It is not just that, as a matter of their personal experience, Melville was able to describe actual labour whereas Gaskell—along with other misnamed 'industrial' novelists in Britain—could give us only the domestic sickbed or the riot at the factory gates. It is also a matter of instinctive identifications: unlike Gaskell, Melville has no occasion to recoil from his 'monsters', the crew and the whale. His impatience with the anti-democratic rhetoric of popular monstrosity is highlighted in the repartee of his idealized mariner Jack Chase in *White-Jacket.* The

ship's poetaster Lemsford bewails the philistinism of a public which ignores him:

> 'Blast them, Jack, what they call the public is a monster, like the idol we saw in Owhyhee, with the head of a jackass, the body of a baboon, and the tail of a scorpion!'

> 'I don't like that,' said Jack; 'when I'm ashore, I myself am part of the public.'[23]

The difference is resolved by an evasive distinction between public and people, but Melville's democratic reservation still stands, signalling his suspicion of the traditionally reactionary uses to which the 'monstrous' has been put, and reminding us of his own place within the monstrous body of democracy. Himself a renegade, castaway, and deserter, Melville can give the outcasts and victims of industrial Prometheanism a human voice, while Gaskell silences them or relegates them to a faltering infancy.

The point at which Elizabeth Gaskell transforms her workers from reasonable beings into Gothic banditti in *Mary Barton* has a certain ironic significance. During the negotiations between the employers and a trade union delegation, Mary's prospective seducer Harry Carson vigorously opposes the workers' right to organize, and scribbles a caricature of the lean and hungry delegates for the amusement of his fellow-capitalists. This cartoon is later picked up by one of the workmen, and it inflames them to the point of drawing lots for Carson's assassination. Although we are meant to take Carson's caricature as another sign of his callous insensitivity, a portrayal of the workers of just the kind that Gaskell wants to supersede in her own work, it comes instead to set the tone of Gaskell's subsequent treatment of her workers: in her portrayal of working-class organization as a murderous conspiracy Gaskell herself degenerates into literary 'caricature'. Such contradictions in her treatment of the working class revolve around the ambivalence of her central and repeated insistence upon the mutual dependence between masters and men. As it appears in her other 'industrial' novel, *North and South,* Gaskell's argument formulates a Christian paternalist qualification to the *laissez-faire* doctrines of Manchester: Margaret Hale tells the employer Thornton that 'the most isolated of your Darkshire Egos has dependants clinging to him on all sides; he cannot shake them off . . . '[24] Through her heroine Gaskell espouses here what could be called the official morality of the Victorian novel, chiding liberal individualism in the name of social responsibility. But the reminder of Christian brotherhood has its more sinister underside, which Gaskell's appeal to the Frankenstein myth in *Mary Barton* brings into focus. For if the capitalists truly cannot shake off the terrifying power which they have brought into being (and since they live off its labour, they cannot) then they are saddled, like Victor Frankenstein, with a threatening monster who will never leave them in peace. Gaskell's use of the Frankenstein myth announces the awful recognition by the Victorian bourgeoisie that its prosperity is inescapably haunted.

It is this indelible historical fear that Harry Carson's professional counterparts—the cartoonists of the Victorian press—play upon in their adaptations of Frankenstein's monster. True to the older traditions of the monstrous as a visible vice, they depict in their political allegories a creature who embodies pure brutal menace. The most vicious of their caricatures were reserved for the Irish nationalists, always regarded in Britain as mindless and primitive brutes; but the Frankenstein myth also appears in cartoons which depict the sometimes linked threat of the British working class, as in Tenniel's 'The Brummagem Frankenstein'. Tenniel preserved in his two Frankenstein cartoons the Burkean prophecy which warns that middle-class radicals (here, the Irish nationalist Charles Stewart Parnell and the Liberal orator John Bright) will surely be overwhelmed by the uncontrollable masses they incite. Frankenstein had come to stand as the reflected image of the Victorian bourgeois order as it faced nervously the Irish and the working class stirring into independent political life.

Notes

1 Honoré de Balzac, *The Quest of the Absolute,* trans. Ellen Marriage (London, 1908), 80-2.

2 Goethe's *Faust* itself, in its second part, follows the same path to modern industry, as Berman emphasizes in *All That Is Solid,* 37-86.

3 *Tales of Hoffmann,* trans. R. J. Hollingdale, Stella and Vernon Humphries, and Sally Hayward (Harmondsworth, 1982), 95-6.

4 Nathaniel Hawthorne, *Selected Tales and Sketches,* ed. Hyatt H. Waggoner (New York, 1964), 193.

5 Nathaniel Hawthorne. *The Blithedale Romance* (Harmondsworth, 1983), 55 (ch. 7).

6 Ibid., 218 (ch. 25).

7 Leo Marx, *The Machine in the Garden: Technology and the Pastoral Ideal in America.* (New York, 1967), 267-9.

8 Ralph Waldo Emerson, *Selected Essays,* ed. Larzer Ziff (Harmondsworth, 1982), 84-5.

9 Ralph Waldo Emerson, *Poems* (Boston, 1904), 78.

10 Henry David Thoreau, *Walden, and Civil Disobedience* (Harmondsworth, 1983), 136, 99, 76, 80.

11 *The Writings of Margaret Fuller,* ed. Mason Wade (New York, 1941), 359-60.

12 Herman Melville, *Billy Budd, Sailor and Other Stories,* ed. Harold Beaver (Harmondsworth, 1967), 213.

13 *Moby Dick,* Harold Beaver's Penguin edition (Harmondsworth, 1972).

14 Herman Melville, *White-Jacket,* ed. Hennig Cohen (New York, 1967), 246 (ch. 61).

15 Ibid., 215 (ch. 52).

16 H. Bruce Franklin, *The Victim as Criminal and Artist: Literature from the American Prison* (New York, 1978), 31-2.

17 Melville, *White-Jacket,* 296 (ch. 71).

18 Charles Olson, *Call Me Ishmael* (New York, 1947), 59.

19 Melville was of course not a Marxist but a radical democrat of a sceptical disposition. However, the common objection to Marxist readings of *Moby Dick*—that Melville also celebrates capitalist industry's heroic achievements as well as condemning its recklessness—is quite misplaced, since the same is true of Marx and Engels themselves in their *Communist Manifesto.*

20 Elizabeth Gaskell, *Mary Barton: A Tale of Manchester Life,* ed. Stephen Gill (Harmondsworth, 1970), 37.

21 Despite such confident expositions of economic fact against the childish imaginings of the workers, Gaskell claims in her Preface that she knows 'nothing of Political Economy, or the theories of trade' (*Mary Barton: A Tale of Manchester Life*, 38), soon after remarking upon the 'unhappy state of things between those so bound to each other by common interests, as the employers and the employed must ever be' (*Mary Barton: A Tale of Manchester Life*, 37). The illusion of disinterestedness here in taking for granted the common interest of contending classes is a perfect instance of ideological blindness.

22 Cf. the inverted *pietà* which Gaskell contrives at the end of the riot scene in Chapter 22 of her *North and South.*

23 Melville, *White-Jacket,* 191-2 (ch. 45).

24 Elizabeth Gaskell, *North and South,* ed. Dorothy Collin (Harmondsworth, 1970), 169.

Cecelia Tichi

SOURCE: "Looking Backward, Looking Forward," in *Shifting Gears: Technology, Literature, Culture in Modernist America,* The University of North Carolina Press, 1987, pp. 97-117.

[In the excerpt that follows, Tichi discusses the figure of the engineer in late nineteenth-century American culture and literature, focusing on works by Edward Bellamy, Thorstein Veblen, and Henry Adams.]

> It is a great profession. There is the fascination of watching a figment of the imagination emerge through the aid of science to a plan on paper. Then it moves to realization in stone or metal or energy. Then it brings jobs and homes to men. Then it elevates the standards of living and adds to the comforts of life. That is the engineer's high privilege.

Herbert Hoover, *Memoirs,* 1951

In Sinclair Lewis's novel *Dodsworth* (1929) young Sam Dodsworth, a graduate of Yale and "Massachusetts Tech," peers over Long Island Sound to reflect on his post-college plans to be "a civil engineer . . . riding a mountain trail, two thousand sheer feet above a steaming valley." Instead, Dodsworth works on his mechanical drawing, convinced in 1903 that the new-fangled automobile ought to be streamlined instead of boxy and that he is the man to make the design change "in the urgent new motor industry." A quarter century later in Paris this same Dodsworth, a successful engineer and manufacturer of automobiles ("the first man to advocate four-wheel brakes"), stands contemplating the Cathedral of Notre Dame and feels a kinship with the artisans who built it centuries ago. Reflecting on his achievement, he goes even further to claim identity as an artist of the twentieth century. Like painters and writers and composers, "he had created something," for "every one of the twenty million motors on the roads of America had been influenced by his vision . . . of long, clean stream-lines" (12-17, 133, 228-29).

Lewis's Dodsworth was attuned to the times. From the turn of the century through the 1920s countless American youngsters yearned to master the secrets of technology and to become engineers, whom one writer called "true poets, makers whose creations touch the imagination and move the world" (Maclaurin xxv). By the late nineteenth century the engineer's signature was everywhere on the American landscape, in railroads, bridges, and tall buildings, in tunnels and in systems for water, gas, and electricity. As the historian Samuel Eliot Morison recalled in his memoir, *One Boy's Boston,* his boyhood "opened [in 1887] with the horsecar and . . . closed [in 1910] with the Cadillac and the airplane" (81).

As engineers made their presence felt in the American scene, they began to figure prominently in imaginative literature. Yet critics and analysts have been oddly blind to their presence. Students of American texts, avid seekers of national types, have failed to recognize the engineer's presence or to notice the embodiment of engineering values either in popular or enduring literature. Other American occupational types—doctors, lawyers, ministers, businessmen—have become our familiars from the novels of Ernest Hemingway, Herman Melville, William Dean Howells, and Theodore Dreiser. The characteristics of those figures, pro and con, are taken into account in college classroom lectures and in scholarly journal articles. In this sense the missing engineer is simply an empty frame in the national gallery of occupational portraits.

But the issue is more complex than that. It surpasses mere occupation to concern itself with national myth and ideology in an era of industrialization and pervasive technology. It calls to mind the precedent set by the study of another national type, the cowboy, a symbol of rugged individualism, egalitarianism, and heroism in the western dime novels of the nineteenth century. By the turn of the century, as Alan Trachtenberg points out, the cowboy reflected the post-Civil War incorporation of America, becoming the guardian of the private property of the conservative ruling class (*Incorporation of America* 21-25). Reflecting social change, the cowboy has compelled attention as a symbolic figure who can be shown to embody distinct values in the American experience. He reflects cultural change even as he participates in the myth and ideology of the nation.

So does the engineer, this invisible man of American studies who appeared as the hero in over one hundred silent movies and in best-selling novels approaching five million copies in sales between 1897 and 1920. From Edward Bellamy's *Looking Backward* (1888) through *The Education of Henry Adams* (1906) and the writings of Thorstein Veblen, the engineer appears as a crucial figure in modern American civilization. He is in Emerson's sense the representative man for the era, a symbol of efficiency, stability, functionalism, and power. In the imaginative literature of industrialized America he figures as a new hero who enacts the values of civilization. He is at once visionary and pragmatic.

Even writers who cast him in minor roles exploit these qualities. Dreiser does so, for instance, in the figure of the electrical engineer, Robert Ames. In *Sister Carrie* Ames is the one man *not* dazzled by luxury ablaze in incandescent restaurant lights. Carrie thinks the young engineer a "scholar" who is both "innocent and clean," and "wiser, saner, and brighter" than her lovers, the traveling salesman and the failed restauranteur (291-94, 361, 389). For once she is right, since Dreiser

Charles Dickens depicted social changes caused by industrialization.

endows Ames with unusual analytical powers. The young engineer criticizes wasteful consumption, critiques current literature, and, sexually unmoved by Carrie, foresees her potential as an actress because he recognizes in her facial features the objectification of popular longing. Ames is the ethical man of clarifying vision, and he is the only figure in the novel who transcends the materialistic romanticism that holds all others in a tight, even fatal, grip.

Dreiser's engineer, once identified, beckons us toward similar engineer character-types in imaginative writings. He alerts us to the possibility that a knowledge of literature and culture is incomplete without the recognition of the figure in popular and enduring texts. To scrutinize industrialized, technological America without due regard for the engineer is like studying the idea of the American West without attention to the cowboy, or agrarianism without noticing the farmer. Each is indispensable to an adequate understanding of ideology and of the values that underlie social change and define an era.

Engineering, moreover, has important aesthetic implications, as Sinclair Lewis suggests in Sam Dodsworth's drive to supplant the horseless carriage with the sculptured automotive streamline, the very line we heard Ezra Pound praise for its vibrant efficiency. In fact,

Dodsworth's claim to be a modern artist is authentic and authoritative. It suggests the basis on which the engineer could become a role model for twentieth-century artists, including poets and novelists. In an age in which machine manufacture took precedence over handicrafts and artisanry, the engineer was the new kind of author. He created efficient, functional, componentpart designs. He set a new example for the twentieth-century artist, no longer a craftsman fashioning unique objects from raw materials, but a designer committed to the functional, efficient arrangement of prefabricated components into a total design. Ezra Pound emphasized that language is "made out of concrete things . . . arranged" in precise relations to each other (*SL* 49; *SP* 41). It is fair to say that engineering values entered the national literature virtually as a matter of course, once the national landscape burgeoned with engineers' achievements.

It is essential to recognize the ways in which engineers and their work were presented to the American public. A masculine figure in a male profession, the spokesman for a gear-and-girder world, the engineer became a vital American symbol between the 1890s and 1920s. In popular fiction, as we shall see, he signified stability in a changing world. He was technology's human face, providing reassurance that the world of gears and girders combined rationality with humanity. And he represented the power of civilization in the contemporary moment. Popular texts present the engineer as the descendant of once-powerful ministers and statesmen; his is ethical *and* utilitarian power. In an industrial era, in a gear-and-girder world, the engineer wears the mantle of civilizing power and ethical judgment.

As we shall see, the engineer is also a critical figure in the enduring imaginative literature of the era. To understand why, we must revisit Edward Bellamy and Thorstein Veblen. They insist that the engineer poses a compelling and powerful alternative to the profit-minded businessman or industrialist. We must also examine the writings of Henry Adams. His respect for the achievement and potential of engineers has so far not been recognized, though it is compatible with the popular images of engineers and helps to anticipate the election of America's only engineer president. Herbert Hoover. All these strands so interconnect that the engineer needs full and separate treatment.

In sheer numbers and geographical range the growth of the engineering profession signaled its cultural importance in the United States of the late nineteenth and early twentieth centuries. In 1917 New York's City College planned its School of Technology for five hundred engineering students, only to find it enroll over five thousand students by the late 1920s. The phenomenon was not only urban. A handful of engineers' biographies suggests that engineering attracted youth from logging towns of the Pacific Northwest to the Finger Lakes region of upstate New York to rural Idaho and to the very shadow of the Brooklyn Bridge teeming with the hyphenated, immigrant Americans. Engineering lured its (overwhelmingly male) students from diverse households—that of the Methodist minister whose watchwords were "peace and order," of the lower East Side laborer's family, of Idaho farmers whose children interrupted their university training in engineering to help their families with urgent farm-work (Ratigan, Kimball, Vauclain, Hammond).

The allure of engineering surfaces in American fiction of the time, reflecting the breadth of its popularity. In Abraham Cahan's *The Rise of David Levinsky* (1917) a young New York City clothing manufacturer saves money in order to "take up medicine, engineering, or law" (168). In an early Edna Ferber novel, *Roast Beef, Medium* (1913), the college-age son of the heroine exclaims, "Mother, you know how wild I am about machines, and motors, and engineering" (74). And in Robert Herrick's *Together* (1908) the young engineer gets the opportunity to work on the Panama Canal, saying, "They have interesting problems down there. It is really big work, you know. A man might do something worth while." Ferber's young man cries, "Professions! Why, you talk about the romance of a civil engineer's life!" (296-97).

That romance was served up in a towering book stack of children's literature of the 1910s and 1920s. Readers of H. Irving Hancock's series on *Grammar School Boys* and *High School Boys* could follow the young-sters into their grown-up heroic exploits in a four-volume *Young Engineers* series (in Colorado, in Arizona, in Nevada, in Mexico). Those same readers could venture into the war zone in James R. Driscoll's *The Brighton Boys with the Engineers at Castigny,* all the while keeping abreast of Victor Appleton's *Tom Swift* books whose titles suggest the excitement of the fantastic yet plausible new technologies: *Tom Swift and His Motor Cycle, Tom Swift and His Motor Boat* (*and* his airship, submarine, wireless message, sky racer, electric rifle, wizard camera, photo telephone, etc., each a separate full-length novel).

Tom Swift's followers received lessons in mechanics along with vicarious adventures. Their appetites for invention and engineering were surely whetted by this fictional mix of technology and adventure. When Tom's plane engine fails in mid-air in *Tom Swift and His Air Glider* (1912), for instance, the boy inventor is forced to land in a rural field where he pokes "among the numerous cogs, wheels, and levers," then diagnoses the problem: the magneto is broken because the bear-ings and contact surfaces are fused and crystallized. Here the action stops for a narrator's lesson in me-chanics. "The magneto of an aeroplane performs a service similar to one in an automobile; it provides the spark that explodes the charge of gas in the cylinders"

(12). The narrator restarts the extraordinary engine of a plot, which features a Siberian quest for the platinum necessary for Tom's magneto and other machinery.

It is not known how many American boys were first lured into engineering through adventure books like the *Tom Swift* series. But it is probable that many of these readers realized their fantasies of technology in play with A. C. Gilbert's Erector Sets, which, as we saw, featured the small electric motors and square gird-ers that could be bolted together to form machines and structures. Boys who attained a certain level of inge-nuity in their models were awarded diplomas certify-ing them as Engineers or Master Engineers of the Gilbert Institute of Engineering. The Erector instruc-tion manual of 1915 boasted that "Erector is the only builder with girders that resemble the real structural material used in the great sky-scrapers, offices, facto-ries, and public buildings." It promised, "You can build derricks—machine shops—battleships—aeroplanes—duplicates of celebrated bridges, arches, etc. that can be operated with the electric motor." In his autobiog-raphy A. C. Gilbert recounted that over the years hun-dreds of engineers had written to tell him that their professional commitment began in boyhood with an Erector Set.

In part such boyhood interest accounts for the findings of William F. Book, who surveyed six thousand high school seniors for vocational preference and published the results in 1922. The occupation favored by 31 percent of the boys was engineering. It eclipsed agri-culture by seven percentage points and showed the prestige of technology (*Intelligence* 139-42). Back in 1870 Ralph Waldo Emerson had described the Amer-ican farmer minding a "machine of colossal propor-tions." "The earth," wrote Emerson, "is a machine which yields almost gratuitous service to every appli-cation of intellect" ("The Farmer" 404-5). Struggling to dignify the farmer, Emerson came close to the credo of the engineer, set forth in 1828 by the British bridge and rail designer, Thomas Telford, in the charter of the British Institute of Civil Engineering: "engineering is the science of controlling the forces and utilizing the materials of nature for the benefit of man" (qtd. in Beyer 419). In 1872 in a post-Civil War sermon Henry Ward Beecher looked into the American future and proclaimed that "the higher instincts, when civilized, become engineers' forces." By the turn of the century many agreed (qtd. in H. N. Smith x-xi).

The imagination of Americans warmed to engineers and engineering values for complex reasons. To some extent the "romance" that thrilled Ferber's young man came from popular contemporary images of such mas-sive projects as the Panama Canal (1902-14), the Wil-son Dam on the Tennessee River (1922-26), and the Alaska Railroad (1914-23). Engineers made so many indelible marks on the American scene that even in

1869 the *New York Times* reported the "revolution in every mode and attribute of [American] life." The *Times* defined this "revolution" through technological achievements: "the dissolving and recomposing of materials, the utilization of natural forces, the wonders of chemistry, the feats of engineering, the triumphs of machinery . . . the steamship, the locomotive, the telegraph, the iron bridge, the Bessemer process, the machinery of agriculture, of water supply, of illumination, or weaving, or printing . . . or turning power into infinite channels, and the machinery that makes machinery" (qtd. in Merritt 32).

Very slowly, in the 1860s and 1870s, the American public came to recognize that individual engineers and their growing profession were responsible for this "revolution" whose breadth can be measured, in brief, in statistics. The *United States Census Reports* from 1850 to 1880 indicates that engineering was the fastest-growing profession, increasing sixteen times over thirty years. (The numbers of physicians and clergymen, by contrast, just more than doubled.) In 1850 there were 512 civil engineers, in 1880, 8,261, with the heaviest concentration of them in urban, industrial centers. (Merritt 9-11; D. F. Noble 38-39).

Many engineers were schooled, in those years, in informal apprenticeships on the shop floor, but formal engineering education increased at the land-grant colleges as a direct result of the first Morrill Act of 1862. That law mandated land to be set aside in each state for the support of a "College of Agriculture and Mechanic Arts." Institutions like Cornell University, the Pennsylvania State College, and the University of Idaho joined the older polytechnic institutions (Rensselaer, the Polytechnic College of the State of Pennsylvania, the Massachusetts Institute of Technology) and such additional centers as the University of Michigan, the Columbia School of Mines, and the Lawrence Scientific School at Harvard to provide education for the more than 3,800 engineering graduates of the 1880s. One historian reports, "In the third quarter of the nineteenth century the most rapid and extensive development of American higher institutions of learning took place within the so-called polytechnic education." By 1900 there were approximately 45,000 engineers, by 1930, 23,000, a fivefold increase (Merritt 11).

The public, nevertheless, largely overlooked the engineer himself in those latter decades of the nineteenth century, even if engineering achievements were ubiquitous. Perhaps, as one historian of the period argues, engineers' work so well accorded with the goals and objectives of established groups that the people who spoke for them—farmers, clergymen, educators—appropriated technological achievements and reformulated them in schemes congruent with their own beliefs. Thus the railroad promised farmers higher land-and-crop values, while its passenger service promised to

sinew the nation in Christian brotherhood. In poetry Walt Whitman (whose brother was chief engineer of the St. Louis waterworks) argued that "chef-d'oeuvres of engineering" endured only as the objectification of the nation's "personal qualities," of its "muscle and pluck" (Merritt 23-25; Whitman 188).

Engineering "muscle" was amply evident in the final decade of the nineteenth century, when steel-framed bridges arose to span the rivers and bays of the eastern seaboard, the rivers of the Ohio Valley, and the Mississippi itself (following the stunning example of the Eads Bridge at St. Louis, 1867-74). Every major city boasted the tall, steel-framed buildings made possible by fabricated steel and by the elevator powered by electric motors. Newspapers and magazines kept readers abreast of these phenomenal engineering feats, which much of the population experienced at firsthand in such major cities as Chicago, Pittsburgh, and New York, and in smaller locales like Sioux City, Iowa; Marietta, Ohio; Tyrone, Kentucky; and Nebraska City, Nebraska. Sinclair Lewis marked the trend in his fictional mid-size American city, Zenith, whose office buildings are "austere towers of steel and cement and limestone, sturdy as cliffs and delicate as silver rods" (*Babbitt* 5).

As these structures reshaped the American scene, the engineer became the exemplar of technological power and began to appear, at last, as a new kind of American hero in popular fiction. Yet he was more than a dashing figure of industrial age romance and adventure, the director of "the terrific chorus of steel and stone and glass" (Huneker 39-40). In the American imagination he was also much more than a boys' role model for the strenuous life urged by Theodore Roosevelt, the Young Men's Christian Association, and the scouting movement.

The figure of the engineer apparently satisfied other, deep psychological needs that were specific to the new age. The enginee played a critical role in an America that was trying to surmount its anxieties about instability. He became vital to a nation striving to achieve efficiency while ridding itself of the dreaded waste. In 1883 the soon-to-be mayor of New York City, Abram Hewitt, spoke directly to this point in his address at the opening ceremonies of the Brooklyn Bridge. The structure "looks like a motionless mass of masonry and metal," Hewitt observed. "But as a matter of fact it is instinct with motion. . . . It is an aggregation of unstable elements, changing with every change in the temperature and every movement of the heavenly bodies." Hewitt then posed the challenge central to engineering and, by extension, to American society itself. "The problem was, out of these unstable elements, to produce absolute stability" (308-9).

Absolute stability: that, in the politician Hewitt's view, was the enviable societal goal, which he saw successfully realized, materially, in the engineering of John A. and Colonel Washington Roebling. For Hewitt, their bridge satisfied the yearnings documented in so many contemporary American writings, even if few believed that stability could be "absolute." As Oliver Wendell Holmes wrote, "Our stability is but balance, and wisdom lies in masterful administration of the unforeseen" (qtd. in Fitch, *Engineering and Civilization* 329). A broad spectrum of the public looked to the engineers to provide this mastery, to bring a fast-changing culture into balance or stability just as the Robelings' calculations brought stone and steel into the dynamic equipoise of the Brooklyn Bridge.

The engineer was the exponent of efficiency and the slayer of that dragon, waste. In the age of pervasive machine technology he was a messianic figure, at least a priestly one. His values—efficiency, organization, production, functional and elegant design—enabled Americans once again to expect national salvation. The engineer renewed the spiritual mission embedded for over two and a half centuries in the national experience. He promised, so it seemed, to lead industrialized America directly into the millennium.

Bellamy's best-selling *Looking Backward 2000-1887* (1888), once again compels attention, this time because the novel heralded a new millennial vision and signaled a popular endorsement of the engineering mentality in America. Like Washington Irving's story of Rip Van Winkle, *Looking Backward* uses the ploy of time-change to develop its themes. The central figure, a Bostonian named Julian West, awakens from a trance-induced sleep of more than a century to be reborn in the American future of the year 2000. Sheltered in the futuristic household of Dr. and Mrs. Leete and nurtured by their lovely daughter, Edith, Julian West also finds himself in a new America of full employment, material abundance, efficiency, social stability and harmony, and technological sophistication. Vanished is West's familiar, late-nineteenth-century Boston (and America) of instability, class tension, waste, strikes, misery, and extremes of wealth and poverty.

The novel tells the story of West's gradual conversion of faith to a utopian America-2000. Under Dr. Leete's tutelage he comes to reject his lifelong beliefs in the nineteenth-century status quo, to become angry at its inequities even as he participates in the daily life of Boston-2000, shopping, dining, strolling—and falling in love with Edith Leete.

In fact, Bellamy sets up his plot with Edith Leete's allure and with West's insatiable, amnesiac craving to have the American metamorphosis explained to him as he copes with his sudden double identity. His readers, citizens themselves of an imperfect world, share the Bostonian's skepticism about the cultural transformation. Bellamy exploits both the attraction and the resistance of his audience, its optimism and its defense against gullibility.

Generically, *Looking Backward* is both a stock-in-trade romance and a reformist tract. The sage father-doctor, Leete, becomes the interlocutor for a story whose philosophical base is Christian socialism and whose religious presumption of brotherhood is a version of Emerson's Transcendentalism. The doctor must first prove to his visitor that this new city is in fact Boston. From a roofed gallery of the Leete house they behold Boston-2000:

> Miles of broad streets, shaded by trees and lined with fine buildings, for the most part not in continuous blocks but set in larger or smaller enclosures, stretched in every direction. Every quarter contained large open squares filled with trees, along which statues glistened and fountains flashed in the late-afternoon sun. Public buildings of a colossal size and architectural grandeur unparalleled in my day raised their stately piles on every side. (55)

Julian West exclaims that he surely has never seen this or a comparable city before (though Bellamy's post-1893 readers might know that nearly five million Americans saw exactly that city in Chicago's Jackson Park, where the World's Columbian Exposition featured its unified White City in the "wedding cake" Beaux Arts architectural style) (Badger 109). But West recognizes Boston's topography, and from that moment knows he must confront the truth of his time travel.

Looking Backward is largely the story of Julian West's conversion to the socialist principles of nationalism. He is Bellamy's specimen of the nineteenth-century gentleman whose sensitivity to injustice is channeled at last into belief in the feasibility of social change. Gradually during strolls, shopping trips, sojourns to restaurants, and in hours-long talks with Dr. Leete the young man recognizes the barbarism of his era and comes to understand that individuals like himself can redeem an inhuman social order.

Meanwhile the new, enlightened West succumbs inevitably to the charms of Edith Leete, who is sensitive to his suffering and, coincidentally, bears the same name as West's Boston-1887 fiancée. An element of mystery is cleared with the revelation that Edith Leete is that very fiancée's own granddaughter. The bloodlines are intact, and West can pledge his troth to the new Edith. He is not, after all, a stranger in a strange land—though his fitness for Boston-2000 is sorely tested in a dream scene late in the novel when the new Julian West revisits the old Boston, finds it unendurably grotesque and cruel, yet cannot persuade his friends and acquaintances that together they can reform this "Golgotha."

The nightmare from which West awakens is really the certification of his citizenship in Boston-2000 and the reader's own injunction to take reformist action. The vital center of *Looking Backward,* however, is the American millennium made possible by a research-and-development office of American engineers. At heart a socialist reformer, Bellamy paid the dues of a mystery writer and romancer. But the author clearly got his deepest satisfaction from the engineering of the American future.

Bellamy was not, it must be said, an engineer. But his Christian mysticism was overlaid with logical habits of mind and a pragmatic approach to problems of all kinds. Bellamy even considered fiction in this light, saying that "nothing outside of the exact sciences has to be so logical as the thread of a story, if it is to be acceptable" (qtd. in Kasson 259). In boyhood he yearned to become a cadet at that citadel of American engineering, West Point. Failing the physical examination in 1867, he enrolled at Union College in Schenectady, New York, for one year of independent study in philosophy and political economy.

The year at Union was perhaps crucial. The college had enjoyed unusual, long-standing faculty and administrative leadership in the field of engineering. The outspoken William Mitchell Gillespie took charge of the civil engineering course in 1845, published two treatises on surveying and road construction at mid-century, and went on to translate and publish a portion of Auguste Comte's *Cours de philosophie positive,* a work Bellamy reportedly studied at Union. If this very young collegian was, at that time, far from reinventing the United States of America within the framework of a novel, it is possible that the tone set by figures like Gillespie and his successor, Cady Staley, enabled Bellamy to embrace the idea of systematic, utilitarian, practical application of thought to all problems of American life.

Newspaper journalism eventually became Bellamy's route to the functional intellectualism of *Looking Backward.* By his mid-1830s he had studied German socialism and law, and was also a cub reporter for William Cullen Bryant's *New York Evening Post,* a newspaper involved in reform issues like sanitary regulation and tenement problems. In 1872, at his father's suggestion, Edward returned to his Chickopee Falls, Massachusetts, hometown to become an editorial writer and book reviewer for the *Springfield Union,* and five years later to form a partnership with his brother to publish their own paper, the *Springfield Daily News.* Married, the father of two children, his health always precarious, Bellamy nevertheless drove himself with reformist ardor. His editorials of the mid-1870s are revealing: "Overworked Children in Our Mills," "Riches and Rottenness," "Wastes and Burdens of Society." Meanwhile, he wrote novels and short stories, some two dozen of which appeared in periodicals like the *Century,* the *Atlantic Monthly, Harper's,* and *Scrib-*

ner's. William Dean Howells, who was then the nation's foremost literary critic and editor, admired Bellamy's fictional romances (though he remained silent on the young writer's tendency to solve characters' psychological problems with the kind of plot gimmicks soon to be featured in O. Henry's stories). Bellamy, nevertheless, so well mastered the techniques of fiction that in *Looking Backward* he held readers rapt while expounding the very social theories which a mass audience had found tedious in other writers (introduction to *Looking Backward* 7-27).

Looking Backward piques readers' interest in part because its advanced technologies (electric lights, electronic broadcasting, indoor climate control, credit cards, enclosed shopping malls) make Bellamy seem a canny futurist. The novel has compelled attention for its political vision of a socialist, America, one that transforms an American "Black Hole of Calcutta" into a "paradise of order, equity, and felicity." This bloodless revolution occurs when competing, ruthless capitalist corporations, trusts, syndicates, and pools merge into one Great Trust operating for the mutual benefit of all citizens who are organized into an Industrial Army.

The novel's appealing argument is that every class, "rich and poor, cultured and ignorant, old and young, weak and strong, men and women" can recognize the mutual advantage to be had in sharing equally in the production and distribution of wealth. In economic theory, as readers have noticed, Bellamy was indebted to Henry George's *Progress and Poverty* (1879) with its "single-tax" system based on agrarian socialism. George closed his book with a futuristic glimpse of "the Golden Age . . . the city of God on earth" (522). *Looking Backward* presents that American millennium in full function.

Bellamy's images reveal his engineering bias. He looked backward (and askance at) the nineteenth century, scorning its society as a badly designed, precarious structure. It is "a pyramid poised on its apex . . maintained upright . . . by an elaborate system of constantly renewed props and buttresses and guy-ropes in the form of laws." Twenty thousand new annual state and federal legislative acts fail to buttress it. The props break down or become "ineffectual through some shifting of the strain." The structure threatens to topple while America-2000, in fortunate contrast, "rests on its base" (156).

That base is an engineered structure, even if Bellamy reverts to images from nature to invoke the pyramidal stability of the "everlasting hills" and to laud America's communal union as a "mighty heaven-touching tree whose leaves are its people." Overlooking the distinction made by engineers themselves between structures and machines, he praises America-2000 for its elegant simplicity of design. He assures us that "the machine which [the modern Washington functionaries] direct is indeed vast, but so logical in its principles and direct and simple in its workings, that it all but runs itself." In contrast, Bellamy criticizes the nineteenth century for its cumbersome, intricate design of the sort soon to be identified with Rube Goldberg. ("There is not with us, as with you," says Dr. Leete, "any complex machinery to get out of order and magnify a thousand times the original mistake.") As for the engineers of America-2000, they are eligible, along with great authors, artists, physicians, and inventors, for the highest of all national honors. Their bridges and transportation systems are categorically as valuable and aesthetic as performances and exhibitions in theaters, art galleries, and music halls (183, 140, 174, 130, 177).

Bellamy's engineering ethos, however, surpasses figures of speech and his validation of engineering as a prestigious contribution to America-2000. His alliance with the "functional intellectuals" is best revealed in his zest for the efficient systemization of every aspect of American life. The officers in his Industrial Army have indeed learned to "control the forces and utilize the materials of nature for the benefit of man." Urban design, including water and sewerage systems and climate control, for instance, are presupposed. Citizens need not even get wet in a storm, thanks to a retractable canopy—a device of public-health significance at a time when physicians prescribed travel to congenial climes and when a sophisticate like William Dean Howells thought that harsh climes could be ameliorated if, for the cost of a medium-sized war, the jet-stream currents were redirected by razing the Alaskan mountains (*Through the Eye of the Needle* 163).

Readers of *Looking Backward* hear Dr. Leete expound at length on the Boston-2000 systemization of education, domestic labor, economics, book and newspaper publishing. But Bellamy waxes warmest in his engineering of the social order. The population of the entire nation is reconstituted in the Industrial Army, which is led by the "highest-class men" but enrolls everyone, male and female, for three entry-level years of manual labor in service to the nation. Thereafter the competition for advancement is intense. In place of monetary incentives there are elaborate prizes, privileges, and honorable mentions at all levels, together with manipulations of rank in an elaborate guild system culminating in an elite officer corps. The army as well as the presidency is emphatically apolitical, insulated from partisan politics by an electorate of retirees who, after age forty-five, are mustered out of the army and are free to cultivate new interests for the remaining decades of their lives. Repeatedly Bellamy emphasizes the humane motivation of the army, unified by "the solidarity of the race and the brotherhood of man," even if dissenters find themselves on bread and water in solitary confinement (111).

Readers who disagree on the political and psychological ramifications of the Industrial Army must concur on one point. Bellamy's is an America by design. To read Dr. Leete's lengthy monologues on the structure of the army is to recognize both Bellamy's commitment to the amelioration of social conditions and his engineering ethos. His scheme for a new social order anticipates the broadening of professional engineers' concerns in the United States in the early twentieth century. As one essayist, an engineer, wrote in 1922, "It is of fundamental significance that the American engineering profession has of late considerably widened the scope" of its effort. Now, says the writer, engineering is not only "the science of controlling the forces and utilizing the materials of nature for the benefit of man"—but also *the art of organizing and of directing human activities in connection therewith*" (Beyer 419).

Bellamy's America-2000, in fact, heralded the work of Frederick Winslow Taylor. Like Bellamy, Taylor argued that maximal national prosperity depended upon the utmost efficiency of the individual engaged in the work best suited to his natural abilities. Taylor, too, envisioned the abundance of low-cost consumer goods and presupposed that the interests of workers and managers—in fact, of the entire society—meshed like gears. As one reader remarks, Taylor could have been a general in Bellamy's army (Kasson 197).

Looking Backward inspired a welter of utopian and dystopian novels in an era notorious for political corruption, corporate power, and social upheaval. Significant in literary and political study, the novel is also a landmark in the history of technology and culture in the United States. As a serious book for a mass audience it proclaimed the power of technology to solve the most vexing and debilitating national problems, those both moral and material. Its sale of over 500,000 copies in the several years following publication, together with the formation of some five hundred politically activist Bellamy Clubs, signifies the public readiness to welcome engineering and its values into every area of national life. To bring humane order from chaotic instability, to banish waste and achieve efficiency, to serve others in benevolent disinterest—these were the promises of Bellamy's engineered America. They represented the future, even if Bellamy conservatively chose a minister, not an engineer, to deliver the eloquent peroration on America-2000 toward the closing of his book.

Bellamy and his readers may seem naive one century later. In hindsight both author and audience appear unaware of the totalitarian implications of America-2000. Both, it seems, mistook the attainment of comfort for the achievement of happiness. Both overestimated the ability of engineering to bring about the industrial-age millennium, as the presidency of the engineer Herbert Hoover was to make painfully clear by the early 1930s.

But the extraordinary popularity of Bellamy's novel through the 1890s is significant in another way. *Looking Backward* announced that engineering had come of age in the imaginations of Americans. Henceforth it would be a discrete yet integral part of the national consciousness. Thus in 1905 William James's Harvard University colleague, Hugo Munsterberg, wrote that "the utilitarians," embracing science and technology, comprised fully one half of the American character (354-59). By 1914 Van Wyck Brooks wrote that men merely dilated over vague catchwords like democracy and patriotism, reserving "careful thought and intellectual contact" for "engineering, finance, advertising, and trade" (166). In 1918 George Santayana praised the vigor of young philosophers by comparing their minds to those of doctors, engineers, or social reformers (102). When the cultural analyst, Harold Stearns, enlisted writers to undertake "a critical examination of our [American] civilization" in the early 1920s, he invited the engineer Otto S. Beyer, Jr., to join such figures as Lewis Mumford, H. L. Mencken, Van Wyck Brooks, Conrad Aiken, and Ring Lardner. Their anthology, *Civilization in the United States,* featured Beyer's essay, "Engineering," along with those on topics like "The City," "The Literary Life," "The Law," and on racial minorities, sex, sports, and medicine—all issues that American intellectuals thought crucial for the invigoration of the national culture.

In fact, the popular usage of the very term "engineer" through the 1920s shows a continuing regard for a profession valued for expertise, authority, and power. In *The American Language* H. L. Mencken satirizes the many borrowings of the word with his characteristic scorn for pretension. He begins, "I once knew an ancient bill-sticker, attached to a Baltimore theatre, who boasted the sonorous title of *chief lithographer,* Today, in all probability, he would be called a *lithographic-engineer,*" (289-91).

Mencken shows just how probable as he surveys Americans' efforts to dignify their mundane jobs with the imprimatur of engineering. There is the bedding manufacturer "who first became a *mattress-engineer* and then promoted himself to the lofty dignity of *sleep-engineer.*" There is the "beautician who burst out as an *appearance-engineer,* and the *demolition-engineers* who were once content to be house-wreckers." Mencken relishes the "*sanitary-engineers* who had an earlier incarnation as garbage-men," and the "*wedding-engineer,* a technician employed by florists to dress churches for hymeneal orgies." He spoofs the "*packing-engineer,* a scientist who crates clocks, radios, and chinaware for shipment," and the "*income-engineer,* an insurance solicitor in a new false-face." Doubtless he would have scorned Edward Bernays's definition of

public relations, the field Bernays virtually founded in the 1920s, as "the engineering of consent" (*Boston Globe* [June 27, 1984]: 72).

In any case, as much as Mencken relished his own satire, the egregious examples multiplied and outran his willingness to sustain what Sinclair Lewis dubbed his "gay anarchy" (*Dodsworth* 133). He resorted at last to the researcher's format, listing as data some sixty-five engineering euphemisms that include "a *printing-e,* a *furniture-e.,* a *photographic-e.,* a *financial-e.* (stock-market tipster), a *paint-e.,* a *clothing-e., wrapping-e.* (a dealer in wrapping paper), a *matrimonial-e.*"

The source of Mencken's humor was, understandably, an irritant to the professional engineers, at least one of whom kept a scrupulous tally of the pseudo-professionals. In a revealing footnote Mencken says that Theodore J. Hoover, dean of the School of Engineering at Stanford University, combed *Who's Who in Engineering* to report in 1935 that entrants listed themselves under 2,518 different engineering titles, most well suited to the satirist's barbs at the American "Booboisie."

Mencken's jibe at America's linguistic sins underscores a serious point. The self-styled engineers not only sought higher status but revealed, inadvertently, what engineers represented to the public. The beautician and the mattress manufacturer who paraded themselves as engineers did so with every expectation of gaining customers' respect and approval as specialists and professionals. In proclaiming themselves to be engineers, these and similar individuals reveal the positive connotations surrounding the very term "engineer" in earlier twentieth-century America. . . .

Works Cited

Adams, Henry. *The Education of Henry Adams.* Edited by Ernest Samuels. 1907. Reprint. Boston: Houghton Mifflin, 1973.

Appleton, Victor. *Tom Swift and His Air Glider.* New York: Grosset and Dunlap, 1912.

Badger, R. Reid. *The Great American Fair: The World's Columbian Exposition and American Culture.* Chicago: Nelson Hall, 1979.

Bellamy, Edward. *Looking Backward 2000–1887.* 1888. Reprint. Introduction by Cecelia Tichi. New York: Penguin, 1982.

Beyer, O[tto] S. "Engineering." In *Civilization in the United States,* edited by Harold E. Stearns, pp. 417-26. New York: Harcourt, Brace and Co., 1922.

Book, William F. *The Intelligence of High School Seniors.* New York: Macmillan, 1922.

Brooks, Van Wyck. *America's Coming of Age.* New York: Huebsch, 1914.

Cahan, Abraham. *The Rise of David Levinsky.* 1917. Reprint. New York: Harper and Row, 1966.

Dreiser, Theodore. *Sister Carrie.* 1900. Reprint. New York: Holt, Rinehart and Winston, 1957.

Emerson, Ralph Waldo. "The Farmer." In *Society and Solitude,* pp. 139-49. Boston: Fields, Osgood, 1870.

Ferber, Edna. *Roast Beef, Medium.* New York: Frederick A. Stokes, 1913.

Fitch, James Kip. *Engineering and Western Civilization.* New York: McGraw-Hill, 1951.

George, Henry. *Progress and Poverty.* 1879. Reprint. New York: Robert Schalkenbach Foundation, 1951.

Hammond, John H. *The Autobiography of John Hays Hammond.* 2 vols. New York: Farrar and Rinehart, 1935.

Hancock, H. Irving. *The Young Engineers in Mexico.* Akron, Ohio: Saalfield, 1913.

———. *The Young Engineers in Nevada.* Philadelphia: Henry Altemus, 1913.

Herrick, Robert. *Together.* New York: Grosset and Dunlap, 1908.

Hewitt, Abram S. *Selected Writings of Abram S. Hewitt.* Edited by Allan Nevins. New York: Columbia University Press, 1937.

Howells, William Dean. *Through the Eye of the Needle.* New York: Harper and Brothers, 1907.

Huneker, James. *New Cosmopolis.* New York: Scribner's, 1915.

James, William. "The Energies of Men." In *Essays on Faith and Morals.* New York: New American Library, 1962.

———. *Principles of Psychology.* 2 vols. New York: Holt, 1890.

Kasson, John. *Civilizing the Machine: Technology and Republican Values in America, 1776-1900.* 1976. Reprint. New York: Penguin, 1977.

Kimball, Dexter S. *I Remember.* New York: McGraw-Hill, 1953.

Lewis, Sinclair. *Babbitt.* 1922. Reprint. New York: New American Library, 1961.

———. *Dodsworth.* 1929. Reprint. New York: New American Library, 1967.

Maclaurin, Richard C., ed. *The Mechanic Arts.* Vol. 1. Boston: Hall and Locke, 1911.

Mencken, H[enry] L[ouis]. *The American Language: An Inquiry into the Development of English in the United States.* 4th ed. New York: Knopf, 1936.

Merritt, Raymond H. *Engineering in American Society 1850-1875.* Lexington: University Press of Kentucky, 1969.

Morison, Samuel Eliot. *One Boy's Boston 1887-1901.* 1962. Reprint. Boston: Northeastern University Press, 1983.

Mumford, Lewis. "The Economics of Contemporary Decoration." *Creative Art* 4 (January 1929): xix-xxii.

———. *My Works and Days.* New York: Harcourt Brace Jovanovich, 1979.

———. *Sticks and Stones: A Study of American Architecture and Civilization.* New York: Norton, 1924.

Munsterberg, Hugo. *The Americans.* London: Williams and Norgate, 1905.

Noble, David F. *America by Design: Science, Technology, and the Rise of Corporate Capitalism.* New York: Oxford University Press, 1977.

Pound, Ezra. *Selected Letters 1907-1941.* 1950. Reprint. New York: New Directions, 1971.

———. *Selected Poems.* New York: New Directions, 1957.

———. *Selected Prose 1909-1965.* New York: New Directions, 1975.

Ratigan, William. *Highways Over Broad Waters: Life and Times of David B. Steinman, Bridgebuilder.* Grand Rapids, Mich.: Eerdmans, 1959.

Santayana, George. *The Genteel Tradition: Nine Essays by George Santayana.* Edited by Douglas L. Wilson. Cambridge, Mass.: Harvard University Press, 1967.

Smith, Henry Nash, ed. *Popular Culture and Industrialization 1865-1890.* New York: New York University Press, 1967.

Stearns, Harold, ed. *Civilization in the United States.* New York: Harcourt Brace and Co., 1922.

Taylor, Frederick W. *Scientific Management Comprising Shop Management, The Principles of Scientific Management, Testimony before the House Special Committee.* New York: Harper and Brothers, 1947.

Trachtenberg. Alan. *The Incorporation of America: Culture and Society in the Gilded Age.* New York: Hill and Wang, 1982.

Vauclain, Samuel M., with Earl May. *Steaming Up!* New York: Brewer and Warren, 1930.

Whitman, Walt. *Leaves of Grass.* Edited by Sculley Bradley and Harold W. Blodgett. New York: Norton, 1973.

Miles Orvell

SOURCE: "Literature and the Authority of Technology," in *Literature and Science as Modes of Expression,* edited by Frederick Amrine, Kluwer Academic Publishers, 1989, pp. 169-75.

[*In the following excerpt, Orvell examines Whitman's treatment of technology and his influence on such modern writers as John Dos Passos and James Agee.*]

Whitman, who is the starting point for modern American literature in so many ways, took it upon himself in *Democratic Vistas* (1871) to define the character of American culture in a way that has had continuing relevance throughout the twentieth century: "America demands a poetry that is bold, modern, and all-surrounding and kosmical, as she is herself. It must in no respect ignore science or the modern, but inspire itself with science and the modern. It must bend its vision toward the future, more than the past". Starting with the close observation of nature, the poet works by analogies, by indirections; his genius lies in the "image-making faculty, coping with material creation, and rivaling, almost triumphing over it". Thus, as Whitman describes it, the poet or artist is making a kind of facsimile world, a world that rivals the creation, and indeed—in a curious phrase—almost triumphs over it; inspired by "science or the modern", Whitman posits an analogy between artistic creation and the technological process that situates him at a particular juncture in American culture, the beginning of the modern vision.

For Whitman was writing at a moment when the force of technology was being acutely recognized as a vigorous determinant of social direction, transforming the material fabric of society in starkly visible ways, and displacing even the traditional social power of poetry and the arts; what defines Whitman's response as "modern" is precisely his effort to absorb the meaning of technology—even if only in some vague way—into

his aesthetic process, and it is a strategy that I want to track to its culmination in the work of John Dos Passos and James Agee.

We can better understand the pressure behind such a strategy by looking briefly at the post-Civil War period in America, when the revolutionary powers of technology were first being consistently articulated within the culture, and in a way that might well put the arts on the defensive. Consider, for example, the review written by the Reverend John C. Kimball, following his visit to the Eleventh Exhibition of the Charitable Mechanic Association in Boston in 1869. Kimball sees the machine, as did many others, as man's servant, and as an egalitarian force, making available to the masses what had previously been the luxuries of the aristocracy. But what is most interesting from the present point of view is that Kimball sets machinery against the arts as rivals for our allegiance. Arguing against those who hold that "painting and sculpture, philosophy and poetry, embody somehow grander truths" than the mechanical arts, Kimball sounds like Plato reborn in the Promethean fire of American industry. The arts, for all their grandeur, Kimball claims, are "only of themselves an imitation, or, at most, an idealization, of the outside of things, only a surface expression of ideas. There is an element of falsity runs through them all". Machinery, says Kimball, "is not imitation, but the embodiment, of real forces, laws, and principles, which are made to act". In order for inventions to work, "they must not only seem, but be. A lie in them is absolutely fatal. What would be the worth of a sewing machine, however highly ornamented, which, like a picture, only looked as if it sewed?" To Kimball, in short, machines act upon things, the arts provide merely pictures of things.

One doesn't want to belabor Kimball's ontological confusions, which find their comic *reductio ad absurdum* in Rube Goldberg's improbable machines; but how interesting that Kimball felt some kind of choice and even comparison between the machine and the arts was necessary. (We are reminded, perhaps, that artisan [skilled laborer] and artist [original creator] share a common root.) It is as if the practical and the aesthetic were competing within the culture for influence and ascendancy. The enthusiasm of a Kimball—and he was representative of a widespread attitude—could well cause the writer either to retreat into a cloistered aestheticism (as did many) or else attempt in some other way to come to grips with the changed material conditions of society. And yet, that very effort to absorb the pressures of the modern, of technology, could result in works that are peculiarly, though interestingly, muddled, especially at the end of the nineteenth century. No wonder Mark Twain—who registered acutely so many cultural conflicts—would write a book as conflicted as *A Connecticut Yankee in King Arthur's Court,* which begins as a vindication of technological rationality in the face of benighted European superstitions and social habit and ends in a nightmarish vision of technology run amok. And other writers too at the end of the century—Dreiser and Norris, for example—would feel the attraction of scientific and technological forces within American society, which they would yet try to assimilate within a vocabulary and worldview which was in many ways romantic and mystical.

With the modernist writers of the early twentieth century—beginning with Ezra Pound—technology takes on immediate and profound importance. And Pound's influence on a younger generation of writers who attain maturity in the 'teens and 'twenties—most notably Eliot, Williams, and Moore—has been well documented (see Tichi). But even someone like Willa Cather—whom we think of as a traditionalist, alienated from the modern world of technology and bureaucracy, looking backward to an idealized, organic civilization—even Cather had absorbed by 1925 much of the ethos of the modernists. For in the same work in which she can condemn science as giving us nothing but sleights of hand (*The Professor's House*), she celebrates the virtues of a functional style in a manner that relates her to technological values. As the professor annotates Tom Outland's diary, in which the discovery of the Blue Mesa civilization is detailed, he appreciates a beauty in Outland's minute descriptions of the tools, pottery, and cloth: "If words had cost money, Tom couldn't have used them more sparingly. The adjectives were purely descriptive, relating to form and colour, and were used to present the objects under consideration, not the young explorer's emotions". Yet through the austerity of the style, Cather explains, one feels the discoverer's excitement.

Cather's description of Outland's style is a perfect description of Hemingway's style, with its economies of diction and rhythm, its clarity, its sense of emotional pressure under control; and it closely resembles as well the rules that Ezra Pound had formulated over a decade earlier in *Poetry* magazine as "A Few Don'ts": "Use no superfluous word, no adjective which does not reveal something. . . . Use either no ornament or good ornament. . . . Consider the way of the scientists rather than the way of an advertising agent for a new soap. The scientist does not expect to be acclaimed as a great scientist until he has *discovered* something".

Still, there is an instructive difference between Pound and Cather. Where Cather associates her functionalist style with the putative organic civilization of the Indian, the younger Pound is more clearly borrowing the prestige and language of science, and his formulation leads to Williams' later notion that "A poem is a small (or large) machine made of words". But this modernist ideal, which so clearly invokes the authority of technology, conceives of the poem as an object, a machine-like object, in a somewhat static sense. The poem

has a thing-like objectivity, it is a functional system, an integral design of part and whole in which no part is redundant; but it is essentially a thing to look at, rather than, for example, an instrument for knowing the world.

In order to see how far the authority of technology could carry the writer, we must turn to John Dos Passos and James Agee, who, in their work during the 'thirties, in different ways, sought to develop a mode of writing that established an even deeper relationship to technology, and one that goes back for its inspiration to Walt Whitman.

Dos Passos' clearest formulation of his views in this respect comes in a 1935 speech he delivered at the American Writers' Congress, "The Writer as Technician". For Dos Passos, the professional writer is involved in a process of "discovery and invention", a process "not very different from that of scientific discovery and invention". Here is Dos Passos the modernist speaking, who in fact invented, in the structure of *USA,* the most elaborate novel—machine of its time, a four-part mechanism of fictional narratives, biographies, newsreels, and autobiographical fragments. But it is Dos Passos' view of the writer's relation to society that is particularly interesting in this context: "In his relation to society a professional writer is a technician just as much as an electrical engineer is" (1935). The authority that Dos Passos thus claims is borrowed from the larger authority of technology—with its objectivity, its rational solution to problems of disorder and waste, its claims to efficiency—all of which were so compelling in the Depression.

Yet at the same time, Dos Passos wants to preserve the traditional vatic role of the writer as prophet, as seer, a Whitmanesque role that places him in opposition to the domination of machinery. For the successful literary work, according to Dos Passos, will have an influence on "ways of thinking to the point of changing and rebuilding the language, which is the mind of the group". Far from being a mere technician, then, the writer lays claim to a special authority: "At this particular moment in history, when machinery and institutions have so outgrown the ability of the mind to dominate them, we need bold and original thought more than ever. It is the business of writers to supply that thought, and not to make of themselves figureheads in political conflicts" (1935). The technician here has become the poet-legislator. At the bottom of Dos Passos' conception of the writer's role is the implication that the literary work can embody a special way of knowing the world.

In *USA* that special knowledge is carried in the "Camera Eye" sections, which provide a personal, subjective, autobiographical perspective on the panorama that otherwise unfolds in the novel. In thus naming these autobiographical units Dos Passos was doubtless attempting to capitalize on the aesthetic authority of photography during the early decades of the century as an instrument for objectively registering the visual world; and probably too he was borrowing the political authority of the moving picture camera that was a part of the influential Soviet documentary cinema movement (Kino-Pravda) anchored by Dziga Vertov. (And incidentally he was reversing Whitman's earlier scorn for the medium, when the latter had said, in *Democratic Vistas* that the artist's process of creation was "No useless attempt to repeat the material creation, by daguerreotyping the exact likeness by mortal mental means".) Using the camera as symbol, Dos Passos invoked the objectivity of the machine, its capacity to record literally the world before the lens; but he was also invoking, obviously, the process of seeing, which was, he argued, a subjective process.

The key passage is in "Camera Eye 47": "from the upsidedown image on the retina painstakingly out of color shape words remembered light and dark straining" (1946) The implied sense of vision itself as something that must be turned right side up, interpreted, was a persistent part of Dos Passos' epistemology: "Your two eyes are an accurate stereoscopic camera, sure enough", he wrote in "Satire as a Way of Seeing" (1937), "but the process by which the upsidedown image on the retina takes effect on the brain entails a certain amount of unconscious selection. What you see depends to a great extent on subjective distortion and elimination which determines the varied impacts on the nervous system of speed of line, emotions of color, touchvalues of form. Seeing is a process of imagination" (1964). The artist is thus constructing his vision, his eye formed by the climate of visual stimuli in the culture at large. Combining the objectivity of the camera with the subjectivity of constructed vision, the artist unites the technological and the artistic.

For James Agee, the camera was also a crucial model for writing, and it is explicitly developed as such in his documentary (or anti-documentary) portrait of three Alabama tenant farmers and their families, *Let Us Now Praise Famous Men*. Aiming for an authentic representation of the thing itself, Agee was acutely aware of the limitations of language, which, he held, must inevitably sag beneath the weight of naturalistic description. The visual image, in its wordless immediacy, could avoid that problem. "One reason I so deeply care for the camera is just this. So far as it goes (which is, in its own realm, as absolute anyhow as the traveling distance of words or sound), and handled cleanly and literally in its own terms, as an ice-cold, some ways limited, some ways more capable, eye, it is, like the phonograph record and like scientific instruments and unlike any other leverage of art, incapable of recording anything but absolute, dry truth". Of course, Agee does not assume that the camera is in everyone's hands a recorder of truth: it

was Walker Evans, his collaborator, he had in mind, and not, for example, Margaret Bourke-White.

Agee invokes Evans' images—which are printed as part of *Famous Men*—on several occasions, either to supplement his prose descriptions or to replace them, but in fact Agee's prose inevitably has qualities nowhere visible (or possible) in Evans' or any photographer's image. Yet even allowing for the difference in medium, and allowing for the differences in style between Agee and Evans (which I will not go into here), Agee's invocation of the camera forms the basis for his whole moral aesthetic: a deep and self-conscious respect for the actual lives he is depicting. *Famous Men* sums up not only the documentary impulse of the 'thirties, with its urge to encompass the social reality of life in Depression America, but also the modernist urge to invent forms that would reflect the new scientific and technological conditions of knowledge and that would embody, self-consciously, our experience of the world. And here I might add that Agee's constant—and for some readers irritating—intrusion of himself into the exposition is a deliberate strategy, not unlike Dos Passos' use of the "Camera Eye" sections in *USA*. Both books are really as much about their authors as about their subjects; and they both thus make a virtue of Heisenberg's uncertainty principle, which declares that the observer himself is an inevitable function in the calculus of observation, that the eye of the seer makes the thing seen.

Out of the artist's complex sensibility and his attunement to the age would arise, in Agee's words, "the beginning of somewhat new forms, of which the still and moving cameras are the strongest instruments and symbols. It would be an art and a way of seeing existence based, let us say, on an intersection of astronomical physics, geology, biology, and (including psychology) anthropology, known and spoken of not in scientific but in human terms". Whatever else he may have had in mind, Agee was doubtless thinking of the book he was at that moment writing—*Let Us Now Praise Famous Men*—and his words have application as well to the multi-faceted constructions of Dos Passos. And too, Agee's words respond to Whitman's challenge of the previous century, to write a poetry that is "bold, modern, and all-surrounding and kosmical, as America is herself", a poetry that is inspired by science and the modern.

Whether or not they were gaining an audience commensurate with their goals, Dos Passos and Agee were defining in their works a literature that would span the complementary impulses of the technological and the aesthetic. In depicting the artist as an engineer, or as a new kind of scientist, they are not only borrowing the new mystique of science and technology; they are also bringing together in the single person of the writer the components of American culture that were sundered by the John Kimballs, and that Van Wyck Brooks had worried about at the start of the modern period, in *America's Coming of Age*—the technical and the theoretical, the scientific and the artistic, the practical and the spiritual. The work of these modernists thus accepted Whitman's challenge of accurately defining "material creation" in a culture that was coming more and more, through the screen of mass culture, to thrive on caricatures of itself.

Bibliography

Agee, J. and Evans, W.: *Let Us Now Praise Famous Men,* Houghton Miffin, New York, 1960.

Cather, W.: *The Professor's House,* Knopf, New York, 1925.

Dos Passos, J.: *The Big Money, USA,* Houghton Mifflin, Boston, 1946.

————: 'Satire as a Way of Seeing', in his *Occasions and Protests,* Henry Regnery, Chicago, 1964, pp. 20-32.

————: 'The Writer as Technician', in *American Writer's Congress* (ed. by H. Hart), International Publishers, New York, 1935.

Kimball, J.: 'Machinery as a Gospel Worker', *Unitarian Christian Examiner,* November 1869, pp. 323-4.

Pound, E.: 'A Few Don'ts', in *Prose Keys to Modern Poetry* (ed. by K. Shapiro), Harper & Row, New York, 1962, pp. 106-7.

Tichi, C: *Shifting Gears: Literature, Technology, Culture in Modernist America,* Univ. of North Carolina Press, Chapel Hill, N. C., 1987.

Whitman, W.: 'Democratic Vistas', in *Leaves of Grass and Selected Prose* (ed. by J. Kouwenhoven), Modern Library, New York, 1950.

Williams, W.: 'Author's Introduction' to *The Wedge,* in *Selected Essays,* New Directions, New York, 1969.

FURTHER READING

Buckley, J. F. "Living in the Iron Mills: A Tempering of Nineteenth-Century America's Orphic Poet." *Journal of American Culture* 16, No. 1 (Spring 1993): 67-72.
  Discusses Rebecca Harding Davis's "realistic view of America" in the midst of war, transcendental idealism, and nationalistic fervor.

Chesterton, G. K. *The Victorian Age in Literature.* London: Oxford University Press, 1966, 120 p.
  Broad-ranging thematic and historical study of the major Victorian poets and novelists, originally published in 1912.

Jennings, Humphrey. *Pandaemonium 1660-1886: The Coming of the Machine as Seen by Contemporary Observers.* Edited by Mary-Lou Jennings and Charles Madge. New York: Free Press, 1985, 376 p.
  Excerpted poetry and prose, fiction and nonfiction, by writers of the eighteenth and nineteenth centuries, reflecting the impact of industrialism upon British life and culture.

Johnson, Patricia E. "*Hard Times* and the Structure of Industrialism: The Novel as Factory." *Studies in the Novel* XXI, No. 2 (Summer 1989): 128-37.
  Examines Dickens's symbolic use of the factory, focusing on his "critique of the interlocking structures—economic, social, and political—of industrial capitalism."

Marx, Leo. *The Machine in the Garden: Technology and the Pastoral Ideal in America.* London: Oxford University Press, 1964, 387 p.
  A comprehensive analysis of the various effects of industrialism on American culture and literature.

Mumford, Lewis. *Technics and Civilization.* New York: Harcourt, Brace and Co., 1934, 480 p.
  Analyzes the inception and development of the Industrial Revolution from an historical and cultural studies perspective.

O'Brien, Robert Lincoln. "Machinery and English Style." *The Atlantic Monthly* XCIV, No. 564 (October 1904): 464-72.
  Analyzes the effect of inventions such as the typewriter and the telegraph on the "form and substance" of language.

Seltzer, Mark. *Bodies and Machines.* New York: Routledge, 1992, 230 p.
  Discusses how "persons, bodies, and technologies are made and represented in turn-of-the-century American culture and beyond."

The Knickerbocker Group

INTRODUCTION

At the turn of the nineteenth century, New York had exceeded Boston as a center of population and social activity. At the hub of the city's and the nation's literary life were the Knickerbockers, a loose association of professional and amateur literati. It was perhaps their greatest luminary, Washington Irving, who had made famous the name "Knickerbocker" in the persona of Diedrich Knickerbocker, narrator of *A History of New York* (1809). These writers' activity spans the period from around 1807, the year their original literary journal, *Salmagundi,* was first published, to 1865, when the last issue of *The Knickerbocker Magazine,* their final representative publication, appeared. But the first third of the century was the period in which the Knickerbockers achieved their greatest popular notoriety and critical acclaim. It was then that the three original and most illustrious Knickerbockers—Irving, James Fenimore Cooper, and William Cullen Bryant—flourished, leaving their permanent mark on American letters. The genius and success of Irving and Cooper especially stimulated the talent and ambition of a number of lesser lights who would help carry on the Knickerbocker name through the middle of the century. Of these writers, spanning the entire Knickerbocker period, the more prominent were James Kirke Paulding, Joseph Rodman Drake, Fitz-Greene Halleck, Gulian Verplanck, John Howard Payne, Samuel Woodworth, and George P. Morris.

The members of the group were associated chiefly by social class, literary sensibility, the social and intellectual confines of New York City, and a respect for each other's work. With no intention of organizing themselves into a formal school, they published the representative journals mentioned above in which their own and others' writings regularly appeared. As a group, the Knickerbockers were remarkably prolific, publishing in a broad range of literary genres: journalism, editorship, literary criticism, travel sketches that included the American and Canadian frontiers as well as the conventional Old World cities, novels, short stories, dramas, operas, and translations from the classics. After their heyday, the Knickerbockers' popularity steadily declined until, a generation after Irving, Cooper, and Bryant, their work was largely forgotten or ignored.

Twentieth-century critical appreciation has focused mainly on the Knickerbockers' literary criticism and their own literary art. It is generally agreed that the best of Knickerbocker criticism helped raise the standards of literary criticism in the early nineteenth century, which was narrowly moralistic and often ruled by the reviewer's personal or political regard for the author. A wide array of critical opinion existed among the Knickerbockers, ranging within two broad literary attitudes. The most common in the early period of Knickerbocker literature was the eighteenth-century neo-classical attitude in the tradition of Alexander Pope, Samuel Johnson, and Joseph Addison, which extolled disciplined and judicial analysis of the merits of a work according to exacting rules that were supposed to determine good literature. Others of the Knickerbockers adopted the new Romantic standard of criticism, following the English Romantics such as William Wordsworth, Charles Lamb, William Hazlitt, and Thomas De Quincey. They distrusted the rational and analytical and inclined much more to the critic's subjective appreciation of a work, relying in their judgments on the impression a work made. In the 1830s and 1840s, Romantic, impressionistic criticism was becoming increasingly common, but it was tempered by the growing influence in America of German criticism as reflected in the writings of Thomas Carlyle and Samuel Taylor Coleridge in England; it strove to include both the analytical and the impressionistic and was supposed to achieve a balance between the two extremes.

Knickerbocker literature varies widely in form, subject, and style. One finds classical gravity as well as the absurdities and fatuities of modern burlesque, or the realistic and urbane attitudes of the neo-classical outlook along with the maudlin sentiments and naturalism of the romantic outlook. But certain unmistakable influences from England gave the Knickerbocker literature, at different periods, a common identity. In the early stages of its development, Knickerbocker literature was indebted, not surprisingly, to eighteenth-century writers like Pope, Addison, Oliver Goldsmith, and Johnson; in its middle years it imbibed heavily the influence of Walter Scott, Lord Byron, and Lamb among others; and in its decline, Charles Dickens, Benjamin Disraeli, and lesser writers prevailed. An identity emerged as well from the considerable influence the individual Knickerbockers, especially Irving and Cooper, exerted on one another. They shared common interests, read many of the same books—including each others'—and wrote for the same journals, all of which helped produce, in broad outline at least, a common character. Their love of humor, especially satire, foreign places, and landscapes and their basic conservatism, especially in Cooper and Paulding, pervade their writings so much so as to be almost traditional in Knickerbocker literature.

In spite of the Knickerbockers' use of the English models they knew so well and their mutual influence, they demonstrated a considerable degree of independence and originality and were powerful forces in the creation of a native literary tradition. Irving's contribution is the most remarkable. His sketchbooks—including *The Sketch Book of Geoffrey Crayon, Gent* (1819-20) and *Bracebridge Hall* (1822)—were largely responsible for establishing a new and peculiarly American literary genre, the short story, because they exceeded in quality and popularity everything of its kind. The Knickerbockers often wrote contemptuously of the predominance of British influence in American letters, despite and because of their own indebtedness, and many tried to foster a genuinely national literature by choosing specifically American themes, subjects, and language, particularly from the frontier. For such authors as James Kirke Paulding, it was a supreme embarrassment that American writers looked to England at all for their inspiration.

Though their contribution to American literature was considerable, it was a contribution appreciated by almost exclusively twentieth-century critics, in whose estimation they nevertheless remain only minor figures in American literary history, with the exception of Irving and Cooper.

REPRESENTATIVE WORKS

James Gordon Brooks
  The Rivals of Este, and Other Poems (poetry) 1829

William Cullen Bryant
  "The Skeleton's Cave" (short story) 1832; published in *Tales of the Glauber-Spa*
  Letters of a Traveller; or, Notes of Things Seen in Europe and America (travel sketches) 1850
  Discourse on the Life and Genius of Cooper (criticism) 1852
  A Discourse on the Life, Character, and Genius of Washington Irving (criticism) 1860
  Letters from the East (travel sketches) 1869
  A Popular History of the United States from the First Discovery of the Western Hemisphere . . . to the End of the First Century of the Union of the States. 4 vols. (history) 1876-81
  The Poetical Works of William Cullen Bryant (poetry) 1878

Lewis Gaylord Clark
  The Knickerbocker Sketch-Book (short stories) 1845

The Poetical Writings of Lewis Gaylord Clark (poetry) 1846
  Knick-Knacks from an Editor's Table (essays) 1852

McDonald Clarke
  The Gossip; or, A Laugh with the Ladies, a Grin at the Gentlemen, and Burlesques on Byron, a Sentimental Satire (poetry) 1823
  Sketches (short stories) 1826
  Poems of McDonald Clarke (poetry) 1836

James Fenimore Cooper
  The Last of the Mohicans (novel) 1826
  Notions of the Americans (travel essay) 1828
  A Letter to His Countrymen (essay) 1834
  The Monikins (satire) 1835
  The American Democrat; or, Hints on the Social and Civic Relations of the United States of America (essay) 1838
  The Pathfinder; or, The Inland Sea (novel) 1840
  The Deerslayer; or, The First War Path (novel) 1841
  Satanstoe; or, The Littlepage Manuscripts (novel) 1845
  The Sea Lions; or, The Lost Sealers (novel) 1849

William Cox
  Crayon Sketches (essays) 1833

Theodore Sedgwick Fay
  Dreams and Reveries of a Quiet Man (familiar essays) 1832
  Norman Leslie (novel) 1835
  Sydney Clifton (novel) 1839
  The Countess Ida (novel) 1840
  Hoboken, A Romance (novel) 1843
  Ulric; or, The Voices (poetry) 1851
  The Three Germanys (travel sketches) 1889

Fitz-Greene Halleck
  The Poetical Works of Fitz-Greene Halleck (poetry) 1847
  The Poetical Writings of Fitz-Greene Halleck, with Extracts from those of Joseph Rodman Drake (poetry) 1869

Charles Fenno Hoffman
  Wild Scenes in the Forest and Prairie (travel and nature sketches) 1839
  Greyslayer: A Romance of the Mohawk (novel) 1840
  The Poems of Charles Fenno Hoffman (poetry) 1873

Washington Irving
  Salmagundi; or, The Whim-Whams and Opinions of Launcelot Langstaff, Esq., and Others [with William Irving and James Kirke Paulding] (satirical essays) 1807-08
  A History of New York [as Diedrich Knickerbocker] (historical parody) 1809

The Sketch Book of Geoffrey Crayon, Gent [as Geoffrey Crayon] (short stories) 1819-20
Bracebridge Hall [as Geoffrey Crayon] (sketches) 1822
Tale of a Traveller [as Geoffrey Crayon] (travel sketches) 1824
A Tour on the Prairies (travel sketches) 1835
The Life of George Washington (biography) 1855-59

William Legget
Journals of the Ocean (travel sketches) 1826
Tales and Sketches (sketches) 1829
"The Block House" [published in *Tales of the Glauber-Spa*] (sketches) 1829
A Collection of the Political Writings of William Leggett (political essays) 1840

George Pope Morris
Brier Cliff (play) 1935 [first produced on stage in 1826]
The Songs and Ballads of George P. Morris (musical verse) 1846
Poems by George P. Morris (poetry) 1853

James Kirke Paulding
Salmagundi; or, The Whim-Whams and Opinions of Launcelot Langstaff, Esq., and Others [with William and Washington Irving] (satirical essays) 1807-08
The Diverting History of John Bull and Brother Jonathan [as Hector Bull-us] (satire) 1812
The United States and England (history) 1815
The Backwoodsman (poetry) 1818
Salmagundi; Second Series [as Launcelot Langstaff] (essays) 1819-20
Koningsmarke, the Long Finne: A Story of the New World (novel) 1823
John Bull in America; or, The Munchausen (satire) 1825
Tales of the Good Woman (short stories) 1829
The Old Continental; or, The Price of Liberty (novel) 1846

John Howard Payne
Lovers' Vows (play) 1806 [performed]
Juvenile Poems (poetry) 1813
Thérèse, The Orphan of Geneva (play) 1821 [performed]
Richelieu (play) 1826 [performed]

Robert Charles Sands
Yamoyden (poetry) 1820
The Talisman. 3 vols. [editor with William Cullen Bryant and Gulian Verplanck] 1827-29
The Writings of Robert C. Sands, in Prose and Verse, with a Memoir of the Author (poetry and essays) 1834

Gulian Crommelin Verplanck
The Bucktail Bards (poetry) 1819
The Talisman. 3 vols. [editor with Bryant and Sands] 1827-29
Discourses and Addresses on Subjects of American History, Arts, and Literature (lectures) 1833
Shakespeare's Plays: With His Life. 3 vols. [editor] 1845

Nathaniel Parker Willis
Fugitive Poetry (poetry) 1829
Melanie and Other Poems (poetry) 1835
Pencillings by the Way (travel sketches) 1835-36
Bianca Visconti; or, The Heart Overtasked (play) 1839; published in *Two Ways of Dying for a Husband*
Paul Fane; or, Parts of a Life Else Untold (novel) 1857

Samuel Woodworth
Beasts at Law (poetry) 1811
The Deed of Gift. A Comic Opera (opera) 1822
Lafayette, or The Castle of Olmutz (play) 1824
Sunday Morning Reflections (essays) 1839

OVERVIEWS

The Nation, New York

SOURCE: "Knickerbocker Literature," in *The Nation*, New York, Vol. V, No. 127, December 5, 1867, pp. 459-61.

[*This unsigned essay from 1867 provides a brief, first-hand look at the critical regard for the Knickerbockers and their writings, revealing how, only a generation after their own time, the writings of the Knickerbockers were largely forgotten or dismissed by the critics.*]

Fitz Greene Halleck, who left us the other day, was a writer whose works are a favorable specimen of what, speaking roughly, may be called the Knickerbocker literature. Of the school of writers which produced this literature it is true to say that it was composed of authors whom we all remember as forgotten. Their names are well enough remembered, but the present generation knows little of them except their names, that they very properly acknowledged Washington Irving as their leader and master, and that they lived in or about New York. Charles Fenno Hoffman was one of them, James Kirke Paulding was another, Halleck and Joseph Rodman Drake were two more, and besides these there were Robert C. Sands, John Sanderson, the two Clarks—Willis Gaylord and Lewis Gaylord—Nathaniel Parker Willis, perhaps, and, in a sense, Cooper the novelist. Two men, for a time classed among these by the popular voice, are Mr. Bancroft and Mr. Bryant;

but these have both escaped. Mr. Bryant deserved his good fortune. For what saddens him a man can hardly return gratitude; but respect, very genuine if not profound, every reader of Mr. Bryant's poems must, it seems to us, accord their author. The spirit of his poetry is melancholic almost to sombreness; there is in it nothing to delight. It might be compared to a chill wind which blows softly—not out of graveyards; it possesses hardly so much of human interest as that—which blows over graves that have long been forgotten, where lies, undistinguished from the common earth, the dust of disappeared races—unremembered nations and tribes resolved into earth. From such a soil grow all Mr. Bryant's lonesome, sad flowers of poetry. But though the impression produced by his poetry is not a pleasant one, and therefore not in the highest sense pleasing, still it is powerful, and he produces it of himself. Small faults of imitation he has, but the aspect of nature of which we have spoken—nature as seen from a solitary Indian mound sepulchre—is his own property, and at once he becomes independent of the Knickerbockers. Mr. Bancroft—who is to American history what Mr. Paulding is to American *belles-lettres* literature—came to New York from New England too late to be thoroughly identified with the old Knickerbocker people. A good many other names might be added to those we have mentioned, but they would be names, and no more at all, meaning nothing to this generation.

Doctor Rufus Wilmot Griswold, however, ought not to be passed by in silence, being, as he was, the Knickerbocker Boswell of our Knickerbocker Johnsons, in whose books they are perhaps more plainly to be seen than in any of their own works. Cotton Mather, during his sojourn here below, or above, produced three hundred and eighty-two books big and little; then comes Doctor Griswold, and praises him as "the first American Fellow of the Royal Society." It seems to us that in this critical judgment on so extremely literary an American as Mather was we find the clue which, if any clue were needed, would more surely than any other lead us to the right appreciation of the Knickerbocker literature. Indeed, it is so true as to be truismatically true that to the end of their days the writers who produced it were colonists and provincials; as literary men they had no right to any Fourth of July. Provincial they were even in the often-made assertion of their political independence and nationality, as any one may see to his abundant satisfaction who will look into the works of Paulding and see how that author, "lying supinely on his back," as somebody makes Patrick Henry say, "while his enemy binds him hand and foot"—writing stiffly in the manner of Swift with the matter of Paulding—insisted, with much illtemper, not that America was America, but that it was not England, was much better than England and bigger than England; that the Mississippi is a larger river than the Thames; that *The Quarterly Review* was not infallible,

and in a variety of ways rapped British knuckles with a yardstick that after all was British. The case was of a less inflammatory character, but, perhaps, even more hopeless, when Paulding and his compeers were not engaged in being patriotic. As Doctor Griswold flatteringly says, Mr. Hoffman was our Knickerbocker Moore—with the breadth of the Atlantic between him and the Irish one; Mr. Cooper was Scott whenever he could be, so far as he could be, and was himself only when he came to backwoods and prairies which Sir Walter had not seen; Verplanck and Sanderson had not, to be sure, remembered enough, but certainly they had not forgotten enough of the essayists of Queen Anne's time and the reviewers of *The Edinburgh*. Willis's reputation is dead, not because he was essentially an imitator but because he was essentially a slight man in his books. But even though Willis did not reflect English literature, he was driven to putting into his books English literary men and English society. At any rate he did so, and found his account in it. Drake died young, but lived long enough to imitate the versification of Byron and Moore, and to make it pretty evident that he would never have emancipated himself. Lewis Gaylord Clark came again to the surface the other day after a perfectly characteristic fashion—a fashion characteristic, at any rate, of the school of which he was one, not, perhaps, characteristic of him; we know next to nothing about him—in a letter written *à propos* of Mr. Dickens's arrival. Of course Mr. Samuel Rogers figured in it; so did the library at Sunnyside, Sidney Smith, Henry Brevoort, Mr. Bryant, and Mr. Halleck. "I think," says Mr. Clark, "it was Mr. Bryant who, in this connection, mentioned the fact to Rogers that Halleck when in England had passed his house near Hyde Park. 'Tell him,' said Rogers, 'when he is next in England that the author of "Marco Bozzaris" must not pass my house again; he must come in.'" We love to think that probably Doctor Griswold had heard this anecdote a couple of hundred times. It would have done him such a world of good. "Rogers's house," he would say to himself, "and near Hyde Park! Rogers knew him as the author of 'Marco Bozzaris!'" And we can imagine with what scorn he would have gazed on the young person who after that declined to believe Mr. Halleck "one of the first poets of the age." He would have leaned back in his chair and proceeded to relate that "Mr. Bryant once said to Rogers, the poet-banker, that Mr. Halleck"—and so on. Then, it is possible, he grasped his pen firmly, and continued his biography of the poet: "One evening in the spring of 1819, as Halleck was on the way home from his place of business, he stopped at a coffee-house then much frequented by young men, in the vicinity of Columbia College. A shower had just fallen, and a brilliant sunset was distinguished by a rainbow of unusual magnificence. In a group about the door half-a-dozen had told what they would wish, could their wishes be realized, when Halleck said, looking at the glorious spectacle above the horizon: 'If I could have any wish, it should be to lie in the lap of that rainbow and read 'Tom Campbell.' A handsome young fellow standing near suddenly turned to him and exclaimed, 'You and I must be friends.'"

It was Joseph Rodman Drake who, thus impressed by a bit of imagery worthy of his own "Culprit Fay," thus proffered friendship, which was accepted on the spot. We have no need to imagine what sort of a man it was who could form the wish above recorded; it is still possible to turn to Halleck's works and discern plainly what Campbell, with the help of others, made of him. "Gem of the crimson-colored even," Campbell says, "Companion of retiring day," and Halleck follows after with "Twilight;" Byron, without at all meaning it, wrote "Fanny." Scott and Scott's parodists wrote for him "Alnwick Castle;" "Burns" Halleck himself had a finger in, and it was he, too, who wrote the energetic and obsolescent "Marco Bozzaris." Parts of the last-mentioned poem are, however, hardly yet obsolescent, and will hardly become so. It is the only poem of his in which he for a little while forgot himself—a feat of great difficulty for him; by which is meant not that he habitually carried undue self-consciousness into his poetry; but when he forgot himself he had to forget so many people.

The imitative character of Irving, also, the head and front of the school, is very generally, though it is not yet universally, recognized. There are still among us men of the generation whose hearts glowed within them when *The Edinburgh* praised "Bracebridge Hall," and who confuse the pleasure they got from Irving's works with the patriotic pleasure they got from the reviews of them. And then, unoriginal as he is, yet, speaking carefully, one would not so readily say of him that, born near the Tappan Zee, he closely imitated Addison, as one would say that he was a sort of a kind of an Addison—to speak after the New England fashion—who, by the bad accident of birth, happened to see the light in these Western wilds. As has often been said, his humor is imitative of the humor of the Anne-Augustan age; but it has a local color, and less often a local flavor, which proves it the fruit not of a graft merely, but of a tree in some respects *sui generis*. With this not very great amount of eulogy his admirers will be obliged, we suppose, to rest content; that seems to be the opinion on which criticism has for some time settled. For our own part, we should make this much abatement of the praise just given—his humor was constantly alloyed by a coarseness, sometimes with a knowing air half-concealed, sometimes not concealed at all, from which Addison kept himself more pure.

What has been said of the essentially imitative and colonial character of our Knickerbocker authors is not to be said, as nothing is to be said, without some limitations. Not much, however, is necessary in the way of limitation. Mr. Willis, for example, was the author

of one or two little poems which possess the underived beauty of natural sentiments expressed in fine verse. Mr. Paulding is recognizable as an American patriot. Cooper, among his many utterly unreadable books, has one or two in which are one or two characters that are original with him, and that may be supposed natural. It is hard to tell. Indiscriminate praise was heaped on him; all of it that came from the other side of the water was bestowed by ignorant critics; most of it given him here was given by patriotically enthusiastic men, the mass of whom, we suppose, were as ignorant as their English brethren of the true Indian and true backwoodsman. We know nobody who gets through the books twice. However, the characters we have mentioned are, in a way, a success, and are, beyond a doubt, of Cooper's invention, unless we say that the backwoodsman was a discovery rather than an invention. What is true of Willis is to a less extent true of Morris, and so on of some of the others. But it remains true, too, that imitation was the life and breath of the Knickerbocker literature, and that it is now pretty much dead.

A few writers still linger among us who have sat at meat with the masters and disciples of it, and keep alive for a while longer its traditions in their own memories and the memories of the rest of us. Indeed, one or two of the disciples themselves are with us yet, and Halleck, but just gone, was even a master. Mr. L. G. Clark, who once edited *The Knickerbocker Magazine*—"Maga" and "Knick" they used to call it, with jocoseness—is, *ex officio,* of that other world. Mr. Tuckerman appears to be a connecting link between that one and ours. Mr. D. G. Mitchell smacks of it, and there are several other contemporary writers who, by some inexplicable, or explicable, association of ideas suggest to us the old days, though it would not be possible to bring them within our definition of the Knickerbocker author, or to make his description apply at all accurately to them.

Beyond a doubt it would be wrong to pass upon these writers whom we have been glancing at a sentence of unmitigated condemnation. They were once the boast of their countrymen while yet Longfellow, Emerson, Hawthorne, Lowell, all our really best men, were considered but 'prentice hands, and while it was unsuspected that almost our only really good names in literature—names that have, at any rate, thrown into utter eclipse the renown of the Knickerbocker men—were those of writers who knew not Irving. Once, we say, they were very eminent, and they have since so thoroughly lost their former distinction that we do not know where to look for a case parallel to theirs. The master of them all died after Sumter was fired on, and already it seems as if he had lived two hundred years ago. But nevertheless they served a most useful purpose. They were our first crop—to borrow a figure—and very properly were ploughed in, and though nothing of the same sort has come up since, and we may be permitted to hope that nothing of just the same sort will ever again come up, yet certainly they did something toward fertilizing the soil from the products of which we are now getting a part of our food. Certainly they cherished in our not wholly civilized community a love for things not materialistic. Halleck, for instance, if he did but little for literature pure and simple, did more and better for American civilization than if he had wholly devoted himself to "the cotton trade and sugar line" or to his duties as John Jacob Astor's agent. Our young men in Wall street and the streets adjacent may better trust themselves to his influence, though he never "swung a railroad," as they say in the West, than to the influence of Commodore Vanderbilt, if we may name names, in whose eyes business, it would seem, is war, and the war-cry is *vœ victis*. It cannot be expected of the average critic of to-day to say that as literary men our Knickerbocker literature is a very fine thing or a very valuable thing, but as Americans, if we are not sorry that it exists no longer, we may very well be glad that it once existed.

George Edward Woodberry

SOURCE: "Knickerbocker Era of American Letters," in *Harper's Magazine*, Vol. CV, No. 629, October, 1902, pp. 677-83.

[*In this brief essay, Woodberry discusses the Knickerbocker era of American letters in its heyday under the bright lights of Washington Irving, James Fenimore Cooper, and William Cullen Bryant, and afterward under the lesser lights who presided over the decline of that era. The critic touches generally upon the literary conditions and atmosphere in early America and early New York that helped give the work of the Knickerbockers its general character, as well as upon the features that distinguished them as literary artists.*]

Father Knickerbocker was the first literary creation of our country. The little old man in the old black coat and cocked hat who strayed from his lodgings, and was near being advertised for by the police of that day, and who left behind him the curious history that was to be sold for his debts, was destined by the spirit of humor to be the eldest child of our originality, and he proved his title deeds of true birth so well that the estate of New York proudly received and owned him, and gave him the island and river realm, and took to itself and its belongings the name of its droll saint. He was a myth, like all our types; for American genius has never yet created a man or a woman so much of nature's stamp as to live in our memories and affections like one of ourselves, as Uncle Toby or Hamlet or Pickwick does; but, like all true myths, he had a root in the soil. It was characteristically American, premonitory of a land of many races, that this Dutch grotesque, so pure in his racial strain as to incorporate

all the old traditional blood in his small figure, should have issued from a brain half Scotch and half English, the first-born of Irving's invention; but Diedrich Knickerbocker could hardly have seen himself in Dutch eyes, and so from the very first it was the blending of the stocks that gave literary consciousness and set up the reactions that breed imagination and humor.

The city, nevertheless, was pure-blooded in those early days, at least by comparison with its later conglomerations; and it was, in fact, the expression of local pride of race in Dr. Mitchell's *Picture of New York* that gave occasion to the graceless half-breed, this young Irving, to amuse himself and the town with its author's vanity and heaviness. The Knickerbocker *History* was the sort of broad travesty that the victim calls coarse caricature and it might not have survived so long and so acceptably if the victorious English race had not grown with the city and continued the local temper that most enjoyed the humor. Certainly the old Dutch town cannot be credited with producing Irving, except on the theory of opposites; it furnished the material, but the hand that wrought it was English by blood and breeding. It belonged to the situation that the observer should be of a different kind; the subject gained by his aloofness from it. If one to the manner born could never have seen the broad humor of it, neither could he have touched the Knickerbocker world with that luminous sentiment which by another smile of fortune made Rip Van Winkle immortal. Individuality has played an uncommonly large part in our literature, and its part is always greater than is usually allowed; and, after all, Irving created this past; he was the medium through whom it became visible; and it still lies there in the atmosphere of his genius, not in the crudity of its own bygone fact. He found the old Dutch life there in the little city, and up and down the waterways, in his cheerful, tender, and warm youth; he laughed at it and smiled on it; and what it was to his imagination it came to be as reality almost historic to his countrymen.

It is all a colonial dream, like Longfellow's Acadie; and the witchery of literature has changed it into a horizon of our past where it broods forever over the reaches of the Hudson north ward. Hawthorne's Puritan past is not more evasive; but a broad difference is marked by the contrast of *The Scarlet Letter* and *The Legend of Sleepy Hollow*; the absence of the moral element is felt in the latter; and a grosser habit of life, creature comfort, a harmless but unspiritual superstition, a human warmth, a social comradery, are prominent in Irving's lucubrations, and these are traits of the community ripened and sweetened in him. Irving must have been a charming boy, and in his young days he laid the bases of his life in good cheer, happy cordiality, the amiableness of a sensitive and pleasurable temperament, which he developed in the kindly and hospitable homes of the city. He was all his days a social creature, and loved society, masculine and feminine; and going from New York to a long European experience of social life, he returned to be one of the finest types of a man so bred, fit to be one of the historic literary figures of a commercial and cosmopolitan city.

Irving, however, thorough American of his day though he was, bore but little relation to the life of the nation. He was indebted to his country for some impulses of his genius and much material which he reworked into books; but he gave more than he received. Our early literary poverty is illustrated by the gifts he brought. He was a pioneer of letters, but our literary pioneers, instead of penetrating further into the virgin wilderness, had to hark back to the old lands, and come again with piratical treasures; and in this he was only the first of a long line of Continental adventurers. Much of American literary experience, which comes to us in our few classics, was gained on foreign soil; and, in fact, it must be acknowledged that, like some young wines, American genius has been much improved by crossing the seas. Irving was the first example. Commerce naturally leads to travel, and he went out as a man in trade to stay a few months. He remained seventeen years. It was not merely that he received there an aristocratic social training and opportunity peculiarly adapted to ripen his graces—and the graces of his style and nature are essentially social graces—but subjects were given to him and his sympathies drawn out and loosed by both his English and his Spanish residences.

Sentiment and romance were more to him than humor, and grew to be more with years; and in the old lands his mind found that to cling to and clamber over that otherwise might not have come to support his wandering and sympathetic mood. Genius he had, the nature and the faculty of an imaginative writer; what he needed was not power, but opportunity; and at every new chance of life he answered to the time and place, and succeeded. He alone of men not English-born has added fascination to English shrines and given them that new light that the poet brings; and he has linked his name indissolubly for all English-reading people with the Alhambra and Granada. It was because of his American birth that he wrote of Columbus, and perhaps some subtle imaginative sympathy always underlies the attraction of Spain, which is so marked, for American writers; but it was not unfitting that in his volumes of travel sketches the romantic after-glow of Spain should bloom in our western sky. By such works, more than by his English scenes, which will always seem an undivided part of English literature, he gave to our early literature a romantic horizon, though found in the history and legend of a far country, which it had hitherto lacked; and it is a striking phenomenon to find our writers, on whom the skies shut down round the shores of the New World, lifting up and opening out

Washington Irving, creator of Diedrich Knickerbocker.

these prospects into the picturesque distance of earth's space and the romantic remoteness of history, as if our literary genius were gone on a voyage of discovery. It shows the expansion of the national mind, the cessation of the exiguous exile of the colonial days, the beginning of our reunion with the nations of the world, which still goes on; and in this reunion, necessary for our oneness with man, literature led the way in these romantic affections of our first travelled man of letters, Irving, in whose wake the others followed.

The third point of contact that Irving's genius found with the larger life of his native land was in the realm of exploration. It was long now since the human tide had swept from the shores and inlets of the sea through the great forests and down the Appalachian slopes and broken in broad streams upon the open prairie; and the adventures were already threading the thin trails of the desert and high mountain solitudes. Here was the new and unused material of national experience, and to this day its riches have gone to waste, so far as literature is concerned. Irving, however, on his late return home, was struck with admiration at the vast progress made into the western wilderness; and he perceived its literary utility. A journey he made in the southwest gave him the near view he always needed to stimulate his descriptive power and to wake his eye for incident, and in his *Tour of the Prairies* he wrote down our best literary impression of the actual scene. It was no more than a traveller's journal, but it remains unique and interesting. Unfortunately his temperament was not such as to respond with creative power over this new world.

The theme did not pass beyond the realistic stage of treatment, just as in the case of Poe, who also saw the subject in his *Julius Rodman,* though Irving's handling far surpasses Poe's by virtue of his personality and the charm that radiates from it. Even less in *Astoria* and *Captain Bonneville* did Irving win the heart from this western mystery. The matter remained crude, fine in its facts, but unimaginative, unwakened, unbreathed-on by the spirit that giveth life. The Americanization of the wilderness was going on, but its literature was like that of the settlement of the coast in the earlier time, a mass of contemporary, rudely recorded experience and memory; the routes of the furtraders still led only to and from the Astor counting-room; Irving observed and noted, and made a book or two of the discovery, but his imagination was not of the sort to draw out the romance of it, for it had no element of the past, and the past was his mother muse.

It was the second writer who sprang up in the old city of New York, Cooper, who was to create in this broad field of national expansion, though in narrowly limited ways far from adequate to the vast sweep and variety of its immensely efficient life. Cooper subdued for literature the forest and the sea, and brought them into the mind's domain; but it was rather as parts of nature than as the theatre of men. The power of the scenery is most felt in his work, and prevails over the human element. It is a just perspective, nevertheless, and true to the emotion of the time and place.

He began very naturally. His first interest was in character, the personality that he immortalized as Harvey Birch, and in the events so near in memory to him and so close in locality, the Revolutionary scene as it was in Westchester; and out of these he made a historical tale that was the corner-stone of a great literary reputation. But it was not long before he went deeper into the sources of his own experience for theme and feeling, and his most characteristic work was a part of himself, and that self which had shared most widely in the novel and broad experience of American life. He had grown up under the shadow of the wild forest and in the sunlight of the lake and clearing, in close contact with nature all his boyish days; familiarity with the forest gave him at a later time of youth the open secret of the sea, so much the same are the ground tones of nature; and ceasing to be midshipman and lieutenant, he had, so to speak, made the rounds of the great elements in whose primitive simplicities he set his story. There was something of the artist in him, but

nothing of the poet, and he felt the impressiveness of nature, its opposition to society and law and man, as our common humanity feels them, not in Wordsworthian aloofness and spiritual interpretation, but as a real presence, an actuality, a thing of fact. His popular vogue in France was prepared for him by a pre-established harmony between the eloquent French dream of the life of nature and his narrative where nature still brooded as in a lake, so near was he to her presence; but what was to the foreigner a new Areadia only, an illusion of the heart, was to him a [familiar] world.

Being a novelist, he concentrated this vague emotion of the free majesty of nature in a character of fiction, Leather Stocking, one of the great original types of romanticism in the past century. Yet Leather Stocking, like Knickerbocker, is pure myth, though with a root in the soil too; an incarnation of the forest border, a blend of nature and man in a human form, thoroughly vitalized, impressive, emotional, an ideal figure. It is characteristic of our greater writers, even our humorists, to be nearer to the American idea than to anything concretely American. The infusion of grandeur—the word is not inappropriate—in Cooper's work is what gives it distinction, and most in its most imaginative portions. It is true that he invented the sea novel, as was not unnatural in view of his experience of our maritime life and of the great place of that life in our national activity and consciousness; and he used colonial, Revolutionary, and border history out of our stores to weave incident, plot, and scene; but it is not these things that make him national, but the American breath that fills his works; and where this is least, the scene grows mean, petty, awkward, inept, feeble; and where it is greatest, there the life is found, in *The Pathfinder, The Deerslayer, The Prairie.* He was abroad, like Irving, for many years, and gained thereby, perhaps through contrast and detachment merely, a truer conception and deeper admiration of democracy, its principles, aims, and energies; but he was national, when Irving was international; and if Irving, in his literary relation to his country, is rather thought of as an influence upon it, Cooper was its effluence, the American spirit in forest, sea, and man taking on form, feature, and emotion first in his world, sentimentalized, idealized, pictorial though it was. The best that literature achieves is a new dream; this was the first dream of American life, broad and various, in its great new solitudes of sea and land.

Irving and Cooper were the two writers of the first rank in our letters. Sharply contrasted in their careers as well as in character, and curiously overlapping in their experience and writings, neither of them was a true product of the city, or bound to it except in ephemeral ways. The one beloved, the other hated, their reputations were alike national. American literature, which was in no sense provincial, began with them. A third great name, which is as large in tradition, at least, is linked with theirs in the city's literary fame. Bryant was a New-Englander by birth and remained one in nature all his life, but his name lingers where he had his career, in the metropolis. It belongs to a city in which, of all the cities of the earth, nativity is the least seal of citizenship to appropriate justly the works of its foster-children; and Bryant illustrates, as a New-Yorker, its assimilation of the sons of all the nation. In the Niagara of life that forever pours into its vast human basin there has been a constant current from New England, important in the city's life and control. What Beecher was in religion, Bryant was in poetry, an infusion of highly liberalized moral power. Irving said there was nothing Puritanical in him, nor had he any sympathy with Puritanism; and Cooper hated the New England type, though he was pietistic to an uncommon degree. Between them they represented the temper of the New York community on both its worldly and evangelical side. Bryant, however, offers a sharp contrast to them, for he had precisely that depth of moral power that was his heritage from Puritanism, and marked in the next generation the literature of New England, setting it off from the literature of New York. Depth, penetration, intensity, all that religious fervor fosters and spirituality develops, was what Irving and Cooper could lay no claim to. In Bryant something of this, in an early, primitive, and simple form of liberalism, came into the city, though it was not naturalized there. So lonely is it, indeed, that it is almost impossible for the mind to identify Bryant the poet with Bryant the editor. He himself kept the two lives distinct, and his distance and coldness was the aloofness of the poet in him from the world about him.

It is hard in any case to localize Bryant, not merely in the city, but in America, because he is so elemental in his natural piety. That something Druidical that there is in his aspect sets him apart; he was a seer, or what we fancy a seer to be, in his verse, a priest of the holy affections of the heart in communion with nature's God, one whose point of view and attitude suggest the early ministration of adoring Magians, the intuition of Indian sages, or the meditations of Greek philosophers. A sensitive mind can hardly rid itself of this old world or early world impression in respect to Bryant. The hills and skies of Berkshire had roofed a temple for him, and the forest aisled it, and wherever he moved he was within the divine precincts. Eternity was always in the same room with him. It was this sense of grandeur in nature and man, the perpetual presence of a cosmic relation, that dignified his verse and made its large impression; even his little blue gentian has the atmosphere of the whole sky. He was a master of true style, as refined in its plainness as was Irving's in its grace. If he was not national in a comprehensive sense, he was national in the sense that something that went to the making of the nation went to the making of him; the New England stock which had spread into the west and veined the continent with its spirit as ore veins the

rock was of the same stuff as himself, and the rare manifestation of its fundamental religious feeling in his pure and uncovenanted poetry was the same as in Channing's universality. Present taste may forget his work for a time, but its old American- spirit has the lasting power of a horizon peak; from those uplands he came, and some of the songs sung there the nation will long carry in its heart. He was the last of the early triad of our greater writers, and his presence is still a memory in the city streets; but the city that was greater for his presence, as for that of Irving and Cooper who had passed away before him, is also greater for their memory.

Between the greater and the lesser gods of the city there is a broad gulf fixed. Irving, Cooper, and Bryant were on the American scale; they were national figures. There were almost none who could be described as second to them. Every metropolis, however, breeds its own race of local writers, like mites in a cheese, numerous and active, the literary coteries of their moment. To name one of them, there was Willis; he was gigantic in his contemporaneousness. He is shrunk now, as forgotten as a fashion-plate, though once the cynosure of the literary town. He was the man that Irving by his richer nature escaped being, the talented, clever, frivolous, sentimental, graceful artifice of a man, the town-gentleman of literature; he was the male counterpart of Fanny Fern and Grace Greenwood; he outlasted his vogue, like an old beau, and was the superannuated literary journalist. Yet in no other city was he so much at home as here, and in the memoirs of the town he would fill a picturesque and rightful place. A court would have embalmed him, but in a democracy his oblivion is scaled.

One or two other early names had a sad fortune in other ways. Drake and Halleck stand for our boyish precocity; death nipped the one trade sterilized the other; there is a mortuary suggestion in the memory of both. Halleck long survived, a fine outside of a man, with the ghost of a dead poet stalking about in him, a curious experience to those who met him, with his old-fashioned courtesy and the wonder of his unliterary survival. Of the elder generation these are the names that bring back the old times, Willis, Drake, and Halleck; and they all suggest the community in a more neighborly way than the national writers.

There was a culture in the old city, and a taste for letters such as grows up where there are educated men of the professions and a college to breed them. The slight influence of Columbia, however, and the main fact that it developed professional and technical schools instead of academic power, point to the controlling factor in the city's life, its preoccupation with practical and material interests. Literature was bound in such a modern community to be bottomed on commerce; whatever else it might be, it was first an article of trade to be used as news, circulated in magazines, sold in books. It has become, at present, largely an incident of advertising. New York was a great distributing centre, and editors, publishers, and writers multiplied exceedingly. The result was as inevitable here as in London or Paris, but the absence of a literary past and of a society of high-bred variety made a vast difference in the tone and in the product. Parnassus became a receding sentimental memory, fit for a child's wonder-book like Hawthorne's; but Bohemia was thronged, and its denizens grew like mushrooms in a cellar. There was, too, from the beginning, something bibulous and carnivorous in the current literary life; the salon did not flourish, but there was always a Bread-and-Cheese Club in the city, and indeed its literary legend from the days of Irving's youthful suppers, not excluding its greater names, might be interestingly and continuously told by a series of memories of its convivial haunts. The men who frequented them and kept each other in countenance were as mortal, for the most part, as Pfaff's, for instance, once the Mermaid of the town wits. Such resorts, too, are hot-houses for the development of clever lads; and literature suffered by the overproduction of small minds. When in the history of letters gregariousness begins, one may look out for mediocrity. Great writers have found themselves in exile, in prison, in solitudes of all sorts; and great books are especially written in the country. Literature, too, is naturally exogamous; it marries with the remote, the foreign, the strange, and requires to be fertilized from without; but Bohemia, shut in its own petty frivolities, breeds the race of those manikins of Manhattan whose fame Holmes gibed at as having reached Harlem. Open Griswold and find their works; open Poe's *Literati* and find their epitaphs; of such is the kingdom of the Bohemians the world over. Such a race is incidental to a metropolitan literature. Nor were they altogether inferior men; many of them led useful lives and won local eminence; some even achieved the honors of diplomacy. They contributed much to their own gayety, and enlivened life with mutual admiration and contempt. Poe stirred up the swarm considerably. But no satire embalmed them in amber, and they are forgotten even by their own successors.

The city grew to be, through these middle years of the century, an ever-increasing mart of literary trade. The people, with their schools and Sunday-schools and habits of home reading, were to be supplied with information and entertainment; and New York, like Philadelphia, became a great manufactory of books. The law of demand and supply, however, has a limited scope in literature; it can develop quantity, but not quality. Textbooks, encyclopedias, popular knowledge, travel, and story all spawned in great numbers; but the literature of creation and culture continued to be sparse. It might have been thought that the literature of amusement, at least, would have flourished,

and songs and plays have abounded; in fact, they did not exist except in the mediocre state. This infertility of the metropolis in the lasting forms of literature brings home to us the almost incredible famine of the time more sharply than even the tales that are told of the lack of expectation of any appreciation felt by the first great writers.

Irving's discovery that he could live by literature was a surprise to him; he had begun with an experiment rather than an ambition, and, having thus found his humor, he went on to make trial of sentiment, pathos, and romance. Cooper had no confidence, scarcely a hope, that an American novel would be accepted by his own countrymen. They had become so used to their lack of native productions as to mistake it for a permanent state. It was almost an accident that Cooper ever finished *The Spy,* and he did it much as the writer of a poem of classic rank to-day would complete it, in the scorn of circumstance and probably in ignorance of its reception.

The success of the greater writers was immediate and great; the city gave them dinners and has reared their statues, and was proud of them at the time in a truly civic way; but a cold obstruction of genius has set in ever since. The lesser writers approached them only on their feeblest side. Perhaps the bulk of emotional writing in every kind was of the sentimental sort. The men produced a good deal of it, but the women revelled and languished in it. "Ben Bolt," the popular concert-hall tune of its day, was a fair example of its masculine form; and such writers as Mrs. Osgood and the Cary sisters illustrate its feminine modes. Sentimentality is apt to seem very foolish to the next generation in its words, but in character it survives with a more realistic impression; and in Poe, in his relations to these literary women, one sees the contemporary type. He was mated with Willis as the dark with the sunny, and as misery with mirth. He enchanted the poetesses, and was enchanted, finding in each one a new lost *Lenore*. All his female figures, in their slightly varied monotone, *Annabel* and *Annie,* are in the realm of this sentimentality gone maudlin in him, as it had gone silly in others. It was most wholesome when it stayed nearest to nature and domestic life; but here, too, it was feeble and lachrymose. The breath of the civil war put an end to it for the time; but even that great passion left few traces of itself in our letters. The writings of Dickens favored sentimentality, and much more the poems of Mrs. Browning and the early verse of Tennyson. We had our "little Dickenses," but it is significant of the temperament of our literature that we had not even a "little" Thackeray. Just above this level there was here and there a cultivated author, reminiscent of sentiment in its purer forms—of Lamb and Irving, for example—of whose small number Curtis stands eminent for cheerfulness, intrinsic winningness, and unfailing grace. He was the last of the line that began with Irving, through which the literary history of the city can be traced as if in lineal descent. In him sentiment was what it should always be, a touch, not the element itself.

It is quite in the order of things that in a literature so purely romantic as our own has been in the greater writers, sentimentality should characterize those of lesser rank, for it naturally attends romanticism as an inferior satellite. It has all vanished now, and left *Lenore* and *Annie* and *Annabel* its lone survivors. We are a romantic and sentimental nation, as is well known, and we are also a nation of efficiency. The literary energies of the nation, apart from its genius, have been immense, in reality; they have gone almost wholly into popular education in its varied forms, and in no city upon such a scale as in New York. The magazines and the great dailies exhibit this activity in the most striking ways, both for variety and distinction; and on the side of literature, in the usual sense, from the days of the old *Mirror, Knickerbocker,* and *Democratic,* the growth has been steady, and has carried periodical writing to its height of popular efficiency both for compass and power. The multitude of writers in the service have been substantially occupied with the production of news in the broadest sense. The poem and the essay have been rather a thing conceded than demanded, and make a small part in the whole; but the news of the artistic, literary, and scientific worlds— fact, event, personality, theory, and performance—all this has been provided in great bulk. The writers strive to engage attention, to interest, and the matter of prime interest in such a city is the news of the various world. Even in the imaginative field something of the same sort is to be observed in the usual themes and motives. The popularity of the detective story, for example, and of Japanese or other foreign backgrounds, and of the novel of adventure; and the travel and animal sketches, and the like, have an element of news; and the entire popularization of knowledge belongs in the same region of interest.

Thought, reflection, meditation, except on political and social subjects, does not flourish; that brooding on life and experience out of which the greatest literature emerges has not been found, whatever the reason may be, and in fact it is rather a matter of original endowment than of the environment. The literary craft, however, if it lacked genius, has been characterized by facile and versatile talent, and its product has been very great in mass and of vast utility. In no other city is the power of the printed word more impressive. The effective literature of the city is in reality, and has long been, its great dailies; they are for the later time what the sermons of the old clergy were in New England, the mental sphere of the community; and in them are to be found all the elements of literature except the qualities that secure permanence.

Hamilton Wright Mabie on the youthful conduct of the Knickerbockers:

[Washington] Irving had loitered and dreamed on the water-front as a boy when he ought to have been at his books; and now, at the gateway of his career, the literary temperament turned him toward congenial fellowship rather than arduous study. There was plenty of material for comradeship in the town; and young men of spirit instinctively gathered about him. It was a very kindly and wholesome Bohemia in which they disported themselves in the halcyon days of a fleeting youth. They regarded themselves as "men about town" of the deepest dye, but it was a very innocent town in which they amused themselves, and they all bore honorable names in later and more serious years.

Henry Ogden, Henry Brevoort, James K. Paulding, John and Gouverneur Kemble, Peter and Washington Irving, the leaders of this vivacious company, were members of families who had long been foremost in the social life of the city, and they were far from being the "roistering blades" they fondly thought themselves to be. They were young men of spirit, generous tastes, and no little cultivation. They combined with great success devotion to literature and social activity. Irving speaks of himself as "a champion at the tea-parties," and the "nine worthies," or "lads of Kilkenny," as he called them, shone in the society of what was then known as "the gentler sex" no less than on the festive occasions when they celebrated their youth in private revels. . . .

Hamilton Wright Mabie, in The Writers of Knickerbocker New York, *The Grolier Club of the City of New York, 1912.*

Kendall B. Taft

SOURCE: Introduction to *Minor Knickerbockers,* American Book Company, 1947, pp. xliii-cx.

[*In the following excerpt, Taft provides a thoroughly documented examination of those Knickerbockers who succeeded the founders of the Group (Washington Irving, James Fenimore Cooper, and William Cullen Bryant), discussing their theories and standards as well as their own work as the principal literary critics and writers of early nineteenth-century America.*]

LITERARY THEORIES

In describing the contributions of the Knickerbocker writers to American literary thought, historians have tended to use such epithets as "timid," "insular," "moralistic," "genteel," "bourgeois," "uncritical," and "sterile."[1] Perhaps the vision of a cultural wasteland evoked by such terms is not without a basis in fact, but the picture, in certain important aspects, needs to be modified. although it is probably true that more and better literary criticism came out of New England—especially during its remarkable "flowering" in the late thirties, the forties, and the fifties[2]—New York's share in the intellectual development of the new nation should not therefore be denigrated.

Granting that there were few critical giants in New York during the Knickerbocker period, one may with some justice maintain that the literary criticism produced was more extensive, more varied, and—possibly—more influential than has commonly been admitted. In the matter of critical periodicals, alone, New York was not inferior to other centers of literary activity: between 1817 and 1840 there were at least twenty such publications established in the city,[3] and the more general magazines, such as the *Mirror* and the *Knickerbocker,* devoted much of their space to literary notices, book reviews, and critical articles. It is true that relatively few volumes of formal literary criticism (by American authors) were published in New York during the period, but the same generalization can be made, of course, for the country as a whole. For statements of critical theory, the student of our pre-Civil War literature must depend largely on periodicals, prefaces, satires, and remarks made in letters, public lectures, and recorded conversations.

Critical standards in Knickerbocker New York, as elsewhere in the United States, were of the most diverse kinds, coming, as they did, from many sources. On its lower levels, indeed, Knickerbocker criticism may be said to have had no standards. This was particularly true in the first quarter of the nineteenth century, when critical or even semi-critical periodicals were relatively scarce and when the literature itself was striving, somewhat painfully, to outgrow its adolescence. In these earlier years there were occasional attempts on the part of reviewers—and others—to render judgments based on some kind of general principles, but such attempts were often confused or puerile, or both. In these earlier years, also, what may be called pseudo-criticism flourished—literary notices and book reviews prompted almost solely by feelings of friendship or of enmity for the author. The feelings might be either personal[4] or political;[5] whatever the basis, the "criticism" produced was likely to be a nonsensical farrago, consisting of fulsome flattery, at one extreme, and virulent abuse, at the other. This kind of reviewing, it hardly needs to be said, had not disappeared by 1825, or by 1835, for that matter. By the thirties, however, the better periodicals were frowning upon the practice,[6] and reviewing based on at least elementary critical standards tended to be the rule, rather than the exception.

It may be desirable at this point to survey, briefly, the various attitudes toward the purpose of literature—and, incidentally, toward the function of criticism—expressed by the Knickerbocker writers who did concern themselves with critical standards. One does not have to read between the lines to detect several steps or stages in the Knickerbocker approach to critical theory.

As might be expected, the principle of moral utility had a prominent place among the dicta of the earlier critics. That religious, moral, and economic objections to the arts persisted well into the nineteenth century is, of course, a truism. It is not surprising, then, that advocates of literature, and of the arts generally, often thought it necessary to take a defensive or a conciliatory attitude. Typical of this attitude are some remarks made by Gulian C. Verplanck, in 1824, at the opening of the tenth exhibition of the American Academy of the Fine Arts:

> Among a people situated like this, to whom comparative freedom from those more pressing cares of life, which weigh heavily and incessantly upon the most numerous class of society in many other countries, leaves much leisure, is it not wise, is it not prudent, is it not consonant to the nature of man, to provide for him some occupations and objects, far lower, we willingly admit, than the exercise of his religious and social duties and affections, but as far above the vicious gratification of grosser appetites—something, that, while it engages and employs his faculties in innocence, at the same time invigorates his mind, and enlarges his conceptions?

> Whatever utility in this regard may be justly claimed for elegant literature, or speculative science, may, on the same grounds, be ascribed to taste and knowledge in the fine arts. If, however, some stern and severe moralist should yet doubt whether society derives any real benefit from either source, we may at least ask him, if the time thus employed is not well redeemed from coarse sensuality, from the calumnies and slanders of malicious insolence, from ostentatious luxury, from the dull, dull round of fashionable amusement, or from the feverish strife of personal ambition?[7]

And in reviewing Catharine Sedgwick's *Redwood,* in the same year, George Pope Morris reflected a similar attitude when he said:

> . . . this excellent novel receives increased value from the pure spirit of morality which breathes through every page. She [the author] places before us our blessed religion, in her most winning garb. . . . The story displays the permanent pleasures of morality, and the inevitable degradation of vice.[8]

Eleven years later, the editors of the *Mirror* were much pleased to find their "own opinion as to the utility of fictitious writings" confirmed by the Reverend Sharon Turner, whose *Sacred History of the World* contained such observations as:

The peculiar susceptibility of the young mind to poetry, to works of felling, to imaginative narrations, and to reading or hearing of romantic incidents, or of supernatural fictions, is striking; and this is so natural and so universal . . . that we cannot err in presuming that it is an effect which was intended to take place. . . . My belief is, that all romantic fiction, which does not actually and purposely paint and praise vice and vicious characters, and seek to make them attractive or imitated, acts advantageously on the mind, and especially on the well-educated spirit, and most certainly adds to the happiness of life.[9]

The ideas expressed by Verplanck, Morris, and Turner are duplicated throughout the period in many reviews, articles, and books. So often are they duplicated, in fact, that they give a moralistic tinge to the whole body of Knickerbocker criticism. It would be fruitless to argue that the New York critics did not share in the literary gentility[10] common to the time, but it may be suggested that this was precisely the attitude forced upon them by the religio-moral objections already mentioned. Before "profane" literature could be criticized from any artistic viewpoint, it had to be granted the right to exist. Hence the insistence of authors, editors, and critics upon the moral value of literature. Hence their frequent—and, one is tempted to add, shrewdly calculated—remarks on poetry, fiction, and drama as valuable adjuncts to the "pure spirit of morality" and to "our blessed religion."[11]

Related to the principle of moral utility is the notion (it can hardly be called a principle) that the excellence of a work of art depends upon the "moral character" of its creator. A few of the Knickerbocker critics made this notion an article of their literary faith,[12] but others dismissed it as a fallacy long since exploded.[13] William Cox expressed a fairly general attitude on this question when he objected to having "the obloquy attached to Byron as a man . . . most unjustly brought to bear upon his works, whenever the latter did not, in themselves, furnish matter sufficient for vindictive censure."[14]

Also akin to the principle of moral utility is the doctrine of the social responsibility of the artist. As the New York critics expounded this doctrine, it had one major implication: since literature may influence the thoughts and the conduct of many readers, it is the obligation of the writer to express—and of course to exemplify—the "highest principles" of religion, morality, patriotism, and so on. "Literature," said one writer, " . . . is perhaps the most powerful of agents upon human character. . . . It most exalts and purifies; or corrupts and destroys. Hence, the importance of the ingredients and complexion of books, particularly the popular or favourite species such as tales and romances."[15] The same idea is implicit in a comment made by the anonymous reviewer of a volume of Samuel Wood-

worth's verse: "It is exactly what *American* poetry always ought to be—patriotic, moral, chaste, and republican."[16] And it is explicit in Verplanck's statement:

> The author or artist who has the power of pleasing, has committed to his charge a vast control over the tastes, feelings, and sentiments of all within his reach. But he is himself re-acted upon by those whom he influences. He that hopes to please must accommodate his talent to the tastes and habits of those whom he addresses.[17]

Deferent though the New York writers were to the readymade principle of moral utility and its corollaries, they were, in general, much more interested in other aspects of literature. Although they frequently gave homage to the idea of its moral value, they paid more attention to its other values—amusement, escape, instruction,[18] and artistry. In placing emphasis on these other values, they distinguished themselves from their New England contemporaries, whose main critical concern was likely to be either ethical or philosophical.[19]

Shortly before he came to New York as an associate editor of the *Mirror,* N. P. Willis published some hints to writers for periodicals. "Do not be grave," he said. "It is one of the great faults of American magazine writers. Periodical readers expect to be amused, and would exchange all the dignity of a number for a witticism."[20] Willis's avowal of amusement as a legitimate function of literature was echoed frequently by other New York writers. "I have seen enough of the world, and of the people of the world," remarked Paulding, "to know that, beautiful as wisdom is, if she would only sometimes condescend to smile, she would be irresistible."[21] The pages of the *Mirror* and the *Knickerbocker* were always open to amusing verse, sketches, tales, and articles, and the editors of these most representative of New York periodicals consistently defended the value of "light reading."[22] The Knickerbocker love of social amusement, of gaiety and conviviality, has already been noted;[23] it was only natural that something of the same spirit should appear in the attitude toward literature. Nor was it especially remarkable that many of the local writers should take a somewhat self-conscious delight in the "literature of pleasure . . . at a time when, Lowell said, all New England was a pulpit."[24]

On the possibilities of literature as escape, the New York writers were almost unanimous in agreement. One of the chief values of good literature, said Verplanck, is that it "emancipates the soul from the bondage of the world, lifting it above the desires, the cares, the meanness, and the follies of the present."[25] According to Samuel Woodworth, "this tangible, physical world, with a few exceptions, is a miserable place. . . . But the world of mind, of fancy, of imagination, of invention, oh, that is truly delightful!"[26] Even Halleck, who jeered at many of the current sentimentalities, declared that

> . . . the weary heart can find repose
> From its own pains in fiction's joys or woes.[27]

William Cox epitomized a general point of view when he wrote:

> My blessing on books! the quietest of friends, the most unobtrusive of companions; the healthy man's enjoyment, and the sick man's solace! When all goes well and merrily they are a pleasure—when it is otherwise, a consolation. Better than the physician can they "minister to a mind diseased"; and if they cannot "pluck from the memory a rooted sorrow," they are at least "a sweet oblivious antidote" to a thousand petty cares and small vexations, that might fret and irritate—and then corrode and fester in many minds, were it not for the sweet companionship of books![28]

Although they admitted the potentialities of literature as an escape from the dullness and vexations of everyday life, the Knickerbocker writers also recognized that certain kinds of literary expression might have a very immediate, practical value. The literature of politics, of commerce, of theology, of history, of science, of manual instruction—all these and other types of instructive writing were read, reviewed, and admired. Most of the Knickerbocker writers commented at one time or another on the pre-eminently "practical genius" of New York City.[29] When Willis came down from Boston, in 1831, he was impressed by the fact that "the one broad and long picture stamped upon the face of every street, creature, and countenance" in New York was *"gain."* And yet he was "agreeably disappointed" to discover that the mercantile society of the city possessed many cultured men and an equal number of charming, accomplished women. "Every day," he said, "I have stumbled . . . upon some self-cultivated and unsuspected scholar, with whom a book was a topic to be mentioned in a suppressed tone, but still a topic well understood and well talked upon."[30] Lecture courses were popular in the city throughout the Knickerbocker period,[31] and other efforts toward self-improvement were encouraged. In such an environment it was to be expected that the literature of practical knowledge would thrive. As early as 1817, Paulding observed this tendency, and remarked: "Aided by the vast magazine of knowledge contained in books accessible to every one at this present time, the aspiring genius has ample means and opportunities for self-cultivation, the best of all possible cultivation."[32]

It was toward problems of artistry, however, that the Knickerbocker writers—especially those who ventured into the field of criticism—directed their most frequent remarks. That much of their criticism was crude, stum-

bling, and, from the standpoint of the twentieth century, jejune, does not alter the main fact: the New York writers were more interested in the *art* of literature than in (what to them were) its secondary or incidental characteristics. This does not mean that they thought of literature—that is, of *belles-lettres*—as something divorced from life.[33] Nor does it mean that there were no dissenting voices among them; there was Cooper, for instance, who used the novel mainly as a medium for social criticism and apparently believed that literary art was less important than a "message."[34] It is of considerable significance that few of Cooper's New York contemporaries understood his intention or agreed with his thesis.[35] As we have seen, the Knickerbocker critics sometimes raised the questions: What morally useful end does this work serve? Does it inculcate the "highest principles of truth and virtue"? Is it, perhaps, designed merely to "amuse an idle hour"? Or does it convey some form of useful knowledge? But far more often they asked: How well, artistically, has the author performed his task? Their answers to this last question reflect a variety of critical standards.[36]

Probably the most common critical attitude was one inherited from the eighteenth century. Criticism should be judicial: an author's excellencies and defects should be weighed, and if the merits exceed the faults, the work may be pronounced good.[37] Many of the Knickerbocker critics agreed with Addison, however, in believing that more attention should be given to excellencies than to defects. Writing an article on criticism in 1831, Theodore S. Fay approvingly quoted Addison's statement:

> "A true critic ought to dwell rather upon excellencies than imperfections, to discover the concealed beauties of a writer, and communicate to the world such things as are worth their observation. The most exquisite words, and finest strokes of an author, are those which very often appear the most doubtful and exceptionable to a man who wants a relish for polite learning; and they are these, which a sour undistinguishing critic generally attacks with the greatest violence."[38]

A number of years later, C. F. Hoffman expressed very much the same idea when he remarked: "That criticism is most true which rather *seeks* the good than the evil, albeit not to shun our defects or to deny them where they exist. A book, like a man, should be judged by its goodness rather than its badness, unless the latter predominate, when it must soon condemn itself."[39] It was Hoffman, also, who commented on an inherent weakness of judicial—or, indeed, of any other—criticism as practiced in America during the early nineteenth century.

> The standard of criticism adopted in this country [he said], is, for the most part, equally unjust, and

incorrect. Our criticism is comparative, not absolute! We praise a book, because we fancy that it bears some faint resemblance to some other book be praised in London—for a similar reason we condemn another—and we betide the author, whose book we can compare to nothing.[40]

Hoffman did not bother to distinguish carefully between absolute and comparative criticism, nor did he suggest ways in which absolute standards might be achieved.[41] But Edward S. Gould,[42] a contemporary of Hoffman's, was more explicit. He not only indicated some of the principles upon which a competent judicial critic should proceed, but gave an example of "the perfection to which [such] criticism may attain." According to Gould:

[Our critics] *evince* no interest in the welfare of our literature, by expending time or talent in its revision. Their criticisms are, for the most part, *superficial* in every particular. They very seldom descend to the *analysis* of merit and demerit, in detail. They give no *reasons* why this is pronounced excellent; or that, execrable. They deal chiefly in general terms, and hyperbole; seize some one prominent feature, and make that the criterion for their verdict; and, by means of extracts, fill up a large space with the sentiments of the author, which should be occupied by their own. . . . But . . . it is still incontrovertibly true, that criticism is itself a high department of literature, and capable of displaying a degree of intellectual power equal to almost any kind of writing whatever. Johnson's Review of Milton may, perhaps, be cited as a proof of the perfection to which criticism may attain, and of the talent it may embody. It is an illustrious specimen of impartial analysis both of the defects and the beauties of an author; and it transmits to the reader in distant ages the privilege of studying that great master of verse with the comprehensive intelligence and the disciplined judgment of Johnson's gigantick mind.[43]

Gould gives a none too flattering account of American critical writing in 1836,[44] but his article—with its emphasis on a reasoned "analysis of merit and demerit" and its reference to the "comprehensive intelligence" and "disciplined judgment" of Johnson—exhibits his admiration for the neo-classical ideal of judicial criticism. And, despite Gould's strictures, it is clear that many of his New York contemporaries shared this admiration.[45] Even when they condemned the social and political morality of the English neo-classicists, some of the Knickerbocker writers were still able to admire their literary and critical ability.[46] In any event, and whatever its immediate background in British literary culture,[47] much of the criticism published in New York during the Knickerbocker period may be described as judicial criticism.

Some of the Knickerbockers, however, had small use for measured judgments of writers and literature. Dis-

trusting the analytical methods of traditional criticism, they were inclined to rely more on "feeling" than on intellectual appraisal; to them, the emotional effect produced was more important than the instrument used. Like their more judicial compeers, they were concerned with problems of artistry, but in a less precise way. In short, their criticism was subjective, impressionistic, and appreciative.

This kind of criticism appeared with increasing frequency in the thirties and forties, although it was not altogether lacking in the earlier part of the period. Washington Irving, Professor Pochmann tells us, "was, by and large, a sympathetic impressionist before impressionism became popular."[48] Appreciative criticism as practiced by the English romanticists was slow to gain a wide audience in this country,[49] but such writers as Lamb, Hazlitt, and DeQuincey had individual admirers here and there, and, more important still, romanticism was "in the air" in America well before 1830. It was but a step from political and religious liberalism to literary individualism:[50] the practice of a criticism based on personal tastes, feelings, and reactions was certain to attract some of the New York writers who had grown to maturity in the age of Byron and Shelley.

"The volume before us," said a reviewer of George Hill's *The Ruins of Athens,* "might have been better. There are points obviously open to improvement, a few thoughts which should have been omitted, others capable of enlargement, and, in one or two instances, imitations . . . which are injudicious, and may provoke the wrath of the stop-watch people; but there are also numerous passages of fervid fancy and graceful simple feeling, which, we trust, will not be overlooked by the reading public."[51]

When the reviewer made these comments, he was not only speaking to a sentimental generation—although he was obviously doing that. He was also speaking for himself. He was saying, in effect: "I like this book of verse. Even though judicial critics may not approve, it appeals to my sensibilities, and you—the reader—will probably feel the same way about it." This is not a lofty critical standard, perhaps, but it was from some such assumption as this that the great bulk of early subjective criticism proceeded. It offered a convenient formula for the criticism of romance, especially of sentimental romance, and it was bound to appeal to those writers who shrank from the formalities of judicial analysis.

Of the minor Knickerbockers, the most successful practitioners of impressionism were Willis, Cox, and Fay. To the pages of his *American Monthly Magazine* (1829-31) Willis contributed numerous appreciative essays on books and authors,[52] and his later literary comments were of the same general variety.[53] A fairly typical

Willis review begins: "We love this rambling, familiar gossip. It is the undress of the mind. There are few people who possess the talent of graceful trifling, either in writing or conversation. Study may make anything but this. It is like *naïveté* in character,—nature let alone."[54] And his attitude toward the purpose of criticism is rather clearly indicated in this statement: "For myself, I am free to confess I am one of those who like to take the first taste of an author in a good review. I look upon the reviewer as a sensible friend, who came before me to the feast, and recommends me the dish that has most pleased him."[55] William Cox, although endowed with subtler literary perceptions than Willis, had a similar attitude toward criticism.[56] His own critical essays, usually devoted to giving his personal reactions to the books he had read or the plays he had seen, were often warmly appreciative.[57] On reading these essays, one of Cox's New York contemporaries was reminded of "the poetical eloquence of Hazlitt, and the quaint humour and eccentric tastes of Charles Lamb."[58] Theodore Fay, a slighter figure than either Willis or Cox, was inclined at times to be judicial in his estimates of literature,[59] but in some of his critical writing he made use of the impressionist technique. This tendency reveals itself, for instance, when he says, in a review of Irving's *Alhambra:* "The reader must admire the works of Washington Irving as the perfection of refined and elegant writing. He will scarce detect a word out of place—a deficiency, or a superfluity. He will find imagination chastened by taste—humor purified by delicacy, and blended with pathos. In perusing them, many will have smiles on their lips and tears in their eyes."[60]

In the latter part of the period critical theory and practice show signs of greater maturity, especially in the approach to problems of artistry. Influenced, perhaps, by the German theories of expressionistic criticism through their reading of Coleridge and Carlyle,[61] certain New York writers began to develop a "new" critical philosophy. An inclination to discard the "rules" of the older judicial criticism was paralleled by a growing distrust of mere impressionism. There were increasingly frequent demands for a complete criticism—a criticism that would take into account not only the outward form of a literary work but also its inner significance, its motivation, its "essence." This quest is adumbrated, in 1835, in a *Mirror* editorial on the subject of criticism. "The critic who reviews a book," said the writer, " . . . should first discover what the author proposed and intended to perform, and then examine how he has fulfilled his undertaking. He may indeed go farther than this; he may discuss the question whether that which the author undertook to do was right and proper to be done; but nothing can be more unjust, or more absurd, than to censure the non-performance of what was never undertaken; to find fault because a certain purpose is not effected, which formed no part of the author's plan and for which he has made no

effort."[62] Only a few years later, in an article on the poetry of Charles Sprague, there appeared a more cogent and far more complete statement of the need for an inclusive criticism. The writer, looking for a guide to a just appraisal of the poet's work, found it in Carlyle's statement of "the principles of German criticism":

> Carlyle in his Essay on German literature, gives a clear sketch of the principles of German criticism. "It is not," says he, "a question concerning the qualities of diction, the coherence of metaphors, the fitness of sentiments, the general logical truth, in a work of art, as it was some half century ago, among most criticks; neither is it a question mainly of a psychological sort, to be answered by discovering, and delineating the peculiar nature of the poet from his poetry, as is usual with the best of our own criticks at present; but it is, not indeed exclusively, but inclusively of these two other questions, properly and ultimately, a question of the *essence and peculiar life of the poetry itself.* The first of these questions, as we see it answered, for instance, in the criticisms of Johnson and Kames, relates, strictly speaking, to the garment of poetry; the second, indeed, to its *body* and material existence, a much higher point; but only the last to its *soul* and spiritual existence, by which alone, can the body in its movements and phases be informed with significance and rational life."

> This is true criticism. It gives the author his just deserts. It considers, rather the ideas, than the words in which they are clothed; it examines, more the correctness of opinion, the originality and brilliancy of thought, the beauty of sentiment, than the coherence of metaphor, or even the sequence of logick. Such a critick must possess the *"mens divinier,"* not merely a knowledge of the rules of Kames and Blair—he must have a kindred feeling with the poet—he must be a poet, and not a cold calculating measurer and inspector of words and sentences.[63]

The drift toward a more comprehensive criticism was manifested, also, in the increasing tendency to preface articles and reviews with a summary statement of the principles by which the work or the writer is being criticized. By the end of our period, it was no longer safe for a critic to assume that he could "express his function as a mere *attitude.*"[64] Thus we find James Lawson,[65] in an article on the poetry of Halleck, specifying his critical point of view: "To estimate the poet justly, it is necessary to consider, first, the quality of his mind, and the depth of its resources; second, his enthusiasm, his invention, and truth in delineation; and lastly, the language in which he expresses his thoughts and emotions. In these, so essential to the great poet, few indeed have reached a high degree of excellence."[66] Thus, too, we find Charles Fenno Hoffman writing, in a spirited defense of Scott's poetry: "If creative power be the first great element of poetry, and if such thorough mastery of the reader that he shall believe he is reading a mere animated description of things that belong to all poets in common, be the highest test of skill, 'The Lady of the Lake' is one of the most perfect poems ever written. For it is a creation which every one reads as an actual narrative done into verse, which verse is constantly calling up poetic feeling without the reader's ever dreaming that it is poetry itself."[67] One does not have to agree with these opinions to recognize that they are more original, more thoughtful, and more mature than the critical dicta current in the first two or three decades of the century.

About the various forms of literature the Knickerbockers, collectively, had a great deal to say.[68] It will be possible here to give only a brief resumé of their theories of poetry, drama, and fiction.

In their thinking about poetry, as in their general literary thought, they were of course influenced by many forces. At the beginning of the period, English neo-classical attitudes toward the form and function of poetry were prevalent, although undergoing modification through the precept and example of certain pre-romantic poets and aestheticians.[69] In the middle years (*ca.* 1820-35), the poetry of Scott, Byron, Campbell, and, to a lesser extent, Moore, furnished touchstones for evaluating verse. The latter part of the period was marked by the broadening influence of such poets, prosodists, and critics as Coleridge, Wordsworth, and Carlyle.[70] These influences from England were supplemented by those that worked from within—the influences that either had a strong infusion of native opinion or were distinctively American.

Paulding and Woodworth, both born well before the close of the eighteenth century, derived many of their ideas about poetry from neo-classical theory. Paulding, especially, felt at home among the champions of good sense and of the heroic couplet. He was no doubt thinking of the clarity of Pope and Goldsmith, whom he admired above all "modern" poets, when he said: "The basis of all good poetry as well as all good writing is common sense."[71] He expanded this notion somewhat in two other statements: (1) "One of the best tests of poetry is to turn it into plain prose, and see how it looks in its nakedness. At present, it is a mere fine lady dressed up in such a profusion of incongruous ornaments, that it is impossible to tell what are her real proportions, or what nature has actually done for her."[72] (2) "I believe the perfection of a work of genius to consist in the symmetry and harmony of its parts, the purity of the design, the chastity of its embellishments, and the nice judgment with which the whole is put together."[73] Paulding believed, clearly enough, that all the other possible qualities of poetry should be subordinate to clarity; order, and design. Woodworth, unlike Paulding, admired Byron and such sentimental poets as Thomas Campbell and James Montgomery,[74] but his

theory of poetry was distinctly neo-classical. In poetry, he said, "genius without method, is like passion without reason, or feeling without judgment—for ever running into wild and extravagant vagaries—exciting admiration without imparting pleasure."[75] Taking Edward Bysshe's *Art of Poetry* (1702) as a model,[76] he once designed a "Poet's Prompter," in the introduction to which appear such remarks as "the feet of English verse . . . are distinguished by *accent* instead of *quantity* (though sometimes by *both*)," and "every perfect English verse, whether it be long or short, must belong to one or the other of two *accentual scales*—corresponding to the *iambic* and the *anapaestic* of the ancients."[77] The examples included in the "Prompter" were chosen with two main objects in view: "That every couplet, or triplet, should exhibit examples of *perfect rhymes*"; and "that every sentiment, allusion, simile, description, &c. should tend to improve the intellect, refine the taste, and amend the heart."[78] Woodworth, although not untouched by the new romantic impulses, in his poetic theory was obviously an inheritor of eighteenth century "sense and sensibility."

Neither Halleck nor Drake made any extended comments on the theory of poetry, although both were intensely interested in the art of the poet, and they often discussed verse and versification in the years of their close companionship.[79] We know that Drake admired Coleridge and Keats long before their poetry was generally popular in America,[80] that he had a high regard for the poetic function,[81] and that he was interested in experimenting with a variety of techniques and subject matters.[82] Halleck indicated his fundamental attitude on poetic theory when he said that "expression" was, in his opinion, "the *attribute* of genius, especially in poetry, 'the vision and the faculty divine.'"[83] N. F. Adkins, in commenting on this attitude, gives a corroboratory anecdote:

> It was apparently a poet's ability to emotionalize the fact—to transform events by the subtle power of the imagination—which Halleck regarded as the supreme test of the art. "'They are still trying to define poetry,'" Halleck once remarked in a conversation with Bayard Taylor. "'It can be explained in a word: it's simply the opposite of reason! Reason is based on fact; and fact is not poetry. A poet has nothing to do with the facts of things, for he must continually deny them!' 'Will you give me an illustration?'" asked Taylor. "'Certainly,'" replied the poet, "and then quoted, not from Campbell, or Byron, or Moore, as I was expecting, but these lines from Wordsworth's 'Song at the Feast of Brougham Castle':
>
> Armor, rusting on his walls
> On the blood of Clifford calls;—
> 'Quell the Scot!' exclaims the lance—
> 'Bear me to the heart of France!'
> Is the longing of the shield.

"'There!' Halleck exclaimed: 'was ever anything more irrational than the lance exclaiming and the shield longing?—but what poetry it is!'"[84]

"Halleck has not adopted a poetic creed, and worshipped by it," said James Lawson; "he never seeks to explore the hidden sources of thought or action, but seems contented with the effect."[85] But Bryant recognized that Halleck was "familiar with those general rules and principles which are the basis of metrical harmony. . . . You will find in no poet, passages which flow with a more sweet and liquid smoothness; but he knows very well that to make this smoothness perceived, and to prevent it from degenerating into monotony, occasional roughnesses must be interposed."[86]

Willis, whose tastes in literature though wide-ranging were somewhat precious, thought that poetry should be the expression of a sensitive nature. He admired a fine turn of phrase, an unusual figure of speech, a delicately conveyed sentiment.[87] Fairly early in his writing career, he gave this impressionistic definition of poetry: "The poet hears music in common sounds, and sees loveliness by the wayside. There is not a change in the sky, nor a noise of the water, nor a sweet human voice, which does not bring him pleasure. He sees all the light and hears all the music about him— and this is poetry.[88] As he grew older, his attitude did not change greatly. H. A. Beers has pointed out that Willis's mind was not conspicuously analytical, that "his bright fancy played over the surface of things."[89] Although he often remarked on those poems and poets that pleased him,[90] he seldom did more than remark. His definition of poetry, given above, may be set beside his much later comment: "In the daily life of every human being, I am inclined to think, there is a background of poetry, . . . something *around us beyond what is seen and saleable*."[91] He was content, in general, to practice versification without working out a theory either of poetry or of prosody.[92]

Charles Fenno Hoffman was less nebulous. We have already noted his observation on the creative power and technical skill displayed in Scott's poetry.[93] In various other essays and reviews he made clear his conviction that poetry should have powerful emotional appeal, that it should create what Coleridge called "that willing suspension of disbelief for the moment, which constitutes poetic faith.[94] In a review of Moore's *Life of Byron*, Hoffman made a strong plea for greater originality and enthusiasm in poetry. "Why did not the revolution in France," he asked, " . . . produce one [poem] that will live? Why has not the glorious struggle of Poland called forth one decent ode?" The answer, he thought, was not difficult to find. "Why? Because one-half of the young disciples of the Nine, in the world, are pre-engaged in recording their own love-lorn miseries in rhyme, and the other half scoffing at

every thing like enthusiasm; because there is no precedent for such a thing."[95] An equally strong statement— probably Hoffman's best statement of poetic theory— appeared in his brief analysis of contemporary New England verse:

> A nicety of execution, a carefulness of arrangement, and a very decided moral aim and tone are demanded by the social requisitions of that section of the land. And in such qualities we are seldom disappointed by the acknowledged poets of New England. On the other hand, they are deficient, to our thinking, in naturalness and spontaneity. Art predominates in their verse. There is more of intellectual force than of poetic emotion; and the play of fancy shows itself rather in ingenuity of expression than warmth of imagery. Their poetry, instead of being the uncontrollable utterance of an o'ermastering sentiment—the lyric gush of feelings—appears to be calmly and thoughtfully elaborated. An over-consciousness is evident.[96]

William Cox was an avid reader of verse, although he rarely wrote it. To him, the imaginative, romantic elements of poetry were the most important. "Take the spiritual from poetry," he remarked on one occasion, "and what do you leave but a mass of stagnant words— a few sensual, satirical, or evanescent rhymes? It would be literally divorcing soul and body."[97] He thought that England and America, being "the greatest manufacturing and commercial nations in the world," should cherish their superstitions and traditions, and should "encourage a love for the romantic in poetry, as the best counterbalance to the flat and practical modes of thinking likely to be generated by their triumphs in mechanics."[98] He commented, now and then, on specific matters of poetic practice, as, for example, when he called attention to Coleridge's skillful use of verbal repetition in "The Ancient Mariner,"[99] and when he deplored the absurdity of the senseless imitator—"a small mind playing the egotist, and describing the agony of its feelings at the same time that it is hunting for a rhyme, and seeing that the line contains the requisite number of syllables."[100] But Cox was, professedly, no more than an amateur in poetry; his remarks are significant only inasmuch as they reflect the opinions of a professional journalist and critic.

Like their British contemporaries, the Knickerbocker poets used a wide variety of metres and stanza forms. An early preference for the heroic couplet[101] soon gave way to all sorts of experimentation with metrical and stanzaic patterns. The magazine verse of the period exhibits an unusual range of forms, as does the work of individual poets when collected between covers. Miltonic and Wordsworthian blank verse contends with lyric forms out of Moore and Campbell, octosyllabics *à la* Scott, Spenserians and ottava rimas in the manner of *Childe Harold, Don Juan,* and *Beppo,* and ballad metres from any number of sources.[102] The versification of the New York poets was imitative, to be sure, but where in America was it not? Throughout the period, there was much emphasis upon "regularity" of measure and "perfection" of rhyme.[103] When, in "The Field of the Grounded Arms," Halleck tried a "daring" experiment in the unrhymed Horatian stanza, he was severely chastised by most of the reviewers.[104] Neither they nor readers generally were yet ready for anything that approached free verse.[105] Critical prejudice against the sonnet, also, was fairly general until about 1835, but this prejudice[106] did not keep poets from using the form, and by 1840 or so it was well established.[107] The New York writers made no remarkable contributions to American prosody, perhaps,[108] but, despite their imitative tendency and for all their limitations, they fostered a healthy experimental attitude toward verse form.[109]

On theatrical performances, the New York newspapers and magazines published literally hundreds of critiques made up mostly of remarks on scenery, costume, actors, and acting. But relatively little critical writing was directed at the drama as a literary form. Even Shakespeare was usually discussed as a dramatic poet, with emphasis on his poetry rather than on his dramatic artistry. Occasionally, however, there were articles on plays and playwrights—articles with a backward look toward the Elizabethan and, more rarely, the Restoration dramatists.[110] Occasionally, also, a native play was commented on, and the playwright commended for his skill in characterization and dialogue. A review in the *Mirror* of Custis's *Pocahontas* (1830) is exceptional in that it analyzes the play in some detail, and calls attention to its bombastic speeches, lack of probability, bad grammar, and poorly defined characters.[111] Of the Knickerbocker critics, William Cox was almost the only one who was consistently interested in the drama as literature, and even his interest was as much theatrical as literary.[112] The dearth of good dramatic criticism during the Knickerbocker period may be ascribed largely to the fact that the native drama had not yet established itself as a respectable literary form.[113]

Fiction fared considerably better. By 1820, though the pulpit still denounced and stern moralists still grumbled, the novel had become an accepted fact in American cultural life.[114] Any lingering hope the objectors may have had that their warnings would be heeded was dispelled by the spectacular rise to popularity of Scott's novels, and, a little later, of Cooper's.[115]

The work of these novelists was a godsend to critics, for it provided them at once with a point of departure and a standard of comparison. Writing in 1836, Edward S. Gould had little reason to fear contradiction when he asserted that "Walter Scott, by universal consent, is the monarch and master of modern fiction," or when he ranked Cooper first among American novel-

ists.[116] William Cox, in 1833, noted that Scott, "like the Bay of Naples," had been "a standard for small comparisons," and that the advocates of inferior novelists had been "endeavoring to exalt their particular favorites by insinuating that 'the northern magician would have to look well to his laurels,' or that 'the great unknown must be content to bear a rival near his throne.'" Such comparisons were impertinent, he thought, for had not Scott "done more for literature, both in quantity and quality, with the single exception of Shakespeare, than any man since Noah left the ark?"[117] The writer answered this question to his own satisfaction, if not to ours; but the point is, of course, that Cox, a fairly discerning minor critic, was expressing a general attitude. Not until the early forties, when Dickens' fame shone bright, was Scott's prestige seriously threatened. Among the New York writers at least, Cooper's pre-eminence was almost equally secure.[118] Halleck called Cooper "the colonel of the [American] literary regiment,"[119] and Lewis Gaylord Clark, in writing to Francis Parkman, implied that he was giving the highest praise when he said "the closing scene [of your sketch] is worthy of Cooper's pen."[120]

Although some of the Knickerbocker writers felt that novels—especially "popular" novels—merited scant critical attention,[121] others were convinced that the novel, "that species of invention which alone could body forth the infinite variety of modern society," was not only an important literary form but one requiring "all that the mind has ever possessed of original power."[122] At any rate, novels were frequently and copiously reviewed, with regard to their artistry as well as their moral purpose and their Americanism.[123]

There was, as might be supposed, no general agreement on the question of style. To judge from a cross-section of critical opinion, it would appear that the Knickerbocker writers thought the style of fiction should be simple but not too plain,[124] dignified but not unwieldy,[125] fresh and original but not eccentric.[126] Paulding, in 1817, objected to the extravagant, inflated style of writing then current,[127] and he was supported in this objection by various later writers.[128] "Words, phrases and paragraphs, and even pages, wholly superfluous, swell the magnitude of many modern works," said one anonymous critic.[129] T. S. Fay deplored the constant use of trite figures of speech,[130] and William Cox spoke scornfully of the novelist Bulwer's tendency to write "page after page of description, filled with dashes, italics, adjectives and epithets."[131] Consciously or not, a reviewer of *The Dutchman's Fireside* (1831), in commenting on Paulding's characteristic traits as a writer, summarized many of the Knickerbocker ideas about the style of prose fiction:

> His [Paulding's] dialogue is full of spirit and colloquial ease, and [is marked by] the total absence of display or, affectation. The style of his works is

almost as various as the themes he discusses, or the objects he describes, . . . and, generally speaking, it is always happily adapted to the subject. Without being labored, highly polished, or ambitious, it is clear and energetic, occasionally, and we have sometimes thought designedly so, a little careless, as if in wilful opposition to the taste of the times. Though not dealing much in the pathetic, there are touches of feeling which sufficiently indicate that, if he has chosen the walks of humor, it is not from want of power to address the deeper passions.[132]

Dullness was recognized as a cardinal fault in a work of fiction,[133] but, on the other hand, many critics believed that a novelist should not attempt to attract readers by mere sensationalism.[134] Paulding waged a long warfare against "high-seasoned [fictional] dishes of foreign cookery, most especially bloodpuddings, plentifully spiced and sauced with adultery, seduction, poisoning, stabbing, suicide and all other sublime excesses of genius."[135] His theory of "rational fictions,"[136] although not much heeded by the popular novelists of the time, was echoed in many an article and review. John Inman,[137] for instance, warned novelists that they could not hope for critical approval if they failed to adhere to the "realities of life and achievement."[138] And G. P. Morris commended Miss Sedgwick's *Redwood* because, incidental to its other virtues, it was a "plain tale," without "the brilliancy of exuberant figure" and unadorned by "the wonders of romance."[139] The injunction to "copy nature," William Cox thought, could be carried too far: it might result in a feebler realism than that achieved by the novelist who understands the principle of selection. "To copy nature in her everyday forms," he said, "is neither difficult nor desirable. To report the slip-slop conversation of a tea-table is to copy nature, and the more literal the copy the less the skill required; but to be *true* to nature—to anticipate her, and make human beings in extraordinary situations and agitated by strong and conflicting passions, act and speak as she would make them act and speak in such situations—to make them do and say that which the reader has no conception of beforehand, but which, the moment he has read it, flashes upon him as the only thing they ought or could have done and said, is a power that few mortals are gifted with."[140] Another critic, reviewing Cooper's novels written before 1831, maintained that a great writer of fiction "must unite, with the knack of describing what he has seen, the power to invent; the faculty of judgment to arrange; and the combination of all the constituents of a consummate intellect, in bringing about, by striking and natural means, a striking yet natural catastrophe."[141]

The short story and the essay[142] received rather limited critical treatment. Although the short prose narrative—usually called "the tale" during this period[143]—was widely popular after the publication of *The Sketch Book,*[144] it was slow to gain serious attention from the critics. The theory and practice of the modern short

story followed in the wake of Hawthorne and Poe;[145] before their influence became general, there was a tendency to regard the tale as an interesting but fragmentary accomplishment. The genuinely ambitious writer, it was often suggested, would attempt something "more sustained"—presumably a novel.[146] One of the earlier and more discriminating comments on the tale as a literary form appeared, somewhat casually, in a brief review:

> Those compositions which pass under the name of tales, as distinguished from novels, require talents of a peculiar kind to insure success. They are not, it is true, so great an effort on the whole, nor do they perhaps require powers of so great an order as the novel;—they do not admit of the same complete development of character—the same fulness and variety of description, nor in general of that large mixture of dialogue, which gives to modern novels such a dramatic air. They require, however, greater vivacity of narration, and more point and polish of style; a little occasional tediousness is not so readily forgiven, and some negligence and heaviness of manner, is not so easily overlooked. To construct the plot of a tale, is perhaps a matter of as much invention and difficulty, as to construct that of a novel,—the chief difference lies in the execution. One is the miniature, the other the full-length picture; it is the former, therefore, which requires the highest and most delicate finish.[147]

Toward the end of the Knickerbocker period, in an enthusiastic appraisal of Poe's *Tales of the Grotesque and Arabesque,* L. F. Tasistro[148] made a similar though less elaborate distinction. "The tale," he remarked, "although not so encumbered with plot and incidents, belongs to the same class of composition [as the novel], and all that it has to depend upon for usefulness or effect, is its truth of principle, its fidelity to nature, and the tact and talent with which that truth is told and that fidelity is preserved."[149] Tasistro's offhand assumption that the tale might be mentioned in the same breath with the novel—of which he had a very high opinion—indicates how the critical attitude toward the short story was changing. Increased respect for the form is shown also in the comment of another New York writer: "Mr. Hawthorne is the author of a volume of excellent prose sketches, bearing the title of 'Twice-told Tales.' . . . Hawthorne will, before many years, be acknowledged one of the most remarkable and gifted writers of his day."[150]

In the prolonged struggle for a national literature,[151] the New York writers took an active part. Of the larger aspects of this struggle it is enough to say here that it has been continuous from the time of the Revolution, that it has been greatly stimulated by certain events or tendencies in the developing pattern of American life, and that it has inspired a variety of critical reactions.[152] With the War of 1812, the demand for a national literature became especially vociferous. This demand had only one of its expressions, therefore, and not its beginning, in Emerson's "The American Scholar" (1837); it perhaps reached its apogee in 1855 in Whitman's preface to *Leaves of Grass*.

Not all the Knickerbocker writers believed that America should have a distinctive literature or that American materials, exclusively, should be used by native authors. Halleck, for instance, in referring to some writings by two of his contemporaries, was careful to call them "American specimens of English literature." He went on to say: "I have been emphatic in using the word *English* in place of *American* literature, because I have never been able to define what '*American Literature*' means."[153] And Thatcher Payne,[154] writing in 1824 on America's lack of traditions and romantic associations, observed that "more poetry is to be made out of the humblest hillock upon the surface of the long inhabited regions of the other continent, than out of the whole American chain of Appalaches, Alleghanies, and Andes."[155]

The general tendency, however, was quite otherwise. Stung by Payne's remarks, Robert C. Sands made a prompt and vigorous rejoinder. In an essay entitled "Domestic Literature," after admitting that "our national associations are few," he insisted that the "local associations are many and of deep interest." He cited several American writings in which these local associations had been used effectively, and then declared, with emphasis:

> I contend . . . that a writer of talents among our own people should devote his abilities and apply his acquirements to subjects of domestic interest; exclusively so, so far forth as his opportunities admit. Why should we do what others have done well before, and be content, at best, but with the praise of successful imitation? . . . The literature of a nation is its common property, and one of the strongest bonds of common feeling. More particularly does it become so when the subject is domestic. The fame of an author who is universally admired is part of the inheritance of every individual citizen of his country. He adds another ligament to the ties which bind a people together; and in so doing, although the immediate object of his efforts may have only been to amuse his readers, he becomes the benefactor of his country.[156]

Sands had of course been anticipated in his major ideas by various other writers.[157] Probably the most outspoken and undeviating of all the Knickerbockers in his insistence upon the use of native themes and freedom from European influences was James Kirke Paulding. His pronounced American bias appears in almost all his writings,[158] but his concern for an independent national literature finds direct expression in *The Backwoodsman* (1818) and the essay "National Literature"

(1820). In the first of these, Paulding addressed the American muse bluntly:

> Neglected Muse of this our Western clime,
> How long in servile, imitative rhyme,
> Wilt thou thy stifled energies enchain,
> And tread the worn-out path still o'er again![159]

Equally forthright were his comments in the essay on "National Literature": "It appears to me that the young [American] candidate for the prize of genius . . . has but one path open to fame. . . . By freeing himself from the habit of servile imitation; by daring to think and feel, and express his feelings; by dwelling on scenes and events connected with our pride and our affections; by indulging in those little peculiarities of thought, feeling, and expression which belong to every nation; by borrowing from nature, and not from those who disfigure or burlesque her—he may and will in time destroy the ascendancy of foreign taste and opinions, and elevate his own in the place of them. These causes lead to the final establishment of a national literature, and give that air and character of originality which it is sure to acquire, unless it is debased and expatriated by a habit of servile imitation."[160] Paulding never abandoned the campaign: in his last novel, *The Puritan and His Daughter* (1849), he still lamented the influence of foreign literature[161] and once more exemplified his favorite fictional theme—American history.

Joseph Rodman Drake was also an ardent nationalist. In "The Culprit Fay," written in 1816, he undertook to show that American scenery could be used in a romantically conceived poem,[162] and in "To a Friend" (written *ca.* 1817) he called on Fitz-Greene Halleck to forsake trivial, imitative themes and to employ his talents upon native subjects.[163] Samuel Woodworth, likewise, was emphatic in his Americanism. In his editorial work, as well as in his verse, plays, and fiction, he labored for the cause of national letters. A contemporary reviewer of Woodworth's *Poems* (1818) noted that his verses contained "Americanisms and American allusions," and congratulated him on being "no copier of foreign poets and foreign ideas."[164] Woodworth himself called attention to the fact that his novel *The Champions of Freedom* was "of domestic manufacture" and could not "displease the eye of a patriot."[165] In introducing the *Literary Casket* to the public, he remarked, with characteristic optimism: " . . . the march of literature in our happy country is scarcely less wonderful than the growth of our physical and political greatness."[166]

When Woodworth and Morris founded the *New-York Mirror* in the summer of 1823, they dedicated it to the encouragement of domestic literature.[167] Throughout most of its relatively long life, the *Mirror* continued to give preference to American writers and American writing; as it remarked editorially in 1840: "The New-

York Mirror . . . encourages native genius and industry to an extent which certainly entitles it to the support of those who would foster talent of indigenous growth."[168] The *Knickerbocker Magazine* aspired to become "a sympathetic literary medium for talented literary aspirants of every geographical section of America—'to be a ready and convenient channel into which every little rill of mind may pour its tributary stream.'"[169] In an early number of the *Knickerbocker* the editor declared that "the formation of a literature of our own—*a National American Literature*—is the dearest idol of our heart,"[170] while other early issues contained Timothy Flint's article on national literature[171] and S. D. Langtree's injunction to Irving to abandon foreign themes.[172]

Charles Fenno Hoffman, first editor of the *Knickerbocker,* was another champion of nationalism. In his varied journalistic career, he gave himself unreservedly to advancing the reputation of American literature and encouraging American authors. In 1835, when he assumed the editorship of the *American Monthly Magazine,* he announced that this periodical would "consist wholly of original material"—tales, sketches, essays, and reviews of "such new works as may possess a national character from originating at home, or may have a bearing upon taste and opinions on this side of the Atlantic. In a word, every effort will be made to give the work an original and strongly-marked American character."[173] Two years later, he wrote to R. M. Bird that he had been "endeavoring to build up a periodical which should in every sense of the word be a *National One*"—one that would counteract the denationalizing influence of the foreign periodicals with which the country was being flooded.[174] He admitted that his reviews were sometimes colored by a desire to stimulate and protect the growth of domestic literature;[175] in any event, he would not supinely consult foreign opinion before pronouncing a native book good or bad.[176]

As has been said, the critical demand for a national literature continued long after the close of the Knickerbocker period. In the early decades of the nineteenth century, however, the New York writers, almost without exception,[177] defended the use of native materials. More important, in its ultimate effect, was their eager participation in the effort to establish a literature that would adequately represent the varied life, the scenic grandeur, and the cherished ideals of the America they knew.

THE LITERATURE

Only an uncritical reader or historian would care to dogmatize about the general characteristics of Knickerbocker literature. Shaped by many forces, produced by numerous individuals, and revealing a wide range of forms and interests, it presents a constantly shifting pattern. In it are mingled the grave and the gay, the satirical and the sentimental, the imitative and the original, the fatuous and the sophisticated. And yet, with all these disparate qualities, it possesses a kind of homogeneity and is marked by at least a few distinguishing traits.

It may be said, for one thing, that practically all the Knickerbocker writers—and, of course, their writings—were influenced in one way or another by antecedent or contemporary British authors. Through Paulding spoke the voices of Pope, Goldsmith, and Fielding; Woodworth echoed Thomas Gray, James Montgomery, Robert Tannahill, and various others; many of Halleck's verbal melodies were anticipated in the poems of Campbell, Moore, and Byron; Drake's poetic ear was attuned to the rhythms of Burns, Coleridge, and Campbell; Fay, as an essayist, followed haltingly in the footsteps of Addison; Cox and Willis Clark drew much of their literary sustenance from Charles Lamb; Cornelius Mathews warmed his hands before the fire of Dickens. So it went. Lacking a well established native tradition, in their search for models the New York writers usually turned, as was natural enough, to the "foreign" literature they knew best. Even when the subject matter was mainly of local interest or the theme distinctively American, the form was likely to be patterned upon a British archetype.

In the early stages of its development, the Knickerbocker literature was especially indebted to such eighteenth century writers as Pope, Addison, Goldsmith, and Johnson;[178] in its middle years it was profoundly affected by the writings of Scott, Byron, Moore, Campbell, and Lamb;[179] and its decline was coincident with the increasing influence of Dickens, Bulwer, Disraeli, and a number of lesser writers. Non-English authors undoubtedly had a share in the forming of Knickerbocker literary expression,[180] but in extent and continuity the influence of the British writers just named was hardly exceeded by any of these.

As might be supposed, the New York men of letters exerted considerable influence on each other. Having many common interests, reading very much the same books, contributing to the same periodicals, they were inevitably led to the exploration of parallel—or at least similar—literary veins. The prestige gained by some of their confreres also had its effect. Irving's success, for example, stimulated a number of his less talented townsmen[181] to attempt Irvingesque prose. The contemporary fame of Halleck's verses was great enough to ensure their being imitated,[182] and a like observation may be made about Bryant's poems and Cooper's novels.[183]

For all its derivativeness, and in spite of the cultural and literary interrelationships of its authors, the Knickerbocker literature possesses both variety and originality.

Its variety will be obvious to anyone who troubles to leaf through the pages of the many books, magazines, and newspapers that comprise the literary record of the period. Its originality, although perhaps less obvious, is none the less real. Paulding, Halleck, Drake, Payne, Willis, Cox, Hoffman—to name only a few of the minor figures—were all gifted with inventiveness, freshness of fancy, and zest for phrase making. None of them, it may be, achieved Bryant's singleness of purpose, Cooper's imaginative fecundity, or Irving's sheer virtuosity, but in their respective ways they all engaged in that essentially creative act which, as one critic has said, "adds to the sum of existences."[184] Slight though these contributions may have been, they were still contributions, and they came at a time when American letters would have been far poorer without them.

In adapting to their own uses the forms and thought patterns of British literature, the Knickerbockers showed a certain degree of independence and originality. This tendency was magnified on those frequent occasions when they were confronted with the frankly contemptuous attitude of some British writers and reviews toward all things American. For a period of nearly twenty-five years (*ca.* 1812-1835) the New York *littérateurs* spent much of their energy in verbal combat with Great Britain.[185] Chief strategist in this "paper war with England" was J. K. Paulding,[186] but many of the other Knickerbocker writers shared in the campaign.[187] Even Halleck felt impelled, in 1822, to write some violent lines beginning:

> Growl, critics of England, growl on, ye hired
>   hounds
>   Of a pitiful court! at America's name,
> For as long as that name through your vassal-
>   air sounds,
>   It must crimson your cheeks with the
>   blushes of shame.[188]

Although Irving[189] and others counselled moderation, many of the Knickerbockers could neither overlook nor forgive the harsh comments on America they found in British periodicals and in books by British travellers.[190] It is possible that the New York writers were unduly sensitive and that they were plagued by a feeling of inferiority,[191] but in any event the Anglo-American controversy provided them with no small amount of literary capital.

As has already been suggested,[192] the tone for much of the early New York literature was established by *Salmagundi* and *Knickerbocker's History.* Produced in part by a strongly felt town spirit, this jesting, serio-comic, satiric tone was destined to outlast the conditions that engendered it, so that in time it dwindled into faint vibrations of mere whimsy and "cuteness."[193] For some thirty years, however, satire enlivened and brightened the Knickerbocker literary scene. Most of its early

appearances were unabashedly eighteenth century in form and mood. Just as *Salmagundi* was indebted to the *Spectator,* to *The Citizen of the World,* and to earlier native attempts in the same genre,[194] and just as *A History of New York* leaned upon Fielding, Sterne, Swift, and others,[195] so did Woodworth's *New-Haven* (1809) depend upon Pope and the Connecticut Wits, his *Beasts at Law* (1811), upon *Hudibras* and *M'Fingal,* and his *Quarter-Day* (1812), upon Thomson and Cowper.[196] So, too, did Paulding's *Diverting History of John Bull and Brother Jonathan* (1812) draw upon Addison, Goldsmith, and Swift, as well as Hopkinson's *A Pretty Story,*[197] while the indebtedness of Verplanck's *The Bucktail Bards* to neo-classic satire is at once evident.[198] After 1815 newer influences, notably those of John Wolcot ("Peter Pindar"), James and Horatio Smith, J. H. Frere, and Lord Byron,[199] began to make themselves felt, but by this time or a little later the Knickerbocker love of humor, especially of satire, had become almost a tradition.[200] The "Croaker" poems and *Fanny* appeared in the same year as *The Bucktail Bards* (1819), to be followed in fairly rapid succession by S. B. H. Judah's *Gotham and the Gothamites* (1823), McDonald Clarke's *The Gossip* (1823), Paulding's *Koningsmarke* (1823) and *John Bull in America* (1825), Woodworth's "Fashions" (1825), and Isaac Starr Clason's *Horace in New-York* (1826).[201]

The New York newspapers and magazines fostered the taste for satire by opening their columns to almost every conceivable variety of skit, parody, burlesque, travesty, and caricature.[202] Such writings, directed mainly at the current passing show of events, personages, and follies, had an immediate journalistic value that editors were quick to recognize. By the same token, most of these writings were foredoomed to brief renown and early oblivion. But in their time they contributed to the mirth of a generation of readers, and they helped to give to Knickerbocker letters a spirit of adolescent gaiety and verve.

This spirit was, indeed, characteristic of much of the Knickerbocker writing, whether satirical or not. Its authors were young or youngish men;[203] the town was engaged in the youthful process of growth; and the nation itself was still relatively new—and conscious of its newness. There was, in addition, a discernible aura of amateurism about many of the New York writers.

In the early days of the republic, even in a cosmopolitan center such as New York was becoming, the mere poet, the mere novelist, the mere playwright or biographer, was an unusual if not an unknown figure. Unless a man were a professional journalist,[204] he did not ordinarily depend upon his pen for a livelihood. Among the Knickerbockers, William Irving, Henry Brevoort, Halleck, and P. M. Wetmore were businessmen; S. L. Mitchill and Drake were physicians; Anthony Bleecker was an attorney; Clement Moore, a teacher, with inherited wealth; Verplanck, a lawyer and teacher. With these men, as with numerous others, writing was an avocation, not a career.[205] The journalists, to be sure, took a more professional attitude toward their literary work, but they, like the self-acknowledged dilettantes although for somewhat different reasons, found it difficult to devote themselves wholeheartedly to creative expression. Ambitious though some of them were for literary fame, the environment in which they worked was hardly favorable to the production of masterpieces.[206] Much of their writing was done on the spur of the moment—under journalistic pressure or to meet the demands of a particular occasion.[207] This writing was often amusing, spirited, and robust, but it was not likely to be either profound or permanently interesting.

It may be somewhat gratuitous, at this point, to remark that the Knickerbocker writers flourished in a time of transition. Behind them (to borrow some of Joaquin Miller's swelling rhetoric) lay the gray Azores of neoclassicism; before them and around them were the shoreless seas of romanticism. Consequently, many of them tended to face in two directions at once, with results that were not always happy. It is more than probable that the writers themselves were not fully aware of the divergent forces at work within their *milieu* and, hence, upon them as individuals. Like their less articulate fellow townsmen, they responded to the time-spirit in such ways as their various temperaments dictated. Thus we find in the literature of the period a continual conflict between romantic vagueness and neoclassic precision, between romantic idealism and realistic disenchantment, between romantic sentimentality and rationalistic restraint.[208]

Though the satirical or realistic attitudes of many of the Knickerbocker authors saved them from the more maudlin types of sentimentality, none wholly escaped the infection. Inheritors of eighteenth century sensibility, they were also assailed by the epidemic of emotional fervor that accompanied the new romanticism and the new humanitarianism.[209] As contributors to the gift books, annuals, and home magazines—all edited primarily for a feminine audience—they were compelled to genuflect before the gods of coyness, propriety, and bathos.[210] As editors they made concessions to what one of their number called the "mawkish sentimentality" of the day.[211] As poets, essayists, and tellers of tales, they were mainly concerned "with the *feelings* of humanity, with emotion rather than reason, with the heart rather than the head."[212] Some of them, making no effort to hide their predilection for the immoderate, the suspiring, the tearful, spoke in accents that reveal their kinship with the confirmed sentimentalists of all times and every land.[213]

But the soil that nourished this exoticism, this extreme sensibility, bore other and hardier growths. Within the hothouse of sentimentality all was exaggerated, warmly moist, faintly mildewed; outside and beyond were the rushing wind, the cool rain, the beating sun, the clean smell of the pines. The soil was the same, but the atmosphere was different. And in this fresher, lighter air developed a sturdy realism.

A few of the Knickerbocker writers were realists by conviction: literature, they thought, should present a credible picture of life. They admired those literary artists who eschewed improbable situations, specious characters, extravagant emotions, lurid sensationalism. Paulding, for instance, in both theory and practice upheld the standard of "common sense."[214] His realism, it is true, was more nearly a survival than an anticipation, for Paulding's literary idols were the neoclassic Olympians. But the significant fact is that he *was* a realist—an influential exponent of restraint, reasonableness, and fidelity to nature. The native writer, he insisted, could achieve fidelity to nature only by using the backgrounds, incidents, characters, and feelings that were parts of the common American experience.[215] This doctrine he exemplified in a notable succession of short stories, novels, and other writings.

At least partly through Paulding's efforts, the attention of other New York writers was directed to the literary possibilities of local color material.[216] Whether influenced by Paulding or not, when the Knickerbocker authors portrayed typical aspects of the local scene, local character, or local dialect, they generally aimed at verisimilitude.[217] This tendency they carried over into their delineations of the frontier and the frontiersman,[218] as well as into their handling of native humor.[219] Although they undoubtedly emphasized the eccentric characters, the unconventional speech, and the picturesque scenery of the rustic settlement and the backwoods, they were nevertheless interested in these things as characteristic features of American life. Through their varied use of indigenous materials, the Knickerbockers played a part in the development of local color and realism.

While the New York literature was reaching out in the manifold directions that have been described, the city itself was changing. Between 1810 and 1840 the population had more than tripled: from an overgrown town of fewer than one hundred thousand inhabitants, Manhattan had developed into a crowding city of over three hundred thousand.[220] This great growth was accompanied by an increased cosmopolitanism and a corresponding diminution of the town spirit that had brought into being much of the Knickerbocker literature.[221] "Old New York" was rapidly becoming a memory—a vanished dream yearned over by aged or aging men. Gone, or going, were the old landmarks, the old manners, the old camaraderie, the old friends.

Commenting on this change, in 1839, Samuel Woodworth said mournfully: "The friends of my youth, with very few exceptions, have all gone off the stage of life, or have become old men, so different from what they once were that they do not seem like the same individuals; and most of them who survive are so completely absorbed in *politics,* that they have not time to attend to the calls of friendship, or the pleasures of literature."[222] Three years later Woodworth himself entered the vast silence that had already engulfed Drake and Sands and Leggett and Brooks and Willis Clark and many others.

Those who remained were, for the most part, engaged in either journalistic or non-literary pursuits. They, like the general reading public of the forties, were looking to a new generation of writers—younger writers who could better adapt their talents to new conditions and new tastes. The great day of the gift book, of the Godey hero and heroine, of Hawthorne's "damned mob of scribbling women,"[223] had arrived. To the seemingly insatiable demand for sentimental or sensational verse and prose, market-wise editors like Lewis Clark, or Morris and Willis, acceded with relatively faint protests. Times had changed, and they knew it. On one hand, the old Knickerbocker favorites were being replaced by popular authors, men and women, who were at once less masculine and more "fashionable," less local in their interests and more turgid in style. On the other hand, they were swiftly losing ground to more formidable adversaries. The leaders of New England's cultural renaissance were rising in public esteem: as their fame increased, that of the Knickerbockers declined. Those readers who demanded from literature something more than mere entertainment were attracted by the moral earnestness and the inspirational philosophy of the New England writers. In retrospect (from the vantage point of, say, 1845) the Knickerbockers began to seem antiquated—too exclusively concerned with local matters, too largely dependent on satire and an outmoded wit, too conspicuously lacking in solid intellectual interests.[224] And in America's Victorian age, then imminent—an age marked by the triumph of middle-class morality, the rise of evangelical religion, the emergence of an industrial economy, the growth of a feminized culture—writers other than the New York contemporaries of Irving and Cooper were to play the leading parts.

In their own day, however, several of those whom we now call the "minor" Knickerbockers were anything but insignificant. For this reason, even though much of their work can remain comfortably forgotten, it may be worth while to look briefly at some of their individual accomplishments.

The writings of James Kirke Paulding invite special attention. A caustic apologist for the American way of life, Paulding dissipated part of his literary energy in tilting at John Bull, but this was only one phase of his career as an author. The truth is that Paulding was an extremely versatile writer. Fluent, contentious, wryly humorous, he not only contributed generously to periodical literature,[225] but also appeared before the public as the author of five novels, two volumes of verse, two plays, a life of Washington, and more than a dozen volumes of essays, sketches, satires, and other miscellany. To his writing Paulding brought an active, inquiring, slowly matured mind, a moderately broad background of reading, some definite ideas on both literature and society, and an admirable clarity of perception. These qualities, together with fluency and vigor of expression, were enough to ensure the approval of his contemporaries. Unfortunately for his after-fame, he had neither the creative gifts of the great writer nor the patience and technical skill of the first-rate artist. Careless structure and melodramatic claptrap mar the effectiveness of even his best novels, such as *Koningsmarke, The Dutchman's Fireside,* and *The Old Continental.* His other fictions, despite their author's tendency toward realism and his interesting use of local color, are often clumsily contrived and unconvincing. With all their faults, however, many of his narratives have a vitality that is but partially obscured by inept workmanship.[226]

Even had he written no fiction, Paulding would still be memorable as satirist and social critic. An outspoken individualist with strong Jeffersonian physiocratic leanings, he was a shrewd observer of democracy and its workings. He did not hesitate to call for correction when he thought it was needed, but he was equally quick to defend America against the attacks of stupid or envious or presumptuous foreigners. Although he deplored the chicaneries of practical politics, he climaxed an honorable career of public service by becoming Secretary of the Navy in Van Buren's cabinet. His abiding faith in America and in its political and social democracy is revealed in almost everything he wrote, perhaps most directly in *Letters from the South.* In this work, in *A Sketch of Old England,* in *The Merry Tales of the Three Wise Men of Gotham,* and on many other pages by the same author are abundant proofs of his independent, vigorous mind and resolute character.

If Paulding was a "versatile American,"[227] Samuel Woodworth may be thought of as a literary jack-of-all-trades. The greater part of his work, like the man, has long been forgotten: of his numerous and varied writings, only "The Old Oaken Bucket" achieved even an anonymous immortality. But New Yorkers of the Knickerbocker era knew him as the author of verse, novels, essays, short stories, and plays, and as the editor—for short periods, at least—of eleven different newspapers and magazines. Much of his writing was a by-product of his career in journalism and was not regarded, even by its author, as having any permanent value. Several of his lyrics, written to well-known melodies, caught the popular fancy for a season, however, and two or three—including "The Bucket" and "The Hunters of

Kentucky"—lingered on in the somewhat anomalous realm of the folk song. His plays made a modest contribution to the stock of native drama, and one of them, *The Forest Rose,* served to establish the Yankee character on the American stage.[228] Perhaps the kindest words that can be said about *The Champions of Freedom* (1816), his only novel to appear in book form,[229] are that it is a devoutly patriotic early example of the American historical romance, anticipating Cooper's *The Spy* by five years.

Of New England yeoman stock, largely self-educated, a printer by trade, Woodworth spoke for and to the common people.[230] His acquaintance with toil and poverty was not at all academic; his sympathy for the weak, the underprivileged, the persecuted, was no mere sentimental pose. His democracy, his love of liberty, his religious faith,[231] his humanitarianism—all these traits of character are reflected in Woodworth's literary expression. That he was a man of good will can hardly be doubted. But it must also be recorded that his writing was, in general, the work of an artisan rather than that of an artist.

For Gulian Crommelin Verplanck, writing was mainly incidental to a career as lawyer, teacher, and politician. The early satires prompted by his quarrel with DeWitt Clinton are the most spirited of his many productions in verse and prose[232] His later writings, although presenting their author in the rôles of moralist, theologian, legal theorist, antiquarian, and scholar, are weighted down by a pompous, pseudo-elegant rhetoric. Verplanck's cultural and practical interests moved him to take up the pen on numerous occasions, first and last, but it is to be feared that his spirit rarely ignited; certainly it burned with no hard, gemlike flame.[233] Yet he conscientiously served his city and state in a number of ways,[234] and he made good use of his critical abilities when he undertook the task of editing Shakespeare's plays for American readers.[235]

"Whoever undertakes the examination of Halleck's poetical character, will naturally wish for a greater number of examples from which to collect an estimate of his powers. He has given us only samples of what he can do. His verses are like passages of some mighty choral melody, heard in the brief interval between the opening and shutting of the doors of a temple. Why does he not more frequently employ the powers with which he is so eminently gifted? . . . He will excel himself, if he applies his powers, with an earnest and resolute purpose, to the work which justice to his own fame demands of him."[236] Thus spoke Bryant, in 1836. His question was to remain unanswered, his admonition unheeded, for in the remaining three decades of his life Halleck rarely used the poetic powers with which he was "so eminently gifted." Indeed, he was never committed to a life of letters.[237] The greater part of his verse writing was done between 1819 and 1827,

but even through this relatively prolific period Halleck continued to regard himself as a businessman who dabbled in poetry. That he consistently maintained this amateur attitude tends to disarm serious criticism of his work. It is also one of the minor tragedies of American literary history.

For Fitz-Greene Halleck possessed genuine poetic talents. Had he devoted himself to a mastery of the poet's art, had there been added to those traits described by P. H. Boynton as "his nicety of taste, his keen eye, his fund of humor, and his frankness"[238] a desire for lasting literary fame, he might have become a major figure. The times and his own temperament conspired against him. Notwithstanding the extravagant praise heaped on him by some of his contemporaries,[239] Halleck was, and remains, a minor poet.

But in his casual way and within his self-imposed limits, he performed cleverly. He had a quick wit, an adroit satirical touch, a gift for the serio-comic, and a verbal felicity not often encountered in our early literature. The author of *Fanny* and co-author of the "Croaker" poems had few real competitors in the field of jaunty verse satire until Lowell appeared. Halleck's familiar verse, such as "Alnwick Castle," "A Poet's Daughter," and "The Winds of March Are Humming," if it did nothing else, helped to prepare the way for Holmes's popular success in that genre. And some of his more serious efforts—"On the Death of Joseph Rodman Drake," "Marco Bozzaris," "Burns," "The Field of the Grounded Arms"—although less famous than they once were, may still be read not merely as examples of this or that literary influence but for their intrinsic merit.

Halleck's friend and collaborator in the "Croaker" series, Joseph Rodman Drake, was another gifted amateur. During his lifetime (he died at twenty-five, seemingly indifferent to literary reputation),[240] young Dr. Drake was known to only a few intimates as a writer of verse. The posthumous publication of his poems, first in periodicals and then in volume form,[241] brought exclamations of delight from many American critics,[242] and gave Drake a secure place among the Knickerbocker poets. Later generations of students have been aware of his part in the "Croakers," and literary historians have usually given at least a perfunctory nod to "The Culprit Fay" and "The American Flag.[243] Drake's output was both small and uneven, but his best work shows that he had metrical dexterity, a bright fancy, and a keen sense of color, movement, and sound. Fully conscious of his own imperfect achievement, yet ardently nationalistic, he cherished the hope that other native poets would do justice to the themes and scenes of "nature's loveliest land."[244]

Although born in New York City and befriended by many of the Knickerbocker writers, John Howard Payne somehow seems remote from the group with which his name is often associated. This impression of aloofness no doubt results from the fact that Payne not only lived abroad for years but worked largely with foreign materials. His plays, however, were popular in the city of his birth, and when, in 1832, he returned from a twenty years' sojourn in Europe, the New York men of letters greeted him with great cordiality.[245] As it developed, Payne's return to America coincided with the end of his career as a playwright; his most important contributions to dramatic writing were made, therefore, while he was living in a foreign environment. Payne's genius, as his contemporaries were aware, was that of a skilled adapter, a brilliant reshaper of plot, character, and dialogue. "It does not appear," said T. S. Fay, "that . . . Payne has . . . been favored with many opportunities for those more enduring and exclusively original efforts which make a man's name immortal." But Fay also recognized that Payne was early New York's most talented man of the theatre, and acclaimed him, fittingly enough, as the author of "the most popular tragedy (Brutus), comedy (Charles the Second), melodrama (Thérèse), opera (Clari), and song (Sweet Home), of the day in which they respectively appeared."[246]

Quite unlike Payne, Robert Charles Sands lived and worked in almost daily contact with the Knickerbocker scene. A graduate of Columbia and a member of the New York bar, he abandoned the law to identify himself with the literary life of the town. Before his death at the age of thirty-three he had become locally renowned as versifier, essayist, short story writer, magazine editor, and journalist.[247] As editor of the short-lived *Atlantic Magazine,* he strongly advocated literary nationalism; in his contributions to this and other periodicals, and in his writing, generally, he exemplified the use of native materials. He was a fluent, vigorous, masculine writer of prose, as a reading of "The Man Who Burnt John Rogers" or "Boyuca" or "Mr. Green" will reveal.[248] The last-named tale, an amusing satire, is marked by the same eccentric and somewhat extravagant humor that appears in his mock-heroic "Monody on Samuel Patch."[249] His serious verse, although bearing the signs of hasty composition, is occasionally affecting and almost always energetic. During his too brief career, Sands brought a quickening, vital force into Knickerbocker letters.

So, also, did William Leggett. Some of Leggett's productions—especially his early efforts in verse and literary criticism—may be charitably overlooked; they are the work of a young man who had not yet found his calling. Though shapeless and prolix, his tales of the frontier and the sea, based on firsthand observation, are decidedly the most impressive of these early ventures. Not until he turned to journalism, however, did Leggett's real abilities manifest themselves. In his few years as assistant editor of the *Evening Post* and editor of the *Plaindealer* he showed himself to be one of the most fearless newspaper writers of the period. From June, 1834, to October, 1835, with Bryant abroad, Leggett was chief editor of the *Post.* It was at this time that he "disgraced the once respectable columns of that well-known paper by the most profligate and disorganizing sentiments"—if we are to believe the testimony of that arch-conservative, Philip Hone.[250] Leggett's "profligate and disorganizing sentiments" were, it seems: (1) he favored a wide extension of the suffrage; (2) he opposed the rechartering of the Bank of the United States; (3) he deplored special privileges of all kinds; and (4) he insisted that the principle of freedom of speech should apply to abolitionists.[251] In the editorial columns of the *Plaindealer* he carried on his bold, high-minded campaign to "make government . . . not the dispenser of privileges to a few for their efforts in subverting the rights of the many, but the beneficent promoter of the equal happiness of all."[252] It is clear that William Leggett was no mere political agitator or rabble rouser. He was, rather, as V. L. Parrington has observed, "a man of immense vitality and boundless sympathies, to whom social justice was a religion."[253]

Certain parallels may be drawn between Leggett's career and that of James Gordon Brooks. Nearly of an age, both men first attracted attention by their writing of verse and critical essays; both of them gained further experience through magazine editing; and both devoted their latest years to journalism. Dedicated, like Leggett, to the ideal of social and political equality, Brooks in 1830 established a daily paper, the *Sentinel,* in which he proposed to "sustain the interests and promote the moral and general advancement of the mechanic classes."[254] Brooks's verse, once greatly admired,[255] now seems limited in range and derivative in manner—Byron diluted with generous draughts of Campbell and the "graveyard" poets. But it also serves as a reminder, if any is needed, that the romantic ferment was unmistakably at work.

Somewhat different influences appear in the verse of George Pope Morris. Like Woodworth, Morris was a writer of popular songs. "Morris's heart," said his friend Willis, "is at the level of most other people's and his poetry flows out by that door. . . . Ninety-nine people in a hundred, taken as they come in the census, would find more to admire in Morris's songs than in the writings of any other American poet."[256] Most of Morris's lyrics are brief, simply phrased, and unaffectedly sentimental: he seems to have had no higher aim than to continue the songwriting tradition of Burns and Moore, or perhaps even less pretentiously, that of Robert Tannahill, William Motherwell, and Felicia Hemans. Quite apart from his popular songs, his successful Revolutionary War play, *Brier Cliff* (produced in 1826), and his occasional skits in prose,[257] Morris played a significant rôle in Knickerbocker literature as editor of the *New-York Mirror.* In a day when the existence of periodicals was notably transient, he kept the *Mirror* alive for twenty years, thus providing a medium of literary expression for scores of local writers. The *Mirror,* under Morris's direction, lived up to its name by reflecting a great many of the current interests, and it also had a widespread influence on other American periodicals.

Among the frequent contributors to the *Mirror* was William Cox, a British subject who lived in New York for several years and maintained his contacts with Knickerbocker letters even after he had returned to England. While residing in New York, he supplied the *Mirror* with vivacious dramatic criticisms, book reviews, and familiar essays—many of which were brought together in 1833 and published as *Crayon Sketches, by an Amateur.*[258] In his essays Cox perhaps rather self-consciously adopted the tone and the mannerisms of Lamb and Irving. He was nevertheless a keen, humorous observer and a facile writer; his work deserves more attention than it has hitherto received.

Another author whose name is often associated with the *New-York Mirror* is Nathaniel Parker Willis. Though born, reared, and educated in New England, and cosmopolitan by nature, Willis in 1831 allied himself with Knickerbocker literary activity by becoming an associate editor of the *Mirror;* from this time until his death in 1867 he was generally thought of as a New York writer. Early in his career he learned that fame can be accompanied by misrepresentation, malicious envy, and virulent abuse. Over the years, his literary output was prodigious, but much of his writing was hastily done and trivial, the frothiest kind of journalism. Willis was skilled in gauging the flow and ebb of popular tastes, in touching the proper notes of flippancy or sentiment, and in becoming—as he might have said—*en rapport* with his readers. These traits made him a brilliant magazinist and a successful editor, but they did little to sustain his later reputation.

In some parts of his work, however, Willis showed that he had larger gifts. He could—and did—write sparkling *vers de société,* as well as an occasional serious poem of some merit. He was the author of two competently written and successful romantic plays, *Bianca Visconti* and *Tortesa the Usurer.*[259] He made numerous contributions to the stock of early impressionistic criticism.[260] In his informal essays he wrote easily and pleasantly about a great many things, ranging all the way from gossipy descriptions of the London literati and British society to colloquially phrased sketches of the homely tasks and earthy wisdom of the American farmer. It is easy to dismiss Willis as a poseur, as an elegant trifler whose album pieces were dear to the hearts of a sentimental and slightly simpleminded generation. But the man's best work refuses to be dismissed in this offhand manner; it may not be profound—any more than Willis himself was profound—but it is at least alive.

About the time that Willis launched his spectacular career, Charles Fenno Hoffman, a "native son" of Manhattan, began to make anonymous contributions to various New York newspapers and magazines. When his literary life ended, some twenty years later, Hoffman was anything but an anonymous figure, for in the interim he had been editor of the *Knickerbocker,* the *American Monthly Magazine,* and the *Literary World,* associate editor of the *New-York American,* the *Mirror,* and other periodicals, and he had gained recognition as poet, novelist, and nature writer. He had taken an active part, furthermore, in the struggle for literary nationalism,[261] as well as in the agitation for an effective copyright law.[262] Hoffman's intense Americanism and his almost equally ardent romanticism appear side by side in the greater part of his writing, whether verse, descriptive sketch, criticism, or fiction. His stories are sometimes couched in extravagant though sonorous rhetoric, perhaps most obviously in *Greyslaer,* a melodramatic historical romance. Even his simpler tales, such as "The Man in the Reservoir,"[263] are not altogether free from this tendency toward rant, while his travel letters and other descriptive writings are full of lush passages. His verse, also, shows that whatever else he may have learned from his reading of Scott and Moore and Byron, he did not learn restraint. Of all the Knickerbockers, Hoffman seems to have been the most complete convert to the principles and practice of romanticism.

When Theodore Sedgwick Fay's first novel, *Norman Leslie,* was published in October, 1835, its author was already well known in New York literary circles as an associate editor of the *Mirror,* as a sentimental essayist and genial satirist, and as the writer of a collection of sketches called *Dreams and Reveries of a Quiet Man.* The novel, unfortunately, was to be remembered almost solely as the object of one of Poe's most vicious critical attacks[264]—an attack to which Fay eventually made a stinging rejoinder.[265] This was but a single episode in the long life of the author of *Norman Leslie,* for Fay went on to write three more novels and various other works; outliving most of his contemporaries by many years, he died in Germany in 1898.[266] During the Knickerbocker period he spoke out strongly for the creation of a distinctive national literature, for the use of native materials, and for the democratic way of life. More than once he expressed the conviction that America, with its love of liberty and its simple republicanism, enjoyed unique blessings.[267]

In time, the voices of Fay and his fellow New Yorkers were blurred, muted, drowned out by the roar of the machines and the rumblings of civil war. They come to us faintly now, as though from another world. For theirs are the voices of a youthful literature—uncertain, blatant, awkward, idealistic, naive, pompous, derisive, tender. Its faults are the faults of youth, but its strength, too, is the buoyant strength of youth, dedicated to singing the American song and proclaiming the American faith.

Notes

1 Vernon L. Parrington, *Main Currents in American Thought,* II, 1927, 195-200; S.T. Williams, *Life of Washington Irving,* II, 52-54; William Charvat, *The Origins of American Critical Thought, 1810-1835* (Philadelphia, 1936), pp. 201-203; Bernard Smith, *Forces in American Criticism* (New York, 1939), pp. 53-55.

2 See Van Wyck Brooks, *The Flowering of New England,* 1936, pp. 172-195, *et passim;* and F. O. Matthiessen, *American Renaissance* (New York, 1941), pp. 12-13, 66-67, *et passim.*

3 My list includes: *American Monthly Magazine and Critical Review* (1817-19), *Literary and Scientific Repository* (1820-22), *Literary Casket and Pocket Magazine* (1821-22), *Minerva* (1822-25), *Atlantic Magazine* (1824-25), *American Athenaeum* (1825-26), *New-York Review and Atheneum Magazine* (1825-26), *New-York Literary Gazette and Phi Beta Kappa Repository* (1825-26), *New-York Literary Gazette and American Athenaeum* (1826-27), *United States Review and Literary Gazette* (1826-27), *Parthenon* (1827), *Critic* (1828-29), *American Monthly Magazine* (1833-38), *Literary and Theological Review* (1834-39), *New-York Review* (1837-42), *United States Magazine and Democratic Review* (1841-59), *Literary and Scientific Review* (1839-40), *Expositor* (1839), *New-York Literary Gazette* (1839), and *Arcturus* (1840-42). I do not mean to imply that this list of periodicals established is in itself an index of achievement in criticism, but it does reveal a continuity of interest. As their titles show, several of these periodicals divided their pages between literary and other matter, and some of the early magazines were largely eclectic.

4 *New-York Mirror,* XIV, 119 (October 8, 1836): "How few writers of the present day judge of an author by his book, and how many foreign considerations influence them when recording their opinion of his talents and the merits of his work! How little of honest criticism we have; how much censure is pronounced where the author, and not the book, is the object; and how much commendation bestowed from personal motives and private regards! How very wrong and base all this is!" Cf. Mott, *History of American Magazines,* 1741-1850, pp. 405-407.

5 For an extensive discussion of the influence of politics upon the reviews of a writer's work, see Dorothy Waples, *The Whig Myth of James Fenimore Cooper* (New Haven, 1938).

6 The *Mirror's* objection, quoted [in footnote 4], is typical.

7 *Discourses and Addresses on Subjects of American History, Arts, and Literature,* pp. 150-151.

8 *New-York Mirror,* I, 380 (June 26, 1824).

9 *Ibid.,* XII, 259 (February 14, 1835). Turner went on to quote some remarks he had seen in a recent periodical: "'The connexion between the want of religious principle, and the want of poetical feeling, is seen in Hume and Gibbon; they had, radically, unpoetical minds. Revealed religion is especially poetical. . . . It brings us into a new world—a world of overpowering interest, of the sublimest views, and of the tenderest and purest feelings. With Christians, a poetical view of things is a duty. . . . The virtues peculiarly Christian are also essentially poetical.'"

10 Bernard Smith has pointed out that when "the function of the critic to make the artist toe the moral mark of the time" is no longer debated, "the concept of moral utility is known in criticism as *gentility*" (*Forces in American Criticism,* p. 40).

11 I do not doubt that many writers were quite sincere when they insisted, as did Verplanck, on the need for "a sound, an undefiled, and wholesome literature"—a literature directed to the "best ends of truth and virtue" (*Discourses and Addresses,* p. 249). But these writers were surely not unaware that they were—however circuitously—defending their own right to practice the *art* of letters when they underscored the "moral value" of literature.

12 See, for example, Solyman Brown, *An Essay on American Poetry* (New Haven, 1818), p. 26; and [Joseph Price], "Immoral Publications," *New-York Mirror,* XIII, 339 (April 23, 1836).

13 William Leggett, among these others, explicitly rejected the idea that an artist must be a "good" man. See *The Political Writings of William Leggett* (New York, 1840), II, 261-262.

14 "Byron," *New-York Mirror,* XIV, 356 (May 6, 1837).

15 "Fashionable Books," *New-York Mirror,* VIII, 7 (July 10, 1830).

16 *New-York Mirror,* VIII, 141 (November 6, 1830). The reviewer italicized *American,* indicating that his bias was nationalistic as well as moralistic.

17 *Discourse and Addresses,* p. 248. On another occasion, Verplanck quoted, with approval, from one of the *Discourses* of Sir Joshua Reynolds: "'Every artist ought well to remember, that he deserves just so much encouragement in the state, as he makes himself a member of it virtuously useful, and contributes in his sphere to the general purpose and perfection of society'" (*Ibid.,* p. 153).

[18] Other than moral instruction, although that was, of course, comprised in the term as used by most nineteenth century critics.

[19] See Smith, *Forces in American Criticism,* pp. 41-54; and Charvat, *Origins of American Critical Thought,* pp. 173-201. As Dr. Charvat points out (p. 195), Willis's *American Monthly Magazine* (1829-1831) was unique among New England critical periodicals in that its criticisms were often devoted "to enjoyment rather than analysis and judgement." Naturally enough, Willis felt more "at home" in New York than he did in Boston.

[20] *American Monthly Magazine* (Boston), I, 866 (March, 1830). Reprinted in *New-York Mirror,* XIII, 213 (January 2, 1836).

[21] "The Politician," *Tales of the Good Woman* (New York, 1836), II, 191. Originally published in *Chronicles of the City of Gotham* (New York, 1830).

[22] A characteristic comment is that in the *Mirror,* XI, 295 (March 15, 1834): "We would say to the long-faced critic—Dost thou think because thou art profound, there shall be no more light reading?"

[23] See above, p. xxi.

[24] Hamilton Wright Mabie, *The Writers of Knickerbocker New York,* 1912, p. 117. Cf. Adkins, *Fitz-Greene Halleck,* pp. 80, 125.

[25] *Discourses and Addresses,* p. 249.

[26] "Memoirs of a Sensitive Man about Town," *New-York Mirror,* XI, 97-98 (September 28, 1833).

[27] "Address at the Opening of a New Theatre" (1831), *Poetical Writings of Fitz-Greene Halleck,* ed. J. G. Wilson (New York, 1869), p. 201.

[28] "Books and Readers," *New-York Mirror,* XIII, 254 (February 6, 1836). See also "Traveling—Mentally and Bodily," Selections following, p. 278.

[29] See above, pp. xx, xxviii.

[30] *New-York Mirror,* IX, 100 (October 1, 1831).

[31] The annual series of lectures sponsored, 1827 *et seq.,* by the Mercantile Library Association, may be cited.

[32] *Letters from the South* (New York, 1835), I, 223. Originally published in 1817. For further comments on the production of "useful" literature, see Francis, *Old New York,* pp. 362-363; Goodrich, *Recollections of a Lifetime,* II, 380-382; and Verplanck, *Discourses and Addresses,* p. 204.

[33] Witness their share in the struggle for literary nationalism. See below, p. lxxx *et seq.*

[34] See R. E. Spiller, Introduction, *James Fenimore Cooper* (New York, 1936), pp. xxv-xxix, lvii-lxv, lxxvii-lxxxiii.

[35] *Ibid.,* p. lxxx. Cf. the review of *The Water Witch* in the *New-York Mirror,* VIII, 190 (December 18, 1830): "Mr. Cooper is certainly incorrigible. Most of the critics in the country opened in full cry against the errors of his former productions; yet here is another novel, in which they are all repeated; here is the same mannerism in style—the same awkwardness and heaviness in the conversations—the same ill-judged and badly drawn characters."

[36] As I suggest [previously], the critical judgments of the period are sometimes hopelessly confused. Such confusion is to be expected, when one considers the diverse cultural forces at work in America during the years from 1800 to 1840 or 1850. See Jones, *America and French Culture,* chaps. II and III, but especially pp. 53-76.

[37] Judicial criticism is not, of course, confined to the eighteenth century. It was from the critical practice of that century, nevertheless, that the Knickerbockers derived much of their theory.

[38] "Criticism," *New-York Mirror,* IX, 61 (August 27, 1831). Cf. the *Mirror,* IX, 319 (April 7, 1832), where the same passage from Addison is quoted, again with approval.

[39] "A Spicy Cut-up of an Author," *Literary World,* III, 41 (February 19, 1848).

[40] *American Monthly Magazine* (New York), V, 11 (March, 1835). Quoted by Barnes, *Charles Fenno Hoffman,* p. 97. It should be noted, here, that Hoffman was less interested in establishing absolute standards of criticism than he was in emancipating American literary opinion from what he called the "leadingstrings of Europe."

[41] Unless he was implying that an American criticism independent of European influences would be "absolute."

[42] Now remembered almost solely, and somewhat unjustly, as the "Cassio" who assailed J. F. Cooper. See Waples, *The Whig Myth of James Fenimore Cooper,* pp. 90-111, *et passim.*

[43] "American Criticism on American Authors," *New-York Mirror,* XIII, 322 (April 9, 1836). Reprinted from the *Literary and Theological Review* for March, 1836. The italics are Gould's.

[44] But see the replies to Gould's article in the *New-Yorker*, I, 65-66 (April 23, 1836), and the *Mirror*, XIII, 327 (April 9, 1836). For a summary of part of Gould's essay, see Mott, *History of American Magazines, 1741-1850*, pp. 405-406.

[45] Paulding, for instance, thought Dryden "the best critic of modern times." See Selections following, p. 16. It seems to me that A. L. Herold, in his *James Kirke Paulding*, does not sufficiently emphasize Paulding's essential kinship with the English neo-classicists. His faith in reason, his lifelong preference for the heroic couplet, his emphasis on common sense, his admiration of Dryden, Pope, and other "older" writers, his basic anti-romanticism—all these and other qualities of Paulding's mind and temperament were more or less directly derived from the eighteenth century intellectual atmosphere of his formative years.

[46] See, e.g., William Dunlap's review of Croker's edition of Boswell's *Life of Johnson, New-York Mirror*, XI, 82 (September 14, 1833).

[47] William Charvat argues that early American critical theory and practice were derived largely from the Scotch rhetoricians and aestheticians—Kames, Blair, Alison, and their disciples (*Origins of American Critical Thought*, pp. 27-58). I have found little evidence that the New York critics were profoundly influenced by the Scotch theorists, although some of them may have been, through their reading of the quarterlies and of the critical writings of Thomas Campbell and James Montgomery. But, throughout the period, the English neo-classicists are much more frequently named, quoted, and cited as authorities. In 1833, upon the appearance of Abraham Mills's textbook editions of Kames's *Elements of Criticism*, Blair's *Lectures on Rhetoric*, and Alison's *Essays . . . on Taste*, a reviewer for the *Mirror* spoke of them as "celebrated" and "much praised," but displayed no great acquaintance with the volumes under review (*New-York Mirror*, X, 395 [June 15, 1833]). As I suggest elsewhere in this introduction, the sources of American literary thought are exceedingly complex; no single thesis that I know of provides a satisfactory resolution of this complexity.

[48] Introduction, *Washington Irving*, p. lxxvii. See Irving's "The Mutability of Literature" in *The Sketch Book*. The diverse critical standards of the period are interestingly exemplified in the three principal Knickerbocker men of letters. Irving, in such critical writing as he did, tended toward impressionism; Bryant, whose original neo-classicism was modified by a species of romantic liberalism (see W. P. Hudson, "Archibald Alison and William Cullen Bryant," *American Literature*, XII, 59-68 [March, 1940]), adopted a judicial attitude in his critical essays; and Cooper's critical interest was mainly social or sociological. Here is striking confirmation of the fact that although *milieu* is

important in the study of a writer or a period, differences in individual temperament must also be taken into account.

[49] Charvat, *op. cit.*, pp. 117-120. Cf. Julia Power, *Shelley in America in the Nineteenth Century* (Lincoln, Nebraska, 1940), pp. 9-11, *et passim*.

[50] It must be admitted that it was sometimes a rather long step. The phenomenon of the liberal—or even radical—thinker in politics and religion who is conservative in matters of art and literary taste has often been commented on. There were, of course, such individuals among the Knickerbockers.

[51] *New-York Mirror*, IX, 66 (September 3, 1831). The reviewer also raised a question: "Shall we sit down to a little gift from one such [as this author], with a cold critic's frown, and ferret out a mischosen word, or snap at a sentence . . . because it has not all the polish which the student's closet labor might have imparted?" Cf. T. S. Fay's definition of a critic—"a large dog, that goes unchained, and barks at every thing he does not comprehend" (*Dreams and Reveries of a Quiet Man*, I, 178).

[52] K. L. Daughrity, *The Life and Work of Nathaniel Parker Willis, 1806-1836* (Unpublished University of Virginia Doctoral Dissertation, 1935), chaps. V and VI. Cf. Charvat, *op. cit.*, p. 166.

[53] Willis's reviews were not always sympathetic. See, e.g., his criticism of Paulding, reprinted from the *Corsair*, in *Southern Literary Messenger*, V, 415-417 (June, 1839).

[54] Quoted in Beers, *Nathaniel Parker Willis*, pp. 87-88. Willis was here reviewing Lady Sydney Morgan's *Book of the Boudoir*. Beers remarks that Willis "had a natural instinct for journalism, and he soon acquired by practice that personal, sympathetic attitude toward his readers, and that ready adjustment of himself to the public taste, which made him the most popular magazinist of his day and defined at once his success and his limitations."

[55] *À l'Abri, or, the Tent Pitch'd* (New York, 1839), p. 147.

[56] Cox expressed his general attitude in an article written shortly after the death of Sir Walter Scott. In an early paragraph of this essay, Cox says: "I would fain pay a portion of my tribute of thankfulness for the many, many hours of pure pleasure his works have afforded me, in a few scattered remarks, though it almost looks like presumption to do so. Criticism is out of the question. Criticism, as far as Scott is concerned, should now . . . go to sleep, at least for a while" (*Crayon Sketches* [New York, 1833], II, 236). It is

evident that the kind of "criticism" Cox was objecting to was the judicial type, or "formal, frigid criticism," as he called it.

[57] See, e.g., "A Few of the Inconveniences of Seeing Shakespeare Acted," *Crayon Sketches,* I, 41-54; "Bulwer and Walter Scott," *ibid.,* I, 77-95; "Sir Walter Scott," *ibid.,* II, 233-246; "Washington Irving," *New-York Mirror,* VII, 348 (May 8, 1830); "Byron," *ibid.,* XIV, 356-357 (May 6, 1837). Cf. Washington Irving's "Desultory Thoughts on Criticism" (1839), in *Biographies and Miscellanies,* ed. P. M. Irving.

[58] G. C. Verplanck, "Memoir of the Late Robert C. Sands," *New-York Mirror,* XI, 251 (February 8, 1834). Cf. *Knickerbocker,* XXXIX, 373 (April, 1852).

[59] See his article, "Criticism," *New-York Mirror,* IX, 60-61 (August 27, 1831).

[60] *Dreams and Reveries of a Quiet Man,* II, 151. Note that Fay here mingles judicial analysis (of a sort) with sentimental impressionism. Such mixtures are by no means rare in the criticism of the period.

[61] By 1835, Coleridge was generally accepted in New York literary circles as both poet and critic. See *New-York Mirror,* VII, 185 (December 19, 1829); and *ibid.,* XIII, 31 (July 25, 1835). Of Carlyle, there was still considerable doubt—perhaps because of his relationship with the New England transcendentalists—but his writings were read (see above, p. xlii) and his influence was undoubtedly felt. In 1841, an American edition of his *German Romance* caused a New York reviewer to exclaim: "Mr. Carlyle's wonderful genius is as conspicuous in these translations as in his original works, and it is as well employed, for it opens to the English reader copious sources of amusement and instruction which were before locked up in a foreign . . . language" (*New-York Mirror,* XIX, 175 [May 29, 1841]). Both Coleridge and Carlyle, of course, exerted an indirect influence on the period through the writings of various American disciples. On Carlyle's early influence in this country, see W. S. Vance, "Carlyle in America before *Sartor Resartus,*" *American Literature,* VII, 363-375 (January, 1936); and George Kummer, "Anonymity and Carlyle's Early Reputation in America," *ibid.,* VIII, 297-299 (November, 1936).

[62] *New-York Mirror,* XII, 335 (April 18, 1835).

[63] "The Poetry of Charles Sprague," *New-York Mirror,* XVI, 253 (February 2, 1839). J. E. Spingarn, in commenting on the development of German expressionist criticism, quotes very much the same passage from Carlyle's essay, and remarks: "I am afraid that no German critic wholly realized this ideal; but it was at least the achievement of the Germans that they enunciated the doctrine, even if they did not always adequately illustrate it in practice" (*Creative Criticism* [New York, 1917], pp. 20-21). It may be added that the *Mirror* critic's "ideal" was considerably above his practice.

[64] The quoted words are used by Bernard Smith in speaking of the widespread acceptance of the doctrine of moral utility (*Forces in American Criticism,* p. 40).

[65] New York journalist, business man, and occasional writer (1799-1880). He was the author of *Tales and Sketches by a Cosmopolite* (1830), of *Giordano,* a play (1832), and of a considerable amount of verse and criticism.

[66] *Southern Literary Messenger,* VIII, [2]44 (April, 1842).

[67] *Evening Gazette* (New York), June 9, 1845. Quoted by Barnes, *Charles Fenno Hoffman,* p. 101.

[68] The literary theories of Irving, Cooper, and Bryant are briefly but adequately treated in the individual volumes devoted to them in this series. Bryant's prosodic theories and practice are discussed in Allen, *American Prosody,* pp. 28-55; and Irving's literary theories in Williams, *Life of Washington Irving, passim.*

[69] G. W. Allen summarizes (*American Prosody,* p. 54) the important influences on American verse at the beginning of the nineteenth century thus: "In all there were five movements in English poetry which could not fail to influence American versification in one way or another: (1) The revival of blank verse and the creation of a new poetic style, as in Thomson's *Seasons;* (2) the related 'Miltonic school,' with the revival of interest in the octosyllabic couplet and blank verse, as practiced by Parnell, Young, Blair, and others; (3) the 'imitators of Spenser,' in the work of Shenstone, Akenside, Beattie, and others; (4) the work of the 'antiquaries,' notably Percy's *Reliques,* Macpherson's *Ossian,* and Chatterton's *Rowley Poems;* and (5) finally, *Lyrical Ballads.*"

[70] The influence of Coleridge and Wordsworth was felt before 1835, as was that of Southey, Shelley, and Keats. But the wider influence of almost all the English romantic poets, save Byron, came in the late thirties, the forties, and the fifties.

[71] In a letter written in February, 1847. Quoted by Herold, *James Kirke Paulding,* p. 120.

[72] *Ibid.*

[73] *A Sketch of Old England* (New York, 1822), I, 218. Quoted by Herold, *op. cit.,* p. 118.

[74] K. B. Taft, *Samuel Woodworth* (Unpublished University of Chicago Doctoral Dissertation, 1936), pp. 112-115.

[75] "Art of Poetry," *Parthenon,* I, 23 (August 29, 1827).

[76] Woodworth mentions Bysshe by name and quotes from his *Art of Poetry.*

[77] *Parthenon,* I, 39 (September 5, 1827). Woodworth qualifies his rigid insistence upon iambs and anapaests by allowing that other kinds of feet "may be *occasionally* introduced, for the same purpose that *discords* are admitted into music—to heighten the effect by contrast, or to produce some incidental or some extraordinary *expression.*" Cf. Bryant's remark that Robert C. Sands "understood how to roughen his verse with skill, and to vary its modulation" (quoted in *New-York Mirror,* XI, 251 [February 8, 1834] from the *Knickerbocker* for January, 1833). See also Bryant's "On the Use of Trisyllabic Feet in Iambic Verse" (1819), conveniently accessible in Tremaine McDowell, *William Cullen Bryant: Representative Selections* (New York, 1935), pp. 158-164.

[78] *Parthenon,* I, 23 (August 29, 1827).

[79] See Adkins, *Fitz-Greene Halleck,* p. 50; and Pleadwell, *Life and Works of Joseph Rodman Drake,* pp. 41-44, 136-137.

[80] Pleadwell, *op. cit.,* p. 117. See also the note on "The Culprit Fay" in the present volume, p. 389.

[81] See "To a Friend," Selections following, p. 209.

[82] "The Culprit Fay" is a good example of this interest.

[83] J. G. Wilson, *Life and Letters of Fitz-Greene Halleck* (New York, 1869), p. 560.

[84] *Fitz-Greene Halleck,* p. 199. The anecdote first appeared in *North American Review,* CXXV, 65 (July, 1877).

[85] *Southern Literary Messenger,* VIII, [2]45 (April, 1842).

[86] "The Writings of Fitz-Greene Halleck," *New-York Mirror,* XIV, 97 (September 24, 1836).

[87] See *À l'Abri,* pp. 111-112, 169-172.

[88] "Unwritten Poetry," *The Legendary* (Boston, 1828), I, 37.

[89] *Nathaniel Parker Willis,* p. 108.

[90] Daughrity, *Life and Work of Nathaniel Parker Willis,* p. 206.

[91] *The Convalescent* (New York, 1859), pp. 48-49.

[92] Wills did, however, make some very specific comments on the art of prose.

[93] See above, p. lxiii.

[94] *Biographia Literaria* (1817), chap. XIV.

[95] *New-York Mirror,* IX, 381 (June 2, 1832). Reprinted from the *New-York American.*

[96] *Literary World,* II, 553 (January 8, 1848). Quoted by Barnes, *Charles Fenno Hoffman,* p. 103.

[97] "Grave Speculations," *New-York Mirror,* XVI, 269 (February 16, 1839)

[98] "On the Decay of the Supernatural," *New-York Mirror,* XVII, 108 (September 28, 1839).

[99] "Repetitions," *New-York Mirror,* XV, 20 (July 15, 1837).

[100] *Crayon Sketches,* II, 102.

[101] See Bleecker's "Jungfrau Spaiger's Apostrophe to Her Cat," Paulding's *The Backwoodsman,* and Verplanck's *The Bucktail Bards,* Selections following.

[102] Most of the forms mentioned are illustrated in the Selections.

[103] In 1835, the editors of the *Mirror* rejected some verses because they were "nothing more than unmeaning prose, cut up into lines, without the least regard even to measure" (*New-York Mirror,* XII, 335 [April 18, 1835]). Remarks of this kind are common, with the censure most frequently directed at faulty metre and imperfect rhyme.

[104] Writing to Halleck in January, 1836, Willis Gaylord Clark said: "I like less than any other piece [in your volume], 'The Field of the Grounded Arms.' It is full of thought and rich language, but you will forgive me, if I think even harmony would have improved it" (*Letters of Willis Gaylord Clark and Lewis Gaylord Clark,* ed. L. W. Dunlap [New York, 1940], p. 35). Cf. Adkins, *Fitz-Greene Halleck,* pp. 231-235. See the poem itself, Selections following, p. 129, and note, p. 386.

[105] There were, however, numerous experiments with irregular forms of verse, even in the twenties and thirties. See, e.g., the Skeltonic verses of Isaac Starr Clason's "To a Moscheto," in *Horace in New-York* (New York, 1826), pp. 9-10. J. G. Percival openly advocated license in poetic form in the preface to his *Prometheus,* Part II (New Haven, 1822); see Charvat, *American Critical Thought,* pp. 100-101.

[106] See Woodworth's "A Sonnet on Sonnets," Selections following, p. 60, and note, p. 381.

[107] See Charvat, *op. cit.,* p. 109. In *The Sonnet in American Literature* (Philadelphia, 1930) L. G. Sterner gives a general survey of the history of the sonnet in this country. But cf. H. Carter Davidson, "The Sonnet in Seven Early American Magazines and Newspapers," *American Literature,* IV, 180-187 (May, 1932).

[108] See Allen, *American Prosody,* p. 87.

[109] If this statement needs further qualification, it can be supplied by adding the phrase "according to their light." It is hardly to be expected that the Knickerbocker poets and critics would welcome radical departures from standard prosodic theory and practice.

[110] *The Literary and Scientific Repository,* the *Atlantic Magazine,* the *New-York Review and Atheneum Magazine,* the *Mirror,* and the *Knickerbocker,* among others, published such articles. This interest in the older dramatists was undoubtedly stimulated by German and English romantic criticism.

[111] *New-York Mirror,* VIII, 131 (October 30, 1830).

[112] See *Crayon Sketches* for examples of Cox's dramatic criticism. Attention may also be called to Paulding's various remarks on dramatic writing. See his *A Sketch of Old England,* I, 211-226; and "American Drama," *American Quarterly Review,* I, 331-357 (June, 1827).

[113] See Mott, *History of American Magazines,* 1741-1850, pp. 165-170, 427-431; and Charvat, *American Critical Thought,* pp. 120-133. In the *Plaindealer* for March 11, 1837, William Leggett found it necessary to defend the drama and the theatre from the attacks that were still being made on moral, religious, and economic grounds. See *Political Writings of William Leggett,* II, 256-265.

[114] See Brown, *The Sentimental Novel in America,* chap. I. For the earlier attitude, see G. H. Orians, "Censure of Fiction in American Romances and Magazines, 1789-1810," *Publications of the Modern Language Association,* LII, 195-214 (March, 1937).

[115] G. H. Orians, "The Romance Ferment after *Waverley,*" *American Literature,* III, 408-431 (January, 1932).

[116] *New-York Mirror,* XIII, 330 (April 16, 1836). Gould *was* contradicted, however, by the editors of the *Mirror,* who thought that Paulding should be accorded first place among American writers of fiction. Gould's appraisal was, of course, much the more commonly accepted one.

[117] *Crayon Sketches,* I, 79-81. For a dissenting opinion on the relative greatness of Scott, see Paulding, *A Sketch of Old England,* II, 149; for another, based on considerably different grounds, see James Fenimore Cooper, *Gleanings in Europe: England,* ed. R. E. Spiller (New York, 1930), p. 153.

[118] As Dorothy Waples suggests in *The Whig Myth of James Fenimore Cooper,* there were fluctuations in Cooper's popularity, as well as severe attacks upon him. But when the whole period is taken into account, it is clear that Cooper was generally regarded as the leading American novelist of the day.

[119] Wilson, *Bryant and His Friends,* p. 238. Halleck made this remark about Cooper in the course of a conversation with Wilson; he went on to say: "Irving [is] lieutenant-colonel; Bryant, the major; while Longfellow, Whittier, Holmes, Dana, and myself may be considered captains." Cf. Halleck's comments on Cooper in the first two stanzas of "Red Jacket," Selections following, p. 132.

[120] *Letters of Willis Gaylord Clark and Lewis Gaylord Clark,* p. 122. Clark was writing (February 18, 1845) to Parkman about "The Scalp Hunter," which the future historian had submitted to the *Knickerbocker.*

[121] One reviewer remarked: "A *critique,* in the true sense of the word, is neither required nor deserved by the popular novels of the day" (*New-York Mirror,* XII, 238 [January 24, 1835]).

[122] L. F. Tasistro, in a review of Poe's *Tales of the Grotesque and Arabesque, New-York Mirror,* XVII, 215 (December 28, 1839).

[123] The problem of moral utility has been discussed above, pp. xlvi-xlix. On the matter of literary nationalism, see below, pp. lxxx-lxxxv.

[124] See the review of Morris Mattson's *Paul Ulric, New-York Mirror,* XIII, 198 (December 19, 1835).

[125] Cooper was often censured for his cumbersome style. See, e.g., the review of *The Water Witch* cited above, footnote 164.

[126] Hawthorne was complimented on his "singularly beautiful and original" style (*New-York Mirror,* XVI, 263 [February 9, 1839]). C. F. Hoffman praised Melville for the "fresh, graceful, and animated style" of *Typee* (*Gazette & Times,* March 30, 1846; quoted by Barnes, *Charles Fenno Hoffman,* p. 104); but a reviewer for the *Knickerbocker* (XXXV, 448 [May, 1850]) was disturbed by certain Carlylean and Emersonian tendencies in *White Jacket.*

[127] *Letters from the South,* I, 248; quoted by Herold, *James Kirke Paulding,* pp. 117-118.

[128] See, e.g., William Cox's burlesque of the extravagances of sentimental romance, "The Victim of Sensibility," *New-York Mirror*, VII, 308-309 (April 3, 1830); and a similar parody on pretentious style, "The Fly Market Loafer," *ibid.*, IX, 253-254 (February II, 1832).

[129] *New-York Mirror*, XV, 189 (December 9, 1837).

[130] *Dreams and Reveries of a Quiet Man*, I, 39-45.

[131] *Crayon Sketches*, I, 83.

[132] *New-York Mirror*, VIII, 380 (June 4, 1831).

[133] A reviewer of Bird's *Nick of the Woods* (probably C. F. Hoffman) remarked: "The three great requisites of a novel we believe to be interest—interest—interest. And with this, Nick of the Woods is supplied in a very high degree" (*New-York Mirror*, XIV, 327 [April 8, 1837]).

[134] This was clearly a reaction to an increasing tendency in the popular fiction of the day. The novels of Bulwer, greatly admired in some respects, were often censured for their extravagances in episode, characterization, and plot.

[135] Dedication to *The Puritan and His Daughter* (New York, 1849). See also his essay "Blood-Pudding Literature," which prefaces the second volume of the same novel.

[136] See "National Literature," Selections following, p. 15.

[137] New York miscellaneous writer (1805-1850), and editor or associate editor of various newspapers and magazines, including a brief period with the *Mirror*. He was a brother of Henry Inman, the portrait painter.

[138] "A Caution to Novelists," *New-York Mirror*, XIV, 372 (May 20, 1837).

[139] *New-York Mirror*, I, 380 (June 26, 1824). Cf. Bryant's review of the same novel, *North American Review*, XX, 245-272 (April, 1825).

[140] *Crayon Sketches*, I, 89-90. Cox thought that Scott possessed the power he described, whereas Bulwer lacked it.

[141] "The Works of the Author of *The Spy*," *New-York Mirror*, VIII, 254 (February 12, 1831).

[142] Perhaps the best comments on the essay are those of N. P. Willis. See his remarks on magazine article writing, *American Monthly Magazine*, I, 866-867 (March, 1830); on the same subject in *À l'Abri*, p. 144; and, on the revival of the essay form, in *Hurry-graphs*, pp. 251-252. Willis thought that a good essay should be brief, spirited, original in its handling of a subject, and amusing but not impudent. He had high regard for the essays of Lamb and of Irving. C. F. Hoffman, incidentally, believed that Willis's own essays were "superior in elegance and spirit to those of any other American Writer except Washington Irving" (quoted by Barnes, *Charles Fenno Hoffman*, p. 89). William Cox, like Willis, greatly admired the essays of Lamb and Irving. Attention has already been called (see above, p. lx) to Verplanck's comparison of Cox's essays to those of Lamb and Hazlitt.

[143] In 1834, a magazine editor noted the need for a distinctive name to apply to the writer of tales—and his product. See "A Philological Deficiency," *New-York Mirror*, XII, 159 (November 15, 1834).

[144] See Williams, *Life of Washington Irving*, II, 277-278. For Irving's own statement of his reasons for adopting the short story form, see *Letters of Washington Irving to Henry Brevoort*, p. 399.

[145] See Charvat, *American Critical Thought*, pp. 160-162. Cf. Pochmann, *Washington Irving*, p. lxviii.

[146] A reviewer of *Tales of Glauber-Spa* (1832), for example, remarked that William Leggett's contribution to that work and his other tales and sketches were excellent, but that he should "accomplish a larger work of the same description, which shall do more honor to him and to his country, than the best of such less ambitious flights as the one before us" (*New-York Mirror*, X, 151 [November 10, 1832]).

[147] In a review of *National Tales*, ed. George Houston (New York, 1825), in the *New-York Review and Atheneum Magazine*, II, 37 (December, 1825).

[148] Louis Fitzgerald Tasistro (ca. 1807-1868), Irish-born actor, versifier, and journalist, was editor in 1839 of the *Expositor*, a New York literary weekly.

[149] *New-York Mirror*, XVII, 215 (December 28, 1839).

[150] *Ibid.*, XVI, 263 (February 9, 1839).

[151] There has been a large amount of scholarly writing on this and related topics. Representative articles are: N. M. Ashby, "Aliment for Genius," *American Literature*, VIII, 371-378 (January, 1937); R. W. Bolwell, "Concerning the Study of Nationalism in American Literature," *ibid.*, X, 405-416 (January, 1939); H. H. Clark, "Nationalism in American Literature," *University of Toronto Quarterly*, II, 491-519 (July, 1933); J. C. McCloskey, "The Campaign of Periodicals after the War of 1812 for National American Literature," *Publications of the Modern Language Association*, L, 262-273 (March, 1935); W. E. Sedgwick, "The Materials

for an American Literature: A Critical Problem of the Early Nineteenth Century," *Harvard Studies and Notes in Philology and Literature,* XVII, 141-162 (1935); and B. T. Spencer, "A National Literature, 1837-1855," *American Literature,* VIII, 125-159 (May, 1936).

[152] See the articles by Bolwell and Spencer, cited above.

[153] Wilson, *Life Letters of Fitz-Greene Halleck,* pp. 262-263. Halleck made these remarks only a few weeks before his death, in 1867, in a letter to J. G. Wilson. It should not be overlooked that in his younger days he often—and consciously—used distinctively American subjects (see "The Field of the Grounded Arms" and "Red Jacket," Selections following), or that he had a share in "the paper war with England" (see below, p. lxxxviii).

[154] New York lawyer and occasional writer (1796-1863), brother of John Howard Payne.

[155] *Atlantic Magazine,* I, 19 (May, 1824).

[156] *Writings of Robert C. Sands* (New York, 1834), I, 103-115. This essay was originally published in the *Atlantic Magazine,* I, 130-139 (June, 1824).

[157] See, for example, J. G. Palfrey's review of Sands's own poem, *Yamoyden* (written in collaboration with J. W. Eastburn), in *North American Review,* XII, 480-485 (April, 1821).

[158] See N. F. Adkins, "James K. Paulding's *Lion of the West,*" *American Literature,* III, 249 (November, 1931); and Herold, *James Kirke Paulding, passim.*

[159] See the rest of this introductory section of *The Backwoodsman,* Selections following, p. 14.

[160] See the complete essay, Selections following, p. 15.

[161] See the quotation given above, p. lxxvi, and footnote 264.

[162] Pleadwell, *Life and Works of Joseph Rodman Drake,* pp. 134-139.

[163] See "To a Friend," Selections following, p. 209.

[164] *Analectic Magazine,* XII, 69 (July, 1818). Another reviewer of the same volume, however, in reading some of Woodworth's stanzas was reminded of Campbell and Montgomery (*American Monthly Magazine,* III, 167 [July, 1818]).

[165] *The Champions of Freedom* (New York, 1816), I, viii.

[166] *Literary Casket and Pocket Magazine,* I, 3 (April, 1821). He said the same thing, six years later, in the *Parthenon,* I, 40 (September 5, 1827).

[167] *New-York Mirror,* I, 1 (August 2, 1823).

[168] *Ibid.,* XVIII, 15 (July 4, 1840). The editor went on to say: "It does not, however, neglect exotic productions; but culls, from time to time, with studious care, the roses and laurels that have sprung in a foreign soil." Thus did the periodical extenuate its then increasing eclecticism.

[169] Spivey, *The Knickerbocker Magazine,* 1833-1865, p. 380. Dr. Spivey here quotes from an editorial statement in the *Knickerbocker,* II, 487 (December, 1833).

[170] *Knickerbocker,* II, 5 (July, 1833).

[171] *Ibid.,* II, 161-168 (September, 1833).

[172] *Ibid.,* III, 136 (February, 1834).

[173] Quoted by Barnes, *Charles Fenno Hoffman,* p. 69.

[174] *Ibid.,* p. 81. See also above, p. lv.

[175] *Ibid.,* pp. 105, 213.

[176] *Ibid.,* p. 97.

[177] In addition to those discussed above, various other Knickerbocker writers advocated nationalism, in one form or another. Among them were Mitchill, Verplanck, Fay, Willis, Lewis Gaylord Clark (and his brother), and, a little later, Cornelius Mathews. On the part played by Mathews in the struggle for literary nationalism, see Spencer, *op. cit.,* pp. 136-137.

[178] The influence of Pope was particularly pervasive in the early satirical verse. See below, p. xc.

[179] Although the echoings of Scott, Byron, Moore, and Campbell are palpable, and have frequently been noted, the extensive influence of Lamb has received relatively scant attention. But as early as 1839, in commenting on this influence, N. P. Willis could say, retrospectively: "The writings of all our young authors were tinctured with imitation of his [Lamb's] style" (*À l'Abri,* p. 120).

[180] Non-English influences are perhaps especially noticeable in the work of Washington Irving. See Williams and McDowell, "Introduction," *Knickerbocker's History of New York,* pp. xxxviii-xlvi; Pochmann, *Washington Irving,* pp. lxiii-lxvi; and Williams, *Life of Washington Irving, passim.* Many aspects of the whole problem of non-English influences upon early American literature await and deserve investigation.

[181] Among them were Paulding, Fay, Cox, Sands, and Hoffman.

[182] Barnes, *Charles Fenno Hoffman,* p. 31; Taft, *Samuel Woodworth,* pp. 114, 122; Adkins, *Fitz-Greene Halleck, passim.*

[183] Contemporary reviewers of the poems of J. G. Brooks and Alfred B. Street perceived the indebtedness of these versifiers to Bryant. Noted with some frequency, also, was the apparent influence of Cooper on certain tales by Paulding, Hoffman, and Leggett.

[184] R. G. Moulton, *The Modern Study of Literature* (Chicago, 1915), p. 16.

[185] An excellent account of some phases of the Anglo-American controversy will be found in Mesick, *The English Traveller in America,* pp. 270-290. See also R. E. Spiller, "Brother Jonathan to John Bull," *South Atlantic Quarterly,* XXVI, 346-358 (October, 1927); the same author's *The American in England* (New York, 1926), pp. 300-345; and Nevins, *American Social History as Recorded by British Travellers, passim.*

[186] See his *The Diverting History of John Bull and Brother Jonathan* (1812), *The United States and England* (1815), *Letters from the South* (1817), *A Sketch of Old England by a New-England Man* (1822), *John Bull in America* (1825); and Herold, *James Kirke Paulding,* pp. 46-65.

[187] Among the participants were S. L. Mitchill, Woodworth, Sands, Leggett, Morris, Hoffman, and Fay.

[188] The entire poem, "To the Critics of England," is given in Wilson, *Life and Letters of Fitz-Greene Halleck,* pp. 257-258. Halleck's verses were addressed, in particular, to certain writers for the *Quarterly Review* (London). See Adkins, *Fitz-Greene Halleck,* p. 138.

[189] See "English Writers on America" in *The Sketch Book.*

[190] See Fay's satire on Mrs. Trollope's *Domestic Manners of the Americans,* Selections following, p. 339, and note, p. 398.

[191] Williams, *Life of Washington Irving,* I, 77.

[192] See above, pp. xv and li.

[193] Exemplified in what may very properly be called the lucubrations of Thomas Ward (1807-1873), author of *Passaic: A Group of Poems Touching that River* (1842), and contributor under the pen-name "Flaccus" to the *Knickerbocker Magazine.*

[194] Williams, *Life of Washington Irving,* II, 263-267.

[195] *Ibid.,* I, 114-115. See also Williams and McDowell, "Introduction," *A History of New York,* pp. xxxviii-xliii.

[196] Taft, *Samuel Woodworth,* pp. 112-119, 121.

[197] Herold, *James Kirke Paulding,* pp. 39-42. Cf. G. E. Hastings, "John Bull and His American Descendants," *American Literature,* I, 40-68 (March, 1929).

[198] See Selections following, p. 70.

[199] Adkins, *Fitz-Greene Halleck,* pp. 81-84, 104-115. See also Leonard, *Byron and Byronism in America, passim.*

[200] Adkins, (*op. cit.,* p. 125) quotes a Philadelphia reviewer of *Fanny,* who remarked: "In New York they make a man jocose in spite of himself—at least, whether he be so inclined or not. An excellent, amiable, and intelligent set of people, they certainly are in that town, but ever since they have had to boast of 'Salmagundi' and 'Knickerbocker' as indigenous productions—a propensity to satire and burlesque has been their besetting sin; the passion has been a perfect *mania,* and they have laughed at their own caricature in every variety of shape. No wonder, therefore, if a poet should find it difficult either to escape the infection (*contagion* it would be called there), or to resist the current" (*Literary Gazette,* I, 209 [April 7, 1821]).

[201] These are only a few of the satires and burlesques published in New York during the Knickerbocker period. The Anglo-American controversy produced a large number of satires, as did the various political quarrels of the era. Among the later satires by New York writers, mention may be made here of Paulding's *Merry Tales of the Three Wise Men of Gotham* (1826), *The New Mirror for Travellers* (1828), *Chronicles of the City of Gotham* (1830), and *The Bucktails; or, Americans in England* (published 1847), of Sands's "Mr. Green" (in *Tales of Glauber-Spa,* 1832), of the several satiric sketches in Fay's *Dreams and Reveries of a Quiet Man* (1832) and Cox's *Crayon Sketches* (1833), of Anna Cora Mowatt's *Reviewers Reviewed* (1837), of F. W. Shelton's *Trollopiad* (1837), of Laughton Osborne's *Vision of Rubeta* (1838), of the anonymous *St. Jonathan: The Lay of a Scald* (1838) and *Richardsiana* (1841), of Park Benjamin's *Poetry: A Satire* (1842) and *Infatuation* (1844), and of Cornelius Mathews's *The Career of Puffer Hopkins* (1842).

[202] *The Bucktail Bards* and many of the "Croaker" poems, for example, were originally published in newspapers. Most of Fay's and Cox's satires were first printed in the *New-York Mirror,* and *The Career of Puffer Hopkins* ran through numerous issues of *Arcturus.* Even such decorous journals as the *New-York*

Review and Atheneum Magazine occasionally welcomed satiric verse and articles.

[203] When *Salmagundi* was published, Washington Irving was twenty-four, Paulding twenty-nine; Woodworth was twenty-five when his *New-Haven* appeared; Halleck was twenty-nine and Drake twenty-four when they wrote the "Croaker" poems; Morris was twenty-one when he and Woodworth established the *Mirror;* Willis on joining the *Mirror* staff at the age of twenty-five was already an experienced journalist and a well known writer; Payne was only fifteen when his first play was produced and published; Fay, Cox, and Sands were all active in New York journalism before reaching their twenty-fifth birthdays.

[204] Of the minor Knickerbockers represented in the Selections following, more than half were active at various times in the editing of newspapers or magazines, or both. Among those who may be thought of as "professional journalists" are Woodworth, Sands, Leggett, Brooks, Morris, Cox, Willis, Hoffman, Fay, Mellen, the brothers Clark, Benjamin, and Mathews.

[205] See Adkins, *Fitz-Greene Halleck,* p. 128.

[206] One may only speculate on the possible effect of such an environment upon Emerson, or Thoreau, or Melville, or Hawthorne. Melville, of course, lived in New York after 1847, when the Knickerbocker period had ended. It should be remembered also that in his most productive years he had little to do with the hurly-burly of commerce, politics, or journalism.

[207] The social activities of the day—convivial gatherings, club meetings, public dinners, and the like—inspired the writing of many occasional pieces, most often in verse. Celebrations of holidays and of "milestones" in the life of the city prompted innumerable compositions, as did the theatrical benefits, the recurrent prize contests, and the openings of new theatres.

[208] N. F. Adkins comments sanely (*Fitz-Greene Halleck,* pp. 207-214) on these conflicts as they appear in the personality and the writings of Halleck. Such conflicts are apparent, in various combinations, in the work of other Knickerbocker writers. See C. G. Laird, "Tragedy and Irony in *Knickerbocker's History,*" *American Literature,* XII, 157-172 (May, 1940).

[209] For an account of the numerous ways in which this emotional fervor manifested itself, see Branch, *The Sentimental Years,* especially chaps. IV-VI. See also Brown, *The Sentimental Novel in America, passim;* Tremaine McDowell, "Sensibility in the Eighteenth Century American Novel," *Studies in Philology,* XXIV, 383-402 (July, 1927); and R. E. Watters, *The Vogue and Influence of Samuel Richardson in America*

(Unpublished University of Wisconsin Doctoral Dissertation, 1941).

[210] "It was logical . . . that the gift books should be highly sentimental and exotic. Lords and ladies, far-off lands, and a somewhat impossibly glorious national history were normal products of romanticism as well as a means of transcending middle class existence. Tender and genteel verse satisfied emotional longings, unrealistic engravings the visual" (Thompson, *American Literary Annuals & Gift Books,* p. 5). Cf. Mott, *History of American Magazines, 1741-1850,* pp. 139-144, 348-354; and Beers, *Nathaniel Parker Willis,* pp. 77-80.

[211] *New-York Mirror,* VII, 287 (March 13, 1830).

[212] Taft, *Samuel Woodworth,* p. 122. Woodworth, like Washington Irving and various others, exhibited an early interest in the writing of satire, but drifted, amiably enough, into the placid current of sentimentality.

[213] In this category may be placed Woodworth, Morris, Willis, the Clarks, and a good many of their contemporaries, both masculine and feminine.

[214] See above, pp. lvi, n., and lxv.

[215] See "National Literature" and "Of the Vulgar, and in What It Principally Consists," Selections following, pp. 15 and 19.

[216] One should not overlook the probable influence of Washington Irving's handling of local color in such stories as "Rip Van Winkle" and "The Legend of Sleepy Hollow," but, as A. L. Herold has pointed out (*James Kirke Paulding,* pp. 1-2), Paulding's use of similar material was both more extensive and more realistic.

[217] Examples of this tendency may be found in the work of practically all the minor Knickerbockers. Even those writers who treated emotions and ideas sentimentally or plot melodramatically were likely to become realistic when they presented local color material. See, e.g., T. S. Fay's sketch of a polling place at election time, *New-York Mirror,* VII, 148 (November 14, 1829); Woodworth's description of moving day in New York, *Poetical Works of Samuel Woodworth,* II, 53-54; or Willis's account of a September morning's activities on his farm, *À l'Abri,* pp. 165-168. But cf. Cooper's introduction to *The Pioneers* (1850 ed.), in which he says that a "rigid adhesion to truth, an indispensable requisite in history and travels, destroys the charm of fiction; for all that is necessary to be conveyed to the mind by the latter had better be done by delineation of principles, and of characters in their classes, than by a too fastidious attention to originals."

[218] See Woodworth's "The Hunters of Kentucky" and the chapter from Hoffman's *A Winter in the West,*

Selections following, pp. 56 and 319. Other treatments of the frontier character and scene appear in Leggett's "The Block House" (1832), Hoffman's *Wild Scenes in the Forest and Prairie* (1839), and Paulding's *The Backwoodsman* (1818), *The Lion of the West* (produced 1831), and *Westward Ho!* (1832).

219 Walter Blair, *Native American Humor* (New York, 1937), pp. 16, 30-31, 38, 82-85, *et passim.*

220 The population figure for Greater New York in 1840 was 391,114; for Manhattan alone, 312,710. See the census table for Manhattan on p. xvii, above.

221 See above, p. xviii.

222 *Sunday Morning Reflections* (New York, 1839), p. 46.

223 Caroline Ticknor, *Hawthorne and His Publisher* (Boston, 1913), p. 141.

224 Cf. Adkins, *Fitz-Greene Halleck,* p. 304.

225 See the lists in Herold, *James Kirke Paulding,* pp. 88-92, 153-157.

226 Cf. Parrington, *Main Currents in American Thought,* II, 219-221.

227 This is the subtitle of Herold's biography of Paulding.

228 See O. S. Coad, "The Plays of Samuel Woodworth," *Sewanee Review,* XXVII, 166-169 (April-June, 1919); and Quinn, *History of the American Drama from the Beginning to the Civil War,* pp. 294-295.

229 Several other long narratives by Woodworth were serialized in magazines. Among them were *Magnanimity* (1819) and *Resignation* (1820), both published in the *Ladies' Literary Cabinet.*

230 Cf. R. W. Griswold, *The Poets and Poetry of America* (11th ed.; Philadelphia, 1851), p. 84: "[Woodworth] was the poet of the 'common people,' and was happy in the belief that 'The Bucket' was read by multitudes who never heard of 'Thanatopsis.'"

231 Over a period of many years Woodworth was active in the affairs of the General Convention of the New Church (Swedenborgian) and of its Society in New York City. He edited two New Church periodicals—the *Halcyon Luminary* (1812-13) and the *New-Jerusalem Missionary* (1823-24). A collection of his essays on religious topics, *Sunday Morning Reflections,* was published in 1839. Unlike most of his contemporaries among New York men of letters, Woodworth seems to have been deeply concerned with religious questions.

For many of the other Knickerbockers, religion was apparently a matter of form, of occasional church attendance, and of having the "proper" sentiments. A census of the writers included in the present collection shows that about half of them were communicants of the Protestant Episcopal church, while others had Unitarian, Presbyterian, or Lutheran affiliations. The writings of Paulding, Verplanck, and others reveal that they were fundamentally deistic in their religious thinking. Cf. Williams, *Life of Washington Irving,* I, 15-16.

232 See the passage from *The Bucktail Bards,* Selections following, p. 70, and note, p. 381. For a list of Verplanck's writings, see S. K. Harvey, "A Bibliography of the Miscellaneous Prose of Gulian Crommelin Verplanck," *American Literature,* VIII, 199-203 (May, 1936).

233 In speaking of Verplanck's testy reaction to *Knickerbocker's History of New York,* S. T. Williams remarks: "Verplanck was oracularly secure in family, wealth, and in the unimpeachable heaviness of his own pounding humor. Uncompanionable and cold, he was the last person to appreciate the spirit of Knickerbocker; 'too much of a frog, Sir,' said Ogilvie, the orator, 'too much of a frog!'" (*Life of Washington Irving,* II, 276). See above, p. xvi.

234 See the biographical sketch of Verplanck in the present volume, p. 68.

235 A. V. R. Westfall, *American Shakespearean Criticism: 1607-1865* (New York, 1939), pp. 128-136; E. C. Dunn, *Shakespeare in America* (New York, 1939), p. 292. See also R. B. Falk, *Representative American Criticism of Shakespeare, 1830-1885* (Unpublished University of Wisconsin Doctoral Dissertation, 1940).

236 "The Writings of Fitz-Greene Halleck," *New-York Mirror,* XIV, 97 (September 24, 1836).

237 See Adkins, *Fitz-Greene Halleck,* pp. 178-184, 217-218, 255-256 266, 285, *et passim.*

238 *American Poetry* (New York, 1918), p. 629.

239 Adkins, *op. cit.,* pp. 148-149, 219-238.

240 Pleadwell, *Life and Works of Joseph Rodman Drake,* pp. 92-94.

241 The first collected edition of Drake's poems appeared in 1835.

242 See the review in the *New-York Mirror,* XIII, 164-165 (November 21, 1835). Poe, characteristically, refused to join in the chorus of praise. See *Southern Literary Messenger,* II, 326-336 (April, 1836).

[243] Both these poems will be found in the Selections following. For brief but sympathetic comments by W. E. Leonard, see the accompanying notes, pp. 388 and 391.

[244] See "To a Friend," Selections following, p. 209.

[245] See Harrison, *John Howard Payne*, pp. 126-136. Cf. *New-York Mirror*, X, 39 (August 4, 1832); *ibid.*, X, 182 (December 8, 1832).

[246] "Memoir of John Howard Payne," *New-York Mirror*, X, 174 (December 1, 1832). Cf. Quinn, *History of the American Drama from the Beginning to the Civil War*, pp. 186-187.

[247] See the biographical sketch of Sands given below, p. 224.

[248] "The Man Who Burnt John Rogers" appeared originally in the *Atlantic Magazine* for October, 1824; "Boyuca" and "Mr. Green," in *Tales of Glauber-Spa* (1832).

[249] See Selections following, p. 230.

[250] See Hone's *Diary*, I, 240.

[251] *Political Writings of William Leggett, passim.*

[252] *Ibid.*, II, 326. See "The Morals of Politics," Selections following, p. 246.

[253] *Main Currents in American Thought*, II, 243.

[254] *New-York Mirror*, VII, 223 (January 16, 1830).

[255] See, e.g., *Letters of Willis Gaylord Clark and Lewis Gaylord Clark*, pp. 23-24; *New-York Mirror*, V, 229-230 (January 26, 1828); *Critic*, I, 161 (January 3, 1829); Wilson, *Life and Letters of Fitz-Greene Halleck*, p. 162.

[256] *Hurry-graphs*, p. 254. In the same article, Willis remarked that Morris could, "at any moment, get fifty dollars for a song unread, when the whole remainder of the American Parnassus could not sell one to the same buyer for a shilling." Cf. *United States Review*, XXXV, 473-492 (June, 1855).

[257] See "The Little Frenchman and His Water Lots," Selections following, p. 257.

[258] This work has sometimes mistakenly been ascribed to T. S. Fay, who was merely its editor.

[259] See Quinn, *History of the American Drama . . . to the Civil War*, pp. 255-259.

[260] See above, p. lix.

[261] See above, p. lxxxiv.

[262] Barnes, *Charles Fenno Hoffman*, pp. 109-112.

[263] See Selections following, p. 326.

[264] In the *Southern Literary Messenger*, II, 54-57 (December, 1835).

[265] See "The Successful Novel," Selections following, p. 342, and accompanying note, p. 398.

[266] See the biographical sketch of Fay in the present volume, p. 334.

[267] See, e.g., "Republicanism of Americans Abroad," *New-York Mirror*, XIII, 169 (November 28, 1835); "Rich and Poor People," *ibid.*, XV, 404 (June 16, 1838).

An excerpt from *Diedrich Knickerbocker's A History of New York*:

It was sometime, if I recollect right, in the early part of the Fall of 1808, that a stranger applied for lodgings at the Independent Columbian Hotel in Mulberry Street, of which I am landlord. . . .

During the whole time that he stayed with us, we found him a very worthy good sort of an old gentleman, though a little queer in his ways. He would keep in his room for days together, and if any of the children cried or made a noise about his door, he would bounce out in a great passion, with his hands full of papers, and say something about "deranging his ideas," which made my wife believe sometimes that he was not altogether *compos*. Indeed there was more than one reason to make her think so, for his room was always covered with scraps of paper and old mouldy books, laying about at sixes and sevens, which he would never let any body touch; for he said he had laid them all away in their proper places, so that he might know where to find them; though for that matter, he was half his time worrying about the house in search of some book or writing which he had carefully put out of the way. I shall never forget what a pother he once made, because my wife cleaned out his room when his back was turned, and put every thing to rights; for he swore he should never be able to get his papers in order again in a twelvemonth—Upon this my wife ventured to ask him what he did with so many books and papers, and he told her that he was "seeking for immortality," which made her think more than ever, that the poor old gentleman's head was a little cracked.

Washington Irving, in Diedrich Knickerbocker's A History of New York, *edited by Stanley Williams and Tremaine McDowell, Harcourt, Brace and Company, 1927.*

KNICKERBOCKER PERIODICALS

William Irving, James Kirke Paulding, and Washington Irving

SOURCE: "Publisher's Notice. Shakespeare Gallery, New York. Saturday, January 24, 1807," in *Salmagundi; or, The Whimwhams and Opinions of Launcelot Langstaff, Esq., and Others,* G. P. Putnam's Sons, 1860.

[*In this 1807 preface to the Knickerbockers' magazine* Salmagundi *(reprinted in book form in 1860) the editors display the wit and playfulness characteristic of the writing in that magazine and indicative of the spirit of cultured amusement in which the editors wished it to be regarded by their reading public.*]

As everybody knows, or ought to know, what a Salmagund is, we shall spare ourselves the trouble of an explanation; besides, we despise trouble as we do everything low and mean, and hold the man who would incur it unnecessarily as an object worthy our highest pity and contempt. Neither will we puzzle our heads to give an account of ourselves, for two reasons; first, because it is nobody's business; secondly, because if it were, we do not hold ourselves bound to attend to anybody's business but our own; and even *that* we take the liberty of neglecting when it suits our inclination. To these we might add a third, that very few men *can* give a tolerable account of themselves, let them try ever so hard; but this reason we candidly avow, would not hold good with ourselves.

There are, however, two or three pieces of information which we bestow gratis on the public, chiefly because it suits our own pleasure and convenience that they should be known, and partly because we do not wish that there should be any ill will between us at the commencement of our acquaintance.

Our intention is simply to instruct the young, reform the old, correct the town, and castigate the age; this is an arduous task, and therefore we undertake it with confidence. We intend for this purpose to present a striking picture of the town; and as everybody is anxious to see his own phiz on canvas, however stupid or ugly it may be, we have no doubt but the whole town will flock to our exhibition. Our picture will necessarily include a vast variety of figures; and should any gentlemen or lady be displeased with the inveterate truth of their likenesses, they may ease their spleen by laughing at those of their neighbors—this being what *we* understand by *poetical justice.*

Like all true and able editors, we consider ourselves infallible; and therefore, with the customary diffidence of our brethren of the quill, we shall take the liberty of interfering in all matters either of a public or a private

nature. We are critics, amateurs, dilettanti, and cognoscenti; and as we know "by the pricking of our thumbs," that every opinion which we may advance in either of those characters will be correct, we are determined, though it may be questioned, contradicted, or even controverted, yet it shall never be revoked.

We beg the public particularly to understand that we solicit no patronage. We are determined, on the contrary, that the patronage shall be entirely on our side. We have nothing to do with the pecuniary concerns of the paper; its success will yield us neither pride nor profit—nor will its failure occasion to us either loss or mortification. We advise the public, therefore, to purchase our numbers merely for their own sakes; if they do not, let them settle the affair with their consciences and posterity.

To conclude, we invite all editors of newspapers and literary journals to praise us heartily in advance, as we assure them that we intend to deserve their praises. To our next-door neighbor, "Town,"[1] we hold out a band of amity, declaring to him that, after ours, his paper will stand the best chance for immortality. We proffer an exchange of civilities: he shall furnish us with notices of epic poems and tobacco; and we in return will enrich him with original speculations on all manner of subjects, together with "the rummaging of my grandfather's mahogany chest of drawers," "the life and amours of mine Uncle John," "anecdotes of the Cockloft family," and learned quotations from that unheard of writer of folios, *Linkum Fidelius.*

Notes

[1] The title of a newspaper published in New York, the columns of which, among other miscellaneous topics, occasionally contained strictures on the performances at the theatres.—*Paris Ed.*

Amos L. Herold

SOURCE: "Salmagundi and Other Literary Experiments," in *James Kirke Paulding: Versatile American,* Columbia University Press, 1926, pp. 30-45.

[*In this excerpt, Herold explains the origin, success, and character of the popular, witty New York literary magazine* Salmagundi, *which the Knickerbockers produced in 1807 and had for a brief year established as the* Punch *of American letters and journalism.*]

In the annals of the United States few years are more noteworthy than 1807. In that year Congress recognized the development of a strong anti-slavery sentiment by prohibiting the importation of African slaves; and the new republic safely weathered the seditious movement headed by Aaron Burr, whose arrest culminated in a spectacular trial at Richmond, Virginia. The romantic Robert Fulton, fresh from foreign travels, revolutionized water traffic by perfecting the steamboat; and the embargo act encouraged American manufacturing. In literature, a group of youthful New York wits broke with the tradition of formal prose an won a notable success in the Salmagundi papers. Just as the *Lyrical Ballads* of 1798 marked a new era in English poetry, so did the *Salmagundi* of 1807 mark the beginning of a simpler fashion in American prose.

On January 24, 1807, up-to-date New Yorkers found themselves eagerly buying and discussing a little, yellowbacked, thirty-page pamphlet that could be easily carried in a man's coat pocket or in a lady's purse. It bore the whimsical title, *Salmagundi; or, The Whim-Whams and Opinions of Launcelot Langstaff, Esq. and Others.* Beneath the name there was a fantastic quotation, mocking the English literary practice of quoting choice bits of Latin as mottoes, and striking the keynote of the periodical. In the introductory article the unnamed authors jocularly announced their purpose "to instruct the young, reform the old, correct the town, and castigate the age; this is an arduous task, and therefore we undertake it with confidence. We intend for this purpose to present a striking picture of the town; and as everybody is anxious to see his own phiz on canvas, however stupid or ugly it may be, we have no doubt but the whole town will flock to our exhibition." Both the authors and the publisher professed a sublime contempt for the pecuniary success of the paper, which would appear at irregular intervals to suit the convenience of the authors; as laughing philosophers, they were eager to entertain their readers and to conceal themselves behind pseudonyms. The first number ended effectively with humorous accounts of recent New York theatrical performances and dancing assemblies. The second, dated February 4, continued the wit of the first, and introduced the humorous bachelor, Pindar Cockloft, who made rhymes on the follies of the new fashions. In the third there appeared the first of nine serial letters on New York attributed to a fictitious Tripolitan named Mustapha Rub-a-Dub Keli Khan, recently a prisoner in the city. Thereafter, the principal topics were the Cockloft family, English travelers in America, fashions, theaters, descriptions of nature, character sketches, Pindar Cockloft's verses, a chapter on the ancient city of Gotham, and other miscellanies. Since number twenty, the last, was published on January 25, 1808, the pamphlets on an average appeared every two or three weeks.

Audacious and spiced with wit, *Salmagundi* became an immediate success. Cleverly advertised and expectantly awaited, many of the separate numbers passed through several editions; a bound copy in a Boston library contains individual numbers in the fourth and fifth editions. With each number the public interest increased; 800 copies at a shilling apiece were sold in a day—a record for that time. Its fame extended to other cities; the authors were astonished at the success of their venture. The publisher, David Longwroth, secured a copyright, and before it expired in 1822, Paulding estimated that the sales amounted to ten or fifteen thousand dollars. Paulding and Irving, however, received only one hundred dollars apiece, and the publication was abruptly discontinued, because the authors and the publisher could not amicably adjust their sublime contempt for the financial gains. John Lambert, an Englishman, who was then in New York and who edited the London edition of 1811, states in his excellent preface that the numbers received "unprecedented applause and passed through several editions during the course of their publication." Since Longworth issued the second American edition in 1814 and the third in 1820, it is evident that *Salmagundi* could subsist without the aid of Irving's later masterpieces. Altogether, down to 1902, it had attained at least thirty-four editions—nineteen American, thirteen English, one French, and one Swedish. Of these, the English with one exception appeared in the first half of the century, indicating lively British curiosity about American affairs; and most of the American editions appeared in the second half of the century, indicating a native revival of interest in early New York. On an average, then, *Salmagundi,* either in separate or in collected editions, has been republished every three years since it first greeted New Yorkers.

This novel periodical elicited some noteworthy contemporary comments both abroad and at home. In England, John Lambert, characterizing it as "a dish of real American cookery," stated: "The distinguishing feature of the Salmagundian Essays is humorous satire, which runs through the whole work like veins of rich ore in the bowels of the earth. These essays partake more of the broad humour and satirical wit of Rabelais and Swift than the refined morality of Addison and Johnson; their chief aim is to raise a laugh at the expense of folly and absurdity."[1] In a friendly critique *The Monthly Review* of London welcomed *Salmagundi* as a commendable specimen of American literature, praised the descriptions and character sketches, and granted that the authors "certainly excel in an adroit species of irony."[2] Still more significant are the opinion and prediction of Sir Walter Scott, recorded in a letter to Washington Irving, dated December 4, 1819: "Knickerbocker and Salmagundi are more exclusively American [than *The Sketch-Book*], and may not be quite so well suited for our meridian. But they are so excellent in their way, that if the public attention could be once turned on them I am confident that they would become popular."[3] At home, the *North American Review,* while praising the early numbers of *The Sketch-Book,* reverted to *Salmagundi,* stated that its fortunate appearance in New York prevented its being looked out of countenance and talked down by supercilious people, and acknowledged that it was "the ablest work of wit and humour which we had produced."[4]

These disinterested commendations, verified by time, are best explained by the fact that *Salmagundi* was written by three wits and published by a fourth. The authorship was so well concealed that John Lambert could hear only whispers of a lawyer and two merchants, and even as late as March, 1832, the editor of the *New York Mirror* after careful enquiry felt the need of publishing an authentic statement, assigning all the poetry and two of the prose articles to William Irving and the rest in about equal but unidentified parts to Washington Irving and James K. Paulding.[5] Of course, in literary circles the Irving-Paulding combination was previously known. For some years the authors had been intermittently writing for the newspapers. Washington Irving at twenty-four had recently returned from a two-year trip to Europe, had passed the bar examination, and was popular in New York and Philadelphia society; Paulding, past twenty-eight, was a handsome young man, alert and satirical. Between them *Salmagundi* arose. P. M. Irving states that Washington proposed the plan of the publication to Paulding, who readily fell in with it, wrote his part, and was in full charge when Irving went to Burr's trial in Richmond. Later, they were joined by William Irving, who completed the trio of wits and wrote the verse.

To determine the authorship of the separate Salmagundi papers is a knotty problem. They have always been published together, and no author ever fully indicated his share. In fact, Paulding stated in the Harper edition of his works (1835) that the essays were so literally joint productions that it would be difficult to assign to each his exact part. P. M. Irving, however, upon the authority of the chief writers, credits the six poems and two of the Mustapha letters (in Nos. 5 and 14) to William Irving, and assigns the rest of the essays, a few specifically, to Washington Irving and to Paulding, with the statement that Paulding's share in the work, though it could not be accurately discriminated, was equal to Washington Irving's.[6] He credits Paulding with beginning and writing (in Nos. 3 and 18) two of the Mustapha letters, which as a whole became very popular and were probably suggested by Goldsmith's *The Citizen of the World;* to Paulding he also assigns the Langstaff article in No. 1, the second and third in No. 2, "Mine Uncle John" in No. 11, and the New Year essay in No. 20. In addition, it is highly probable from internal evidences of style and theme that Paulding wrote the prose sketches of the Cockloft family in Nos. 6, 9, 12, and 14, and the essays "On Style," "A Retrospect," "On Greatness," "Style at Ballston," and "Autumnal Reflections." In the composition of the character sketches, especially the sketch of Aunt Charity (No. 9), Irving may have participated.

To its eccentric publisher, David Longworth, who was also a bookdealer, collector of plays, and exhibitor of paintings, proper credit is due. He used to gratify his taste and reduce his bank account by publishing handsome literary collections, but he would reimburse himself as proprietor of the New York City directory. In him business sense and literary taste mingled in the right proportions to make a successful advertiser; his book shop in Park Row near the theater he called the Shakespeare Gallery in honor of Boydell's engravings on exhibition there, and of a huge painting, on the front of his shop, of the crowning of Shakespeare. In the directory for 1804, he ran a witty advertisement, declaring that he was determined to be silent about his business and to let people discover it for themselves. The next year he versified his accomplishments, thus celebrating the directory:

"The people liked it wondrous well,
Both high and low degree,
For there each one, in black and white,
His own dear name might see.

"It told his neighbor's dwelling place
To each enquiring elf;
And, what was more important still,
Told where he lived himself.

* * * *

"This song the minstrel often sung,
Which did his hearers please,
And though it brought him little fame,
It brought him bread and cheese."

It is significant that in Evergreen's account of Langstaff (No. 8) and "Sketches from Nature" (No. 15), Washington Irving chose Paulding for his subject. Though Irving allowed his imagination and humor to play with the facts, he drew a substantially true sketch of his friend, characterizing him as "rich in many of the sterling qualities of our nature," gifted with a vivacious and satirical fancy, and viewing the world as a solitary spectator. "And trust me, gentle folk," Irving concludes, "his are the whim-whams of a courteous gentleman full of most excellent qualities; honourable in his disposition, independent in his sentiments, and of unbounded good nature, as may be seen through all his works." In "Sketches from Nature," Irving pictures Paulding (Langstaff) dreaming and discoursing by a riverside. The essay is Irving's recognition of Paulding's rooted love of nature, a love somewhat melancholy then but becoming joyful. In Paulding he sees a thinker, who had written beautifully of his observations of nature.

But *Salmagundi* will never be a classic. "The work," Irving wrote to Brevoort in 1819, "was pardonable as a juvenile production, but it is full of errors, puerilities, and imperfections. I was in hopes it would gradually have gone down into oblivion,"—an opinion that P. M. Irving justly called rigorous and oversensitive. In 1824, Paulding came nearer the truth in a letter to his friend: "I don't hold this early bantling of ours in such utter contempt as you do, and can't help viewing it in the light of a careless popular thing that will always be read in spite of its faults, perhaps in consequence of these very faults." The modern reader may wonder how it could excite so much interest a century ago; certainly its satires on the dandies and follies of 1807 have little appeal nowadays. Indeed, excepting the Mustapha letters and two or three character sketches, the first volume is hardly more than good modern journalism. The authors, however, improved by practice, and, having captivated the town with the witty audacity of the early numbers and acquired greater confidence in their own powers, showed both humor and sense in the second volume. Here are the character sketches of "Mine Uncle John" and "The Little Man in Black," true predecessors of Paulding's "Cobus Yerks" and Irving's "The Stout Gentleman"; here are pleasant descriptions of nature; here we find Paulding affirming that there are two kinds of greatness—"one conferred by heaven—the exalted nobility of the soul;—the other, a spurious distinction, engendered by the mob and lavished upon its favourites." Here we discover Irving's humorous chapter upon the ancient city of Gotham, and here, too, Mustapha's eloquent letter on fame in Irving's best manner, concluding,

> "Alas! alas! said I to myself, how mutable are the foundations on which our proudest hopes of future fame are reposed! He who imagines he has secured to himself the meed of deathless renown, indulges in deluding visions, which only bespeak the vanity of the dreamer. The storied obelisk—the triumphant arch,—the swelling dome, shall crumble into dust, and the names they would preserve from oblivion shall often pass away, before their own duration is accomplished."

The writers owed something to Steele, Addison, and Goldsmith, to Swift and Rabelais; but much more to their own vivacity and native wit, to their determination to write entertainingly and let their intelligence play over the panorama around them, to their relish for eccentric characters, to their dislike of the pompous prose style then fashionable in America, and to the practice of using the language of real men though it should be abrupt and slangy. Irving and Paulding even then had individual styles, though less well marked than later: the former was romantic, humorous, courteous, and vivacious; the latter, realistic, satirical, civil, and jocose. They reflected the gayety, prosperity, sanity, and liberality of New York.

Salmagundi, however, should be contrasted, not compared, with *The Spectator,* because *The Spectator* was composed by mature, experienced authors, scholarly, refined, and wise, and it was their masterpiece. *Salmagundi,* on the other hand, was the spontaneous creation of two youthful writers, whose strength lay, not in deep, rich thought, nor in a finished style, but in their vivacity, good humor, originality, and wish to entertain. *The Spectator* may be likened to a sprightly widow of thirty-five, sophisticated, dignified, yet, like the Mona Lisa, captivating all eyes and winning a train of admirers. But *Salmagundi* resembles an American girl of sixteen, light-hearted, rejoicing in health, witty and self-reliant, smiling infectiously, shocking her maiden aunts yet doing no wrong.

The success of *Salmagundi* stimulated the literary ambitions of the authors. Like prospectors in a new land, they had discovered literary gold, and though the title of the first venture passed to the publisher through their indifference, they were encouraged to undertake other literary adventures, which ultimately attracted international attention. In 1809, Irving, writing in the humorously exaggerated style of the Mustapha letters, published his comical history of the New York Dutch; and ten years later, when he was dejected by financial disasters, the memory of the *Salmagundi* and *Knickerbocker* success helped him to decide, in the face of family opposition, to enter the literary profession resolutely and wholeheartedly. Paulding, thereafter, writing alone and developing slowly yet steadily and surely, continued his literary experiments, sometimes succeeding, sometimes failing, but ultimately winning distinction and praise on both sides of the Atlantic. Down to 1820, he wrote six separate books in prose and verse, surpassing Irving in quantity by four volumes but falling decidedly behind him in quality. The merit of Irving's *The Sketch-Book* (1819-20) Paulding did not approach until he wrote ten years later his tales and novels of the New York Dutch. This delay was due partly to his political activities, partly to his engaging in the literary war against England, and partly to a hasty use of inferior literary matter. Meanwhile, Irving searched Europe and America for rich material to nourish his humor and imagination.

Of the period from 1808 to 1812 in Paulding's life we know little. It lies between the conclusion of *Salmagundi* and the publication of his first independent work. He was still supporting himself, probably writing for the newspapers, and penning verses in imitation of Milton's "L'Allegro." In 1809, we get a glimpse of him reading the *Knickerbocker History.* In November, 1810, he may have seen the actor, George Frederick Cooke, appear in *Richard III* and captivate the town so long as he remained sober. In the summer of 1812, Paulding proposed a second joint work to Irving, who agreed to it, but nothing came of the suggestion. In December, Paulding visited Washington, D.C.

Earlier in the same year, following Irving's success in humorous history and probably taking a few hints from Francis Hopkinson's *A Pretty Story* (1774) or Jeremy Belknap's *The Foresters* (1792), he wrote and published the first of his John Bull satires. In *The Diverting History of John Bull and Brother Jonathan* (Philadelphia, 1812), Paulding came near striking off a little masterpiece of political satire. Falling short of this, the story was published the next year in London with favorable comments on its quaint humor and lively portrayal of character. A third edition appeared in Philadelphia in 1827, and eight years later in his collected works the author revised the original and added several brief chapters on the recent English travelers in America. The story was last published inauspiciously in 1867.

The original edition, an insignificant little book of 135 pages (18mo), divided into sixteen short chapters, sets forth, in the manner of *Gulliver's Travels*, the settlement and growth of the English colonies in America, and the development through revolt and severance of an independent nation. For humorous effect, the setting is so minimized that the Atlantic Ocean becomes a millpond; England, a little island in it; the thirteen colonies, thirteen prosperous farms. In like manner, the participants are reduced to represent a family and its neighbors, and the American Revolution becomes a boxing bout between father Bull and son Jonathan. Literally, then, the narrative records the ups and downs of a family, whose members, John Bull and Mrs. Bull, their youngest son Jonathan and Mrs. Jonathan, are well-marked characters. Their differences are aggravated by an active and troublesome neighbor (Napoleon), called Beau Napperty.

This good-natured but unpolished satire shows unmistakably that Paulding was keenly interested in the political developments that immediately preceded and followed the American Revolution, and that the facts were so familiar to him that he could play with them in a politico-satirical allegory. While the narrative is sometimes inconsistent and is deficient in detailed structure, yet it is fairly well sustained and scarcely ever marred by digressions. The author had a sharp eye both for national and sectional idiosyncrasies and follies, and for sane action and sound common sense. Fickle and perverse Mrs. Bull and fickle and perverse Mrs. Jonathan represent, respectively and appropriately, the English Parliament and the American Congress, which are even now diverting. The author's style, though humorously countrified and unpolished, at its best somewhat resembles that of Swift in racy simplicity and directness.

The satire begins in this fashion (edition of 1835):

John Bull was a choleric old fellow, who held a good manor in the middle of a great millpond, and which, by reason of its being quite surrounded by water, was generally called *Bullock Island*. Bull was an ingenious man, an exceeding good blacksmith, a dexterous cutler, and a notable weaver and pot-baker besides. He also brewed capital porter, ale, and small beer, and was, in fact, a sort of jack of all trades, and good bottle-companion, and passably honest as times go.

But what tarnished all these qualities was a devilish quarrelsome, overbearing disposition, which was always getting him into some scrape or other. The truth is, he never heard of a quarrel going on among his neighbours, but his fingers itched to be in the thickest of them; so that he was hardly ever seen without a broken head, a black eye, or a bloody nose. Such was Squire Bull, as he was commonly called by the country people his neighbours—one of those odd, testy, grumbling, boasting old codgers, that never get credit for what they are, because they are always pretending to be what they are not.

Mrs. Jonathan, representing the American Congress, is thus depicted:

The honest truth of the matter is, that she was one of the most whimsical, cross-grained, contradictory, and bedevilled termagants, that ever fell to the lot of mortal man. Though composed of but one body, she had as many minds as she could hold, and was almost always of at least *seventeen* different opinions. Her face had all the appearance of one of your patchwork coverlets, and the different parts seemed to be collected from all quarters of the globe. She had an eastern squint of the eye, a northern aspect, and a southern *complexion.* Then her language resembled the confusion of Babel; at one time she talked like a Frogmorean, at another like Bull's wife herself; sometimes she talked half French half English, and very rarely she talked like Brother Jonathan's wife.

Paulding's representation of New England's opposition to the War of 1812 and of her threatened secession, as well as certain reflections on New York's lethargy in contributing funds for the war, elicited a commentary and reply in the same year entitled *The Beauties of Brother Bull-Us by his loving Sister Bull-A* (New York). The anonymous author points out certain coarse phraseology and sentiments, and endeavors to clear New England from Paulding's discreditable imputations, which, however, were true. One of the author's statements indicates that 2000 copies of Paulding's satire were published.

Among his experiments in this decade were two volumes of verse. . . . The first, a poem in five cantos entitled *The Lay of the Scottish Fiddle* and written to parody Walter Scott's verse stories, was published at Philadelphia in 1813, and the next year in London. Its descriptions and humor have some merit, but the story is obscure and uninteresting. The second, which was named *The Backwoodsman* and published in 1818, was more carefully wrought, but it failed to enhance the author's reputation. He also wrote the first draft of a play. He had not yet learned to tell a story effectively either in prose or in verse, and, unlike Cooper, he had no intimate knowledge of frontier life.

Early in 1813, Paulding upon Irving's invitation became a contributor to *The Analectic Magazine,* a monthly miscellany consisting of reprinted British articles and contributions from native authors, published in Philadelphia by Moses Thomas. After two years, Irving resigned the editorship, but Paulding wrote for it regularly until the end of 1816. Fifteen of his thirty articles were sketches of the naval commanders in the War of 1812 and accounts of the naval controversies that followed. Bryant in his discourse on Washington Irving stated that these sketches, accompanied by portraits, were a popular feature of the magazine. Like a safety valve, they allowed Paulding's patriotism and rising anti-British feeling to escape harmlessly. They also contain some valuable historical data. Having only meager knowledge of some of the commanders, however, the author fell into the unfortunate habit of padding his sketches with rhetorical phrases and patriotic sentiments, which led Irving to wish that his friend would divorce himself from the magazine.[7] Probably the best are the accounts of "John Paul Jones" and "The Navy," in which the author advocated a strong American fleet.

The remaining articles are less ephemeral. In a review of Charles Phillips' *The Emerald Isle,* Paulding likened the then fashionable narrative poem with long explanatory notes to "that multifarious variety of broken chairs, ancient bureaus, wornout tables, and other precious remains of antiquity, which every good housewife thinks it necessary to scour up, and carry along with her in her periodical migrations." In "The Idea of a True Patriot," an ironical essay, which Halleck admired and praised,[8] he satirized those false patriots who would sacrifice private virtue and seek only their own profit, reminding the reader of Samuel Johnson's famous dictum that patriotism is the last resort of a scoundrel. In "Americanisms," he humorously maintained America's inalienable right to modify and develop the American language. Among his original narratives are "Walbridge," which is partly autobiographical, "The Lost Traveler," and "The Adventures of Henry Bird," the true story of a Virginian who settled in Ohio. Bird was captured by the Indians, was carried to Canada, and after several years was ransomed for a gallon of rum. He came to Washington to seek relief for sixty captured white women, and related his personal experiences to Paulding in the summer of 1815. Paulding indulged his fancy for fairies, ghosts, and mythology in "May-Day" and "Cupid and Hymen—An Allegory." In the latter, a beautiful thing, Jove sends Cupid

and Hymen to bless mankind; but mankind banish Cupid, who ascends to Venus, while Hymen, the mortal, remains, his glory and loveliness departed.

Of Paulding's manner of life and associations early in 1815 one gets a pleasant glimpse from Hiram Paulding, a relative, then a boy of eighteen, who later became an admiral in the American navy. "At the close of the war with England," [wrote Hiram in 1873]

> I left Lake Champlain and found myself in New York without employment . . . and, in my earnest desire to join the fleet then nearly ready to sail, sought the friendly interest of James K. Paulding, who with Washington Irving, Commodore Decatur, Lieut. Jack Nicholson, Henry Brevoort, one of the literary clique, and some others lived with Mrs. Bradish, whose house fronted the Battery, forming a joyous fraternity.[9]

By 1815 Paulding's writings, though anonymous and chiefly political, had attracted considerable attention. For three years, as we have seen, he had been a contributor to *The Analectic Magazine* of Philadelphia, making a naval record of the War of 1812 and at times taking a fling at the British travelers and critics of America. His good-natured *John Bull and Brother Jonathan* had been republished and favorably reviewed in England; his narrative poem, *The Lay of the Scottish Fiddle,* had won the double distinction of a republication in London and a merciless scalping in *The Quarterly Review* for January, 1814. In the same number C. J. Ingersoll's *Inchiquin's Letters* (1810), a favorable account of the United States, occasioned another unmitigated censure of America, which with the savage review of his own poem heated Paulding's wrath to the boiling point. Immediately he began to assemble material for a systematic defence of the United States, and published it early in 1815 under the title *The United States and England.* Whatever effect this argumentative thunderbolt may have had on the relations between the two nations just then making peace, it had far-reaching influence on the author's future work. It was favorably reviewed and quoted by American publications, and it caught the admiring eye of President Madison, who at once set about finding a federal position worthy of the author's acceptance. Accordingly, in April, 1815, Paulding was appointed secretary of the newly created Board of Navy Commissioners at an annual salary not to exceed two thousand dollars, and began an eight-year residence in the pioneer city of Washington.

Notes

[1] Introductory Essay to London edition of 1811.

[2] Vol. 65, pp. 418-424, August, 1811.

[3] P. M. Irving's *Life and Letters of Washington Irving,* Vol. 1, p. 444.

[4] Vol. 9, p. 334, September, 1819.

[5] *New York Mirror,* Vol. 9, p. 295.

[6] P. M. Irving's *Life and Letters of Washington Irving,* Vol. 1, p. 178.

[7] *Letters of Washington Irving to Henry Brevoort,* Vol. I, p. 174.

[8] *Putnam's Magazine* for February, 1868, Vol. 11, p. 238.

[9] *Life of Hiram Paulding* by Rebecca Paulding Meade (1910), p. 296.

An excerpt from James Kirke Paulding's "National Literature" (1820):

The favourite, yet almost hopeless object of my old age, is to see this attempt [at creating a national literature] consummated. For this purpose, it is my delight to furnish occasionally such hints as may turn the attention of those who have leisure, health, youth, genius, and opportunities, to domestic subjects on which to exercise their powers. Let them not be disheartened, even should they sink into a temporary oblivion in the outset. This country is not destined to be always behind in the race of literary glory. The time will assuredly come, when that same freedom of thought and action which has given such a spur to our genius in other respects, will achieve similar wonders in literature. It is then that our early specimens will be sought after with avidity, and that those who led the way in the rugged discouraging path will be honoured, as we begin to honour the adventurous spirits who first sought, explored, and cleared this western wilderness.

James Kirke Paulding, in Minor Knickerbockers, *American Book Company, 1947.*

Perry Miller

SOURCE: "Knickerbocker Whiggery," in *The Raven and the Whale,* Harcourt, Brace & Company, 1956, pp. 23-35.

[*In this excerpt, Miller examines the Knickerbocker writers' explicit conservatism and how it manifested itself in their art and criticism, particularly their fierce nationalism and cultural nativism which, Miller explains, they had to espouse in the full knowledge of their own and their country's literary and cultural debt to England.*]

The first fact [Lewis Gaylord] Clark's gossip pages [in the *Knickerbocker*] make clear is that his band [of New Yorkers] were, to a man, Whigs. Secondly, they were professing Christians, most of them Episcopalians, apt to be "high-church" in complexion, partisans of Bishop Hobart. Clark professed from the beginning that he would avoid party rancor "and occupy a broad, neutral literary ground, on which all parties in politics, and men of all creeds in religion, might meet like brothers," but only a Whig could conceive such neutralism. While maintaining the apolitical pose, the *Knickerbocker* never lost a chance to extol the genius of Daniel Webster:

> As the most impetuous sweeps of passion in him are pervaded and informed and guided by intellect, so the most earnest struggles of intellect seem to be calmed and made gentle in their vehemence, by a more essential rationality of taste.

While this is not explicitly a Party avowal, it is, more importantly, the proclamation of an aesthetic code which could come most easily from a Whig commitment. As for economics, whenever the journal ventured into that realm it made emphatic its hostility to all forms of radicalism. It would print "Mocha Dick" as an adventure story, but also quote with approval Edward Everett's justification for the capitalistic structure of the fishery. Fifty thousand dollars, said Everett, is the cost of fitting out a ship which procures for the masses cheap and commodious light. True, the investor does get a return; nevertheless he is a public servant: "Before he can pocket his six per cent., he has trimmed the lamp of the cottager who borrows an hour from evening to complete her day's labor, and has lighted the taper of the pale and thought-worn student, who is 'outwatching the bear,' over some ancient volume."

On religious and moral issues the *Knickerbocker*'s orthodoxy came frankly, sometimes (considering Clark's profession of good manners) brutally, to the front. It steadily denounced the immorality of French writers—Madame de Staël, George Sand, Balzac, and above all Hugo—contrasting them with such a truly American novelist as John Pendleton Kennedy: from his *Rob of the Bowl* "we rise with a stronger detestation of vice, and a new love of virtue; which makes us love our country and our fellow creatures better." The Knickerbockers tried not to step unnecessarily on the toes of their New England friends, but as loyal New Yorkers (especially those who came from New England) they had to dissociate themselves from any taint of Puritanism, calling it a religious radicalism happily being replaced throughout America by "a conservative and redeeming influence."

This phrase and others like it, so frequently repeated in the *Knickerbocker,* show that the magazine is one of those avatars within which a precious group of conservatives achieved, for the moment, a modicum of stability. We must, to be sure, acknowledge one factor which abridges the representative value of this particular company of conservative literati, which makes them more creatures of their time and place than spokesmen for any continuing tradition. They grew up (except Dr. Francis) after the three demigods of American literature had been enthroned; they had to live all their lives under these shadows. Clark born in 1808, Kimball in 1816, Cozzens in 1818, Bristed in 1820—let us add Duyckinck in 1816, Melville and Whitman in 1819—by the time any of them was twenty, Irving, Bryant, and Cooper dominated the scene. The Knickerbockers, being conservatives, had no way of staging a literary revolt; they were inwardly restive, secretly or unconsciously discontented with forms the mighty three had popularized, but they had to endure frustration, and so took out their resentment on other ideas and on lesser persons.

These conservatives were profoundly ambitious for literary fame and for American fame: the three Rhadamanthine figures blocked every path. What else was there to do in humor and sketch but to follow Irving, what else in American poetry but to echo Bryant, how otherwise in fiction use American themes—the only two we had, the forest and the sea—except by imitating Cooper? The three had won their mastery in the 1820's; by 1840 they were, spiritually speaking, remote, inaccessible. Bryant was indeed publishing the *Post* and was always available to chair a dinner for Dickens or for international copyright, but he was more a civic institution than a man (his monumental reserve kept him from being, in any helpful sense, a participant in the dreams of youth). Irving, when not in Spain, lived up the Hudson at "Sunnyside," an object of pilgrimage in a nation that lacked shrines. Visitors carried away what they thought were locks of his hair (he wore a wig). He belonged to the New York of *The Salmagundi Papers;* the difference between the city of 1810 and of 1840, even more of 1850, was immense. Cooper, fortified in Cooperstown, came to the city so seldom as to be in effect a legend.

Americans—especially conservatives—were proud of this triumvirate, but could begrudge the admiration. The three were, alas, *universally* admired; no voice could be raised in protest, even in mild criticism, without incurring the charge of treason. A young author could hardly seek novelty in another field without by implication calling in question sanctified standards. Even political differences, which dragged everybody else down to the ordinary level, did not diminish these colossi. The *Democratic Review* could not let its anger against Irving for going over to the Whigs prevent it from saying, in 1847, that to him the American people were beholden for the elevated character of their literature: "His name maintains a conceded pre-eminence,

James Fenimore Cooper, one of the original Knickerbockers.

as distinct and decided, as the unanimity with which it is accorded is singular and unprecedented." By the same token, Clark had to overlook the *Post*'s editorials, and say in 1854 that for a quarter of a century Bryant's recorded emotions had been so interwoven with those of later generations that Bryant not so much described as *caused* them. But what then was left for younger writers, burning with patriotism, especially those convinced that if Jackson and Van Buren were to be prevented from ruining the country something further and fresher had to be said?

Cooper had come perilously close—wantonly it seemed—to sacrificing his divinity. We wonder how far Melville considered the lesson. In 1850 Melville gratefully remembered that a decade before he had enjoyed *The Red Rover;* at Cooper's death, he testified that upon his own boyhood Cooper exerted a vivid and "awakening" power. Cooper was a friend of Uncle Peter Gansevoort, and none in Albany could be ignorant of what happens to a popular novelist who falls out of line with the populace, or of the indignities heaped upon even "our National Novelist," as Melville called him. Just as *Moby-Dick* was coming out, Melville wrote Rufus Griswold a letter for the Cooper memorial meeting: he had long been pained that Cooper's fame received even a temporary clouding "from some very paltry accidents, incident, more or less, to the general career of letters." Possibly Melville had digested the moral; his assertion that Cooper possessed no weakness except the infallible indices of greatness, that "he was a great, robust-souled man, all whose merits are not even yet fully appreciated," may indicate that he too was prepared to grapple with unpopularity. Whether or no, Melville's letter tells much about the difficulties of growing up as an American novelist under the blighting majesty of Fenimore Cooper.

Cooper and Irving had, between them, proved that the world would read an American book. "When I was a boy," Kimball wrote to Richard Bentley, the London publisher, "it was thought the *acme* of literary fame to be noticed by an English critic. It was this which made Cooper & Irving so renowned *at home*." But Cooper, having first assuaged the nation's sense of inferiority, came back from Europe to the Jacksonian era and castigated it for having become a society of vulgarians, cheap editors, bragging hucksters, village gossips, utterly deficient in style and in manners. A cry went up from his admirers which promptly turned into a howl of rage. The story of his fight with the newspapers is familiar; what is less appreciated is the fact that by deviating from the enshrined "romance" into a satirical novel, Cooper affronted at one and the same time two orthodoxies—such as in Europe no writer had to face—the aesthetic and the patriotic. He excited the accusation that a romancer who puts the errors and follies of his country into a novel sins against both form and the flag.

"Is there," Clark asked in December, 1838, "cause for an *American* to represent the mass of his countrymen as fools or clowns?—to speak slightingly of our scenery, and disparagingly, nay contemptuously, of our society?" The violence of the reaction frightened Irving; if Cooper could be so dethroned, what security had he? Scott and Byron, Irving wrote in the *Knickerbocker* for August, 1839, are scarce cold in their graves before "criticism" is questioning their magic powers; in this country that same upstart "criticism" is unsaying all that has been said of our greatest genius. "If, then, such reverses in opinion as to matters of taste can be so readily brought about, when may an author feel himself secure?" What seems to have eluded his fellow Knickerbockers is the implication, in which Irving may appear most American, that we would do better without any criticism at all. To have a national author whom nobody dared to criticize was suffocating, but to have one whom everybody criticized was disaster.

Fortunately—or, if you view it that way, unfortunately—Cooper recovered himself, and the Knickerbockers could finish out their days burning tapers to a restored trinity. Cooper returned to Natty Bumppo, and so spared the nation the agony of self-criticism. "Most

gladly," said Clark in April, 1840, upon receiving *The Pathfinder*, "do we welcome Mr. Cooper back to the field wherein he won his early laurels." Once more the chorus arose from city and farm, the baton firmly clutched in Clark's fist: "the wide, solemn forest," "the lake embosomed in its recesses," "the wild and boundless ocean," "the idealizing faculty," "the elevation and lustre of romance." Criticism regained its office, which was to expatiate upon "the influences which in the silent mighty regions of the west act upon the character of man till they inspire it insensibly with a force and sublimity kindred to their own." Clark wrote this sentence in March, 1848, after the Mexican War, which he heartily disliked, had added several million square miles of silent mighty regions to the public domain.

Cooper's near escape from obloquy casts a bright light into the hidden recesses of the Knickerbocker—which is to say, the conservative—mentality. Powerful as were the Olympian three in shaping that mind, still more determining had been Scott and Byron. The New Yorkers were fated to live with an insoluble problem: they had to insist upon the native and original quality of Irving, Bryant, and Cooper, and to imitate them, which required a certain cultivation of their own unique individuality; yet at the same time they had to pay homage to Scott and Byron—and, after about 1840, to Wordsworth. In that sense, these metropolitans were committed from birth, with no prospect of release, to what historians call "romanticism."

In poetry, this commitment created no serious discord within either their heads or hearts. Though reluctant to recognize the greatness of Wordsworth, the town literati as happily appropriated the lyricism of Byron and Scott as did the gift books and annuals. Clark published hundreds of verses in which the lilting melody entirely displaced any preoccupation with thought; he immediately recognized Longfellow as master of the mode. Frequently verses of this sort were addressed to Byron himself, as when the Reverend Walter Colton, a chaplain in the Navy, described Byron as an orb that has set but still flashes a lurid light above the horizon:

> As if some comet, plunging from its height,
> Should pause upon the ocean's boiling surge;
> And, in defiance of its, darksome doom,
> Light for itself a fierce volcanic tomb!

You could write or read such verse in Nassau Street without any feeling of contradiction between the individuality of the place and the literary fashion.

With Scott, the New York literati had more trouble. The Wizard of the North charmed their youth; they were as much bewitched as Southern planters. But Scott established the supremacy of the "romance," which, beginning with *Waverley,* he sharply distinguished as a genre distinct from the novel. Echoing Scott, Simms explained it: the romance is an epic, approximates the poem or myth, has infinitely more in common with these three forms than with the novel; it does not confine itself to what is known or even to what is probable. Cooper never had anything but a snort of impatience for those who accused his Indians of being unreal; he was not writing novels about their squalor and misery, he was composing romances "to present the *beau-idéal* of their characters." From the first years of his editorship, Clark was not only conscious of the distinction, but dutifully proclaimed the romance to be the supreme art form of the age, that in which American literature had already found expression and in which it would forever be expressed. Clark was committed to that judgment which John McVickar (Columbia's "Professor of Moral, Intellectual, and Political Philosophy, Rhetoric and Belles Lettres") delivered at the city's memorial service for Scott in 1832: Scott paints man as he truly is because Scott "tells a story, in short, just as an excited child would tell it—if his language answered to his conceptions." This, said McVickar, and officially all the metropolis had to concur, is what fidelity to "Nature" means.

There was no possibility for this generation of Knickerbockers, having constantly before them the example of the three great Americans, behind whom loomed the three monumental Englishmen, to imagine even for a moment obeying any other rule than that of "Nature." Once Cooper had been restored to good standing, Clark could explain wherein Cooper proved his genius: "He was called upon first to drive away the atmosphere of familiarity that surrounded and degraded the landscape, and then to breathe through all the region from his own resources of fancy and feeling the roseate air of romance." Still, occasional indiscretions betray a temperament forced into an orthodoxy something less than congenial. Clark and his followers had difficulty uttering the standard clichés about the romance; they would often contrive that "Nature" should extend protection to less romantic qualities, as when Clark said of Daniel Thompson's *The Green Mountain Boys:* "there is a freshness in his descriptions, and a tone of reality about his incidents, which exhibit less of imagination than of nature." In their heart of hearts they were not worshipers of rural landscape, they did not want to range the wilderness with Natty Bumppo, they were not savages. What they wanted was that Nassau Street and Gramercy Park be rated equivalents of Fleet Street and Grosvenor Square; they did not really believe that familiarity degraded these urban localities and that New York needed to be fumigated by the roseate air of romance. They found in themselves a perverse appetite for the individuality which was theirs, even though it was no *"beau-idéal";* however, they were ashamed to reveal their propensity, and besides had learned from the experience of Cooper that to indulge it in such a novel as *Home as Found* was suicidal.

Thus, while Clark paid lip-service to Scott, one feels that he got a secret satisfaction in giving space, in October, 1838, to Cooper's attack upon Lockhart's *Life of Scott.* This almost completed the wreck of Cooper's reputation—to George Templeton Strong it proved Cooper "meanly malignant enough for anything"—but a civil war among the gods of the romance gave mortals a chance to breathe. Cooper advanced the dangerous thesis that Scott was in fact no romancer at all, that his strength lay in *vraisemblance,* and that by trying to conceal his one and only gift, he showed himself, as he did in social conduct, a hypocrite, a snob, and a fawner upon dukes and duchesses. If this were true, then an American might not always be required in the name of Scott to write as an excited child, and under the standard of honest *vraisemblance* he might be let off romancing about familiar scenes.

Meanwhile, the Knickerbockers knew what they did like: they reveled in Southey's *The Doctor,* admired Hazlitt as essayist (ignoring his radicalism), loved Leigh Hunt, worshiped De Quincey, and idolatrously adored Charles Lamb. This was the literature they wanted to reproduce in America, this cockney wit, this elegance; not Bryant and Cooper, and not Irving except in so far as he (they thought) pertained to it. The *Essays* of Elia, said Clark, are infused with a "conservative, vital principle." In 1853, when the battle was both lost and won, Duyckinck was to say of Cozzens's *Prismatics:* "There is a peculiar style of book, genial, humorous, and warm-hearted, which a race of New Yorkers seems sent into the world specially to keep up." This was their mission, though they had a hard time discovering it; they were summoned by their elders to a grandeur for which not only were they unfitted but which they inwardly thought histrionic. If they never quite came to maturity, the fault was not entirely theirs: their resistance to maturity was their way of proving themselves Americans.

They did, let us note, find allies in their cryptic revolt. In the first year of his incumbency, Clark greeted the *New-York Mirror* and its editors, George P. Morris (composer of ballads, remembered, if at all, for "Woodman, Spare That Tree") and Nathaniel P. Willis, New York's best effort toward a *flâneur.* Clark kept up his friendship with the *Mirror* after it came into the hands of Hiram Fuller (both Fuller and Willis, Gothamite scandalmongers, being New Englanders). The invincible, even though hesitant, urbanism of the *Knickerbocker* mind enabled Clark, long before he knew the name of Thackeray, to welcome the *Yellowplush Papers,* just as, throughout his editorship, he maintained convivial relations with William Trotter Porter and the *Spirit of the Times.* The myth persists that Porter's sporting journal was disdained by genteel Americans, that his pioneering ventures into native American humor went unappreciated by all but gentry of the track. "The Editor's Table" quoted the *Spirit of the Times* at length, always with approbation. In Clark's column for February, 1852, appears the story of a man who wished he owned half a baying dog so that he could shoot his half. By their latent anti-romanticism, Clark, Cozzens, and Kimball reach confusedly toward Mark Twain.

However, let no one suppose for a moment that because they were Whigs and would-be *boulevardiers,* they were one iota less nationalistic than the raging Jacksonians. Wherefore they were enmeshed in a web of contradiction that fell upon every literary patriot in the decades after Old Hickory: to declare the cultural independence of the United States was to commit its creative energies to celebrating the physical expanse of the continent—the mountains, lakes, prairies, rivers. Even persons who preferred the city to the country, who detested fields and streams, were obliged, if they would be considered patriots, to celebrate "Nature."

In the 1830's the *Knickerbocker* contains a large element of patriotic naturalism, the sea stories being part of it. One of the earliest pieces to attract, by reprints, the attention of the nation was James Brooks's "Our Own Country," which in 1835 told America that God had spoken His promise to the Republic through the sublimity of the landscape:

> It resounds all along the crags of the Alleghanies.
> It is uttered in the thunder of Niagara. It is heard in
> the roar of two oceans, from the great Pacific to the
> rocky ramparts of the Bay of Fundy. His finger has
> written it in the broad expanse of our Inland Seas,
> and traced it out by the mighty Father of Waters.

In the *Knickerbocker* as everywhere else in American journalism, the thesis was that we should automatically create a big literature because we were a big country; inevitably bigness became a catalogue of mountains and rivers, always including Niagara Falls. In New York as in Concord, the injunction for the "scholar" was to follow Nature, but in Nassau Street or in Brooklyn this command more glibly translated itself into the standard inventory: "from the roar of Niagara, and the vast melancholy sweep of the Mississippi . . . gather laurels for immortality."

Since eloquence of this variety pointedly disappears from the *Knickerbocker* in the 1840's, I suspect that Clark's heart was never wholly in it. Be that as it may, there were, for urban and conservative New Yorkers, advantages in promoting national naturalism. In its name a stand could be taken against "foreign" corruptions. French immorality could be rejected without bringing down an accusation of provinciality. More importantly, full hostility could be expressed to Germany and all its works. There was nothing more characteristic of all New York intellectuals than their instinctive, their spontaneous detestation of the very idea of Germany. And along with it, they could not abide the "transcendentalism" of New England. Herman Melville had a mind, but nobody to educate it; on his own he acquired a passion for ideas, and then tried to enter a world where taste was respected, wit admired, erudition praised, but ideas themselves—well, those might turn out to be "German" and "transcendental." If so, they were to be ridiculed and, wherever possible, stamped out.

Clark struggled for years with the problem of Emerson; he never failed to point out that Emerson was no Christian. Though a cultivated New Yorker might be ultimately obliged to concede some merit to Emerson as a stylist, he certainly never spoke anything but contempt of Bronson Alcott, Theodore Parker, or others among the hobgoblins, even though he was sorely tried when Margaret Fuller in 1844 came to town and as literary editor of the *Tribune* proved a match for the best metropolitan brains. One thing, if nothing else, seemed clear in New York that was not at all clear in New England: identifying the literary prospects of the country with the natural scenery did not mean endorsing the inane twaddle of the Alcotts, who "consider German *fog* a necessary appendage of their profound thinking." There was no sympathy in the *Knickerbocker,* Clark said, apropos of Theodore Parker, for those "who would reduce the inspired writings to a level with the ordinary compositions of men; who would take away the solace of religion from the undoubting believer, wearied with the cares and trials of life, or turning his eyes toward heaven from the bed of death."

Mixed with this New York hostility to transcendentalism is a certain amount of New York's ingrained dislike of New England, nowhere more vigorous than among transplanted New Englanders. Time and again we perceive that on the New York side there is a barely concealed, often not concealed, sense of inferiority. Hence there were immense gratifications in heaping abuse upon New England transcendentalists; but these had to be compensated by professions of cordial admiration for those civilized New Englanders who rejected Emerson's philosophy, who wrote poetry for the masses, turned Byronic lyricism to the purposes of morality, and set the mold of literary form. The Knickerbocker group would disregard Lowell's abolitionism, Longfellow's poems on slavery (had they done this on purely critical grounds we should admire them more), and even Whittier's politics, in order to pay their respects to these "respectable" New Englanders. Clark's loyalty to every author he had ever published reinforced his esteem for Longfellow; he praised Longfellow's exquisite moral sense and was delighted with *Hyperion* because it was a venture into the "ultra-German style" only in order to exorcise it. Likewise it was the sane and solid Hawthorne who appealed to Knickerbockers; reviewing *Twice-Told Tales* in 1837 and comparing it with Longfellow's *Outre-Mer,* Clark said that in both Nature is the only guide; therefore they approach the standard of Washington Irving. In fact, Clark gave Hawthorne the highest accolade in his bestowal: the *Tales* are "Lamb-like." These being the qualities which New York would import from New England, even as the city strove to erect barriers against the heresies of Concord and Brook Farm, we are not surprised that the *Knickerbocker* recognized a kindred spirit in Dr. Oliver Wendell Holmes and never, all the time Clark was editor, wavered in its devotion to him.

Dr. Holmes was a joy because he openly ridiculed the notion that native American literature would roar with all the winds of the Alleghenies and bellow with the sound of Niagara. He was a city man, and though he paid his respects to nature, he had no patience with Naturalism. But for some reason it was more difficult in New York than in Boston to be so cheerfully urban, to be unimpressed by the Mississippi. Part of the difficulty was that the cult of Nature called not only for exulting in the vastness of the continent, but for putting the meanings of the landscape into words, and words inevitably became ideas. If the Knickerbocker set could have remained happy with their boyhood allegiance to Scott, they would not have worried about Emerson; but they were uncomfortable even when most severely criticizing—a fact that seemed in itself a treason to Irving. And then, in the 1830's, as Clark took the helm of the *Knickerbocker,* such intellectuals as New York boasted were further worried because they found themselves unable to resist the lure, which they knew was insidious, of Edward Bulwer.

These patriotic Americans protested that Bulwer's romances—*Pelham, Paul Clifford, Ernest Maltravers*—gave simple republicans false notions about aristocracy. Actually, what most disturbed the Knickerbockers was Bulwer's shameless admission that he composed romances according to an *a priori* scheme, that he wrote not at all as an excited child. They might be furtively moving away from Scott, but, being worshipers of Charles Lamb, they could regard Bulwer's pronouncements only as scandalous. He was brazen about *Ernest Maltravers:* it is constructed, he said, upon "an interior philosophical design." The hero is not so much a person as the embodiment of "Genius"; the heroine, from whom he is separated and to whom he finds his way back, is "Nature." Bulwer hardly helped the cause of "premeditated conception" by having Genius beget an unpremeditated and illegitimate child upon Nature. The trouble was that, fulminate as Clark might, he could not stop American women (and they made up most of the reading public) from reveling in Bulwer. As Harriet Martineau said in 1836: "I question whether it is possible to pass half a day in general society without hearing him mentioned." The "morality" of his books was a constant theme of discussion, from the most sensitive of the clergy down to the schoolboy. And why should not all social classes read the fascinating

Bulwer, since they could get uncopyrighted editions so cheaply?

Clark assumed direction of the *Knickerbocker* at a time of crisis: much as he hated Jackson, the real danger, with the influence of Scott declining, was that the popular literature would demonstrate how "corruption and refinement go hand in hand." This would be to enhance manners "utterly and irreconcilably opposed to those of this country." Clark banked upon the demands of the business world to keep American men from dissipation, because they have to be bright and early at their offices; "fortunately we have no women too high or too low, to be exonerated from domestic duties." But literature would have to assist. Business, after all, was producing wealth, and sooner or later the children of wealth would be tempted: the wives would hire servants. Considering what happened to the romance in the hands of Bulwer, Clark was ready to proclaim: "the age of chivalry is no more, and the chivalrous romances have had their day." But the conservative mentality required more sustenance than the pitifully few works that American writers, contending against a flood of uncopyrighted imports, could provide.

In 1836 assistance came, not from American Nature, but from urban London. The fact that the solution to the American problem was provided from abroad did not disturb Whig intellectuals. Here, it seemed, was the way in which we, by frank imitation, could reconcile Christian sentiment with a technique that could safely abandon the outmoded romances of Scott and Cooper, which could remain faithful to universal Nature and yet permit writers to treat, without embarrassment, the individualities of cities. American literature would be saved by Charles Dickens.

At first Clark did not even know the name of his Messiah; in December, 1836, he could say only that *Pickwick Papers* were a remedy against blue devils, ennui, or dyspepsia. The next February he called the still unknown author the best of philosophers. A year later, "Mr. Dickens" is the most accurate disciple of Nature in modern literature, for he treats humble characters without being ashamed of them. By November, 1839, Dickens becomes the master spirit of the age: he is great in satire and description, "while his calm philosophy, his love of nature, and of poor humanity, as warmly commend him to the *hearts* of his readers." Here was deliverance from premeditation and the intellect. The nineteen-year-old George Strong never so much enjoyed a work of fiction as *Nicholas Nickleby:* "It has been drop by drop, and each drop glorious."

Men like Clark and Strong responded to Dickens not because they were tired businessmen seeking relaxation; they were conscientious, literate Americans, trying to comprehend themselves and their universe. Here they found a synthesis beyond the reach of the head, a synthesis of the heart such as would protect conservatives against the divisive and infidel tendencies of the intellect. No matter that it came, uncopyrighted, from London, or that Dickens was a reformer (the things he wanted reformed in England were already reformed in America); what was our strident nationalism, with all its boisterous talk of mountains and Niagara and colossal whales, compared to this basically conserving humanity? Henceforth let the writer who strove in America for originality take warning. It would not be enough that he excel Irving in humor, Bryant in landscape, Cooper in action: he would now be measured by the standard of Dickens; he would suffer should he fall short of what conservative Americans took to be Dickensian naturalness, morality, and universal wholesomeness.

WRITERS AND ARTISTS

James T. Callow

SOURCE: "Landscape: Similar Techniques and Mutual Publications," in *Kindred Spirits: Knickerbocker Writers and American Artists, 1807-1855,* The University of North Carolina Press, 1967, pp. 144-72.

[*In this excerpt, Callow demonstrates how the Knickerbocker writers and the American painters of the Hudson River School, as a result of their philosophical and aesthetic affinities, used similar methods in their work to portray (especially American) landscapes— even to the point of collaboration on certain picture books.*]

The Knickerbocker writers and the American painters used analogous methods to develop their landscapes. To some extent this overlapping of techniques arose from the social contact afforded by The Bread and Cheese Club and its successor, The Sketch Club. Members were usually artists who at some time in their lives painted landscapes, or authors who, like Bryant and Cooper, wrote about landscapes. What at first was merely fraternization soon became a broad spiritual affinity between large numbers of painters and writers, all striving for the same goals and employing similar procedures to reach them. It was only natural that they sometimes joined forces to produce landscape gift books.

Similar Techniques

Although individual authors undoubtedly had their own favorite painters' tricks,[1] the Knickerbockers and the Hudson River School resembled each other most in their use of the panoramic view, composition, accessories, and contrast. In some cases these techniques appear to be contradictory, but all were resolved in the largeness of their context and the multiplicity of their purposes. Motivated by religion, aesthetics, nationalism, regionalism, romanticism, and a dozen other forces, few American artists could have been satisfied with a single method of expression.

Little attempt will be made to discover the original ownership of these techniques. During the early nineteenth century, painters and writers were in such close contact and borrowed so freely from each other that an effective procedure could hardly have remained the property of any one group for more than a few years. Furthermore, almost all of the landscape methods employed by the Knickerbockers had not been invented by them, but were inherited from earlier poets, like Freneau, whose sun was setting as theirs was rising. To some extent the same thing might be said of the Hudson River School, since its techniques were foreshadowed in certain primitive paintings.[2] Suffice it to say, then, that the Knickerbockers and the American painters frequently saw nature through each other's eyes and sometimes forgot to distinguish between the pen and the brush.

THE PANORAMIC APPROACH. The panorama was one of the most interesting devices shared by the artists and writers. An importation from Europe, this technique had for its immediate purpose the inclusion of more landscape than an observer could take in without moving his head from side to side. This was accomplished at first by covering the walls of a rotunda with a series of canvases such as John Vanderlyn's "View of the Palace and Gardens of Versailles," exhibited in a circular structure called the New York Rotunda. As it progressed, however, the panorama encompassed larger areas, made possible by simply stitching paintings together and showing them as moving pictures. Several panoramas of this type, designed to celebrate the scenery of the Mississippi River, are still preserved; and in many contemporary reviews we have descriptions of others.[3] Both moving and circular panoramas, as well as scenes of more modified wide-angle proportions, appear in the landscape works of the Knickerbockers and the Hudson River School.

The panoramic viewpoint was utilized by American artists for several reasons. First, it achieved drama and excitement by placing the observer in an unusual position. Paintings such as Doughty's "On the Banks of the Susquehanna" and Cole's "Destruction," from "The Course of Empire," appeal psychologically to the onlooker, who is flattered at being allowed to command acres of land temporarily his own. Like the eighteenth-century "spectator"—in the fourth book of Cowper's *Task,* for example—he enjoys an enlarged vision of life. Secondly, panoramas reflected the notion that America was vast beyond exhaustion, a place of horizons without limit.[4] Thus, as the frontier spread westward, the panorama followed. Trumbull's inclusive views of Niagara Falls, and Cole's near-boundless "Oxbow" were later supplemented with similar treatments of the West in the paintings of Bierstadt and Moran.

In Knickerbocker literature, sweeping descriptions of scenery were used for like reasons. Rip Van Winkle's perch high in the Catskills became a psychological release from the frustrations of an unhappy marriage. Readers of *The Alhambra* felt giddy but important as they were conducted to the tower of Comares and invited to gaze at the almost endless vistas to the north, the south, and the west.[5] Cooper, who believed that the lofty view "astonishes, and . . . excites the feelings,"[6] mixed it with the panorama to describe the Valley of the Mohawk in *Notions of the Americans,*[7] Lake George in *The Last of the Mohicans,*[8] the Valley of the Susquehanna in *Home as Found,*[9] and the area surrounding the specklike ruins of Fort William Henry in *Satanstoe.*[10] Of course, the dramatic position of the onlooker could tend toward the sublime by placing him in vicarious danger and therefore introducing the Burkean element of terror. Most Knickerbocker works came far from succeeding with this effect, however.[11] If anyone achieved true sublimity with the panorama it was Bryant, and his was of a different sort. "Thanatopsis," "The Prairies," and "The Flood of Years" contain an exciting mental liberation so closely integrated with the panoramic view that one cannot be sure which is the cause, which the effect. Surely these poetic visions are genuine panoramas of the mind, for they contain neither physical-spatial nor chronological boundaries. Completely free, the poet soars out of his own country into the past and future.

In addition to these various psychological uses, the literary panorama served as a way of impressing readers with the vastness of native scenery. Bryant employed it in "Monument Mountain" to prove that the American landscape was a huge melting pot large enough to blend the picturesque and the beautiful. Joseph Rodman Drake advised his friend Halleck to become a national poet by seating himself on "Appalachia's brow," where he could absorb the immensity of nature and stimulate his imagination.[12] Fortified with this counsel, Halleck adopted the technique to describe Weehawken and succeeded in filling his readers with a sense of patriotism as they cautiously peered over the edge of a cliff to see "ocean, and earth, and heaven, burst" before their eyes.[13] The nationalistic tone of such verses might be more accurately termed regionalistic, but it should be remembered that nationalism and regionalism meant the same thing in the days of the Knickerbockers, the microcosm standing for the macrocosm, and praise of many local scenes cumulatively proving the value of one vast, national landscape.

Two Knickerbocker writings were especially connected with the moving panorama. The first of these was *A Trip to Niagara* (1828), a three-act play written by William Dunlap "at the request of the Managers [of the Bowery Theatre], and intended by them as a kind of running accompaniment to the more important product of the Scene-painter."[14] Although it comprises an effective plea for tolerance on the part of foreign travelers toward America, the subject matter of *A Trip to Niagara* is subordinated to its panoramic background. At the beginning of the second act, the following paintings were shown as the players were made to journey up the Hudson:

DIORAMA, OR MOVING SCENERY

The steam boat is seen as passing up the river.

Scene 1. Harbour of New York. Governor's Island, Ships at anchor.
2. Frigate at anchor. Jersey City.
3. Hoboken.
4. Weehawk.
5. Palisades.
6. Approaching storm.
7. Storm.
8. Boats passing through a fog.
9. Clearing away and rainbow. Caldwell's landing. Boat stops.
10. Highlands.
11. Buttermilk Falls.
12. West Point. Sun setting.
13. Highlands continued.
14. Newburgh by moonlight.
15. Island near Newburgh.
16. Catskill Mountains in distance, and Mountain House.
17. Continuation of scenery.
18. Catskill landing.[15]

Apparently Dunlap restricted himself merely to writing the play: According to the advertisements, the scenery was painted by Jones, Gordon, and Reinagle, with the assistance of Haddock, White, and Leslie—obscure figures in the history of American painting.[16] *A Trip to Niagara* was quite popular, and on one occasion the diorama alone was presented as an afterpiece.[17]

A Pen-and-Ink Panorama of New York City (1853), written by Cornelius Mathews, was an extremely clever adaptation of the moving panorama for literary purposes. Regional in tone, this little book of essays, character sketches, and scenic views was designed to give its readers the feeling that they were actually present at the showing of a mid-century panorama. Thus Mathews addressed his audience with familiar patter:

In the little canvass I propose to open before you, ladies and gentlemen, I have attempted to paint a

home picture. The seven colors of the rainbow have been pretty freely used, I may say, quite exhausted, by previous artists; there is little more to be done with them. We have had panoramas of the Thames, of California, the Mississippi, the Holy Land, gorgeous with all the tints of the palette. What, then, is left to me, that I too invite you to a panoramic exhibition? There is a single unemployed color, common writing-ink, and for a pencil, the old . . . grey goose-quill. With the aid of these, and your kind indulgence, I shall endeavor to body forth something for your entertainment, by unrolling before you the streets and characters of a great city. . . . In an hour or two we will accomplish lengths and breadths of this town which it should take you, unaided, twenty years, more or less, to traverse. . . . I invite you, ladies and gentlemen, to bear me company.[18]

Mathews never allowed this illusion of reality to disappear. With each change of scene there was a carefully planned transition. For example:

> In town again, with eyes sharpened by our holiday— let us follow our panorama as it moves along. Ladies and gentlemen, you have probably seen several historical paintings, and read a number of historical romances in your time with profound admiration! Will you be good enough to look this way at

> THE NEW YORK FIREMAN.

> Mark the picture before you. It is the morning of a wide and fierce conflagration. The clouds are dull and sullen. . . .[19]

The ending of the book is equally consistent: "Ladies and gentlemen, the Pen-and-Ink Panorama of New York City is closed—I am much obliged to you for your attendance, and hope to have the pleasure of meeting you again."[20] But the "audience" never gave this charming work the recognition it deserved.

The panoramic technique was employed quite sparingly by the Knickerbockers, who never used it to the extent that Walt Whitman did. In the novel it could exist only as a unit dependent on the more important ingredients of character analysis and plot development. In poetry it never replaced the popular microscopic point of view in the tradition of Burns's "To a Mouse."[21] On the other hand, the panoramic method was landscape's "Sunday best" and was useful for achieving a sense of vastness considered necessary for sublimity. Above all, it was employed by the Knickerbockers in much of their better work and served well to express the exalted notions of nature which they shared with American painters.

COMPOSITION. In compositional techniques the writers of New York and the members of the Hudson River School were romantic realists, romantic because they arranged and selected their details for singleness of effect and mood, a unity which mirrored the all-ordering hand of God, and realists because they documented their landscapes with almost microscopic thoroughness, portraying each detail with infinite care and always applying that famous touchstone, truth to nature.[22] Coleridge's dictum that each part must be pleasurable but no single part more pleasurable than the whole was usually their ideal, yet it must be recorded that they sometimes failed to achieve it. The first third of Bryant's "Monument Mountain," for example, embodies such a minute portrayal of nature that the reader disregards Bryant's contention that all things were "mingled in harmony"[23] and asks himself instead: Is the story of the lover's leap, comprising the last twothirds of the poem, an anecdote to embellish the landscape, or is the landscape description merely introduction to the anecdote? Is "Monument Mountain" primarily a descriptive or a narrative poem? Bryant seems to have lost his usual awareness of the whole, the sense of form which has helped him to survive even the close gaze of modern criticism.[24]

The painters also lapsed into compositional blunders at times. But the fact that these errors were caught and condemned by the reviewers of the day shows that an ideal of unity existed. Even offenses by the much-respected Thomas Cole were not allowed to go unnoticed. "Falls of Nunda," one of Cole's minor landscapes was put to rest by these remarks in *The New-York Mirror:* "This may be true to nature; but a more confused higgledy-piggledy picture we don't desire to see. Such a commingling of reds, and yellows, and browns, and mists, and cascades, and clouds, and cliffs! If it hadn't been for the house and the sky we should have thought the picture upside down."[25] Cole's pupil Frederick E. Church received like treatment from *The Knickerbocker* magazine. "CHURCH is much the same as ever," complained the reviewer; for "his pictures are frittered up in detail, which, though true by itself, yet lacks the unity and repose of nature."[26] Realism of parts was no excuse for confusion of the whole.

A few examples will serve to illustrate the methods by which the Knickerbockers composed for unity in their landscapes. The first is from Willis' *Pencillings by the Way:*

> A lovely scene lay before me when I turned to look back. The valley . . . is as round as a bowl, with an edge of mountain-tops absolutely even all around the horizon. It slopes down from every side to the centre, as if it had been measured and hollowed by art; and there is not a fence to be seen from one side to the other, and scarcely a tree, but one green and almost unbroken carpet of verdure, swelling up in broad green slopes to the top. . . . St. Bris is a little handful of stone buildings around an old church; just such a thing as a painter would throw

into a picture—and the different-colored grain, and here and there a ploughed patch of rich yellow earth, and the road crossing the hollow from hill to hill like a white band; and then for the life of the scene, the group of Italians . . . and the peasants in their broad straw hats, scattered over the fields.[27]

Here the unifying device is the mountains, enclosing the valley and framing the many details included in the description—the building, the church, the grain, the patches of ploughed earth, the road, and, finally, the human accessories. This technique of the "closed" scene had been used by the Hudson River School from its beginning and may be found in the watercolors of William Guy Wall, a forerunner of native landscape painters.[28]

This urge to arrange is evident in Willis' declaration that "all . . . rivers, . . . to be seen to advantage, . . . should form the middle, not the foreground of the picture,"[29] and it is what makes Willis' description of the Silver Cascade almost as effective as the engraving of Doughty's picture which accompanies it: "The ear is suddenly saluted by soft dashings of this sweetest of cascades; and a glance upwards reveals its silver streams issuing from the loftiest crests of the mountain, and leaping from crag to crag, or spread in a broad thin sheet of liquid light over the edge of some projecting ledge, till it reaches the road, across which it passes, forming a still and transparent pool immediately beneath, before it joins the Saco in the depths of the gorge."[30] In both instances, in the letterpress and in the engraving, the cascade has been used to achieve totality of impression. All other details are subordinated to it.

To capture this unity the Knickerbockers sometimes rearranged the elements of an actual scene as any painter would. Thus Cooper explained that the landscapes of *The Deerslayer* were accurate "in all but precise position." He had carefully drawn rocks, shoals, rivers, bays, mountains, and "all the other accessories" from real models but had shuffled them around to some extent. An important shoal, for example, he had moved a little to the northeast.[31] Such procedures were just as allowable to Cooper and his fellow writers as they were to any member of the Hudson River School, for the goal of unity was common to both literature and painting. If neither group had sacrificed petty detail to this more important end, neither would have achieved true artistry. But such was not the case, and both groups by seeking unity through a blend of romantic and realistic techniques, naturally created arranged pictures with marked resemblances.

HUMAN ACCESSORIES. Both groups also employed man as an accessory in their landscapes. Minor gods and goddesses, sylphs, satyrs, and centaurs were no longer fashionable. Instead of such figures, nineteenth-century paintings and writings contained Indians, woodsmen, and townsfolk out for an airing. A few dehumanized landscapes were occasionally produced (Cole's "The Maid of the Mist" and Drake's "The Culprit Fay," for example), but these must be considered oddities at a time when man had become the chief landscape accessory.

Human beings were used in four different ways, each method strictly determined by the function of the picture. In the first place, man was introduced for technical purposes. He provided a foreground in Allston's "Moonlit Landscape"; he became a point of contact between spectator and scene, leading the eye into a "depth of space" in Morse's "View from Apple Hill";[32] he served to concentrate light and to develop the contrast of mild activity and static nature in Stanley's "Western Landscape." Among the writers, N. P. Willis made the most use of the human accessory for technical purposes, even going so far as to select the workers on his grounds at Idlewild for their picturesque appearances.[33] His acquaintance with many painters had given him a sharp, analytical eye.

> Every new group changed and embellished the glorious combination of rock, foliage and water below me [at Trenton Falls], and I studied their dresses and attitudes as you would criticise them in a picture. The men with their two sticks of legs, and angular hats, looked abominably, of course. I was glad when they were out of the perspective. But the ladies of each party, with their flowing skirts, veils lifted by the wind, picturesque bonnets and parasols, were charming outlines as heighteners to the effect. . . . In the course of the morning, one lady came along . . . and, for her use, the gentleman who was with her carried a *crimson shawl,* flung over his shoulder. You would need to be an artist to understand how much that one shawl embellished the scene. It concentrated the light of the whole ravine. . . .[34]

This conviction of the picturesqueness of humanized landscape prompted Willis and the artist Bartlett to "people" one hundred and fifteen of the one hundred and nineteen engravings in their *American Scenery.*

A second type of landscape employed man to convey a sense of enjoyment, a method which is apparent in Henry Inman's "Picnic in the Catskills," Asher Durand's "Sunday Morning," and E. C. Coates's "View of New York Harbor." Here nature is pictured in its pastoral sense, as capable of transmitting simple pleasure apart from any spiritual therapy. In these scenes man is happy to have stolen away from the cares of the world. Alfred Billings Street's "A Forest Walk," although perhaps too closely resembling Marvell's "The Garden," is a telling example of this motif in the literature of New York:

> Here stretch'd, the pleasant turf I press,
> In luxury of idleness;
> Sun-streaks, and glancing wings, and sky
> Spotted with cloud-shapes, charm my eye;
> While murmuring grass, and waving trees
> Their leaf-harps sounding to the breeze
> And water-tones that tinkle near
> Blend their sweet music to my ear;
> And by the changing shades alone
> The passage of the hours is known.[35]

Although the artists and writers depicted men in groups as well as by themselves, the literary treatments of this subject often showed the author alone, passing freely amidst the scenes of nature, as in Drake's "Bronx" or Bryant's "Green River."

A third type of landscape arose as the poet or painter transformed man's simple enjoyment into a sense of wonder or awe in the face of nature's marvels. In such cases a single human being was usually employed, as in Cooper's *Leatherstocking Tales* or Doughty's "In Nature's Wonderland."[36] A few of the artists at times rejected such tricks and eliminated man entirely.[37] There was probably a nationalistic motive behind this omission, a desire to exhibit the superiority of American over European scenery by showing that some areas in this country had never known the contaminating presence of man and civilization. "The Falls of the Mongaup" and "The Callicoon in Autumn," by Alfred Billings Street, present parallel examples of this method in Knickerbocker writings.

Finally, man was used as an accessory in landscapes of terror and desolation.[38] This was the most ambitious method because the painter or writer tried to create sublimity by injecting the element of horror into his art, in other words, by pursuing man with nature. Thus the painters portrayed man as either fleeing from nature (Catlin's "View on Missouri, Prairie Meadows Burning") or overcome by it (J. Shaw's "The Deluge"). The writers employed similar techniques for Gothic effects. In "A Forest Hymn," Bryant pictured himself as "annihilated" by a "mighty oak."[39] Willis personified the waters of Niagara as a dying man in order to lend the interest of the man-against-nature theme to his description of a scene which had already been exploited by others.[40] There were other examples of Gothic landscapes, such as "The Hunter's Flight" and "The Lost Hunter" by Alfred Billings Street and "Sonnet—Frost" by Park Benjamin. Perhaps the most effective was Bryant's "Midsummer" with its deliberately harsh sounds and spondee-impeded lines:

> A power is on the earth and in the air
>   From which the vital spirit shrinks afraid,
>   And shelters him, in nooks of deepest shade,
> From the hot steam and from the fiery glare.

> Look forth upon the earth—her thousand
>   plants
>   Are smitten; even the dark sun-loving maize
>   Faints in the field beneath the torrid blaze;
> The herd beside the shaded fountain pants;
> For life is driven from all the landscape
>   brown;
>   The bird has sought his tree, the snake his den,
>   The trout floats dead in the hot stream, and men
> Drop by the sun-stroke in the populous town;
>   As if the Day of Fire had dawned, and sent
>   Its deadly breath into the firmament.[41]

This sonnet is chiefly a landscape poem with man as an accessory even though his entrance is saved for the dramatic ending, the treatment progressing up a kind of ladder of being: first vegetable, then animal, then man—each in its turn overcome by nature. Through the religious terror introduced in the last two lines, the poet has striven for sublimity.

The painters and writers could at times give man a rather dignified place in their landscapes, at other times relegate him to diminutive proportions. These methods appeared simultaneously because of the wide variety of purposes behind nineteenth-century literature and art. Landscape was expected to please, instruct, soothe, spiritualize, and terrorize. Each function dictated a special technique and variations in the use of man.

CONTRASTED LANDSCAPES. Another device shared by writers and painters was the "before and after" technique of contrasting two or more landscapes in separate stanzas, chapters, books, or canvases. When Asher Durand exploited the device in "The Morning of Life" and "The Evening of Life" (1840), his friend Thomas Cole had already done so in "The Course of Empire" (1836), "The Departure" and "The Return" (1837), and "Past" and "Present" (1838). Cole devoted another four canvases to "The Voyage of Life" (1840) and was working on "The Cross of the World," a series of five pictures, when he died. Moreover, he had plans for at least three other groups: "Sowing and Reaping," "The World's Mirror," and "Future Course of Empire."

Alfred Billings Street and James Fenimore Cooper also experimented with this technique. In "A Contrast," a short poem of two stanzas, Street presented a sharp double-picture of a frontier landscape and a civilized landscape. The first stanza might have been painted by any Hudson River artist:

> A LAKE is slumbering in the wild-wood depths,
> Picturing naught upon its polish'd glass
> But the long stretching and contracting shades
> That change as change the hours: its sullen
>   tones
> Blending but with the forest's daylight songs
> And midnight howlings; o'er the leafy waste

Curls a light thread of smoke—a hunter's fire;
And mid the lilies' floating golden globes,
Spangling the margin, where the ripples play
And melt in silver, rocks his bark canoe.[42]

In the next stanza, however, we are told that years have passed and the scene is changed: much of the forest had been replaced with meadows; a village and gardens now stand where the hunter had comped; the sky is filled with the spires of churches, the domes of schools, and the roofs of houses. The single canoe has given way to "swift keels." In short, the hand of man has transformed a picturesque forest scene into the beauty of a cultivated and civilized landscape. But in contrasts such as these it was necessary to depict variety only amidst sameness; therefore, in the second stanza Street retained both the forest and the lake so that the reader might have familiar points of reference, the same context, in other words, in which to discover dissimilarities. There are not two landscapes; there is only an altered one.[43] This same retention of context may be found in "The Evening of Life." Durand pictured the aged shepherd sitting upon the base of a ruined column which, in "The Morning of Life," had probably been a section of the classical temple in the background.

Cooper's anti-rent series, comprised of *Satanstoe* (1845), *The Chainbearer* (1845), and *The Redskins* (1846), contains numerous examples of contrasted landscapes seen by three generations of the Littlepage family. Each novel has such contrasts *within* it,[44] but there are also contrasts *between* the novels. Thus a "before picture" in *Satanstoe* may have its "after picture" in *The Chainbearer* or even in *The Redskins*. For example, amid the heart of "a vast forest edifice" depicted in *Satanstoe*, Corny Littlepage discovers the scalped bodies of the surveyor Mr. Traverse and his two chainbearers. So carefully drawn is "this wide, gloomy" setting, in which "a sombre light prevailed, . . . rendering everything mellow and grave," that the Gothic landscape takes firm hold of the reader's memory.[45] The use of this same setting in *The Chainbearer* is, therefore, quite effective. Mordaunt Littlepage, Corny's son, is led like his father to this spot in the forest. It has changed in only one respect: it now contains a ruin—a human skeleton.

To show the evils of provincialism certain townscapes are also contrasted in this series. Rather cleverly, Cooper paints no townscapes in *The Chainbearer,* and as a result differences are greatly heightened. There is no easy transitional stage. First, in *Satanstoe* we see the New York of 1751, then the Albany of 1758; two books later—with a leap that takes us from the colonial period right into the middle of the nineteenth century—we come upon the same towns during the 1840's.[46]

But more important is the three-way contrast involving Ravensnest, the frontier settlement established by Herman Mordaunt, Corny Littlepage's father-in-law, and inherited successively by Corny's son Mordaunt and grandson Hugh Roger Littlepage. At first Ravensnest is nothing more than a few clearings in the wilderness, "neither very large nor very inviting."[47] Never an admirer of land filled with stumps and girdled trees, Cooper devoted only a few lines in *Satanstoe* to describing the terrain and an equal amount to the Old Nest House, which was later besieged by the Indians.[48] In *The Chainbearer,* however, he not only portrayed the landscape in full[49] but did so with the vocabulary of a painter. Looking down upon the scene, he saw "a foreground of open land, dotted with cottages and barns, mostly of logs, beautified by flourishing orchards, and garnished with broad meadows, or enriched by fields, in which the corn was waving under the currents of a light summer air." Several roads and a hamlet with its inn, store, school, and mills comprised the middle distance, and "the back-ground of this picture . . . was the 'boundless woods.'" The forest is represented as mysterious and therefore might be considered sublime. But more pertinent here are the abundant contrasts in the entire landscape with its indigenous mixture of the beautiful and the picturesque, the open and the closed, the light and the dark. Besides these internal contrasts there is the contrast between this view of Ravensnest and that found in *Satanstoe*. The stumps had now "nearly all disappeared from the fields," and Cooper delighted in their absence, compensating for it by picturing Herman Mordaunt's Old Nest House as a ruin, "mouldering, and . . . gone far into decay." The house had associations too, since it had once withstood an Indian attack. A third canvas was supplied in *The Redskins*. By this time Ravensnest had become a thriving frontier community. With dexterity, however, as if to avoid treating those inhabitants who had turned against their landlord, Cooper narrowed his focus from the panoramic sweep of *The Chainbearer* to a close-up of the Nest House and its immediate grounds. Here was a picture of aristocratic bliss, the original log Nest House having been replaced by one of stone, replete with stables, coachman, and extensive, parklike grounds, kept trim by a thousand grazing sheep.[50]

One of the purposes of the anti-rent novels was to prove that the property of the Littlepages, probably in reality Cooper's own property, had belonged to the family for at least three generations and that, as a result, the present landlord's title to it was indisputable. Therefore, it harmonized with Cooper's plan to give the Ravensnest area the stamp of age. This he neatly accomplished by decorating the grounds, so to speak, with two human ruins, the Indian Susquesus and the Negro Jaap, both of whom were over a century old and had been associated with all three landlords. Both, in fact, but especially the Indian, had been with Corny Littlepage and later with his son Mordaunt as they came upon the various landscapes in *Satanstoe* and *The Chainbearer*. Thus in all three novels they formed the continuing point of reference, the similarity in dissimilarity which rendered the contrast between the books meaningful. Furthermore, these two men were employed to enforce contrast within the single landscape itself. When put in with the soft, sylvan scenery of the Ravensnest of *The Redskins,* they achieved the same juxtaposition of the beautiful and the picturesque that belonged to a parallel landscape in *The Chainbearer*. One might compare the topography of *The Redskins* with that of the Englishman Richard Wilson's pictures if it were not for the abiding but subordinated wildness inherent in Cooper's scene.

Like Cole's landscapes of contrast, Cooper's books were saturated with theme; the idea behind the series which might be entitled "The Course of Ravensnest" was the recession and advance of men's minds. Each new generation of the landholding Littlepages frees itself from the shackles of provincial thinking while each new generation of renters is more tightly wrapped not only in the chains of provincialism but also in those of anti-rentism, to Cooper the vilest theory ever invented to destroy the rights of property. Thus the landscapes themselves, progressing always from a primitive to a civilized state, represent both parallel and contrast. In the case of the Littlepages, they parallel on the physical level a mental progression. In the case of the tenants, there is no parallel, only contrast between the attainment of material prosperity and the loss of spiritual integrity. To this irony of situation is added a final, telling contrast as Susquesus puts the antirenters to shame by demonstrating that he, an uncivilized Indian, has recognized the rights of property, while they, supposedly civilized beings, have not. This talking ruin, already covered with the symbolism of antiquity, takes on even more meaning as a spokesman for democratic principles that protect the individual as well as the masses.

In *The Crater* (1847) one again finds Cooper using similar methods to puncture the belief in pseudo-progress. Since parallels between *The Crater* and Cole's "The Course of Empire" have been thoroughly analyzed elsewhere,[51] there is little need to discuss the subject here. Suffice it to say that Cooper, like Cole, adopted the role of prophet, declaring in *The Crater* that the present course of civilization would eventually call down the punishment of God, administered through nature, and that, like Cole, he developed his theme in a series of contrasted landscapes. Because he mentions "The Course of Empire" in the final chapter of this novel and because he praises Cole at another time for this series,[52] he undoubtedly borrowed his general design from the painter although other sources for ideas in *The Crater* have also been discovered.[53]

The Sea Lions (1849) contains further evidence of Cole's influence on Cooper. It, too, was composed of many different elements; the author drew upon various written accounts of Antarctic voyages as well as upon his own exposure to the sealing industry and familiarity with Alpine landscapes. Yet, as Thomas Philbrick suggests,[54] the framework for this novel was probably inspired by the second and third pictures in Cole's "Voyage of Life" series. Like the youth in these paintings, the hero of *The Sea Lions* (Roswell Gardiner) takes a voyage which symbolizes his spiritual progress, and while he moves from youth to middle age, he learns that his own powers are not enough to reach heaven, that he must also have faith. Cooper, in other words, was not only using Cole's methods but also repeating his conclusions.

Cooper and Cole were by no means the only Americans to be fascinated with the downfall of nations or to compare nature's mutation to man's. Some Americans, however, were so deeply imbued with democratic faith that they could interpret prophetic messages of empire's decay as visions of republic's bloom. To them it was the manifest destiny of the United States to prosper where other nations failed. A writer in the *Mirror,* for example, could optimistically interpret "The Course of Empire": "The climax in the course of man's progress, which Mr. Cole has here represented, is *that* which *has been,* and was founded on the usurpation of the strong over the weak: the perfection which man is hereafter to attain, will be based upon more stable foundations: political equality; the rights of man; the democratick principle; *the sovereignty of the people.*"[55]

Yet Cooper and Cole stand alone as masters of the contrasted landscape because they were more deeply discontented and pessimistic than most of their fellow artists. Cooper's strong-mindedness is apparent in all his works, and his acute dissatisfaction with the America of his day is well known. Cole, however, has traditionally been thought of more or less as an ardent American and a cheerful romanticist. But, as Kenneth LaBudde has noted, Cole was at heart a pessimist about time and country:

> Thomas Cole's criticisms of his society were probably shaped in part by the position it accorded him as an artist. His idea of the role he should play was not realized, and this contributed, no doubt, to his pessimistic frame of mind. Indeed, it may have been the largest single cause for the tenor of his outlook. He had hoped to have a volume of his verse published and he would have liked to have been recognized as an architect of monumental structures, but his major disappointment was not being able to be a painter of great art as he saw that art to be.[56]

Cooper and Cole, not close friends, not living for that matter in very similar environments, were kindred spirits nevertheless. Both were horrified by the increasing materialism of American society, and both found a panacea for it in Christianity. That both used parallel methods to develop their themes is, therefore, not surprising.

This survey of the techniques employed by Knickerbocker writers and American painters should prove, if nothing else, that these men were true artists, motivated by a high purpose. Whether they took the panoramic approach, used the human accessory, composed their pictures with a brand of selective realism, or created sharply contrasted scenes in order to criticize society, they did so with a single worthy goal in mind—to strengthen the bonds between God, man, and nature, and thus to fashion a spiritually functional art.

Mutual Publications

It was inevitable that with this much in common they would work on joint projects. The results of their co-operation were four gift books and a magazine, all devoted to landscape but varying in historical significance and commercial appeal. Such undertakings were for the aggressive, not the timid, since publication of any kind in the early nineteenth century was a precarious business, and sales were never insured.[57] Furthermore, the ineffectiveness of copyright laws gave pirated rather than native works a special attraction to publishers. Successful, original landscape books were therefore rare.[58] At least two such works, however, may be attributed to the Knickerbockers.

THE AMERICAN LANDSCAPE. The first joint production limited to native scenery, illustrated by an American, written by a Knickerbocker, and published in New York was *The American Landscape* (1830). Asher Durand engraved all but one of the seven illustrations for this pioneer volume. His friend Bryant composed most of the letterpress, which matched original paintings and drawings by Durand, Cole, Bennett, and Weir. The publishers planned extending "the work to ten numbers," each with "six views, in quarto, . . . to appear at intervals of six months, or oftener if possible."[59] But the first number proved to be the last,[60] although three of its engravings—"Weehawken," "Falls of the Sawkill," and "The Delaware Water-Gap"—were later reissued with their letterpress in *The New-York Mirror*.[61]

The reasons for the failure of *The American Landscape* are somewhat obscure. In many ways it promised success. Although it might be considered a continuation of *The Talisman* series, it abandoned the humor of these volumes[62] and approached its problem seriously. Its nationalistic tone was especially suitable to the temper of its day. The "Prospectus" read: "Nature is not less liberal of the characteristics of beauty and sublimity in the new world, than in the old"—an appealingly chauvinistic statement,[63] supplemented by

Bryant's observation that native scenery contains "enough of the lovely, the majestic, and the romantic, to entitle it to be ranked with that of any country."[64] The text of *The American Landscape* was written by a man whose reputation was firmly established, and was illustrated by the country's leading engraver. Neither Bryant nor Durand could have been accused of hack work: the straightforward prose, hardly as lively as Willis' or Irving's, was nonetheless appropriate to the informative nature of the publication. The plates, although small, were carefully executed and are rather highly valued by some of today's art historians.[65] Lastly, both text and illustrations stressed aspects of American scenery that were most appealing in the early nineteenth century. Lake Winnipiseogee was associated with the romantic Indian,[66] and Fort Putnam was described as a "venerable ruin of massive military architecture, . . . fraught with recollections of heroism, liberty, and virtue."[67] Above all, the popular concern for documentation was strictly adhered to; Bryant was careful to inform his readers of the exact point from which each picture was made, and "the proprietors" vowed that "*characteristic features will, in all cases, be truly and correctly copied.*"[68]

But the fate of pioneer works was unpredictable, and the failure of *The American Landscape* seems to have been due mostly to external circumstances rather than to lack of merit. First, its small, gray plates could hardly compete with the larger, colored views of William Wall's *Hudson River Portfolio,* issued five years earlier than *The American Landscape*.[69] Secondly, it probably was not merchandised with any great enthusiasm by Elam Bliss, its publisher, who had already met with only limited success in the publication of The Sketch Club's *Talisman* series.[70] Thirdly, it appeared at a very precarious time. Although the fervor of the public was gradually being stirred up by the writers of the day, as yet the great wave of enthusiasm for nature which was to culminate in the National Park movement was only a promising ripple. The success or failure of landscape publications could hardly be predicted, and while one book might find buyers, another might not.

Had *The American Landscape* been published fifteen years later, it might have thrived. Bryant's dry comment that "it would be easier to find a series of good views of the scenery of China or Southern India, than of the United States"[71] would have been as true in 1845 as it was in 1830. No American book in the first half of the nineteenth century covered the scenery of the entire United States. Perhaps *The American Landscape* would have done so, even with its modest regional beginning, had its life not been cut short by public apathy, but the need for such a publication was not yet felt by more than a few.

AMERICAN SCENERY. *American Scenery* (1840), written by Nathaniel Parker Willis and illustrated by William

Henry Bartlett, was the most ambitious undertaking of the entire Knickerbocker period. Embodying two hundred and forty-six pages of text and one hundred and nineteen engravings, it was a bulky work, especially if its owner had its two volumes bound under one cover. The book's scope was limited to the northeastern part of the United States, but in this area was enough diversity of landscape to prevent the engraved views from becoming monotonous. The purpose of *American Scenery* was twofold: The illustrations were assembled to allow "those whose lot is domestic and retired" to enjoy the benefits of travel "at little cost and pains."[72] The letterpress was written to make each engraving meaningful by matching it with a legend, a poem, an anecdote, or a descriptive essay, chosen for its associational value.

American Scenery was a Knickerbocker production only in a limited sense. Willis, its editor, had been a New Yorker for almost a decade, but Bartlett, its illustrator, was an Englishman;[73] the book itself was published in London.[74] Only the two engravings made after pictures by Thomas Doughty cannot be traced to Bartlett's watercolors. On the other hand, because of its editorship, contents, and influence, the book is American in a very real sense.

Today, more than one hundred years after its publication, the value of *American Scenery* has been recognized but partially. True, it is an expensive book; a foxed copy now sells for about $25, but this is due largely to the possibilities of grangerizing. When hand-colored and framed, its plates fetch from $6 to $30 and are sold even in department stores. *American Scenery* has retained its popularity because of Bartlett's illustrations, not Willis' text. This is unfortunate because the letterpress contains some of Willis' best writing, despite Henry Beers's remark that it is "hack work" of "little . . . purely literary interest."[75] What the author did not write for himself he compiled with skill from a wide range of chroniclers and poets. Actually, Willis imagined a worthy goal and achieved it, shaping *American Scenery* into a vast storehouse of association-enhanced landscape, and an authentic, colorful record of America's folklore, legend, and history. Equal credit should be given to Bartlett and Willis alike for this enterprise.

CANADIAN SCENERY. *Canadian Scenery* (1840),[76] another fireside travel work by Willis and Bartlett, was a two-volume companion of *American Scenery,* which it resembled in bulk, format, and, presumably, popularity. Since Willis borrowed most of the letterpress from various authorities on Canadian life and history, whom he acknowledged in a footnote of general indebtedness,[77] he can be praised only for his editorial acumen. Original or not, the text of *Canadian Scenery* is still valuable for its wealth of historical and legendary matter—two hundred and forty-four pages in all—much

of it concerned with the North American Indian.[78] By uncovering its associations, Willis performed almost as great a service for the Canadian landscape as he had for the scenery of the northeastern United States.

The real charm of *Canadian Scenery* comes not from Willis' text, however, but from Bartlett's illustrations. This English artist seems to have felt more at home in Canada. His drawing appears bolder; his ability to capture the romance of a scene greater in this book than in *American Scenery.* "Raft in a Squall, on Lake St. Peter" surpasses in its impact, most nineteenth-century engraved seascapes; "Les Marches Naturelles" and "A Forest Scene" place one solidly in the midst of nature, their moodiness heightened by contrast with the documentary quality of Bartlett's architectural and genre views. Because of its numerous fine engravings and authentic text, *Canadian Scenery* was a significant work, next to *American Scenery* the most ambitious effort at artistic collaboration in the Knickerbocker period.[79]

THE HOME BOOK OF THE PICTURESQUE. With *The Home Book of the Picturesque* (1852),[80] production of landscape gift books during the Knickerbocker period reached its climax. Its one hundred and eightyeight pages encompassed letterpress by the leading writers of New York and engravings after pictures by major Hudson River School artists, so that everything about this book was either native or regional, including the publisher, George P. Putnam. One had to pay $7 for a cloth-bound copy, $10 for morocco, and $16 for a volume with India proofs,[81] but even these were bargain prices which allowed purchasers to support their country's arts.

The engravings were small but splendid vignettes executed by Henry Beckwith, John Halpin, Samuel Valentine Hunt, and John Kirk, all respectable practitioners of their craft. A list of the painters from whose pictures the engravings were made includes both the older and younger members of the Hudson River School: Thomas Cole, Asher Durand, and Robert Weir, plus Beckwith, who engraved his own picture of "The Bay of New York," Jaspar F. Cropsey, Thomas Addison Richards, Frederick E. Church, and Régis Gignoux. The superiority of *The Home Book of the Picturesque* was due, however, not to its inclusiveness or bulk (it contained only thirteen plates), but to its consistently high quality of illustrations,[82] especially notable since, at the time of its publication, the usual American gift book was a congeries of secondhand engravings, pirated text, and trite sentimentality of the Botanical School type. No Fanny Fern wrote for this volume; the publisher therefore chose his pictures to explain the American landscape, not to provoke emotional outbursts over plagued heroines.

The letterpress was both varied and meaty, beginning in scholarly fashion with Elias Lyman Magoon's formal attempt to prove the spiritual benefits of land-scape. Another selection, Fenimore Cooper's "American and European Scenery Compared," was a blunt essay, devoid of chauvinism, conceding "to Europe much the boldest scenery . . . [to] America the freshness of a promising youth."[83] A shorter piece contained Irving's desultory observations on national landscape and some recollections of his boyhood in the New York area. Bryant discussed "The Valley of the Housatonic," and Willis wrote about "The Highland Terrace, above West Point."[84] Representing the younger writers were Susan Fenimore Cooper, Bayard Taylor, Henry T. Tuckerman, Mary E. Field, and Alfred Billings Street. George Washington Bethune provided a fitting close to the volume with his "Art in the United States," predicting the establishment of a national gallery. Although no writer did his best work in these pages, each contributed to the anthology's over-all richness, due largely to the lively interest these authors took in the American landscape, an enthusiasm matched by the artists whose pictures they illustrated.

PICTURESQUE AMERICA. Years after the Hudson River School had declined and most of the Knickerbocker writers had died, William Cullen Bryant edited *Picturesque America* (1872), another landscape gift book which deserves mention here. The poet's contribution may be given in his own words: "I edited the work, it is true. Somebody must edit such a publication, and I do not see why I should not do it as well as another. Every part of it, except a few of the first sheets, passed through my hands; and I do not remember that I was ever more weary of any literary task, for the mere description of places is the most tedious of all reading. It was my business to correct the language, omit superfluous passages, and see that no nonsense crept into the text; and this I did as faithfully as I knew how."[85] In this mass of letterpress, over eleven hundred large pages, Bryant must have been happy to come upon essays by Thomas Bangs Thorpe, John Esten Cooke, and Constance Fenimore Woolson.

Although he did not select the hundreds of excellent illustrations in *Picturesque America,* Bryant was probably delighted with those which recalled friendships of earlier days: James M. Hart's "The Adirondack Woods" had the delicate serenity of Asher Durand's "Monument Mountain," and J. D. Woodward's "Connecticut Valley from Mount Tom" was reminiscent of Thomas Cole's panoramic "Oxbow." The old spirit—druidical, topographical, associational—lingered on the pages of this belated Knickerbocker book. Its old editor, destined to live only six more years, having once failed with *The American Landscape,* was too tired to be proud of the acclaim which met his latest effort.

Picturesque America was the first major landscape publication edited by a Knickerbocker writer to treat of the entire United States and, in this sense, was quite new. *The American Landscape, The Home Book of the Picturesque,* and even *American Scenery* had been limited to the northern and eastern part of this country. *Picturesque America* with its descriptions and views of the Rocky Mountains, the Golden Gate, and the coast of Florida, achieved a coverage that the pioneer works had been denied because of insufficient public support and the immaturity of native publishing. Unfortunately, few of the Knickerbockers still lived to enjoy this eloquent tribute to America's vastness.

Paradoxically enough, this study of nature demonstrates the importance of man. Certain techniques were used and gift books were published so that man might benefit from the experience of those who had devoted their lives to analyzing scenery. Panoramic and compositional techniques, for example, taught that even in vastness God can create and men can find unity, harmony, and order. Human accessories in painted and printed views allowed man to look at himself in a mirror to discover his relationship to nature, which could delight, awe, and terrorize. By paying special attention to landscapes of contrast he could learn that his own life and the lives of his empires have, like nature, periods of blight and bloom. Finally, the publication of attractive landscape gift books helped him to review the lessons he had been taught by the Knickerbockers and their fellow artists, who never lost sight of the fact that they were men talking to men—about nature.

Notes

[1] See, for example, Donald A. Ringe, "Chiaroscuro as an Artistic Device in Cooper's Fiction," pp. 349-57.

[2] See F. Sweet, p. 14; Sears, p. xvii.

[3] See Perry T. Rathbone (ed.), *Mississippi Panorama.* For a survey of the panorama in American painting, see Wolfgang Born, *American Landscape Painting: An Interpretation,* pp. 75-117. Several New York magazines took an interest in panoramas which were exhibited locally. See "The Departure of the Israelites from Egypt," *The Knickerbocker,* V (Feb., 1835), 171-72; "Belshazzar's Feast," *The Knickerbocker,* V (April, 1835), 359; "Moving Diorama," *The Knickerbocker,* VI (July, 1835), 83; "Peristrephick Dioramas," *The New-York Mirror,* XIII (July 25, 1835), 31; "Hannington's Peristrephic Diorama," *The New-York Mirror,* XIII (Aug. 29, 1835), 71; "The New Panorama," *The New-York Mirror,* XVI (Aug. 18, 1838), 63; "Catherwood's Panorama of Thebes," *The New-York Mirror,* XVI (April 13, 1839), 335. Cf., however, the displeasure of an anonymous critic in "Monthly Record of Current Events," *Harper's New Monthly Magazine,* II (April, 1851), 705.

[4] Born, p. 80.

[5] Washington Irving, *The Alhambra,* pp. 124-32.

[6] *Excursions in Switzerland,* p. 186.

[7] I, 248-49.

[8] See Howard M. Jones, "James Fenimore Cooper and the Hudson River School," p. 249.

[9] I, 141-43.

[10] See James Fenimore Cooper, *Satanstoe,* pp. 101-2.

[11] Some interesting approaches in poetry and prose were Richard Haywarde [Frederick S. Cozzens], "Thoughts from the Top of Trinity," *The Knickerbocker,* XXXII (July, 1848), 38-40; Bryant, "Monument Mountain," *Poetical Works,* I, 103; Halleck, "Fanny," *Poetical Writings,* p. 130 (stanza xcv).

[12] Joseph R. Drake, "To a Friend," *The Culprit Fay and Other Poems,* p. 42.

[13] Halleck, "Fanny," *Poetical Writings,* pp. 130-31.

[14] Dunlap, *A Trip to Niagara,* p. iii.

[15] *Ibid.,* pp. 26-27.

[16] See George C. D. Odell, *Annals of the New York Stage,* III, 407. The Christian names of only two of these painters, Duke White and John L. Leslie, are certain. The original paintings from which the scenery was executed are attributed to Wall, probably William Guy Wall, in "Fine Arts: The Diorama at the Bowery Theatre," *The Critic,* I (Dec. 13, 1828), 104. See Born, p. 90, for possible far-reaching effects of this diorama.

[17] See Odell, III, 408. An appreciative contemporary review was "Mr. Dunlap's Play of a Trip to Niagara," *The New-York Mirror,* VI (Dec. 20, 1828), 191. Earlier instances of moving scenery on the New York stage are given in "A Trip to Niagara," *The New-York Mirror,* VI (Nov. 22, 1828), 159.

[18] Cornelius Mathews, *A Pen-and-Ink Panorama of New York City,* pp. 5-7.

[19] *Ibid.,* pp. 92-93. Also see p. 173.

[20] *Ibid.,* p. 209.

[21] See, for instance, Bryant's "To the Fringed Gentian," "To a Mosquito," and "The Yellow Violet," as well as C. F. Hoffman's "The Brook and the Pine," Edward Sanford's "Address to a Mosquito," and William P. Hawes's "Song of the Hermit Trout." The last two poems were collected in a useful anthology of writings by Gothamites: *The New-York Book of Poetry,* pp. 11-14, 46.

[22] See E. Clark, *History of the National Academy of Design,* p. 49. Paul Shepard, Jr., has analyzed 60 paintings of the Hudson River School by comparing them with the actual sites from which they were taken. His study shows quite conclusively that these artists were not literal transcribers of nature but that they frequently moved mountains, elevated foregrounds, depressed middle distances, and inserted waterfalls to suit their compositions. See especially Shepard, pp. 85-89, for a comparison of Kaaterskill Clove, an area in the Catskills and the site of Durand's "Kindred Spirits," with the painting itself.

[23] Bryant, *Poetical Works,* I, 102.

[24] See George Arms, *The Fields Were Green,* p. 19.

[25] "National Academy of Design," *The New-York Mirror,* XIX (May 15, 1841), 159.

[26] "National Academy of Design," *The Knickerbocker,* XXXIX (June, 1852), 567.

[27] Willis, *Pencillings,* p. 35.

[28] See Donald A. Shelley, "William Guy Wall and His Watercolors," p. 37.

[29] Willis, *American Scenery,* I, 24.

[30] *Ibid.,* II, 29.

[31] James Fenimore Cooper, *The Deerslayer,* p. x. The wording of this passage is slightly different in the "New Edition."

[32] Born, p. 36.

[33] See Willis, *Out-Doors at Idlewild,* pp. 104-5.

[34] Willis, *Rural Letters,* pp. 351-52.

[35] Street, *Poems,* p. 93.

[36] The following pictures exhibit various degrees of this method: William Dunlap, "View of Niagara Falls," William Wall, "Hudson River from West Point," Thomas Doughty, "In the Catskills," Thomas Cole, "The Pass Called 'The Notch of the White Mountains,'" and William Bartlett, "Caterskill Falls."

[37] See Thomas Cole, "Mountain Sunrise" and "Landscape with Tree Trunks," Thomas Doughty, "Mountain Torrent," Thomas Birch, "Upper Hudson," Asher Durand, "Monument Mountain" and "North Mountain Reservation, South Orange, New Jersey," John W.

Casilear, "Moonlight," John F. Kensett, "Glimpse of Lake George," and William Hart, "Autumn in the Catskills."

[38] For the literary influences on the American vogue of solitary and gloomy landscapes, see G. Harrison Orians, "The Rise of Romanticism," pp. 223-25. Other background is in Shepard, pp. 47-49.

[39] Bryant, *Poetical Works,* I, 132.

[40] See Willis, *American Scenery,* I, 33.

[41] Bryant, *Poetical Works,* I, 172.

[42] Street, *Poems,* p. 100.

[43] *Ibid.* For a similar use of contrast, see Anthony Bleecker's "Trenton Falls, near Utica," collected in *The New-York Book of Poetry,* pp. 110-11.

[44] See Donald Ringe's analysis of *Satanstoe* in his "James Fenimore Cooper and Thomas Cole: An Analogous Technique," pp. 31-36.

[45] Cooper, *Satanstoe,* II, 157-58.

[46] For New York City, cf. *Satanstoe,* I, 32, 34-35, 100-2 to *Redskins,* I, 54-56; for Albany, cf. *Satanstoe,* I, 156, 161-65, 200 to *Redskins,* I, 74-75.

[47] Cooper, *Satanstoe,* II, 74.

[48] *Ibid.,* II, 77.

[49] Cooper, *The Chainbearer,* I, 113-14.

[50] Cooper, *The Redskins,* I, 118, 156-59.

[51] Ringe, "Cooper and Cole," pp. 18-30.

[52] See Noble, p. 224.

[53] See Harold H. Scudder, "Cooper's *The Crater,*" pp. 109-26; W. B. Gates, "Cooper's *The Crater* and Two Explorers," pp. 243-46. Another possible germ of this novel is in Cooper, *Gleanings in Europe: Italy,* I, 224.

[54] *James Fenimore Cooper and the Development of American Sea Fiction,* pp. 233-37.

[55] "The Third of Mr. Cole's Five Pictures," *The New-York Mirror,* XIV (Nov. 4, 1836), 150. For equations of man's mutation and nature's, see Irving, *Bracebridge Hall,* p. 12; Prosper M. Wetmore, *Lexington, with Other Fugitive Poems,* p. 72; Halleck, "Twilight," *Poetical Writings,* pp. 36-37; Bryant, "Ruins of Italica," *Poetical Works,* II, 283; Willis, *American Scenery,* I, 33.

Interest in the cyclical interpretation of history appears in B., "Downfall of Nations," *The Knickerbocker,* VI (July, 1835), 44-53; Bryant, *Letters of a Traveller: Second Series,* pp. 15-16.

[56] LaBudde, p. 159.

[57] MS letter, Irving to Cole, New York, Sept. 15, 1835, Cole Papers, New York State Library, is an example of preliminary arrangements for the publication of such landscape books.

[58] These are surveyed in Frank Weitenkampf, "Early American Landscape Prints," pp. 40-68.

[59] A. B. Durand and E. Wade, Jun., "Prospectus of the American Landscape," in Bryant and Durand, *The American Landscape,* No. 1, p. 4.

[60] The *Mirror*'s statement that *The American Landscape* "was not put into circulation" appears to be inaccurate. See "Falls of the Sawkill," *The New-York Mirror,* X (May 25, 1833), 369.

[61] *The New-York Mirror,* X (April 20, 1833), 329; X (May 25, 1833), 369; XI (June 7, 1834), 385 respectively. The engravings faced these pages of text. The *Mirror* also reprinted, without engravings, three other descriptions from *The American Landscape,* with several very short and minor additions and changes in wording: "Catskill Mountains," *The New-York Mirror,* X (Oct. 17, 1832), 133; "Weehawken," X (Nov. 3, 1832), 142; and, with the third paragraph of Bryant's text omitted, "The Delaware Water-Gap," X (Dec. 1, 1832), 174.

[62] Bryant II, pp. 180-81; MS letters, Bryant to Verplanck, New York, Feb. 23, March 5, 1830, Bryant-Verplanck Correspondence, Berg Collection, New York Public Library.

[63] Bryant and Durand, p. 3.

[64] *Ibid.,* p. 6.

[65] See Virgil Barker, *American Painting,* p. 511; Larkin, p. 143; and, for the most specific analysis, Richardson, p. 169. The nineteenth century was apparently not quite so enthusiastic. See "The American Landscape," *The New-York Mirror,* VIII (Jan. 8, 1831), 214; Durand, *A. B. Durand,* p. 73.

[66] Bryant and Durand, p. 15.

[67] *Ibid.,* pp. 11-12.

[68] *Ibid.,* p. 4.

[69] See Weitenkampf, p. 65.

70 This lack of enterprise became especially apparent when Bliss published Bryant's poetry in 1832. Finding approximately 100 copies of this edition still for sale, Bryant remarked: "Bliss *sells* as slow as Old Rapid in the play *sleeps*. Any other bookseller would have got off the whole before this time; but he is a good creature . . ." (letter to Dana, quoted in Godwin, I, 285).

71 Bryant and Durand, p. 6.

72 Willis, *American Scenery*, I, iv.

73 Information on Bartlett may be found in Bartlett Cowdrey, "William Henry Bartlett and the American Scene," pp. 388-400, and in Sears, pp. 1-2. Willis mentions Bartlett in *Rural Letters*, pp. 41-42, 114-17, 130; *Hurry-Graphs*, p. 78.

74 At a later date, however, a shorter, 92-page edition was published in America: N. P. Willis, *Picturesque American Scenery: A Series of Twenty-Five Beautiful Steel Engravings* (1883). In this edition, a few engravings after Thomas Moran and George L. Brown were added to those after Bartlett.

75 Beers, p. 247.

76 Some background material for the writing of this book is given in Beers, pp. 244, 247-48.

77 See N. P. Willis, *Canadian Scenery*, I, 1 n.

78 See Daughrity, pp. 136-37.

79 Willis also worked with Bartlett on a book of Irish landscape but wrote very little of its text: N. P. Willis and J. Sterling Coyne, *The Scenery and Antiquities of Ireland*. A much smaller and less significant work, replete with wood engravings after various minor artists, was N. P. Willis (ed.), *Trenton Falls, Picturesque and Descriptive*. Willis was actually co-author of this book, not merely its editor. Thirty-three pages consisted of an essay written by John Sherman in 1827; the remaining 56 pages of text were Willis'.

80 Reissued as *Home Authors and Home Artists, or American Scenery, Art, and Literature* (n.d.).

81 See Thompson, p. 128.

82 For some background material, including a letter to Putnam from his close friend John F. Kensett, who was displeased with the engraving of his picture, see George H. Putnam, *George Palmer Putnam: A Memoir*, pp. 192-93.

83 *Home Book of the Picturesque*, p. 69.

84 This essay was reprinted in Willis, *Out-Doors at Idlewild*, pp. 1-25.

85 Letter from Bryant to Dr. Dewey, quoted in Godwin, II, 347.

Works Cited

Arms, George. *The Fields Were Green: A New View of Bryant, Whittier, Holmes, Lowell, and Longfellow, with a Selection of Their Poems*. Stanford: Stanford University Press, 1953.

Barker, Virgil. *American Painting: History and Interpretation*. New York: Macmillan Co., 1951.

Beers, Henry A. *Nathaniel Parker Willis*. ("American Men of Letters.") Boston: Houghton, Mifflin & Co., 1885.

Born, Wolfgang. *American Landscape Painting: An Interpretation*. New Haven: Yale University Press, 1948.

Bryant, William Cullen. *Letters of a Traveller: Second Series*. New York: D. Appleton & Co., 1860.

———. *The Poetical Works of William Cullen Bryant*, ed. Parke Godwin. 2 vols. New York: D. Appleton & Co., 1883.

———, and Asher Brown Durand. *The American Landscape, No. I, Containing the Following Views: Weehawken, Catskill Mountains, Fort Putnam, Delaware Water-Gap, Falls of the Sawkill, Winnipiseogee Lake. Engraved from Original and Accurate Drawings; Executed from Nature Expressly for This Work, and from Well Authenticated Pictures; with Historical and Topographical Illustrations*. New York: Elam Bliss, 1830.

Clark, Eliot. *History of the National Academy of Design*. New York: Columbia University Press, 1954.

Cooper, James Fenimore. *Cooper's Novels*. 65 vols. in 33. New Ed. New York: Sringer & Townsend [1849], 1852-1854. With the exception of *Wyandotte* and *The Deerslayer*, all of Cooper's novels cited in the preceding [excerpt] have been taken from this edition.

———. *The Deerslayer, or The First War-Path*. Mohawk Ed. New York: G. P. Putnam's Sons, n.d.

———. *Excursions in Switzerland*. Paris: Baudry's European Library, 1836.

[Cooper, James Fenimore.] *Gleanings in Europe: Italy*. 2 vols. Philadelphia: Carey, Lea, & Blanchard, 1838.

————. *James Fenimore Cooper: Representative Selections, with Introduction, Bibliography, and Notes by Robert E. Spiller,* ed. Robert E. Spiller. ("American Writers Series.") New York: American Book Co., 1936.

————. *Notions of the Americans Picked up by a Travelling Bachelor.* 2 vols. New York: Stringer & Townsend, 1850.

Cowdrey, Mary Bartlett. "William Henry Bartlett and the American Scene," *New York History,* XXII (Oct., 1941), 388-400.

Daughrity, Kenneth Leroy. "The Life and Work of Nathaniel Parker Willis: 1806-1836." Unpublished Ph.D. dissertation, University of Virginia, 1935.

Drake, Joseph Rodman. *The Culprit Fay and Other Poems.* New York: Van Norden & King, 1847.

Dunlap, William. *A Trip to Niagara; or Travellers in America. A Farce, in Three Acts.* New York: E. B. Clayton, 1830.

Durand, John. *The Life and Times of A. B. Durand.* New York: Charles Scribner's Sons, 1894.

Gates, W. B. "Cooper's *The Crater* and Two Explorers," *American Literature,* XXIII (May, 1951), 243-46.

Godwin, Parke. *A Biography of William Cullen Bryant, with Extracts from His Private Correspondence.* 2 vols. New York: D. Appleton & Co., 1883.

Halleck, Fitz-Greene. *The Poetical Writings of Fitz-Greene Halleck, with Extracts from Those of Joseph Rodman Drake,* ed. James Grant Wilson. New York: D. Appleton & Co., 1869.

The Home Book of the Picturesque: or American Scenery, Art, and Literature. New York: G. P. Putnam, 1852.

Irving, Washington. *The Alhambra.* Hudson Ed. New York: G. P. Putnam's Sons [1880].

————. *Bracebridge Hall.* Hudson Ed. New York: G. P. Putnam's Sons, 1892.

Jones, Howard Mumford. "James Fenimore Cooper and the Hudson River School," *Magazine of Art,* XLV (Oct., 1952), 243-51.

LaBudde, Kenneth J. "The Mind of Thomas Cole." Unpublished Ph.D. dissertation, University of Minnesota, 1954.

Larkin, Oliver W. *Art and Life in America.* New York: Rinehart & Co., 1949.

Mathews, Cornelius. *A Pen-and-Ink Panorama of New York City.* New York: John S. Taylor, 1853.

The New-York Book of Poetry. [Ed. Charles Fenno Hoffman.] New York: G. Dearborn, 1837.

Noble, Louis L. *The Course of Empire, Voyage of Life, and Other Pictures of Thomas Cole, N. A., with Selections from His Letters and Miscellaneous Writings: Illustrative of His Life, Character, and Genius.* New York: Cornish, Lamport & Co., 1853.

Odell, George C. D. *Annals of the New York Stage.* Vol. III: *1821-1834.* New York: Columbia University Press, 1928.

Orians, G. Harrison. "The Rise of Romanticism: 1805-1855," in *Transitions in American Literary History* (ed. Harry Hayden Clark; Durham, N.C.: Duke University Press, 1953), pp. 163-244.

Philbrick, Thomas. *James Fenimore Cooper and the Development of American Sea Fiction.* Cambridge, Mass.: Harvard University Press, 1961.

Putnam, George Haven. *George Palmer Putnam: A Memoir. . . .* New York: G. P. Putnam's Sons, 1912.

Rathbone, Perry T. (ed.), *Mississippi Panorama.* New ed. rev. St. Louis: City Art Museum of St. Louis, 1950.

Richardson, E. P. *Painting in America: The Story of 450 Years.* New York: Thomas Y. Crowell, 1956.

Ringe, Donald A. "Chiaroscuro as an Artistic Device in Cooper's Fiction," *PMLA,* LXXVIII (Sept., 1963), 349-57.

————. "James Fenimore Cooper and Thomas Cole: An Analogous Technique," *American Literature,* XXX (March, 1958), 26-36.

Scudder, Harold H. "Cooper's *The Crater,*" *American Literature,* XIX (March, 1947), 109-26.

Sears, Clara Endicott. *Highlights among the Hudson River Artists.* Boston: Houghton Mifflin Co., 1947.

Shelley, Donald A. "William Guy Wall and His Watercolors," *The New-York Historical Society Quarterly,* XXXI (Jan., 1947), 25-45.

Shepard, Paul H., Jr. "American Attitudes toward the Landscape in New England and the West, 1830-1870." Unpublished Ph.D. dissertation, Yale University, 1954.

Street, Alfred B. *The Poems of Alfred B. Street.* Complete Ed. New York: Clark & Austin, 1845.

Sweet, Frederick A. *The Hudson River School and the Early American Landscape Tradition.* New York: Whitney Museum of American Art & The Art Institute of Chicago, 1945.

Thompson, Ralph,. *American Literary Annuals & Gift Books.* New York: H. W. Wilson Co., 1936.

Weitenkampf, Frank. "Early American Landscape Prints," *Art Quarterly,* VIII (Winter, 1945), 40-68.

Wetmore, Prosper Montgomery. *Lexington, with Other Fugitive Poems.* New York: Carvill, 1830.

Willis, Nathaniel Parker. *American Scenery; or, Land, Lake, and River: Illustrations of Transatlantic Nature.* 2 vols. London: George Virtue, 1840.

————. *Canadian Scenery . . . Illustrated in a Series of Views by W. H. Bartlett.* 2 vols. London: George Virtue, 1840.

————. *Hurry-Graphs, or Sketches of Scenery, Celebrities and Society, Taken from Life.* Detroit: Kerr, Doughty, & Lapham, 1853.

————. *Out-Doors at Idlewild; or, The Shaping of a Home on the Banks of the Hudson.* New York: Charles Scribner, 1855.

————. *Pencillings by the Way: Written during Some Years of Residence and Travel in France, Italy, Greece, Asia Minor, Turkey, and England.* "The First Complete Edition." New York: Morris & Willis, 1844.

————. *Rural Letters.* New York: Baker & Scribner, 1849.

———— (ed.). *Trenton Falls, Picturesque and Descriptive: . . . Embracing the Original Essay of John Sherman. . . .* New York: George P. Putnam, 1851.

————, and J. Sterling Coyne. *The Scenery and Antiquities of Ireland. Illustrated by Drawings from W. H. Bartlett. The Literary Portion of the Work by N. P. Willis and J. Sterling Coyne, Esqs.* London: George Virtue, 1842.

FURTHER READING

Aderman, Ralph M. *Critical Essays on Washington Irving.* Boston: G. K. Hall & Co., 1990, 276 p.
> Covering a period of 180 years, contains a broad selection of critical essays on the work of Washington Irving.

Adkins, Nelson Frederick. *Fitz-Greene Halleck: An Early Knickerbocker Wit and Poet.* New Haven: Yale University Press, 1930, 461 p.
> A critical biography of one of the most popular and respected members of the Knickerbockers; it is also an excellent study of the whole of Knickerbocker literature and of the literary tradition in which Halleck wrote.

Arms, George. "Bryant." In *The Fields Were Green: A View of Bryant, Whittier, Holmes, Lowell, and Longfellow, with a Selection of Their Poems,* pp. 9-32. Stanford: Stanford University Press, 1953.
> A critical study of Bryant that re-evaluates his true literary merit as one of America's minor poets who has been unjustly neglected by twentieth-century criticism.

Current-Garcia, Eugene. "Soundings and Alarums: The Beginnings of Short Fiction in America." *Midwest Quarterly* XVII, No. 4 (Summer 1976): 311-28.
> A survey of the short story in the United States that affirms *The Sketch Book* as the first accomplished example of the genre.

Dayton, Abram C. *Last Days of Knickerbocker Life in New York.* New York: George W. Harlan, Publisher, 1882, 275 p.
> Written by one of the last of the Knickerbockers, it provides a picture of the social and literary milieu in New York at the end of the Knickerbocker era.

Fox, Dixon Ryan. "Yankee Culture in New York." In *Yankees and Yorkers,* pp. 199-223. New York: Ira J. Friedman, Inc., 1940.
> Explores the tension between the Dutch and New England cultures in New York City, explaining how it affected certain Knickerbocker writers, viz. James Fenimore Cooper and Charles Fenno Hoffman, in their characterizations of "Yankees" and New England culture in their work.

Hedges, William L. "The Knickerbocker History as Knickerbocker's 'History.'" In *The Old and New World Romanticism of Washington Irving,* edited by Stanley Brodwin, pp. 153-66. New York: Greenwood Press, 1986.
> Pointing out Irving's use of irony, burlesque, and even the absurd, Hedges argues that Irving's chief design in his 1809 work was simply his readers' amusement.

————. *Washington Irving: An American Study, 1802-1832.* The Grouchen College Series. Baltimore: Johns Hopkins Press, 1965, 274 p.

A study of Irving's relevance to American literary history that attempts to define Irving's major contributions and his relation to his intellectual milieu.

July, Robert W. *The Essential New Yorker: Gulian Crommelin Verplanck.* Durham: Duke University Press, 1951, 313 p.

A biography of one of the lesser Knickerbockers who was at once a well-known, accomplished man of letters and a successful politician of the Whig Party.

The Knickerbocker Gallery: A Testimonial to the Editor of the Knickerbocker Magazine. New York: Samuel Hueston, 1855, 505 p.

A commemorative collection of writings contributed by *Knickerbocker* writers in honor of their editor, L. G. Clark.

Mabie, Hamilton Wright. *The Writers of Knickerbocker New York.* New York: The Grolier Club, 1912, 121 p.

A descriptive, chronological account of the Knickerbocker writers and their work, publications, and associations.

Mott, Frank Luther. "*The Knickerbocker Magazine.*" In *A History of American Magazines: 1741-1850,* pp. 606-14. Cambridge: Harvard University Press, 1957.

Discusses *The Knickerbocker*—one of the most beloved American magazines of its day—under Lewis Gaylord Clarke's editorship, giving an account of its history, character, literary tastes and standards, and contributors.

Myers, Andrew B., ed. *1860-1974: A Century of Commentary on the Works of Washington Irving.* Tarrytown, NY: Sleepy Hollow Restorations, 1976, 504 p.

Comprises forty-five biographical and critical essays written between 1860 and 1974, including essays by Bryant, Longfellow, George Curtis, and William Hedges.

Ringe, Donald A. "Kindred Spirits: Bryant and Cole." *American Quarterly* VI, No. 3 (Fall 1954): 233-44.

Compares Bryant's aesthetic theory and practice as a poet with that of his closest friend, Thomas Cole, a painter of the Hudson River School, to reveal the connection between the two artists.

Rubin-Dorsky, Jeffrey. "Washington Irving and the Genesis of the Fictional Sketch." *Early American Literature* 21, No. 3 (Winter 1986/87): 226-47.

Demonstrates how Irving appropriated the popular form of the travel sketch, transforming what was crude documentary into a fictional narrative that was descriptively rich and emotionally intense.

Springer, Haskell. "Washington Irving and the Knickerbocker Group." In *Columbia Literary History of the United States,* edited by Emory Elliott, pp. 229-39. New York: Columbia University Press, 1988.

Presents Washington Irving as a critical and transitional figure in the development of a specifically American literary consciousness and tradition.

Taft, Kendall B. *Minor Knickerbockers.* New York: American Book Company, 1947, 410 p.

A representative selection of the works of the minor members of the Knickerbocker group with a critical introduction, extensive bibliography, notes, and biographical sketches of each member.

Williams, Stanley, and Tremaine McDowell. "Introduction." In *Diedrich Knickerbocker's "A History of New York"* by Washington Irving, edited by Stanley Williams and Tremaine McDowell, pp. ix-lxxiii. New York: Harcourt Brace and Co., 1927.

Explains the origin, influences, probable sources of the work, the many difficulties in interpreting it as history, and its specific literary qualities and characteristics.

The Novel of Manners

INTRODUCTION

Although the novel of manners has always defied easy definition, literary historians seem to have arrived at a consensus on at least three elements: it originated in England, Jane Austen was the quintessential producer of the form, and its subject is the set of social conventions of a particular class in a particular time and place. The growth of the novel of manners appears to have been centered in the nineteenth century, although some critics place its emergence earlier, in the works of Henry Fielding (1707-1754) or Samuel Richardson (1689-1761); others insist it survives well into the twentieth century in the works of F. Scott Fitzgerald (1896-1940) and Sinclair Lewis (1885-1951). If critics agree on England as the country of origin, there is considerable disagreement on whether the form exists at all in America. And the class whose social relations are scrutinized in the novel of manners could be the aristocracy, but it is more likely the gentry, the emerging middle class, or even the lower class.

Changes in English society in the nineteenth century that eroded the boundaries between these various groups provided the background for the emergence of the novel of manners. Industrialization, urbanization, and revolutions in transportation and communication were accompanied by profound changes in the social hierarchy. As the aristocracy lost power to industrial and business interests, the standard markers for determining an individual's position in society were becoming increasingly unreliable. In some sense, the novel of manners emerged to clear up this uncertainty by offering detailed renderings of how the various groups behaved in everyday situations, and by both describing and prescribing codes of conduct. Many works contrasted the customs of the various groups, examining not only class and economic differences, but also the differences between city and countryside, between an earlier agrarian culture and a contemporary industrial order, and between England and America.

This apparent necessity to compare the conventions of two or more groups led some early critics to insist that the novel of manners was not suited to American literature. They proclaimed the United States a homogeneous, classless society where no distinctions between citizens existed. Some asserted that the manners of all groups were identical; others insisted that American manners were nonexistent, claiming that Americans were too preoccupied with taming the wilderness and settling the land to develop any standard rules of conduct. More recent literary historians have disagreed with this assessment, insisting that concern with American manners and mores can be traced at least as far back as James Fenimore Cooper's time (1789-1851).

The novel of manners is dominated by women—as authors, as subjects, and often as intended audience—and for this reason has occasionally been dismissed as trivial. William Forsyth (1871), for example, tempers his praise of Jane Austen's novels by criticizing the constant "husband-hunting" by Austen's female characters. But although the focus of the novel of manners—domestic life, matrimony, and social behavior—tends to be narrow, the "manners" being studied very often have far wider implications beyond the pouring of tea and the search for the proper mate. Adherence to good manners in these texts is not only a reliable indicator of one's social standing, but is intended to serve as an indicator of good morals as well.

The novel of manners often deals with gender issues as well, as the accepted standards for both manners and morals differ markedly between men and women. Regardless of the social class under study, there are frequently two distinct sets of codes in operation, and as many feminist critics point out, the ideals prescribed for women were often a source of anxiety for nineteenth-century women writers—an anxiety that plays itself out in the novels. In many woman-authored texts, the interaction of individual characters with the social conventions of their cultures is not a happy one, and the conventions themselves are as likely to be satirized as celebrated.

REPRESENTATIVE WORKS

Jane Austen
Sense and Sensibility   1811
Pride and Prejudice   1813
Emma   1816

Charlotte Brontë
Jane Eyre   1847
Shirley   1849
Villette   1853

Edward Bulwer-Lytton
The Caxtons   1848-49

James Fenimore Cooper
 Satanstoe 1845
 The Chainbearer 1845
 The Redskins 1846

Charles Dickens
 Great Expectations 1860-61

Benjamin Disraeli
 Sybil, or the Two Nations 1845

Maria Edgeworth
 Castle Rackrent 1800
 Belinda 1801
 Leonora 1806

George Eliot
 Adam Bede 1859
 The Mill on the Floss 1860
 Felix Holt 1866

F. Scott Fitzgerald
 The Great Gatsby 1925
 Tender Is the Night 1934

Elizabeth Cleghorn Gaskell
 Mary Barton 1848
 North and South 1855
 Wives and Daughters 1866

William Dean Howells
 The Rise of Silas Lapham 1885

Henry James
 The American 1877
 Daisy Miller 1878
 Portrait of a Lady 1881

Sinclair Lewis
 Main Street 1920

Catharine M. Sedgwick
 Clarence 1830
 Married or Single? 1857

William Makepeace Thackeray
 Vanity Fair 1847-48

Anthony Trollope
 He Knew He Was Right 1869
 Phineas Finn 1869
 Lady Anna 1874

Edith Wharton
 The House of Mirth 1905
 The Age of Innocence 1920

Charlotte Mary Yonge
 The Heir of Redclyffe 1853

SOCIAL AND POLITICAL ORDER

Richard Faber

SOURCE: "Ordered Estates," in *Proper Stations: Class in Victorian Fiction*, Faber & Faber, 1971, pp. 16-22.

[*In the essay that follows, Faber discusses how the works of such novelists as George Eliot, Elizabeth Gaskell, and Anthony Trollope reflected the changes in nineteenth-century English society brought about by industrialization and urbanization.*]

Looking back from the middle years of the century novelists could recall a pastoral England, where the country still bulked larger than the towns and where every village was an island. In each distinct community the squire and/or the parson represented the gentry. Below them were the well-to-do farmers and the rural professional men—doctors, lawyers and, more humbly, schoolmasters. Below them, again, the rural artisans and tradesmen (carpenters, blacksmiths, wheelwrights, saddlers, weavers, shopkeepers) and, finally, the labourers who often lived and ate in the farms where they worked. Where there was a big house the servants would form a community of their own, observing its own hierarchy. The village innkeeper might be (as in *Adam Bede*) a former butler of the squire's. The Parish Clerk helped the Rector to maintain the dignity of the Church, which radiated more or less benevolently, but without excessive heat.

George Eliot brings out most pungently the contrast in village and country town life between the turn of the century and her own time. Her recollections have a gently idyllic glow and convey a touch of nostalgia for patriarchal stability. Perhaps this stability was partly illusory and belonged to a child's world rather than to the actual world of late eighteenth-century England. There was never a time, even in the eighteenth century, when social relations stood still. In so far as they had found a balance it was one that, in the country, lasted substantially until George Eliot's death and even later. She says, writing of 1799 in *Adam Bede:* '. . . in those days the keenest of bucolic minds felt a whispering awe at the sight of the gentry . . .' But this awe was not very much less potent in the middle of the nineteenth century. There were parts of England where it was still to be reckoned with in the twentieth century.

There had certainly been some decline in feudal spirit between the Napoleonic Wars and the mid-Victorian era, but not to a revolutionary extent; the structure of rural society remained basically the same throughout the eighteenth and nineteenth centuries. The real contrast between the countryside of, say 1800 and 1850 lay in material, rather than social, conditions: the greater intensity of cultivation, the greater absorption of the countryside for urban and industrial use, and above all the greater ease of communication. It was the railways, rather than any social revolution, that changed the rural life that George Eliot had glimpsed in her childhood: the theme of the Railway Revolution is a frequent and stirring *leit-motiv* in Victorian fiction. Ease of communication disturbed parochial self-sufficiency and diffused fashions and ideas. Clergymen began to torture themselves and their parishioners with points of doctrine. In refined provincial circles there was a serious striving after culture. Hospitality became more elegant and conversation more virtuous; the well-to-do ate and drank rather less heavily than they had before.

These changes in manners did not affect the social balance of the nation as a whole, so much as did the growth of the towns and of industrial activity. During the period covered in this book England changed from a predominantly rural country to a predominantly urban one. In 1851 the Census showed half the population—which then stood at 18 million—as urban. After this date the population continued to expand rapidly and the large towns became more and more important.

Mrs. Gaskell's *North and South* brings out more sharply than any other novel the contrast between the life of the traditional England and that of the new manufacturing towns. Aristocratic influence was overwhelming in the former, even after the Reform Bill of 1832. In the latter it seldom counted for much, in practical terms, and sometimes for nothing. Wealth and power, rather than gentility, were the standards of the new manufacturing society—as they have been in most parts of the United States and still tend to be in the industrial North today. The working classes may have feared or respected their masters; but they did not owe them a traditional reverence. The masters sometimes treated their men humanely and sometimes not; but their understanding of economic laws (*Hard Times* gives a powerful, if exaggerated, picture of their attitude) tended to put paternalism at a discount.

Disraeli's *Sybil,* published in 1845, set out to startle by announcing the co-existence of two nations in early Victorian England:

> Two nations, between whom there is no intercourse and no sympathy; who are as ignorant of each other's habits, thoughts and feelings, as if they were dwellers in different zones, or inhabitants of different planets; who are formed by a different breeding, are fed by a different food, are ordered by different manners, and are not governed by the same laws.

Disraeli was referring to the Rich and the Poor—and indeed the difference between an aristocrat and an industrial worker of the time was entirely what he claimed. But there were many sorts of rich and many sorts of poor. Perhaps a truer contrast would have been between the new industrial nation (of all classes) and the older nation which still surrounded it and from which it had sprung.

Much of the wealth and more of the enterprise of the country was concentrated in the industrial towns; but they did not set the social tone. Although the inhabitants of these towns were quick to forget their rural origins, some of the traditional sense of rank was bound to linger. In *Hard Times* Dickens pictures Mrs. Sparsit—a decayed, though majestic, gentlewoman—as malevolently keeping house in an industrial town for the self-made Mr. Bounderby, who deeply appreciates her lady-like qualities. Mr. Gradgrind, the rigid economist, is in league with Mr. Bounderby. We are told that 'the Gradgrind school . . . liked fine gentlemen; they pretended that they did not, but they did. They became exhausted in imitation of them; and they yaw-yawed in their speech like them . . .' Dickens suggests a kind of unholy alliance between manufacturers and aristocrats, in which each tried to make use of the other. The former had wealth and power, in their own sphere, but could not help being impressed by the latter.

Mr. Thornton, the manufacturer in Mrs. Gaskell's *North and South,* has a sturdy independence. He sets little store by the values of 'the South', respects hard work and material success, and boasts that the manufacturing working-man 'may raise himself into the power and position of a master by his own exertions and behaviour'. But he is ready to describe the impoverished Hale family to his mother as 'a gentleman and ladies'. Manufacturers were not necessarily above having their sons educated at aristocratic public schools, even when, like Mr. Millbank in Disraeli's *Coningsby,* they were of a 'democratic bent' and disapproved of them. Their sons or grandsons might use their money, like the returning 'nabobs' of the eighteenth century, to acquire landed property and, with it, social respectability of the older type. Thus Lord Minchampstead, in Kingsley's *Yeast,* was a mill-owner and coal-owner before he became a landed proprietor 'as the summit of his own and his compeers' ambition'; his dissenting, self-made, father had said to him: 'I have made a gentleman of you, you must make a nobleman of yourself.'

If the new manufacturing class was wealthy, the land-owners had not yet been hit by the bad harvests and cheap American corn of the seventies and they kept their heads above water in the middle of the nineteenth century. Agriculture was seldom a very paying investment;[1] but owners of non-agricultural land shared in the general prosperity. As to power, the manufacturers certainly enjoyed it in their own towns and businesses, and their needs and attitudes strongly affected national policies. But the government of the countryside, and of the nation as a whole, remained in the hands of the aristocracy and gentry. Rank had perhaps governed society more absolutely in the eighteenth century and had adopted a haughtier style. Thackeray at least was under that impression, when he wrote in *The Virginians* of the middle eighteenth century that 'in those times, when the distinction of ranks yet obtained, to be high and distant with his inferiors, brought no unpopularity to a gentleman'. Lord St. George, in Trollope's *Vicar of Bullhampton,* had moved with the times and would disturb his father by reminding him that 'in these days'—presumably the late sixties—'marquises were not very different from other people, except in this, that they perhaps might have more money.' But, if the manifestations of rank had become more discreet, its superiority was still very widely accepted. Although the intellectual and artistic life of the country was less firmly under aristocratic patronage than it had been in the eighteenth century, landed families still dominated Parliament and London society, as well as their own counties or parishes, and they still set fashions in dress and behaviour. Cobden wrote to a friend in 1858:

> During my experience the higher classes never stood so high in relative social and political rank compared with the other classes as at present. The middle classes have been content with the very crumbs from their table . . .

Thus, in spite of the emergence of new forces and classes, and in spite of the increasing diversity of English life, the old social system continued and flourished. It even reacted to change by developing a greater self-consciousness and rigidity. All readers of mid-Victorian fiction must be impressed by the sense which it conveys of a society both intricate and stable. Even Dickens, who found so much in society to dislike, gives an impression of solidity and permanence in the social order. There was certainly a time, in 'the hungry forties', when novelists became aware of dangerous divisions in society and when the distress, or resentment, of the poor seemed to threaten revolution. This was the time of the 'social protest' novel: Disraeli's *Sybil* (1845), Mrs. Gaskell's *Mary Barton* (1848), Kingsley's *Alton Locke* (1850) and *Yeast* (1851). But the resentment was gradually alleviated by governmental concessions, by the removal of abuses and by greater economic security; Chartism petered out; there was no revolution. By the time of the late fifties and sixties (the period of Trollope's best novels) the essential stability of society seems to be taken for granted in current fiction. There are still abuses to correct; there is still scope for a gradual evolution; but there is no danger of any rapid or drastic overhaul. In *Phineas Redux* Trollope notes that the differences between the two English parliamentary parties are really very small: 'Who desires among us to put down the Queen, or to repudiate the National Debt, or to destroy religious worship, or even to disturb the ranks of society?'

It was in the sixties that Sir Hugo Mallinger, of George Eliot's *Daniel Deronda,* 'carried out his plan of spending part of the autumn at Diplow' and spread

> some cheerfulness in the neighbourhood among all ranks and persons concerned, from the stately homes of Brackenshaw and Quetsham to the respectable shop-parlours in Wancester. For Sir Hugo was a man who liked to show himself and be affable, a Liberal of good lineage, who confided entirely in Reform as not likely to make any serious difference in English habits of feeling, one of which undoubtedly is the liking to behold society well fenced and adorned with hereditary rank. Hence he made Diplow a most agreeable house, extending his invitations to old Wancester solicitors and young village curates, but also taking some care in the combination of his guests, and not feeding all the common poultry together, so that they should think their meal no particular compliment.

It is a combination of complexity and stability, of vigour and strict form, that seems to confer on mid-Victorian society its classic quality—the sense that what preceded (however attractive in its simplicity) was a preparation and that what followed (however refreshing in its informality) must be a dissolution.

How much the form was created by the novelists themselves: how much they helped to establish and perpetuate the social distinctions that they portrayed: it is impossible to say. At least the socially conservative Trollope seems likely to have had some influence of this kind. Yet, though his novels may have confirmed his middle-class and upper-class readers in their social attitudes, he was himself obliged to describe a world that was familiar and agreeable to them. In his *Autobiography* he complains about the reception of his novel *Lady Anna:*

> In it a young girl, who is really a lady of high rank and great wealth, though in her youth she enjoyed none of the privileges of wealth or rank, marries a tailor who had been good to her, and whom she had loved when she was poor and neglected. A fine young noble lover is provided for her, and all the charms of sweet living with nice people are thrown in her way, in order that she may be made to give up the tailor. And the charms are very powerful with her. But the feeling that she is bound by her troth to the man who had always been true to her overcomes everything—and she marries the tailor. It was my wish of course to justify her in doing so, and to carry my readers along with me in my sympathy with her. But everybody found fault with me for marrying her to the tailor.

It would be unfair not to continue the quotation. Trollope goes on to say: 'What would they have said if I had allowed her to jilt the tailor and marry the good-looking young lord?' The most satisfactory solution would presumably have been for the tailor to die, or to perform a heroic act of self-renunciation, leaving the girl free to marry her noble lover with a clear conscience. But, in *Lady Anna,* Trollope was too much of a realist for that. As it was, he recognized, with truth, that Victorian sentiment called for as much nourishment as Victorian snobbery. Coronets were important; but so, in a different, and no doubt more basic, way were kind hearts. So much was this so, that the Victorian might even need to be reassured that, *pace* Dickens, 'Hearts just as brave and fair may beat in Belgrave Square as in the lowly air of Seven Dials'[3] or, as Thackeray puts it in *Philip:* 'Because people are rich, they are not of necessity ogres. Because they are gentlemen and ladies of good degree, are in easy circumstances, and have a generous education, it does not follow that they are heartless and will turn their back on a friend.'

[It] has to be remembered that, for most Victorians, inequality on earth was to be completed or compensated by a different kind of inequality after death. Rank conferred its temporary distinction; but equality in the sight of God would ensure that, in the long run, virtue met with its reward. The intelligent Lady Harriet, in Mrs. Gaskell's *Wives and Daughters,* is very conscious of her position and apt to be a bit disdainful of some of her inferiors. But she tells Molly Gibson: 'I don't set myself up in solid things as any better than my neighbours.' . . .

Notes

[1] Cf. *English Landed Society in the Nineteenth Century* by F. M. L. Thompson.

[2] Cf. Robert Blake's *Disraeli* (p. 273): 'As late as 1870 four hundred peers were reckoned to own over one-sixth of the whole surface of the country. It is not surprising that Cabinet and Parliament, lower as well as upper House, were overwhelmingly aristocratic in composition.'

[3] W. S. Gilbert: *Iolanthe* (1882).

T. B. Tomlinson

SOURCE: "Love and Politics in the English Novel, 1840s-1860s," in *The English Middle-Class Novel,* Barnes & Noble Books, 1976, pp. 69-82.

[*In the essay below, Tomlinson examines works by Benjamin Disraeli, Elizabeth Gaskell, and George Eliot and finds in them a mix of the personal and the political that is less than successful; the love stories are overly sentimental and the politics are oversimplified.*]

The title of this chapter is in a sense fraudulent: 'Small politics and less love' would be nearer the mark for Disraeli, Mrs. Gaskell, and the George Eliot of *Felix Holt.* Each of the novels I want to consider here is minor, and each of them seems to me badly flawed. Compared with the best of English literature, these are not about either love or politics in any full sense of those words. They must, therefore, be very untrustworthy evidence of what love and politics might really have meant either in the period generally or, if it comes to that, in the lives of these authors.

Nevertheless, and with the possible exception of Trollope, these are the nineteenth-century novelists in English who most specifically engage with political issues. I don't myself count Trollope as a political novelist, because even the Finn/Palliser series, close though it is to the parliamentary scene, seems to me more interested in the general moral dilemma that Palliser's career, for instance, figures: for Plantagenet Palliser, to act in the world is essential and honourable; but honour cannot survive dirtying one's hands in the business of the world. Phineas Finn comes to feel much the same in the end, and I don't think it would have made very much difference to these men, or to Trollope (despite his consuming interest in the House of Commons), if the 'business of the world' had been trade and commerce instead of rigged elections and party managers. But in other novels of the period politics, political economy and trade unions loom large. There are in fact too many political novels to discuss here—nominally a list might include, for instance, Kay-Shuttleworth's dreadful effusion, *Scarsdale*—but a fair selection from among the better ones of the period would be: Mrs. Gaskell's *Mary Barton* (1848) and *North and South* (which appeared in *Household Words* 1854-5); Disraeli's *Sybil* (1845); and George Eliot's *Felix Holt* (1866).

The question that interests me most about these is how and why did they fail? I do not believe it is simply that politics is intractable material for literature (it certainly wasn't for the Shakespeare of *Henry IV,* for instance). Nor do the kinds of weaknesses here seem simply weaknesses of and in the individual novelists concerned. There is a more general malaise than that operating, I think, and though it escapes final or complete diagnosis, one might approach an understanding of it by considering the persistent disjunction in these novels between politics on the one hand, and the rather unconvincing love-stories very much on the other. There is at least one other consideration that should be weighed in with this, though I don't want to do more than mention it in passing here: each of these novelists must have been cut off by the conditions of nineteenth-century middle-class life, education and aspirations from the popular movements they wrote about. If Disraeli's education, for instance, took place largely by reading in his father's library, he nevertheless had a library to read in beyond the dreams of the self-educated minority of the working class he and others describe in their fiction. The novelists' approach had to be to some degree academic, and this can only have increased their difficulties in the already difficult enough business of trying to write fiction that might make essentially personal emotions and affairs impinge on public ones.

On the other hand, I don't think that the novelists' lack of direct contact with working-class life and politics, debilitating though this must have been, was the only, or even the main, factor operating against them. Looking first at Mrs. Gaskell's two novels (though they are in fact a few years later in time than Disraeli's), and thinking still in largely political and sociological terms: one thing about these that deserves notice first of all is that they seem to have stirred up more political or quasi-political controversy than they warranted. Most reviewers accepted the sentimental love-affairs for the most part uncritically, but took offence at Mrs. Gaskell's interest in artisans and the working class. For instance, she was accused in *The Edinburgh Review* of April 1849, in an unsigned article in fact by W. R. Greg, of 'a sincere, though sometimes too exclusive and indiscriminating, sympathy with artisans'. Others joined in the complaint, but in fact there is no substance in it: her novels are full of doctrines of co-operation and self-help of precisely the kind advocated by the *Edinburgh* itself in its review of *Mary Barton,* and tend merely to protest against abuses, never against the wage-system itself or the existence of the employer class.

Indeed, I am inclined to think it might have helped her novels had Mrs. Gaskell been a shade less conventional, a shade more outrageous in her political and sociological thinking. There are interesting and convincing sections in both novels on trade unions, working-class conditions and so on, but even these seem—at least given the hindsight of a hundred years and more—rather settled, rather unquestioning of basic nineteenth-century assumptions about self-help, and about co-operation between artisans (who must, however, keep their place) and employers (who also rarely speculate beyond the local conditions and events they know). Had Mrs. Gaskell's political thinking been freer, I suspect that it would have been easier for her to make it relevant to the other, more personal and domestic, concerns in her novels.

Mary Barton for instance, though written during the 'hungry forties', and gloomier in tone than *North and South,* is if anything less radical in outlook than, say, James P. Kay's 1832 pamphlet on Manchester, or dozens of the reports that came in to Chadwick from his local doctors and poor-law officers:

> As they passed, women from their doors tossed household slops of *every* description into the gutter. . . . Our friends were not dainty, but even they picked their way, till they got to some steps leading down to a small area, where a person standing would have his head about one foot below the level of the street. . . . You went down one step even from the foul area into a cellar in which a family of human beings lived. It was very dark inside. The window-panes, many of them, were broken and stuffed with rags. . . . no-one can be surprised that on going into the cellar inhabited by Davenport, the smell was so foetid as almost to knock the two men down. . . . they began to penetrate the thick darkness of the place, and to see three or four little children rolling on the damp, nay wet brick floor, through which the stagnant, filthy moisture of the street oozed up; the fireplace was empty and black; the wife sat on her husband's lair [bed], and cried in the dark loneliness. (ch. VI)

The protest here against the injustice of working-class conditions in the industrial Midlands is obviously fair, and it is supported by literally hundreds of contemporary accounts, including of course those of Engels in his report on Manchester. But one's suspicions that, in context, Mrs. Gaskell's protest may suffer not from any radicalism but from her unthinking and basically sentimental conservatism, are born out by her handling of events generally in the novel. For example, after giving this and other perfectly clear instances of a system that condemns human beings to a sub-human existence, the novel nevertheless concludes that master and servant may, *without any prior change in the system or in the living conditions of the men and their families,* be brought together in and by a kind of Christian humanism. In the end of the novel Barton, the by now broken and disillusioned trade-union delegate, meets Carson, the employer and the man whose son Barton has murdered. Under the stress of emotion class barriers break down; or rather, we are asked to believe that they might:

> The eyes of John Barton grew dim with tears. Rich and poor, masters and men, were then brothers in the deep suffering of the heart; for was not this the very anguish he had felt for little Tom, in years so long gone by . . . ?
>
> . . . . .
>
> The mourner before him was no longer the employer; a being of another race, eternally placed in antagonistic attitude; going through the world glittering like gold, with a stony heart within, which knew no sorrow but through the accidents of Trade; no longer the enemy, the oppressor, but a very poor and desolate man. (ch. XXXV)

Writing in this softly sentimental prose, Mrs. Gaskell almost makes it sound as if murder is the price we must pay for better class relations. And the moral tale that follows only makes matters worse: a little girl forgives a rough labouring lad for pushing her, with the words (italics Mrs. Gaskell's or her editor's) *'He did not know what he was doing, did you little boy?'*

North and South is I think a better novel than *Mary Barton,* and in part it is better because Mrs. Gaskell's enquiry into the phenomenon of industrial magnate *versus* working men, though still fairly conventional and limited, is by now slightly freer. The over-all pattern follows directly from her rather sentimental hopes at the end of *Mary Barton,* but here the writing is sturdier and more interesting. In *North and South* Mrs. Gaskell is determined to bring the tough but likeably honest mill-owner, Thornton, to a better understanding of his men; and the men (notably the bluff, radically minded Higgins) to a better understanding of their free-enterprising master. The novel does this of course mainly through the heroine's influence, but also by forcing Thornton to ask himself tougher questions than he has done in his life to date. 'What do you want money for?' demands Mr. Bell (Margaret's—the heroine's—godfather and fellow of an Oxford college). The question, though ironically put and only half serious from Mr. Bell, is a faint precursor of Gudrun's famous question about Gerald in *Women in Love:* 'Where does his *go* go to?' Thornton's answer—unlike Gerald, he has the question put to him directly—is strongly enough shaped by Mrs. Gaskell to give a clear, and in its unambitious way quite convincing, account of her hero's and to a large extent her own sympathies. (Thornton is by no means merely a mouthpiece for Mrs. Gaskell's view, but such irony as is directed against him in this scene leaves his views about work and industry pretty much undisturbed.) These sympathies are neither so radically questioning nor so despairing of industrial society as Lawrence's, and they are, at least in this novel written in the more prosperous fifties, firmly in favour of a vigorous individualism in labourer and master alike. As such they seem both inoffensive and quite strongly put:

> 'But I belong to Teutonic blood . . . we do not look upon life as a time for enjoyment, but as a time for action and exertion. Our glory and our beauty arise out of our inward strength, which makes us victorious over material resistance, and over greater difficulties still. We are Teutonic up here in Darkshire in another way. We hate to have laws made for us at a distance. We wish people would allow us to right ourselves, instead of continually meddling, with their imperfect legislation. We stand up for self-government, and oppose centralization.' (ch. XI)

The larger interest of Mrs. Gaskell's political novels however is not so much in her own political position as, once again, in the enormous gap that identifying this reveals between the love-stories in her books on the one hand, and her attack on contemporary problems and abuses on the other. The love-stories, particularly that of Mary Barton's love for Jem Wilson, are in outline very like those of countless popular novels of the time.[1] Mrs. Gaskell's, like those of the popular novel and indeed, if it comes to that, those of many of the greater nineteenth-century novelists, are generally affairs that flourish on ill-chance, separation, difficulties of degree and circumstances that force lovers apart before they can be united; and through it all the lovers lean yearningly on the very circumstances that part them or put difficulties in their way. In other words they, and Mrs. Gaskell, thoroughly enjoy the pains of misunderstanding and separation. And if this sort of nostalgia is more marked in Mrs. Gaskell than it is in Hardy, whose name obviously looms in any such discussion, it is so precisely because of the remarkable dichotomy between love and politics, at least in these two books of hers.

The most uncomfortable example of this tendency is Mary's totally unconvincing change of heart in favour of Jem in *Mary Barton.* Mary has for some time been dazzled by the local mill-owner's rakish son, but in the course of a few minutes' anguish, and after a pretty mawkish appeal from Jem, she drops Carson. 'What were these hollow vanities to her, now that she had discovered the passionate secret of her soul?' This is not just a technical slip or a moment of bad writing that one could happily forget, because in fact it governs the course of the succeeding tale in which Jem, who has rushed off without hearing Mary's declaration, and who despairs of her until she pleads for him in court at the end, leaves the district hurriedly and is wrongly but with some colour accused of Carson's murder. All the time it is Mary's father, driven to opium by hunger and despair at the failure of the trade-union petition to London, who, drawing the killer's lot in a working-men's ballot, has killed young Carson. Mary's character is improved—redeemed from flightiness, though she was always good at heart—by and in the *angst* of her apparently unrequited love for Jem; and the impetus of most of the second half of the novel, its own emotional charge as well as Mary's and Jem's, is diverted to this heroic stand of Mary's in the face of circumstance and of Jem's estrangement. The conditions that caused Carson's murder are left gradually behind—almost forgotten, indeed, except for the death-bed repentance-reconciliation scene between Mr. Carson and John Barton.

North and South is emotionally tougher than this, and less of its energy is diverted into the masochistic pleasures of an apparently tragic separation that ends happily for the lovers. In *North and South* the mutual suspicion of a pride and prejudice kind between Thornton and Margaret (the proud daughter of an ex-Anglican minister who has given up his ministry) is psychologically well done. Margaret's initial rejection of the whole notion of trade and the cotton-spinning town of Milton is made a real challenge to Thornton, in that it forces him to think as well as feel differently about industry and its purpose in life. But again there is the dependence on self-sacrifice and on unlikely chance separating the lovers. Margaret's estrangement from Thornton is increased when he sees her meeting a strange man (in fact it is her brother, whose life she is trying to save); yet despite this she offers him all her new-found money (left to her by the Oxford don) when he is financially endangered by his own honesty and some bad years in trade. These circumstances produce again that nostalgia and *angst,* so inseparable from one's remembrance of nineteenth-century tales in verse and prose, that bedevils incipient maturity. In Margaret, Mrs. Gaskell has sketched a credibly strong-willed and intelligent woman but one who, quite *in*credibly, has more fainting-fits, illnesses, spells of weeping than any other heroine in reasonably mature fiction. It is as if Mrs. Gaskell will not allow genuine independence and spirit without melting sentiment to make up for it. Whatever the reason, sentimentality spoils any real development of the critique of industrialism ('What do you want money for?') begun so interestingly earlier in the book.

And always, side by side with love-affairs of this kind, but only very insecurely related to them, Mrs. Gaskell has what under the circumstances becomes too often a potpourri of topical questions and issues—debates and talks about all the problems, or a good many of them, of the 1840s and 1850s. Into *North and South* alone she manages to cram the agricultural poor in the South; the doctrine of self-help; drink and opium as the refuge of the poor; atheism; ill-health and death caused by factory conditions; the tyranny of the majority in trade-union affairs, and so on. In *Mary Barton* she even has, in a speech of John Barton's, a version of the labour theory of value: 'I say, our labour's our capital, and we ought to draw interest on that.'[2] All these were, and many of them still are, real issues, and at her best Mrs. Gaskell dramatises them well. But even at her best she can do no more than dramatise or illustrate a particular, and usually fairly localised, issue (for example, Higgins giving up drink for self-help—quite credibly, in fact). There is no possibility of or room for expansion or questioning or exploration, because the scenes so 'dramatised' have nowhere to go in terms of the governing stories, the increasingly threatening love-affairs of Margaret and Thornton, Jem and Mary. The love-stories are loosely conventional, and grow apart from any urgent questioning of industrialism or politics; in turn, questions of politics therefore remain under-developed, at points little more than illustrations of well-known abuses that are documented equally well in journals and reports of the time.

If this split between an informed but truncated enquiry into sociological and political issues on the one hand, and thinly conventional love-stories on the other, were an isolated phenomenon, peculiar to Mrs. Gaskell alone, it would not merit longer attention than simply the great regret one has for an intelligent novelist whose work is persistently flawed by what amounts to a fault of character in herself. But the more one looks at nineteenth-century novels, the more it becomes obvious that here is a case of an overriding convention hindering rather than helping literature. Indeed, the love-convention affects major novelists as well, and as Denis de Rougemont has suggested, love-stories of the kind Mrs. Gaskell uses are much more than *simply* a literary convention or convenience.[3] Like most phenomena worthy of notice for good or ill in literature, this 'convention' is clearly rooted in human nature, rather than just in literary 'style' or form.

I want to consider some of the implications of Rougemont's thesis more fully in a moment. Before doing so it is essential to notice that all the other novels I have picked out, admittedly rather summarily, for discussion exhibit startlingly similar patterns of behaviour in their characters; and again these stories of frustrated love grow more or less irrelevantly apart from the political issues raised in the books. The result is that the personal love-stories tend to lose substance, to become *merely* personal anguish; the political and sociological enquiries tend to be, if not always impersonal, then at least undeveloped because they have no driving, compelling human action to work with or clash against.

Disraeli's *Sybil* is very much a case in point. Obviously knowledgeable about contemporary England, Disraeli gives accurate accounts of the disorganised nature of the Chartist groups in the 1830s and 1840s, and a slightly sentimentalised portrait of one of the 'moral force' leaders ('Gerard' in the novel), vainly opposing the 'physical force' tactics of some of his comrades. Disraeli sees very clearly the inevitability of the collapse of Chartism: it is doomed from the beginning by its own divided and confused aims and leadership, while at the same time, on the 'establishment' side, it faces a mixture of some sympathy (too weak to do more than encourage the men to present petitions that must fail), some apathy (the petition to Parliament is politely ignored by most), and superior force. In addition, he gives slightly stiffly written but credible pictures of working men's houses in the crowded lanes of 'Marney', each with its damp or flooded floors inside and its dunghill immediately outside; and he shows northern strike-parties of the late 1830s and 1840s, often starting out (as others have testified) with peaceful intentions, but as often inflamed to violence by a mixture of opposition from the soldiers and rabble-rousing speeches from demagogues ('Bishop Hatton' in the novel, a drunken, savage mobster with some brute energy and appeal). Finally in this vein, Disraeli details the effects of the 'truck' system: workmen's wives and children have to take part of the husband's wages in 'tommy' (food and clothing bought at shops controlled or owned by the masters). Generally the best bacon, food, clothing goes to the 'butties' (who keep the shops), and nothing is left for the men but over-priced, under-weight goods.

All this is accurately described by Disraeli, though it tells one nothing that other accounts of Chartism and of conditions in Lancashire and Yorkshire at the time could not reveal equally well. The facts are not really in dispute. However, Disraeli's attempts to develop his account of the 'condition of England' beyond mere fact-finding are bedevilled by two things: first, his over-simple and nostalgic yearning for a past alliance and condition that never in fact existed, but that Disraeli wants to restore:

> In the selfish strife of factions, two great existences have been blotted out of the history of England—The Monarch and the Multitude; as the power of the Crown has diminished, the privileges of the People have disappeared; till at length the sceptre has become a pageant, and its subject has degenerated again into a serf. (Book VI, ch. 13)

Going along with this nostalgia for a past that must in fact have been much more brutal and much more inequitable than Disraeli is willing to allow, and indeed preventing him from breaking out of his own nostalgic dream of a perfect alliance between Church, monarchy and commons, is the story of the love of Egremont, younger brother of the mean and bullying Lord Marney, for Sybil, daughter of Gerard. Sybil wants to reinstate her father in his ancient rights to land—his family lost them with the dissolution of the monasteries under Henry VIII—and then rejoin a sisterhood with whom she is staying at the beginning of the novel. She is saved from a police attack on a secret Chartist meeting by Egremont (she has gone there to try and warn her father), and finally marries him instead of the sisterhood. In all this the threatened separation of Egremont and Sybil (they belong of course to opposite sides in 'the two nations' of modern England) produces an all-too-familiar note of anxious melodrama and sentimentality. Overstraining the notion of separation and threatening tragedy, Disraeli's prose—at its best factual though uninspired—at times adopts the weirdest contortions of false neo-feudalism. Sybil's rigorous purity, for instance, results in dialogue like this terrible *mélange* of colloquial and 'literary' English:

> 'Call it what you will, Walter,' replied Stephen; 'but if I ever gain the opportunity of fully carrying the principle of association into practice, I will sing *Nunc me dimittas*.'

> '*Nunc me dimittas*,' burst forth the Religious, in a voice of thrilling melody, and she pursued for some minutes the divine canticle. Her companions gazed on her with an air of affectionate reverence as she

sang; each instant the stars becoming brighter, the wide moor assuming a darker hue.

> 'Now, tell me, Stephen,' said the Religious, turning her head and looking round with a smile, 'think you not it would be a fairer lot to bide this night at some kind monastery, than to be hastening now to that least picturesque of all creations, a railway station . . . ?'

> 'You must regain our lands for us, Stephen,' said the Religious; 'promise me, my father, that I shall raise a holy house for pious women, if that ever hap. (Book II, ch. 8)

If there is a touch of intended humour in all this from England's future Prime Minister, it is only uncertainly and waveringly there. The fake old-English affected by Sybil is intended solemnly and seriously, and the humour, if it is there at all, only glances briefly and not at all slightingly at her. Disraeli's notion of this religious life is flimsy, and his notion of the love between Sybil and Egremont, which takes precedence later in the novel, is equally so. In such a setting, and with the novel's structure based largely on the unworldly lives and loves of Sybil and Egremont, it is not surprising that the 'political' element never develops beyond a hopelessly impractical neo-feudalism on the one hand—a vague aspiration towards 'community' instead of the mere gregariousness of modern cities—and on the other much more interesting but still limited notations of contemporary conditions.

George Eliot is quite obviously the most intelligent novelist in this group. The clear and sympathetic but unsentimental eye with which she gives us Mrs. Transome's imprisonment and isolation in a masculine world is beyond the range of anything in Mrs. Gaskell, Disraeli, or even Trollope. Indeed, even to call this society 'a masculine world' is misleading, though true in an over-all summarising sense. George Eliot's creation of the life and world of Matthew Jermyn, and of Jermyn fighting against his illegitimate son Harold Transome, is subtler than summarising terms can possibly suggest. As she says herself, Mrs. Transome is a captive in a man's world, and the male dominance she cannot fight once Harold has returned to England (unaware of his birth but determined to get control of affairs and in addition to ruin his mother's man of business, Jermyn) is indeed a large factor, both in George Eliot's account of society and in her account of Mrs. Transome's increasing loneliness. But though Jermyn is a scoundrel, he is far from the conventional villain of melodrama, merely seducing women and then using his power over property and money affairs to ruin them further; and he is also far from being unconvincingly 'masculine' in the way mere villains often are. ('How now, my pretty wench . . .' is a turn of phrase and personality that goes as far up the scale as

Hardy's Alec d'Urberville, but which George Eliot is never even tempted to use.) Jermyn's relations with Mrs. Transome include from the start both a dominance over her and a dependence on her finer nature. And a similar intelligence governs most of the characterisation of Harold Transome. Clearly George Eliot knew and shaped very well the sense in which a man like this can be—perhaps, in such a society and given a more determined clear-mindedness than other men, *has* to be—insensitively unaware of an intelligent woman's interest in life and in those affairs of business and property that Harold simply assumes she neither knows nor cares about. But George Eliot also knows the sense in which such a man may well behave decently and sensitively towards women, even though his quite genuine decency is at the same time serving his own ends (compare his courtship of Esther, in which Harold very often shows a genuine kindness to her and to Felix Holt which, as he well knows, will also heighten him in Esther's estimation).

All this, despite some minor flaws, could be documented easily from the clear, assured writing in that part of *Felix Holt* which concerns Mrs. Transome, Harold and Jermyn. It means that there, as of course much more largely in her greater novels, George Eliot's interest in 'society' (including her interest in the politics of the period after the 1831 election) has been made subservient to ends that are less clearly summarisable, but far more interesting, than any imagined by Disraeli or Mrs. Gaskell.

Nevertheless *Felix Holt* viewed as a whole is weak, structurally thin. This in itself might not be significant—a George Eliot is entitled to her failures, or comparative failures—but what is significant is that the weaknesses in *Felix Holt* are remarkably similar to ones that consistently limit or warp other political novels in the period. The story of Felix Holt and Esther bears distressing resemblances in tone and outlook to stories like that of Disraeli's Sybil and Egremont, or Mrs. Gaskell's Mary Barton and the good artisan Jem Wilson. In all three cases the authors, in order to further the love affairs that lift the main characters clear of the dirt of politics and local conditions, give us the men, and to some extent the women, as both exceptional *and* idealised. Gerald, alone in the working-class milieu of *Sybil,* is against factionalism and violence; and he is alone because his nature is simply too pure to be relevant to the Chartist politics he is supposedly engaged in. Jem, alone of the artisans who influence the story in *Mary Barton,* has the purity of motive to save money and strike out on his own as a foreman/inventor, free alike from the squalor and the trade-union pressures that attack other men. More singleminded than either of these, Felix Holt, the son of a quack doctor, deliberately throws away his chance to rise in the world to stay in and with the working class as a clock and watch repairer. The trouble is that

the way in which he does this is so idealised that neither his advice, nor his life as he lives it, can touch either working-class conditions or the men he has devoted his life to:

> He was considerably taller, his head and neck were more massive, and the expression of his mouth and eyes was something very different from the mere acuteness and rather hard-lipped antagonism of the trades-union man. Felix Holt's face had the look of habitual meditative abstraction from objects of mere personal vanity or desire, which is the peculiar stamp of culture, and makes a very roughly-cut face worthy to be called 'the human face divine.' Even lions and dogs know a distinction between men's glances; and doubtless those Duffield men, in the expectation with which they looked up at Felix, were unconsciously influenced by the grandeur of his full yet firm mouth, and the calm clearness of his grey eyes . . . (ch. XXX)

This is belittling and contemptuous of the men; it also underlines the noble shagginess and impetuous but other-worldly purity in Felix that 'redeem' his rough-cut features, lift him out of the working-class world he is allegedly part of and devoted to serve, and further the love between him and the reformed, no longer girlish Esther. The whole drive of the Felix/Esther stand in the novel is towards a love that thrives on obstacles and separation—

> And Felix wished Esther to know that her love was dear to him as the beloved dead are dear. He felt that they must not marry—that they would ruin each other's lives. But he had longed for her to know fully that his will to be always apart from her was renunciation, not an easy preference. (ch. XXXII)

These last two passages are practically a translation into novel terms of the Rougemont thesis about the inevitable course of love in Western society (a searching for obstacles rather than fulfilment, and union desired only in death or in some other transcendental state of being). And though this state of mind can be handled much more powerfully by some novelists, here the difference in tone between these passages and almost any on Mrs. Transome, or on Jermyn and Harold, is obvious. The sugared isolation of Felix and Esther's stand has infected George Eliot's prose itself, and clearly has her backing. It leads, as similar tendencies do in *Mary Barton,* to a plea in open court by the heroine for her lover. George Eliot's prose at this point (the trial) shows glimpses of the conceptual intelligence that underpins her great work, and this is, even in its relatively weak form, beyond Mrs. Gaskell's range; but otherwise the two women are not far apart when writing scenes of this nature:

> When a woman feels purely and nobly, that ardour of hers which breaks through formulas too rigorously

urged on men by daily practical needs, makes one of her most precious influences. . . . Some of that ardour which has flashed out and illuminated all poetry and history was burning to-day in the bosom of sweet Esther Lyon. In this, at least, her woman's lot was perfect: that the man she loved was her hero; that her woman's passion and her reverence for rarest goodness rushed together in an undivided current. And to-day they were making one danger, one terror, one irresistible impulse for her heart. (ch. XLVI)

Why should George Eliot's intelligence fail her, or be in abeyance, at precisely *this* point, and at others like it, in the novel? Even the more purely reflective prose of the novel is often, at such moments, irritatingly mannered, as if George Eliot were nervously aware that some stiffening was needed ('We have all felt the presence of . . .'; '. . . all of us—whether men or women—are liable to this weakness . . .'). The question is unanswerable in any full or complete terms, because one can only guess at factors of personality that must have been there, and that so disastrously combined with tendencies in the literature and society around her to produce such an absence of the rigour that determines the key scenes with Mrs. Transome, and such a corresponding access of escapist sentimentality and buttonholing mannerism. Perhaps the closest one can get—and this is certainly not any full 'answer' to the question—is to point again to the gulf between the tendencies evident in the Felix/Esther conjunction on the one hand, and the political and sociological circumstances this conjunction allegedly arises from on the other. Whole sections of *Felix Holt* make dull reading because the circumstances of the 1831 election campaign and its aftermath—the details about a 're-formed' parliament, the parties that are voting and bolstering their candidates, the unfranchised workers' role in this—as well as the circumstances of nonconformist chapels (the book's rather rigidly minded 're-ligious' interest)—all these are cut off from the increasingly idealised love of Felix and Esther. As with Disraeli and Mrs. Gaskell, these surrounding circumstances tend to remain either dully factual or, at best, interesting illustrations or dramatisations of essentially documentary material.

The sense in which this disjunction may provide a partial 'answer' to the question why George Eliot's intelligence failed her is that the gap between the transcendentalist love-story and the circumstances of Felix Holt's actual life points once again to a general failure rather than to a particular or local one (of 'characterisation', 'plot development', and so on). Tendencies in the age, and in George Eliot herself, to separate idealism—even simple emotion—from fact and reason were so strong that evidently even her intelligence was swamped in at least this novel. As Rougemont would put it in still more general terms: there is evidently a strong tendency, perhaps infecting Western society as

a whole, for love ('passion') to cut loose from the practicalities of life, because it has become an emotion that only feeds on itself and must therefore end, at least in the most extreme cases, by feeding on death, the one absolute left that it can trust. George Eliot does not give Felix or Esther a tragic end (the Rougemont thesis fits Mrs. Gaskell's *Ruth* much more completely),[4] but the overt idealisation combines with a long series of nostalgically treated separations, misunderstandings, failures between Felix and Esther to make his diagnosis relevant. Indeed the general cast of their story, in which absence and separation are longed for at least as much as successful consummation, would seem to expect an apocalyptic or tragic ending rather than the ending George Eliot in fact gives, with Felix freed, married to Esther, and living quietly in a village away from Treby Magna and its Reform politics. The drive of the story being what it is, such an ending is only possible by substituting for death and tragedy a sentimental transcendentalism that puts the lovers beyond the range both of their own passions and of the worldly interests and politics the novel started out to investigate.

'In the seventeenth century a dissociation of sensibility set in, from which we have never recovered . . .' T. S. Eliot's famous statement has of course been challenged in a number of ways, but personally I think it is substantially right, and certainly applicable to the sort of situations revealed by and in the nineteenth-century novels discussed and referred to . . . [here]. Furthermore, Eliot's diagnosis can be linked both with Rougemont's thesis, and with D. H. Lawrence's comments on a Western civilisation in which, as he sees it, the impersonal intelligence has become divorced from the therefore too personal 'self'. One could add Blake, more gnomically but if anything still more trenchantly:

> Those who restrain Desire, do so because theirs is weak enough to be restrained; and the restrainer or Reason usurps its place and governs the unwilling.

> And being restrained, it by degrees becomes passive, till it is only the shadow of Desire. (*The Marriage of Heaven and Hell*)

The trouble is that Blake's own later writings in the rest of the Prophetic Books seem for the most part too cloudy to suggest any solution, or to adumbrate any true 'marriage' between the opposites he contemplates. And as the nineteenth century goes on, and develops into the twentieth century, even the best writing seems at times distorted by the dichotomy that makes for instance the intelligence of J. S. Mill rather dryly forbidding, the emotionalism of most of Victorian poetry and some parts of the Victorian and indeed twentieth-century novel rather gushingly unthinking. Dickens is one case in point here, and Lawrence is another; but even *Middlemarch,* solid and secure though it is in most respects, has the embarrassingly thin Dorothea/ Will Ladislaw sections.

The 'Two Nations' split is indeed a threat, therefore, in nineteenth- and even early twentieth-century England; though to be fully meaningful the phrase has to be extended beyond Disraeli's original sense to include one or more of the senses sketched by Blake, Lawrence and Eliot. In this situation, what the novel at its best can and does do (though at the cost of virtually abandoning any specific commitment to politics or government as a major theme) is impart to wider spheres of enquiry the sort of resilience in dramatising personal affairs that George Eliot achieved in the Mrs. Transome episodes of *Felix Holt. Middlemarch* itself is the clearest case of a novel in which this sort of writing ('political' in a sense, but also personal) is spread through a multiplicity of groups and situations within a middle-class society. . . .

Notes

[1] For some examples, see John W. Dodds, *The Age of Paradox* (Gollancz, 1953); and Margaret Dalziel, *Popular Fiction 100 Years Ago,* (Cohen, 1957).

[2] Though this is no extraordinary prescience on Mrs. Gaskell's part, since the 'theory' was, in one form or another, common in pre-Marxist England. Margaret Cole credits Robert Owen with formulating the notion 'long before Marx' in her book *Robert Owen of New Lanark* (Batchworth Press, 1953) p. 2. And even *laissez-faire* economists like Ricardo showed a clear and strong feeling for labour as a source of value.

[3] Denis de Rougemont, *Passion and Society,* translated by Montgomery Belgion from the earlier version in French (Faber, 1956).

[4] In *Ruth* the seduced but innocently pure heroine dies from the saintly act of nursing her rakish lover through typhus.

DOMESTIC ORDER

William Forsyth

SOURCE: "Goldsmith: Jane Austen," in *The Novels and Novelists of the Eighteenth Century, An Illustration of the Manners and Morals of the Age,* D. Appleton & Company, 1871, pp. 322-30.

[*In the following excerpt, Forsyth praises Jane Austen's portrayals of English domestic life, though he protests, nonetheless, the excessive attention her characters devote to matters of matrimony.*]

Strictly speaking, [the] charming writer [Jane Austen] belongs to the present century, for her first *publication* took place in 1811. But three of her novels were written several years before, and two of them had been offered in vain to the booksellers. Fully to appreciate the excellence of Miss Austen's works, one ought to have some acquaintance with the state of the literature of fiction at the time she began to write. Besides the gloomy horrors of the Radcliffe school, there was a flood of weak and vapid novels which deluged the libraries with trash.

In Hannah More's *Cœlebs* the hero questions two young ladies on the subject of books, and one of them says that she had read *Tears of Sensibility,* and *Rosa Matilda,* and *Sympathy of Souls,* and *Too Civil by Half,* and *The Sorrows of Werter,* and *The Stranger,* and *The Orphans of Snowdon.* "'Yes, sir,' joined in the younger sister, who had not risen to so high a pitch of literature, 'and we have read *Perfidy Punished,* and *Jemmy and Jenny Jessamy,* and *The Fortunate Footman,* and *The Illustrious Chambermaid.*" I do not think that these were much worse, in point of morality, than many of the novels which now appear, and of which the incidents seem to be taken from the records of the Police Courts and the Divorce Courts; but the misfortune was, that at that time, a young lady had very little choice, and her mind must feed upon such garbage, or abstain from novel-reading altogether.

It is wonderful to think that Jane Austen, a young woman, the daughter of a country clergyman, brought up in absolute retirement, should, by the intuitive force of genius, have been able to produce a series of fictions which, in a knowledge of the anatomy of the human heart, in purity and gracefulness of style, and in individuality of character, have never been surpassed.[1] We are introduced, at once, into the domestic life of England at the close of the century, and find that in her pages it does not much differ from that of the present day—the periwigs and swords have disappeared, and the habits of society are much the same as now. But still there are some differences which it is curious to observe, considering how short, in point of time, is the distance that separates us from the writer, and that there are still living persons who remember her. She is fond of introducing clergymen into her stories, and in some of them they are the heroes of the tale. But theology, and indeed religion, is kept entirely in the background. The type is rather secular than religious. But it is far higher and more refined than in the conceptions of the earlier novelists, although not so refined as it appears in the pages of a distinguished writer of the present day—I mean Anthony Trollope—who excels in the description of sleek Canons and polished Archdeacons, and courtly Bishops. The Reverend Josiah Crawley, perpetual curate of Hogglestock, would, in the hands of Fielding or Smollett, have been represented as smoking tobacco in the kitchen, drinking beer in the ale-house, and involved in very questionable scenes; but with all his poverty and obstinacy, he is a perfect gentleman and an accomplished scholar. The line which is now more strictly drawn as to the amusements in which the clergy allow themselves to indulge, was, in Miss Austen's time, more flexible—and although in *Mansfield Park* the young clergyman, Edmund Bertram, has some misgivings as to the propriety of taking part in private theatricals, it is thought quite a matter of course that clergymen should dance at public balls, as the Rev. Mr. Tilney, in *Northanger Abbey,* does at Bath. And the view taken of a clergyman's duties was very superficial. With a snug parsonage and decent income it seems to have been supposed that nothing more was incumbent upon him than to preach a few sermons, and he might enjoy the pleasures of life with as little restriction as if he were a layman.

In *Persuasion* we have the following recommendation of a living:

> 'And a very good living it was,' Charles added; 'only five-and-twenty miles from Uppercross, and in a very fine country—fine part of Dorsetshire. In the centre of some of the best preserves in the kingdom, surrounded by three great proprietors, each more careful and jealous than the other.'

In *Sense and Sensibility,* Robert Ferrars laughs at the idea of his brother Edward becoming a clergyman.

> The idea of Edward's being a clergyman, and living in a small parsonage-house, diverted him beyond measure; and when to that was added the fanciful imagery of Edward reading prayers in a white surplice, and publishing the banns of marriage between John Smith and Mary Bacon, he could conceive nothing more ridiculous.

And in *Mansfield Park,* the elder brother of Edmund Bertram says, when Edmund is about to be ordained: "Seven hundred a year is a fine thing for a younger brother; and as, of course, he will live at home, it will be all for his *menus plaisirs;* and a sermon at Christmas and Easter, I suppose, will be the sum total of all the sacrifice." It is, however, only fair to state that Edmund has a higher and more worthy conception of the duties of a clergyman.

The vice of drunkenness hardly appears in Miss Austen's novels; but she represents the Rev. Mr. Elton as flustered with wine, if not quite tipsy, when he surprises Emma by a declaration of his attachment as they drive home together in a carriage after a dinner-party. And in another of her novels she speaks of a clergyman "breathing of wine" as he passes from the dining-room to the drawing-room to join the ladies.

In her novels, Jane Austen often depicted ladies and gentlemen of the landed gentry.

We are told by the Rev. Austen Leigh, in the sketch he has lately published of Miss Austen's life, that she was never in love. It is difficult to believe this; but, if so, it is an additional proof of her wonderful acquaintance with the human heart, that she was able to write,

> In maiden meditation fancy-free,

and yet to describe love in all its mysteries and effects, with a subtlety of analysis and skill which make her almost unapproachable among novelists. Where shall we find elsewhere such touching pictures of concealed and aching attachment, where all hope seems to be struck dead, as in Fanny Price in *Mansfield Park,* in Elinor Dashwood in *Sense and Sensibility,* and in Anne Elliot in *Persuasion*? The last heroine, one of the most charming of Miss Austen's characters, says to Captain Harville, "All the privilege I claim for my own sex (it is not a very enviable one, you need not covet it), is that of loving longest, when existence or when hope is gone." And how finely contrasted with the gnawing tooth of this "worm i' the bud" is the half-formed love of Elizabeth Bennet for Mr. Darcy in *Pride and Prejudice,* and the undisguised and artless love of Catherine Morland for Mr. Tilney in *Northanger Abbey*!

One thing, however, that strikes us in these novels is the excessive and obtrusive eagerness of all the minor heroines to get married. Are we to think that husband-hunting was the sole object in life of daughters, and the sole object for which mothers existed? *Pride and Prejudice* opens with the sentence that when a single man of good fortune settles in a neighborhood the maxim that he must be in want of a wife "is so well fixed in the minds of the surrounding families that he is considered as the rightful property of some one or other of their daughters." And when the Rev. Mr. Collins, who, it must be admitted, is intended as a fool, comes to visit his cousins with the intention of proposing to one of them, the first words he speaks in the presence of the young ladies, the Miss Bennets, is to assure them that he comes prepared to admire them. Here "he was interrupted by a summons to dinner; and the girls smiled on each other." As to Mrs. Bennet, she thinks, and dreams, and speaks of nothing else but getting her girls married. And the last chapter tells us that "happy for all her maternal feelings was the day on which Mrs. Bennet *got rid* of her two most deserving daughters" by marriage.

The story of *Emma* is nothing but match-making from beginning to end, and a very charming story indeed it is. In *Sense and Sensibility* Marianne Dashwood, who represents sensibility as opposed to her sister Elinor's sense, happens to fall and sprain her ankle, and is carried by a stranger to her mother's house. Sir John Middleton calls soon afterward, and on being asked about the unknown by Elinor answers, "Yes, yes, he is well worth catching, I can tell you, Miss Dashwood; he has a pretty little estate of his own in Somersetshire besides; and if I were you I would not give him up to my younger sister, in spite of all this tumbling down-hills." In *Northanger Abbey,* the heroine, Catherine Morland, dances twice in the Lower Rooms at Bath with a young clergyman, whom she has never seen before; and her friend Miss Thorpe, to whom she mentions the circumstance, immediately assumes that she has fallen desperately in love with him—exclaiming, when his sister is pointed out to her, "But where is her all-conquering brother? Is he in the room? Point him out to me this instant if he is. I die to see him." This is the speech of a silly girl, but from the general tone of the characters in these novels it would really seem as if it were thought that no man could look twice at a woman, or show her ordinary civility, without falling in love with her; or that, at all events, every woman was entitled to construe the commonest attentions as declarations of attachment.

I feel that I am treading on delicate ground, and my opinion on such a subject is perhaps worth little; but I cannot believe that, except among those who are known by the *sobriquet* of "Belgravian mothers," young women at the present day are so brought up. That they should desire to be happily married is most reasonable, and that they should fall in love is most natural; but this is something very different from the constant husband-hunting which we see displayed in Miss Austen's novels. For the change that has taken place in this respect several reasons may be assigned. In the first place, there is generally nowadays among gentlewomen a greater degree of modesty and reserve; they are also better educated, and do not feed their minds with such trash as the old circulating libraries supplied. In the next, their resources are greatly multiplied, and they can find in works of charity and benevolence, in visiting the sick and ministering to the wants of the poor, means of occupation and outlets for their affections, which were practically unknown to young women of a former generation.

Notes

[1] The late Sir George Lewis coupled the names of Defoe and Miss Austen together as writers of fiction, "which observes all the canons of probability."—See his *Credibility of Early Roman History,* vol. ii. p. 489.

Vineta Colby

SOURCE: "Ut Pictura Poesis: The Novel of Domestic Realism as Genre," in *Yesterday's Woman: Domestic Realism in the English Novel,* Princeton University Press, 1974, pp. 9-40.

[*In the following excerpt, Colby both explores the link between the bourgeois genre painting and the domestic novel, and traces the nineteenth-century transition from the male-dominated romance to the female-centered domestic novel—with its increasing reliance on detailed descriptions of everyday scenes and activities.*]

The working relationship between the artist and the novelist was never closer than during the period in which the domestic novel flourished. Dickens gave much personal attention to the illustration of his novels. Some novelists, like Thackeray and George Du Maurier, illustrated their own work. Other novelists wrote art criticism professionally—Henry James, Mrs. Oliphant, and Thackeray again. These and still other novelists—Charlotte Brontë, George Eliot—introduced painters as characters and discussed painting in their novels. What caught the artist's imagination and moved his heart was much the same as what inspired the novelist—domestic life, portrayed in the simple reality of its day-to-day course. "The heroic, and peace be with it! has been deposed," Thackeray proclaimed in 1843, "and our artists, in place, cultivate the pathetic and the familiar."[1] In 1855, viewing a Paris exhibition of English painting, Baudelaire was struck by its "intimate glimpses of home," and another visitor to the show, Richard Redgrave, observed that to walk from the salon containing French and other continental paintings into the British gallery "was to pass at once from the midst of warfare and its incidents, from passion, strife and bloodshed, from martyrdoms and suffering, to the peaceful scenes of home."[2]

Bourgeois genre painting, as Mario Praz has written, had "an addiction to narrative." Other styles of painting—religious, allegorical, and symbolical—that draw upon mythology, epic, and history transcend mere circumstantiality. They invite multiple interpretations, but offer no simple explanations. Genre, however, is drawn from the everyday reality that can be described, explained, accounted for. It is therefore anecdotal.[3] This woman is reading a letter, taking a music lesson, nursing a child, preparing a meal, dressing in a cluttered and shabby bedroom. She is an ordinary woman—not the Virgin receiving the Annunciation or holding the Christ child. We are free to speculate: does she have a lover? what was she doing a moment before? what is she thinking about? Victorian novelists were especially attracted to this style of painting because of its air of "truth," its concern with subjects that could be instantly recognized and verified by the experience of the viewer. "Dutch realism" is a recurring phrase in nineteenth-century art and literary criticism. In *Adam Bede* George Eliot cited it as justification for her whole approach to fiction:

> It is for this rare, precious quality of truthfulness that I delight in many Dutch paintings, which lofty-minded people despise. I find a source of delicious sympathy in these faithful pictures of a monotonous homely existence, which has been the fate of so many more among my fellow-mortals than a life of pomp or of absolute indigence, of tragic suffering or of world-stirring actions. (Ch. 17).

Among the "lofty-minded" was Henry James, novelist and art critic, deploring, as many others did and still do, the excesses of genre—its sentimentality, triviality, and banality—every bit as much the plague of the novels as of the paintings. It is significant that James's condemnation embraces the novel as well. Reviewing the Royal Academy's exhibition of 1877, he observed:

> The pictures, with very few exceptions, are 'subjects'; they belong to what the French call the anecdotical class . . . they are subjects addressed to a taste of a particularly unimaginative and unaesthetic order—to the taste of the British merchant and paterfamilias and his excellently regulated family. What this taste appears to demand of a picture is that it shall have a taking title, like a three-volume novel or an article in a magazine; that it shall embody in its lower flights some comfortable incident of the daily life of our period, suggestive more especially of its gentilities and proprieties and familiar moralities, and in its loftier scope some picturesque episode of history or fiction which may be substantiated by a long explanatory extract in the catalogue.[4]

Whether for aesthetic good or bad, genre, Biedermeier, domestic realism swept over Germany and France in the early nineteenth century as powerfully as the countervailing force of romanticism had swept Europe in the last decades of the eighteenth century. In England its effects on painting were pervasive and long-lasting. Its effects on the novel were more curiously mixed. A newly emerging art form, the realistic English novel was in a state of rapid evolution and development throughout the nineteenth century. It was plastic and flexible. Its history was far shorter than that of painting and its public vastly larger. To draw close parallels between the two art forms, however inviting such efforts may be, is perilous. Far too many histories and critical studies of the nineteenth-century novel make reductive and simplistic generalizations about its bourgeois-sentimental character. *The Vicar of Wakefield,* a kind of archetype of the domestic novel, illustrates the pitfalls of the genre approach. Is it, as it appears to be, a glorification of home, family, and church? Or is it, as we may also read it, an acid-etched satire on those same honored institutions? Its implications are less profound than those of the Book of Job, from which Goldsmith took his theme, but no less ambiguous. Genre painting is a fixed scene on canvas. We may speculate on the action and circumstances involved, but we usually know what we see. Fiction, however, involving the complexities and ambiguities of language and concept, is open-ended and resists critical generalizations.

A novel of wit written by a notoriously sophisticated man of letters, *The Vicar of Wakefield*'s enduring popularity cannot be accounted for only by its simple sentimental appeal. [The] elements of domestic realism—privacy, enclosure and warmth, precision of detail—. . . are more than accidental literary effects. Goldsmith knew the nature of the public for whom he wrote and the nature of the society about which he was writing. *The Vicar* was widely imitated in lower-class fiction up through the mid-nineteenth century. Working-class readers, crowded into industrial towns, in dreary slums and dingy factories, devoured pastoral-domestic idylls of rustic life. Titles like *The Cottage Girl, The Pride of the Village, The Maid of the Village,* or the *Farmer's Daughter* dot the bestseller lists of the 1840's.[5] Although that same public was reading a variety of fictional genres—latter-day romances and gothic tales—the modest attractions of domestic fiction seem to have had special staying powers. The mass public was at last discovering what realistic novelists from Defoe onwards had known, namely, the pleasure of recognition and identification, the appeal of homely detail, precise and specific and recognizable to the average reader. One of the shrewdest and most perceptive witnesses to nineteenth-century cultural developments was Harriet Martineau, who, writing of her youth, attributed the great success of Miss Mitford's sketches of rural life, *Our Village* (1824-1832), to her exploitation of "that new style of 'graphic description' to which literature owes a great deal":

> In my childhood, there was no such thing known, in the works of the day, as 'graphic description,' and most people delighted as much as I did in Mrs. Ratcliffe's [sic] gorgeous or luscious generalities— just as we admired in picture galleries landscapes all misty and glowing indefinitely with bright colours—yellow sunrises and purple and crimson sunsets,—because we had no conception of detail like Miss Austen's in manners and Miss Mitford's in scenery, or of Millais' and Wilkie's analogous life pictures, or Rosa Bonheur's adventurous Hayfield at noon-tide. Miss Austen had claims to other and greater honours; but she and Miss Mitford deserve no small gratitude for rescuing us from the folly and bad taste of slovenly indefiniteness in delineation.[6]

Homely descriptive detail became increasingly graphic in the early nineteenth century. In the most popular novelist of the period, Sir Walter Scott, it served the special function of recreating the dead past of history with activities and interests recognizable in the living reality of his readers. Scott resolved, he wrote in his introduction to *Waverley,* to throw the force of his narrative on

> those passions common to men in all stages of society, and which have alike agitated the human heart, whether it be throbbed under the steel corselet of the fifteenth century, the brocaded coat of the eighteenth, or the blue frock and white dimity waistcoat of the present day.

Sharing almost equal time with his battling knights in armor, feuding clansmen in tartan, and dramatic highland scenery, are the "broth, onions, cheese" and the roasted yearling lamb—"It was set upon its legs, with a bunch of parsley in its mouth, and was probably exhibited in that form to gratify the pride of the cook, who piqued himself more on the plenty than on the elegance of his master's table" (*Waverley,* Ch. 20). Jeanie Deans, that noblest and homeliest of Scott's heroines, is as remarkable for her cheese-making and the contents of her pantry ("in which she kept her honey, her sugar, her pots of jelly, her vials of the more ordinary medicines") as for her integrity and courage. The daily living habits of the rugged Highlanders were in fact a subject of endless fascination to Scott and, evidently, to his readers. In *Old Mortality* we get a faithful account of the dinner offered to the Laird of Milnwood's domestics:

> . . . old Robin, who was butler, valet-de-chambre, footman, gardener, and what not, in the house of

Milnwood, placed on the table an immense charger of broth, thickened with oatmeal and colewort, in which ocean of liquid was indistinctly discovered, by close observers, two or three short ribs of lean mutton sailing to and fro. Two huge baskets, one of bread made of barley and pease, and one of oatcakes, flanked this standing dish. A large boiled salmon would now-a-days have indicated more liberal housekeeping; but at that period salmon was caught in such plenty in the considerable rivers in Scotland, that instead of being accounted a delicacy, it was generally applied to feed the servants . . . (Ch. 8).

Rob Roy, a veritable travelogue of the wild remote regions of the north, balances the flamboyantly romantic adventures of its hero with documentation on the realities of life in a rough highland public house:

> The interior presented a view which seemed singular enough to southern eyes. The fire, fed with blazing turf and branches of dried wood, blazed merrily in the centre; but the smoke, having no means to escape but through a hole in the roof, eddied round the rafters of the cottage, and hung in sable folds at the height of about five feet from the floor. The space beneath was kept pretty clear, by innumerable currents of air which rushed towards the fire from the broken panel of basketwork which served as a door, from two square holes, designed as ostensible windows, through one of which was thrust a plaid, and through the other a tattered great-coat; and moreover, through various less distinguishable apertures, in the walls of the tenement, which, being built of round stones and turf, cemented by mud, let in the atmosphere at innumerable crevices. (Ch. 28).

Jane Austen, on the other hand, seems to revert to the eighteenth century with its fondness for typology and generalization. Much as we *think* we know her world— landscapes, interiors, and the habits and activities of her characters—we discover that she gave scant space to physical description of any kind. Pemberley, Rosings, Mansfield Park are magnificent houses, but we know surprisingly little about their details—their size, furnishings, numbers and arrangements of rooms. Nevertheless, Jane Austen utilized the techniques of domestic realism. Having so thoroughly mastered her art, with a few economical strokes she achieved what lesser novelists needed paragraphs for. "She stimulates us to supply what is not there," Virginia Woolf observed, or, as Margaret Lane points out, " . . . she takes such an immediate grasp of our attention, so firmly trains our imagination on to her characters and the exact social milieu in which they have their being, that our inner eye obediently supplies everything that she has economically left out."[7] The eye for domestic detail, for example, with which she sees the squalor of Fanny Price's home in Portsmouth is cruelly perceptive:

> She sat in a blaze of oppressive heat, in a cloud of moving dust; and her eyes could only wander from

the walls, marked by her father's head, to the table cut and knotched by her brothers, where stood the tea-board never thoroughly cleaned, the cups and saucers wiped in streaks, the milk a mixture of motes floating in thin blue, and the bread and butter growing every minute more greasy than even Rebecca's hands had first produced it. (*Mansfield Park*, III, ch. 15).

She characterizes with domestic detail: fussy, talkative but loving Miss Bates worries about her niece's failing appetite:

> . . . and she really eats nothing—makes such a shocking breakfast, you would be quite frightened if you saw it. I dare not let my mother know how little she eats—so I say one thing and then I say another, and it passes off. But about the middle of the day she gets hungry, and there is nothing she likes so well as these baked apples, and they are extremely wholesome, for I took the opportunity the other day of asking Mr. Perry; I happened to meet him in the street. Not that I had any doubt before—I have so often heard Mr. Woodhouse recommend a baked apple. I believe it is the only way that Mr. Woodhouse thinks the fruit thoroughly wholesome. We have apple-dumplings, however, very often. Patty makes an excellent apple-dumpling. (*Emma*, II, ch. 9).

In her domestic arrangements practical Charlotte Collins reveals her determination to make the best of her marriage to an insufferable bore. She chooses a small back room for her private parlor:

> Elizabeth at first had rather wondered that Charlotte should not prefer the dining parlour for common use; it was a better sized room, and had a pleasanter aspect; but she soon saw that her friend had an excellent reason for what she did, for Mr. Collins would undoubtedly have been much less in his own apartment, had they sat in one equally lively; and she gave Charlotte credit for the arrangement. (*Pride and Prejudice*, II, ch. 7).

The use of itemized domestic description for social "placing," for satire, for special effects of all kinds, was firmly established by the first quarter of the nineteenth century. Long before Dickens lampooned the bourgeois prosperity of the Podsnaps, Susan Ferrier in *Destiny* (1831) impaled the Ribleys, a London couple "whose household gods were all united in one, and that one—comfort," with an inventory of the furnishings of their drawing-room:

> . . . with its little serpentine sofas and formal circle of chairs; its small elaborate mirrors, stuck half-way up the wall; its high mantelpiece, decorated with branching girandoles and Dresden shepherds and shepherdesses; its Brussels carpet, with festoons of roses; its small bare satin-wood tables; its tall

twin fire-screens, embroidered forty years ago by Mrs. Ribley's own hands; not a vestige of a book or work, or any such lumber was to be seen in this room, appropriate solely to the purpose of sitting in bolt upright . . . . (Ch. 72)

With catalogues and price lists of fashionable London shops and menus of exclusive clubs and dinner parties, Mrs. Gore set her Regency aristocrats and parvenus firmly in their scene. Maria Edgeworth placed her socially ambitious Irish Lady Clonbrony, trying to make an entree into fashionable London society, with the advice of her interior decorator, Mr. Soho,

> the first architectural upholsterer of the age": "You fill up your angles here with *encoinières*—round your walls with the *Turkish tent drapery*—a fancy of my own—in apricot cloth, or crimson velvet, suppose, or *en flute,* in crimson satin draperies, fanned and riched with gold fringes, *en suite*—intermediate spaces, Apollo's heads with gold rays . . . . (*The Absentee*, ch. 2)

Descriptive detail, however, is merely a utility device of the fiction of domestic realism. It serves the needs of the novelist who is seeking to portray a way of life, a milieu in which his characters can move. The impression of family life that stamps itself upon the reader of the pastoral, idyllic opening pages of *The Vicar of Wakefield* is graphic but unreal because the family is not engaged in believable activity. They are described in detail but not in motion. In many late-eighteenth- and early-nineteenth-century family portraits we notice that everyone is either engaged in some appropriate activity or so represented as to suggest his or her identification with specific duties and activities—the mother with a baby in her lap while older children cling to her skirts, the father holding a book or an implement identifying his line of work, the children with balls or toys, sometimes even the family cat ready to pounce on a caged bird or the dog caught silently in the act of yapping.[8] We have a sense of life arrested, caught in a moment of normal activity and about to resume that activity the moment that the sitting ends. These are not Keats's "Cold Pastoral," frozen in sculpture. Goldsmith himself ridiculed the allegorical posturing of the Vicar's family when they sat stiffly for their family portrait—his wife as Venus "with a stomacher richly set with diamonds and her two little ones as Cupids by her side, while I, in my gown and band, was to present her with books on the Whistonian controversy" (Ch. 16). When he attempted to draw their "life picture," the family was at tea—engaged, in other words, in ordinary domestic activity:

> On these occasions, our two little ones always read for us. . . . Sometimes, to give variety to our amusements, the girls sung to the guitar; and while they thus formed a little concert, my wife and I

would stroll down the sloping field that was embellished with bluebells and centaury, talk of our children with rapture, and enjoy the breeze that wafted both health and harmony. (Ch. 5).

These painterly details appear in strikingly similar ways in the nineteenth-century domestic novel. One of the best and most popular domestic novelists, Charlotte Yonge, writing almost a century later than Goldsmith, places her family in nature with more individualized detail but the same painter's eye for a "conversation piece"—light, sky, a landscape background with laboring farmers, a foreground peopled with her characters, each engaged in some typical action or inaction:

It was a glorious day in June, the sky of pure deep dazzling blue, the sunshine glowing with brightness, but with cheerful freshness in the air that took away all sultriness, the sun tending westward in his long day's career, and casting welcome shadows from the tall firs and horse-chestnuts that shaded the lawn. A long rank of haymakers—men and women—proceeded with their rakes, the white shirt-sleeves, straw bonnets, and ruddy faces, radiant in the bath of sunshine, while in the shady end of the field were idler haymakers among the fragrant piles, Charles half lying on grass, with his back against a tall haycock; Mrs. Edmondstone sitting on another, book in hand; Laura sketching the busy scene, the sun glancing through the chequered shade on her glossy curls; Philip stretched out at full length, hat and neck-tie off, luxuriating in the cool repose after a dusty walk from Broadstone; and a little way off, Amabel and Charlotte, pretending to make hay, but really building nests with it, throwing it at each other, and playing as heartily as the heat would allow. (*The Heir of Redclyffe,* ch. 7).

The happiest family in all of George Eliot's fiction, the Garths, are painted in similar activity: "He found the family group, dogs and cats included, under the great appletree in the orchard." While one son reads aloud from *Ivanhoe,* the younger children frolic in the grass:

Ben, bouncing across the grass with Brownie at his heels, and seeing the kitten dragging the knitting by a lengthening line of wool, shouted and clapped his hands; Brownie barked, the kitten, desperate, jumped on the tea-table and upset the milk, then jumped down again and swept half the cherries with it; and Ben, snatching up the half-knitted sock-top, fitted it over the kitten's head as a new source of madness, while Letty arriving cried out to her mother against this cruelty—it was a history as full of sensation as 'This is the house that Jack built'. (*Middlemarch,* Bk. VI, ch. 57).

The Victorians liked interior domestic scenes even better than outdoor ones. The sense of warmth, intimacy, privacy, and security, is very striking—both in painted family portraits and in literary ones: the group

sitting near the fire or around the parlor table, the home their castle (Wemmick even builds a moat around his cottage in *Great Expectations*). There seems to be a special affinity between such cozy interiors and novel-reading itself. In her preface to *Emilia Wyndham* (1846), a kind of apology and justification for novels, Anne Marsh-Caldwell paints an idyllic domestic scene the center of which is a novel:

It is a beautiful sight, when the winter wind is raving and howling, the snow and sleet falling upon the windowpane,—servants comfortably sitting over the hearth, and horses snugly sheltered in the stables,—to see, instead of a group of young ladies dressed for the incessant succession of evening parties, too often to return home wearied, dissatisfied, unimproved and out of humour—it is a beautiful sight to behold the blazing fire, the happy circle assembled, the embroidery-frames, or the poor-clothes basket, or the drawing materials brought out; and sweet female forms, surrounded with all the attractive neatness which renders the Englishman's home his paradise, gathered round; while the father rests in his arm-chair, and the brother, or, perhaps the mother, or maybe one of the fair creatures themselves, produces to the bright eyes beaming with pleasure the new novel of the day.

Charlotte Yonge's numerous May family (eleven children) crowd into a sitting-room described so faithfully that it needs only a frame to be imagined as a painting:

It was such a room as is often to be found in old country town houses, the two large windows looking out on a broad old-fashioned street, through heavy framework, and panes of glass scratched with various names and initials. The walls were painted blue, the skirting almost a third of the height, and so wide at the top as to form a narrow shelf. The fireplace, constructed in the days when fires were made to give as little heat as possible, was ornamented with blue and white Dutch tiles bearing marvellous representations of Scripture history, and was protected by a very tall green guard; the chairs were much of the same date, solid and heavy, the seats in faded carpet-work . . . but there was a large table in the middle of the room, with three desks on it: a small one, and a light cane chair by each window; and loaded book-cases. (*The Daisy Chain,* Ch. 1)

Here the Mays assemble to share their joys and griefs, cut off from the outside world, intimate, private, and—in spite of their troubles—secure in their sense of family unity:

Ethel, on coming in, found Flora making tea, her father leaning back in his great chair in silence, Richard diligently cutting bread, and Blanche sitting on Mr. Wilmot's knee, chattering fast and confidentially. Flora made Harry dispense the cups, and called everyone to their places; Ethel timidly glanced at her father's face as he rose and came into the light. She thought the lines and hollows were more marked than ever . . . . (Ch. 14)

Faithful and circumstantial as all this detail is, mere "photographic" reproduction of life was never the aim of domestic realism. No matter how sharply the novelist observed or how conscientiously he recorded his observations, he was doomed to failure unless he had those other talents for selectivity, arrangement, and characterization that breathe life into fiction. Tired hacks—Mrs. Gore occasionally and Theodore Hook more frequently—puffed out their formula-fabricated three deckers with descriptions remarkable for camera-like fidelity but little else. Theodore Hook in particular had both microscopic and panoramic lenses but rarely used them to artistic purpose. Describing a character dining in a low-class London inn, he counts the spots on the tablecloth:

> He then proceeded to exhibit a pewter tea-pot, with a Davenanted spout, a small jug, containing three or four tablespoonsful of a light-blue liquid, professing to be milk, which, with some half-dozen lumps of dingy sugar, recumbent in a basin, and attended thereon by a pair of brown japanned tongs, shared the board with a bit of salt butter, and a French roll, three inches long by two inches in circumference. ("Passion and Principle," in *Sayings and Doings* [1825])

Hook was very likely one of the novelists George Henry Lewes had in mind when in 1865 he complained about the vogue for "detailism," which purports to be realism but is actually "false art . . . a preference for the Familiar, under the misleading notion of adherence to Nature." The "rage for realism," he warns, is healthy "in as far as it insists on truth," but it becomes unhealthy

> . . . in as far as it confounds truth with familiarity, and predominance of unessential details. There are other truths besides coats and waistcoats, pots and pans, drawing-rooms and suburban villas. . . . And the painter who devotes years to a work representing modern life, yet calls for even more attention to a waistcoat than to the face of a philosopher, may exhibit truth of detail which will delight the tailor-mind, but he is defective in artistic truth, because he ought to be representing something higher than waistcoats. . . .[9]

Some years later, in "The Art of Fiction," Henry James issued a similar warning against the confusion of mere detailism with realism:

> It goes without saying that you will not write a good novel unless you possess the sense of reality; but it will be difficult to give you a recipe for calling that sense into being. Humanity is immense, and

reality has myriad forms; the most one can affirm is that some of the flowers of fiction have the odour of it, and others have not.

The "illusion of life," James continues, "the air of reality," is "the supreme virtue of a novel." If he could not offer the formula for achieving it, he did at least name its main element—"solidity of specification." It is the solidity of detail, not the quantity, that distinguishes great novels of domestic realism from lesser ones. It is the ring of homely truth that we hear in Miss Phoebe, in Mrs. Gaskell's *Wives and Daughters,* describing her excitement at an unexpected visit from an aristocratic lady:

> 'Oh, dear, Molly! If you're not in a hurry to go to bed, let me sit down quietly and tell you all about it; for my heart jumps into my mouth still when I think of how I was caught. She—that is, her ladyship—left the carriage at "The George" and took to her feet to go shopping—just as you or I may have done many a time in our lives. And sister was taking her forty winks; and I was sitting with my gown up above my knees and my feet on the fender, pulling out my grandmother's lace which I'd been washing. The worst has yet to be told. I'd taken off my cap, for I thought it was getting dusk and no would come, and there was I in my black silk skull-cap, when Nancy put her head in, and whispered, "There's a lady downstairs—a real grand one by her talk"; and in there came Lady Harriet, so sweet and pretty in her ways, it was some time before I forgot I had never a cap on.' (Ch. 14)

"Solidity of specification" is the power by which the novelist somehow convinces us of the presence of life. We feel it in a single gesture, like Hetty Sorrel's kissing her arms at a moment when, abandoned and contemplating suicide, she finds shelter in a sheepfold:

> She reached the opposite gate, and felt her way along its rails, and the rails of the sheepfold, till her hand encountered the pricking of the gorsy wall. Delicious sensation! She had found the shelter; she groped her way, touching the prickly gorse, to the door, and pushed it open. It was an ill-smelling, close place, but warm, and there was straw on the ground: Hetty sank down on the straw with a sense of escape. Tears came—she had never shed tears before since she left Windsor—tears and sobs of hysterical joy that she had still hold of life, that she was still on the familiar earth, with the sheep near her. The very consciousness of her own limbs was a delight to her; she turned up her sleeves, and kissed her arms with the passionate love of life. (*Adam Bede,* Ch. 37)

For George Eliot homely, realistic detail provides the material out of which she constructs the total social and conceptual reality of her novels. It no longer functions for the single purpose of sentimental decoration, but for a complex of purposes. Dutch genre painting, which she so admired, may have inspired those magnificent rustic and family scenes in *Adam Bede* and also individual portraits—the aged Martin Poyser, for example,

> . . . his head hanging forward a little, and his elbows pushed backward so as to allow the whole of his fore-arm to rest on the arm of the chair. His blue handkerchief was spread over his knees, as was usual indoors, when it was not hanging over his head; and he sat watching what went forward with the quiet *outward* glance of healthy old age . . . . (Ch. 14)

But domestic realism achieves cumulative effects in her work that go far beyond the pictorial. Out of the domestic scene she constructs an entire social order—like the Dodson world in *The Mill on the Floss:*

> There were particular ways of doing everything in that family; particular ways of bleaching the linen, of making the cowslip wine, curing the hams, and keeping the bottled gooseberries; so that no daughter of that house could be indifferent to the privilege of having been born a Dodson, rather than a Gibson or a Watson. . . . In short, there was in this family a peculiar tradition as to what was the right thing in household management and social demeanour, and the only bitter circumstance attending this superiority was a painful inability to approve the condiments or the conduct of families ungoverned by the Dodson tradition. (Bk. I, ch. 6)

For the Dodsons domestic life defines social standing. The manner in which domestic chores are performed, food prepared, linen arranged, is ritualistic and symbolic. It represents their sense of values; indeed, it is their religion:

> The religion of the Dodsons consisted in revering whatever was customary and respectable. . . . A Dodson would not be taxed with the omission of anything that was becoming, or that belonged to that eternal fitness of things which was plainly indicated in the practice of the most substantial parishioners, and in the family traditions—such as obedience to parents, faithfulness to kindred, industry, rigid honesty, thrift, the thorough scouring of wooden and copper utensils, the hoarding of coins likely to disappear from the currency, the production of first-rate commodities for the market, and the general preference for whatever was homemade. (Bk. IV, ch. 1)

. . . . .

As the novel moved away from romance—or toward romance in totally new forms with domesticated heroes and "adventures" drawn from everyday life—it became increasingly bourgeois and feminine. The term "novel" had already been identified with "familiar" domestic life in Clara Reeve's often-quoted definition from *The Progress of Romance* in 1785: "The Romance in lofty language, describes what never happened nor is likely to happen. The Novel gives a familiar relation of such things, as pass every day before our eyes."

During the transitional period, as we have noted, Sir Walter Scott adapted his romantic-historical themes to the demands of a new fiction-reading market. In abandoning narrative poetry for the novel he tacitly acknowledged the changing nature of his public. As his contemporary, the once-eminent bluestocking Mrs. Anna Laetitia Barbauld, editor of a fifty-volume collection "The British Novelists" (1810), pointed out in her prefatory essay "On the Origin and Progress of Novel-Writing," poetry "requires in the reader a certain elevation of mind and a practised ear." But novel-reading, she admitted somewhat apologetically, "is the cheapest of pleasures: it is a domestic pleasure." It demands no education beyond literacy and offers no higher reward than amusement. Its natural audience is therefore women and its area the home. Humble as the novel is, however ("A collection of Novels has a better chance of giving pleasure than of gaining respect"), its effects are far-reaching because it touches the reader's feelings and moral sensibilities. Therefore, Mrs. Barbauld argues, the novelist has a higher responsibility than is at first apparent. In the young and impressionable particularly, novels

> awaken a sense of finer feelings than the commerce of ordinary life inspires . . . they mix with the natural passions of our nature all that is tender in virtuous affection; all that is estimable in high principle and unshaken constancy; all that grace, delicacy, and sentiment can bestow of touching and attractive.

Thus without elevating the novel to the ranks of great literature, Mrs. Barbauld cautiously reconciles its end—entertainment—with the higher moral purposes of art. She had a powerful ally in Scott, who in the *Quarterly Review* of October 1815 hailed Jane Austen's *Emma* as a fresh new kind of novel, a happy successor to the exhausted romance:

> The substitute for these excitements, which had lost much of their poignancy by the repeated and injudicious use of them, was the art of copying from nature as she really exists in the common walks of life, and presenting to the reader, instead of the splendid scenes of an imaginary world, a correct and striking representation of that which is daily taking place around him.

The two most remarkable qualities of this "new novel" were fidelity to the experiences of ordinary living and sensitivity to the feelings and emotions aroused in and produced by ordinary life. When Thackeray's Laura

Bell advised Pendennis to write "good kind books with gentle thoughts" (Ch. 66), she was speaking as a woman, not a literary pundit. But her advice was sound. Intuitively she grasped the nature of the market. As early as 1777 the omnipresent Mrs. Hannah More had observed the fitness of women for writing faithfully and feelingly about real life:

> The merit of this kind of writing consists in the *vraisemblance* to real life, as to the events themselves, with a certain elevation in the narrative, which places them, if not above what is natural, yet above what is common. It further consists in the art of interesting the tender feelings by a pathetic representation of those minute, endearing, domestic circumstances, which take captive the soul before it has time to shield itself with an armour of reflection. To amuse rather than to instruct, or to instruct indirectly by short inferences, drawn from a long concatenation of circumstances, is at once the business of this sort of composition, and one of the characteristics of female genius.[10]

Even earlier Rousseau in *Emile* (1762) had discovered from his analysis of the female character her "natural gift" for human insight and sensibility. He was not concerned with her application of this gift to literature. On the contrary, he felt that she could best use it in her home, educating her children. Science, all abstract and speculative knowledge, were beyond her grasp. But if she followed Rousseau's advice by confining her duties to the more practical work of leading and directing men—her husband and her children—in their moral development, she might also obliquely be preparing herself for the career of a novelist:

> A woman's thoughts, beyond the range of her immediate duties, should be directed to the study of men, or the acquirement of that agreeable learning whose sole end is the formation of taste. . . . The men will have a better philosophy of the human heart, but she will read more accurately in the heart of men. Women should discover, so to speak, an experimental morality, man should reduce it to a system. (Bk. v)

Critics and novelists alike were no doubt patronizing and condescending in their commendation of women novelists. Until the domestic novel achieved its full stature as literature in the mid-nineteenth century, its practitioners were inevitably looked down upon. Writers like the Brontës assumed masculine pen-names to assure an objective critical reception for their work. Serious men novelists like Bulwer and Disraeli drew their material from high society and political life or from history, following the respected example of Scott. Others, like Charles Kingsley, took up specific reform causes, producing novels of social realism and crusading for political and social change. By the 1840's,

however, not only were younger men novelists like Dickens and Thackeray turning to domestic subjects, but the established Bulwer launched himself into domestic realism with a family novel, *The Caxtons* (1848-1849), announcing in his preface that his plot has been drawn from

> the records of ordinary life . . . a simple Family picture. And thus, in any appeal to the sympathies of the human heart, the common household affections occupy the place of those livelier or larger passions which usually (and not unjustly) arrogate the foreground in Romantic composition.

Bulwer was both a taste-maker and a barometer of changes in popular taste. His success in all the popular fictional forms—historical novels, society novels, crime novels, novels of the supernatural—had been remarkable, but there was a noticeable decline of interest in these as mid-century approached. When in 1855 a young Cambridge student, Fitzjames Stephen, could define the novel as "a fictitious biography," the age of realism had arrived.[11] In the next decade a critic of considerable reputation, E. S. Dallas, repeated that definition and added the final link to domestic realism: "A novel may be described as gossip etherealized, family talk generalised." Dallas noted the anti-romantic and anti-heroic drift of the novel, citing Thackeray as the supreme example of the "new" novelist who, by reducing the heroic proportions of his individual characters, gave them new importance and dignity as human beings. With heroes and heroic action eliminated, the role of women becomes vastly more significant, Dallas observes.

> Now all the more important characters seem to be women. Our novelists have suddenly discovered that the feminine character is an unworked mine of wealth. . . . This is all the more natural, seeing that most of our novelists just now seem to belong to the fair sex. But their masculine rivals follow in the same track.

The result, inevitably, is "the ascendancy of domestic ideas, and the assertion of the individual, not as a hero, but as a family man—not as a heroine, but as an angel in the house."[12]

Since the realistic domestic novel allowed little room for lofty philosophizing and profound erudition (all commentators agreed that if novels were to be realistic they must faithfully reproduce ordinary life and speech) or for spectacular scenery and action, it was considered appropriate for women, with their limited education and experience, to be novelists. The "silver-fork" novelist T. H. Lister, reviewing Mrs. Gore's *Women as They Are* in the *Edinburgh Review* in 1830, even conceded their superiority to men in this field:

There are some things which women do better than men; and of these, perhaps, novel-writing is one. Naturally endowed with greater delicacy of taste and feeling, with a moral sense not blunted and debased by those contaminations to which men are exposed, leading lives rather of observation than of action, with leisure to attend to the minutiae of conduct, and more subtle developments of character, they are peculiarly qualified for the task of exhibiting faithfully and pleasingly the various phases of domestic life, and those varieties which chequer the surface of society.[13]

Women themselves were prompt to admit that they had made a virtue of necessity. Confined to the home circle, like Rousseau's model wife-mother, they cultivated close observation, introspection, analysis. What better training for a novelist's career? Men, boasting of their knowledge of the world, "know mankind only as they appear in one or two particular habits," Mrs. Elizabeth Hamilton wrote in 1808. They are too actively engaged in life to study "that infinite variety which in reality exists. . . ." But women, scrutinizing "little particulars," observe more and better, " . . . as I am persuaded that a single week spent *tête-à-tête* with a person, in their own house, gives a more thorough insight into the mind and disposition than would in years be obtained in the common intercourse of society."[14] Herself a novelist as well as a once-celebrated philosopher and educator, Mrs. Hamilton seems to offer the *raison d'être* of the female-dominated domestic novel. For its "Poetics," its working critical principles, we may look to two other women, novelists and writers of some reputation in their day— Anne Marsh-Caldwell (1791-1874) and Sarah Stickney Ellis (1812-1872), the latter famous for a series of non-fiction books with echo titles: *The Women of England* (1838), *The Daughters of England* (1842), *The Wives of England* (1843), and *The Mothers of England* (1843).

Mrs. Marsh, mother of seven children, wrote eighteen novels of which only one, *Emilia Wyndham,* survives in flickering memory. Harriet Martineau admired her work and wrote an introduction to another of her books, *The Two Old Men's Tales* (1834), for which, she reported in her *Autobiography,* Mrs. Marsh received "high and well deserved fame." Whatever immortality *Emilia Wyndham* has is the result not of the novel itself but of the preface its author wrote for it. The plot concerns an ardent young girl who learns, first from her mother's teaching and then from the experience of life itself, that one's heroism is challenged and displayed not in lofty romantic adventures, but in "the heavy, wearying every-day evils of every-day actual life . . . combining patience, perseverance, endurance, gentleness, and disinterestedness." Significantly, the novel is dedicated to William Wordsworth, "the fine influences" of whose poetry have contributed to the moral life of "countless numbers."

The Preface to *Emilia Wyndham* is an essay on the realistic domestic novel. Mrs. Marsh firmly rejects fables and fantasy:

> The novel must not trench upon the confines of either the allegory or the fable; its essential, its indisputable quality is, that it should convey the sense of reality— that the people we read of should be to us as actual beings and persons—that we should believe in them.

Credibility is necessary in order that the moral teachings of the novel be effective. We cannot expect readers to believe in the characters of *The Faerie Queene,* she points out; therefore, "the divine poem is uninteresting and cast aside." But we can believe in "the tale of life," where the novelist's object is to connect actions and their consequences. Long before E. M. Forster, Mrs. Marsh urged, "Only connect":

> The object, therefore, of the novelist should be, not so much to illustrate a particular moral maxim, as to *point the tale of life*—to bring actions and their consequences, passions, principles, and their results, into that sort of connexion, which, though it certainly and inevitably takes place in actual life, escapes the careless, or, perhaps, undiscerning eye of the reader of the vast volume amid the multiplicity of circumstances in which it is involved. It is for the writer of fiction, without ever over-stepping the bounds of *easy* probability, to bring . . . causes and their consequences into obvious connexion.

When the novel performs this, its proper function, it finds its proper audience in the home. We have already quoted from this preface Mrs. Marsh's depiction of a cozy family scene—a storm raging outside, parents, children, and servants gathered around the fire, eager to hear one of them read aloud from "the new novel of the day." That saccharin-sprinkled vision should not dazzle or becloud our perception of Mrs. Marsh's critical shrewdness. She knew her medium and her audience. Though she emphasized the moral-didactic function of the domestic novel, she also recognized its need to interest and entertain the volatile "fair creatures," the young daughters of the family, every bit as much as its need to meet with the approval of the Englishman and his matron-wife:

> What life, what animation, diffuses itself, as the strange tale proceeds! What sighs—what tears—what anxieties—what smiles!—as the storm-tossed traveller over life's restless ocean reaches the desired haven at last. How the honest heart glows with new aspirations after better things to come for its own inner life—as the loveliness of virtuous self-sacrifice, the grandeur of true heroism, the beauty of sweetness, and temper, and gentleness, and love, are displayed as in a living picture!

A sterner moral critic, yet an equally enthusiastic advocate of the domestic novel, Sarah Stickney (later

Mrs. Ellis) prefaced her *Pictures of Private Life* (note that the title suggests both painting and domesticity) in 1833 with a similar "Apology for Fiction," drawing a firm line between that fiction which offers "lawful" and that which offers "unlawful" pleasure. Unlawful is "whatever weakens your reason, impairs the tenderness of your conscience, obscures your sense of God, or takes off the relish of spiritual things." Turning her severe scrutiny to specifics of novel-writing, she rules out such "abuses" as

> the delineation of unnatural characters, by the combination of such qualities as never did, and never could exist in one human being; and the placing such creatures of the imagination in scenes and circumstances, where the common sympathies of our nature find no place.

She accepts, however, that fiction in which characters are

> drawn from the scenes of every-day life, animated with our feelings, weak with our frailties, led into our difficulties, surrounded by our temptations, and altogether involved in a succession of the same causes and effects which influence our lives. . . .

In such fiction the more exact the descriptive detail the better. The painter who wishes to exhibit to the public "a personification of old age" would not simply paint an old woman in a cottage. To complete his idea he would "place before our eyes" the interior of her house—furniture, spinning wheel, kettle, cat. "Now, though such an old woman . . . never did exist, yet the picture may be true." By analogous means, the novelist evokes a living reality out of imagined details. He has the additional advantage over the painter of being able to add moral teaching to his picture by creating a plot in which virtue may be tested, other characters introduced to demonstrate actions opposed to virtue, all arranged for the purpose "of tracing causes to their effects." In the scale of moral teaching, Mrs. Ellis points out,

> some preach virtue, some only practise it, some make a picture of it, and some a poem, and some . . . adorn it in the garb of fiction, that it may ensure a welcome, where it would not otherwise obtain an entrance. . . . Fiction may be compared to a key, which opens many minds that would be closed against a sermon.

The assumption of order and rationality involved in such teaching, in assuming that actions are connected and that effects have causes that may be traced and consequences that may be properly inferred, is basically anti-romantic. The novel of domestic realism was, in fact, born in reaction to romanticism. Yet even as it rejected and negated those qualities

of the remote and exotic, the self-indulgent emotionalism that readers associated with romanticism, it cultivated sentimentality, sensibility, idealism, and spirituality—qualities that are themselves incompatible with the hard core of realism as we generally use the term. Domestic realism in the nineteenth-century English novel may be described, then, as an attempt to substitute one kind of romanticism for another, or at best to transcend the coarser everyday reality and see it in a softer, more idealized glow. It was an effort, relatively short-lived but vigorous while it lasted, to persuade the public that there was an alternative to the romantic ideal. In one of her most popular books, *The Daughters of England,* Mrs. Ellis argued that readers could be persuaded to reject the Corsairs of Byron and the Isles of Greece and even the gypsies of Sir Walter Scott for alternative attractions in "the page of actual life." There, "beneath the parental roof, or mixing with the fireside circle by the homely hearth, there are often feelings as deep, and hearts as warm, and experience as richly fraught with interest, as ever glowed in verse, or lived in story" (Ch. 5).

By "story" Mrs. Ellis meant romance. The domestic novel that was emerging in the early 1840's when she wrote that sentence was of an apparently if not really different order. Within another generation it had become the established and favorite popular literary genre. In 1874 an article titled "The Domestic Novel," published in the magazine *The Argosy,* proclaimed that "novels to-day seem to occupy the same place in literature that the plays of Shakespeare and Ben Jonson and Marlowe held in the Elizabethan era." Attributing their popularity largely to the influence of women readers who had demanded the elimination of the "gross coarseness of language and customs" of the eighteenth-century novel, the writer hails Jane Austen as a forerunner ("Her region, and in it she reigns unequalled, is that of the commonplace") and, among contemporaries, Thackeray ("whose pictures of English life and manners are without rival in their way"), Trollope, Bulwer (for his "most delightful domestic novel *What Will He Do With It?*"), Dickens (with some reservations about his preoccupation with "low life"), and George Eliot (though *Middlemarch* is "rather too transcendental")—"Doubtless a great change has taken place in the last few years. No one now speaks of novels in the same style of indifferent contempt that was the fashion not long ago. . . . Where are we to look, if not to novels, for the truest and most highly finished pictures of English life?" [15]

The Victorian novel was often described in contemporary reviews as a "picture," but by mid-century the term was conceived far more broadly than a mere literal reproduction of scenes and activities of daily life. A better approximation might be the medieval *specu-*

lum, a reflecting mirror, with all the philosophical connotations of speculative, reflective thought. The novelists were commentators on life, not photographers or reporters. Though they drew from the details that today journalism and photography command, to the degree that they were creative artists they also selected, filtered, and arranged their detail to serve their philosophical, ideological, and aesthetic purposes. Focussed in the English painter's eye as in the English novelist's eye was a small, orderly, regular, and somehow purposeful and logical world. Reverend Primrose's beautifully ordered little family of 1766 was menaced and came perilously near collapse, but Goldsmith's readers up through the mid-nineteenth century could follow the Primroses' misfortunes with serenity, confident that, however miraculously, all would be restored to right. The major and later Victorian novelists were less secure. Working under the demands of "truth," they had to concede occasional defeats and allow for disappointment, frustration, and compromise. But even their most realistically "truthful" novels end with a consoling sense of resignation to some higher meaning and purpose in life. Lucy Snowe accepts and is almost exalted by her lover's death. Pip buries his lost expectations and his love for Estella in solid, constructive work. Young Clive Newcome, frustrated both in love and in his ambitions to be a great painter, learns how to accept life by witnessing his father's humble acceptance of death. Dorothea Brooke will never be a Saint Theresa or an Antigone, but she will find satisfaction in her second marriage, performing useful "unhistoric acts" in an "imperfect social state." When, however, in the second half of the century, the sense of connected experience and purposeful existence was itself challenged, when established institutions and values were exposed to new and often shattering pressures, painters began to see broken images through reflected light, and novelists of artistic integrity, still concerned with "truth," could no longer find their subjects in the enclosed unit of the home, the family, or the small community. Domestic realism, as the early Victorian novelists practiced it, was a sturdy, serviceable genre that left its mark on the fiction of the second half of the century, but as a literary genre it had run its course.

Notes

[1] "Letters on the Fine Arts," *Stray Papers,* ed. Lewis Melville (Philadelphia, n.d.), p. 214.

[2] Graham Reynolds, *Victorian Painting* (London, 1966), p. 94.

[3] *The Hero in Eclipse in Victorian Fiction* (Oxford, 1956); *Mnemosyne: The Parallel Between Literature and the Arts* (Princeton, 1970), Ch. 1; and *Conver-sation Pieces: A Survey of the Informal Group Portrait in Europe and America* (University Park, Pa., 1971).

[4] "The Picture Season in London," in *The Painter's Eye,* ed. John L. Sweeney (Cambridge, Mass., 1956), p. 148.

[5] Louis James, *Fiction for the Working Man* (Oxford, 1963), p. 103.

[6] *Autobiography,* ed. Maria Weston Chapman (Boston, 1878), I, 315-16.

[7] "Jane Austen," in *The Common Reader* (London, 1925), p. 174; *Purely for Pleasure* (London, 1966), p. 102. See also Karl Kroeber, *Styles in Fictional Structure* (Princeton, 1971). On the basis of tabulations of word usage, Professor Kroeber confirms that Jane Austen uses little physical description, but he also demonstrates, through a close analysis of her style as it relates to theme and characterization, that her art "consists of subtle complexities . . . presented in a simple, lucid, even conventionalized manner". (p. 19)

[8] See, for example, Hogarth's portrait of the Graham family in the Tate Gallery. Of these paintings in general Mario Praz writes: "In the conversation piece the environment is depicted with an attention to detail no less scrupulous than we find practised in the portrayal of the sitters, and this gives to the picture a *Stimmung,* an intimate feeling which is not shared to an appreciable degree by the group scene, isolated or presented against a summarily indicated background as it is". (*Conversation Pieces,* p. 56)

[9] *The Principles of Success in Literature,* ed. Fred N. Scott (third ed., New York, 1891), pp. 83-84. These articles were originally published in *The Fortnightly Review* in 1865.

[10] *Essays on Various Subjects Principally Designed for Young Ladies* (New ed., Chiswick, 1820), p. xv.

[11] "The Relation of Novels to Life," in *Cambridge Essays* (Cambridge, 1855), pp. 149-50.

[12] *The Gay Science* (London, 1866), II, Ch. 17, "The Ethical Current."

[13] The review is attributed to Lister in the *Wellesley Index.*

[14] *Memoirs of the Late Mrs. Elizabeth Hamilton.* By Miss [E. O.] Benger (London, 1818), I, 251-52.

[15] 18 (July-December, 1874), pp. 291-97.

Henry James, in a review of Eliot's *Felix Holt* (1866):

In our opinion, then, neither *Felix Holt*, nor *Adam Bede*, nor *Romola*, is a master-piece. . . . They belong to a kind of writing in which the English tongue has the good fortune to abound—that clever, voluble, bright-colored novel of manners which began with the present century under the auspices of Miss Edgeworth and Miss Austen. George Eliot is stronger in degree than either of these writers, but she is not different in kind. She brings to her task a richer mind, but she uses it in very much the same way. With a certain masculine comprehensiveness which they lack, she is eventually a feminine—a delightfully feminine—writer. . . . George Eliot has the exquisitely good taste on a small scale, the absence of taste on a large (the vulgar plot of *Felix Holt* exemplifies this deficiency), the unbroken current of feeling and, we may add, of expression, which distinguish the feminine mind. That she should be offered a higher place than she has earned, is easily explained by the charm which such gifts as hers in such abundance are sure to exercise.

Henry James, in Literary Criticism: Essays on Literature, American Writers, English Writers, *Vol. I,* The Library of America, 1984.

Monica Correa Fryckstedt

SOURCE: "Defining the Domestic Genre: English Women Novelists of the 1850s," in *Tulsa Studies in Women's Literature*, Vol. 6, No. 1, Spring, 1987, pp. 9-25.

[*In the essay that follows, Fryckstedt looks at the prescriptive nature of the minor domestic novel in the 1850s, with its presentation to a young female reading audience of the ideal woman—pure, submissive, and devoted to duty.*]

When Harriet Martineau's *Deerbrook* was published in 1839 it struck the reading public as a pioneering novel. Conditioned by the romances and fashionable novels of high life by Bulwer-Lytton, Disraeli, Lister, Lady Bury, and Mrs. Gore, novel readers were unprepared for a domestic love story, with a village apothecary for its hero, which glorified the values of family and home. *Deerbrook* was bourgeois and unromantic, and it was precisely for this reason—because the novel was "laid in middle life"[1]—that the publisher John Murray declined it. Although English domestic fiction may trace its origin to *The Vicar of Wakefield* (1766), Miss Martineau established, as Vineta Colby phrases it, "the domestic love story as a valid literary genre"[2] in the form in which the mid-Victorians were to know it. With its emphasis on submission to the will of God, fulfillment of duty,

self-sacrifice, and endurance, *Deerbrook* is the archetype of a genre that was to reach its height in novels by Dickens, Thackeray, Mrs. Gaskell, Trollope, and George Eliot.

One of the first to follow this new development in fiction was Mrs. Anne Marsh whose *Emilia Wyndham* (1846) centered on home and family and preached the homespun virtues of endurance, perseverance, and submission. In a preface that she wrote for the 1848 edition of the novel, she set down what were to remain for over a decade the main principles governing this new genre. It was the novel's task, she stated, "to paint the ideal of loveliness and goodness" and to remind its women readers of "how noble a thing is a well-disciplined heart," "how beautiful are duties conscientiously performed" and "how widespread the influence of good."[3]

There are several reasons for seeing 1849 as a watershed in the literary tastes of the British reading public. Not only did a reviewer in *Fraser's* announce in April of that year that fashionable novels, i.e., novels of high society, had at last become "most *un*-fashionable,"[4] but at this time, Bulwer-Lytton, the established author of society novels, crime novels, and historical novels, turned to domestic realism with *The Caxtons* (1848-49). Bulwer-Lytton was, as one critic claims, "both a taste-maker and a barometer of changes in popular taste,"[5] and when he discarded romance for domesticity, there was no doubt about readers' preferences. Moreover, in 1849, when three of the most popular "queens" of the circulating libraries during the 1850s began their careers as novelists, they all adopted the novel of domestic realism as their genre: Margaret Oliphant with *Passages in the Life of Mrs. Margaret Maitland*, Dinah Mulock (later Mrs. Craik) with *The Ogilvies*, and Anne Manning with *Mary Powell*.

In fact, one of the main characteristic of the 1850s is precisely the host of women novelists who then emerged. Talented enough, as George Henry Lewes stated, to write "the best novels," women invaded what had hitherto been regarded as a male domain, and, half jokingly, half in despair, Lewes claimed that his "idea of a perfect woman is of one who can write but won't."[6] Drawing its incidents from daily life and depicting middle-class characters, the domestic novel was, to use Vineta Colby's phrase, "female-dominated."[7] The growing number of women readers turning to Mudie's Select Library for the latest domestic novel had a large range of novelists at their disposal: Anne Marsh, Anne Manning, Charlotte Yonge, Dinah Mulock Craik, Margaret Oliphant, Geraldine Jewsbury, Holme Lee, Julia Kavanagh, Emma Worboise, Selina Bunbury; Lady Georgiana Fullerton, Hesba Stretton, Katherine Macquoid, and Georgiana Craik all supplied wholesome family stories.

R. C. Terry's argument that "an age is often to be better appreciated by what is no longer read than by its standard works still on the shelves,"[8] is highly applicable to the 1850s. Whereas the major domestic fiction, Dickens, Thackeray, Gaskell, Trollope, and Eliot, has been thoroughly examined, the minor domestic novel, which flourished during this decade, remains largely an unmapped territory. Read and admired by the large reading public as well as by major novelists, popular domestic novels are interesting today because they help us to see the major authors in clearer perspective: these novels shaped styles and created attitudes that were taken for granted by the readers of the 1850s, and they show, as Kathleen Tillotson points out, "what expectations had been built up in the minds of the readers and hence how far the great novelists could afford to defeat these expectations."[9] If we want to understand a significant phase of Victorian fiction, we cannot afford to overlook the minor domestic novels, produced mainly by women for women, which enjoyed such popularity at the time. . . .

The object of the domestic novel was usually to describe love ending in marriage. The reason for this was, as the critic David Masson explained in 1859, that "the novel-reading age" in women so often fell between the ages of eighteen and twenty-five.[10] Another contemporary critic pointed to the crucial importance of marriage in a woman's life: "a happy marriage," he stated, "is to a woman what success in any of the careers of life is to a man," for, he added, "it is almost the only profession which society . . . opens to her."[11]

The salient characteristic of domestic fiction was its moral message. Dinah Mulock Craik voiced a common belief when she called the novel "one of the most important moral agents of the community." The novelist, she argued, "creeps innocently on our family-table in the shape of those three well-thumbed library volumes" and "slowly but surely . . . his opinions, ideas, feelings, impress themselves upon us."[12] Most novel readers were women, and the lessons taught aimed at upholding the prescribed code of behavior for women, for from novels girls learned, Trollope wrote, "what is expected of them, and what they are to expect when lovers come." By novels, the *Saturday Review* observed, a woman actually "regulates her conduct."[13]

Frequently constructed as an illustration of a passage of Scripture, domestic novels instilled precepts such as "They will be done," "Do unto others," "Bear thy burdens," and "Do thy duty," lessons primarily directed at the impressionable minds of young women readers for whom it was particularly important to learn submission, endurance, and resignation in order to conform to the womanly ideal. In Emma Worboise's *The Wife's Trials* (1858) an old spinster sums up her life on her deathbed in this manner: "The sweetest of

human ties was not for me, I could never be wife and mother. . . . I bowed my head in resignation to the Almighty will, saying from my inmost heart 'Thy will be done.'"[14] Similarly, a dying lady in Mrs. Hubback's *The Old Vicarage* resignedly reveals her impending death to her stepdaughter: "'His will be done,' said Mrs. Duncan, raising her eyes, and fixing them on the glowing west."[15] Few fictional characters, however, surpass Mrs. Craik's Lord Cairnforth in patiently enduring his fate as a complete invalid: indeed, "the lesson of the Earl's whole life" was, the author tells us, "'Thy will be done!'"[16] The moral message may seem meek and mawkish in the extreme to a modern reader, but a Victorian woman could hardly learn endurance too early. Not only was it her "duty to strive for contentment," as Charlotte Yonge's heroine Violet declares,[17] it was, as another heroine puts it, her duty to thank God "for the burden that had been laid upon her."[18] Georgiana Craik's Mildred never tries to escape from her duty to "bear what God said she *must*" (326). Similarly Mrs. Hubback's Hilary, who feels unequal to shouldering the responsibilities after her stepmother's death, finds strength in the Biblical saying: "Nay, but it was her duty! it was *God's* will, and as such, it could not be too hard; her burden would not be greater than she could bear" (*The Old Vicarage,* I, 18).

In the struggle between duty and love, duty was always presented as the right course of action. Mrs. Craik's John Halifax speaks on behalf of the whole genre when he states that "one right alone I hold superior to the right of love,—duty."[19] And so noble is Captain Hepburn's love in *The Old Vicarage* that he refuses to take his fiancé away from her blind father. Filial duty comes before love: "Do you think I could tempt you away?" he asks, "or that I could look for happiness with you, if it was bought at the price of neglecting your first duty?" (II, 169).

The center of the submissive heroine's life was, of course, the home. In *Emilia Wyndham* (1846) Mrs. Marsh had presented the Victorian concept of a happy home. Dreaming of making Emilia his wife, Mr. Danby, the hero, "thought of her as the clam . . . the gentle, with her quiet smile, presiding at his table, and making *his* tea, and in his own home!"[20] Mrs. Craik's novels also idealize the Victorian home as a sanctuary, guarded by the angel in the house from the tumult and wickedness of the outside world. Returning from the Crimean War, her Dr. Urquhart perceives the home as nothing less than earthly bliss:

> I suddenly entered this snug little "home." The fire, the tea-table, the neatly-dressed daughters. . . . Certainly, to one who has been much abroad, there is a great charm in the sweet looks of a thorough English woman by her own fireside.[21]

Moreover, Mrs. Craik contributed to raising hopes in young women about having a home of their own.

"Every woman," the narrator states in *Christian's Mistake,* "has among the various ideals of happiness, good to make, if never to enjoy, one special ideal—that great necessity of every tender heart,—Home."[22]

That a woman only acquired her supreme status in society by becoming a wife is reflected in the halo of sanctity attached to wifehood in domestic fiction. With respect and reverence Mrs. Craik's John Halifax, for instance, explains to his closest friend that "if ever Ursula Marsh marries she will be my wife—*my* wife" (149). In Mrs. Craik's *Christian's Mistake* the words "my wife" ring like a magic formula when the husband protects his young wife from her new relatives' pestering in this manner:

> "She is my wife!" said Dr. Grey, so suddenly and decisively that even Christian [the heroine] . . . involuntarily started. *My wife.* He said only those two words, yet somehow they brought a tear in her eye. The sense of protection, so new and strange, was also pleasant. She could have fought her own battles . . . but when he stood there, with his hand on her shoulder, simply saying those words, which implied, or ought to imply, everything that man is to woman, and everything that woman needs, she became no longer warlike and indignant, but humble, passive, and content. (80-81)

As the sensation novel mania swept across England in the 1860s introducing heroines who were bigamists, liars, flirts, and adulteresses, it became even more urgent for domestic novelists to glorify the purity of the wife. Christian Grey in Mrs. Craik's *Christian's Mistake* is one of the domestic heroines who must have appeared a blatant anachronism in the eyes of many while drawing the admiration of conservative readers who yearned for respectability and propriety:

> Christian Grey was a wife. Therefore, both as wife and woman, it never occurred to her as the remotest possibility that she could indulge in one tender thought of any man not her husband, or allow any man to lift up the least corner of that veil of matronly dignity with which every married woman, under whatever circumstances she has married or whatever may befall her afterwards, ought to enwrap herself for ever. (197-98)

Heroines were not only paragons of virtue, but their angelic appearance was also a reflection of their maidenly modesty and nobility of soul. When Mrs. Hubback's Hilary receives a proposal from the man of her heart, "she could not answer, except by the quivering lip and drooping eyelid, which spoke of strong, but suppressed emotion" (*The Old Vicarage,* II, 312), and equally stereotyped is the description of Miss Manning's Clarinda Singlehart: in spite of her "sweet mouth, good forehead, fine eyebrow, serene eye,"

there was nothing in her face to equal "the soul that shone through it."[23]

Only the most wholesome kind of reading, of course, was suitable for the angelic heroine. Emma Worboise's Lilian "never read a common novel," but selected prose writers of "undoubted merit" like "Charlotte Brontë, Mrs. Marsh, Mrs. Gaskell and Miss Mulock [Mrs. Craik]," and Henrietta Keddie's Phemie Millar would not dream of touching "Eugène Sue, or George Sand, not even a translation."[24] For many a heroine, however, nothing less than the Bible sufficed to give her comfort and teach her contentment. Alone at Christmas, Holme Lee's Maude Talbot, whose life has been ruined by excessive pride, ponders over her lost love. Seeking for mental balance, she resorts to the Bible, "her last hope of all: she is no longer comfortless."[25]

Through her purity the heroine exerted a purifying influence on her surroundings, particularly on the man she loved. Again the early domestic novel *Emilia Wyndham* established a pattern when Mrs. Marsh's hero accustomed himself to regard Emilia "as a sort of tutelary angel, attached to his life, under whose divine influence he was to become all that it is best for man to be" (235). When Charlotte Yonge's Arthur Martindale wonders "what would become of the world if wives were not better than their husbands" (*Heartsease,* II, 186), he voices an assumption generally shared by domestic novelists. For Holme Lee's Gilbert Massenger the fever-stricken Helen was "his good angel," for she showed him a life "overshadowed by the acknowledged love and power of God."[26] The gambler and drunkard Philip Romney in Georgiana Craik's *Mildred* was saved from a profligate life in the London slums by the heroine's ennobling love. Her hand, he claims, has been "the first angel's hand that has ever stooped down to touch me," and only "through faith in her love" (188) would he be saved from his wicked life.

Weary of the many predictable, insipid heroines of domestic fiction, a modern reader is immediately heartened by the few who depart from the womanly ideal subscribed to in the 1850s. Such exceptional heroines prove not only that minor fiction may have redeeming qualities, but, more importantly, that the incipient debate on the woman question had occasional repercussions even on the generally conventional domestic novel. At a time when Margaret Fuller's *Woman in the Nineteenth Century* (1845) and Fredrika Bremer's *Hertha* (1855) were making women slowly aware of their right to education and to independence from male dominance, a note of protest and mild revolt made itself sporadically felt in the domestic novel, long considered the tame genre of fiction. Thus in Margaret Oliphant's *Passages in the Life of Mrs. Margaret Maitland* (1849), a young girl boldly questions her position as a middle-class woman that prevents her from earning a living:

If I could have changed places with Claud . . . who can be independent always; whereas, we poor girls— is it not strange, aunt? Men are honoured in all ranks for labouring in an honest avocation, while women must reverse the saying of the unjust steward, "I cannot beg, and to work I am ashamed."[27]

The only pleasure available to Julia Kavanagh's Rachel Gray, a meek girl, resigned to God's will, is to meditate in her garret. Resenting her inability to behave like other girls, her stepmother never quite guesses what an odd girl Rachel is:

What if her mother [stepmother] should suspect that she had gone up for the purpose of thinking? Mrs. Gray had no such suspicion, fortunately; else she would surely have been horror-struck at the monstrous idea, that Rachel would actually dare to think! The very extravagance of the supposition saved Rachel. It was not to be thought of.[28]

Mrs. Marsh's otherwise traditional *Margaret and Her Bridesmaids* (1856) exhibits a very interesting heroine. The untamed, spontaneous little Lotty has an integrity and independence of mind that recall Jane Eyre. Refusing to conform to the passive and meek role prescribed for women, she anticipates heroines more common in the late Victorian period. Her suitor Philip is torn between his desire to own Lotty and his admiration for her wild, unconventional character. His reaction reflects the confusion and loss of foothold that the Victorian male experienced when confronted with the new kind of woman who was slowly beginning to emerge:

She was not to be happy but through him; she was to see with his eyes, hear with his ears, speak with his mouth. And yet he acknowledged to himself, that it was her free, independent mind; her noble, truthful heart, her frank, happy temper, that made her so adorable to him. And how was he to make two such incongruities meet?[29]

Six years before George Eliot brought Maggie Tulliver before the world in *The Mill on the Floss* (1860), Henrietta Keddie created Phemie Millar, a Scottish girl, who was too intellectual for her uncongenial home and endowed with "a nature gifted beyond the common" (I, 16). Had she been a boy, she would have been trained for the bar, but being the daughter of a fishcurer, she pined in solitude, longing for an "intellectual Samson" to appear. Since *Phemie Millar* is a poorly constructed novel that barely holds the modern reader's interest throughout its three volumes, it is all the more surprising to encounter such a refreshing heroine as Phemie. Capable of discussing the topics of the day "like a man," she appeared odd and unfeminine in the eyes of the villagers. But, Phemie rebelliously wondered, "were reading and thinking so great a crime in

a girl?" (I, 86). The conflict between her desire to marry and get a home of her own and her reluctance to have her mind and spirit crushed by a narrow-minded husband comprises the best part of the novel:

to undertake the burden with Niels Farquharson— to spend her life by his side, confining herself to his range of thought and feeling, banishing the bright dreams, the intense longings, the bold guesses, even the cloudy mysteries, that were beyond his sphere? Impossible! it would be a species of self-destruction, robbing the world of its greenness and beauty. (I, 309)

It is possible that, consciously or unconsciously, George Eliot drew on her memory of Phemie Millar when she created Maggie Tulliver. Phemie is an example of how a heroine in minor fiction both provided a stepping stone between major heroines and anticipated women characters in later novels. In her assertion of her integrity, Phemie is akin to Jane Eyre as well as to Maggie Tulliver, while foreshadowing, in some respects, George Gissing's Monica Widdowson (in *The Odd Women*), trapped with an uncongenial husband, and Virginia Woolf's Katherine Hilbery in *Night and Day,* reluctant to sacrifice her independence and be molded by her future husband.

Whereas an investigation of Mudie's catalogues and advertisements indicates the popularity of domestic fiction, an exploration of contemporary reviews will enable one to understand *why* the mid-Victorians were so attracted to the host of women writers who thrived in the 1850s. From the very beginning Mrs. Oliphant won success with her entertaining and highly moral novels for which readers had an insatiable appetite. Reviewers admired the domestic realism of *Margaret Maitland,* her first novel. "Quiet and still in the depths of its most exciting scenes," *Fraser's Magazine* noted, "everything passes before us like the business of real life."[30] But while the novel's pathos, sentimentality, and overt didacticism make it appear dated today, "the *morale* [sic] of the story" is precisely what appealed to Mrs. Oliphant's contemporaries, for, as the *North British Review* pointed out, it "glides through troubles and tribulations into a quiet haven of rest at last."[31] Twenty years after its publication, *Margaret Maitland* still struck readers as the epitome of quiet, wholesome domestic fiction. Discussing the large variety of genres that came under the heading of "novel," one journal called attention to the gulf that lay between Miss Braddon's notorious sensation novel *Lady Audley's Secret* and *Margaret Maitland,* holding up the latter as nothing less than "a beautiful sermon in action on pure and holy living."[32]

In the 1850s, before Mrs. Oliphant had begun her Carlingford novels, which were to bring her fame, Dinah Mulock Craik was as a rule rated above her, and the *Academy* declared that her novels "were more widely read than are the productions of any other writer after Dickens" (October 22, 1887, p. 269). In 1856 Mrs. Craik published what was to become a minor classic, *John Halifax, Gentleman,* the novel by whose title she chose to be known throughout her career. The protagonist is a self-made man whose integrity, intelligence, and industry bring success, and clearly the quiet resignation and unshaken faith in God of John and his wife Ursula had enormous attractions for mid-Victorian readers. Surveying the novelists of the 1850s, the critic and novelist John Cordy Jeaffreson concluded that "as a painter of domestic life, and a delineator of rural manners," Mrs. Craik "is unequalled."[33] The many editions of *John Halifax,* including English editions for Swedish secondary schools as late as 1918, prove that Mrs. Craik's Christian ideals of goodness, duty, and endurance were still valid half a century later. In the 1860s, when Miss Braddon and Mrs. Henry Wood invaded the literary market, conservative critics looked back with nostalgia to the "healthy" novels that had flourished in the 1850s, but they found consolation in the fact that in Mrs. Craik's novels the moral message remained largely unchanged. Her novels not only survived the onrush of sensationalism in the 1860s, but they appealed to a sizable reading public even at the close of the century. For, as the *Academy* explained in 1887, "so long as the social views and individual ideals therein faithfully represented are those dominant among our middle classes, so long will Mrs. Craik hold her place" (October 22, 1887, p. 269).

Few writers wrote purer novels than Charlotte Yonge. Her *The Heir of Redclyffe* (1853) established a pattern of endurance, self-sacrifice, duty, and honesty that made it one of the most influential novels of the day. Unlike Mrs. Gaskell's *Ruth,* focusing on a fallen woman and her illegitimate son, which was published the same year, *The Heir of Redclyffe* could be safely entrusted to any young woman. In Miss Yonge's novel there was no juggling with right and wrong, no questioning, no element of sordidness, and the *Saturday Review* contended that "she has had considerable influence on the youthful and most impressible portion of the reading community" (August 20, 1864, p. 250). Like John Halifax, Sir Guy Morville stands out as a paragon of goodness who confirmed the mid-Victorian belief in the nobility of man. "In the presence of such," *Fraser's* writes, "we feel that we are communing with fellow-creatures belonging to a higher order of beings, yet so linked with our own as to compel us to rise into their purer atmosphere."[34]

The mid-Victorian view of the contemporary literary scene was based upon a different hierarchy than the one we have come to apply when we look at the fiction of the last century. This is particularly important to remember in the case of even less important novelists than the three above. Few may now have heard of, much less read, Holme Lee, Julia Kavanagh, and Henrietta Keddie, yet they were highly regarded by their contemporaries and attracted readers as late as the turn of the century when Mudie circulated 25, 14, and 53 respectively of their novels. By placing the review of Holme Lee's *Thorney Hall* before that of Mrs. Gaskell's *North and South* in the "New Novels" section on April 7, 1855, solely devoted to these two novels, the *Athenaeum* indicated the high regard Holme Lee enjoyed among contemporary readers.

Started upon her career by Charles Dickens who took an interest in one of her rejected manuscripts[35] and a regular contributor to his *Household Words,* Miss Harriet parr published numerous novels under the pseudonym "Holme Lee." It is hardly a coincidence that "Holme Lee" and "homely" are homonyms, for the atmosphere pervading her fiction is indeed homely. That her novels *Maude Talbot* (1854), *Thorney Hall* (1855), and *Gilbert Massenger* (1855) have not dated as much as, for instance, Mrs. Hubback's *The Old Vicarage* or Miss Manning's *Clarinda Singlehart* can only be ascribed to the author's talent for telling a story. Turning on the issue of hereditary insanity, *Gilbert Massenger* was widely praised when it appeared. While the *Spectator* claimed that its principal trait was "great power of delineation" (March 4, 1854, p. 255), other critics drew attention to its impeccable moral tone: George Eliot stated in the prestigious *Westminster Review* that Holme Lee had "excellent moral taste," and the *Saturday Review* found it "a book which, read by a thoughtful youth, might serve to determine the course of his whole future life."[36] Thus Holme Lee's popularity arose from her ability to create readable novels with plots that hold the readers' attention while propagating mid-Victorian standards of renunciation, self-sacrifice, honor, and duty.

Although the domestic fiction of Julia Kavanagh has much in common with that of Mrs. Hubback, Miss Manning, Miss Pardoe, and Georgiana Craik, she produced novels that display more talent than theirs. Successfully delineating the details of French provincial life in *Adele* (1858) and *Seven Years* (1860), her real forte lay, as the *Irish Monthly* pointed out, in her "capabilities of touching the chords of pathos, and her tender sympathy with sorrow and suffering."[37] It was above all her talent to deal with humble and simple material in a charming and touching way that ensured her popularity in the 1850s. Even George Eliot found her *Rachel Gray* (1855) "commendable," since it "occupies ground which is very far from being exhausted" and "widens our sympathies . . . with every-day sorrows of our commonplace fellow-men."[38] Anticipating major novelists in subject matter, *Rachel Gray* affords an insight, as early as 1855, into the daily problems of the shopkeeping class in "low" London surroundings.

Few novelists perhaps illustrate better the predominant taste for domestic fiction among the educated classes than Mrs. Marsh. Her *Emilia Wyndham* (1846) was regarded as a trend-setter in which the heroine combined "patience, perseverance, endurance, gentleness, and disinterestedness," qualities that, according to the *New Monthly Magazine,* constituted "the heroism of our day."[39] Mrs. Marsh's "purity of purpose" and "earnestness of moral aim," according to the reviewer, made readers leave her books with "a sense of being bettered by the intercourse."[40] The *Dublin University Magazine* even took her success as "a favourable attestation to the soundness of our public opinion."[41] Consequently, to the mid-Victorians, the popularity of her novels vouchsafed the sanity of the moral climate of the nation.

Calling the 1850s the heyday of English domestic fiction can only be justified if we regard it from a quantitative rather than a qualitative perspective. Whereas Trollope, Gaskell, and Eliot continued to write domestic novels well into the 1860s and 1870s, exemplified by major works like *Wives and Daughters* and *Middlemarch,* the 1850s were the decade in which the genre attracted the largest number of minor talents. Women churning out novels to earn a living, or merely to break the boredom of leisure, universally wrote domestic love stories and, if successful, found an avid reading public awaiting their morally impeccable products. In the 1860s on the other hand, aspiring writers were most likely to try their hand at sensation novels, imitating Miss Braddon and Mrs. Henry Wood. What was it then that made the 1850s *the* decade of minor domestic fiction? A brief look at the scientific, literary, and social climate of the time may bring us closer to an answer.

As we have seen, 1849 was a watershed in the climate of popular taste: the reading public then preferred the wholesome bourgeois love-story, whether in the shape of Bulwer-Lytton's *The Caxtons* or of the first novels of the new novelists, Mrs. Oliphant, Mrs. Craik, or Miss Manning. The year 1859 was another watershed in the scientific, religious, and literary history of England, and it is not without reason that Appleman, Madden, and Wolff call their book, devoted solely to that year, *1859: Entering an Age of Crisis.*[42] Dynamic changes took place in science and philosophy, beginning with Darwin's *On The Origin of Species* (1859) and Mill's *On Liberty* (1859). Darwin was thought, as Basil Willey states, "To have banished from the world the idea of God as Creator and Designer, and to have substituted the notion of 'blind chance,' thus undermining the basis of religious belief."[43] Darwin's scientific theories were an undeniable dissolver of faith in the 1860s, and the atmosphere of unquestioning belief in God, the very foundation of the religious message of minor domestic novels, no longer obtained. The publication of *Adam Bede* and *The Ordeal of Richard Feverel* in 1859 signaled a new interest in the psychological make-up of characters. Novelists tended more and more to analyze their fictional characters, probing under the respectable surface where "un-Christian" feelings of revolt, passion, and ambition were replacing submission, faith, and endurance. Consequently, the 1850s strike us as the calm before the storm, as the decade in which the tenets of Christian faith and the code of duty and resignation still ruled supreme, as the decade in which the mass public was still content to admire the simple loving natures of the heroines and the noble and lofty ideals of the heroes of minor domestic novels. During this calm, however, traditional values were gradually beginning to be threatened, and it is possible that, rushing to their defense, domestic novelists manipulated their readers into believing in a perfect calm, while, in fact, discordant notes were disturbing the harmony. But only in the relatively stable moral climate that prevailed before England entered the "age of crisis" could such a manipulation have been successful: in the 1860s no clever maneuvering would have deluded readers into believing in a calm that no longer existed.

The popularity of the genre in the 1850s must also be seen against the social background. The plots and settings of domestic fiction reflected the everyday life of the rapidly growing number of middle-class women readers who took pleasure in recognizing their own problems and in identifying themselves with the heroines of these novels. The 1850s was perhaps the last decade in which the great majority of women were still content to make home, husband, and children their whole sphere. Of course, Margaret Fuller, Fredrika Bremer, and Frances Power Cobbe had planted a germ of protest against woman's traditional role, and the opening of Queen's College in 1848 for educating women as teachers had sprung from an awareness of women's deficient education, but the inroads on the womanly ideal were as yet sporadic. In a sense then, the 1850s represented the calm before the storm, for in the 1860s and 1870s when higher education was opened up for women; when they could obtain professional training as nurses, clerks, telegraph operators, and printers; when women edited magazines like the *Argosy* and the *Belgravia;* when women ran their own press, the Victoria Press; when women were constantly reminded by the public debate that they had minds, intellects, and aspirations that they had a right to gratify; when journals and novels insisted that women need not marry to become first-class citizens or remain in loveless marriages; when women needed no longer tolerate faithless husbands with a "Thy will be done" as their only consolation, or thank God for the burden He had laid upon them; in short, when the new woman emerged, the code of renunciation and submission, propagated in domestic novels, was seriously challenged and attacked as outmoded and destructive.

Little known today, even to professional students of Victorian fiction, the minor women novelists of the

1850s contributed to a genre that enjoyed enormous popularity during that decade. Although there was a significant shift of taste in the 1860s when most readers were drawn away from the tame precincts of the domestic novel to spicier regions, there were still readers, judging from Mudie's catalogues, who continued to read domestic love stories to the end of the Victorian period. It is in fact remarkable that they did survive in such numbers. They did so because they reminded readers of what in retrospect seemed a more stable society in which men and women had their given roles. Perhaps novels like *Rachel Gray* and *Clarinda Singlehart* were also bought or borrowed by parents who, themselves preferring Ouida's and Rhoda Broughton's "wicked" novels for literary entertainment, wanted their offspring to imbibe the values that had prevailed in their own youth, values to which they subscribed at least sentimentally, although it became harder to believe in their validity in a world that was changing beyond recognition.

Notes

[1] Harriet Martineau, *Autobiography,* IV, 4, quoted in Kathleen Tillotson, *Novels of the Eighteen-Forties* (1954; rpt. London: Oxford University Press, 1962), p. 83. *Deerbrook* was finally published by Moxon.

[2] Vineta Colby, *Yesterday's Woman: Domestic Realism in the English Novel* (Princeton: Princeton University Press, 1974), p. 256.

[3] [Anne Marsh], *Emilia Wyndham* (1846; rpt. London: Colburn's Standard Novel Series, 1848), pp. vii and viii.

[4] *Fraser's Magazine,* 39 (April 1849), 419, quoted in Tillotson, p. 87.

[5] Colby, p. 33.

[6] "Vivian" [G. H. Lewes], "A Gentle Hint to Writing-Women," *Leader,* 1 (1850), 189.

[7] Colby, p. 4.

[8] R.C. Terry, *Victorian Popular Fiction, 1860-80* (London: Macmillan, 1983), p. 166.

[9] Tillotson, p. 4.

[10] David Masson, *British Novelists and Their Styles* (Cambridge: Macmillan, 1859), p. 296.

[11] Sir [James] Fitzjames Stephen, "The Relation of Novels to Life" in *Cambridge Essays* (London: Parker, 1855), p. 171.

[12] [D. M. Craik], "To Novelists and a Novelist," *Macmillan's Magazine,* 3 (1861), 442.

[13] Anthony Trollope, "Novel-Reading," *Nineteenth Century,* 5 (1879), 39, and "Novels, Past and Present," *Saturday Review,* April 14, 1866, p. 440.

[14] [Emma Worboise], *The Wife's Trials: A Tale* (London; Thickbroom Brothers, 1858), p. 122.

[15] Mrs. Hubback, *The Old Vicarage: A Novel* (London: Skeet, 1856), I, 3. Subsequent references are cited parenthetically in the text.

[16] [D. M. Craik], *A Noble Life* (Leipzig: Tauchnitz, 1865), p. 227.

[17] Charlotte Yonge, *Heartsease; or, the Brother's Wife* (Leipzig: Tauchnitz, 1855), I, 198. Subsequent references are cited parenthetically in the text.

[18] Georgiana M. Craik, *Mildred* (Leipzig: Tauchnitz, 1868), p. 294. Subsequent references are cited parenthetically in the text.

[19] [D. M. Craik], *John Halifax,* Gentleman (1856; rpt. London: Dent, 1969), p. 383. Subsequent references are cited parenthetically in the text.

[20] [Anne Marsh], *Emilia Wyndham* (1846; rpt. London: Simms and M'Intyre, 1850), p. 126.

[21] [D. M. Craik], *A Life for a Life* (Leipzig: Tauchnitz, 1859), I, 112.

[22] [D. M. Craik], *Christian's Mistake* (Leipzig: Tauchnitz, 1865), p. 95. Subsequent references are cited parenthetically in the text.

[23] [Anne Manning], *Some Account of Mrs. Clarinda Singlehart* (London: Hall, Virtue, 1855), p. 20.

[24] [Henrietta Keddie], *Phemie Millar* (London: Hurst & Blackett, 1854), II, 49. Subsequent references are cited parenthetically in the text.

[25] Holme Lee, *Maude Talbot* (London: Smith, Elder, 1854), III, 291.

[26] Holme Lee, *Gilbert Massenger* (London: Smith, Elder, 1855), p. 215.

[27] [Margaret Oliphant], *Passages in the Life of Mrs. Margaret Maitland of Sunnyside. Written by Herself* (1849; rpt. New York: D. Appleton, 1851), p. 37.

[28] Julia Kavanagh, *Rachel Gray. A Tale Founded on Fact* (1855; rpt. Leipzig: Tauchnitz, 1856), p. 59.

[29] [Anne Marsh], *Margaret and Her Bridesmaids* (London: Hurst & Blackett, 1856), II, 200.

[30] "A Triad of Novels," *Fraser's Magazine*, 42 (1850), 586.

[31] "Recent Works of Fiction," *North British Review*, 15 (1851), 429 and 427 respectively.

[32] "The Works of Mrs. Oliphant," *British Quarterly Review*, 49 (1868), 304.

[33] John Cordy Jeaffreson, *Novels and Novelists from Elizabeth to Victoria* (London: Hurst & Blackett, 1858), II, 380.

[34] "Heartsease; or, the Brother's Wife," *Fraser's Magazine*, 50 (1854), 503.

[35] *Literary Year Book and Bookman's Directory* (London, 1901), pp. 101-02.

[36] [George Eliot], "Belles Lettres," *Westminster Review*, 65 (1856), 300, and *Saturday Review*, May 3, 1856, p. 21.

[37] [Mrs. C. Martin], "The Late Julia Kavanagh," *Irish Monthly*, 6 (1878), 97.

[38] [George Eliot], "Rachel Gray," *Leader*, January 5, 1856, p. 19.

[39] "Female Novelists. Mrs. Marsh Caldwell," *New Monthly Magazine*, 96 (1852), 316.

[40] "Female Novelists," *New Monthly Magazine*, 315.

[41] "Mrs. Marsh Caldwell," *Dublin University Magazine*, 34 (1849), 575.

[42] Terry also sees 1859-60 as "a watershed in popular fiction," p. 15.

[43] Basil Willey, "Darwin and Clerical Orthodoxy," in *1859: Entering an Age of Crisis*, p. 52.

David Castronovo on the English country gentleman:

The country gentleman's function was to give life coherence and stability. The medium by means of which he acted out his role was the landed estate. For it was his duty to preserve his property as the visible symbol of the social order and to see that life on the land gave each member of the community his place in the social hierarchy. The gentleman had to preserve a continuity with the past; he had to live up to the achievements and contributions of his ancestors. At the same time he had to consider his descendants; he had to leave his properties intact; his reputation for honesty and integrity would also reflect on those who came after him.

David Castronovo, in The English Gentleman: Images and Ideals in Literature and Society, *Ungar Publishing Company, 1987.*

DEPICTIONS OF GENDER

Patricia Beer

SOURCE: "Chapter III," in *Reader, I Married Him: A Study of the Women Characters of Jane Austen, Charlotte Brontë, Elizabeth Gaskell and George Eliot*, Barnes & Noble Books, 1974, pp. 84-93.

[*In the following excerpt, Beer compares Jane Austen's female characters with those of Charlotte Brontë, revealing the changing nature of women's relationship to work and to marriage in the first half of the nineteenth century.*]

Between the publication of Jane Austen's *Persuasion* and Charlotte Brontë's *Jane Eyre* great social changes occurred. They had begun in Jane Austen's time, of course, and she had apparently not taken much notice of them, but by 1847, the date of the publication of *Jane Eyre*, they could no longer be ignored and in any case Charlotte Brontë had no wish to ignore them. Mr Suckling's fling at the slave trade turned, with her, into serious author's comment.

In her novels she not only shows the changes brought about by the growth and spread of the industrial revolution but tends to approve of them, as in this passage from the end of *Shirley*, where Robert Moore, the mill-owner, reprieved from the threat of bankruptcy by the repeal of the Orders in Council, prophesies a bright future.

> I can line yonder barren Hollow with lines of cottages, and rows of cottage-gardens . . . The copse shall be firewood ere five years elapse: the beautiful wild ravine shall be a smooth descent; the green natural terrace shall be a paved street: there shall be cottages in the dark ravine, and cottages on the lonely slopes: the rough pebbled track shall be an even, firm, broad, black, sooty road, bedded with the cinders from my mill: and my mill shall fill its present yard . . . I will get an act for enclosing Nunnely Common, and parcelling it out into farms . . . The houseless, the starving, the unemployed, shall come to Hollow's Mill from far and near.

The tone is apocalyptic. Caroline, Moore's future wife, does protest a little, but she knows quite well that progress must come before prettiness. And at the end the narrator confirms it all.

> The other day I passed up the Hollow, which tradition says was once green, and lone, and wild; and there I saw the manufacturer's day-dreams embodied in substantial stone and brick and ashes—the cinder-black highway, the cottages, and the cottage gardens; there I saw a mighty mill, and a chimney, ambitious as the tower of Babel.[1]

However unattractive some of these details may be, the tone is the quietly elegiac voice of acceptance and its rhythm hauntingly recalls the conclusion of *Wuthering Heights.*

We think of those two romantic preservationists, Fanny Price and Marianne Dashwood: Fanny with her general suspicion of Mr Repton's improvements and Marianne with her distress at the idea of the dead leaves of Norland being swept up and her preference for a picturesquely ragged village community to a tidy prosperous one. Though Jane Austen is laughing at Marianne's exaggeration and a little at Fanny's sentiment, both girls are her heroines and she does not really dissociate herself from them. She, too, liked things as they were.

The difference between the attitudes of the two authors, on this and on other issues, particularly the Woman Question, sprang partly from a difference of class. Jane Austen and Charlotte Brontë were both daughters of clergymen, but there, socially, the resemblance ended. Patrick Brontë had social pretensions—he changed his name from Brunty—but he was a self-made man of humble origins, whom Haworth provided with none of the polished society which might have made his manners more relaxed and easy. And Branwell Brontë established a positively downward trend with the unambitious work he undertook (imagine any of Jane Austen's brothers as a booking clerk on the railway) and the low company he preferred to keep. The family was poor and the girls, though their school friendships brought and kept them in touch with people of wealth and property, had to go out to work.

It was a similarly insecure background that Charlotte Brontë gave her heroines. They come from much the same social class as Jane Austen's heroines, at least from its lower echelons. Caroline Helstone, for example, the portionless niece of a country vicar, is on much the same footing as Emma Watson. Two of them, Jane Eyre and Lucy Snowe, have fallen from relatively high estate. They are all ladies of course. Jane, in spite of her lowly status and unimpressive looks, is still recognised by the servants as a social superior; as Bessie says, 'You are genteel enough, you look like a lady'[2] and even Hannah, when every circumstance works to mislead her, concludes, 'You look a raight down dacent little crater',[3] her egalitarian North Country way of saying much the same thing. Lucy Snowe can, if she chooses, mix with the de Bassompierres on terms of equality. Shirely Keeldar, when Sir Philip Nunnely seems about to propose, meets with no more opposition from his mother than Elizabeth Bennet does from Lady Catherine de Bourgh.

But there is the question of work. Jane Austen's women for the most part live unthinkingly on the labour of others. The dark world of paid employment—and it is consistently presented as gloomy—casts its shadow over only a few of them. But Charlotte Brontë's most important women characters have to work. And this necessity looms so large as to affect her presentation of women as a whole. Work gives Jane Eyre, Lucy Snowe and Frances Henri greater freedom of a sort, and however unwelcome, than their more sheltered sisters in the drawing rooms of Mansfield Park and Pemberley. It gives them wider experience, however unpleasant, and more urgent and realistic needs. It certainly brings them face to face with the Woman Question.

Charlotte Brontë's own passionate nature with all its aspirations and consequent frustrations would no doubt have burst through Godmersham Park as it did through Haworth, and it is impossible to do more than suggest where her views came from. But it is possible to define them and particularly, of course, her views on the status of women, without having to decide on their exact source. A comparison of certain passages from her novels with essentially similar ones from the work of Jane Austen will begin to demonstrate Charlotte Brontë's strikingly different attitude.

Firstly: two scenes where a gentleman reads Shakespeare aloud to the ladies. In *Mansfield Park* Henry Crawford, chiefly to further his pursuit of Fanny, declaims with excellent effect some passages from *Henry VIII.* Fanny has been reading it to her aunt before his arrival but there is no question of her continuing now. The ladies listen and their only response to the performance can be praise. Henry dominates the scene completely and would do so even if Lady Bertram were more talkative and Fanny less determined to give him no encouragement.

In *Shirley* Caroline Helstone, spending an evening at Hollow's Cottage, formally though they are her distant cousins, with Robert and Hortense Moore, takes the initiative in suggesting reading aloud, chooses the play, *Coriolanus,* and, brushing aside Hortense's hint that 'when the gentleman of a family reads, the ladies should always sew', joins Robert in the reading, catechises him about it afterwards and draws rather outspoken morals from it with a view to improving his character.[4] Yet Caroline is no Elizabeth Bennet; she is more like Fanny Price.

Secondly: two sustained passages of which amateur acting is the subject. We know from *Mansfield Park* what Jane Austen thought of it and particularly her horror at the indelicacy of women taking parts which called on them to display themselves in front of young men to whom they were not married and to utter sentiments of love, even if it was only maternal love, in public. A great deal of the early part of *Mansfield Park* depends on this theme, and the evils resulting from the performance of *Lover's Vows* are the worst the author can devise.

In *Villette* there are absolutely none of these 'modest loathings'. Even the conventional Mme Beck, even the hidebound M. Paul, see nothing wrong in women appearing on the stage in front of a considerable audience including a number of strange men. Some of the girls take men's parts and are expected to wear trousers. The play they are presenting is all about love and flirtation. In taking part Lucy has nothing worse than shyness to overcome, not principle—though she refuses to wear trousers—and when it comes to the point she throws herself into the rôle and thoroughly enjoys herself.[5]

And thirdly: two quite different views of feminine accomplishments. As we have seen, Jane Austen presents them as lures to catch men. The scene in *Emma* where the heroine plans to paint Harriet's portrait as a means of securing Mr Elton for her is a good example. Emma draws and paints purely for social and sexual reasons; when there is no such motive she puts the apparatus away. There is no question of her doing it to please or express herself.

In *Jane Eyre* the subject is seen in quite a new light. Jane's standard of performance is no better than Emma's but her motivation is superior. In the course of her first conversation with Mr Rochester she shows her pictures to him and they are described to the reader.[6] They sound rather dreadful but they are genuine expressions of a personal vision pursued for its own sake, with diligence and as much technique as the artist can command, by a girl who, though lonely and deprived, respects and cherishes her own individuality. Her later attempts to subdue her feelings for Mr Rochester, when it really does seem that he is going to marry Blanche Ingram, are touching and brave. She draws a portrait of the sumptuous Blanche and another of her thin plain self;[7] not a way to produce great art, probably, but a higher impetus than the wish to catch a man.

Here, we might be tempted to think, is a leader, a leader in the cause of feminism, and after reading *Shirley* with its clarion calls about the fatuousness of what women are expected to do and be and its glimpses of their possible scope, we might be completely convinced. But we should be finally disappointed. Charlotte Brontë writes of individuals, each with her own frustrations and her own solution to them. She does not think in terms of a cause and can see no body of women to lead. It is the same as with her social attitudes in general; she can see no more organised way of helping the poor than the easy Cheeryble Brothers-type of hand-out that Shirley administers or Robert Moore's preference for hiring rather than firing as he works his way up to being a rich mill-owner.

Worse than this, Charlotte Brontë is a lost leader. In the spirit and independence of its heroine the whole of *Shirley* demonstrates the potential of woman, but at the end the heroine dwindles into a tiresome neurotic who keeps putting off her wedding day for no good reason and who, when asked to shoulder any responsibility, simply says, 'Go to Mr. Moore; ask Mr. Moore'.

The limitations and hardships of the only work available to middle-class women, that is, governessing or school teaching, are presented explicitly by Charlotte Brontë. Teaching in a school is made to seem not too bad. Lucy Snowe, Frances Henri and Jane Eyre—in her last years at Lowood and after she had escaped from Thornfield and is put in charge of a village school by St John Rivers—all have a certain independence and scope, and are supported by the hope, realised in the case of Frances and Lucy, of owning schools of their own and becoming powerful and prosperous like Mlle Reuter and Mme Beck. But governessing can be truly terrible. The novels contain eloquent emotional passages on the subject; situation is not enough, there is direct and forcible comment.

Jane Austen has already shown us something of governessing, representing it as a sort of leprosy or cancer; rather strangely in view of the fact that one governess, Miss Taylor, has an extremely happy home with the Woodhouses, on terms of family intimacy, her health the first object with Mr Woodhouse and her subservient status no bar to her making an eligible marriage. Jane Fairfax's reprieve from going as a governess is made to seem like a reprieve from hanging. Charlotte Lucas marries a lout to escape this even worse fate. Emma Watson, repudiating with all the courage of a pretty young girl the idea of marrying for money, says she would rather go as a governess and she can imagine nothing worse.

Charlotte Brontë goes further. The words of Mrs Pryor in *Shirley* are quite blood-curdling; she quotes extensively the very phrases that most wounded her in the circumstances she is describing.

> I was early given to understand that 'as I was not their equal', so I could not expect 'to have their sympathy'. It was in no sort concealed from me that I was held a 'burden and restraint in society'. The gentlemen, I found, regarded me as a 'tabooed woman', to whom 'they were interdicted from granting the usual privileges of the sex', and yet who 'annoyed them by frequently crossing their path'. The ladies too made it plain that they thought me a 'bore'. The servants, it was signified, 'detested me'; *why,* I could never clearly comprehend. My pupils, I was told, 'however much they might love me, and however deep soever the interest I might take in them, could not be my friends'. It was intimated that I must 'live alone, and never transgress the invisible but rigid line which established the difference between me and my employers'. My life in this house was sedentary, solitary, constrained, joyless, toilsome.[8]

This is fine, paranoid stuff and though it is part of the characterisation—Mrs Pryor has marked paranoid tendencies—it is meant to sound like serious reportage as well. Mrs Pryor forgets that her life as Shirley Keeldar's governess has been remarkably pleasant, but so does Charlotte Brontë seem to forget, when recounting the spiteful remarks of the Thornfield house party about governesses, that Jane is having a peaceful, reasonably happy time teaching Adèle.

The attitude of the men is significant. When Mr Rochester and Jane become engaged he exclaims imperiously: 'You will give up your governessing slavery at once.'[9] What was quite suitable for an unknown young woman is not good enough for his future wife, however bigamous he may be. One is reminded of Mr Willcox in *Howard's End* who was calmly ready to sell a house for a boys' preparatory school which he considered too damp for himself and his family. It is an essential part of Paul Emanuel's wooing of Lucy that he should set her up as the proprietress of a school rather than leave her as an employed teacher.

But with all this dire talk we are shown that there are worse things than governessing. One is boredom and the feeling that life is slipping away with nothing worthwhile done. Caroline is so driven by the frustrations of her life ('It is scarcely *living* to measure time as I do at the Rectory. The hours pass, and I get them over somehow, but I do not *live*',)[10] that she asks her uncle for permission to go as a governess. Mr Helstone, his mind working on the same lines as Mr Rochester's and Paul Emanuel's, gives her the strongest reason he can for not complying: 'I will not have it said that my niece is a governess.' The conversation ends as follows:

> 'Put all crotchets out of your head, and run away and amuse yourself.'
>
> 'What with? My doll?' asked Caroline to herself as she quitted the room.[11]

As distressing as the ennui and the sense of futility of an unmarried girl is the torment of the unhappily married woman; in this case, too, teaching is a soft option as even Mrs Pryor acknowledges.

> My new name sheltered me: I resumed under its screen my old occupation of teaching. At first, it scarcely procured me the means of sustaining life; but how savoury was hunger when I fasted in peace! How safe seemed the darkness and chill of an unkindled hearth, when no lurid reflection from terror crimsoned its desolation! How serene was solitude, when I feared not the irruption of violence and vice.[12]

And a third worse evil for a woman than having to teach is a loss of self respect in an illicit union. Jane Eyre is eloquent on this point.

> Whether is it better, I ask, to be a slave in a fool's paradise at Marseilles—fevered with delusive bliss one hour—suffocating with the bitterest tears of remorse and shame the next—or to be a village-schoolmistress, free and honest, in a breezy mountain nook in the healthy heart of England?[13]

At times, in *Shirley,* we seem to be on the brink of some eulogy of work as a positive pleasure and an opportunity for women, some noble forward-looking idea of occupation more elevated and more honourable than governessing. But it all boils down to the same dreary concept of work being marginally better than aimlessness. Caroline talking to Shirley uses very strong language indeed about both alternatives, and gives the conversation an unpleasant twist by refuting the conventional cant about the evils of women working with an argument even more reactionary.

> 'Caroline', demanded Miss Keeldar abruptly, 'don't you wish you had a profession—a trade?'
>
> 'I wish it fifty times a day. As it is, I often wonder what I came into the world for. I long to have something absorbing and compulsory to fill my head and hands, and to occupy my thoughts.'
>
> 'Can labour alone make a human being happy?'
>
> 'No; but it can give varieties of pain, and prevent us from breaking our hearts with a single tyrant master-torture. Besides successful labour has its recompense; a vacant, weary, lonely, hopeless life has none.'
>
> 'But hard labour and learned professions, they say, make women masculine, coarse, unwomanly.'
>
> 'And what does it signify, whether unmarried and never-to-be-married women are unattractive and inelegant, or not?—provided only they are decent, decorous, and neat, it is enough. The utmost which ought to be required of old maids, in the way of appearance, is that they should not absolutely offend men's eyes as they pass them in the street; for the rest, they should be allowed without too much scorn, to be as absorbed, grave, plain-looking, and plain-dressed as they please.'[14]

Marriage, as Jane Austen pointed out, is a woman's pleasantest preservative from want, and many of her women characters are gratefully conscious of this aspect of their unions. Charlotte Brontë's heroines are not compelled to fall back on marriage for financial independence; she takes care to provide for them first. Jane Eyre is left a fortune. (One is reminded of Margaret Dashwood's ridiculous wish that someone would leave all three of them a large fortune apiece.) It must give Jane great satisfaction to tell Mr Rochester that she is quite rich, sir. If you won't let me live with you, I can build a house of my own close up to your door, and you may come and sit in my parlour when you want company of an evening.[15]

Lucy Snowe who, we understand, never marries is put firmly on the path to prosperity and it is the man who wishes to marry her who makes her financially independent of him. Caroline Helstone's future is made secure by Mrs Pryor's offer to provide for her, some time before Robert Moore at last proposes. Shirley Keeldar is, of course, rich from start to finish.

The fact that the heroines do have a viable alternative to marriage makes their decision and their eagerness to marry more significant. Kate Millett's interesting but contrived account of *Villette*[16] seems to overlook this fact. Lucy is *not* free at the end of the book; she does not rise above the lures of marriage and wisely choose to refrain from it. Her future husband is drowned, by Charlotte Brontë, and she is an unhappy and deprived woman for the rest of her life.

The heroines need to have somebody of their own. Lucy Snowe, indulging her modest dreams of setting up a school and becoming independent, continues:

> But afterwards, is there nothing more for me in life— no true home—nothing to be dearer to me than myself, and by its paramount preciousness to draw from me better things than I care to culture for myself only? Nothing at whose feet I can willingly lay down the whole burden of human egotism, and gloriously take up the nobler charge of labouring and living for others?[17]

Later in the book when Paulina, inspired by happiness into more insufferable condescension than usual, says patronisingly to Lucy:

> But ours, Lucy, is a beautiful life, or it will be; and you shall share it;

Lucy very properly and roundly replies:

> I shall share no man's or woman's life in this world, as you understand sharing. I think I have one friend of my own, but am not sure, and till I *am* sure, I live solitary.[18]

The important difference is that when the heroines do decide on the man they want to marry they are absolutely whole-hearted, with no reservations whatever about suitability. . . .

Notes

[1] *Shirley,* ch. 37.

[2] *Jane Eyre,* ch. 10.

[3] Ibid., ch. 29.

[4] *Shirley,* ch. 6.

[5] *Villette,* ch. 14.

[6] *Jane Eyre,* ch. 13.

[7] Ibid., ch. 16.

[8] *Shirley,* ch. 21.

[9] *Jane Eyre,* ch. 24.

[10] *Shirley,* ch. 21.

[11] Ibid., ch. 11.

[12] Ibid., ch. 24.

[13] *Jane Eyre,* ch. 31.

[14] *Shirley,* ch. 12.

[15] *Jane Eyre,* ch. 37.

[16] *Sexual Politics,* ch. 3.

[17] *Villette,* ch. 31.

[18] Ibid., ch. 37.

Maureen T. Reddy

SOURCE: "Men, Women, and Manners in *Wives and Daughters,*" in *Reading and Writing Women's Lives: A Study of the Novel of Manners,* UMI Research Press, 1990, pp. 67-85.

[In the following study of Elizabeth Gaskell's Wives and Daughters, *Reddy reveals the limited impact of nineteenth-century social change on the lives of women who were, for the most part, still restricted by their dependence on men.]*

Six months before coining the term *novel of manners* in a review of *Felix Holt,* Henry James described Elizabeth Gaskell's *Wives and Daughters* as "one of the very best novels of its kind" ("Mrs. Gaskell" 153). But what "kind" is that? Although James's comment begs this question, the elements of *Wives and Daughters* that he singles out for particular praise are strikingly similar to those he later identifies as placing George Eliot's *Felix Holt* within the tradition of the novel of manners. For instance, James comments extensively on Gaskell's skillful use of many "modest domestic facts," asserting that these details are essential to her art: her heroine Molly Gibson is "a product, to a cer-

Walter Scott, in an unsigned review of Austen's *Emma* (March 1816):

Accordingly a style of novel has arisen, within the last fifteen or twenty years, differing . . . in the points upon which the interest hinges; neither alarming our credulity nor amusing our imagination by wild variety of incident, or by those pictures of romantic affection and sensibility, which were formerly as certain attributes of fictitious characters as they are of rare occurrence among those who actually live and die. The substitute for these excitements, which had lost much of their poignancy by the repeated and injudicious use of them, was the art of copying from nature as she really exists in the common walks of life, and presenting to the reader, instead of the splendid scenes of an imaginary world, a correct and striking representation of that which is daily taking place around him.

In adventuring upon this task, the author makes obvious sacrifices, and encounters peculiar difficulty. . . . [He] who paints a scene of common occurrence, places his composition within that extensive range of criticism which general experience offers to every reader. The resemblance of a statue of Hercules we must take on the artist's judgement; but every one can criticize that which is presented as the portrait of a friend, or neighbour. . . . The portrait must have spirit and character, as well as resemblance; and being deprived of all that, according to Bayes, goes 'to elevate and surprize,' it must make amends by displaying depth of knowledge and dexterity of execution. We, therefore, bestow no mean compliment upon the author of *Emma*, when we say that, keeping close to common incidents, and to such characters as occupy the ordinary walks of life, she has produced sketches of such spirit and originality, that we never miss the excitation which depends upon a narrative of uncommon events, arising from the consideration of minds, manners, and sentiments, greatly above our own.

Walter Scott, in Jane Austen: The Critical Heritage, *edited by B. C. Southam, Barnes & Noble Inc., 1968.*

tain extent, of clean frocks and French lessons" and of all the other "modest domestic facts" Gaskell presents (156). Here, James seems to suggest that Molly's character is largely determined by her environment, and that if we wish to understand Molly—or any other character in *Wives and Daughters*—we must first understand the social forces that help shape her. Implicit in this view is a definition of the novel of manners as a genre in which the social world and the individual character are equally important and mutually dependent, a definition James would later employ in his review of *Felix Holt*.

In this later review, James suggests that the novel of manners is the "natural" province of the woman novelist, for reasons Richard Faber states more directly over a century later; of the Victorians, Faber notes, "the women novelists are, within the limits of their experience, the most reliable guides to the Victorian social labyrinth" (14). Disguised as a compliment, this remark is actually damning, for it denies the art of women novelists, implying that they are mere "observers," not creators or shapers of their fiction. And what are the "limits" to which Faber refers? He does not define them, but we can infer from the context that the limits are those of the domestic world, the underlying assumption being that the domestic world is always smaller, less important than the political world, missing the truth that the domestic is itself political, always and everywhere.

Later critics have tended to treat *Felix Holt* as a social problem novel, with affinities to Charlotte Brontë's *Shirley* and to Gaskell's *Mary Barton* and *North and South,* a position that accords well with the often-made but seldom-articulated assumption that the social-problem novel and the novel of manners are two distinct, mutually exclusive categories.[1] I would argue, however, that novels of manners very often are social-problem novels, and that *Wives and Daughters,* like *Felix Holt, Shirley, Mary Barton,* and *North and South,* is both. Granted that *Wives and Daughters* has no single, obvious social issue at its heart that would correspond to the "arguments" of Gaskell's so-called social-problem novels—nothing so clearly defined as the plight of the industrial working classes in *Mary Barton* and *North and South,* or the sexual double standard in *Ruth*—I nevertheless believe it is more useful to think of it in relation to this group of novels than to treat it as more directly comparable to *Cranford* or to *Cousin Phillis.*[2] In *Wives and Daughters,* the social problem is actually the entire society itself, which Gaskell explores in terms of manners. The central question is this: How is the individual, especially the individual woman, to find a way to live in a society that seems hostile to individual desires, and in which members even of the *same* class cannot agree upon the proper relation of the individual to society, much less upon how one expresses that relationship in one's daily conduct? The society Gaskell examines is characterized by often subtle but nevertheless substantial conflict and disorder.

As Lionel Trilling points out in "Manners, Morals, and the Novel," the focus of the novel of manners is the problem of reality, explored through close observation of the shifts and conflicts of social classes, as expressed in their manners, what Trilling calls a culture's "hum and buzz of implication" (200). Setting *Wives and Daughters* back forty years, during the period of her own childhood and adolescence, in fact, enabled Gaskell to comment explicitly on manners that were old-fashioned even at the time of writing, and also to comment implicitly on the present.[3] Gaskell wrote *Wives and Daughters* during 1864-65, a time when there was much

Maria Edgeworth contributed notably to the development of the English novel of manners.

debate about further parliamentary reform; the early 1860s seem to have been close in spirit to the mid-to-late 1820s, the time in which the novel is set. In the 1820s and very early 1830s, there had been considerable talk of parliamentary reform, and a number of other reforms had actually been enacted. By the mid 1830s, the middle classes not only were the source of political power in England but also had established themselves as the nation's moral conscience and the guardians of its manners, with parliamentary reform quickly followed by other reforms important to the urban community of Dissenters within which Gaskell made her adult life: the end of colonial slavery, the factory act, the municipal corporations act, and so on. Although Gaskell does not comment directly on these events in *Wives and Daughters,* they form the background of the novel: in addition to the coming election, there are rumors of a railroad branch for Hollingford (with all that such an event implies), and Gaskell relies on her audience's awareness of political changes to provide a context for her story. The awareness of social change that Gaskell here demonstrates acquires its depth and resonance from a lively engagement with the social and political changes of the two parallel periods with which she works. *Wives and Daughters* presents a society desperately seeking order in the midst

of perceived chaos—some members of that society clinging to old and inadequate ways of understanding the world, others actively seeking a new order, and still others responding with confusion and withdrawal.

Tracing the maturation of one young woman, Molly Gibson, *Wives and Daughters* takes as its subject the enormous changes disturbing English society. Molly is likable but unremarkable; her ordinariness, her utter normality, is an important part of Gaskell's strategy: it prevents the reader from explaining away Molly's dissatisfaction and confusion as the predictable result of an extraordinary woman's equally predictable conflict with the conventional mores of her society. Molly's dilemma—determining how to live the best life within a cruelly limiting society—is shared by *all* women, Gaskell suggests.

Many critics agree that *Wives and Daughters* falls somewhere within the tradition of the novel of manners,[4] but there is disagreement concerning just where within that tradition the novel belongs. Some say that *Wives and Daughters* establishes Gaskell as the Victorian heir to Jane Austen through its description of a world made stable by the general acceptance of social standards and of class distinctions (Wright 209-17), with individuals knowing how they are expected to behave and learning to fulfill social expectations (Pollard 227), whereas others see a stronger connection between Gaskell and Henry James, noting the irremediable tensions between the individuals and their society in *Wives and Daughters* (Craik 207-8 and Duthie 42). I would argue that the novel is far more ambiguous than either of these positions fully acknowledges: some elements of the society Gaskell describes are indeed orderly and stable, and some characters do uphold traditional class distinctions and social standards, but other elements of the society are in disorder—many characters are confused by the cultural changes they observe, some find themselves in conflict with established social standards, and several entirely reject old notions of rank. Most importantly, the spirit with which the heroine apparently—and it is only *apparently*—comes into accord with her society differs radically from that of the typical Austen heroine.

Placing *Wives and Daughters* within the tradition of the novel of manners of course assumes that there *is* such a tradition, an assumption Henry James made when he gave the tradition a name in 1866 and one that critics still make today, without seeming to realize that the genre, if indeed it is one, has never been fully defined (and perhaps never can be), as Barbara Brothers and Bege Bowers point out. . . . The fifth edition of the *Oxford Companion to English Literature* recognizes "epistolary novel," "fashionable novel," "historical novel," "memoir-novel," "oriental novel," and "sentiment, novel of," but has no entry for the novel of manners. This oversight is repeated by some literary handbooks, suggesting either that various handbook editors believe there is no such thing as the novel of manners or that the novel of manners is so well understood that it requires no definition (the latter possibility seems right for the *Oxford Companion,* which also excludes "novel," offering instead "novel, rise of the"). Nevertheless, critics speak of the "tradition" of the genre, as if that tradition were not a matter of dispute. In this essay, I use *novel of manners* to describe those fictional narratives that explore the shaping of individual character by social forces, the self expressing itself in some relation to the values of the society as embodied in its conventions, including but not limited to conversation, dress, and gesture. Gaskell's particular perspective on the extent to which social forces shape the self varies according to the subject's gender, with female characters generally experiencing more extreme dissonance with their society than do similarly placed male characters and therefore resorting to more varied and complex strategies for reconciling felt needs with social demands.

There are two distinct movements in *Wives and Daughters:* one that emphasizes the new possibilities opening for men as the result of shifts in the balance of power, and a second, or counter, movement that emphasizes the continuing restrictions on, the lack of possibilities for, women. The men that Gaskell depicts are to some extent able to shape their own lives, whereas the women must all learn to accommodate themselves to the shapes their lives are given by their relationships with men. Even though Gaskell did not invent the novel's title, the way it draws attention to women's relationships underscores the difficulties awaiting any young woman who hopes for autonomy and self-fulfillment. The contrast between the meanings of adulthood for men and for women is pointed: men are expected to move into the world as self-sufficient individuals, but women may move only from dependence on fathers to what is frequently a still more onerous dependence on husbands. The novel's title appears to define the only socially acceptable roles available to women (Lansbury 109), but the role the novel shows to be most important is the missing term of the title: "mothers," as Stoneman also notes (173). This absence is emblematic both of the absence of mothering that Molly experiences and of the erasure of the mother in the society Gaskell explores, absences that are of crucial significance to the novel's concern with manners.

I want to go back now to look more closely at Gaskell's focus on manners and at the values those manners reflect—the "hum and buzz of implication" of the complex culture Gaskell describes. Trilling says that the novel is born in reaction to snobbery, in an attempt to expose the truth hidden behind a society's carefully constructed illusion of appearances (203). In *Wives and Daughters,* more so than in any of her earlier novels, Gaskell is careful to draw attention to the gap between appearances and reality through dialogue that incorporates explicit commentary on shifting relationships between classes and on individual struggles either to identify with a particular class or to reject the values of the class to which the world assigns one. The longest speeches in the novel concern manners, in the sense of outward behavior, and they are made by the male characters and by the most intellectually limited female characters (Mrs. Gibson and the Misses Browning), all of whom advocate female submission to established social standards, adhering to the ideology of the "pleasing female" (Stoneman 173). . . .

One movement of the novel traces the rise of the middle classes and the decline of the aristocracy, a development important mostly for men. By novel's end, the aristocracy's influence has waned considerably, with only the most limited characters—all of them women—caring much about their doings. Osborne Hamley's fall from grace and eventual death are part of this thematic pattern. The eldest son of the local squire, Osborne in appearance and in tastes suggests a move upward from the squirearchy to the aristocracy, a move Gaskell portrays also as a feminization; he is interested in the land only as a source of wealth and of social position, finds dealing directly with the Hamley tenants distasteful, writes sentimental poetry, is "delicate" and fine in appearance and fastidious in his tastes (106). Osborne seems bred for idleness; when his allowance is cut and he is faced with the prospect of having to earn his own living, Osborne cannot think of a single skill that would earn him adequate money, a predicament that parallels the difficulties of women. Significantly, Osborne dies of an unspecified wasting disease—as does his mother, who shares his appearance and tastes—which seems a strain of that "idle women's illness" so common in Victorian novels. . . .

There is evidence in Gaskell's letters that she originally intended Squire Hamley to be a yeoman (no. 550), but she changed her mind, thereby altering the structure of the work, and made him a squire who is, nonetheless, yeomanlike in his love of the land, his lack of education, his total distrust of the city, and his insistence that the ancient order is the best, indeed the only entirely imaginable structure for society. Gaskell's decision to change the class of this character is revealing, as the shift enabled her to limit her attention to representatives of the different segments of those classes that ruled England both before the first Reform Act and after it. Squire Hamley reminds us of the traditional basis of power and status, the land, and his worsening economic situation and increasing confusion stand in direct contrast to the ascendancy and confidence of the new man, Robert Gibson, a propertyless professional representative of the class that became the source of political power after the Reform Act.

Of course, it is men only who are directly involved in these shifts of power: women remain disenfranchised, excluded from the public arena. This gender-based distinction makes women of the middle and upper classes especially suitable subjects for novels of manners, which generally investigate the domestic sphere, the domain of women. *Wives and Daughters* sharply contrasts the very different social roles of men and of women. Subtitled "An Every-Day Story," the novel gives a great deal of careful attention to what one does in everyday life, to how one fills one's days. The men of the novel, with the important exception of Osborne Hamley, are busy with useful work of some type, but the women are a different story; freed from domestic work by virtue of their privileged class (even the comparatively poor Brownings have a servant), prohibited by the mores of that same class from working for pay, the women have trouble finding anything to do, and therefore devote much of their time to analyzing behavior and speculating about feeling.[5] The story the novel tells of women's lives is far more radical than is the story woven from the men's lives, for the former encodes a social critique so far-reaching as to challenge the basis of the society Gaskell dissects. I think those critics who describe *Wives and Daughters* as more conservative and "less ideologically questioning" than Gaskell's earlier novels—who see Gaskell in her final book accepting "social creeds and institutions," to quote Shirley Foster's representative remark (176)—miss the significance of the doubled plot and theme, the clear separation of the sexes.

Much of the novel concerns the relationship of manners to class and the ways in which social class affects the individual life. Three characters—Hyacinth Gibson, Squire Hamley, and Lady Harriet Cumnor—say quite a lot about issues of class. Interestingly, these three people, with their widely divergent views, share a single audience: Molly Gibson, who is herself nearly classless because of her peculiar position as the motherless daughter of a country general practitioner. That Gaskell chose to make her central character the daughter of a general practitioner and planned to marry her to the scientific Roger Hamley draws our attention to the theme of professional accomplishments determining men's status in the new order to come. The medical man who preceded Gibson as the local g.p. was treated as an inferior by the county families, usually sent to eat in the kitchen with the servants when attending the Cumnors at the Towers, and generally ignored socially. When Gibson first arrives in Hollingford, it seems that he, too, will be relegated to a servant's role, but he is not; instead, he is frequently invited to dine at the Towers and treated as an equal by Lord Hollingford. The main reason for this treatment is that Gibson is a "man of science," to use Gaskell's term, not merely a medical hired hand, and Lord Hollingford has a great interest in science—in

fact, one of his dinner parties is described as a gathering of the "freemasonry" of science.

Another reason, unmentioned by Gaskell but certainly contributing to her characterization of Gibson, is the shift in medical men's status still working itself out in the first half of the nineteenth century. Until mid-century, medical men were not uniformly true professionals, because of the lack of widely shared standards, and they tended to fall into one of three main groups: surgeons who practiced obstetrics, frequently considered lower class because they worked with their hands; "consultants" who held appointments at London hospitals, made a great deal of money, and were certainly gentlemen by birth and education; and, in the middle, general practitioners, country physicians who often performed surgery and served as midwives as part of their practices. During the debates that carried over to mid-century, consultants several times tried to exclude general practitioners from the profession. There was considerable confusion about the social class of the country doctor: did he take his standing from his birth? His competence? His own achievements and education? On the whole, his social standing was ambiguous.

Molly, the daughter of a general practitioner whose origins are unknown but who has considerable personal polish and an admirable intellect, is unplaceable. Socially, she is clearly superior to the Misses Browning, the spinsters who represent the old middle classes, yet inferior to the Cumnors and even to the Hamleys; she and her father form their own class. Molly is invited to visit at Hamley Hall and at the Towers, in both cases first because the families like Mr. Gibson and then because they grow to care for Molly herself. Molly associates with, but is not of, the various classes described in the novel; she is permanently outside all such placing. Molly's ambiguous class standing is central to the novel's plot because an important part of her education is her observation, and either acceptance or rejection, of the differing codes of conduct of several classes. Feeling instinctively that Molly is not really one of them enables people to speak more openly to her than they might to one of their peers or to someone clearly superior or inferior in class. Also contributing to Molly's suitability as an audience are her youth and the sense that she might end up fitting in anywhere at all. Lady Harriet, for instance, seems to forget that Molly might consider herself a member of the same class as the Brownings, rudely discoursing on "that sort of person" to Molly. By novel's end, Molly sees clearly the multiple ways in which each established vantage point on the world serves to stifle the individual and to limit—artificially—possibilities for happiness. Molly is the character who most intensely experiences the disorder of the transitional period in which she lives. However, unlike Roger, who can go off to Africa and thereby escape the restrictions of social class,

Molly has no options for escape except, briefly, an illness that threatens to end her life entirely. . . .

Just as women's position in society remains static, so are women's manners portrayed as unchanging. The "freemasonry of science," with all that it symbolizes, is not open to women, who cannot hope that people will look beyond their manners in order to judge them on the basis of their achievements, as they would judge a Lord Hollingford, a Roger Hamley, or a Mr. Gibson. Because there are so few avenues of achievement open to them, women remain at the mercy of a stifling, dehumanizing social code. To violate this code, or even to *appear* to violate it, puts a woman outside her society entirely, where she cannot hope to survive. Given women's economic dependence on men, to make oneself ineligible for marriage by becoming the subject of scandal is to commit social and economic suicide if one is female. Gaskell is critical of the sexual double standard but seems unable, or unwilling, to imagine genuine changes.

Gaskell does, however, see clearly that the society in which Molly lives encourages dishonesty in women by reckoning their manners more important than their morals. In this way, Mrs. Gibson's basic flaw—her lack of a moral center, of a real self—is one that reflects the social training offered women of all classes. As Patsy Stoneman shrewdly points out, Mrs. Gibson's moral bankruptcy is the logical result of her dedication to the notion of the "pleasing female," an ideology into which she, like other women, has been carefully socialized (173-74). The surprise is not that Mrs. Gibson worships appearances but that some other women somehow manage to escape superficiality and to maintain inner selves. Whatever else we might say about her, Mrs. Gibson grasps the basic facts of the society that made her.

Molly, too, comes to understand these facts, although she refuses to be entirely the product of her society. In Molly's case, knowledge is symbolized by a wasting illness. She becomes progressively weaker, having fallen ill while visiting Hamley Hall after Mrs. Hamley's death, a visit marked by the strain of keeping up a false reserve toward Roger for the sake of appearances, and her father seems to doubt that she will survive the illness. Her illness, after which she is acknowledged to be a woman, no longer a girl, can be read as a response to her recognition of the severe limitations imposed on women, just as her earlier identification with men can be seen as an attempt to circumvent those as yet only half-perceived limits. We may also think of the illness as a process of infantile regression, signifying Molly's desire both for a reunion with her dead mother and for an escape from the rules that regulate adult womanhood. Her recovery, which is incomplete at the end of the book, suggests an acceptance of the limitations and a willingness to try for whatever measure of happiness may be possible; it

suggests also a turning away from the dead mother toward her more acceptable adult substitute: the man that Molly loves, Roger Hamley.

The fact that the novel is unfinished—Gaskell wrote *Wives and Daughters* as a serial for the monthly *Cornhill Magazine* and died before completing the final installment—is peculiarly appropriate. Gaskell's text breaks off with Roger's setting off to complete his research in Africa, hoping to return to ask Molly to marry him; at this point, however, no understanding has been reached between them, and Molly does not know Roger loves her. Although her editor, Frederick Greenwood, wrote a conclusion for *Wives and Daughters* in which he told how Gaskell planned to end the novel, using her letters and conversations as a guide and making it clear that Gaskell intended for Molly and Roger to marry, the lack of closure is more consistent with the rest of this novel than any formal closure would be. We feel certain that the men of the novel will evolve new and useful ways of dealing with their society, and will come into harmony with it because that society will be of their own creation. Women, however, will remain enclosed by the one social institution that most directly affects them—marriage—and will have no power to change its public meaning. Continuing conflict with their society can only destroy those women who engage in it, but complete acceptance of that society has the same result: three of the women who fully accept social conventions—Mrs. Gibson, Mrs. Hamley, and Lady Cumnor—suffer wasting but unspecified illnesses much like the one from which Molly is recuperating when the novel breaks off. There seems to be no way for women to achieve actual happiness within the confines of their society, and this social problem seems insoluble.

Notes

[1] See, for example, Millett, 341-42. . . .

[2] Patsy Stoneman alone among critics writing on Gaskell offers a model for reading her novels as part of an integrated whole; most critics divide Gaskell's works into social problem or "lady novelist" categories.

[3] Angus Easson makes a similar point, 187.

[4] See Craik (211) and Pollard (225).

[5] Spacks also notes this, 88-89.

Works Cited

Brothers, Barbara and Bege K. Bowers. "Introduction: What Is a Novel of Manners?" *Reading and Writing Women's Lives.* Ed. Brothers and Bowers. Ann Arbor: UMI Research Press, 1990.

Craik, W. A. *Elizabeth Gaskell and the English Provincial Novel*. London: Methuen, 1975.

Duthie, Enid L. *The Themes of Elizabeth Gaskell*. Totowa, N. J.: Rowman, 1980.

Easson, Angus. *Elizabeth Gaskell*. London: Routledge, 1979.

Faber, Richard. *Proper Stations: Class in Victorian Fiction*. London: Faber, 1971.

Foster, Shirley. *Victorian Women's Fiction: Marriage, Freedom, and the Individual*. Totowa, N.J.: Barnes; London: Croom, 1985.

Gaskell, Elizabeth. *The Letters of Mrs. Gaskell*. Ed. J. A. V. Chapple and Arthur Pollard. Cambridge: Harvard UP, 1979.

————. *Wives and Daughters: An Every-Day Story*. 1866. Ed. Frank Glover Smith. Middlesex: Penguin, 1975.

James, Henry. "Mrs. Gaskell." In *Notes and Reviews*. 1921. Freeport, N. Y.: Books for Libraries, 1968. 153-59.

Lansbury, Coral. *Elizabeth Gaskell*. Twayne's English Authors Series 371. Boston: Twayne, 1984.

Millett, Fred B., ed. *A History of English Literature* [by William Vaughn Moody and Robert Morss Lovett]. 8th ed. New York: Scribner's, 1964.

Pollard, Arthur. *Mrs Gaskell: Novelist and Biographer*. Manchester: Manchester UP, 1965.

Spacks, Patricia Meyer. *The Female Imagination*. New York: Knopf, 1975.

Stoneman, Patsy. *Elizabeth Gaskell*. Key Women Writers. Bloomington: Indiana UP, 1987.

Trilling, Lionel. "Manners, Morals, and the Novel." *The Liberal Imagination: Essays on Literature and Society*. 1950. Garden City, N. Y.: Anchor-Doubleday, 1957. 199-215.

Wright, Edgar. *Mrs. Gaskell: The Basis for Reassessment*. London: Oxford UP, 1965.

THE AMERICAN NOVEL OF MANNERS

James W. Tuttleton

SOURCE: "The Sociological Matrix of the Novel of Manners," in *The Novel of Manners in America*, The University of North Carolina Press, 1972, pp. 7-19.

[*In the excerpt below, Tuttleton recounts and refutes claims that the novel of manners is not a viable form in American literature.*]

The charge that the novel is dead, so often heard in the literary criticism of the 1950s, is today a dead issue.

There is one type of novel, though, which is generally held to be deader than usual—especially in this country. And when, in our recent criticism, writers have reflected on the death of the American novel, they have usually meant a certain kind of novel—the American novel of manners. The obituaries pronounced by our critics upon this kind of novel are primarily oversimplifications of a point of view expressed by Lionel Trilling in his provocative essay "Manners, Morals, and the Novel." . . . Trilling's description of "manners" is of such interest that it deserves to be quoted in full:

> What I understand by manners, then, is a culture's hum and buzz of implication. I mean the whole evanescent context in which its explicit statements are made. It is that part of a culture which is made up of half-uttered or unutterable expressions of value. They are hinted at by small actions, sometimes by the arts of dress or decoration, sometimes by tone, gesture, emphasis, or rhythm, sometimes by the words that are used with a special frequency or a special meaning. They are the things that separate them from the people of another culture. They make the part of a culture which is not art, or religion, or morals, or politics, and yet it relates to all these highly formulated departments of culture. It is modified by them; it modifies them; it is generated by them; it generates them. In this part of culture assumption rules, which is often so much stronger than reason.[1]

I find this a brilliant observation about the content of the novels of manners considered in this study. But let me declare at the outset that I do not consider satisfactory some of the critical observations which have been inferred from it—namely, that American society has no hum and buzz; that we have never had in this country a hierarchy of social classes; that we have never had and do not now have a variety of manners and mores—those small actions, arts, gestures, emphases, and rhythms that express value; that, consequently, the novel of manners never really established itself in America; and that our best writers are therefore idea-oriented symbolic romancers. When Richard Chase claims in *The American Novel and Its Tradition* that American "novels" are inferior to our prose romances and that only second- or third-rate writers spend time on novels, he means that our novels of manners and their authors are inferior. Are we compelled to regard only our romances as great books? In view of the extraordinary achievement of *The Portrait of a Lady, The American, The House of Mirth,* and *The Great*

Gatsby, it is remarkable that some of our critics have concluded that "we do not have the novel that touches significantly on society, on manners."[2]

To understand this issue of the relation of the American novel to our society—it has had a long and controversial history—requires of us assent to the proposition that, as James somewhere remarked, "kinds" are the very life of literature, and truth and strength come from the complete recognition of them. We need also to be aware of some aspects of the history of the American romance and of a special kind of American novel . . . —the American novel of manners.

Dr. Johnson once observed that one of the maxims of civil law is that definitions are hazardous. This maxim holds true in the field of literary criticism. Although no "kind" or genre of literature has been more difficult to define than the novel of manners, formulating an acceptable definition of it is the first order of business. Without a satisfactory definition, misunderstanding rather than enlightenment is the result; and along with misunderstanding usually comes irrelevant arguments about whether America is capable of producing a novel of manners.

To formulate a definition of the American novel of manners, let us regard as polarities the concept of the individual and the concept of the group, of society. Neither of these extremes can of course be the focus of the novel. Yet every novel locates itself somewhere between these extremes. If the novel deals largely with the self, personal experience, or the individual consciousness, the result will be a work which gravitates toward autobiography or "lyric or informal philosophy." If the self is refined out of existence in favor of social documentations, the result is history or chronicle. As Mark Schorer puts it: "The problem of the novel has always been to distinguish between these two, the self and society, and at the same time to find suitable structures that will present them together. . . . The novel seems to exist at a point where we can recognize the intersection of the stream of social history and the stream of the soul. This intersection gives the form its dialectical field, provides the source of those generic tensions that make it possible at all."[3] Near the center of this convergence, where the streams of the self and of social history intersect, is the novel of manners. It is probably not amiss to say that the form emphasizes social history more than lyric, confessional, or autobiographical statement.

Perhaps a useful test of the definition of the novel of manners—to borrow a term from Irving Howe's definition of the political novel—is its "inclusiveness," rather than its narrowness, for narrow definitions have provoked some of the controversies which always attend a discussion of this genre. If we are inclusive, we may define the novel of manners as a novel in which the closeness of manners and character is of itself interesting enough to justify an examination of their relationship. By a novel of manners I mean a novel in which the manners, social customs, folkways, conventions, traditions, and mores of a given social group at a given time and place play a dominant role in the lives of fictional characters, exert control over their thought and behavior, and constitute a determinant upon the actions in which they are engaged, and in which these manners and customs are detailed realistically—with, in fact, a premium upon the exactness of their representation.

The representation of manners may be without authorial prejudice, in which case the novelist merely concerns himself, without comment, with his society's hum and buzz of implication. But more often the portrait of manners is put to the service of an ideological argument. The center of the novel of manners, that is, may be an idea or an issue—for example, the idea of social mobility, of class conflict, of professional ambition, of matchmaking, of divorce. But if, in the development of such "ideas," significant attention is paid to a realistic notation of the customs and conventions of the society in which these ideas arise and are acted out, then we are dealing with a novel of manners. That a novel is "about" a subject does not necessarily disqualify it as a novel of manners. Jane Austen's *Pride and Prejudice,* for example, is "about" the problem of finding suitable husbands for a household of girls; and Scott Fitzgerald's *The Great Gatsby* is "about" the failure of the American dream. But enough attention is directed to the traditions of the early nineteenth-century English middle class, in the one, and to jazz-age manners and mores, in the other, to justify our examination of both of them as novels of manners. A useful extension of this definition, therefore, would be to say that the analysis of manners yields, from the point of view of this definition, profitable insights into the meaning of the novel without any distortion of its total significance.

Since the novel of manners inclines more toward social history than toward subjective psychologies or autobiography, it is, in a fundamental sense, sociologically oriented. That is, the novelist of manners is in some sense a "sociologist" who manipulates his data in terms of a narrative rather than a scientific or "logical" framework. This fact need not prejudice our attitude toward the novelist of manners or the genre created by his observation and notation. Many good novels survive the freight of social documentation intrinsic to the form. The influence of Comte's positivism is clearly evident in George Eliot's best studies of manners in midland England, yet we are never bothered by it. With the rise of sociology as a "science," in fact, novelists discovered a new set of tools for dissecting man in society. Many worthwhile novels have in fact major characters who are sociologists, anthropologists, or students of these disciplines—for example, Edith Wharton's Ralph Marvell of *The Custom of the Country;* Sinclair Lewis's Carol Kennicott of *Main Street,* who studied sociology at college; William Dean Howells's protagonist in *The Vacation of the Kelwyns,* a professor of historical sociology at Harvard; and Marquand's Malcolm Bryant, a sociologist in *Point of No Return* who has come to Clyde, Massachusetts, to analyze its social structure.

If we look to sociology for a systematic analysis of society, we soon find ourselves dealing with five areas of social experience which may be described as follows: "Firstly, a set of social conventions and taboos regarding relations between the sexes, between parents and children, as well as people's behavior in the company of their fellowmen. Secondly, a set of commonly, or at any rate widely accepted ethical standards. Thirdly, a set of religious and philosophical beliefs, or more often a miscellany of such beliefs, concerning the position and role of man in the universe. Fourthly, a given type of economic organization, with a greater or lesser emphasis on the importance of material possessions. Lastly, the political structure of a given community, embodying certain conceptions of government, of the individual's position in the state, and of international relations."[4]

The first category, "a set of social conventions and taboos," is of course the most important area of human experience for the novel of manners. For manners represent the expression, in positive and negative form, of the assumptions of society at a given time and place. Dramatic violations of commonly held ethical values are also endemic to the novel of manners. (Sometimes morals and manners are so inextricably mixed that we cannot tell whether characters act as they do because they think it is morally right or because it is socially proper. And in the novels of Henry James we cannot always be sure that there is any difference.) From the sociological point of view, in fact, a system of ethics merely represents the crystallization of the folkways of a society. Religious or philosophical beliefs are less important to the novel of manners, but if religious or philosophical assumptions did not subtly affect the behavior of fictional characters, the novel of manners would be other than it is. Economic considerations also play a less significant role in the development of the novel of manners, though wealth is often a particularly useful device for the freedom it provides a novelist in dramatizing certain social values. Whenever religious, philosophical, or economic "ideas" tend to be blown up out of proportion, the novel of manners becomes something else—the propaganda novel advocating religious opinions, philosophical systems, or economic dogmas. This point also applies to political considerations in the novel: if they become obtrusive, not merely a part of the fabric of the fictive social world,

the novel becomes something other than a novel of manners—it becomes a radical or political novel.

To put it another way, the novel of manners is primarily concerned with social conventions as they impinge upon character. These other concerns are less central to it, but they help to define the ethos of the society portrayed, they provide a body of assumptions about experience which underlie its social code, and they affect the thought and behavior of fictional characters. To return to the analogy offered by Mark Schorer, as long as the impulse of the novelist does not push him too far toward propaganda or the extreme of chronicle or history, I see him as writing the novel of manners. . . .

"Society," as used in this study, ordinarily refers to the structure of "classes," cliques, or groups by which specific American communities are organized. More particularly, "society" may refer to whatever group is presumed by the author to constitute the class defining itself through "polite manners," such as the commercial aristocracy of Edith Wharton's Old New York or the Brahmin patriciate of Marquand's New England. In a novel of manners, the illusion of society may be generated in two ways. First, the sense of society may be created by a vast number of characters who sprawl and swarm across the printed page and who, by very mass and number, give the novel the illusion of social density, of that "substantiality" characteristic of actual society. Novelists like Balzac, Proust, Thackeray, and O'Hara develop the illusion of society by this documentary technique. On the other hand, society may be merely felt as an abstract force; that is, the novel may deal with only a few individuals who embody various social attitudes. Howells was this kind of novelist—he liked to focus on three or four characters whose conflicting manners stand for the values of the social classes to which they belong.

What is important to this genre is that there be for analysis groups with recognizable and differentiable manners and conventions. These groups need not be stable, in the sense of enduring for centuries (e.g., the English or French hereditary aristocracy). They need not even be typical of the general culture of a particular country (e.g., James's American colony in Rome). For the novel of manners it is necessary only that there be groups large enough to have developed a set of differing conventions which express their values and permanent enough for the writer's notation of their manners. Frequently the most successful novels of manners treat classes which have existed briefly or during transitional periods when one group is in the process of decay while another is rising to supplant it. Hence it need not be assumed that the novel of manners features only an aristocratic class in conflict with the bourgeoisie; any stratified groups will do. In America, Cable found such groups in New Orleans; Ellen

Glasgow in Richmond; J. P. Marquand in New England; Louis Auchincloss in New York; John O'Hara in the mid-Pennsylvania coal district; and Edith Wharton in New York. To deny the reality of these distinctive groups as "social classes" is largely to miss the point of the social analysis contained in the fiction of these writers. Their fiction suggests that, once and for all, the criterion for distinguishing the novel of manners is execution—what James would have called "treatment"—rather than subject matter.

The novel of manners in America has not always been a popular genre with our writers. And any discussion of this form must deal with two objections which frequently attend it. One has to do with the alleged superiority of symbolic romances over the realistic novel. In part, this objection . . . is an extension of the old theory of a hierarchy of literary genres. The other objection is based on the claim that America lacks the social differences which are the sine qua non of the novel of manners. Can the novel of manners flourish in a democratic country which supposedly lacks adequate social density and a clearly stratified and stable class structure? A surprisingly large number of serious novelists and critics of the past century and a half have contended that American social experience is and has been too meager and limited to nourish a fiction that portrays men involved in the social world and perhaps even establishing through it their personal identities. A concomitant argument is often put this way: The absence of clear and stable class lines prohibits a meaningful portrayal of American manners—everybody has middle-class manners; without a diversity of manners based on class distinctions there can be no contrasts in the values, customs, or traditions of fictional characters; and without such contrasts, there can be no intrinsic interest, conflict, or "solidity of specification" in the portrait of American society. As W. M. Frohock has ironically phrased it: "At first glance the syllogism seems unattackable: only a firmly (but not too firmly) stratified society can furnish the materials of which novels are made; the society of the United States is not firmly stratified; therefore the novel in the United States is out of the question. And the corollary is that the best we can hope for is romances."[5]

Both of these objections, in their earliest form, appear as a general criticism of what was once called "the poverty for the artist of native American materials." This issue is no longer as relevant as it was a century ago, but if we know what some of our writers and critics have felt about American society, we may be better able to understand the dilemma they saw themselves as confronting.

James Fenimore Cooper was the first major novelist to indict America on the grounds of its cultural poverty. His observation is my point of departure because he first isolated the issue, and he articulated it so fully

that most subsequent references to America's social thinness are mere repetitions, mostly thoughtless, of views Cooper presented in 1828:

> The second obstacle against which American literature has to contend [the first was the pirating and copyright problem], is in the poverty of materials. There is scarcely an ore which contributes to the wealth of the author, that is found, here, in veins as rich as in Europe. There are no annals for the historian; no follies (beyond the most vulgar and commonplace) for the satirist; no manners for the dramatist; no obscure fictions for the writer of romance; no gross and hardy offences against decorum for the moralist; nor any of the rich artificial auxiliaries of poetry. The weakest hand can extract a spark from the flint, but it would baffle the strength of a giant to attempt kindling a flame with a pudding-stone. I very well know there are theorists who assume that the society and institutions of this country are, or ought to be, particularly favourable to novelties and variety. But the experience of one month, in these States, is sufficient to show any observant man the falsity of their position. The effect of a promiscuous assemblage any where, is to create a standard of deportment; and great liberty permits every one to aim its attainment. I have never seen a nation so much alike in my life, as the people of the United States, and what is more, they are not only like each other, but they are remarkably like that which common sense tells them they ought to resemble. No doubt, traits of character that are a little peculiar, without, however, being either very poetical, or very rich, are to be found in remote districts; but they are rare, and not always happy exceptions.[6]

This passage, expressing Cooper's characteristic ambivalence toward our "national conformity," is suspect in the very rhetorical extravagance of his description of our social dullness. The fact is that the example of his own fiction belies the assumptions here expressed. *Home As Found* and *The Pioneers,* for example, are rich in the depiction of native manners, national follies, and social offenses. But it cannot be escaped that Cooper *believed* that the character of American society prevented his writing the *roman de moeurs,* even though he wanted to. Under the inspiration of Scott, therefore, he took his characters out of the drawing room and trailed them into the woods. It should not be forgotten, however, that even in the Leatherstocking series, the real issues are sometimes social issues masked in the adventure of the romance genre. In *The Pathfinder,* for example, Cooper's real purpose is to explore the question of whether a man of the hunter class (however much a "nature's gentleman") can find settlement happiness married to a girl whose manners have been polished by real ladies—the wives of the garrison officers.

But Cooper was not alone in pointing out the deficiencies in American society for the novelist. In "Some

Reflections on American Manners" in *Democracy in America,* Alexis de Tocqueville, one of the most perceptive foreign critics of American ways, remarked in 1835 that in a new democratic society, the forms of social experience are so transitory that even if a code of good breeding were formulated no one could enforce it. "Every man therefore behaves after his own fashion, and there is always a certain incoherence in the manners of such times, because they are molded upon the feelings and notions of each individual rather than upon an ideal model proposed for general imitation." The absence of an authoritative code might make for more sincerity and openness in the American character, but Tocqueville felt that "the effect of democracy is not exactly to give men any particular manners, but to prevent them from having manners at all."[7] This alleged absence of observable manners, however beneficial to the political citizen, Cooper regarded as fatal to the novelist because it deprived him of the raw material of his social portrait.

Some of their contemporaries, however, argued that it was an easier task to draw the portrait of American manners than Cooper and Tocqueville admitted. Social witnesses of the stature of William Cullen Bryant, John Neal, and William Hickling Prescott argued that American society, for all its apparent formlessness, still offered a rich field for fiction. As Bryant observed in his 1825 review of Catharine Maria Sedgwick's *Redwood,* American social novels do not need the European class of idle aristocrats who "have leisure for that intrigue, those plottings and counter plottings, which are necessary to give a sufficient degree of action and eventfulness to the novel of real life."[8] Though lacking a class with "polite manners," he argued, the annals of our people "are abundantly fertile in interesting occurrences, for all the purposes of the novelists." Since "distinctions of rank, and the amusements of elegant idleness, are but the surface of society," the American novelist is uniquely capable of dramatizing character through the representation of different manners. "Whoever will take the pains to pursue this subject into its particulars," Bryant observed, "will be surprised at the infinite variety of forms of character, which spring up under the institutions of our country." Bryant went on to suggest the "innumerable and diverse influences upon the manners and temper of our people": the variety of religious creeds, geographical differences (North and South, East and West, seacoast and interior, province and metropolis), diversifications in manners produced by massive immigrations, and the like. "When we consider all these innumerable differences of character, native and foreign," he concluded, "this infinite variety of pursuits and objects, this endless diversity of change of fortunes, and behold them gathered and grouped into one vast assemblage in our own country, we shall feel little pride in the sagacity or the

skill of that native author, who asks for a richer or a wider field of observation."[9]

Put in this way, nineteenth-century America does seem to have been an immensely rich source of social materials for the novelist. Bryant makes us wonder seriously whether Cooper's social vision was as perspicuous as we might wish. I do not mean to say that early American novelists did not face formidable obstacles. They surely did. But the problem of the "materials" was less crucial than the artist's felt need for those "romantic associations" which these materials could not provide. By this I mean that some of our early novelists seriously resented the notion that fiction ought to deal with the actualities of American life. A strictly realistic portrait of men's ordinary lives was held inferior because it made "few demands upon the imagination." Writing novels based on everyday actualities was merely imitating, unimaginatively, what men did. And what men did in this country, in the early years of the republic, was mainly a variety of disagreeable things incident to clearing and settling the country.

More and more our writers fixated on the need for "romantic settings" to evoke aesthetic emotions. Isaac Mitchell even went to the extreme of creating a medieval castle for Long Island in his *Alonzo and Melissa* (1804). "Romance" and "novel" cannot be defined too precisely, but the differences between them were so important to early American writers that to understand the relation of the American novel of manners to American fiction, we would do well to consider them.

The basic differences, as they develop in the eighteenth and nineteenth centuries, are loosely as follows. The novel was held to be a "truthful" representation of ordinary reality; it detailed with satisfactory realism the actualities of the social world. The romance, on the other hand, less committed to the realities of ordinary life, sought to leave "the powers of fancy at liberty to expatiate through the boundless realms of invention."[10] In the romance, in other words, invention rather than observation or description was valued. The novel emphasized character as revealed in everyday life—in the religious, business, political, moral, and social relationships of people. The romance, however, was concerned very little with the interaction of men in society; in fact, in the romance social relations were often so thinly represented that the characters seem less complex, less rounded, and therefore less credible as "real people." In the romance, the representation of character often resulted in abstractions or idealizations of social types—gentlemen, heroes, villains, soldiers, aristocrats. In the novel, extremes of characterization were avoided in favor of multidimensional or rounded characters, most of them drawn from the middle class.

The novel usually did not have a complicated plot, heroic action, or improbabilities. Plotting in the romance, however, was often elaborately worked out on the basis of coincidence or chance and was, if not incredible, often implausible. In many respects, the romance extended into prose some of the characteristics of the medieval verse romance, from which it derived not only its name but its tendency toward the "poetic," the legendary, and the highly imaginative, wonderful scenes of the distant past or the strange and faraway. Since it is "less committed to the immediate rendition of reality than the novel," as Chase has observed, "the romance will more freely veer toward mythic, allegorical, and symbolic forms."[11]

Clara Reeve's early history of prose fiction, *The Progress of Romance,* defined what in 1785 was understood to be the nature of the novel:

> The Novel is a picture of real life and manners, and of the time in which it is written. . . . The Novel gives a familiar relation of such things, as pass every day before our eyes, such as may happen to our friend, or to ourselves; and the perfection of it, is to represent every scene, in so easy and natural a manner, and to make them appear so probable, as to deceive us into a persuasion (at least while we are reading) that all is real, until we are affected by the joys or distresses, of the persons in the story, as if they were our own.[12]

This definition will not of course do any more. It stands as a generally reliable definition of the novel of manners, though, except for the claim that the novel must deal with the time in which it is written. There is no reason why a novel of manners reflecting all of these qualities may not be laid in the past, say (like *Waverley*) "sixty years since."

Notes

[1] Trilling, "Manners, Morals, and the Novel," in his *The Liberal Imagination* (Garden City, N. Y., 1950), pp. 200-201.

[2] Chase, *American Novel and Its Tradition,* (Garden City, N. Y., 1957), pp. 157-59; Trilling, "Manners, Morals, and the Novel," p. 207.

[3] Mark Schorer, "Foreword: Self and Society," in *Society and Self in the Novel: English Institute Essays, 1955* (New York, 1956), pp. viii-ix.

[4] W. Witte, "The Sociological Approach to Literature," *Modern Language Review* 36 (1951): 87-88.

[5] W. M. Frohock, *Strangers to This Ground,* (Dallas, 1961), p. 28.

[6] James Fenimore Cooper, *Notions of the Americans, Picked Up by a Travelling Bachelor,* ed. Robert E. Spiller, 2 vols. (New York, 1963), 2:108-9.

[7] Alexis de Tocqueville, *Democracy in America,* ed. Phillips Bradley, 2 vols. (New York, 1958), 2:229-30.

[8] William Cullen Bryant, review of *Redwood* by Catherine M. Sedgwick, *North American Review* 20 (April 1825); reprinted in *William Cullen Bryant: Representative Selections,* ed. Tremaine McDowell (New York, 1935), pp. 182-83.

[9] Ibid.

[10] Horace Walpole, "*The Castle of Otranto,*" in *Shorter Novels: Eighteenth Century,* ed. Philip Henderson (London, 1930), p. 102.

[11] Chase, *American Novel and Its Tradition,* p. 13.

[12] Clara Reeve, *The Progress of Romance,* Facsimile Text Society, ser. 1, vol. 4 (1785; reprint ed. New York, 1930), p. 111.

Lionel Trilling on the American novel of manners (1947):

[The] novel in America diverges from its classic intention, which . . . is the investigation of the problem of reality beginning in the social field. The fact is that American writers of genius have not turned their minds to society. . . . In America in the nineteenth century, Henry James was alone in knowing that to scale the moral and aesthetic heights in the novel one had to use the ladder of social observation.

There is a famous passage in James's life of Hawthorne in which James enumerates the things which are lacking to give the American novel the thick social texture of the English novel—no state; barely a specific national name; no sovereign; no court; no aristocracy; no church; no clergy; no army; no diplomatic service; no country gentlemen; no palaces; no castles; no manors; no old country houses; no parsonages; no thatched cottages; no ivied ruins; no cathedrals; no great universities; no public schools; no political society; no sporting class—no Epsom, no Ascot! That is, no sufficiency of means for the display of a variety of manners, no opportunity for the novelist to do his job of searching out reality, not enough complication of appearance to make the job interesting. Another great American novelist of very different temperament had said much the same thing some decades before: James Fenimore Cooper found that American manners were too simple and dull to nourish the novelist.

Lionel Trilling, in The Liberal Imagination: Essays on Literature and Society, *Harcourt Brace Jovanovich, 1979.*

Gordon Milne

SOURCE: "The Beginnings," in *The Sense of Society: A History of the American Novel of Manners,* Fairleigh Dickinson University Press, 1977, pp. 19-42.

[*In the following essay, Milne explores the development of the American novel of manners from the late eighteenth century to the Civil War, examining the works of H. H. Brackenridge, James Fenimore Cooper, Catharine Maria Sedgwick, John Pendleton Kennedy, and John Esten Cooke.*]

The American novel of manners originates at the end of the eighteenth century, at the time when the novel in general began to take hold in America. H. H. Brackenridge's *Modern Chivalry* (1792-1815) stands as a replica, in a very rudimentary sense, of the work of his English contemporary, Jane Austen. This many-volumed affair, a loose imitation of *Don Quixote* in its detailing the adventures of its hero, Captain Farrago, and his servant Teague O'Regan, achieves its importance primarily as a vigorous satire on the customs of the America of Brackenridge's era. In his survey of both the backwoods (of Pennsylvania) and the cities (Philadelphia and Washington), Brackenridge comments frankly on a number of aspects of American society.

His targets include matters of politics (whiskey settles elections in the back countries, business interests, in the cities), the medical profession (which is filled with quack doctors), the law (which is filled with pedantic and/or corrupt lawyers), and the social swing (bogtrotter Teague O'Regan, cuts a swath at a President's levee in Washington). About these matters Brackenridge writes in a style that is for the most part witty and entertaining, intermingles classical allusion and racy diction in an easy manner, and neatly maintains his lightly scoffing stance.

Modern Chivalry does not really qualify as a novel of manners, however, for, aside from its "social scene" focus and satiric method, it lacks the components of the form. Indeed, it barely qualifies as a novel. Brackenridge is really concerned with presenting a series of essays on an assortment of topics, and his picaresque adventure pattern only partially conceals the "essayizing" and does not convert the work into a sustained piece of fiction.

A forerunner Brackenridge may be, but it seems more accurate to call his successor, James Fenimore Cooper, the first genuine—or almost genuine—American novelist of manners. Cooper's reputation is based, to be sure, on his creation of the archetypal American romance, the Leatherstocking saga, but a number of his novels fall into the "social criticism" category and, as such, are close to the manners genre. One does well to remember that his first novel, *Precaution* (1820), was

a story of English high society, and that later works like *Homeward Bound* (1838), *Home As Found* (1838), and the Littlepage Manuscript series stress a social thesis, the significant role of the landed gentry class. Even in the Leatherstocking tales one can observe Cooper defending the "patroon" aristocracy at the expense of a leveling democracy, assigning to them a place at the top of the social-and-political ladder as "wise" leaders. Much of his work, as a whole or in part, describes—one should really say "glamorizes"—their way of life. . . .

It is in the Littlepage trilogy—*Satanstoe* (1845), *The Chainbearer* (1845), and *The Redskins* (1846)—that Cooper most precisely hews to the manners line. The three novels are intended, in the first place, as a social history, a defense of the landed gentry as representing the ideal of the gentleman, who will promote the law and order that exemplify American democracy at its best. The Littlepages and the Mordaunts, colonial gentry of English ancestry (those of Dutch descent rank a little below), are at the forefront, seen as they found an estate in the then unsettled northern New York woods. Almost immediately, however, the Littlepage-Mordaunt security is threatened by leveling demagogues, as personified by the tribe of Newcomes and by Aaron Thousandacres, a believer in "unrestrained" democracy. The issue is brought to a head in the antirent wars, which serve as the background to *The Redskins;* in these the "levelers" refuse to pay rent to the landowners, insisting that every man should be allowed to possess whatever land he wants or needs. Cooper, throughout the series, has taken an opposing view. The Littlepage class exhibits a democratic spirit (e.g., Mordaunt Littlepage's recognition of the poor but perceptive chainbearer, Andries Coejemans, as a gentleman and his equal) but refuses to carry "democracy" to the free-for-all extreme. The landowners deserve, as Cooper sees it, their legitimately obtained possessions. Moreover, they deserve the highest position in the American social structure—owed to them, not on the basis of wealth and social grace, but as a reward for virtue and talent—and they will accept this position "with Christian humility and deep submission of the self to the moral laws of the universe." Cooper argues vehemently, as Donald Ringe points out, that "a social organization is after all but a reflection of the moral principles upon which it is based."[1]

In the course of the trilogy Cooper instructs the reader about a number of social issues: the role of the landed proprietor, cultural differences between England and America, American class distinctions, and so on. Freely mixing the social commentary with the adventure-love story plots, he outlines a "chronicle of manners" (the label he himself applies in his preface to *Satanstoe*—adding that "every such has a certain value"), one filled with reference to customs and habits in various social spheres.

Satanstoe, in particular, is given over to a portrayal of the way of life of New York's colonial aristocracy, providing, along with this, comparisons among the colonies (e.g., New York vs. New England) and among people of different racial strains (English vs. Dutch), and affording glimpses of other classes and of special types (the Negro, the Indian) as well. The opening sequences of the novel establish this sort of picture, as the narrator, Corny Littlepage, carefully "places" himself for the reader: "We happened to be in a part of Westchester in which were none of the very large estates." The Littlepages, one learns, belong to the "haute bourgeoisie," located between the aristocracy and the higher classes of yeomanry; they have a very adequate establishment at Satanstoe, not to mention the 40,000 acres in the North that will become the estate of "Ravensnest," and the male members of the family have served in the Assembly and the militia and are "well connected." Corny Littlepage has been brought up in a genteel and comfortable environment, first tutored by the Reverend Thomas Worden, rector of St. Jude's—and the American version of the English hunting parson type—then attending Nassau Hall. A sociable atmosphere prevails at Satanstoe, witnessed on the occasions of the visits of Colonel Van Valkenburgh, when hot flip facilitates the conversation, encouraging talk about cockfights and horse racing, and even about religion (when a man is really good, religion only does him harm, says the Colonel). Contrasts are made between the solid but stolid Dutch and the more graceful English-descended Americans, who are less averse to "education" and therefore more informed and polished.

The jolly country living is paralleled in New York City, as Corny Littlepage and Dirck Van Valkenburgh find out as they pay a visit to relatives there. Stopping en route at a country inn, they partake of a lavish dinner of ham, potatoes, boiled eggs, beefsteak, pickles, cole slaw, apple pie, and cider, hearty and appetizing fare, if less elaborate than the turtle soup and oysters they will have at urban banquets to come. In New York the provincials take note of town and country differences, of how, for example, Aunt Legge sups at half past eight, a little later "than my mother, as being more fashionable and genteel." Aunt Legge always dresses for dinner, too, even though she may dine on a cold dumpling. Dinner at the Mordaunts' is even more formal, involving many courses, a removal of the cloth, a series of toasts, and a separation of the ladies and the gentlemen, and we are made aware of "that peculiar air of metropolitan superiority" that strikes the "provincial ignorance" of Corny.

Cooper obviously enjoys describing "old New York," still a relatively small town, where people walk rather than ride, and where everyone participates in the "Pinkster," the "great Saturnalia" of the blacks, featuring sideshows and the drinking of "white wine" (buttermilk). Various social usages are noted: the servant-

companion relationship among the upper classes, the vogue for "things French among us," the habit of addressing the British soldiers quartered in the city as "Mr." rather than by their titles ("such things never occurring in the better circles"), and the interest in the drama, spurred on by the garrison of British soldiers, who perform Addison's *Cato* and Farquhar's *The Beaux Stratagem.*

Cooper then turns his attention to the "inland" city of Albany, its inhabitants and their customs. A more relaxed and informal pattern prevails in Albany, partly because of the town's location in the "interior," says the author, and partly because most of the people are of Dutch rather than English descent and thus more free and easy, perfectly willing to condone a twenty-year-old "man" indulging in the sport of sledding on the town's hills, or robbing, as a prank, a family of its supper. Rector Worden one observes, looks down on the Albany Dutch "in a very natural, metropolitan sort of way," preferring the company of the English officers, a more sophisticated group. They—and the English Americans—would not be inclined to patronize the fortune teller Mother Doortje, as do the less worldly Dutch. If Jason Newcome proves an exception, he, it must be remembered, is a New Englander rather than a New Yorker, and indeed of the lower middle class, and, as such, one who "had not much notion of the fitness of things in matters of taste."

When the novel's scene shifts for a final time, to the remote northern settlements, a strong sense of "locale" is imparted to the reader again. As the group of principals depart from Albany for the backwoods, the girls assume veils of green (as protective coloring), and the men put on buckskin (with the exceptions of Jason Newcome and Mr. Worden, the latter keeping to his clerical garb). Now, too, the cast of characters includes surveyors, chainbearers, and Indian guides, and the manner of living begins to verge on the primitive. To be sure, the loghouse dwelling into which the principals settle has "five apartments," and is a forerunner of the one-day-to-be provincial Littlepage "estate" of Ravensnest.

The author's handling of setting does much to authenticate the social background of *Satanstoe.* The pleasant pictures of the comfortable but not lavish country home of the Littlepages and of the more elegant town house of the Mordaunts suggest their class and role. A strong feeling of local color permeates the New York City scenes, with landmarks like Wall Street, Trinity Church, and the Battery appearing, and hilly Albany, dotted with neat Dutch edifices characterized by stoops and gables, is vividly drawn as well. The familiar Cooper "big nature" backdrops crop up, too, in the later stages of the book—for example the breaking up of the ice on the Hudson, and the forest clearings in the area of Lake George.

The book's social commentary contributes to the authentication process, particularly Cooper's discussion of American types, from the intelligent and firmly upright "English" Corny Littlepage, to the physically attractive but less bright "Dutch" Dirck Van Valkenburgh, to the narrow and greedy New Englander Jason Newcome, to the Negro Jaap, to the Indian Susquesus. Cooper also formulates a number of English-American contrasts, and it is worth noting that, though depicting the titled Englishman Bulstrode flatteringly, he bestows the hand of the American "heiress" Anneke Mordaunt on Littlepage rather than on Bulstrode. The latter, as Anneke says at one point, will function better at the head of his officers' mess than in the snug Dutch parlor of her cousin Mrs. Van der Hayden, where the "colony hospitality, colony good-will, colony plainness" are more suited to Corny Littlepage. Americans, according to Cooper, need not "ape" the British; their culture, even their language, is their own.

Though generally a charming book, *Satanstoe* suffers from a number of technical flaws. The author, as usual, structures his work loosely, mixing adventure with love story, genre painting with political debate, and, in this case, adding many a description of manners. Though his flair for storytelling makes itself evident in a number of gripping episodes, his tendency toward the prolix slows the book down as a whole. His "beau idéal" concept of characterization—Anneke Mordaunt and Mary Wallace are "lovely and delicate girls" even on an ice floe in a rampaging river—also seems a deterrent feature. Exceptions do exist, like the virile, fun-loving, but unstable Guert Ten Eyck or the sociable "Loping Dominie" Worden, but as a rule Cooper glamorizes his leading characters. Conversely, he paints his villains too darkly. Jason Newcome should not be *quite* so sneaky, materialistic, narrow, hypocritical, and lacking in taste. The Cooper stylistic habits of confused syntax, periphrasis, and stilted dialogue do not, needless to say, serve him well, either. If he writes less clumsily and with less "giftbook flossiness" in *Satanstoe* than elsewhere, he still does not often approximate the sparkling phrasing of later novelists of manners.

The remaining two novels in the Littlepage trilogy, *The Chainbearer* and *The Redskins,* reveal less concern with summoning up the way of life of the landed class and ignore, for the most part, details of dress, food and drink, deportment, and custom. Cooper continues to theorize, to be sure, about the function of the landed proprietor and indeed devotes himself increasingly to the antirent issue. In *The Chainbearer* much is said about the "gentleman," as about leveling democracy and majority rule, and there are passing comments on American-European distinctions. In regard to the latter, Cooper distributes praise and blame on both sides, attacking "Yankee" provinciality that can lead to mock-refinement (e.g., the Littlepage neighbors

object to the name *Satanstoe* as undignified), but defending the naturalness of the American girl, as opposed to her artificial European counterpart.

He has more to say on this topic in *The Redskins* (mostly because his protagonist, Hugh Littlepage, has traveled in Europe for a number of years and thus has a "vantagepoint"), tending, in this latter novel, to favor the Europeans. "New world" inhabitants should visit the "Old," says Cooper firmly, for travel acts as a decided corrective to narrow self-adulation. The traveler would recognize, he feels, that society in America "in its ordinary meaning" is not as well ordered, tasteful, well mannered, agreeable, instructive, and useful as that in almost any European country. The American watering places, for example, seem to Hugh Littlepage "very much inferior" to most of those abroad, and Americans would do well, he suggests, to adopt many of the trans-atlantic customs, especially those of the British. America, he admits, has at least one or two advantages, such as the absence of a peasant class, and even of the "mercenary" spirit (that is, "two men might be bought in any European country for one here").

The Chainbearer discusses on a number of occasions what Cooper means by the terms *lady* and *gentleman.* Dismissing birth and wealth ("the vulgar, almost invariably, in this country, reduce the standard of distinction to mere money") as proper claims,[2] he stresses the following characteristics: taste, manners, opinions that are based on intelligence and cultivation, a refusal to stoop to meanness, generosity, superiority to scandal, and a truthfulness that stems from self-respect. People like his protagonist, Mordaunt Littlepage, clearly encompass the list, as does the young lady, Ursula Malbone, whom Mordaunt marries. Though very poor, even reduced to helping her uncle as a surveyor, Ursula was born and educated as a lady. Education is central in Cooper's scheme of things ("the wife of an educated man," he notes, "should be an educated woman"), and, because of the lack of it, the chainbearer, Andries Coejemans, "is and is not a gentleman." Coejemans *"is"* because he possesses what is even more central, a belief in and ability to recognize principles. He contrasts sharply in this respect with someone like Aaron Thousandacres, for whom all sense of right was concentrated in selfishness. Wherever firm moral fiber appears—in the yeoman, in the servant, in the Indian—a "good specimen" of man will be found. Only among the "gentry," however, do *all* the characteristics of the gentleman appear, and thus it is that Mordaunt's father can state that "nothing contributes so much to the civilization of a country as to dot it with a gentry," the effect produced by "one gentleman's family in a neighborhood, in the way of manners, tastes, general intelligence and civilization at large," being of substantial proportions.

While echoing this thesis ("the aristocrat means, in the parlance of the country, no other than a man of gentlemanlike tastes, habits, opinions and associations"), *The Redskins* defines less and describes more, supplying more information than *The Chainbearer* about the practices and habits of the aristocracy. One hears of its cultural interests, like the theater (though it is "pretty much all farces"), of its church (Episcopalian—and with a canopy over the Littlepage pew), of its clothes (Hugh and his uncle keep "a supply of country attire at the 'Nest"; no man, Cooper has declared in *The Chainbearer,* assumes the "wardrobe of a gentleman without having certain pretensions to the character"), of its dinners (good habits at the table are "conventionalities that belong to the fundamental principles of civilized society"), and of its homes (e.g., Ravensnest, "a respectable New York country dwelling"). Such are the links that "connect cultivated society together"—and separate it from the "Heirs of New York merchants getting rid of their portion in riotous living," as also from the covetous antirenters, and from the "demagogues and editors." Cooper contentedly places on the top rung of the "social ladder" the "Patroon" contingent, those who are "equal" in "social position, connections, education and similarity of habits, thoughts, and, if you will, prejudices."

Since he employs the genre of manners only as a secondary focus[3]—after the adventure, after the love story, after the sociopolitical criticism—and since he lacks some of the necessary attributes of the novelist of manners, most notably, a smooth and suave style and a tone of reasonably detached irony, Cooper initiates the genre imperfectly. One can appreciate, however, his providing the impetus, a much stronger one than that which stemmed from Brackenridge.

Among his contemporaries, a few writers also attempted to kindle the spark—the New Englander, Catharine Maria Sedgwick, for one, and the two Southerners, John Pendleton Kennedy and John Esten Cooke. If making but partial and not very adequate contributions, still, they lent assistance in keeping the tradition alive.

Kennedy and Cooke, like so many other later Southern novelists, relied upon the historical romance as their formula, a type into which might be easily inserted, however, some manners embellishments, especially in the form of local-color touches. Kennedy's *Swallow Barn* (1832) illustrates this in its reproduction of life on a Virginia plantation, the Meriwether estate of Swallow Barn. Although pursuing two lines of plot, a litigation issue and a love affair, Kennedy seems more preoccupied with summoning up a vision of the feudal South, of graceful living in the hunting country. The vision certainly has its charms, yet these are gently minimized by the vein of satire that runs throughout the book. Kennedy mocks the chivalric ideal in his account of the courting of romantic Bel Tracy by down-

to-earth Ned Hazard, and he lightly undercuts some Southern types and traditions, such as the landed gentleman model, Frank Meriwether; the "girlish" Prudence Meriwether who is so devoted to "good works"; Chub, the dogmatic schoolmaster; and the generally provincial (Richmond is the center of the universe) and stultified Virginians. In its nimble mockery *Swallow Barn* anticipates, to a degree, the subsequent more severe indictment of nostalgic regionalism to be found in the work of Ellen Glasgow.

Cooke's *Virginia Comedians* (1854) also depends on an ancestral home for its background, this being Effingham Hall, a "stately edifice near Williamsburg." In the vicinity of the Hall events like governors' balls and fox hunts take place, and there are also festal days devoted to wrestling and running matches, ballad singing and fiddler contests, as well as formal picnics and regimental musters. The book's cast of characters includes conventional types, too, like the worldly clergyman and the class-conscious gentleman. *Less* conventional figures are present as well, actors and theater managers (Mr. Hallam of the *Virginia Company of Comedians*), and yeoman farmers, and the book contains some derogatory remarks about the "Influential classes," "aristocracy" and "feudalism," together with frequent defenses of the acting profession and of the unfairly maligned "poor playing girl." Despite the presence of some fresh types and of some refreshing commentary, however, *Virginia Comedians* does not really veer very far away from a standard tale of entertainment, filled with the customary elements of sentimental romance, low comedy, and suspense.

More in keeping with the manners format—perhaps because it was written thirty years later, and thus in the James-Howells era—is Cooke's *Fanchette* (1883). Shifting his locale slightly northward, to Washington and the Eastern Shore of Maryland, and eschewing a historical setting in favor of the contemporary period, Cooke turns his book into something less characteristically "southern" than *Virginia Comedians*. Issues of politics, journalism, the theater, religion, and economics now interest him, and these are discussed against the background of a fairly cosmopolitan society. Some sense of the Washington social scene is established—"Vanity Fair in full blast"—with contrasts drawn between the old-rich like the Delanceys and the new-rich like the Ordmores. The former can produce "good company seated at a good dinner," whereas the latter stage less selective receptions, in a drawing room that was "as magnificent as great wealth and questionable taste could make it." Those attending such dinners and receptions may vary from journalists like Waring ("a flâneur . . . but under the trifler is the honest gentleman"), to cultivated men of leisure like Armyn, to the "gentleman adventurer," Prince Seminoff, determined to marry a rich American girl. Many members of the "best society" of Washington have country houses in

Maryland in the vicinity of the Chesapeake Bay, Armyn owning "Montrose," an imposing dwelling with "every mark of age," and the Delanceys inhabiting "Bayside," a "handsome country house" nearby. A "very social and affectionate society" exists on the Eastern Shore, so Cooke reports, the "best features of the old regime" lingering there and making "life attractive."

Fanchette devotes itself for the most part to a suspenseful plot involving the titular character, a young actress with a mysterious background. After a rather inordinate amount of intrigue, the book ends happily with Fanchette—who, actress or no, is a "perfect lady"—being permitted to make a proper marriage. Indeed, four weddings take place before the close of the book. As this suggests, the element of romance is uppermost in the novel, and the treatment of it, one has to say, is conventional and uninspiring. The book is enlivened, however, by the sprightliness of the heroine and by the author's sense of humor, and the authorial reflections on materialism (and its effect on politics in Washington in particular) and on the drama command the interest of the present-day reader.

The author most readily matched with Cooper as an incipient novelist of manners is Catharine Maria Sedgwick. Born into the upper class, she chose to describe it in her novels and indeed to defend it, provided that it exemplified an aristocracy of talent and virtue rather than one simply of birth or wealth. Though Miss Sedgwick could envision an approaching "American Utopia endowed with unlimited social grace,"[4] if such an aristocracy prevailed, she entertained serious doubts about the possibility, as her often tart thrusts at the higher social spheres in novels like *Clarence* (1830) and *Married or Single?* (1857) suggest.

Clarence is based on a town-and-country contrast, the rural gentry, Mr. Clarence and his daughter Gertrude, juxtaposed with New York City society, personified chiefly by Mrs. Layton. The former are well-read and well traveled individuals (in addition to being well supplied with money), who possess moderation and humility and thus act with delicacy in social situations. The latter, her graceful manners, spirited conversation, and engaging ways notwithstanding, is prone to self-indulgence and needless expenditure and to decided carelessness about principles. Miss Sedgwick says again and again that money corrupts (the "perils of a fortune") and presents numerous examples besides that of Mrs. Layton: the Browns, with their "nouveau riche immense parlor" and "costly, ill-assorted and cumbrous furniture"; Mrs. Stanley, "a rich, motherless, uneducated, unintellectual woman" and therefore "very pitiable"; Mr. Morley, obsequious to the affluent and fashionable and determined to marry among them; Major Daisy, a shallow social arbiter ("an Areopagite in the female fashionable world"); and Miss Patty Sprague,

the "walking, talking chronicle of the floating events of the day," who is quick to associate with those on the way up, quick to forget those on the way down. Exceptions, apart from the Clarences, do exist, notably Mrs. Roscoe and her son Gerald, and the Marion family. The latter, one notes, have a Southern bucolic background; the rural gentry has the edge again.[5]

Miss Sedgwick fires away from the first page to the last: at the belles and dandies ("living personifications of their prototypes in the tailor's window, dignified, self-complacent morons"), the gossiping and too-dress-conscious matrons, the gambling and speculating husbands operating in their "bank-note world," the businesslike pursuit of pleasure and the avoidance of intellectual interests,[6] and the purely mercenary view of marriage. In the words of Mr. Clarence, the New York social scene is marked by vacuity, flippancy, superficial accomplishments, idle competitions, and useless and wasteful expenditure. Such, he adds, are the sins and follies of every commercial city, and, though he (and his creator) would not wish to "condemn en masse the class of fashionable society," he makes it clear that this "polite world" does not represent "the most elevated and virtuous class."

Clarence touches on other issues of manners, such as the role of women (the author declaring, for one thing, that talent is demanded in "housewifery" just as in other "departments of life"), the rites of hospitality, and the importance of setting (the air of luxury and refinement in Mrs. Layton's establishment is commended as going "beyond that usually produced by the union of fortune and fashion"). The book also contains a passage caricaturing the impercipient British traveler in America, one who draws inane and often faulty English-American parallels. Captain Edmund Stuart, the example in this instance, labels Benjamin West an English painter and even remarks that his name may not have reached America yet, "owing probably to the ignorance of the fine arts here."

Its well-directed satire aside, *Clarence* represents hard going for the present-day reader, for much of its author's energy is expended in unfolding a highly melodramatic and sentimental plot; the characters are carelessly motivated and/or dull; structural arrangements seem slipshod (letters are thrown in at random to convey necessary exposition); and the style is marred by epithets on the "crown matrimonial," "manly bosom" order.

In her later novel, *Married or Single?*, Miss Sedgwick spends most of her time discussing the question posed in her title, whether a married or a single life is preferable for a woman. After a sterling defense of the latter position, she allows her heroine to marry at the novel's end—once she has found the "right" man. Developing this discussion against a New York aristocracy background once again, Miss Sedgwick also satirizes once again, but more incidentally than she had in *Clarence*. So occupied is she in riding her thesis, that a woman's single life can be useful and dignified and is certainly preferable to a "bankrupt marriage," that she rarely delivers a satiric shaft.

When she does so, her targets recall those found in *Clarence*—the frivolous belle who thinks of feathers, lace, and fringe, but never of books; the Anglophile "lauding anything English";[7] and the arriviste Adeline Clapp, ignorant of conventions and with no proper instincts, the "fashionable" lady assiduously pursuing an empty social round, from morning reception to evening ball. As in *Clarence,* too, she utilizes foil characters, Grace Herbert contra Anne Carlton, corresponding to Gertrude Clarence contra Mrs. Layton. Anne Carlton epitomizes the socialite, pretty to look at and perfectly dressed, but flippant and shallow, materialistic and loosely principled. Grace, on the other hand, though too impetuous and more than a little worldly ("At twenty-two one can't turn hermit," she says, "and parties and receptions and their edifying accessories make up our social life, you know"), is intelligent, sensitive, and firmly principled. Eventually she is rewarded for possessing these more positive traits; she escapes the clutches of the wealthy but corrupt man-about-town, Horace Copley, and attaches herself to the sturdy lawyer, Archibald Lisle, her equal in morals and—after his experiencing a European sojourn of a year or two—in manners as well. He has moved from his "narrow social sphere" into her world of "high breeding." Of course, Grace is still defending the single life even as she ventures upon marriage.

Married or Single? gives the reader a good deal of information about the "fashionable quarter" of New York, its materialism, coldness (e.g., Madam Copley), vanity and levity, and its easy morality. The benefits to be found—good dinners, tolerable operas, "practiced manners"—do not compensate. At one stage of the novel, Miss Sedgwick permits herself a severe tirade:

> A creature of Grace's rare gifts is about as well adapted to the fashionable world of New York as a first-rate ship would be to the artificial lake of a pleasure-ground. In other civilized countries, where a privileged class is sustained by rank, individuality of character is cultivated and developed in brilliant accomplishments that enamel society. But . . . who hopes to meet our poets, artists, historians at the "most brilliant party of the season"? Our society is characterized by monotony, infinite tediousness of mediocrity, a vulgar and childish struggle for insipid celebrities, celebrity for fine dress, palatial house, costly furniture and showy equipage. [p. 159]

Citing the recently published *Potiphar Papers,* Miss Sedgwick echoes the indictment of its author, George

William Curtis, against New York society, with its parvenu emphasis on luxury at the expense of taste.

No more than *Clarence* is *Married or Single?* an artistic triumph, unfortunately. An exhausting two-volume affair; it piles intrigue upon intrigue, provides not one but two pathetic deaths of young ladies and one of a child as well, employs coincidence with abandon, idealizes its principal characters and caricatures others, and relies heavily on pompous dialogue. The presence of one or two interesting characters like Mrs. Tallis, an occasional witty remark ("persons of Grace's temperament are apt to mistake impulses for inspirations"), and the appropriately directed satiric attacks only partially redress the balance.

One has to conclude that the American novel of manners in the pre-Civil War era does not reach artistic heights. The polish and skill of a Thackeray, whom Miss Sedgwick speaks, in *Married or Single?,* of wishing to call to her aid, are generally lacking. Happily, they were soon to be supplied by James and Howells.

The question of artistry aside, the Coopers and Sedgwicks, Kennedys and Cookes, can still be praised for recognizing the value of social satire as novelistic material and for, in this and other ways, utilizing the genre of manners, thus keeping the tradition alive.[8]

Notes

[1] Donald A. Ringe, *James Fenimore Cooper* (New York: Twayne Publishers, Inc., 1962), p. 121.

[2] The reader would be inclined to argue that Cooper does not really dismiss the claim of "birth." One remembers that Ursula Malbone is a lady "by birth," as is Mary Warren, the heroine of *The Redskins*. Mary, like Ursula, is, though poor, rewarded with the hand of the protagonist, Hugh Littlepage, for she is educated as well as well born, refined as well as principled. Like many another Cooper heroine, she has everything!

[3] *Autobiography of a Pocket Handkerchief* is the one exception.

[4] Edward H. Foster, *Catharine Maria Sedgwick* (New York: Twayne Publishers, Inc., 1974), p. 99.

[5] Vulgar little ladies like Mrs. Upton can be found in the country, however, and, as Mr. Clarence says, with wry amusement, to his daughter, six distinct social ranks exist in the village of Clarenceville.

[6] Mrs. Layton, for example, attends lectures and the opera merely to be seen, and Gerald Roscoe's mind, "enriched with elegant acquisitions," is regarded as an embellishment but hardly a necessity. Miss Sedgwick

anticipates later novelists of manners in her assignment of antiintellectualism to "society."

[7] Unlike the Anglophile, Walter Herbert does not want his niece, Grace, to marry an Englishman, for she would be received on sufferance in England, whereas in America she is a "queen in her own right."

[8] One observes the comment of Edward H. Foster that, "aside from various works by Cooper and Miss Sedgwick, very few good works of fiction were explicitly devoted to a study of manners in pre-Civil War America." He goes on to say that "there are women who industriously wrote domestic novels in which much attention was given to manners. . . . but few authors of distinction attempted this particular kind of fiction. Perhaps the very lack of a class, or at least a highly influential class, which based its principles upon a life of manners precluded the possible development of a tradition of novels of manners in the half-century before the Civil War" (Foster, *Catharine Maria Sedgwick,* p. 104.).

FURTHER READING

Baker, Ernest A. "Some Women Novelists." In *The History of the English Novel,* Volume 10: *Yesterday,* pp. 199-243. London: H. F. & G. Witherby, 1939.
    Argues that the female novelists of the nineteenth century may appropriately be studied as a group because of their common, "distinctively feminine," sensibility, although the critic concedes it would be "absurd" to do the same with the era's male authors.

Bushnell, Nelson S. "Susan Ferrier's *Marriage* as Novel of Manners." In *Studies in Scottish Literature* V (July 1967-April 1968): 216-28.
    Discusses how Ferrier's 1818 novel of manners contrasts the customs of the Scottish Highlands with the manners of the English community at Bath; according to the critic, the former are viewed with affection, the latter with disdain.

Castronovo, David. *The English Gentleman: Images and Ideals in Literature and Society.* New York: Ungar, 1987, 171 p.
    Studies the role of the nineteenth-century English gentleman in life as well as in literature; the ideal is based as much on duty as on privilege.

Chase, Richard. "Three Novels of Manners." In *The American Novel and Its Tradition,* pp. 157-84. Garden City, NY: Doubleday, 1957.
    Maintains that the American novel of manners, unlike its European counterpart, is for the most part the work of second-rate authors; when the American form *does* achieve greatness, it is usually because the work is a romance first and only secondarily a novel of manners. Chase examines F. Scott Fitzgerald's *The Great Gatsby,* G. W. Cable's *The Grandissimes,* and William Dean Howells's *The Vacation of the Kelwyns.*

Crabtree, Paul R. "Propriety, *Grandison,* and the Novel of Manners." In *Modern Language Quarterly* 41, No. 2 (June 1980): 151-61.
    Treats the last novel of Samuel Richardson—*Sir Charles Grandison*—as a novel of manners, signaling a shift in focus from the spiritual dilemmas of Puritanism to the practical application of moral issues to everyday conduct.

Craik, W. A. *Elizabeth Gaskell and the English Provincial Novel.* London: Methuen, 1975, 277 p.
    Examines Gaskell's five full-length novels as well as the author's development over the course of her career and her place in the literary canon.

Darnell, Donald. *James Fenimore Cooper: Novelist of Manners.* Newark: University of Delaware Press, 1993, 142 p.
    Analyzes fifteen of Cooper's novels and finds the manners formula at work throughout—not only in the Littlepage Trilogy and other works that are widely recognized as novels of manners—but even in the Leatherstocking tales.

Foster, Shirley. *Victorian Women's Fiction: Marriage, Freedom and the Individual.* London: Croom Helm, 1985, 240 p.
    Discusses how many of the women writers of the nineteenth-century domestic novel had mixed feelings about their era's glorification of women as wives and mothers. According to Foster, this contradiction is apparent in their fiction, which seems to alternately endorse and condemn the rigidity of those prescribed roles.

Gilbert, Sandra M. and Susan Gubar. *The Madwoman in the Attic: The Woman Writer and the Nineteenth-Century Literary Imagination.* New Haven: Yale University Press, 1979, 719 p.
    Explores the anxieties of the nineteenth-century woman writer struggling to exist in a field dominated and defined by males. Gilbert and Gubar point out representations of confinement and enclosure and fantasies of escape in the works of Jane Austen, Charlotte Brontë, George Eliot, and others.

Gilmour, Robin. *The Idea of the Gentleman in the Victorian Novel.* London: George Allen & Unwin, 1981, 190 p.
    Studies the preoccupation with the notion of the "gentleman" in Victorian English society and literature, indicating that the culture's hopes and aspirations, contradictions and anxieties, can all be read in the constantly changing definition of the term.

Godden, Richard. "Some Slight Shifts in the Manner of the Novel of Manners." In *Henry James: Fiction as History*, edited by Ian F. A. Bell, pp. 156-83. London: Vision, 1984.

   Analyzes the historical and economic context of Henry James's *The Bostonians* (1886).

Hapke, Laura. "He Stoops to Conquer: Redeeming the Fallen Woman in the Fiction of Dickens, Gaskell and Their Contemporaries." *The Victorian Newsletter*, No. 69 (Spring 1986): 16-22.

   Through an examination of the social problem novels of Charles Dickens, Elizabeth Gaskell, Anthony Trollope, and others, Hapke looks at the mid-nineteenth century controversy over who was better suited to rescue and redeem society's "fallen" women—men, or other women.

Hierth, Harrison E. "The Class Novel." In *The CEA Critic* XXVII, No. 3 (December 1964): 1, 3-4.

   Compares Edith Wharton's 1905 novel *The House of Mirth* with John O'Hara's 1934 work *Appointment in Samarra*; both deal with class distinctions and the high price society exacts from individuals who fail to abide by the prescribed rules of behavior.

Letwin, Shirley Robin. "Birth and Rank," pp. 123-34. In *The Gentleman in Trollope: Individuality and Moral Conduct*. Cambridge, Mass.: Harvard University Press, 1982.

   Finds evidence supporting both sides of the nature/nurture controversy as it applies to the nineteenth-century gentleman.

Millgate, Michael. *American Social Fiction: James to Cozzens*. New York: Barnes & Noble, 1964, 217 p.

   Examines the representation of the American businessman in the American social novels during the years 1877 to 1957.

Mizener, Arthur. "The Novel of Manners in America." In *The Kenyon Review* 12, No. 1 (Winter 1950): 1-19.

   Argues that the difficulty of producing quality twentieth-century novels of manners in America lies in achieving the proper balance between the individual and the socio-political realms.

Morgan, Charlotte E. *The Rise of the Novel of Manners: A Study of English Prose Fiction Between 1600 and 1740*. New York: Russell & Russell, 1963, 271 p.

   Claims that the early nineteenth-century reaction to the immorality of earlier times led to a general concern about good conduct—a fitting context for the rise of the novel of manners.

Poovey, Mary. *The Proper Lady and the Woman Writer: Ideology as Style in the Works of Mary Wollstonecraft, Mary Shelley, and Jane Austen*. Chicago: University of Chicago Press, 1984, 287 p.

   Examines the works of Austen, Wollstonecraft, and Shelley, focusing on how each gained the personal and professional autonomy necessary to become successful writers in an age that expected women to be modest, self-effacing, dependent, and most of all, "proper."

Price, Martin. "Manners, Morals, and Jane Austen." In *Nineteenth-Century Fiction* 30, No. 3 (December 1975): 261-80.

   Discusses Jane Austen's fiction as a series of schematic drawings as opposed to the minutely-detailed reproductions of domestic life often associated with the novel of manners; the more abstract quality of her representations enables the reader to see the moral implications behind the manners being displayed.

Stovel, Bruce. "Subjective to Objective: A Career Pattern in Jane Austen, George Eliot, and Contemporary Women Novelists." In *Ariel* 18, No. 1 (January 1987): 53-61.

   Traces how the literary careers of Austen, Eliot, Margaret Drabble, and Barbara Pym progress from novels that are narrow and personal to those that have both a broader social scope and a more objective stance.

Trilling, Lionel. "Manners, Morals, and the Novel." In *The Liberal Imagination: Essays on Literature and Society*, pp. 193-209. New York: Harcourt Brace Jovanovich, 1979.

   Discusses the conflicting sets of cultural codes that constitute manners as they appear in the novels popular with the "reading class."

Wiesenfarth, Joseph. *Gothic Manners and the Classic English Novel*. Madison: University of Wisconsin Press, 1988, 235 p.

   Makes a case for a hybrid form that combines the features of the Gothic novel and the novel of manners—a form Wiesenfarth dubs the "novel of Gothic manners" and which includes *Middlemarch, The Portrait of a Lady,* and *Jude the Obscure*.

How to Use This Index

The main references

list all author entries in the following Gale Literary Criticism series:

BLC = *Black Literature Criticism*
CLC = *Contemporary Literary Criticism*
CLR = *Children's Literature Review*
CMLC = *Classical and Medieval Literature Criticism*
DA = *DISCovering Authors*
DAB = *DISCovering Authors: British*
DAC = *DISCovering Authors: Canadian*
DAM = *DISCovering Authors Modules*
   DRAM: *Dramatists module*
   MST: *Most-studied authors module*
   MULT: *Multicultural authors module*
   NOV: *Novelists module*
   POET: *Poets module*
   POP: *Popular/genre writers module*

DC = *Drama Criticism*
HLC = *Hispanic Literature Criticism*
LC = *Literature Criticism from 1400 to 1800*
NCLC = *Nineteenth-Century Literature Criticism*
PC = *Poetry Criticism*
SSC = *Short Story Criticism*
TCLC = *Twentieth-Century Literary Criticism*
WLC = *World Literature Criticism, 1500 to the Present*

The cross-references

list all author entries in the following Gale biographical and literary sources:

AAYA = *Authors & Artists for Young Adults*
AITN = *Authors in the News*
BEST = *Bestsellers*
BW = *Black Writers*
CA = *Contemporary Authors*
CAAS = *Contemporary Authors Autobiography Series*
CABS = *Contemporary Authors Bibliographical Series*
CANR = *Contemporary Authors New Revision Series*
CAP = *Contemporary Authors Permanent Series*
CDALB = *Concise Dictionary of American Literary Biography*
CDBLB = *Concise Dictionary of British Literary Biography*

DLB = *Dictionary of Literary Biography*
DLBD = *Dictionary of Literary Biography Documentary Series*
DLBY = *Dictionary of Literary Biography Yearbook*
HW = *Hispanic Writers*
JRDA = *Junior DISCovering Authors*
MAICYA = *Major Authors and Illustrators for Children and Young Adults*
MTCW = *Major 20th-Century Writers*
NNAL = *Native North American Literature*
SAAS = *Something about the Author Autobiography Series*
SATA = *Something about the Author*
YABC = *Yesterday's Authors of Books for Children*

Literary Criticism Series
Cumulative Author Index

A. E. . . . . TCLC 3, 10
See also Russell, George William

Abasiyanik, Sait Faik 1906-1954
See Sait Faik
See also CA 123

Abbey, Edward 1927-1989 . . . . . . CLC 36, 59
See also CA 45-48; 128; CANR 2, 41

Abbott, Lee K(ittredge) 1947- . . . . . . CLC 48
See also CA 124; CANR 51; DLB 130

Abe, Kobo 1924-1993 . . . . . CLC 8, 22, 53, 81
See also CA 65-68; 140; CANR 24;
DAM NOV; MTCW

Abelard, Peter c. 1079-c. 1142 . . . CMLC 11
See also DLB 115

Abell, Kjeld 1901-1961 . . . . CLC 15
See also CA 111

Abish, Walter 1931- . . . . CLC 22
See also CA 101; CANR 37; DLB 130

Abrahams, Peter (Henry) 1919- . . . . . CLC 4
See also BW 1; CA 57-60; CANR 26;
DLB 117; MTCW

Abrams, M(eyer) H(oward) 1912- . . . CLC 24
See also CA 57-60; CANR 13, 33; DLB 67

Abse, Dannie 1923- . . . . CLC 7, 29; DAB
See also CA 53-56; CAAS 1; CANR 4, 46;
DAM POET; DLB 27

Achebe, (Albert) Chinua(lumogu)
1930- . . . . . CLC 1, 3, 5, 7, 11, 26, 51, 75;
BLC; DA; DAB; DAC; WLC
See also AAYA 15; BW 2; CA 1-4R;
CANR 6, 26, 47; CLR 20; DAM MST,
MULT, NOV; DLB 117; MAICYA;
MTCW; SATA 40; SATA-Brief 38

Acker, Kathy 1948- . . . . CLC 45
See also CA 117; 122

Ackroyd, Peter 1949- . . . . CLC 34, 52
See also CA 123; 127; CANR 51; DLB 155;
INT 127

Acorn, Milton 1923- . . . . CLC 15; DAC
See also CA 103; DLB 53; INT 103

Adamov, Arthur 1908-1970 . . . . . . CLC 4, 25
See also CA 17-18; 25-28R; CAP 2;
DAM DRAM; MTCW

Adams, Alice (Boyd) 1926- . . . CLC 6, 13, 46
See also CA 81-84; CANR 26, 53;
DLBY 86; INT CANR-26; MTCW

Adams, Andy 1859-1935 . . . . TCLC 56
See also YABC 1

Adams, Douglas (Noel) 1952- . . . CLC 27, 60
See also AAYA 4; BEST 89:3; CA 106;
CANR 34; DAM POP; DLBY 83; JRDA

Adams, Francis 1862-1893 . . . . NCLC 33

Adams, Henry (Brooks)
1838-1918 . . . . . . TCLC 4, 52; DA; DAB;
DAC
See also CA 104; 133; DAM MST; DLB 12,
47

Adams, Richard (George)
1920- . . . . CLC 4, 5, 18
See also AAYA 16; AITN 1, 2; CA 49-52;
CANR 3, 35; CLR 20; DAM NOV;
JRDA; MAICYA; MTCW; SATA 7, 69

Adamson, Joy(-Friederike Victoria)
1910-1980 . . . . CLC 17
See also CA 69-72; 93-96; CANR 22;
MTCW; SATA 11; SATA-Obit 22

Adcock, Fleur 1934- . . . . CLC 41
See also CA 25-28R; CAAS 23; CANR 11,
34; DLB 40

Addams, Charles (Samuel)
1912-1988 . . . . CLC 30
See also CA 61-64; 126; CANR 12

Addison, Joseph 1672-1719 . . . . LC 18
See also CDBLB 1660-1789; DLB 101

Adler, Alfred (F.) 1870-1937 . . . . . . TCLC 61
See also CA 119

Adler, C(arole) S(chwerdtfeger)
1932- . . . . CLC 35
See also AAYA 4; CA 89-92; CANR 19,
40; JRDA; MAICYA; SAAS 15;
SATA 26, 63

Adler, Renata 1938- . . . . CLC 8, 31
See also CA 49-52; CANR 5, 22, 52;
MTCW

Ady, Endre 1877-1919 . . . . TCLC 11
See also CA 107

Aeschylus
525B.C.-456B.C. . . . . CMLC 11; DA;
DAB; DAC
See also DAM DRAM, MST

Afton, Effie
See Harper, Frances Ellen Watkins

Agapida, Fray Antonio
See Irving, Washington

Agee, James (Rufus)
1909-1955 . . . . TCLC 1, 19
See also AITN 1; CA 108; 148;
CDALB 1941-1968; DAM NOV; DLB 2,
26, 152

Aghill, Gordon
See Silverberg, Robert

Agnon, S(hmuel) Y(osef Halevi)
1888-1970 . . . . CLC 4, 8, 14
See also CA 17-18; 25-28R; CAP 2; MTCW

Agrippa von Nettesheim, Henry Cornelius
1486-1535 . . . . LC 27

Aherne, Owen
See Cassill, R(onald) V(erlin)

Ai 1947- . . . . CLC 4, 14, 69
See also CA 85-88; CAAS 13; DLB 120

Aickman, Robert (Fordyce)
1914-1981 . . . . CLC 57
See also CA 5-8R; CANR 3

Aiken, Conrad (Potter)
1889-1973 . . . CLC 1, 3, 5, 10, 52; SSC 9
See also CA 5-8R; 45-48; CANR 4;
CDALB 1929-1941; DAM NOV, POET;
DLB 9, 45, 102; MTCW; SATA 3, 30

Aiken, Joan (Delano) 1924- . . . . CLC 35
See also AAYA 1; CA 9-12R; CANR 4, 23,
34; CLR 1, 19; DLB 161; JRDA;
MAICYA; MTCW; SAAS 1; SATA 2,
30, 73

Ainsworth, William Harrison
1805-1882 . . . . NCLC 13
See also DLB 21; SATA 24

Aitmatov, Chingiz (Torekulovich)
1928- . . . . CLC 71
See also CA 103; CANR 38; MTCW;
SATA 56

Akers, Floyd
See Baum, L(yman) Frank

Akhmadulina, Bella Akhatovna
1937- . . . . CLC 53
See also CA 65-68; DAM POET

Akhmatova, Anna
1888-1966 . . . . CLC 11, 25, 64; PC 2
See also CA 19-20; 25-28R; CANR 35;
CAP 1; DAM POET; MTCW

Aksakov, Sergei Timofeyvich
1791-1859 . . . . NCLC 2

Aksenov, Vassily
See Aksyonov, Vassily (Pavlovich)

Aksyonov, Vassily (Pavlovich)
1932- . . . . CLC 22, 37
See also CA 53-56; CANR 12, 48

Akutagawa Ryunosuke
1892-1927 . . . . TCLC 16
See also CA 117

Alain 1868-1951 . . . . TCLC 41

Alain-Fournier . . . . TCLC 6
See also Fournier, Henri Alban
See also DLB 65

Alarcon, Pedro Antonio de
1833-1891 . . . . NCLC 1

Alas (y Urena), Leopoldo (Enrique Garcia)
1852-1901 . . . . TCLC 29
See also CA 113; 131; HW

Albee, Edward (Franklin III)
1928- . . . . . . CLC 1, 2, 3, 5, 9, 11, 13, 25,
53, 86; DA; DAB; DAC; WLC
See also AITN 1; CA 5-8R; CABS 3;
CANR 8; CDALB 1941-1968;
DAM DRAM, MST; DLB 7;
INT CANR-8; MTCW

Alberti, Rafael 1902- . . . . CLC 7
See also CA 85-88; DLB 108

Albert the Great 1200(?)-1280 . . . . CMLC 16
See also DLB 115

Alcala-Galiano, Juan Valera y
See Valera y Alcala-Galiano, Juan

Alcott, Amos Bronson 1799-1888 .. NCLC 1
See also DLB 1

Alcott, Louisa May
1832-1888 . . . . NCLC 6; DA; DAB;
DAC; WLC
See also CDALB 1865-1917; CLR 1, 38;
DAM MST, NOV; DLB 1, 42, 79; JRDA;
MAICYA; YABC 1

Aldanov, M. A.
See Aldanov, Mark (Alexandrovich)

Aldanov, Mark (Alexandrovich)
1886(?)-1957 . . . . TCLC 23
See also CA 118

Aldington, Richard 1892-1962 . . . . . . CLC 49
See also CA 85-88; CANR 45; DLB 20, 36,
100, 149

Aldiss, Brian W(ilson)
1925- . . . . CLC 5, 14, 40
See also CA 5-8R; CAAS 2; CANR 5, 28;
DAM NOV; DLB 14; MTCW; SATA 34

Alegria, Claribel 1924- . . . . CLC 75
See also CA 131; CAAS 15; DAM MULT;
DLB 145; HW

Alegria, Fernando 1918- . . . . CLC 57
See also CA 9-12R; CANR 5, 32; HW

Aleichem, Sholom . . . . TCLC 1, 35
See also Rabinovitch, Sholem

Aleixandre, Vicente
1898-1984 . . . . CLC 9, 36; PC 15
See also CA 85-88; 114; CANR 26;
DAM POET; DLB 108; HW; MTCW

Alepoudelis, Odysseus
See Elytis, Odysseus

Aleshkovsky, Joseph 1929-
See Aleshkovsky, Yuz
See also CA 121; 128

Aleshkovsky, Yuz . . . . CLC 44
See also Aleshkovsky, Joseph

Alexander, Lloyd (Chudley) 1924- . . CLC 35
See also AAYA 1; CA 1-4R; CANR 1, 24,
38; CLR 1, 5; DLB 52; JRDA; MAICYA;
MTCW; SAAS 19; SATA 3, 49, 81

Alfau, Felipe 1902- . . . . CLC 66
See also CA 137

Alger, Horatio, Jr. 1832-1899 . . . . . NCLC 8
See also DLB 42; SATA 16

Algren, Nelson 1909-1981 . . . . CLC 4, 10, 33
See also CA 13-16R; 103; CANR 20;
CDALB 1941-1968; DLB 9; DLBY 81,
82; MTCW

Ali, Ahmed 1910- . . . . CLC 69
See also CA 25-28R; CANR 15, 34

Alighieri, Dante 1265-1321 . . . . CMLC 3, 18

Allan, John B.
See Westlake, Donald E(dwin)

Allen, Edward 1948- . . . . CLC 59

Allen, Paula Gunn 1939- . . . . CLC 84
See also CA 112; 143; DAM MULT;
NNAL

Allen, Roland
See Ayckbourn, Alan

Allen, Sarah A.
See Hopkins, Pauline Elizabeth

Allen, Woody 1935- . . . . CLC 16, 52
See also AAYA 10; CA 33-36R; CANR 27,
38; DAM POP; DLB 44; MTCW

Allende, Isabel 1942- . . . . CLC 39, 57; HLC
See also AAYA 18; CA 125; 130;
CANR 51; DAM MULT, NOV;
DLB 145; HW; INT 130; MTCW

Alleyn, Ellen
See Rossetti, Christina (Georgina)

Allingham, Margery (Louise)
1904-1966 . . . . CLC 19
See also CA 5-8R; 25-28R; CANR 4;
DLB 77; MTCW

Allingham, William 1824-1889 . . . NCLC 25
See also DLB 35

Allison, Dorothy E. 1949- . . . . CLC 78
See also CA 140

Allston, Washington 1779-1843 . . . . NCLC 2
See also DLB 1

Almedingen, E. M. . . . . CLC 12
See also Almedingen, Martha Edith von
See also SATA 3

Almedingen, Martha Edith von 1898-1971
See Almedingen, E. M.
See also CA 1-4R; CANR 1

Almqvist, Carl Jonas Love
1793-1866 . . . . NCLC 42

Alonso, Damaso 1898-1990 . . . . CLC 14
See also CA 110; 131; 130; DLB 108; HW

Alov
See Gogol, Nikolai (Vasilyevich)

Alta 1942- . . . . CLC 19
See also CA 57-60

Alter, Robert B(ernard) 1935- . . . . . . CLC 34
See also CA 49-52; CANR 1, 47

Alther, Lisa 1944- . . . . CLC 7, 41
See also CA 65-68; CANR 12, 30, 51;
MTCW

Altman, Robert 1925- . . . . CLC 16
See also CA 73-76; CANR 43

Alvarez, A(lfred) 1929- . . . . CLC 5, 13
See also CA 1-4R; CANR 3, 33; DLB 14,
40

Alvarez, Alejandro Rodriguez 1903-1965
See Casona, Alejandro
See also CA 131; 93-96; HW

Alvarez, Julia 1950- . . . . CLC 93
See also CA 147

Alvaro, Corrado 1896-1956 . . . . TCLC 60

Amado, Jorge 1912- . . . . . CLC 13, 40; HLC
See also CA 77-80; CANR 35;
DAM MULT, NOV; DLB 113; MTCW

Ambler, Eric 1909- . . . . CLC 4, 6, 9
See also CA 9-12R; CANR 7, 38; DLB 77;
MTCW

Amichai, Yehuda 1924- . . . . . . CLC 9, 22, 57
See also CA 85-88; CANR 46; MTCW

Amiel, Henri Frederic 1821-1881 . . NCLC 4

Amis, Kingsley (William)
1922-1995 . . . . . CLC 1, 2, 3, 5, 8, 13, 40,
44; DA; DAB; DAC
See also AITN 2; CA 9-12R; 150; CANR 8,
28; CDBLB 1945-1960; DAM MST,
NOV; DLB 15, 27, 100, 139;
INT CANR-8; MTCW

Amis, Martin (Louis)
1949- . . . . CLC 4, 9, 38, 62
See also BEST 90:3; CA 65-68; CANR 8,
27; DLB 14; INT CANR-27

Ammons, A(rchie) R(andolph)
1926- . . . CLC 2, 3, 5, 8, 9, 25, 57; PC 16
See also AITN 1; CA 9-12R; CANR 6, 36,
51; DAM POET; DLB 5, 165; MTCW

Amo, Tauraatua i
See Adams, Henry (Brooks)

Anand, Mulk Raj 1905- . . . . CLC 23, 93
See also CA 65-68; CANR 32; DAM NOV;
MTCW

Anatol
See Schnitzler, Arthur

Anaya, Rudolfo A(lfonso)
1937- . . . . CLC 23; HLC
See also CA 45-48; CAAS 4; CANR 1, 32,
51; DAM MULT, NOV; DLB 82; HW 1;
MTCW

Andersen, Hans Christian
1805-1875 . . . . NCLC 7; DA; DAB;
DAC; SSC 6; WLC
See also CLR 6; DAM MST, POP;
MAICYA; YABC 1

Anderson, C. Farley
See Mencken, H(enry) L(ouis); Nathan,
George Jean

Anderson, Jessica (Margaret) Queale
. . . . CLC 37
See also CA 9-12R; CANR 4

Anderson, Jon (Victor) 1940- . . . . CLC 9
See also CA 25-28R; CANR 20;
DAM POET

Anderson, Lindsay (Gordon)
1923-1994 . . . . CLC 20
See also CA 125; 128; 146

Anderson, Maxwell 1888-1959 . . . . . TCLC 2
See also CA 105; DAM DRAM; DLB 7

Anderson, Poul (William) 1926- . . . . CLC 15
See also AAYA 5; CA 1-4R; CAAS 2;
CANR 2, 15, 34; DLB 8; INT CANR-15;
MTCW; SATA-Brief 39

Anderson, Robert (Woodruff)
1917- . . . . CLC 23
See also AITN 1; CA 21-24R; CANR 32;
DAM DRAM; DLB 7

Anderson, Sherwood
1876-1941 . . . . TCLC 1, 10, 24; DA;
DAB; DAC; SSC 1; WLC
See also CA 104; 121; CDALB 1917-1929;
DAM MST, NOV; DLB 4, 9, 86;
DLBD 1; MTCW

Andier, Pierre
See Desnos, Robert

Andouard
See Giraudoux, (Hippolyte) Jean

Andrade, Carlos Drummond de . . . . . . CLC 18
See also Drummond de Andrade, Carlos

Author Index

Baldwin, James (Arthur)
1924-1987 ...... **CLC 1, 2, 3, 4, 5, 8, 13, 15, 17, 42, 50, 67, 90; BLC; DA; DAB; DAC; DC 1; SSC 10; WLC**
See also AAYA 4; BW 1; CA 1-4R; 124; CABS 1; CANR 3, 24; CDALB 1941-1968; DAM MST, MULT, NOV, POP; DLB 2, 7, 33; DLBY 87; MTCW; SATA 9; SATA-Obit 54

Ballard, J(ames) G(raham)
1930- .... **CLC 3, 6, 14, 36; SSC 1**
See also AAYA 3; CA 5-8R; CANR 15, 39; DAM NOV, POP; DLB 14; MTCW

Balmont, Konstantin (Dmitriyevich)
1867-1943 .... **TCLC 11**
See also CA 109

Balzac, Honore de
1799-1850 .... **NCLC 5, 35, 53; DA; DAB; DAC; SSC 5; WLC**
See also DAM MST, NOV; DLB 119

Bambara, Toni Cade
1939-1995 ...... **CLC 19, 88; BLC; DA; DAC**
See also AAYA 5; BW 2; CA 29-32R; 150; CANR 24, 49; DAM MST, MULT; DLB 38; MTCW

Bamdad, A.
See Shamlu, Ahmad

Banat, D. R.
See Bradbury, Ray (Douglas)

Bancroft, Laura
See Baum, L(yman) Frank

Banim, John   1798-1842 .... **NCLC 13**
See also DLB 116, 158, 159

Banim, Michael   1796-1874 ...... **NCLC 13**
See also DLB 158, 159

Banks, Iain
See Banks, Iain M(enzies)

Banks, Iain M(enzies)   1954- .... **CLC 34**
See also CA 123; 128; INT 128

Banks, Lynne Reid .... **CLC 23**
See also Reid Banks, Lynne
See also AAYA 6

Banks, Russell   1940- .... **CLC 37, 72**
See also CA 65-68; CAAS 15; CANR 19, 52; DLB 130

Banville, John   1945- .... **CLC 46**
See also CA 117; 128; DLB 14; INT 128

Banville, Theodore (Faullain) de
1832-1891 .... **NCLC 9**

Baraka, Amiri
1934- .... **CLC 1, 2, 3, 5, 10, 14, 33; BLC; DA; DAC; DC 6; PC 4**
See also Jones, LeRoi
See also BW 2; CA 21-24R; CABS 3; CANR 27, 38; CDALB 1941-1968; DAM MST, MULT, POET, POP; DLB 5, 7, 16, 38; DLBD 8; MTCW

Barbauld, Anna Laetitia
1743-1825 .... **NCLC 50**
See also DLB 107, 109, 142, 158

Barbellion, W. N. P. .... **TCLC 24**
See also Cummings, Bruce F(rederick)

Barbera, Jack (Vincent)   1945- ...... **CLC 44**
See also CA 110; CANR 45

Barbey d'Aurevilly, Jules Amedee
1808-1889 .... **NCLC 1; SSC 17**
See also DLB 119

Barbusse, Henri   1873-1935 .... **TCLC 5**
See also CA 105; DLB 65

Barclay, Bill
See Moorcock, Michael (John)

Barclay, William Ewert
See Moorcock, Michael (John)

Barea, Arturo   1897-1957 .... **TCLC 14**
See also CA 111

Barfoot, Joan   1946- .... **CLC 18**
See also CA 105

Baring, Maurice   1874-1945 .... **TCLC 8**
See also CA 105; DLB 34

Barker, Clive   1952- .... **CLC 52**
See also AAYA 10; BEST 90:3; CA 121; 129; DAM POP; INT 129; MTCW

Barker, George Granville
1913-1991 .... **CLC 8, 48**
See also CA 9-12R; 135; CANR 7, 38; DAM POET; DLB 20; MTCW

Barker, Harley Granville
See Granville-Barker, Harley
See also DLB 10

Barker, Howard   1946- .... **CLC 37**
See also CA 102; DLB 13

Barker, Pat(ricia)   1943- .... **CLC 32, 94**
See also CA 117; 122; CANR 50; INT 122

Barlow, Joel   1754-1812 .... **NCLC 23**
See also DLB 37

Barnard, Mary (Ethel)   1909- .... **CLC 48**
See also CA 21-22; CAP 2

Barnes, Djuna
1892-1982 ... **CLC 3, 4, 8, 11, 29; SSC 3**
See also CA 9-12R; 107; CANR 16; DLB 4, 9, 45; MTCW

Barnes, Julian   1946- .... **CLC 42; DAB**
See also CA 102; CANR 19; DLBY 93

Barnes, Peter   1931- .... **CLC 5, 56**
See also CA 65-68; CAAS 12; CANR 33, 34; DLB 13; MTCW

Baroja (y Nessi), Pio
1872-1956 .... **TCLC 8; HLC**
See also CA 104

Baron, David
See Pinter, Harold

Baron Corvo
See Rolfe, Frederick (William Serafino Austin Lewis Mary)

Barondess, Sue K(aufman)
1926-1977 .... **CLC 8**
See also Kaufman, Sue
See also CA 1-4R; 69-72; CANR 1

Baron de Teive
See Pessoa, Fernando (Antonio Nogueira)

Barres, Maurice   1862-1923 .... **TCLC 47**
See also DLB 123

Barreto, Afonso Henrique de Lima
See Lima Barreto, Afonso Henrique de

Barrett, (Roger) Syd   1946- .... **CLC 35**

Barrett, William (Christopher)
1913-1992 .... **CLC 27**
See also CA 13-16R; 139; CANR 11; INT CANR-11

Barrie, J(ames) M(atthew)
1860-1937 .... **TCLC 2; DAB**
See also CA 104; 136; CDBLB 1890-1914; CLR 16; DAM DRAM; DLB 10, 141, 156; MAICYA; YABC 1

Barrington, Michael
See Moorcock, Michael (John)

Barrol, Grady
See Bograd, Larry

Barry, Mike
See Malzberg, Barry N(athaniel)

Barry, Philip   1896-1949 .... **TCLC 11**
See also CA 109; DLB 7

Bart, Andre Schwarz
See Schwarz-Bart, Andre

Barth, John (Simmons)
1930- ...... **CLC 1, 2, 3, 5, 7, 9, 10, 14, 27, 51, 89; SSC 10**
See also AITN 1, 2; CA 1-4R; CABS 1; CANR 5, 23, 49; DAM NOV; DLB 2; MTCW

Barthelme, Donald
1931-1989 ...... **CLC 1, 2, 3, 5, 6, 8, 13, 23, 46, 59; SSC 2**
See also CA 21-24R; 129; CANR 20; DAM NOV; DLB 2; DLBY 80, 89; MTCW; SATA 7; SATA-Obit 62

Barthelme, Frederick   1943- .... **CLC 36**
See also CA 114; 122; DLBY 85; INT 122

Barthes, Roland (Gerard)
1915-1980 .... **CLC 24, 83**
See also CA 130; 97-100; MTCW

Barzun, Jacques (Martin)   1907- .... **CLC 51**
See also CA 61-64; CANR 22

Bashevis, Isaac
See Singer, Isaac Bashevis

Bashkirtseff, Marie   1859-1884 ... **NCLC 27**

Basho
See Matsuo Basho

Bass, Kingsley B., Jr.
See Bullins, Ed

Bass, Rick   1958- .... **CLC 79**
See also CA 126; CANR 53

Bassani, Giorgio   1916- .... **CLC 9**
See also CA 65-68; CANR 33; DLB 128; MTCW

Bastos, Augusto (Antonio) Roa
See Roa Bastos, Augusto (Antonio)

Bataille, Georges   1897-1962 .... **CLC 29**
See also CA 101; 89-92

Bates, H(erbert) E(rnest)
1905-1974 ...... **CLC 46; DAB; SSC 10**
See also CA 93-96; 45-48; CANR 34; DAM POP; DLB 162; MTCW

Bauchart
See Camus, Albert

Baudelaire, Charles
1821-1867 .... **NCLC 6, 29, 55; DA; DAB; DAC; PC 1; SSC 18; WLC**
See also DAM MST, POET

Baudrillard, Jean   1929- .... **CLC 60**

Booth, Philip 1925-.............. **CLC 23**
See also CA 5-8R; CANR 5; DLBY 82

Booth, Wayne C(layson) 1921- ..... **CLC 24**
See also CA 1-4R; CAAS 5; CANR 3, 43;
DLB 67

Borchert, Wolfgang 1921-1947 ..... **TCLC 5**
See also CA 104; DLB 69, 124

Borel, Petrus 1809-1859........ **NCLC 41**

Borges, Jorge Luis
1899-1986 ... **CLC 1, 2, 3, 4, 6, 8, 9, 10,
13, 19, 44, 48, 83; DA; DAB; DAC;
HLC; SSC 4; WLC**
See also CA 21-24R; CANR 19, 33;
DAM MST, MULT; DLB 113; DLBY 86;
HW; MTCW

Borowski, Tadeusz 1922-1951...... **TCLC 9**
See also CA 106

Borrow, George (Henry)
1803-1881 .... **NCLC 9**
See also DLB 21, 55, 166

Bosman, Herman Charles
1905-1951 .... **TCLC 49**

Bosschere, Jean de 1878(?)-1953... **TCLC 19**
See also CA 115

Boswell, James
1740-1795 ...... **LC 4; DA; DAB; DAC;
WLC**
See also CDBLB 1660-1789; DAM MST;
DLB 104, 142

Bottoms, David 1949-............. **CLC 53**
See also CA 105; CANR 22; DLB 120;
DLBY 83

Boucicault, Dion 1820-1890...... **NCLC 41**

Boucolon, Maryse 1937(?)-
See Conde, Maryse
See also CA 110; CANR 30, 53

Bourget, Paul (Charles Joseph)
1852-1935 .... **TCLC 12**
See also CA 107; DLB 123

Bourjaily, Vance (Nye) 1922- .... **CLC 8, 62**
See also CA 1-4R; CAAS 1; CANR 2;
DLB 2, 143

Bourne, Randolph S(illiman)
1886-1918 .... **TCLC 16**
See also CA 117; DLB 63

Bova, Ben(jamin William) 1932-.... **CLC 45**
See also AAYA 16; CA 5-8R; CAAS 18;
CANR 11; CLR 3; DLBY 81;
INT CANR-11; MAICYA; MTCW;
SATA 6, 68

Bowen, Elizabeth (Dorothea Cole)
1899-1973 ...... **CLC 1, 3, 6, 11, 15, 22;
SSC 3**
See also CA 17-18; 41-44R; CANR 35;
CAP 2; CDBLB 1945-1960; DAM NOV;
DLB 15, 162; MTCW

Bowering, George 1935-........ **CLC 15, 47**
See also CA 21-24R; CAAS 16; CANR 10;
DLB 53

Bowering, Marilyn R(uthe) 1949-... **CLC 32**
See also CA 101; CANR 49

Bowers, Edgar 1924- .... **CLC 9**
See also CA 5-8R; CANR 24; DLB 5

Bowie, David .... **CLC 17**
See also Jones, David Robert

Bowles, Jane (Sydney)
1917-1973 .... **CLC 3, 68**
See also CA 19-20; 41-44R; CAP 2

Bowles, Paul (Frederick)
1910- .... **CLC 1, 2, 19, 53; SSC 3**
See also CA 1-4R; CAAS 1; CANR 1, 19,
50; DLB 5, 6; MTCW

Box, Edgar
See Vidal, Gore

Boyd, Nancy
See Millay, Edna St. Vincent

Boyd, William 1952-........ **CLC 28, 53, 70**
See also CA 114; 120; CANR 51

Boyle, Kay
1902-1992 ..... **CLC 1, 5, 19, 58; SSC 5**
See also CA 13-16R; 140; CAAS 1;
CANR 29; DLB 4, 9, 48, 86; DLBY 93;
MTCW

Boyle, Mark
See Kienzle, William X(avier)

Boyle, Patrick 1905-1982......... **CLC 19**
See also CA 127

Boyle, T. C. 1948-
See Boyle, T(homas) Coraghessan

Boyle, T(homas) Coraghessan
1948- .... **CLC 36, 55, 90; SSC 16**
See also BEST 90:4; CA 120; CANR 44;
DAM POP; DLBY 86

Boz
See Dickens, Charles (John Huffam)

Brackenridge, Hugh Henry
1748-1816 .... **NCLC 7**
See also DLB 11, 37

Bradbury, Edward P.
See Moorcock, Michael (John)

Bradbury, Malcolm (Stanley)
1932- .... **CLC 32, 61**
See also CA 1-4R; CANR 1, 33;
DAM NOV; DLB 14; MTCW

Bradbury, Ray (Douglas)
1920- .... **CLC 1, 3, 10, 15, 42; DA;
DAB; DAC; WLC**
See also AAYA 15; AITN 1, 2; CA 1-4R;
CANR 2, 30; CDALB 1968-1988;
DAM MST, NOV, POP; DLB 2, 8;
INT CANR-30; MTCW; SATA 11, 64

Bradford, Gamaliel 1863-1932..... **TCLC 36**
See also DLB 17

Bradley, David (Henry, Jr.)
1950- .... **CLC 23; BLC**
See also BW 1; CA 104; CANR 26;
DAM MULT; DLB 33

Bradley, John Ed(mund, Jr.)
1958- .... **CLC 55**
See also CA 139

Bradley, Marion Zimmer 1930-..... **CLC 30**
See also AAYA 9; CA 57-60; CAAS 10;
CANR 7, 31, 51; DAM POP; DLB 8;
MTCW

Bradstreet, Anne
1612(?)-1672 ...... **LC 4, 30; DA; DAC;
PC 10**
See also CDALB 1640-1865; DAM MST,
POET; DLB 24

Brady, Joan 1939- .... **CLC 86**
See also CA 141

Bragg, Melvyn 1939- .... **CLC 10**
See also BEST 89:3; CA 57-60; CANR 10,
48; DLB 14

Braine, John (Gerard)
1922-1986 .... **CLC 1, 3, 41**
See also CA 1-4R; 120; CANR 1, 33;
CDBLB 1945-1960; DLB 15; DLBY 86;
MTCW

Brammer, William 1930(?)-1978 .... **CLC 31**
See also CA 77-80

Brancati, Vitaliano 1907-1954..... **TCLC 12**
See also CA 109

Brancato, Robin F(idler) 1936- ..... **CLC 35**
See also AAYA 9; CA 69-72; CANR 11,
45; CLR 32; JRDA; SAAS 9; SATA 23

Brand, Max
See Faust, Frederick (Schiller)

Brand, Millen 1906-1980.......... **CLC 7**
See also CA 21-24R; 97-100

Branden, Barbara .... **CLC 44**
See also CA 148

Brandes, Georg (Morris Cohen)
1842-1927 .... **TCLC 10**
See also CA 105

Brandys, Kazimierz 1916- .... **CLC 62**

Branley, Franklyn M(ansfield)
1915- .... **CLC 21**
See also CA 33-36R; CANR 14, 39;
CLR 13; MAICYA; SAAS 16; SATA 4,
68

Brathwaite, Edward Kamau 1930-... **CLC 11**
See also BW 2; CA 25-28R; CANR 11, 26,
47; DAM POET; DLB 125

Brautigan, Richard (Gary)
1935-1984 .... **CLC 1, 3, 5, 9, 12, 34, 42**
See also CA 53-56; 113; CANR 34;
DAM NOV; DLB 2, 5; DLBY 80, 84;
MTCW; SATA 56

Brave Bird, Mary 1953-
See Crow Dog, Mary
See also NNAL

Braverman, Kate 1950- .... **CLC 67**
See also CA 89-92

Brecht, Bertolt
1898-1956 ...... **TCLC 1, 6, 13, 35; DA;
DAB; DAC; DC 3; WLC**
See also CA 104; 133; DAM DRAM, MST;
DLB 56, 124; MTCW

Brecht, Eugen Berthold Friedrich
See Brecht, Bertolt

Bremer, Fredrika 1801-1865 ..... **NCLC 11**

Brennan, Christopher John
1870-1932 .... **TCLC 17**
See also CA 117

Brennan, Maeve 1917-............. **CLC 5**
See also CA 81-84

Brentano, Clemens (Maria)
1778-1842 .... **NCLC 1**
See also DLB 90

Brent of Bin Bin
See Franklin, (Stella Maraia Sarah) Miles

Brenton, Howard 1942- .... **CLC 31**
See also CA 69-72; CANR 33; DLB 13;
MTCW

Brulls, Christian
    See Simenon, Georges (Jacques Christian)

Brunner, John (Kilian Houston)
        1934-1995 .... **CLC 8, 10**
    See also CA 1-4R; 149; CAAS 8; CANR 2,
        37; DAM POP; MTCW

Bruno, Giordano 1548-1600........ **LC 27**

Brutus, Dennis 1924- .... **CLC 43; BLC**
    See also BW 2; CA 49-52; CAAS 14;
        CANR 2, 27, 42; DAM MULT, POET;
        DLB 117

Bryan, C(ourtlandt) D(ixon) B(arnes)
        1936- .... **CLC 29**
    See also CA 73-76; CANR 13;
        INT CANR-13

Bryan, Michael
    See Moore, Brian

Bryant, William Cullen
        1794-1878 ..... **NCLC 6, 46; DA; DAB;
                                                DAC**
    See also CDALB 1640-1865; DAM MST,
        POET; DLB 3, 43, 59

Bryusov, Valery Yakovlevich
        1873-1924 .... **TCLC 10**
    See also CA 107

Buchan, John 1875-1940 ... **TCLC 41; DAB**
    See also CA 108; 145; DAM POP; DLB 34,
        70, 156; YABC 2

Buchanan, George 1506-1582 .... **LC 4**

Buchheim, Lothar-Guenther 1918- ... **CLC 6**
    See also CA 85-88

Buchner, (Karl) Georg
        1813-1837 .... **NCLC 26**

Buchwald, Art(hur) 1925-......... **CLC 33**
    See also AITN 1; CA 5-8R; CANR 21;
        MTCW; SATA 10

Buck, Pearl S(ydenstricker)
        1892-1973 .... **CLC 7, 11, 18; DA; DAB;
                                                DAC**
    See also AITN 1; CA 1-4R; 41-44R;
        CANR 1, 34; DAM MST, NOV; DLB 9,
        102; MTCW; SATA 1, 25

Buckler, Ernest 1908-1984.... **CLC 13; DAC**
    See also CA 11-12; 114; CAP 1;
        DAM MST; DLB 68; SATA 47

Buckley, Vincent (Thomas)
        1925-1988 .... **CLC 57**
    See also CA 101

Buckley, William F(rank), Jr.
        1925- .... **CLC 7, 18, 37**
    See also AITN 1; CA 1-4R; CANR 1, 24,
        53; DAM POP; DLB 137; DLBY 80;
        INT CANR-24; MTCW

Buechner, (Carl) Frederick
        1926- .... **CLC 2, 4, 6, 9**
    See also CA 13-16R; CANR 11, 39;
        DAM NOV; DLBY 80; INT CANR-11;
        MTCW

Buell, John (Edward) 1927-........ **CLC 10**
    See also CA 1-4R; DLB 53

Buero Vallejo, Antonio 1916- ... **CLC 15, 46**
    See also CA 106; CANR 24, 49; HW;
        MTCW

Bufalino, Gesualdo 1920(?)-....... **CLC 74**

Bugayev, Boris Nikolayevich 1880-1934
    See Bely, Andrey
    See also CA 104

Bukowski, Charles
        1920-1994 .... **CLC 2, 5, 9, 41, 82**
    See also CA 17-20R; 144; CANR 40;
        DAM NOV, POET; DLB 5, 130; MTCW

Bulgakov, Mikhail (Afanas'evich)
        1891-1940 .... **TCLC 2, 16; SSC 18**
    See also CA 105; DAM DRAM, NOV

Bulgya, Alexander Alexandrovich
        1901-1956 .... **TCLC 53**
    See also Fadeyev, Alexander
    See also CA 117

Bullins, Ed 1935-.. **CLC 1, 5, 7; BLC; DC 6**
    See also BW 2; CA 49-52; CAAS 16;
        CANR 24, 46; DAM DRAM, MULT;
        DLB 7, 38; MTCW

Bulwer-Lytton, Edward (George Earle Lytton)
        1803-1873 .... **NCLC 1, 45**
    See also DLB 21

Bunin, Ivan Alexeyevich
        1870-1953 .... **TCLC 6; SSC 5**
    See also CA 104

Bunting, Basil 1900-1985.... **CLC 10, 39, 47**
    See also CA 53-56; 115; CANR 7;
        DAM POET; DLB 20

Bunuel, Luis 1900-1983 .. **CLC 16, 80; HLC**
    See also CA 101; 110; CANR 32;
        DAM MULT; HW

Bunyan, John
        1628-1688 ...... **LC 4; DA; DAB; DAC;
                                                WLC**
    See also CDBLB 1660-1789; DAM MST;
        DLB 39

Burckhardt, Jacob (Christoph)
        1818-1897 .... **NCLC 49**

Burford, Eleanor
    See Hibbert, Eleanor Alice Burford

Burgess, Anthony
        **CLC 1, 2, 4, 5, 8, 10, 13, 15, 22, 40, 62,
                                                81, 94; DAB**
    See also Wilson, John (Anthony) Burgess
    See also AITN 1; CDBLB 1960 to Present;
        DLB 14

Burke, Edmund
        1729(?)-1797 .... **LC 7; DA; DAB; DAC;
                                                WLC**
    See also DAM MST; DLB 104

Burke, Kenneth (Duva)
        1897-1993 .... **CLC 2, 24**
    See also CA 5-8R; 143; CANR 39; DLB 45,
        63; MTCW

Burke, Leda
    See Garnett, David

Burke, Ralph
    See Silverberg, Robert

Burke, Thomas 1886-1945....... **TCLC 63**
    See also CA 113

Burney, Fanny 1752-1840 .... **NCLC 12, 54**
    See also DLB 39

Burns, Robert 1759-1796........... **PC 6**
    See also CDBLB 1789-1832; DA; DAB;
        DAC; DAM MST, POET; DLB 109;
        WLC

Burns, Tex
    See L'Amour, Louis (Dearborn)

Burnshaw, Stanley 1906-..... **CLC 3, 13, 44**
    See also CA 9-12R; DLB 48

Burr, Anne 1937- .... **CLC 6**
    See also CA 25-28R

Burroughs, Edgar Rice
        1875-1950 .... **TCLC 2, 32**
    See also AAYA 11; CA 104; 132;
        DAM NOV; DLB 8; MTCW; SATA 41

Burroughs, William S(eward)
        1914- .... **CLC 1, 2, 5, 15, 22, 42, 75;
                                                DA; DAB; DAC; WLC**
    See also AITN 2; CA 9-12R; CANR 20, 52;
        DAM MST, NOV, POP; DLB 2, 8, 16,
        152; DLBY 81; MTCW

Burton, Richard F. 1821-1890.... **NCLC 42**
    See also DLB 55

Busch, Frederick 1941- ... **CLC 7, 10, 18, 47**
    See also CA 33-36R; CAAS 1; CANR 45;
        DLB 6

Bush, Ronald 1946- .... **CLC 34**
    See also CA 136

Bustos, F(rancisco)
    See Borges, Jorge Luis

Bustos Domecq, H(onorio)
    See Bioy Casares, Adolfo; Borges, Jorge
        Luis

Butler, Octavia E(stelle) 1947- ..... **CLC 38**
    See also AAYA 18; BW 2; CA 73-76;
        CANR 12, 24, 38; DAM MULT, POP;
        DLB 33; MTCW; SATA 84

Butler, Robert Olen (Jr.) 1945-..... **CLC 81**
    See also CA 112; DAM POP; INT 112

Butler, Samuel 1612-1680 .... **LC 16**
    See also DLB 101, 126

Butler, Samuel
        1835-1902 ...... **TCLC 1, 33; DA; DAB;
                                                DAC; WLC**
    See also CA 143; CDBLB 1890-1914;
        DAM MST, NOV; DLB 18, 57

Butler, Walter C.
    See Faust, Frederick (Schiller)

Butor, Michel (Marie Francois)
        1926- .... **CLC 1, 3, 8, 11, 15**
    See also CA 9-12R; CANR 33; DLB 83;
        MTCW

Buzo, Alexander (John) 1944-...... **CLC 61**
    See also CA 97-100; CANR 17, 39

Buzzati, Dino 1906-1972 .... **CLC 36**
    See also CA 33-36R

Byars, Betsy (Cromer) 1928-....... **CLC 35**
    See also CA 33-36R; CANR 18, 36; CLR 1,
        16; DLB 52; INT CANR-18; JRDA;
        MAICYA; MTCW; SAAS 1; SATA 4,
        46, 80

Byatt, A(ntonia) S(usan Drabble)
        1936- .... **CLC 19, 65**
    See also CA 13-16R; CANR 13, 33, 50;
        DAM NOV, POP; DLB 14; MTCW

Byrne, David 1952-............... **CLC 26**
    See also CA 127

Byrne, John Keyes 1926-
    See Leonard, Hugh
    See also CA 102; INT 102

Byron, George Gordon (Noel)
1788-1824 . . . . . **NCLC 2, 12; DA; DAB;**
DAC; PC 16; WLC
See also CDBLB 1789-1832; DAM MST,
POET; DLB 96, 110

C. 3. 3.
See Wilde, Oscar (Fingal O'Flahertie Wills)

Caballero, Fernan 1796-1877 . . . . . **NCLC 10**

Cabell, James Branch 1879-1958 . . . **TCLC 6**
See also CA 105; DLB 9, 78

Cable, George Washington
1844-1925 . . . . **TCLC 4; SSC 4**
See also CA 104; DLB 12, 74; DLBD 13

Cabral de Melo Neto, Joao 1920- . . . **CLC 76**
See also CA 151; DAM MULT

Cabrera Infante, G(uillermo)
1929- . . . . **CLC 5, 25, 45; HLC**
See also CA 85-88; CANR 29;
DAM MULT; DLB 113; HW; MTCW

Cade, Toni
See Bambara, Toni Cade

Cadmus and Harmonia
See Buchan, John

Caedmon fl. 658-680 . . . . **CMLC 7**
See also DLB 146

Caeiro, Alberto
See Pessoa, Fernando (Antonio Nogueira)

Cage, John (Milton, Jr.) 1912- . . . . . **CLC 41**
See also CA 13-16R; CANR 9;
INT CANR-9

Cain, G.
See Cabrera Infante, G(uillermo)

Cain, Guillermo
See Cabrera Infante, G(uillermo)

Cain, James M(allahan)
1892-1977 . . . . **CLC 3, 11, 28**
See also AITN 1; CA 17-20R; 73-76;
CANR 8, 34; MTCW

Caine, Mark
See Raphael, Frederic (Michael)

Calasso, Roberto 1941- . . . . **CLC 81**
See also CA 143

Calderon de la Barca, Pedro
1600-1681 . . . . **LC 23; DC 3**

Caldwell, Erskine (Preston)
1903-1987 . . . . **CLC 1, 8, 14, 50, 60;**
SSC 19
See also AITN 1; CA 1-4R; 121; CAAS 1;
CANR 2, 33; DAM NOV; DLB 9, 86;
MTCW

Caldwell, (Janet Miriam) Taylor (Holland)
1900-1985 . . . . **CLC 2, 28, 39**
See also CA 5-8R; 116; CANR 5;
DAM NOV, POP

Calhoun, John Caldwell
1782-1850 . . . . **NCLC 15**
See also DLB 3

Calisher, Hortense
1911- . . . . **CLC 2, 4, 8, 38; SSC 15**
See also CA 1-4R; CANR 1, 22;
DAM NOV; DLB 2; INT CANR-22;
MTCW

Callaghan, Morley Edward
1903-1990 . . . . . **CLC 3, 14, 41, 65; DAC**
See also CA 9-12R; 132; CANR 33;
DAM MST; DLB 68; MTCW

Callimachus
c. 305B.C.-c. 240B.C. . . . . **CMLC 18**

Calvino, Italo
1923-1985 . . . . . **CLC 5, 8, 11, 22, 33, 39,**
73; SSC 3
See also CA 85-88; 116; CANR 23;
DAM NOV; MTCW

Cameron, Carey 1952- . . . . **CLC 59**
See also CA 135

Cameron, Peter 1959- . . . . **CLC 44**
See also CA 125; CANR 50

Campana, Dino 1885-1932 . . . . **TCLC 20**
See also CA 117; DLB 114

Campanella, Tommaso 1568-1639 . . . . **LC 32**

Campbell, John W(ood, Jr.)
1910-1971 . . . . **CLC 32**
See also CA 21-22; 29-32R; CANR 34;
CAP 2; DLB 8; MTCW

Campbell, Joseph 1904-1987 . . . . **CLC 69**
See also AAYA 3; BEST 89:2; CA 1-4R;
124; CANR 3, 28; MTCW

Campbell, Maria 1940- . . . . . . **CLC 85; DAC**
See also CA 102; NNAL

Campbell, (John) Ramsey
1946- . . . . **CLC 42; SSC 19**
See also CA 57-60; CANR 7; INT CANR-7

Campbell, (Ignatius) Roy (Dunnachie)
1901-1957 . . . . **TCLC 5**
See also CA 104; DLB 20

Campbell, Thomas 1777-1844 . . . . **NCLC 19**
See also DLB 93; 144

Campbell, Wilfred . . . . **TCLC 9**
See also Campbell, William

Campbell, William 1858(?)-1918
See Campbell, Wilfred
See also CA 106; DLB 92

Campion, Jane . . . . **CLC 95**
See also CA 138

Campos, Alvaro de
See Pessoa, Fernando (Antonio Nogueira)

Camus, Albert
1913-1960 . . . . **CLC 1, 2, 4, 9, 11, 14, 32,**
63, 69; DA; DAB; DAC; DC 2; SSC 9;
WLC
See also CA 89-92; DAM DRAM, MST,
NOV; DLB 72; MTCW

Canby, Vincent 1924- . . . . **CLC 13**
See also CA 81-84

Cancale
See Desnos, Robert

Canetti, Elias
1905-1994 . . . . **CLC 3, 14, 25, 75, 86**
See also CA 21-24R; 146; CANR 23;
DLB 85, 124; MTCW

Canin, Ethan 1960- . . . . **CLC 55**
See also CA 131; 135

Cannon, Curt
See Hunter, Evan

Cape, Judith
See Page, P(atricia) K(athleen)

Capek, Karel
1890-1938 . . . . . . **TCLC 6, 37; DA; DAB;**
DAC; DC 1; WLC
See also CA 104; 140; DAM DRAM, MST,
NOV

Capote, Truman
1924-1984 . . . . . . **CLC 1, 3, 8, 13, 19, 34,**
38, 58; DA; DAB; DAC; SSC 2; WLC
See also CA 5-8R; 113; CANR 18;
CDALB 1941-1968; DAM MST, NOV,
POP; DLB 2; DLBY 80, 84; MTCW

Capra, Frank 1897-1991 . . . . **CLC 16**
See also CA 61-64; 135

Caputo, Philip 1941- . . . . **CLC 32**
See also CA 73-76; CANR 40

Card, Orson Scott 1951- . . . . **CLC 44, 47, 50**
See also AAYA 11; CA 102; CANR 27, 47;
DAM POP; INT CANR-27; MTCW;
SATA 83

Cardenal, Ernesto 1925- . . . . . **CLC 31; HLC**
See also CA 49-52; CANR 2, 32;
DAM MULT, POET; HW; MTCW

Cardozo, Benjamin N(athan)
1870-1938 . . . . **TCLC 65**
See also CA 117

Carducci, Giosue 1835-1907 . . . . . . **TCLC 32**

Carew, Thomas 1595(?)-1640 . . . . **LC 13**
See also DLB 126

Carey, Ernestine Gilbreth 1908- . . . . **CLC 17**
See also CA 5-8R; SATA 2

Carey, Peter 1943- . . . . **CLC 40, 55**
See also CA 123; 127; CANR 53; INT 127;
MTCW

Carleton, William 1794-1869 . . . . . . **NCLC 3**
See also DLB 159

Carlisle, Henry (Coffin) 1926- . . . . . . **CLC 33**
See also CA 13-16R; CANR 15

Carlsen, Chris
See Holdstock, Robert P.

Carlson, Ron(ald F.) 1947- . . . . **CLC 54**
See also CA 105; CANR 27

Carlyle, Thomas
1795-1881 . . **NCLC 22; DA; DAB; DAC**
See also CDBLB 1789-1832; DAM MST;
DLB 55; 144

Carman, (William) Bliss
1861-1929 . . . . **TCLC 7; DAC**
See also CA 104; DLB 92

Carnegie, Dale 1888-1955 . . . . **TCLC 53**

Carossa, Hans 1878-1956 . . . . **TCLC 48**
See also DLB 66

Carpenter, Don(ald Richard)
1931-1995 . . . . **CLC 41**
See also CA 45-48; 149; CANR 1

Carpentier (y Valmont), Alejo
1904-1980 . . . . **CLC 8, 11, 38; HLC**
See also CA 65-68; 97-100; CANR 11;
DAM MULT; DLB 113; HW

Carr, Caleb 1955(?)- . . . . **CLC 86**
See also CA 147

Carr, Emily 1871-1945 . . . . **TCLC 32**
See also DLB 68

Carr, John Dickson 1906-1977 . . . . . . **CLC 3**
See also CA 49-52; 69-72; CANR 3, 33;
MTCW

Carr, Philippa
See Hibbert, Eleanor Alice Burford

Carr, Virginia Spencer 1929-...... **CLC 34**
See also CA 61-64; DLB 111

Carrere, Emmanuel 1957- .... **CLC 89**

Carrier, Roch 1937-..... **CLC 13, 78; DAC**
See also CA 130; DAM MST; DLB 53

Carroll, James P. 1943(?)-......... **CLC 38**
See also CA 81-84

Carroll, Jim 1951- .... **CLC 35**
See also AAYA 17; CA 45-48; CANR 42

Carroll, Lewis .... **NCLC 2, 53; WLC**
See also Dodgson, Charles Lutwidge
See also CDBLB 1832-1890; CLR 2, 18;
DLB 18, 163; JRDA

Carroll, Paul Vincent 1900-1968.... **CLC 10**
See also CA 9-12R; 25-28R; DLB 10

Carruth, Hayden
1921- ...... **CLC 4, 7, 10, 18, 84; PC 10**
See also CA 9-12R; CANR 4, 38; DLB 5,
165; INT CANR-4; MTCW; SATA 47

Carson, Rachel Louise 1907-1964... **CLC 71**
See also CA 77-80; CANR 35; DAM POP;
MTCW; SATA 23

Carter, Angela (Olive)
1940-1992 ...... **CLC 5, 41, 76; SSC 13**
See also CA 53-56; 136; CANR 12, 36;
DLB 14; MTCW; SATA 66;
SATA-Obit 70

Carter, Nick
See Smith, Martin Cruz

Carver, Raymond
1938-1988 ... **CLC 22, 36, 53, 55; SSC 8**
See also CA 33-36R; 126; CANR 17, 34;
DAM NOV; DLB 130; DLBY 84, 88;
MTCW

Cary, Elizabeth, Lady Falkland
1585-1639 .... **LC 30**

Cary, (Arthur) Joyce (Lunel)
1888-1957 .... **TCLC 1, 29**
See also CA 104; CDBLB 1914-1945;
DLB 15, 100

Casanova de Seingalt, Giovanni Jacopo
1725-1798 .... **LC 13**

Casares, Adolfo Bioy
See Bioy Casares, Adolfo

Casely-Hayford, J(oseph) E(phraim)
1866-1930 ....**TCLC 24; BLC**
See also BW 2; CA 123; DAM MULT

Casey, John (Dudley) 1939-....... **CLC 59**
See also BEST 90:2; CA 69-72; CANR 23

Casey, Michael 1947-............. **CLC 2**
See also CA 65-68; DLB 5

Casey, Patrick
See Thurman, Wallace (Henry)

Casey, Warren (Peter) 1935-1988... **CLC 12**
See also CA 101; 127; INT 101

Casona, Alejandro................ **CLC 49**
See also Alvarez, Alejandro Rodriguez

Cassavetes, John 1929-1989....... **CLC 20**
See also CA 85-88; 127

Cassill, R(onald) V(erlin) 1919-... **CLC 4, 23**
See also CA 9-12R; CAAS 1; CANR 7, 45;
DLB 6

Cassirer, Ernst 1874-1945 .... **TCLC 61**

Cassity, (Allen) Turner 1929- .... **CLC 6, 42**
See also CA 17-20R; CAAS 8; CANR 11;
DLB 105

Castaneda, Carlos 1931(?)-......... **CLC 12**
See also CA 25-28R; CANR 32; HW;
MTCW

Castedo, Elena 1937-............. **CLC 65**
See also CA 132

Castedo-Ellerman, Elena
See Castedo, Elena

Castellanos, Rosario
1925-1974 .... **CLC 66; HLC**
See also CA 131; 53-56; DAM MULT;
DLB 113; HW

Castelvetro, Lodovico 1505-1571..... **LC 12**

Castiglione, Baldassare 1478-1529 ... **LC 12**

Castle, Robert
See Hamilton, Edmond

Castro, Guillen de 1569-1631........ **LC 19**

Castro, Rosalia de 1837-1885 ..... **NCLC 3**
See also DAM MULT

Cather, Willa
See Cather, Willa Sibert

Cather, Willa Sibert
1873-1947 .... **TCLC 1, 11, 31; DA;**
DAB; DAC; SSC 2; WLC
See also CA 104; 128; CDALB 1865-1917;
DAM MST, NOV; DLB 9, 54, 78;
DLBD 1; MTCW; SATA 30

Catton, (Charles) Bruce
1899-1978 .... **CLC 35**
See also AITN 1; CA 5-8R; 81-84;
CANR 7; DLB 17; SATA 2;
SATA-Obit 24

Catullus c. 84B.C.-c. 54B.C. ..... **CMLC 18**

Cauldwell, Frank
See King, Francis (Henry)

Caunitz, William J. 1933- .... **CLC 34**
See also BEST 89:3; CA 125; 130; INT 130

Causley, Charles (Stanley) 1917-..... **CLC 7**
See also CA 9-12R; CANR 5, 35; CLR 30;
DLB 27; MTCW; SATA 3, 66

Caute, David 1936-............... **CLC 29**
See also CA 1-4R; CAAS 4; CANR 1, 33;
DAM NOV; DLB 14

Cavafy, C(onstantine) P(eter)
1863-1933 .... **TCLC 2, 7**
See also Kavafis, Konstantinos Petrou
See also CA 148; DAM POET

Cavallo, Evelyn
See Spark, Muriel (Sarah)

Cavanna, Betty .... **CLC 12**
See also Harrison, Elizabeth Cavanna
See also JRDA; MAICYA; SAAS 4;
SATA 1, 30

Cavendish, Margaret Lucas
1623-1673 .... **LC 30**
See also DLB 131

Caxton, William 1421(?)-1491(?)..... **LC 17**

Cayrol, Jean 1911-................ **CLC 11**
See also CA 89-92; DLB 83

Cela, Camilo Jose
1916- .... **CLC 4, 13, 59; HLC**
See also BEST 90:2; CA 21-24R; CAAS 10;
CANR 21, 32; DAM MULT; DLBY 89;
HW; MTCW

Celan, Paul ...... **CLC 10, 19, 53, 82; PC 10**
See also Antschel, Paul
See also DLB 69

Celine, Louis-Ferdinand
.... **CLC 1, 3, 4, 7, 9, 15, 47**
See also Destouches, Louis-Ferdinand
See also DLB 72

Cellini, Benvenuto 1500-1571 .... **LC 7**

Cendrars, Blaise .... **CLC 18**
See also Sauser-Hall, Frederic

Cernuda (y Bidon), Luis
1902-1963 .... **CLC 54**
See also CA 131; 89-92; DAM POET;
DLB 134; HW

Cervantes (Saavedra), Miguel de
1547-1616 .... **LC 6, 23; DA; DAB;**
DAC; SSC 12; WLC
See also DAM MST, NOV

Cesaire, Aime (Fernand)
1913- .... **CLC 19, 32; BLC**
See also BW 2; CA 65-68; CANR 24, 43;
DAM MULT, POET; MTCW

Chabon, Michael 1965(?)- .... **CLC 55**
See also CA 139

Chabrol, Claude 1930-............. **CLC 16**
See also CA 110

Challans, Mary 1905-1983
See Renault, Mary
See also CA 81-84; 111; SATA 23;
SATA-Obit 36

Challis, George
See Faust, Frederick (Schiller)

Chambers, Aidan 1934-........... **CLC 35**
See also CA 25-28R; CANR 12, 31; JRDA;
MAICYA; SAAS 12; SATA 1, 69

Chambers, James 1948-
See Cliff, Jimmy
See also CA 124

Chambers, Jessie
See Lawrence, D(avid) H(erbert Richards)

Chambers, Robert W. 1865-1933... **TCLC 41**

Chandler, Raymond (Thornton)
1888-1959 .... **TCLC 1, 7; SSC 23**
See also CA 104; 129; CDALB 1929-1941;
DLBD 6; MTCW

Chang, Jung 1952- .... **CLC 71**
See also CA 142

Channing, William Ellery
1780-1842 .... **NCLC 17**
See also DLB 1, 59

Chaplin, Charles Spencer
1889-1977 .... **CLC 16**
See also Chaplin, Charlie
See also CA 81-84; 73-76

Chaplin, Charlie
See Chaplin, Charles Spencer
See also DLB 44

Chapman, George 1559(?)-1634...... **LC 22**
See also DAM DRAM; DLB 62, 121

Clancy, Tom. . . . . **CLC 45**
See also Clancy, Thomas L., Jr.
See also AAYA 9; BEST 89:1, 90:1;
DAM NOV, POP

Clare, John 1793-1864 . . . . . **NCLC 9; DAB**
See also DAM POET; DLB 55, 96

Clarin
See Alas (y Urena), Leopoldo (Enrique
Garcia)

Clark, Al C.
See Goines, Donald

Clark, (Robert) Brian 1932- . . . . **CLC 29**
See also CA 41-44R

Clark, Curt
See Westlake, Donald E(dwin)

Clark, Eleanor 1913-1996 . . . . **CLC 5, 19**
See also CA 9-12R; 151; CANR 41; DLB 6

Clark, J. P.
See Clark, John Pepper
See also DLB 117

Clark, John Pepper
1935- . . . . **CLC 38; BLC; DC 5**
See also Clark, J. P.
See also BW 1; CA 65-68; CANR 16;
DAM DRAM, MULT

Clark, M. R.
See Clark, Mavis Thorpe

Clark, Mavis Thorpe 1909- . . . . **CLC 12**
See also CA 57-60; CANR 8, 37; CLR 30;
MAICYA; SAAS 5; SATA 8, 74

Clark, Walter Van Tilburg
1909-1971 . . . . **CLC 28**
See also CA 9-12R; 33-36R; DLB 9;
SATA 8

Clarke, Arthur C(harles)
1917- . . . . . . **CLC 1, 4, 13, 18, 35; SSC 3**
See also AAYA 4; CA 1-4R; CANR 2, 28;
DAM POP; JRDA; MAICYA; MTCW;
SATA 13, 70

Clarke, Austin 1896-1974. . . . . **CLC 6, 9**
See also CA 29-32; 49-52; CAP 2;
DAM POET; DLB 10, 20

Clarke, Austin C(hesterfield)
1934- . . . . **CLC 8, 53; BLC; DAC**
See also BW 1; CA 25-28R; CAAS 16;
CANR 14, 32; DAM MULT; DLB 53,
125

Clarke, Gillian 1937- . . . . **CLC 61**
See also CA 106; DLB 40

Clarke, Marcus (Andrew Hislop)
1846-1881 . . . . **NCLC 19**

Clarke, Shirley 1925- . . . . **CLC 16**

Clash, The
See Headon, (Nicky) Topper; Jones, Mick;
Simonon, Paul; Strummer, Joe

Claudel, Paul (Louis Charles Marie)
1868-1955 . . . . **TCLC 2, 10**
See also CA 104

Clavell, James (duMaresq)
1925-1994 . . . . **CLC 6, 25, 87**
See also CA 25-28R; 146; CANR 26, 48;
DAM NOV, POP; MTCW

Cleaver, (Leroy) Eldridge
1935- . . . . **CLC 30; BLC**
See also BW 1; CA 21-24R; CANR 16;
DAM MULT

Cleese, John (Marwood) 1939- . . . . . **CLC 21**
See also Monty Python
See also CA 112; 116; CANR 35; MTCW

Cleishbotham, Jebediah
See Scott, Walter

Cleland, John 1710-1789 . . . . **LC 2**
See also DLB 39

Clemens, Samuel Langhorne 1835-1910
See Twain, Mark
See also CA 104; 135; CDALB 1865-1917;
DA; DAB; DAC; DAM MST, NOV;
DLB 11, 12, 23, 64, 74; JRDA;
MAICYA; YABC 2

Cleophil
See Congreve, William

Clerihew, E.
See Bentley, E(dmund) C(lerihew)

Clerk, N. W.
See Lewis, C(live) S(taples)

Cliff, Jimmy. . . . . **CLC 21**
See also Chambers, James

Clifton, (Thelma) Lucille
1936- . . . . **CLC 19, 66; BLC**
See also BW 2; CA 49-52; CANR 2, 24, 42;
CLR 5; DAM MULT, POET; DLB 5, 41;
MAICYA; MTCW; SATA 20, 69

Clinton, Dirk
See Silverberg, Robert

Clough, Arthur Hugh 1819-1861. . **NCLC 27**
See also DLB 32

Clutha, Janet Paterson Frame 1924-
See Frame, Janet
See also CA 1-4R; CANR 2, 36; MTCW

Clyne, Terence
See Blatty, William Peter

Cobalt, Martin
See Mayne, William (James Carter)

Cobbett, William 1763-1835 . . . . . **NCLC 49**
See also DLB 43, 107, 158

Coburn, D(onald) L(ee) 1938- . . . . . . **CLC 10**
See also CA 89-92

Cocteau, Jean (Maurice Eugene Clement)
1889-1963 . . . . **CLC 1, 8, 15, 16, 43; DA;
DAB; DAC; WLC**
See also CA 25-28; CANR 40; CAP 2;
DAM DRAM, MST, NOV; DLB 65;
MTCW

Codrescu, Andrei 1946- . . . . **CLC 46**
See also CA 33-36R; CAAS 19; CANR 13,
34, 53; DAM POET

Coe, Max
See Bourne, Randolph S(illiman)

Coe, Tucker
See Westlake, Donald E(dwin)

Coetzee, J(ohn) M(ichael)
1940- . . . . **CLC 23, 33, 66**
See also CA 77-80; CANR 41; DAM NOV;
MTCW

Coffey, Brian
See Koontz, Dean R(ay)

Cohan, George M. 1878-1942 . . . . . **TCLC 60**

Cohen, Arthur A(llen)
1928-1986 . . . . **CLC 7, 31**
See also CA 1-4R; 120; CANR 1, 17, 42;
DLB 28

Cohen, Leonard (Norman)
1934- . . . . **CLC 3, 38; DAC**
See also CA 21-24R; CANR 14;
DAM MST; DLB 53; MTCW

Cohen, Matt 1942- . . . . **CLC 19; DAC**
See also CA 61-64; CAAS 18; CANR 40;
DLB 53

Cohen-Solal, Annie 19(?)- . . . . **CLC 50**

Colegate, Isabel 1931- . . . . **CLC 36**
See also CA 17-20R; CANR 8, 22; DLB 14;
INT CANR-22; MTCW

Coleman, Emmett
See Reed, Ishmael

Coleridge, Samuel Taylor
1772-1834 . . . . . **NCLC 9, 54; DA; DAB;
DAC; PC 11; WLC**
See also CDBLB 1789-1832; DAM MST,
POET; DLB 93, 107

Coleridge, Sara 1802-1852. . . . . . **NCLC 31**

Coles, Don 1928- . . . . **CLC 46**
See also CA 115; CANR 38

Colette, (Sidonie-Gabrielle)
1873-1954 . . . . . . **TCLC 1, 5, 16; SSC 10**
See also CA 104; 131; DAM NOV; DLB 65;
MTCW

Collett, (Jacobine) Camilla (Wergeland)
1813-1895 . . . . **NCLC 22**

Collier, Christopher 1930- . . . . **CLC 30**
See also AAYA 13; CA 33-36R; CANR 13,
33; JRDA; MAICYA; SATA 16, 70

Collier, James L(incoln) 1928- . . . . . **CLC 30**
See also AAYA 13; CA 9-12R; CANR 4,
33; CLR 3; DAM POP; JRDA;
MAICYA; SAAS 21; SATA 8, 70

Collier, Jeremy 1650-1726. . . . . **LC 6**

Collier, John 1901-1980. . . . . **SSC 19**
See also CA 65-68; 97-100; CANR 10;
DLB 77

Collins, Hunt
See Hunter, Evan

Collins, Linda 1931- . . . . **CLC 44**
See also CA 125

Collins, (William) Wilkie
1824-1889 . . . . **NCLC 1, 18**
See also CDBLB 1832-1890; DLB 18, 70,
159

Collins, William 1721-1759 . . . . **LC 4**
See also DAM POET; DLB 109

Collodi, Carlo 1826-1890. . . . . . . **NCLC 54**
See also Lorenzini, Carlo
See also CLR 5

Colman, George
See Glassco, John

Colt, Winchester Remington
See Hubbard, L(afayette) Ron(ald)

Colter, Cyrus 1910- . . . . **CLC 58**
See also BW 1; CA 65-68; CANR 10;
DLB 33

Colton, James
See Hansen, Joseph

Cox, William Trevor 1928- . . . **CLC 9, 14, 71**
See also Trevor, William
See also CA 9-12R; CANR 4, 37;
DAM NOV; DLB 14; INT CANR-37;
MTCW

Coyne, P. J.
See Masters, Hilary

Cozzens, James Gould
1903-1978 . . . . **CLC 1, 4, 11, 92**
See also CA 9-12R; 81-84; CANR 19;
CDALB 1941-1968; DLB 9; DLBD 2;
DLBY 84; MTCW

Crabbe, George 1754-1832 . . . . . . **NCLC 26**
See also DLB 93

Craddock, Charles Egbert
See Murfree, Mary Noailles

Craig, A. A.
See Anderson, Poul (William)

Craik, Dinah Maria (Mulock)
1826-1887 . . . . **NCLC 38**
See also DLB 35, 163; MAICYA; SATA 34

Cram, Ralph Adams 1863-1942 . . . . **TCLC 45**

Crane, (Harold) Hart
1899-1932 . . . . . . **TCLC 2, 5; DA; DAB;
DAC; PC 3; WLC**
See also CA 104; 127; CDALB 1917-1929;
DAM MST, POET; DLB 4, 48; MTCW

Crane, R(onald) S(almon)
1886-1967 . . . . **CLC 27**
See also CA 85-88; DLB 63

Crane, Stephen (Townley)
1871-1900 . . . . **TCLC 11, 17, 32; DA;
DAB; DAC; SSC 7; WLC**
See also CA 109; 140; CDALB 1865-1917;
DAM MST, NOV, POET; DLB 12, 54,
78; YABC 2

Crase, Douglas 1944- . . . . **CLC 58**
See also CA 106

Crashaw, Richard 1612(?)-1649 . . . . . . **LC 24**
See also DLB 126

Craven, Margaret
1901-1980 . . . . **CLC 17; DAC**
See also CA 103

Crawford, F(rancis) Marion
1854-1909 . . . . **TCLC 10**
See also CA 107; DLB 71

Crawford, Isabella Valancy
1850-1887 . . . . **NCLC 12**
See also DLB 92

Crayon, Geoffrey
See Irving, Washington

Creasey, John 1908-1973 . . . . **CLC 11**
See also CA 5-8R; 41-44R; CANR 8;
DLB 77; MTCW

Crebillon, Claude Prosper Jolyot de (fils)
1707-1777 . . . . **LC 28**

Credo
See Creasey, John

Creeley, Robert (White)
1926- . . . . . **CLC 1, 2, 4, 8, 11, 15, 36, 78**
See also CA 1-4R; CAAS 10; CANR 23, 43;
DAM POET; DLB 5, 16; MTCW

Crews, Harry (Eugene)
1935- . . . . **CLC 6, 23, 49**
See also AITN 1; CA 25-28R; CANR 20;
DLB 6, 143; MTCW

Crichton, (John) Michael
1942- . . . . **CLC 2, 6, 54, 90**
See also AAYA 10; AITN 2; CA 25-28R;
CANR 13, 40; DAM NOV, POP;
DLBY 81; INT CANR-13; JRDA;
MTCW; SATA 9, 88

Crispin, Edmund . . . . **CLC 22**
See also Montgomery, (Robert) Bruce
See also DLB 87

Cristofer, Michael 1945(?)- . . . . **CLC 28**
See also CA 110; DAM DRAM; DLB 7

Croce, Benedetto 1866-1952 . . . . . . **TCLC 37**
See also CA 120

Crockett, David 1786-1836 . . . . **NCLC 8**
See also DLB 3, 11

Crockett, Davy
See Crockett, David

Crofts, Freeman Wills
1879-1957 . . . . **TCLC 55**
See also CA 115; DLB 77

Croker, John Wilson 1780-1857 . . **NCLC 10**
See also DLB 110

Crommelynck, Fernand 1885-1970 . . **CLC 75**
See also CA 89-92

Cronin, A(rchibald) J(oseph)
1896-1981 . . . . **CLC 32**
See also CA 1-4R; 102; CANR 5; SATA 47;
SATA-Obit 25

Cross, Amanda
See Heilbrun, Carolyn G(old)

Crothers, Rachel 1878(?)-1958 . . . . . **TCLC 19**
See also CA 113; DLB 7

Croves, Hal
See Traven, B.

Crow Dog, Mary . . . . **CLC 93**
See also Brave Bird, Mary

Crowfield, Christopher
See Stowe, Harriet (Elizabeth) Beecher

Crowley, Aleister . . . . **TCLC 7**
See also Crowley, Edward Alexander

Crowley, Edward Alexander 1875-1947
See Crowley, Aleister
See also CA 104

Crowley, John 1942- . . . . **CLC 57**
See also CA 61-64; CANR 43; DLBY 82;
SATA 65

Crud
See Crumb, R(obert)

Crumarums
See Crumb, R(obert)

Crumb, R(obert) 1943- . . . . **CLC 17**
See also CA 106

Crumbum
See Crumb, R(obert)

Crumski
See Crumb, R(obert)

Crum the Bum
See Crumb, R(obert)

Crunk
See Crumb, R(obert)

Crustt
See Crumb, R(obert)

Cryer, Gretchen (Kiger) 1935- . . . . . . **CLC 21**
See also CA 114; 123

Csath, Geza 1887-1919 . . . . **TCLC 13**
See also CA 111

Cudlip, David 1933- . . . . **CLC 34**

Cullen, Countee
1903-1946 . . . . . . **TCLC 4, 37; BLC; DA;
DAC**
See also BW 1; CA 108; 124;
CDALB 1917-1929; DAM MST, MULT,
POET; DLB 4, 48, 51; MTCW; SATA 18

Cum, R.
See Crumb, R(obert)

Cummings, Bruce F(rederick) 1889-1919
See Barbellion, W. N. P.
See also CA 123

Cummings, E(dward) E(stlin)
1894-1962 . . . . . . **CLC 1, 3, 8, 12, 15, 68;
DA; DAB; DAC; PC 5; WLC 2**
See also CA 73-76; CANR 31;
CDALB 1929-1941; DAM MST, POET;
DLB 4, 48; MTCW

Cunha, Euclides (Rodrigues Pimenta) da
1866-1909 . . . . **TCLC 24**
See also CA 123

Cunningham, E. V.
See Fast, Howard (Melvin)

Cunningham, J(ames) V(incent)
1911-1985 . . . . **CLC 3, 31**
See also CA 1-4R; 115; CANR 1; DLB 5

Cunningham, Julia (Woolfolk)
1916- . . . . **CLC 12**
See also CA 9-12R; CANR 4, 19, 36;
JRDA; MAICYA; SAAS 2; SATA 1, 26

Cunningham, Michael 1952- . . . . **CLC 34**
See also CA 136

Cunninghame Graham, R(obert) B(ontine)
1852-1936 . . . . **TCLC 19**
See also Graham, R(obert) B(ontine)
Cunninghame
See also CA 119; DLB 98

Currie, Ellen 19(?)- . . . . **CLC 44**

Curtin, Philip
See Lowndes, Marie Adelaide (Belloc)

Curtis, Price
See Ellison, Harlan (Jay)

Cutrate, Joe
See Spiegelman, Art

Czaczkes, Shmuel Yosef
See Agnon, S(hmuel) Y(osef Halevi)

Dabrowska, Maria (Szumska)
1889-1965 . . . . **CLC 15**
See also CA 106

Dabydeen, David 1955- . . . . **CLC 34**
See also BW 1; CA 125

Dacey, Philip 1939- . . . . **CLC 51**
See also CA 37-40R; CAAS 17; CANR 14,
32; DLB 105

Dagerman, Stig (Halvard)
1923-1954 . . . . **TCLC 17**
See also CA 117

Dahl, Roald
　　1916-1990 . . . . . . **CLC 1, 6, 18, 79; DAB;**
　　　　　　　　　　　　　　　　　　　　　　DAC
　　See also AAYA 15; CA 1-4R; 133;
　　CANR 6, 32, 37; CLR 1, 7, 41;
　　DAM MST, NOV, POP; DLB 139;
　　JRDA; MAICYA; MTCW; SATA 1, 26,
　　73; SATA-Obit 65

Dahlberg, Edward 1900-1977 . . . **CLC 1, 7, 14**
　　See also CA 9-12R; 69-72; CANR 31;
　　DLB 48; MTCW

Dale, Colin . . . . **TCLC 18**
　　See also Lawrence, T(homas) E(dward)

Dale, George E.
　　See Asimov, Isaac

Daly, Elizabeth 1878-1967 . . . . **CLC 52**
　　See also CA 23-24; 25-28R; CAP 2

Daly, Maureen 1921- . . . . **CLC 17**
　　See also AAYA 5; CANR 37; JRDA;
　　MAICYA; SAAS 1; SATA 2

Damas, Leon-Gontran 1912-1978 . . . **CLC 84**
　　See also BW 1; CA 125; 73-76

Dana, Richard Henry Sr.
　　1787-1879 . . . . **NCLC 53**

Daniel, Samuel 1562(?)-1619 . . . . **LC 24**
　　See also DLB 62

Daniels, Brett
　　See Adler, Renata

Dannay, Frederic 1905-1982 . . . . **CLC 11**
　　See also Queen, Ellery
　　See also CA 1-4R; 107; CANR 1, 39;
　　DAM POP; DLB 137; MTCW

D'Annunzio, Gabriele
　　1863-1938 . . . . **TCLC 6, 40**
　　See also CA 104

Danois, N. le
　　See Gourmont, Remy (-Marie-Charles) de

d'Antibes, Germain
　　See Simenon, Georges (Jacques Christian)

Danticat, Edwidge 1969- . . . . **CLC 94**
　　See also CA 152

Danvers, Dennis 1947- . . . . **CLC 70**

Danziger, Paula 1944- . . . . **CLC 21**
　　See also AAYA 4; CA 112; 115; CANR 37;
　　CLR 20; JRDA; MAICYA; SATA 36,
　　63; SATA-Brief 30

Da Ponte, Lorenzo 1749-1838 . . . . **NCLC 50**

Dario, Ruben
　　1867-1916 . . . . **TCLC 4; HLC; PC 15**
　　See also CA 131; DAM MULT; HW;
　　MTCW

Darley, George 1795-1846 . . . . **NCLC 2**
　　See also DLB 96

Darwin, Charles 1809-1882 . . . . . . **NCLC 57**
　　See also DLB 57, 166

Daryush, Elizabeth 1887-1977 . . . . **CLC 6, 19**
　　See also CA 49-52; CANR 3; DLB 20

Dashwood, Edmee Elizabeth Monica de la
　　　Pasture 1890-1943
　　See Delafield, E. M.
　　See also CA 119

Daudet, (Louis Marie) Alphonse
　　1840-1897 . . . . **NCLC 1**
　　See also DLB 123

Daumal, Rene 1908-1944 . . . . **TCLC 14**
　　See also CA 114

Davenport, Guy (Mattison, Jr.)
　　1927- . . . . **CLC 6, 14, 38; SSC 16**
　　See also CA 33-36R; CANR 23; DLB 130

Davidson, Avram 1923-
　　See Queen, Ellery
　　See also CA 101; CANR 26; DLB 8

Davidson, Donald (Grady)
　　1893-1968 . . . . **CLC 2, 13, 19**
　　See also CA 5-8R; 25-28R; CANR 4;
　　DLB 45

Davidson, Hugh
　　See Hamilton, Edmond

Davidson, John 1857-1909 . . . . **TCLC 24**
　　See also CA 118; DLB 19

Davidson, Sara 1943- . . . . **CLC 9**
　　See also CA 81-84; CANR 44

Davie, Donald (Alfred)
　　1922-1995 . . . . **CLC 5, 8, 10, 31**
　　See also CA 1-4R; 149; CAAS 3; CANR 1,
　　44; DLB 27; MTCW

Davies, Ray(mond Douglas) 1944- . . **CLC 21**
　　See also CA 116; 146

Davies, Rhys 1903-1978 . . . . **CLC 23**
　　See also CA 9-12R; 81-84; CANR 4;
　　DLB 139

Davies, (William) Robertson
　　1913-1995 . . . . . **CLC 2, 7, 13, 25, 42, 75,**
　　　　　　　　　　91; CLC 2; DA; DAB; DAC; WLC
　　See also BEST 89:2; CA 33-36R; 150;
　　CANR 17, 42; DAM MST, NOV, POP;
　　DLB 68; INT CANR-17; MTCW

Davies, W(illiam) H(enry)
　　1871-1940 . . . . **TCLC 5**
　　See also CA 104; DLB 19

Davies, Walter C.
　　See Kornbluth, C(yril) M.

Davis, Angela (Yvonne) 1944- . . . . . . **CLC 77**
　　See also BW 2; CA 57-60; CANR 10;
　　DAM MULT

Davis, B. Lynch
　　See Bioy Casares, Adolfo; Borges, Jorge
　　Luis

Davis, Gordon
　　See Hunt, E(verette) Howard, (Jr.)

Davis, Harold Lenoir 1896-1960 . . . . **CLC 49**
　　See also CA 89-92; DLB 9

Davis, Rebecca (Blaine) Harding
　　1831-1910 . . . . **TCLC 6**
　　See also CA 104; DLB 74

Davis, Richard Harding
　　1864-1916 . . . . **TCLC 24**
　　See also CA 114; DLB 12, 23, 78, 79;
　　DLBD 13

Davison, Frank Dalby 1893-1970 . . . **CLC 15**
　　See also CA 116

Davison, Lawrence H.
　　See Lawrence, D(avid) H(erbert Richards)

Davison, Peter (Hubert) 1928- . . . . . **CLC 28**
　　See also CA 9-12R; CAAS 4; CANR 3, 43;
　　DLB 5

Davys, Mary 1674-1732 . . . . **LC 1**
　　See also DLB 39

Dawson, Fielding 1930- . . . . **CLC 6**
　　See also CA 85-88; DLB 130

Dawson, Peter
　　See Faust, Frederick (Schiller)

Day, Clarence (Shepard, Jr.)
　　1874-1935 . . . . **TCLC 25**
　　See also CA 108; DLB 11

Day, Thomas 1748-1789 . . . . **LC 1**
　　See also DLB 39; YABC 1

Day Lewis, C(ecil)
　　1904-1972 . . . . **CLC 1, 6, 10; PC 11**
　　See also Blake, Nicholas
　　See also CA 13-16; 33-36R; CANR 34;
　　CAP 1; DAM POET; DLB 15, 20;
　　MTCW

Dazai, Osamu . . . . **TCLC 11**
　　See also Tsushima, Shuji

de Andrade, Carlos Drummond
　　See Drummond de Andrade, Carlos

Deane, Norman
　　See Creasey, John

de Beauvoir, Simone (Lucie Ernestine Marie
　　　Bertrand)
　　See Beauvoir, Simone (Lucie Ernestine
　　Marie Bertrand) de

de Brissac, Malcolm
　　See Dickinson, Peter (Malcolm)

de Chardin, Pierre Teilhard
　　See Teilhard de Chardin, (Marie Joseph)
　　Pierre

Dee, John 1527-1608 . . . . **LC 20**

Deer, Sandra 1940- . . . . **CLC 45**

De Ferrari, Gabriella 1941- . . . . **CLC 65**
　　See also CA 146

Defoe, Daniel
　　1660(?)-1731 . . . . **LC 1; DA; DAB; DAC;**
　　　　　　　　　　　　　　　　　　　　　　WLC
　　See also CDBLB 1660-1789; DAM MST,
　　NOV; DLB 39, 95, 101; JRDA;
　　MAICYA; SATA 22

de Gourmont, Remy(-Marie-Charles)
　　See Gourmont, Remy (-Marie-Charles) de

de Hartog, Jan 1914- . . . . **CLC 19**
　　See also CA 1-4R; CANR 1

de Hostos, E. M.
　　See Hostos (y Bonilla), Eugenio Maria de

de Hostos, Eugenio M.
　　See Hostos (y Bonilla), Eugenio Maria de

Deighton, Len . . . . **CLC 4, 7, 22, 46**
　　See also Deighton, Leonard Cyril
　　See also AAYA 6; BEST 89:2;
　　CDBLB 1960 to Present; DLB 87

Deighton, Leonard Cyril 1929-
　　See Deighton, Len
　　See also CA 9-12R; CANR 19, 33;
　　DAM NOV, POP; MTCW

Dekker, Thomas 1572(?)-1632 . . . . **LC 22**
　　See also CDBLB Before 1660;
　　DAM DRAM; DLB 62

Delafield, E. M. 1890-1943 . . . . **TCLC 61**
　　See also Dashwood, Edmee Elizabeth
　　Monica de la Pasture
　　See also DLB 34

de la Mare, Walter (John)
　　1873-1956 .... **TCLC 4, 53; DAB; DAC;**
　　　　　　　　　　　　　SSC 14; WLC
　　See also CDBLB 1914-1945; CLR 23;
　　　DAM MST, POET; DLB 162; SATA 16

Delaney, Franey
　　See O'Hara, John (Henry)

Delaney, Shelagh 1939- .... **CLC 29**
　　See also CA 17-20R; CANR 30;
　　　CDBLB 1960 to Present; DAM DRAM;
　　　DLB 13; MTCW

Delany, Mary (Granville Pendarves)
　　1700-1788 .... **LC 12**

Delany, Samuel R(ay, Jr.)
　　1942- .... **CLC 8, 14, 38; BLC**
　　See also BW 2; CA 81-84; CANR 27, 43;
　　　DAM MULT; DLB 8, 33; MTCW

De La Ramee, (Marie) Louise 1839-1908
　　See Ouida
　　See also SATA 20

de la Roche, Mazo 1879-1961 ...... **CLC 14**
　　See also CA 85-88; CANR 30; DLB 68;
　　　SATA 64

Delbanco, Nicholas (Franklin)
　　1942- .... **CLC 6, 13**
　　See also CA 17-20R; CAAS 2; CANR 29;
　　　DLB 6

del Castillo, Michel 1933- .... **CLC 38**
　　See also CA 109

Deledda, Grazia (Cosima)
　　1875(?)-1936 .... **TCLC 23**
　　See also CA 123

Delibes, Miguel .... **CLC 8, 18**
　　See also Delibes Setien, Miguel

Delibes Setien, Miguel 1920-
　　See Delibes, Miguel
　　See also CA 45-48; CANR 1, 32; HW;
　　　MTCW

DeLillo, Don
　　1936- ..... **CLC 8, 10, 13, 27, 39, 54, 76**
　　See also BEST 89:1; CA 81-84; CANR 21;
　　　DAM NOV, POP; DLB 6; MTCW

de Lisser, H. G.
　　See De Lisser, Herbert George
　　See also DLB 117

De Lisser, Herbert George
　　1878-1944 .... **TCLC 12**
　　See also de Lisser, H. G.
　　See also BW 2; CA 109

Deloria, Vine (Victor), Jr. 1933- .... **CLC 21**
　　See also CA 53-56; CANR 5, 20, 48;
　　　DAM MULT; MTCW; NNAL; SATA 21

Del Vecchio, John M(ichael)
　　1947- .... **CLC 29**
　　See also CA 110; DLBD 9

de Man, Paul (Adolph Michel)
　　1919-1983 .... **CLC 55**
　　See also CA 128; 111; DLB 67; MTCW

De Marinis, Rick 1934- .... **CLC 54**
　　See also CA 57-60; CAAS 24; CANR 9, 25,
　　　50

Dembry, R. Emmet
　　See Murfree, Mary Noailles

Demby, William 1922- .... **CLC 53; BLC**
　　See also BW 1; CA 81-84; DAM MULT;
　　　DLB 33

Demijohn, Thom
　　See Disch, Thomas M(ichael)

de Montherlant, Henry (Milon)
　　See Montherlant, Henry (Milon) de

Demosthenes 384B.C.-322B.C. .... **CMLC 13**

de Natale, Francine
　　See Malzberg, Barry N(athaniel)

Denby, Edwin (Orr) 1903-1983 ..... **CLC 48**
　　See also CA 138; 110

Denis, Julio
　　See Cortazar, Julio

Denmark, Harrison
　　See Zelazny, Roger (Joseph)

Dennis, John 1658-1734 .... **LC 11**
　　See also DLB 101

Dennis, Nigel (Forbes) 1912-1989 .... **CLC 8**
　　See also CA 25-28R; 129; DLB 13, 15;
　　　MTCW

De Palma, Brian (Russell) 1940- .... **CLC 20**
　　See also CA 109

De Quincey, Thomas 1785-1859 ... **NCLC 4**
　　See also CDBLB 1789-1832; DLB 110; 144

Deren, Eleanora 1908(?)-1961
　　See Deren, Maya
　　See also CA 111

Deren, Maya .... **CLC 16**
　　See also Deren, Eleanora

Derleth, August (William)
　　1909-1971 .... **CLC 31**
　　See also CA 1-4R; 29-32R; CANR 4;
　　　DLB 9; SATA 5

Der Nister 1884-1950 .... **TCLC 56**

de Routisie, Albert
　　See Aragon, Louis

Derrida, Jacques 1930- .... **CLC 24, 87**
　　See also CA 124; 127

Derry Down Derry
　　See Lear, Edward

Dersonnes, Jacques
　　See Simenon, Georges (Jacques Christian)

Desai, Anita 1937- ...... **CLC 19, 37; DAB**
　　See also CA 81-84; CANR 33, 53;
　　　DAM NOV; MTCW; SATA 63

de Saint-Luc, Jean
　　See Glassco, John

de Saint Roman, Arnaud
　　See Aragon, Louis

Descartes, Rene 1596-1650 .... **LC 20**

De Sica, Vittorio 1901(?)-1974 ..... **CLC 20**
　　See also CA 117

Desnos, Robert 1900-1945 .... **TCLC 22**
　　See also CA 121; 151

Destouches, Louis-Ferdinand
　　1894-1961 .... **CLC 9, 15**
　　See also Celine, Louis-Ferdinand
　　See also CA 85-88; CANR 28; MTCW

Deutsch, Babette 1895-1982 .... **CLC 18**
　　See also CA 1-4R; 108; CANR 4; DLB 45;
　　　SATA 1; SATA-Obit 33

Devenant, William 1606-1649 ...... **LC 13**

Devkota, Laxmiprasad
　　1909-1959 .... **TCLC 23**
　　See also CA 123

De Voto, Bernard (Augustine)
　　1897-1955 .... **TCLC 29**
　　See also CA 113; DLB 9

De Vries, Peter
　　1910-1993 .... **CLC 1, 2, 3, 7, 10, 28, 46**
　　See also CA 17-20R; 142; CANR 41;
　　　DAM NOV; DLB 6; DLBY 82; MTCW

Dexter, John
　　See Bradley, Marion Zimmer

Dexter, Martin
　　See Faust, Frederick (Schiller)

Dexter, Pete 1943- .... **CLC 34, 55**
　　See also BEST 89:2; CA 127; 131;
　　　DAM POP; INT 131; MTCW

Diamano, Silmang
　　See Senghor, Leopold Sedar

Diamond, Neil 1941- .... **CLC 30**
　　See also CA 108

Diaz del Castillo, Bernal 1496-1584 .. **LC 31**

di Bassetto, Corno
　　See Shaw, George Bernard

Dick, Philip K(indred)
　　1928-1982 .... **CLC 10, 30, 72**
　　See also CA 49-52; 106; CANR 2, 16;
　　　DAM NOV, POP; DLB 8; MTCW

Dickens, Charles (John Huffam)
　　1812-1870 ..... **NCLC 3, 8, 18, 26, 37,**
　　　　　　　50; DA; DAB; DAC; SSC 17; WLC
　　See also CDBLB 1832-1890; DAM MST,
　　　NOV; DLB 21, 55, 70, 159, 166; JRDA;
　　　MAICYA; SATA 15

Dickey, James (Lafayette)
　　1923- .... **CLC 1, 2, 4, 7, 10, 15, 47**
　　See also AITN 1, 2; CA 9-12R; CABS 2;
　　　CANR 10, 48; CDALB 1968-1988;
　　　DAM NOV, POET, POP; DLB 5;
　　　DLBD 7; DLBY 82, 93; INT CANR-10;
　　　MTCW

Dickey, William 1928-1994 ...... **CLC 3, 28**
　　See also CA 9-12R; 145; CANR 24; DLB 5

Dickinson, Charles 1951- .... **CLC 49**
　　See also CA 128

Dickinson, Emily (Elizabeth)
　　1830-1886 .... **NCLC 21; DA; DAB;**
　　　　　　　　　　　DAC; PC 1; WLC
　　See also CDALB 1865-1917; DAM MST,
　　　POET; DLB 1; SATA 29

Dickinson, Peter (Malcolm)
　　1927- .... **CLC 12, 35**
　　See also AAYA 9; CA 41-44R; CANR 31;
　　　CLR 29; DLB 87, 161; JRDA; MAICYA;
　　　SATA 5, 62

Dickson, Carr
　　See Carr, John Dickson

Dickson, Carter
　　See Carr, John Dickson

Diderot, Denis 1713-1784 .... **LC 26**

Didion, Joan 1934- ..... **CLC 1, 3, 8, 14, 32**
　　See also AITN 1; CA 5-8R; CANR 14, 52;
　　　CDALB 1968-1988; DAM NOV; DLB 2;
　　　DLBY 81, 86; MTCW

Dietrich, Robert
　　See Hunt, E(verette) Howard, (Jr.)

Dillard, Annie 1945- .... **CLC 9, 60**
See also AAYA 6; CA 49-52; CANR 3, 43;
DAM NOV; DLBY 80; MTCW;
SATA 10

Dillard, R(ichard) H(enry) W(ilde)
1937- .... **CLC 5**
See also CA 21-24R; CAAS 7; CANR 10;
DLB 5

Dillon, Eilis 1920-1994 .... **CLC 17**
See also CA 9-12R; 147; CAAS 3; CANR 4,
38; CLR 26; MAICYA; SATA 2, 74;
SATA-Obit 83

Dimont, Penelope
See Mortimer, Penelope (Ruth)

Dinesen, Isak .... **CLC 10, 29, 95; SSC 7**
See also Blixen, Karen (Christentze
Dinesen)

Ding Ling .... **CLC 68**
See also Chiang Pin-chin

Disch, Thomas M(ichael) 1940- ... **CLC 7, 36**
See also AAYA 17; CA 21-24R; CAAS 4;
CANR 17, 36; CLR 18; DLB 8;
MAICYA; MTCW; SAAS 15; SATA 54

Disch, Tom
See Disch, Thomas M(ichael)

d'Isly, Georges
See Simenon, Georges (Jacques Christian)

Disraeli, Benjamin 1804-1881 .. **NCLC 2, 39**
See also DLB 21, 55

Ditcum, Steve
See Crumb, R(obert)

Dixon, Paige
See Corcoran, Barbara

Dixon, Stephen 1936- ..... **CLC 52; SSC 16**
See also CA 89-92; CANR 17, 40; DLB 130

Dobell, Sydney Thompson
1824-1874 .... **NCLC 43**
See also DLB 32

Doblin, Alfred .... **TCLC 13**
See also Doeblin, Alfred

Dobrolyubov, Nikolai Alexandrovich
1836-1861 .... **NCLC 5**

Dobyns, Stephen 1941- .... **CLC 37**
See also CA 45-48; CANR 2, 18

Doctorow, E(dgar) L(aurence)
1931- ..... **CLC 6, 11, 15, 18, 37, 44, 65**
See also AITN 2; BEST 89:3; CA 45-48;
CANR 2, 33, 51; CDALB 1968-1988;
DAM NOV, POP; DLB 2, 28; DLBY 80;
MTCW

Dodgson, Charles Lutwidge 1832-1898
See Carroll, Lewis
See also CLR 2; DA; DAB; DAC;
DAM MST, NOV, POET; MAICYA;
YABC 2

Dodson, Owen (Vincent)
1914-1983 .... **CLC 79; BLC**
See also BW 1; CA 65-68; 110; CANR 24;
DAM MULT; DLB 76

Doeblin, Alfred 1878-1957 .... **TCLC 13**
See also Doblin, Alfred
See also CA 110; 141; DLB 66

Doerr, Harriet 1910- .... **CLC 34**
See also CA 117; 122; CANR 47; INT 122

Domecq, H(onorio) Bustos
See Bioy Casares, Adolfo; Borges, Jorge
Luis

Domini, Rey
See Lorde, Audre (Geraldine)

Dominique
See Proust, (Valentin-Louis-George-Eugene-)
Marcel

Don, A
See Stephen, Leslie

Donaldson, Stephen R. 1947- .... **CLC 46**
See also CA 89-92; CANR 13; DAM POP;
INT CANR-13

Donleavy, J(ames) P(atrick)
1926- .... **CLC 1, 4, 6, 10, 45**
See also AITN 2; CA 9-12R; CANR 24, 49;
DLB 6; INT CANR-24; MTCW

Donne, John
1572-1631 .... **LC 10, 24; DA; DAB;**
                              DAC; PC 1
See also CDBLB Before 1660; DAM MST,
POET; DLB 121, 151

Donnell, David 1939(?)- .... **CLC 34**

Donoghue, P. S.
See Hunt, E(verette) Howard, (Jr.)

Donoso (Yanez), Jose
1924- .... **CLC 4, 8, 11, 32; HLC**
See also CA 81-84; CANR 32;
DAM MULT; DLB 113; HW; MTCW

Donovan, John 1928-1992 .... **CLC 35**
See also CA 97-100; 137; CLR 3;
MAICYA; SATA 72; SATA-Brief 29

Don Roberto
See Cunninghame Graham, R(obert)
B(ontine)

Doolittle, Hilda
1886-1961 ..... **CLC 3, 8, 14, 31, 34, 73;**
                              DA; DAC; PC 5; WLC
See also H. D.
See also CA 97-100; CANR 35; DAM MST,
POET; DLB 4, 45; MTCW

Dorfman, Ariel 1942- .... **CLC 48, 77; HLC**
See also CA 124; 130; DAM MULT; HW;
INT 130

Dorn, Edward (Merton) 1929- ... **CLC 10, 18**
See also CA 93-96; CANR 42; DLB 5;
INT 93-96

Dorsan, Luc
See Simenon, Georges (Jacques Christian)

Dorsange, Jean
See Simenon, Georges (Jacques Christian)

Dos Passos, John (Roderigo)
1896-1970 ...... **CLC 1, 4, 8, 11, 15, 25,**
                       34, 82; DA; DAB; DAC; WLC
See also CA 1-4R; 29-32R; CANR 3;
CDALB 1929-1941; DAM MST, NOV;
DLB 4, 9; DLBD 1; MTCW

Dossage, Jean
See Simenon, Georges (Jacques Christian)

Dostoevsky, Fedor Mikhailovich
1821-1881 ...... **NCLC 2, 7, 21, 33, 43;**
                       DA; DAB; DAC; SSC 2; WLC
See also DAM MST, NOV

Doughty, Charles M(ontagu)
1843-1926 .... **TCLC 27**
See also CA 115; DLB 19, 57

Douglas, Ellen .... **CLC 73**
See also Haxton, Josephine Ayres;
Williamson, Ellen Douglas

Douglas, Gavin 1475(?)-1522 .... **LC 20**

Douglas, Keith 1920-1944 .... **TCLC 40**
See also DLB 27

Douglas, Leonard
See Bradbury, Ray (Douglas)

Douglas, Michael
See Crichton, (John) Michael

Douglass, Frederick
1817(?)-1895 .... **NCLC 7, 55; BLC; DA;**
                              DAC; WLC
See also CDALB 1640-1865; DAM MST,
MULT; DLB 1, 43, 50, 79; SATA 29

Dourado, (Waldomiro Freitas) Autran
1926- .... **CLC 23, 60**
See also CA 25-28R; CANR 34

Dourado, Waldomiro Autran
See Dourado, (Waldomiro Freitas) Autran

Dove, Rita (Frances)
1952- .... **CLC 50, 81; PC 6**
See also BW 2; CA 109; CAAS 19;
CANR 27, 42; DAM MULT, POET;
DLB 120

Dowell, Coleman 1925-1985 .... **CLC 60**
See also CA 25-28R; 117; CANR 10;
DLB 130

Dowson, Ernest (Christopher)
1867-1900 .... **TCLC 4**
See also CA 105; 150; DLB 19, 135

Doyle, A. Conan
See Doyle, Arthur Conan

Doyle, Arthur Conan
1859-1930 .... **TCLC 7; DA; DAB;**
                              DAC; SSC 12; WLC
See also AAYA 14; CA 104; 122;
CDBLB 1890-1914; DAM MST, NOV;
DLB 18, 70, 156; MTCW; SATA 24

Doyle, Conan
See Doyle, Arthur Conan

Doyle, John
See Graves, Robert (von Ranke)

Doyle, Roddy 1958(?)- .... **CLC 81**
See also AAYA 14; CA 143

Doyle, Sir A. Conan
See Doyle, Arthur Conan

Doyle, Sir Arthur Conan
See Doyle, Arthur Conan

Dr. A
See Asimov, Isaac; Silverstein, Alvin

Drabble, Margaret
1939- .... **CLC 2, 3, 5, 8, 10, 22, 53;**
                              DAB; DAC
See also CA 13-16R; CANR 18, 35;
CDBLB 1960 to Present; DAM MST,
NOV, POP; DLB 14, 155; MTCW;
SATA 48

Drapier, M. B.
See Swift, Jonathan

Drayham, James
See Mencken, H(enry) L(ouis)

Drayton, Michael 1563-1631 .... **LC 8**

Dreadstone, Carl
See Campbell, (John) Ramsey

Dreiser, Theodore (Herman Albert)
    1871-1945 ...... **TCLC 10, 18, 35; DA;**
                                    DAC; WLC
    See also CA 106; 132; CDALB 1865-1917;
        DAM MST, NOV; DLB 9, 12, 102, 137;
        DLBD 1; MTCW

Drexler, Rosalyn 1926- .... **CLC 2, 6**
    See also CA 81-84

Dreyer, Carl Theodor 1889-1968.... **CLC 16**
    See also CA 116

Drieu la Rochelle, Pierre(-Eugene)
    1893-1945 .... **TCLC 21**
    See also CA 117; DLB 72

Drinkwater, John 1882-1937..... **TCLC 57**
    See also CA 109; 149; DLB 10, 19, 149

Drop Shot
    See Cable, George Washington

Droste-Hulshoff, Annette Freiin von
    1797-1848 .... **NCLC 3**
    See also DLB 133

Drummond, Walter
    See Silverberg, Robert

Drummond, William Henry
    1854-1907 .... **TCLC 25**
    See also DLB 92

Drummond de Andrade, Carlos
    1902-1987 .... **CLC 18**
    See also Andrade, Carlos Drummond de
    See also CA 132; 123

Drury, Allen (Stuart) 1918-........ **CLC 37**
    See also CA 57-60; CANR 18, 52;
        INT CANR-18

Dryden, John
    1631-1700 .... **LC 3, 21; DA; DAB;**
                                    DAC; DC 3; WLC
    See also CDBLB 1660-1789; DAM DRAM,
        MST, POET; DLB 80, 101, 131

Duberman, Martin 1930-.......... **CLC 8**
    See also CA 1-4R; CANR 2

Dubie, Norman (Evans) 1945-..... **CLC 36**
    See also CA 69-72; CANR 12; DLB 120

Du Bois, W(illiam) E(dward) B(urghardt)
    1868-1963 ...... **CLC 1, 2, 13, 64; BLC;**
                                    DA; DAC; WLC
    See also BW 1; CA 85-88; CANR 34;
        CDALB 1865-1917; DAM MST, MULT,
        NOV; DLB 47, 50, 91; MTCW; SATA 42

Dubus, Andre 1936-... **CLC 13, 36; SSC 15**
    See also CA 21-24R; CANR 17; DLB 130;
        INT CANR-17

Duca Minimo
    See D'Annunzio, Gabriele

Ducharme, Rejean 1941- .... **CLC 74**
    See also DLB 60

Duclos, Charles Pinot 1704-1772 ..... **LC 1**

Dudek, Louis 1918- .... **CLC 11, 19**
    See also CA 45-48; CAAS 14; CANR 1;
        DLB 88

Duerrenmatt, Friedrich
    1921-1990 ...... **CLC 1, 4, 8, 11, 15, 43**
    See also CA 17-20R; CANR 33;
        DAM DRAM; DLB 69, 124; MTCW

Duffy, Bruce (?)-................. **CLC 50**

Duffy, Maureen 1933- .... **CLC 37**
    See also CA 25-28R; CANR 33; DLB 14;
        MTCW

Dugan, Alan 1923-............. **CLC 2, 6**
    See also CA 81-84; DLB 5

du Gard, Roger Martin
    See Martin du Gard, Roger

Duhamel, Georges 1884-1966 .... **CLC 8**
    See also CA 81-84; 25-28R; CANR 35;
        DLB 65; MTCW

Dujardin, Edouard (Emile Louis)
    1861-1949 .... **TCLC 13**
    See also CA 109; DLB 123

Dumas, Alexandre (Davy de la Pailleterie)
    1802-1870 .... **NCLC 11; DA; DAB;**
                                    DAC; WLC
    See also DAM MST, NOV; DLB 119;
        SATA 18

Dumas, Alexandre
    1824-1895 .... **NCLC 9; DC 1**

Dumas, Claudine
    See Malzberg, Barry N(athaniel)

Dumas, Henry L. 1934-1968 ..... **CLC 6, 62**
    See also BW 1; CA 85-88; DLB 41

du Maurier, Daphne
    1907-1989 .... **CLC 6, 11, 59; DAB;**
                                    DAC; SSC 18
    See also CA 5-8R; 128; CANR 6;
        DAM MST, POP; MTCW; SATA 27;
        SATA-Obit 60

Dunbar, Paul Laurence
    1872-1906 ...... **TCLC 2, 12; BLC; DA;**
                                    DAC; PC 5; SSC 8; WLC
    See also BW 1; CA 104; 124;
        CDALB 1865-1917; DAM MST, MULT,
        POET; DLB 50, 54, 78; SATA 34

Dunbar, William 1460(?)-1530(?) .... **LC 20**
    See also DLB 132, 146

Duncan, Lois 1934-............... **CLC 26**
    See also AAYA 4; CA 1-4R; CANR 2, 23,
        36; CLR 29; JRDA; MAICYA; SAAS 2;
        SATA 1, 36, 75

Duncan, Robert (Edward)
    1919-1988 .... **CLC 1, 2, 4, 7, 15, 41, 55;**
                                    PC 2
    See also CA 9-12R; 124; CANR 28;
        DAM POET; DLB 5, 16; MTCW

Duncan, Sara Jeannette
    1861-1922 .... **TCLC 60**
    See also DLB 92

Dunlap, William 1766-1839 ...... **NCLC 2**
    See also DLB 30, 37, 59

Dunn, Douglas (Eaglesham)
    1942- .... **CLC 6, 40**
    See also CA 45-48; CANR 2, 33; DLB 40;
        MTCW

Dunn, Katherine (Karen) 1945-..... **CLC 71**
    See also CA 33-36R

Dunn, Stephen 1939- .... **CLC 36**
    See also CA 33-36R; CANR 12, 48, 53;
        DLB 105

Dunne, Finley Peter 1867-1936.... **TCLC 28**
    See also CA 108; DLB 11, 23

Dunne, John Gregory 1932-........ **CLC 28**
    See also CA 25-28R; CANR 14, 50;
        DLBY 80

Dunsany, Edward John Moreton Drax
    Plunkett 1878-1957
    See Dunsany, Lord
    See also CA 104; 148; DLB 10

Dunsany, Lord................ **TCLC 2, 59**
    See also Dunsany, Edward John Moreton
        Drax Plunkett
    See also DLB 77, 153, 156

du Perry, Jean
    See Simenon, Georges (Jacques Christian)

Durang, Christopher (Ferdinand)
    1949- .... **CLC 27, 38**
    See also CA 105; CANR 50

Duras, Marguerite
    1914-1996 .. **CLC 3, 6, 11, 20, 34, 40, 68**
    See also CA 25-28R; 151; CANR 50;
        DLB 83; MTCW

Durban, (Rosa) Pam 1947-......... **CLC 39**
    See also CA 123

Durcan, Paul 1944-............. **CLC 43, 70**
    See also CA 134; DAM POET

Durkheim, Emile 1858-1917 ...... **TCLC 55**

Durrell, Lawrence (George)
    1912-1990 .... **CLC 1, 4, 6, 8, 13, 27, 41**
    See also CA 9-12R; 132; CANR 40;
        CDBLB 1945-1960; DAM NOV; DLB 15,
        27; DLBY 90; MTCW

Durrenmatt, Friedrich
    See Duerrenmatt, Friedrich

Dutt, Toru 1856-1877........... **NCLC 29**

Dwight, Timothy 1752-1817...... **NCLC 13**
    See also DLB 37

Dworkin, Andrea 1946-........... **CLC 43**
    See also CA 77-80; CAAS 21; CANR 16,
        39; INT CANR-16; MTCW

Dwyer, Deanna
    See Koontz, Dean R(ay)

Dwyer, K. R.
    See Koontz, Dean R(ay)

Dylan, Bob 1941- ...... **CLC 3, 4, 6, 12, 77**
    See also CA 41-44R; DLB 16

Eagleton, Terence (Francis) 1943-
    See Eagleton, Terry
    See also CA 57-60; CANR 7, 23; MTCW

Eagleton, Terry................ **CLC 63**
    See also Eagleton, Terence (Francis)

Early, Jack
    See Scoppettone, Sandra

East, Michael
    See West, Morris L(anglo)

Eastaway, Edward
    See Thomas, (Philip) Edward

Eastlake, William (Derry) 1917-..... **CLC 8**
    See also CA 5-8R; CAAS 1; CANR 5;
        DLB 6; INT CANR-5

Eastman, Charles A(lexander)
    1858-1939 .... **TCLC 55**
    See also DAM MULT; NNAL; YABC 1

Eberhart, Richard (Ghormley)
    1904- .... **CLC 3, 11, 19, 56**
    See also CA 1-4R; CANR 2;
        CDALB 1941-1968; DAM POET;
        DLB 48; MTCW

Eberstadt, Fernanda 1960-........ **CLC 39**
See also CA 136

Echegaray (y Eizaguirre), Jose (Maria Waldo)
1832-1916 .... **TCLC 4**
See also CA 104; CANR 32; HW; MTCW

Echeverria, (Jose) Esteban (Antonino)
1805-1851 .... **NCLC 18**

Echo
See Proust, (Valentin-Louis-George-Eugene-)
Marcel

Eckert, Allan W. 1931- .... **CLC 17**
See also AAYA 18; CA 13-16R; CANR 14,
45; INT CANR-14; SAAS 21; SATA 29;
SATA-Brief 27

Eckhart, Meister 1260(?)-1328(?) .. **CMLC 9**
See also DLB 115

Eckmar, F. R.
See de Hartog, Jan

Eco, Umberto 1932-........... **CLC 28, 60**
See also BEST 90:1; CA 77-80; CANR 12,
33; DAM NOV, POP; MTCW

Eddison, E(ric) R(ucker)
1882-1945 .... **TCLC 15**
See also CA 109

Edel, (Joseph) Leon 1907-...... **CLC 29, 34**
See also CA 1-4R; CANR 1, 22; DLB 103;
INT CANR-22

Eden, Emily 1797-1869 .... **NCLC 10**

Edgar, David 1948-............... **CLC 42**
See also CA 57-60; CANR 12;
DAM DRAM; DLB 13; MTCW

Edgerton, Clyde (Carlyle) 1944- .... **CLC 39**
See also AAYA 17; CA 118; 134; INT 134

Edgeworth, Maria 1768-1849... **NCLC 1, 51**
See also DLB 116, 159, 163; SATA 21

Edmonds, Paul
See Kuttner, Henry

Edmonds, Walter D(umaux) 1903- .. **CLC 35**
See also CA 5-8R; CANR 2; DLB 9;
MAICYA; SAAS 4; SATA 1, 27

Edmondson, Wallace
See Ellison, Harlan (Jay)

Edson, Russell.................... **CLC 13**
See also CA 33-36R

Edwards, Bronwen Elizabeth
See Rose, Wendy

Edwards, G(erald) B(asil)
1899-1976 .... **CLC 25**
See also CA 110

Edwards, Gus 1939-.............. **CLC 43**
See also CA 108; INT 108

Edwards, Jonathan
1703-1758 .... **LC 7; DA; DAC**
See also DAM MST; DLB 24

Efron, Marina Ivanovna Tsvetaeva
See Tsvetaeva (Efron), Marina (Ivanovna)

Ehle, John (Marsden, Jr.) 1925-.... **CLC 27**
See also CA 9-12R

Ehrenbourg, Ilya (Grigoryevich)
See Ehrenburg, Ilya (Grigoryevich)

Ehrenburg, Ilya (Grigoryevich)
1891-1967 .... **CLC 18, 34, 62**
See also CA 102; 25-28R

Ehrenburg, Ilyo (Grigoryevich)
See Ehrenburg, Ilya (Grigoryevich)

Eich, Guenter 1907-1972 .... **CLC 15**
See also CA 111; 93-96; DLB 69, 124

Eichendorff, Joseph Freiherr von
1788-1857 .... **NCLC 8**
See also DLB 90

Eigner, Larry...................... **CLC 9**
See also Eigner, Laurence (Joel)
See also CAAS 23; DLB 5

Eigner, Laurence (Joel) 1927-1996
See Eigner, Larry
See also CA 9-12R; 151; CANR 6

Einstein, Albert 1879-1955 .... **TCLC 65**
See also CA 121; 133; MTCW

Eiseley, Loren Corey 1907-1977 ..... **CLC 7**
See also AAYA 5; CA 1-4R; 73-76;
CANR 6

Eisenstadt, Jill 1963- .... **CLC 50**
See also CA 140

Eisenstein, Sergei (Mikhailovich)
1898-1948 .... **TCLC 57**
See also CA 114; 149

Eisner, Simon
See Kornbluth, C(yril) M.

Ekeloef, (Bengt) Gunnar
1907-1968 .... **CLC 27**
See also CA 123; 25-28R; DAM POET

Ekelof, (Bengt) Gunnar
See Ekeloef, (Bengt) Gunnar

Ekwensi, C. O. D.
See Ekwensi, Cyprian (Odiatu Duaka)

Ekwensi, Cyprian (Odiatu Duaka)
1921- .... **CLC 4; BLC**
See also BW 2; CA 29-32R; CANR 18, 42;
DAM MULT; DLB 117; MTCW;
SATA 66

Elaine........................ **TCLC 18**
See also Leverson, Ada

El Crummo
See Crumb, R(obert)

Elia
See Lamb, Charles

Eliade, Mircea 1907-1986 .... **CLC 19**
See also CA 65-68; 119; CANR 30; MTCW

Eliot, A. D.
See Jewett, (Theodora) Sarah Orne

Eliot, Alice
See Jewett, (Theodora) Sarah Orne

Eliot, Dan
See Silverberg, Robert

Eliot, George
1819-1880 ..... **NCLC 4, 13, 23, 41, 49;
DA; DAB; DAC; WLC**
See also CDBLB 1832-1890; DAM MST,
NOV; DLB 21, 35, 55

Eliot, John 1604-1690 .... **LC 5**
See also DLB 24

Eliot, T(homas) S(tearns)
1888-1965 ..... **CLC 1, 2, 3, 6, 9, 10, 13,
15, 24, 34, 41, 55, 57; DA; DAB; DAC;
PC 5; WLC 2**
See also CA 5-8R; 25-28R; CANR 41;
CDALB 1929-1941; DAM DRAM, MST,
POET; DLB 7, 10, 45, 63; DLBY 88;
MTCW

Elizabeth 1866-1941............. **TCLC 41**

Elkin, Stanley L(awrence)
1930-1995 ...... **CLC 4, 6, 9, 14, 27, 51,
91; SSC 12**
See also CA 9-12R; 148; CANR 8, 46;
DAM NOV, POP; DLB 2, 28; DLBY 80;
INT CANR-8; MTCW

Elledge, Scott.................... **CLC 34**

Elliott, Don
See Silverberg, Robert

Elliott, George P(aul) 1918-1980..... **CLC 2**
See also CA 1-4R; 97-100; CANR 2

Elliott, Janice 1931-............... **CLC 47**
See also CA 13-16R; CANR 8, 29; DLB 14

Elliott, Sumner Locke 1917-1991 ... **CLC 38**
See also CA 5-8R; 134; CANR 2, 21

Elliott, William
See Bradbury, Ray (Douglas)

Ellis, A. E........................ **CLC 7**

Ellis, Alice Thomas................ **CLC 40**
See also Haycraft, Anna

Ellis, Bret Easton 1964-......... **CLC 39, 71**
See also AAYA 2; CA 118; 123; CANR 51;
DAM POP; INT 123

Ellis, (Henry) Havelock
1859-1939 .... **TCLC 14**
See also CA 109

Ellis, Landon
See Ellison, Harlan (Jay)

Ellis, Trey 1962-................. **CLC 55**
See also CA 146

Ellison, Harlan (Jay)
1934- .... **CLC 1, 13, 42; SSC 14**
See also CA 5-8R; CANR 5, 46;
DAM POP; DLB 8; INT CANR-5;
MTCW

Ellison, Ralph (Waldo)
1914-1994 .... **CLC 1, 3, 11, 54, 86;
BLC; DA; DAB; DAC; WLC**
See also BW 1; CA 9-12R; 145; CANR 24,
53; CDALB 1941-1968; DAM MST,
MULT, NOV; DLB 2, 76; DLBY 94;
MTCW

Ellmann, Lucy (Elizabeth) 1956-.... **CLC 61**
See also CA 128

Ellmann, Richard (David)
1918-1987 .... **CLC 50**
See also BEST 89:2; CA 1-4R; 122;
CANR 2, 28; DLB 103; DLBY 87;
MTCW

Elman, Richard 1934-............. **CLC 19**
See also CA 17-20R; CAAS 3; CANR 47

Elron
See Hubbard, L(afayette) Ron(ald)

Eluard, Paul.................. **TCLC 7, 41**
See also Grindel, Eugene

Elyot, Sir Thomas 1490(?)-1546 ..... **LC 11**

Elytis, Odysseus 1911-1996..... **CLC 15, 49**
See also CA 102; 151; DAM POET; MTCW

Emecheta, (Florence Onye) Buchi
1944-............... **CLC 14, 48; BLC**
See also BW 2; CA 81-84; CANR 27;
DAM MULT; DLB 117; MTCW;
SATA 66

Emerson, Ralph Waldo
1803-1882..... **NCLC 1, 38; DA; DAB;
DAC; WLC**
See also CDALB 1640-1865; DAM MST,
POET; DLB 1, 59, 73

Eminescu, Mihail 1850-1889..... **NCLC 33**

Empson, William
1906-1984........ **CLC 3, 8, 19, 33, 34**
See also CA 17-20R; 112; CANR 31;
DLB 20; MTCW

Enchi Fumiko (Ueda) 1905-1986.... **CLC 31**
See also CA 129; 121

Ende, Michael (Andreas Helmuth)
1929-1995.................. **CLC 31**
See also CA 118; 124; 149; CANR 36;
CLR 14; DLB 75; MAICYA; SATA 61;
SATA-Brief 42; SATA-Obit 86

Endo, Shusaku 1923-..... **CLC 7, 14, 19, 54**
See also CA 29-32R; CANR 21;
DAM NOV; MTCW

Engel, Marian 1933-1985......... **CLC 36**
See also CA 25-28R; CANR 12; DLB 53;
INT CANR-12

Engelhardt, Frederick
See Hubbard, L(afayette) Ron(ald)

Enright, D(ennis) J(oseph)
1920-................... **CLC 4, 8, 31**
See also CA 1-4R; CANR 1, 42; DLB 27;
SATA 25

Enzensberger, Hans Magnus
1929-...................... **CLC 43**
See also CA 116; 119

Ephron, Nora 1941-.......... **CLC 17, 31**
See also AITN 2; CA 65-68; CANR 12, 39

Epsilon
See Betjeman, John

Epstein, Daniel Mark 1948-........ **CLC 7**
See also CA 49-52; CANR 2, 53

Epstein, Jacob 1956-............. **CLC 19**
See also CA 114

Epstein, Joseph 1937-............. **CLC 39**
See also CA 112; 119; CANR 50

Epstein, Leslie 1938-............. **CLC 27**
See also CA 73-76; CAAS 12; CANR 23

Equiano, Olaudah
1745(?)-1797............. **LC 16; BLC**
See also DAM MULT; DLB 37, 50

Erasmus, Desiderius 1469(?)-1536.... **LC 16**

Erdman, Paul E(mil) 1932-........ **CLC 25**
See also AITN 1; CA 61-64; CANR 13, 43

Erdrich, Louise 1954-........... **CLC 39, 54**
See also AAYA 10; BEST 89:1; CA 114;
CANR 41; DAM MULT, NOV, POP;
DLB 152; MTCW; NNAL

Erenburg, Ilya (Grigoryevich)
See Ehrenburg, Ilya (Grigoryevich)

Erickson, Stephen Michael 1950-
See Erickson, Steve
See also CA 129

Erickson, Steve................... **CLC 64**
See also Erickson, Stephen Michael

Ericson, Walter
See Fast, Howard (Melvin)

Eriksson, Buntel
See Bergman, (Ernst) Ingmar

Ernaux, Annie 1940-............. **CLC 88**
See also CA 147

Eschenbach, Wolfram von
See Wolfram von Eschenbach

Eseki, Bruno
See Mphahlele, Ezekiel

Esenin, Sergei (Alexandrovich)
1895-1925................... **TCLC 4**
See also CA 104

Eshleman, Clayton 1935-........... **CLC 7**
See also CA 33-36R; CAAS 6; DLB 5

Espriella, Don Manuel Alvarez
See Southey, Robert

Espriu, Salvador 1913-1985........ **CLC 9**
See also CA 115; DLB 134

Espronceda, Jose de 1808-1842... **NCLC 39**

Esse, James
See Stephens, James

Esterbrook, Tom
See Hubbard, L(afayette) Ron(ald)

Estleman, Loren D. 1952-........ **CLC 48**
See also CA 85-88; CANR 27; DAM NOV,
POP; INT CANR-27; MTCW

Eugenides, Jeffrey 1960(?)-........ **CLC 81**
See also CA 144

Euripides c. 485B.C.-406B.C......... **DC 4**
See also DA; DAB; DAC; DAM DRAM,
MST

Evan, Evin
See Faust, Frederick (Schiller)

Evans, Evan
See Faust, Frederick (Schiller)

Evans, Marian
See Eliot, George

Evans, Mary Ann
See Eliot, George

Evarts, Esther
See Benson, Sally

Everett, Percival L. 1956-......... **CLC 57**
See also BW 2; CA 129

Everson, R(onald) G(ilmour)
1903-...................... **CLC 27**
See also CA 17-20R; DLB 88

Everson, William (Oliver)
1912-1994................ **CLC 1, 5, 14**
See also CA 9-12R; 145; CANR 20; DLB 5,
16; MTCW

Evtushenko, Evgenii Aleksandrovich
See Yevtushenko, Yevgeny (Alexandrovich)

Ewart, Gavin (Buchanan)
1916-1995............... **CLC 13, 46**
See also CA 89-92; 150; CANR 17, 46;
DLB 40; MTCW

Ewers, Hanns Heinz 1871-1943... **TCLC 12**
See also CA 109; 149

Ewing, Frederick R.
See Sturgeon, Theodore (Hamilton)

Exley, Frederick (Earl)
1929-1992................ **CLC 6, 11**
See also AITN 2; CA 81-84; 138; DLB 143;
DLBY 81

Eynhardt, Guillermo
See Quiroga, Horacio (Sylvestre)

Ezekiel, Nissim 1924-............. **CLC 61**
See also CA 61-64

Ezekiel, Tish O'Dowd 1943-....... **CLC 34**
See also CA 129

Fadeyev, A.
See Bulgya, Alexander Alexandrovich

Fadeyev, Alexander.............. **TCLC 53
See also Bulgya, Alexander Alexandrovich

Fagen, Donald 1948-............. **CLC 26**

Fainzilberg, Ilya Arnoldovich 1897-1937
See Ilf, Ilya
See also CA 120

Fair, Ronald L. 1932-............. **CLC 18**
See also BW 1; CA 69-72; CANR 25;
DLB 33

Fairbairns, Zoe (Ann) 1948-....... **CLC 32**
See also CA 103; CANR 21

Falco, Gian
See Papini, Giovanni

Falconer, James
See Kirkup, James

Falconer, Kenneth
See Kornbluth, C(yril) M.

Falkland, Samuel
See Heijermans, Herman

Fallaci, Oriana 1930-............. **CLC 11**
See also CA 77-80; CANR 15; MTCW

Faludy, George 1913-............. **CLC 42**
See also CA 21-24R

Faludy, Gyoergy
See Faludy, George

Fanon, Frantz 1925-1961..... **CLC 74; BLC**
See also BW 1; CA 116; 89-92;
DAM MULT

Fanshawe, Ann 1625-1680.......... **LC 11**

Fante, John (Thomas) 1911-1983... **CLC 60**
See also CA 69-72; 109; CANR 23;
DLB 130; DLBY 83

Farah, Nuruddin 1945-....... **CLC 53; BLC**
See also BW 2; CA 106; DAM MULT;
DLB 125

Fargue, Leon-Paul 1876(?)-1947... **TCLC 11**
See also CA 109

Farigoule, Louis
See Romains, Jules

Farina, Richard 1936(?)-1966....... **CLC 9**
See also CA 81-84; 25-28R

Farley, Walter (Lorimer)
1915-1989.................. **CLC 17**
See also CA 17-20R; CANR 8, 29; DLB 22;
JRDA; MAICYA; SATA 2, 43

Farmer, Philip Jose   1918- .... **CLC 1, 19**
See also CA 1-4R; CANR 4, 35; DLB 8;
MTCW

Farquhar, George   1677-1707 .... **LC 21**
See also DAM DRAM; DLB 84

Farrell, J(ames) G(ordon)
1935-1979 .... **CLC 6**
See also CA 73-76; 89-92; CANR 36;
DLB 14; MTCW

Farrell, James T(homas)
1904-1979 ..... **CLC 1, 4, 8, 11, 66**
See also CA 5-8R; 89-92; CANR 9; DLB 4,
9, 86; DLBD 2; MTCW

Farren, Richard J.
See Betjeman, John

Farren, Richard M.
See Betjeman, John

Fassbinder, Rainer Werner
1946-1982 .... **CLC 20**
See also CA 93-96; 106; CANR 31

Fast, Howard (Melvin)   1914- ...... **CLC 23**
See also AAYA 16; CA 1-4R; CAAS 18;
CANR 1, 33; DAM NOV; DLB 9;
INT CANR-33; SATA 7

Faulcon, Robert
See Holdstock, Robert P.

Faulkner, William (Cuthbert)
1897-1962 ..... **CLC 1, 3, 6, 8, 9, 11, 14,
18, 28, 52, 68; DA; DAB; DAC; SSC 1;
WLC**
See also AAYA 7; CA 81-84; CANR 33;
CDALB 1929-1941; DAM MST, NOV;
DLB 9, 11, 44, 102; DLBD 2; DLBY 86;
MTCW

Fauset, Jessie Redmon
1884(?)-1961 .... **CLC 19, 54; BLC**
See also BW 1; CA 109; DAM MULT;
DLB 51

Faust, Frederick (Schiller)
1892-1944(?) .... **TCLC 49**
See also CA 108; DAM POP

Faust, Irvin   1924- .... **CLC 8**
See also CA 33-36R; CANR 28; DLB 2, 28;
DLBY 80

Fawkes, Guy
See Benchley, Robert (Charles)

Fearing, Kenneth (Flexner)
1902-1961 .... **CLC 51**
See also CA 93-96; DLB 9

Fecamps, Elise
See Creasey, John

Federman, Raymond   1928- ...... **CLC 6, 47**
See also CA 17-20R; CAAS 8; CANR 10,
43; DLBY 80

Federspiel, J(uerg) F.   1931- .... **CLC 42**
See also CA 146

Feiffer, Jules (Ralph)   1929- .... **CLC 2, 8, 64**
See also AAYA 3; CA 17-20R; CANR 30;
DAM DRAM; DLB 7, 44;
INT CANR-30; MTCW; SATA 8, 61

Feige, Hermann Albert Otto Maximilian
See Traven, B.

Feinberg, David B.   1956-1994 ...... **CLC 59**
See also CA 135; 147

Feinstein, Elaine   1930- .... **CLC 36**
See also CA 69-72; CAAS 1; CANR 31;
DLB 14, 40; MTCW

Feldman, Irving (Mordecai)   1928-.... **CLC 7**
See also CA 1-4R; CANR 1

Fellini, Federico   1920-1993 ..... **CLC 16, 85**
See also CA 65-68; 143; CANR 33

Felsen, Henry Gregor   1916- .... **CLC 17**
See also CA 1-4R; CANR 1; SAAS 2;
SATA 1

Fenton, James Martin   1949- .... **CLC 32**
See also CA 102; DLB 40

Ferber, Edna   1887-1968 .... **CLC 18, 93**
See also AITN 1; CA 5-8R; 25-28R; DLB 9,
28, 86; MTCW; SATA 7

Ferguson, Helen
See Kavan, Anna

Ferguson, Samuel   1810-1886 ..... **NCLC 33**
See also DLB 32

Fergusson, Robert   1750-1774 .... **LC 29**
See also DLB 109

Ferling, Lawrence
See Ferlinghetti, Lawrence (Monsanto)

Ferlinghetti, Lawrence (Monsanto)
1919(?)- .... **CLC 2, 6, 10, 27; PC 1**
See also CA 5-8R; CANR 3, 41;
CDALB 1941-1968; DAM POET; DLB 5,
16; MTCW

Fernandez, Vicente Garcia Huidobro
See Huidobro Fernandez, Vicente Garcia

Ferrer, Gabriel (Francisco Victor) Miro
See Miro (Ferrer), Gabriel (Francisco
Victor)

Ferrier, Susan (Edmonstone)
1782-1854 .... **NCLC 8**
See also DLB 116

Ferrigno, Robert   1948(?)- .... **CLC 65**
See also CA 140

Ferron, Jacques   1921-1985 ... **CLC 94; DAC**
See also CA 117; 129; DLB 60

Feuchtwanger, Lion   1884-1958 ..... **TCLC 3**
See also CA 104; DLB 66

Feuillet, Octave   1821-1890 ...... **NCLC 45**

Feydeau, Georges (Leon Jules Marie)
1862-1921 .... **TCLC 22**
See also CA 113; DAM DRAM

Ficino, Marsilio   1433-1499 .... **LC 12**

Fiedeler, Hans
See Doeblin, Alfred

Fiedler, Leslie A(aron)
1917- .... **CLC 4, 13, 24**
See also CA 9-12R; CANR 7; DLB 28, 67;
MTCW

Field, Andrew   1938- .... **CLC 44**
See also CA 97-100; CANR 25

Field, Eugene   1850-1895 .... **NCLC 3**
See also DLB 23, 42, 140; DLBD 13;
MAICYA; SATA 16

Field, Gans T.
See Wellman, Manly Wade

Field, Michael .... **TCLC 43**

Field, Peter
See Hobson, Laura Z(ametkin)

Fielding, Henry
1707-1754 ...... **LC 1; DA; DAB; DAC;
WLC**
See also CDBLB 1660-1789; DAM DRAM,
MST, NOV; DLB 39, 84, 101

Fielding, Sarah   1710-1768 .... **LC 1**
See also DLB 39

Fierstein, Harvey (Forbes)   1954- ... **CLC 33**
See also CA 123; 129; DAM DRAM, POP

Figes, Eva   1932- .... **CLC 31**
See also CA 53-56; CANR 4, 44; DLB 14

Finch, Robert (Duer Claydon)
1900- .... **CLC 18**
See also CA 57-60; CANR 9, 24, 49;
DLB 88

Findley, Timothy   1930- ...... **CLC 27; DAC**
See also CA 25-28R; CANR 12, 42;
DAM MST; DLB 53

Fink, William
See Mencken, H(enry) L(ouis)

Firbank, Louis   1942-
See Reed, Lou
See also CA 117

Firbank, (Arthur Annesley) Ronald
1886-1926 .... **TCLC 1**
See also CA 104; DLB 36

Fisher, M(ary) F(rances) K(ennedy)
1908-1992 .... **CLC 76, 87**
See also CA 77-80; 138; CANR 44

Fisher, Roy   1930- .... **CLC 25**
See also CA 81-84; CAAS 10; CANR 16;
DLB 40

Fisher, Rudolph
1897-1934 .... **TCLC 11; BLC**
See also BW 1; CA 107; 124; DAM MULT;
DLB 51, 102

Fisher, Vardis (Alvero)   1895-1968.... **CLC 7**
See also CA 5-8R; 25-28R; DLB 9

Fiske, Tarleton
See Bloch, Robert (Albert)

Fitch, Clarke
See Sinclair, Upton (Beall)

Fitch, John IV
See Cormier, Robert (Edmund)

Fitzgerald, Captain Hugh
See Baum, L(yman) Frank

FitzGerald, Edward   1809-1883 .... **NCLC 9**
See also DLB 32

Fitzgerald, F(rancis) Scott (Key)
1896-1940 .... **TCLC 1, 6, 14, 28, 55;
DA; DAB; DAC; SSC 6; WLC**
See also AITN 1; CA 110; 123;
CDALB 1917-1929; DAM MST, NOV;
DLB 4, 9, 86; DLBD 1; DLBY 81;
MTCW

Fitzgerald, Penelope   1916-... **CLC 19, 51, 61**
See also CA 85-88; CAAS 10; DLB 14

Fitzgerald, Robert (Stuart)
1910-1985 .... **CLC 39**
See also CA 1-4R; 114; CANR 1; DLBY 80

FitzGerald, Robert D(avid)
1902-1987 .... **CLC 19**
See also CA 17-20R

Fitzgerald, Zelda (Sayre)
1900-1948 . . . . **TCLC 52**
See also CA 117; 126; DLBY 84

Flanagan, Thomas (James Bonner)
1923- . . . . **CLC 25, 52**
See also CA 108; DLBY 80; INT 108;
MTCW

Flaubert, Gustave
1821-1880 . . . . **NCLC 2, 10, 19; DA;
DAB; DAC; SSC 11; WLC**
See also DAM MST, NOV; DLB 119

Flecker, Herman Elroy
See Flecker, (Herman) James Elroy

Flecker, (Herman) James Elroy
1884-1915 . . . . **TCLC 43**
See also CA 109; 150; DLB 10, 19

Fleming, Ian (Lancaster)
1908-1964 . . . . **CLC 3, 30**
See also CA 5-8R; CDBLB 1945-1960;
DAM POP; DLB 87; MTCW; SATA 9

Fleming, Thomas (James) 1927- . . . . **CLC 37**
See also CA 5-8R; CANR 10;
INT CANR-10; SATA 8

Fletcher, John 1579-1625 . . . . . . **LC 33; DC 6**
See also CDBLB Before 1660; DLB 58

Fletcher, John Gould 1886-1950 . . . **TCLC 35**
See also CA 107; DLB 4, 45

Fleur, Paul
See Pohl, Frederik

Flooglebuckle, Al
See Spiegelman, Art

Flying Officer X
See Bates, H(erbert) E(rnest)

Fo, Dario 1926- . . . . **CLC 32**
See also CA 116; 128; DAM DRAM;
MTCW

Fogarty, Jonathan Titulescu Esq.
See Farrell, James T(homas)

Folke, Will
See Bloch, Robert (Albert)

Follett, Ken(neth Martin) 1949- . . . . **CLC 18**
See also AAYA 6; BEST 89:4; CA 81-84;
CANR 13, 33; DAM NOV, POP;
DLB 87; DLBY 81; INT CANR-33;
MTCW

Fontane, Theodor 1819-1898 . . . . . **NCLC 26**
See also DLB 129

Foote, Horton 1916- . . . . **CLC 51, 91**
See also CA 73-76; CANR 34, 51;
DAM DRAM; DLB 26; INT CANR-34

Foote, Shelby 1916- . . . . **CLC 75**
See also CA 5-8R; CANR 3, 45;
DAM NOV, POP; DLB 2, 17

Forbes, Esther 1891-1967 . . . . **CLC 12**
See also AAYA 17; CA 13-14; 25-28R;
CAP 1; CLR 27; DLB 22; JRDA;
MAICYA; SATA 2

Forche, Carolyn (Louise)
1950- . . . . **CLC 25, 83, 86; PC 10**
See also CA 109; 117; CANR 50;
DAM POET; DLB 5; INT 117

Ford, Elbur
See Hibbert, Eleanor Alice Burford

Ford, Ford Madox
1873-1939 . . . . **TCLC 1, 15, 39, 57**
See also CA 104; 132; CDBLB 1914-1945;
DAM NOV; DLB 162; MTCW

Ford, John 1895-1973 . . . . **CLC 16**
See also CA 45-48

Ford, Richard 1944- . . . . **CLC 46**
See also CA 69-72; CANR 11, 47

Ford, Webster
See Masters, Edgar Lee

Foreman, Richard 1937- . . . . **CLC 50**
See also CA 65-68; CANR 32

Forester, C(ecil) S(cott)
1899-1966 . . . . **CLC 35**
See also CA 73-76; 25-28R; SATA 13

Forez
See Mauriac, Francois (Charles)

Forman, James Douglas 1932- . . . . . . **CLC 21**
See also AAYA 17; CA 9-12R; CANR 4,
19, 42; JRDA; MAICYA; SATA 8, 70

Fornes, Maria Irene 1930- . . . . . . **CLC 39, 61**
See also CA 25-28R; CANR 28; DLB 7;
HW; INT CANR-28; MTCW

Forrest, Leon 1937- . . . . **CLC 4**
See also BW 2; CA 89-92; CAAS 7;
CANR 25, 52; DLB 33

Forster, E(dward) M(organ)
1879-1970 . . . . . **CLC 1, 2, 3, 4, 9, 10, 13,
15, 22, 45, 77; DA; DAB; DAC; WLC**
See also AAYA 2; CA 13-14; 25-28R;
CANR 45; CAP 1; CDBLB 1914-1945;
DAM MST, NOV; DLB 34, 98, 162;
DLBD 10; MTCW; SATA 57

Forster, John 1812-1876 . . . . **NCLC 11**
See also DLB 144

Forsyth, Frederick 1938- . . . . . . **CLC 2, 5, 36**
See also BEST 89:4; CA 85-88; CANR 38;
DAM NOV, POP; DLB 87; MTCW

Forten, Charlotte L. . . . . **TCLC 16; BLC**
See also Grimke, Charlotte L(ottie) Forten
See also DLB 50

Foscolo, Ugo 1778-1827 . . . . **NCLC 8**

Fosse, Bob . . . . **CLC 20**
See also Fosse, Robert Louis

Fosse, Robert Louis 1927-1987
See Fosse, Bob
See also CA 110; 123

Foster, Stephen Collins
1826-1864 . . . . **NCLC 26**

Foucault, Michel
1926-1984 . . . . **CLC 31, 34, 69**
See also CA 105; 113; CANR 34; MTCW

Fouque, Friedrich (Heinrich Karl) de la Motte
1777-1843 . . . . **NCLC 2**
See also DLB 90

Fourier, Charles 1772-1837 . . . . . . **NCLC 51**

Fournier, Henri Alban 1886-1914
See Alain-Fournier
See also CA 104

Fournier, Pierre 1916- . . . . **CLC 11**
See also Gascar, Pierre
See also CA 89-92; CANR 16, 40

Fowles, John
1926- . . . . . . **CLC 1, 2, 3, 4, 6, 9, 10, 15,
33, 87; DAB; DAC**
See also CA 5-8R; CANR 25; CDBLB 1960
to Present; DAM MST; DLB 14, 139;
MTCW; SATA 22

Fox, Paula 1923- . . . . **CLC 2, 8**
See also AAYA 3; CA 73-76; CANR 20,
36; CLR 1; DLB 52; JRDA; MAICYA;
MTCW; SATA 17, 60

Fox, William Price (Jr.) 1926- . . . . . **CLC 22**
See also CA 17-20R; CAAS 19; CANR 11;
DLB 2; DLBY 81

Foxe, John 1516(?)-1587 . . . . **LC 14**

Frame, Janet . . . . **CLC 2, 3, 6, 22, 66**
See also Clutha, Janet Paterson Frame

France, Anatole . . . . **TCLC 9**
See also Thibault, Jacques Anatole Francois
See also DLB 123

Francis, Claude 19(?)- . . . . **CLC 50**

Francis, Dick 1920- . . . . **CLC 2, 22, 42**
See also AAYA 5; BEST 89:3; CA 5-8R;
CANR 9, 42; CDBLB 1960 to Present;
DAM POP; DLB 87; INT CANR-9;
MTCW

Francis, Robert (Churchill)
1901-1987 . . . . **CLC 15**
See also CA 1-4R; 123; CANR 1

Frank, Anne(lies Marie)
1929-1945 . . . . **TCLC 17; DA; DAB;
DAC; WLC**
See also AAYA 12; CA 113; 133;
DAM MST; MTCW; SATA 87;
SATA-Brief 42

Frank, Elizabeth 1945- . . . . **CLC 39**
See also CA 121; 126; INT 126

Frankl, Viktor E(mil) 1905- . . . . **CLC 93**
See also CA 65-68

Franklin, Benjamin
See Hasek, Jaroslav (Matej Frantisek)

Franklin, Benjamin
1706-1790 . . . . . **LC 25; DA; DAB; DAC**
See also CDALB 1640-1865; DAM MST;
DLB 24, 43, 73

Franklin, (Stella Maraia Sarah) Miles
1879-1954 . . . . **TCLC 7**
See also CA 104

Fraser, (Lady) Antonia (Pakenham)
1932- . . . . **CLC 32**
See also CA 85-88; CANR 44; MTCW;
SATA-Brief 32

Fraser, George MacDonald 1925- . . . . **CLC 7**
See also CA 45-48; CANR 2, 48

Fraser, Sylvia 1935- . . . . **CLC 64**
See also CA 45-48; CANR 1, 16

Frayn, Michael 1933- . . . . . . **CLC 3, 7, 31, 47**
See also CA 5-8R; CANR 30;
DAM DRAM, NOV; DLB 13, 14;
MTCW

Fraze, Candida (Merrill) 1945- . . . . . **CLC 50**
See also CA 126

Frazer, J(ames) G(eorge)
1854-1941 . . . . **TCLC 32**
See also CA 118

Garcia Lorca, Federico
1898-1936 . . . **TCLC 1, 7, 49; DA; DAB;
DAC; DC 2; HLC; PC 3; WLC**
See also CA 104; 131; DAM DRAM, MST,
MULT, POET; DLB 108; HW; MTCW

Garcia Marquez, Gabriel (Jose)
1928- . . . . **CLC 2, 3, 8, 10, 15, 27, 47, 55,
68; DA; DAB; DAC; HLC; SSC 8; WLC**
See also AAYA 3; BEST 89:1, 90:4;
CA 33-36R; CANR 10, 28, 50;
DAM MST, MULT, NOV, POP;
DLB 113; HW; MTCW

Gard, Janice
See Latham, Jean Lee

Gard, Roger Martin du
See Martin du Gard, Roger

Gardam, Jane 1928- . . . . **CLC 43**
See also CA 49-52; CANR 2, 18, 33;
CLR 12; DLB 14, 161; MAICYA;
MTCW; SAAS 9; SATA 39, 76;
SATA-Brief 28

Gardner, Herb(ert) 1934- . . . . **CLC 44**
See also CA 149

Gardner, John (Champlin), Jr.
1933-1982 . . . . . **CLC 2, 3, 5, 7, 8, 10, 18,
28, 34; SSC 7**
See also AITN 1; CA 65-68; 107;
CANR 33; DAM NOV, POP; DLB 2;
DLBY 82; MTCW; SATA 40;
SATA-Obit 31

Gardner, John (Edmund) 1926- . . . . . **CLC 30**
See also CA 103; CANR 15; DAM POP;
MTCW

Gardner, Miriam
See Bradley, Marion Zimmer

Gardner, Noel
See Kuttner, Henry

Gardons, S. S.
See Snodgrass, W(illiam) D(e Witt)

Garfield, Leon 1921- . . . . **CLC 12**
See also AAYA 8; CA 17-20R; CANR 38,
41; CLR 21; DLB 161; JRDA; MAICYA;
SATA 1, 32, 76

Garland, (Hannibal) Hamlin
1860-1940 . . . . **TCLC 3; SSC 18**
See also CA 104; DLB 12, 71, 78

Garneau, (Hector de) Saint-Denys
1912-1943 . . . . **TCLC 13**
See also CA 111; DLB 88

Garner, Alan 1934- . . . . **CLC 17; DAB**
See also AAYA 18; CA 73-76; CANR 15;
CLR 20; DAM POP; DLB 161;
MAICYA; MTCW; SATA 18, 69

Garner, Hugh 1913-1979 . . . . **CLC 13**
See also CA 69-72; CANR 31; DLB 68

Garnett, David 1892-1981 . . . . **CLC 3**
See also CA 5-8R; 103; CANR 17; DLB 34

Garos, Stephanie
See Katz, Steve

Garrett, George (Palmer)
1929- . . . . **CLC 3, 11, 51**
See also CA 1-4R; CAAS 5; CANR 1, 42;
DLB 2, 5, 130, 152; DLBY 83

Garrick, David 1717-1779 . . . . **LC 15**
See also DAM DRAM; DLB 84

Garrigue, Jean 1914-1972 . . . . **CLC 2, 8**
See also CA 5-8R; 37-40R; CANR 20

Garrison, Frederick
See Sinclair, Upton (Beall)

Garth, Will
See Hamilton, Edmond; Kuttner, Henry

Garvey, Marcus (Moziah, Jr.)
1887-1940 . . . . **TCLC 41; BLC**
See also BW 1; CA 120; 124; DAM MULT

Gary, Romain . . . . **CLC 25**
See also Kacew, Romain
See also DLB 83

Gascar, Pierre . . . . **CLC 11**
See also Fournier, Pierre

Gascoyne, David (Emery) 1916- . . . . **CLC 45**
See also CA 65-68; CANR 10, 28; DLB 20;
MTCW

Gaskell, Elizabeth Cleghorn
1810-1865 . . . . **NCLC 5; DAB**
See also CDBLB 1832-1890; DAM MST;
DLB 21, 144, 159

Gass, William H(oward)
1924- . . . **CLC 1, 2, 8, 11, 15, 39; SSC 12**
See also CA 17-20R; CANR 30; DLB 2;
MTCW

Gasset, Jose Ortega y
See Ortega y Gasset, Jose

Gates, Henry Louis, Jr. 1950- . . . . . . **CLC 65**
See also BW 2; CA 109; CANR 25, 53;
DAM MULT; DLB 67

Gautier, Theophile
1811-1872 . . . . **NCLC 1; SSC 20**
See also DAM POET; DLB 119

Gawsworth, John
See Bates, H(erbert) E(rnest)

Gay, Oliver
See Gogarty, Oliver St. John

Gaye, Marvin (Penze) 1939-1984 . . . **CLC 26**
See also CA 112

Gebler, Carlo (Ernest) 1954- . . . . **CLC 39**
See also CA 119; 133

Gee, Maggie (Mary) 1948- . . . . **CLC 57**
See also CA 130

Gee, Maurice (Gough) 1931- . . . . **CLC 29**
See also CA 97-100; SATA 46

Gelbart, Larry (Simon) 1923- . . . **CLC 21, 61**
See also CA 73-76; CANR 45

Gelber, Jack 1932- . . . . **CLC 1, 6, 14, 79**
See also CA 1-4R; CANR 2; DLB 7

Gellhorn, Martha (Ellis) 1908- . . **CLC 14, 60**
See also CA 77-80; CANR 44; DLBY 82

Genet, Jean
1910-1986 . . . **CLC 1, 2, 5, 10, 14, 44, 46**
See also CA 13-16R; CANR 18;
DAM DRAM; DLB 72; DLBY 86;
MTCW

Gent, Peter 1942- . . . . **CLC 29**
See also AITN 1; CA 89-92; DLBY 82

Gentlewoman in New England, A
See Bradstreet, Anne

Gentlewoman in Those Parts, A
See Bradstreet, Anne

George, Jean Craighead 1919- . . . . . . **CLC 35**
See also AAYA 8; CA 5-8R; CANR 25;
CLR 1; DLB 52; JRDA; MAICYA;
SATA 2, 68

George, Stefan (Anton)
1868-1933 . . . . **TCLC 2, 14**
See also CA 104

Georges, Georges Martin
See Simenon, Georges (Jacques Christian)

Gerhardi, William Alexander
See Gerhardie, William Alexander

Gerhardie, William Alexander
1895-1977 . . . . **CLC 5**
See also CA 25-28R; 73-76; CANR 18;
DLB 36

Gerstler, Amy 1956- . . . . **CLC 70**
See also CA 146

Gertler, T. . . . . **CLC 34**
See also CA 116; 121; INT 121

Ghalib . . . . **NCLC 39**
See also Ghalib, Hsadullah Khan

Ghalib, Hsadullah Khan 1797-1869
See Ghalib
See also DAM POET

Ghelderode, Michel de
1898-1962 . . . . **CLC 6, 11**
See also CA 85-88; CANR 40;
DAM DRAM

Ghiselin, Brewster 1903- . . . . **CLC 23**
See also CA 13-16R; CAAS 10; CANR 13

Ghose, Zulfikar 1935- . . . . **CLC 42**
See also CA 65-68

Ghosh, Amitav 1956- . . . . **CLC 44**
See also CA 147

Giacosa, Giuseppe 1847-1906 . . . . . . **TCLC 7**
See also CA 104

Gibb, Lee
See Waterhouse, Keith (Spencer)

Gibbon, Lewis Grassic . . . . **TCLC 4**
See also Mitchell, James Leslie

Gibbons, Kaye 1960- . . . . **CLC 50, 88**
See also CA 151; DAM POP

Gibran, Kahlil
1883-1931 . . . . **TCLC 1, 9; PC 9**
See also CA 104; 150; DAM POET, POP

Gibran, Khalil
See Gibran, Kahlil

Gibson, William
1914- . . . . **CLC 23; DA; DAB; DAC**
See also CA 9-12R; CANR 9, 42;
DAM DRAM, MST; DLB 7; SATA 66

Gibson, William (Ford) 1948- . . . **CLC 39, 63**
See also AAYA 12; CA 126; 133;
CANR 52; DAM POP

Gide, Andre (Paul Guillaume)
1869-1951 . . . . **TCLC 5, 12, 36; DA;
DAB; DAC; SSC 13; WLC**
See also CA 104; 124; DAM MST, NOV;
DLB 65; MTCW

Gifford, Barry (Colby) 1946- . . . . **CLC 34**
See also CA 65-68; CANR 9, 30, 40

Gilbert, W(illiam) S(chwenck)
1836-1911 . . . . **TCLC 3**
See also CA 104; DAM DRAM, POET;
SATA 36

Gordon, Adam Lindsay
　1833-1870 . . . . **NCLC 21**

Gordon, Caroline
　1895-1981 . . . **CLC 6, 13, 29, 83; SSC 15**
　See also CA 11-12; 103; CANR 36; CAP 1;
　DLB 4, 9, 102; DLBY 81; MTCW

Gordon, Charles William 1860-1937
　See Connor, Ralph
　See also CA 109

Gordon, Mary (Catherine)
　1949- . . . . **CLC 13, 22**
　See also CA 102; CANR 44; DLB 6;
　DLBY 81; INT 102; MTCW

Gordon, Sol 1923- . . . . **CLC 26**
　See also CA 53-56; CANR 4; SATA 11

Gordone, Charles 1925-1995 . . . . . **CLC 1, 4**
　See also BW 1; CA 93-96; 150;
　DAM DRAM; DLB 7; INT 93-96;
　MTCW

Gorenko, Anna Andreevna
　See Akhmatova, Anna

Gorky, Maxim . . . . **TCLC 8; DAB; WLC**
　See also Peshkov, Alexei Maximovich

Goryan, Sirak
　See Saroyan, William

Gosse, Edmund (William)
　1849-1928 . . . . **TCLC 28**
　See also CA 117; DLB 57, 144

Gotlieb, Phyllis Fay (Bloom)
　1926- . . . . **CLC 18**
　See also CA 13-16R; CANR 7; DLB 88

Gottesman, S. D.
　See Kornbluth, C(yril) M.; Pohl, Frederik

Gottfried von Strassburg
　fl. c. 1210- . . . . **CMLC 10**
　See also DLB 138

Gould, Lois . . . . **CLC 4, 10**
　See also CA 77-80; CANR 29; MTCW

Gourmont, Remy (-Marie-Charles) de
　1858-1915 . . . . **TCLC 17**
　See also CA 109; 150

Govier, Katherine 1948- . . . . **CLC 51**
　See also CA 101; CANR 18, 40

Goyen, (Charles) William
　1915-1983 . . . . **CLC 5, 8, 14, 40**
　See also AITN 2; CA 5-8R; 110; CANR 6;
　DLB 2; DLBY 83; INT CANR-6

Goytisolo, Juan
　1931- . . . . **CLC 5, 10, 23; HLC**
　See also CA 85-88; CANR 32;
　DAM MULT; HW; MTCW

Gozzano, Guido 1883-1916 . . . . **PC 10**
　See also DLB 114

Gozzi, (Conte) Carlo 1720-1806 . . **NCLC 23**

Grabbe, Christian Dietrich
　1801-1836 . . . . **NCLC 2**
　See also DLB 133

Grace, Patricia 1937- . . . . **CLC 56**

Gracian y Morales, Baltasar
　1601-1658 . . . . **LC 15**

Gracq, Julien . . . . **CLC 11, 48**
　See also Poirier, Louis
　See also DLB 83

Grade, Chaim 1910-1982 . . . . **CLC 10**
　See also CA 93-96; 107

Graduate of Oxford, A
　See Ruskin, John

Graham, John
　See Phillips, David Graham

Graham, Jorie 1951- . . . . **CLC 48**
　See also CA 1?1; DLB 120

Graham, R(obert) B(ontine) Cunninghame
　See Cunninghame Graham, R(obert)
　B(ontine)
　See also DLB 98, 135

Graham, Robert
　See Haldeman, Joe (William)

Graham, Tom
　See Lewis, (Harry) Sinclair

Graham, W(illiam) S(ydney)
　1918-1986 . . . . **CLC 29**
　See also CA 73-76; 118; DLB 20

Graham, Winston (Mawdsley)
　1910- . . . . **CLC 23**
　See also CA 49-52; CANR 2, 22, 45;
　DLB 77

Grahame, Kenneth
　1859-1932 . . . . **TCLC 64; DAB**
　See also CA 108; 136; CLR 5; DLB 34, 141;
　MAICYA; YABC 1

Grant, Skeeter
　See Spiegelman, Art

Granville-Barker, Harley
　1877-1946 . . . . **TCLC 2**
　See also Barker, Harley Granville
　See also CA 104; DAM DRAM

Grass, Guenter (Wilhelm)
　1927- . . . . . **CLC 1, 2, 4, 6, 11, 15, 22, 32,**
　　　　　　　　　49, 88; DA; DAB; DAC; WLC
　See also CA 13-16R; CANR 20;
　DAM MST, NOV; DLB 75, 124; MTCW

Gratton, Thomas
　See Hulme, T(homas) E(rnest)

Grau, Shirley Ann
　1929- . . . . **CLC 4, 9; SSC 15**
　See also CA 89-92; CANR 22; DLB 2;
　INT CANR-22; MTCW

Gravel, Fern
　See Hall, James Norman

Graver, Elizabeth 1964- . . . . **CLC 70**
　See also CA 135

Graves, Richard Perceval 1945- . . . . **CLC 44**
　See also CA 65-68; CANR 9, 26, 51

Graves, Robert (von Ranke)
　1895-1985 . . . . . . **CLC 1, 2, 6, 11, 39, 44,**
　　　　　　　　　　　　　　45; DAB; DAC; PC 6
　See also CA 5-8R; 117; CANR 5, 36;
　CDBLB 1914-1945; DAM MST, POET;
　DLB 20, 100; DLBY 85; MTCW;
　SATA 45

Graves, Valerie
　See Bradley, Marion Zimmer

Gray, Alasdair (James) 1934- . . . . . . **CLC 41**
　See also CA 126; CANR 47; INT 126;
　MTCW

Gray, Amlin 1946- . . . . **CLC 29**
　See also CA 138

Gray, Francine du Plessix 1930- . . . . **CLC 22**
　See also BEST 90:3; CA 61-64; CAAS 2;
　CANR 11, 33; DAM NOV;
　INT CANR-11; MTCW

Gray, John (Henry) 1866-1934 . . . . **TCLC 19**
　See also CA 119

Gray, Simon (James Holliday)
　1936- . . . . **CLC 9, 14, 36**
　See also AITN 1; CA 21-24R; CAAS 3;
　CANR 32; DLB 13; MTCW

Gray, Spalding 1941- . . . . **CLC 49**
　See also CA 128; DAM POP

Gray, Thomas
　1716-1771 . . . . . . **LC 4; DA; DAB; DAC;**
　　　　　　　　　　　　　　PC 2; WLC
　See also CDBLB 1660-1789; DAM MST;
　DLB 109

Grayson, David
　See Baker, Ray Stannard

Grayson, Richard (A.) 1951- . . . . **CLC 38**
　See also CA 85-88; CANR 14, 31

Greeley, Andrew M(oran) 1928- . . . . **CLC 28**
　See also CA 5-8R; CAAS 7; CANR 7, 43;
　DAM POP; MTCW

Green, Anna Katharine
　1846-1935 . . . . **TCLC 63**
　See also CA 112

Green, Brian
　See Card, Orson Scott

Green, Hannah
　See Greenberg, Joanne (Goldenberg)

Green, Hannah . . . . **CLC 3**
　See also CA 73-76

Green, Henry . . . . **CLC 2, 13**
　See also Yorke, Henry Vincent
　See also DLB 15

Green, Julian (Hartridge) 1900-
　See Green, Julien
　See also CA 21-24R; CANR 33; DLB 4, 72;
　MTCW

Green, Julien . . . . **CLC 3, 11, 77**
　See also Green, Julian (Hartridge)

Green, Paul (Eliot) 1894-1981 . . . . . . **CLC 25**
　See also AITN 1; CA 5-8R; 103; CANR 3;
　DAM DRAM; DLB 7, 9; DLBY 81

Greenberg, Ivan 1908-1973
　See Rahv, Philip
　See also CA 85-88

Greenberg, Joanne (Goldenberg)
　1932- . . . . **CLC 7, 30**
　See also AAYA 12; CA 5-8R; CANR 14,
　32; SATA 25

Greenberg, Richard 1959(?)- . . . . **CLC 57**
　See also CA 138

Greene, Bette 1934- . . . . **CLC 30**
　See also AAYA 7; CA 53-56; CANR 4;
　CLR 2; JRDA; MAICYA; SAAS 16;
　SATA 8

Greene, Gael . . . . **CLC 8**
　See also CA 13-16R; CANR 10

Greene, Graham
    1904-1991 .... **CLC 1, 3, 6, 9, 14, 18, 27,**
        37, 70, 72; DA; DAB; DAC; WLC
    See also AITN 2; CA 13-16R; 133;
    CANR 35; CDBLB 1945-1960;
    DAM MST, NOV; DLB 13, 15, 77, 100,
    162; DLBY 91; MTCW; SATA 20

Greer, Richard
    See Silverberg, Robert

Gregor, Arthur 1923- .... **CLC 9**
    See also CA 25-28R; CAAS 10; CANR 11;
    SATA 36

Gregor, Lee
    See Pohl, Frederik

Gregory, Isabella Augusta (Persse)
    1852-1932 .... **TCLC 1**
    See also CA 104; DLB 10

Gregory, J. Dennis
    See Williams, John A(lfred)

Grendon, Stephen
    See Derleth, August (William)

Grenville, Kate 1950- .... **CLC 61**
    See also CA 118; CANR 53

Grenville, Pelham
    See Wodehouse, P(elham) G(renville)

Greve, Felix Paul (Berthold Friedrich)
    1879-1948
    See Grove, Frederick Philip
    See also CA 104; 141; DAC; DAM MST

Grey, Zane 1872-1939 .... **TCLC 6**
    See also CA 104; 132; DAM POP; DLB 9;
    MTCW

Grieg, (Johan) Nordahl (Brun)
    1902-1943 .... **TCLC 10**
    See also CA 107

Grieve, C(hristopher) M(urray)
    1892-1978 .... **CLC 11, 19**
    See also MacDiarmid, Hugh; Pteleon
    See also CA 5-8R; 85-88; CANR 33;
    DAM POET; MTCW

Griffin, Gerald 1803-1840 .... **NCLC 7**
    See also DLB 159

Griffin, John Howard 1920-1980.... **CLC 68**
    See also AITN 1; CA 1-4R; 101; CANR 2

Griffin, Peter 1942- .... **CLC 39**
    See also CA 136

Griffiths, Trevor 1935-........ **CLC 13, 52**
    See also CA 97-100; CANR 45; DLB 13

Grigson, Geoffrey (Edward Harvey)
    1905-1985 .... **CLC 7, 39**
    See also CA 25-28R; 118; CANR 20, 33;
    DLB 27; MTCW

Grillparzer, Franz 1791-1872...... **NCLC 1**
    See also DLB 133

Grimble, Reverend Charles James
    See Eliot, T(homas) S(tearns)

Grimke, Charlotte L(ottie) Forten
    1837(?)-1914
    See Forten, Charlotte L.
    See also BW 1; CA 117; 124; DAM MULT,
    POET

Grimm, Jacob Ludwig Karl
    1785-1863 .... **NCLC 3**
    See also DLB 90; MAICYA; SATA 22

Grimm, Wilhelm Karl 1786-1859 .. **NCLC 3**
    See also DLB 90; MAICYA; SATA 22

Grimmelshausen, Johann Jakob Christoffel
    von 1621-1676 .... **LC 6**

Grindel, Eugene 1895-1952
    See Eluard, Paul
    See also CA 104

Grisham, John 1955- .... **CLC 84**
    See also AAYA 14; CA 138; CANR 47;
    DAM POP

Grossman, David 1954- .... **CLC 67**
    See also CA 138

Grossman, Vasily (Semenovich)
    1905-1964 .... **CLC 41**
    See also CA 124; 130; MTCW

Grove, Frederick Philip .... **TCLC 4**
    See also Greve, Felix Paul (Berthold
    Friedrich)
    See also DLB 92

Grubb
    See Crumb, R(obert)

Grumbach, Doris (Isaac)
    1918- .... **CLC 13, 22, 64**
    See also CA 5-8R; CAAS 2; CANR 9, 42;
    INT CANR-9

Grundtvig, Nicolai Frederik Severin
    1783-1872 .... **NCLC 1**

Grunge
    See Crumb, R(obert)

Grunwald, Lisa 1959- .... **CLC 44**
    See also CA 120

Guare, John 1938- .... **CLC 8, 14, 29, 67**
    See also CA 73-76; CANR 21;
    DAM DRAM; DLB 7; MTCW

Gudjonsson, Halldor Kiljan 1902-
    See Laxness, Halldor
    See also CA 103

Guenter, Erich
    See Eich, Guenter

Guest, Barbara 1920- .... **CLC 34**
    See also CA 25-28R; CANR 11, 44; DLB 5

Guest, Judith (Ann) 1936- .... **CLC 8, 30**
    See also AAYA 7; CA 77-80; CANR 15;
    DAM NOV, POP; INT CANR-15;
    MTCW

Guevara, Che .... **CLC 87; HLC**
    See also Guevara (Serna), Ernesto

Guevara (Serna), Ernesto 1928-1967
    See Guevara, Che
    See also CA 127; 111; DAM MULT; HW

Guild, Nicholas M. 1944-......... **CLC 33**
    See also CA 93-96

Guillemin, Jacques
    See Sartre, Jean-Paul

Guillen, Jorge 1893-1984.......... **CLC 11**
    See also CA 89-92; 112; DAM MULT,
    POET; DLB 108; HW

Guillen, Nicolas (Cristobal)
    1902-1989 ..... **CLC 48, 79; BLC; HLC**
    See also BW 2; CA 116; 125; 129;
    DAM MST, MULT, POET; HW

Guillevic, (Eugene) 1907-.......... **CLC 33**
    See also CA 93-96

Guillois
    See Desnos, Robert

Guillois, Valentin
    See Desnos, Robert

Guiney, Louise Imogen
    1861-1920 .... **TCLC 41**
    See also DLB 54

Guiraldes, Ricardo (Guillermo)
    1886-1927 .... **TCLC 39**
    See also CA 131; HW; MTCW

Gumilev, Nikolai Stephanovich
    1886-1921 .... **TCLC 60**

Gunesekera, Romesh............... **CLC 91**

Gunn, Bill .... **CLC 5**
    See also Gunn, William Harrison
    See also DLB 38

Gunn, Thom(son William)
    1929- .... **CLC 3, 6, 18, 32, 81**
    See also CA 17-20R; CANR 9, 33;
    CDBLB 1960 to Present; DAM POET;
    DLB 27; INT CANR-33; MTCW

Gunn, William Harrison 1934(?)-1989
    See Gunn, Bill
    See also AITN 1; BW 1; CA 13-16R; 128;
    CANR 12, 25

Gunnars, Kristjana 1948-.......... **CLC 69**
    See also CA 113; DLB 60

Gurganus, Allan 1947- .... **CLC 70**
    See also BEST 90:1; CA 135; DAM POP

Gurney, A(lbert) R(amsdell), Jr.
    1930- .... **CLC 32, 50, 54**
    See also CA 77-80; CANR 32;
    DAM DRAM

Gurney, Ivor (Bertie) 1890-1937 ... **TCLC 33**

Gurney, Peter
    See Gurney, A(lbert) R(amsdell), Jr.

Guro, Elena 1877-1913........... **TCLC 56**

Gustafson, Ralph (Barker) 1909-.... **CLC 36**
    See also CA 21-24R; CANR 8, 45; DLB 88

Gut, Gom
    See Simenon, Georges (Jacques Christian)

Guterson, David 1956- .... **CLC 91**
    See also CA 132

Guthrie, A(lfred) B(ertram), Jr.
    1901-1991 .... **CLC 23**
    See also CA 57-60; 134; CANR 24; DLB 6;
    SATA 62; SATA-Obit 67

Guthrie, Isobel
    See Grieve, C(hristopher) M(urray)

Guthrie, Woodrow Wilson 1912-1967
    See Guthrie, Woody
    See also CA 113; 93-96

Guthrie, Woody.................. **CLC 35**
    See also Guthrie, Woodrow Wilson

Guy, Rosa (Cuthbert) 1928-........ **CLC 26**
    See also AAYA 4; BW 2; CA 17-20R;
    CANR 14, 34; CLR 13; DLB 33; JRDA;
    MAICYA; SATA 14, 62

Gwendolyn
    See Bennett, (Enoch) Arnold

H. D. .... **CLC 3, 8, 14, 31, 34, 73; PC 5**
    See also Doolittle, Hilda

H. de V.
    See Buchan, John

Haavikko, Paavo Juhani
  1931- . . . . **CLC 18, 34**
  See also CA 106

Habbema, Koos
  See Heijermans, Herman

Hacker, Marilyn
  1942- . . . . **CLC 5, 9, 23, 72, 91**
  See also CA 77-80; DAM POET; DLB 120

Haggard, H(enry) Rider
  1856-1925 . . . . **TCLC 11**
  See also CA 108; 148; DLB 70, 156;
  SATA 16

Hagiwara Sakutaro 1886-1942 . . . . **TCLC 60**

Haig, Fenil
  See Ford, Ford Madox

Haig-Brown, Roderick (Langmere)
  1908-1976 . . . . **CLC 21**
  See also CA 5-8R; 69-72; CANR 4, 38;
  CLR 31; DLB 88; MAICYA; SATA 12

Hailey, Arthur 1920- . . . . **CLC 5**
  See also AITN 2; BEST 90:3; CA 1-4R;
  CANR 2, 36; DAM NOV, POP; DLB 88;
  DLBY 82; MTCW

Hailey, Elizabeth Forsythe 1938- . . . **CLC 40**
  See also CA 93-96; CAAS 1; CANR 15, 48;
  INT CANR-15

Haines, John (Meade) 1924- . . . . **CLC 58**
  See also CA 17-20R; CANR 13, 34; DLB 5

Hakluyt, Richard 1552-1616 . . . . **LC 31**

Haldeman, Joe (William) 1943- . . . . . **CLC 61**
  See also CA 53-56; CANR 6; DLB 8;
  INT CANR-6

Haley, Alex(ander Murray Palmer)
  1921-1992 . . . . **CLC 8, 12, 76; BLC; DA;
                                    DAB; DAC**
  See also BW 2; CA 77-80; 136; DAM MST,
  MULT, POP; DLB 38; MTCW

Haliburton, Thomas Chandler
  1796-1865 . . . . **NCLC 15**
  See also DLB 11, 99

Hall, Donald (Andrew, Jr.)
  1928- . . . . **CLC 1, 13, 37, 59**
  See also CA 5-8R; CAAS 7; CANR 2, 44;
  DAM POET; DLB 5; SATA 23

Hall, Frederic Sauser
  See Sauser-Hall, Frederic

Hall, James
  See Kuttner, Henry

Hall, James Norman 1887-1951 . . . **TCLC 23**
  See also CA 123; SATA 21

Hall, (Marguerite) Radclyffe
  1886-1943 . . . . **TCLC 12**
  See also CA 110; 150

Hall, Rodney 1935- . . . . **CLC 51**
  See also CA 109

Halleck, Fitz-Greene 1790-1867 . . **NCLC 47**
  See also DLB 3

Halliday, Michael
  See Creasey, John

Halpern, Daniel 1945- . . . . **CLC 14**
  See also CA 33-36R

Hamburger, Michael (Peter Leopold)
  1924- . . . . **CLC 5, 14**
  See also CA 5-8R; CAAS 4; CANR 2, 47;
  DLB 27

Hamill, Pete 1935- . . . . **CLC 10**
  See also CA 25-28R; CANR 18

Hamilton, Alexander
  1755(?)-1804 . . . . **NCLC 49**
  See also DLB 37

Hamilton, Clive
  See Lewis, C(live) S(taples)

Hamilton, Edmond 1904-1977 . . . . **CLC 1**
  See also CA 1-4R; CANR 3; DLB 8

Hamilton, Eugene (Jacob) Lee
  See Lee-Hamilton, Eugene (Jacob)

Hamilton, Franklin
  See Silverberg, Robert

Hamilton, Gail
  See Corcoran, Barbara

Hamilton, Mollie
  See Kaye, M(ary) M(argaret)

Hamilton, (Anthony Walter) Patrick
  1904-1962 . . . . **CLC 51**
  See also CA 113; DLB 10

Hamilton, Virginia 1936- . . . . **CLC 26**
  See also AAYA 2; BW 2; CA 25-28R;
  CANR 20, 37; CLR 1, 11, 40;
  DAM MULT; DLB 33, 52;
  INT CANR-20; JRDA; MAICYA;
  MTCW; SATA 4, 56, 79

Hammett, (Samuel) Dashiell
  1894-1961 . . . . **CLC 3, 5, 10, 19, 47;
                                                  SSC 17**
  See also AITN 1; CA 81-84; CANR 42;
  CDALB 1929-1941; DLBD 6; MTCW

Hammon, Jupiter
  1711(?)-1800(?) . . . **NCLC 5; BLC; PC 16**
  See also DAM MULT, POET; DLB 31, 50

Hammond, Keith
  See Kuttner, Henry

Hamner, Earl (Henry), Jr. 1923- . . . **CLC 12**
  See also AITN 2; CA 73-76; DLB 6

Hampton, Christopher (James)
  1946- . . . . **CLC 4**
  See also CA 25-28R; DLB 13; MTCW

Hamsun, Knut . . . . **TCLC 2, 14, 49**
  See also Pedersen, Knut

Handke, Peter 1942- . . **CLC 5, 8, 10, 15, 38**
  See also CA 77-80; CANR 33;
  DAM DRAM, NOV; DLB 85, 124;
  MTCW

Hanley, James 1901-1985 . . . **CLC 3, 5, 8, 13**
  See also CA 73-76; 117; CANR 36; MTCW

Hannah, Barry 1942- . . . . **CLC 23, 38, 90**
  See also CA 108; 110; CANR 43; DLB 6;
  INT 110; MTCW

Hannon, Ezra
  See Hunter, Evan

Hansberry, Lorraine (Vivian)
  1930-1965 . . . . . . **CLC 17, 62; BLC; DA;
                                        DAB; DAC; DC 2**
  See also BW 1; CA 109; 25-28R; CABS 3;
  CDALB 1941-1968; DAM DRAM, MST,
  MULT; DLB 7, 38; MTCW

Hansen, Joseph 1923- . . . . **CLC 38**
  See also CA 29-32R; CAAS 17; CANR 16,
  44; INT CANR-16

Hansen, Martin A. 1909-1955 . . . . . **TCLC 32**

Hanson, Kenneth O(stlin) 1922- . . . . **CLC 13**
  See also CA 53-56; CANR 7

Hardwick, Elizabeth 1916- . . . . **CLC 13**
  See also CA 5-8R; CANR 3, 32;
  DAM NOV; DLB 6; MTCW

Hardy, Thomas
  1840-1928 . . . . . . **TCLC 4, 10, 18, 32, 48,
  53; DA; DAB; DAC; PC 8; SSC 2; WLC**
  See also CA 104; 123; CDBLB 1890-1914;
  DAM MST, NOV, POET; DLB 18, 19,
  135; MTCW

Hare, David 1947- . . . . **CLC 29, 58**
  See also CA 97-100; CANR 39; DLB 13;
  MTCW

Harford, Henry
  See Hudson, W(illiam) H(enry)

Hargrave, Leonie
  See Disch, Thomas M(ichael)

Harjo, Joy 1951- . . . . **CLC 83**
  See also CA 114; CANR 35; DAM MULT;
  DLB 120; NNAL

Harlan, Louis R(udolph) 1922- . . . . . **CLC 34**
  See also CA 21-24R; CANR 25

Harling, Robert 1951(?)- . . . . **CLC 53**
  See also CA 147

Harmon, William (Ruth) 1938- . . . . . **CLC 38**
  See also CA 33-36R; CANR 14, 32, 35;
  SATA 65

Harper, F. E. W.
  See Harper, Frances Ellen Watkins

Harper, Frances E. W.
  See Harper, Frances Ellen Watkins

Harper, Frances E. Watkins
  See Harper, Frances Ellen Watkins

Harper, Frances Ellen
  See Harper, Frances Ellen Watkins

Harper, Frances Ellen Watkins
  1825-1911 . . . . **TCLC 14; BLC**
  See also BW 1; CA 111; 125; DAM MULT,
  POET; DLB 50

Harper, Michael S(teven) 1938- . . . **CLC 7, 22**
  See also BW 1; CA 33-36R; CANR 24;
  DLB 41

Harper, Mrs. F. E. W.
  See Harper, Frances Ellen Watkins

Harris, Christie (Lucy) Irwin
  1907- . . . . **CLC 12**
  See also CA 5-8R; CANR 6; DLB 88;
  JRDA; MAICYA; SAAS 10; SATA 6, 74

Harris, Frank 1856-1931 . . . . **TCLC 24**
  See also CA 109; 150; DLB 156

Harris, George Washington
  1814-1869 . . . . **NCLC 23**
  See also DLB 3, 11

Harris, Joel Chandler
  1848-1908 . . . . **TCLC 2; SSC 19**
  See also CA 104; 137; DLB 11, 23, 42, 78,
  91; MAICYA; YABC 1

**Harris, John (Wyndham Parkes Lucas)
  Beynon** 1903-1969
  See Wyndham, John
  See also CA 102; 89-92

Harris, MacDonald . . . . **CLC 9**
  See also Heiney, Donald (William)

Heller, Joseph
1923- .... **CLC 1, 3, 5, 8, 11, 36, 63; DA; DAB; DAC; WLC**
See also AITN 1; CA 5-8R; CABS 1; CANR 8, 42; DAM MST, NOV, POP; DLB 2, 28; DLBY 80; INT CANR-8; MTCW

Hellman, Lillian (Florence)
1906-1984 ...... **CLC 2, 4, 8, 14, 18, 34, 44, 52; DC 1**
See also AITN 1, 2; CA 13-16R; 112; CANR 33; DAM DRAM; DLB 7; DLBY 84; MTCW

Helprin, Mark 1947- ..... **CLC 7, 10, 22, 32**
See also CA 81-84; CANR 47; DAM NOV, POP; DLBY 85; MTCW

Helvetius, Claude-Adrien
1715-1771 .... **LC 26**

Helyar, Jane Penelope Josephine 1933-
See Poole, Josephine
See also CA 21-24R; CANR 10, 26; SATA 82

Hemans, Felicia 1793-1835 ...... **NCLC 29**
See also DLB 96

Hemingway, Ernest (Miller)
1899-1961 .... **CLC 1, 3, 6, 8, 10, 13, 19, 30, 34, 39, 41, 44, 50, 61, 80; DA; DAB; DAC; SSC 1; WLC**
See also CA 77-80; CANR 34; CDALB 1917-1929; DAM MST, NOV; DLB 4, 9, 102; DLBD 1; DLBY 81, 87; MTCW

Hempel, Amy 1951- .... **CLC 39**
See also CA 118; 137

Henderson, F. C.
See Mencken, H(enry) L(ouis)

Henderson, Sylvia
See Ashton-Warner, Sylvia (Constance)

Henley, Beth .... **CLC 23; DC 6**
See also Henley, Elizabeth Becker
See also CABS 3; DLBY 86

Henley, Elizabeth Becker 1952-
See Henley, Beth
See also CA 107; CANR 32; DAM DRAM, MST; MTCW

Henley, William Ernest
1849-1903 .... **TCLC 8**
See also CA 105; DLB 19

Hennissart, Martha
See Lathen, Emma
See also CA 85-88

Henry, O. .... **TCLC 1, 19; SSC 5; WLC**
See also Porter, William Sydney

Henry, Patrick 1736-1799 .... **LC 25**

Henryson, Robert 1430(?)-1506(?). .... **LC 20**
See also DLB 146

Henry VIII 1491-1547 .... **LC 10**

Henschke, Alfred
See Klabund

Hentoff, Nat(han Irving) 1925- ..... **CLC 26**
See also AAYA 4; CA 1-4R; CAAS 6; CANR 5, 25; CLR 1; INT CANR-25; JRDA; MAICYA; SATA 42, 69; SATA-Brief 27

Heppenstall, (John) Rayner
1911-1981 .... **CLC 10**
See also CA 1-4R; 103; CANR 29

Herbert, Frank (Patrick)
1920-1986 .... **CLC 12, 23, 35, 44, 85**
See also CA 53-56; 118; CANR 5, 43; DAM POP; DLB 8; INT CANR-5; MTCW; SATA 9, 37; SATA-Obit 47

Herbert, George
1593-1633 .... **LC 24; DAB; PC 4**
See also CDBLB Before 1660; DAM POET; DLB 126

Herbert, Zbigniew 1924- .... **CLC 9, 43**
See also CA 89-92; CANR 36; DAM POET; MTCW

Herbst, Josephine (Frey)
1897-1969 .... **CLC 34**
See also CA 5-8R; 25-28R; DLB 9

Hergesheimer, Joseph
1880-1954 .... **TCLC 11**
See also CA 109; DLB 102, 9

Herlihy, James Leo 1927-1993 ...... **CLC 6**
See also CA 1-4R; 143; CANR 2

Hermogenes fl. c. 175- .... **CMLC 6**

Hernandez, Jose 1834-1886 ...... **NCLC 17**

Herodotus c. 484B.C.-429B.C. .... **CMLC 17**

Herrick, Robert
1591-1674 ..... **LC 13; DA; DAB; DAC; PC 9**
See also DAM MST, POP; DLB 126

Herring, Guilles
See Somerville, Edith

Herriot, James 1916-1995 .... **CLC 12**
See also Wight, James Alfred
See also AAYA 1; CA 148; CANR 40; DAM POP; SATA 86

Herrmann, Dorothy 1941- .... **CLC 44**
See also CA 107

Herrmann, Taffy
See Herrmann, Dorothy

Hersey, John (Richard)
1914-1993 ...... **CLC 1, 2, 7, 9, 40, 81**
See also CA 17-20R; 140; CANR 33; DAM POP; DLB 6; MTCW; SATA 25; SATA-Obit 76

Herzen, Aleksandr Ivanovich
1812-1870 .... **NCLC 10**

Herzl, Theodor 1860-1904 .... **TCLC 36**

Herzog, Werner 1942- .... **CLC 16**
See also CA 89-92

Hesiod c. 8th cent. B.C.- .... **CMLC 5**

Hesse, Hermann
1877-1962 .... **CLC 1, 2, 3, 6, 11, 17, 25, 69; DA; DAB; DAC; SSC 9; WLC**
See also CA 17-18; CAP 2; DAM MST, NOV; DLB 66; MTCW; SATA 50

Hewes, Cady
See De Voto, Bernard (Augustine)

Heyen, William 1940- .... **CLC 13, 18**
See also CA 33-36R; CAAS 9; DLB 5

Heyerdahl, Thor 1914- .... **CLC 26**
See also CA 5-8R; CANR 5, 22; MTCW; SATA 2, 52

Heym, Georg (Theodor Franz Arthur)
1887-1912 .... **TCLC 9**
See also CA 106

Heym, Stefan 1913- .... **CLC 41**
See also CA 9-12R; CANR 4; DLB 69

Heyse, Paul (Johann Ludwig von)
1830-1914 .... **TCLC 8**
See also CA 104; DLB 129

Heyward, (Edwin) DuBose
1885-1940 .... **TCLC 59**
See also CA 108; DLB 7, 9, 45; SATA 21

Hibbert, Eleanor Alice Burford
1906-1993 .... **CLC 7**
See also BEST 90:4; CA 17-20R; 140; CANR 9, 28; DAM POP; SATA 2; SATA-Obit 74

Hichens, Robert S. 1864-1950 ..... **TCLC 64**
See also DLB 153

Higgins, George V(incent)
1939- .... **CLC 4, 7, 10, 18**
See also CA 77-80; CAAS 5; CANR 17, 51; DLB 2; DLBY 81; INT CANR-17; MTCW

Higginson, Thomas Wentworth
1823-1911 .... **TCLC 36**
See also DLB 1, 64

Highet, Helen
See MacInnes, Helen (Clark)

Highsmith, (Mary) Patricia
1921-1995 .... **CLC 2, 4, 14, 42**
See also CA 1-4R; 147; CANR 1, 20, 48; DAM NOV, POP; MTCW

Highwater, Jamake (Mamake)
1942(?)- .... **CLC 12**
See also AAYA 7; CA 65-68; CAAS 7; CANR 10, 34; CLR 17; DLB 52; DLBY 85; JRDA; MAICYA; SATA 32, 69; SATA-Brief 30

Highway, Tomson 1951- ...... **CLC 92; DAC**
See also CA 151; DAM MULT; NNAL

Higuchi, Ichiyo 1872-1896 .... **NCLC 49**

Hijuelos, Oscar 1951- ...... **CLC 65; HLC**
See also BEST 90:1; CA 123; CANR 50; DAM MULT, POP; DLB 145; HW

Hikmet, Nazim 1902(?)-1963 .... **CLC 40**
See also CA 141; 93-96

Hildesheimer, Wolfgang
1916-1991 .... **CLC 49**
See also CA 101; 135; DLB 69, 124

Hill, Geoffrey (William)
1932- .... **CLC 5, 8, 18, 45**
See also CA 81-84; CANR 21; CDBLB 1960 to Present; DAM POET; DLB 40; MTCW

Hill, George Roy 1921- .... **CLC 26**
See also CA 110; 122

Hill, John
See Koontz, Dean R(ay)

Hill, Susan (Elizabeth)
1942- .... **CLC 4; DAB**
See also CA 33-36R; CANR 29; DAM MST, NOV; DLB 14, 139; MTCW

Hillerman, Tony 1925- .... **CLC 62**
See also AAYA 6; BEST 89:1; CA 29-32R; CANR 21, 42; DAM POP; SATA 6

Horgan, Paul (George Vincent O'Shaughnessy)
1903-1995 . . . . **CLC 9, 53**
See also CA 13-16R; 147; CANR 9, 35;
DAM NOV; DLB 102; DLBY 85;
INT CANR-9; MTCW; SATA 13;
SATA-Obit 84

Horn, Peter
See Kuttner, Henry

Hornem, Horace Esq.
See Byron, George Gordon (Noel)

Hornung, E(rnest) W(illiam)
1866-1921 . . . . **TCLC 59**
See also CA 108; DLB 70

Horovitz, Israel (Arthur) 1939- . . . . . **CLC 56**
See also CA 33-36R; CANR 46;
DAM DRAM; DLB 7

Horvath, Odon von
See Horvath, Oedoen von
See also DLB 85, 124

Horvath, Oedoen von 1901-1938 . . . **TCLC 45**
See also Horvath, Odon von
See also CA 118

Horwitz, Julius 1920-1986 . . . . **CLC 14**
See also CA 9-12R; 119; CANR 12

Hospital, Janette Turner 1942- . . . . . **CLC 42**
See also CA 108; CANR 48

Hostos, E. M. de
See Hostos (y Bonilla), Eugenio Maria de

Hostos, Eugenio M. de
See Hostos (y Bonilla), Eugenio Maria de

Hostos, Eugenio Maria
See Hostos (y Bonilla), Eugenio Maria de

Hostos (y Bonilla), Eugenio Maria de
1839-1903 . . . . **TCLC 24**
See also CA 123; 131; HW

Houdini
See Lovecraft, H(oward) P(hillips)

Hougan, Carolyn 1943- . . . . **CLC 34**
See also CA 139

Household, Geoffrey (Edward West)
1900-1988 . . . . **CLC 11**
See also CA 77-80; 126; DLB 87; SATA 14;
SATA-Obit 59

Housman, A(lfred) E(dward)
1859-1936 . . . . . . **TCLC 1, 10; DA; DAB;**
DAC; PC 2
See also CA 104; 125; DAM MST, POET;
DLB 19; MTCW

Housman, Laurence 1865-1959 . . . . . **TCLC 7**
See also CA 106; DLB 10; SATA 25

Howard, Elizabeth Jane 1923- . . . **CLC 7, 29**
See also CA 5-8R; CANR 8

Howard, Maureen 1930- . . . . . **CLC 5, 14, 46**
See also CA 53-56; CANR 31; DLBY 83;
INT CANR-31; MTCW

Howard, Richard 1929- . . . . . . **CLC 7, 10, 47**
See also AITN 1; CA 85-88; CANR 25;
DLB 5; INT CANR-25

Howard, Robert Ervin 1906-1936 . . . **TCLC 8**
See also CA 105

Howard, Warren F.
See Pohl, Frederik

Howe, Fanny 1940- . . . . **CLC 47**
See also CA 117; SATA-Brief 52

Howe, Irving 1920-1993 . . . . **CLC 85**
See also CA 9-12R; 141; CANR 21, 50;
DLB 67; MTCW

Howe, Julia Ward 1819-1910 . . . . . **TCLC 21**
See also CA 117; DLB 1

Howe, Susan 1937- . . . . **CLC 72**
See also DLB 120

Howe, Tina 1937- . . . . **CLC 48**
See also CA 109

Howell, James 1594(?)-1666 . . . . **LC 13**
See also DLB 151

Howells, W. D.
See Howells, William Dean

Howells, William D.
See Howells, William Dean

Howells, William Dean
1837-1920 . . . . **TCLC 7, 17, 41**
See also CA 104; 134; CDALB 1865-1917;
DLB 12, 64, 74, 79

Howes, Barbara 1914-1996 . . . . **CLC 15**
See also CA 9-12R; 151; CAAS 3;
CANR 53; SATA 5

Hrabal, Bohumil 1914- . . . . **CLC 13, 67**
See also CA 106; CAAS 12

Hsun, Lu
See Lu Hsun

Hubbard, L(afayette) Ron(ald)
1911-1986 . . . . **CLC 43**
See also CA 77-80; 118; CANR 52;
DAM POP

Huch, Ricarda (Octavia)
1864-1947 . . . . **TCLC 13**
See also CA 111; DLB 66

Huddle, David 1942- . . . . **CLC 49**
See also CA 57-60; CAAS 20; DLB 130

Hudson, Jeffrey
See Crichton, (John) Michael

Hudson, W(illiam) H(enry)
1841-1922 . . . . **TCLC 29**
See also CA 115; DLB 98, 153; SATA 35

Hueffer, Ford Madox
See Ford, Ford Madox

Hughart, Barry 1934- . . . . **CLC 39**
See also CA 137

Hughes, Colin
See Creasey, John

Hughes, David (John) 1930- . . . . **CLC 48**
See also CA 116; 129; DLB 14

Hughes, Edward James
See Hughes, Ted
See also DAM MST, POET

Hughes, (James) Langston
1902-1967 . . . . . **CLC 1, 5, 10, 15, 35, 44;**
BLC; DA; DAB; DAC; DC 3; PC 1;
SSC 6; WLC
See also AAYA 12; BW 1; CA 1-4R;
25-28R; CANR 1, 34; CDALB 1929-1941;
CLR 17; DAM DRAM, MST, MULT,
POET; DLB 4, 7, 48, 51, 86; JRDA;
MAICYA; MTCW; SATA 4, 33

Hughes, Richard (Arthur Warren)
1900-1976 . . . . **CLC 1, 11**
See also CA 5-8R; 65-68; CANR 4;
DAM NOV; DLB 15, 161; MTCW;
SATA 8; SATA-Obit 25

Hughes, Ted
1930- . . . . **CLC 2, 4, 9, 14, 37; DAB;**
DAC; PC 7
See also Hughes, Edward James
See also CA 1-4R; CANR 1, 33; CLR 3;
DLB 40, 161; MAICYA; MTCW;
SATA 49; SATA-Brief 27

Hugo, Richard F(ranklin)
1923-1982 . . . . **CLC 6, 18, 32**
See also CA 49-52; 108; CANR 3;
DAM POET; DLB 5

Hugo, Victor (Marie)
1802-1885 . . . . **NCLC 3, 10, 21; DA;**
DAB; DAC; WLC
See also DAM DRAM, MST, NOV, POET;
DLB 119; SATA 47

Huidobro, Vicente
See Huidobro Fernandez, Vicente Garcia

Huidobro Fernandez, Vicente Garcia
1893-1948 . . . . **TCLC 31**
See also CA 131; HW

Hulme, Keri 1947- . . . . **CLC 39**
See also CA 125; INT 125

Hulme, T(homas) E(rnest)
1883-1917 . . . . **TCLC 21**
See also CA 117; DLB 19

Hume, David 1711-1776 . . . . **LC 7**
See also DLB 104

Humphrey, William 1924- . . . . **CLC 45**
See also CA 77-80; DLB 6

Humphreys, Emyr Owen 1919- . . . . . **CLC 47**
See also CA 5-8R; CANR 3, 24; DLB 15

Humphreys, Josephine 1945- . . . . **CLC 34, 57**
See also CA 121; 127; INT 127

Huneker, James Gibbons
1857-1921 . . . . **TCLC 65**
See also DLB 71

Hungerford, Pixie
See Brinsmead, H(esba) F(ay)

Hunt, E(verette) Howard, (Jr.)
1918- . . . . **CLC 3**
See also AITN 1; CA 45-48; CANR 2, 47

Hunt, Kyle
See Creasey, John

Hunt, (James Henry) Leigh
1784-1859 . . . . **NCLC 1**
See also DAM POET

Hunt, Marsha 1946- . . . . **CLC 70**
See also BW 2; CA 143

Hunt, Violet 1866-1942 . . . . **TCLC 53**
See also DLB 162

Hunter, E. Waldo
See Sturgeon, Theodore (Hamilton)

Hunter, Evan 1926- . . . . **CLC 11, 31**
See also CA 5-8R; CANR 5, 38;
DAM POP; DLBY 82; INT CANR-5;
MTCW; SATA 25

Hunter, Kristin (Eggleston) 1931- . . . **CLC 35**
See also AITN 1; BW 1; CA 13-16R;
CANR 13; CLR 3; DLB 33;
INT CANR-13; MAICYA; SAAS 10;
SATA 12

Hunter, Mollie 1922- . . . . **CLC 21**
See also McIlwraith, Maureen Mollie
Hunter
See also AAYA 13; CANR 37; CLR 25;
DLB 161; JRDA; MAICYA; SAAS 7;
SATA 54

Hunter, Robert (?)-1734 . . . . **LC 7**

Hurston, Zora Neale
1903-1960 . . . . **CLC 7, 30, 61; BLC; DA;**
DAC; SSC 4
See also AAYA 15; BW 1; CA 85-88;
DAM MST, MULT, NOV; DLB 51, 86;
MTCW

Huston, John (Marcellus)
1906-1987 . . . . **CLC 20**
See also CA 73-76; 123; CANR 34; DLB 26

Hustvedt, Siri 1955- . . . . **CLC 76**
See also CA 137

Hutten, Ulrich von 1488-1523 . . . . . . **LC 16**

Huxley, Aldous (Leonard)
1894-1963 . . . . . **CLC 1, 3, 4, 5, 8, 11, 18,**
35, 79; DA; DAB; DAC; WLC
See also AAYA 11; CA 85-88; CANR 44;
CDBLB 1914-1945; DAM MST, NOV;
DLB 36, 100, 162; MTCW; SATA 63

Huysmans, Charles Marie Georges
1848-1907
See Huysmans, Joris-Karl
See also CA 104

Huysmans, Joris-Karl . . . . **TCLC 7**
See also Huysmans, Charles Marie Georges
See also DLB 123

Hwang, David Henry
1957- . . . . **CLC 55; DC 4**
See also CA 127; 132; DAM DRAM;
INT 132

Hyde, Anthony 1946- . . . . **CLC 42**
See also CA 136

Hyde, Margaret O(ldroyd) 1917- . . . **CLC 21**
See also CA 1-4R; CANR 1, 36; CLR 23;
JRDA; MAICYA; SAAS 8; SATA 1, 42,
76

Hynes, James 1956(?)- . . . . **CLC 65**

Ian, Janis 1951- . . . . **CLC 21**
See also CA 105

Ibanez, Vicente Blasco
See Blasco Ibanez, Vicente

Ibarguengoitia, Jorge 1928-1983 . . . . **CLC 37**
See also CA 124; 113; HW

Ibsen, Henrik (Johan)
1828-1906 . . . . **TCLC 2, 8, 16, 37, 52;**
DA; DAB; DAC; DC 2; WLC
See also CA 104; 141; DAM DRAM, MST

Ibuse Masuji 1898-1993 . . . . **CLC 22**
See also CA 127; 141

Ichikawa, Kon 1915- . . . . **CLC 20**
See also CA 121

Idle, Eric 1943- . . . . **CLC 21**
See also Monty Python
See also CA 116; CANR 35

Ignatow, David 1914- . . . . . . **CLC 4, 7, 14, 40**
See also CA 9-12R; CAAS 3; CANR 31;
DLB 5

Ihimaera, Witi 1944- . . . . **CLC 46**
See also CA 77-80

Ilf, Ilya . . . . **TCLC 21**
See also Fainzilberg, Ilya Arnoldovich

Illyes, Gyula 1902-1983 . . . . **PC 16**
See also CA 114; 109

Immermann, Karl (Lebrecht)
1796-1840 . . . . **NCLC 4, 49**
See also DLB 133

Inclan, Ramon (Maria) del Valle
See Valle-Inclan, Ramon (Maria) del

Infante, G(uillermo) Cabrera
See Cabrera Infante, G(uillermo)

Ingalls, Rachel (Holmes) 1940- . . . . . **CLC 42**
See also CA 123; 127

Ingamells, Rex 1913-1955 . . . . **TCLC 35**

Inge, William Motter
1913-1973 . . . . **CLC 1, 8, 19**
See also CA 9-12R; CDALB 1941-1968;
DAM DRAM; DLB 7; MTCW

Ingelow, Jean 1820-1897 . . . . **NCLC 39**
See also DLB 35, 163; SATA 33

Ingram, Willis J.
See Harris, Mark

Innaurato, Albert (F.) 1948(?)- . . **CLC 21, 60**
See also CA 115; 122; INT 122

Innes, Michael
See Stewart, J(ohn) I(nnes) M(ackintosh)

Ionesco, Eugene
1909-1994 . . . . **CLC 1, 4, 6, 9, 11, 15, 41,**
86; DA; DAB; DAC; WLC
See also CA 9-12R; 144; DAM DRAM,
MST; MTCW; SATA 7; SATA-Obit 79

Iqbal, Muhammad 1873-1938 . . . . . **TCLC 28**

Ireland, Patrick
See O'Doherty, Brian

Iron, Ralph
See Schreiner, Olive (Emilie Albertina)

Irving, John (Winslow)
1942- . . . . **CLC 13, 23, 38**
See also AAYA 8; BEST 89:3; CA 25-28R;
CANR 28; DAM NOV, POP; DLB 6;
DLBY 82; MTCW

Irving, Washington
1783-1859 . . . . . **NCLC 2, 19; DA; DAB;**
SSC 2; WLC
See also CDALB 1640-1865; DAM MST;
DLB 3, 11, 30, 59, 73, 74; YABC 2

Irwin, P. K.
See Page, P(atricia) K(athleen)

Isaacs, Susan 1943- . . . . **CLC 32**
See also BEST 89:1; CA 89-92; CANR 20,
41; DAM POP; INT CANR-20; MTCW

Isherwood, Christopher (William Bradshaw)
1904-1986 . . . . **CLC 1, 9, 11, 14, 44**
See also CA 13-16R; 117; CANR 35;
DAM DRAM, NOV; DLB 15; DLBY 86;
MTCW

Ishiguro, Kazuo 1954- . . . . . . **CLC 27, 56, 59**
See also BEST 90:2; CA 120; CANR 49;
DAM NOV; MTCW

Ishikawa, Takuboku
1886(?)-1912 . . . . **TCLC 15; PC 10**
See also CA 113; DAM POET

Iskander, Fazil 1929- . . . . **CLC 47**
See also CA 102

Isler, Alan . . . . **CLC 91**

Ivan IV 1530-1584 . . . . **LC 17**

Ivanov, Vyacheslav Ivanovich
1866-1949 . . . . **TCLC 33**
See also CA 122

Ivask, Ivar Vidrik 1927-1992 . . . . . . **CLC 14**
See also CA 37-40R; 139; CANR 24

Ives, Morgan
See Bradley, Marion Zimmer

J. R. S.
See Gogarty, Oliver St. John

Jabran, Kahlil
See Gibran, Kahlil

Jabran, Khalil
See Gibran, Kahlil

Jackson, Daniel
See Wingrove, David (John)

Jackson, Jesse 1908-1983 . . . . **CLC 12**
See also BW 1; CA 25-28R; 109; CANR 27;
CLR 28; MAICYA; SATA 2, 29;
SATA-Obit 48

Jackson, Laura (Riding) 1901-1991
See Riding, Laura
See also CA 65-68; 135; CANR 28; DLB 48

Jackson, Sam
See Trumbo, Dalton

Jackson, Sara
See Wingrove, David (John)

Jackson, Shirley
1919-1965 . . . . **CLC 11, 60, 87; DA;**
DAC; SSC 9; WLC
See also AAYA 9; CA 1-4R; 25-28R;
CANR 4, 52; CDALB 1941-1968;
DAM MST; DLB 6; SATA 2

Jacob, (Cyprien-)Max 1876-1944 . . . **TCLC 6**
See also CA 104

Jacobs, Jim 1942- . . . . **CLC 12**
See also CA 97-100; INT 97-100

Jacobs, W(illiam) W(ymark)
1863-1943 . . . . **TCLC 22**
See also CA 121; DLB 135

Jacobsen, Jens Peter 1847-1885 . . **NCLC 34**

Jacobsen, Josephine 1908- . . . . **CLC 48**
See also CA 33-36R; CAAS 18; CANR 23,
48

Jacobson, Dan 1929- . . . . **CLC 4, 14**
See also CA 1-4R; CANR 2, 25; DLB 14;
MTCW

Jacqueline
See Carpentier (y Valmont), Alejo

Jagger, Mick 1944- . . . . **CLC 17**

Jakes, John (William) 1932- . . . . **CLC 29**
See also BEST 89:4; CA 57-60; CANR 10,
43; DAM NOV, POP; DLBY 83;
INT CANR-10; MTCW; SATA 62

James, Andrew
See Kirkup, James

James, C(yril) L(ionel) R(obert)
1901-1989 . . . . **CLC 33**
See also BW 2; CA 117; 125; 128; DLB 125;
MTCW

James, Daniel (Lewis) 1911-1988
See Santiago, Danny
See also CA 125

James, Dynely
See Mayne, William (James Carter)

James, Henry Sr. 1811-1882 ..... **NCLC 53**

James, Henry
1843-1916 ...... **TCLC 2, 11, 24, 40, 47,**
64; DA; DAB; DAC; SSC 8; WLC
See also CA 104; 132; CDALB 1865-1917;
DAM MST, NOV; DLB 12, 71, 74;
DLBD 13; MTCW

James, M. R.
See James, Montague (Rhodes)
See also DLB 156

James, Montague (Rhodes)
1862-1936 .... **TCLC 6; SSC 16**
See also CA 104

James, P. D. .... **CLC 18, 46**
See also White, Phyllis Dorothy James
See also BEST 90:2; CDBLB 1960 to
Present; DLB 87

James, Philip
See Moorcock, Michael (John)

James, William 1842-1910 ..... **TCLC 15, 32**
See also CA 109

James I 1394-1437 .... **LC 20**

Jameson, Anna 1794-1860 ...... **NCLC 43**
See also DLB 99, 166

Jami, Nur al-Din 'Abd al-Rahman
1414-1492 .... **LC 9**

Jandl, Ernst 1925- .... **CLC 34**

Janowitz, Tama 1957- .... **CLC 43**
See also CA 106; CANR 52; DAM POP

Japrisot, Sebastien 1931- .... **CLC 90**

Jarrell, Randall
1914-1965 .... **CLC 1, 2, 6, 9, 13, 49**
See also CA 5-8R; 25-28R; CABS 2;
CANR 6, 34; CDALB 1941-1968; CLR 6;
DAM POET; DLB 48, 52; MAICYA;
MTCW; SATA 7

Jarry, Alfred
1873-1907 .... **TCLC 2, 14; SSC 20**
See also CA 104; DAM DRAM

Jarvis, E. K.
See Bloch, Robert (Albert); Ellison, Harlan
(Jay); Silverberg, Robert

Jeake, Samuel, Jr.
See Aiken, Conrad (Potter)

Jean Paul 1763-1825 .... **NCLC 7**

Jefferies, (John) Richard
1848-1887 .... **NCLC 47**
See also DLB 98, 141; SATA 16

Jeffers, (John) Robinson
1887-1962 ... **CLC 2, 3, 11, 15, 54; DA;**
DAC; WLC
See also CA 85-88; CANR 35;
CDALB 1917-1929; DAM MST, POET;
DLB 45; MTCW

Jefferson, Janet
See Mencken, H(enry) L(ouis)

Jefferson, Thomas 1743-1826 .... **NCLC 11**
See also CDALB 1640-1865; DLB 31

Jeffrey, Francis 1773-1850 .... **NCLC 33**
See also DLB 107

Jelakowitch, Ivan
See Heijermans, Herman

Jellicoe, (Patricia) Ann 1927- ...... **CLC 27**
See also CA 85-88; DLB 13

Jen, Gish .... **CLC 70**
See also Jen, Lillian

Jen, Lillian 1956(?)-
See Jen, Gish
See also CA 135

Jenkins, (John) Robin 1912- .... **CLC 52**
See also CA 1-4R; CANR 1; DLB 14

Jennings, Elizabeth (Joan)
1926- .... **CLC 5, 14**
See also CA 61-64; CAAS 5; CANR 8, 39;
DLB 27; MTCW; SATA 66

Jennings, Waylon 1937- .... **CLC 21**

Jensen, Johannes V. 1873-1950 .... **TCLC 41**

Jensen, Laura (Linnea) 1948- ...... **CLC 37**
See also CA 103

Jerome, Jerome K(lapka)
1859-1927 .... **TCLC 23**
See also CA 119; DLB 10, 34, 135

Jerrold, Douglas William
1803-1857 .... **NCLC 2**
See also DLB 158, 159

Jewett, (Theodora) Sarah Orne
1849-1909 .... **TCLC 1, 22; SSC 6**
See also CA 108; 127; DLB 12, 74;
SATA 15

Jewsbury, Geraldine (Endsor)
1812-1880 .... **NCLC 22**
See also DLB 21

Jhabvala, Ruth Prawer
1927- .... **CLC 4, 8, 29, 94; DAB**
See also CA 1-4R; CANR 2, 29, 51;
DAM NOV; DLB 139; INT CANR-29;
MTCW

Jibran, Kahlil
See Gibran, Kahlil

Jibran, Khalil
See Gibran, Kahlil

Jiles, Paulette 1943- .... **CLC 13, 58**
See also CA 101

Jimenez (Mantecon), Juan Ramon
1881-1958 .... **TCLC 4; HLC; PC 7**
See also CA 104; 131; DAM MULT,
POET; DLB 134; HW; MTCW

Jimenez, Ramon
See Jimenez (Mantecon), Juan Ramon

Jimenez Mantecon, Juan
See Jimenez (Mantecon), Juan Ramon

Joel, Billy .... **CLC 26**
See also Joel, William Martin

Joel, William Martin 1949-
See Joel, Billy
See also CA 108

John of the Cross, St. 1542-1591 .... **LC 18**

Johnson, B(ryan) S(tanley William)
1933-1973 .... **CLC 6, 9**
See also CA 9-12R; 53-56; CANR 9;
DLB 14, 40

Johnson, Benj. F. of Boo
See Riley, James Whitcomb

Johnson, Benjamin F. of Boo
See Riley, James Whitcomb

Johnson, Charles (Richard)
1948- .... **CLC 7, 51, 65; BLC**
See also BW 2; CA 116; CAAS 18;
CANR 42; DAM MULT; DLB 33

Johnson, Denis 1949- .... **CLC 52**
See also CA 117; 121; DLB 120

Johnson, Diane 1934- .... **CLC 5, 13, 48**
See also CA 41-44R; CANR 17, 40;
DLBY 80; INT CANR-17; MTCW

Johnson, Eyvind (Olof Verner)
1900-1976 .... **CLC 14**
See also CA 73-76; 69-72; CANR 34

Johnson, J. R.
See James, C(yril) L(ionel) R(obert)

Johnson, James Weldon
1871-1938 .... **TCLC 3, 19; BLC**
See also BW 1; CA 104; 125;
CDALB 1917-1929; CLR 32;
DAM MULT, POET; DLB 51; MTCW;
SATA 31

Johnson, Joyce 1935- .... **CLC 58**
See also CA 125; 129

Johnson, Lionel (Pigot)
1867-1902 .... **TCLC 19**
See also CA 117; DLB 19

Johnson, Mel
See Malzberg, Barry N(athaniel)

Johnson, Pamela Hansford
1912-1981 .... **CLC 1, 7, 27**
See also CA 1-4R; 104; CANR 2, 28;
DLB 15; MTCW

Johnson, Samuel
1709-1784 ..... **LC 15; DA; DAB; DAC;**
WLC
See also CDBLB 1660-1789; DAM MST;
DLB 39, 95, 104, 142

Johnson, Uwe
1934-1984 .... **CLC 5, 10, 15, 40**
See also CA 1-4R; 112; CANR 1, 39;
DLB 75; MTCW

Johnston, George (Benson) 1913- ... **CLC 51**
See also CA 1-4R; CANR 5, 20; DLB 88

Johnston, Jennifer 1930- .... **CLC 7**
See also CA 85-88; DLB 14

Jolley, (Monica) Elizabeth
1923- .... **CLC 46; SSC 19**
See also CA 127; CAAS 13

Jones, Arthur Llewellyn 1863-1947
See Machen, Arthur
See also CA 104

Jones, D(ouglas) G(ordon) 1929- .... **CLC 10**
See also CA 29-32R; CANR 13; DLB 53

Jones, David (Michael)
1895-1974 .... **CLC 2, 4, 7, 13, 42**
See also CA 9-12R; 53-56; CANR 28;
CDBLB 1945-1960; DLB 20, 100; MTCW

Jones, David Robert 1947-
See Bowie, David
See also CA 103

Jones, Diana Wynne 1934- .... **CLC 26**
See also AAYA 12; CA 49-52; CANR 4,
26; CLR 23; DLB 161; JRDA; MAICYA;
SAAS 7; SATA 9, 70

Jones, Edward P. 1950- .... **CLC 76**
See also BW 2; CA 142

Kazan, Elia 1909- .... **CLC 6, 16, 63**
See also CA 21-24R; CANR 32

Kazantzakis, Nikos
1883(?)-1957 .... **TCLC 2, 5, 33**
See also CA 105; 132; MTCW

Kazin, Alfred 1915- .... **CLC 34, 38**
See also CA 1-4R; CAAS 7; CANR 1, 45;
DLB 67

Keane, Mary Nesta (Skrine) 1904-1996
See Keane, Molly
See also CA 108; 114; 151

Keane, Molly .... **CLC 31**
See also Keane, Mary Nesta (Skrine)
See also INT 114

Keates, Jonathan 19(?)- .... **CLC 34**

Keaton, Buster 1895-1966 .... **CLC 20**

Keats, John
1795-1821 .... **NCLC 8; DA; DAB;**
DAC; PC 1; WLC
See also CDBLB 1789-1832; DAM MST,
POET; DLB 96, 110

Keene, Donald 1922- .... **CLC 34**
See also CA 1-4R; CANR 5

Keillor, Garrison .... **CLC 40**
See also Keillor, Gary (Edward)
See also AAYA 2; BEST 89:3; DLBY 87;
SATA 58

Keillor, Gary (Edward) 1942-
See Keillor, Garrison
See also CA 111; 117; CANR 36;
DAM POP; MTCW

Keith, Michael
See Hubbard, L(afayette) Ron(ald)

Keller, Gottfried 1819-1890 .... **NCLC 2**
See also DLB 129

Kellerman, Jonathan 1949- .... **CLC 44**
See also BEST 90:1; CA 106; CANR 29, 51;
DAM POP; INT CANR-29

Kelley, William Melvin 1937- ...... **CLC 22**
See also BW 1; CA 77-80; CANR 27;
DLB 33

Kellogg, Marjorie 1922- .... **CLC 2**
See also CA 81-84

Kellow, Kathleen
See Hibbert, Eleanor Alice Burford

Kelly, M(ilton) T(erry) 1947- ...... **CLC 55**
See also CA 97-100; CAAS 22; CANR 19,
43

Kelman, James 1946- .... **CLC 58, 86**
See also CA 148

Kemal, Yashar 1923- .... **CLC 14, 29**
See also CA 89-92; CANR 44

Kemble, Fanny 1809-1893 .... **NCLC 18**
See also DLB 32

Kemelman, Harry 1908- .... **CLC 2**
See also AITN 1; CA 9-12R; CANR 6;
DLB 28

Kempe, Margery 1373(?)-1440(?) ..... **LC 6**
See also DLB 146

Kempis, Thomas a 1380-1471 .... **LC 11**

Kendall, Henry 1839-1882 .... **NCLC 12**

Keneally, Thomas (Michael)
1935- ...... **CLC 5, 8, 10, 14, 19, 27, 43**
See also CA 85-88; CANR 10, 50;
DAM NOV; MTCW

Kennedy, Adrienne (Lita)
1931- .... **CLC 66; BLC; DC 5**
See also BW 2; CA 103; CAAS 20; CABS 3;
CANR 26, 53; DAM MULT; DLB 38

Kennedy, John Pendleton
1795-1870 .... **NCLC 2**
See also DLB 3

Kennedy, Joseph Charles 1929-
See Kennedy, X. J.
See also CA 1-4R; CANR 4, 30, 40;
SATA 14, 86

Kennedy, William 1928- ... **CLC 6, 28, 34, 53**
See also AAYA 1; CA 85-88; CANR 14,
31; DAM NOV; DLB 143; DLBY 85;
INT CANR-31; MTCW; SATA 57

Kennedy, X. J. .... **CLC 8, 42**
See also Kennedy, Joseph Charles
See also CAAS 9; CLR 27; DLB 5;
SAAS 22

Kenny, Maurice (Francis) 1929- .... **CLC 87**
See also CA 144; CAAS 22; DAM MULT;
NNAL

Kent, Kelvin
See Kuttner, Henry

Kenton, Maxwell
See Southern, Terry

Kenyon, Robert O.
See Kuttner, Henry

Kerouac, Jack ..... **CLC 1, 2, 3, 5, 14, 29, 61**
See also Kerouac, Jean-Louis Lebris de
See also CDALB 1941-1968; DLB 2, 16;
DLBD 3; DLBY 95

Kerouac, Jean-Louis Lebris de 1922-1969
See Kerouac, Jack
See also AITN 1; CA 5-8R; 25-28R;
CANR 26; DA; DAB; DAC; DAM MST,
NOV, POET, POP; MTCW; WLC

Kerr, Jean 1923- .... **CLC 22**
See also CA 5-8R; CANR 7; INT CANR-7

Kerr, M. E. .... **CLC 12, 35**
See also Meaker, Marijane (Agnes)
See also AAYA 2; CLR 29; SAAS 1

Kerr, Robert .... **CLC 55**

Kerrigan, (Thomas) Anthony
1918- .... **CLC 4, 6**
See also CA 49-52; CAAS 11; CANR 4

Kerry, Lois
See Duncan, Lois

Kesey, Ken (Elton)
1935- ...... **CLC 1, 3, 6, 11, 46, 64; DA;**
DAB; DAC; WLC
See also CA 1-4R; CANR 22, 38;
CDALB 1968-1988; DAM MST, NOV,
POP; DLB 2, 16; MTCW; SATA 66

Kesselring, Joseph (Otto)
1902-1967 .... **CLC 45**
See also CA 150; DAM DRAM, MST

Kessler, Jascha (Frederick) 1929- .... **CLC 4**
See also CA 17-20R; CANR 8, 48

Kettelkamp, Larry (Dale) 1933- .... **CLC 12**
See also CA 29-32R; CANR 16; SAAS 3;
SATA 2

Key, Ellen 1849-1926 .... **TCLC 65**

Keyber, Conny
See Fielding, Henry

Keyes, Daniel 1927- .... **CLC 80; DA; DAC**
See also CA 17-20R; CANR 10, 26;
DAM MST, NOV; SATA 37

Keynes, John Maynard
1883-1946 .... **TCLC 64**
See also CA 114; DLBD 10

Khanshendel, Chiron
See Rose, Wendy

Khayyam, Omar
1048-1131 .... **CMLC 11; PC 8**
See also DAM POET

Kherdian, David 1931- .... **CLC 6, 9**
See also CA 21-24R; CAAS 2; CANR 39;
CLR 24; JRDA; MAICYA; SATA 16, 74

Khlebnikov, Velimir .... **TCLC 20**
See also Khlebnikov, Viktor Vladimirovich

Khlebnikov, Viktor Vladimirovich 1885-1922
See Khlebnikov, Velimir
See also CA 117

Khodasevich, Vladislav (Felitsianovich)
1886-1939 .... **TCLC 15**
See also CA 115

Kielland, Alexander Lange
1849-1906 .... **TCLC 5**
See also CA 104

Kiely, Benedict 1919- .... **CLC 23, 43**
See also CA 1-4R; CANR 2; DLB 15

Kienzle, William X(avier) 1928- .... **CLC 25**
See also CA 93-96; CAAS 1; CANR 9, 31;
DAM POP; INT CANR-31; MTCW

Kierkegaard, Soren 1813-1855.... **NCLC 34**

Killens, John Oliver 1916-1987..... **CLC 10**
See also BW 2; CA 77-80; 123; CAAS 2;
CANR 26; DLB 33

Killigrew, Anne 1660-1685........... **LC 4**
See also DLB 131

Kim
See Simenon, Georges (Jacques Christian)

Kincaid, Jamaica 1949- ... **CLC 43, 68; BLC**
See also AAYA 13; BW 2; CA 125;
CANR 47; DAM MULT, NOV;
DLB 157

King, Francis (Henry) 1923- ..... **CLC 8, 53**
See also CA 1-4R; CANR 1, 33;
DAM NOV; DLB 15, 139; MTCW

King, Martin Luther, Jr.
1929-1968 .... **CLC 83; BLC; DA; DAB;**
DAC
See also BW 2; CA 25-28; CANR 27, 44;
CAP 2; DAM MST, MULT; MTCW;
SATA 14

King, Stephen (Edwin)
1947- ...... **CLC 12, 26, 37, 61; SSC 17**
See also AAYA 1, 17; BEST 90:1;
CA 61-64; CANR 1, 30, 52; DAM NOV,
POP; DLB 143; DLBY 80; JRDA;
MTCW; SATA 9, 55

King, Steve
See King, Stephen (Edwin)

King, Thomas 1943- .... **CLC 89; DAC**
See also CA 144; DAM MULT; NNAL

Kristeva, Julia 1941- . . . . **CLC 77**

Kristofferson, Kris 1936- . . . . **CLC 26**
See also CA 104

Krizanc, John 1956- . . . . **CLC 57**

Krleza, Miroslav 1893-1981 . . . . **CLC 8**
See also CA 97-100; 105; CANR 50;
DLB 147

Kroetsch, Robert
1927- . . . . **CLC 5, 23, 57; DAC**
See also CA 17-20R; CANR 8, 38;
DAM POET; DLB 53; MTCW

Kroetz, Franz
See Kroetz, Franz Xaver

Kroetz, Franz Xaver 1946- . . . . **CLC 41**
See also CA 130

Kroker, Arthur 1945- . . . . **CLC 77**

Kropotkin, Peter (Aleksieevich)
1842-1921 . . . . **TCLC 36**
See also CA 119

Krotkov, Yuri 1917- . . . . **CLC 19**
See also CA 102

Krumb
See Crumb, R(obert)

Krumgold, Joseph (Quincy)
1908-1980 . . . . **CLC 12**
See also CA 9-12R; 101; CANR 7;
MAICYA; SATA 1, 48; SATA-Obit 23

Krumwitz
See Crumb, R(obert)

Krutch, Joseph Wood 1893-1970 . . . . **CLC 24**
See also CA 1-4R; 25-28R; CANR 4;
DLB 63

Krutzch, Gus
See Eliot, T(homas) S(tearns)

Krylov, Ivan Andreevich
1768(?)-1844 . . . . **NCLC 1**
See also DLB 150

Kubin, Alfred (Leopold Isidor)
1877-1959 . . . . **TCLC 23**
See also CA 112; 149; DLB 81

Kubrick, Stanley 1928- . . . . **CLC 16**
See also CA 81-84; CANR 33; DLB 26

Kumin, Maxine (Winokur)
1925- . . . . **CLC 5, 13, 28; PC 15**
See also AITN 2; CA 1-4R; CAAS 8;
CANR 1, 21; DAM POET; DLB 5;
MTCW; SATA 12

Kundera, Milan
1929- . . . . **CLC 4, 9, 19, 32, 68**
See also AAYA 2; CA 85-88; CANR 19,
52; DAM NOV; MTCW

Kunene, Mazisi (Raymond) 1930- . . . **CLC 85**
See also BW 1; CA 125; DLB 117

Kunitz, Stanley (Jasspon)
1905- . . . . **CLC 6, 11, 14**
See also CA 41-44R; CANR 26; DLB 48;
INT CANR-26; MTCW

Kunze, Reiner 1933- . . . . **CLC 10**
See also CA 93-96; DLB 75

Kuprin, Aleksandr Ivanovich
1870-1938 . . . . **TCLC 5**
See also CA 104

Kureishi, Hanif 1954(?)- . . . . **CLC 64**
See also CA 139

Kurosawa, Akira 1910- . . . . **CLC 16**
See also AAYA 11; CA 101; CANR 46;
DAM MULT

Kushner, Tony 1957(?)- . . . . **CLC 81**
See also CA 144; DAM DRAM

Kuttner, Henry 1915-1958 . . . . **TCLC 10**
See also CA 107; DLB 8

Kuzma, Greg 1944- . . . . **CLC 7**
See also CA 33-36R

Kuzmin, Mikhail 1872(?)-1936 . . . . **TCLC 40**

Kyd, Thomas 1558-1594 . . . . . . **LC 22; DC 3**
See also DAM DRAM; DLB 62

Kyprianos, Iossif
See Samarakis, Antonis

La Bruyere, Jean de 1645-1696 . . . . . . **LC 17**

Lacan, Jacques (Marie Emile)
1901-1981 . . . . **CLC 75**
See also CA 121; 104

Laclos, Pierre Ambroise Francois Choderlos
de 1741-1803 . . . . **NCLC 4**

Lacolere, Francois
See Aragon, Louis

La Colere, Francois
See Aragon, Louis

La Deshabilleuse
See Simenon, Georges (Jacques Christian)

Lady Gregory
See Gregory, Isabella Augusta (Persse)

Lady of Quality, A
See Bagnold, Enid

La Fayette, Marie (Madelaine Pioche de la
Vergne Comtes 1634-1693 . . . . **LC 2**

Lafayette, Rene
See Hubbard, L(afayette) Ron(ald)

Laforgue, Jules
1860-1887 . . . . **NCLC 5, 53; PC 14;**
SSC 20

Lagerkvist, Paer (Fabian)
1891-1974 . . . . **CLC 7, 10, 13, 54**
See also Lagerkvist, Par
See also CA 85-88; 49-52; DAM DRAM,
NOV; MTCW

Lagerkvist, Par . . . . **SSC 12**
See also Lagerkvist, Paer (Fabian)

Lagerloef, Selma (Ottiliana Lovisa)
1858-1940 . . . . **TCLC 4, 36**
See also Lagerlof, Selma (Ottiliana Lovisa)
See also CA 108; SATA 15

Lagerlof, Selma (Ottiliana Lovisa)
See Lagerloef, Selma (Ottiliana Lovisa)
See also CLR 7; SATA 15

La Guma, (Justin) Alex(ander)
1925-1985 . . . . **CLC 19**
See also BW 1; CA 49-52; 118; CANR 25;
DAM NOV; DLB 117; MTCW

Laidlaw, A. K.
See Grieve, C(hristopher) M(urray)

Lainez, Manuel Mujica
See Mujica Lainez, Manuel
See also HW

Laing, R(onald) D(avid)
1927-1989 . . . . **CLC 95**
See also CA 107; 129; CANR 34; MTCW

Lamartine, Alphonse (Marie Louis Prat) de
1790-1869 . . . . **NCLC 11; PC 16**
See also DAM POET

Lamb, Charles
1775-1834 . . . . **NCLC 10; DA; DAB;**
DAC; WLC
See also CDBLB 1789-1832; DAM MST;
DLB 93, 107, 163; SATA 17

Lamb, Lady Caroline 1785-1828 . . **NCLC 38**
See also DLB 116

Lamming, George (William)
1927- . . . . **CLC 2, 4, 66; BLC**
See also BW 2; CA 85-88; CANR 26;
DAM MULT; DLB 125; MTCW

L'Amour, Louis (Dearborn)
1908-1988 . . . . **CLC 25, 55**
See also AAYA 16; AITN 2; BEST 89:2;
CA 1-4R; 125; CANR 3, 25, 40;
DAM NOV, POP; DLBY 80; MTCW

Lampedusa, Giuseppe (Tomasi) di . . . **TCLC 13**
See also Tomasi di Lampedusa, Giuseppe

Lampman, Archibald 1861-1899 . . **NCLC 25**
See also DLB 92

Lancaster, Bruce 1896-1963 . . . . **CLC 36**
See also CA 9-10; CAP 1; SATA 9

Landau, Mark Alexandrovich
See Aldanov, Mark (Alexandrovich)

Landau-Aldanov, Mark Alexandrovich
See Aldanov, Mark (Alexandrovich)

Landis, John 1950- . . . . **CLC 26**
See also CA 112; 122

Landolfi, Tommaso 1908-1979 . . . **CLC 11, 49**
See also CA 127; 117

Landon, Letitia Elizabeth
1802-1838 . . . . **NCLC 15**
See also DLB 96

Landor, Walter Savage
1775-1864 . . . . **NCLC 14**
See also DLB 93, 107

Landwirth, Heinz 1927-
See Lind, Jakov
See also CA 9-12R; CANR 7

Lane, Patrick 1939- . . . . **CLC 25**
See also CA 97-100; DAM POET; DLB 53;
INT 97-100

Lang, Andrew 1844-1912 . . . . **TCLC 16**
See also CA 114; 137; DLB 98, 141;
MAICYA; SATA 16

Lang, Fritz 1890-1976 . . . . **CLC 20**
See also CA 77-80; 69-72; CANR 30

Lange, John
See Crichton, (John) Michael

Langer, Elinor 1939- . . . . **CLC 34**
See also CA 121

Langland, William
1330(?)-1400(?) . . . . . . **LC 19; DA; DAB;**
DAC
See also DAM MST, POET; DLB 146

Langstaff, Launcelot
See Irving, Washington

Lanier, Sidney 1842-1881 . . . . **NCLC 6**
See also DAM POET; DLB 64; DLBD 13;
MAICYA; SATA 18

Lanyer, Aemilia 1569-1645 . . . . . . **LC 10, 30**
See also DLB 121

Lee, Willy
    See Burroughs, William S(eward)

Lee-Hamilton, Eugene (Jacob)
    1845-1907 . . . . **TCLC 22**
    See also CA 117

Leet, Judith   1935- . . . . **CLC 11**

Le Fanu, Joseph Sheridan
    1814-1873 . . . . **NCLC 9; SSC 14**
    See also DAM POP; DLB 21, 70, 159

Leffland, Ella   1931- . . . . **CLC 19**
    See also CA 29-32R; CANR 35; DLBY 84;
    INT CANR-35; SATA 65

Leger, Alexis
    See Leger, (Marie-Rene Auguste) Alexis
        Saint-Leger

Leger, (Marie-Rene Auguste) Alexis
    Saint-Leger   1887-1975. . . . . . . **CLC 11**
    See also Perse, St.-John
    See also CA 13-16R; 61-64; CANR 43;
    DAM POET; MTCW

Leger, Saintleger
    See Leger, (Marie-Rene Auguste) Alexis
        Saint-Leger

Le Guin, Ursula K(roeber)
    1929- . . . . . . **CLC 8, 13, 22, 45, 71; DAB;**
                                    DAC; SSC 12
    See also AAYA 9; AITN 1; CA 21-24R;
    CANR 9, 32, 52; CDALB 1968-1988;
    CLR 3, 28; DAM MST, POP; DLB 8, 52;
    INT CANR-32; JRDA; MAICYA;
    MTCW; SATA 4, 52

Lehmann, Rosamond (Nina)
    1901-1990 . . . . **CLC 5**
    See also CA 77-80; 131; CANR 8; DLB 15

Leiber, Fritz (Reuter, Jr.)
    1910-1992 . . . . **CLC 25**
    See also CA 45-48; 139; CANR 2, 40;
    DLB 8; MTCW; SATA 45;
    SATA-Obit 73

Leimbach, Martha   1963-
    See Leimbach, Marti
    See also CA 130

Leimbach, Marti . . . . **CLC 65**
    See also Leimbach, Martha

Leino, Eino . . . . **TCLC 24**
    See also Loennbohm, Armas Eino Leopold

Leiris, Michel (Julien)   1901-1990 . . . **CLC 61**
    See also CA 119; 128; 132

Leithauser, Brad   1953- . . . . **CLC 27**
    See also CA 107; CANR 27; DLB 120

Lelchuk, Alan   1938- . . . . **CLC 5**
    See also CA 45-48; CAAS 20; CANR 1

Lem, Stanislaw   1921- . . . . **CLC 8, 15, 40**
    See also CA 105; CAAS 1; CANR 32;
    MTCW

Lemann, Nancy   1956- . . . . **CLC 39**
    See also CA 118; 136

Lemonnier, (Antoine Louis) Camille
    1844-1913 . . . . **TCLC 22**
    See also CA 121

Lenau, Nikolaus   1802-1850 . . . . . . **NCLC 16**

L'Engle, Madeleine (Camp Franklin)
    1918- . . . . **CLC 12**
    See also AAYA 1; AITN 2; CA 1-4R;
    CANR 3, 21, 39; CLR 1, 14; DAM POP;
    DLB 52; JRDA; MAICYA; MTCW;
    SAAS 15; SATA 1, 27, 75

Lengyel, Jozsef   1896-1975 . . . . **CLC 7**
    See also CA 85-88; 57-60

Lennon, John (Ono)
    1940-1980 . . . . **CLC 12, 35**
    See also CA 102

Lennox, Charlotte Ramsay
    1729(?)-1804 . . . . **NCLC 23**
    See also DLB 39

Lentricchia, Frank (Jr.)   1940- . . . . . . **CLC 34**
    See also CA 25-28R; CANR 19

Lenz, Siegfried   1926- . . . . **CLC 27**
    See also CA 89-92; DLB 75

Leonard, Elmore (John, Jr.)
    1925- . . . . **CLC 28, 34, 71**
    See also AITN 1; BEST 89:1, 90:4;
    CA 81-84; CANR 12, 28, 53; DAM POP;
    INT CANR-28; MTCW

Leonard, Hugh . . . . **CLC 19**
    See also Byrne, John Keyes
    See also DLB 13

Leonov, Leonid (Maximovich)
    1899-1994 . . . . **CLC 92**
    See also CA 129; DAM NOV; MTCW

Leopardi, (Conte) Giacomo
    1798-1837 . . . . **NCLC 22**

Le Reveler
    See Artaud, Antonin (Marie Joseph)

Lerman, Eleanor   1952- . . . . **CLC 9**
    See also CA 85-88

Lerman, Rhoda   1936- . . . . **CLC 56**
    See also CA 49-52

Lermontov, Mikhail Yuryevich
    1814-1841 . . . . **NCLC 47**

Leroux, Gaston   1868-1927 . . . . **TCLC 25**
    See also CA 108; 136; SATA 65

Lesage, Alain-Rene   1668-1747 . . . . . . **LC 28**

Leskov, Nikolai (Semyonovich)
    1831-1895 . . . . **NCLC 25**

Lessing, Doris (May)
    1919- . . . . . **CLC 1, 2, 3, 6, 10, 15, 22, 40,**
                              94; DA; DAB; DAC; SSC 6
    See also CA 9-12R; CAAS 14; CANR 33;
    CDBLB 1960 to Present; DAM MST,
    NOV; DLB 15, 139; DLBY 85; MTCW

Lessing, Gotthold Ephraim
    1729-1781 . . . . **LC 8**
    See also DLB 97

Lester, Richard   1932- . . . . **CLC 20**

Lever, Charles (James)
    1806-1872 . . . . **NCLC 23**
    See also DLB 21

Leverson, Ada   1865(?)-1936(?) . . . . **TCLC 18**
    See also Elaine
    See also CA 117; DLB 153

Levertov, Denise
    1923- . . . . . . **CLC 1, 2, 3, 5, 8, 15, 28, 66;**
                                        PC 11
    See also CA 1-4R; CAAS 19; CANR 3, 29,
    50; DAM POET; DLB 5, 165;
    INT CANR-29; MTCW

Levi, Jonathan . . . . **CLC 76**

Levi, Peter (Chad Tigar)   1931- . . . . . **CLC 41**
    See also CA 5-8R; CANR 34; DLB 40

Levi, Primo
    1919-1987 . . . . **CLC 37, 50; SSC 12**
    See also CA 13-16R; 122; CANR 12, 33;
    MTCW

Levin, Ira   1929- . . . . **CLC 3, 6**
    See also CA 21-24R; CANR 17, 44;
    DAM POP; MTCW; SATA 66

Levin, Meyer   1905-1981 . . . . **CLC 7**
    See also AITN 1; CA 9-12R; 104;
    CANR 15; DAM POP; DLB 9, 28;
    DLBY 81; SATA 21; SATA-Obit 27

Levine, Norman   1924- . . . . **CLC 54**
    See also CA 73-76; CAAS 23; CANR 14;
    DLB 88

Levine, Philip   1928- . . **CLC 2, 4, 5, 9, 14, 33**
    See also CA 9-12R; CANR 9, 37, 52;
    DAM POET; DLB 5

Levinson, Deirdre   1931- . . . . **CLC 49**
    See also CA 73-76

Levi-Strauss, Claude   1908- . . . . **CLC 38**
    See also CA 1-4R; CANR 6, 32; MTCW

Levitin, Sonia (Wolff)   1934- . . . . **CLC 17**
    See also AAYA 13; CA 29-32R; CANR 14,
    32; JRDA; MAICYA; SAAS 2; SATA 4,
    68

Levon, O. U.
    See Kesey, Ken (Elton)

Lewes, George Henry
    1817-1878 . . . . **NCLC 25**
    See also DLB 55, 144

Lewis, Alun   1915-1944 . . . . **TCLC 3**
    See also CA 104; DLB 20, 162

Lewis, C. Day
    See Day Lewis, C(ecil)

Lewis, C(live) S(taples)
    1898-1963 . . . . . **CLC 1, 3, 6, 14, 27; DA;**
                                    DAB; DAC; WLC
    See also AAYA 3; CA 81-84; CANR 33;
    CDBLB 1945-1960; CLR 3, 27;
    DAM MST, NOV, POP; DLB 15, 100,
    160; JRDA; MAICYA; MTCW;
    SATA 13

Lewis, Janet   1899- . . . . **CLC 41**
    See also Winters, Janet Lewis
    See also CA 9-12R; CANR 29; CAP 1;
    DLBY 87

Lewis, Matthew Gregory
    1775-1818 . . . . **NCLC 11**
    See also DLB 39, 158

Lewis, (Harry) Sinclair
    1885-1951 . . . . . **TCLC 4, 13, 23, 39; DA;**
                                    DAB; DAC; WLC
    See also CA 104; 133; CDALB 1917-1929;
    DAM MST, NOV; DLB 9, 102; DLBD 1;
    MTCW

Lord, Bette Bao 1938- . . . . **CLC 23**
See also BEST 90:3; CA 107; CANR 41;
INT 107; SATA 58

Lord Auch
See Bataille, Georges

Lord Byron
See Byron, George Gordon (Noel)

Lorde, Audre (Geraldine)
1934-1992 . . . . **CLC 18, 71; BLC; PC 12**
See also BW 1; CA 25-28R; 142; CANR 16,
26, 46; DAM MULT, POET; DLB 41;
MTCW

Lord Jeffrey
See Jeffrey, Francis

Lorenzini, Carlo 1826-1890
See Collodi, Carlo
See also MAICYA; SATA 29

Lorenzo, Heberto Padilla
See Padilla (Lorenzo), Heberto

Loris
See Hofmannsthal, Hugo von

Loti, Pierre . . . . **TCLC 11**
See also Viaud, (Louis Marie) Julien
See also DLB 123

Louie, David Wong 1954- . . . . **CLC 70**
See also CA 139

Louis, Father M.
See Merton, Thomas

Lovecraft, H(oward) P(hillips)
1890-1937 . . . . **TCLC 4, 22; SSC 3**
See also AAYA 14; CA 104; 133;
DAM POP; MTCW

Lovelace, Earl 1935- . . . . **CLC 51**
See also BW 2; CA 77-80; CANR 41;
DLB 125; MTCW

Lovelace, Richard 1618-1657 . . . . **LC 24**
See also DLB 131

Lowell, Amy 1874-1925 . . **TCLC 1, 8; PC 13**
See also CA 104; 151; DAM POET;
DLB 54, 140

Lowell, James Russell 1819-1891 . . **NCLC 2**
See also CDALB 1640-1865; DLB 1, 11, 64,
79

Lowell, Robert (Traill Spence, Jr.)
1917-1977 . . . **CLC 1, 2, 3, 4, 5, 8, 9, 11,
15, 37; DA; DAB; DAC; PC 3; WLC**
See also CA 9-12R; 73-76; CABS 2;
CANR 26; DAM MST, NOV; DLB 5;
MTCW

Lowndes, Marie Adelaide (Belloc)
1868-1947 . . . . **TCLC 12**
See also CA 107; DLB 70

Lowry, (Clarence) Malcolm
1909-1957 . . . . **TCLC 6, 40**
See also CA 105; 131; CDBLB 1945-1960;
DLB 15; MTCW

Lowry, Mina Gertrude 1882-1966
See Loy, Mina
See also CA 113

Loxsmith, John
See Brunner, John (Kilian Houston)

Loy, Mina . . . . **CLC 28; PC 16**
See also Lowry, Mina Gertrude
See also DAM POET; DLB 4, 54

Loyson-Bridet
See Schwob, (Mayer Andre) Marcel

Lucas, Craig 1951- . . . . **CLC 64**
See also CA 137

Lucas, George 1944- . . . . **CLC 16**
See also AAYA 1; CA 77-80; CANR 30;
SATA 56

Lucas, Hans
See Godard, Jean-Luc

Lucas, Victoria
See Plath, Sylvia

Ludlam, Charles 1943-1987 . . . . . **CLC 46, 50**
See also CA 85-88; 122

Ludlum, Robert 1927- . . . . **CLC 22, 43**
See also AAYA 10; BEST 89:1, 90:3;
CA 33-36R; CANR 25, 41; DAM NOV,
POP; DLBY 82; MTCW

Ludwig, Ken . . . . **CLC 60**

Ludwig, Otto 1813-1865 . . . . **NCLC 4**
See also DLB 129

Lugones, Leopoldo 1874-1938 . . . . . **TCLC 15**
See also CA 116; 131; HW

Lu Hsun 1881-1936 . . . . . . **TCLC 3; SSC 20**
See also Shu-Jen, Chou

Lukacs, George . . . . **CLC 24**
See also Lukacs, Gyorgy (Szegeny von)

Lukacs, Gyorgy (Szegeny von) 1885-1971
See Lukacs, George
See also CA 101; 29-32R

Luke, Peter (Ambrose Cyprian)
1919-1995 . . . . **CLC 38**
See also CA 81-84; 147; DLB 13

Lunar, Dennis
See Mungo, Raymond

Lurie, Alison 1926- . . . . **CLC 4, 5, 18, 39**
See also CA 1-4R; CANR 2, 17, 50; DLB 2;
MTCW; SATA 46

Lustig, Arnost 1926- . . . . **CLC 56**
See also AAYA 3; CA 69-72; CANR 47;
SATA 56

Luther, Martin 1483-1546 . . . . **LC 9**

Luxemburg, Rosa 1870(?)-1919 . . . . **TCLC 63**
See also CA 118

Luzi, Mario 1914- . . . . **CLC 13**
See also CA 61-64; CANR 9; DLB 128

L'Ymagier
See Gourmont, Remy (-Marie-Charles) de

Lynch, B. Suarez
See Bioy Casares, Adolfo; Borges, Jorge
Luis

Lynch, David (K.) 1946- . . . . **CLC 66**
See also CA 124; 129

Lynch, James
See Andreyev, Leonid (Nikolaevich)

Lynch Davis, B.
See Bioy Casares, Adolfo; Borges, Jorge
Luis

Lyndsay, Sir David 1490-1555 . . . . . . **LC 20**

Lynn, Kenneth S(chuyler) 1923- . . . **CLC 50**
See also CA 1-4R; CANR 3, 27

Lynx
See West, Rebecca

Lyons, Marcus
See Blish, James (Benjamin)

Lyre, Pinchbeck
See Sassoon, Siegfried (Lorraine)

Lytle, Andrew (Nelson) 1902-1995 . . **CLC 22**
See also CA 9-12R; 150; DLB 6; DLBY 95

Lyttelton, George 1709-1773 . . . . **LC 10**

Maas, Peter 1929- . . . . **CLC 29**
See also CA 93-96; INT 93-96

Macaulay, Rose 1881-1958 . . . . . **TCLC 7, 44**
See also CA 104; DLB 36

Macaulay, Thomas Babington
1800-1859 . . . . **NCLC 42**
See also CDBLB 1832-1890; DLB 32, 55

MacBeth, George (Mann)
1932-1992 . . . . **CLC 2, 5, 9**
See also CA 25-28R; 136; DLB 40; MTCW;
SATA 4; SATA-Obit 70

MacCaig, Norman (Alexander)
1910- . . . . **CLC 36; DAB**
See also CA 9-12R; CANR 3, 34;
DAM POET; DLB 27

MacCarthy, (Sir Charles Otto) Desmond
1877-1952 . . . . **TCLC 36**

MacDiarmid, Hugh
. . . . **CLC 2, 4, 11, 19, 63; PC 9**
See also Grieve, C(hristopher) M(urray)
See also CDBLB 1945-1960; DLB 20

MacDonald, Anson
See Heinlein, Robert A(nson)

Macdonald, Cynthia 1928- . . . . . . **CLC 13, 19**
See also CA 49-52; CANR 4, 44; DLB 105

MacDonald, George 1824-1905 . . . . . **TCLC 9**
See also CA 106; 137; DLB 18, 163;
MAICYA; SATA 33

Macdonald, John
See Millar, Kenneth

MacDonald, John D(ann)
1916-1986 . . . . **CLC 3, 27, 44**
See also CA 1-4R; 121; CANR 1, 19;
DAM NOV, POP; DLB 8; DLBY 86;
MTCW

Macdonald, John Ross
See Millar, Kenneth

Macdonald, Ross . . . . . **CLC 1, 2, 3, 14, 34, 41**
See also Millar, Kenneth
See also DLBD 6

MacDougal, John
See Blish, James (Benjamin)

MacEwen, Gwendolyn (Margaret)
1941-1987 . . . . **CLC 13, 55**
See also CA 9-12R; 124; CANR 7, 22;
DLB 53; SATA 50; SATA-Obit 55

Macha, Karel Hynek 1810-1846 . . **NCLC 46**

Machado (y Ruiz), Antonio
1875-1939 . . . . **TCLC 3**
See also CA 104; DLB 108

Machado de Assis, Joaquim Maria
1839-1908 . . . . **TCLC 10; BLC**
See also CA 107

Machen, Arthur . . . . **TCLC 4; SSC 20**
See also Jones, Arthur Llewellyn
See also DLB 36, 156

Maniere, J.-E.
See Giraudoux, (Hippolyte) Jean

Manley, (Mary) Delariviere
1672(?)-1724 . . . . **LC 1**
See also DLB 39, 80

Mann, Abel
See Creasey, John

Mann, (Luiz) Heinrich 1871-1950. . . **TCLC 9**
See also CA 106; DLB 66

Mann, (Paul) Thomas
1875-1955 . . . . **TCLC 2, 8, 14, 21, 35, 44,**
60; DA; DAB; DAC; SSC 5; WLC
See also CA 104; 128; DAM MST, NOV;
DLB 66; MTCW

Mannheim, Karl 1893-1947 . . . . . . **TCLC 65**

Manning, David
See Faust, Frederick (Schiller)

Manning, Frederic 1887(?)-1935 . . . **TCLC 25**
See also CA 124

Manning, Olivia 1915-1980 . . . . . . **CLC 5, 19**
See also CA 5-8R; 101; CANR 29; MTCW

Mano, D. Keith 1942- . . . . **CLC 2, 10**
See also CA 25-28R; CAAS 6; CANR 26;
DLB 6

Mansfield, Katherine
. . **TCLC 2, 8, 39; DAB; SSC 9, 23; WLC**
See also Beauchamp, Kathleen Mansfield
See also DLB 162

Manso, Peter 1940- . . . . **CLC 39**
See also CA 29-32R; CANR 44

Mantecon, Juan Jimenez
See Jimenez (Mantecon), Juan Ramon

Manton, Peter
See Creasey, John

Man Without a Spleen, A
See Chekhov, Anton (Pavlovich)

Manzoni, Alessandro 1785-1873 . . **NCLC 29**

Mapu, Abraham (ben Jekutiel)
1808-1867 . . . . **NCLC 18**

Mara, Sally
See Queneau, Raymond

Marat, Jean Paul 1743-1793 . . . . **LC 10**

Marcel, Gabriel Honore
1889-1973 . . . . **CLC 15**
See also CA 102; 45-48; MTCW

Marchbanks, Samuel
See Davies, (William) Robertson

Marchi, Giacomo
See Bassani, Giorgio

Margulies, Donald . . . . **CLC 76**

Marie de France c. 12th cent. -. . . . **CMLC 8**

Marie de l'Incarnation 1599-1672 . . . . **LC 10**

Mariner, Scott
See Pohl, Frederik

Marinetti, Filippo Tommaso
1876-1944 . . . . **TCLC 10**
See also CA 107; DLB 114

Marivaux, Pierre Carlet de Chamblain de
1688-1763 . . . . **LC 4**

Markandaya, Kamala . . . . **CLC 8, 38**
See also Taylor, Kamala (Purnaiya)

Markfield, Wallace 1926- . . . . **CLC 8**
See also CA 69-72; CAAS 3; DLB 2, 28

Markham, Edwin 1852-1940 . . . . . **TCLC 47**
See also DLB 54

Markham, Robert
See Amis, Kingsley (William)

Marks, J
See Highwater, Jamake (Mamake)

Marks-Highwater, J
See Highwater, Jamake (Mamake)

Markson, David M(errill) 1927- . . . . **CLC 67**
See also CA 49-52; CANR 1

Marley, Bob . . . . **CLC 17**
See also Marley, Robert Nesta

Marley, Robert Nesta 1945-1981
See Marley, Bob
See also CA 107; 103

Marlowe, Christopher
1564-1593 . . . . . **LC 22; DA; DAB; DAC;**
DC 1; WLC
See also CDBLB Before 1660;
DAM DRAM, MST; DLB 62

Marmontel, Jean-Francois
1723-1799 . . . . **LC 2**

Marquand, John P(hillips)
1893-1960 . . . . **CLC 2, 10**
See also CA 85-88; DLB 9, 102

Marquez, Gabriel (Jose) Garcia
See Garcia Marquez, Gabriel (Jose)

Marquis, Don(ald Robert Perry)
1878-1937 . . . . **TCLC 7**
See also CA 104; DLB 11, 25

Marric, J. J.
See Creasey, John

Marrow, Bernard
See Moore, Brian

Marryat, Frederick 1792-1848 . . . . **NCLC 3**
See also DLB 21, 163

Marsden, James
See Creasey, John

Marsh, (Edith) Ngaio
1899-1982 . . . . **CLC 7, 53**
See also CA 9-12R; CANR 6; DAM POP;
DLB 77; MTCW

Marshall, Garry 1934- . . . . **CLC 17**
See also AAYA 3; CA 111; SATA 60

Marshall, Paule
1929- . . . . **CLC 27, 72; BLC; SSC 3**
See also BW 2; CA 77-80; CANR 25;
DAM MULT; DLB 157; MTCW

Marsten, Richard
See Hunter, Evan

Marston, John 1576-1634 . . . . **LC 33**
See also DAM DRAM; DLB 58

Martha, Henry
See Harris, Mark

Martial c. 40-c. 104 . . . . **PC 10**

Martin, Ken
See Hubbard, L(afayette) Ron(ald)

Martin, Richard
See Creasey, John

Martin, Steve 1945- . . . . **CLC 30**
See also CA 97-100; CANR 30; MTCW

Martin, Valerie 1948- . . . . **CLC 89**
See also BEST 90:2; CA 85-88; CANR 49

Martin, Violet Florence
1862-1915 . . . . **TCLC 51**

Martin, Webber
See Silverberg, Robert

Martindale, Patrick Victor
See White, Patrick (Victor Martindale)

Martin du Gard, Roger
1881-1958 . . . . **TCLC 24**
See also CA 118; DLB 65

Martineau, Harriet 1802-1876. . . . **NCLC 26**
See also DLB 21, 55, 159, 163, 166;
YABC 2

Martines, Julia
See O'Faolain, Julia

Martinez, Jacinto Benavente y
See Benavente (y Martinez), Jacinto

Martinez Ruiz, Jose 1873-1967
See Azorin; Ruiz, Jose Martinez
See also CA 93-96; HW

Martinez Sierra, Gregorio
1881-1947 . . . . **TCLC 6**
See also CA 115

Martinez Sierra, Maria (de la O'LeJarraga)
1874-1974 . . . . **TCLC 6**
See also CA 115

Martinsen, Martin
See Follett, Ken(neth Martin)

Martinson, Harry (Edmund)
1904-1978 . . . . **CLC 14**
See also CA 77-80; CANR 34

Marut, Ret
See Traven, B.

Marut, Robert
See Traven, B.

Marvell, Andrew
1621-1678 . . . . . . **LC 4; DA; DAB; DAC;**
PC 10; WLC
See also CDBLB 1660-1789; DAM MST,
POET; DLB 131

Marx, Karl (Heinrich)
1818-1883 . . . . **NCLC 17**
See also DLB 129

Masaoka Shiki . . . . **TCLC 18**
See also Masaoka Tsunenori

Masaoka Tsunenori 1867-1902
See Masaoka Shiki
See also CA 117

Masefield, John (Edward)
1878-1967 . . . . **CLC 11, 47**
See also CA 19-20; 25-28R; CANR 33;
CAP 2; CDBLB 1890-1914; DAM POET;
DLB 10, 19, 153, 160; MTCW; SATA 19

Maso, Carole 19(?)- . . . . **CLC 44**

Mason, Bobbie Ann
1940- . . . . **CLC 28, 43, 82; SSC 4**
See also AAYA 5; CA 53-56; CANR 11,
31; DLBY 87; INT CANR-31; MTCW

Mason, Ernst
See Pohl, Frederik

Mason, Lee W.
See Malzberg, Barry N(athaniel)

Mason, Nick 1945- . . . . **CLC 35**

Mason, Tally
See Derleth, August (William)

Author Index

Newman, Edwin (Harold) 1919- .... **CLC 14**
See also AITN 1; CA 69-72; CANR 5

Newman, John Henry
1801-1890 .... **NCLC 38**
See also DLB 18, 32, 55

Newton, Suzanne 1936- .... **CLC 35**
See also CA 41-44R; CANR 14; JRDA;
SATA 5, 77

Nexo, Martin Andersen
1869-1954 .... **TCLC 43**

Nezval, Vitezslav 1900-1958 ...... **TCLC 44**
See also CA 123

Ng, Fae Myenne 1957(?)- .... **CLC 81**
See also CA 146

Ngema, Mbongeni 1955- .... **CLC 57**
See also BW 2; CA 143

Ngugi, James T(hiong'o) .... **CLC 3, 7, 13**
See also Ngugi wa Thiong'o

Ngugi wa Thiong'o 1938- ..... **CLC 36; BLC**
See also Ngugi, James T(hiong'o)
See also BW 2; CA 81-84; CANR 27;
DAM MULT, NOV; DLB 125; MTCW

Nichol, B(arrie) P(hillip)
1944-1988 .... **CLC 18**
See also CA 53-56; DLB 53; SATA 66

Nichols, John (Treadwell) 1940- .... **CLC 38**
See also CA 9-12R; CAAS 2; CANR 6;
DLBY 82

Nichols, Leigh
See Koontz, Dean R(ay)

Nichols, Peter (Richard)
1927- .... **CLC 5, 36, 65**
See also CA 104; CANR 33; DLB 13;
MTCW

Nicolas, F. R. E.
See Freeling, Nicolas

Niedecker, Lorine 1903-1970.... **CLC 10, 42**
See also CA 25-28; CAP 2; DAM POET;
DLB 48

Nietzsche, Friedrich (Wilhelm)
1844-1900 .... **TCLC 10, 18, 55**
See also CA 107; 121; DLB 129

Nievo, Ippolito 1831-1861 .... **NCLC 22**

Nightingale, Anne Redmon 1943-
See Redmon, Anne
See also CA 103

Nik. T. O.
See Annensky, Innokenty Fyodorovich

Nin, Anais
1903-1977 ...... **CLC 1, 4, 8, 11, 14, 60;
SSC 10**
See also AITN 2; CA 13-16R; 69-72;
CANR 22, 53; DAM NOV, POP; DLB 2,
4, 152; MTCW

Nishiwaki, Junzaburo 1894-1982 .... **PC 15**
See also CA 107

Nissenson, Hugh 1933- .... **CLC 4, 9**
See also CA 17-20R; CANR 27; DLB 28

Niven, Larry .... **CLC 8**
See also Niven, Laurence Van Cott
See also DLB 8

Niven, Laurence Van Cott 1938-
See Niven, Larry
See also CA 21-24R; CAAS 12; CANR 14,
44; DAM POP; MTCW

Nixon, Agnes Eckhardt 1927- ...... **CLC 21**
See also CA 110

Nizan, Paul 1905-1940 .... **TCLC 40**
See also DLB 72

Nkosi, Lewis 1936- .... **CLC 45; BLC**
See also BW 1; CA 65-68; CANR 27;
DAM MULT; DLB 157

Nodier, (Jean) Charles (Emmanuel)
1780-1844 .... **NCLC 19**
See also DLB 119

Nolan, Christopher 1965- .... **CLC 58**
See also CA 111

Noon, Jeff 1957- .... **CLC 91**
See also CA 148

Norden, Charles
See Durrell, Lawrence (George)

Nordhoff, Charles (Bernard)
1887-1947 .... **TCLC 23**
See also CA 108; DLB 9; SATA 23

Norfolk, Lawrence 1963- .... **CLC 76**
See also CA 144

Norman, Marsha 1947- .... **CLC 28**
See also CA 105; CABS 3; CANR 41;
DAM DRAM; DLBY 84

Norris, Benjamin Franklin, Jr.
1870-1902 .... **TCLC 24**
See also Norris, Frank
See also CA 110

Norris, Frank
See Norris, Benjamin Franklin, Jr.
See also CDALB 1865-1917; DLB 12, 71

Norris, Leslie 1921- .... **CLC 14**
See also CA 11-12; CANR 14; CAP 1;
DLB 27

North, Andrew
See Norton, Andre

North, Anthony
See Koontz, Dean R(ay)

North, Captain George
See Stevenson, Robert Louis (Balfour)

North, Milou
See Erdrich, Louise

Northrup, B. A.
See Hubbard, L(afayette) Ron(ald)

North Staffs
See Hulme, T(homas) E(rnest)

Norton, Alice Mary
See Norton, Andre
See also MAICYA; SATA 1, 43

Norton, Andre 1912- .... **CLC 12**
See also Norton, Alice Mary
See also AAYA 14; CA 1-4R; CANR 2, 31;
DLB 8, 52; JRDA; MTCW

Norton, Caroline 1808-1877 ...... **NCLC 47**
See also DLB 21, 159

Norway, Nevil Shute 1899-1960
See Shute, Nevil
See also CA 102; 93-96

Norwid, Cyprian Kamil
1821-1883 .... **NCLC 17**

Nosille, Nabrah
See Ellison, Harlan (Jay)

Nossack, Hans Erich 1901-1978 ..... **CLC 6**
See also CA 93-96; 85-88; DLB 69

Nostradamus 1503-1566 .... **LC 27**

Nosu, Chuji
See Ozu, Yasujiro

Notenburg, Eleanora (Genrikhovna) von
See Guro, Elena

Nova, Craig 1945- .... **CLC 7, 31**
See also CA 45-48; CANR 2, 53

Novak, Joseph
See Kosinski, Jerzy (Nikodem)

Novalis 1772-1801 .... **NCLC 13**
See also DLB 90

Nowlan, Alden (Albert)
1933-1983 .... **CLC 15; DAC**
See also CA 9-12R; CANR 5; DAM MST;
DLB 53

Noyes, Alfred 1880-1958 .... **TCLC 7**
See also CA 104; DLB 20

Nunn, Kem 19(?)- .... **CLC 34**

Nye, Robert 1939- .... **CLC 13, 42**
See also CA 33-36R; CANR 29;
DAM NOV; DLB 14; MTCW; SATA 6

Nyro, Laura 1947- .... **CLC 17**

Oates, Joyce Carol
1938- ...... **CLC 1, 2, 3, 6, 9, 11, 15, 19,
33, 52; DA; DAB; DAC; SSC 6; WLC**
See also AAYA 15; AITN 1; BEST 89:2;
CA 5-8R; CANR 25, 45;
CDALB 1968-1988; DAM MST, NOV,
POP; DLB 2, 5, 130; DLBY 81;
INT CANR-25; MTCW

O'Brien, Darcy 1939- .... **CLC 11**
See also CA 21-24R; CANR 8

O'Brien, E. G.
See Clarke, Arthur C(harles)

O'Brien, Edna
1936- ... **CLC 3, 5, 8, 13, 36, 65; SSC 10**
See also CA 1-4R; CANR 6, 41;
CDBLB 1960 to Present; DAM NOV;
DLB 14; MTCW

O'Brien, Fitz-James 1828-1862... **NCLC 21**
See also DLB 74

O'Brien, Flann .... **CLC 1, 4, 5, 7, 10, 47**
See also O Nuallain, Brian

O'Brien, Richard 1942- .... **CLC 17**
See also CA 124

O'Brien, Tim 1946- .... **CLC 7, 19, 40**
See also AAYA 16; CA 85-88; CANR 40;
DAM POP; DLB 152; DLBD 9;
DLBY 80

Obstfelder, Sigbjoern 1866-1900 ... **TCLC 23**
See also CA 123

O'Casey, Sean
1880-1964 ...... **CLC 1, 5, 9, 11, 15, 88;
DAB; DAC**
See also CA 89-92; CDBLB 1914-1945;
DAM DRAM, MST; DLB 10; MTCW

O'Cathasaigh, Sean
See O'Casey, Sean

Ochs, Phil 1940-1976 .... **CLC 17**
See also CA 65-68

O'Connor, Edwin (Greene)
1918-1968 .... **CLC 14**
See also CA 93-96; 25-28R

O'Connor, (Mary) Flannery
1925-1964 .... **CLC 1, 2, 3, 6, 10, 13, 15,
21, 66; DA; DAB; DAC; SSC 1, 23; WLC**
See also AAYA 7; CA 1-4R; CANR 3, 41;
CDALB 1941-1968; DAM MST, NOV;
DLB 2, 152; DLBD 12; DLBY 80;
MTCW

O'Connor, Frank . . . . **CLC 23; SSC 5**
See also O'Donovan, Michael John
See also DLB 162

O'Dell, Scott 1898-1989. . . . . **CLC 30**
See also AAYA 3; CA 61-64; 129;
CANR 12, 30; CLR 1, 16; DLB 52;
JRDA; MAICYA; SATA 12, 60

Odets, Clifford
1906-1963 . . . . **CLC 2, 28; DC 6**
See also CA 85-88; DAM DRAM; DLB 7,
26; MTCW

O'Doherty, Brian 1934- . . . . **CLC 76**
See also CA 105

O'Donnell, K. M.
See Malzberg, Barry N(athaniel)

O'Donnell, Lawrence
See Kuttner, Henry

O'Donovan, Michael John
1903-1966 . . . . **CLC 14**
See also O'Connor, Frank
See also CA 93-96

Oe, Kenzaburo
1935- . . . . **CLC 10, 36, 86; SSC 20**
See also CA 97-100; CANR 36, 50;
DAM NOV; DLBY 94; MTCW

O'Faolain, Julia 1932- . . . . **CLC 6, 19, 47**
See also CA 81-84; CAAS 2; CANR 12;
DLB 14; MTCW

O'Faolain, Sean
1900-1991 . . . . **CLC 1, 7, 14, 32, 70;
SSC 13**
See also CA 61-64; 134; CANR 12;
DLB 15, 162; MTCW

O'Flaherty, Liam
1896-1984 . . . . **CLC 5, 34; SSC 6**
See also CA 101; 113; CANR 35; DLB 36,
162; DLBY 84; MTCW

Ogilvy, Gavin
See Barrie, J(ames) M(atthew)

O'Grady, Standish James
1846-1928 . . . . **TCLC 5**
See also CA 104

O'Grady, Timothy 1951- . . . . **CLC 59**
See also CA 138

O'Hara, Frank
1926-1966 . . . . **CLC 2, 5, 13, 78**
See also CA 9-12R; 25-28R; CANR 33;
DAM POET; DLB 5, 16; MTCW

O'Hara, John (Henry)
1905-1970 . . . . **CLC 1, 2, 3, 6, 11, 42;
SSC 15**
See also CA 5-8R; 25-28R; CANR 31;
CDALB 1929-1941; DAM NOV; DLB 9,
86; DLBD 2; MTCW

O Hehir, Diana 1922- . . . . **CLC 41**
See also CA 93-96

Okigbo, Christopher (Ifenayichukwu)
1932-1967 . . . . . . **CLC 25, 84; BLC; PC 7**
See also BW 1; CA 77-80; DAM MULT,
POET; DLB 125; MTCW

Okri, Ben 1959- . . . . **CLC 87**
See also BW 2; CA 130; 138; DLB 157;
INT 138

Olds, Sharon 1942- . . . . **CLC 32, 39, 85**
See also CA 101; CANR 18, 41;
DAM POET; DLB 120

Oldstyle, Jonathan
See Irving, Washington

Olesha, Yuri (Karlovich)
1899-1960 . . . . **CLC 8**
See also CA 85-88

Oliphant, Laurence
1829(?)-1888 . . . . **NCLC 47**
See also DLB 18, 166

Oliphant, Margaret (Oliphant Wilson)
1828-1897 . . . . **NCLC 11**
See also DLB 18, 159

Oliver, Mary 1935- . . . . **CLC 19, 34**
See also CA 21-24R; CANR 9, 43; DLB 5

Olivier, Laurence (Kerr)
1907-1989 . . . . **CLC 20**
See also CA 111; 150; 129

Olsen, Tillie
1913- . . . . . **CLC 4, 13; DA; DAB; DAC;
SSC 11**
See also CA 1-4R; CANR 1, 43;
DAM MST; DLB 28; DLBY 80; MTCW

Olson, Charles (John)
1910-1970 . . . . . **CLC 1, 2, 5, 6, 9, 11, 29**
See also CA 13-16; 25-28R; CABS 2;
CANR 35; CAP 1; DAM POET; DLB 5,
16; MTCW

Olson, Toby 1937- . . . . **CLC 28**
See also CA 65-68; CANR 9, 31

Olyesha, Yuri
See Olesha, Yuri (Karlovich)

Ondaatje, (Philip) Michael
1943- . . . **CLC 14, 29, 51, 76; DAB; DAC**
See also CA 77-80; CANR 42; DAM MST;
DLB 60

Oneal, Elizabeth 1934-
See Oneal, Zibby
See also CA 106; CANR 28; MAICYA;
SATA 30, 82

Oneal, Zibby . . . . **CLC 30**
See also Oneal, Elizabeth
See also AAYA 5; CLR 13; JRDA

O'Neill, Eugene (Gladstone)
1888-1953 . . . . . . **TCLC 1, 6, 27, 49; DA;
DAB; DAC; WLC**
See also AITN 1; CA 110; 132;
CDALB 1929-1941; DAM DRAM, MST;
DLB 7; MTCW

Onetti, Juan Carlos
1909-1994 . . . . **CLC 7, 10; SSC 23**
See also CA 85-88; 145; CANR 32;
DAM MULT, NOV; DLB 113; HW;
MTCW

O Nuallain, Brian 1911-1966
See O'Brien, Flann
See also CA 21-22; 25-28R; CAP 2

Oppen, George 1908-1984 . . . . **CLC 7, 13, 34**
See also CA 13-16R; 113; CANR 8; DLB 5,
165

Oppenheim, E(dward) Phillips
1866-1946 . . . . **TCLC 45**
See also CA 111; DLB 70

Orlovitz, Gil 1918-1973 . . . . **CLC 22**
See also CA 77-80; 45-48; DLB 2, 5

Orris
See Ingelow, Jean

Ortega y Gasset, Jose
1883-1955 . . . . **TCLC 9; HLC**
See also CA 106; 130; DAM MULT; HW;
MTCW

Ortese, Anna Maria 1914- . . . . **CLC 89**

Ortiz, Simon J(oseph) 1941- . . . . **CLC 45**
See also CA 134; DAM MULT, POET;
DLB 120; NNAL

Orton, Joe . . . . **CLC 4, 13, 43; DC 3**
See also Orton, John Kingsley
See also CDBLB 1960 to Present; DLB 13

Orton, John Kingsley 1933-1967
See Orton, Joe
See also CA 85-88; CANR 35;
DAM DRAM; MTCW

Orwell, George
. . . . **TCLC 2, 6, 15, 31, 51; DAB; WLC**
See also Blair, Eric (Arthur)
See also CDBLB 1945-1960; DLB 15, 98

Osborne, David
See Silverberg, Robert

Osborne, George
See Silverberg, Robert

Osborne, John (James)
1929-1994 . . . . . **CLC 1, 2, 5, 11, 45; DA;
DAB; DAC; WLC**
See also CA 13-16R; 147; CANR 21;
CDBLB 1945-1960; DAM DRAM, MST;
DLB 13; MTCW

Osborne, Lawrence 1958- . . . . **CLC 50**

Oshima, Nagisa 1932- . . . . **CLC 20**
See also CA 116; 121

Oskison, John Milton
1874-1947 . . . . **TCLC 35**
See also CA 144; DAM MULT; NNAL

Ossoli, Sarah Margaret (Fuller marchesa d')
1810-1850
See Fuller, Margaret
See also SATA 25

Ostrovsky, Alexander
1823-1886 . . . . **NCLC 30, 57**

Otero, Blas de 1916-1979. . . . . **CLC 11**
See also CA 89-92; DLB 134

Otto, Whitney 1955-. . . . . **CLC 70**
See also CA 140

Ouida . . . . **TCLC 43**
See also De La Ramee, (Marie) Louise
See also DLB 18, 156

Ousmane, Sembene 1923- . . . . **CLC 66; BLC**
See also BW 1; CA 117; 125; MTCW

Ovid 43B.C.-18(?). . . . . **CMLC 7; PC 2**
See also DAM POET

Owen, Hugh
See Faust, Frederick (Schiller)

Owen, Wilfred (Edward Salter)
1893-1918 . . . . . . **TCLC 5, 27; DA; DAB; DAC; WLC**
See also CA 104; 141; CDBLB 1914-1945; DAM MST, POET; DLB 20

Owens, Rochelle 1936-. . . . . **CLC 8**
See also CA 17-20R; CAAS 2; CANR 39

Oz, Amos 1939- . . . **CLC 5, 8, 11, 27, 33, 54**
See also CA 53-56; CANR 27, 47; DAM NOV; MTCW

Ozick, Cynthia
1928- . . . . **CLC 3, 7, 28, 62; SSC 15**
See also BEST 90:1; CA 17-20R; CANR 23; DAM NOV, POP; DLB 28, 152; DLBY 82; INT CANR-23; MTCW

Ozu, Yasujiro 1903-1963 . . . . **CLC 16**
See also CA 112

Pacheco, C.
See Pessoa, Fernando (Antonio Nogueira)

Pa Chin . . . . **CLC 18**
See also Li Fei-kan

Pack, Robert 1929-. . . . . **CLC 13**
See also CA 1-4R; CANR 3, 44; DLB 5

Padgett, Lewis
See Kuttner, Henry

Padilla (Lorenzo), Heberto 1932-. . . **CLC 38**
See also AITN 1; CA 123; 131; HW

Page, Jimmy 1944-. . . . . **CLC 12**

Page, Louise 1955-. . . . . **CLC 40**
See also CA 140

Page, P(atricia) K(athleen)
1916- . . . . **CLC 7, 18; DAC; PC 12**
See also CA 53-56; CANR 4, 22; DAM MST; DLB 68; MTCW

Page, Thomas Nelson 1853-1922. . . . **SSC 23**
See also CA 118; DLB 12, 78; DLBD 13

Paget, Violet 1856-1935
See Lee, Vernon
See also CA 104

Paget-Lowe, Henry
See Lovecraft, H(oward) P(hillips)

Paglia, Camille (Anna) 1947-. . . . . . . **CLC 68**
See also CA 140

Paige, Richard
See Koontz, Dean R(ay)

Pakenham, Antonia
See Fraser, (Lady) Antonia (Pakenham)

Palamas, Kostes 1859-1943 . . . . **TCLC 5**
See also CA 105

Palazzeschi, Aldo 1885-1974 . . . . . . **CLC 11**
See also CA 89-92; 53-56; DLB 114

Paley, Grace 1922-. . . . **CLC 4, 6, 37; SSC 8**
See also CA 25-28R; CANR 13, 46; DAM POP; DLB 28; INT CANR-13; MTCW

Palin, Michael (Edward) 1943-. . . . . **CLC 21**
See also Monty Python
See also CA 107; CANR 35; SATA 67

Palliser, Charles 1947-. . . . . **CLC 65**
See also CA 136

Palma, Ricardo 1833-1919. . . . . . . **TCLC 29**

Pancake, Breece Dexter 1952-1979
See Pancake, Breece D'J
See also CA 123; 109

Pancake, Breece D'J. . . . . **CLC 29**
See also Pancake, Breece Dexter
See also DLB 130

Panko, Rudy
See Gogol, Nikolai (Vasilyevich)

Papadiamantis, Alexandros
1851-1911 . . . . **TCLC 29**

Papadiamantopoulos, Johannes 1856-1910
See Moreas, Jean
See also CA 117

Papini, Giovanni 1881-1956. . . . . . **TCLC 22**
See also CA 121

Paracelsus 1493-1541. . . . . **LC 14**

Parasol, Peter
See Stevens, Wallace

Parfenie, Maria
See Codrescu, Andrei

Parini, Jay (Lee) 1948- . . . . **CLC 54**
See also CA 97-100; CAAS 16; CANR 32

Park, Jordan
See Kornbluth, C(yril) M.; Pohl, Frederik

Parker, Bert
See Ellison, Harlan (Jay)

Parker, Dorothy (Rothschild)
1893-1967 . . . . **CLC 15, 68; SSC 2**
See also CA 19-20; 25-28R; CAP 2; DAM POET; DLB 11, 45, 86; MTCW

Parker, Robert B(rown) 1932-. . . . . . **CLC 27**
See also BEST 89:4; CA 49-52; CANR 1, 26, 52; DAM NOV, POP; INT CANR-26; MTCW

Parkin, Frank 1940-. . . . . **CLC 43**
See also CA 147

Parkman, Francis, Jr.
1823-1893 . . . . **NCLC 12**
See also DLB 1, 30

Parks, Gordon (Alexander Buchanan)
1912- . . . . **CLC 1, 16; BLC**
See also AITN 2; BW 2; CA 41-44R; CANR 26; DAM MULT; DLB 33; SATA 8

Parnell, Thomas 1679-1718 . . . . **LC 3**
See also DLB 94

Parra, Nicanor 1914-. . . . . **CLC 2; HLC**
See also CA 85-88; CANR 32; DAM MULT; HW; MTCW

Parrish, Mary Frances
See Fisher, M(ary) F(rances) K(ennedy)

Parson
See Coleridge, Samuel Taylor

Parson Lot
See Kingsley, Charles

Partridge, Anthony
See Oppenheim, E(dward) Phillips

Pascoli, Giovanni 1855-1912 . . . . . **TCLC 45**

Pasolini, Pier Paolo
1922-1975 . . . . **CLC 20, 37**
See also CA 93-96; 61-64; DLB 128; MTCW

Pasquini
See Silone, Ignazio

Pastan, Linda (Olenik) 1932- . . . . . . **CLC 27**
See also CA 61-64; CANR 18, 40; DAM POET; DLB 5

Pasternak, Boris (Leonidovich)
1890-1960 . . . . . . **CLC 7, 10, 18, 63; DA; DAB; DAC; PC 6; WLC**
See also CA 127; 116; DAM MST, NOV, POET; MTCW

Patchen, Kenneth 1911-1972. . . **CLC 1, 2, 18**
See also CA 1-4R; 33-36R; CANR 3, 35; DAM POET; DLB 16, 48; MTCW

Pater, Walter (Horatio)
1839-1894 . . . . **NCLC 7**
See also CDBLB 1832-1890; DLB 57, 156

Paterson, A(ndrew) B(arton)
1864-1941 . . . . **TCLC 32**

Paterson, Katherine (Womeldorf)
1932-. . . . . **CLC 12, 30**
See also AAYA 1; CA 21-24R; CANR 28; CLR 7; DLB 52; JRDA; MAICYA; MTCW; SATA 13, 53

Patmore, Coventry Kersey Dighton
1823-1896 . . . . **NCLC 9**
See also DLB 35, 98

Paton, Alan (Stewart)
1903-1988 . . . . . . **CLC 4, 10, 25, 55; DA; DAB; DAC; WLC**
See also CA 13-16; 125; CANR 22; CAP 1; DAM MST, NOV; MTCW; SATA 11; SATA-Obit 56

Paton Walsh, Gillian 1937-
See Walsh, Jill Paton
See also CANR 38; JRDA; MAICYA; SAAS 3; SATA 4, 72

Paulding, James Kirke 1778-1860. . **NCLC 2**
See also DLB 3, 59, 74

Paulin, Thomas Neilson 1949-
See Paulin, Tom
See also CA 123; 128

Paulin, Tom. **CLC 37**
See also Paulin, Thomas Neilson
See also DLB 40

Paustovsky, Konstantin (Georgievich)
1892-1968 . . . . **CLC 40**
See also CA 93-96; 25-28R

Pavese, Cesare
1908-1950 . . . . . **TCLC 3; PC 13; SSC 19**
See also CA 104; DLB 128

Pavic, Milorad 1929-. . . . . **CLC 60**
See also CA 136

Payne, Alan
See Jakes, John (William)

Paz, Gil
See Lugones, Leopoldo

Paz, Octavio
1914- . . . . **CLC 3, 4, 6, 10, 19, 51, 65; DA; DAB; DAC; HLC; PC 1; WLC**
See also CA 73-76; CANR 32; DAM MST, MULT, POET; DLBY 90; HW; MTCW

Peacock, Molly 1947-. . . . . **CLC 60**
See also CA 103; CAAS 21; CANR 52; DLB 120

Peacock, Thomas Love
1785-1866 . . . . **NCLC 22**
See also DLB 96, 116

Peake, Mervyn 1911-1968. . . . . . . **CLC 7, 54**
See also CA 5-8R; 25-28R; CANR 3; DLB 15, 160; MTCW; SATA 23

Pearce, Philippa .... **CLC 21**
See also Christie, (Ann) Philippa
See also CLR 9; DLB 161; MAICYA;
SATA 1, 67

Pearl, Eric
See Elman, Richard

Pearson, T(homas) R(eid) 1956- .... **CLC 39**
See also CA 120; 130; INT 130

Peck, Dale 1967- .... **CLC 81**
See also CA 146

Peck, John 1941- .... **CLC 3**
See also CA 49-52; CANR 3

Peck, Richard (Wayne) 1934- ...... **CLC 21**
See also AAYA 1; CA 85-88; CANR 19,
38; CLR 15; INT CANR-19; JRDA;
MAICYA; SAAS 2; SATA 18, 55

Peck, Robert Newton
1928- .... **CLC 17; DA; DAC**
See also AAYA 3; CA 81-84; CANR 31;
DAM MST; JRDA; MAICYA; SAAS 1;
SATA 21, 62

Peckinpah, (David) Sam(uel)
1925-1984 .... **CLC 20**
See also CA 109; 114

Pedersen, Knut 1859-1952
See Hamsun, Knut
See also CA 104; 119; MTCW

Peeslake, Gaffer
See Durrell, Lawrence (George)

Peguy, Charles Pierre
1873-1914 .... **TCLC 10**
See also CA 107

Pena, Ramon del Valle y
See Valle-Inclan, Ramon (Maria) del

Pendennis, Arthur Esquir
See Thackeray, William Makepeace

Penn, William 1644-1718 .... **LC 25**
See also DLB 24

Pepys, Samuel
1633-1703 ..... **LC 11; DA; DAB; DAC;
WLC**
See also CDBLB 1660-1789; DAM MST;
DLB 101

Percy, Walker
1916-1990 .... **CLC 2, 3, 6, 8, 14, 18, 47,
65**
See also CA 1-4R; 131; CANR 1, 23;
DAM NOV, POP; DLB 2; DLBY 80, 90;
MTCW

Perec, Georges 1936-1982 .... **CLC 56**
See also CA 141; DLB 83

Pereda (y Sanchez de Porrua), Jose Maria de
1833-1906 .... **TCLC 16**
See also CA 117

Pereda y Porrua, Jose Maria de
See Pereda (y Sanchez de Porrua), Jose
Maria de

Peregoy, George Weems
See Mencken, H(enry) L(ouis)

Perelman, S(idney) J(oseph)
1904-1979 ... **CLC 3, 5, 9, 15, 23, 44, 49**
See also AITN 1, 2; CA 73-76; 89-92;
CANR 18; DAM DRAM; DLB 11, 44;
MTCW

Peret, Benjamin 1899-1959 ...... **TCLC 20**
See also CA 117

Peretz, Isaac Loeb 1851(?)-1915 ... **TCLC 16**
See also CA 109

Peretz, Yitzkhok Leibush
See Peretz, Isaac Loeb

Perez Galdos, Benito 1843-1920 ... **TCLC 27**
See also CA 125; HW

Perrault, Charles 1628-1703 .... **LC 2**
See also MAICYA; SATA 25

Perry, Brighton
See Sherwood, Robert E(mmet)

Perse, St.-John .... **CLC 4, 11, 46**
See also Leger, (Marie-Rene Auguste) Alexis
Saint-Leger

Perutz, Leo 1882-1957 .... **TCLC 60**
See also DLB 81

Peseenz, Tulio F.
See Lopez y Fuentes, Gregorio

Pesetsky, Bette 1932- .... **CLC 28**
See also CA 133; DLB 130

Peshkov, Alexei Maximovich 1868-1936
See Gorky, Maxim
See also CA 105; 141; DA; DAC;
DAM DRAM, MST, NOV

Pessoa, Fernando (Antonio Nogueira)
1888-1935 .... **TCLC 27; HLC**
See also CA 125

Peterkin, Julia Mood 1880-1961 .... **CLC 31**
See also CA 102; DLB 9

Peters, Joan K. 1945- .... **CLC 39**

Peters, Robert L(ouis) 1924- ...... **CLC 7**
See also CA 13-16R; CAAS 8; DLB 105

Petofi, Sandor 1823-1849 .... **NCLC 21**

Petrakis, Harry Mark 1923- .... **CLC 3**
See also CA 9-12R; CANR 4, 30

Petrarch 1304-1374 .... **PC 8**
See also DAM POET

Petrov, Evgeny .... **TCLC 21**
See also Kataev, Evgeny Petrovich

Petry, Ann (Lane) 1908- ...... **CLC 1, 7, 18**
See also BW 1; CA 5-8R; CAAS 6;
CANR 4, 46; CLR 12; DLB 76; JRDA;
MAICYA; MTCW; SATA 5

Petursson, Halligrimur 1614-1674 .... **LC 8**

Philips, Katherine 1632-1664 .... **LC 30**
See also DLB 131

Philipson, Morris H. 1926- .... **CLC 53**
See also CA 1-4R; CANR 4

Phillips, David Graham
1867-1911 .... **TCLC 44**
See also CA 108; DLB 9, 12

Phillips, Jack
See Sandburg, Carl (August)

Phillips, Jayne Anne
1952- .... **CLC 15, 33; SSC 16**
See also CA 101; CANR 24, 50; DLBY 80;
INT CANR-24; MTCW

Phillips, Richard
See Dick, Philip K(indred)

Phillips, Robert (Schaeffer) 1938- ... **CLC 28**
See also CA 17-20R; CAAS 13; CANR 8;
DLB 105

Phillips, Ward
See Lovecraft, H(oward) P(hillips)

Piccolo, Lucio 1901-1969 .... **CLC 13**
See also CA 97-100; DLB 114

Pickthall, Marjorie L(owry) C(hristie)
1883-1922 .... **TCLC 21**
See also CA 107; DLB 92

Pico della Mirandola, Giovanni
1463-1494 .... **LC 15**

Piercy, Marge
1936- .... **CLC 3, 6, 14, 18, 27, 62**
See also CA 21-24R; CAAS 1; CANR 13,
43; DLB 120; MTCW

Piers, Robert
See Anthony, Piers

Pieyre de Mandiargues, Andre 1909-1991
See Mandiargues, Andre Pieyre de
See also CA 103; 136; CANR 22

Pilnyak, Boris .... **TCLC 23**
See also Vogau, Boris Andreyevich

Pincherle, Alberto 1907-1990 ... **CLC 11, 18**
See also Moravia, Alberto
See also CA 25-28R; 132; CANR 33;
DAM NOV; MTCW

Pinckney, Darryl 1953- .... **CLC 76**
See also BW 2; CA 143

Pindar 518B.C.-446B.C. .... **CMLC 12**

Pineda, Cecile 1942- .... **CLC 39**
See also CA 118

Pinero, Arthur Wing 1855-1934 ... **TCLC 32**
See also CA 110; DAM DRAM; DLB 10

Pinero, Miguel (Antonio Gomez)
1946-1988 .... **CLC 4, 55**
See also CA 61-64; 125; CANR 29; HW

Pinget, Robert 1919- .... **CLC 7, 13, 37**
See also CA 85-88; DLB 83

Pink Floyd
See Barrett, (Roger) Syd; Gilmour, David;
Mason, Nick; Waters, Roger; Wright,
Rick

Pinkney, Edward 1802-1828 ..... **NCLC 31**

Pinkwater, Daniel Manus 1941- .... **CLC 35**
See also Pinkwater, Manus
See also AAYA 1; CA 29-32R; CANR 12,
38; CLR 4; JRDA; MAICYA; SAAS 3;
SATA 46, 76

Pinkwater, Manus
See Pinkwater, Daniel Manus
See also SATA 8

Pinsky, Robert 1940- ..... **CLC 9, 19, 38, 94**
See also CA 29-32R; CAAS 4;
DAM POET; DLBY 82

Pinta, Harold
See Pinter, Harold

Pinter, Harold
1930- ..... **CLC 1, 3, 6, 9, 11, 15, 27, 58,
73; DA; DAB; DAC; WLC**
See also CA 5-8R; CANR 33; CDBLB 1960
to Present; DAM DRAM, MST; DLB 13;
MTCW

Piozzi, Hester Lynch (Thrale)
1741-1821 .... **NCLC 57**
See also DLB 104, 142

Pirandello, Luigi
1867-1936 . . . . . . **TCLC 4, 29; DA; DAB; DAC; DC 5; SSC 22; WLC**
See also CA 104; DAM DRAM, MST

Pirsig, Robert M(aynard)
1928- . . . . **CLC 4, 6, 73**
See also CA 53-56; CANR 42; DAM POP; MTCW; SATA 39

Pisarev, Dmitry Ivanovich
1840-1868 . . . . **NCLC 25**

Pix, Mary (Griffith) 1666-1709 . . . . . . **LC 8**
See also DLB 80

Pixerecourt, Guilbert de
1773-1844 . . . . **NCLC 39**

Plaidy, Jean
See Hibbert, Eleanor Alice Burford

Planche, James Robinson
1796-1880 . . . . **NCLC 42**

Plant, Robert 1948- . . . . **CLC 12**

Plante, David (Robert)
1940- . . . . **CLC 7, 23, 38**
See also CA 37-40R; CANR 12, 36; DAM NOV; DLBY 83; INT CANR-12; MTCW

Plath, Sylvia
1932-1963 . . . . . **CLC 1, 2, 3, 5, 9, 11, 14, 17, 50, 51, 62; DA; DAB; DAC; PC 1; WLC**
See also AAYA 13; CA 19-20; CANR 34; CAP 2; CDALB 1941-1968; DAM MST, POET; DLB 5, 6, 152; MTCW

Plato
428(?)B.C.-348(?)B.C.. . . . . **CMLC 8; DA; DAB; DAC**
See also DAM MST

Platonov, Andrei . . . . **TCLC 14**
See also Klimentov, Andrei Platonovich

Platt, Kin 1911- . . . . **CLC 26**
See also AAYA 11; CA 17-20R; CANR 11; JRDA; SAAS 17; SATA 21, 86

Plautus c. 251B.C.-184B.C. . . . . **DC 6**

Plick et Plock
See Simenon, Georges (Jacques Christian)

Plimpton, George (Ames) 1927- . . . . . **CLC 36**
See also AITN 1; CA 21-24R; CANR 32; MTCW; SATA 10

Plomer, William Charles Franklin
1903-1973 . . . . **CLC 4, 8**
See also CA 21-22; CANR 34; CAP 2; DLB 20, 162; MTCW; SATA 24

Plowman, Piers
See Kavanagh, Patrick (Joseph)

Plum, J.
See Wodehouse, P(elham) G(renville)

Plumly, Stanley (Ross) 1939- . . . . . . **CLC 33**
See also CA 108; 110; DLB 5; INT 110

Plumpe, Friedrich Wilhelm
1888-1931 . . . . **TCLC 53**
See also CA 112

Poe, Edgar Allan
1809-1849 . . . . **NCLC 1, 16, 55; DA; DAB; DAC; PC 1; SSC 1, 22; WLC**
See also AAYA 14; CDALB 1640-1865; DAM MST, POET; DLB 3, 59, 73, 74; SATA 23

Poet of Titchfield Street, The
See Pound, Ezra (Weston Loomis)

Pohl, Frederik 1919- . . . . **CLC 18**
See also CA 61-64; CAAS 1; CANR 11, 37; DLB 8; INT CANR-11; MTCW; SATA 24

Poirier, Louis 1910-
See Gracq, Julien
See also CA 122; 126

Poitier, Sidney 1927- . . . . **CLC 26**
See also BW 1; CA 117

Polanski, Roman 1933- . . . . **CLC 16**
See also CA 77-80

Poliakoff, Stephen 1952- . . . . **CLC 38**
See also CA 106; DLB 13

Police, The
See Copeland, Stewart (Armstrong); Summers, Andrew James; Sumner, Gordon Matthew

Polidori, John William
1795-1821 . . . . **NCLC 51**
See also DLB 116

Pollitt, Katha 1949- . . . . **CLC 28**
See also CA 120; 122; MTCW

Pollock, (Mary) Sharon
1936- . . . . **CLC 50; DAC**
See also CA 141; DAM DRAM, MST; DLB 60

Polo, Marco 1254-1324 . . . . **CMLC 15**

Polonsky, Abraham (Lincoln)
1910- . . . . **CLC 92**
See also CA 104; DLB 26; INT 104

Polybius c. 200B.C.-c. 118B.C. . . . . **CMLC 17**

Pomerance, Bernard 1940- . . . . **CLC 13**
See also CA 101; CANR 49; DAM DRAM

Ponge, Francis (Jean Gaston Alfred)
1899-1988 . . . . **CLC 6, 18**
See also CA 85-88; 126; CANR 40; DAM POET

Pontoppidan, Henrik 1857-1943 . . . **TCLC 29**

Poole, Josephine . . . . **CLC 17**
See also Helyar, Jane Penelope Josephine
See also SAAS 2; SATA 5

Popa, Vasko 1922-1991 . . . . **CLC 19**
See also CA 112; 148

Pope, Alexander
1688-1744 . . . . . . **LC 3; DA; DAB; DAC; WLC**
See also CDBLB 1660-1789; DAM MST, POET; DLB 95, 101

Porter, Connie (Rose) 1959(?)- . . . . . **CLC 70**
See also BW 2; CA 142; SATA 81

Porter, Gene(va Grace) Stratton
1863(?)-1924 . . . . **TCLC 21**
See also CA 112

Porter, Katherine Anne
1890-1980 . . . . . . **CLC 1, 3, 7, 10, 13, 15, 27; DA; DAB; DAC; SSC 4**
See also AITN 2; CA 1-4R; 101; CANR 1; DAM MST, NOV; DLB 4, 9, 102; DLBD 12; DLBY 80; MTCW; SATA 39; SATA-Obit 23

Porter, Peter (Neville Frederick)
1929- . . . . **CLC 5, 13, 33**
See also CA 85-88; DLB 40

Porter, William Sydney 1862-1910
See Henry, O.
See also CA 104; 131; CDALB 1865-1917; DA; DAB; DAC; DAM MST; DLB 12, 78, 79; MTCW; YABC 2

Portillo (y Pacheco), Jose Lopez
See Lopez Portillo (y Pacheco), Jose

Post, Melville Davisson
1869-1930 . . . . **TCLC 39**
See also CA 110

Potok, Chaim 1929- . . . . . . **CLC 2, 7, 14, 26**
See also AAYA 15; AITN 1, 2; CA 17-20R; CANR 19, 35; DAM NOV; DLB 28, 152; INT CANR-19; MTCW; SATA 33

Potter, Beatrice
See Webb, (Martha) Beatrice (Potter)
See also MAICYA

Potter, Dennis (Christopher George)
1935-1994 . . . . **CLC 58, 86**
See also CA 107; 145; CANR 33; MTCW

Pound, Ezra (Weston Loomis)
1885-1972 . . . . . . **CLC 1, 2, 3, 4, 5, 7, 10, 13, 18, 34, 48, 50; DA; DAB; DAC; PC 4; WLC**
See also CA 5-8R; 37-40R; CANR 40; CDALB 1917-1929; DAM MST, POET; DLB 4, 45, 63; MTCW

Povod, Reinaldo 1959-1994 . . . . **CLC 44**
See also CA 136; 146

Powell, Adam Clayton, Jr.
1908-1972 . . . . **CLC 89; BLC**
See also BW 1; CA 102; 33-36R; DAM MULT

Powell, Anthony (Dymoke)
1905- . . . . **CLC 1, 3, 7, 9, 10, 31**
See also CA 1-4R; CANR 1, 32; CDBLB 1945-1960; DLB 15; MTCW

Powell, Dawn 1897-1965 . . . . **CLC 66**
See also CA 5-8R

Powell, Padgett 1952- . . . . **CLC 34**
See also CA 126

Power, Susan . . . . **CLC 91**

Powers, J(ames) F(arl)
1917- . . . . **CLC 1, 4, 8, 57; SSC 4**
See also CA 1-4R; CANR 2; DLB 130; MTCW

Powers, John J(ames) 1945-
See Powers, John R.
See also CA 69-72

Powers, John R. . . . . **CLC 66**
See also Powers, John J(ames)

Powers, Richard (S.) 1957- . . . . **CLC 93**
See also CA 148

Pownall, David 1938- . . . . **CLC 10**
See also CA 89-92; CAAS 18; CANR 49; DLB 14

Powys, John Cowper
1872-1963 . . . . **CLC 7, 9, 15, 46**
See also CA 85-88; DLB 15; MTCW

Powys, T(heodore) F(rancis)
1875-1953 . . . . **TCLC 9**
See also CA 106; DLB 36, 162

Prager, Emily 1952- . . . . **CLC 56**

Pratt, E(dwin) J(ohn)
1883(?)-1964 . . . . **CLC 19; DAC**
See also CA 141; 93-96; DAM POET;
DLB 92

Premchand . . . . **TCLC 21**
See also Srivastava, Dhanpat Rai

Preussler, Otfried 1923- . . . . **CLC 17**
See also CA 77-80; SATA 24

Prevert, Jacques (Henri Marie)
1900-1977 . . . . **CLC 15**
See also CA 77-80; 69-72; CANR 29;
MTCW; SATA-Obit 30

Prevost, Abbe (Antoine Francois)
1697-1763 . . . . **LC 1**

Price, (Edward) Reynolds
1933- . . **CLC 3, 6, 13, 43, 50, 63; SSC 22**
See also CA 1-4R; CANR 1, 37;
DAM NOV; DLB 2; INT CANR-37

Price, Richard 1949- . . . . **CLC 6, 12**
See also CA 49-52; CANR 3; DLBY 81

Prichard, Katharine Susannah
1883-1969 . . . . **CLC 46**
See also CA 11-12; CANR 33; CAP 1;
MTCW; SATA 66

Priestley, J(ohn) B(oynton)
1894-1984 . . . . **CLC 2, 5, 9, 34**
See also CA 9-12R; 113; CANR 33;
CDBLB 1914-1945; DAM DRAM, NOV;
DLB 10, 34, 77, 100, 139; DLBY 84;
MTCW

Prince 1958(?)- . . . . **CLC 35**

Prince, F(rank) T(empleton) 1912- . . **CLC 22**
See also CA 101; CANR 43; DLB 20

Prince Kropotkin
See Kropotkin, Peter (Alekseievich)

Prior, Matthew 1664-1721 . . . . **LC 4**
See also DLB 95

Pritchard, William H(arrison)
1932- . . . . **CLC 34**
See also CA 65-68; CANR 23; DLB 111

Pritchett, V(ictor) S(awdon)
1900- . . . . **CLC 5, 13, 15, 41; SSC 14**
See also CA 61-64; CANR 31; DAM NOV;
DLB 15, 139; MTCW

Private 19022
See Manning, Frederic

Probst, Mark 1925- . . . . **CLC 59**
See also CA 130

Prokosch, Frederic 1908-1989 . . . . **CLC 4, 48**
See also CA 73-76; 128; DLB 48

Prophet, The
See Dreiser, Theodore (Herman Albert)

Prose, Francine 1947- . . . . **CLC 45**
See also CA 109; 112; CANR 46

Proudhon
See Cunha, Euclides (Rodrigues Pimenta) da

Proulx, E. Annie 1935- . . . . **CLC 81**

Proust, (Valentin-Louis-George-Eugene-)
Marcel
1871-1922 . . . . **TCLC 7, 13, 33; DA;**
DAB; DAC; WLC
See also CA 104; 120; DAM MST, NOV;
DLB 65; MTCW

Prowler, Harley
See Masters, Edgar Lee

Prus, Boleslaw 1845-1912 . . . . **TCLC 48**

Pryor, Richard (Franklin Lenox Thomas)
1940- . . . . **CLC 26**
See also CA 122

Przybyszewski, Stanislaw
1868-1927 . . . . **TCLC 36**
See also DLB 66

Pteleon
See Grieve, C(hristopher) M(urray)
See also DAM POET

Puckett, Lute
See Masters, Edgar Lee

Puig, Manuel
1932-1990 . . . **CLC 3, 5, 10, 28, 65; HLC**
See also CA 45-48; CANR 2, 32;
DAM MULT; DLB 113; HW; MTCW

Purdy, Al(fred Wellington)
1918- . . . . **CLC 3, 6, 14, 50; DAC**
See also CA 81-84; CAAS 17; CANR 42;
DAM MST, POET; DLB 88

Purdy, James (Amos)
1923- . . . . **CLC 2, 4, 10, 28, 52**
See also CA 33-36R; CAAS 1; CANR 19,
51; DLB 2; INT CANR-19; MTCW

Pure, Simon
See Swinnerton, Frank Arthur

Pushkin, Alexander (Sergeyevich)
1799-1837 . . . . . **NCLC 3, 27; DA; DAB;**
DAC; PC 10; WLC
See also DAM DRAM, MST, POET;
SATA 61

P'u Sung-ling 1640-1715 . . . . **LC 3**

Putnam, Arthur Lee
See Alger, Horatio, Jr.

Puzo, Mario 1920- . . . . **CLC 1, 2, 6, 36**
See also CA 65-68; CANR 4, 42;
DAM NOV, POP; DLB 6; MTCW

Pym, Barbara (Mary Crampton)
1913-1980 . . . . **CLC 13, 19, 37**
See also CA 13-14; 97-100; CANR 13, 34;
CAP 1; DLB 14; DLBY 87; MTCW

Pynchon, Thomas (Ruggles, Jr.)
1937- . . . . . **CLC 2, 3, 6, 9, 11, 18, 33, 62,**
72; DA; DAB; DAC; SSC 14; WLC
See also BEST 90:2; CA 17-20R; CANR 22,
46; DAM MST, NOV, POP; DLB 2;
MTCW

Qian Zhongshu
See Ch'ien Chung-shu

Qroll
See Dagerman, Stig (Halvard)

Quarrington, Paul (Lewis) 1953- . . . . **CLC 65**
See also CA 129

Quasimodo, Salvatore 1901-1968 . . . **CLC 10**
See also CA 13-16; 25-28R; CAP 1;
DLB 114; MTCW

Quay, Stephen 1947- . . . . **CLC 95**

Quay, The Brothers
See Quay, Stephen; Quay, Timothy

Quay, Timothy 1947- . . . . **CLC 95**

Queen, Ellery . . . . **CLC 3, 11**
See also Dannay, Frederic; Davidson,
Avram; Lee, Manfred B(ennington);
Sturgeon, Theodore (Hamilton); Vance,
John Holbrook

Queen, Ellery, Jr.
See Dannay, Frederic; Lee, Manfred
B(ennington)

Queneau, Raymond
1903-1976 . . . . **CLC 2, 5, 10, 42**
See also CA 77-80; 69-72; CANR 32;
DLB 72; MTCW

Quevedo, Francisco de 1580-1645 . . . . **LC 23**

Quiller-Couch, Arthur Thomas
1863-1944 . . . . **TCLC 53**
See also CA 118; DLB 135, 153

Quin, Ann (Marie) 1936-1973 . . . . **CLC 6**
See also CA 9-12R; 45-48; DLB 14

Quinn, Martin
See Smith, Martin Cruz

Quinn, Peter 1947- . . . . **CLC 91**

Quinn, Simon
See Smith, Martin Cruz

Quiroga, Horacio (Sylvestre)
1878-1937 . . . . **TCLC 20; HLC**
See also CA 117; 131; DAM MULT; HW;
MTCW

Quoirez, Francoise 1935- . . . . **CLC 9**
See also Sagan, Francoise
See also CA 49-52; CANR 6, 39; MTCW

Raabe, Wilhelm 1831-1910 . . . . **TCLC 45**
See also DLB 129

Rabe, David (William) 1940- . . . **CLC 4, 8, 33**
See also CA 85-88; CABS 3; DAM DRAM;
DLB 7

Rabelais, Francois
1483-1553 . . . . . . **LC 5; DA; DAB; DAC;**
WLC
See also DAM MST

Rabinovitch, Sholem 1859-1916
See Aleichem, Sholom
See also CA 104

Racine, Jean 1639-1699 . . . . **LC 28; DAB**
See also DAM MST

Radcliffe, Ann (Ward)
1764-1823 . . . . **NCLC 6, 55**
See also DLB 39

Radiguet, Raymond 1903-1923 . . . . **TCLC 29**
See also DLB 65

Radnoti, Miklos 1909-1944 . . . . **TCLC 16**
See also CA 118

Rado, James 1939- . . . . **CLC 17**
See also CA 105

Radvanyi, Netty 1900-1983
See Seghers, Anna
See also CA 85-88; 110

Rae, Ben
See Griffiths, Trevor

Raeburn, John (Hay) 1941- . . . . **CLC 34**
See also CA 57-60

Ragni, Gerome 1942-1991 . . . . **CLC 17**
See also CA 105; 134

Rahv, Philip 1908-1973 . . . . **CLC 24**
See also Greenberg, Ivan
See also DLB 137

Raine, Craig 1944- . . . . **CLC 32**
See also CA 108; CANR 29, 51; DLB 40

Raine, Kathleen (Jessie) 1908- . . . **CLC 7, 45**
  See also CA 85-88; CANR 46; DLB 20;
  MTCW

Rainis, Janis 1865-1929 . . . . **TCLC 29**

Rakosi, Carl . . . . **CLC 47**
  See also Rawley, Callman
  See also CAAS 5

Raleigh, Richard
  See Lovecraft, H(oward) P(hillips)

Raleigh, Sir Walter 1554(?)-1618 . . . . **LC 31**
  See also CDBLB Before 1660

Rallentando, H. P.
  See Sayers, Dorothy L(eigh)

Ramal, Walter
  See de la Mare, Walter (John)

Ramon, Juan
  See Jimenez (Mantecon), Juan Ramon

Ramos, Graciliano 1892-1953 . . . . . **TCLC 32**

Rampersad, Arnold 1941- . . . . **CLC 44**
  See also BW 2; CA 127; 133; DLB 111;
  INT 133

Rampling, Anne
  See Rice, Anne

Ramsay, Allan 1684(?)-1758 . . . . **LC 29**
  See also DLB 95

Ramuz, Charles-Ferdinand
  1878-1947 . . . . **TCLC 33**

Rand, Ayn
  1905-1982 . . . . . . **CLC 3, 30, 44, 79; DA;
                                        DAC; WLC**
  See also AAYA 10; CA 13-16R; 105;
  CANR 27; DAM MST, NOV, POP;
  MTCW

Randall, Dudley (Felker)
  1914- . . . . **CLC 1; BLC**
  See also BW 1; CA 25-28R; CANR 23;
  DAM MULT; DLB 41

Randall, Robert
  See Silverberg, Robert

Ranger, Ken
  See Creasey, John

Ransom, John Crowe
  1888-1974 . . . . **CLC 2, 4, 5, 11, 24**
  See also CA 5-8R; 49-52; CANR 6, 34;
  DAM POET; DLB 45, 63; MTCW

Rao, Raja 1909- . . . . **CLC 25, 56**
  See also CA 73-76; CANR 51; DAM NOV;
  MTCW

Raphael, Frederic (Michael)
  1931- . . . . **CLC 2, 14**
  See also CA 1-4R; CANR 1; DLB 14

Ratcliffe, James P.
  See Mencken, H(enry) L(ouis)

Rathbone, Julian 1935- . . . . **CLC 41**
  See also CA 101; CANR 34

Rattigan, Terence (Mervyn)
  1911-1977 . . . . **CLC 7**
  See also CA 85-88; 73-76;
  CDBLB 1945-1960; DAM DRAM;
  DLB 13; MTCW

Ratushinskaya, Irina 1954- . . . . **CLC 54**
  See also CA 129

Raven, Simon (Arthur Noel)
  1927- . . . . **CLC 14**
  See also CA 81-84

Rawley, Callman 1903-
  See Rakosi, Carl
  See also CA 21-24R; CANR 12, 32

Rawlings, Marjorie Kinnan
  1896-1953 . . . . **TCLC 4**
  See also CA 104; 137; DLB 9, 22, 102;
  JRDA; MAICYA; YABC 1

Ray, Satyajit 1921-1992 . . . . **CLC 16, 76**
  See also CA 114; 137; DAM MULT

Read, Herbert Edward 1893-1968 . . . . **CLC 4**
  See also CA 85-88; 25-28R; DLB 20, 149

Read, Piers Paul 1941- . . . . . . **CLC 4, 10, 25**
  See also CA 21-24R; CANR 38; DLB 14;
  SATA 21

Reade, Charles 1814-1884 . . . . **NCLC 2**
  See also DLB 21

Reade, Hamish
  See Gray, Simon (James Holliday)

Reading, Peter 1946- . . . . **CLC 47**
  See also CA 103; CANR 46; DLB 40

Reaney, James 1926- . . . . **CLC 13; DAC**
  See also CA 41-44R; CAAS 15; CANR 42;
  DAM MST; DLB 68; SATA 43

Rebreanu, Liviu 1885-1944 . . . . **TCLC 28**

Rechy, John (Francisco)
  1934- . . . . **CLC 1, 7, 14, 18; HLC**
  See also CA 5-8R; CAAS 4; CANR 6, 32;
  DAM MULT; DLB 122; DLBY 82; HW;
  INT CANR-6

Redcam, Tom 1870-1933 . . . . **TCLC 25**

Reddin, Keith . . . . **CLC 67**

Redgrove, Peter (William)
  1932- . . . . **CLC 6, 41**
  See also CA 1-4R; CANR 3, 39; DLB 40

Redmon, Anne . . . . **CLC 22**
  See also Nightingale, Anne Redmon
  See also DLBY 86

Reed, Eliot
  See Ambler, Eric

Reed, Ishmael
  1938- . . . **CLC 2, 3, 5, 6, 13, 32, 60; BLC**
  See also BW 2; CA 21-24R; CANR 25, 48;
  DAM MULT; DLB 2, 5, 33; DLBD 8;
  MTCW

Reed, John (Silas) 1887-1920 . . . . . . **TCLC 9**
  See also CA 106

Reed, Lou . . . . **CLC 21**
  See also Firbank, Louis

Reeve, Clara 1729-1807 . . . . **NCLC 19**
  See also DLB 39

Reich, Wilhelm 1897-1957 . . . . **TCLC 57**

Reid, Christopher (John) 1949- . . . . . **CLC 33**
  See also CA 140; DLB 40

Reid, Desmond
  See Moorcock, Michael (John)

Reid Banks, Lynne 1929-
  See Banks, Lynne Reid
  See also CA 1-4R; CANR 6, 22, 38;
  CLR 24; JRDA; MAICYA; SATA 22, 75

Reilly, William K.
  See Creasey, John

Reiner, Max
  See Caldwell, (Janet Miriam) Taylor
  (Holland)

Reis, Ricardo
  See Pessoa, Fernando (Antonio Nogueira)

Remarque, Erich Maria
  1898-1970 . . . . **CLC 21; DA; DAB; DAC**
  See also CA 77-80; 29-32R; DAM MST,
  NOV; DLB 56; MTCW

Remizov, A.
  See Remizov, Aleksei (Mikhailovich)

Remizov, A. M.
  See Remizov, Aleksei (Mikhailovich)

Remizov, Aleksei (Mikhailovich)
  1877-1957 . . . . **TCLC 27**
  See also CA 125; 133

Renan, Joseph Ernest
  1823-1892 . . . . **NCLC 26**

Renard, Jules 1864-1910 . . . . **TCLC 17**
  See also CA 117

Renault, Mary . . . . **CLC 3, 11, 17**
  See also Challans, Mary
  See also DLBY 83

Rendell, Ruth (Barbara) 1930- . . **CLC 28, 48**
  See also Vine, Barbara
  See also CA 109; CANR 32, 52;
  DAM POP; DLB 87; INT CANR-32;
  MTCW

Renoir, Jean 1894-1979 . . . . **CLC 20**
  See also CA 129; 85-88

Resnais, Alain 1922- . . . . **CLC 16**

Reverdy, Pierre 1889-1960 . . . . **CLC 53**
  See also CA 97-100; 89-92

Rexroth, Kenneth
  1905-1982 . . . . . . **CLC 1, 2, 6, 11, 22, 49**
  See also CA 5-8R; 107; CANR 14, 34;
  CDALB 1941-1968; DAM POET;
  DLB 16, 48, 165; DLBY 82;
  INT CANR-14; MTCW

Reyes, Alfonso 1889-1959 . . . . **TCLC 33**
  See also CA 131; HW

Reyes y Basoalto, Ricardo Eliecer Neftali
  See Neruda, Pablo

Reymont, Wladyslaw (Stanislaw)
  1868(?)-1925 . . . . **TCLC 5**
  See also CA 104

Reynolds, Jonathan 1942- . . . . **CLC 6, 38**
  See also CA 65-68; CANR 28

Reynolds, Joshua 1723-1792 . . . . **LC 15**
  See also DLB 104

Reynolds, Michael Shane 1937- . . . . **CLC 44**
  See also CA 65-68; CANR 9

Reznikoff, Charles 1894-1976 . . . . . . **CLC 9**
  See also CA 33-36; 61-64; CAP 2; DLB 28,
  45

Rezzori (d'Arezzo), Gregor von
  1914- . . . . **CLC 25**
  See also CA 122; 136

Rhine, Richard
  See Silverstein, Alvin

Rhodes, Eugene Manlove
  1869-1934 . . . . **TCLC 53**

R'hoone
  See Balzac, Honore de

Rhys, Jean
        1890(?)-1979 .... **CLC 2, 4, 6, 14, 19, 51;**
                                                SSC 21
        See also CA 25-28R; 85-88; CANR 35;
        CDBLB 1945-1960; DAM NOV; DLB 36,
        117, 162; MTCW

Ribeiro, Darcy 1922- .... **CLC 34**
        See also CA 33-36R

Ribeiro, Joao Ubaldo (Osorio Pimentel)
        1941- .... **CLC 10, 67**
        See also CA 81-84

Ribman, Ronald (Burt) 1932- .... **CLC 7**
        See also CA 21-24R; CANR 46

Ricci, Nino 1959- .... **CLC 70**
        See also CA 137

Rice, Anne 1941- .... **CLC 41**
        See also AAYA 9; BEST 89:2; CA 65-68;
        CANR 12, 36, 53; DAM POP

Rice, Elmer (Leopold)
        1892-1967 .... **CLC 7, 49**
        See also CA 21-22; 25-28R; CAP 2;
        DAM DRAM; DLB 4, 7; MTCW

Rice, Tim(othy Miles Bindon)
        1944- .... **CLC 21**
        See also CA 103; CANR 46

Rich, Adrienne (Cecile)
        1929- .... **CLC 3, 6, 7, 11, 18, 36, 73, 76;**
                                                PC 5
        See also CA 9-12R; CANR 20, 53;
        DAM POET; DLB 5, 67; MTCW

Rich, Barbara
        See Graves, Robert (von Ranke)

Rich, Robert
        See Trumbo, Dalton

Richard, Keith .... **CLC 17**
        See also Richards, Keith

Richards, David Adams
        1950- .... **CLC 59; DAC**
        See also CA 93-96; DLB 53

Richards, I(vor) A(rmstrong)
        1893-1979 .... **CLC 14, 24**
        See also CA 41-44R; 89-92; CANR 34;
        DLB 27

Richards, Keith 1943-
        See Richard, Keith
        See also CA 107

Richardson, Anne
        See Roiphe, Anne (Richardson)

Richardson, Dorothy Miller
        1873-1957 .... **TCLC 3**
        See also CA 104; DLB 36

Richardson, Ethel Florence (Lindesay)
        1870-1946
        See Richardson, Henry Handel
        See also CA 105

Richardson, Henry Handel .... **TCLC 4**
        See also Richardson, Ethel Florence
        (Lindesay)

Richardson, John
        1796-1852 .... **NCLC 55; DAC**
        See also DLB 99

Richardson, Samuel
        1689-1761 ...... **LC 1; DA; DAB; DAC;**
                                                WLC
        See also CDBLB 1660-1789; DAM MST,
        NOV; DLB 39

Richler, Mordecai
        1931- .... **CLC 3, 5, 9, 13, 18, 46, 70;**
                                                DAC
        See also AITN 1; CA 65-68; CANR 31;
        CLR 17; DAM MST, NOV; DLB 53;
        MAICYA; MTCW; SATA 44;
        SATA-Brief 27

Richter, Conrad (Michael)
        1890-1968 .... **CLC 30**
        See also CA 5-8R; 25-28R; CANR 23;
        DLB 9; MTCW; SATA 3

Ricostranza, Tom
        See Ellis, Trey

Riddell, J. H. 1832-1906 .... **TCLC 40**

Riding, Laura .... **CLC 3, 7**
        See also Jackson, Laura (Riding)

Riefenstahl, Berta Helene Amalia 1902-
        See Riefenstahl, Leni
        See also CA 108

Riefenstahl, Leni .... **CLC 16**
        See also Riefenstahl, Berta Helene Amalia

Riffe, Ernest
        See Bergman, (Ernst) Ingmar

Riggs, (Rolla) Lynn 1899-1954 .... **TCLC 56**
        See also CA 144; DAM MULT; NNAL

Riley, James Whitcomb
        1849-1916 .... **TCLC 51**
        See also CA 118; 137; DAM POET;
        MAICYA; SATA 17

Riley, Tex
        See Creasey, John

Rilke, Rainer Maria
        1875-1926 .... **TCLC 1, 6, 19; PC 2**
        See also CA 104; 132; DAM POET;
        DLB 81; MTCW

Rimbaud, (Jean Nicolas) Arthur
        1854-1891 ..... **NCLC 4, 35; DA; DAB;**
                                                DAC; PC 3; WLC
        See also DAM MST, POET

Rinehart, Mary Roberts
        1876-1958 .... **TCLC 52**
        See also CA 108

Ringmaster, The
        See Mencken, H(enry) L(ouis)

Ringwood, Gwen(dolyn Margaret) Pharis
        1910-1984 .... **CLC 48**
        See also CA 148; 112; DLB 88

Rio, Michel 19(?)- .... **CLC 43**

Ritsos, Giannes
        See Ritsos, Yannis

Ritsos, Yannis 1909-1990..... **CLC 6, 13, 31**
        See also CA 77-80; 133; CANR 39; MTCW

Ritter, Erika 1948(?)- .... **CLC 52**

Rivera, Jose Eustasio 1889-1928... **TCLC 35**
        See also HW

Rivers, Conrad Kent 1933-1968...... **CLC 1**
        See also BW 1; CA 85-88; DLB 41

Rivers, Elfrida
        See Bradley, Marion Zimmer

Riverside, John
        See Heinlein, Robert A(nson)

Rizal, Jose 1861-1896.......... **NCLC 27**

Roa Bastos, Augusto (Antonio)
        1917- .... **CLC 45; HLC**
        See also CA 131; DAM MULT; DLB 113;
        HW

Robbe-Grillet, Alain
        1922- ...... **CLC 1, 2, 4, 6, 8, 10, 14, 43**
        See also CA 9-12R; CANR 33; DLB 83;
        MTCW

Robbins, Harold 1916-............. **CLC 5**
        See also CA 73-76; CANR 26; DAM NOV;
        MTCW

Robbins, Thomas Eugene 1936-
        See Robbins, Tom
        See also CA 81-84; CANR 29; DAM NOV,
        POP; MTCW

Robbins, Tom .... **CLC 9, 32, 64**
        See also Robbins, Thomas Eugene
        See also BEST 90:3; DLBY 80

Robbins, Trina 1938- .... **CLC 21**
        See also CA 128

Roberts, Charles G(eorge) D(ouglas)
        1860-1943 .... **TCLC 8**
        See also CA 105; CLR 33; DLB 92;
        SATA 88; SATA-Brief 29

Roberts, Kate 1891-1985 .... **CLC 15**
        See also CA 107; 116

Roberts, Keith (John Kingston)
        1935- .... **CLC 14**
        See also CA 25-28R; CANR 46

Roberts, Kenneth (Lewis)
        1885-1957 .... **TCLC 23**
        See also CA 109; DLB 9

Roberts, Michele (B.) 1949-........ **CLC 48**
        See also CA 115

Robertson, Ellis
        See Ellison, Harlan (Jay); Silverberg, Robert

Robertson, Thomas William
        1829-1871 .... **NCLC 35**
        See also DAM DRAM

Robinson, Edwin Arlington
        1869-1935 .... **TCLC 5; DA; DAC; PC 1**
        See also CA 104; 133; CDALB 1865-1917;
        DAM MST, POET; DLB 54; MTCW

Robinson, Henry Crabb
        1775-1867 .... **NCLC 15**
        See also DLB 107

Robinson, Jill 1936-.............. **CLC 10**
        See also CA 102; INT 102

Robinson, Kim Stanley 1952- ...... **CLC 34**
        See also CA 126

Robinson, Lloyd
        See Silverberg, Robert

Robinson, Marilynne 1944- .... **CLC 25**
        See also CA 116

Robinson, Smokey .... **CLC 21**
        See also Robinson, William, Jr.

Robinson, William, Jr. 1940-
        See Robinson, Smokey
        See also CA 116

Robison, Mary 1949- .... **CLC 42**
        See also CA 113; 116; DLB 130; INT 116

Rod, Edouard 1857-1910 .... **TCLC 52**

Roddenberry, Eugene Wesley 1921-1991
See Roddenberry, Gene
See also CA 110; 135; CANR 37; SATA 45;
SATA-Obit 69

Roddenberry, Gene .... **CLC 17**
See also Roddenberry, Eugene Wesley
See also AAYA 5; SATA-Obit 69

Rodgers, Mary 1931- .... **CLC 12**
See also CA 49-52; CANR 8; CLR 20;
INT CANR-8; JRDA; MAICYA;
SATA 8

Rodgers, W(illiam) R(obert)
1909-1969 .... **CLC 7**
See also CA 85-88; DLB 20

Rodman, Eric
See Silverberg, Robert

Rodman, Howard 1920(?)-1985 ..... **CLC 65**
See also CA 118

Rodman, Maia
See Wojciechowska, Maia (Teresa)

Rodriguez, Claudio 1934- .... **CLC 10**
See also DLB 134

Roelvaag, O(le) E(dvart)
1876-1931 .... **TCLC 17**
See also CA 117; DLB 9

Roethke, Theodore (Huebner)
1908-1963 ...... **CLC 1, 3, 8, 11, 19, 46;**
PC 15
See also CA 81-84; CABS 2;
CDALB 1941-1968; DAM POET; DLB 5;
MTCW

Rogers, Thomas Hunton 1927- ..... **CLC 57**
See also CA 89-92; INT 89-92

Rogers, Will(iam Penn Adair)
1879-1935 .... **TCLC 8**
See also CA 105; 144; DAM MULT;
DLB 11; NNAL

Rogin, Gilbert 1929- .... **CLC 18**
See also CA 65-68; CANR 15

Rohan, Koda .... **TCLC 22**
See also Koda Shigeyuki

Rohmer, Eric .... **CLC 16**
See also Scherer, Jean-Marie Maurice

Rohmer, Sax .... **TCLC 28**
See also Ward, Arthur Henry Sarsfield
See also DLB 70

Roiphe, Anne (Richardson)
1935- .... **CLC 3, 9**
See also CA 89-92; CANR 45; DLBY 80;
INT 89-92

Rojas, Fernando de 1465-1541 ...... **LC 23**

Rolfe, Frederick (William Serafino Austin
Lewis Mary) 1860-1913 ...... **TCLC 12**
See also CA 107; DLB 34, 156

Rolland, Romain 1866-1944 .... **TCLC 23**
See also CA 118; DLB 65

Rolvaag, O(le) E(dvart)
See Roelvaag, O(le) E(dvart)

Romain Arnaud, Saint
See Aragon, Louis

Romains, Jules 1885-1972 .... **CLC 7**
See also CA 85-88; CANR 34; DLB 65;
MTCW

Romero, Jose Ruben 1890-1952 ... **TCLC 14**
See also CA 114; 131; HW

Ronsard, Pierre de
1524-1585 .... **LC 6; PC 11**

Rooke, Leon 1934- .... **CLC 25, 34**
See also CA 25-28R; CANR 23, 53;
DAM POP

Roper, William 1498-1578 .... **LC 10**

Roquelaure, A. N.
See Rice, Anne

Rosa, Joao Guimaraes 1908-1967 ... **CLC 23**
See also CA 89-92; DLB 113

Rose, Wendy 1948- .... **CLC 85; PC 13**
See also CA 53-56; CANR 5, 51;
DAM MULT; NNAL; SATA 12

Rosen, Richard (Dean) 1949- .... **CLC 39**
See also CA 77-80; INT CANR-30

Rosenberg, Isaac 1890-1918 ...... **TCLC 12**
See also CA 107; DLB 20

Rosenblatt, Joe .... **CLC 15**
See also Rosenblatt, Joseph

Rosenblatt, Joseph 1933-
See Rosenblatt, Joe
See also CA 89-92; INT 89-92

Rosenfeld, Samuel 1896-1963
See Tzara, Tristan
See also CA 89-92

Rosenthal, M(acha) L(ouis) 1917- ... **CLC 28**
See also CA 1-4R; CAAS 6; CANR 4, 51;
DLB 5; SATA 59

Ross, Barnaby
See Dannay, Frederic

Ross, Bernard L.
See Follett, Ken(neth Martin)

Ross, J. H.
See Lawrence, T(homas) E(dward)

Ross, Martin
See Martin, Violet Florence
See also DLB 135

Ross, (James) Sinclair
1908- .... **CLC 13; DAC**
See also CA 73-76; DAM MST; DLB 88

Rossetti, Christina (Georgina)
1830-1894 ..... **NCLC 2, 50; DA; DAB;**
DAC; PC 7; WLC
See also DAM MST, POET; DLB 35, 163;
MAICYA; SATA 20

Rossetti, Dante Gabriel
1828-1882 .... **NCLC 4; DA; DAB;**
DAC; WLC
See also CDBLB 1832-1890; DAM MST,
POET; DLB 35

Rossner, Judith (Perelman)
1935- .... **CLC 6, 9, 29**
See also AITN 2; BEST 90:3; CA 17-20R;
CANR 18, 51; DLB 6; INT CANR-18;
MTCW

Rostand, Edmond (Eugene Alexis)
1868-1918 ..... **TCLC 6, 37; DA; DAB;**
DAC
See also CA 104; 126; DAM DRAM, MST;
MTCW

Roth, Henry 1906-1995 .... **CLC 2, 6, 11**
See also CA 11-12; 149; CANR 38; CAP 1;
DLB 28; MTCW

Roth, Joseph 1894-1939 .... **TCLC 33**
See also DLB 85

Roth, Philip (Milton)
1933- ...... **CLC 1, 2, 3, 4, 6, 9, 15, 22,**
31, 47, 66, 86; DA; DAB; DAC; WLC
See also BEST 90:3; CA 1-4R; CANR 1, 22,
36; CDALB 1968-1988; DAM MST,
NOV, POP; DLB 2, 28; DLBY 82;
MTCW

Rothenberg, Jerome 1931- .... **CLC 6, 57**
See also CA 45-48; CANR 1; DLB 5

Roumain, Jacques (Jean Baptiste)
1907-1944 .... **TCLC 19; BLC**
See also BW 1; CA 117; 125; DAM MULT

Rourke, Constance (Mayfield)
1885-1941 .... **TCLC 12**
See also CA 107; YABC 1

Rousseau, Jean-Baptiste 1671-1741 ... **LC 9**

Rousseau, Jean-Jacques
1712-1778 ..... **LC 14; DA; DAB; DAC;**
WLC
See also DAM MST

Roussel, Raymond 1877-1933 ..... **TCLC 20**
See also CA 117

Rovit, Earl (Herbert) 1927- .... **CLC 7**
See also CA 5-8R; CANR 12

Rowe, Nicholas 1674-1718 .... **LC 8**
See also DLB 84

Rowley, Ames Dorrance
See Lovecraft, H(oward) P(hillips)

Rowson, Susanna Haswell
1762(?)-1824 .... **NCLC 5**
See also DLB 37

Roy, Gabrielle
1909-1983 ..... **CLC 10, 14; DAB; DAC**
See also CA 53-56; 110; CANR 5;
DAM MST; DLB 68; MTCW

Rozewicz, Tadeusz 1921- .... **CLC 9, 23**
See also CA 108; CANR 36; DAM POET;
MTCW

Ruark, Gibbons 1941- .... **CLC 3**
See also CA 33-36R; CAAS 23; CANR 14,
31; DLB 120

Rubens, Bernice (Ruth) 1923- ... **CLC 19, 31**
See also CA 25-28R; CANR 33; DLB 14;
MTCW

Rudkin, (James) David 1936- ...... **CLC 14**
See also CA 89-92; DLB 13

Rudnik, Raphael 1933- .... **CLC 7**
See also CA 29-32R

Ruffian, M.
See Hasek, Jaroslav (Matej Frantisek)

Ruiz, Jose Martinez .... **CLC 11**
See also Martinez Ruiz, Jose

Rukeyser, Muriel
1913-1980 .... **CLC 6, 10, 15, 27; PC 12**
See also CA 5-8R; 93-96; CANR 26;
DAM POET; DLB 48; MTCW;
SATA-Obit 22

Rule, Jane (Vance) 1931- .... **CLC 27**
See also CA 25-28R; CAAS 18; CANR 12;
DLB 60

Rulfo, Juan 1918-1986 .... **CLC 8, 80; HLC**
See also CA 85-88; 118; CANR 26;
DAM MULT; DLB 113; HW; MTCW

Runeberg, Johan 1804-1877 ...... **NCLC 41**

Runyon, (Alfred) Damon
1884(?)-1946 . . . . **TCLC 10**
See also CA 107; DLB 11, 86

Rush, Norman 1933- . . . . **CLC 44**
See also CA 121; 126; INT 126

Rushdie, (Ahmed) Salman
1947- . . . . . . **CLC 23, 31, 55; DAB; DAC**
See also BEST 89:3; CA 108; 111;
CANR 33; DAM MST, NOV, POP;
INT 111; MTCW

Rushforth, Peter (Scott) 1945- . . . . . **CLC 19**
See also CA 101

Ruskin, John 1819-1900 . . . . **TCLC 63**
See also CA 114; 129; CDBLB 1832-1890;
DLB 55, 163; SATA 24

Russ, Joanna 1937- . . . . **CLC 15**
See also CA 25-28R; CANR 11, 31; DLB 8;
MTCW

Russell, George William 1867-1935
See A. E.
See also CA 104; CDBLB 1890-1914;
DAM POET

Russell, (Henry) Ken(neth Alfred)
1927- . . . . **CLC 16**
See also CA 105

Russell, Willy 1947- . . . . **CLC 60**

Rutherford, Mark . . . . **TCLC 25**
See also White, William Hale
See also DLB 18

Ruyslinck, Ward 1929- . . . . **CLC 14**
See also Belser, Reimond Karel Maria de

Ryan, Cornelius (John) 1920-1974 . . . **CLC 7**
See also CA 69-72; 53-56; CANR 38

Ryan, Michael 1946- . . . . **CLC 65**
See also CA 49-52; DLBY 82

Rybakov, Anatoli (Naumovich)
1911- . . . . **CLC 23, 53**
See also CA 126; 135; SATA 79

Ryder, Jonathan
See Ludlum, Robert

Ryga, George 1932-1987 . . . . . **CLC 14; DAC**
See also CA 101; 124; CANR 43;
DAM MST; DLB 60

S. S.
See Sassoon, Siegfried (Lorraine)

Saba, Umberto 1883-1957 . . . . **TCLC 33**
See also CA 144; DLB 114

Sabatini, Rafael 1875-1950 . . . . **TCLC 47**

Sabato, Ernesto (R.)
1911- . . . . **CLC 10, 23; HLC**
See also CA 97-100; CANR 32;
DAM MULT; DLB 145; HW; MTCW

Sacastru, Martin
See Bioy Casares, Adolfo

Sacher-Masoch, Leopold von
1836(?)-1895 . . . . **NCLC 31**

Sachs, Marilyn (Stickle) 1927- . . . . . **CLC 35**
See also AAYA 2; CA 17-20R; CANR 13,
47; CLR 2; JRDA; MAICYA; SAAS 2;
SATA 3, 68

Sachs, Nelly 1891-1970 . . . . **CLC 14**
See also CA 17-18; 25-28R; CAP 2

Sackler, Howard (Oliver)
1929-1982 . . . . **CLC 14**
See also CA 61-64; 108; CANR 30; DLB 7

Sacks, Oliver (Wolf) 1933- . . . . **CLC 67**
See also CA 53-56; CANR 28, 50;
INT CANR-28; MTCW

Sade, Donatien Alphonse Francois Comte
1740-1814 . . . . **NCLC 47**

Sadoff, Ira 1945- . . . . **CLC 9**
See also CA 53-56; CANR 5, 21; DLB 120

Saetone
See Camus, Albert

Safire, William 1929- . . . . **CLC 10**
See also CA 17-20R; CANR 31

Sagan, Carl (Edward) 1934- . . . . **CLC 30**
See also AAYA 2; CA 25-28R; CANR 11,
36; MTCW; SATA 58

Sagan, Francoise . . . . **CLC 3, 6, 9, 17, 36**
See also Quoirez, Francoise
See also DLB 83

Sahgal, Nayantara (Pandit) 1927- . . . **CLC 41**
See also CA 9-12R; CANR 11

Saint, H(arry) F. 1941- . . . . **CLC 50**
See also CA 127

St. Aubin de Teran, Lisa 1953-
See Teran, Lisa St. Aubin de
See also CA 118; 126; INT 126

Sainte-Beuve, Charles Augustin
1804-1869 . . . . **NCLC 5**

Saint-Exupery, Antoine (Jean Baptiste Marie Roger) de
1900-1944 . . . . **TCLC 2, 56; WLC**
See also CA 108; 132; CLR 10; DAM NOV;
DLB 72; MAICYA; MTCW; SATA 20

St. John, David
See Hunt, E(verette) Howard, (Jr.)

Saint-John Perse
See Leger, (Marie-Rene Auguste) Alexis
Saint-Leger

Saintsbury, George (Edward Bateman)
1845-1933 . . . . **TCLC 31**
See also DLB 57, 149

Sait Faik . . . . **TCLC 23**
See also Abasiyanik, Sait Faik

Saki . . . . **TCLC 3; SSC 12**
See also Munro, H(ector) H(ugh)

Sala, George Augustus . . . . **NCLC 46**

Salama, Hannu 1936- . . . . **CLC 18**

Salamanca, J(ack) R(ichard)
1922- . . . . **CLC 4, 15**
See also CA 25-28R

Sale, J. Kirkpatrick
See Sale, Kirkpatrick

Sale, Kirkpatrick 1937- . . . . **CLC 68**
See also CA 13-16R; CANR 10

Salinas, Luis Omar 1937- . . . **CLC 90; HLC**
See also CA 131; DAM MULT; DLB 82;
HW

Salinas (y Serrano), Pedro
1891(?)-1951 . . . . **TCLC 17**
See also CA 117; DLB 134

Salinger, J(erome) D(avid)
1919- . . . . . . **CLC 1, 3, 8, 12, 55, 56; DA;
DAB; DAC; SSC 2; WLC**
See also AAYA 2; CA 5-8R; CANR 39;
CDALB 1941-1968; CLR 18; DAM MST,
NOV, POP; DLB 2, 102; MAICYA;
MTCW; SATA 67

Salisbury, John
See Caute, David

Salter, James 1925- . . . . **CLC 7, 52, 59**
See also CA 73-76; DLB 130

Saltus, Edgar (Everton)
1855-1921 . . . . **TCLC 8**
See also CA 105

Saltykov, Mikhail Evgrafovich
1826-1889 . . . . **NCLC 16**

Samarakis, Antonis 1919- . . . . **CLC 5**
See also CA 25-28R; CAAS 16; CANR 36

Sanchez, Florencio 1875-1910 . . . . . **TCLC 37**
See also HW

Sanchez, Luis Rafael 1936- . . . . **CLC 23**
See also CA 128; DLB 145; HW

Sanchez, Sonia 1934- . . . **CLC 5; BLC; PC 9**
See also BW 2; CA 33-36R; CANR 24, 49;
CLR 18; DAM MULT; DLB 41;
DLBD 8; MAICYA; MTCW; SATA 22

Sand, George
1804-1876 . . . . **NCLC 2, 42, 57; DA;
DAB; DAC; WLC**
See also DAM MST, NOV; DLB 119

Sandburg, Carl (August)
1878-1967 . . . . **CLC 1, 4, 10, 15, 35; DA;
DAB; DAC; PC 2; WLC**
See also CA 5-8R; 25-28R; CANR 35;
CDALB 1865-1917; DAM MST, POET;
DLB 17, 54; MAICYA; MTCW; SATA 8

Sandburg, Charles
See Sandburg, Carl (August)

Sandburg, Charles A.
See Sandburg, Carl (August)

Sanders, (James) Ed(ward) 1939- . . . **CLC 53**
See also CA 13-16R; CAAS 21; CANR 13,
44; DLB 16

Sanders, Lawrence 1920- . . . . **CLC 41**
See also BEST 89:4; CA 81-84; CANR 33;
DAM POP; MTCW

Sanders, Noah
See Blount, Roy (Alton), Jr.

Sanders, Winston P.
See Anderson, Poul (William)

Sandoz, Mari(e Susette)
1896-1966 . . . . **CLC 28**
See also CA 1-4R; 25-28R; CANR 17;
DLB 9; MTCW; SATA 5

Saner, Reg(inald Anthony) 1931- . . . . **CLC 9**
See also CA 65-68

Sannazaro, Jacopo 1456(?)-1530 . . . . . . **LC 8**

Sansom, William
1912-1976 . . . . **CLC 2, 6; SSC 21**
See also CA 5-8R; 65-68; CANR 42;
DAM NOV; DLB 139; MTCW

Santayana, George 1863-1952 . . . . . **TCLC 40**
See also CA 115; DLB 54, 71; DLBD 13

Scott, Evelyn 1893-1963. . . . . **CLC 43**
See also CA 104; 112; DLB 9, 48

Scott, F(rancis) R(eginald)
1899-1985 . . . . **CLC 22**
See also CA 101; 114; DLB 88; INT 101

Scott, Frank
See Scott, F(rancis) R(eginald)

Scott, Joanna 1960- . . . . **CLC 50**
See also CA 126; CANR 53

Scott, Paul (Mark) 1920-1978. . . . **CLC 9, 60**
See also CA 81-84; 77-80; CANR 33;
DLB 14; MTCW

Scott, Walter
1771-1832 . . . . **NCLC 15; DA; DAB;
DAC; PC 13; WLC**
See also CDBLB 1789-1832; DAM MST,
NOV, POET; DLB 93, 107, 116, 144, 159;
YABC 2

Scribe, (Augustin) Eugene
1791-1861 . . . . **NCLC 16; DC 5**
See also DAM DRAM

Scrum, R.
See Crumb, R(obert)

Scudery, Madeleine de 1607-1701. . . . . **LC 2**

Scum
See Crumb, R(obert)

Scumbag, Little Bobby
See Crumb, R(obert)

Seabrook, John
See Hubbard, L(afayette) Ron(ald)

Sealy, I. Allan 1951- . . . . **CLC 55**

Search, Alexander
See Pessoa, Fernando (Antonio Nogueira)

Sebastian, Lee
See Silverberg, Robert

Sebastian Owl
See Thompson, Hunter S(tockton)

Sebestyen, Ouida 1924- . . . . **CLC 30**
See also AAYA 8; CA 107; CANR 40;
CLR 17; JRDA; MAICYA; SAAS 10;
SATA 39

Secundus, H. Scriblerus
See Fielding, Henry

Sedges, John
See Buck, Pearl S(ydenstricker)

Sedgwick, Catharine Maria
1789-1867 . . . . **NCLC 19**
See also DLB 1, 74

Seelye, John 1931- . . . . **CLC 7**

Seferiades, Giorgos Stylianou 1900-1971
See Seferis, George
See also CA 5-8R; 33-36R; CANR 5, 36;
MTCW

Seferis, George . . . . **CLC 5, 11**
See also Seferiades, Giorgos Stylianou

Segal, Erich (Wolf) 1937- . . . . **CLC 3, 10**
See also BEST 89:1; CA 25-28R; CANR 20,
36; DAM POP; DLBY 86;
INT CANR-20; MTCW

Seger, Bob 1945- . . . . **CLC 35**

Seghers, Anna . . . . **CLC 7**
See also Radvanyi, Netty
See also DLB 69

Seidel, Frederick (Lewis) 1936- . . . . . **CLC 18**
See also CA 13-16R; CANR 8; DLBY 84

Seifert, Jaroslav
1901-1986 . . . . **CLC 34, 44, 93**
See also CA 127; MTCW

Sei Shonagon c. 966-1017(?) . . . . . . **CMLC 6**

Selby, Hubert, Jr.
1928- . . . . **CLC 1, 2, 4, 8; SSC 20**
See also CA 13-16R; CANR 33; DLB 2

Selzer, Richard 1928- . . . . **CLC 74**
See also CA 65-68; CANR 14

Sembene, Ousmane
See Ousmane, Sembene

Senancour, Etienne Pivert de
1770-1846 . . . . **NCLC 16**
See also DLB 119

Sender, Ramon (Jose)
1902-1982 . . . . **CLC 8; HLC**
See also CA 5-8R; 105; CANR 8;
DAM MULT; HW; MTCW

Seneca, Lucius Annaeus
4B.C.-65. . . . . **CMLC 6; DC 5**
See also DAM DRAM

Senghor, Leopold Sedar
1906- . . . . **CLC 54; BLC**
See also BW 2; CA 116; 125; CANR 47;
DAM MULT, POET; MTCW

Serling, (Edward) Rod(man)
1924-1975 . . . . **CLC 30**
See also AAYA 14; AITN 1; CA 65-68;
57-60; DLB 26

Serna, Ramon Gomez de la
See Gomez de la Serna, Ramon

Serpieres
See Guillevic, (Eugene)

Service, Robert
See Service, Robert W(illiam)
See also DAB; DLB 92

Service, Robert W(illiam)
1874(?)-1958 . . . . . . **TCLC 15; DA; DAC;
WLC**
See also Service, Robert
See also CA 115; 140; DAM MST, POET;
SATA 20

Seth, Vikram 1952- . . . . **CLC 43, 90**
See also CA 121; 127; CANR 50;
DAM MULT; DLB 120; INT 127

Seton, Cynthia Propper
1926-1982 . . . . **CLC 27**
See also CA 5-8R; 108; CANR 7

Seton, Ernest (Evan) Thompson
1860-1946 . . . . **TCLC 31**
See also CA 109; DLB 92; DLBD 13;
JRDA; SATA 18

Seton-Thompson, Ernest
See Seton, Ernest (Evan) Thompson

Settle, Mary Lee 1918- . . . . **CLC 19, 61**
See also CA 89-92; CAAS 1; CANR 44;
DLB 6; INT 89-92

Seuphor, Michel
See Arp, Jean

**Sevigne, Marie (de Rabutin-Chantal) Marquise
de** 1626-1696 . . . . **LC 11**

Sexton, Anne (Harvey)
1928-1974 . . . . **CLC 2, 4, 6, 8, 10, 15, 53;
DA; DAB; DAC; PC 2; WLC**
See also CA 1-4R; 53-56; CABS 2;
CANR 3, 36; CDALB 1941-1968;
DAM MST, POET; DLB 5; MTCW;
SATA 10

Shaara, Michael (Joseph, Jr.)
1929-1988 . . . . **CLC 15**
See also AITN 1; CA 102; 125; CANR 52;
DAM POP; DLBY 83

Shackleton, C. C.
See Aldiss, Brian W(ilson)

Shacochis, Bob . . . . **CLC 39**
See also Shacochis, Robert G.

Shacochis, Robert G. 1951-
See Shacochis, Bob
See also CA 119; 124; INT 124

Shaffer, Anthony (Joshua) 1926- . . . . **CLC 19**
See also CA 110; 116; DAM DRAM;
DLB 13

Shaffer, Peter (Levin)
1926- . . . . . . **CLC 5, 14, 18, 37, 60; DAB**
See also CA 25-28R; CANR 25, 47;
CDBLB 1960 to Present; DAM DRAM,
MST; DLB 13; MTCW

Shakey, Bernard
See Young, Neil

Shalamov, Varlam (Tikhonovich)
1907(?)-1982 . . . . **CLC 18**
See also CA 129; 105

Shamlu, Ahmad 1925- . . . . **CLC 10**

Shammas, Anton 1951- . . . . **CLC 55**

Shange, Ntozake
1948- . . . . **CLC 8, 25, 38, 74; BLC; DC 3**
See also AAYA 9; BW 2; CA 85-88;
CABS 3; CANR 27, 48; DAM DRAM,
MULT; DLB 38; MTCW

Shanley, John Patrick 1950- . . . . **CLC 75**
See also CA 128; 133

Shapcott, Thomas W(illiam) 1935- . . **CLC 38**
See also CA 69-72; CANR 49

Shapiro, Jane . . . . **CLC 76**

Shapiro, Karl (Jay) 1913- . . **CLC 4, 8, 15, 53**
See also CA 1-4R; CAAS 6; CANR 1, 36;
DLB 48; MTCW

Sharp, William 1855-1905 . . . . **TCLC 39**
See also DLB 156

Sharpe, Thomas Ridley 1928-
See Sharpe, Tom
See also CA 114; 122; INT 122

Sharpe, Tom . . . . **CLC 36**
See also Sharpe, Thomas Ridley
See also DLB 14

Shaw, Bernard . . . . **TCLC 45**
See also Shaw, George Bernard
See also BW 1

Shaw, G. Bernard
See Shaw, George Bernard

Shaw, George Bernard
  1856-1950 . . . **TCLC 3, 9, 21; DA; DAB;**
                                DAC; WLC
  See also Shaw, Bernard
  See also CA 104; 128; CDBLB 1914-1945;
  DAM DRAM, MST; DLB 10, 57;
  MTCW

Shaw, Henry Wheeler
  1818-1885 . . . . **NCLC 15**
  See also DLB 11

Shaw, Irwin 1913-1984 . . . . . . **CLC 7, 23, 34**
  See also AITN 1; CA 13-16R; 112;
  CANR 21; CDALB 1941-1968;
  DAM DRAM, POP; DLB 6, 102;
  DLBY 84; MTCW

Shaw, Robert 1927-1978 . . . . **CLC 5**
  See also AITN 1; CA 1-4R; 81-84;
  CANR 4; DLB 13, 14

Shaw, T. E.
  See Lawrence, T(homas) E(dward)

Shawn, Wallace 1943- . . . . **CLC 41**
  See also CA 112

Shea, Lisa 1953- . . . . **CLC 86**
  See also CA 147

Sheed, Wilfrid (John Joseph)
  1930- . . . . **CLC 2, 4, 10, 53**
  See also CA 65-68; CANR 30; DLB 6;
  MTCW

Sheldon, Alice Hastings Bradley
  1915(?)-1987
  See Tiptree, James, Jr.
  See also CA 108; 122; CANR 34; INT 108;
  MTCW

Sheldon, John
  See Bloch, Robert (Albert)

Shelley, Mary Wollstonecraft (Godwin)
  1797-1851 . . . . **NCLC 14; DA; DAB;**
                                       DAC; WLC
  See also CDBLB 1789-1832; DAM MST,
  NOV; DLB 110, 116, 159; SATA 29

Shelley, Percy Bysshe
  1792-1822 . . . . **NCLC 18; DA; DAB;**
                               DAC; PC 14; WLC
  See also CDBLB 1789-1832; DAM MST,
  POET; DLB 96, 110, 158

Shepard, Jim 1956- . . . . **CLC 36**
  See also CA 137

Shepard, Lucius 1947- . . . . **CLC 34**
  See also CA 128; 141

Shepard, Sam
  1943- . . . . **CLC 4, 6, 17, 34, 41, 44; DC 5**
  See also AAYA 1; CA 69-72; CABS 3;
  CANR 22; DAM DRAM; DLB 7;
  MTCW

Shepherd, Michael
  See Ludlum, Robert

Sherburne, Zoa (Morin) 1912- . . . . . . **CLC 30**
  See also AAYA 13; CA 1-4R; CANR 3, 37;
  MAICYA; SAAS 18; SATA 3

Sheridan, Frances 1724-1766 . . . . **LC 7**
  See also DLB 39, 84

Sheridan, Richard Brinsley
  1751-1816 . . . . **NCLC 5; DA; DAB;**
                               DAC; DC 1; WLC
  See also CDBLB 1660-1789; DAM DRAM,
  MST; DLB 89

Sherman, Jonathan Marc . . . . **CLC 55**

Sherman, Martin 1941(?)- . . . . **CLC 19**
  See also CA 116; 123

Sherwin, Judith Johnson 1936- . . . **CLC 7, 15**
  See also CA 25-28R; CANR 34

Sherwood, Frances 1940- . . . . **CLC 81**
  See also CA 146

Sherwood, Robert E(mmet)
  1896-1955 . . . . **TCLC 3**
  See also CA 104; DAM DRAM; DLB 7, 26

Shestov, Lev 1866-1938 . . . . **TCLC 56**

Shevchenko, Taras 1814-1861 . . . . **NCLC 54**

Shiel, M(atthew) P(hipps)
  1865-1947 . . . . **TCLC 8**
  See also CA 106; DLB 153

Shields, Carol 1935- . . . . **CLC 91; DAC**
  See also CA 81-84; CANR 51

Shiga, Naoya 1883-1971 . . . **CLC 33; SSC 23**
  See also CA 101; 33-36R

Shilts, Randy 1951-1994 . . . . **CLC 85**
  See also CA 115; 127; 144; CANR 45;
  INT 127

Shimazaki, Haruki 1872-1943
  See Shimazaki Toson
  See also CA 105; 134

Shimazaki Toson . . . . **TCLC 5**
  See also Shimazaki, Haruki

Sholokhov, Mikhail (Aleksandrovich)
  1905-1984 . . . . **CLC 7, 15**
  See also CA 101; 112; MTCW;
  SATA-Obit 36

Shone, Patric
  See Hanley, James

Shreve, Susan Richards 1939- . . . . . . **CLC 23**
  See also CA 49-52; CAAS 5; CANR 5, 38;
  MAICYA; SATA 46; SATA-Brief 41

Shue, Larry 1946-1985 . . . . **CLC 52**
  See also CA 145; 117; DAM DRAM

Shu-Jen, Chou 1881-1936
  See Lu Hsun
  See also CA 104

Shulman, Alix Kates 1932- . . . . . . **CLC 2, 10**
  See also CA 29-32R; CANR 43; SATA 7

Shuster, Joe 1914- . . . . **CLC 21**

Shute, Nevil . . . . **CLC 30**
  See also Norway, Nevil Shute

Shuttle, Penelope (Diane) 1947- . . . . . **CLC 7**
  See also CA 93-96; CANR 39; DLB 14, 40

Sidney, Mary 1561-1621 . . . . **LC 19**

Sidney, Sir Philip
  1554-1586 . . . . . **LC 19; DA; DAB; DAC**
  See also CDBLB Before 1660; DAM MST,
  POET; DLB 167

Siegel, Jerome 1914-1996 . . . . **CLC 21**
  See also CA 116; 151

Siegel, Jerry
  See Siegel, Jerome

Sienkiewicz, Henryk (Adam Alexander Pius)
  1846-1916 . . . . **TCLC 3**
  See also CA 104; 134

Sierra, Gregorio Martinez
  See Martinez Sierra, Gregorio

Sierra, Maria (de la O'LeJarraga) Martinez
  See Martinez Sierra, Maria (de la
  O'LeJarraga)

Sigal, Clancy 1926- . . . . **CLC 7**
  See also CA 1-4R

Sigourney, Lydia Howard (Huntley)
  1791-1865 . . . . **NCLC 21**
  See also DLB 1, 42, 73

Siguenza y Gongora, Carlos de
  1645-1700 . . . . **LC 8**

Sigurjonsson, Johann 1880-1919 . . . **TCLC 27**

Sikelianos, Angelos 1884-1951 . . . . **TCLC 39**

Silkin, Jon 1930- . . . . **CLC 2, 6, 43**
  See also CA 5-8R; CAAS 5; DLB 27

Silko, Leslie (Marmon)
  1948- . . . . **CLC 23, 74; DA; DAC**
  See also AAYA 14; CA 115; 122;
  CANR 45; DAM MST, MULT, POP;
  DLB 143; NNAL

Sillanpaa, Frans Eemil 1888-1964 . . . **CLC 19**
  See also CA 129; 93-96; MTCW

Sillitoe, Alan
  1928- . . . . **CLC 1, 3, 6, 10, 19, 57**
  See also AITN 1; CA 9-12R; CAAS 2;
  CANR 8, 26; CDBLB 1960 to Present;
  DLB 14, 139; MTCW; SATA 61

Silone, Ignazio 1900-1978 . . . . **CLC 4**
  See also CA 25-28; 81-84; CANR 34;
  CAP 2; MTCW

Silver, Joan Micklin 1935- . . . . **CLC 20**
  See also CA 114; 121; INT 121

Silver, Nicholas
  See Faust, Frederick (Schiller)

Silverberg, Robert 1935- . . . . **CLC 7**
  See also CA 1-4R; CAAS 3; CANR 1, 20,
  36; DAM POP; DLB 8; INT CANR-20;
  MAICYA; MTCW; SATA 13

Silverstein, Alvin 1933- . . . . **CLC 17**
  See also CA 49-52; CANR 2; CLR 25;
  JRDA; MAICYA; SATA 8, 69

Silverstein, Virginia B(arbara Opshelor)
  1937- . . . . **CLC 17**
  See also CA 49-52; CANR 2; CLR 25;
  JRDA; MAICYA; SATA 8, 69

Sim, Georges
  See Simenon, Georges (Jacques Christian)

Simak, Clifford D(onald)
  1904-1988 . . . . **CLC 1, 55**
  See also CA 1-4R; 125; CANR 1, 35;
  DLB 8; MTCW; SATA-Obit 56

Simenon, Georges (Jacques Christian)
  1903-1989 . . . . **CLC 1, 2, 3, 8, 18, 47**
  See also CA 85-88; 129; CANR 35;
  DAM POP; DLB 72; DLBY 89; MTCW

Simic, Charles 1938- . . . **CLC 6, 9, 22, 49, 68**
  See also CA 29-32R; CAAS 4; CANR 12,
  33, 52; DAM POET; DLB 105

Simmel, Georg 1858-1918 . . . . **TCLC 64**

Simmons, Charles (Paul) 1924- . . . . . **CLC 57**
  See also CA 89-92; INT 89-92

Simmons, Dan 1948- . . . . **CLC 44**
  See also AAYA 16; CA 138; CANR 53;
  DAM POP

Simmons, James (Stewart Alexander)
1933- . . . . CLC 43
See also CA 105; CAAS 21; DLB 40

Simms, William Gilmore
1806-1870 . . . . NCLC 3
See also DLB 3, 30, 59, 73

Simon, Carly 1945- . . . . CLC 26
See also CA 105

Simon, Claude 1913- . . . . . . CLC 4, 9, 15, 39
See also CA 89-92; CANR 33; DAM NOV;
DLB 83; MTCW

Simon, (Marvin) Neil
1927- . . . . CLC 6, 11, 31, 39, 70
See also AITN 1; CA 21-24R; CANR 26;
DAM DRAM; DLB 7; MTCW

Simon, Paul 1942(?)- . . . . CLC 17
See also CA 116

Simonon, Paul 1956(?)- . . . . CLC 30

Simpson, Harriette
See Arnow, Harriette (Louisa) Simpson

Simpson, Louis (Aston Marantz)
1923- . . . . CLC 4, 7, 9, 32
See also CA 1-4R; CAAS 4; CANR 1;
DAM·POET; DLB 5; MTCW

Simpson, Mona (Elizabeth) 1957- . . . CLC 44
See also CA 122; 135

Simpson, N(orman) F(rederick)
1919- . . . . CLC 29
See also CA 13-16R; DLB 13

Sinclair, Andrew (Annandale)
1935- . . . . CLC 2, 14
See also CA 9-12R; CAAS 5; CANR 14, 38;
DLB 14; MTCW

Sinclair, Emil
See Hesse, Hermann

Sinclair, Iain 1943- . . . . CLC 76
See also CA 132

Sinclair, Iain MacGregor
See Sinclair, Iain

Sinclair, Mary Amelia St. Clair 1865(?)-1946
See Sinclair, May
See also CA 104

Sinclair, May . . . . TCLC 3, 11
See also Sinclair, Mary Amelia St. Clair
See also DLB 36, 135

Sinclair, Upton (Beall)
1878-1968 . . . . . . CLC 1, 11, 15, 63; DA;
DAB; DAC; WLC
See also CA 5-8R; 25-28R; CANR 7;
CDALB 1929-1941; DAM MST, NOV;
DLB 9; INT CANR-7; MTCW; SATA 9

Singer, Isaac
See Singer, Isaac Bashevis

Singer, Isaac Bashevis
1904-1991 . . . . CLC 1, 3, 6, 9, 11, 15, 23,
38, 69; DA; DAB; DAC; SSC 3; WLC
See also AITN 1, 2; CA 1-4R; 134;
CANR 1, 39; CDALB 1941-1968; CLR 1;
DAM MST, NOV; DLB 6, 28, 52;
DLBY 91; JRDA; MAICYA; MTCW;
SATA 3, 27; SATA-Obit 68

Singer, Israel Joshua 1893-1944 . . . TCLC 33

Singh, Khushwant 1915- . . . . CLC 11
See also CA 9-12R; CAAS 9; CANR 6

Sinjohn, John
See Galsworthy, John

Sinyavsky, Andrei (Donatevich)
1925- . . . . CLC 8
See also CA 85-88

Sirin, V.
See Nabokov, Vladimir (Vladimirovich)

Sissman, L(ouis) E(dward)
1928-1976 . . . . CLC 9, 18
See also CA 21-24R; 65-68; CANR 13;
DLB 5

Sisson, C(harles) H(ubert) 1914- . . . . . CLC 8
See also CA 1-4R; CAAS 3; CANR 3, 48;
DLB 27

Sitwell, Dame Edith
1887-1964 . . . . CLC 2, 9, 67; PC 3
See also CA 9-12R; CANR 35;
CDBLB 1945-1960; DAM POET;
DLB 20; MTCW

Sjoewall, Maj 1935- . . . . CLC 7
See also CA 65-68

Sjowall, Maj
See Sjoewall, Maj

Skelton, Robin 1925- . . . . CLC 13
See also AITN 2; CA 5-8R; CAAS 5;
CANR 28; DLB 27, 53

Skolimowski, Jerzy 1938- . . . . CLC 20
See also CA 128

Skram, Amalie (Bertha)
1847-1905 . . . . TCLC 25

Skvorecky, Josef (Vaclav)
1924- . . . . CLC 15, 39, 69; DAC
See also CA 61-64; CAAS 1; CANR 10, 34;
DAM NOV; MTCW

Slade, Bernard . . . . CLC 11, 46
See also Newbound, Bernard Slade
See also CAAS 9; DLB 53

Slaughter, Carolyn 1946- . . . . CLC 56
See also CA 85-88

Slaughter, Frank G(ill) 1908- . . . . . . CLC 29
See also AITN 2; CA 5-8R; CANR 5;
INT CANR-5

Slavitt, David R(ytman) 1935- . . . . CLC 5, 14
See also CA 21-24R; CAAS 3; CANR 41;
DLB 5, 6

Slesinger, Tess 1905-1945 . . . . TCLC 10
See also CA 107; DLB 102

Slessor, Kenneth 1901-1971 . . . . CLC 14
See also CA 102; 89-92

Slowacki, Juliusz 1809-1849 . . . . . NCLC 15

Smart, Christopher
1722-1771 . . . . LC 3; PC 13
See also DAM POET; DLB 109

Smart, Elizabeth 1913-1986 . . . . CLC 54
See also CA 81-84; 118; DLB 88

Smiley, Jane (Graves) 1949- . . . . CLC 53, 76
See also CA 104; CANR 30, 50;
DAM POP; INT CANR-30

Smith, A(rthur) J(ames) M(arshall)
1902-1980 . . . . CLC 15; DAC
See also CA 1-4R; 102; CANR 4; DLB 88

Smith, Anna Deavere 1950- . . . . CLC 86
See also CA 133

Smith, Betty (Wehner) 1896-1972 . . . CLC 19
See also CA 5-8R; 33-36R; DLBY 82;
SATA 6

Smith, Charlotte (Turner)
1749-1806 . . . . NCLC 23
See also DLB 39, 109

Smith, Clark Ashton 1893-1961 . . . . CLC 43
See also CA 143

Smith, Dave . . . . CLC 22, 42
See also Smith, David (Jeddie)
See also CAAS 7; DLB 5

Smith, David (Jeddie) 1942-
See Smith, Dave
See also CA 49-52; CANR 1; DAM POET

Smith, Florence Margaret 1902-1971
See Smith, Stevie
See also CA 17-18; 29-32R; CANR 35;
CAP 2; DAM POET; MTCW

Smith, Iain Crichton 1928- . . . . CLC 64
See also CA 21-24R; DLB 40, 139

Smith, John 1580(?)-1631 . . . . LC 9

Smith, Johnston
See Crane, Stephen (Townley)

Smith, Joseph, Jr. 1805-1844 . . . . NCLC 53

Smith, Lee 1944- . . . . CLC 25, 73
See also CA 114; 119; CANR 46; DLB 143;
DLBY 83; INT 119

Smith, Martin
See Smith, Martin Cruz

Smith, Martin Cruz 1942- . . . . CLC 25
See also BEST 89:4; CA 85-88; CANR 6,
23, 43; DAM MULT, POP;
INT CANR-23; NNAL

Smith, Mary-Ann Tirone 1944- . . . . . CLC 39
See also CA 118; 136

Smith, Patti 1946- . . . . CLC 12
See also CA 93-96

Smith, Pauline (Urmson)
1882-1959 . . . . TCLC 25

Smith, Rosamond
See Oates, Joyce Carol

Smith, Sheila Kaye
See Kaye-Smith, Sheila

Smith, Stevie . . . . . . CLC 3, 8, 25, 44; PC 12
See also Smith, Florence Margaret
See also DLB 20

Smith, Wilbur (Addison) 1933- . . . . . CLC 33
See also CA 13-16R; CANR 7, 46; MTCW

Smith, William Jay 1918- . . . . CLC 6
See also CA 5-8R; CANR 44; DLB 5;
MAICYA; SAAS 22; SATA 2, 68

Smith, Woodrow Wilson
See Kuttner, Henry

Smolenskin, Peretz 1842-1885 . . . . NCLC 30

Smollett, Tobias (George) 1721-1771 . . LC 2
See also CDBLB 1660-1789; DLB 39, 104

Snodgrass, W(illiam) D(e Witt)
1926- . . . . CLC 2, 6, 10, 18, 68
See also CA 1-4R; CANR 6, 36;
DAM POET; DLB 5; MTCW

Stowe, Harriet (Elizabeth) Beecher
1811-1896 . . . . . **NCLC 3, 50; DA; DAB;**
DAC; WLC
See also CDALB 1865-1917; DAM MST,
NOV; DLB 1, 12, 42, 74; JRDA;
MAICYA; YABC 1

Strachey, (Giles) Lytton
1880-1932 . . . . **TCLC 12**
See also CA 110; DLB 149; DLBD 10

Strand, Mark 1934- . . . . . . **CLC 6, 18, 41, 71**
See also CA 21-24R; CANR 40;
DAM POET; DLB 5; SATA 41

Straub, Peter (Francis) 1943- . . . . . . **CLC 28**
See also BEST 89:1; CA 85-88; CANR 28;
DAM POP; DLBY 84; MTCW

Strauss, Botho 1944- . . . . **CLC 22**
See also DLB 124

Streatfeild, (Mary) Noel
1895(?)-1986 . . . . **CLC 21**
See also CA 81-84; 120; CANR 31;
CLR 17; DLB 160; MAICYA; SATA 20;
SATA-Obit 48

Stribling, T(homas) S(igismund)
1881-1965 . . . . **CLC 23**
See also CA 107; DLB 9

Strindberg, (Johan) August
1849-1912 . . . . . . **TCLC 1, 8, 21, 47; DA;**
DAB; DAC; WLC
See also CA 104; 135; DAM DRAM, MST

Stringer, Arthur 1874-1950 . . . . . . **TCLC 37**
See also DLB 92

Stringer, David
See Roberts, Keith (John Kingston)

Strugatskii, Arkadii (Natanovich)
1925-1991 . . . . **CLC 27**
See also CA 106; 135

Strugatskii, Boris (Natanovich)
1933- . . . . **CLC 27**
See also CA 106

Strummer, Joe 1953(?)- . . . . **CLC 30**

Stuart, Don A.
See Campbell, John W(ood, Jr.)

Stuart, Ian
See MacLean, Alistair (Stuart)

Stuart, Jesse (Hilton)
1906-1984 . . . . **CLC 1, 8, 11, 14, 34**
See also CA 5-8R; 112; CANR 31; DLB 9,
48, 102; DLBY 84; SATA 2;
SATA-Obit 36

Sturgeon, Theodore (Hamilton)
1918-1985 . . . . **CLC 22, 39**
See also Queen, Ellery
See also CA 81-84; 116; CANR 32; DLB 8;
DLBY 85; MTCW

Sturges, Preston 1898-1959 . . . . . . **TCLC 48**
See also CA 114; 149; DLB 26

Styron, William
1925- . . . . . . **CLC 1, 3, 5, 11, 15, 60**
See also BEST 90:4; CA 5-8R; CANR 6, 33;
CDALB 1968-1988; DAM NOV, POP;
DLB 2, 143; DLBY 80; INT CANR-6;
MTCW

Suarez Lynch, B.
See Bioy Casares, Adolfo; Borges, Jorge
Luis

Su Chien 1884-1918
See Su Man-shu
See also CA 123

Suckow, Ruth 1892-1960 . . . . **SSC 18**
See also CA 113; DLB 9, 102

Sudermann, Hermann 1857-1928 . . **TCLC 15**
See also CA 107; DLB 118

Sue, Eugene 1804-1857 . . . . **NCLC 1**
See also DLB 119

Sueskind, Patrick 1949- . . . . **CLC 44**
See also Suskind, Patrick

Sukenick, Ronald 1932- . . . . . **CLC 3, 4, 6, 48**
See also CA 25-28R; CAAS 8; CANR 32;
DLBY 81

Suknaski, Andrew 1942- . . . . **CLC 19**
See also CA 101; DLB 53

Sullivan, Vernon
See Vian, Boris

Sully Prudhomme 1839-1907 . . . . . . **TCLC 31**

Su Man-shu . . . . **TCLC 24**
See also Su Chien

Summerforest, Ivy B.
See Kirkup, James

Summers, Andrew James 1942- . . . . . **CLC 26**

Summers, Andy
See Summers, Andrew James

Summers, Hollis (Spurgeon, Jr.)
1916- . . . . **CLC 10**
See also CA 5-8R; CANR 3; DLB 6

Summers, (Alphonsus Joseph-Mary Augustus)
Montague 1880-1948 . . . . **TCLC 16**
See also CA 118

Sumner, Gordon Matthew 1951- . . . . **CLC 26**

Surtees, Robert Smith
1803-1864 . . . . **NCLC 14**
See also DLB 21

Susann, Jacqueline 1921-1974 . . . . . . **CLC 3**
See also AITN 1; CA 65-68; 53-56; MTCW

Su Shih 1036-1101 . . . . **CMLC 15**

Suskind, Patrick
See Sueskind, Patrick
See also CA 145

Sutcliff, Rosemary
1920-1992 . . . . **CLC 26; DAB; DAC**
See also AAYA 10; CA 5-8R; 139;
CANR 37; CLR 1, 37; DAM MST, POP;
JRDA; MAICYA; SATA 6, 44, 78;
SATA-Obit 73

Sutro, Alfred 1863-1933 . . . . **TCLC 6**
See also CA 105; DLB 10

Sutton, Henry
See Slavitt, David R(ytman)

Svevo, Italo . . . . **TCLC 2, 35**
See also Schmitz, Aron Hector

Swados, Elizabeth (A.) 1951- . . . . **CLC 12**
See also CA 97-100; CANR 49; INT 97-100

Swados, Harvey 1920-1972 . . . . **CLC 5**
See also CA 5-8R; 37-40R; CANR 6;
DLB 2

Swan, Gladys 1934- . . . . **CLC 69**
See also CA 101; CANR 17, 39

Swarthout, Glendon (Fred)
1918-1992 . . . . **CLC 35**
See also CA 1-4R; 139; CANR 1, 47;
SATA 26

Sweet, Sarah C.
See Jewett, (Theodora) Sarah Orne

Swenson, May
1919-1989 . . . . **CLC 4, 14, 61; DA; DAB;**
DAC; PC 14
See also CA 5-8R; 130; CANR 36;
DAM MST, POET; DLB 5; MTCW;
SATA 15

Swift, Augustus
See Lovecraft, H(oward) P(hillips)

Swift, Graham (Colin) 1949- . . . . **CLC 41, 88**
See also CA 117; 122; CANR 46

Swift, Jonathan
1667-1745 . . . . . . **LC 1; DA; DAB; DAC;**
PC 9; WLC
See also CDBLB 1660-1789; DAM MST,
NOV, POET; DLB 39, 95, 101; SATA 19

Swinburne, Algernon Charles
1837-1909 . . . . . . **TCLC 8, 36; DA; DAB;**
DAC; WLC
See also CA 105; 140; CDBLB 1832-1890;
DAM MST, POET; DLB 35, 57

Swinfen, Ann . . . . **CLC 34**

Swinnerton, Frank Arthur
1884-1982 . . . . **CLC 31**
See also CA 108; DLB 34

Swithen, John
See King, Stephen (Edwin)

Sylvia
See Ashton-Warner, Sylvia (Constance)

Symmes, Robert Edward
See Duncan, Robert (Edward)

Symonds, John Addington
1840-1893 . . . . **NCLC 34**
See also DLB 57, 144

Symons, Arthur 1865-1945 . . . . **TCLC 11**
See also CA 107; DLB 19, 57, 149

Symons, Julian (Gustave)
1912-1994 . . . . **CLC 2, 14, 32**
See also CA 49-52; 147; CAAS 3; CANR 3,
33; DLB 87, 155; DLBY 92; MTCW

Synge, (Edmund) J(ohn) M(illington)
1871-1909 . . . . **TCLC 6, 37; DC 2**
See also CA 104; 141; CDBLB 1890-1914;
DAM DRAM; DLB 10, 19

Syruc, J.
See Milosz, Czeslaw

Szirtes, George 1948- . . . . **CLC 46**
See also CA 109; CANR 27

Tabori, George 1914- . . . . **CLC 19**
See also CA 49-52; CANR 4

Tagore, Rabindranath
1861-1941 . . . . **TCLC 3, 53; PC 8**
See also CA 104; 120; DAM DRAM,
POET; MTCW

Taine, Hippolyte Adolphe
1828-1893 . . . . **NCLC 15**

Talese, Gay 1932- . . . . **CLC 37**
See also AITN 1; CA 1-4R; CANR 9;
INT CANR-9; MTCW

Tallent, Elizabeth (Ann) 1954- ..... **CLC 45**
See also CA 117; DLB 130

Tally, Ted 1952- .... **CLC 42**
See also CA 120; 124; INT 124

Tamayo y Baus, Manuel
1829-1898 .... **NCLC 1**

Tammsaare, A(nton) H(ansen)
1878-1940 .... **TCLC 27**

Tan, Amy 1952- .... **CLC 59**
See also AAYA 9; BEST 89:3; CA 136;
DAM MULT, NOV, POP; SATA 75

Tandem, Felix
See Spitteler, Carl (Friedrich Georg)

Tanizaki, Jun'ichiro
1886-1965 ...... **CLC 8, 14, 28; SSC 21**
See also CA 93-96; 25-28R

Tanner, William
See Amis, Kingsley (William)

Tao Lao
See Storni, Alfonsina

Tarassoff, Lev
See Troyat, Henri

Tarbell, Ida M(inerva)
1857-1944 .... **TCLC 40**
See also CA 122; DLB 47

Tarkington, (Newton) Booth
1869-1946 .... **TCLC 9**
See also CA 110; 143; DLB 9, 102;
SATA 17

Tarkovsky, Andrei (Arsenyevich)
1932-1986 .... **CLC 75**
See also CA 127

Tartt, Donna 1964(?)- .... **CLC 76**
See also CA 142

Tasso, Torquato 1544-1595 .... **LC 5**

Tate, (John Orley) Allen
1899-1979 .... **CLC 2, 4, 6, 9, 11, 14, 24**
See also CA 5-8R; 85-88; CANR 32;
DLB 4, 45, 63; MTCW

Tate, Ellalice
See Hibbert, Eleanor Alice Burford

Tate, James (Vincent) 1943- ... **CLC 2, 6, 25**
See also CA 21-24R; CANR 29; DLB 5

Tavel, Ronald 1940- .... **CLC 6**
See also CA 21-24R; CANR 33

Taylor, C(ecil) P(hilip) 1929-1981... **CLC 27**
See also CA 25-28R; 105; CANR 47

Taylor, Edward
1642(?)-1729 ... **LC 11; DA; DAB; DAC**
See also DAM MST, POET; DLB 24

Taylor, Eleanor Ross 1920- .... **CLC 5**
See also CA 81-84

Taylor, Elizabeth 1912-1975 ... **CLC 2, 4, 29**
See also CA 13-16R; CANR 9; DLB 139;
MTCW; SATA 13

Taylor, Henry (Splawn) 1942- ...... **CLC 44**
See also CA 33-36R; CAAS 7; CANR 31;
DLB 5

Taylor, Kamala (Purnaiya) 1924-
See Markandaya, Kamala
See also CA 77-80

Taylor, Mildred D. .... **CLC 21**
See also AAYA 10; BW 1; CA 85-88;
CANR 25; CLR 9; DLB 52; JRDA;
MAICYA; SAAS 5; SATA 15, 70

Taylor, Peter (Hillsman)
1917-1994 ..... **CLC 1, 4, 18, 37, 44, 50,
71; SSC 10**
See also CA 13-16R; 147; CANR 9, 50;
DLBY 81, 94; INT CANR-9; MTCW

Taylor, Robert Lewis 1912- .... **CLC 14**
See also CA 1-4R; CANR 3; SATA 10

Tchekhov, Anton
See Chekhov, Anton (Pavlovich)

Teasdale, Sara 1884-1933......... **TCLC 4**
See also CA 104; DLB 45; SATA 32

Tegner, Esaias 1782-1846........ **NCLC 2**

Teilhard de Chardin, (Marie Joseph) Pierre
1881-1955 .... **TCLC 9**
See also CA 105

Temple, Ann
See Mortimer, Penelope (Ruth)

Tennant, Emma (Christina)
1937- .... **CLC 13, 52**
See also CA 65-68; CAAS 9; CANR 10, 38;
DLB 14

Tenneshaw, S. M.
See Silverberg, Robert

Tennyson, Alfred
1809-1892 .... **NCLC 30; DA; DAB;
DAC; PC 6; WLC**
See also CDBLB 1832-1890; DAM MST,
POET; DLB 32

Teran, Lisa St. Aubin de .... **CLC 36**
See also St. Aubin de Teran, Lisa

Terence 195(?)B.C.-159B.C...... **CMLC 14**

Teresa de Jesus, St. 1515-1582 ...... **LC 18**

Terkel, Louis 1912-
See Terkel, Studs
See also CA 57-60; CANR 18, 45; MTCW

Terkel, Studs .... **CLC 38**
See also Terkel, Louis
See also AITN 1

Terry, C. V.
See Slaughter, Frank G(ill)

Terry, Megan 1932- .... **CLC 19**
See also CA 77-80; CABS 3; CANR 43;
DLB 7

Tertz, Abram
See Sinyavsky, Andrei (Donatevich)

Tesich, Steve 1943(?)-.......... **CLC 40, 69**
See also CA 105; DLBY 83

Teternikov, Fyodor Kuzmich 1863-1927
See Sologub, Fyodor
See also CA 104

Tevis, Walter 1928-1984 .... **CLC 42**
See also CA 113

Tey, Josephine................. **TCLC 14**
See also Mackintosh, Elizabeth
See also DLB 77

Thackeray, William Makepeace
1811-1863 .... **NCLC 5, 14, 22, 43; DA;
DAB; DAC; WLC**
See also CDBLB 1832-1890; DAM MST,
NOV; DLB 21, 55, 159, 163; SATA 23

Thakura, Ravindranatha
See Tagore, Rabindranath

Tharoor, Shashi 1956- .... **CLC 70**
See also CA 141

Thelwell, Michael Miles 1939- ..... **CLC 22**
See also BW 2; CA 101

Theobald, Lewis, Jr.
See Lovecraft, H(oward) P(hillips)

Theodorescu, Ion N. 1880-1967
See Arghezi, Tudor
See also CA 116

Theriault, Yves 1915-1983.... **CLC 79; DAC**
See also CA 102; DAM MST; DLB 88

Theroux, Alexander (Louis)
1939- .... **CLC 2, 25**
See also CA 85-88; CANR 20

Theroux, Paul (Edward)
1941- .... **CLC 5, 8, 11, 15, 28, 46**
See also BEST 89:4; CA 33-36R; CANR 20,
45; DAM POP; DLB 2; MTCW;
SATA 44

Thesen, Sharon 1946-............. **CLC 56**

Thevenin, Denis
See Duhamel, Georges

Thibault, Jacques Anatole Francois
1844-1924
See France, Anatole
See also CA 106; 127; DAM NOV; MTCW

Thiele, Colin (Milton) 1920- .... **CLC 17**
See also CA 29-32R; CANR 12, 28, 53;
CLR 27; MAICYA; SAAS 2; SATA 14,
72

Thomas, Audrey (Callahan)
1935- .... **CLC 7, 13, 37; SSC 20**
See also AITN 2; CA 21-24R; CAAS 19;
CANR 36; DLB 60; MTCW

Thomas, D(onald) M(ichael)
1935- .... **CLC 13, 22, 31**
See also CA 61-64; CAAS 11; CANR 17,
45; CDBLB 1960 to Present; DLB 40;
INT CANR-17; MTCW

Thomas, Dylan (Marlais)
1914-1953 ... **TCLC 1, 8, 45; DA; DAB;
DAC; PC 2; SSC 3; WLC**
See also CA 104; 120; CDBLB 1945-1960;
DAM DRAM, MST, POET; DLB 13, 20,
139; MTCW; SATA 60

Thomas, (Philip) Edward
1878-1917 .... **TCLC 10**
See also CA 106; DAM POET; DLB 19

Thomas, Joyce Carol 1938-........ **CLC 35**
See also AAYA 12; BW 2; CA 113; 116;
CANR 48; CLR 19; DLB 33; INT 116;
JRDA; MAICYA; MTCW; SAAS 7;
SATA 40, 78

Thomas, Lewis 1913-1993 .... **CLC 35**
See also CA 85-88; 143; CANR 38; MTCW

Thomas, Paul
See Mann, (Paul) Thomas

Thomas, Piri 1928-............. **CLC 17**
See also CA 73-76; HW

Thomas, R(onald) S(tuart)
1913- .... **CLC 6, 13, 48; DAB**
See also CA 89-92; CAAS 4; CANR 30;
CDBLB 1960 to Present; DAM POET;
DLB 27; MTCW

Thomas, Ross (Elmore) 1926-1995 . . **CLC 39**
See also CA 33-36R; 150; CANR 22

Thompson, Francis Clegg
See Mencken, H(enry) L(ouis)

Thompson, Francis Joseph
1859-1907 . . . . **TCLC 4**
See also CA 104; CDBLB 1890-1914;
DLB 19

Thompson, Hunter S(tockton)
1939- . . . . **CLC 9, 17, 40**
See also BEST 89:1; CA 17-20R; CANR 23,
46; DAM POP; MTCW

Thompson, James Myers
See Thompson, Jim (Myers)

Thompson, Jim (Myers)
1906-1977(?) . . . . **CLC 69**
See also CA 140

Thompson, Judith . . . . **CLC 39**

Thomson, James 1700-1748 . . . . . . **LC 16, 29**
See also DAM POET; DLB 95

Thomson, James 1834-1882 . . . . . . **NCLC 18**
See also DAM POET; DLB 35

Thoreau, Henry David
1817-1862 . . . . . **NCLC 7, 21; DA; DAB;
DAC; WLC**
See also CDALB 1640-1865; DAM MST;
DLB 1

Thornton, Hall
See Silverberg, Robert

Thucydides c. 455B.C.-399B.C. . . . . **CMLC 17**

Thurber, James (Grover)
1894-1961 . . . . **CLC 5, 11, 25; DA; DAB;
DAC; SSC 1**
See also CA 73-76; CANR 17, 39;
CDALB 1929-1941; DAM DRAM, MST,
NOV; DLB 4, 11, 22, 102; MAICYA;
MTCW; SATA 13

Thurman, Wallace (Henry)
1902-1934 . . . . **TCLC 6; BLC**
See also BW 1; CA 104; 124; DAM MULT;
DLB 51

Ticheburn, Cheviot
See Ainsworth, William Harrison

Tieck, (Johann) Ludwig
1773-1853 . . . . **NCLC 5, 46**
See also DLB 90

Tiger, Derry
See Ellison, Harlan (Jay)

Tilghman, Christopher 1948(?)- . . . . . **CLC 65**

Tillinghast, Richard (Williford)
1940- . . . . **CLC 29**
See also CA 29-32R; CAAS 23; CANR 26,
51

Timrod, Henry 1828-1867 . . . . **NCLC 25**
See also DLB 3

Tindall, Gillian 1938- . . . . **CLC 7**
See also CA 21-24R; CANR 11

Tiptree, James, Jr. . . . . **CLC 48, 50**
See also Sheldon, Alice Hastings Bradley
See also DLB 8

Titmarsh, Michael Angelo
See Thackeray, William Makepeace

**Tocqueville, Alexis (Charles Henri Maurice
Clerel Comte)** 1805-1859 . . . . . **NCLC 7**

Tolkien, J(ohn) R(onald) R(euel)
1892-1973 . . . . **CLC 1, 2, 3, 8, 12, 38;
DA; DAB; DAC; WLC**
See also AAYA 10; AITN 1; CA 17-18;
45-48; CANR 36; CAP 2;
CDBLB 1914-1945; DAM MST, NOV,
POP; DLB 15, 160; JRDA; MAICYA;
MTCW; SATA 2, 32; SATA-Obit 24

Toller, Ernst 1893-1939 . . . . **TCLC 10**
See also CA 107; DLB 124

Tolson, M. B.
See Tolson, Melvin B(eaunorus)

Tolson, Melvin B(eaunorus)
1898(?)-1966 . . . . **CLC 36; BLC**
See also BW 1; CA 124; 89-92;
DAM MULT, POET; DLB 48, 76

Tolstoi, Aleksei Nikolaevich
See Tolstoy, Alexey Nikolaevich

Tolstoy, Alexey Nikolaevich
1882-1945 . . . . **TCLC 18**
See also CA 107

Tolstoy, Count Leo
See Tolstoy, Leo (Nikolaevich)

Tolstoy, Leo (Nikolaevich)
1828-1910 . . . . . . **TCLC 4, 11, 17, 28, 44;
DA; DAB; DAC; SSC 9; WLC**
See also CA 104; 123; DAM MST, NOV;
SATA 26

Tomasi di Lampedusa, Giuseppe 1896-1957
See Lampedusa, Giuseppe (Tomasi) di
See also CA 111

Tomlin, Lily . . . . **CLC 17**
See also Tomlin, Mary Jean

Tomlin, Mary Jean 1939(?)-
See Tomlin, Lily
See also CA 117

Tomlinson, (Alfred) Charles
1927- . . . . **CLC 2, 4, 6, 13, 45**
See also CA 5-8R; CANR 33; DAM POET;
DLB 40

Tonson, Jacob
See Bennett, (Enoch) Arnold

Toole, John Kennedy
1937-1969 . . . . **CLC 19, 64**
See also CA 104; DLBY 81

Toomer, Jean
1894-1967 . . . . . . **CLC 1, 4, 13, 22; BLC;
PC 7; SSC 1**
See also BW 1; CA 85-88;
CDALB 1917-1929; DAM MULT;
DLB 45, 51; MTCW

Torley, Luke
See Blish, James (Benjamin)

Tornimparte, Alessandra
See Ginzburg, Natalia

Torre, Raoul della
See Mencken, H(enry) L(ouis)

Torrey, E(dwin) Fuller 1937- . . . . . . **CLC 34**
See also CA 119

Torsvan, Ben Traven
See Traven, B.

Torsvan, Benno Traven
See Traven, B.

Torsvan, Berick Traven
See Traven, B.

Torsvan, Berwick Traven
See Traven, B.

Torsvan, Bruno Traven
See Traven, B.

Torsvan, Traven
See Traven, B.

Tournier, Michel (Edouard)
1924- . . . . **CLC 6, 23, 36, 95**
See also CA 49-52; CANR 3, 36; DLB 83;
MTCW; SATA 23

Tournimparte, Alessandra
See Ginzburg, Natalia

Towers, Ivar
See Kornbluth, C(yril) M.

Towne, Robert (Burton) 1936(?)- . . . . **CLC 87**
See also CA 108; DLB 44

Townsend, Sue 1946- . . **CLC 61; DAB; DAC**
See also CA 119; 127; INT 127; MTCW;
SATA 55; SATA-Brief 48

Townshend, Peter (Dennis Blandford)
1945- . . . . **CLC 17, 42**
See also CA 107

Tozzi, Federigo 1883-1920 . . . . **TCLC 31**

Traill, Catharine Parr
1802-1899 . . . . **NCLC 31**
See also DLB 99

Trakl, Georg 1887-1914 . . . . **TCLC 5**
See also CA 104

Transtroemer, Tomas (Goesta)
1931- . . . . **CLC 52, 65**
See also CA 117; 129; CAAS 17;
DAM POET

Transtromer, Tomas Gosta
See Transtroemer, Tomas (Goesta)

Traven, B. (?)-1969 . . . . **CLC 8, 11**
See also CA 19-20; 25-28R; CAP 2; DLB 9,
56; MTCW

Treitel, Jonathan 1959- . . . . **CLC 70**

Tremain, Rose 1943- . . . . **CLC 42**
See also CA 97-100; CANR 44; DLB 14

Tremblay, Michel 1942- . . . . . . **CLC 29; DAC**
See also CA 116; 128; DAM MST; DLB 60;
MTCW

Trevanian . . . . **CLC 29**
See also Whitaker, Rod(ney)

Trevor, Glen
See Hilton, James

Trevor, William
1928- . . . . . **CLC 7, 9, 14, 25, 71; SSC 21**
See also Cox, William Trevor
See also DLB 14, 139

Trifonov, Yuri (Valentinovich)
1925-1981 . . . . **CLC 45**
See also CA 126; 103; MTCW

Trilling, Lionel 1905-1975 . . . . **CLC 9, 11, 24**
See also CA 9-12R; 61-64; CANR 10;
DLB 28, 63; INT CANR-10; MTCW

Trimball, W. H.
See Mencken, H(enry) L(ouis)

Tristan
See Gomez de la Serna, Ramon

Tristram
See Housman, A(lfred) E(dward)

Trogdon, William (Lewis) 1939-
See Heat-Moon, William Least
See also CA 115; 119; CANR 47; INT 119

Trollope, Anthony
1815-1882 ..... **NCLC 6, 33; DA; DAB;**
DAC; WLC
See also CDBLB 1832-1890; DAM MST,
NOV; DLB 21, 57, 159; SATA 22

Trollope, Frances 1779-1863 ..... **NCLC 30**
See also DLB 21, 166

Trotsky, Leon 1879-1940 .... **TCLC 22**
See also CA 118

Trotter (Cockburn), Catharine
1679-1749 .... **LC 8**
See also DLB 84

Trout, Kilgore
See Farmer, Philip Jose

Trow, George W. S. 1943- .... **CLC 52**
See also CA 126

Troyat, Henri 1911- .... **CLC 23**
See also CA 45-48; CANR 2, 33; MTCW

Trudeau, G(arretson) B(eekman) 1948-
See Trudeau, Garry B.
See also CA 81-84; CANR 31; SATA 35

Trudeau, Garry B. .... **CLC 12**
See also Trudeau, G(arretson) B(eekman)
See also AAYA 10; AITN 2

Truffaut, Francois 1932-1984 ...... **CLC 20**
See also CA 81-84; 113; CANR 34

Trumbo, Dalton 1905-1976 .... **CLC 19**
See also CA 21-24R; 69-72; CANR 10;
DLB 26

Trumbull, John 1750-1831 .... **NCLC 30**
See also DLB 31

Trundlett, Helen B.
See Eliot, T(homas) S(tearns)

Tryon, Thomas 1926-1991 .... **CLC 3, 11**
See also AITN 1; CA 29-32R; 135;
CANR 32; DAM POP; MTCW

Tryon, Tom
See Tryon, Thomas

Ts'ao Hsueh-ch'in 1715(?)-1763 .... **LC 1**

Tsushima, Shuji 1909-1948
See Dazai, Osamu
See also CA 107

Tsvetaeva (Efron), Marina (Ivanovna)
1892-1941 .... **TCLC 7, 35; PC 14**
See also CA 104; 128; MTCW

Tuck, Lily 1938- .... **CLC 70**
See also CA 139

Tu Fu 712-770 .... **PC 9**
See also DAM MULT

Tunis, John R(oberts) 1889-1975 ... **CLC 12**
See also CA 61-64; DLB 22; JRDA;
MAICYA; SATA 37; SATA-Brief 30

Tuohy, Frank .... **CLC 37**
See also Tuohy, John Francis
See also DLB 14, 139

Tuohy, John Francis 1925-
See Tuohy, Frank
See also CA 5-8R; CANR 3, 47

Turco, Lewis (Putnam) 1934- ... **CLC 11, 63**
See also CA 13-16R; CAAS 22; CANR 24,
51; DLBY 84

Turgenev, Ivan
1818-1883 .... **NCLC 21; DA; DAB;**
DAC; SSC 7; WLC
See also DAM MST, NOV

Turgot, Anne-Robert-Jacques
1727-1781 .... **LC 26**

Turner, Frederick 1943- .... **CLC 48**
See also CA 73-76; CAAS 10; CANR 12,
30; DLB 40

Tutu, Desmond M(pilo)
1931- .... **CLC 80; BLC**
See also BW 1; CA 125; DAM MULT

Tutuola, Amos 1920- ... **CLC 5, 14, 29; BLC**
See also BW 2; CA 9-12R; CANR 27;
DAM MULT; DLB 125; MTCW

Twain, Mark
..... **TCLC 6, 12, 19, 36, 48, 59; SSC 6;**
WLC
See also Clemens, Samuel Langhorne
See also DLB 11, 12, 23, 64, 74

Tyler, Anne
1941- .... **CLC 7, 11, 18, 28, 44, 59**
See also AAYA 18; BEST 89:1; CA 9-12R;
CANR 11, 33, 53; DAM NOV, POP;
DLB 6, 143; DLBY 82; MTCW; SATA 7

Tyler, Royall 1757-1826 .... **NCLC 3**
See also DLB 37

Tynan, Katharine 1861-1931 .... **TCLC 3**
See also CA 104; DLB 153

Tyutchev, Fyodor 1803-1873 ..... **NCLC 34**

Tzara, Tristan .... **CLC 47**
See also Rosenfeld, Samuel
See also DAM POET

Uhry, Alfred 1936- .... **CLC 55**
See also CA 127; 133; DAM DRAM, POP;
INT 133

Ulf, Haerved
See Strindberg, (Johan) August

Ulf, Harved
See Strindberg, (Johan) August

Ulibarri, Sabine R(eyes) 1919- ..... **CLC 83**
See also CA 131; DAM MULT; DLB 82;
HW

Unamuno (y Jugo), Miguel de
1864-1936 .... **TCLC 2, 9; HLC; SSC 11**
See also CA 104; 131; DAM MULT, NOV;
DLB 108; HW; MTCW

Undercliffe, Errol
See Campbell, (John) Ramsey

Underwood, Miles
See Glassco, John

Undset, Sigrid
1882-1949 .... **TCLC 3; DA; DAB;**
DAC; WLC
See also CA 104; 129; DAM MST, NOV;
MTCW

Ungaretti, Giuseppe
1888-1970 .... **CLC 7, 11, 15**
See also CA 19-20; 25-28R; CAP 2;
DLB 114

Unger, Douglas 1952- .... **CLC 34**
See also CA 130

Unsworth, Barry (Forster) 1930- .... **CLC 76**
See also CA 25-28R; CANR 30

Updike, John (Hoyer)
1932- ...... **CLC 1, 2, 3, 5, 7, 9, 13, 15,**
23, 34, 43, 70; DA; DAB; DAC; SSC 13;
WLC
See also CA 1-4R; CABS 1; CANR 4, 33,
51; CDALB 1968-1988; DAM MST,
NOV, POET, POP; DLB 2, 5, 143;
DLBD 3; DLBY 80, 82; MTCW

Upshaw, Margaret Mitchell
See Mitchell, Margaret (Munnerlyn)

Upton, Mark
See Sanders, Lawrence

Urdang, Constance (Henriette)
1922- .... **CLC 47**
See also CA 21-24R; CANR 9, 24

Uriel, Henry
See Faust, Frederick (Schiller)

Uris, Leon (Marcus) 1924- .... **CLC 7, 32**
See also AITN 1, 2; BEST 89:2; CA 1-4R;
CANR 1, 40; DAM NOV, POP; MTCW;
SATA 49

Urmuz
See Codrescu, Andrei

Urquhart, Jane 1949- .... **CLC 90; DAC**
See also CA 113; CANR 32

Ustinov, Peter (Alexander) 1921- .... **CLC 1**
See also AITN 1; CA 13-16R; CANR 25,
51; DLB 13

Vaculik, Ludvik 1926- .... **CLC 7**
See also CA 53-56

Valdez, Luis (Miguel)
1940- .... **CLC 84; HLC**
See also CA 101; CANR 32; DAM MULT;
DLB 122; HW

Valenzuela, Luisa 1938- ... **CLC 31; SSC 14**
See also CA 101; CANR 32; DAM MULT;
DLB 113; HW

Valera y Alcala-Galiano, Juan
1824-1905 .... **TCLC 10**
See also CA 106

Valery, (Ambroise) Paul (Toussaint Jules)
1871-1945 .... **TCLC 4, 15; PC 9**
See also CA 104; 122; DAM POET; MTCW

Valle-Inclan, Ramon (Maria) del
1866-1936 .... **TCLC 5; HLC**
See also CA 106; DAM MULT; DLB 134

Vallejo, Antonio Buero
See Buero Vallejo, Antonio

Vallejo, Cesar (Abraham)
1892-1938 .... **TCLC 3, 56; HLC**
See also CA 105; DAM MULT; HW

Valle Y Pena, Ramon del
See Valle-Inclan, Ramon (Maria) del

Van Ash, Cay 1918- .... **CLC 34**

Vanbrugh, Sir John 1664-1726 ...... **LC 21**
See also DAM DRAM; DLB 80

Van Campen, Karl
See Campbell, John W(ood, Jr.)

Vance, Gerald
See Silverberg, Robert

Vance, Jack .... **CLC 35**
See also Vance, John Holbrook
See also DLB 8

Vance, John Holbrook 1916-
See Queen, Ellery; Vance, Jack
See also CA 29-32R; CANR 17; MTCW

**Van Den Bogarde, Derek Jules Gaspard Ulric
Niven** 1921-
See Bogarde, Dirk
See also CA 77-80

Vandenburgh, Jane . . . . **CLC 59**

Vanderhaeghe, Guy 1951- . . . . **CLC 41**
See also CA 113

van der Post, Laurens (Jan) 1906- . . . **CLC 5**
See also CA 5-8R; CANR 35

van de Wetering, Janwillem 1931- . . **CLC 47**
See also CA 49-52; CANR 4

Van Dine, S. S. . . . . **TCLC 23**
See also Wright, Willard Huntington

Van Doren, Carl (Clinton)
1885-1950 . . . . **TCLC 18**
See also CA 111

Van Doren, Mark 1894-1972 . . . . . **CLC 6, 10**
See also CA 1-4R; 37-40R; CANR 3;
DLB 45; MTCW

Van Druten, John (William)
1901-1957 . . . . **TCLC 2**
See also CA 104; DLB 10

Van Duyn, Mona (Jane)
1921- . . . . **CLC 3, 7, 63**
See also CA 9-12R; CANR 7, 38;
DAM POET; DLB 5

Van Dyne, Edith
See Baum, L(yman) Frank

van Itallie, Jean-Claude 1936- . . . . **CLC 3**
See also CA 45-48; CAAS 2; CANR 1, 48;
DLB 7

van Ostaijen, Paul 1896-1928 . . . . . **TCLC 33**

Van Peebles, Melvin 1932- . . . . . . **CLC 2, 20**
See also BW 2; CA 85-88; CANR 27;
DAM MULT

Vansittart, Peter 1920- . . . . **CLC 42**
See also CA 1-4R; CANR 3, 49

Van Vechten, Carl 1880-1964 . . . . . . **CLC 33**
See also CA 89-92; DLB 4, 9, 51

Van Vogt, A(lfred) E(lton) 1912- . . . . . **CLC 1**
See also CA 21-24R; CANR 28; DLB 8;
SATA 14

Varda, Agnes 1928- . . . . **CLC 16**
See also CA 116; 122

Vargas Llosa, (Jorge) Mario (Pedro)
1936- . . . . **CLC 3, 6, 9, 10, 15, 31, 42, 85;
DA; DAB; DAC; HLC**
See also CA 73-76; CANR 18, 32, 42;
DAM MST, MULT, NOV; DLB 145;
HW; MTCW

Vasiliu, Gheorghe 1881-1957
See Bacovia, George
See also CA 123

Vassa, Gustavus
See Equiano, Olaudah

Vassilikos, Vassilis 1933- . . . . **CLC 4, 8**
See also CA 81-84

Vaughan, Henry 1621-1695 . . . . **LC 27**
See also DLB 131

Vaughn, Stephanie . . . . **CLC 62**

Vazov, Ivan (Minchov)
1850-1921 . . . . **TCLC 25**
See also CA 121; DLB 147

Veblen, Thorstein (Bunde)
1857-1929 . . . . **TCLC 31**
See also CA 115

Vega, Lope de 1562-1635 . . . . **LC 23**

Venison, Alfred
See Pound, Ezra (Weston Loomis)

Verdi, Marie de
See Mencken, H(enry) L(ouis)

Verdu, Matilde
See Cela, Camilo Jose

Verga, Giovanni (Carmelo)
1840-1922 . . . . **TCLC 3; SSC 21**
See also CA 104; 123

Vergil
70B.C.-19B.C. . . . . . . **CMLC 9; DA; DAB;
DAC; PC 12**
See also DAM MST, POET

Verhaeren, Emile (Adolphe Gustave)
1855-1916 . . . . **TCLC 12**
See also CA 109

Verlaine, Paul (Marie)
1844-1896 . . . . **NCLC 2, 51; PC 2**
See also DAM POET

Verne, Jules (Gabriel)
1828-1905 . . . . **TCLC 6, 52**
See also AAYA 16; CA 110; 131; DLB 123;
JRDA; MAICYA; SATA 21

Very, Jones 1813-1880 . . . . **NCLC 9**
See also DLB 1

Vesaas, Tarjei 1897-1970 . . . . **CLC 48**
See also CA 29-32R

Vialis, Gaston
See Simenon, Georges (Jacques Christian)

Vian, Boris 1920-1959 . . . . **TCLC 9**
See also CA 106; DLB 72

Viaud, (Louis Marie) Julien 1850-1923
See Loti, Pierre
See also CA 107

Vicar, Henry
See Felsen, Henry Gregor

Vicker, Angus
See Felsen, Henry Gregor

Vidal, Gore
1925- . . . . . **CLC 2, 4, 6, 8, 10, 22, 33, 72**
See also AITN 1; BEST 90:2; CA 5-8R;
CANR 13, 45; DAM NOV, POP; DLB 6,
152; INT CANR-13; MTCW

Viereck, Peter (Robert Edwin)
1916- . . . . **CLC 4**
See also CA 1-4R; CANR 1, 47; DLB 5

Vigny, Alfred (Victor) de
1797-1863 . . . . **NCLC 7**
See also DAM POET; DLB 119

Vilakazi, Benedict Wallet
1906-1947 . . . . **TCLC 37**

**Villiers de l'Isle Adam, Jean Marie Mathias
Philippe Auguste Comte**
1838-1889 . . . . **NCLC 3; SSC 14**
See also DLB 123

Villon, Francois 1431-1463(?) . . . . **PC 13**

Vinci, Leonardo da 1452-1519 . . . . . . **LC 12**

Vine, Barbara . . . . **CLC 50**
See also Rendell, Ruth (Barbara)
See also BEST 90:4

Vinge, Joan D(ennison) 1948- . . . . . **CLC 30**
See also CA 93-96; SATA 36

Violis, G.
See Simenon, Georges (Jacques Christian)

Visconti, Luchino 1906-1976 . . . . . . **CLC 16**
See also CA 81-84; 65-68; CANR 39

Vittorini, Elio 1908-1966 . . . . . . **CLC 6, 9, 14**
See also CA 133; 25-28R

Vizinczey, Stephen 1933- . . . . **CLC 40**
See also CA 128; INT 128

Vliet, R(ussell) G(ordon)
1929-1984 . . . . **CLC 22**
See also CA 37-40R; 112; CANR 18

Vogau, Boris Andreyevich 1894-1937(?)
See Pilnyak, Boris
See also CA 123

Vogel, Paula A(nne) 1951- . . . . **CLC 76**
See also CA 108

Voight, Ellen Bryant 1943- . . . . **CLC 54**
See also CA 69-72; CANR 11, 29; DLB 120

Voigt, Cynthia 1942- . . . . **CLC 30**
See also AAYA 3; CA 106; CANR 18, 37,
40; CLR 13; INT CANR-18; JRDA;
MAICYA; SATA 48, 79; SATA-Brief 33

Voinovich, Vladimir (Nikolaevich)
1932- . . . . **CLC 10, 49**
See also CA 81-84; CAAS 12; CANR 33;
MTCW

Vollmann, William T. 1959- . . . . **CLC 89**
See also CA 134; DAM NOV, POP

Voloshinov, V. N.
See Bakhtin, Mikhail Mikhailovich

Voltaire
1694-1778 . . . . . **LC 14; DA; DAB; DAC;
SSC 12; WLC**
See also DAM DRAM, MST

von Daeniken, Erich 1935- . . . . **CLC 30**
See also AITN 1; CA 37-40R; CANR 17,
44

von Daniken, Erich
See von Daeniken, Erich

von Heidenstam, (Carl Gustaf) Verner
See Heidenstam, (Carl Gustaf) Verner von

von Heyse, Paul (Johann Ludwig)
See Heyse, Paul (Johann Ludwig von)

von Hofmannsthal, Hugo
See Hofmannsthal, Hugo von

von Horvath, Odon
See Horvath, Oedoen von

von Horvath, Oedoen
See Horvath, Oedoen von

von Liliencron, (Friedrich Adolf Axel) Detlev
See Liliencron, (Friedrich Adolf Axel)
Detlev von

Vonnegut, Kurt, Jr.
1922- . . . . . . **CLC 1, 2, 3, 4, 5, 8, 12, 22,
40, 60; DA; DAB; DAC; SSC 8; WLC**
See also AAYA 6; AITN 1; BEST 90:4;
CA 1-4R; CANR 1, 25, 49;
CDALB 1968-1988; DAM MST, NOV,
POP; DLB 2, 8, 152; DLBD 3; DLBY 80;
MTCW

Von Rachen, Kurt
See Hubbard, L(afayette) Ron(ald)

von Rezzori (d'Arezzo), Gregor
See Rezzori (d'Arezzo), Gregor von

von Sternberg, Josef
See Sternberg, Josef von

Vorster, Gordon 1924-............ CLC 34
See also CA 133

Vosce, Trudie
See Ozick, Cynthia

Voznesensky, Andrei (Andreievich)
1933-................. CLC 1, 15, 57
See also CA 89-92; CANR 37;
DAM POET; MTCW

Waddington, Miriam 1917-........ CLC 28
See also CA 21-24R; CANR 12, 30;
DLB 68

Wagman, Fredrica 1937-............ CLC 7
See also CA 97-100; INT 97-100

Wagner, Richard 1813-1883....... NCLC 9
See also DLB 129

Wagner-Martin, Linda 1936-....... CLC 50

Wagoner, David (Russell)
1926-................... CLC 3, 5, 15
See also CA 1-4R; CAAS 3; CANR 2;
DLB 5; SATA 14

Wah, Fred(erick James) 1939-...... CLC 44
See also CA 107; 141; DLB 60

Wahloo, Per 1926-1975 .... CLC 7
See also CA 61-64

Wahloo, Peter
See Wahloo, Per

Wain, John (Barrington)
1925-1994 .... CLC 2, 11, 15, 46
See also CA 5-8R; 145; CAAS 4; CANR 23;
CDBLB 1960 to Present; DLB 15, 27,
139, 155; MTCW

Wajda, Andrzej 1926-............ CLC 16
See also CA 102

Wakefield, Dan 1932-.............. CLC 7
See also CA 21-24R; CAAS 7

Wakoski, Diane
1937-..... CLC 2, 4, 7, 9, 11, 40; PC 15
See also CA 13-16R; CAAS 1; CANR 9;
DAM POET; DLB 5; INT CANR-9

Wakoski-Sherbell, Diane
See Wakoski, Diane

Walcott, Derek (Alton)
1930-.... CLC 2, 4, 9, 14, 25, 42, 67, 76;
BLC; DAB; DAC
See also BW 2; CA 89-92; CANR 26, 47;
DAM MST, MULT, POET; DLB 117;
DLBY 81; MTCW

Waldman, Anne 1945-............. CLC 7
See also CA 37-40R; CAAS 17; CANR 34;
DLB 16

Waldo, E. Hunter
See Sturgeon, Theodore (Hamilton)

Waldo, Edward Hamilton
See Sturgeon, Theodore (Hamilton)

Walker, Alice (Malsenior)
1944-....... CLC 5, 6, 9, 19, 27, 46, 58;
BLC; DA; DAB; DAC; SSC 5
See also AAYA 3; BEST 89:4; BW 2;
CA 37-40R; CANR 9, 27, 49;
CDALB 1968-1988; DAM MST, MULT,
NOV, POET, POP; DLB 6, 33, 143;
INT CANR-27; MTCW; SATA 31

Walker, David Harry 1911-1992.... CLC 14
See also CA 1-4R; 137; CANR 1; SATA 8;
SATA-Obit 71

Walker, Edward Joseph 1934-
See Walker, Ted
See also CA 21-24R; CANR 12, 28, 53

Walker, George F.
1947-........ CLC 44, 61; DAB; DAC
See also CA 103; CANR 21, 43;
DAM MST; DLB 60

Walker, Joseph A. 1935-.......... CLC 19
See also BW 1; CA 89-92; CANR 26;
DAM DRAM, MST; DLB 38

Walker, Margaret (Abigail)
1915-................. CLC 1, 6; BLC
See also BW 2; CA 73-76; CANR 26;
DAM MULT; DLB 76, 152; MTCW

Walker, Ted..................... CLC 13
See also Walker, Edward Joseph
See also DLB 40

Wallace, David Foster 1962-....... CLC 50
See also CA 132

Wallace, Dexter
See Masters, Edgar Lee

Wallace, (Richard Horatio) Edgar
1875-1932 .... TCLC 57
See also CA 115; DLB 70

Wallace, Irving 1916-1990...... CLC 7, 13
See also AITN 1; CA 1-4R; 132; CAAS 1;
CANR 1, 27; DAM NOV, POP;
INT CANR-27; MTCW

Wallant, Edward Lewis
1926-1962 .... CLC 5, 10
See also CA 1-4R; CANR 22; DLB 2, 28,
143; MTCW

Walley, Byron
See Card, Orson Scott

Walpole, Horace 1717-1797.......... LC 2
See also DLB 39, 104

Walpole, Hugh (Seymour)
1884-1941 .... TCLC 5
See also CA 104; DLB 34

Walser, Martin 1927-............. CLC 27
See also CA 57-60; CANR 8, 46; DLB 75,
124

Walser, Robert
1878-1956 .... TCLC 18; SSC 20
See also CA 118; DLB 66

Walsh, Jill Paton................. CLC 35
See also Paton Walsh, Gillian
See also AAYA 11; CLR 2; DLB 161;
SAAS 3

Walter, Villiam Christian
See Andersen, Hans Christian

Wambaugh, Joseph (Aloysius, Jr.)
1937-..................... CLC 3, 18
See also AITN 1; BEST 89:3; CA 33-36R;
CANR 42; DAM NOV, POP; DLB 6;
DLBY 83; MTCW

Ward, Arthur Henry Sarsfield 1883-1959
See Rohmer, Sax
See also CA 108

Ward, Douglas Turner 1930-....... CLC 19
See also BW 1; CA 81-84; CANR 27;
DLB 7, 38

Ward, Mary Augusta
See Ward, Mrs. Humphry

Ward, Mrs. Humphry
1851-1920 .... TCLC 55
See also DLB 18

Ward, Peter
See Faust, Frederick (Schiller)

Warhol, Andy 1928(?)-1987........ CLC 20
See also AAYA 12; BEST 89:4; CA 89-92;
121; CANR 34

Warner, Francis (Robert le Plastrier)
1937-..................... CLC 14
See also CA 53-56; CANR 11

Warner, Marina 1946-............ CLC 59
See also CA 65-68; CANR 21

Warner, Rex (Ernest) 1905-1986.... CLC 45
See also CA 89-92; 119; DLB 15

Warner, Susan (Bogert)
1819-1885 .... NCLC 31
See also DLB 3, 42

Warner, Sylvia (Constance) Ashton
See Ashton-Warner, Sylvia (Constance)

Warner, Sylvia Townsend
1893-1978 .... CLC 7, 19; SSC 23
See also CA 61-64; 77-80; CANR 16;
DLB 34, 139; MTCW

Warren, Mercy Otis 1728-1814... NCLC 13
See also DLB 31

Warren, Robert Penn
1905-1989 .... CLC 1, 4, 6, 8, 10, 13, 18,
39, 53, 59; DA; DAB; DAC; SSC 4; WLC
See also AITN 1; CA 13-16R; 129;
CANR 10, 47; CDALB 1968-1988;
DAM MST, NOV, POET; DLB 2, 48,
152; DLBY 80, 89; INT CANR-10;
MTCW; SATA 46; SATA-Obit 63

Warshofsky, Isaac
See Singer, Isaac Bashevis

Warton, Thomas 1728-1790........ LC 15
See also DAM POET; DLB 104, 109

Waruk, Kona
See Harris, (Theodore) Wilson

Warung, Price 1855-1911........ TCLC 45

Warwick, Jarvis
See Garner, Hugh

Washington, Alex
See Harris, Mark

Washington, Booker T(aliaferro)
1856-1915 .... TCLC 10; BLC
See also BW 1; CA 114; 125; DAM MULT;
SATA 28

Washington, George 1732-1799...... LC 25
See also DLB 31

Wassermann, (Karl) Jakob
1873-1934 . . . . **TCLC 6**
See also CA 104; DLB 66

Wasserstein, Wendy
1950- . . . . **CLC 32, 59, 90; DC 4**
See also CA 121; 129; CABS 3; CANR 53;
DAM DRAM; INT 129

Waterhouse, Keith (Spencer)
1929- . . . . **CLC 47**
See also CA 5-8R; CANR 38; DLB 13, 15;
MTCW

Waters, Frank (Joseph)
1902-1995 . . . . **CLC 88**
See also CA 5-8R; 149; CAAS 13; CANR 3,
18; DLBY 86

Waters, Roger 1944- . . . . **CLC 35**

Watkins, Frances Ellen
See Harper, Frances Ellen Watkins

Watkins, Gerrold
See Malzberg, Barry N(athaniel)

Watkins, Gloria 1955(?)-
See hooks, bell
See also BW 2; CA 143

Watkins, Paul 1964- . . . . **CLC 55**
See also CA 132

Watkins, Vernon Phillips
1906-1967 . . . . **CLC 43**
See also CA 9-10; 25-28R; CAP 1; DLB 20

Watson, Irving S.
See Mencken, H(enry) L(ouis)

Watson, John H.
See Farmer, Philip Jose

Watson, Richard F.
See Silverberg, Robert

Waugh, Auberon (Alexander) 1939- . . **CLC 7**
See also CA 45-48; CANR 6, 22; DLB 14

Waugh, Evelyn (Arthur St. John)
1903-1966 . . . . . . **CLC 1, 3, 8, 13, 19, 27,
44; DA; DAB; DAC; WLC**
See also CA 85-88; 25-28R; CANR 22;
CDBLB 1914-1945; DAM MST, NOV,
POP; DLB 15, 162; MTCW

Waugh, Harriet 1944- . . . . **CLC 6**
See also CA 85-88; CANR 22

Ways, C. R.
See Blount, Roy (Alton), Jr.

Waystaff, Simon
See Swift, Jonathan

Webb, (Martha) Beatrice (Potter)
1858-1943 . . . . **TCLC 22**
See also Potter, Beatrice
See also CA 117

Webb, Charles (Richard) 1939- . . . . . . **CLC 7**
See also CA 25-28R

Webb, James H(enry), Jr. 1946- . . . . **CLC 22**
See also CA 81-84

Webb, Mary (Gladys Meredith)
1881-1927 . . . . **TCLC 24**
See also CA 123; DLB 34

Webb, Mrs. Sidney
See Webb, (Martha) Beatrice (Potter)

Webb, Phyllis 1927- . . . . **CLC 18**
See also CA 104; CANR 23; DLB 53

Webb, Sidney (James)
1859-1947 . . . . **TCLC 22**
See also CA 117

Webber, Andrew Lloyd . . . . **CLC 21**
See also Lloyd Webber, Andrew

Weber, Lenora Mattingly
1895-1971 . . . . **CLC 12**
See also CA 19-20; 29-32R; CAP 1;
SATA 2; SATA-Obit 26

Webster, John
1579(?)-1634(?) . . . . . . **LC 33; DA; DAB;
DAC; DC 2; WLC**
See also CDBLB Before 1660;
DAM DRAM, MST; DLB 58

Webster, Noah 1758-1843 . . . . **NCLC 30**

Wedekind, (Benjamin) Frank(lin)
1864-1918 . . . . **TCLC 7**
See also CA 104; DAM DRAM; DLB 118

Weidman, Jerome 1913- . . . . **CLC 7**
See also AITN 2; CA 1-4R; CANR 1;
DLB 28

Weil, Simone (Adolphine)
1909-1943 . . . . **TCLC 23**
See also CA 117

Weinstein, Nathan
See West, Nathanael

Weinstein, Nathan von Wallenstein
See West, Nathanael

Weir, Peter (Lindsay) 1944- . . . . **CLC 20**
See also CA 113; 123

Weiss, Peter (Ulrich)
1916-1982 . . . . **CLC 3, 15, 51**
See also CA 45-48; 106; CANR 3;
DAM DRAM; DLB 69, 124

Weiss, Theodore (Russell)
1916- . . . . **CLC 3, 8, 14**
See also CA 9-12R; CAAS 2; CANR 46;
DLB 5

Welch, (Maurice) Denton
1915-1948 . . . . **TCLC 22**
See also CA 121; 148

Welch, James 1940- . . . . **CLC 6, 14, 52**
See also CA 85-88; CANR 42;
DAM MULT, POP; NNAL

Weldon, Fay
1933- . . . . **CLC 6, 9, 11, 19, 36, 59**
See also CA 21-24R; CANR 16, 46;
CDBLB 1960 to Present; DAM POP;
DLB 14; INT CANR-16; MTCW

Wellek, Rene 1903-1995 . . . . **CLC 28**
See also CA 5-8R; 150; CAAS 7; CANR 8;
DLB 63; INT CANR-8

Weller, Michael 1942- . . . . **CLC 10, 53**
See also CA 85-88

Weller, Paul 1958- . . . . **CLC 26**

Wellershoff, Dieter 1925- . . . . **CLC 46**
See also CA 89-92; CANR 16, 37

Welles, (George) Orson
1915-1985 . . . . **CLC 20, 80**
See also CA 93-96; 117

Wellman, Mac 1945- . . . . **CLC 65**

Wellman, Manly Wade 1903-1986 . . **CLC 49**
See also CA 1-4R; 118; CANR 6, 16, 44;
SATA 6; SATA-Obit 47

Wells, Carolyn 1869(?)-1942 . . . . . . **TCLC 35**
See also CA 113; DLB 11

Wells, H(erbert) G(eorge)
1866-1946 . . . . **TCLC 6, 12, 19; DA;
DAB; DAC; SSC 6; WLC**
See also AAYA 18; CA 110; 121;
CDBLB 1914-1945; DAM MST, NOV;
DLB 34, 70, 156; MTCW; SATA 20

Wells, Rosemary 1943- . . . . **CLC 12**
See also AAYA 13; CA 85-88; CANR 48;
CLR 16; MAICYA; SAAS 1; SATA 18,
69

Welty, Eudora
1909- . . . . . . **CLC 1, 2, 5, 14, 22, 33; DA;
DAB; DAC; SSC 1; WLC**
See also CA 9-12R; CABS 1; CANR 32;
CDALB 1941-1968; DAM MST, NOV;
DLB 2, 102, 143; DLBD 12; DLBY 87;
MTCW

Wen I-to 1899-1946 . . . . **TCLC 28**

Wentworth, Robert
See Hamilton, Edmond

Werfel, Franz (V.) 1890-1945 . . . . . . **TCLC 8**
See also CA 104; DLB 81, 124

Wergeland, Henrik Arnold
1808-1845 . . . . **NCLC 5**

Wersba, Barbara 1932- . . . . **CLC 30**
See also AAYA 2; CA 29-32R; CANR 16,
38; CLR 3; DLB 52; JRDA; MAICYA;
SAAS 2; SATA 1, 58

Wertmueller, Lina 1928- . . . . **CLC 16**
See also CA 97-100; CANR 39

Wescott, Glenway 1901-1987 . . . . . . **CLC 13**
See also CA 13-16R; 121; CANR 23;
DLB 4, 9, 102

Wesker, Arnold 1932- . . **CLC 3, 5, 42; DAB**
See also CA 1-4R; CAAS 7; CANR 1, 33;
CDBLB 1960 to Present; DAM DRAM;
DLB 13; MTCW

Wesley, Richard (Errol) 1945- . . . . **CLC 7**
See also BW 1; CA 57-60; CANR 27;
DLB 38

Wessel, Johan Herman 1742-1785 . . . . **LC 7**

West, Anthony (Panther)
1914-1987 . . . . **CLC 50**
See also CA 45-48; 124; CANR 3, 19;
DLB 15

West, C. P.
See Wodehouse, P(elham) G(renville)

West, (Mary) Jessamyn
1902-1984 . . . . **CLC 7, 17**
See also CA 9-12R; 112; CANR 27; DLB 6;
DLBY 84; MTCW; SATA-Obit 37

West, Morris L(anglo) 1916- . . . . . **CLC 6, 33**
See also CA 5-8R; CANR 24, 49; MTCW

West, Nathanael
1903-1940 . . . . . **TCLC 1, 14, 44; SSC 16**
See also CA 104; 125; CDALB 1929-1941;
DLB 4, 9, 28; MTCW

West, Owen
See Koontz, Dean R(ay)

West, Paul 1930- . . . . **CLC 7, 14**
See also CA 13-16R; CAAS 7; CANR 22,
53; DLB 14; INT CANR-22

West, Rebecca 1892-1983 .. **CLC 7, 9, 31, 50**
See also CA 5-8R; 109; CANR 19; DLB 36;
DLBY 83; MTCW

Westall, Robert (Atkinson)
1929-1993 .... **CLC 17**
See also AAYA 12; CA 69-72; 141;
CANR 18; CLR 13; JRDA; MAICYA;
SAAS 2; SATA 23, 69; SATA-Obit 75

Westlake, Donald E(dwin)
1933- .... **CLC 7, 33**
See also CA 17-20R; CAAS 13; CANR 16,
44; DAM POP; INT CANR-16

Westmacott, Mary
See Christie, Agatha (Mary Clarissa)

Weston, Allen
See Norton, Andre

Wetcheek, J. L.
See Feuchtwanger, Lion

Wetering, Janwillem van de
See van de Wetering, Janwillem

Wetherell, Elizabeth
See Warner, Susan (Bogert)

Whale, James 1889-1957 .... **TCLC 63**

Whalen, Philip 1923- .... **CLC 6, 29**
See also CA 9-12R; CANR 5, 39; DLB 16

Wharton, Edith (Newbold Jones)
1862-1937 ...... **TCLC 3, 9, 27, 53; DA;
DAB; DAC; SSC 6; WLC**
See also CA 104; 132; CDALB 1865-1917;
DAM MST, NOV; DLB 4, 9, 12, 78;
DLBD 13; MTCW

Wharton, James
See Mencken, H(enry) L(ouis)

Wharton, William (a pseudonym)
.... **CLC 18, 37**
See also CA 93-96; DLBY 80; INT 93-96

Wheatley (Peters), Phillis
1754(?)-1784 .... **LC 3; BLC; DA; DAC;
PC 3; WLC**
See also CDALB 1640-1865; DAM MST,
MULT, POET; DLB 31, 50

Wheelock, John Hall 1886-1978 .... **CLC 14**
See also CA 13-16R; 77-80; CANR 14;
DLB 45

White, E(lwyn) B(rooks)
1899-1985 .... **CLC 10, 34, 39**
See also AITN 2; CA 13-16R; 116;
CANR 16, 37; CLR 1, 21; DAM POP;
DLB 11, 22; MAICYA; MTCW;
SATA 2, 29; SATA-Obit 44

White, Edmund (Valentine III)
1940- .... **CLC 27**
See also AAYA 7; CA 45-48; CANR 3, 19,
36; DAM POP; MTCW

White, Patrick (Victor Martindale)
1912-1990 .. **CLC 3, 4, 5, 7, 9, 18, 65, 69**
See also CA 81-84; 132; CANR 43; MTCW

White, Phyllis Dorothy James 1920-
See James, P. D.
See also CA 21-24R; CANR 17, 43;
DAM POP; MTCW

White, T(erence) H(anbury)
1906-1964 .... **CLC 30**
See also CA 73-76; CANR 37; DLB 160;
JRDA; MAICYA; SATA 12

White, Terence de Vere
1912-1994 .... **CLC 49**
See also CA 49-52; 145; CANR 3

White, Walter F(rancis)
1893-1955 .... **TCLC 15**
See also White, Walter
See also BW 1; CA 115; 124; DLB 51

White, William Hale 1831-1913
See Rutherford, Mark
See also CA 121

Whitehead, E(dward) A(nthony)
1933- .... **CLC 5**
See also CA 65-68

Whitemore, Hugh (John) 1936- ..... **CLC 37**
See also CA 132; INT 132

Whitman, Sarah Helen (Power)
1803-1878 .... **NCLC 19**
See also DLB 1

Whitman, Walt(er)
1819-1892 ..... **NCLC 4, 31; DA; DAB;
DAC; PC 3; WLC**
See also CDALB 1640-1865; DAM MST,
POET; DLB 3, 64; SATA 20

Whitney, Phyllis A(yame) 1903- .... **CLC 42**
See also AITN 2; BEST 90:3; CA 1-4R;
CANR 3, 25, 38; DAM POP; JRDA;
MAICYA; SATA 1, 30

Whittemore, (Edward) Reed (Jr.)
1919- .... **CLC 4**
See also CA 9-12R; CAAS 8; CANR 4;
DLB 5

Whittier, John Greenleaf
1807-1892 .... **NCLC 8, 57**
See also CDALB 1640-1865; DAM POET;
DLB 1

Whittlebot, Hernia
See Coward, Noel (Peirce)

Wicker, Thomas Grey 1926-
See Wicker, Tom
See also CA 65-68; CANR 21, 46

Wicker, Tom .... **CLC 7**
See also Wicker, Thomas Grey

Wideman, John Edgar
1941- .... **CLC 5, 34, 36, 67; BLC**
See also BW 2; CA 85-88; CANR 14, 42;
DAM MULT; DLB 33, 143

Wiebe, Rudy (Henry)
1934- .... **CLC 6, 11, 14; DAC**
See also CA 37-40R; CANR 42;
DAM MST; DLB 60

Wieland, Christoph Martin
1733-1813 .... **NCLC 17**
See also DLB 97

Wiene, Robert 1881-1938 .... **TCLC 56**

Wieners, John 1934- .... **CLC 7**
See also CA 13-16R; DLB 16

Wiesel, Elie(zer)
1928- ...... **CLC 3, 5, 11, 37; DA; DAB;
DAC**
See also AAYA 7; AITN 1; CA 5-8R;
CAAS 4; CANR 8, 40; DAM MST,
NOV; DLB 83; DLBY 87; INT CANR-8;
MTCW; SATA 56

Wiggins, Marianne 1947- .... **CLC 57**
See also BEST 89:3; CA 130

Wight, James Alfred 1916-
See Herriot, James
See also CA 77-80; SATA 55;
SATA-Brief 44

Wilbur, Richard (Purdy)
1921- ... **CLC 3, 6, 9, 14, 53; DA; DAB;
DAC**
See also CA 1-4R; CABS 2; CANR 2, 29;
DAM MST, POET; DLB 5;
INT CANR-29; MTCW; SATA 9

Wild, Peter 1940- .... **CLC 14**
See also CA 37-40R; DLB 5

Wilde, Oscar (Fingal O'Flahertie Wills)
1854(?)-1900 .... **TCLC 1, 8, 23, 41; DA;
DAB; DAC; SSC 11; WLC**
See also CA 104; 119; CDBLB 1890-1914;
DAM DRAM, MST, NOV; DLB 10, 19,
34, 57, 141, 156; SATA 24

Wilder, Billy .... **CLC 20**
See also Wilder, Samuel
See also DLB 26

Wilder, Samuel 1906-
See Wilder, Billy
See also CA 89-92

Wilder, Thornton (Niven)
1897-1975 ...... **CLC 1, 5, 6, 10, 15, 35,
82; DA; DAB; DAC; DC 1; WLC**
See also AITN 2; CA 13-16R; 61-64;
CANR 40; DAM DRAM, MST, NOV;
DLB 4, 7, 9; MTCW

Wilding, Michael 1942- .... **CLC 73**
See also CA 104; CANR 24, 49

Wiley, Richard 1944- .... **CLC 44**
See also CA 121; 129

Wilhelm, Kate .... **CLC 7**
See also Wilhelm, Katie Gertrude
See also CAAS 5; DLB 8; INT CANR-17

Wilhelm, Katie Gertrude 1928-
See Wilhelm, Kate
See also CA 37-40R; CANR 17, 36; MTCW

Wilkins, Mary
See Freeman, Mary Eleanor Wilkins

Willard, Nancy 1936- .... **CLC 7, 37**
See also CA 89-92; CANR 10, 39; CLR 5;
DLB 5, 52; MAICYA; MTCW;
SATA 37, 71; SATA-Brief 30

Williams, C(harles) K(enneth)
1936- .... **CLC 33, 56**
See also CA 37-40R; DAM POET; DLB 5

Williams, Charles
See Collier, James L(incoln)

Williams, Charles (Walter Stansby)
1886-1945 .... **TCLC 1, 11**
See also CA 104; DLB 100, 153

Williams, (George) Emlyn
1905-1987 .... **CLC 15**
See also CA 104; 123; CANR 36;
DAM DRAM; DLB 10, 77; MTCW

Williams, Hugo 1942- .... **CLC 42**
See also CA 17-20R; CANR 45; DLB 40

Williams, J. Walker
See Wodehouse, P(elham) G(renville)

Williams, John A(lfred)
1925- . . . . **CLC 5, 13; BLC**
See also BW 2; CA 53-56; CAAS 3;
CANR 6, 26, 51; DAM MULT; DLB 2,
33; INT CANR-6

Williams, Jonathan (Chamberlain)
1929- . . . . **CLC 13**
See also CA 9-12R; CAAS 12; CANR 8;
DLB 5

Williams, Joy   1944- . . . . **CLC 31**
See also CA 41-44R; CANR 22, 48

Williams, Norman   1952- . . . . **CLC 39**
See also CA 118

Williams, Sherley Anne
1944- . . . . **CLC 89; BLC**
See also BW 2; CA 73-76; CANR 25;
DAM MULT, POET; DLB 41;
INT CANR-25; SATA 78

Williams, Shirley
See Williams, Sherley Anne

Williams, Tennessee
1911-1983 . . . . . **CLC 1, 2, 5, 7, 8, 11, 15,
19, 30, 39, 45, 71; DA; DAB; DAC;
DC 4; WLC**
See also AITN 1, 2; CA 5-8R; 108;
CABS 3; CANR 31; CDALB 1941-1968;
DAM DRAM, MST; DLB 7; DLBD 4;
DLBY 83; MTCW

Williams, Thomas (Alonzo)
1926-1990 . . . . **CLC 14**
See also CA 1-4R; 132; CANR 2

Williams, William C.
See Williams, William Carlos

Williams, William Carlos
1883-1963 . . . . **CLC 1, 2, 5, 9, 13, 22, 42,
67; DA; DAB; DAC; PC 7**
See also CA 89-92; CANR 34;
CDALB 1917-1929; DAM MST, POET;
DLB 4, 16, 54, 86; MTCW

Williamson, David (Keith)   1942- . . . . **CLC 56**
See also CA 103; CANR 41

Williamson, Ellen Douglas   1905-1984
See Douglas, Ellen
See also CA 17-20R; 114; CANR 39

Williamson, Jack . . . . **CLC 29**
See also Williamson, John Stewart
See also CAAS 8; DLB 8

Williamson, John Stewart   1908-
See Williamson, Jack
See also CA 17-20R; CANR 23

Willie, Frederick
See Lovecraft, H(oward) P(hillips)

Willingham, Calder (Baynard, Jr.)
1922-1995 . . . . **CLC 5, 51**
See also CA 5-8R; 147; CANR 3; DLB 2,
44; MTCW

Willis, Charles
See Clarke, Arthur C(harles)

Willy
See Colette, (Sidonie-Gabrielle)

Willy, Colette
See Colette, (Sidonie-Gabrielle)

Wilson, A(ndrew) N(orman)   1950- . . **CLC 33**
See also CA 112; 122; DLB 14, 155

Wilson, Angus (Frank Johnstone)
1913-1991 . . **CLC 2, 3, 5, 25, 34; SSC 21**
See also CA 5-8R; 134; CANR 21; DLB 15,
139, 155; MTCW

Wilson, August
1945- . . . . **CLC 39, 50, 63; BLC; DA;
DAB; DAC; DC 2**
See also AAYA 16; BW 2; CA 115; 122;
CANR 42; DAM DRAM, MST, MULT;
MTCW

Wilson, Brian   1942- . . . . **CLC 12**

Wilson, Colin   1931- . . . . **CLC 3, 14**
See also CA 1-4R; CAAS 5; CANR 1, 22,
33; DLB 14; MTCW

Wilson, Dirk
See Pohl, Frederik

Wilson, Edmund
1895-1972 . . . . **CLC 1, 2, 3, 8, 24**
See also CA 1-4R; 37-40R; CANR 1, 46;
DLB 63; MTCW

Wilson, Ethel Davis (Bryant)
1888(?)-1980 . . . . **CLC 13; DAC**
See also CA 102; DAM POET; DLB 68;
MTCW

Wilson, John   1785-1854. . . . . **NCLC 5**

Wilson, John (Anthony) Burgess   1917-1993
See Burgess, Anthony
See also CA 1-4R; 143; CANR 2, 46; DAC;
DAM NOV; MTCW

Wilson, Lanford   1937- . . . . **CLC 7, 14, 36**
See also CA 17-20R; CABS 3; CANR 45;
DAM DRAM; DLB 7

Wilson, Robert M.   1944- . . . . **CLC 7, 9**
See also CA 49-52; CANR 2, 41; MTCW

Wilson, Robert McLiam   1964- . . . . . **CLC 59**
See also CA 132

Wilson, Sloan   1920- . . . . **CLC 32**
See also CA 1-4R; CANR 1, 44

Wilson, Snoo   1948- . . . . **CLC 33**
See also CA 69-72

Wilson, William S(mith)   1932- . . . . . **CLC 49**
See also CA 81-84

Winchilsea, Anne (Kingsmill) Finch Counte
1661-1720 . . . . **LC 3**

Windham, Basil
See Wodehouse, P(elham) G(renville)

Wingrove, David (John)   1954- . . . . . . **CLC 68**
See also CA 133

Winters, Janet Lewis . . . . **CLC 41**
See also Lewis, Janet
See also DLBY 87

Winters, (Arthur) Yvor
1900-1968 . . . . **CLC 4, 8, 32**
See also CA 11-12; 25-28R; CAP 1;
DLB 48; MTCW

Winterson, Jeanette   1959- . . . . **CLC 64**
See also CA 136; DAM POP

Winthrop, John   1588-1649. . . . . **LC 31**
See also DLB 24, 30

Wiseman, Frederick   1930- . . . . **CLC 20**

Wister, Owen   1860-1938 . . . . **TCLC 21**
See also CA 108; DLB 9, 78; SATA 62

Witkacy
See Witkiewicz, Stanislaw Ignacy

Witkiewicz, Stanislaw Ignacy
1885-1939 . . . . **TCLC 8**
See also CA 105

Wittgenstein, Ludwig (Josef Johann)
1889-1951 . . . . **TCLC 59**
See also CA 113

Wittig, Monique   1935(?)- . . . . **CLC 22**
See also CA 116; 135; DLB 83

Wittlin, Józef   1896-1976 . . . . **CLC 25**
See also CA 49-52; 65-68; CANR 3

Wodehouse, P(elham) G(renville)
1881-1975 . . . **CLC 1, 2, 5, 10, 22; DAB;
DAC; SSC 2**
See also AITN 2; CA 45-48; 57-60;
CANR 3, 33; CDBLB 1914-1945;
DAM NOV; DLB 34, 162; MTCW;
SATA 22

Woiwode, L.
See Woiwode, Larry (Alfred)

Woiwode, Larry (Alfred)   1941- . . . **CLC 6, 10**
See also CA 73-76; CANR 16; DLB 6;
INT CANR-16

Wojciechowska, Maia (Teresa)
1927- . . . . **CLC 26**
See also AAYA 8; CA 9-12R; CANR 4, 41;
CLR 1; JRDA; MAICYA; SAAS 1;
SATA 1, 28, 83

Wolf, Christa   1929- . . . . **CLC 14, 29, 58**
See also CA 85-88; CANR 45; DLB 75;
MTCW

Wolfe, Gene (Rodman)   1931-. . . . . . . **CLC 25**
See also CA 57-60; CAAS 9; CANR 6, 32;
DAM POP; DLB 8

Wolfe, George C.   1954- . . . . **CLC 49**
See also CA 149

Wolfe, Thomas (Clayton)
1900-1938 . . . . . **TCLC 4, 13, 29, 61; DA;
DAB; DAC; WLC**
See also CA 104; 132; CDALB 1929-1941;
DAM MST, NOV; DLB 9, 102; DLBD 2;
DLBY 85; MTCW

Wolfe, Thomas Kennerly, Jr.   1931-
See Wolfe, Tom
See also CA 13-16R; CANR 9, 33;
DAM POP; INT CANR-9; MTCW

Wolfe, Tom . . . . **CLC 1, 2, 9, 15, 35, 51**
See also Wolfe, Thomas Kennerly, Jr.
See also AAYA 8; AITN 2; BEST 89:1;
DLB 152

Wolff, Geoffrey (Ansell)   1937- . . . . . **CLC 41**
See also CA 29-32R; CANR 29, 43

Wolff, Sonia
See Levitin, Sonia (Wolff)

Wolff, Tobias (Jonathan Ansell)
1945- . . . . **CLC 39, 64**
See also AAYA 16; BEST 90:2; CA 114;
117; CAAS 22; DLB 130; INT 117

Wolfram von Eschenbach
c. 1170-c. 1220 . . . . **CMLC 5**
See also DLB 138

Wolitzer, Hilma   1930- . . . . **CLC 17**
See also CA 65-68; CANR 18, 40;
INT CANR-18; SATA 31

Wollstonecraft, Mary   1759-1797 . . . . . . **LC 5**
See also CDBLB 1789-1832; DLB 39, 104,
158

Literary Criticism Series
Cumulative Topic Index

This index lists all topic entries in Gale's *Classical and Medieval Literature Criticism, Contemporary Literary Criticism, Literature Criticism from 1400 to 1800, Nineteenth-Century Literature Criticism,* and *Twentieth-Century Literary Criticism.*

NCLC Cumulative Nationality Index

Nationality Index

ISBN 0-8103-7005-0